Our land a-bounds in na-tures gifts Of beau...

Then here he raised Old Eng-land's flag, The stan-dard of the brave.

In hist'ry's page, let ev'ry stage Ad-vance Aus-tra-lia fair.

"With all her faults we love her still" "Bri-tan-nia rules the wave."

In joy-ful strains then let us sing Ad-vance Aus-tra-lia fair.

3.
Beneath our radiant Southern Cross,
We'll toil with hearts and hands,
To make our youthful Commonwealth
Renowned of all the lands;
For loyal sons beyond the seas
We've boundless plains to share,
With courage let us all combine
To "Advance Australia Fair."
In joyful strains, etc.,

4.
Shou'd foreign foe e'er sight our coast,
Or dare a foot to land,
We'll rouse to arms like sires of yore
To guard our native strand;
Britannia then shall surely know,
Beyond wide ocean's roll,
Her sons in fair Australia's land
Still keep a British soul.
In joyful strains, etc.

"'Advance Australa Fair' is now our National Anthem."—*The Premier, May, 1907.*

THE OXFORD
COMPANION TO
AUSTRALIAN
MUSIC

THE OXFORD
COMPANION TO
AUSTRALIAN
MUSIC

EDITED BY
WARREN BEBBINGTON

Melbourne
OXFORD UNIVERSITY PRESS
Oxford   Auckland   New York

OXFORD UNIVERSITY PRESS AUSTRALIA

Oxford   New York
Athens   Auckland   Bangkok   Bombay
Calcutta   Cape Town   Dar es Salaam   Delhi
Florence   Hong Kong   Istanbul   Karachi
Kuala Lumpur   Madras   Madrid   Melbourne
Mexico City   Nairobi   Paris   Port Moresby
Singapore   Taipei   Tokyo   Toronto
and associated companies in
Berlin   Ibadan

OXFORD is a trade mark of Oxford University Press

National Library of Australia
Cataloguing-in-Publication data:

Bebbington, Warren A., 1952– .
The Oxford Companion to Australian Music

 ISBN 0 19 553432 8.

 1. Music – Australia – Encyclopaedias. 2. Music –
 Australia – Bio-bibliography. 3. Musicians – Australia
 – Biography. I. Bebbington, Warren Arthur

780.99403

Edited by Venetia Somerset
Text design by Derrick Stone
Cover design by Anitra Blackford
Cover photograph: Dame Joan Sutherland in the title
   role of Donizetti's *Lucrezia Borgia*, an Opera Australia
   (formerly the Australian Opera) production, 1977.
Typeset by Desktop Concepts P/L, Melbourne
Printed by Australian Print Group
Published by Oxford University Press,
253 Normanby Road, South Melbourne, Australia

PREFACE

The *Oxford Companion to Australian Music* is a reference work which should be of interest to music lovers as well as of use to students and scholars. To date there has been no universally available volume combining an account of Australia's music with biographical information about its musicians, a critical guide to their works, publishers and recordings, and a key to the sources and growing research literature in the field. To produce such a work, and thereby help bring Australian music to much wider attention, has been my aim.

Australia's musical life has been very diverse, and it seems to me the view of it among scholars has often been too narrow. The following pages deliberately range across a wide spectrum, from ancient Aboriginal traditions and European-derived orchestral, operatic and concert music, to Australian folk, jazz, country, popular, rock, electronic and experimental music. The volume covers the music not only of the mainstream audience but also of Australia's religious denominations and recent migrant communities. Special attention is given to the distinctive features of Australian musical life, its reliance on public support via government grants, festivals and changeable civic sympathies rather than on ecclesiastical, aristocratic or private patronage; its unquenchable appetite for eisteddfods, choral societies and bands, and fickleness towards intrepid opera companies and orchestras; the shadow cast by European traditions and an easy openness to foreign influence; the vicissitudes of its attitude to composers; the late development of music criticism and scholarship; and the role, at least until the advent of radio, of its widely dispersed regional cities and towns, with their many local societies and competitions. Accordingly, Australian music has been broadly defined here as that music made in Australia or by Australians. The first part of such a definition can be troublesome: foreign musicians like conductor Nicolai Malko, who resided in Australia for a period but whose career belongs substantially elsewhere, or Sir Malcolm Sargent, who toured Australia extensively, present an ambiguous category, and are recorded here only to the extent that they contributed to Australian musical life. The second part is more perplexing: such Australians as Percy Grainger, Peggy Glanville-Hicks and Arthur Benjamin, who spent most of their careers abroad, frequently had less of a role in Australian musical life than in the countries of their adoption, but they are recorded here more generously, especially if they themselves continued to claim their achievements as Australian.

Entries on individuals comprise half the *Companion*. They principally encompass composers and performers, but also many teachers, instrument-makers, lyricists, critics, scholars, impresarios, and administrators. In each case the aim has been to supply basic biographical information, summary description of the output and some measure of appreciation. Clearly there has been selection and weighting in the preparation of these entries: not every established Australian musical figure has been included, and some have been discussed in far greater detail than others. The composer biographies, for example, are not as numerous as they might be in a composition directory; obviously, to achieve the breadth of coverage I wanted, space in each category had to be constrained. A variety of judgments for inclusion was made: among performers for example, the jazzmen (indeed, most are men) are generally those most consistently involved in public performance within Australia, while the opera singers (interestingly, most are women) are generally those with most success abroad. In both cases this usually means artists with careers that span many years; yet the pop and rock singers are generally those with chart success, although this may mean careers that were only momentary. Yet the choice and varied length of entries is not always the result of a judgment on relative importance of individuals. For some subjects information has been difficult to discover, some careers are more conducive to summary than others, and in a few instances the writing was affected by problems in obtaining the co-operation of contributors or living subjects, despite persistent requests and correspondence over an extended period. To have excluded all living subjects, as sometimes occurs in a national reference work, would have simplified matters, but would have been absurd in a Companion to a musical life as young as Australia's. Nevertheless I have limited entries on living subjects here: especially where a subject's output and the assessment of it are likely to undergo significant change I have often opted for a conservative coverage.

The other half of the *Companion*, including most of the longer articles, encompasses musical works, institutions, genres, instruments, terms, and some of the historical or other cultural contexts within which Australian musicians can be placed. For musical works a reader should generally consult the composer entries, many of which include lists of works providing details of instrumentation, date of composition (with number of acts and name of librettist in the case of operas), date of publication and recording information. For some well-known folk-songs, popular songs, operas or ballets there are also separate entries, but these are limited to works like *Jim Jones*, *The Wild Colonial Boy* or *I Still Call Australia Home* which are of special national significance, like *Sun Music*, *Voss* or *Bran Nue Dae* which achieved a place in the repertory of major companies, or like Antill's *Corroboree*, The Seekers' *A World Of Our Own* or Nathan's *Don John of Austria* which attracted considerable public notice in their own day. For genres and terms I have aimed at readers unfamiliar with Australian music who might need basic information on matters encountered in its study. These entries have been consciously focused towards Australia: thus the entries about Ragtime, Yodelling, and Organ-building, for example, give only summary information on their foreign origins and deliberately emphasise their adaptation and creation in Australia.

Most entries are supported at their ends by reference to reading, to current recordings, and often to research literature or source materials. It is inevitable that a book of this scope and magnitude is much indebted to the work of others, ranging from standard reference works such as the *Australian Dictionary of Biography* to many specialist studies of individual topics. Population figures are those of the *Australian Census 1991*, and positions for popular music in 'the charts' are generally those of Barnes et al., *Top 40 Research 1956–1977* or Kent's *Australian Chart Book 1970–1992* as appropriate (see *Charts*). It is impossible to list all works consulted in the preparation of the *Companion*, but the most significant sources are generally acknowledged in the 'Further Reference' lists at the end of each entry.

I conceived a plan of entries for the *Companion* in 1991. My view was that clear editorial guidelines would control and stimulate the kind of information gathered and the way it was presented, and I specified such matters as entry construction and text styles in a set of 'Guidelines to Contributors' at the outset. My associate Jennifer Hill developed and greatly expanded the master lists of headwords in 1992–93, and a group of advisers was then invited to review and amend lists in several areas. About a third of the entries (but nearly two-thirds of the copy) was then commissioned to contributors, and my associate Royston Gustavson spent much of 1994–96 seeking authors and gathering and checking their work. Two research assistants were engaged to collect source data for many of the minor entries early in 1996, and with their material I wrote the bulk of the remaining entries myself, as well as editing the work of the contributors, during a sabbatical leave later that year. In the process, considerable effort was made to check the accuracy of the facts included here, although it must be pointed out that in many areas of Australian music and music history definitive studies are yet to emerge, and some errors or faults of emphasis are unavoidable. Naturally, I will welcome any suggestions and corrections for future revisions and editions.

WARREN BEBBINGTON
University of Melbourne, 1997

ACKNOWLEDGMENTS

For the breadth of what follows, I am greatly indebted to an array of people who gave generously of their time. To all the contributors who took such an interest in the project, I am grateful; their names are listed in the Directory on the following pages. One who deserves special mention is Dr Bruce Johnson, University of NSW, who contributed over 160 entries on jazz topics—a quite remarkable feat; in preparing these entries, he would wish me to acknowledge especially the assistance of the subjects themselves in many places, the generous assistance of Eric Myers (NSW and National Jazz Co-ordinator), and of Bill Haesler (2MBS–FM jazz broadcaster). Dr Johnson was one of a group of contributors who also assisted me by reviewing parts of the master list, providing advice or suggesting contributors in their areas; the members of this group have their names repeated under Advisers in the Directory that follows. The Opera Australia staff answered many enquiries about singers; Kenneth Hince (Melbourne) provided helpful details about music critics; Max Cooke (Monash University), John Painter and Vernon Hill (Canberra School of Music) filled in many blanks about pianists, string and wind players respectively; and Robert Browne (Australian Flute Guild) was of particular assistance for flautists. Rock discographer Chris Spencer answered various questions about rock music from his extensive files and Kathy Bail, editor of *Rolling Stone*, suggested several rock authors. Nick Erby (Tamworth), Dallas Briggs (BAL Marketing, Tamworth), Eric Watson (Selection Records, Casino NSW) and Hadley Records, Tamworth, all gave invaluable help over the country music entries. Alan Musgrove (Victorian Folklife Association) and Edna Gardner (Victorian Folk Music Club) generously shared their knowledge of folk music. I am also grateful to the many musicians (or in some instances their descendants) who had special knowledge or are subjects of some entries and responded to requests for assistance, generously supplying in many cases more information than I was able to use.

In the Centre for Studies in Australian Music, Faculty of Music, University of Melbourne, I would like to thank Jennifer Hill, who gathered much of the data from which the larger part of the headword list was later distilled, assembled lists of the source material which form the core of Further Reference for many of the biographical entries, and suggested many advisers and authors with specialised knowledge; Royston Gustavson, who located many contributors, supervised the commissioning process, assembled the contributions, checked the Further Reference lists, circulated numerous questionnaires by mail, and helped with a host of other matters; Carolyn Muntz and Jennifer Royle, who worked so thoroughly at assembling data from which a great many short entries were written; Dr Kerry Murphy, who found many research students from her Musicological Research Methods class to take on small tasks; Dr Brenton Broadstock, who kindly provided access to the lists of composers he had compiled for his book *Sound Ideas*; and the Centre Co-ordinator, Dr Suzanne Robinson, who patiently provided facilities and support. The staff of the Music Branch, Baillieu Library, University of Melbourne, Evelyn Portek, Gail Wissmann, Lena Vigilante, Christine Webster and Anja Weise, had endless tolerance for even my most unreasonable requests. My mother Thelma Bebbington read the entire manuscript and made many helpful suggestions. At home my wife Barbara was a constant source of support, while Anne Watson helped in ways too numerous to mention. At Oxford University Press, I always appreciated the unfailing courtesy and interest of my publisher, Peter Rose.

Many individuals and institutions provided pictorial material. Their courtesy is acknowledged in the captions to the illustrations. I would also like to acknowledge the assistance of the Hanson-Dyer Bequest, University of Melbourne, whose generous grant facilitated the first year of work on the project; the Australian Research Council, whose several grants helped in the last three years; and the University of Melbourne for allowing me sabbatical leave in 1996 to complete the volume.

W.B.

HOW TO USE THE COMPANION

1. Alphabetisation

In this *Companion,* entries are alphabetised A to Z by surname for individuals (**Sutherland, Dame Joan**) and by first word for ensembles and other subjects, but not under an English definite or indefinite article (**Seekers, The**). For individuals, the alphabetisation proceeds by the most commonly known name, often a stage name or nickname, rather than by the birth name: **Barnard, Bob (Robert)** before **Barnard, Len (Leonard)**. The alphabetisation ignores apostrophes and diacritical marks (such as ö, ñ), and proceeds word by word (**I Still Call Australia Home** before **Illing, Rosamund**). **Mc** is treated as Mac and **Saint** as St. Entries beginning with numbers are alphabetised as if the numbers were spelled out (**3DB Orchestra** as Three DB Orchestra). Several subjects with the same name are numbered chronologically: **Sydney Symphony Orchestra (1); Sydney Symphony Orchestra (2).** Two or more family members with entries are grouped as a family with each member numbered from the eldest: **Carandini.** Family of theatrical performers. **(1) Gerolamo Carandini; (2) Marie Carandini;** etc.

2. Arrangement of headwords

Headwords are given in bold. Individuals commonly known by a stage or professional name are listed with their birth-names in square brackets: **Lamond, Toni** [Lawman, Patricia Lamond]. Where the stage name abbreviates a first name, the given names follow in parentheses: **Burrows, Don (Donald Vernon)**. Elements in a person's name generally unused are presented in parentheses: **Wallace, W(illiam) Vincent** means that W. Vincent Wallace is the normal form. Nicknames are presented in quotation marks within parentheses: **McNamara, Ian ('Macca')**, unless the nickname is also the stage name: **Dawson, 'Smoky' (Herbert Henry)**. Pseudonyms or pen-names appear in quotation marks in square brackets: **Prerauer, Maria** ['Marietta'].

3. Names of institutions

In headwords, an institution is listed under its current name, but in entries is referred to by the name used at the time under discussion; hence the national opera company is under **Opera Australia**, but entries discussing its work before 1970 refer to the Elizabethan Theatre Trust Opera Co., and 1970–96 to the Australian Opera. The company changed its name to Opera Australia as this book went to press.

4. Place-names

For places other than capital cities abbreviated state names are given ('Bendigo, Vic.'); for places outside Australia, country names are given where helpful ('Cambridge, Mass., USA'); English county names are given where they are judged to be helpful.

5. Abbreviations

Abbreviations have been used for frequently mentioned musical institutions and terms, but they may be spelt out in an entry where sense demands it. The key to these appears under Abbreviations §1 below. Musical instruments are abbreviated in the lists of composer's works according to the list in Abbreviations §2.

6. Cross-references

References leading a reader to another related entry are indicated by ★ or at the end of an entry by the use of 'See' followed by the entry title in italics or a general indication of further relevant entries. Cross-references have been used only for subjects where an entry might not obviously be warranted, but not where it could reasonably be expected: readers are therefore encouraged to see if a subject not indicated by a cross-reference nevertheless has its own entry.

7. Further Reference

Further Reference sections comprising lists of works, recordings and further reading have been included at the end of an entry where more extended material of particular significance to the topic exists. In these lists abbreviations have been used for frequently mentioned books, journals and libraries (see Abbreviations §3 below).

DIRECTORY OF CONTRIBUTORS

Unattributed entries are by the editor

Staff and Advisers

Research Associates
  Royston Gustavson
  Jennifer Hill
Research Assistants
  Carolyn Muntz
  Jennifer Royle
Advisers
  Michael Atherton
  Ros Bandt
  Doreen Bridges
  Peter Burgis
  Geoffrey Cox
  Joel Crotty
  Kay Dreyfus
  Jennifer Hill
  John Holmes
  Ian Holtham
  Bruce Johnson
  Grace Koch
  Harold Love
  Sally Macarthur
  John Maidment
  Thérèse Radic
  Graeme Smith
  Robin Stevens
  Jill Stubington
  Chris Wallace-Crabbe
  Stephen Wild

Authors

Noel Ancell
  Melbourne
Bronwen Arthur
  Department of Music
  University of Queensland
Michael Atherton
  Professor of Music
  Nepean Campus
  University of Western Sydney
Ros Bandt
  Music Department
  Monash University
Michael Barkl
  Illawarra Institute of Technology

Linda Barwick
  University of Hong Kong
Georgina Binns
  Music Librarian
  Monash University
Hilary Blackshaw
  Faculty of Music
  University of Melbourne

Robert Boughen
  St John's Anglican Cathedral
  Brisbane
Warren Bourne
  Department of Music Studies
  University of Adelaide
Marcus Breen
  Melbourne
Doreen Bridges
  Sydney
Brenton Broadstock
  Faculty of Music
  University of Melbourne
Jeff Brownrigg
  National Film and Sound Archive
  Canberra
Michael Burden
  New College
  Oxford, UK
Peter Burgis
  Port Macquarie
Ian Burk
  St Andrew's Anglican Church
  Brighton, Melbourne
Warren Burt
  Canberra School of Music
  Australian National University
Duncan Bythell
  Department of History
  University of Durham, UK
Peter Campbell
  Canberra School of Music
  Australian National University
Donald Cave
  St Francis Monastery
  Melbourne
Lyle Chan
  Soundscapes
  Sydney
William Chappell
  Melbourne
John Cleary
  Religious Affairs Department
  Australian Broadcasting Corporation
  Sydney
John Colborne-Veel
  Fellowship of Australian Composers
  Sydney
Aaron Corn
  Faculty of Music
  University of Melbourne
Geoffrey Cox
  Department of Visual and Performing Arts
  Mercy Campus
  Australian Catholic University

Rita Crews
    Armidale
Joel Crotty
    Department of Music
    Monash University
Naomi Cumming
    Faculty of Music
    University of Melbourne
Amanda Cummins
    Faculty of Music
    University of Melbourne
Peter Dart
    Trinity Grammar School
    Sydney
Jim Davidson
    Victoria University of Technology
Jenny Dawson
    Department of Music
    University of Queensland
Tamsin Donaldson
    Australian Institute of Aboriginal and
        Torres Strait Islander Studies
    Canberra
Kay Dreyfus
    Department of Music
    Monash University
Peter Dunbar-Hall
    Sydney Conservatorium of Music
    University of Sydney
Jane Edwards
    Department of Music
    University of Queensland
Denise Erdonmez Grocke
    Faculty of Music
    University of Melbourne
Catherine Falk
    Faculty of Music
    University of Melbourne
Jean Farrant
    Western Australian Conservatorium of
        Music
Anne-Marie Forbes
    Department of Music
    University of Queensland
Helen Gagliano
    Faculty of Music
    University of Melbourne
Phillip Gearing
    Department of Music
    University of Southern Queensland
Monique Geitenbeek
    Department of Music
    Monash University
Malcolm Gillies
    Professor of Music
    University of Queensland
Dianne Gome
    Department of Music
    Mercy Campus
    Australian Catholic University
Leonie Goodwin
    Faculty of Music
    University of Melbourne

Peter Gore-Symes
    James Cook University
Tony Gould
    School of Music
    Victorian College of the Arts
John Griffiths
    Professor of Music and
        Director, Early Music Studio
    University of Melbourne
Margaret Gummow
    Department of Music
    University of Sydney
Royston Gustavson
    Centre for Studies in Australian Music
    University of Melbourne
Thomas Hall
    Department of Music
    University of Sussex, UK
Wayne Hancock
    Adelaide
Graham Hardie
    Department of Music
    University of Sydney
Kelvin Hastie
    Sydney
Barbara Hebden
    Courier-Mail
    Brisbane
Thomas Heywood
    Faculty of Music
    University of Melbourne
Flinder Hiew
    Faculty of Music
    University of Melbourne
Jennifer Hill
    Centre for Studies in Australian
        Music
    University of Melbourne
Kenneth Hince
    Euroa Fine Books
    Euroa
Howard Hollis
    St Paul's Anglican Cathedral
    Melbourne
John Holmes
    Canberra
Ian Holtham
    Faculty of Music
    University of Melbourne
Gregg Howard
    Queensland Conservatorium
        of Music
David Hugo
    Strehlow Research Centre
    Alice Springs
Le Tuan Hung
    Research Associate
    Australia Asia Foundation
Ya Hui Hung
    Faculty of Music
    University of Melbourne
Catherine Ingram
    Melbourne

Lilla Ito-Hongo
  Faculty of Music
  University of Melbourne
Bruce Johnson
  Department of English
  University of New South Wales
Margaret Kartomi
  Professor of Music
  Monash University
Lyndell King
  Faculty of Music
  University of Melbourne
Steven Knopoff
  Centre for Aboriginal Studies in Music
  University of Adelaide
Grace Koch
  Australian Institute of Aboriginal and
      Torres Strait Islander Studies
  Canberra
Bronia Kornhauser
  Australian Archive of Jewish Music
  Department of Music
  Monash University
Helen Lancaster
  Central Queensland Conservatorium of Music
  Central Queensland University
Natasha Langford
  Faculty of Music
  University of Melbourne
Sarah Larkin
  Faculty of Music
  University of Melbourne
Helen Reeves Lawrence
  Canberra School of Music
  Australian National University
Chris Lesser
  Melbourne
Tom Liolios
  Faculty of Music
  University of Melbourne
Harold Love
  Professor of English
  Monash University
Alastair McAllister
  Melbourne
Sally Macarthur
  Faculty of Visual and Performing Arts
  Nepean Campus
  University of Western Sydney
Peter McCallum
  Sydney Conservatorium of Music
Andrew McCredie
  Munich-Nymphenberg
  Germany
Belinda McKay
  Queensland Studies Centre
  Griffith University
Neil McKelvie
  Professor of Organic Chemistry
  City College
  City University of New York, USA
Beverley Maclellan
  Melbourne

Isobel McLennan
  Department of Music
  Monash University
Michael McNab
  Faculty of Music
  University of Melbourne
Adrian McNeil
  Department of Music
  Monash University
Roslyn Maguire
  Sydney
John Maidment
  Organ Historical Trust of Australia
Allan Marett
  Professor of Music
  University of Hong Kong
Christopher Mark
  Department of Music
  University of Surrey, UK
Christopher Martin
  Faculty of Music
  University of Melbourne
Emma Matthews
  Faculty of Music
  University of Melbourne
Robert Maynard
  Australian Broadcasting Corporation
  Adelaide
Cyrus Meher-Homji
  Soundscapes
  Sydney
Alan Moffat
  St John's Anglican Cathedral
  Brisbane
James Moffat
  Sydney
Kylie Moloney
  Faculty of Music
  University of Melbourne
Richard Moyle
  Archive of Maori and Pacific Music
  University of Auckland
Carolyn Muntz
  Faculty of Music
  University of Melbourne
Alan Musgrove
  Melbourne
Diane Napthali
  Sydney
Kathleen Nelson
  Sydney Conservatorium of Music
  University of Sydney
Nigel Nettheim
  Sydney
Karl Neuenfeldt
  Department of Music
  University of Newcastle
Philip Nunn
  Ealing Abbey
  London, UK
Peter Nussey
  Dragon Enterprises
  Brisbane

Clive O'Connell
    Xavier College
    Melbourne
Kathleen Oien
    Australian Institute of Aboriginal and
        Torres Strait Islander Studies
    Canberra
Jennifer Oldfield
    Faculty of Music
    University of Melbourne
Moffatt Oxenbould
    Artistic Director
    Opera Australia
    Sydney
Faye Patton
    Melbourne
Helen Payne
    Department of Music Studies
    University of Adelaide
Robert Peterson
    Brisbane
Rose Peterson
    Faculty of Music
    University of Melbourne
Bruce Petherick
    Faculty of Music
    University of Melbourne
Pauline Petrus
    Melbourne
Graham Pont
    Professor of General Studies
    University of New South Wales
Thérèse Radic
    Centre for Studies in Australian Music
    University of Melbourne
Jennifer Rakauskas
    Department of Music
    University of Queensland
Amanda Reynolds
    Canberra School of Music
    Australian National University
Marianne Rigby
    Faculty of Music
    University of Melbourne
Peter Roberts
    Boorowa, NSW
Suzanne Robinson
    Centre for Studies in Australian Music
    University of Melbourne
Peter Roennfeldt
    Queensland Conservatorium of Music
Philippa Roylance
    Faculty of Education
    University of Central Queensland
Jennifer Royle
    Faculty of Music
    University of Melbourne
Graeme Rushworth
    Sydney
Robin Ryan
    Department of Music
    Monash Univerity

Thomas Sammut
    Faculty of Music
    University of Melbourne
Melinda Sawers
    Faculty of Music
    University of Melbourne
Natascha Schmidt
    Faculty of Music
    University of Melbourne
Aubrey Schrader
    Faculty of Music
    University of Melbourne
Margaret Seares
    Department of Music
    University of Western Australia
John Semmens
    Ballarat
Alessandro Servadei
    Grainger Museum
    University of Melbourne
Fiona Shade
    Faculty of Music
    University of Melbourne
Nikola Sharp
    Faculty of Music
    University of Melbourne
Patricia Shaw
    Department of Music
    Mercy Campus
    Australian Catholic University
Kerri-Ann Sheppard
    Tasmanian Conservatorium of Music
Michael Shmith
    Director of Communications
    Australian Ballet, Melbourne
Adrienne Simpson
    Wellington, New Zealand
Christopher Sinclair
    Melbourne
Graeme Smith
    Department of Music
    Monash University
Russell Smith
    Mount Nelson, Tasmania
Jane Southcott
    Faculty of Education
    Gippsland Campus
    Monash University
Gordon Spearritt
    Maleney, Queensland
Jessica Spiccia
    Department of Music
    University of Melbourne
Leon Stemler
    Tasmanian Conservatorium of Music
Catherine Stevens
    Faculty of Music
    University of Melbourne
Robin Stevens
    Associate Professor of Music Education
    Geelong Campus
    Deakin University

Janice Stockigt
    Australian Music Examinations Board
Helen Stowasser
    Associate Professor of Music Education
    University of Western Australia
David Swale
    Walkerville, SA
David Symons
    Department of Music
    University of Western Australia
Julja Szuster
    Department for the Arts and Cultural
        Development
    South Australia
Rachel Tew
    Brisbane
Lesleigh Thompson
    Faculty of Music
    University of Melbourne
Patricia Thorpe
    Department of Music
    University of Western Australia
Peter Tregear
    King's College
    Cambridge, UK
Demeter Tsounis
    Department of Music Studies
    University of Adelaide
J. Neville Turner
    Faculty of Law
    Monash University
Myfanwy Turpin
    Department of Linguistics
    Australian National University

William van Pinxteren
    Melbourne
Kerry Vann
    Department of Music
    University of Queensland
Richard Waterhouse
    Associate Professor of History
    University of Sydney
Eric Watson
    Selection Records
    Casino, NSW
Katrina Watson
    Faculty of Music
    University of Melbourne
Sarah Weiss
    Director
    Gamelan Kyai Kebo Giro
    University of Sydney
John Weretka
    Faculty of Music
    University of Melbourne
John Whiteoak
    La Trobe University
    Melbourne
Eric Wicks
    Melbourne
Stephen Wild
    Australian Institute of Aboriginal and
        Torres Strait Islander Studies
    Canberra
Noel Wilmott
    Department of Music
    University of Queensland

ABBREVIATIONS

1. General

Standard abbreviations are used in the text for Australian states, months of the year, and music degrees.

★ indicates that this subject is covered by a separate entry.

ABC	Australian Broadcasting Corporation (*formerly* Commission)
ACMA	Australasian Country Music Awards
AIAS	Australian Institute of Aboriginal Studies (renamed AIATSIS in 1989)
AIATSIS	Australian Institution of Aboriginal and Torres Strait Islander Studies
AMEB	Australian Music Examinations Board
AMusA	Associate in Music, Australia
ANU	Australian National University
APRA	Australasian Performing Right Association
ARIA	Australian Recording Industry Association
arr.	arranged, arranger
ASME	Australian Society for Music Education
b	born
BBC	British Broadcasting Corporation
c.	*circa*
CAAMA	Central Australian Aboriginal Media Association
CASM	Centre for Aboriginal Studies in Music
CD	compact disc
choreog.	choreographed, choreographer
Co.	Company
coll.	collector
comp.	compiled, compiler
cond.	conducted, conductor
CUP	Cambridge University Press
d	died
dir.	directed, director
ed.	edited, editor
edn	edition
EP	extended play
fl.	*floruit* (flourished)
FMusA	Fellowship in Music, Australia
ISCM	International Society for Contemporary Music
ISME	International Society for Music Education
LMusA	Licentiate in Music, Australia
LP	long play
ms(s)	manuscript(s)
MUP	Melbourne University Press
NIDA	National Institute of Dramatic Art
n.d.	no date
n.p.	no publisher/place of publication
nr	near
obit.	obituary
op.	opus
OUP	Oxford University Press
pop.	population
pub.	published
rec.	recorded
rev.	revised
SBS	Special Broadcasting Service
trad.	traditional
UNSWP	University of New South Wales Press
unpub.	unpublished
UQP	University of Queensland Press

2. Lists of Works

Where lists of musical works or recordings are given, abbreviations are used for vocal and instrumental parts.

A	alto voice
B	bass voice
Bar	baritone voice
bn	bassoon
ch	choir
cl	clarinet
Ct	countertenor voice
db	double bass
elec	electronic
ens	ensemble
fl	flute
gui	guitar
hn	horn
hp	harp
hpd	harpsichord
inst	instrument
kbd	keyboard
Mez	mezzo-soprano voice
nar	narrator
ob	oboe
orch	orchestra
org	organ
perc	percussion
pf	piano
pic	piccolo
qrt	quartet
rec	recorder
S	soprano voice
SATB	mixed chorus
sax	saxophone
str	strings
synth	synthesiser
T	tenor voice
tba	tuba
tpt	trumpet
trbn	trombone
v, vv	voice, voices
va	viola
vc	violoncello
vn	violin

3. Further Reference

In the lists of further reference, abbreviations are used for commonly cited books, journals, and libraries.

ADB
Australian Dictionary of Biography, 14+ vols, ed. John Ritchie (Melbourne: MUP, 1966–).

ADMR
Australian Directory of Music Research, ed. Philip J. Drummond (Sydney: Australia Music Centre, 1978).

AJME
Australian Journal of Music Education, 1967– .

AMN
Australian Musical News, 1911–63.

APRAJ
Australasian Performing Rights Association Journal, 1969– .

AthertonA
Atherton, Michael, *Australian Made, Australian Played: Handcrafted Musical Instruments from the Didjeridu to the Synthesiser* (Sydney: UNSWP, 1990).

BakerA
Baker, Glenn A., ed., *Australian Made: Gonna Have a Good Time Tonight* (Sydney: Fontana/Collins, 1987).

BissetB
Bisset, Andrew, *Black Roots White Flowers: A History of Jazz in Australia,* rev. edn (Sydney: ABC, 1987).

BrewerD
Brewer, F. C., *Drama and Music in NSW* (Sydney: Government Printer, 1892).

BrisbaneE
Brisbane, Katherine, ed., *Entertaining Australia: An Illustrated History* (Sydney: Currency Press, 1991).

BroadstockS
Broadstock, Brenton, *Sound Ideas: Australian Composers Born Since 1950* (Sydney: Australian Music Centre, 1995).

CallawayA
Callaway, Frank and David Tunley, *Australian Composition in the Twentieth Century* (Melbourne: OUP, 1978).

CA
Contemporary Australians 1995–96, ed. Lee White (Melbourne: Reed Reference Australia, 1995)

CAnl
Canberra, National Library of Australia.

ClareB
Clare, John, *Bodgie, Dada and the Cult of Cool* (Sydney: UNSWP, 1995).

CohenI
Cohen, Aaron I., *International Encyclopedia of Women Composers,* 2nd edn, 2 vols (New York: Books & Music, 1987).

ContemporaryC
Contemporary Composers, ed. Brian Morton and Pamela Collins (Chicago: St James Press, 1992).

CoupeN
Coupe, Stuart and Glenn A. Baker, *The New Rock'n'Roll: The A–Z of Rock in the '80s* (London: Omnibus Press, c.1983).

DPA
Dictionary of Performing Arts in Australia, 2 vols, ed. Ann Atkinson, Lindsay Knight and Margaret McPhee (Sydney: Allen & Unwin, 1996–).

EAA
Encyclopaedia of Aboriginal Australia, 2 vols, ed. David Horton (Canberra: Aboriginal Studies Press, 1994).

EdwardsG
Edwards, Ron, *Great Australian Folk Songs* (Adelaide, 1976; reprint Sydney: Ure Smith, 1991). Contains his *Index of Australian Folk Songs,* 3rd edn.

GlennonA
Glennon, James, *Australian Music and Musicians* (Adelaide: Rigby, 1968).

GroveD
New Grove Dictionary of Music and Musicians, 20 vols, ed. Stanley Sadie (London: Macmillan, 1980).

GroveI
New Grove Dictionary of Musical Instruments, 3 vols, ed. Stanley Sadie (London: Macmillan, 1984).

GroveJ
New Grove Dictionary of Jazz, 2 vols, ed. Barry Kernfeld (London: Macmillan, 1988).

GroveO
New Grove Dictionary of Opera, 4 vols, ed. Stanley Sadie (London: Macmillan, 1992).

GroveW
New Grove Dictionary of Women Composers, ed. Julie Anne Sadie and Rhian Samuel (London: Macmillan, 1994).

GuinnessP
Guinness Encyclopedia of Popular Music, 4 vols, ed. Colin Larkin (Enfield, Middlesex: Guinness Publishing, 1992).

HolmesC
Holmes, John, *Conductors On Record* (London: Gollancz, 1982).

JA
Jazz: The Australian Contemporary Music Magazine, 1981– .

JenkinsT
Jenkins, John, *Twenty-Two Contemporary Australian Composers* (Melbourne: NMA Publications, 1988).

LattaA
Latta, David, *Australian Country Music* (Sydney: Random House, 1991).

LePageW
LePage, Jane Weiner, *Women Composers, Conductors, and Musicians of the Twentieth Century: Selected Biographies,* vol. 3 (Metuchen, NJ: Scarecrow Press, 1988).

LimbacherF
Limbacher, James, ed, *Film Music from Violins to Video* (Metuchen, NJ: Scarecrow Press, 1974; *Keeping Score: Film Music 1972–1979* (Metuchen, NJ: Scarecrow Press, 1981); *Keeping Score: Film and Television Music 1980–1988,* with H. Stephen Wright (Metuchen, NJ: Scarecrow Press, 1991).

MA
Musicology Australia, 1985–; previously *Musicology,* 1964–82.

McCredieM
McCredie, Andrew D. *Musical Composition in Australia* (Canberra: Australian Government Advisory Board, 1969).

McGrathA — McGrath, Noel, *Australian Encyclopaedia of Rock and Pop* (Adelaide: Rigby, 1984).

MackenzieS — Mackenzie, Barbara and Findlay Mackenzie, *Singers of Australia from Melba to Sutherland* (Melbourne: Lansdowne Press, 1967).

ManifoldP — Manifold, John, comp., *Penguin Australian Song Book* (Ringwood, Vic.: Penguin, 1964).

MarsiI — Marsi, Lina, *Index to the Australian Musical News 1911–1963* (Melbourne: Lima Press, 1990).

MeredithF — Meredith, John and Hugh Anderson. *Folks Songs of Australia and the Men and Women Who Sang Them*, vol. 1 (Sydney, 1967; reprint Sydney: UNSWP, 1985); vol. 2, with Roger Covell and Patricia Brown (Sydney: UNSWP, 1987).

MMA — *Miscellanea Musicologica*, 1966– .

MonashB — *Monash Biographical Dictionary of 20th Century Australia*, ed. John Arnold and Deirdre Morris (Melbourne: Reed Reference Publishing, 1994).

MoresbyA — Moresby, Isabelle, *Australia Makes Music* (Melbourne: Longmans, 1948).

MoyleA — Moyle, Alice M., *Aboriginal Sound Instruments* (Canberra: AIAS, 1978).

Msl — Melbourne, State Library of Victoria.

MurdochA — Murdoch, James, *Australia's Contemporary Composers* (Melbourne: Macmillan, 1972).

OrchardM — Orchard, W. Arundel, *Music in Australia: More Than 150 Years of Development* (Melbourne: Georgian House, 1952).

OxfordF — *Oxford Companion to Australian Folklore*, ed. Gwenda Beed Davey and Graham Seal (Melbourne: OUP, 1993).

OxfordJ — *Oxford Companion to Australian Jazz* by Bruce Johnson (Melbourne: OUP, 1987).

OxfordL — *Oxford Companion to Australian Literature*, 2nd edn, ed. William H. Wilde, Joy Hooton and Barry Andrews (Melbourne: OUP, 1994).

ParsonsC — Parsons, Philip, ed., with Victoria Chance, *Companion to Theatre in Australia* (Sydney: Currency Press/CUP, 1995).

PlushD — Plush, Vincent, 'Discography of Music by Australian Composers', *Studies in Music* 6 (1972), 68–85; 7 (1973) 91–3.

PorterS — Porter, Hal, *Stars of the Australian Stage and Screen* (Adelaide: Rigby, 1965).

PVgm — Parkville, Grainger Museum, University of Melbourne.

RadicS — Radic, Thérèse, comp., *Songs of Australian Working Life* (Elwood, Vic.: Greenhouse, 1989).

RadicT — Radic, Thérèse, comp., *A Treasury of Favourite Australian Songs* (Melbourne.: Currey O'Neil, 1983).

SA — *Sounds Australian*, 1987– ; previously *Australia Music Centre Quarterly News*, 1983–84, and *AMC News*, 1984–87.

SMA — *Studies in Music*, 1967–92.

SMH — *Sydney Morning Herald*.

SmithB — Smith, Jazzer, ed., *The Book of Australian Country Music* (Sydney: BFT Publishing, 1984).

SnellA — Snell, Kenneth R., *Australian Popular Music: Composer Index* (Melbourne: Quick Trick Press, 1987).

SpencerA — Spencer, Chris, *Australian Rock Discograph* (Golden Square, Vic.: Moonlight Publishing, 1990). *Australian Rock Discography 1990–1994*. Golden Square, Vic.: Moonlight Publishing, 1995).

SpencerW — Spencer, Chris and Zbig Nowara, *Who's Who of Australian Rock*, 4th edn (Knoxfield, Vic.: Five Mile Press, 1996).

StubingtonC — Stubington, Jill, *Collecting Folk Music in Australia* (Sydney: UNSWP, 1989).

WatsonC — Watson, Eric, *Country Music in Australia*, vol. 1, 2nd rev. edn (Sydney: Rodeo Publications, 1976); vol. 2 (Sydney: Cornstalk Publishing, 1983).

WilliamsA — Williams, Mike, *The Australian Jazz Explosion* (Sydney: Angus & Robertson, 1981).

WWA — *Who's Who in Australia* 32nd edn (Melbourne: Information Australia, 1996).

A

A. The note universally used in tuning instruments, internationally standardised at *a'*=440 Hz in 1939. Tuning forks brought to Australia by bandsmen in the 1820s have yet to be studied, but English organs installed at Hobart and Sydney in the 1840s seem to have had a pitch about a quarter-tone below the present standard. It is not likely that Australia was much affected by the widespread European application of the *diapason normal* (*a'* =435) from 1859. The Hill & Son, London, organs found in Australian town halls and cathedrals in the 1890s used a higher pitch (up to *a'* =452), which would have brightened many oratorio performances and recitals; indeed, the Sydney Town Hall instrument installed in 1890 proved too high for the local instrumentalists and could not be comfortably used with an orchestra until adjusted in 1903. The opera orchestras were evidently closer to European practice, although the *Quinlan Opera Co. brought its own organ in 1912 to accommodate the 'new low pitch' they preferred.

ABC Concerto Competition. See *ABC Instrumental and Vocal Competition*.

ABC Countdown Awards. Rock music awards (1979–87) made by the ABC TV rock music program *Countdown*. With divisions for awards by the industry and by popular vote, the categories gradually increased to over 17, including songwriters, performers, producers, videos, albums, album-cover designers, international artists, and new talent. See *Awards*.

ABC Instrumental and Vocal Competition. Eminent national solo performance contest funded by the ABC. Its origins are in a concerto competition Bernard *Heinze ran in Victoria from 1940, using the Melbourne Symphony Orchestra to accompany the finalists; from 1944 ABC Concerto Competitions were held in each state, and from 1950 the state winners competed in a Commonwealth final. From 1968 the competition was divided into instrumental and vocal divisions and renamed the ABC Concerto and Vocal Competitions

(later Instrumental and Vocal Competition); a section for the ACT was added in 1978; and the instrumental division was divided into keyboard, orchestral strings and other instrument sections in 1982. From 1988 it was renamed the *Young Performers' Award. Early Commonwealth winners included singers Neil Warren-Smith, Nance Grant, and Yvonne Minton, pianists Max Olding and Roger Woodward, and violinist Charmian Gadd, but the competition has acquired such prestige that the winning of a state section final can also prove a powerful catalyst to a performer's career.

ABC News Theme. The orchestral fanfare *Majestic Fanfares* by Charles Williams (in its original or a reorchestrated version by Richard Mills) has been used as the theme to introduce national ABC radio news since 1952.

Aboriginal Islander Dance Theatre (AIDT). Sydney-based contemporary dance company specialising in repertoire influenced by Australian indigenous dance and cultures; dancers are drawn from the National Aboriginal and Islander Skills Development Association (NAISDA) College. Active since 1976, AIDT was formally launched as a professional performing company in 1991 under the directorship of Raymond Blanco, and has made extensive national and international tours, including to Asia, Europe, South America and the UK.

P. DUNBAR-HALL

Aboriginal Music.
1. Origins and Traditional Culture. 2. Music in Traditional Culture. 3. Structure of Traditional Music. 4. Contemporary Music and Musical Culture. 5. Conclusion.

1. Origins and Traditional Culture. The Australian Aborigines are now considered by prehistorians to have occupied the continent of Australia for at least 40 000 years. Until about 8000 years ago, the continental land mass included New Guinea and Tasmania. The geographical separation of New Guinea and Australia and the later migration of Austronesian-speaking people into Melanesia eventually resulted in a cultural division, although human contact was maintained via the inhabitants of the Torres Strait Islands. The Aboriginal culture of Tasmania, separated from the mainland by a much longer stretch of open ocean with few intervening islands, diverged from mainland culture over the intervening 8000 years to the extent that for long the question of a different or the same origin of the Tasmanians was a major issue in Australian prehistory.

Australian Aborigines were hunter-gatherers; that is, they neither domesticated plants nor herded animals, and they were unable to maintain large stable concentrations of population over most of the continent. The typical local organisation consisted of semi-nomadic bands of several closely related families which occasionally coalesced into larger gatherings for ceremonial and general social purposes. Despite many cultural similarities throughout the continent, Australian Aboriginal society developed regional differences due to several factors of which environmental variation was no doubt important. Because of its long isolation from the mainland, Tasmanian Aboriginal culture had some distinctive features, for example in stone tool technology and, according to Alice M. *Moyle, in songs (preserved in some of the earliest Australian sound recordings). However, Tasmanian Aboriginal culture was an early victim of European invasion and little is known about earlier forms of social organisation, religion and language there. Similarly, the Aboriginal cultures of south-eastern and south-western mainland Australia, the areas of the earliest and most intense European settlement, were severely disrupted during the nineteenth century. Most reliable information on Aboriginal culture prior to the European invasion relates to the northern and central regions of the country.

The most common estimate of the number of languages spoken in Australia in 1788 is between 200 and 250, most of them probably descended from a single parent language. In addition to everyday spoken languages, special forms of language are used in communication between particular categories of kin (for example between mother-in-law and son-in-law), in certain kinds of ritual contexts (for example between novices and their ritual guardians), in speech-making, and in songs.

There is enough similarity of basic religious concepts and practices among Australian Aborigines for R.M. and C.H. Berndt to write of 'one religion, with different, independent, local "churches"'. The central concept of Aboriginal religion is usually translated as 'the Dreaming', a spiritual dimension of existence lying beyond and determining the features of the physical, biological and social world. It is populated by spirit beings which are named after and have the prototypical characteristics of categories of phenomena in the material world, for example of rain, species of trees, rocks, species of animals, species of plants, and humans of particular sex, age, and ritual statuses. These spirit beings are associated with tracks across the countryside, and with sacred sites located at points

along the tracks where they paused to rest, to carry out activities full of significance for the material world, and to deposit spiritual power. Sometimes a spirit being stayed and was metamorphosed at such a site, and can be seen today as a rocky outcrop, a hill, a stand of trees, or some other notable natural feature.

The Dreaming is activated in the material world by ritual action, which is seen as imperative to maintain the continuity of life. There is a similarity of types of religious rites across all of Aboriginal society. Rites performed primarily for the purpose of maintaining fertility of the country and of society, usually referred to as 'increase rites', are traditionally among the most common and perhaps the most often performed. Initiation rites, especially for boys, are performed in all Aboriginal societies and in some areas are the most elaborate rites. Rites associated with death (mortuary rites) are often performed some years after the death of a person and their purpose is primarily to assist the spirit of the deceased to find its resting place with the spirits of previously deceased Ancestors. Cult ceremonies are innovative and often integrative and give rise to deities transcending local concerns; they attract allegiance over a wider area than other rites, but they wax and wane over a finite period of time. There is a class of rites that are so specifically instrumental in their purpose that they may be referred to as 'magical.' These include magical rites to attract a person of the opposite sex ('love magic'), rites to induce rain, rites to heal, and rites to ensorcel. There are rites to manage conflict, such as rites of diplomacy between neighbouring groups and rites to ease tension between kin whose relationship involves inherent conflict. Finally, some rituals have public entertainment as their main purpose; these are commonly called corroborees after the Aboriginal name given to such rites in the original language spoken around Sydney.

2. Music in Traditional Culture. (i) Sources of Music. As a general rule, all innovation is believed to belong to the Dreaming Ancestors who created songs, dances, visual designs, ceremonies and ceremonial objects which were at the same time a celebration of and the means of sustaining the creation. Songs are not merely 'made with the brain' (as non-Aboriginal songs are said by Aboriginal people to be) but are direct communications of the Ancestors.

Most songs in the Aboriginal repertoire are said to have been handed to the first people by the Ancestors, and subsequently to have been handed down through the generations. But 'new' songs may be added to the repertoire by the spirits of recently deceased kin or by other, non-genealogical, spirits. Usually new songs are taught by a spirit to a person while he or she is removed from social life, such as when a person is sick, or asleep, or merely camping apart from the rest of the community.

New songs often refer to historical events and figures in the recent past, although they are couched in similar language and musical structure to old songs, and they may be identified with particular ancestral figures. In central

Australia these songs die with their receiver and they must be newly received by close kin of the deceased. In the process of being received again, the original historical references become more distant and begin to take on a mythical quality. In two regions at least, the Kimberley region of north-west Australia and the ★Tiwi region of Melville and Bathurst Islands off the coast of Arnhem Land, the predominant belief that new songs are created spiritually does not hold. In the Kimberleys, according to A. Moyle, some songs are believed to have been 'made with the brain', that is, made up by human beings, while according to Andrée Grau, the Tiwi believe all songs are created by human beings, not by ancestral spirits, and there is strong encouragement for everyone to participate in song-making. It is possible that in south-eastern Australia also, some songs were believed to be created by living human beings, since extant songs quite directly address historical events.

Whatever the ultimate relationship between new songs and old songs, they tend to be dichotomised at any particular time. Called *purlapa* among the Warlpiri Aborigines of central Australia and *inma* among the Pitjantjatjara of the Western Desert, new songs are open to all: men and women, adults and children, Aboriginal and non-Aboriginal may at least listen to them. In the case of the Warlpiri, *purlapa* are the only songs that men and women sing together. By contrast, songs that are believed to have been handed down directly from the Ancestors are surrounded by restrictions: they may be sung and some even heard only by the members of one sex, and uninitiated children may not hear the most restricted songs. In central and eastern Arnhem Land the dichotomisation of old and new songs takes on a different character. The whole society is divided into two named moieties, one of which has responsibility for new songs, so that in its repertoire are found songs about diesel-powered motor boats, introduced food and introduced plants and animals. In the other moiety's repertoire are found songs only about items which existed before European settlement.

(ii) Sacred and Secular Music.

In central Australia and the Western Desert all songs have religious reference and sources. However, a hierarchy of sacredness may be said to exist, with some songs closer to being secular than others. Sociologically, sacredness has to do with being set apart from ordinary life and being endowed with mystery and awe. Thus songs which are least bounded with restrictions on their performance—for example Warlpiri *purlapa*—are the most secular, and those surrounded with the most stringent restrictions—for example cult songs and some initiation songs —are the most sacred. Some song types belong between these two extremes, generally those which may by heard by members of the opposite sex but not performed by them. In some cases songs of the intermediate types may be sung by men and accompanied by women's dancing. In central and eastern Arnhem Land, songs about topical events and gossip songs are closer to the Western concept of secular songs. Although they are received from spirits and their poetic imagery is borrowed from the more sacred clan songs (*manikay*), their relationship with the spiritual world is tenuous.

(iii) Women's and Men's Music.

Ritual life in central Australia and the Western Desert tends to be more segregated than in most regions of Australia. Women have a rich ceremonial life with their own sacred sites, ancestral Dreaming tracks, myths, songs, dances and visual designs. With the advent of European settlement on their land, it appears that women's ceremonial life may have suffered greater disruption than men's, although undoubtedly both men and women were forced to modify and reconstruct traditions. Women and men each have a strong and largely independent ceremonial tradition: except for songs performed by members of both sexes together (e.g. Warlpiri *purlapa*), neither a man nor a woman would dare to sing the songs belonging to the other sex in public.

Central Australia and the Western Desert contrast quite markedly with both Arnhem Land and the Tiwi Aborigines of Melville and Bathurst Islands in this respect. In Arnhem Land, men have a virtual monopoly on the performance of songs. The only song-like expression exclusively reserved for women consists of crying songs performed on the death of kin. Crying songs use the words of the clan songs performed by specialist male singers, but the pitch and rhythmic structures are entirely different and the occasions on which they may be performed are narrowly restricted to mourning. Women's performance role within ceremonial life is largely restricted to dancing, while men sing, make ceremonial designs and sculptures, and dance. In contrast, Tiwi women and men perform equally, according to Grau, and there is virtually no sexual segregation in ceremonial life. Tiwi women and Tiwi men are both composers of new songs and creators of new dances.

(iv) Children's Music.

If universally adults make music, so too, children universally imitate them. A relevant question, however, is whether adults recognise children's musical imitations as music. Among the Warlpiri Aborigines, for example, groups of children perform what an outside observer would probably recognise as music; that is, they have recognisable melodies and song texts and the singing is accompanied by some kind of percussive rhythm. On a superficial level the children's 'music' is similar to, though a simplified version of, that of adults in the community. However, adult members of the Warlpiri community do not recognise children's performances as music. One reason for this is that children's music does not have a spiritual origin and is merely made up by children. The situation is quite different in north-east Arnhem Land, where Richard Waterman noted that children are the most prolific of song composers, and the songs are believed by adults to have their source in the Dreaming. Clearly here, songs created by children are included in the adult conception of music.

Margaret *Kartomi has distinguished between three kinds of children's music: music created by children, music created by adults for performance by children, and music created by adults for performance to children. Although Warlpiri children create and perform their own music (unrecognised by adults as music), adults do not create music specifically for children to perform or specifically for performance by adults to children. It may be that children do perform songs created by adults which they hear at open ceremonies, and that some adults sing songs to children, for example to put them to sleep. But in the case of the Warlpiri it would be erroneous to classify such songs as 'songs for children' or 'lullabies', for they are not their primary purposes and they are not classified by the Warlpiri in this way.

The Pitjantjatjara of the Western Desert, however, do have songs created by adults specifically for children, who perform them in play ceremonies (*tjitjiku inma*) imitative of adult ceremonies. Later, when the boys have grown up, they learn and perform the adult versions of these songs. Also among the Pitjantjatjara, both women and men sing songs to lull their children to sleep; these songs are said to be structurally more like women's songs than men's, although they are performed in a distinctive 'lullaby' style. A similar phenomenon has been reported among other Aboriginal language communities.

3. Structure of Traditional Music. (i) Sound Components.
Australian Aboriginal music is mainly a vocal tradition, but there are few musical occasions which do not include some kind of non-vocal sound component. Torres Strait Islanders played jew's harp, panpipes, and notched flute as solo instruments, but their music is no longer regularly heard.

Of the four main classes of musical instruments in the Sachs/Hornbostel system of classification—idiophones, membranophones, aerophones and chordophones—only the first three occur in Aboriginal Australia. Idiophones, the sound produced by the vibrating body of the instrument itself, are the most ubiquitous. Clapsticks of one kind or another accompanied singing throughout the continent in the past and still do where these traditions are intact. The rhythmic sound is produced usually by clapping two sticks together, one held in each hand. The most distinctively Australian variant is the clapping together of the tips of two boomerangs, each held at its centre and struck against each other by rotating the wrists in opposite directions. Clapsticks are played in several widely distributed rhythmic patterns, such as evenly spaced clicks at either fast or slow speeds, pairs of clicks separated by a rest, or three evenly spaced clicks followed by a rest. A tremolo effect is created by rapidly repeated striking together of sticks and requires considerable manual dexterity, particularly with paired boomerangs. Other idiophones include a rasp (a notched stick rubbed rhythmically by another stick) played in the north-west of the country, and a seed-pod rattle held one in each hand by dancers in Cape York Peninsula and Torres Strait.

Membranophones, the sound produced by the vibration of a stretched membrane, occur only on Cape York Peninsula and the Torres Strait Islands. Drums in the Torres Strait are of the Papuan type—long-waisted, made from a single piece of wood, a snake-skin membrane at one end and open at the other end. The membrane is struck by hand, the drum held horizontally, in a series of regular beats or rolls. Drumming on the mainland opposite was almost certainly derived from the Torres Strait, and is today mainly used in contemporary 'Island' music (see below).

The outstanding example of an aerophone in Australia is the didjeridu, a wooden or bamboo trumpet measuring usually one to one and a half metres in length. The tradition of didjeridu playing belonged mainly to the central and western north coast of Australia, from Arnhem Land in the Northern Territory to the Kimberley district in the north of Western Australia. A bamboo type is made by burning out the sectional membranes of a length of bamboo, while a wooden instrument is made of a tree branch hollowed out first by termites and finished off by the maker. The basic sound is produced by holding the tube to the mouth and buzzing the lips. The sound can be modified by varying the shape of the mouth cavity, by tonguing techniques, by changing the wind pressure, by tightening the lips to produce a higher pitch, and by combining it with a variety of vocal sounds produced by the player. All of these techniques are used to create a remarkable range of different sounds which may be put together in dazzling displays of rhythm and tone colour. Other aerophones have been reported in Australia but none are now extant.

Aboriginal musical performances often include several sound components, including body percussion—handclapping, lap-slapping, buttocks-slapping—and other sounds produced by both singers and dancers—ritual calls, lip vibrations, ululations, grunts, shouts, and the abrasive rustling of eucalyptus branches tied to the dancers' legs—as well as the vocal and instrumental sounds described above. By no means all of these sounds are used at the one time, but as in other areas of their lives Australian Aborigines exhibit a remarkable ability to create variety from limited means.

(ii) Central Australia and the Western Desert.
Knowledge of the structure of traditional songs is mainly based on the songs of central and northern Australia, since the sample of traditional songs from southern Australia, particularly south-eastern and south-western Australia, is too limited. Evidence indicates, however, that traditional songs from most parts of Australia occurred in series, although recordings of songs from south-eastern Australia appear to indicate that each song may have existed as an independent entity.

The song structure of central Australia and the Western Desert is the classic case. Terminology needs clarification if misunderstanding and confusion are to be avoided. A song is an abstract construct consisting of a melodic contour, a text, a rhythmic pattern to which the text is sung, a rhythmic accompaniment, and rules of performance. In central Australia, however, the outcomes on any two occasions may be rather more different than in Western music. The important point is that a number of songs are conceptually, textually, musically and in performance linked together in a series. All of the song texts in a series relate to the same Dreaming, or to a single ancestral spirit or several closely linked ancestral spirits, and the series is known by the name of the Dreaming. Thus there are Kangaroo song series, Rain song series and Boomerang song series, named after the Kangaroo Ancestor, the Rain Ancestor and the Boomerang Ancestor respectively. All songs in the same song series have the same melodic contour, so that a song series is known by at least the common melodic contour and the closely related texts. The number of songs in a series varies, but it is not uncommon for a single series to have more than a hundred songs.

The songs of a song series follow the travelling of an ancestral Spirit. As the Ancestor travelled it created sites (e.g. a rocky outcrop, or a lake, or a stand of trees) and then sang about them to create the present song series. In the performance of the series, the songs should be sung in the order in which the Ancestor created them; that is, the songs follow the ancestral track. Some Ancestors travelled across language borders, so that different language communities may share the same song series, creating spiritual ties between them. The language of the texts may also change across linguistic boundaries, although because song words are often both archaic and arcane it is usually of little practical consequence.

Each song has a fixed text with the words sung in a fixed order. There is often repetition of segments of the text such as *aabb* or *abb*, each segment consisting of several words. The text, and each part of the text (word or segment), is set to a fixed rhythm so that one may refer to a textual/rhythmic pattern. The rhythm consists of a sequence of long and short durations usually with a long duration on the last syllable of each word. The complete textual/rhythmic pattern of a song is repeated cyclically several times during the performance of the song until the melody is completed. An example of a textual/rhythmic pattern is as follows:

waluwalulaa laangkangkarraa
waluwalulaa laangkangkarraa
wanirri ngayingnyangkarraa
wanirri ngayingnyangkarraa

(Warlpiri Yam *purlapa* from central Australia. A double vowel represents a long duration, a single vowel a short duration. All of the short durations are of the same length, the long durations vary in length. A loose translation of the text is:

At a rocky water hole the Ancestors are decorated
with ritual fluff from the head down
[in preparation for dancing].)

That is: *aabb*. Linda Barwick identified the common types of melodic contour as follows:

1. A single descent, ranging from a fifth to an octave, preceded by a short introduction around the highest tone of the descent and a coda around the lowest tone of the descent.
2. A double descent bounded by an introduction and a coda.
3. A series of descents bounded by an introduction and a coda, each descent separated by a transitional section similar to the introduction.
4. A series of double descents bounded by an introduction and a coda, each double descent separated by a transitional section.

In the case of double descents, one is usually more elaborated than the other and is referred to as the main descent.

It is establishing the rules of matching the melodic contour with the textual/rhythmic pattern that most occupies the minds of ethnomusicologists. Different textual/rhythmic patterns vary in total duration, and the number of times a particular textual/rhythmic pattern is repeated in a song varies from one performance to another. These two facts mean that the melodic contour is compressed or expanded to accommodate the varying total durations of repeated textual/rhythmic patterns. Further, a song performance may begin at different points in the rhythmic/textual pattern, for example the first performance of the pattern may be *aabb* or *abba* or *bbaa* or *baab* depending on where in the pattern the singing begins. Since performances are usually by groups of singers, how is this all accomplished?

The first relevant fact in understanding how the textual/rhythmic pattern is matched with the melodic contour is that each performance has a song-leader who establishes where in the textual/rhythmic pattern the performance will begin by beginning the singing; at critical points in the song performance, particularly the beginnings of descents, the song-leader leads the other singers. However, the matching is not only dependent on the choices of the song-leader since there are constraints within which these choices are made. It became clear mainly through the work of ethnomusicologist Catherine *Ellis that it was in the descent, or the main descent in the case of double descents, where the matching principles were the most crucial. However, Guy Tunstill described different principles operating in different song series. For example, the main descent may be sung over a complete rhythmic/textual pattern plus one unit (or word) in all the songs of one song series, but in another it may be sung over a fixed number of words irrespective of the number of words in particular songs. Even different performances of the same song may follow different principles, highlighting different structural features of the textual/rhythmic pattern. Indeed the matching of melodic and textual/rhythmic aspects of central Australian song in performance demands a sophisticated understanding of and creativity within the complex structure of these seemingly simple musical entities.

(iii) Arnhem Land and north-western Australia. Arnhem Land may be defined as the whole of the central northern peninsula of the continent, or as that part (approximately the eastern half) of the peninsula that was set aside as Aboriginal reserve land and is now freehold Aboriginal land under the *Land Rights (Northern Territory) Act 1976*. Aboriginal Arnhem Land has at least two (and Jill Stubington argued three) distinct musical styles: eastern Arnhem Land style, western Arnhem Land style, and (if a third is accepted) central Arnhem Land style. The central style is closer to the eastern style than to the western style. The western style extends beyond Aboriginal-owned Arnhem Land and even further west than Arnhem Land in the broadest sense into the Kimberley region; Alan Marett has referred to this musical region as 'north-western Australia'.

It is convenient to begin with the central Arnhem Land style. As in central Australia, songs are organised into song series, called here *manikay*, which are sung at initiation ceremonies, mortuary ceremonies, ceremonies of diplomacy or gift exchange, or merely for entertainment, usually at night. *Manikay* may also accompany dancing. Each *manikay* is named and is owned by a clan or a consortium of clans. A single clan may own more than one *manikay*, but unlike the case in central Australia, each *manikay* celebrates a number of ancestral beings or subjects. When a *manikay* is performed, several verses of each subject (or ancestral being) are normally sung before the singer progresses to the next subject. The number of subjects in a single *manikay* varies between about 20 and 40. Again unlike central Australia, where songs are normally performed by a group of singers, in central Arnhem Land songs are normally sung by one singer who is a specialist in that particular *manikay*. The singer accompanies himself with clapsticks and is accompanied by a didjeridu player.

The concept of a song is even more problematic here. Each subject consists of a repertoire of musical and textual phrases, a set of clapstick patterns, and didjeridu patterns. Within certain constraints, the singer creates a musical item from these phrases and patterns, while for the next item of the same subject he will use different phrases to emphasise different aspects of the subject. Each item may be thought of as a verse of the subject, 'verse' here only having meaning within a particular performance, since in no two performances will the verses be the same.

Each verse consists of at least two parts and sometimes three. Part 1 is an introduction performed by the singer with clapsticks and introducing the subject to be sung and the tempo in which it will be sung. Part 2 is the main part, performed by the singer with clapsticks, and accompanied by the didjeridu which imitates the rhythmic patterns of the vocal melody. Melodically, part 2 consists of a series of sections separated by rests, a refrain, and a terminating pattern. The refrain effectively divides the main part into

two. Part 3, which is not performed in every verse, is an unaccompanied vocal coda sung unmetrically.

The verses of a subject are identifiable textually and musically (melodically, rhythmically, by clapstick patterns, by didjeridu patterns, by refrains and by terminating figures). However, Clunies Ross and ★Wild, and Anderson showed that they vary according to whether or not they are accompanied by dancing, to the kind of dancing they accompany, and to the ceremonial context in which they are performed, as well as to other variables.

In eastern Arnhem Land, songs are also organised into series, also called *manikay*. Here, however, *manikay* are often not named except by reference to the name of the owning clan and the kind of environment the songs are about, for example, forest, freshwater or saltwater. Whereas in central Arnhem Land each *manikay* has songs about several environments (sea and land songs are commonly identified), in eastern Arnhem Land a single *manikay* concerns only a single environment. Although the overall form of *manikay* is the same in central and eastern Arnhem Land, in the latter several occurrences of the refrain divide the verse into a multipartite structure rather than a bipartite structure as in central Arnhem Land. Melodically, the central Arnhem Land style is freer and often has a wider range than the eastern Arnhem Land style, but in the latter there is a greater variety of stick patterns and the didjeridu playing is much more virtuosic. The subjects of an eastern Arnhem Land *manikay* seem to be less well defined and less stable, each performance of a verse being more like a new composition than is the case in central Arnhem Land. In summary, Stubington showed that eastern Arnhem land and central Arnhem Land musical styles are similar but show differences in the details of organisation.

In western Arnhem Land, or north-western Australia, the nearest equivalent genres to *manikay* include *gunborg* and *wangga*. These are public genres and are used for essentially the same purposes as *manikay* (e.g. initiation ceremonies, mortuary ceremonies, public entertainments). But they are individually owned rather than clan-owned, and are received from the same kinds of spirits as are *purlapa* in Central Australia. The tradition of song specialists (or 'songmen' as they are always traditionally men), which was noted in central and eastern Arnhem Land, appears to be more developed in western Arnhem Land. As well as singing for ceremonies and for entertainment, a songman may command a troupe of dancers and supporting musicians (didjeridu players and clapstick players). Songmen trade song series between themselves.

Recent work on *wangga* by Marett indicates that the equivalent of a song series consists of the songs received from a spirit by a single songman over a period of time which are currently in his repertoire. The individual songs are melodically more elaborate than in central and eastern Arnhem Land, formally sectionalised with instrumental interludes (clapsticks and didjeridu), and relatively fixed. There are frequently more than one pair of clapsticks, played by other than the singer, accompanying the singing and playing different interlocking rhythms. Song texts sometimes consist of burden syllables only, other song texts consist of words used in everyday speech, while still others are a mixture of burden syllables and ordinary words. Unlike central and eastern Arnhem Land where the fundamental tone and an overtone about a tenth above the fundamental are alternated, only the fundamental tone of the didjeridu is used in western Arnhem Land, the rhythmic interest being sustained by variations in volume, tonguing techniques and differences in coloration.

In comparing these three regional styles in Arnhem Land and north-western Australia, it seems clear that the western tradition and the eastern tradition are the two extremes, and the central tradition, while being more closely identified with the eastern, is nonetheless transitional between east and west. It is in the east that the dazzling didjeridu technique has been developed and perfected, while in central Arnhem Land the didjeridu technique is far less impressive and more like the western style. But in central Arnhem Land the melody is more developed, although not as well developed as in western Arnhem Land and north-western Australia. Composition and formal repeatable structure is much more closely approximated in the western tradition than in the eastern, where creativity is focused on improvisation within a very loose framework. In central Arnhem Land, form and the framework of improvisation are much more defined and fixed than in eastern Arnhem Land, although not as much as in western Arnhem Land and north-western Australia. It is noteworthy that songmen in central Arnhem Land often also sing in the western Arnhem Land style.

(iv) Cape York Peninsula. Western and eastern Cape York musical styles appear to be quite different. In western Cape York, A. Moyle distinguished three broad song types: clan songs, shake-a-leg songs, and Island songs. Island songs (or Island music) are a contemporary genre shared with Torres Strait Islanders (see §4(i) below). Clan songs and shake-a-leg songs are sacred and secular songs respectively to the extent that a sacred and secular division can be maintained.

Among the clan songs, which will be discussed first, two main traditions have been documented: *apalach* (or *apledj*) and *wanam*, which concern clan territories north and south of the Kendall River respectively. The musical styles of the two are similar. As elsewhere, individual clan songs belong to series, each series recounting stories of Ancestors who created the country and laid down the patterns of life and culture. The two series (*apalach* and *wanam*) contain songs whose texts are in the several languages belonging to the owning clans. The specialist singers sing in all languages of the series and about the territories of all the owning clans, without having to seek the permission of the clan owners. J. von Sturmer has suggested that the powerful position of specialist singers is related to the supra-clan political organisation of the region, and it is almost certainly related to the 'big man'

complex here whereby political allegiance is courted by politically ambitious and able operators. Gifted dancers are also highly valued.

The music itself is characterised by a narrow vocal range, generally two tones a second apart or even in some cases an inflected monotone. Musical interest is maintained by performance of a range of non-melodic sounds which accompany and punctuate the vocal melody: handclapping, paired sticks beaten together, boomerang clapsticks, shouts, cries, growls, foot-stamping, high-pitched and piercing calls. The singer is assisted by others in producing these non-melodic sounds. The melody is characteristically divided into short sections of only a few seconds each, terminated by sequences of calls, shouts and so forth. Women's songs are narrow ranged and unaccompanied. Women also performing 'crying songs', which are embellished and extended melodic figures, hummed at a relatively high pitch. Because of the narrow melodic range of the singing, A. Moyle has suggested that these songs are part of a broader musical region that includes eastern Arnhem Land on the other side of the Gulf of Carpentaria. The tradition of song specialists might be another feature that the two areas have in common.

Shake-a-leg songs are essentially dance-songs performed by male singers young and old. Like *wangga* in western Arnhem Land, they are individually owned, and are bartered and exchanged over considerable distances. The songs vary considerably in range and melodic structure. The beat is always clearly marked, sometimes reinforced by beating a skin drum, or by beating a metal drum with sticks, or by hitting together paired boomerang clapsticks. A. Moyle wrote of these dances:

The climax of the dance, which consists of jumping and bounding with quivering limbs, comes at the conclusion of each dancer's individual entry into the ring. At this point there is an increase in the tempo of jumping and of the loud and rhythmic expirations of breath by the rest of the group.

In eastern Cape York, in the rainforest region around the town of Cairns, songs have a melodic range of between a fifth and an octave. According to G. Koch, song texts are made up of lines of equal numbers of syllables, concluded either by a vocal rest or an identifying syllable such as *nga* or *dang*. The vocal rests divide the song into melodic sections of unequal lengths, consisting of different numbers of lines. Songs have fixed texts, although different song performances are begun on different text lines. Songs are organised into series, each song having the same melody. Singing is accompanied by paired sticks.

4. Contemporary Music and Musical Culture. (i) Island Music. When the London Missionary Society first descended upon the Torres Strait Islanders in 1871 they brought with them preachers from the Loyalty Islands, and in a second wave in the 1890s from Samoa and Niue. Frowning upon the traditional songs and dances of the Torres Strait Islanders and learning from their success in suppressing local music and dance traditions in the rest of the Pacific, the missionaries encouraged the adoption of the Pacific Islands style of vocal music, which is a mixture of Protestant hymn style and local Polynesian music. Probably a local Torres Strait Islands traditional component was added to create a distinctive variant of Pacific Islands music. From the Torres Strait, Island music, as it became known, was introduced to Cape York Peninsula Aboriginal communities.

Island music consists of group singing with an accompaniment on guitar or ukulele, skin drum, sometimes a metal container such as a flour drum struck with sticks, hand-clapping and sometimes seed-pod rattles, held by the dancers who usually perform with the singers and instrumentalists. The range of the melody often exceeds an octave, the scale is generally diatonic, and the voices sing in triadic harmony. However, according to M. Hata, there are distinctive features which distinguish it from European Protestant hymns. The harmony generally consists of the three basic chords tonic, dominant and subdominant, but the parts often move in parallel octaves, fourths and fifths, the seventh note of the diatonic scale often lacks the function of a leading note, the fourth note of the scale is often augmented, the harmony may be above or below the melody, and cadences characteristically end on the tonic unison, tonic octaves or the tonic chord lacking the third. (See *Torres Strait*.)

On Cape York, a clear distinction is made between traditional Aboriginal music ('old payten' songs) and Island music. The term 'old payten' is thought to be derived from the English 'old-fashioned.' Another variant is 'old paintin' songs, thought to refer to the fact that the bodies of the dancers accompanying traditional Aboriginal singing are painted with Dreaming designs. The dancers accompanying Island singing are not painted with designs but wear a distinctive costume. 'Old payten' songs are either permanently in the repertoire, handed down from the Dreaming, or pre-existent songs received from Ancestors, as elsewhere in Australia. Island songs, on the other hand, are consciously 'thought up' or composed in the Western sense. Unlike the case of 'old payten' songs, the music accompanying Island songs may be sung by the dancers as well as by the instrumental musicians and the audience. Island music and dance are most commonly performed at public ceremonies such as house openings, sports days and other public festivals. An element of rivalry in performances among teams of dancers has been reported to occur at Lockhart River on west Cape York. P. Black and G. Koch wrote: 'Each team is named from a mythological figure associated with initiation ceremonies, and each has its own practice area, song repertoire and dance stories.' Songs are owned by individual teams, composed by a living composer or handed down patrilineally.

(ii) *Christian Music.* Christianity has been a major force in the lives of generations of the indigenous peoples of Australia, and Christian music has been an important part of their musical experience. The most characteristic Christian music performed by Aboriginal people consists of fundamentalist, evangelical Protestant songs commonly called 'gospel music'. Today, Aboriginal gospel music ranges from choral music performed by Aboriginal choirs in the remotest communities of central Australia to solo songs with guitar accompaniment sung in rural areas of eastern Australia. Examples of the former have been issued commercially on a compact cassette by Imparja Records, a subsidiary of CAAMA, as 'Aboriginal Choirs of central Australia' in which six central Australian community choirs are represented. Most, but not all, of the songs have Christian themes. An example of the latter is represented on a compact cassette called 'Today's the Day' which consists of Christian songs sung by Aboriginal singer Tim Edwards.

Traditional Aboriginal music has also been harnessed to express Christian themes. In central Australian Warlpiri Aboriginal communities, a genre called 'Jesus *purlapa*' has emerged. Christian texts in Warlpiri language have been set to traditional music by Warlpiri Christians. The songs have been created in series, for example the Christmas *purlapa*, Easter *purlapa* and Creed *purlapa*. They are sung by groups of singers, men and women together, accompanied by the playing of boomerang clapsticks by the male singers and by body percussion produced by the women. Dances may also accompany the singing of Jesus *purlapa*, the bodies of the dancers being painted and decorated in traditional style. Shields painted with Christian motifs are carried by the dancers.

(iii) *Popular Music.* There have been three phases of Aboriginal adoption of introduced genres of popular music. In the first phase, in the nineteenth century, Aboriginal people of rural eastern Australia adopted the popular song styles (and dances) introduced from the British Isles (English, Scottish and Irish) whence most early European settlers came. The Australian repertoire developed a character of its own and became known as 'bush music'. Characteristically, the singing was accompanied by button accordion, fiddle and harmonica. As shown by C. Sullivan, while most bush music eventually retreated to the urban folk music clubs as a specialist interest, Aboriginal people continued to perform it as a popular genre in rural areas right up to the present day.

The second phase of Aboriginal adoption of introduced popular music occurred in the twentieth century with the universal popularisation of American country music. Country music, predominantly accompanied by guitar played by the singer, was adopted enthusiastically in rural Australia as a symbol of country life, particularly of cattle and sheep grazing. Aboriginal workers played a major role in the development of the Australian pastoral industry, and country music held a natural attraction for Aboriginal musicians. An early Aboriginal composer of country music was Dougie ★Young, who lived in western New South Wales and was recorded and brought to the attention of a wider audience in the 1950s by J. Beckett. His songs expressed in a self-mocking way the painful and hopeless experiences of Aboriginal people in rural towns where discrimination against them was pervasive. Themes of the songs included getting drunk, being in and out of jail frequently, chronic unemployment, and unstable relationships. Country music is still very popular among rural Aboriginal people.

The third phase of the Aboriginal adoption of introduced popular genres of music was the use of various forms of urban youth music—rock and reggae in particular. This came about with the increasing urbanisation of the Aboriginal population in the last few decades. Rock music and especially Jamaican-derived reggae are the medium of expression of frustration and anger which urban Aboriginal youth experience acutely, with the prevalence of cultural confusion and alienation, poor education, unemployment and poverty. Reggae appeals to urban Aboriginal youth because of its associations with international Black solidarity, and a number of Aboriginal reggae bands emerged during the 1980s. Another form of Jamaican popular music—calypso—has been adopted by an Aboriginal band *Kuckles based in the north-west coastal town of Broome. This band and its music provided the basis of the first Aboriginal musical *Bran Nue Dae* which premiered at the Perth Festival in early 1990 and was subsequently performed in other major cities around the country. The most recent and most stunning success among Aboriginal rock bands has been *Yothu Yindi. Based in north-east Arnhem Land, Yothu Yindi's music is perhaps the most successful fusion yet of Western popular music and traditional Aboriginal music.

Two institutions have played a major role in the recent development of Aboriginal popular music—the Centre for Aboriginal Studies in Music (CASM) and the Central Australian Aboriginal Media Association (CAAMA). CASM was established in 1975 within the University of Adelaide and was originally intended as a music school for urban Aboriginal youth in SA. It has subsequently become a national institution. Its curriculum includes traditional Aboriginal musical performance from central Australia (taught by singers from remote communities), Western musical performance, and theoretical, historical and ethnomusicological courses. Some early rock and reggae bands emerged from this centre, and it has been a continuing source of training for Aboriginal musicians. CAAMA had a humble beginning in Alice Springs c.1980 with the broadcasting of a weekly radio program to the town's large Aboriginal community. A decade later it owned and operated a complete radio station, and became the major shareholder in a satellite broadcast television station which reaches the whole of the central third of Australia. CAAMA broadcasts have played a large part in popularising Aboriginal musicians, and it has used its recording studio to produce commercial cassettes of Aboriginal musicians on its own label. Although a few Aboriginal bands have been promoted by major record companies, CAAMA has given many Aboriginal musi-

cians their first opportunities in the commercial field. Other Aboriginal and Islander media associations have been established in the wake of CAAMA's success.

5. Conclusion. Traditionally, Aboriginal and Islander music varied significantly from region to region. While the major division was between Aboriginal and Islander music, as it was in culture and language generally, nevertheless being so close together geographically there were inevitably mutual influences and borrowings, and the differences between Aboriginal music on Cape York and that of the Torres Strait Islands were probably no greater than between the music of central Australia and Arnhem Land. While Aboriginal and Islander music and culture generally were undoubtedly long influenced by the music and culture of visitors from islands to the north of the continent, foreign influences since the advent of European settlement of Australia in 1788 and subsequent non-European immigration have been increasingly more overwhelming. In some areas, indigenous traditions have changed only slowly. In others, indigenous people have adopted and developed new traditions, such as rock and reggae. In still other areas, Aboriginal and Islander traditions have mixed with introduced elements, such as Island music and Jesus *purlapa*. It is not possible to draw boundaries around these areas: in the remotest communities the local youth perform rock music in their own languages, and in urban communities of large cities young Aborigines learn older styles from the remote centre and north of the continent.

Some observers and participants alike are pessimistic about the continuity of a distinctive Aboriginal musical tradition. Others believe that Aboriginal and Islander people will continue to express their identity, their life experiences and their beliefs through music, as they have always done.

See also *Alyawarra; Arandic; Bundjalong; Burarra; Daly River; Dyirbal; Kaytetye; Kukatja; Pintupi; Tiwi; Warlpiri; Yolngu;* and entries under individual place-names.

FURTHER REFERENCE
Discography
Aboriginal Sound Instruments (AIAS 14, 1981); Archie Roach, *Charcoal Lane* (Mushroom 30386, 1990); *Bunggridj-bunggridj: Wangga Songs by Alan Maralung, Northern Australia* (International Institute for Traditional Music, Smithsonian Folkways 40430, 1993); *Djambidj: An Aboriginal Song Series from Northern Australia* (AIAS 16, 1982); *Goyulan the Morning Star* (AIAS 18, 1988); *Modern Music of Torres Strait* (AIAS 15, 1981); *Songs of Aboriginal Australia* (AIAS 17, 1987); *Songs from North Queensland* (AIAS 12, 1966); *Songs from the Northern Territory* (AIAS, 1-5, 1964); *Songs from the Kimberleys* (AIAS 13, 1968); *Stompem Ground: Highlights from the 1992 Kimberley Aboriginal Arts and Cultural Festival* (ABC 518 0202, 1993); *The Songs of Dougie Young* (National Library of Australia, Aboriginal Studies Press 19, 1994); Tiddas. *Sing About Life* (Id Phonogram 518 3482, 1993); *Traditional Music of Torres Strait* (AIAS 11, 1972); Yothu Yindi. *Tribal Voice* (Mushroom 30602, 1992).

Select Bibliography

Anderson, G., Mularra: A Clan Song Series from Central Arnhem Land, PhD, Univ. of Sydney, 1992.

Barwick, L., 'Creative (Ir)regularities: The Intermeshing of Text and Melody in Performance of Central Australian Song', *Australian Aboriginal Studies* (1989) 1, 12–28.

Beckett, J., 'Aborigines Make Music', Quadrant 2 (1957–58), 32–42.

___, 'The Land Where the Crow Flies Backward', *Quadrant* 9 (1965), 38–43.

___, and T.A. Jones, *Traditional Music of Torres Strait* (Canberra: AIAS, 1972).

___, with E. Bani, S. Townson, K. Mabo, and D. Ober, *Modern Music of Torres Strait* (Canberra: AIAS, 1981).

Bell, D., *Daughters of the Dreaming* (Melbourne: McPhee Gribble, Allen & Unwin, 1983).

Breen, M., ed., *Our Place, Our Music* (Canberra: Aboriginal Studies Press, 1989).

Clunies Ross, M., T. Donaldson, and S. Wild, eds, *Songs of Aboriginal Australia*. Oceania Monographs No. 32 (Sydney: University of Sydney, 1987).

___, and J. Mundrugmundrug, *Goyulan The Morning Star* (Canberra: AIAS, 1988).

___, and S. Wild, *Djambidj: An Aboriginal Song Series from Northern Australia* (Canberra: AIAS, 1982).

___, and S. Wild, 'Formal Performance: The Relations of Tune, Text and Dance in Arnhem Land Clan Songs', *Ethnomusicology* 28 (1984), 209–35.

Elkin, A.P., and T.A. Jones, *Arnhem Land Music (North Australia)*. Oceania Monographs No. 9 (Sydney: University of Sydney, 1953–57).

Ellis, C., *Aboriginal Music: Education for Living* (Brisbane: University of Queensland Press, 1985).

Grau, A., Dreaming, Dancing, Kinship. The Study of Yoi, The Dance of the Tiwi of Melville and Bathurst Islands, North Australia, PhD, The Queen's University, Belfast, 1983.

Gummow, M., Aboriginal Songs from the Bundjalung and Gidabal Areas of South-eastern Australia, PhD, Univ. of Sydney, 1992.

Hata, M., 'Melody and Harmony in Modern Music in Torres Strait'. Paper presented at Symposium of the International Musicological Society, Melbourne, 1988.

Kartomi, M., 'Childlikeness in Play Songs: A Case Study Among the Pitjantjara at Yalata, South Australia', *Miscellanea Musicologica* 11 (1980), 172–214.

___, 'Songs of Some Aboriginal Children's Play Ceremonies', *SMA* 15 (1981), 1–35.

___, 'Delineation of Lullaby Style in Three Areas of Aboriginal Australia', in *Problems and Solutions: Occasional Essays in Musicology Presented to Alice M. Moyle*, ed. J. Kassler and J. Stubington (Sydney: Hale & Iremonger, 1984), 59–93.

Keogh, R., '*Nurlu* Songs from the West Kimberley: An Introduction', *Australian Aboriginal Studies* (1989) 1, 2–11.

___, Nurlu Songs of the West Kimberleys, PhD, Univ. of Sydney, 1990.

Koch, G., and P. Black, 'Koko-Bera Island Style Music', *Aboriginal History* 7 (1983), 157–72.

Marett, A., and L. Barwick, *Bunggridj-bunggridj: Wangga Songs from Northern Australia by Alan Maralung* (Berlin and Washington, International Institute for Traditional Music, Smithsonian Folkways, 1993).

Moyle, A.M., 'Bara and Mamariga Songs on Groote Eylandt', *MA* 1 (1964), 15–24.

___, *Songs from North Queensland* (Canberra: AIAS, 1966).

___, 'Tasmanian Music. An Impasse?', *Queen Victoria Museum Records* 26 (1968).

___, *Songs from the Kimberleys* (Canberra: AIAS, 1968).

___, 'Aboriginal Music on Cape York', *MA* 3 (1968–69), 1–20.

___, *Songs from the Northern Territory*. Rev. edn (Canberra: AIAS, 1974).

___, North Australian Music: A Taxonomic Approach to the Study of Aboriginal Song Performances, PhD, Monash Univ., 1974.

___, ed, *Music and Dance of Aboriginal Australia and the South Pacific. The Effects of Documentation on the Living Tradition*. Oceania Monographs No. 41 (Sydney: University of Sydney, 1992).

Moyle, R.M., *Songs of the Pintupi: Musical Life in a Central Australian Society* (Canberra: AIAS, 1979).

___. 'Songs, Ceremonies and Sites: The Agharringa Case', in *Aborigines, Land and Land Rights,* ed. N. Peterson and M. Langton (Canberra: AIAS, 1983, 66–93).

___, *Alyawarra Music: Songs and Society in a Central Australian Community* (Canberra, AIAS, 1986).

Stubington, J., Yolngu *Manikay*: Modern Performances of Australian Aboriginal Clan Songs, PhD, Monash Univ., 1978.

Stubington, J., and P. Dunbar-Hall, 'Yothu Yindi's "Treaty": *Ganma* in Music', *Popular Music* 13/3 (1994), 243–59.

Sullivan, C., 'Non-tribal Dance Music and Song: From First Contact to Citizen Rights', *Australian Aboriginal Studies* (1988) 1, 64–7.

Waterman, R.A., 'Music in Australian Aboriginal Culture: Some Sociological and Psychological Implications', *Journal of Music Therapy* 5 (1955), 40–9.

Wild, S., Walbiri Music and Dance in their Social and Cultural Nexus, PhD, Indiana Univ., 1975.

___, 'Warlpiri Music and Culture: Meaning in a Central Australian Song Series', in *Problems and Solutions: Occasional Essays in Musicology Presented to Alice M. Moyle*, ed. J. Kassler and J. Stubington (Sydney: Hale & Iremonger, 1984), 186–203.

STEPHEN A. WILD

Abravanel, Maurice [de]   (*b* Thessaloniki, Greece, 6 Jan. 1903; *d* Salt Lake City, USA, 1993), conductor. Abravanel studied medicine at Lausanne, Switzerland, then music with Weill in Berlin, where he first conducted. After conducting in several German cities he became conductor for Balanchine's ballet company in Paris and London, conducted at the New York Metropolitan Opera (1936–39), the Chicago Opera (1940–41) and on Broadway (1941–49). He toured Australia with the British National Opera Co. (1934), returning in 1935–36 and finally in 1946 to conduct a series of orchestral concerts in Sydney with an *ad hoc* orchestra sponsored by the *Daily Telegraph*. In 1947 he became musical director of the Utah Symphony Orchestra, his tenure there being the longest of any conductor with an orchestra in the United States.   J.L. HOLMES

AC/DC. Hard rock band formed at Melbourne in 1974, originally comprised of Ronald Belford 'Bon' Scott (vocals, *b* Kirriemuir, Scotland, 1946; *d* London, 1980), Angus Young (lead guitar, *b* Glasgow 1959), Malcolm Young (rhythm guitar, *b* Glasgow 1953), Phil Rudd (drums, *b* Melbourne 1954) and Mark Evans (bass, *b* Melbourne 1957). Angus and Malcolm Young emigrated with their family from Scotland to Australia in 1963, where their older brother George found musical success as a member of the *Easybeats. The original AC/DC membership did not settle until 1974 in Melbourne, but national success soon followed with the release of their *High Voltage* and *TNT* albums in 1975, which both charted well. The group's appearances on *Countdown* also helped to establish several of their most important trademarks: an uncompromising approach to hard rock, songs dealing mainly with sex, alcohol and the life-view of hard rockers, and Angus Young's persona as a recalcitrant schoolboy, dressed in shorts and a cap.

Cliff Williams (*b* Ramford, England, 1949) replaced Evans on bass in 1977, and the group first achieved major international success in 1979 with the album *Highway to Hell,* which charted strongly both in the USA and the UK. Their success was dealt a blow when Scott died after a night of heavy drinking; nevertheless the band's comeback album *Back in Black* (1980), with Brian Johnston (*b* Newcastle, England, 1947) replacing Scott, reached No. 1 on the Australian and UK charts, and No. 4 in the US. In 1983 Rudd was replaced on drums by Simon Wright (*b* 1963), who was in turn replaced by Chris Slade (*b* 1946) in 1990.

With their rebellious image and an aggressive guitar-based sound, the group achieved international success which reached a peak during the early 1980s, and they remain Australia's best known rock band abroad. Throughout the 1980s and 90s, AC/DC have remained a formidable international success, regularly releasing albums and touring around the world.

FURTHER REFERENCE
Recordings include *High Voltage* (1975, rec. Albert, distributed EMI 477082-2); *Highway to Hell* (1979, Albert/EMI 477088-2); *Back in Black* (1980, Albert/EMI 477089-2); *For Those About to Rock* (1981, Albert/EMI 477090-2); *Blow Up Your Video* (1988, Albert/EMI 477094-2); *Live* (1992, EMI 470014-2). For a discography, see *SpencerA*. See also *McGrathA*; *SpencerW*.
                                    WILLIAM VAN PINXTEREN

Acheson, Merv(yn) Fletcher (*b* Sydney, 31 Mar. 1922; *d* Sydney, 11 Aug. 1987), jazz saxophonist, leader. Acheson started violin with his father, a dance band musician, but switched to tenor saxophone in 1933 after a sporting injury. From the age of 15 he was playing profes-

sionally with George Fuller's dance band and became prominent in after-hours jazz sessions. He enlisted in the army following the outbreak of war and served in entertainment units until going AWOL and resuming playing in Sydney. A shooting incident in 1944 led to prison sentences (120 days for the AWOL, nine months for the shooting) in Goulburn Gaol, where he formed a band. After the war he resumed nightclub and pit work, including in Melbourne in 1948. Liberalised licensing laws in NSW from 1955 provided him with numerous restaurant and pub residencies, including the Criterion (1958–65). Apart from leading his own groups, Acheson worked in bands led by Dick *Hughes (1979–85) and Alan *Geddes (1984–86), until retiring in ill health in 1986. He was also active in jazz journalism from 1938 and held senior offices in the NSW branch of the Musicians' Union. Although his playing was firmly lodged in the mainstream tradition, Acheson influenced younger musicians of extraordinarily varied styles. He was a legendary figure in Australian jazz, and the durability of his reputation was attested to by his winning major polls on his instrument 25 years apart: *Tempo* (1946) and *Music Maker* (1971).

FURTHER REFERENCE
Recordings include *Merv Acheson 60th Birthday Concert*, Dick Hughes Famous Five with Merv Acheson (1982, 2MBS-FM Jazz-1). His reminiscences are serialised in 13 instalments in *JA* (Mar./Apr. 1982 to Summer/Autumn 1986). See also *BissetB*; *GroveJ*; *OxfordJ*; John Clare, 'A Footnote on Merv Acheson', *JA* (Jan./Feb. 1982), 31; Bruce Johnson, 'Merv Acheson: Half a Century's Dedication', *Stereo FM Radio: 2MBS-FM Program Guide* (Mar. 1987), 10–11.   BRUCE JOHNSON

Ackland, Essie Adele (*b* Woollahra, Sydney, 27 Mar. 1896; *d* Mosman, Sydney, 14 Feb. 1975), contralto. She studied at the NSW State Conservatorium with Roland Foster, taking further lessons with Joseph Bradley and Mme Emily Marks. After various notable local performances, she toured Australasia with Belgian cellist Jean Gerardy in 1923. She sailed for London in March 1925, there marrying baritone Reginald Joseph Morphew in February 1926. Befriended by Ada Crossley, she became a prominent oratorio and concert performer, notably at the Crystal Palace massed choral concerts. Browning Mummery introduced her to HMV for whom she made 40 best-selling discs, chiefly as a ballad-singer. She toured Australia for the ABC in 1937, finally returning to Sydney in November 1947, and retired in February 1949.

FURTHER REFERENCE
Her papers are in *CAnl*. See also K. Moignard, *ADB*, 13; *BrisbaneE*. For an index to references in *AMN* see *MarsiI*.
                                    KAY DREYFUS

Adelaide, pop. (1991) 1 023 597, capital of South Australia, situated at the base of the Mount Lofty Ranges, inland from the Gulf of St Vincent. Founded by the South

Australian Association on principles of colonisation developed by E.G. Wakefield, Adelaide received its first assisted migrants in 1836, and no convicts were allowed to be transported. Approximately 12 000 Aborigines are thought to have lived in SA before European settlement, but numbers declined sharply in the 19th century.

1. 1836–84. The initial settlement of English Protestant migrants was soon complemented by German Lutheran settlers, and by 1891 it is estimated that German descent accounted for 9 per cent of South Australia's population. The first Governor of SA, John Hindmarsh, also brought the first piano to Adelaide, floated ashore on a raft and carted to Government House, a tiny cottage on the site of the present Festival Centre. In 1839 a London organist, Charles Platts, advertised himself as a 'professor of pianoforte', was later appointed organist of Trinity Church and opened the colony's first music shop, selling sheet music and instruments. An extensive industry of composing and publishing for a domestic market grew up around the piano: songs, galops, waltzes, polkas and other dances with titles such as *Adelaide March,* or *Adelaide Schottische.*

The Royal Theatre, the first venue for theatre opened April 1838, seating 400, and although a theatre orchestra was planned the venture was short-lived, a characteristic fate in several early theatres. The first documented performance of music-theatre was Henry Bishop's *Rob Roy* in December 1839 and the pattern of entertainments using songs, dances and musical numbers interspersed in spoken dialogue was the mainstay throughout the first two decades. Not until 1856 did George Coppin bring his Melbourne English Opera Co. from Melbourne to give Adelaide's first season of opera, including *Lucia di Lammermoor* and *La Sonnambula.* Adelaide became part of the circuit for travelling opera companies in Australia, Lyster's companies alone playing nine seasons between 1865 and 1880. No resident company was established.

Professional concert life began in February 1849 with Charles Platts (piano) and George Bennett (violin) playing arrangements of Handel and Beethoven overtures, vocal ballads and trios. Bennett organised concerts in the 1840s held in hotels, music stores, theatres and offices, followed by S.V. Wallace (brother of Vincent Wallace) and Frederick Ellard from Sydney giving 16 concerts in 1850, including orchestral works with more than 35 players. Later visitors included Catherine Hayes (1854), Miska Hauer (1855–57), Anne Bishop (1856, 1868, 1869) and Ilma de Murska (1875).

The first attempt to establish a permanent orchestra occurred in 1879–80, when the Adelaide Orchestra Society, including paid professionals, prepared for a series of concerts to be conducted by George Oughton. A concert was given 27 May 1880, but the society's finances collapsed. More successful was the Adelaide String Quartet Club, which promoted chamber music by Haydn, Mozart, Beethoven, Schubert as well as songs, opera and

oratorio excerpts in 1880–85 (one further season was held in 1891). Brass and military bands were widely established; one of the earliest was the Adelaide Town Band formed in March 1848 and led by Henry Witton, a local music teacher and amateur composer. By 1884 40 such bands are known to have been formed in Adelaide and surrounding districts, including the establishment that year of the SA Police Band.

Choral singing was formally established in November 1842 with the founding of the Adelaide Choral Society. Early conductors included Wallace and Carl ★Linger, the latter leading the first Adelaide performance of *Messiah* on 14 April 1859. In the 1850s other societies were formed and regular concerts of choral music became a prominent feature of the city. The German community also supported choral groups, several of which were consolidated under Linger's conductorship as the Adelaider Liedertafel in September 1858. Anglican and Methodist churches (the main denominations in SA) established firm traditions of music. Holy Trinity Anglican on North Terrace had acquired an early reed organ in 1841; the first pipe organ was built by Marshall for St John's Anglican Church in Halifax Street in 1848. The predominantly German-speaking Lutheran churches established strong musical practices and encouraged the construction of organs in their churches, the Barossa Valley instruments of Daniel Lemke (1832–97) being especially fine.

The first significant composer in Adelaide was Carl Linger (1810–62) who arrived from Berlin in August 1849. He successfully combined the musical traditions of his German education with the English society of his adopted city, a confluence nicely symbolised by his music for Caroline Carleton's *Song of Australia* (1859). Little of his music has been recovered, but the *Six Interludes* for orchestra, songs and motets suggest a competent composer familiar with the language of Haydn and Mozart and with trends in early nineteenth-century choral music for the Church. The music of Carl Puttmann (1843–99) and Edward Smith Hall (*b* 1855), in common with most of the music known to have been composed by Adelaide musicians in this early period, has failed to survive.

2. 1884–1960. With the appointment of Sir William ★Robinson as governor (1883–88), the colony gained a powerful patron of music with his own modest claim to composition. Conversations between Robinson, Sir Thomas Elder and the city council led to the funding of a chair of music at the University of Adelaide and the appointment of Joshua ★Ives as first professor, taking up his duties in 1885. Two years previously Immanuel ★Reimann (*b* Hahndorf, 1859) had returned to Adelaide from studies in Berlin under Scharwenka and Bischoff to open the Adelaide College of Music along the lines of a German conservatorium, the first professional music school in Australia. Cecil Sharp, working in Adelaide 1883–93, was co-director from 1889. Excellent teachers were appointed to the college, including August

★Heinicke (*b* 1863 Dresden), a violinist and conductor who set up Adelaide's first semi-professional orchestra in 1891. A further Elder bequest in 1897 led to the permanent founding of the Elder professorship and the ★Elder Conservatorium, created by taking over the staff and facilities of Reimann's College. Construction of the Elder Hall (opened September 1900) consolidated the place of music in the university.

In music-theatre, a shift in taste away from grand opera to the lighter operetta was reflected in the repertoires of companies touring in the years after 1880. The interwar years saw little change in this pattern, only the Elder Conservatorium opera class offering regular student productions after the appointment of George Carey in 1924, and these too faded after 1934. In the subsequent decade little opera was seen, but the postwar recovery was rapid, with the re-establishment of the opera class and the return of J.C. Williamson's Italian Grand Opera in 1949. A pool of experienced singers was developed, leading to the formation of the Intimate Opera Group in 1957, the precursor of the city's later permanent opera companies. Organised and financed by local singers led by John Worthley, Intimate Opera performed an adventurous and mid-20th-century repertoire with strong community support.

Heinicke's orchestras included the Heinicke Grand Orchestra (1891–97), the Conservatorium Grand Orchestra (1898–1910) and the Adelaide Grand Orchestra (1911–14), but he retired from active musical life with the onslaught of anti-German sentiments during World War I, a circumstance that disrupted much of Adelaide's musical tradition. The focus of concert life shifted to the Elder Conservatorium after 1900, both in chamber music and in orchestral playing. The Elder String Quartet was formed in 1918 and was maintained continuously until 1964; and the SA Orchestra was formed in 1920, but this ensemble collapsed with the onset of the Depression. Adelaide benefited from the establishment of the ABC and its policy of sponsoring performing groups; William ★Cade was appointed to conduct a wireless chorus from 1929 and a studio orchestra from 1934, which in 1936 was called the Adelaide Symphony Orchestra with a complement of at least 50 players. The Musica Viva Ensemble arrived in 1948 and the new Elder professor, John ★Bishop (appointed 1948) established the University Music Society in 1954.

The strong choral tradition of the 19th century continued unabated. Harold ★Davies (Elder professor 1919–47) formed the Adelaide Bach Society in 1901; the Adelaide Philharmonic Choir (1937–79), Adelaide Choral Society (1886–*c*.1910, re-established 1922–79) and Harmony Choir (1947–present) also presented oratorio and large-scale repertoire, usually with orchestral accompaniment. The only professional group was the Adelaide Singers (1946–76), an outstanding ensemble that long survived the loss of similar ensembles elsewhere in Australia. The choir pursued a vigorous policy of performing new music, playing and commissioning Aus-

tralian composers such as Banks, Brumby, Butterley, Gross, Henderson, Penberthy, Werder and Williamson. Among new organs may be noted the contribution of J.E. Dodd, who provided the first Elder Hall organ in 1901: his instruments are regarded as fine examples of late Romantic organ-building.

Composers active *c*.1900 included E.R.G.W. Andrews, whose 1887 *Adelaide Jubilee Cantata* is one of the few surviving scores, Harold Davies, first doctor of music from the University of Adelaide in 1902, Moritz ★Heuzenroeder, who composed five operas (all lost: but probably German *Singspiel* or operetta), Cecil Sharp, Ernest Mitchell, H. Winsloe Hall, and Joshua Ives, reputed to have written the first symphony in Adelaide in 1901. The composition course at the Elder Conservatorium guaranteed a steady stream of graduates, but the content of the teaching was deeply conservative. Almost no contemporary music was performed or taught in Adelaide until after World War II. Composers who studied at the Elder included Hooper ★Brewster Jones (1887–1949), Alexander ★Burnard (1900–71), Horace Perkins (1901–86) and Duncan McKie (1904–82). Burnard left in 1935 to join the staff of the NSW State Conservatorium and another graduate also moved to Sydney a year later, the composer and pianist Miriam ★Hyde (*b* 1913).

Several of these composers supplemented their Adelaide coursework with London studies, an experience which did little to alleviate conservative styles acquired as students. The unswerving allegiance to 19th-century idioms, however attractive and earnest, and deserving of some performance recognition, relegates their music to a souvenir of times long past. Claims for modernity have been made for the music of Brewster Jones, who left sonatas and short piano pieces, songs, an opera *Deirdre of the Sorrows*, piano concertos, the symphonic poem *Australia Felix* and chamber works.

3. 1960–present. The founding of the Festival of Arts in 1960 provided not only a focus for arts activity but regularly presented new music from Europe, America and Australia. Bishop started a visiting composers scheme at the University of Adelaide in 1962: the first incumbent, the Dutch composer Henk Badings, laid the groundwork for an electronic music studio at the conservatorium, and succeeding visitors (Hopkins 1964, ★Tahourdin 1965, Maxwell Davies 1966, Veress 1967, Feld 1968, 1969, Rands 1972, Cary 1974, ★Lumsdaine 1976) were influential.

A further impetus was the opening of the Festival Centre in 1974, built at a cost of $20 million. The decade of the 1970s was marked by extensive patronage of the arts by the government led by Don Dunstan, which created new opportunities in performance, composition and music education. Complementing the Adelaide Festival, the Fringe Festival since 1974 hosted experimental and radical music events that might not otherwise have occurred. Youth arts received encouragement with the start of the Come Out Festival in 1975, enabling students to participate in a variety of musical activities. In 1992 John Russell and Brenton Langbein established the Barossa Music Festival, which developed a unique mix of chamber music, folk and ethnic performance, blended with heritage values, food and wine. Wider exposure to world music was brought to Adelaide from 1992 by the WOMADelaide event.

Through the 1960s the partnership between the university and the Intimate Opera Group, together with the opera component of festival programs, remained the mainstay of opera. In 1973 New Opera, South Australia was formed from the nucleus of experience, singers and administrative staff developed by Intimate Opera. The company created a nationwide reputation for small-scale music-theatre with a strong commitment to 20th-century works and Australian composers. Increasing costs forced a restructuring in 1976 as the State Opera of SA, from whence it emerged as a regional opera company concentrating on Mozart and 19th-century repertoire, although productions for the Adelaide Festival were more adventurous.

The proliferation of small, specialised ensembles included the University of Adelaide Wind Quintet (established 1964), Musica Antiqua (1973), Adelaide String Quartet (1972), Adelaide Chamber Orchestra (1976), Australian String Quartet (1985) and Lights (1991). The ABC's Adelaide Symphony Orchestra (renamed from 1975), after a period of declining support in the later 1970s while using the Festival Theatre as its main venue, widened the scope of its concert series and returned to the Adelaide Town Hall in the 1990s, with effective results. The absence of a purpose-built concert hall has continued to be a serious lack in the profile of the city's performance spaces.

The Adelaide Chorus was formed from the amalgamation of the Adelaide Philharmonic Choir and Adelaide Choral Society in 1980 and has continued the tradition of large-scale choral pieces. Other groups to have emerged include the Corinthian Singers (1963), Graduate Singers (1977) and Adelaide Chamber Singers (1985). Three major organs were also constructed in Adelaide embodying recent trends in the aesthetics and technology of organ-building: the Rieger (Austria 1979) in the Festival Theatre, Casavant (Canada 1979) in Elder Hall and Walker (England 1990) in the Adelaide Town Hall.

The policy of visiting composers and later appointments in composition at the University of Adelaide (Peter Tahourdin 1969–73, Richard ★Meale 1969–87, Tristram ★Cary 1974–85, Malcolm ★Fox 1974, Peter Brideoake 1976, and Graeme ★Koehne 1987), together with initiatives such as the John Bishop Memorial Fund (begun 1965) and the ASME composition awards (begun 1973) all served to bring Adelaide into the orbit of new composition that was characterising the emergence of contemporary styles in the eastern states. Music-theatre works composed in Adelaide included Martin Wesley-Smith's *Pi in the Sky* (1971) and *Boojum!* (1986), Fox's *Sid the Serpent*

Who Wanted to Sing (1977) and *The Iron Man* (1987), Meale's *Voss* (1986), Ralph Middenway's *Barossa* (1988), and Koehne's *Love Burns* (1992). Major orchestral works are the second symphony of Peters (1964–65), Bozidar Kos's *Metamorphosis for Orchestra* (1978), Meale's *Viridian* (1979), Koehne's *Rain Forest* (1982) and Cary's *Dancing Girls: Four Mobiles for Orchestra* (1991).

Younger composers in the 1990s are an eclectic group, looking to conservative, minimalist and mildly experimentalist styles from America for much of their work. They include Quentin Grant, John Hines, Becky Llewellyn, John Polglase and Stephen Whittington.

FURTHER REFERENCE

Anderson, H. 'Virtue in a Wilderness: Cecil Sharp's Australian Sojourn, 1882–1892', *Folk Music Journal* 6 (1994), 617–52.

Brewster-Jones, H., 'Pioneers and Problems: South Australia's Musical History', *AMN* 27/3 (Oct 1936), 1–3, 28–33.

Cooper, J., The Foundation of Culture in Adelaide: A Study of the First Colonists' Transplantation of Ideas and Art: 1836–1857, MA, Univ. of Adelaide, 1970.

Holmes, R., *Through the Opera Glass: A Chronological Register of Opera Performed in South Australia 1836 to 1988* (Adelaide: Friends of the State Opera of South Australia, 1991).

Krips, M., A History of Music in South Australia before 1900, BA(Hons), Univ. of Adelaide, 1974.

McCredie, A.D., ed., *From Colonel Light Into the Footlights: The Performing Arts in South Australia from 1836 to the Present* (Adelaide: Pagel, 1988).

Naylor, B. Organ Building in South Australia, MA, Univ. of Adelaide, 1973.

Roennfeldt, P., 'A History of the First Hundred Years of Lutheran Church Music in South Australia', *MMA* 12 (1987), 161–6.

Szuster, J., 'Dollars and Sense: Music Funding in South Australia', *SA* 43 (1994), 29–30.

WARREN BOURNE

Adelaide Aboriginal Orchestra. Established in 1971, the Adelaide Aboriginal Orchestra was a vehicle for teaching Western music to urban Aboriginal adults and schoolchildren. It was part of the Program for Training Music for South Australian Aboriginal People, which was co-ordinated by Catherine J. ★Ellis, lecturer in ethnomusicology at the University of Adelaide. This program was the precursor of the university's CASM. The music training for the orchestra used traditional tribal teaching methods, such as group music-making with experienced players and tutors sitting beside beginners. By 1977 the orchestra was no longer in operation. JULJA I. SZUSTER

Adelaide Chamber Orchestra. Formed as a string group in 1976, it has developed into a part-time chamber orchestra with a reputation for fine playing of traditional repertoire, interspersed with commissioned works by Australian composers. It receives core support from the State Government, offers an annual subscription season of about five concerts, and appears at the Adelaide Festival, the Barossa Music Festival and other events. The current artistic director is Richard Mills.

FURTHER REFERENCE
Recordings include Mozart, Piano Concerto K.414, Daniel Blumenthal, pf (Move, MS 3952).

Adelaide College of Music. Founded in 1883 by Immanuel Reimann, it was the first practical music school in Australia. A privately owned enterprise, it offered piano lessons with Reimann, organ and theory tuition with Cecil *Sharp (1889–90), singing with Frederick Bevan, and string tuition with Hermann *Heinicke (violin), and Gerard Vollmar (cello). In 1897 it was absorbed into the University of Adelaide as the basis of the Elder Conservatorium, with the Elder professor Joshua *Ives as director.

FURTHER REFERENCE
Maud Karpeles, *Cecil Sharp: His Life and Work* (London: Routledge, 1967).

Adelaide Festival. Held every two years during the month of March since its inception in 1960, the festival has offered a broad artistic program incorporating music, theatre, dance, visual arts and literature. A distinctive feature of the festival has been its array of different artistic directors: the founding artistic director was John *Bishop, Elder professor of music at the University of Adelaide, and other notable artistic directors since have included Robert Helpmann, Louis van Eyssen, Anthony *Steel (director of five festivals), Lord Harewood, Christopher Hunt and Barrie Kosky. An associated Fringe Festival has emerged in recent years.

FURTHER REFERENCE
Whitelock, D. *Festival! the Story of the Adelaide Festival of Arts* (Adelaide: D. Whitelock, 1980).   JULJA SZUSTER

Adelaide String Quartet Club. Formed in 1880 to give subscription concerts in Adelaide of 'the best chamber music', it also sought to perform works never previously heard there. From 1880 to 1885 six concert seasons were held; the club's activities then ceased until 1891 when a final season was offered. Viennese Classical chamber music provided the core programming, with Beethoven being the most performed composer. Probably to encourage audience growth, vocal music was introduced after the second season. Prominent club members included John Grainger (father of Percy), Jules Meilhan and Cecil *Sharp. By the 1890s the club's role had been transferred to the concerts of the Adelaide College of Music.

FURTHER REFERENCE
Kathleen E. Nelson, 'The Adelaide String Quartet Club and "the vocal element" 1880–1891', *MMA* 15 1988, 143–52.
KATHLEEN NELSON

Adelaide Symphony Orchestra. South Australia's full-time orchestra, founded in 1936 as the ABC's Adelaide radio orchestra, and known as the South Australian Symphony Orchestra 1949–74. Funded by the ABC and the SA Government, the orchestra has 68 players and gives regular subscription concerts at the Adelaide Town Hall; it accompanies opera and ballet performances in the Adelaide Festival Theatre. Henry *Krips conducted the orchestra for 23 years, and therefore had a significant influence on Adelaide's musical life during the 1950s and 1960s. Conductors have included William *Cade (1936–48), Krips (1949–72), Elyakum Shapirra (1976–78), Nicholas *Braithwaite (1987–91) and David Porcelijn (1992–).

FURTHER REFERENCE
Recordings include Bartók and Szymanowski Violin Concertos, cond. O. Hadari (ABC 426 479); *French Organ Concertos,* cond. N. Braithwaite, S. Preston, org (ABC 432 529); and *Trombone Concertos,* cond. N. Braithwaite, P. Thomas, W. Tyrrell, trbn (ABC 438 825). See also Charles Buttrose, *Playing for Australia: A Story about ABC Orchestras and Music in Australia* (Sydney: ABC/Macmillan, 1982).   JULJA SZUSTER

Advance Australia Fair. Since 1974 the *national anthem of Australia, attributed to Peter Dodds McCormick (1834–1916), musician and teacher. From its first known public performance at a Loyal Orange Lodge ceremony in Sydney on 12 July 1878, it became a popular song which was sung in schools; it was sung at the inauguration of the Commonwealth of Australia in 1901 and often referred to by politicians as the national anthem, despite the official anthem being *God Save the Queen*. Originally published as a three-verse song under the pseudonym 'Amicus', its published versions did not include McCormick's name until around 1907. Various claims have been made that it was based on German folksong, or written by a schoolteacher, John McFarlane, a contemporary of McCormick's, but it is difficult to establish the truth from the little evidence available. It became the official anthem after a public opinion poll in its favour, but its acceptance was not universal and *God Save the Queen* was reintroduced in 1976. In 1984 it was reinstated (the first two verses only) as the official anthem, and remains so today.

FURTHER REFERENCE
Warren Bebbington, 'Who wrote "Advance Australia Fair"?' *Canberra Times*, 26 Jan. 1985; Georgina Binns, Patriotic and Nationalistic Song in Australia to 1919: A Study of the Popular Sheet Music Genre, MMus, Univ. Melbourne, 1989; Jim Fletcher, 'Peter Dodds McCormick', *ADB*, 10.
GEORGINA BINNS

Adventures of Barry McKenzie, The. Song by Peter Best, text by Barry Humphries. Written as the theme for the Bruce Beresford film of that name (Longford Productions, 1972), based on the comic strip by Nicholas Garland and Barry Humphries, which portrays the satirical exploits of a beer-swilling, uncouth Australian 'ocker' on his visit to London.

Aeroplane Jelly.   See *I Love Aeroplane Jelly.*

Affair, The.   Opera in one act by Felix Werder (1969), libretto by Leonard Radic. Set in Canberra during the turbulent years of the Whitlam Labor government, it is a political satire. First performed by the Australian Opera at the Sydney Opera House on 14 March 1974.

Affley, Declan James   (*b* Cardiff, Wales, 1939; *d* 27 June 1985), folk musician. Playing clarinet from the age of eight, he studied at the Royal Welsh College of Music and joined the British merchant navy at 16. He came to Australia in 1960 and through Brian Mooney, Don Ayrton and others began learning Irish and Australian folk-songs and performing at the Troubadour and the Wentworth Park Hotel, Sydney, and at Traynor's folk club and the Dan O'Connell Hotel, Melbourne. He taught himself guitar, fiddle, banjo and whistle, and (from 1970) focused on *uilleann* pipes; in 1969 he brought together The Wild Colonial Boys. He toured Ireland with an Australian show, *The Restless Years* (1972), then toured NZ, New Guinea and Indonesia (1984), and appeared at folk festivals, as well as on radio and television before his untimely death.

With an excellent singing voice, he was one of the few players of the Irish pipes in Australia and contributed greatly to the traditional folk ballad literature. The Australian Folk Trust Declan Affley Award for songwriting is made at the annual National Folk Festival.

FURTHER REFERENCE
Recordings include *Rake And Rambling Man* (1967, Score FOL 404) and the posthumous *Declan Affley* (Sandstock LPTAR 020). See also *OxfordF.*

African Music.   In Australia, locally produced African music is a fairly recent development, arising in the mid- to late 1970s. As it exists today, the music can be said to fall into one of two general categories: traditional music played on traditional instruments, and popular music using mainly guitars, keyboards, bass, kit drums and percussion. Most of the traditional music derives from one of three areas in Africa: the north-eastern (Ethiopia and Somalia); the southern (South Africa); and the west coast (Ghana, Nigeria, Senegambia). Because the popular music form employs instrumentation similar to Western popular music, and does not require formalised dance responses, it sits more comfortably with the language of Australian popular culture, and is therefore more prevalent than the traditional forms. The African popular music forms most

common in Australia can be broadly identified as Soukous from Zaire, Soweto Township Beat-Jive from South Africa, and Highlife from Ghana.

African music was brought to Australia by African migrants; in the diasporic setting, individuals or ensembles play music from their homeland, and perform either for the general public or for their local ethnic community. There is also adoption of African music, usually at public performances, by local musicians who do not necessarily belong to the ethnic group with which the music is associated. Ensembles in this category may or may not include Africans. In either case the resultant music may be a literal reproduction of the original form or a newly composed or newly arranged form, using the musical principles of African culture.   CHRIS LESSER

Agamemnon.   Opera in one act by Felix Werder after Aeschylus. Originally broadcast on the ABC in 1967, it was first stage in a revised version at the Grant Street Theatre, Melbourne on 1 June 1977.

Agents.   Artist managements for classical music are scarce in Australia, and chiefly centred in Sydney. Most notable are Virginia Braden (Arts Management), Marguerite Pepper and Kevin Jacobson. Raymond Myers (Avere Artists) in Sydney and Jenifer Eddy in Melbourne specialise in representing vocalists. For popular music there are over 100 managements in Australia, of which Michael Gudinsky's Premier Harbour is perhaps the largest and most comprehensive; some of the others most active are Bedford and Pearce, ATA Allstar and Ray Evans in Sydney, and Australian Concert Entertainment, Loud and Clear, and Glen Wheatley in Melbourne.

Agnew, (Robert) Roy Ewing.   (*b* Sydney, 23 Aug. 1891; *d* Sydney, 12 Nov. 1944), composer, pianist. In Australia he studied piano with Daisy Miller, piano/theory with Emanuel de Beaupuis and composition with Alfred Hill. A Sydney benefit concert in 1923 raised funds to send him to England for further training and exposure to a wider field of music, and there he studied composition/orchestration with Gerrard Williams. Well received by London audiences, he gave many public performances of his own works, and his compositions were regularly reviewed in the *Musical Times.* Returning to Australia in 1928, he married Kathleen Olive O'Connor in 1930. He was in England for recitals in London and Glasgow and broadcasts for BBC, then settled in Australia in 1934, and was engaged by the ABC for a concert tour of all capitals, playing about 60 of his own works. He hosted an ABC radio program of contemporary music (1938–43) which included works by Hindemith, Ireland, Bax, Honegger and Scriabin. An AMEB examiner from 1943, he joined the piano teaching staff of the NSW Conservatorium in

1944. Well respected and popular as a composer/performer, with many of his works recorded by the ABC, his style is forthright if conservative, with a complex harmonic vocabulary tending towards Romanticism. His prolific compositional output includes songs, 70 piano miniatures, and the tone-poem *The Breaking of the Drought*. Seven sonatas, written 1920–40, represent the best of his idiomatic piano writing.

WORKS (Selective)
Principal publishers: Augener, OUP, Curwen, Allans. Most ms works available in facsimile from the Australian Music Centre, Sydney, or on microfilm from the Mitchell Library, Sydney.
Orchestral   *The Breaking of the Drought*, orch, v (1928).
Songs   *O moonlight deep and tender* (1913), *Beloved stoop down thro' the clinging dark* (1913), *Dirge* (1924), *Dusk* (1926), *Infant Joy* (1926), *Beauty* (1935), *The flowers of sleep* (1935), *Invocation* (n.d.), *Hie Away* (n.d.), *I don't like beetles* (n.d.), *To a dead violet* (n.d.), *The World's Wanderers* (n.d.), Two Songs without Words, v, cl (n.d.).
Piano   *c.*75 works, *Will o' the Wisp* (ms, n.d.), Nocturne (ms, n.d.), *Australian Forest Scenes* (1913), Sonata *Ossianic* ms partly lost (*c.*1918), Symphonic Poem *La Belle Dame Sans Merci* (*c.*1920), *Deirdre's Lament* (1922), *Poem No. 1* (1922), *Poem No. 2: To the Sunshine* (1922), *Etude* (1924), *Pangbourne Fields* (1925), *Prelude No. 3: The Wind* (1925), *An Autumn Morning* (1927), *Capriccio* (1927), *A Dance Impression* (1927), *Fantasie Sonata* (*c.*1927), *Sonata Poem* (*c.*1929), *Three Preludes* (1927), *Contrasts* (1929), *A May Day* (1927), Two Pieces (n.d.), *Prelude No. 4* (1927), *Rhapsody* (1928), *Rural Sketches* (1927), *Three Poems* (1927), *Three Lyrics* (1927), Two Pieces (1927), *The Windy Hill* (1928), *Rabbit Hill* (1928), *Elf Dance* (c.1928), *Sonata* (1929), *Drifting Mists* (*c.*1931), Two Pieces (*c.*1931), *Toccata* (1933), *Before Dawn* (1935), *Noontide* (1935), *Trains* (1935), *Youthful Fancies* (1936), *Holiday Suite* (1937), *Sonata Ballade* (1937), Sonata Legend *Capricornia* (1940), *Album Leaf* (1949), *Sea Surge* (1949), *Green Valley* pf duet (1932), *The Village Fair* pf duet (n.d.).

FURTHER REFERENCE
Recordings include *The Piano Music of Roy Agnew: The Complete Sonatas and Selected Miniatures*, Larry Sitsky, pf (1991, MBS 23); *Retrospect*, Larry Sitsky, pf (1995, Tall Poppies 049). A list of ABC tapes of his works to 1972 is in *PlushD*. See also *AMN* 1 Sept. 1935; Rita Crews, An Analytical Study of the Piano Works of Roy Agnew, Margaret Sutherland and Dulcie Holland, including Biographical Material, PhD, Univ. New England, 1994; *GlennonA*, 139; Dorothy Helmrich, *ADB*, 7; Faith Johnson, The Piano Music of Roy Agnew, MMus, Univ. WA, 1981; Fiona McGregor, The Career of Roy Agnew and his Impact on Australian Music Life, BMus IV, NSW State Conservatorium of Music, 1987; *MoresbyA*, 130–32.   RITA CREWS

Ahern, David Anthony   (*b* Sydney, 2 Nov. 1947; *d* Sydney, 30 Jan. 1988), composer. He studied composition privately with Nigel Butterley, then Richard Meale, and while only 18 came to prominence with two orchestral works, the static, brilliantly coloured *After Mallarmé* (Uni-

versal Edn, 1966) and *Ned Kelly Music* (Southern Music, 1967), which with its non-traditional instrumental techniques created a sensation at the Sydney Proms in 1968. He studied with Stockhausen at Cologne and Cornelius Cardew at London, and on return to Australia in 1970 was for a time at the centre of Sydney's musical avant-garde, appearing with his acoustic and electronic improvisation group A-Z Music (later Teletopa) and writing vivid articles about new music for the *Daily Telegraph* and *Music Now*. He taught at Sydney College of the Arts from 1977, but never recaptured his first success before his untimely death.

FURTHER REFERENCE
Recordings include *After Mallarmé*, Sydney Symphony Orchestra, cond. J. Hopkins (1969, World Record Club WRC 4930); *Ned Kelly Music*, Sydney Symphony Orchestra, cond. J. Hopkins (1968, ABC RRC 401). His writings include 'Now Music', *Music Now* 1/2 (1969) and 'Stockhausen in Australia', *Music Now* 1/4 (1971). See also *MonashB*; *MurdochA*; *PlushD*; Helen Golden, 'Ahern: The Music of New Sounds', *Sydney Magazine* 1 (Spring 1970).

Air Supply.   Soft-rock band formed in 1975 around the partnership of Russell Hitchcock (vocals) and Graham Russell (vocals, guitar), who met while performing in the Australian production of *Jesus Christ Superstar*. In 1976 they signed with CBS Records and released Russell's song *Love and Other Bruises*. Attaining a gold record with their debut album *Air Supply* only three months after its release, the group was chosen to support Rod Stewart on his 1977 Australian tour. A second Australian hit followed with *Do What You Do*. International recognition was achieved when they were invited to perform at the 1977 CBS convention in London, and once again as Rod Stewart's support act on his 1977 American tour. The group's second album, *The Whole Thing's Started*, again featured Russell's compositions, but did not attain the same chart success as the first. Signing with a new label, Big Time Phonograph Recording Co., the pivotal *Life Support* album was released as a picture disc in 1979, drawing instant local and international acclaim. Russell's *Lost In Love* single from the album was an Australian chart success, and subsequently the group signed a deal with Arista Records which saw the song released in the USA, where it reached No. 1 in the charts, being the first of a succession of singles to enter the American Top Five: *All Out of Love*, *Every Woman In the World*, *The One That You Love*, *Here I Am*, *Sweet Dreams*, *Even the Nights Are Better* and *Making Love Out of Nothing at All*.

As a major force in the international charts of the early 1980s, Air Supply is one of the most successful groups to have emerged from Australian rock. Although Russell and Hitchcock were its nucleus and other members changed, it was an adept performing unit, being voted best group for 1981 at the American Music Awards. Disbanding in

1988, the group reunited to celebrate its 20th anniversary with an Australian tour in 1996.

FURTHER REFERENCE

Recordings include *Air Supply* (1977, CBS), *The Whole Thing's Started* (1977, CBS), *Life Support* (1978, Wizard), *Lost in Love* (1980, Wizard), *The One That You Love* (1981, Big Time), *Now And Forever* (1982, Big Time), *Hearts in Motion* (1986), *Lonely Is The Night* (1986, Arista). Compilations: *Making Love … The Best Of Air Supply* (1983), *Greatest Hits* (1988, Big Time). A discography is in *SpencerA*. See also *APRAJ* 2/10 (1982), 2–5; *BMI Musicworld* 2 (1981), 28–9; Donald Clarke, ed., *The Penguin Encyclopedia of Popular Music* (London: Penguin, 1989); *GuinnessP*, Phil Hardy and Dave Laing, *The Faber Companion to 20th-Century Popular Music* (London: Faber, 1990); *McGrathA*; *SpencerW*; *Sun* 14 Nov. 1985; *Sunday Herald-Sun* 28 Apr. 1996.

EMMA MATTHEWS

Akhurst, William Mower (*b* London, 29 Dec. 1822; *d* at sea, 6 June 1878), playwright, journalist. After writing and producing for stage shows at Cremorne Gardens, London, he came to Australia in 1849. He worked as a journalist at Adelaide then moved to Melbourne as music critic for the *Herald* in 1853. In Melbourne he wrote at least 40 stage works, mostly burlesques, pantomimes, minstrel shows and farce, some adaptations of London works and many containing music. He wrote *Harlequin Arabian Nights* for Lyster's Opera Co. in 1862, and adapted Offenbach's *Un marie à la porte* as *The Wrong Side of the Door* in 1868. He dabbled in composition, a ballad, polka and waltz appearing in the *Illustrated Melbourne Post* (1863–64). He returned to London in 1869, where he continued to write for the stage, but with his health failing set out for Australia again in 1878, only to die at sea.

FURTHER REFERENCE

ParsonsC; *IrvinD*.

Albert, J. & Sons. Music retail and publishing firm established by Jacques Albert. Arriving in Sydney in 1884, Albert established Albert's Music Warehouse in suburban Newtown in 1890. His son Michel François (Frank) entered the business in 1894, when it became J. Albèrt & Sons and moved to 470 George Street, and later 118 King Street. They sold violins, guitars, mandolins, organettes, autoharps, concertinas, cornets, bagpipes and mouthorgans as well as sheet music described as the 'catchiest, ticklish, side-splitting and sweetest ever published'. Albert's developed a line of mouthorgans, including the Woolloomooloo Warbler and the Boomerang series, and in 1897 sold 40 000 of them. Jacques Albert retired in 1896 to write books on diet and leisure and Frank assumed the business.

By 1914 Albert's was one of the leading retailers of instruments and sheet music, publishing tutors, songsters and albums under the Boomerang name. Boomerang House at 137 King Street was completed in 1916 and provided seven storeys of showrooms, offices, and studios for tuition and practice. Albert's was a partner in the Australian Broadcasting Company from 1929 and, in 1933, when that contract expired, acquired the licence for 2UW in Sydney. In the same year the retailing arm of the business was dismantled in favour of publishing, buying the Australian copyrights of hundreds of popular Tin Pan Alley songs and publishing Australian popular composers such as Jack ★Lumsdaine and Joe ★Slater. Albert was a founding director of APRA, and in 1944 endowed a chair of music at the University of Sydney.

From the late 1960s Albert's continued to publish Australian composers such as Colin Brumby, Ross Edwards, Nigel Butterley and Margaret Sutherland and employed the highly successful songwriters Harry ★Vanda and George Young, who produced 20 Top 10 singles for John Paul Young, AC/DC and The Angels. Frank Albert died in 1962 and his second son, Alexis (knighted in 1972), assumed management of the company; many of the successes of the 1960s and 70s were the result of the acumen of Alexis's son Ted, who died in 1990. In the 1980s the company acquired a network of FM radio stations which it sold in 1995 for $62 million. The foundation of the company's successes was its understanding of the market for popular culture.

FURTHER REFERENCE

For Michel François (Frank) Albert, see *ADB*, 7.

SUZANNE ROBINSON

Albert Street Conservatorium. See *Melba Memorial Conservatorium*.

Albury-Wodonga, pop. (1991) 39 975. Urban centre comprised of two cities on the Murray River (the Victoria–NSW border), settled on the north side in 1839 and on the south (as Belvoir) in 1852, but not connected by bridge until 1861. The town developed a lively musical life from its early days. Two-manual Fincham organs were installed at St Matthew's church in 1876 and St Patrick's in 1892, bells chimed from the post office from 1878, and the local families of the growing agricultural trading community sang in church choirs, competing for the choral cup at the Albury Eisteddfod, which had expanded to four days by 1936. The Albury Choral Society was established in 1947 and a city orchestra was proposed in 1951. Lively amateur operetta productions emerged, playing at the Albury Civic Centre, opened in 1964. Since 1973, when the centre was extended into a Civic Theatre complex, locally produced musicals have been regularly performed in the 177-seat theatre and concerts occasionally in the flat-floored 1500-seat hall.

Alcestis. Music-theatre in three acts by G.W.L. Marshall-Hall (1898) to Euripides' drama. Intended as incidental music to the play, the elaborate musical setting for solos, chorus and orchestra made the work closer to opera than drama. It was first performed by Trinity College, University of Melbourne, at the Melbourne Town Hall on 22 July 1898, then at the Stadttheater, Meissen, Germany, in 1913. Ms in *PVgm*.

Alda, Frances Jeanne [Fanny Jane Davis] (*b* Christchurch, NZ, 31 May 1879; *d* Venice, 18 Sept. 1952), soprano. Brought up in Melbourne by her grandparents, Fanny and Martin ★Simonsen, she began singing professionally in 1897. In 1902 she left Australia to study with Marchesi in Paris. After her European debut at the Opéra-Comique in 1904 she appeared at the Monnaie, Brussels (1904–7), Covent Garden (1906) and La Scala (1908) before becoming a member of the Metropolitan Opera, New York (1908–29). A noted interpreter of lyrical roles such as Manon Lescaut, Mimì and Desdemona, she was also a successful recording artist and recitalist. She toured Australasia in 1927.

FURTHER REFERENCE
Her memoirs are *Men, Women and Tenors* (Boston: Houghton Mifflin, 1937). A discography is in Aida Favia-Artsay, 'Frances Alda', *The Record Collector* 6/10 (1951), 221–33. See also: Adrienne Simpson, 'Frances Alda' in *Opera in New Zealand—Aspects of History and Performance,* ed. A. Simpson (Wellington: Witham Press, 1990), 91–104; idem, 'New Zealand's Most Famous Daughter', *Women's Studies Journal* 5/1 (1989), 61–73; idem and Peter Downes, *Southern Voices* (Auckland: Reed, 1992).
ADRIENNE SIMPSON

Alder, Warwick Alan (*b* Newcastle, NSW, 26 Nov. 1959), jazz trumpeter. He took lessons from Reg Bishop and later John Hoffman. Moving to Sydney in 1979, he graduated from the NSW Conservatorium jazz program in 1981. With Serge ★Ermoll and James ★Morrison he was co-founder of Now's The Time (1985). A founder member of John Pochée's Ten Part Invention (1986), he was also with Improviso (1993) and Cathy Harley (1995), and toured Australia and the USA with Australian Jazz Orchestra (1988). Also giving lecture-recitals for Musica Viva throughout Australia, he has taught at the NSW State Conservatorium, and played support for visitors including Joe Williams and Buddy de Franco. He won the Critics and Broadcasters best trumpeter award, 1993.

FURTHER REFERENCE
Recordings include *Ten Part Invention* (1987, ABC/Phonogram 846 729-2); *Now's The Time* (1990, rooArt Jazz 846310-2); *Tall Stories,* Ten Part Invention (1993, Rufus/Polygram RF006); *Rhythm of the Heart,* The Bob Bertles Quintet (1995, Rufus Polygram RF 017). See also review in *Australasian Jazz 'n' Blues* 2/1 (1995), 16.
BRUCE JOHNSON

Alexander, Ruth née Kurtz (*b* Wellington, nr Wichita, Kansas, USA, 29 Apr. 1914), music teacher. After studies in piano at Kansas State University, she toured as an accompanist, but when an illness affected her left arm she began teaching music in schools. Marrying an Australian, she settled at Melbourne in 1943, teaching at Melbourne Church of England Girls' Grammar School and lecturing in music education at the University of Melbourne Conservatorium (1943–53). Impressed by the orchestral music camps founded in Michigan by Joseph E. Maddy, she joined with John ★Bishop and Dr Percy ★Jones to initiate similar camps in Australia (from 1948); due in no small measure to her organising skills, these grew into the National Music Camp Association (today ★Youth Music Australia) and the Australian Youth Orchestra, with which she was deeply involved until her retirement in 1978. An energetic and vivid teacher of great personal warmth, she was a founder of one of Australia's most important music education movements. She was honoured with the Sir Bernard Heinze Memorial Award in 1987.

FURTHER REFERENCE
Christopher Symons, *John Bishop: A Life for Music* (Melbourne: Hyland House, 1989), 135–49.

Alice Springs, pop. (1991) 20 448. Desert town on the Stuart Highway in the NT, half-way between Adelaide and Darwin, founded as a telegraph post in 1871. For the many transport drivers and tourists who pass through there is the annual Country Music Festival and regular shows by the outback balladist Ted ★Egan, an influential presence in the town since the 1950s. For Aborigines throughout the surrounding region there is CAAMA, founded in 1980, which through its radio and television stations broadcasts a blossoming array of Aboriginal bands and choirs, and releases recordings on its Imparja label. The town's remote location has meant that visits from first-class performers have been irregular, if less so since the Araluen Centre for Arts opened with a fully equipped 500-seat theatre in 1984. Local musical activity is surprisingly intense for a community of this size: there is a Town Band, Desert Harmony Chorus, Junior Singers, Country Music Association and Central Australian Folk Society, while the Alice Springs Music Teachers' Association presents regular recitals and the Centralian Eisteddfod is held each May.

Allan, Cameron (*b* Melbourne, 1955), film composer. He studied at the NSW Conservatorium. His scores for the SA Theatre Co. productions of *As You Like It* (1975), *Malfi,* and *Kingdom of Earth* (1976), established him as a notable theatre composer, although he is best known for his contribution to feature films between 1976 and 1988, and for his work as a music producer. He formed the Regular record label with the manager of Mental as Anything, Martin Fabinyi, and has been involved with the production of numerous LP recordings. Allan's film scores include *Summer of Secrets* (1976), *Stir* (1980), *Hoodwink* (1981),

Heatwave (1982), *Emoh Ruo* (1985), *Going Sane* (1987), and *Pandemonium* (1988). He is currently living in the USA.

L. THOMPSON

Allan, George Leavis   (*b* London, 3 Sept. 1826, *d* St Kilda, Melbourne, 1 Apr. 1897), music retailer, publisher, singing master. Trained in Britain in Hullah's 'fixed-doh' method of teaching music, he emigrated to Australia in 1852, and was the first singing master appointed by the Denominational Schools Board, Victoria, in 1853. He was later principal singing master for the Victorian Board of Education, and in 1862 joined the Melbourne music warehouse of Wilkie and Webster, becoming a partner and later its sole proprietor. The business became Allan & Co. in 1881, by which time it was the largest music retailer and publisher in the southern hemisphere, a position it retained under Allan's son and successors for a century. Allan championed many Melbourne musical activities, publishing educational and domestic music, and continued to be influential in school music as an examiner of prospective music teachers.

FURTHER REFERENCE

Kenneth Hince, *ADB*, 3; P. Game, *The Music Sellers* (Melbourne: Hawthorne Press, 1976).

R. S. STEVENS

Allans Music   Music publishing and retail firm established by George Leavis *Allan, who joined the Melbourne music-sellers Wilkie & Webster in 1862 and in 1875 became sole proprietor. In 1877 Allan's took over a three-storey showroom in Collins Street and stocked instruments to the value of £27 000, including pianos by Broadwood, Collard, Erard and Cramer, as well as Alexandre Harmoniums, Albert Clarionets and 'the finest cabinet organs in the world', Smith American Organs. Teaching rooms were available and the store provided a box-office for concerts and the theatre. Allan visited leading European instrument-makers in 1879, and on his return issued a music catalogue advertising publications from leading London publishers as well as local works by Henri Ketten, Signor Giorza and Alberto Zelman Sr. Undeterred by a major fire in 1889, Allan's became a limited liability company. Allan's son, George Clark (1860–1934), became a partner in 1881 and managing director in 1897. George C. Allan was responsible for bringing the conductor Frederick Cowen to Australia for the 1888 Exhibition and for arranging the first concert of the Marshall-Hall orchestra in 1892. Allan's also produced an Australian music yearbook, which by 1900 was selling 100 000 copies a year.

Charles *Tait (1869–1933), a director from 1896, became joint managing director *c*.1905. Believing that sheet music sales would stimulate sales of pianos, Tait built up the publishing arm of the business. In 1906 the company began publishing in arrangement with the AMEB and in 1911 established a periodical, the *Australian Musical News*. In 1922 the manager of Allan's asked Alex Kynoch,

a Scot who had worked in newspapers, to set up a printing works which then printed exclusively for Allan's. At this time songs written by Jack *O'Hagan, an Allan's employee, sold up to 100 000 copies and prompted the sales of pianos and player-pianos, true to Tait's prediction.

At the peak of the boom in sales of player-pianos, in 1922 Allan's went into partnership with *Wertheim, the Melbourne piano-maker, but withdrew from the partnership in 1930; a further piano-manufacturing venture also failed. The Depression affected sales of instruments and sheet music, and from then on Allan's depended mainly on sales of educational music. In 1936 the company merged with the Sydney firm of *Nicholson's. After another fire in 1955 the Collins Street building was replaced at a cost of £500 000; the store was modernised in 1970, with recordings taking over the ground floor. By 1976 Allan's had 15 branches, including Geelong, Bendigo, Adelaide, Hobart and Launceston, and a turnover of $7 million. The company was taken over by *Brash Holdings in that year. It continues to distribute publications to music stores in Australia and Asia and in 1995 relocated to premises in Bourke Street.

FURTHER REFERENCE

P. Game, *The Music Sellers* (Melbourne: Hawthorne Press, 1976).

SUZANNE ROBINSON

Allen Brothers.   See *Allen, Peter.*

Allen, Christie   [June Allen] (*b* Essex, England, 1959), pop singer. She settled in Australia at Bunbury, WA, in the late 1960s. After singing lessons she joined Pendulum at the age of 18, and in collaboration with Terry Britten (formerly of The Twilights) made her debut single *You Know That I Love You* (Mushroom) in 1978. Briefly a huge success with teenagers, she had five Top 40 hits in 1979–80 and toured nationally with her Hot Band in the same year; her single, *Goosebumps*, was No. 3 in the charts in 1979, while *Falling In Love With Only You* and the albums *Magic Rhythm* (1979) and *Detour* (1980) also did well. She won Countdown awards in 1979 and 1980.

FURTHER REFERENCE

Recordings include *Goosebumps* (1978, Mushroom K7608), *Falling In Love With Only You* (1979, Mushroom K7400), *Magic Rhythm* (1979 Mushroom L37075), and *Detour* (1980 Mushroom L37489). For discography, see *SpencerA*. See also *McGrathA*; *SpencerW.*

Allen, Peter   [Peter Woolnough] (*b* Tenterfield, NSW, 10 Feb. 1944; *d* San Diego, California, 18 June 1992), songwriter, stage entertainer. Raised in an all-female household in Armidale, NSW, Allen displayed an early talent for piano and dance. His war-veteran father, a violent alcoholic, shot himself in 1947 and Allen moved with his mother to Lismore. Influenced by the tours of Little

Richard and Jerry Lee Lewis, he took his piano, song and dance act to Surfers Paradise, Queensland, and Sydney and acquired a partner, Chris Bell: they later became the Allen Brothers, appearing in 1959 on Australian *Bandstand* and then touring South-East Asia. Judy Garland discovered them at the Hong Kong Hilton in 1964 and adopted them for her tours; Garland's daughter Liza Minelli and Allen were married in 1967. In 1970 Allen separated from Minelli and from Bell and began a separate career in the USA as a solo cabaret performer and songwriter. Recordings followed including the successful Olivia Newton-John performance of *I Honestly Love You* written with Jeff Barry. Helen Reddy also recorded some of his songs, and he co-wrote *Arthur's Theme (The Best That You can Do)*, the Oscar-winning song, in 1981. He had a successful one-man show on Broadway in 1979 and appeared at Radio City Music Hall in 1982, but the Broadway Musical *Legs Diamond,* in which he starred in 1988, was a flop; he performed regularly in Sydney and Melbourne cabarets, on visits from the USA. He died of AIDS in San Diego after returning there from Surfers Paradise for treatment.

Allen's performing style combined uninhibited spectacle with infectious good humour, and a pleasant voice. His successes included the outrageous Latin-American *I Go to Rio,* but it is his reflective, introspective songs which are most likely to be remembered, including *Tenterfield Saddler* and *I Still Call Australia Home,* which both exhibit an unsentimental nostalgia.

FURTHER REFERENCE
Obit. in *Herald-Sun,* Melbourne, 20 June 1992. His recordings include: *Tenterfield Saddler* (1972, Festival 36495), *Continental American* (1974, Festival 35410), *Taught by Experts* (1977, Festival 35873), *I Could Have Been a Sailor* (1978, Festival 36767), *Bicoastal,* (1980, Festival 37428), *Its Time for Peter Allen* (1982, Festival 45763/4), *Legs Diamond* (1989, RCA), *Making Every Moment Count* (1990, RCA/BMG). See also: Peter Beilby and Michael Roberts, eds, *Australian Music Directory* (Melbourne: Australian Music Directory, 1981); *GuinnessP*; Nicholas Patti, 'Peter Allen', in *Contemporary Musicians: Profiles of People in Music,* ed. Julia M. Rubiner (Detroit: Gale, 1994); Arnold Shaw, *Dictionary of American Pop/Rock* (New York: Schirmer, 1982).

AUBREY SCHRADER

Allman, (George) Faunce (*b* Yass, NSW, 27 Dec. 1883; *d* Sydney, 16 Feb. 1967), organist, music educator. Allman completed his education at Sydney Church of England Grammar School (Shore) where he had music lessons from Gordon Burnside. Organist and choirmaster at St James', King Street, Sydney, 1907–61, he was an examiner for the AMEB from 1915, a teacher of organ at the NSW Conservatorium of Music 1924–61, conductor of the Sydney University Musical Society 1927–57, and University of Sydney organist 1936–62. He was director of music at Presbyterian Ladies' College Croydon from 1930, then at Sydney Church of England Grammar

School 1947–57. A founder and for seven terms president of the Musical Association of NSW, he was conductor of the Sydney University Graduates' Choir 1952–62. Allman possessed real musical erudition and inspired generations of Sydney students with a love of all that was finest in music. An honorary DLitt was conferred on him by the University of Sydney in 1961 in recognition of his contribution to music.

FURTHER REFERENCE
Graeme D. Rushworth, *Historic Organs of New South Wales* (Sydney: Hale & Iremonger, 1988), 407–8.

GRAEME RUSHWORTH

Allman, Robert Edward Joseph   (*b* Melbourne, 8 June 1927), baritone. While working as a salesman he took lessons with Horace Stevens at the University of Melbourne Conservatorium and Marjory Smith in Sydney, making early appearances in concert and with the Australian National Theatre Movement Opera Co. from 1952. Dominique Modesti auditioned him in Melbourne and brought him to Paris to study, 1955–56. He made his debut at Covent Garden in 1957, singing with the company until 1960. He then settled in Germany, appearing in all its major houses, and becoming principal baritone at the Cologne Opera 1962–67. Returning periodically to Australia for the Elizabethan Theatre Trust Opera Co., and for the Sutherland-Williamson Opera Co. (1965), as well as filling guest engagements in New Orleans and South Africa, and at Sadler's Wells and Glyndebourne, he joined the Australian Opera in 1971. With a vast, rich and powerful tone, his roles encompassed Rigoletto, Macbeth, Scarpia, Iago, Nabucco, Sharpless, Jochanaan in *Salome,* Simon Boccanegra and Amonasro, and he made many concert appearances.

FURTHER REFERENCE
Recordings include Pizarro in the Glyndebourne *Fidelio* (1980, IMP video SL2004). See also *CA* (1995–96); *MackenzieS,* 220–22; Roger Covell, *GroveO*; *WWA* (1996); *CA* (1995–96).

Alpen, Hugo   (*b* Kellinghusen, Germany, 26 Oct. 1842; *d* Sydney, 20 June 1917), music educator, composer. He studied with Jacques Schmidt in Germany and with Charles *Horsley in Australia. Settling at Melbourne in 1858, he was a choral conductor, pianist and public school singing master in rural NSW, before succeeding James Fisher as singing master at teacher training colleges in Sydney; he was superintendent of music in the NSW Department of Public Instruction 1884–1908. He developed a movable-doh staff notation method of teaching music for NSW schools almost a decade before similar developments in English education. Composing several school cantatas, including *Arbor Day Cantata* (1891), he also wrote patriotic songs and sacred works and published school song-books.

FURTHER REFERENCE
R.S. Stevens, 'Hugo Alpen—New South Wales Superintendent of Music, 1884–1908', *Unicorn* 19/3 (Sept. 1993), 93–6.

R. S. STEVENS

Althoff, Ernie   (*b* Mildura, Vic., 22 May 1950), composer. He studied science at the University of Melbourne 1969–70 and graphic design at the Caulfield Institute of Technology 1971–74, then became active at the Clifton Hill Community Music Centre from 1978 to 1983. He was composer-in-residence at Monash University in 1991 and sculptural exhibitor at the Fifth Australian Sculpture Triennial at the National Gallery of Victoria, 1993. His works, many of which involve the use of 'low' technology and original instruments, include *Music Machines* (1987), *51 Flexibles for Gramophone Users* (1989), *Music for Seven Metal Machines* (1990), *The Bamboo Orchestra* (1988), *Thirty More* (1992), *Speleology* (1992), and *Victoria Market* (1993).

FURTHER REFERENCE
Recordings include *51 Flexibles for Gramophone,* elec (Canberra School of Music CSM 6); *The Long and the Short of It* (NMA 007B). His writings include 'The Bamboo Orchestra', *Experimental Musical Instruments* 5 (1989), 9–13, and 'The Sonic Installation as a Compositional Tool and More', *SA* 45 (Autumn 1995), 34–6. See also *AthertonA*; *BroadstockS*; *JenkinsT*; L. Wendt, 'Sentient Percussion: Ernie Althoff's Music Machines', *Continuum* 8/1 (1994), 445–55.

MICHAEL BARKL

Alyawarra.   People of the Elkedra, Sandover and Bundey Rivers, central Australian desert. Living in the cultural security of two settlements within their traditional country and a further two close by, the Alyawarra have maintained a strong traditional life away from areas of major European influence.

Most ritual (and its attendant song and dance) occurs during the wet summer season, and each year whole communities travel one or more times to neighbouring settlements for the complex of *apulha* initiation rituals which occupies several days and nights of segregated and integrated activities. Throughout the year, men's patrilineally owned *ngirtilingkwa* rituals ensure an ongoing supply of edible flora and fauna, and women's *awulya* ceremonies promote personal bodily health and spiritual attachment to conception locations. These segregated rituals require periodic maintenance of the physical integrity of associated ancestral sites, a duty eased by both geographical proximity and vehicular transport. Residence on traditional land also means that vehicular travel—whether for pleasure, food or formal visitation—involves constant visual contact with traditional land and landmarks, and thereby renewed spiritual contact with the 'totemic landscape' of metamorphosed Dreaming Ancestors.

In common with neighbouring desert groups, Alyawarra songs are organised into series sung in unison, accompanied by idiophones, and rhythmically organised into isorhythmic units. In a culture where the elderly are respected or even feared for their accumulated wisdom, the performance frequency of rituals is directly related to the potency they are believed to embody, so that the more secret the ritual, the less frequently it is performed, a principle which allows elders to retain their authority without serious challenge from younger participants. As an added difficulty to the rapid learning of a secret ritual, the associated songs contain the greatest rhythmic complexity, whereas public rituals, which are enacted most frequently, use less complex songs and are therefore learned more easily.

In a small community, maintaining a stable population is a matter of frequent discussion and concern. When people leave the community, or are temporarily absent, or die, the ownership and performance of ritual is affected, and transferring or extending ritual ownership, particularly from one generation to another, may involve negotiated access or one-off resolutions rather than reliance on dogmatic adherence to a single 'traditional' transmission principle. See also *Aboriginal Music* §2.

FURTHER REFERENCE
Richard M. Moyle, *Alyawarra Music: Songs and Society in a Central Australian Community* (Canberra: AIAS, 1986).

RICHARD MOYLE

Amadio.   Family of four generations of musicians. Fortunato Amadio, from an Italian musical family, emigrated to Australia; his son, Anthony Amadio, was also a musician and father of Harold (1), John (2) and Adrian.

(1) Harold Amadio   (*b* Sydney, 1884; *d* Sydney, 1945), clarinettist. He learned clarinet from his father Anthony Amadio, and played in silent film orchestras in his twenties. He married Florence Beer and was father and music tutor of Clive (3), Leon (4) and Neville. His eldest son Harry was a fine pianist before an accident claimed his fingers and ended his musical career.

(2) John Bell Amadio   (*b* Christchurch, NZ, 1886, *d* Hobart, 1964), flautist. With his brother Harold he had his first lessons from his father and played in silent film ensembles in his twenties. He toured Britain, Europe and America and made many recordings. Winning international acclaim as a flautist, he was chosen by Nellie Melba to perform with her in her Australian tour of 1915, and he toured the USA with Florence Austral in 1925, whom he married that year. Four flutes from the John Amadio collection are exhibited at the Powerhouse Museum, Sydney.

(3) Clive Amadio   (*b* Sydney, 1903; *d* Sydney, 1990), clarinettist, saxophonist. He learned clarinet from his father Harold Amadio (1) and played with the Sydney Symphony Orchestra, the Mode Moderne Quintet and taught at the NSW State Conservatorium of Music (Newcastle). During the 1940s and early 50s his light classical music ensemble the Amadio Quintet was the most popular group on ABC radio. He was awarded the AM in 1980.

(4) Leon Amadio   (*b* Sydney, 1903; *d* Sydney, 1993), trumpeter. He had his first lessons from his father Harold Amadio (1) and played trumpet in ABC orchestras. He married Phyllis Leslie and later the Sydney soprano Zena Moller.

(5) Leonard Amadio   (*b* Sydney, 1936), arts administrator. Son of Clive Amadio (3), he was appointed concert manager for ABC Adelaide in 1964, and later founding head of the SA department of the arts in 1981. He served on the boards of various musical organisations and took part in UNESCO missions, including the first Australian cultural delegation to visit China in 1978. He worked with the Adelaide Festival in 1992, having been a member of the festival board for many years. He was honoured with the AM in 1978.

(6) Nadine Amadio   (*b* Sydney), music critic, author. Daughter of Leon Amadio (4), she has been one of Australia's most respected writers on music, noted for her support of Australian contemporary music. For 13 years she was the music critic of the *Australian Financial Review* and later was the arts editor with the Sydney *Sunday Telegraph*. She has a regular column in the ABC magazine *24 Hours*, was an Australian correspondent for European magazines and editor of three arts magazines. She has published 16 books, and since 1981 has been working in films. Ten of these were about painters, composers and other creators: *PGH: A Modern Odyssey*, about the Australian composer Peggy Glanville-Hicks, stimulated new interest in Glanville-Hicks's work and major compositions.

(7) Neville Francis Amadio   (*b* Sydney, 1913), flautist. He attended Fort Street High School, Sydney and the NSW State Conservatorium. He became principal flute in the ABC Sydney radio orchestra, which later became the nucleus of the Sydney Symphony Orchestra. Principal flautist with the Sydney Symphony Orchestra for nearly 50 years until 1979, he was a frequent soloist under such conductors as Sir Thomas Beecham, Sir John Barbirolli, Otto Klemperer and Sir Eugene Goossens. He was also associate artist with many famous singers, including Elisabeth Schwarzkopf, Erna Berger, Rita Streich, Mattiwilda Dodds and Lisa Perli, and has a substantial repertoire, including many new works he introduced to Australia. Teaching flute at the NSW Conservatorium and at national music camps, he was a founding member of Musica Viva and numerous ensembles, including the New Sydney Wind Quintet from 1965. He was awarded the MBE in 1969 and the AM in 1981.

FURTHER REFERENCE
For John Amadio see Mimi Colligan, *ADB*, 7; *GlennonA*, 99. For Neville Amadio, see Ann Carr-Boyd, *GroveD*.

ROBERT PETERSON

Amorous Judge, The.   Opera by Eric *Gross, libretto by L. McGlashan after Heinrich von Kleist, *Der zerbrochene Krug*. First performed at Sydney on 2 April 1965.

Amunda.   Aboriginal rock group based at Alice Springs and active since 1985. The group's name is from the Arrernte term for Alice Springs. With lead singer Paul Ah Chee, they have performed at numerous Aboriginal rock festivals throughout the NT. Their various tours in Australia include the Aboriginal and Islander Music Festival, Port Adelaide, 1992; Australia Day in Sydney, 1993–94; and tours of NSW and Vic. in 1995. Songs cover the Dreamtime, the environment, life in Alice Springs, and social issues.

FURTHER REFERENCE
Recordings include *Better Late Than Never* (1989, Amunda); *Civilised World* (1992, CAAMA 269), *Pedlar Ave* (1995, Stunt 007).   P. DUNBAR-HALL

AMusA.   Associate in Music, Australia. Diploma awarded by the AMEB, originally modelled on the British ARSM, and based on an advanced examination in an instrument, music theory or musicianship, taken after completion of practical and theoretical prerequisites in the Board's higher grade examinations. More than 400 candidates succeed in this popular award each year, mostly gifted musicians in their late teens. See *Australian Music Examinations Board*.

And The Band Played Waltzing Matilda.   Protest song (1972) by Eric *Bogle. Relating a soldier's experience of the Gallipoli campaign (1915), which became the source of Australia's Anzac mythology, the song poignantly comments in traditional bush ballad style on the folly of war. It had only a lukewarm reception at first, but it was placed third in a Brisbane song competition in 1976 and then entered the international protest song repertoire. It has been widely recorded. Published Larrikin Music, Sydney, 1977.

Anderson, Gordon A(thol)   (*b* Melbourne, 1 May 1929; *d* Armidale, NSW, 30 June 1981), musicologist. He taught at Pulteney Grammar School, Adelaide, 1947–56, then studied at the University of Adelaide from 1957 (DMus 1976) and held a research fellowship at Flinders University, SA, from 1970 until his appointment as lecturer (later professor) in music at the University of New England, Armidale, NSW, in 1973. Specialising in the music and poetry of the 13th century, particularly the musico-liturgical interpretation of 13th- and 14th-century motets and the symbolic meaning of their texts, he published over 40 papers on Medieval music in international journals, and made several contributions to the *New Grove Dictionary of Music and Musicians*. He began preparing a 10-volume interpretation and transcription of the complete corpus of Notre Dame monophonic and non-centred polyphonic works and related conductus, the last six volumes of which were completed posthumously. Based on original research in music palaeography and on a comparison of the theoretical writings of contemporary theorists, his works are now standard texts and models of their kind. Anderson was the first Australian scholar to attain eminence as a collector and writer on Medieval European music. Elected president of the Musicological Society of Australia from 1977 to 1978, he was also his university's first fellow of the Australian Academy of the Humanities. Although one of the most respected Medieval scholars of 20th-century musicology, he travelled only once to Europe (1979); he also maintained an interest in jazz until his death.

FURTHER REFERENCE

Obit. in *Armidale Express*, 3 July 1981, and by Leo Treitler in Australian National U. *Humanities Research Centre Bulletin* 27 (Mar. 1982). His principal works were *The Latin Composition in Fascicules VII and VIII of the Nôtre Dame Manuscript Wolfenbüttel Helmstadt 1099 (1206)*, vol. 1 (Brooklyn: Institute of Medieval Music, 1972); *Nôtre-Dame and Related Conductus* (Henryville, Pa: Institute of Medieval Music, 1979); 'Mode and Change of Mode in Nôtre Dame Conductus', *Acta Musicologica* 40 (1968): 92–114; 'Nôtre Dame Bilingual Motets: A Study in the History of Music *ca.* 1215–1245', *MMA* 3 (1968); 50–144.

MARGARET KARTOMI

Anderson, Hugh McDonald (*b* Elmore, Vic., 21 Jan. 1927), folklorist. He studied at Bendigo and Melbourne Teachers' Colleges, then taught in Victorian schools from 1946. Beginning in 1952 he wrote, edited and collaborated on over 60 volumes on Australian folksong, ballad, folklore, biography and criticism, including *Colonial Ballads* (1955), *The Black Bull Chapbooks* (1956), *Goldrush Songster* (1958), *Folksongs of Australia* with John Meredith (1967), and *Farewell to Old England: A Broadside History of Early Australia* (1964). He founded Red Rooster Press (1979), contributed to *Overland* and *Folklife* (UK), and in 1986 conducted an inquiry for the Federal Government which resulted in the report *Folklife: Our Living Heritage*. One of the seminal figures in the study of Australian folk-song and ballad, he has made a major contribution to Australia's knowledge of its early songs, composers and performers.

FURTHER REFERENCE

See also *OxfordF*; *WWA* (1996); *StubingtonC*; *OxfordL*.

Andrews, Shirley (*b* Melbourne, 1915), dance folklorist. After training as a dancer with the Borovansky Ballet, she began researching traditional Australian dance in the 1950s, writing papers and conducting traditional dance workshops. She helped organise the earliest national folk festivals (from 1967). Her major work is *Take Your Partner: Traditional Social Dancing in Colonial Australia* (1974) and her other volumes include *Collector's Choice of Set Tunes, Polkas and Barn Dances for Traditional Dancing in Australia* with Peter Ellis (1986). An important figure in the promotion of traditional dance in Australia, she was honoured with the OAM in 1994 and an Australian Folk Trust Lifetime Achievement Award in 1995.

FURTHER REFERENCE

See also *OxfordF*; *StubingtonC*, 42–3.

Angels, The. Rock band formed in Adelaide (1971) around John Brewster, Rick Brewster and Doc Neeson, originally as the Keystone Angels. Throughout the late 1970s and early 1980s the Angels were one of the most successful rock bands in Australia. They toured extensively and became one of the nation's best live rock acts. The group also toured the USA under the name Angel City. Although their first album, *The Angels* (1977), failed to chart in Australia, subsequent albums charted well, with *No Exit* (1979) reaching No. 8, *Dark Room* (1980) No. 5, *Watch the Red* (1983) No. 6, *Two Minute Warning* (1984) No. 5, *Howling* (1986) No. 6 and *Liveline* (1988) No. 3. Although never musical innovators, they drew large audiences by writing simple songs with easily remembered lyrics. Evidence of their style can be found in their three Top 10 single releases *No Secrets* (1980), *We Gotta Get Out of this Place* (1987) and *Dogs are Talking* (1990). Throughout the late 1980s they sought to attract a new younger audience, and in 1990 their efforts were rewarded when the album *Beyond Salvation* topped the national charts. They continued to record in the 1990s, releasing *Red Back Fever* in 1991.

FURTHER REFERENCE

Recordings include *The Angels* (1977, Albert Productions); *Face to Face* (1978, Albert Productions APLP 031); *No Exit* (1979, Albert Productions APLP 038); *Dark Room* (1980, Epic ELPS 4061); *Night Attack* (1981, Epic ELPS 4258); *Watch the Red* (1983, Epic ELPS 4364); *Two Minute Warning* (1984, Mushroom RML 53154); *Howling* (1986, Mushroom RML 53226); *Liveline* (1988, Mushroom RML 59001/2); *Beyond Salvation* (1990, Mushroom TVL 93327); *Red Back Fever* (1991, Mushroom TVL 93352); *Their Finest Hour—and Then Some* (1992, Albert Productions 472250 2); *Evidence* (1994, Mushroom TVD 93368). See also *GuinnessP*; *SpencerW*.

AARON D.S. CORN

Anglican Chant. English settings for singing the psalms and canticles of the Anglican Church, usually published with pointing, a system of signs developed in England from 1837 that indicate how a text was to be fitted to a given chant. The English pointed psalms and canticles were used in most Australian cathedrals by 1880 and widely in parish churches by the World War I years. But although the music was adapted for *An Australian Prayer Book* after its introduction in 1978 (with the publication of *The New Parish Psalter*, ed. Lionel Dakers and Cyril Taylor (Collins, 1981)) the chants are now difficult to find in use outside the city cathedrals. See *Church Music*.

Antakarinja. People of the desert around Oodnadatta, far northern SA, on the headwaters of the Hamilton, Alberga and Wintinna Rivers, neighbours of *Luritja, Arrernte, and others. Antakarinja and Arrernte people hold Arabana and Wangakanguru stories in trust, while

Antakirinya and Pitjantjatjara own songlines together. Catherine ★Ellis and Linda Barwick have researched and recorded Antakirinja music, especially among women at Indulkana. See *Aboriginal Music*.

FURTHER REFERENCE
Linda Barwick, 'Creative (ir)regularities: The intermeshing of text and melody in performance of Central Australian song', *Australian Aboriginal Studies* 1 (1989), 12–28; Catherine Ellis, 'The Role of the Ethnomusicologist in the Study of Andagarinja Women's Ceremonies', *MMA* 5 (1970), 76–206; idem and Linda Barwick, 'Antikirinja women's song knowledge 1963/1972: Its significance in Antikirinja culture', in P. Brock, ed., *Women Rites and Sites: Aboriginal Women's Cultural Knowledge* (Sydney: Allen & Unwin, 1990), 21–40; idem, and Megan Morais, 'Overlapping time structures in a Central Australian women's ceremony', in P. Austin, ed., *Language and History: Essays in Honour of Luise A. Hercus*, Ser. C-116 (Canberra: Pacific Linguistics, 1992), 101–36.

Anthem.   The first Australian anthem composer of distinction was the Irish cleric G.W. ★Torrance, who came to Melbourne in 1869 and whose numerous anthems were published by Novello & Co. Notable composers since have included Alfred Wheeler, George ★Sampson, Edgar ★Bainton and Paul Paviour. See *Church Music*.

Anthony, Julie   [Julie Lush] (*b* Galga, SA, 24 Aug. 1951), popular music singer. After singing at a local pub, she won a television talent quest in 1970, and appeared in Adelaide clubs and television variety shows. She came to wide attention in the title role of J.C. Williamson's centenary production in 1974, the revival of the 1920s musical *Irene* at Sydney, which she also sang at London in 1976; but vocal problems (1977–79) forced her to return to Australia and resume work in the club circuit, appearing regularly on the Adelaide *Tonight* show. Surgery in Germany (1979) improved matters, and she starred in *The Sound of Music* (1983) and *I Do, I Do* (1988), replaced Judith Durham in the Seekers in 1989–91, and appeared in over 500 TV commercials. A vivid personality with a clear, true voice, she is a great favourite with Australian variety audiences; she has won Mo Awards eight times since 1976, and was honoured with the OBE in 1980 and AM in 1989. Now living at Terranora, NSW, she sings jazz and cabaret, and has appeared with the Don Burrows Quartet.

FURTHER REFERENCE
ParsonsC; *Australian* 12 Feb. 1994; *Australian* 30 Dec. 1995.

Antill, John Henry   (*b* Ashfield, Sydney, 8 Apr. 1904; *d* Sydney, 29 Dec. 1986), composer. After studying music at St Andrew's Cathedral choir school, Sydney (1914–20), then working with the NSW Government Railways as an apprentice mechanical draughtsman until 1925, he decided to pursue a career in music, and enrolled at the NSW State Conservatorium, where he won a scholarship to study composition with Alfred ★Hill, and learnt violin

with Gerald Walenn. After graduating, he played in the NSW State Orchestra and Sydney Symphony Orchestra; he toured with J.C. Williamson's Imperial Opera Co. as conductor, musician and tenor, 1932–33. He was appointed assistant music editor with the ABC in Sydney in 1934, also working as chorusmaster and presentation officer, and was promoted to NSW supervisor of music in 1947, during which year he also initiated the Fellowship of Australian Composers. From 1949 to 1971 he held the position of federal music editor. During his retirement he was active as an adjudicator for the ABC's vocal and instrumental competitions, and in 1971 he was awarded the OBE for services to music.

Antill composed a wide selection of music during his lifetime, including ballets, operas, choral and orchestral works, plus film and incidental music. Most of it has been overlooked and remains unperformed or unpublished, so an overall assessment of his creative output still needs to be made. He is mainly known to the public for a single work: ★*Corroboree* was the first of his compositions to achieve performance, bringing him recognition overseas, as well as in Australia. Representing one of the first attempts by an Australian composer to combine the influence of Aboriginal music with Western musical resources, it was premiered as an orchestral suite in Sydney, 1946, by the Sydney Symphony Orchestra conducted by Eugene Goossens. Winning over the audience immediately with its recognisable Australian identity, it created a sensation and was performed abroad and recorded with the London Symphony Orchestra. Its first production as a complete ballet was in 1950 with the National Theatre Ballet and Sydney Symphony Orchestra.

Overall, Antill's approach to composition and twentieth-century music was conservative. He was more indebted to the readily accessible styles of European orchestral writing of the late 19th and early 20th centuries than to current European musical developments of his time. His strong leaning towards traditional English choral techniques can be attributed to his early musical background. From his studies with Alfred Hill he inherited a docile, melodic approach to composition, yet his fascination with the rhythmic drive of Russian composers from Mussorgsky to Prokofiev is also apparent. His employment as a musician with the ABC led to several commissions to write music for state occasions. But he did not receive the necessary public support to enable him to devote himself entirely to composition, and therefore did not fully realise the enormous creative musical potential that he showed so early in his life.

WORKS (Selective)
Orchestral   *Corroboree* (1946), *Corroboree* Orchestral Suite No. 1 (1946), *Corroboree* Orchestral Suite No. 2 (1950), *Variations for Orchestra* (1953), *Outback Overture* (1953), *Overture for a Momentous Occasion* (1957), *Nullarbor Dream Time*, vn, orch (1956), *A Sentimental Suite for Orchestra* (1955), *Symphony on a City* (1959), *Concerto for Harmonica and Orchestra* (1960), *Concerto/Sonata for*

Harmonica and Orchestra (1960), *Music for a Royal Pageant of Nation-hood* (1963), *Introduction for a Distinguished Occasion* (1981), *Burragorang Dreamtime* (1959), *Paean to the Spirit of Man* (1968), *The Unknown Land*, str orch (1968), *Variations on a theme of Alfred Hill* (1970), *Australian Rhapsody* (n.d.), *Capriccio* (n.d.), *Singing Dust*, str, nar (n.d.), *Gentlemen, Your Partners Please*, settings of five early Australian dances (1977).

Keyboard   *Elegy for a Headmaster*, pf (n.d.), *Pastoral for Dancing*, org (1938).

Opera   *Endymion* (*c.*1920) National Opera of Australia, 1953, *Dorothea* (*c.*1920/21), *Here's Luck* (n.d.), *The Glittering Mask* (*c.*1922), *The Gates of Paradise* (*c.*1924), *The Serpent Woman* (*c.*1937, John Wheeler), *The Music Critic* (1953), *Christmas* (1959), *The First Christmas* (1969, 1, Pat Flower).

Ballets   *The Circus Comes to Town* (*c.*1924), unperformed, *Capriccio* (*c.*1924), Melbourne, *Corroboree* (1946), *Corroboree* (1950/51, Rex Reid), *Corroboree* (1954 and 1970, Beth Dean), *The Sentimental Bloke* (1955, Beth Dean), unperformed, *Wakooka* (1957, Valrene Tweedy), *G'Day Digger* (1958, Beth Dean), *The Birth of the Waratah* and *The First Boomerang* (1959, Beth Dean), *Snowy* (1961, Margaret Barr), *Black Opal* (1961, Dawn Swane), *Burragarong Dreamtime* (1964, Beth Dean), *The Unknown Land* (1958, Coralie Hinkley), *The Song of Hagar* (1970, Ronnie Arnold).

Oratorio   *The Song of Hagar to Abraham the Patriarch* (1958).

Choral   *The Lovers Walk Forsaken* (n.d.), *My Sister the Rain*, women's ch, str (n.d.), *Cradle Song*, women's ch, str (n.d.), *Black Opal*, ch, timp (1961), *Festival Te Deum* (1964), *Snowy*, sops, orch (1961), *Cantate Domino*, SATB, brass, org (1970), *Jubugalee* (1973).

Songs (v and pf unless stated otherwise)   There are more than 100 songs, song arrangements and settings of psalms, including: *Prospector's Song* and *Song of a Silver City* (*c.*1948), *Westbound* (*c.*1948), *Five Australian Lyrics*, bar, pf/str orch (1953), *Barbara's Song* (1953), *Five Songs of Happiness*, v, pf, ob (1953), *Songs of Praise*, 5 psalm settings (*c.*1954), *Songs of Righteousness*, 5 psalm settings (*c.*1954), *In An Old Homestead Garden* (n.d.), *St Andrew's Carol* (1965), *God Came Down at Christmas* (1965), *Christmas Cradle Song* (1965), *Lullaby* ('Nathan's Song') (1974), *The Kurrajong Song* (1976), *George Street Carol* (1983).

FURTHER REFERENCE

Recordings include *Corroboree Suite,* London Symphony Orchestra cond. E. Goossens (Everest, LBR 6003); Harmonica Concerto, Sydney Symphony Orchestra, cond. J. Antill, L. Easton, harmonica (RCA SL 16372). A discography of ABC tapes to 1972 is in *PlushD.* See also: *CallawayA,* Roger Covell, *Australia's Music: Themes of a New Society* (Melbourne: Sun Books, 1967), Beth Dean and Victor Carell, *Gentle Genius: A Life of John Antill* (Sydney: Akron Press, 1987); *MurdochA.*

PAULINE PETRUS

Anu, Christine   (*b* Cairns, Qld, 1971), Torres Strait Islander singer-songwriter, dancer. She studied at the Aboriginal and Islander Dance School in Sydney, then toured with the Bangarra Dance Theatre to England and America and sang with Neil Murray's Rainmakers. Her songs combine contemporary dance and techno styles with traditional music from the Torres Strait Islands; some use traditional Torres Strait Island instruments in conjunction with electronic and rock instruments. She won the ARIA best Aboriginal/Islander release award in 1995 for the album *Stylin' Up*, and was winner of two ARIA awards in 1996: Best Female Artist and Best Indigenous Release *(Come On).*

FURTHER REFERENCE

Recordings include *Last Train* (1993, Mushroom Records D11565); *Sing Your Destiny* (1993, Mushroom Records D11562); *Island Home/Kubla Yaday* (1994, Mushroom Records D11912); *Monkey and the Turtle/Tama Oma* (1994, Mushroom Records D11792); and *Stylin' Up* (1995, Mushroom Records D24345).

P. DUNBAR-HALL.

Apalach (Apledj).   Cape York clan songs. See *Aboriginal Music* §3(iv).

Apology of Bony Anderson, The.   See *Bony Anderson.*

Apt Scholarships, Nelly.   Three scholarships awarded annually (from 1996) to a singer, instrumentalist and conductor to study at the Rubin Academy of Music and Dance, Hebrew University, Jerusalem, Israel. Administered by the Music & Opera Singers Trust, Sydney, from the estate of Nelly Apt, the singing award is open to professionals aged 26–36, based on tape and live competition; the instrumental award is judged through the ABC Young Performers Award and the conducting award through the ABC conducting workshop. Currently the awards provide fares, living expenses and tuition; the singing award is valued at $30 000, the other awards at $15 000 each.

Arandic.   Language family of the Central Australian desert, comprised of the languages Arrernte, Alyawarr, Anmatyerr and Kaytetye. More is known about the traditional music of Arandic people than other groups: Sir Baldwin Spencer recorded Arandic music on wax cylinders in 1901; anthropologist Harold Davies recorded music from the Alice Springs and Oodnadatta region in 1926–29; and detailed notes and recordings of ceremonial and sacred Arandic music were made by T.G.H. Strehlow in 1949–60, including his seminal work *Songs of Central Australia.* Although these collections are central to our knowledge of Arandic music, it is often unclear to which Arandic language they belong. Anmatyerr, Western Arrernte and Eastern Arrernte music in particular has rarely been distinguished.

The vocal lines are accompanied by thigh-clapping and/or clapsticks; didjeridu were never used in this region. There are various genres of sacred music from this region including ceremonial songs, a choral performance sung in unison to maintain the country to which Aboriginal people are inextricably linked, and a solo performance, sung to prevent sickness, to control the natural environment, such as love charms, or to cause harm to an enemy. Ceremonial songs are grouped together to form a song series and each song has the same melodic contour throughout the series. Arandic songs usually have four isorhythmic patterns in each word group and a breath can only be taken once this is completed, making the tempo of each performance crucial. The invariable musical features which have a unifying function are the melodic contour, isorhythm and topic of the song; so that two renditions of a song having the same contour and isorhythm, despite different melodic ornamentation and different words, can both be deemed the same tune. These variable features are an avenue for creativity within the set rhythmic framework.

The vocal ornamentation in Arandic music is typically melismatic. Verses do not have to begin or end on the first and final syllables of the corresponding prose utterance; frequently the final syllable of a verse becomes the initial consonant of the next verse, creating a kind of linguistic anacrusis. Other features which make the language of songs difficult to understand include displacement of speech stresses, and the use of archaic and metaphorical terms. Traditionally, knowledge of these sacred songs meant prestige and access to the powers of the Ancestors, so people paid a heavy price in gifts and painful initiation to be taught them. It is little wonder that the meaning of these ancient songs, imbued with ancestral powers, is enshrined in a language difficult to decipher. See also *Aboriginal Music* §2.

FURTHER REFERENCE

Davies, E.H., 'Aboriginal Songs of Central and Southern Australia', *Oceania* 2 (1932): 454–67.

Ellis, C.J., 'Ornamentation in Australian vocal music', *Ethnomusicology* 7/2 (1963): 88–95.

——, *Aboriginal Music Making: A study of Central Australian Music* (Adelaide: Libraries Board of South Australia, 1964).

——, 'Aboriginal songs of South Australia', *MMA* 1 (1964): 137–90.

——, 'Central and South Australian song styles', *Anthropological Society of South Australia* 4/7 (1966): 2–11.

——, 'Time consciousness of Aboriginal performers', in *Problems and Solutions: Occasional Essays in Musicology presented to Alice M. Moyle,* ed Jamie C. Kassler and Jill Stubington (Sydney: Hale & Iremonger, 1984), pp. 149–83.

——, and Linda Barwick, 'Musical syntax and the problem of meaning in a central Australian songline', *Musicology Australia* 10 (1987): 41–56.

Hale, Ken, 'Remarks on creativity in Aboriginal verse', in *Problems and Solutions: Occasional Essays in Musicology presented to Alice M. Moyle,* ed Jamie C. Kassler and Jill Stubington (Sydney: Hale & Iremonger, 1984), pp. 254–64.

Moyle, Richard *Alyawarra music: songs and society in a Central Australian community* (Canberra: AIAS, 1986).

Strehlow, T. G. H., *Aranda Traditions* (Melbourne: Melbourne University Press, 1947).

——, 'Australian Aboriginal Songs', *Journal of the International Folk Music Council* 7 (1955): 37–40.

——, *Songs of Central Australia* (Sydney: Angus & Robertson, 1971).   MYFANY TURPIN

Archer, Robyn [Robyn Smith] (*b* Adelaide, 18 June 1948), theatre and cabaret singer, entertainer. Beginning as a folk singer while still at school, she sang rock and roll and jazz while training as a teacher at the University of Adelaide. She then taught in schools for three years before leaving to work as a nightclub singer. In 1974–75 she was acclaimed for her performances in productions of Brecht and Weill's *Seven Deadly Sins* and *The Threepenny Opera* in Adelaide, and it was through her Brecht interpretation that her talents first received overseas recognition, when she was invited to perform in a Brecht program at the National Theatre, London, in 1977. Her one-woman cabaret *A Star is Torn* premiered in Melbourne in 1979, subsequently toured Australia, and ran for a year-long season in London's West End. She was an early supporter of the Belvoir Street Theatre co-operative, with her cabaret *Robyn Archer's Scandals* opening there in 1985, but she based herself in London for much of the 1980s. In 1990 she was awarded a three-year creative arts fellowship, was director of the National Festival of Australian Theatre in Canberra 1993–95, and became the first female artistic director of a major Australian arts festival when invited to direct the Adelaide Festival from 1998 to 2000.

Archer has written more than 20 theatre pieces, many notable for their articulate communication of dense intellectual ideas concerning feminism and sexual politics to a popular audience. She has also written a children's book, *Mrs Bottle Burps* (1983, later extended and reworked as a musical), and has recorded several albums. She has been honoured with an honorary doctorate from Flinders University.

FURTHER REFERENCE

Her writings include: *The Robyn Archer Songbook* (Melbourne: McPhee Gribble, 1980); *Pack of Women* (Melbourne: Penguin, 1986); *A Star is Torn* (London: Virago, 1986); *Mrs Bottle Burps* (Sydney: ABC Enterprises, 1990); *Cafe Fledermaus* (Sydney: Currency, 1990).   BRONWEN ARTHUR

Arena, Phillipa ('Tina'), rock singer. Appearing as a child on TV's *Young Talent Time,* she released the single *Turn Up The Beat* in 1987 and had a role in the stage show *Dynamite* (1989). Her *I Need Your Body* and *The Machine's Breaking Down* charted well in 1990 and she appeared in *Joseph and the Amazing Technicolour Dreamcoat* in 1992. Her albums include *Strong As Steel* (1990) and *Chains*, and she has done session work with Ray Price.

FURTHER REFERENCE

Recordings include *Turn Up The Beat* (1987, Avenue); *I Need Your Body* (1990, Avenue); *The Machine's Breaking Down* (1990, Avenue); and *Strong As Steel* (1990, Avenue) For discography, see *SpencerA*. See also *CA* (1995–96); *SpencerW*.

Arensky String Quartet. Resident quartet at the University of Western Australia from 1977. They appeared at the Festival of Perth in 1978 and toured nationally for Musica Viva.

Ariel (1). Rock group (1973–77) built around former Spectrum members Mike Rudd (guitar, vocals) and Bill Putt (bass), with John Mills (keyboard), Tim Gaze (guitar) and Nigel Macara (drums) in 1973; Harvey James (guitar) and John Lee (drums) in 1974; Glyn Mason (guitar, vocals) in 1975; and Tony Slavich (keyboard, vocals) and Ian McLennan (drums) in 1976. They toured with Gary Glitter in 1973, then went to the UK 1974–75. An innovative band with a large following in Melbourne, their debut album *A Strange Fantastic Dream* (1973) pioneered the use of the Moog synthesiser in Australian rock music, while *Goodnight Fiona* (1976) mixed folk, blues and country styles.

FURTHER REFERENCE
Recordings include *A Strange Fantastic Dream* (1973, EMI EMC2508) and *Goodnight Fiona* (1976, CBS SBP 234867). For discography, see *SpencerA*. See also *McGrathA*; *SpencerW.*

Ariel (2). World music trio, comprised of Matthew Doyle (didjeridu, vocals), Riley Lee (shakuhachi), and Michael Atherton (percussion and strings). Playing an array of Western and non-Western stringed, percussion and wind folk instruments, including hand-made and novelty instruments, they present unique performances of cross-cultural repertoire of beguiling rhythm and rich sonority. They have toured for Musica Viva.

Arlen, Albert (*b* Sydney, 1905; *d* 1993) composer, director. After studying piano with Frank *Hutchens at Sydney and at the École Normale, Paris, he was an actor in Britain 1925–40, writing plays and musicals for the London stage and (from 1935) the BBC, including the musicals *High Temperature, Ladies' Night,* and *Dolores.* After war service he produced shows for the RAF entertainment service in the Far East and Australia, mounting his *The Sentimental Bloke* (Chappell, 1961) at Canberra in 1960, which was taken up by J.C. Williamson's the following year. His works included an operetta, *Old Chelsea* (1933), which was staged starring Richard Tauber, the Concerto *El Alamein* (1944) for piano (Ascherberg, Hopewood & Crew, 1945), incidental music for orchestra, the chorus *Song To Canberra* (Chappell, 1959), songs such as *I Heard a Blackbird in a Tree* (Boosey & Hawkes, 1938) and *A Lad went Piping Through the Earth* (Aschenberg, Hopewood & Crew, 1937) and piano works. Peter Dawson recorded his song *The Rivetter.*

FURTHER REFERENCE
His mss are at *CAnl*. Recordings include *El Alamein* Concerto (1945, HMV EB263); *The Rivetter*, Peter Dawson, Bar (Pearl). A list of 13 works appears in *SnellA* and others in the *BBC Piano*

and Organ Catalogue. See also *GlennonA*, 141; Viola Tait, *A Family of Brothers* (Melbourne: Heinemann, 1971), 261–2; 'Albert Arlen', *Musikkens Hvem Hvad Hvor,* Nelly Backhausen and Axel Kjerulf, 3 vols (Copenhagen: Politikens Forlag, 1950).

Armidale, pop. (1991) 21 605. City on a plateau in the New England Ranges, north-eastern NSW, established 1849. Although chiefly a pastoral hub for the district, it has become a regional cultural centre of considerable importance. The two cathedrals installed fine Fincham organs soon after they were completed (St Peter's Cathedral in 1878 and St Mary's in 1900), and music has always been strong in the excellent private schools. The Armidale Municipal Orchestral Society was founded in 1942, mounting a 36-member orchestra conducted by Campbell Howard, lecturer at the Armidale Teachers' College, which toured the region in 1947. The Armidale Choral Society had 35 singers by 1950, presenting such works as *Merrie England* in concert version. The University of New England (established 1954) achieved international note in music during the 1970s under the distinguished medievalist Gordon *Anderson, and was for many years host to an excellent summer school in music, which attracted teachers of national distinction.

Armstrong-Martin Scholarship. See *Australian Singing Competition.*

Arts Councils. Beginning in 1945, all Australian states developed Arts Councils, networks dedicated to the promotion of the arts in their regional centres. With assistance from their state governments, municipal councils and in some instances from the *Australia Council, the Councils have regional arts officers, community organisations and local volunteer committees which co-ordinate civic support for tours and events in their areas.

The scheme began when opera-singer Dorothy *Helmrich devised the Council for Encouraging Music and the Arts at Sydney in 1943, based on the model of the Arts Council of Great Britain. Helmrich eventually obtained education department funding, and in 1945 arranged the first tour of artists to four regional centres in NSW. By 1950 there were 20 centres participating. Today there are six state bodies which meet together as the Arts Councils of Australia. Musica Viva Australia relies heavily on these organisations for its vast regional touring program, and in some centres the Councils have been the principal source of local instrumental teaching: with assistance from the Arts Council of NSW, for example, South West Music Inc. at Deniliquin, NSW, employs 11 teachers who travel to eight towns in the region providing a core of the instrumental tuition, concerts and youth ensembles available in this remote area.

With good will and a great deal of voluntary work, the councils make available a surprisingly rich array of concerts and schools visits by touring artists, residencies, workshops and tuition programs outside the Australian capital cities, often in quite remote areas.

FURTHER REFERENCE
MackenzieS, 136–40.

Asche, Oscar [John Stranger Heiss] (*b* Geelong, Vic., 24 Jan. 1871; *d* Buckinghamshire, England, 23 Mar. 1936), actor-manager. After attending Melbourne Grammar School and studying acting in Norway, he made his London debut in *Man and Woman* (1893) then joined F.R. Benson's touring Shakespeare company. He formed his own company and leased His Majesty's Theatre, London, from 1907, touring Australia in 1909 and again (with *Kismet*) in 1912. His libretto for the musical *A Child of the Storm* (1914) was not a success, but that for Norton's *Chu Chin Chow* (1916) was a triumph in London, playing for five years, and *Cairo* (1921) was also a hit. A vigorous actor and fluent librettist of the exotic theatrical fancies then popular, he also published two novels. J.C. Williamson brought him home to Australia in 1922 to present his musicals and Shakespeare's plays, but after increasing acrimony, he returned to England in 1924.

FURTHER REFERENCE
His memories are *Oscar Asche: His Life by Himself* (London: Hurst & Blackett 1929). See also *ADB*, 7; H. Pearson, *The Last Actor-Manager* (London, 1950), 65–70.

Ashcroft, Johnny (*b* Mount Pritchard, nr Liverpool, NSW, *c*.1927), country music singer-songwriter. His early experience included singing on Sydney Harbour showboats, then he joined the Great Levante Show, a travelling magic and variety show. In 1954 he recorded six songs for the Rodeo label, but his second session was with Philips; his album *Songs of the Western Trail* was one of the earliest country albums on microgroove. In 1957 he began recording on Graeme ★Bell's label, and with Bell he expanded his style to embrace pop, calypso and traditional and progressive jazz. Probably his best-known song is ★*Little Boy Lost* (1960), based on a true incident where a four-year-old boy survived three days in the rugged New England Ranges, NSW. The song was an enormous hit in Australia, and supported by a film clip was released in South Africa, the USA and UK. Since 1972 Ashcroft has appeared with Queensland singer Gay Kayler in the Johnny Ashcroft Show. In 1980 he was recipient of the inaugural Mo award for best male country entertainer.

FURTHER REFERENCE
Recordings include *Ramblin' Blues* (1954, Rodeo R 089); *They're a Weird Mob* (1958, Bell BS 201); *Little Boy Lost* (1960, DO 4128); *Graeme Bell Plays for Johnny Ashcroft* (Bell 156); and *They All Died Game* (MFP 8218). A discography is in *WatsonC*, 2. See also *SmithB*. JENNIFER HILL

Ashdown, Doug (*b* 1947), popular music guitarist, singer-songwriter. Learning banjo from the age of 10, he worked in bands in the UK from the age of 17, then joined the folk group Bobby Bright and the Bowmen at Adelaide in 1965. By the time he made *Something Strange* in 1969 he had released three albums, and *The Age Of Mouse* (1970) was the first studio double LP album in Australia. He moved to Nashville, USA, with Jimmy Stewart as a songwriting team, but finding little success returned to found the record label Billingsgate in 1974, playing sessions for Robyn Archer, Jeff St John and others, and producing records for such artists as Lee ★Conway and Carol Channing. His soft-rock blend of folk and country achieved a success with *Winter In America* (1974), which reached No. 9 in Australia and No. 14 in the US charts in 1976. One of the best-known Australian songwriters, his songs are intelligent acoustic-based works, many quite sentimental. He continues to tour in Australia and abroad.

FURTHER REFERENCE
Recordings include *Something Strange* (1969, Philips); *Saddest Day Of All* (1970, Sweet Peach); *You're The Song* (1977, Infinity); albums *The Age Of Mouse* (1970, Sweet Peach); *Trees* (1977, Billingsgate); *Love Lives* (1983, Larrikin). For discography, see *SpencerA*. See also *GuinnessP*, I, 115; *McGrathA*; *SpencerW*.

Ashe, John (*b* Townsville, Qld, 1907), country music songwriter. After training as an accountant, he began writing poetry and (from 1938) songs, influenced first by the English ballad style, then by Irving Berlin. Slim ★Dusty recorded *Harry the Breaker*, then six more of his songs, and Chad ★Morgan recorded nine. After the war he appeared as a singer of his own songs on the *Australian Amateur Hour* then recorded several LPs. His *The Old Pioneers* won second place at the Irish International Song Festival in 1966, and *The Kookaburra Laughs* and *King of The Road* also became well known. A stylish writer of traditional country ballads about the outback or pioneering days, in all more than 80 of his songs appeared in recordings, film and television.

FURTHER REFERENCE
Recordings include *Aussie Songs With A Laugh* (1960, EMI) and *Fair Dinkum Mate* (RCA). See also Eric Myers, 'John Ashe: 79 Not Out', *APRAJ* 4/2 (Dec. 1986), 51, 9.

Ashmadai. Opera in one act by Clive Douglas (1935) after Byron's *Heaven and Earth*. It won first prize in the ABC Composer's Competition 1935 and was first performed on ABC radio in 1936.

Atherton, Michael (*b* 17 Feb. 1950), multi-instrumentalist, composer. After studying English at the University of New South Wales, he qualified as a music therapist in 1982 and also worked as a freelance performer, playing a range of early instruments and folk instruments from various cultures. He has made numerous appearances as a solo performer and lecturer at festivals and exhibitions, on ABC radio and SBS television, as well as performances and recordings with ★Southern

Crossings, Michael Askill, and ★Ariel. In 1993 he was artist-in-residence at the Australian Museum; with Southern Crossings he appeared at the Brisbane Biennial and toured Japan, India, Mexico, Jamaica and Hawaii (1991–92), and with Ariel he toured South-East Asia and Japan (1994–95). Also active as a composer-arranger, he has written film scores for Film Australia and the ABC. He is currently professor and head of the department of music at the University of Western Sydney (Nepean campus). An excellent communicator and versatile instrumentalist, he presents his research on musical instruments through unusually vivid lecture-demonstrations. His books include *Australian Made … Australian Played …* (1990) and he has published in *The New Grove Dictionary of Music and Musicians* and elsewhere. In 1990 he won the Australian Guild of Screen Composers award for best documentary film music for *Riding the Tiger*.

FURTHER REFERENCE

Recordings include *Radum Scadum* (ABC 838980A); *Windshift* (1990, ABC 842 322); *Solo* (GIRL LP001). His books are *The ABC Book of Musical Instruments* (ABC. Sydney, 2nd edn, 1992); *Australian Made … Australian Played …* (Sydney: UNSWP, 1992); *Self Promotion for the Professional Musician* (Sydney: Australia Council, 1996).

Atlantics. Instrumental rock band formed at Sydney in 1961, comprised chiefly of Theo Penglis and James Skiathitis (guitars), Bosco Bosonac (bass), and Peter Hood (drums). Riding the craze for instrumentals after the release of stereo record-players on the market in 1961, they played mainly Shadows-influenced numbers, without vocals. Signed by CBS in 1962, their first release was *Moon Man* in 1963; this was followed in October of the same year with *Bombora*, which reached No. 5 in the charts, and their next single, *The Crusher*, also did well. They acted as a backing group for Johnny Rebb, Kelly Green, Colin Cooper and Russ Kruger, and a number of their compositions were covered by overseas and local artists. As the fad for instrumentals passed, their popularity waned. A change to include mainly vocal numbers failed to revive the band's fortunes. Although their later records were less successful on the charts, the band continued to release singles and albums, and influenced a number of bands especially in Sydney. They had several releases abroad, both as the Atlantics and under names such as Gift of Love and Nova, which were moderately popular.

FURTHER REFERENCE

Recordings include *Bombora* (1963, CBS BA.221037); *The Crusher* (1963, CBS BA.221059); *Bombora* (1963, CBS BP.233066 (M)); *Now It's Stompin' Time* (1963, CBS BP.233086); *The Explosive Sound Of The Atlantics* (1964, CBS BP.233103). For a discography, see *SpencerA*. See also Geoff Jermy, *Australian Rock Instrumental Discography* (Golden Square, Vic.: Moonlight Publishing, n.d.); *McGrathA*; *SpencerW*.   BRUCE PETHERICK

Aurukun. Aboriginal community at Archer Bay on Cape York, north Queensland. Originally a Moravian mission established by the Presbyterian Church in 1904, Aurukun has featured in the news because of its rich bauxite deposits and legal issues of title to the land. The Wik peoples are the traditional owners of the area, and their ceremonial songs are land-based, describing activities of Dreamtime Ancestors at specific sites. These tend to have a narrow pitch range, sometimes with only two adjacent pitches, and are heavily interspersed with calls. 'Shake-a-leg' songs, accompanied by calls and a wide-legged dance posture, often describe current events. Island dance from the Torres Strait, where dancers sing in harmony, is becoming one of the dominant song styles. See *Aboriginal Music* §3 (iv).

FURTHER REFERENCE

Moyle, A. 'Aboriginal Music on Cape York', *MA* 3 (1968–69); 3–20; idem, *Songs from North Queensland* (Canberra: AIAS, 1978), 12.   GRACE KOCH

AusMusic. Melbourne-based agency established in 1987 as the Australian Contemporary Music Development Co. to educate young people about the Australian rock industry and promote opportunities for careers in the industry. Under the direction of Pete Steedman, it has established a national information network, published a newsletter, arranged tours to schools throughout Australia, mounted an annual rock eisteddfod, and issued kits for schools.

Austral, Florence Mary (*b* Richmond, Melbourne 26 Apr. 1892, *d* Newcastle, NSW, 15 May 1968), dramatic soprano. She studied with George Andrews 1908–13, with Elise ★Wiedermann 1914–19, initially at the Albert Street Conservatorium and later at the University of Melbourne Conservatorium. Her debut was on 16 May 1922 with the British National Opera Company at Covent Garden as Brünnhilde in *Die Walküre*. Appearing regularly with the company at Covent Garden and across Great Britain and also in the international seasons in 1924, 1929 and 1933, she was a frequent recitalist and concert artist in the UK, the USA and Canada. She appeared at the Berlin Staatsoper 15 November 1930, and at the Holland Festivals of 1931 and 1934. Australian tours were in 1930 and 1934–1936, with the Benjamin Fuller Opera Co. in 1934–35, and she taught at the Newcastle Conservatorium from 1952 to 1959.

Regarded as one of the very finest Wagnerian singers of her generation, Florence Austral was easily the most prominent Australian singer on the international stage during the interwar years. Her career was not long and did not fulfil its early promise, being eroded by the sudden onset of multiple sclerosis when she was in her prime. She did win considerable fame and popularity, however, particularly in the UK where her career was centred, and she was warmly received during her American and Canadian tours, which she undertook almost annually between 1925 and 1937.

She is a rare example of a large Wagnerian voice emerging from Australia. This is partly attributed to her Scandinavian ancestry—her father had hailed from Norway—but she was a singer quite unlike any other produced in Australia until that time. She is also among the earliest Australian singers to achieve a major career after having undertaken most of her training in Australia. (Apart from a few months with Gabriele Sibella in New York, she had studied exclusively with Australian based teachers.)

Though regarded exclusively as a Wagnerian, Austral made many excursions beyond this repertoire: her singing of Handel, Verdi, Mozart, Sullivan and Puccini was particularly admired, and can be sampled in her many admirable recordings made by HMV. Brünnhilde was her most famous role; she was also widely applauded as Isolde, Senta, Tosca and the Marschallin. Like many Wagnerian singers she made a serious study of lied. In recital she sang the songs of Schubert, Schumann, Brahms and Richard Strauss among others, to great acclaim. She often appeared in concert with her husband, flautist John ★Amadio, and she appeared with many of the great singers and conductors of her day. Her final years were marred by her worsening illness, and by the early 1960s she was living under straitened circumstances, practically forgotten. She died penniless in a Newcastle nursing home.

FURTHER REFERENCE
Her recordings include *Florence Austral* (Pearl GEMMCD 9146); *Florence Austral: One of the Wonder Voices of the World* (Larrikin LRH 453). See also *MackenzieS*, 146–51; James Moffat, *Florence Austral: One of the Wonder Voices of the World* (Sydney: Currency, 1995); Thérèse Radic, *ADB*, 7; Desmonde Shawe-Taylor, *GroveD*.
                                                              JAMES MOFFAT

Austral String Quartet (1).   Formed in 1909 by Cyril Monk in Sydney, it was originally comprised of Monk and Anton Tschaikov (violins), Vost Janssen (viola) and Gladstone Bell (cello). They played the traditional quartet repertoire, as well as a number of new works by Franck, Chausson, Debussy and Ravel, several of which were received by an uncomprehending Sydney audience. They also played works by local composers; Alfred Hill played with them from 1911 and wrote his *Maori* Quartets and other works for the group. The quartet established good standards and an adventurous repertoire, and paved the way for the ★Verbrugghen Quartet, which arrived in 1916. All but Monk had gone overseas by 1917, and as he presently became leader of Verbrugghen's NSW State Orchestra he discontinued the ensemble.

Austral String Quartet (2).   Formed (1958) by members of the Sydney Symphony Orchestra, comprised of Donald Hazelwood (violin), Ronald Ryder (d 1974, then Peter Ashley, violin), Ronald Cragg (viola) and Gregory Elmaloglou (cello). They played the traditional repertoire but focused on Australian works, making

important interpretations of quartets by Sculthorpe, Werder, Butterley, Banks and others. They toured Australia extensively, and three times abroad, to Britain (1965), North America, Europe, Israel and India (1972), and the USA, Europe and Japan (1975). The foremost chamber ensemble in Australia in the 1960s, they disbanded in 1977. They had recorded for EMI, Festival, the ABC and the World Record Club.

FURTHER REFERENCE
Recordings include L. Sitsky, String Quartet and F. Werder, String Quartet No. 9 (1971, ABC AC 1017); P. Sculthorpe, String Quartets (c.1973, HMV OASD 7563).

Australasian Performing Rights Association (APRA).   Formed in 1926, APRA is the copyright agency for songwriters, composers and publishers in Australia and NZ. Operating under the Copyright Act (1968), it issues licences for public performance, broadcast or other live transmissions of copyright music and distributes the revenues to about 20 000 copyright-owners (copyright in recordings is controlled by AMCOS). It also makes annual APRA Awards for songwriting, composition and recordings, and publishes the *APRA Journal*. See *Copyright and Performing Rights.*

Australele.   Australian-designed 16-string zither with fixed chords somewhat akin to the autoharp, popular before World War II. By pressing red, green or white buttons, chords I, IV, or V were produced. Hailed by its producers as a milestone in musical progress because players required minimal musical tuition, it made little headway abroad and is rarely heard today.

FURTHER REFERENCE
AthertonA, 156–7.

Australia Council.   The principal national arts funding and advisory agency, established by the Federal Government (1975) in Sydney. Its origins are in the Australian Council for the Arts (founded 1968); but the new body, based on the Arts Council of Great Britain, had significantly different principles of organisation and assessment and greatly enlarged funds. It differs from the various state government funding schemes in its 'arm's length' process, which ensures decisions about specific grants are made at a distance from the influence of the government of the day. Grants for music operated first through a Music Board comprised of eminent musicians, then a Performing Arts Board, and (from 1996) a Music Fund. The council has strongly stimulated composition, ensemble development, and performance in Australia, and its 'peer assessment' methods have ensured an uncommon degree of independence from the political sphere in its decisions.

Australia Ensemble.   Formed as the resident ensemble at the University of NSW (1980), the current members are Dene Olding and Dimity Hall (violins), Irena Moro-zova (viola), Julian Smiles (cello), Geoffrey Collins (flute), Catherine McCorkill (clarinet) and David Bollard (piano), to which other players are freely added. Conceived by Roger Covell and Murray Khouri, the ensemble established a reputation for unusual programs juxtaposing traditional chamber works and new Australian works in ever-changing instrumental combinations. They present a subscription concert series, and since 1982 have toured annually, appearing for Musica Viva throughout Australia, as well as in the UK, the USA, Europe, Russia, NZ, South America, and the Far East. An ensemble of reliably excellent standards and stimulating repertoire, their string members also appear as the Goldner String Quartet.

FURTHER REFERENCE
Recordings include *Mozart Arranged* (ABC/Polygram 438199-2), Dallapiccola *Liriche Griche* (1988, Entracte ESCD 6504), and C.Vine, *Café Concertino* (1991, Tall Poppies RT 002).

Australian Association of Musical Instrument Makers. Formed (1981) in Sydney, with branches in the ACT and Queensland but members in most states. Comprised of both professional and amateur instrument-makers, it seeks to advance communication between its members, improve public knowledge of the quality of Australian makers, and holds annual conventions, often associated with small exhibitions of the work of its members.

Australian Ballet. Founded as the national ballet troupe in 1962 by Peggy van Praagh, based on the example and goodwill previously created by the privately owned ★Borovansky Ballet. One of the company's aims was to 'encourage Australian creative artists … choreographers, composers and painters … to contribute to the creation of new ballets', and in its early years the troupe had a strong association with composers, including Nehama Patkin, Les Patching, James Penberthy, Peter Sculthorpe, Peter Tahourdin and Malcolm Williamson. Since 1970, however, only four composers have secured commissions: Graeme Koehne, Geoffrey Madge, Richard Mills and Carl Vine. Van Praagh was joined by Robert Helpmann as joint artistic director in 1965; Helpmann became the sole director in 1974; since then the troupe's directors have been Anne Williams (1976–77), van Praagh again (1978), Marilyn Jones (1979–82), Maina Gielgud (1983–96) and Ross Stretton (since 1997).

FURTHER REFERENCE
Edward H. Pask, *Ballet in Australia* (Melbourne: OUP, 1982).
                                                    JOEL CROTTY

Australian Brandenburg Orchestra. Established at Sydney (1990) to perform Baroque and Classical repertoire on period instruments. Under the

direction of its founder, harpsichordist Paul Dyer, the orchestra draws from a national pool of specialist players. One of the ensemble's practices is to perform from scores and parts in their original notation. Its repertoire includes solo concertos, operatic scenes, symphonies and dance suites by 18th-century composers, and in 1993 the orchestra performed the Australian Opera production of Monteverdi's *L'incoronazione di Poppea*. The orchestra tours nationally performing in the nation's principal concert halls and has strong ties with the ABC and Musica Viva.

FURTHER REFERENCE
Recordings include *Handel Arias and Instrumental Music* (1995, ABC).   JOHN GRIFFITHS

Australian Broadcasting Corporation (ABC). Government statutory authority providing a national radio and television broadcasting service, formerly the Australian Broadcasting Commission (founded 1932). From 1934 the ABC was also a concert organisation, setting up orchestras, bands and choruses for radio broadcasting and soon expanding into subscription concerts in all capital cities. Today the ABC controls the network of Australia's six full-time symphony orchestras.

Advertising is not permitted on ABC stations, and as licence fees are no longer levied for radio or television reception in Australia, the ABC is financed primarily by an annual grant from the Federal Government. This income is supplemented by profits from the ABC's other ventures as a concert entrepreneur and in recent years the ABC has diversified into commercial recordings and publishing, including its music magazine and program guide, *24 Hours*. ABC shops provide a retail outlet for books, recordings and other ABC program-inspired merchandise. Radio Australia, the ABC shortwave service, provides information on domestic and international affairs to overseas listeners.

1. Broadcasting before the ABC. Experiments with radio broadcasting in Australia gained momentum after reports in 1920 of England's first broadcast concert, featuring Nellie Melba. By 1923 the Australian Federal Government regulated the airwaves, offering licensed broadcasters a particular frequency. Stations were divided into A-class and B-class; A-class were funded through the listener licence fees collected by the government, while other stations funded themselves through on-air advertising. Music made up the major part of the programming of the A-class stations, either from gramophone recordings or from live performances in the studio. Australia's first broadcast orchestral concert came from the NSW State Conservatorium in 1929, and by 1930 'the wireless' was firmly established in Australian life.

2. The ABC to 1945. In 1932 A-class radio stations were nationalised under the auspices of the Australian

Broadcasting Commission. These were funded from licence fees, but an increasingly important and financially rewarding function of the ABC was the organisation of studio performances and subscription concerts, with overseas celebrity artists and conductors as a drawcard. By 1936 ABC studio orchestras had been established in all capital cities to provide variety in the broadcast repertoire and concerts, and they were soon joined by studio choruses. The ABC was now challenged for what was considered unfair competition with private concert promotion enterprises. This was resolved with a new statute requiring that the ABC not book concerts or engage artists for a paying public unless all or part of the concert was broadcast.

Neither was popular music overlooked. The ABC National Dance Band was formed in Sydney in 1935 and enjoyed great popularity with listeners, particularly after several national concert tours. During World War II there were patriotic demands for more Australian compositions on air, and in response the 1942 Australian Broadcasting Commission Act required at least two and a half per cent of music played on national or commercial stations to be works by Australian composers.

The ABC's required commitment to Australian music and musicians was addressed not only through quotas and studio ensembles, but also through competitions: an ABC composition competition was established from 1933, and Bernard Heinze's Melbourne Symphony Orchestra concerto competition was developed by William James into the national ABC Concerto and Vocal Competition from 1944. The ABC also built an infrastructure for maintaining and nurturing its listener audience, with orchestral concerts specifically targeted at certain age groups—schools concerts, youth concerts, and the subscription concerts for the musically mature listener. These concert activities were supported by radio programs aimed at edifying the music listener, notably the *Music Lovers' Hour* hosted for many years by A.E. Floyd. The importance of the *Argonauts Club* for young radio listeners in fostering an entire generation of ardent supporters of the ABC and its ventures should not be underestimated.

3. Commission to Corporation. After the war, symphony orchestras were established in each capital city for broadcasting and concert-giving. An amendment to the Act in 1956 raised to five per cent the proportion of music by Australian composers to be played on ABC radio, and also on the new medium of television. Television was seen as entertainment, rather than as having the educative role of radio, and as early as 1959 the teenage audience was wooed with rock and roll in programs like *Six O'Clock Rock* and later *Countdown*. ABC radio remained more serious, and did not move into the rock and roll market until 1975, with the 24-hour Sydney station 2JJ. Television, with FM sound transmission, also offered better reception for music, and the televising of

concerts, opera and ballet became increasingly popular with ABC audiences, especially with the advent of colour transmission in 1975. FM radio broadcasting began in 1976, with the provision of television/FM radio simulcasts offering a new audio experience for ABC viewers.

The ABC became increasingly reliant on government funding (listener licences had become a minor source of revenue and were abolished in 1974) and in spite of careful provisions within the Act, there have been regular controversies over the ABC's independence from government and perceived political interference in its programming. Few decisions were so controversial as the forced closure of Radio 3ZZZ in 1977. Cuts to the ABC budget have often been interpreted as being politically motivated and certainly the fortunes of the ABC are linked to the prevailing ideology of the government of the day. The showbands and radio choruses were progressively disbanded and by the late 1970s the entire structure and objectives of the ABC were under intense government review. The Green Report (1976) heralded a series of cuts and re-evaluations of the ABC and its activities, and the Dix Report (1981), following a public inquiry into the ABC, recommended a major reorganisation, defining the ABC's role as a broadcaster of information. In this light its role as a concert-giving body was seen as superfluous and it was recommended that the ABC divest itself of the symphony orchestras.

In 1983 the government adopted some of the recommendations, including turning the Commission into a Corporation, but the matter of the orchestras continued to be debated through further commissioned reports (the Tribe Report in 1985, the Waks Report in 1992). Internal structural changes to the music department forestalled immediate action on the orchestras, but the Sydney Symphony Orchestra has operated independently as a subsidiary company of the ABC since 1995.

In 1985 ABC Radio National went to air across Australia with the predominantly spoken-word format of its predecessor, Radio 2. Music was the province of the FM regional network (renamed ABC Classic FM in 1994), with recorded concerts a significant element of programming. Concert-giving remains a major part of the ABC's role, with limited corporate sponsorship adding to financial viability. Australian music is prominent in programming, encouraged by commissions and artist-in-residence programs with the ABC orchestras. (See also individual orchestra entries.)

FURTHER REFERENCE

BrisbaneE; Nancye Bridges, *Wonderful Wireless* (Sydney: Methuen, 1983); Sandra Hall, *Supertoy: 20 years of Australian Television* (Melbourne: Sun Books, 1976); Kenneth S. Inglis, *This is the ABC: The Australian Broadcasting Commission 1932–1983* (Melbourne: MUP, 1983); Peter McCallum, 'ABC Concert Music's Special Development "Policy" for Composers in the Commissioning of Australian Orchestral Music', *SA*, 36 (Summer 1992–93), 5–8; Richard Nile, *Media and Cultural Industries in Australia: Publishing and Broadcasting* (London: Sir Robert Menzies Centre for Australian Studies, 1991); Alan Thomas, *Broadcast and be Damned: The ABC's First Two Decades* (Melbourne: MUP, 1980).

A.H. FORBES

Australian Chamber Orchestra. Formed at the NSW State Conservatorium in 1975 by John Painter, it was managed by Musica Viva until 1985 when it became an independent company. With notable success at raising private and corporate sponsorship, the ensemble now has a full-time core of 18 young string players, to which others are added as needed. With the most relentless touring schedule of any ensemble in Australia, it maintains a national profile, presenting subscription seasons in all state capital cities, visiting country centres regularly and touring abroad twice a year. The orchestra has made strong inroads with audiences beyond Australia, and regularly visits major venues in Europe, the USA, South America and Asia. It has released 15 CDs as well as numerous albums; signing an exclusive recording contract with Sony Music in 1991, its first Sony release won an ARIA award in 1992. Since 1989 the artistic director has been Richard Tognetti, under whose dynamic leadership the orchestra plays with an unerring sense of style and energy. It has long sought to enlarge its core to the complete orchestra of full-time players it so thoroughly deserves, but government assistance has so far never extended far enough to make this possible.

FURTHER REFERENCE
Recordings include P. Sculthorpe, orchestral works, cond. C. Nicholls (1987, Southern Cross SCCD 1016); J. Suk, *Serenades*, cond. C. Mackerras (1988, Conifer CDCF 1970); and *Mozart in Delphi,* cond. C. Nicholls (video, Tesha Media).

Australian Crawl. Rock band (1979–85) based in Melbourne, originally comprised James Reyne (vocals), Simon Binks and Brad Robinson (guitar), Paul Williams (bass), and Bill McDonough (drums). They rose quickly from pub band to national status, within months of forming having signed a recording contract with EMI, who produced 11 of their 15 singles, their mini-album *Phalanx* and five of their six albums. Australian Crawl's first single was *Beautiful People* (1979); national success came with their first album *Boys Light Up* (1980), which remained in the Australian charts for over a year. Lead singer Reyne was voted most popular male performer at the ABC *Countdown* Awards (1980, 1981), and the band voted most popular group (1981, 1983). Their third album, *Sons of Beaches* (1982) and the single *Reckless* (1983) both reached No. 1. The band has sold over 500 000 albums. Australian Crawl received awards for four Top 10 albums, and two placements in the Top 25 Australian Albums 1985–87 for *Sirocco* (No. 11) and *Boys Light Up* (No. 19). Their only US album release, *Semantics* (Geffen) had limited success, but in Australia the grass-roots popularity of the band saw them sponsor the 1984 Bells Beach Surfing Festival. By this time, despite the development of a more mature songwriting style, band members began to disperse to pursue musical careers elsewhere. Their last album, released in 1986, was appropriately titled *Last Wave*. In 1996 the band was acknowledged with membership of the ARIA Hall of Fame.

FURTHER REFERENCE
Recordings include *Boys Light Up* (1980, EMI 8147402); *Down Hearted* (1980, EMI); *If This Is Love* (1985, Freestyle); *Phalanx* (1983, EMI 829759400); and albums *Boys Light Up* (1980, EMI 7801982CD); *Sirocco* (1981, EMI 1660472CD); *Between Rock and a Hard Place* (1985, Freestyle); *Final Wave* (1986, EMI), *Sons of Beaches* (EMI 8319802CD). For a discography, see *SpencerA*. See also *McGrathA*; *National Times* 23-29 Sept. 1983; *SpencerW.*

MARIANNE RIGBY

Australian Elizabethan Theatre Trust. Founded following the success of the Royal Command performances given during the visit of Elizabeth II in 1954. Largely the inspiration of H.C. 'Nugget' Coombs, it built on the concepts explored by Gertrude Johnson in her National Theatre Movement in previous years. The Trust aimed to establish a 'theatre of Australians', and looked forward to sharing in a new Elizabethan age—a renaissance in British arts which it was hoped would ornament the reign of the young queen, crowned just two years before.

With government assistance the Trust acquired the Majestic Theatre, Newtown, in 1955, established drama and ballet companies, and formed an Australian Opera Co. in 1956 (renamed the Elizabethan Trust Opera Co. in 1957) with the ambition of becoming the first full-time national opera company in Australia. Other important ventures followed, including the Australian Ballet School, NIDA, the Marionette Theatre of Australia, and the Theatre of the Deaf. At first relying on the ABC orchestras for its productions, the Elizabethan Trust Orchestra was established in 1967, subsequently divided into Melbourne and Sydney ensembles. By this time the Trust was in receipt of substantial government assistance and had become the dominating national force in the theatre arts.

In the opera company, however, the financial and artistic stability remained fragile in the early years, and the artists could not rely on extended work for some years. The opera and ballet ventures were reorganised and made independent as the Australian Opera and Australian Ballet Foundation respectively in 1970; the orchestras followed, renamed the Australian Opera and Ballet Orchestra, Sydney and the State Orchestra of Victoria, Melbourne, in 1987. The Trust now had a much narrower role, its administration of the tax-deductible donation scheme for the performing arts being one of its few remaining national functions. Its ventures in theatrical production and musicals in the late 1980s were a mixed success, although it played an important role in creating the Bell Shakespeare Co. in 1991. Operations were scaled down, and today the Trust operates a Sydney ticketing agency, publishes a newsletter, and organises theatre parties, concerts and functions for its 1250 members.

FURTHER REFERENCE
John Cargher, 'The Trust', *Bravo! 200 Years of Opera in Australia* (Sydney: ABC/Macmillan, 1988), 55–87; *BrisbaneE*, 282ff.

Australian Folk Trust [Folk Trust of Australia]. National body based in Canberra and dedicated to the promotion of folk arts and culture, until 1994 comprised of 10 state and regional folk organisations. Originally organised to allocate the annual national folk festival to a host state, from 1977 it operated a grants program on behalf of the Australia Council for folk arts performance, collection and documentation, and more recently for multicultural dance projects. It also publishes the *National Folk Directory* and the *Journal of the Australian Folk Trust*. Criticised in the past for having too narrow a focus on Anglo-Celtic folk traditions, in 1994–95 the trust took several steps to redefine its activities, broadening its membership to embrace any community-based organisation with an interest in folklife and cultural traditions, and renaming itself the Folk Trust of Australia. In 1996, however, the Australia Council withdrew the funding that had sustained the Trust for nearly 20 years, precipitating a winding up of its activities.

FURTHER REFERENCE
OxfordF.

Australian Hymn Book, The. The most widely used book of songs of praise in Australian churches. Compiled 1968–74 by consultation between the Anglican, Congregationalist, Methodist and Presbyterian churches of Australia, and also used (with a Catholic Supplement) by the Roman Catholic Church, it contains some hymns by Australians, modern British and American songs, as well as many traditional hymns, and was published in 1977 (Sydney: Collins). See *Church Music.*

Australian Institute of Aboriginal and Torres Strait Islander Studies (AIATSIS). Established in Canberra as the Australian Institute of Aboriginal Studies (AIAS) by an Act of Parliament in 1964, it gained its present name through a second Act in 1989. AIATSIS is governed by a council partly elected by its members and partly appointed by the Federal Government. A permanent staff of about 60 and a number of visiting and temporary staff are responsible for its three main programs: conducting and sponsoring research, developing and maintaining a resource collection, and publishing Aboriginal studies titles. Publications on indigenous music have included several books, a series of records/cassettes/CDs, films and videos, and articles published in the Institute's journal *Australian Aboriginal Studies.*

STEPHEN WILD

Australian Jazz Convention. First held in Melbourne in 1946, this is the world's oldest and longest surviving jazz festival, celebrating its 50th anniversary in Melbourne in 1995. Now occupying the period 26–31 December, it emerged from a convergence in Melbourne of revivalist jazz players (especially Graeme *Bell), the communist Eureka Youth League (especially Harry Stein) and radical artists connected with the Contemporary Art Society and the journal *Angry Penguins.* The latter two soon faded, but the event survived as a focal point of the Australian revivalist movement, albeit with expanding stylistic parameters. Since 1950 when it was shifted to Sydney, its venue has moved each year, with rural centres becoming increasingly frequent. The handful of bands at the first Convention had grown to over 300 by 1995, with musicians and delegates exceeding 1 000. Apart from programmed concerts, there are continuous informal jam sessions, and permanent fixtures include an original tunes competition, a picnic and a street parade. Although since 1958 there have been permanent trustees of the surplus funds generated, and later a standing steering committee, each Convention is organised by an autonomous, unpaid committee, operating without commercial or state subsidy. With occasional exceptions, musicians appear gratis, and any group may get a performance simply by paying to register. While this inevitably produces musical unevenness, at best the dissolution of the barriers between performers and audiences constitutes a celebration of musical democracy, embodying an instructive, if ambiguous, lesson about Australian culture.

FURTHER REFERENCE
Recordings include *13th Australian Jazz Convention* (1958, Columbia 33OSX 7618); *The Original Tunes* (1980, Jazznote JNLP 026). See also *BissetB; OxfordJ*; Norman Linehan (ed), *Bob Barnard, Graeme Bell, Bill Haesler, John Sangster on the Australian Jazz Convention* (Sydney: Australian Jazz Convention Trust Fund, 1981).   BRUCE JOHNSON

Australian Jazz Quintet. Formed as a quartet in 1954, it comprised Ontario-based Australians Errol *Buddle, Bryce *Rohde and Jack *Brokensha (vibraphone, drums), with US musician Dick Healey (bass, alto, flute). It became a top-rated group in the USA, outbilling artists like Max Roach and Miles Davis, and the members were frequent poll-winners, individually and collectively. It became a quintet with the addition of bassist Jimmy Gannon, who was succeeded by Australian Jack Lander, then Ed *Gaston. After a tour of Australia in 1958 the band broke up in late 1959, with Brokensha and Healey returning to the USA, followed some years later by Rohde.

FURTHER REFERENCE

Recordings include *The Australian Jazz Quintet Plus One* (1956, Bethlehem BCP 6012). See also *ClareB*; *BissetB*; *GroveJ*; *OxfordJ*.   BRUCE JOHNSON

Australian Journal of Music Education. Biannual journal (founded 1967) of the Australian Society for Music Education. It appeared until No. 32 (1982); then a new series in association with the International Society for Music Education, from 1984. A cumulative index for Nos 1–25 was compiled by Jean Farrant and issued in 1980.

Australian Mechanical Copyright Owners Society (AMCOS). Based in Sydney, it controls the licensing of music for mechanical reproduction, and collects royalties for copyright owners from sound recordings, films, videos. Royalties from performance are collected by ★APRA. See *Copyright and Performing Rights*.

Australian Music Centre. Originally established (1975) as an information agency to document and promote Australian composers at home and abroad, today the centre is a national organisation which facilitates the use of Australian music through an array of publications and services. Relying on Australia Council support, under its founding director James ★Murdoch the centre represented all composers interested in its services without restriction, marketing their scores and performing materials, managing the Australia Council/APRA parts-copying scheme, developing a library and information service, and issuing a newsletter *AMC News*. But as the limits of financial assistance were reached in the mid-1980s a selection process for composers interested in representation status had to be developed.

The impact of the centre sharpened dramatically under Richard ★Letts, executive director 1987–93. The trading name Sounds Australian was adopted, an attractive facsimile format was developed for publishing composers' scores, a house recording label (now Vox Australis) was conceived, educational resource kits on Australian music were commissioned, and the *AMC News* was transformed into a thought-provoking and often outspoken quarterly, *Sounds Australian*. The annual Sounds Australian Awards were inaugurated in 1988, attracting strong media interest and quickly achieving high credibility; inexplicably, none were made after Letts's departure until 1996. A major conduit for information about Australian music, today the centre represents over 250 composers and has 1300 members.

Australian Music Examinations Board (AMEB).
Organisation offering public examinations in music, and in speech and drama. In 1887 a program of public music examinations was initiated by the universities of Adelaide and Melbourne, leading over the next 20 years to the emergence of an agreement between educational authorities in all states, and in 1918 the first full meeting of the AMEB took place in Sydney. A motion put by University of Melbourne professor ★Laver that 'this conference records with much satisfaction the consummation of the Pan-Australian Scheme of Public Examinations, which was initiated by the late Franklin Peterson, Ormond Professor of Music in the University of Melbourne', was unanimously carried. This was the beginning of a federal body whose purpose was the provision of graded assessments for students of music (later, for students of speech and drama also). In 1906 Allans Publishing Melbourne began producing teaching material by arrangement with the examining body.

Today the board consists of representation from each of the signatories to the AMEB constitution, the Universities of Melbourne, Adelaide and Western Australia, the Minister for Education and Training in NSW, the Minister for Education in Queensland, and the Minister for Education and the Arts in Tasmania. A federal office and six state offices, one in each state, co-ordinate all activities and policies of the board. Grade and diploma examinations are available in a wide range of practical and theoretical subjects of speech, instrumental and vocal music. Music syllabus lists are based on repertoire drawn from traditional Western music and contemporary popular music. All syllabus development occurs nationally, involving wide consultation with specialist representatives from each state.

From time to time there has been criticism of the effects of public music examinations upon musical education, and many issues of syllabus orientation and content are debated. Some notable music pedagogues have declined to present their students for such examinations. But irrespective of whether candidates use an examination system or not, the AMEB syllabus lists offer Australian students access to carefully graded, universally recognised repertoire for study. The syllabuses are supported through an extensive publishing program, offering well over 100 titles, publishing with standards and editorial practices determined on the advice of leading Australian publishers and musicologists. The board is committed to the inclusion of works by Australians and New Zealanders in its own publications and in syllabus lists. Assessment of performance of each syllabus is offered throughout urban and rural Australia, as well as an increasing number of countries in the Asia-Pacific region. Grade and diploma examinations are organised by each state. AMEB-approved specialist examiners in the areas of instrumental and vocal music, and speech, are engaged for the purpose of assessment. Juries, including a federal examiner, are appointed for the assessment of Licentiate (★LMusA) and Fellowship (★FMusA) recitals and for all diplomas in written and theoretical subjects.

Many distinguished Australians have been associated with the activities of the AMEB, either as candidates, examiners, syllabus writers, editors or Board members. See *AMusA*; *Music Education*; *Music Theory and Analysis*.

FURTHER REFERENCE
Minutes of AMEB meetings are located in the University of Melbourne Archives.   JANICE B. STOCKIGT

Australian Music Teacher. Bimonthly magazine (founded 1990) of musical events, reviews and articles directed at private music teachers, commercially published in Melbourne, incorporating the *Australian Guitar Journal* from 1991.

Australian Musical News. Monthly magazine published by Allans Music, Melbourne (1911–63) as a news-pictorial digest for Australian musicians and music-lovers. Its subtitles for a time were 'Musical Digest', or 'Theatrical and Dramatic News'. Lina Marsi has published a valuable *Index to the Australian Musical News 1911–1963* (Melbourne: Lima Press, 1990).

Australian National Academy of Music. Founded in 1994 with its administration in South Melbourne, the Academy supplements the work of Australia's music schools by conducting masterclasses and short-term courses in various capital cities for a small number of the most exceptionally gifted young musicians, chiefly orchestral and chamber music players, selected each year from around Australia. Distinguished international staff are chosen from players of the front rank around the world. Funded by the Federal and Victorian Governments, the organisation is affiliated with the University of Melbourne, but does not offer degrees or diplomas. The director is Trevor Green.

Australian National Choral Association (ANCA). Founded (1990) by merger of the Australian Choral Association and the Australian Choral Conductors Association. It has branches in most states, holds regular symposia and workshops with noted choral conductors from abroad, and issues a stimulating quarterly journal *Sing Out*.

Australian Opera   See *Opera Australia*.

Australian Opera and Ballet Orchestra. Theatre orchestra founded (1987) at Sydney, comprised of 69 full-time players. The orchestra's origins are in the Australian Elizabethan Theatre Trust (Sydney) Orchestra, formed in 1967 to accompany the Sydney performances of the Trust's Opera Co. and the Australian Ballet. With significant funding from the Australia Council and the State Government, the orchestra's management was passed to the Australian Opera in 1987 and the present name adopted. The orchestra is fully occupied accompanying the Sydney seasons of Opera Australia and the Australian Ballet. A problem for the orchestra has been the shifting demands of conductors of the two companies it serves, and over the years the orchestra has at times had difficulty establishing a continuity of musical policy. Nevertheless it has achieved admirable standards. The current musical adviser is David Stanhope and the artistic director is Moffatt Oxenbould.

Australian Record Industry Association (ARIA). Agency based at Sydney, comprised of the recording companies. It co-ordinates submissions to government, information about the industry, and makes annual ARIA awards for excellence in various categories of record production.

Australian Singing Competition. Largest and most valuable singing competition in Australia. Held annually for singers under 26 and professionals under 35 who are Australian or NZ citizens. Administered by the Music & Opera Singers Trust, Sydney, principally from the estate of the distinguished singing teacher Marianne Mathy-Frisdane (*d* 1978), it was established as the Marianne Mathy Scholarship in 1982 (the Mathy and Opera Awards from 1986), and with commercial sponsorship a contemporary section was added in 1983–89. Winners have included Jeffrey Black, Miriam Gormley and David Lemke. The awards total over $50 000, most notably the Marianne Mathy Scholarship ($25 000) and the Armstrong-Martin Scholarship ($9000).

Australian Society for Music Education (ASME). Society founded by Frank *Callaway (1967) to encourage and advance music education in Australia at all levels. With chapters in all states, it organises national annual conferences, regular chapter meetings, and issues both state and national newsletters. Under Callaway's leadership in the 1970s, it had over 2000 members, participated in international UNESCO projects, and its biannual journal *Australian Journal for Music Education* contained musical supplements and articles on a very broad array of music education issues. ASME stimulated the growth of other, more specialist teacher societies, but these inevitably diminished its own membership, and today it continues on a somewhat reduced scale, chiefly focusing on the needs of classroom music teachers.

Australian String Quartet. Formed in Adelaide in 1985, comprised of William Hennessy (until 1996) and Elinor Lea (violins), Keith Crellin (viola) and Janis Laurs (cello). Their residency at the Elder Conservatorium and substantial government assistance have allowed them to develop as a full-time ensemble in a way few other Australian quartets have achieved. Appearing regularly for Musica Viva in all capital cities, regional centres and schools, they have undertaken eleven international tours since 1987, including Europe, the USA, Russia, China and NZ. Playing with unfailing elegance, energy and technical polish, they are Australia's most distinguished string quartet. They have focused on the standard quartet repertoire, but have also presented a number of commissioned works by Australian composers.

FURTHER REFERENCE
Recordings include *String Quartets* (ABC/Polygram 442347-2); Mozart, Haydn and Beethoven quartets (ABC 426 805B); complete quartets of Alfred Hill (Marco Polo Records, 1994–).

Australian String Teachers' Association. Society for studio teachers of stringed instruments. They hold seminars and string schools, and have published a quarterly journal, *Australian String Teacher,* from 1976.

Australian Wind Virtuosi. Formed (1979–85) from principal players of the Sydney Symphony Orchestra, it comprised chiefly Janet Webb (flute), Guy Henderson (oboe), Lawrence Dobell (clarinet), Robert Jackson (french horn) and John Cran (bassoon), but expanded as repertoire required. It evolved from the New Sydney Woodwind Quintet, now named more loosely to embrace repertoire beyond the wind quintet. It played regularly for the ABC, its touring including Hong Kong and NZ. Many of the members subsequently appeared as the Sydney Wind Soloists, then the Sydney Soloists.

Australian Youth Orchestra. See *Youth Music Australia.*

Australia's Amateur Hour. Radio talent quest (1937–60) on Sydney's 2UW, sponsored by the Brothers Lever company, first compered by Harry Dearth, then Dick Fair (from 1942) and finally George Dear. It went to 54 commercial stations around the country, and in the postwar years via Radio Australia to troops in Korea and Japan. The show would travel to venues in various cities, contestants received some peremptory coaching before they appeared, and listeners were invited to vote on the acts. One of the top-rating shows on radio, a move to TV was attempted in 1955, but it did not flourish there. The best known and longest running of Australia's radio talent quests, it provided a starting point for a great variety of artists, from comic entertainer Rolf Harris to opera-singer Donald Smith.

FURTHER REFERENCE
Colin Jones *Something in the Air: A History of Radio in Australia* (Kenthurst, NSW: Kangaroo Press, 1995), 64; Jacqueline Kent *Out of the Bakelite Box* (Sydney: ABC Publications, 1983), 151-6.

Avion (Lionheart). Rock group formed in 1983 by the Waller brothers, Randall (guitar, vocals), Kendall (bass, vocals) and John (drums, vocals), with Paul Janell (guitar), Martin Tool (guitar) and Evan Murray (keyboards). Their singles included *I Need You* (1983) and *Ships* (1987), and

their albums included *Avion* (1983) released in the USA before Australia, and *White Noise* (1986, EMI).

FURTHER REFERENCE
Recordings include *I Need You* (1983, RCA 104101), *Ships* (1987, EMI 1912), *Avion* (1983, RCA AFL 14750), and *White Noise* (1986, EMI EMX 430046). For discography, see *Spencer A.* See also *Spencer W.*

Awards. National means of recognition for outstanding musical achievement at first progressed slowly in Australia. After Nellie Melba was created a Dame in 1918, outstanding Australian musicians were regularly honoured in the British imperial honours, then (from 1975) in the Australian honours, but the many specialist awards for musical distinction existing today have developed chiefly since the 1970s.

The *Australian Performing Rights Association (APRA) makes annual awards for songwriting, composition and recording. The *Australian Music Centre makes its Sounds Australian Awards for composition, performance, and recording of Australian work, and the University of Melbourne makes its Sir Bernard Heinze Award to acknowledge an outstanding contribution to Australian music.

In the recording industry the achievement of a gold or platinum record based on sales figures is an important distinction, and the *Australian Recording Industry Association (ARIA) makes awards for recordings. In rock music there was the national *Battle of The Sounds (1966–72), then the King of Pop (from 1967, a series of awards made by popular vote through the magazine *GoSet* until 1970, then *TV Week* until 1979); these became the *ABC *Countdown* Awards (1979–87). A variety of awards have played their part in popular music, most notably the Mo awards and the TV Logies, which include awards for musical performers. The Australasian Country Music Awards (ACMA) of Golden Guitars for composition, performance and recording of country music are made at the Tamworth country music festival. The Australian Film Institute (AFI) includes awards for the most original film music. For distinguished contribution to instrumental teaching the AMEB occasionally awards honorary *FMusA diplomas. A few Australian universities have conferred honorary degrees for distinction in composition, performance or musical scholarship, but Australia has yet to develop the specialist awards for musical scholarship which exist in learned societies abroad.

Axiom. Rock group (1969–71) consisting of already seasoned players, former *Groop members Brian Cadd (organ) and Don Mudie (bass), with Glen Shorrock (vocals), Doug Lavery (drums, then Don Lebler from 1970) and Chris Stockley (guitar). Cadd and Mudie wrote the songs, and after their single *Arkansas Grass* reached No. 7 in the charts in 1969, they toured England and Australia in 1970, making an album, *Fool's Gold*, that featured quite innovative instrumentation, including didjeridu. They had two more Top 10 singles, but failed to make a lasting impact and disbanded in 1971.

FURTHER REFERENCE

Recordings include *Arkansas Grass* (Parlophone A8909) and *Fool's Gold* (Parlophone PC O7561). For discography, see *SpencerA*. See also *McGrathA*; *SpencerW*; *GuinnessP*, I, 135.

Ayers Rock. Rock group (1973–81) of seasoned players, which evolved from a trio of Ray Burton (vocals, guitar), Duncan McGuire (bass, *d* 10 July 1989), and Mark Kennedy (drums), to which were added Jimmy Doyle (guitar, vocals) and Col Loughnan (winds, piano). In 1974 they released their debut album, *Big Red Rock*, a live recording of jazz-influenced rock with notable drum solos from Kennedy. They then went to the USA and recorded *Beyond* in 1975, but personality differences in late 1976 caused a major split; when they recorded *Hot Spell* in 1980 only Doyle remained from the original members.

FURTHER REFERENCE

Recordings include *Big Red Rock* (Mushroom L35354), *Beyond* (Mushroom L35707), and *Hot Spell* (Red Rock Records RRM 6321). For discography, see *SpencerA*. See also *McGrathA*; *SpencerW*; *GuinnessP*, I, 137.

Aztecs, The. See *Thorpe, Billy*.

B

Badger, Harold (*b* Melbourne, 1930), composer, administrator. After studying piano with Lindsay ★Biggins he went to London in 1950, studying composition and conducting with Almyr ★Buesst at the Royal College of Music and with Georges Tzipine. He conducted at York from 1950, returned to Australia to join the ABC music staff in 1953 and conducted for the Victorian Ballet Guild and other groups. He worked as *répétiteur* and conductor of student operas at the University of Melbourne in 1963, and was director of the Melba Memorial Conservatorium 1963–75. A composer of various short orchestral works and chamber music, his *Melbourne Cup* (1962) was the first Australian work commissioned by the Australian Ballet.

FURTHER REFERENCE
His String Quartet No. 1 (1961) was recorded by the Paul McDermott String Quartet (W&G A1635). As conductor his recordings include Dorian Le Gallienne, *Voyageur,* Victorian Ballet Guild Orchestra (1954, W&G AL660). See also *GlennonA*; *HolmesC*.

Baer, Werner (*b* Berlin, 1914; *d* Sydney, 28 Jan. 1992), broadcast administrator, pianist. He studied piano with Artur Schnabel at the Hochschule für Musik, Berlin, and from 1934 worked as a *répétiteur* at the Berlin Stadtsoper and as an organist. Fleeing the Nazis in 1938, he went to Singapore, teaching at the Far Eastern Music School, as well as broadcasting recitals and helping to launch Singapore's first orchestral subscription concerts. After war service in the Australian Army, he taught at the NSW State Conservatorium and was NSW music supervisor for the ABC 1951–79. He was an active vocal adjudicator and coach, and conductor of the Singers of Australia and the Great Synagogue, Sydney. An instinctive yet reflective pianist and at times an irascible character, as a composer he wrote art songs and children's music, including *Under the Coolabah Tree: Songs for Young Australians* (Paling, 1955), and *Salute to Australia: Songs For Australians* (Paling, 1951), which shared the prize in the Australian National Song Competition in 1951. He was honoured with the MBE in 1977, and an annual piano competition with the Federated Music Clubs bears his name.

FURTHER REFERENCE
Obit. in *Musical Opinion* (Apr. 1992), 150–1. See also *APRA*, 2/9 (Dec. 1981).

Bailey, Bert (Albert Edward) ['Albert Edmunds'] (*b* Auckland, NZ, 11 June 1872; *d* 30 Mar. 1953), vaudeville entertainer, writer. He arrived in Sydney in 1879 and worked in vaudeville as a singer, then as an actor for Edmund Duggan's touring company (1889) and as a comedian for William Anderson's troupe (from 1900). With Duggan, as 'Albert Edmunds', he wrote the melodrama *The Squatter's Daughter* (1907), *The Man from the Outback* (1909), then *On Our Selection* after the stories of Steele Rudd (1912), which became a minor classic, performed repeatedly until the 1930s. One of the most successful figures in Australian melodrama and creator of the character Dad Rudd, he presented productions at the King's Theatre, Melbourne (1912–27) and retired in 1940.

FURTHER REFERENCE
Obit. in *SMH* 5 Apr. 1953. His manuscripts are in *CAnl*. See also *ADB*, 7; *IrvinD*; *ParsonsC*.

Bailey, Judy (Judith Mary) (*b* Auckland, NZ, 3 Oct. 1935), jazz pianist, composer. She began learning piano at the age of 10, gaining her ATCL at 16, but thereafter was increasingly jazz-based, becoming arranger-composer for the Auckland Radio Band. She settled in Sydney in 1960 and was active in session work (including with Tommy ★Tycho), and at ★El Rocco, including with Stewie Speer, Don Burrows, Graeme Lyall, Lyn Christie (bass), and John Sangster. In 1974 she formed a quartet with saxophonist Ken James (later Col Loughnan), Ron Philpott, and John Pochée, which she led over the next decade. Active in education establishing schools programs, she has composed for children's radio, television and theatre, and for documentaries, and in 1995 was commissioned to write for the Sydney Children's Choir. She has taught in the Sydney Conservatorium jazz program since its inception (1973), had a term as musical director for the Bennelong Series at the Sydney Opera House from 1978, and has been musical director for Sydney Youth Jazz Ensemble since 1990, for which she wrote *Australiana Suite*. She served on the Music Board of the Australia Council (1982–85), and toured South-East Asia for Musica Viva (1978, 1982 and as soloist, 1986).

Performing for more than 30 years, she is one of the few women with long and successful careers in Australian jazz. She has composed for jazz and orchestral settings, including Don Banks's *Nexus* (1987), her String Quartet (1994), and *Two Minds One Music,* for orchestra and jazz group (in progress). She was the inaugural winner of the APRA award for jazz composition and won a Mo Award in 1992.

FURTHER REFERENCE

Recordings include *You & The Night & The Music* (1964, CBS BP-233126); *My Favourite Things,* Judy Bailey Quartet (1965, CBS BP-233263); *One Moment,* Judy Bailey Quartet (1974, Philips 6357 018); *Colours,* Judy Bailey Quartet (1976, Eureka E-103); *Solo* (1977, Eureka E-107); *Notwithstanding* (1980, Phonogram 510 600–2); *Nexus and Nocturnes* (1987, Vox Australis, VAST 006/2); *Sundail,* Judy Bailey and Friends (1993, ABC/Polygram 514 978–2). An interview with her is in *WilliamsA*, 98–105. See also *ClareB*; *BissetB*; *CA*; *GroveJ*; *OxfordJ*; Eric Myers, 'An Improvised Career', *APRAJ* iv/1 (1986), 6.

BRUCE JOHNSON

Bainton, Edgar Leslie   (*b* London, 14 Feb. 1880; *d* Sydney, 8 Dec. 1956), composer. He was educated at King Henry VIII School at Coventry, and in 1896 won an open scholarship to the Royal College of Music, where he studied under Stanford and Franklin Taylor. In 1901 he was appointed professor of piano and composition at the Newcastle upon Tyne Conservatoire, and became principal in 1912. Visiting Germany in 1914 for the Bayreuth music festival, he was interned in Ruhleben camp with other musicians after the declaration of war. On return to Newcastle, he continued activities as teacher, pianist, composer and conductor of the Newcastle Philharmonic Orchestra. A prolific composer, frequently using late-Romantic harmonic language, his symphony *Before Sunrise* won a Carnegie Trust Award in 1917, and he was elected FRCM and awarded an honorary DMus by the University of Durham. In 1934 he was appointed director of the NSW State Conservatorium in Sydney where he raised the standards of the conservatorium diploma and founded the conservatorium's opera school. In Sydney he played a vital role in the development of musical life, reviving chamber music concerts, increasing the number of orchestral concerts, teaching, playing, examining and lecturing. In addition to conducting performances of his own works, from 1939 he directed an annual Easter performance of Bach's *St Matthew Passion*. At Sydney in 1944 one of his major works, an opera, *The Pearl Tree*, was successfully staged.

FURTHER REFERENCE

Helen Bainton, *ADB*, 7; idem, *Remembered on Waking* (Sydney: Currawong, 1960), which contains a list of works; Eric Blom, *Grove's Dictionary of Music and Musicians*, ed. Eric Blom, 5th edn. (London: Macmillan, 1954); Franz Holford, 'Edgar Bainton (1880–1956)', *The Canon* (Jan. 1957), 198–9; David Tunley, *GroveD*; idem, 'Thoughts on the Music of Edgar Bainton', *Westerly* (June 1963), 55. For an index to various references to Bainton in the *AMN* see *MarsiI*.   THOMAS HEYWOOD

Baker, Glenn A.   (*b* 1952), rock historian, archivist. In his late teens he began writing for Australian rock magazines *Go-Set*, *Tharunka* and *Cosmos*, then while managing various bands in his twenties, most notably ★Ol'55 and Cheek, he also wrote for the mainstream Australian rock periodicals *RAM* and *Juke*. By the 1980s and 90s Baker had become a rock music scholar of international repute. He has compered various television rock programs, written for hundreds of major publications, and compiled albums of songs by various artists from both Australia and overseas. He is also host of the long-running syndicated radio show *Back to the Future*, the resident music expert on Channel 10's *Good Morning Australia*, and thrice winner of the BBC's Rock Brain of the Universe award.

FURTHER REFERENCE

His books include *The New Music* (Sydney: Bay Books, 1980); *The New Rock 'n' Roll* (London: Omnibus, 1983); *The Name Game* (Sydney: Weldon, 1984); *External Combustion* (Sydney: Grahame, 1990); *Perpetual Motion* (Sydney: Allen & Unwin, 1993); and *Faces, Places and Barely Human Races* (Sydney: Random House, 1995). See also *SpencerW*.   AARON D. S. CORN

Baker, Tom (John Thomas)   (*b* Oakdale, California, 14 Sept. 1952), jazz trumpeter, saxophonist. He began piano at the age of six, then trumpet at 15. After arrival in Australia he worked under various leaders, including Nick Boston and Ray ★Price, on trumpet, tuba and vocals. He formed his San Francisco Jazz Band in 1975, and toured widely with it, including to the USA in 1977, before leaving to form a succession of other bands. He has appeared chiefly as a leader or featured guest in Australia and overseas. Adding saxophone to his repertoire in 1981 also marked an expansion of his mainstream style.

FURTHER REFERENCE

Recordings include *Absolutely Positively Tom Baker* (1990, RooArt CD 846311–2). See also *OxfordJ*; Eric Myers, 'Tom Baker: Apostle of Swing', *JA* (Summer/Autumn 1984), 7–12.

BRUCE JOHNSON

Ballad. (1) Traditional ballads are short narrative folksongs, often of uncertain authorship, preserved in the aural tradition and consequently often found in numerous versions. Australia has a sizeable literature of traditional ballads, some dating from convict times. (2) ★Broadside ballads are written-down versions of traditional ballads, published for their topical interest in the 18th and early 19th century in crudely printed handbills. A number of Australian traditional ballads circulated in broadsides in the 19th century. (3) Bush ballads and rural ballads are short narrative songs newly composed by known authors in the traditional ballad style; some date from the mid-19th century, but most from the folk-song revival and country music movement of the 1950s onwards. See *Folk Music*.

Ballad of Kelly's Gang, The. Folk-song of nearly 20 verses. Set to the Irish 'The Wearing of the Green', it is one of several traditional songs to recount with humour and some admiration the exploits of the best-known of Australia's bushrangers, Edward (Ned) Kelly, the Irish Catholic youth who, with his brother Dan, Steve Byrne and Joe Hart was driven by troubles with the authorities into banditry in 1878, was captured and hanged in 1880, his exploits and the home-made suit of armour he wore soon passing into folklore. First collected by A.V. Vennard *c.*1939.

FURTHER REFERENCE
Edition and commentary in *Edwards G*.

Ballad Opera. English farce with interspersed music, often ballads or folk-songs, originating in the 18th century. John Gay's *The Beggar's Opera* (1728), a ballad opera with music by John Pepusch, as well as the various ballad operas of Sir Henry Bishop were among the first works performed on the Australian stage in the 1830s, and remained popular into the 1870s.

Ballarat, pop. (1991) 64 980, city on the Yarrowee River in central Victoria, founded 1851. A road and rail centre for the surrounding agricultural and pastoral district, it is one of the largest inland cities in Australia. Music came to Ballarat with the miners who flocked to the fields after the first discovery of gold in August 1851 and reflected their melting-pot of nationalities. English, Irish, Scotch, Welsh and Cornish blended with Europeans—among whom the Germans were particularly successful—Jews and Americans. The Chinese were present in large numbers (9000 in 1858), attracting attention by their 'excruciating instruments' and outlandish cultural practices. S.T. Gill's sketches of life on the goldfields depict music as integral to the earliest entertainments in the hotels, with the musicians partaking as freely of the comforts of alcohol as the patrons. The theatres (five by the end of 1854, each with its own small band), concert halls and hotels of Main Street, Ballarat East, offered a variety of

entertainments by the mid-1850s: slapstick, melodramas, opera, farce, vaudeville and circus, with French and Italian singers being much in demand. In 1854 Richard Henry Sutton laid the basis of a successful business selling concertinas and other instruments to the miners. Against the profanity and rough transience of this largely bachelor community, the Wesleyans asserted the values of respectability and Sabbath observance and the singing of hymns was heard in their tent church from as early as September 1851. The earliest musical societies, most of them short-lived, are listed in Withers' *History of Ballarat*.

By 1871 Ballarat was a city of about 47 000 people, drawing great benefit from its prosperous pastoral hinterland. Ballarat West became the centre of the city's development after the opening of the railway from Geelong in 1862. Consolidation of cultural life was guided by pioneering individuals for whom public philanthropy was an appropriate expression of worldly success. The values of British upper and middle-class culture were reinterpreted and remade in a liberal-democratic ideal of equality of opportunity. The influence of the Wesleyans, with their emphasis on home and church, was decisive in shaping cultural attitudes, as was the commitment of prominent civic figures. Music was identified with high moral purpose: community harmony, rational recreation and self-improvement. Nowhere are these values better expressed than in the great educative enterprise that is the ★(Royal) South Street Eisteddfod, which established Ballarat's national reputation as a musical city. Originating in a secular self-improvement society in 1879, its development over some 42 years was guided by William Duguid Hill. In addition to the substantial economic benefits it brought to the city as gold declined, South Street gave expression to the public faith in music as an activity open to all and of value to all. In 1964 the Eisteddfod Society purchased the historic Her Majesty's Theatre, which it gave to the city in 1987 and which remains one of the finest small venues for music-theatre performance in Victoria and one of the few restored 19th-century theatres in the country.

Three musical conventions, written large through repetition and given an irresistible competitive edge, sustained South Street as it in turn nourished local music-making practices: the parish concert, the municipal brass band and the church choir. The Eisteddfod also expressed other characteristic features: that the experience and making of music is essentially a communal and collective experience—hence the apparent failure of high art manifestations such as symphony orchestras (local and visiting) and celebrity concerts—and that it is essentially an unpaid activity. Ballarat produced the distinguished opera-singers Evelyn ★Scotney, Elsie ★Morison and Rosina ★Raisbeck, but apart from legions of music teachers and church organists, its musicians did not and do not make a living from music.

Always conservative, 19th-century traditions of home-based music-making persisted at least until the end of

World War II, when the impact of modern technologies transformed many participants into consumers. Against this, however, the value of educating the young has always been perceived and acted upon, whether at school (where choirs and bands flourished), privately (through the music examination systems) or informally (through music shops, within families or groups).

FURTHER REFERENCE

W. Bate, *Lucky City, The First Generation in Ballarat: 1851–1901* (Melbourne: MUP, 1978); idem, *Life After Gold, 20th-Century Ballarat* (Melbourne: MUP, 1993); K. Dreyfus, 'The South Street Eisteddfod and Local Music-making in Ballarat in the 1920s and 1930s', *Victorian Historical Journal* 66/2 (Nov. 1995), 99–121; G. Sutton, *Richard Henry Sutton Esq. 1830–1876* (Melbourne, 1954); H. Love, ed., *The Australian Stage: A Documentary History* (Sydney: NSW University Press, 1984); W.B. Withers, *History of Ballarat* (Ballarat: F.W. Niven & Co., 1870; 2nd edn 1887).

KAY DREYFUS

Ballet and Dance Music.

1. Music for Dance to 1940. 2. 1940s and 50s. 3. 1960s to the Present. 4. Music for Modern Dance.

Many Australian composers have written for theatrical dance. For some a long-term relationship has developed within the choreographic sphere, while for others the occasional collaboration with dancers has mitigated the solitude of composing for the concert platform.

1. Music for Dance to 1940 (i) The Colonial Era. In 1835 the first ballet to be staged in Australia, *The Fair Maid of Perth, or, The Rival Lovers,* was produced at Levey's Theatre Royal, Sydney. In the subsequent years, audiences were introduced to leading works from the European repertoire: *La Sylphide* (in 1845), *La Fille mal gardée* (in 1855) and *Giselle* (in 1855). Although *Giselle* had been a success in Europe, at its Australian premiere it was a flop, for the audiences preferred to see ballet primarily within the context of opera, an attitude which lingered until the tour of Adeline Genee and the Imperial Russian Ballet in 1913. The colonial era saw various visiting troupes or solo dancers touring Australia, sometimes under the guiding hands of the impresarios George Coppin, W.S. Lyster, and J.C. Williamson, and the visiting principals were often supported by resident dancers, who had received training from the local dance schools. Gradually a sense of permanency for theatrical dance in Australia began to emerge; but whether dance was presented in its own right or as a diversion in opera, pantomime, or other theatrical fare, music from local musicians rendered on piano, ensemble or theatre orchestra was always required.

It was during this period that one of the first pieces of choreographic music by an Australian composer was produced: Alfred Hill's Maori-inspired opera *Tapu* (1903) included Maori *haka* and *poi* dances. The novelty of the setting brought the work a modicum of success at the box-office during its Australian and NZ tour of 1903–4. Next came William James's orchestral score for the dance-play *By Candlelight* in 1917, produced in London as a fund-raiser for the war effort. However, no stand-alone choreographic music was written in Australia until the tours by Pavlova in 1926 and 1929 inspired the dance community to organise themselves into a cohesive group.

(ii). The First Ballet Commissions. In the early 1930s the first Australian Ballet was formed under the direction of Louise Lightfoot and Mischa Burlakov. Together they forged a repertoire based on both standard works and original ballets, with scores by Roy Maling (1901–80) and Ramsay Pennicuick (*d* 1968). But this little troupe of amateurs was no competition for Colonel de Basil's Ballets Russes, which toured Australia three times for extended periods between 1936 and 1940. Formed from the remnants of Diaghilev's group (disbanded in 1929), this fully professional company stunned Australian audiences with their sumptuous productions. For the first time many ballet enthusiasts felt they were connected with European chic. The troupe inspired young Australian artists, dancers and musicians, and in response a number of dancers within the company decided to settle in Australia. Of those who decided to stay, Helen Kirsova, Kira Abricossova (later Bousloff) and Edouard Borovansky were to establish their own troupes and schools. This group, together with Australian-born Laurel *Martyn, nurtured ballet to levels not previously achieved in Australia.

2. 1940s and 50s. Kirsova, Bousloff, Borovansky and Martyn sought to collaborate with Australian composers and designers. In particular Martyn, through her *Ballet Guild of Victoria (established 1946), maintained a solid working relationship with musicians. For a decade (1946–56) she commissioned scores, mostly of chamber music, from Dorian *Le Gallienne, Esther *Rofe, Margaret *Sutherland and John Tallis (1911–96). The two ballets with scores by Le Gallienne proved popular at the box-office: *Contes heraldiques* (1946) was a satirical exposé of fairy-tale characters which Le Gallienne enhanced with comical writing and subtle references to Mozart, Bizet and Chopin, while *Voyageur* (1956) was of a more serious nature, revolving around the unrequited love of two water-birds, the musical realisation of their wing movements being hauntingly effective.

Bousloff married the composer James *Penberthy, and together they established the West Australian Ballet Company in 1952. Their interest in Aboriginal culture as a source for creating a national style led to many projects on Aboriginal topics, only a few of which were produced, *Brolga* (1957) and *Kooree and the Mists* (1960) being the most prominent.

The most famous neo-Aboriginal ballet was John Antill's *Corroboree* (1946). Hailed as a success by the critics and public alike at its premiere concert performance with the Sydney Symphony Orchestra under Eugene

Goossens in 1946, the work's balletic intentions were realised by two different choreographers, Rex Reid (in 1950) and Beth Dean (in 1954). Reid interpreted Antill's original stage plan with a series of totemic representations; Dean, on the other hand, dismissed such ideas and wove into the music the story of a native boy's initiation into adulthood, introducing Aboriginal dance movements into her choreography. In both versions the high praise for Antill's music continued. His combination of overtly Aboriginal references—clapsticks, sounds imitative of the didjeridu, and short, tightly knit motifs—with a pronounced rhythmic drive was enough for Goossens and the commentators to announce that *Corroboree* was the way forward for Australian composition. Ironically, after this Antill virtually abandoned Aboriginal subjects, preferring to write his later music in a more conventional style.

Sporadically, Aboriginal subjects for dance have continued to appear in the repertoires of Australian companies up to the present time. The Aboriginal Islander Dance Theatre and Bangarra Dance Theatre combine traditional and Western dance culture, commissioning music which reflects such a fusion, as in David Page's *Pride* (1993) for Bangarra and Tony Lewis's *Mimi* (1988) for AIDT.

One of the most successful companies of the 1940s and 50s was the *Borovansky Ballet. From early on, Borovansky had enjoyed intermittent patronage from the powerful J.C. Williamson organisation, and his troupe consequently had quality theatres and competent orchestras at its disposal. But Borovansky's need to repay his backer with returns at the box-office meant that risk-taking in the form of new, untested productions was something he tended to avoid. On only three occasions did he use original Australian music in his repertoire: twice from Rofe and once from Verdon *Williams.

3. 1960s to the Present. After Borovansky's death in 1959, his company was gradually reorganised and presented its first season as the *Australian Ballet in 1962. Now guaranteed its funding from the Federal Government, the troupe was able to welcome Australian composers in their creation of new works. The first music commission was Harold *Badger's arrangements of 19th-century tunes for the *Melbourne Cup* (1962). In the subsequent seven years of the company's existence, Les Patching (1927–93), Nahama Patkin (b 1939), Penberthy, Peter *Sculthorpe, Peter *Tahourdin and Malcolm *Williamson were commissioned to write ballets. The collaboration between Williamson and choreographer Robert Helpmann for *The Display* (1964) proved so successful that the work entered the company's permanent repertoire, and reappeared intermittently between 1964 and 1983. But the euphoria of a new company championing new music evaporated after 1969, and Classical works became the dominant feature. Since 1970 only four composers have been commissioned by the Australian Ballet for new ballets: Graeme *Koehne, Geoffrey Madge (b 1941), Richard *Mills and Carl *Vine. Of their pro-

ductions, only Mills's *Snugglepot and Cuddlepie* (1988) has maintained itself in the company's repertoire.

Unlike the generous funding of the Australian Ballet, the *Queensland Ballet (established 1960) began rather tentatively. A mixture of newly choreographed 19th-century music and popular standards were its mainstays; only after 20 years of building audiences and gaining credibility with its private and government sponsors was the company in a position to commission new music from Australian composers. In the 1980s it engaged Colin *Brumby, Koehne, Wilfred *Lehmann, David Pyle, Antony Slavich, and Vine. The *West Australian Ballet continued working with original Australian music, realising scores from Brian *Howard, Koehne, Peter Sluik (b 1933), Roger *Smalley, Vine, and Williams.

The *Sydney Dance Company, under the visionary leadership of *Graeme Murphy, has used the talents of a large number of Australian composers. Murphy's desire to fuse contemporary and classical choreography has enabled him and his guest choreographers to commission widely: rock musicians Iva Davies and Bob Kretschmer were engaged to write a score for *Boxes* (1985), jazz musician Judy *Bailey was commissioned to write the music for *Suite for a Lonely Child* (1982), and a Moog synthesiser was featured in *Constant Reach* (1977) by Michael Carlos (b 1948), while Koehne's score for *The Selfish Giant* (1983) was for chamber orchestra. *Poppy* (1978), with music by Vine, and *Nearly beloved* (1986), with a score by Koehne, have been two of the troupe's most popular works with both audiences and critics. Murphy's versatility made him the ideal choice as the choreographer for one of the centrepieces of the Australian bicentenary celebrations in 1988, *Vast* (1988), scored for orchestra by Barry *Conyngham. This massive work, combining dancers from the West Australian Ballet, Queensland Ballet, *Meryl Tankard Australian Dance Theatre and the Sydney Dance Company, depicts the multifaceted Australian social and natural environments. Murphy's collaborative spirit aligns him closely with the modern dance practitioners, many of whom actively seek a creative interaction with composers.

4. Music for Modern Dance Modern dance companies, as opposed to their counterparts in the ballet, are freed from the necessity of interpreting an established repertoire, and as such direct their attention to devising new work. In the 1940s and 50s the foundation of Australian modern dance was being established by troupes centred around Gertrud *Bodenwieser and Margaret Barr. Bodenwieser's musical tastes were conservative and she commissioned composers who wrote in the late-Romantic idiom, such as Marcel Lorber (1900–86) and Werner *Baer. Barr was more adventurous, but the conservatively crafted scores of Arnold Butcher (b 1926) for *Strange Children* (1955) and Antill for *Snowy!* (1961) were probably her most successful essays using original Australian music.

Since the 1960s modern dance has been in a state of flux through the constant reorganisation of its community into—and out of—numerous troupes and collectives. Nanette Hassell, who established Danceworks in 1983 and remained its artistic director for six years, worked closely with the composer Les Gilbert (*b.* 1946) on a number of projects. Gilbert's long association with manipulating environmental sounds was clearly expressed in the sound-track he set down for *Pyralis* (1984). In this work, choreographed by Hassell, he explored the sounds of fire, the environmental resonances of an area recently ravaged by bushfire, and the dancers' own bodies through body-slapping and foot-stamping. The dancers' input into the sound-creation of *Pyralis* was mixed in the studio and thus pre-set for performance.

However, some modern dance choreographers have gone beyond this level of collaboration to be actively engaged in the musical production during the performance. For example, the composers Warren ★Burt and Ros ★Bandt with the dancer-choreographers Shona Innes, Jane Refshauge and Sylvia Staehli worked with Simon Veitch's computer surveillance system 3DIS (Three Dimensional Interactive Space) to create *Fair Exchanges* (1988–89), in which the dancer's movements activated sensors, these in turn generating within the system a series of predetermined sounds.

Irrespective of a company's longevity, a dominant aesthetic has been for modern dance choreographers to champion new music technologies and to seek out composers who have expertise in the areas of electro-acoustics. The generation of new sounds with new movement continues to form in many instances productive coalitions for collaboration.

FURTHER REFERENCE
Joel Crotty, 'From Balletic Binge to Cultural Cringe: Choreographic Music in Australia 1936–1956', in Nicholas Brown et al., eds, *One Hand on the Manuscript* (Canberra: Humanities Research Centre, ANU, 1995), 217–28; Stephen Leek, 'The Music, the Dance', *SA* 29 (Winter 1989) [whole issue]; Edward H. Pask, *Enter the Colonies Dancing* (Melbourne: OUP, 1979); idem, *Ballet in Australia* (Melbourne: OUP, 1982).   JOEL CROTTY

Ballet Victoria. Founded as the Ballet Guild of Victoria in 1946 by Laurel Martyn. From the outset Martyn encouraged a collaborative spirit between dancers, musicians and designers, and in its first decade composers such as Margaret Sutherland, Esther Rofe, Verdon Williams, John Tallis and Dorian Le Gallienne contributed choreographic scores. After 1956, new repertoire was created using pre-existing music. The troupe was renamed the Victorian Ballet Company in 1963 and Ballet Victoria in 1967; it closed after a financially disastrous season in 1976.

FURTHER REFERENCE
Edward H. Pask, *Ballet in Australia* (Melbourne: OUP, 1982); *Brolga* 4 (June 1996); Laurel Martyn, 'Supporting the Arts to Death: The Case of Ballet Victoria', *Meanjin* 36/3 (Oct. 1977), 372–7.   JOEL CROTTY

Bamaga Diptych. Orchestral work by Richard Mills (1986), portraying Bamaga, the settlement in far north Queensland. Recorded by the Queensland Symphony Orchestra, cond. R. Mills (OZM 1002).

Bamford, John ('Ocker') (*b* Adelaide, 10 July 1930; *d* Adelaide 4 Oct. 1985), jazz trombonist. He began his career as a pianist in 1945, then was active in Adelaide dance bands. Proficient on vibraphone, saxophone, vocals, and most notably trombone, he worked in Melbourne 1948–50, then Sydney, becoming prominent in concerts, nightclubs, and session work as an instrumentalist, composer and arranger. In 1957 he won the *Music Maker* poll in the trombone and big band categories. He backed numerous visitors including Stan Kenton, who offered Bamford a permanent trombone chair in his own band. In 1981 he resettled in Adelaide, working with the SA College of Advanced Education and as musical director for radio 5AA Big Band until shortly before his death.

FURTHER REFERENCE
Recordings include *Music Maker 1957 All Stars* (1957, Parlophone PMDO-7511). See also *BissetB; OxfordJ*; Bruce Johnson, 'The Forgotten Ones: John Bamford', *Quarterly Rag* 68/69 (4th Quarter, 1993), 64–7.   BRUCE JOHNSON

Bananas in Pyjamas. Theme song by Carey Blyton for the ABC TV's immensely successful pre-school program, surpassed in popularity in Australia only by the ★Wiggles. It describes the two matching comic characters B1 and B2 chasing their teddy-bear friends. Based on a brass band march standard, it may be heard on *It's Singing Time* (1996, ABC 8146652–4) or in the various *Bananas in Pyjamas* videos.

Bandstand. National television rock and roll show (1958–72) made at Channel 9, Sydney. Modelled on the American *Bandstand* (which it outlived), the format featured guest artists and a sizeable group of regular singers, backed by the resident band Col ★Joye and the Joy Boys. At first couples danced around the singers, reflecting rock music's origin in dance halls; later there were elaborate productions and a 20-piece orchestra. An impeccably well-mannered compère, Brian Henderson (later a TV newsreader), a strict dress code and sophisticated productions conferred a somewhat uncharacteristic gentility on the music, not found in ★*Six O'Clock Rock* or its other competitors. It launched the careers of many early rock and roll singers, including Lonnie ★Lee, Patsy Ann ★Noble, the ★Allen Brothers, the ★Delltones, Judy ★Stone, Frank Ifield and Billy ★Thorpe.

FURTHER REFERENCE
John Byrell, *Bandstand and All That* (Kenthurst, NSW: Kangaroo Press, 1995); Bob Rogers and Denis O'Brien, *Rock'n'Roll Australia: The Australian Pop Scene 1954–1964* (Sydney: Cassell, 1975).

Bandt, Ros (Rosalie Edith) (*b* Geelong, 18 Aug. 1951), sound artist. One of the most individual presences in Australian music, at once composer, performer, inventor, and thinker in unique combination. Trained at Monash University as a schoolteacher, she soon turned to chance music, and her earliest solo and chamber works show the influence of John Cage, whose methods and ideas she studied. A pioneer of interactive sound sculpture in Australia, from 1977 her work began to be exhibited in various city and regional centres; her *Sound Playground* was installed in Brunswick, Melbourne, in 1981. At the same time she had a significant career as a performer, from 1978 playing both medieval instruments in La Romanesca and live improvisations in LIME. Since 1980 she has become increasingly noted in Australia and abroad as a solo performer-composer and sound artist, receiving two Australia Council composer fellowships (1982, 1991). In 1986 she invented an interactive playback system, SSIIPP, which has featured in many of her sound installations. Her compositions include tape pieces, works for environmental sounds and for highly unusual instrumental combinations, often involving pitched percussion, such as zithers, danh tranh, ceramic gongs, whirlies, or her own flagong (constructed of glass microtonal bells). *Stargazer* (1983) is for amplifier, music boxes and tape, *Invading the Landscape* (1983) for brass bells, cymbals and gong, and *Genesis* (1987) for psaltery. She completed doctoral studies in repetitive music processes at Monash University in 1984, and has published in her field.

WORKS (Selective)

Chamber *Variations Too*, after John Cage, fl, synth, graphic score (1974), *Disjointed Quartet*, LIME rec pieces, mime (1980), *Soft & Fragile Music In Glass & Clay*, 32 works, oral tradition art-form (1980), *Let's Go Fishen*, 2 perfs on thongaphones, vv, tape (1984), *From the Greenhouse*, vv, psaltery, tamboura, jew's harp, environmental sound recordings, conch, perc, 80 slides dissolving (1990), *Cobwebs*, zithers, danh tranh, kecapi, psaltery (1990), *Coventry in West Brunswick*, danh tranh, psaltery, tape, environmental recordings, vv, transparencies of a burnt Anglican church (1991), *Ode to Catullus*, rec, nar (1991), *Secluded Ponds*, environmental recordings, perc, gender, flagong, electronic birds, zithers (1993).

Solo Instrumental Variations II, after John Cage, gui (1974), *Meditation*, fl, rec or shakuhachi (1975), *Drifts in Sand*, alto or bass rec (1976), *Flight*, rec (1978), *Loops*, rec, 4 recorders and quadraphonic tape (1982), *Ear Wear*, sound artist/nar, 4 channel tape, transparencies, props (1985–87), *Gulf Song*, v, ceramic gongs, tape (1991), *Night on the Indian Ocean*, glass flagong, environmental tape (1993).

FURTHER REFERENCE

Recordings include *Stargazer* (Move MD3075), *Footsteps: Ros Bandt and Friends* (Move MD3135), and *Genesis* (New Albion Records NAO28CD). Her book is *Sound in Space: Windchimes and Sound Sculptures* (Melbourne: VAC/CAE, 1985). See also *BroadstockS*, 42–7; *CohenI*; *JenkinsT*, 9–18. On her instruments see Warren Burt, 'Instrumental Composition', *AMC News* 9 (Spring 1985), 3–14.

Banks, Don [Donald Oscar] (*b* Melbourne, 25 Oct. 1923; *d* Sydney, 5 Sept. 1980), composer. He played piano from the age of five, showing an early interest in improvisation which was developed from 1938 with fellow high school jazz enthusiasts including Keith Atkins (reeds). He studied composition with A.E.H. Nickson and Dorian Le Gallienne at the University of Melbourne under a Commonwealth Reconstruction Training Scholarship 1947–49, with Matyas Seiber in London 1950–52; with Milton Babbitt in Salzburg at the Seminar in American Studies 1952; with Luigi Dallapiccola in Florence on an Italian Government scholarship 1952–53, and with Luigi Nono on a London Youth and Music scholarship 1956. After war service Banks formed the Don Banks Boptet, a jazz sextet with Banks on piano, in 1946. He lived in London 1950–71 and worked as a copyist, jazz arranger, composer of television commercials, incidental music for television series, documentary films, feature films and concert music. With Margaret Sutherland he established the Australian Musical Association in London, serving as chairman and vice-president. He was director of the Composers' Seminars for the Society for the Promotion of New Music in 1967, 1968 and 1971, founding and executive member of the British Society for Electronic Music, and music director of Goldsmiths' College, University of London, from 1969 to 1971.

Banks visited Australia briefly in 1970 to direct the Composers' Seminar for the Perth Festival and returned permanently in 1972 for a creative arts fellowship at the ANU. He was the first chairman of the Music Board of the Australia Council, 1973, head of composition and electronic music at the Canberra School of Music, 1973–77, and head of the school of composition at the NSW State Conservatorium, 1978–80.

From the late 1930s Banks was associated with the Melbourne jazz community, including Graeme *Bell with whom he performed and made private recordings. With Charlie *Blott and Splinter *Reeves he became active in the postwar Melbourne bop movement, as pioneer composer and pianist, and leading his 'Boptet' in clubs, concerts and radio. In 1949 worked with a visiting Duke Ellington alumnus, the cornettist Rex Stewart. Once he achieved international eminence in 'third stream' and avant-garde composition, he incorporated jazz into his work for concert hall, film and as an educator. Banks was a linchpin of the postwar experiments in Melbourne, leading the earliest bop recording sessions including what is arguably the first Australian bop composition, his 'Feeling Dizzy'. His departure for England contributed significantly to the decline of this phase of Australian jazz history. Upon his return, his position of influence helped to achieve institutional recognition for jazz.

Banks's works, particularly his concertos, made a significant impact in England in the 1960s, while his later 'third stream' music of the early 1970s was an important contribution to the genre. His compositions include *Trio for Horn, Violin and Piano* (1962), *Concerto for Horn and Orchestra* (1965), *Settings from Roget* (1966) for voice and jazz quartet, *Concerto for Violin and Orchestra* (1968), *Prelude, Night Piece and Blues for Two* (1968) for clarinet and piano, *Tirade* (1968) for soprano, harp, piano and three percussion, *Intersections* (1969) for electronic sounds and orchestra, *Meeting Place* (1970) for chamber orchestra, jazz group and synthesiser, *Limbo* (1971), a cantata for three voices, eight instruments and tape, *Nexus* (1971) for symphony orchestra and jazz quintet, *Equation III* (1972) for chamber group, jazz quartet and electronics, and *Prospects* (1974) for orchestra. Banks's concert music displays an exceptionally high degree of craftsmanship in matters of orchestration and musical development. His technical resources ranged from serialism to bebop to electronic music, and the integrity of his work served as an important model to the young composers under his influence after his return to Australia.

WORKS (Selective)
Orchestral and Concerto Four Pieces, orch (1953, Schott), *Episode*, small orch (1958, Schott/B&H), Concerto, solo hn, orch (1965, Schott), *Divisions*, orch (1965, Schott), *Assemblies*, orch (1966, Schott), Concerto, solo vn, orch (1968, Schott), *Dramatic Music*, orch (1969, Schott), *Intersections*, electronic sounds, orch (1969, Schott), *Fanfare and National Anthem*, orch (1970, Schott), *Nexus*, jazz quintet, orch (1971, Schott), *Prospects*, orch (1974, Schott), *Trilogy*, orch (1977, Chester).
Chamber Instrumental Trio, fl, vn, vc (1948), Divertimento, fl, vn, va, vc (1951), Duo, vn, vc (1951), Sonata, vn, pf (1953, Schott), Three Studies, vc, pf (1955, Schott), *Sonata da camera*, chamber ens (1961, Schott), *Elizabethan Miniatures*, fl, lute, viola da gamba, str (1962, Schott), Trio, hn, vn, pf (1962, Schott), *Equation I*, chamber ens, jazz ens (1963, Schott), *Three Episodes*, fl, pf (1964, Schott), *Prologue, Night Piece and Blues for Two*, cl, pf (1968, Schott), *Equation II*, chamber ens, jazz ens (1969, Schott), *Meeting Place*, chamber ens, jazz ens, synth (1970, Schott), *Commentary*, pf, tape (1971, Schott), Four Pieces, 2 vn, va, vc (1971, Schott), *Equation III*, chamber ens, jazz ens, elec (1972, Schott), *Take Eight*, 2 vn, va, vc, jazz ens (1973, Schott), String Quartet, 2 vn, va, vc (1975, ms), Trio, bass cl, elec pf, moog synth (1976, Schott), *4x2x1*, cl, tape (1977 ms).
Solo Instrumental Sonatina in C sharp minor, pf (1949), *Pezzo Dramatico*, pf (1956, Schott), *Sequence*, vc (1967, Schott), *One for Murray*, cl (1977, ms).
Brass Band, Wind Ensemble Music for Wind Band (1971, Schott).
Vocal *Five North Country Folk Songs*, S, pf (1953, Schott), *Five North Country Folk Songs*, S, str (1954, Schott), Psalm 70, S, small orch (1954, Schott), *Three North Country Folk Songs*, S, pf (1955, Schott), *Settings from Roget*, female jazz v, jazz ens (1966, Schott), *Tirade*, medium v, chamber ens (1968, Schott), *Findings Keepings*, SATB, elec bass gui, jazz ens (1969, Novello), *Limbo*, 3 v, chamber

ens, tape (1971, Schott), *Three Short Songs*, female jazz v, jazz ens (1971, Schott), *Walkabout*, children's vv, ens (1972, Schott), *Benedictus*, vv, jazz ens, synth, elec pf, tape (1976, Schott), *An Australian Entertainment*, male ch (1979, ms).
Electronic *Shadows of Space*, 4-channel tape (1972), *Synchronos 72*, tape (1972), *Carillon*, 2-channel tape (1975), *4/5/7*, tape (1976), *Magician's Castle*, tape (1977), *Form*, tape (1979).

FURTHER REFERENCE
Recordings include *Don Banks Orchestra* (1950, Jazzart JA-48); *Four Pieces for String Quartet*, Australian Str Quartet (ABC 426 992); Violin Concerto, Tasmanian Symphony Orchestra, L. Dommett, vn (ABC 426 993); *Trilogy*, Melbourne Symphony Orchestra, cond. R. Mills (ABC 426 807). A discography to 1972 is in *PlushD*. His writings include 'Converging Streams', *Musical Times* 111 (1970): 596–9. See also *CallawayA*; Bruce Johnson, 'Towards a New Cartography: Rethinking Australia's Musical History', in *One Hand on the Manuscript: Music in Australian Cultural History 1930–1960*, ed. Nicholas Brown et al. (Canberra: Humanities Research Centre, 1995), 243–57; K. Luck, Don Banks—Eclectic Craftsman: An Analytical Study of Five Representative Works, BMus(Hons) Univ. Queensland, 1977; W. Mann, 'The Music of Don Banks', *Musical Times* 109 (1968), 719–21; *MurdochA*; *OxfordJ*; John Whiteoak, 'Don Banks: From "Bebop" to Incipient Third Stream Music', *SA* 41 (Autumn 1994), 36–7.

MICHAEL BARKL
with Bruce Johnson

Banks of the Condamine (Riverine), The folksong. Usually set to a tune descended from 'The Banks of the Nile', this widely disseminated traditional song is a dialogue in which a nomadic horse-breaker (in one version a shearer) takes leave of his lover to work for squatters at the Condamine River, near Chinchilla, Queensland. First found in the Hurd Collection (to the tune 'Willey Reilly'), 1894–98, it was published as 'Banks of the Riverine' by A.B. Paterson in *Old Bush Songs* (1912), and at least 10 other variants have been collected, including one to a version of 'I'll Be All Smiles Tonight, Mother'.

FURTHER REFERENCE
Edition and commentary in *EdwardsG; ManifoldP; RadicS*, 11.

Barambah, Maroochy (b Cherbourg, Qld), Aboriginal singer, actor, dancer, storyteller and composer. She studied at the Melba Conservatorium of Music and the Victorian College of the Arts in Melbourne, in 1987 at the National Aboriginal Islander Dance Theatre in Sydney, then at the Elder Conservatorium and the Centre for Aboriginal Studies in Music, University of Adelaide. After appearances in the television series *The Flying Doctors*, *Winner Take All* and *Women of the Sun*, in 1989 she appeared in the opera *Black River* by Andrew Schultz, then in Sydney performances of the Aboriginal musical *Bran Nue Dae*, and she has developed a significant career as a solo popular music artist. Invited to perform at the United

Nations in 1993, her recordings combine traditional material with contemporary popular music styles.

FURTHER REFERENCE
Recordings include *Mongungi* (1994, Daki Budchta Records DBPL 100123-DS).   P. DUNBAR-HALL

Barber, Tony (*b* Perth, 3 Dec. 1943), pop singer. At first an importer, he soon joined Billy ★Thorpe's Aztecs as a rhythm guitarist-songwriter, writing *Blue Day* and *Don't You Know* for them. After the Aztecs disbanded in 1965 he was briefly with Vince Maloney (guitar) as Vince and Tony's Two, then pursued a solo career, and in 1966 his single *Someday* reached No. 7 in the Top 40 charts and *No, No, No* reached No. 21. He released an album *Someday Now* (1966). After his marriage in 1967 he turned to other activities, producing records for Ray Brown, Denise Drysdale and others, writing for *Go-Set* and *Everybody's,* and entering television as a quiz show host.

FURTHER REFERENCE
Recordings include *Someday* (Spin EK1155), *No, No, No* (Spin EK1401), *Someday* and *Now* (1966 Spin EL 31882). For discography, see *SpencerA*. See also *McGrathA*; *SpencerW*.

Bark (Skin Pad, Bundle). Percussion accompaniment played by women to Aboriginal singing in the eastern and south-eastern part of Australia. The pads were made by the players and they were struck either with the hand or by sticks. Early sources document opossum skins rolled into a cylinder which was sometimes filled with shells, rags or earth. The bundles were held between the thighs or on the lap, and sounded an even beat throughout the songs. Aboriginal people along the coast of NSW and Queensland describe women 'beating the pillow' during corroborees. See *Aboriginal Music* §3(i).
    GRACE KOCH

Barkl, Michael Laurence Gordon (*b* Sydney, 9 Aug. 1958), composer. While supporting himself as an electric guitarist, he studied at the NSW State Conservatorium 1977–80, winning the Frank Hutchens Composition Prize and writing a thesis on Donatoni under Richard Toop. He produced four short orchestral works for the ABC in the following years and his piano trio *Rota* (1981) achieved *segnalata* in the International Valentino Bucchi Competition. In 1986 he completed a master's degree in composition with Ann ★Ghandar at the University of New England and was composer-in-residence at Orange, NSW. Aside from a full-length music-theatre piece, *The Animals Noah Forgot* (1988), his works have chiefly been short, such as the chamber work *The Laird of Drumblair* (1987), and show both his knowledge of jazz and a focus on minute detail perhaps absorbed from his Donatoni studies. Since 1987 he has taught at Illawarra Institute of Technology.

FURTHER REFERENCE
His *Ballade* has been recorded by 2MBS–FM and four orchestral works by the ABC. See also *BroadstockS* 48–9, 270–9.

Barklamb, Leslie Raymond (*b* 1905; *d* Melbourne, Sept. 1993), flautist. He was principal flute in the Melbourne Symphony Orchestra, then lecturer at the University of Melbourne Conservatorium, where his students included John ★Wion, David ★Cubbin, Margaret Crawford, Fredrick Shade and many other flautists who went on to prominent careers. A figure of boundless generosity, warmth and humour, he organised numerous flute workshops, master classes and performances, and often offered flute scholarships from his own resources. Popular as an adjudicator, teacher and examiner, he was founder of the Victorian Flute Guild and foundation member of the Australian Flute Guild, and contributed greatly to the popularising of the flute as an instrument for study in Australia. A Barklamb Prize has been established by the AMEB in Melbourne in his memory.

Barlow, Dale (*b* Sydney, 25 Dec. 1959), jazz saxophonist, composer. He learned piano, flute, and clarinet as a child, changing to tenor saxophone at the age of 16. He studied at the NSW Conservatorium jazz course and came to attention in the Young Northside Big Band, which performed at the Monterey Festival in 1978. Forming the Benders, one of the bands that proclaimed a new generation of players in the 1980s, he left Australia in 1982, touring Europe with Peter O'Mara (guitar); then went to New York, studying saxophone, piano and improvisation with David Leibman, George Coleman, Hal Galper, and Barry Harris. From a London base in 1983, he worked in jazz and pop settings in the UK, Europe and New York, with Chet Baker, Gil Evans, Ronnie Scott, Bryan Ferry and others. He joined Cedar Walton in 1984, touring Europe, and composed and played for the London Contemporary Theatre before returning to Australia in 1986. With Paul ★Grabowsky he founded Wizards of Oz, 1987, which toured internationally and recorded the award-winning CD *Soundtrack*. He toured Australia with Australian Jazz Orchestra and returned to New York in 1989, working with Gil Evans and joining Art Blakey's Jazz Messengers, with whom he recorded and toured internationally.

The experience with Blakey consolidated Barlow's reputation as Australia's currently most internationally authoritative composer-performer in the tradition derived from hard bop, but he has also been associated with more experimental and eclectic activities, working with indigenous musicians, orchestral sections, and in free improvisation. At present divides his time between Sydney and overseas bases, mainly New York. In 1988 he received an Australian Bicentennial Music Award.

FURTHER REFERENCE

Recordings include *The Benders: E* (1982, Hot 1002); *Bluesville Time*, Cedar Walton (1985, Criss Cross, Criss 1017); *Soundtrack*, Wizards of Oz (1988, Polygram 834531–2); *One For All*, Art Blakey Jazz Messengers (1990, A & M 395 329–2); *Horn* (1990, Spiral Scratch 0003); *Hipnotation* (1991, Spiral Scratch 0009). See also *ClareB*; *OxfordJ*; Eric Myers, 'The Young Lions: James Morrison and Dale Barlow', *JA* (May/June 1981), 5–8; Eric Myers, 'Dale Barlow', *APRAJ* (Dec. 1992), 21–3; John Shand, 'Apple-Biter: Dale Barlow', *Australasian Jazz 'n' Blues* 2/4 (1995), 14–16.

BRUCE JOHNSON

Barnard, Bob (Robert Graeme)

(*b* Melbourne, 24 Nov. 1933), jazz trumpeter. Starting in brass bands on cornet at the age of 12, his first engagement was with his parents' dance band when he was 14. He joined his brother Len's band, making his first recording on his 16th birthday. When his brother's band dissolved in Brisbane in 1955, he returned to Melbourne. In 1957–58 he was in Sydney with the Ray Price Trio and the Port Jackson Jazz Band, then with saxophonist Kenn Jones's band in Melbourne until moving permanently to Sydney to join Graeme ★Bell (1962–67). He was then mainly active in studio work until he formed his own jazz band with John McCarthy, Alan Geddes (later Laurie Thompson and Len Barnard), trombonist John Costelloe, Wally Wickham, and pianist Chris Taperell in 1974. This band has enjoyed international acclaim, with tours including Australia, Asia, Europe and the USA, where it has frequently played at the Bix Beiderbecke festival. Along with Warren Vaché he played the narrative music for the film *The Gig*. Barnard is the most commanding trumpeter to emerge from Australia's traditional jazz movement. Since winning the *Music Maker* poll in 1952, his authority has remained unchallenged in a broadening stylistic range that developed from his classic Louis Armstrong-inspired beginnings. Now working as an international soloist and freelancing, he leads units of his band for residencies in Sydney, including the Orient Hotel, the Old Push, and the Marble Bar. He was honoured with the AM in 1990, and the Advance Australia Award in 1991.

FURTHER REFERENCE

Recordings include *Len Barnard and his South City Stompers* (1949, Jazzart JA-34); *Len Barnard's Famous Jazz Band* (1955, Swaggie S-1008); *The Naked Dance*, Len Barnard's Jazz Band (1961, Astor ALP-1007); *Classics of Australian Jazz*, Len Barnard's Jazz Band, vol. 1 (1967, Swaggie S-1221); *Lord of the Rings*, vol 1, (1974, EMI EMC.2525/6), vol. 2 (1976, EMI EMC 2548/9), vol. 3 (1977, EMI EMC 2580/1); *Bud Freeman with Bob Barnard's Jazz Band* (1976, Swaggie S-1367); *For Leon Bismark,* John Sangster (1977, Swaggie S-1379); *Music to Midnight*, Bob Barnard with the Kenny Powell Orchestra (1980, ABCL8003); *Partners in Crime*, Ralph Sutton and Bob Barnard (1983, Dialogue SVL 505); *Bob Barnard with the International Set* (1988, Calligraph Records CLGLP 017); *Just Foolin' Around: A Tribute to Louis Armstrong,*

Ricky May and Bob Barnard with the Julian Lee Orchestra (1987, ABC Records L 60027/8). An interview with him is in *WilliamsA*, 22–27. See also *ClareB*; *BissetB*; *GroveJ*; *OxfordJ*; Dick Hughes, 'Is Bob Barnard Australia's greatest Jazz Musician?', *JA* (Dec. 1981), 13; Bruce Johnson, 'Bob Barnard: Excellence and Dedication', *FM Stereo Radio* (Nov. 1986), 6–8.

BRUCE JOHNSON

Barnard, Len (Leonard Arthur)

(*b* Melbourne, 23 Apr. 1929), jazz drummer, leader, arranger. Playing drums with his parents' dance band, he formed his first band, South City Stompers, in 1948, achieving considerable success with various residencies (including Mentone Lifesaving Club, 1949–55), and broadcasting. In 1955, preparing for a planned European tour, his band toured Australia's eastern states, but with a series of misfortunes the tour concluded in Brisbane and the band dissolved. Barnard remained in Brisbane, playing at the Story Bridge Hotel before returning to Melbourne in 1956, where he freelanced and led groups on drums, washboard and piano, including at Jazz Centre 44, and for session work with Frank Smith. From 1970 he worked as a representative for Yamaha musical instruments, until moving to Sydney in 1974, where he began extensive and stylistically wide-ranging freelance work, including with Judy ★Bailey, Col ★Nolan and Ray ★Price among others, as well as with touring packages and in nightclubs. He has been a member of Galapagos Duck, and of the band led by his brother Bob Barnard.

Len Barnard's first band ushered in a significant new phase in the Melbourne traditional jazz movement, and his prolific recording activity documented an array of major jazz musicians, from traditional to mainstream, as well as his own compositions. Currently living in Sydney, he freelances, assembling concert groups, playing in festivals, supporting visitors such as Scott Hamilton and Charlie Byrd, and working with singer Marie Wilson and pianist Kenny Powell. He has been honoured with life membership of the Musicians' Union (1989), in the Montsalvat Roll of Honour (1990), and the Gold Coast Festival Critics' Award (1991).

FURTHER REFERENCE

Recordings include *Len Barnard and his South City Stompers* (1949, Jazzart JA-34); *Len Barnard's Famous Jazz Band* (1955, Swaggie S-1008); *Jazzways With Len Barnard* (1961, World Record Club JS 2); *The Naked Dance* (1961, Astor ALP-1007); *Classics of Australian Jazz vol. 1* (1967, Swaggie S-1221); *The Trouper* (1972, Swaggie S-1302); *Lord of the Rings, vol. 1,* (1974, EMI EMC.2525/6), *vol. 2* (1976, EMI EMC 2548/9), *vol. 3* (1977, EMI EMC 2580/1); *Partners in Crime*, with Ralph Sutton (1983, Dialogue SVL 505); *Drop Me Off At Harlem*, with Danny Moss and Brian Lemon (1984, WEA 2570102); *Easy Street* (1990, Sackville SKCD.2/2040); *The Famous PIX Sessions: Classic Australian Jazz from the Sixties* (1996, Australian Jazz Reissues AJR-001 A&B). His writings include 'The Len Barnard Story',

JA 7 parts (Jan./Feb. 1981–Feb. 1982); 'On The Road With Bob and Errol', *JA* (Mar./Apr. 1983), 22–3; and 'Riffin' With The Scotch', *JA* (Spring 1983), 22–3. See also *ClareB*; *BissetB*; *CA*; *GroveJ*; *OxfordJ*.   BRUCE JOHNSON

Barnes, Jimmy [James Dixon Swan] (*b* Glasgow, Scotland, 28 Apr. 1956), rock singer. The second of six children, he was born James Swan into a working-class family in Glasgow. His parents were not musical, but they did give him some early exposure to the groups and styles, particularly rhythm and blues, which were to leave an impression on his music-making. His singing career was also to draw on his experiences of the Glasgow working-class environment. The family emigrated to Australia under the assisted passenger scheme, arriving in Adelaide on the SS *Strathnaver* on 1 July 1961, eventually settling in the Adelaide suburb of Elizabeth West. An improvement in circumstances which they had hoped for did not eventuate; Barnes's father was employed at various times, but they were soon slipping towards poverty. The divorce of his parents followed, and his mother married Reg Barnes, whose name all the children took except John, the eldest son. It was from John that Jimmy received his first real exposure to the popular music of the day, John having found a talent for drumming and begun playing in the groups Pulse and Hard Time Killing Floor. Despite being talented at school and later taking up an apprenticeship with the SA Railways, Jimmy too found his interest tending towards music and joined the group Tarkus, whose style had been influenced by Deep Purple, Free, and Hendrix.

Barnes's association with Cold Chisel began in 1973, when the group was called Orange. After establishing itself on the Adelaide pub circuit, Cold Chisel moved to Melbourne, and then to Sydney. Disappointed with the group's lack of success, Barnes temporarily joined Feather, later rejoining Cold Chisel, with whom he worked until 1983. WEA signed the group in 1977, and the albums they produced under this contract firmly established them in Australia. An abortive tour to America in 1981 set the tone for Cold Chisel's problems in the world market: they achieved enormous success within Australia, but not outside it. Frictions within the group became evident, despite its successes, and in 1983 they disbanded. After their dissolution Barnes went on to form a successful solo career, fronting the Jimmy Barnes Band. His album *Heat* was released in 1993. Both as lead singer of Cold Chisel and through his own exploration of the hard rock style, Barnes has exercised a profound influence on Australian popular music, and songs like *Working Class Man* have established him as an icon of the rock scene in Australia.

FURTHER REFERENCE
Recordings as lead singer of Cold Chisel: *You're 13* (1978); *Cold Chisel* (1978, Atlantic 6000382); *Breakfast at Sweethearts* (1979, Elektra 6000422); *East* (1980, WEA 6000642); *Swingshift* (1981, Elektra 8000032); *Circus Animals* (1982, Polydor 6001132); *North-*

bound/The Best of Cold Chisel (1983); *Twentieth Century* (1984, Elektra 2503902); *The Barking Spiders Live* (1984, Elektra 2515252); *Radio Songs* (1985); *Razor Songs* (1988, Warner 6001482); *Chisel* (1991, Warner 9031750212). As a solo act: *Bodyswerve* (1984, Festival D19553); *Jimmy Barnes* (1985, Mushroom); *Freight Train Heart* (1988, Geffen RMD 53238); *Barnestorming* (1988, Festival D24521/2); *Two Fires* (1990, Atlantic RMD 51016); *Soul Deep* (1991, Festival RMD 53344); *Heat* (1993, Festival D91050). See also Toby Creswell, *Jimmy Barnes: Too Much Ain't Enough* (Sydney: Random House, 1993); John W. Edwards, *Rock n' Roll 1970 Through 1979: Discographies of All the Performers who Hit the Charts* (Jefferson, North Carolina: McFarland, 1993); *GuinnessP*; Tony Jasper and Derek Oliver, *The International Encyclopædia of Hard Rock and Heavy Metal* (London: Sidgwick & Jackson, 1991); *SpencerW.*

JOHN WERETKA

Barnett, Neville George (*b* London, 3 Mar. 1854; *d* Upper Picton, NSW 26 Sept. 1895), organist. He played organ from the age of 15, taking lessons from E.J. Hopkins, organist of the Temple Church, London, and obtaining his FRCO in 1874. He went to NZ in 1874 and held organist positions in Christchurch, Auckland and Wellington. He arrived in Sydney in 1887 and was soon an organist at St Mary's Cathedral, Sydney, under John ★Delany. He gave recitals, helped complete the cathedral organ, and also worked as a music critic. His works include a mass and a textbook on harmony and music history. He was one of the most able organists in NSW in the late colonial period.

FURTHER REFERENCE
E. Lea-Scarlett, *ADB*, 3.

Barossa Music Festival. Founded in 1990 and held for two weeks each October in the picturesque Barossa Valley, SA. With support from the State Government, the festival presents concerts in the valley's historic churches, wineries and heritage buildings and includes a Barossa Spring Academy, in which students take masterclasses with distinguished visiting artists featured in the festival.

Barossa Valley. Wine-making region in the Mount Lofty Ranges north of Adelaide, settled in 1838. From the outset a Prussian and Silesian community, several organs of German make were installed in churches from 1880. Moritz ★Heuzenroeder taught and conducted in the valley from 1872, writing several operettas in German for the local musical societies. An annual wine festival has been held each March in the Barossa since 1947, and a ★Barossa Music Festival was established in 1990, each October attracting artists of national distinction.

Barrett, Sir James William (*b* Emerald Hill, Melbourne, 27 Feb. 1862; *d* Toorak, Melbourne, 6 Apr. 1945), administrator. A prominent surgeon in Melbourne and from 1931 vice-chancellor then (1935–39) chancellor of the University of Melbourne, he took over management of G.W.L. *Marshall-Hall's orchestral concerts (1902–13) and was a key contributor to Bernard *Heinze's development of the University of Melbourne Conservatorium Symphony Orchestra from 1923 into the major forerunner of the Melbourne Symphony Orchestra. A crucial supporter of Melbourne's orchestral development before World War II, the orchestras he favoured mixed student, amateur and professional players, and he was a vocal opponent of those who, like Alberto *Zelman Jr, advocated fully professional conditions for orchestral players. He wrote a pamphlet *Outline History of Orchestral Music in Melbourne* (Melbourne, 1941).

FURTHER REFERENCE

Obit. in *Age* 7 Apr. 1945. Stephen Murray-Smith, *ADB*, 7; Jim Davidson, *Lyrebird Rising* (Melbourne: MUP, 1994), 121–3.

Bartle, Graham Alfred Reginald (*b* Ballarat, 6 Nov. 1928), music educator. After studies in arts and music at the University of Melbourne he taught in high schools from 1954, becoming the first lecturer in music at the Secondary Teachers' College, Melbourne, in 1962. He was lecturer (later senior lecturer) at the University of Melbourne 1966–93, and its deputy dean from 1978. He conducted Gilbert and Sullivan operas for the Savoy Opera Co., Melbourne (1964–77), founded the Ionian Singers, and has had a long involvement as an examiner for the AMEB. He wrote *Music in Australian Schools* (Melbourne: Aust. Council for Educational Research, 1968), compiled the *International Directory of Music and Music Education Institutions* 2 vols, 2nd edn (Perth: Callaway International Resource Centre for Music Education, 1996) and numerous articles for the *Australian Journal for Music Education* and the *International Journal for Music Education*.

Basement, The. Sydney jazz venue (1973–88, 1993–). It opened at 29 Reiby Place, Sydney, in August 1973 with *Galapagos Duck as the house band, and other groups were presented from November that year. Apart from the occasional traditional-oriented group, the venue provided the first important forum since *El Rocco for progressive jazz experimentation. It featured local and visiting musicians, often in conjunction with the jazz studies program established at the NSW Conservatorium under Howie Smith. When it closed in 1988, it had become Australia's best-known jazz venue. In 1993 the name was revived at a new venue, which continued the populist broadening towards fusion and cabaret which characterised the original venue's later years.

FURTHER REFERENCE

Recordings include *Jazz Co-op* (1974, Philips 6641–225). See also *ClareB*; *BissetB*; *OxfordJ*; Phil Tripp, 'Ten Years of the Basement', *JA* (Spring 1983), 26–7.

BRUCE JOHNSON

Batchelor, Charlie (*b* Bingara, nr Myall Creek, NSW, 1897; *d* May 1984), bush music fiddle player. Inspired by Harry Reeves's bush-dance band, he taught himself fiddle, learning popular and traditional bush-dance tunes by ear. When bush dancing lost its popularity in the 1940s he largely ceased playing, but stimulated by folklorist Chris Sullivan revived his skills and began recording and teaching from 1981, appearing at the Newcastle Folk Festival and Sydney's Bush Music Club in 1983. His work was recorded on tape, video and film before his death.

FURTHER REFERENCE

Stringybark and Greenhide 5/3 (1984) 24–7; *OxfordF*.

Batchelor, Phyllis Eileen (*b* Healesville, Vic., 1 Feb. 1915), composer, pianist. She studied piano with Waldemar Seidel at the University of Melbourne Conservatorium of Music and composition with Fritz Hart at the Albert Street Conservatorium. Later she established herself as a recitalist, accompanist, teacher and composer in Melbourne. Her compositional output is focused on vocal, choral and instrumental chamber music; the predominance of text-based work stems from her abiding interest in word–music relationships. Her numerous songs are Romantically styled with a detailed sense of word-colour, while her flute, violin and piano sonatas have strong virtuosic elements and are worthy of study. She was honoured with the OAM in 1993.

FURTHER REFERENCE

Monique Geitenbeek, 'Composer-pianist Phyllis Batchelor: An Introduction', *SA* 41 (Autumn 1994): 33–4.

JOEL CROTTY

Bathurst, pop. (1991) 24 682. Birthplace of the opera singer Ronal *Jackson, it is set in central-western NSW and was established in 1815, Australia's oldest inland city and the first west of the Great Dividing Range. It was also home to the Wiradjuri, the largest Aboriginal tribe in NSW, who fiercely resisted white settlement until martial law was declared in 1826.

A bell sounded from St Stephen's Presbyterian church from the early days of settlement, but growth was slow until the goldrush of the 1850s. Virtuoso violinist Miska *Hauser visited in 1854, and thought his audience filled with 'reformed felons . . . vice and misery'. Because of the town's remoteness, musical skills were lacking: there may never have been active change-ringers for the sizeable peals of bells installed at All Saints' Cathedral (1854) and the Cathedral of St Michael and St George (1861). Gradually the cathedral organists, such as A.W. Juncker (1885–90), Thomas H. Massey (from 1901), Leicester Johnson (1918–22), developed a more vigorous musical life. A series of groups presenting amateur operetta and oratorios came and went: the Bathurst Philharmonic Society (1883–90), the Bathurst Choral Society which competed vigorously with the Federal Choir (1898–1905), and the Bathurst Musical and Dramatic Society (1918–35). The Bathurst District Band was established in 1885, and were Australian champions in 1909. A fine carillon tower, one of only three in Australia, was built as a war memorial in 1933.

The Bathurst City Hall was built in 1965, where today the Carillon Theatre Society presents a musical each May and the Bathurst Eisteddfod is held each October, serving the surrounding region. The Mitchell Conservatorium, Charles Sturt University, offers music instruction, and the Ronald Dowd National Summer School for Singers attracts singers widely each January.

Batley, Noelene (b Sydney, 25 Dec. 1943), pop singer. Appearing on Sydney radio in childhood, she was signed to Festival Records at the age of 16 and appeared on *Six O'Clock Rock* and *Bandstand* from 1960. The first female artist to have a Top 40 hit in Australia, her *Barefoot Boy* reached No. 5 in the charts in 1960; and with *Rendezvous* in 1961 she became the first female artist to release an LP pop album in Australia. She toured nationally with Johnny O'Keefe, Lonnie Lee and others. After recording an English version of 'Kon Nichi Wa Ahachan' as *Little Treasure From Japan* in 1964 she successfully toured Japan; then, moving into cabaret work, she toured Europe in 1969. She now lives in Miami, USA.

FURTHER REFERENCE
Recordings include *Barefoot Boy* (Rex RS026), *Rendezvous* (Rex RL 30010), *Little Treasure From Japan* (Festival FK 10964). For discography, see *SpencerA*. See also Damian Johnstone in *Collected Stories on Australian Rock and Roll*, ed. David McLean (Sydney: Canetoad Publications, 1991), 17–20; *McGrathA*; *SpencerW*.

Battersby, Jean Agnes (b Drouin, Vic., 12 Mar. 1928), arts administrator. Originally a university language teacher, then a freelance writer and broadcaster, she was executive officer of the Australian Council for the Arts 1968–72 then founding chief executive of the ★Australia Council, 1972–83. Under her guidance, a pattern was set of peer-assessed funding, decided at 'arm's length' from the government, which has prevailed in the arts in Australia ever since. Her publications include *Australian Cultural Policy* (1979) and *The Arts Council Phenomenon* (1981). Since 1987 she has been director of the Australian International Cultural Foundation. She was honoured with the AO in 1986.

FURTHER REFERENCE
MonashB; *WWA* (1996); Andrea Lofthouse, comp. *Who's Who of Australian Women* (Melbourne: Methuen, 1982).

Battle of the Sounds, The. Rock music competition (1966–72), organised by a chocolate company, with regional heats, state semi-finals, and a national final broadcast on commercial radio. Winners included the ★Twilights, the ★Groop and ★Sherbert. The prize involved a trip to the UK and USA, which some winners used to launch their careers abroad.

Bauld, Alison Margaret (b Sydney, 7 May 1944), composer. After studies at NIDA in 1962 she worked as a stage and television actress; she completed a music degree at Sydney University in 1967, then doctoral studies with Elizabeth Lutyens and Hans Keller at York University (PhD, 1974). She became music director at Laban Centre for Dance, Goldsmiths' College, University of London, in 1975, then composer-in-residence NSW State Conservatorium in 1978; since then she has taught at Hollins College, London. Many of her works have been heard in Europe, including at the Aldeburgh, York and Edinburgh Festivals. Her output includes few instrumental works; most have a vocal and dramatic element, such as the music-theatre *In a Dead Brown Land* (1972, set in colonial Australia), or those for solo singer with chamber ensemble, such as *Banquo's Buried* (1982) and *Farewell Already* (1993, after Shakespeare). More recently, she has produced a series of keyboard tutors, *Play Your Way*.

WORKS
Publisher: Novello & Co.

FURTHER REFERENCE
Recordings include *One Pearl* (1991, Oz Music OZM2005); *Banquo's Buried* (1982, Canberra School of Music, CSM 15) and *Farewell Already*, Jane Manning (NMC). See also Jenny Dawson, *ContemporaryC*; Toni Calam and Thérèse Radic, *GroveW*; *CohenI*; Paul Griffiths, 'Alison Bauld', *Musical Times* 1605 (Nov. 1976), 903–4; Nadine Amadio, 'Alison Bauld: A Modern Woman Composer', *Hi-Fi and Music* (Feb. 1979), 72–7.

Bayreuth Scholarship. Awarded annually (since 1973) by application to a singer, *répétiteur*, producer or conductor professionally engaged in opera. Administered by Opera Foundation Australia, it provides fares, accommodation and tuition for two months' study in Germany. Winners have included singers Nance ★Grant, Ronald ★Dowd and Robert ★Gard, and conductors Richard ★Divall and Ronald Peelman.

Beach Inspector and the Mermaid, The. Ballet by James Penberthy (1958). First performed by the WA Ballet at Perth in 1958 and recorded by the WA Symphony Orchestra under Thomas Mayer (1970, Philips 6508002).

Beale. Firm of piano manufacturers founded at Sydney by Octavius Beale (1850–1930). Establishing a business importing sewing machines in 1879, Beale moved into piano manufacture in 1893. He laid out a vast factory at Annandale, Sydney, with a timber seasoning yard, sawmill, veneer factory and electroplating shop as well as an instrument-making plant. He used a production line approach, at his height employing 300 people and producing up to 50 pianos a week. He focused on local timbers, using Queensland walnut for the cases, and pioneering the use of Australian timbers in plywood and veneer. Patenting an 'all-iron tuning system' in 1902, which enabled the piano's tuning pegs to be locked down to prevent slippage, he advertised his instruments as ideally suited to the changeable Australian climate. Some of his 13 children went into his business and continued it after his death, but competition from cheap imported pianos led eventually to a takeover by W.H. *Paling & Co, and production ceased in 1961. Having made about 95 000 instruments, Beale had been the largest piano manufacturer in Australia; many of his instruments are still in use.

FURTHER REFERENCE
AthertonA.

Beath, Betty (*b* Bundaberg, Qld, 19 Nov. 1932), composer. Learning piano from an early age, she was twice a finalist in the ABC Concerto competition in her teens, and studied piano at the NSW State Conservatorium with Frank *Hutchens, then at the Queensland Conservatorium. In 1974, with her husband the writer-illustrator David Cox, she gathered source material in Indonesia on an Australia Council grant, which she used in *Indonesian Triptych* (Goenawan Mohamad, 1977), *Nawang Wulan* (Sastrowardojo, 1980) and other works. She has long taught at St Margaret's Girls' School, Brisbane, and the Queensland Conservatorium, and was resident at North Adams State College, Massachusetts, USA, in 1987. Her music has focused on exquisite sets of miniatures for voice and piano, sometimes with flute or small ensemble, and music-theatre. Her works include *Poems from the Chinese* (medieval texts, 1979), *Songs from the Beast's Choir* (1984) heard at Carnegie Recital Hall, *Asmaradana* (1994) for orchestra and *The Raja who Married an Angel* (1983) for children. Active as an advocate for women composers, she has been an executive member of the International League of Women Composers since 1984.

FURTHER REFERENCE
Her recordings include *Points In A Journey* (Oz Music, OZM 2010); *River Songs* (1992, Jade JADCD1038). See also Jenny Dawson, *ContemporaryC*; Graham Hair and Greta Mary Hair, *GroveW*; *CohenI*.

Beatty, Raymond Wesley (*b* Narrandera, NSW, 22 June 1903; *d* Sydney, 5 Dec. 1973), bass baritone, teacher. After studying with Roland Foster at the NSW State Conservatorium, he sang with the Royal Philharmonic Society, Sydney, and gave recitals from 1926. He went to London in 1930, appearing in regional orchestral concerts and on the BBC, then to the USA, appearing in radio broadcasts. He was with the NZ Broadcasting Co. in 1935, appeared in the 1936 ABC Opera season, singing Don Pasquale, Figaro and Bartolo, and toured Australia and NZ in concerts. After war service he taught at the NSW State Conservatorium 1946–73. A singer noted for his precise diction and robust tone, he sang over 200 *Messiahs* and was a teacher in Sydney of considerable influence.

FURTHER REFERENCE
Martha Ruthlege, *ADB,* 7.

Beaumont, (Edward) Armes (*b* Ingham, Norfolk, England, 15 Dec. 1840; *d* North Melbourne, 17 July 1913), tenor. He arrived at Melbourne in August 1848 and was educated in Fitzroy. Despite receiving limited vocal training, Beaumont's natural abilities soon drew the attention of William and Fred Lyster, who witnessed his debut in a Melbourne performance of Handel's *Messiah* in 1861. Joining Lyster's Opera Co. in 1863, Beaumont drew praise for his rich voice and convincing acting, and was particularly admired in *Faust, Carmen, L'Africaine* and *Maritana.* In February 1867 he was involved in a shooting accident that left his sight seriously damaged. Despite this, he continued to excel in both grand and comic operas, developing a repertoire of some 82 solo roles. A frequent concert and oratorio performer, he sang a record 67 solo performances with the Royal Melbourne Philharmonic Society. After a career spanning 30 years, he retired from public performance in 1894.

FURTHER REFERENCE
Argus 18 July 1913: 5; *BrewerD,* 68; Kenneth Hince, *ADB,* 3; H. Morin Humphreys, *Men of the Time in Australia,* Victorian Series, 2nd edn (Melbourne: McCarron, Bird & Co., 1882), viii-ix.

JENNIFER ROYLE

Bebbington, Warren Arthur (*b* Caulfield, Melbourne, 25 Apr. 1952), administrator, musicologist, conductor. He graduated in piano from the University of Melbourne, and in musicology from Queen's College, New York and City University of New York (PhD, 1984), then was a lecturer at the Canberra School of Music from 1979, professor and dean of music, University of Queensland from 1985, and Ormond professor and dean of the faculty of music, University of Melbourne from 1991. He was a member of the Music Board (then Performing Arts Board) Australia Council (1986–92). As a scholar he has published editions of the works of Haydn (Bärenreiter), J.G. Graun and C.H. Graun (Garland, New York) and edited a volume of essays, *Sound and Reason,* and *The Oxford Companion to Australian Music.*

FURTHER REFERENCE
ADMR; CA (1995–96); *WWA* (1996).

MARGARET KARTOMI

Bebop. The modern jazz movement of the early 1940s, originated in the USA by Dizzy Gillespie, Charlie Parker and others, which superimposed substituted chords on jazz standards and involved improvisations of highly florid melodic lines and complex rhythmic patterns. In Australia it flourished in the immediate postwar years, its exponents including Don *Banks, Wally *Norman, Splinter *Reeves, Bruce *Clarke and Charlie *Blott. See *Jazz*.

Bee Gees, The.   Pop group comprised of Barry Gibb (*b* Douglas, Isle of Man, 1 Sept. 1947, vocals, guitar) and his twin brothers Robin (vocals, bass) and Maurice (*b* Douglas, 22 Dec. 1949, vocals). They emigrated with their parents to Australia in 1958, having performed hit songs of the day at local Saturday morning picture shows since 1956. While performing at the Speedway Circus in Brisbane (1960) for racetrack organiser Bill Good, the Gibb brothers were introduced to disc jockey Bill Gates, who played their tapes on his 4KQ radio show *Clatter Chatter*. An interest in the brothers' music ensued, and Good dubbed the group 'The B. G.'s' after his and Gates's initials. Radio exposure lead to a TV debut on *Anything Goes*, which was followed by regular appearances on BTQ7's *Cotties' Happy Hour* program.

In 1962, the brothers relocated to Sydney, and as the Bee Gees played at the Sydney Stadium supporting Chubby Checker. This year also saw them start their songwriting career, notably producing Col Joye's No. 1 hit *Starlight of Love*. As the Bee Gees went to the UK in January 1967, their 11th single *Spicks and Specks* topped the Australian charts. In February that year they signed a five-year management contract with Robert Stigwood at Brian Epstein's NEMS Enterprises, and in March completed their line-up with drummer Colin Petersen (*b* Kingaroy, Qld, 24 Mar. 1946) and guitarist Vince Melouney (*b* Sydney, 18 Aug. 1945). Their first UK-recorded single *New York Mining Disaster 1941* featured the appealing three-part harmonies led by Barry's distinctive falsetto that became their trademark, and was a global million-seller, reaching No. 12 in the UK and No. 14 in the USA.

A string of hits followed including the UK chart-toppers *Massachusetts* (1967) and *I've Gotta Get a Message to You* (1968). Despite their popularity, internal conflict caused Melouney, Petersen and Robin Gibb to leave the group in 1969, and although Robin returned late in 1970, their UK popularity had waned. The band took on a new funky, disco-oriented direction, producing *Jive Talkin'* (1975) and *You Should Be Dancing* (1976), which topped the US charts. In 1977 Stigwood produced the disco film *Saturday Night Fever* featuring seven Bee Gees songs; the sound-track double album topped the US and UK charts and eventually sold over 30 million copies worldwide, remaining the best-selling film sound-track in recording history. New songs from this album, *How Deep Is Your Love*, *Stayin' Alive* and *Night Fever*, all topped the US chart, as did 1979 hits *Too Much Heaven*, *Tragedy* and *Love You Inside Out*. Continuing to hone their songwriting talents throughout the 1980s, the Bee Gees returned to the UK

charts with the No. 1 hit *You Win Again* in 1987, and became the only band to have topped the charts in each of the 1960s, 70s and 80s.

FURTHER REFERENCE

Recordings include *Barry Gibb and the Bee Gees Sing and Play 14 Barry Gibb Songs* (1965); *Spicks and Specks* (1966); *The Bee Gees First* (1967); *Horizontal* (1968); *Idea* (1968); *Odessa* (1969); *Cucumber Castle* (1970, Spin SEL 933797); *Two Years On* (1970, Spin SEL 934061); *Trafalgar* (1971, Spin SEL 934385); *To Whom It May Concern* (1972, Spins EL 34631); *Life in a Tin Can* (1973, Spins EL 34844); *Mr Natural* (1974, Spin L 35244); *Main Course* (1975, RSO 2394 150); *Children of the World* (1976, RSO 2394 169); *Here at Last . . . Bee Gees Live* (1977, RSO 2658 120); *Saturday Night Fever* (1977, RSO 800 068–2); *Sgt Pepper's Lonely Hearts Club Band* (1978); *Spirits Having Flown* (1979, RSO 2394 216); *Living Eyes* (1981, RSO 2394 301); *Stayin' Alive* (1983, RSO); *ESP* (1987, Warner Bros 25541–1); *One* (1989, Warner Bros 25887–1); *High Civilisation* (1991); *Size isn't Everything* (1993, Polydor 519945–2); *Irresistible Force* (1996). See also *GuinnessP*; *SpencerW*; D. Rees and L. Crampton, eds, *Rock Movers and Shakers* (Santa Barbara, CA: ABC-CLIO, 1991).

AARON D.S. CORN

Bell, Graeme Emerson (*b* Melbourne, 7 Sept. 1914), jazz pianist, leader. He began classical piano at the age of 11, and was converted to jazz by his brother Roger *Bell, with whom he played his first engagement in 1935. By 1941, his band was becoming established in Melbourne through a residency at Leonards Café and was playing at the Contemporary Art Society's annual exhibition, reflecting his interest in radical art and politics. Apart from a period in Queensland in May–November 1943, Bell led his band at its Heidelberg Town Hall residency until June 1944, and as house band of the communist Eureka Youth League's Hot Jazz Society. In 1946 he started a cabaret, the Uptown Club, in the Youth League's premises, and played at the first Australian Jazz Convention, which was largely founded by him with League official Harry Stein. Concerts and recordings at Sydney in 1947 consolidated his national reputation.

With the Youth League's assistance Stein invited the band to Prague for the 1947 World Youth Festival, and its performances there profoundly influenced jazz in Czechoslovakia. The band subsequently went to the UK, where Bell's 'jazz for dancing' policy expanded jazz audiences. Returning to Australia in 1948 to a national ABC tour, he founded the Swaggie jazz label in 1949 and organised an Australian tour for USA cornettist Rex Stewart. Following a second UK and European tour (1950–52), another ABC tour upon their return to Australia, and *Music Maker* poll awards for both the band and Graeme, the band broke up in 1953.

He formed a new band for Combined Services Entertainment tours of Korea and Japan 1954–55, based himself in Brisbane 1955–56, and then settled in Sydney in 1957, opening an art gallery and playing casual engagements. The first of his 'All Stars' in 1962 marked the serious renewal of his jazz career, embracing recording, broadcasting (including his own television show), concert and club work and touring nationally and internationally. In 1975 with an Arts Council grant he visited the USA on a study tour, then established his own record label (Sea Horse) in 1977.

Bell has been central to some of the most significant projects in Australian jazz—the Uptown Club, the Australian Jazz Convention and Swaggie Records. As a bandleader and composer he was pivotal to 'the Australian jazz sound', one of the few distinctive styles to emerge outside the USA. His early activities provided the musical focal point for otherwise disparate forces in Australian music and radical thought, and his work in Europe and the UK represented the most influential export in Australia's jazz history. He is the most significant jazz musician Australia has produced. He was honoured with the Queen's Jubilee Medal, the MBE (1978), and the AO (1990). In 1993 the Annual Bell Lecture was inaugurated in his honour in Sydney.

FURTHER REFERENCE
Recordings include *Czechoslovak Journey,* Graeme Bell and his Dixieland Jazz Band (1973, Supraphon 0 15 1455); *Big Walkabout,* Graeme Bell with his Dixieland Jazz Band, Australian Jazz Band, All Stars [compilation covering 1947–67] (1988 RCA Victor VJL 0625); *Graeme Bell in Holland with the Graeme Bell All Stars* (1982 Sea Horse SHL 004). His autobiography is *Graeme Bell, Australian Jazzman, His Autobiography* (Sydney, Child & Associates, 1988). See also *BissetB*; *CA*; *GroveJ*; *OxfordJ*; *WWA;* Bruce Clunies-Ross, 'An Australian Sound, Jazz in Melbourne and Adelaide 1941–1951', in P. Spearritt & D. Walker, eds, *Australian Popular Culture* (Sydney: Allen & Unwin, 1979), 62–80; Bruce Johnson, 'Graeme Bell at Seventy', *JA* (Winter 1984), 8–11; idem, 'Australian Jazz in Europe, A case study in musical displacement', *Perfect Beat: The Pacific Journal of Research into Contemporary Music and Popular Culture* 2/3 (July 1995), 49–64.

BRUCE JOHNSON

Bell, Roger Emerson   (*b* Melbourne, 4 Jan. 1919), jazz trumpeter, composer. Drawn to jazz in 1932 by hearing American recordings, in 1935 he took drum lessons and played dances with his older brother Graeme ★Bell, whom he converted to jazz. He began playing trumpet in 1938 and from 1939 was a member of the Graeme Bell band, leading it in 1943 during his brother's absence in Queensland in residencies at Heidelberg Town Hall (July), the Palais Royale (September), and for a recording session with Max Kaminsky (then touring Australia with Artie Shaw's US Navy band). He remained with his brother's band until it broke up in 1953. After a year's break he joined Max Collie's band, and in 1958 began a lengthy tenure with the Melbourne Jazz Club house band. In 1963 he revived the band name Pagan Pipers (which he had originally used in 1949), and over the next few years made a series of recordings which document

his own compositions. He has continued to be active with his own groups, notably at festivals. Bell is one of the central figures in the evolution of the 'Australian sound', particularly as a trumpeter, vocalist and prolific composer. Since the mid-1980s he has spent much of his time at Hawks Nest, NSW.

FURTHER REFERENCE
Recordings include *Roger Bell and His Pagan Pipers* (1968, Swaggie S1244). See also *BissetB*; *GroveJ*; *OxfordJ*; Bruce Johnson, 'Is there an Australian jazz?' *JA* Part 1 (Dec. 1981), 6–8, and Part 2 (Feb. 1982), 20–3.

BRUCE JOHNSON

Bells.   The earliest church bells installed in Australia were the eight Whitechapel bells which arrived in 1795, but they were not hung until a belltower was completed at St Phillip's in Sydney in 1807 (they did not carry well, and were replaced in 1858). Eight locally cast bells were hung at the convict church at Port Arthur in 1837; several are now at New Norfolk. At the Benedictine monastery at New Norcia, WA, are four bells hung in Spanish fashion, two of which probably date from the monastery's opening in 1846. By this time bells were becoming common in the settlements, and several churches had peals of good quality: St Mary's Cathedral had a peal from 1843, Trinity Church, Hobart, had a peal from 1847, and St James Old Cathedral, Melbourne, had a peal of six installed in 1852. Today there are 28 ringable peals and about 27 chimes in Australian churches. There are striking bells in the clock towers of only four capital-city and a few regional town halls, but a great many more in the clock towers of post offices, even in remote centres. There are only three carillons. See *Change Ringing*; *Carillons.*

FURTHER REFERENCE
John D. Keating, *Bells in Australia* (Melbourne: MUP, 1977).

Bells of St Mary's, The.   Popular song by expatriate Australian composer A. Emmett Adams, words by Douglas Furber, first published for voice and piano in London (Ascherberg, Hopwood & Crew) in 1917. This sentimental ballad of love and marriage was allegedly inspired by the bells of the parish church of St Mary's, Southampton, England. Its early popularity was boosted with a recording by NZ-born soprano Frances ★Alda (Victor, 1920). Revived in the eponymous 1945 American film starring Bing Crosby and Ingrid Bergman, it became an international hit through Crosby's recording. The refrain is heard, played on cinema organ, in the film *The Godfather* (1972).

JENNIFER HILL

Beloved Vagabond, The.   Musical comedy by Dudley Glass, libretto by Adrian Ross after the romantic novel of W.J. Locke. First performed in Australia by the Frank Thring Co. at the Princess Theatre, Melbourne, in 1934.

Belsazer. Opera in one act, music and libretto by Felix Werder, after Heine. First performed at the Gymnasium, Dortmund, Germany, on 5 October 1988.

Ben Hall. See *Death of Ben Hall*.

Bendigo, pop. (1991) 57 427. City in the central uplands of Vic. 160 km north of Melbourne. Founded as Sandhurst in 1840, it was the site of important goldfields in the 1850s; today it is a centre for the agricultural produce of the region. Predominantly amateur music has flourished in Bendigo since the city's establishment in 1852. There has been a multitude of different ensembles, one of the first being the Sandhurst Philharmonic Society, a choral society with conductor, organist and formal committee founded in 1865. The turn of the century saw an increase in musical activity, some of the larger ensembles including the Liedertafel (1884), the Orchestral Society (*c.*1892), the Bendigo Glee Club (1894) and the Operatic Society (1898), all of which gave regular performances of a high standard; the Glee Club performed Verdi's *Il Trovatore* in 1894. Smaller ensembles and bands of this period included the St Paul's Cathedral Quartet (1895), the Bendigo String Quartet (1899), the Golden City Vocal Quartet (1899), the Choral Society (1913), and the Hopetoun (1898), Eaglehawk (1906) and Bendigo City (1906) bands. The increase in musical activity led to the establishment of the Austral Society competitions in 1898, later becoming the Bendigo Competitions in 1924, which are still held today.

The early 20th century saw the establishment, influenced by local music teacher Edward Allen Bindly, of the Bendigo Conservatorium in 1906, one of the first of its kind in Victoria. Some of Bindly's better-known graduates included the soprano Kate Samuels, later known as Madam Benda, the contralto Erna Mueller, and the pianist William *Murdoch. But Bindly's most famous student was the soprano Amy *Castles who achieved international recognition, performing in most of Europe's great opera houses. There was a brief recess of musical activity during the World War I, when the conservatorium closed and many ensembles disbanded or merged. From the 1920s the orchestral society and the concert orchestra led by the prominent musician Oscar Flight developed. Both these ensembles went into recess during the 1960s and 70s, and were replaced by the Bendigo Symphony Orchestra in 1981. In 1953 the Operatic Society was revived, and performed regularly until the late 1970s when it was replaced by other theatre and community arts musical groups. The Benola Singers, led by Mavis Webster, was founded in 1957 and continues to be successful today, as does the Music Lovers Club (1958) and the Music Advancement Society (1958). From 1953 until the late 1970s the Music for the People Concerts were a very popular institution. Successful musicians to come from Bendigo during this later period have included the popu-

lar music singer Colleen *Hewett, flautist Derek Jones and composer Stephen *Holgate.

At present, there are numerous brass and highland bands, a folk club, the country talent club and rock bands. The Symphony Orchestra still performs, often with the youth orchestra, and there is also a youth choir. Bendigo has a regional arts centre, situated at the Capitol theatre, and a community music co-operative, called Open Stage, all contributing to keeping the music-making tradition alive.

FURTHER REFERENCE

Annals of Bendigo vols 5–8 (1921–88); Keith Cole, *The Benolas: Thirty Years of Making Music* (Bendigo: Benola Choristers, 1987); Anthony Condon, A History of Music in Bendigo, Special Study, Univ. Melbourne, 1966; Frank Cusack, *Bendigo: A History* (Melbourne: Heinemann, 1973); Tsou Nan Chien, Musical Life in Bendigo 1856–1918, MMus, Univ. Melbourne, 1992; Steve Grey, ed., *Decibels: Midland Music Directory* 2 (Aug. 1994).

HILARY BLACKSHAW

Benjamin, Arthur Leslie   (*b* Sydney, 18 Sept. 1893; *d* London, 10 Apr. 1960), pianist, conductor, composer. Initially taught to play piano by his mother, he began organ lessons with George *Sampson in Brisbane at the age of nine. He won an open scholarship from Brisbane Grammar School to the Royal College of Music, London, in 1911, studying composition with Stanford. During World War I, he served with the Royal Fusiliers and the RAF, returning to Australia in 1919 to became professor of piano study at the NSW Conservatorium. In 1921 he went back to England and was to hold the same post at the Royal College of Music from 1925 to 1938. In 1939 he was appointed conductor of the Vancouver Symphony Orchestra. During World War II he conducted and lectured in Canada, afterwards returning to London, where he lived until his death. In 1950, to celebrate his 50th year in music, he was commissioned by the ABC to compose a piano concerto, which he also personally performed in Sydney. In 1956 he was awarded the Cobbett Medal.

As a teacher Benjamin was very highly regarded; his pupils included many notable musicians, among them Benjamin Britten, Muir Mathieson and George Weldon. As a composer he was somewhat underrated in Australia, being better known in England, Canada and the USA. The success of his compositions overseas allowed him to devote much of his later life to writing music. In 1924 he received a Carnegie Award for his *Pastoral Fantasy*; in 1926 he appeared as soloist in a performance of his own Piano Concertino under Sir Henry Wood at Queen's Hall; in 1931 Sir Thomas Beecham conducted his opera *The Devil Take Her*. Benjamin was particularly interested in operatic music and composed *A Tale of Two Cities*, which won the Festival of Britain Opera Competition in 1951, and *Tartuffe*, both full-length operas, a short comic opera called *Prima Donna*, and *Mañana*, written especially for television. He also wrote a symphony, a major choral work, piano concertos, suites, orchestral pieces, songs, and much film music.

But his most popular piece of music was *Jamaican Rumba* (1938), which was so successful that it tended to obscure his more substantial works. On a visit to the West Indies, a folk tune known as *Mattei Rag* attracted Benjamin's attention and he made an orchestral version of it. It was recorded on disc by Heifetz and in its first year sold over 250 000 copies. Overall his music displayed a stylish elegance, his forte being his innate sense of theatre and flair for orchestral writing. Although returning to Australia only briefly once he had left, he always maintained links with his home country and did much to promote Australian composers abroad, including the organisation of Australia House concerts in London.

FURTHER REFERENCE

Recordings include *Jamaican Rumba,* Cleveland Pops Orchestra, cond. Lane (Decca LXT 5304–33); Harmonica Concerto, Royal Philharmonic Orchestra, Larry Adler, harmonica (RCA SB 6786); *Valses caprices,* Gervase de Peyer, cl, Colin Preedy pf (L'Oiseau-lyre SOL 60028). A discography to 1972 is in *PlushD.* See also *CallawayA*; Charles Campbell, *ADB,* 7; Roger Covell, *Australia's Music: Themes of a New Society* (Melbourne: Sun Books, 1967); *MurdochA*; Peter J. Pirie, *GroveD.*

PAULINE PETRUS

Bennelong. Opera (1988) by Barry Conyngham, libretto by Murray Copland, to be acted by puppets. Tells the story of Bennelong, an Aborigine captured in 1789, taken by Governor Phillip to visit England, made go-between in the colony's dealings with local natives, and given a house where the Sydney Opera House now stands (Bennelong Point). Commissioned for the Australian Bicentennial, and first performed by the Australian Chamber Orchestra on tour at Gröningen State Theatre, The Netherlands, on 21 April 1988.

Bennett, Laurie (*b* Sydney, 21 Dec. 1940), jazz drummer. He began drums at the age of 15 and from the early 1960s was becoming active at the Mocambo, Sydney, then at *El Rocco. Primarily a freelancer in club, concert and session work over a broad stylistic range, he has worked and recorded regularly with such artists as Don *Burrows at the Wentworth Supper Club, Bob Bertles (1977), bassist Richard Ochalski (1978–79), singer Nancy Stuart, Bernie McGann, and for fairly lengthy periods with Col *Nolan. He has also led his own groups at the Orient Hotel, Soup Plus and elsewhere, and for Jazz Action Society concerts.

FURTHER REFERENCE

Recordings include *The Don Burrows Quartet* (1971, Cherry Pie CPS-1009); *Arrangements,* Col Nolan Quartet (1976, M7 Records MLF-157); *Nancy Stuart* (1977, 44 Records 44 6357 717); *Bob Barnard with Kenny Powell's Orchestra* (1979, ABC Records L-8003); *Straight Ahead,* Richard Ochalski (1979, 44 Records 44

6357 723); *The Jazz Action Sessions vol. 1* (1983, 2MBS-FM JAZZ-2/3). See also *OxfordJ.*　　　BRUCE JOHNSON

Benson, Lucy Charlotte (*b* Hobart, 1 Mar. 1860; *d* Sandy Bay, Hobart, 14 Oct. 1943), singing teacher, conductor. Daughter of singer Fanny *Lempriere, she played organ from the age of 10, and studied singing at Melbourne with del Sarte and Emery Gould and piano with Thomas Guenett and Frank *Packer. She sang the female lead in *HMS Pinafore* in 1879, then conducted numerous Gilbert and Sullivan performances. After having a family she taught singing at Hobart and formed a choir which won the Bathurst Eisteddfod 1903 and the South Street Competitions in 1905. As a choral conductor, prominent teacher and director of amateur operetta and light opera productions, she was a leading figure in Tasmanian musical life until World War II.

FURTHER REFERENCE

Obit. in Hobart *Mercury* 15 Oct. 1943. See also Diana Large, *ADB,* 7; *OrchardM,* 87.

Benton, Merv (*b* Melbourne, 1945), pop singer. Working in a bank and singing at local dances, he was signed to W&G in 1964 and toured with Billy J. Kramer, the Tamlas and others. Magnetically singing rock and roll standards, his good looks and routinely smart suits made him very popular with young female fans, and he had three Top 20 hits, his single *I Got Burned* reaching No. 13 in the charts in 1965. His debut album *Come On And Get Me* in 1964 was followed by *Sounds Great* and others. But throat problems brought his withdrawal from singing in 1966; he tried miming his work but soon retired from the stage.

FURTHER REFERENCE

Recordings include *I Got Burned* (W&G S2384), *Come On And Get Me* (W&G WGB 1916), *Sounds Great* (1965, W&G WGB 2494). A compilation is *The Fabulous Merv Benton* (1994, Raven RVLP16). For discography, see *SpencerA.* See also *McGrathA*; *SpencerW.*

Berg, Charles (*b* Berlin, 28 Mar. 1917; *d* Sydney, 6 Feb. 1988), accountant, music administrator. Originally a steel works apprentice, he arrived in Australia in 1937 and studied accountancy in Melbourne, eventually becoming director of various companies, representative of the Union Bank of Switzerland, and holder of a large property at Rangers Valley, New England. A keen amateur violinist, he was secretary to Musica Viva from 1947 and president 1955–74, then chairman of the Australian Opera 1974–86. Combining a passion for music with sound business sense, he greatly assisted in the development of these two leading musical organisations. He was honoured with the OBE in 1972 and the AM in 1986.

FURTHER REFERENCE

Obit. in *Age* 8 Feb. 1988. See also *Australian* 25 Jan. 1986.

Bertles, Bob (Robert Anthony) (*b* Mayfield, NSW, 6 Mar. 1939), jazz reed-player, composer, arranger. He began professional jazz work in 1956, and was involved with modernist activities at the Mocambo and ★El Rocco, Sydney. He appeared in clubs, television, and rock music, including with Johnny ★O'Keefe. After periods in Melbourne and Adelaide, he returned to Sydney in 1964, then joined Max ★Merritt in 1967 for five years, including on his international tours. In the UK he played session work with Cliff Richards, Cilla Black and others, and played in Ian Carr's Nucleus. Returning to Sydney in 1976, he joined Col ★Nolan and taught at the NSW Conservatorium. He was in Europe on a study grant, 1980–81; then resumed teaching, session work, and leading and playing with various bands, including Ten Part Invention.

FURTHER REFERENCE
Recordings include *Straight Ahead,* Richard Ochalski (1979, 44 Records 6357723); *Bob Bertles; Moontrane* (1979, Batjazz BAT 2070); *Misty Morning* (1980, Batjazz BAT 2073); *Tall Stories,* Ten Part Invention (1994, Rufus Polygram RF 006); *Rhythm of the Heart,* The Bob Bertles Quintet (1995, Rufus Polygram RF 017). See also *ClareB; BissetB; OxfordJ;* Jim McLeod, 'Out of Sight, Bob Bertles', *Australian Jazz and Blues* 1/6 (1994) 34–5.
BRUCE JOHNSON

Best, Peter (*b* Adelaide, 18 Oct. 1943), film composer. Despite very little involvement or training in music during his school-days, he fostered a keen interest in music and songwriting in particular. He studied arts at the University of Sydney, and his career in film composition grew out of work in the commercial music industry. He soon went on to establish himself as one of Australia's leading film composers, noted particularly for the diversity of his scores. He is the recipient of numerous awards, including AFI best score awards for his work on *The Picture Show Man* (1977), *Rebel* (1985), and more recently *Dad and Dave: On Our Selection,* and APRA score awards for *Crocodile Dundee* (1986), *Crocodile Dundee II* (1988), and *Muriel's Wedding* (1994). His score for the television program *The Heroes* won best original music in the New York International Film and Television Festival. His other scores include: *Barry McKenzie Holds His Own* (1974), *We of the Never Never* (1982), *Goodbye Paradise* (1982), *Bliss* (1985), *Hightide* (1987), *Father* (1990), and *Country Life* (1994), and for television *The Harp in the South* and its sequel *Poor Man's Orange,* the eleven-hour documentary series *Man on the Rim,* and *Blue Murder.*

FURTHER REFERENCE
LimbacherF.   L.THOMPSON

Bice, Olive (*b* Eaglehawk,Vic., 9 June 1939), country music singer. She appeared on Dick Cranbourne's *Hillbilly Hour* at 3DB in her teens, then toured with Reg ★Poole, ★Rick and Thel, and Buddy Weston. A singer

chiefly of traditional country ballads and especially yodels, her repertoire also includes mainstream numbers, such as those by Dolly Parton or Linda Ronstadt. From her Bendigo home she tours extensively with her five children, all musicians, and is a regular at the Mildura and Tamworth Country Music Festivals. She has recorded eight albums and won the Tex Morton Memorial Award in 1994.

FURTHER REFERENCE
Recordings include *Hillbilly Girl With The Blues* (Morning Mist,1981), *Lady of Song* (1982), and *With A Yodel and A Song* (1989). See also *LattaA,* 159; *SmithB,* 238.

Biddell, Kerrie (*b* Sydney, 8 Feb. 1947), jazz singer. She had early success in pop music, including backing Dusty Springfield and singing with the Affair 1968–70, with which she toured England. She was with the ★Daly Wilson Big Band 1970–71, then in the USA, singing in cabaret and session work 1972–73. Returning to Sydney, she was active in session work and had her own television program. She was in the USA again in 1974, then back in Australia playing residencies, tours, festivals, musical theatre, and concerts with Compared to What, Julian Lee, Don Burrows, Judy Bailey, pianist Michael Bartolomei, and Dizzy Gillespie. An artist who eschewed pop music success for work in jazz, she teaches at the NSW Conservatorium jazz program and has won numerous awards for her performances and recordings.

FURTHER REFERENCE
Recordings include *The Daly Wilson Big Band* (1971, Festival SFL-934453); *Only The Beginning,* Kerrie Biddell (1975, EMI EMA-314); *The Tony Ansell Orchestra* (1979, Batjazz BAT-2069); *Kerrie Biddell and Compared to What* (1979, EMI SS-301); *The Singer* (1995, Origin/Polygram OR 015). An interview with her is in *WilliamsA,* 130–5. See also *OxfordJ.*
BRUCE JOHNSON

Biggins, Lindsay (*b* 1904; *d* 13 Jan. 1955), pianist. He won first prize at the South Street Eisteddfod, Ballarat and studied at the University of Melbourne Conservatorium with F.W. Homewood, then in Germany with Max Pauer. He returned to Australia in 1929 and taught at the University of Melbourne Conservatorium, for many years giving educational broadcasts with ABC radio. His *For the Music Student* on 3AW from 1946 often presented listeners with their first experience of new and recent works. An inspiring teacher, gracious and intelligent, he was one of the foremost Australian piano teachers of the middle years of the 20th century; his pupils included Ronald Farren Price and many others who later made careers.

FURTHER REFERENCE
Obit. in *AMN* 45 (Feb. 1955), 2; *AMN* 45 (Mar. 1955), 5; *Melbourne University Gazette* 11/1 (Mar. 1955), 8. See also *OrchardM,* 201; *GlennonA,* 225; *AMN* 10 (1921), 389.

Bill the Bullocky. See *Nine Miles From Gundagai*.

Birthday Party [Boys Next Door]. Rock group (1976–83) formed in Melbourne by Caulfield Grammar School students Nick Cave (vocals), Mick Harvey (guitar), Rowland Howard (guitar), Tracy Pew (bass), and Phil Calvert (drums until 1982, then Mick Harvey). As Boys Next Door they played in the Melbourne alternative rock scene, then in 1980 released their debut album as Birthday Party, and spent periods in the UK, the USA and Europe. Aggressive, abrasive, with opaque songs of violent death or sex, they were an influential band in the post-punk era, releasing such singles as *Mr Clarinet* (1980) and *Release The Bats* (1983). Their album *Prayers On Fire* (1981) was acclaimed by rock critics, but their EP, *The Bad Seed* (1983), with the German experimental band Einsturzende Neubauten, is their most enduring recording. The band dissolved amid drugs, alcohol abuse and rivalries in 1983.

FURTHER REFERENCE
Recordings include *Mr Clarinet* (1980, Missing Link MLS18), *Release The Bats* (1983, Missing Link MISS 3712), *Prayers On Fire* (1981, Missing Link LINK14), *The Bad Seed* (1983, 4AD BAD 301). A compilation is *The Birthday Party* (1944, Shock/Missing Link LINK 30CD). For discography, see *SpencerA*. See also *McGrathA*; *SpencerW*; *CoupeN*; *GuinnessP*, I, 248; Ian McFarlane, 'The Birthday Party', *Prehistoric Sounds* 1/2 (1995), 17–26.

Bishop, John (Lionel Albert Jack)   (*b* Aldinga, SA, 26 Oct. 1903; *d* London, 14 Dec. 1964), conductor, music educator. He studied piano at the Elder Conservatorium, University of Adelaide, from 1919, and in 1922 won an Elder Scholarship to the Royal College of Music, London. In 1928 he went to NZ as conductor of the Wellington Choral Union and the Wellington Philharmonic Orchestra, returning to Australia in 1934. From 1937 as director of music at Scotch College, Melbourne, he transformed the role of music at the school; he also taught piano at the University of Melbourne Conservatorium 1943–47 and conducted the Conservatorium Symphony Orchestra 1940–47. From 1943 he was instrumental, with Ruth ★Alexander and Dr Percy ★Jones, in establishing the National Music Camp Association (now ★Youth Music Australia), and was a driving force as director of the camps for more than a decade. In 1948 he was appointed Elder professor of music and director of the Elder Conservatorium, a position he held until his early death, revitalising the music department, and introducing new courses and staff. As a Carnegie travelling fellow 1952–53, he investigated music education in Britain and America; he formed the Elder String Quartet in 1959 and the University of Adelaide Wind Quintet in 1965. He was the prime mover behind the Adelaide Festival of Arts and its artistic director for the first three Festivals (1960, 1962, 1964).

Bishop was an inspirational teacher and musical leader, who profoundly influenced a generation of young people. His contribution to music and music education in Australia through the creation of the music camp movement and the Adelaide Festival was immense. He was honoured with an honorary DMus from the University of Melbourne in 1963.

FURTHER REFERENCE
Alan Brissenden, *ADB*, 13; Werner Galluser, 'Professor John Bishop: A Bibliography', *MMA* 1 (1966), 8–36; Christopher Symons, *John Bishop A Life for Music* (Melbourne: Hyland House, 1989).

JANE SOUTHCOTT

Black, Jeffrey Douglas   (*b* Brisbane, 6 Sept. 1962), baritone. After studies with Jan Delpratt at the Queensland Conservatorium and Audrey Langford at the National Opera School, London, he made his debut as Mercutio in *Roméo et Juliette* with the Australian Opera in 1985. He joined Covent Garden in the same year, settled in London, and has sung for both companies as well as at Monte Carlo, Glyndebourne, The Netherlands, Munich, Paris, and in major American houses. He returned to Australia in 1994 to sing with the Victoria State Opera and Lyric Opera of Queensland. He has also given numerous concerts and recitals, including with the London Philharmonic and in Australia for the ABC orchestras and in recital with Geoffrey Parsons. At present one of the most regularly heard Australian singers in the world's major opera houses, his roles include the title role in *Barber of Seville*, the Count (*Marriage of Figaro*), Papageno, Guglielmo (*Cosi Fan tutte*), and Harlequin (*Ariadne auf Naxos*).

FURTHER REFERENCE
Recordings include the London Philharmonic Orchestra *Carmina Burana* (1990, EMI CDC 754054-2). See also *CA* (1995–96); *Who's Who in British Opera*, ed. Nicky Adam (Aldershot, UK: Scolar Press, 1993); *CA* (1995/96).

Black Opal.   Ballet by John ★Antill (1961).

Black Sorrows, The.   Soul band formed in Melbourne (1984) by Joe Camilleri (*b* Malta, 1948; guitar, voice, saxophone), Jeff Burstin (guitar), George Butrumlis (piano accordion), Joe Creighton (voice, bass), Sally Ford (saxophone), Steve McTaggart (violin), Richard Sega (bass), and backing vocalists Vika and Linda Bull. At the time of their first Top 10 single release *Chained to the Wheel* (1989), the band's membership had swelled to 14. The Black Sorrows' music can be described as an amalgamation of soul with elements of jazz, Latin big band music, reggae, zydeco, ska, salsa and vocal harmonies derived from the Bull sisters' Tongan heritage.

FURTHER REFERENCE
Recordings include *Sonola* (1984, Spirit L 27118); *Rockin' Zydeco* (1990, Spirit); *A Place in the World* (1986, Spirit JVCLP-2); *Dear Children* (1987, CBS 450924 1); *Hold on to Me* (1989, CBS

462891 1); *Harley and Rose* (1990, CBS 467133 1); *Better Times* (1993, Sony 472149 2); *The Chosen Ones* (1993, Sony 474863 2); *Amazing Stories* (1993, Sony); *Lucky Charm* (1994, Sony 477337 2). See also G. A. Baker, *External Combustion* (Sydney: Grahame, 1990); *SpencerW*.

AARON D. S. CORN

Blair, Harold   (*b* 1924, Cherbourg, nr Murgon, Qld; *d* Melbourne, 1976), tenor. He studied at the Melba Conservatorium of Music, Melbourne, 1945–46, then in the USA 1949–51, originally with Todd Duncan and later with Sara Lee. On the *Australian Amateur Hour* in 1945 he became the first Aboriginal musician to sing on national radio, and in 1951 made a national concert tour of Australia for the ABC. His subsequent career included television and some stage appearances, and the film *A Time to Dream*. In 1957 he represented Australian Aborigines at a Moral Rearmament Conference in the USA, and in 1958–59 he worked at the MRA headquarters in Switzerland and gave recitals throughout Europe. The first and still one of very few Aboriginal artists to appear on the European concert platform, he also taught at the Melba Conservatorium of Music and was strongly involved in activities to improve the conditions of Aborigines.

FURTHER REFERENCE
His recordings include *Australian Aboriginal Songs* (1956, Score POL 003). A documentary of his life is *True Stories: Harold* (1994, ABC TV/Flying Carpet Films). See also Alan T. Duncan, *ADB*, 13; K. Harrison, *Dark Man, White World: A Portrait of Tenor Harold Blair* (Melbourne: Novalit, 1975).

P. DUNBAR-HALL

Blanks, Fred   (*b* Schwabisch-Gmund, Germany, 31 May 1925), music critic. After studying science at the University of Sydney he worked as an industrial chemist and began writing music criticism for the *Australian Jewish News* in 1952 and *Musical Times* in 1955. He has been with the *Sydney Morning Herald* since 1963, and is a popular lecturer on music. An agreeable, readable and longserving critic, he has attempted to measure each performance against appropriate yardsticks in the Australian context rather than against harsher international benchmarks. He was honoured with the AM in 1988.

FURTHER REFERENCE
Fred Blanks, 'Credo of a Critic', *SA, 35* (Spring 1992), 34–5, 53; idem, 'The Education of a Music Critic', *Quadrant* 31/11 (Nov. 1987), 26–8. See also *ADMR*.

Blekbala Mujik.   Aboriginal rock group from Barunga, NT, active since 1986. Led by Peter Apaak Jupurrula Miller, chairman of the Top End Aboriginal Musicians Association, their performances include the Darwin Aboriginal Rock Festival (1989), a tour of the NT and Qld (1991), and appearance on the national tele-

vision show *Hey Hey It's Saturday* (1992). Their albums contain both traditional music and rock songs; in the rock songs the didjeridu is integrated with rock group instruments. Songs by Blekbala Mujik are often in Kriol, and concern local events; *Nitmiluk*, for example, celebrates the return of traditional lands to the Jawoyn people of the NT.

FURTHER REFERENCE
Recordings include *Midnait Mujik* (1990, CAAMA 213); *Nitmiluk!* (1990, CAAMA 209); and *Come-n-Dance* (1993, CAAMA 226).

P. DUNBAR-HALL

Bless This House.   Ballad by May Brahe (1927), lyrics by Helen Taylor. Originally titled 'Bless The House', it did not achieve notable popularity until recorded by John McCormack in 1932, who suggested the change of title. Included in Lax & Smith's listing of 10 000 best-known songs in English-speaking countries, its success rests in large part on the way in which people have appropriated the meaning of the lyrics. In America, Mrs Eisenhower's liking for the text established a connection to the White House, and the song's rather sentimental religiosity has had an enduring appeal. Its two million sheet music sales in the 1930s are balanced by at least 150 recordings (1932–93).

FURTHER REFERENCE
K. Dreyfus and P. Burgis, 'May Brahe Composition Discography', *Australian Record and Music Review* 15 (Oct. 1992), 12–20; 16 (Jan. 1993), 23; K. Dreyfus, 'Capturing the Ear of the Populace: May Brahe and the Domestic Song Market 1912–1953' in *One Hand on the Manuscript*, ed. N. Brown, et al. (Canberra: Humanities Research Centre, ANU, 1995), 45–54; R. Lax and F. Smith, *Great Song Thesaurus*, 2nd edn (New York: OUP, 1989).

KAY DREYFUS

Blose, Daisy.   See *Howard, Jenny*.

Blott, Charlie   (*b* Melbourne, 21 Jan. 1925; *d* Melbourne, 2 Aug. 1988), jazz drummer. He began drumming in his school band, and was attracted to jazz through his family's record collection and the radio. By the early 1940s he was active in the burgeoning jazz scene of wartime Melbourne, playing in both traditional jazz and swing styles. He became central to the Melbourne bop movement of the late 1940s and early 50s but retained his association with traditional jazz. Blott played in bop bands led by Splinter Reeves, Bruce Clarke and others, as well as his own. He contributed significantly to the establishment of Bob Clemens's Jazzart record label and organised jazz concerts. Although Melbourne's intense bop activity declined in the 1950s, Blott's versatility gave him continuing employment in clubs, radio, concerts and recording sessions, and in support of such visiting Americans as Frank Sinatra, Nat King Cole and Gene Krupa. He won the *Music Maker* poll in 1955. A central figure in postwar bop,

Blott was a significant link between the bop era and the later resurgences of the jazz movement in the early 1960s and mid-1970s. The decline of the jazz concerts after the 1950s and the advent of television reduced his high-profile performance opportunities, but he remained active across a wide range of styles until shortly before his death.

FURTHER REFERENCE

Recordings include *Rex Stewart* (1948, Jazzart JA-37); *Splinter Reeves and His Splintet* (1949, Jazzart JA-16); *Don Banks Orchestra* (1950, Jazzart JA-48). See also *BissetB; OxfordJ.*
                                                          BRUCE JOHNSON, JOHN WHITEOAK

Blue Mountains Melody. Musical comedy by Charles Zwar, libretto by J.C. Bancks. Set in the Blue Mountains, NSW, it had an American cabaret flavour. First performed by J.C. Williamsons at Sydney in 1935, starring Cyril Ritchard and Madge Elliot. See *Musical Comedy.*

Bluegrass. American country and western string band style, originated by Bill Monroe in the 1940s, of high-pitched vocals, Scruggs-style banjo, mandolin and fiddle, with tight harmonies, applying jazz and blues techniques often to traditional square dance, ballad or religious melodies. The Rank Strangers have been among the few traditional bluegrass bands in Australia, although elements of the style have been adopted by the Three Chord Wonders, the Flying Emus and others. See *Country Music.*

Blues. Folk music of the American blacks, originating in the American south and developed as urban blues in the 1920s and 30s, chiefly in Chicago. In Australia as in the USA, the blues were a seminal influence in jazz, rhythm and blues, and above all, on rock music. There have, however, been relatively few Australian blues artists and the style has achieved little popularity. ★Chain is an exception, and the blues featuring in the work of Margret ★Road-Knight, Dutch Tilders, Ian Beecroft and few others. See *Jazz, Popular Music.*

Blundell, James (*b* Stanthorpe, Qld, 8 Dec. 1964), popular singer-songwriter. After working as a jackeroo in north Queensland and managing a cattle station in New Guinea, he wrote a drinking ballad *The Gidgee Bug Pub* in 1984 and sang in Sydney pubs and on television. His roots in country music, he won the ACMA Star Maker Quest in 1987, then toured country venues and festivals, winning six ACMA Golden Guitars in quick succession 1988–91. Combining crossover repertoire with unusually good looks, his following has extended well beyond country music into the mainstream audience in Australia and the USA; songs like *The Kimberley Moon* (1990) and *Time On His Hands* (1991) have gained a wide following. His first album, *James Blundell* (1989), won a gold record and *Hand It Down* (1990) was No. 1 in the country music charts for three months; *Touch Of Water* and *Way Out West* (1993) have also been very popular.

FURTHER REFERENCE

Recordings include *James Blundell* (1989, EMI CDP 7918162) and *Hand It Down* (1990, EMI CDP 7947912). See also *LattaA; CA* (1995–96).

Blundell, Owen (*b* Red Hill Station, Tumut, NSW, 22 Mar. 1960), country music singer-songwriter. After winning the Tamworth Country Music Festival yodelling competition in 1983 and 1984, he toured with Reg Poole, Slim Dusty, Smoky Dawson and the Gunbarrel Highwaymen. One of the most successful bush balladists of the younger generation, and a master of more than 50 yodels, he is also a talented songwriter, and won a Tamworth Songwriters Association award in 1986. He has recorded six albums, appeared regularly at country music festivals, and now travels with his Owen Blundell Family Concert.

FURTHER REFERENCE

Recordings, all with Selection records, include *The Snowy Mountain Yodeller* (1988, PCD 704), *Duelling Yodellers* with Rex Dallas (1989, PCD 055), and *Can't Stop Playing Those Sad Songs* (1989, PRC 066). See also *LattaA*, 42–3; Monika Allan, *The Tamworth County Music Festival* (Sydney: Horwitz, Grahame, 1988), 37.

Bobadil. Light opera in three acts by Luscombe ★Searelle, its plot of the Arabian nights genre popular in musicals at the time. First performed at Sydney, 22 Nov 1884.

Bobby and Laurie. Popular music duo (1965–67; 1969–71) of Bobby Bright and Laurie Allen. Bright had been working as a vocalist in Adelaide and Allen was with the Bluejays (organ and vocals); sharing a bill at Melbourne in 1965 they formed a pop duo, developed Everly Brothers-like madcap routines and adopted the long-haired image newly popular since the tour of the Beatles. Their debut single *I Belong With You* reached No. 2 in the charts in 1965 and became a pop classic; they became regulars on the television *Go!!* show and had two more Top 40 hits, including *Hitchhiker* which reached No. 1 in 1966. But after they were given their own show on the ABC their appeal to younger audiences declined, and they disbanded amid friction in 1967. They re-formed as a country music act in 1969, producing country singles such as *Carroll County Accident* (1969).

FURTHER REFERENCE

Recordings include *I Belong With You* (Go!! 5001), *Hitchhiker* (Parlophone A8198), *Carroll County Accident* (1969 RCA 101870). A compilation is *The Very Best Of Bobby And Laurie* (1980, Astor ALPS 1062). For discography, see *SpencerA.* See also *McGrathA; SpencerW.*

Bochsa, Robert Nicholas Charles (*b* Montmédy, France, 9 Aug. 1789; *d* Sydney, 6 Jan. 1856), harpist, conductor. The first virtuoso of the new Erard harp and the harpist to Napoleon and his family, he taught at the Royal

Academy of Music, London, 1822–27 and conducted at the King's Theatre. In 1839 he eloped with soprano Anna Bishop, wife of the composer Sir Henry Bishop, and with her toured the USA and Europe, coming to Sydney in 1855 but dying of dropsy soon after his arrival.

FURTHER REFERENCE
E. Lea-Scarlett, *ADB*, 3.

Bodenwieser Ballet. Viennese-based ballet troupe founded in the early 1920s by Gertrud Bodenwieser. With the situation in Europe in the late 1930s politically unstable, Bodenwieser and a number of her dancers emigrated to Australia, and became one of the first Australian-based troupes to concentrate on performing modern dance. Bodenwieser collaborated with Australian composers, mostly European immigrants such as Marcel Lorber, Werner Baer, Kurt Herweg, Bela Doleskō and Camille Gheysens. After her death in 1959, the performing troupe dissolved and some of its members redirected their attention towards the company's dance school.

FURTHER REFERENCE
Edward H. Pask, *Ballet in Australia* (Melbourne: OUP, 1982); Shoan Dunlop MacTavish, *An Ecstasy of Purpose: The Life and Art of Gertrud Bodenwieser* (Dunedin, NZ: Les Humphrey and Associates, 1987); Elizabeth Russell, 'Gertrud Bodenwieser: the Story of a Style', *Dance Australia* 12 (June-Aug. 1983): 52–6.

JOEL CROTTY

Bogle, Eric (*b* Peebles, Scotland, 23 Sept. 1944) popular singer-songwriter. Playing rock music and then folk music as a teenager, he arrived in Australia in 1969 and worked as a builder's labourer in Canberra, then studied accounting. His folk-style anti-war ballad *And The Band Played Waltzing Matilda* (1972) became an internationally known protest song, and he toured North America, Europe and the UK. In the following years his songs were recorded by Slim Dusty and the Bushwackers, as well as by mainstream artists Rod McKuen, Donovan and others. He has published five song-books and 12 albums, and was honoured with the AM, an APRA award, and a Tamworth Songwriters Association award.

FURTHER REFERENCE
Recordings include albums *Now I'm Easy* (1979, Larrikin LRF 04ITC), *Singing The Spirit Home* (1986, Larrikin LRF 186CD), *Voices In The Wilderness* (1990, Festival D30413) and *Mirrors* (1993, Larrikin CDLRF 282).

Bold Jack Donahue [Donahoo], folk-song. Usually sung to 'Brennan on the Moor', it is one of Australia's oldest traditional songs, recounting the true story of a convicted Irish highwayman, who after transportation to Australia took to the bush with a band of followers in 1826, surviving from robberies until he was killed by police in 1830. It exists in at least five versions: two in

broadsides (1830, *c*.1867); one published by A.B. Paterson in *Old Bush Songs* (1905), a variant collected by John Manifold (1953); others published by A.L. Lloyd (1956) and John Meredith (1957).

FURTHER REFERENCE
Edition and commentary in *EdwardsG*; *ManifoldP*.

Bolleter, Ross (*b* Subiaco, WA, 1946), experimental improviser, teacher. After studies at the University of Western Australia, he played jazz piano in restaurants. With flautist Tos Mahoney in his recording *Openings* (1982), he began to explore more unorthodox techniques, recording tapes of solo improvisations such as *Temple of Joyous Bones* (1985), using prepared piano, piano accordion, or electric piano, and then keyboard in combination with environmental sounds, as in *The Abomination* (1987). He won a WA government grant to devise new keyboard techniques in 1986. A piano teacher of long experience, he wrote *Fostering Creative Improvisation at the Keyboard* (Perth, 1985) and has led various improvisation workshops for children.

FURTHER REFERENCE
Recordings include *Temple of Joyous Bones* (1985, Homegrown Headroom), *The Abomination* (1987, Wasit), and *Nallan Void* for ruined pf (1987, New Albion). See also *JenkinsT*, 19–24.

Bond Family Scholarship for Tenors. Awarded annually (from 1981) after a national competition for tenors resident in Australia for at least one year. Winners included Gregory Tomlinson. Administered by the Opera Foundation Australia until it was withdrawn in 1989, the prize was $15 000.

Bones. Folk-music percussion instrument, a legacy of the visiting American minstrel shows of the 1860s. Matched and boiled bullock ribs are sawn into short lengths and held between the fingers of one hand so that the bones rattle when the hand is shaken.

FURTHER REFERENCE
J.S. Manifold, *The Violin, the Banjo and the Bones* (Ferntree Gully, Vic.: Rams Skull Press, 1957), 13; *GroveI*.

Bonighton, Ian William George (*b* Beaufort, Vic., 4 May 1942; *d* Norwich, England, 30 May, 1975), composer. He studied at the University of Melbourne Conservatorium, 1963–67 and taught there 1968–73, then at the University of East Anglia, UK, 1974–1975. His works include *Cathedral Music I-III*, *Sequenza*, *Music for Sleep* and *De Quattuor Vigilia Noctis* and several major works for organ. Bonighton is remembered for his innovative teaching and his introduction of the avant-garde to Melbourne audiences through the ISCM and the Melbourne Autumn Festival of Organ and Harpsichord. His profound ideas, concentrating on chance elements within specific acoustic environments, were found largely in iso-lation. After his death in a road accident, the interest in his music continued through commemorative recordings sponsored by those for whom he composed, including Douglas Lawrence.

FURTHER REFERENCE
Recordings of his works include 'Cathedral Music I' in *Reverber-ations* (Move Records MS 3008), *Sequenza and other works by Ian Bonighton*, cond. Keith Humble (Move Records MS 3016- 2LP). His principal mss and sketches are in *PVgm*. His writings include: I. Bonighton, 'Electronic Music', in *Conference on Electronic Music* (Melbourne: Music Faculty, Univ. Melbourne, 1972). See also A. McCredie, *Survey of Australian Composition* (Canberra: Australian Government, 1967); *MurdochA*; P. Nunn, The Organ Works of Ian Bonighton (1942–1975): A Description with Analytical Observations, MMus, Univ. Melbourne, 1991.
PHILIP NUNN

Bonwick, Walter (*b* Southwark, London, 21 Nov. 1824; *d* Melbourne, 13 Sept. 1883), teacher, organist, con-ductor. Educated at Borough Road School, London, he was certificated to teach the Hullah singing method in 1841, was sizar at St John's College Cambridge in 1852, and emigrated to Melbourne in 1854. He married Mary Britton at Hawthorn on 15 July 1856. Appointed a singing master by the National Board of Education in 1855, he was later with the Common Schools Board and Education Department until his death. He published the first officially sanctioned song-book in Australia, with program notes, in 1857 and organised public exhibitions of singing, including conducting about 12,000 students in Collins Street during the 1867 royal visit.

FURTHER REFERENCE
B.M. Maclellan, Walter Bonwick and the Place of Music in the Curriculum of the National, Common and State Schools 1854–1883, PhD, Univ. Melbourne, 1995.
BEVERLY MACLELLAN

Bony Anderson. Opera in one act by Barry Conyn-gham, libretto by M. Copland. It was first performed as *The Apology of Bony Anderson* at the University of Mel-bourne in October 1978, then revised under its present title for its performance at the Cell Block Theatre, Sydney, on 30 June 1979.

Bonynge, Richard Alan (*b* Sydney, 29 Sept. 1930), conductor. He studied piano with Lindley Evans at the NSW State Conservatorium and with Herbert Fryer in London, but in 1954 transferred his attention to research into the *bel canto* operatic repertoire and made his debut as a conductor in Rome in 1962 with the Santa Cecilia Orchestra. His operatic debut was with Gounod's *Faust* in Vancouver in 1963. In 1964 he made his debut with San Francisco Opera and Covent Garden, then he appeared at the Metropolitan Opera, New York, with

Lucia di Lammermoor in 1966. He returned to Australia in 1965 as artistic director and chief conductor of the Sutherland–Williamson International Grand Opera Co., and again in 1974 to conduct *Les Contes d'Hoffmann* for the Australian Opera. In 1975 he became musical direc-tor of the Australian Opera, a position he held for the next 10 years, afterwards becoming a regular guest con-ductor. He was artistic and musical director of Vancouver Opera, 1974–78.

Bonynge's career has been principally in the opera house and the recording studio, and he has rarely been heard in the concert hall. His repertoire is extensive, encompassing operas of Handel, Gluck, Cherubini, Pacini, Haydn, Cilea, Leoni, Meyerbeer, Gounod, Delibes, Auber, Thomas, Offenbach and Poulenc as well as the standard repertoire. He has a particular love of operetta and has conducted and recorded works by Johann Strauss Jr, Lehár and Kálmán, as well as several Gilbert and Sulli-van comic operas. He has also made numerous recordings of ballet music, especially French and Russian works of the 19th century. He frequently accompanied his wife, Dame Joan *Sutherland, in recital and has recorded numerous recitals with her and with many of the most renowned singers of his time. His influence on Australia's operatic life since 1965 has been considerable, and he has been an extraordinary advocate and source of support and encouragement for Australian singers.

In 1965 he brought back to Australia a number of expatriate artists as members of the Sutherland–Williamson Company, and throughout his long associa-tion with the Australian Opera he has engaged Australian singers to work with him in Europe and the USA. The Australian Opera's young artists development program was established during his time as musical director and he has remained involved in the training of young singers, *répétiteurs* and conductors. He is a man fascinated by the theatre, and he has brought before the public many neglected works. He was awarded the CBE, the AO, and in France the *Commandeur des Artes et Lettres* (1989).

FURTHER REFERENCE
His writings include *Joan Sutherland and Richard Bonynge with the Australian Opera* (Sydney: The Craftsman House, 1990). See also Brian Adams, *La Stupenda* (Melbourne: Hutchinson, 1980); Rus-sell Braddon, *Joan Sutherland* (Sydney: Collins, 1962); Quaintance Eaton, *Sutherland and Bonynge: An Intimate Biography* (New York: Dodd Mead, 1987); Norma Major, *Joan Sutherland* (London: Queen Anne Press, 1987); Viola Tait, *A Family of Brothers* (Mel-bourne: Heinemann, 1971).
MOFFATT OXENBOULD

Boogie-Woogie. Chicago piano style of the 1920s and 30s, popularised by Jimmy Yancey, Pinetop Smith and others, of percussive, syncopated right-hand phrases played against driving, repeated left-hand patterns. Noted exponents in Australia in the 1940s and 50s included Don *Banks and Dick *Hughes.

Boojum! Music-theatre (1986) by Martin ★Wesley-Smith, libretto by Peter Wesley-Smith, after an annotated version of Lewis Carroll's poem *The Hunting of the Snark*, describing a set of white chess pieces in their search for the elusive snark. Commissioned by the Adelaide Festival, it was first performed before Elizabeth II at the festival in 1986, then rewritten as a concert work in 1988 and recorded by Sydney Philharmonia Motet Choir (1992, Vox Australis VAST 010–2).

Boomerang Clapsticks. Two boomerangs held in the middle and clapped together at the tips as an accompaniment to Aboriginal singing. The beat pattern may consist of even strokes throughout the song or two adjacent strokes followed by a rest in a triple metre. The end of the song or of a significant section of a song may be marked by rapidly rattling the tips of the boomerangs together. Men or women who play the clapsticks usually sing as well. This type of accompaniment has been documented from north Queensland west to the NT and through all of WA. See *Aboriginal Music* §3(i).

GRACE KOCH

Boothby, Guy Newell (*b* Adelaide, 1867; *d* London, 1905), novelist, librettist. Sent to London for his schooling, he returned to work as secretary to the mayor of Adelaide. He wrote librettos for the comic operas of Cecil ★Sharp, including *Sylvia; or the Marquis and the Maid* (1890) and *Dimple's Lovers* (1890). After travelling extensively in Australia and the Far East, he published *On the Wallaby*, then settled in London in 1892, producing 50 works of romantic fiction which were greatly popular. He had little success in London as a playwright.

FURTHER REFERENCE
IrvinD; Paul Depasquale, *Guy Boothby: His Life and Work* (1982); *OxfordL*.

Borich, Kevin (*b* NZ, 1968), rock guitarist. Playing with the Mergers in NZ, he came to Australia with La De Das in 1968, building with them a new trio sound from 1972. After their split in 1975 he formed Kevin Borich Express which toured extensively in the USA, UK and Europe, making such recordings as *Celebration* (1976) and *Kevin Borich Express* (1980). From 1983 he was with the Party Boys, and then formed the Borich-Hunter Band with Marc Hunter (from Dragon) in 1991. With a style influenced by Jimi Hendrix and Robin Trower, he is one of Australia's most significant rock guitarists.

FURTHER REFERENCE
Recordings include *Celebration* (1976, Image ILP 757), *Kevin Borich Express* (1980, Festival L45881/2), and *Kevin Borich Collection* (1993, Mushroom D24509). For discography, see *SpencerA*. See also *McGrathA*; *SpencerW*; *GuinnessP*, I, 298.

Borovansky Ballet. Czech dancer and choreographer Edouard Borovansky had travelled to Australia with the Pavlova troupe in 1929, then with de Basil's Ballets Russes in 1938, after which he decided to remain and establish a ballet school and troupe in Melbourne. In 1944 the J.C. Williamson organisation financially supported Borovansky's troupe, giving the company access to good-quality theatres and resident orchestras, but demanding of Borovansky programs with obvious box-office appeal. Under these conditions Australian music did not become an integral component of the repertoire, and only Esther Rofe and Verdon Williams had ballet scores realised. Borovansky died in 1959 and his troupe survived until 1961. He had proved that a permanent ballet troupe could be maintained in Australia, and his pioneering efforts created the environment in which the government-sponsored Australian Ballet was able to be formed in 1962.

FURTHER REFERENCE
Edward H. Pask, *Ballet in Australia* (Melbourne: OUP, 1982); Frank Salter, *Borovansky* (Sydney: Wildcat Press, 1982).

JOEL CROTTY

Bossa Nova. Brazilian popular music of the late 1950s, featured by Baden Powell, Stan Getz, Herbie Mann, and others, uniting samba and cool jazz in a syncopated 2/4 time. A noted early exponent in Australia was George Golla.

Botany Bay, popular ballad. A parody of traditional convict songs, it appeared in the London musical *Little Jack Sheppard* (1885) and was made famous by the comedian David Belasco James. The text was published in the *Sydney Golden Songster* (1893). Under the same title at least five markedly different versions have been collected, including three in broadsides (*c*.1790, 1820, 1828); one by Cecil Sharp (1914); and one by Ron Edwards (1968).

FURTHER REFERENCE
Edition and commentary in *EdwardsG*; *ManifoldP*.

Boughen, Robert Keith (*b* Brisbane, 13 Oct. 1929), organist. Obtaining his LRSM (later the FRCO and FTCL), he was organist and choirmaster at Scots' Church, Hobart, 1949–50, and after military service he became organist (later director of music) at St John's Cathedral, Brisbane, in 1960. Becoming a prominent personality in Brisbane musical matters, he was conductor of the Queensland State and Municipal Choir (1965–69), guest conductor with the Queensland Symphony Orchestra, Brisbane city organist from 1975, and custodian for the Concert Hall organ of the Queensland Performing Arts Centre from 1987. He was organist and lecturer (then senior lecturer) at the University of Queensland 1977–94, conducting its Pro Musica (1976–79). An organist of great natural gifts, a composer of energetic hymns and liturgical pieces, and an arranger of vibrant, witty choral settings, he was honoured with the OBE in 1987.

FURTHER REFERENCE

His publications include 'Percy Brier', *ADB*, 7. See also *WWA* (1996); *GlennonA*, 238.

Bound for South Australia, sea-shanty, the forlorn song of a South Australian sailor hauling at the capstan far from home. First published in 1888 and revived by Ron Edwards in *Bandicoot Ballads* in 1955; another version was collected by A.L. Lloyd in 1958.

FURTHER REFERENCE

Edition and commentary in *EdwardsG*; *ManifoldP.*

Bourne, Una Mabel (*b* Mudgee, NSW, 23 Oct. 1882; *d* Melbourne, 15 Nov. 1974), pianist, composer. Celebrated as an infant prodigy, she received lessons from Melbourne teacher and conductor Benno Scherek, and by her mid-teens was a soloist in orchestral concerts. In 1905 she undertook studies in Europe, and her success saw her selected as associate artist for Melba's 1907, 1909 and 1912 Australian and NZ tours. Bourne returned to England in 1912 and became a well-established concert pianist and composer of short piano works, several of which were among the 44 recordings she made for HMV before 1930. After touring North America, where she recorded for the American company Duo Art, she returned permanently to Australia in 1939. Based in Melbourne, she established a master school of piano-playing at the Albert Street Conservatorium, and in later years continued to be active in broadcasting, teaching and performance.

FURTHER REFERENCE

Age 19 Nov. 1974; Peter Burgis, *ADB*, 7; *MoresbyA*, 68–74; Thérèse Radic, 'Australian Women in Music', *Lip* 4 (1978/79), 97–110.

JENNIFER ROYLE

Bowyang, Bill. See *Vennard, A.V.*

Boyd, Anne Elizabeth (*b* Sydney, 10 Apr. 1946), composer. She studied flute at the NSW State Conservatorium and composition with Peter Sculthorpe at the University of Sydney, then with Wilfrid Mellers and Bernard Rands for her doctorate at York University. *The Voice of the Phoenix* (1971) brought her notice in Britain, and her works subsequently enjoyed uncommon success, being heard at the Edinburgh, Windsor, Aldeburgh and Hong Kong Arts Festivals, as well as in Australia. She taught at the University of Sussex 1972–77, was founding head of music at the University of Hong Kong (1981–90) and since then has been professor of music, University of Sydney. Her output includes three string quartets, works for flute or wind groups, and several theatre and choral works for children. Lean and precisely ordered, her limpid

scores show the influence of Asian techniques and sounds such as the Javanese gamelan; the Japanese shakuhachi has also made its impression. *The Rose Garden* (1972) is a work of beauty; *Black Sun* (1989) was a response to the Tiananmen Square massacre. She has written articles for *Musical Times*, *Miscellania Musicologica*, *Australian Journal for Music Education* and other journals.

WORKS (Selective)

Principal publisher: Faber Music, London

Opera and Music Theatre: *As Far as Crawls the Toad,* for children, 5 perc (1970); *The Rose Garden*, Mez, ch, instr (Robin Hamilton, 1972); *Mr Fraser* (1976); *The Little Mermaid,* opera for children (2, 1978); *The Beginning of the Day,* opera for children (1980).

Orchestra:*The Voice of the Phoenix* (1971); *Black Sun* (1989); Concerto, fl, str (1992); *Grathawai* (1993).

Choral and Vocal: *Summer Nights,* Ct, harp, str, perc (1976); *As I Crossed a Bridge of Dreams,* 12vv (1975); *As All Waters Flow,* 5vv, instru (1976); *The Death of Captain Cook,* oratorio (1976); *My Name is Tian,* S, fl, va, harp, perc (1979); *The Last of His Tribe,* S,S,A, SSA, pf (1979); *Coal River,* Bar, childrens vv, SATB, brass band, orc (1979); *Cycle of Love,* Ct/C, a fl, vc, pf (1981); *Song of Rain,* for children, SSA (1986).

Chamber: Trio, ob, vn, vc (1967); String Quartet No. 1 *Tu dai oan* (1968); *Hidden in a White Cloud,* fls, vcs, wind quintet (1970); *Metamorphosis of the Solitary Female Phoenix,* wind quintet, pf, perc (1971); *Greetings to Victor McMahon,* 12 fl (1971); *As It Leaves the Bell,* fl, 2 hp, 4 perc (1973); String Quartet No. 2 *Play on the Water* (1973); *Bencharong,* str (1976); *Goldfish Through Summer Rain,* fl, pf (1978); *Angklung II,* vn (1980); *Reed Sun Chill Wind,* fl, pf (1980); *Cloudy Mountain,* fl, pf (1981); *Songs from Telegraph Bay,* instru (1984); *Kakan,* a fl, marimba, pf (1984); *Wind Across Bamboo,* wind quintet (1984); *Bali Moods I,* fl, pf (1987); String Quartet No. 3 (1991).

Piano: *Angklung* (1974); *The Book of Bells* (1980).

FURTHER REFERENCE

Recordings include *Book of the Bells* (Canberra School of Music, CSM 3), *Cycle of Love* (2MBS-FM MBS 21CD), *Bali Moods I, II* (Aust. Music Centre, Cass OO2), and String Quartet No. 1, Oriel String Quartet (1969, ABC RRCS126). Her writings include 'Not for Export', *Musical Times* 111 (Nov. 1970), 1097–1100. See also *CA* (1995/96); Thérèse Radic, *GroveW*; *CohenI*; *Bulletin* 10 July 1990; *SMH* 26 Sept. 1981; Marcia Ruff, 'Anne Boyd', *Lip* (1978–79), 121–2; *MurdochA*, 27–3; Deborah Crisp, Elements of 'gagaku' in the Music of Anne Boyd, BMus(Hons), Univ. Sydney, 1978.

Bracanin, Philip Keith (*b* Kalgoorlie, WA, 26 May 1942), composer, musicologist. After childhood studies in piano and early work as a maths teacher, he took doctoral studies in musicology at the University of Western Australia and became a lecturer (later reader) at the University of Queensland in 1970. Self-taught as a composer, he began writing in earnest in 1974, at first in an atonal idiom, focusing on chamber works, songs and choral music, such as his three *Mescolanza* (1978) and the String Trio. With

Heterophony (1979) he moved to orchestral works, producing in the years since a number of concertos, including two for orchestra (1985, 87), several performed by the Queensland Symphony Orchestra, as well as solo and chamber works on commission for various Queensland artists. Rejecting atonality, these works are frankly melodic and tonal, animated by a thoughtful, personal utterance.

WORKS

Principal publisher: Camden Press (UK).

Orchestral *With and Without* (1973), Trombone Concerto (1977, rev. 1988), *Heterophony* (1979), *Rondellus Suite*, str orch (1980), Piano Concerto (1980), *Sinfonia mescolanza* (1982), Violin Concerto (1983), Concertino pf, str (1983), *A Picture of RC in a Prospect of Blossom* Bar, orch (1985), Concerto for Orch (1986), Clarinet Concerto (1986), Divertimento, chamber orch (1986), *200* (1988), *Muzika za Vigani* chamber orch (1988), Concerto for Orch No. 2 (1989), Cello Concerto (1990), *Dance Poem* (1990), Oboe Concerto, str (1991), Viola Concerto (1991), Guitar Concerto, chamber orch (1991), Alto Saxophone Concerto, str (1991), *Elysian Voyage*, str (1992), Flute and Guitar Concerto, str (1993), *Dance Tableaus*, chamber orch (1993), Symphony No. 1 (ms, 1994), Symphony No. 2 v, SATB, orch. (ms, 1994).

Chamber Music String Quartet No.1 (ms, 1971), *Four by One and a Half*, trbn, pf, str qrt (1974), Piano Quintet (1975), String Quartet No. 2 (1977), *Boutade*, trbn, pf, perc (1981), *Three Pieces*, vn, pf (1976), *Forpasis*, wind quintet (1978), *Mescolanza*, vc, pf (1978), *Mescolanza*, str trio (1980), *Cinque partite*, fl, vc, hpd (1981), Oboe Quartet (1986), Trumpet Concertino, tr, pf (1988), *Tre affetti musicali*, fl, gui (Acona, Italy: Berben Edizioni Musicali, 1989), *Dances Soulful and Sanguine*, cl, va, vc (1990), String Quartet No. 3 (ms, 1993).

Vocal *Selections from Rubaiyat of Omar Khayyam*, SATB, str orch (1976), *From the Roundabout Singing Garden*, SATB, org (1977), *Scherzi musicali*, SATB, cl, pf, db (1977), *Throw me a Heaven around a Child*, song cycle B, pf, (1978) arr. B, gui (ms, 1982), arr. B, chamber orch (ms, 1987), *Chequerboard Music*, SATB, cl, str (1979), *Because we have no Time*, song cycle, B, orch (1981), *A Woman's Question* S, pf (1982), *Four Preludes*, gui (1983), *Lost in a Long Dream*, SATB (1987), *A Quiet Quick Catch of Breath*, 6vv (1987), *Time Flows Not You*, SATB (1991).

Solo Works *Alma luna*, pf (1976), *Sonata mescolanza,* pf (1978), *Toccata mescolanza*, org (1980), *Seven Bagatelles*, pf (1983), *Four Diversions*, gui (1990).

FURTHER REFERENCE

Recordings include Trombone Concerto, Adelaide Symphony Orchestra, cond. N. Braithwaite, W. Tyrrell, trbn (ABC 438 825); *Mescolanza* (1978, Grevillea) and the Clarinet Concerto, Queensland Symphony Orch (ABC 426 424). There are ABC tapes of various other orchestral works. See also Malcolm Gillies, 'The Flight of the Muse: Philip Bracanin as Composer', in *Essays in Honour of David Tunley*, ed. Frank Callaway (Perth: Callaway International Resource Centre for Music Education, 1995), 165–76.

Bradford, Vera (b Melbourne, 5 Sept. 1904), pianist. After lessons with Percy Prout and W. Hornby, she won an AMEB Exhibition in 1922 and entered the University of Melbourne Conservatorium, studying with F.W. Homewood. During her student years she appeared as a soloist at the Melbourne Town Hall and toured Victoria in student concerts; she won the South Street Eisteddfod, Ballarat, and the Australian Natives Association Competition. After teaching piano from 1925 she went to the USA in 1928, studying at North Western University, Chicago. She appeared as a recitalist in the USA and in 1937 as a concerto soloist for the ABC. Teaching at the University of Melbourne Conservatorium from 1938, she gave numerous radio broadcasts and recitals in the eastern states, making recordings in the war years. She toured Europe and the USA in 1945, appeared as a concerto soloist for the ABC in 1950, and continued to give radio broadcasts, and appeared at Wigmore Hall, London, in 1961. An abundantly gifted musician and dedicated teacher, she was one of the best known and most successful pianists in Melbourne. In retirement during the 1970s she founded the Frankston Symphony Orchestra.

FURTHER REFERENCE

Recordings include works of Brahms, Schumann, Ravel and Saint-Saëns (1944, Columbia, not current). Her music collection is at Monash Univ. (Peninsula). See also *AMN*, 14 (June 1925), 41; *AMN*, 52 (Jan. 1962), 14. For an index to other references in *AMN*, see *MarsiI*.

Bradley, Joseph (b Newton, nr Hyde, Cheshire, England, 28 Feb. 1857; d Harrow, England, 3 Mar. 1935), conductor, teacher. He studied with Frederick Bridge, becoming organist at St Paul's Stalybridge, Lancashire, at the age of 12 and obtaining his FRCO in 1873 and Oxford BMus in 1874. He was organist and conductor of the Orchestra at St Thomas's Heaton Norris, Stockport, 1876–80, deputy conductor of the Hallé Orchestra (1881–87), and chorus master of the Glasgow Choral Union (1887–1908). He came to Australia as conductor of the Sydney Philharmonic Society and the Sydney Symphony Orchestra in 1908, presenting the Australian premieres of many choral works, such as the Berlioz *Requiem* (1915). He taught music theory at the NSW State Conservatorium from 1916. Of consummate musicianship but dreaded by students for his strict discipline, he never used a baton, and after losing most of his sight in 1925 continued to conduct from memory. He published *Solfeggio Manual for Teachers* (1919) and retired to England in 1928.

FURTHER REFERENCE

P.F. Leighton, *ADB*, 7.

Brahe, May (Mary) Hannah ['Stanley Dickson', 'Mervyn Banks' etc.] (b Melbourne, 16 Nov. 1884, d Sydney, 14 Aug. 1956), songwriter. Her mother was her first teacher, and her first song, probably written for her mother to sing, was composed at the age of eight. By the time Brahe was 21 she had a husband and two sons (born 1903 and 1905), but her musical studies continued privately with Alicia Rebottaro (vocal techniques) and Mona

McBurney (harmony, orchestration and composition). Regular publication of her songs by Allan & Co., Melbourne, began in 1910. In March 1912 she moved to London on her own, in search of a place in the international song market. Quickly contracted to Enoch & Sons, her first decisive success came in 1915, when Clara Butt performed and recorded *Down Here*. Other successes followed, most spectacularly *★I Passed By Your Window*, published in 1916 as part of the album *Song Pictures*. By 1920 Brahe was a celebrity, but her first husband, Carl Brahe, was killed in a motoring accident in August 1920 and she was left to support her three children—a daughter was born in 1914 when the family was reunited—on her income from composition. She married her second husband, the Australian actor George Morgan, in August 1922. The fourth and last of her children was born in 1925.

In the early 1920s Brahe was publishing an average of one album and eight songs a year. She used nine pseudonyms: Stanley Dickson (*Thanks Be To God*), Mervyn Banks, Donald Crichton, Alison Dodd, Stanton Douglas, Eric Faulkner, Wilbur B. Fox, Henry Lovell and George Pointer. Most recordings of her songs were made at this time. In all, 290 of her 547 songs for which manuscripts survive were published, 248 under her own name. She also wrote three musicals (two with Helen Taylor), two operettas for children and four piano pieces.

In 1927 Enoch & Sons went into liquidation, their catalogue made obsolete by the new craze for dance music. Though Brahe moved immediately to Boosey & Hawkes, her financial loss was severe. In the same year she and Helen Taylor wrote and Boosey & Hawkes published the first version of *★Bless This House*. Since John McCormack recorded it in 1932, *Bless This House* has been recorded at least 150 times, attaining the status of an evergreen and generating substantial income for Brahe's estate through royalties, performing and mechanical rights.

With the outbreak of World War II, Brahe returned to Australia with her youngest son. She continued to compose and publish a few songs, the last of them, *Little Lamb* and *A Leafy Wood*, in the year of her death. Though Brahe's songs were sung and recorded by the great singers of the day, the secret of her success lay in her intuitive feeling for what the public wanted: good lyrics, melody first, simplicity and directness.

FURTHER REFERENCE
A list of many of her published songs is in *SnellA*. A discography is in K. Dreyfus and P. Burgis, 'May Brahe Composition Discography', *Australian Record and Music Review* 15 (Oct. 1992): 12–20; 16 (Jan. 1993), 23. Her mss are in *PVgm*. See also *ADB*, 7; *GroveW*; M. Colligan, 'May Brahe: Australian Composer', *Lip* (1978–9), 114–5; Kay Dreyfus, 'Capturing the ear of the populace: May Brahe and the Domestic Song Market 1912–1953', *One Hand on the Manuscript*, ed. N. Brown, et al. (Canberra: Humanities Research Centre, 1995), 45–54; idem, '"A Woman Composer's Place is in the Parlour": May Brahe, Songwriter', in *Repercussions*, ed. T. Radic (Melbourne: National Centre for Australian Studies, Monash Univ., 1995), 62–5.   KAY DREYFUS

Braithwaite, Daryl (*b* Melbourne, 11 Jan. 1949), popular music singer. He was lead singer of the popular band ★Sherbet (later called the Sherbs) 1969–84. During this time, he also recorded solo albums that were a mixture of standard covers and original songs written by Warren Morgan. Between 1974 and 1979 he recorded seven Top 40 hit singles, but although his rapport with teen audiences throughout the 1970s was sensational, he found it difficult to attract the attention of more mature audiences. With the collapse of the Sherbs in 1984 he retired from music, and it was while working as a labourer that he was encouraged to record again. His comeback album *Edge* (1988) was a great success, topping the charts, while the singles *As the Days Go By* and *One Summer* reached the national Top 10. Like *Edge*, the following album *Rise* (1990) demonstrated his expressive singing and songwriting talents. *Rise* hit No. 2 in the charts, while the single *The Horses* reached No. 1.

FURTHER REFERENCE
Recordings include *The Best of Daryl Braithwaite* (1978, Razzle L 36763); *Out on the Fringe* (1979, Infinity D 19286); *Edge* (1988, CBS 462625 1); *Rise* (1990, CBS 467675 1). See also *GuinnessP*; *SpencerW*.

AARON D.S. CORN

Braithwaite, Nicholas Paul Dallon (*b* London, 26 Aug. 1939), conductor. After studying at the Royal Academy of Music, London, master classes at Bayreuth, and lessons with Hans Swarowsky at Vienna, he became associate principal conductor for the English National Opera 1970–74, musical director of the Glyndebourne Touring Co. 1976–80 then the Stora Teater Opera, Göteborg, 1981–84. He was principal conductor of the Manchester Camerata, 1984–91, and chief conductor of the Tasmanian Symphony Orchestra 1984–86. While chief conductor of the Adelaide Symphony Orchestra 1987–91 he was concurrently appointed dean of music at the Victorian College of the Arts in 1988, but the demands of his conducting career left little time for college work, and he resigned in 1991. A thoroughly professional and musical conductor, he has appeared as guest conductor with all major orchestras in the UK, most ABC orchestras, and various European orchestras.

FURTHER REFERENCE
His recordings include works of Frank Bridge, London Symphony Orch (1979, Lyrita); works of W.S. Bennett, London Philharmonic Orch (1979, Lyrita); and trombone concertos of G. Jacob, P. Bracanin, and N. Currie, Adelaide Symphony Orch (ABC 438825–2). See also *GroveO*; *HolmesC*; *WWA* (1996).

Bran Nue Dae. Musical (1990) in two acts by Jimmy ★Chi and Kuckles. Set in outback Broome, it tells the story of a young Aborigine who, expelled from a missionary school, travels to meet his uncle in Perth, only to become disillusioned with city life and return to the racial harmony of his remote home town. The first musical by an Aborigine about Aboriginal life, it was first performed by the West Australian Theatre Co. at Octagon Theatre, Perth, at the Festival of Perth, 1 March 1990. Chi wrote a cabaret version for touring abroad. Original cast recording (Polygram BND CD 002); published Currency Press/Magabala, Sydney, 1991.

Brandon, Hugh Earle (b Allora, Qld, 24 July 1906; d Brisbane, 19 Apr. 1984), church musician. He studied piano and organ at Trinity College, London, 1926–29, and in Vienna 1930. Organist at Ann Street Presbyterian Church, Brisbane, in 1933, he was organist and choirmaster at St Andrew's Presbyterian Church 1945–78. Appointed to the staff of the University of Queensland in 1945 as an AMEB examiner, he became organiser of music in 1953, then head of the department of music 1956–65, retiring in 1973. Besides his church choirs, Brandon conducted the Bach Society choir 1931–46 and the Queensland University Musical Society 1945–65, setting high standards in the performance of major works, especially of J.S. Bach, Brahms, and Elgar. Through enthusiasm and encouragement he raised the level of AMEB attainment throughout Queensland, particularly in the pre-Conservatorium years.

FURTHER REFERENCE

He published *Fifty Folk Songs* (Melbourne: Allans, 1969) and *12 Studies in Musicianship* (Melbourne: Allans, 1969). See also L. Schloss, Hugh Brandon: His Contribution to Musical Life in Brisbane, BMus(Hons), Univ. Queensland, 1983; N. Wilmott, A History of the Music Department, University of Queensland, 1912–1970, MA(Qual), Univ. Queensland, 1986.

GORDON SPEARRITT

Brashs. Music retailer established in 1862 by Marcus Brasch. An immigrant from NZ, Brash began his business in Melbourne and acquired premises at 108 Elizabeth Street in 1880. After his death in 1894 his wife and son assumed management of the business, and until 1927 the firm concentrated on pianos, player-pianos, organs and piano rolls, its motto being 'Home is not a Home without a Piano'. In the 1930s the company began selling radios and whitegoods, and in 1958 took up publishing. Brash Holdings gradually acquired several leading music retail businesses, assuming control of *Allans in 1976. In 1986 Brashs opened a music and record store in Pitt Street, Sydney, and by 1987 administered 81 stores nationally; severe financial difficulties in the early 1990s led it to the brink of collapse. Since 1994 it has been owned by the Singaporean business of Ong Ben Seng.

SUZANNE ROBINSON

Brass Bands.

1. Musical Significance. 2. Growth and Organisation. 3. Adaption. 4. Brass Band Contests. 5. Decline and Revival.

There are over 600 brass bands in Australia. About half are amateur ensembles formed on the standard 25-piece British brass band pattern, generally members of their state band league. The *Salvation Army has 200 senior and 130 junior brass bands of less regulated instrumentation, the Australian Defence Forces maintain 28 military bands (some of brass, others of concert band instrumentation), and there are also a handful of *Harmonie* bands among the German communities in Sydney and the Barossa Valley in SA.

1. Musical Significance. Brass bands form an important if largely self-contained part of Australian musical life. Between 1880 and 1930, virtually every community from city suburbs to outback country towns could boast at least one band, and no outdoor public ceremony or festivity was complete without a band in attendance to add to the dignity or jollity of the occasion. In addition to officially designated town bands, many voluntary organisations also established and supported their own bands as an adjunct to their particular pattern of activities. Church-based bands—particularly those of the Salvation Army—were a prime example, but labour organisations (such as the Victorian Bootmakers' Trade Union), industrial enterprises (for example, Tooth's Brewery, Sydney) and charitable institutions (for instance, St Vincent's Boys' Home in Melbourne) were among the bodies which generated bands from within their own ranks.

In its heyday, banding was undoubtedly the most popular and pervasive form of amateur instrumental music-making open to Australian men, and tens of thousands of them must have played in a band at some time in their lives. Joining a band gave many their only chance to develop their musical talents, and for the most talented, such as the cornettist and conductor Percy *Code, it meant the first step towards a career in professional music. At the same time, listening to a band provided Australians of all ages and conditions with their easiest access to live, concerted, instrumental music. At a time when recording was rudimentary, radio non-existent, permanent professional orchestras a rarity, and seats in the concert hall and opera house prohibitively expensive, brass band performances—usually given in the open air, and at no charge to the hearer (other than an optional contribution to the collecting tin)—offered ordinary Australians an elementary introduction to the appreciation of serious music.

The eclectic repertoire of brass bands provides the main reason for their popularity. Bands played medleys from the orchestral, theatrical and operatic favourites in their programs, often in mutilated and unauthentic arrangements, transcriptions and selections by their bandmasters. But there were also a considerable number of professional band composers in 19th-century Australia, including Joseph *Reichenberg, George *Sippe, Alfred *Seal, Stephen Hale *Marsh, and Julius *Siede, while various band works were also written by Moritz *Heuzenroeder and Julius *Herz. Their original compositions included simple marches, tuneful descriptive pieces, and technically demanding *aires variées* intended to show off the skills of a principal cornet or euphonium player. Outstanding among later Australian band composers was Alexander Lithgow (1870–1929), who dominated Tasmanian banding for 30 years and who was dubbed 'the Sousa of the Antipodes' because of the popularity of his marches.

2. Growth and Organisation. Military bands were stationed in the Australian colonies from 1800; in Sydney they gave weekly evening concerts at Macquarie Place as well as in the barracks square, at the governor's occasional balls and aboard ships moored in the harbour. Bands competed with one another for favourable comment in the press: units such as the 3rd and 57th Regiment bands were long remembered. In the 1830s these bands supplied the theatres with incidental music, and many of their discharged bandsmen became music teachers.

Civic bands appeared from the 1840s: St Joseph's Total Abstinence Band, Launceston, the oldest band in Australia still functioning, was formed in 1845. A local militia or volunteer band was sometimes merely the town band in another disguise. Nevertheless, although brass bands often sported military-style uniforms, they were essentially civilian bodies in both origins and organisation. Except in the case of the Salvation Army, brass bands were not local branches of some pre-existing national or international body; every band was an independent, self-governing, informal corporation, with its own peculiar origins: it owned its own property, controlled its own membership, and planned and executed its own activities.

The key to independence and survival lay in financial security. Because instruments and uniforms were expensive, a considerable capital outlay was needed to start a new band; but once a band existed, provided it could hold onto its members, it was an income-generating organisation which sold its services to potential hirers. It could normally hope to cover its current running expenses and meet its past debts by a mixture of engagement fees, public collections and subscriptions, and municipal subsidies. An element of patronage or sponsorship—from a local church, a work-group, a wealthy citizens' committee, or a city council—was therefore necessary at the outset. A steady supply of paid engagements required the band to play well, behave in a seemly fashion, and generally satisfy the particular needs of those who hired it. In practice, these requirements imposed few restrictions on a band's freedom of action. The greatest danger for a band lay in imprudent financial management: some bands treated current surplus income as something to be divided up among the players, while others spent lavishly on high-profile but loss-making forays into the world of band contests, or incurred heavy hire-purchase debts to pay for new instruments or uniforms.

A fashion for brass bands swept the country around 1900. The valve systems of most brass band instruments

and the ability to mass-produce them cheaply were perfected in Britain in the 1850s, and simultaneous advances in printing made possible the production of inexpensive sets of band music parts arranged for a standard combination of instruments. Coupled with the opportunities for holding well-supported brass band contests which cheap rail travel presented, this served to foster a massive explosion of banding, particularly in the industrial and mining communities of mainland Britain from 1875. These developments were carried to Australia by successive waves of working-class British emigrants and became a classic reminder of the essentially British-derived character of much Australian culture down to World War II.

Australian bands imported most of their instruments and their music from Britain through firms such as Palings in Sydney, while major Australian brass-band contests brought in British adjudicators when they could. Not surprisingly, regions with a particularly high proportion of immigrants from those parts in Britain where the brass-band tradition was most firmly established, such as the Newcastle coalfield of NSW, or South Australia's 'Little Cornwall', became major centres of Australian banding.

3. Adaptation. If the brass band was originally a British export, it inevitably developed some distinctive characteristics as it took root in a different environment. Photographic evidence, for example, suggests that some Australian bands were more flexible in their instrumentation, and clarinets, saxophones and even string basses can be seen among the cornets and bombardons. By British standards, relatively few Australian bands had the word 'temperance' in their title or were subsidised by private employers. Bands which drew their membership from public employees such as Melbourne's Malvern Tramways or Townsville's Railways band were relatively more common in Australia, as were officially designated town bands, usually enjoying an annual subsidy which paid the bandmaster's salary.

Differences emerge also in the geographic distribution of bands. Remote mining communities seem to have been notably well supplied; thus a strong band tradition developed in Broken Hill, Cobar, Kalgoorlie, and Western Tasmania, as well as around Newcastle and the copper-mining district of SA. But by contrast with Britain, bands seem to have been more important in the state capitals and their suburbs than they were in London. Australian banding also lacked the impetus which the movement in Britain derived from the instrument manufacturers, music publishers, and contest promoters. The implications of this are obvious from the character of the local brass-band press: whereas the *British Bandsmen* and the *Brass Band News* were essentially the advertising vehicles for particular music publishers or contest promoters, the *Australasian Bandsman* (1898–1926) and *Australian Band News* (1909–36) were independent newsletters written by and for active devotees.

Australian bandsmen also had to face a degree of hostility from local professional musicians which was much fiercer than in Britain. Despite the common assumption that brass bands were essentially working-class organisations with strong links with the organised labour movement, it is clear that, in Sydney particularly, the Musicians' Union resented the activities of amateur bandsmen, especially if they took engagements at lower than professional wages or took jobs which would otherwise have gone to professionals.

4. Brass Band Contests. Undoubtedly, brass band contests were a major reason for the movement's widespread popularity with both players and audiences between the 1890s and the 1930s. Contests gave banding both a measure of formal organisation and purpose and a degree of extra-musical excitement which it would otherwise have lacked. Bands were judged partly on their skill in executing elaborate manoeuvres while playing on the march; and vigorous steps had to be taken to ensure honesty by the bands and impartiality by the judges.

By the 1900s most major contests took place under the elaborate rules of state-based Band Associations, which graded the bands into leagues and required them to register their individual players; and a band found guilty of cheating by stiffening its line-up with ineligible guest performers was liable to disqualification. On the contest field itself, British ritual, which isolated the judges in a tent from which the bands could be heard but not seen, was generally observed. In addition to the competitive classes, in which the bands played their chosen test-pieces, most contests also included impressive displays of massed-band playing and marching. Tensions mounted as the moment for declaring the results approached, and the partisan feelings of bandsmen and their followers sometimes led to disorderly scenes when a section of the audience disputed the adjudicator's decision; a near riot broke out in Sydney during the 1931 New South Wales final, when the British adjudicator, Cyril Jenkins, awarded first prize to Townsville Railways Band rather than to the local favourites, Hamilton Citizens.

Although major state contests were usually held in the capital cities, the *Royal South Street Eisteddfod at Ballarat was generally regarded as Australia's premier contest between 1900 and the suspension of its band sections in 1924: to win at Ballarat was the height of an Australian brass band's ambition. In practice, the fortunes of individual bands on the contest field rose and fell: and a run of poor performances could result in dissension, defection, and even disbanding. Among the leading contesters between 1900 and World War II were the City of Newcastle (under William Barkel), Malvern Tramways (under Harry Shugg) and Hamilton Citizens (under J.J. Kelly).

Whether Australia's top bands were equal to those of the mother country was hotly debated, but only once tested. In 1924 Newcastle Steelworks Band under Albert H. Baile undertook a year-long world tour in connection with the British Empire Exhibition at Wembley, during which they won first prize in Britain's oldest contest, the Open Championship at Belle Vue, Manchester. British honour was satisfied a few weeks later when the visitors were beaten into third place in the more prestigious National Championship at London's Crystal Palace.

5. Decline and Revival. In the interwar years dance bands and jazz bands provided exciting new opportunities for instrumentalists, while radio and gramophone expanded the musical awareness of listeners. Brass bands also suffered because unemployment exacerbated the effects of a naturally high turnover of members, while the 1930s Depression brought fewer paid engagements, a reduction of municipal or company subsidies, and the extinction of such famous bands as Newcastle Steelworks and Tooth's Brewery. By 1940 it was clear that contesting was losing its appeal to both bands and the wider public. Inevitably, the war intensified and prolonged the period of decline and contraction.

Yet the brass band did not disappear entirely. Enthusiasts, especially in regions with a deep-rooted band tradition, such as the Hunter Valley, worked hard to revive the movement after 1945. They were helped considerably by the postwar expansion of school bands. Purists regretted the admission of women to bands and the replacement of brass bands by larger concert bands with a more varied instrumentation; but with a ready supply of new recruits from the younger generation, Australian banding took on a new lease of life. There has also been a surge in writing for brass band: composers who have made significant contributions include Percy *Grainger, Allan Pengilly (b 1913), Frank *Wright and Stanley Whitehouse (b 1916), and more recently George *Dreyfus, Brenton *Broadstock (b 1952) and Ronald Hanmer.

Contesting still serves to inspire commitment among players and their immediate supporters, while the assumption that many kinds of outdoor public celebration are incomplete without the presence of a band remains unchallenged.

FURTHER REFERENCE

Bythell, D. 'Class, Community, and Culture: The Case of the Brass Band in Newcastle', *Labour History* 67 (1994), 144–56; idem, 'The Brass Band in Australia: The Transplantation of British Popular Culture 1850–1950', *Bands: The Brass Band Movement in the 19th and 20th Centuries*, ed. Trevor Herbert (Milton Keynes, Open University Press, 1991), 145–64; Cumes, J.W.C., *Their Chastity Was Not Too Rigid: Leisure Times in Early Australia* (Melbourne: Longman Cheshire, 1979); Ericson, Fredrick J., The Bands and Orchestras of Colonial Brisbane, PhD Univ. Queensland, 1987; Herbert, T., ed., *Bands: The Brass Band Movement in the 19th and 20th Centuries* (Milton Keynes: Open University Press, 1991); Madden, D., *A History of Hobart's Brass Bands* (Devonport: C.L. Richmond & Sons, 1986). *Military and Brass Band Music. Catalogues of Australian Compositions*, No. 6 (Sydney: Australian Music Centre, 1977).

DUNCAN BYTHELL

Brewer, F(rancis) C(ampbell) (*b* Stourbridge, England, 1826; *d* Sydney, 23 Nov. 1911), music critic. He came to Australia at the age of eight and worked as a child for the *Port Phillip Patriot*, Melbourne, then went to Sydney, in 1836 apprenticed as a printer and working for the Sydney *Monitor*. He was a printer with the Sydney *Herald* from 1839, eventually becoming a journalist (from 1849), then sub-editor and music critic from 1865. He went to London in 1877 as *Herald* correspondent, then returned to edit the *Echo* (1879–90). At the end of his career he wrote *Drama and Music in NSW* (Sydney, 1892), a valuable account of music and theatre in Sydney during his lifetime. His writing was unskilled and workmanlike, but he was an important chronicler of over 30 years of music and theatre in NSW. From 1893 failing eyesight caused him to abandon writing and he died blind.

FURTHER REFERENCE

Obit. in *Bulletin*, 30 Nov. 1911, 16. See also *IrvinD*; *Australasian*, 6 Sept. 1890, 305.

Brewster-Jones, H(ooper Josse) (*b* Black Rock Plain, SA, 28 June 1887; *d* Adelaide, 8 July 1949), composer. A prodigious child pianist, Brewster-Jones studied initially at the Elder Conservatorium in Adelaide with Bryceson Treharne and later at the Royal College of Music, London, with Bridge and Stanford. After his return to Adelaide in 1909, he became a pivotal figure in South Australia's musical growth. He conducted orchestral concerts from 1915, forming the Brewster Jones Symphony Orchestra, throughout the World War I years the only orchestra in SA. He was active as a composer, pianist and teacher, music critic for the Adelaide *Advertiser* (1935–40) and the *News,* and he generated great interest in modern music through the introduction of many works new to Adelaide audiences. Among his vast output of unpublished compositions,the symphonic poem *Australia Felix*, a string quartet, 73 piano works, songs and chamber works are particularly noteworthy.

FURTHER REFERENCE

Joyce Gibberd, *ADB*, 9; Andrew D. McCredie, 'Hooper Brewster Jones 1887–1949: A Post Centennial Tribute', *MMA* 16 (1989), 19–34; Elizabeth Wood, *GroveD*.

WAYNE HANCOCK (with M. Elphinstone)

Bride Of Fortune, The. Opera in prologue and three acts by Gillian ★Whitehead, libretto by Anna-Maria Dell'oso. First performed at His Majesty's Theatre, Perth, on 18 February 1991. Published Pellinor, Sydney, 1991.

Bridge, Ernie (Ernest Francis) (*b* Hall's Creek, WA, 15 Dec. 1936), politician, country music singer-songwriter. Raised on his family's pastoral property, he founded Open Air Theatre, Hall's Creek in 1967, and was elected to the Hall's Creek Council (1962–79), becoming an inaugural member of the Aboriginal Lands Trust of WA in 1972. An admirer since childhood of Tex Morton, Buddy Williams, and later Slim Dusty, he wrote the song *The Helicopter Ringer* which he recorded in his first album *Kimberley Favourites* in 1979, although until then he had never performed on stage or entered a recording studio. He was elected the first Aboriginal member of the WA Parliament in 1980, becoming Minister for Water Resources, Aboriginal Affairs and the North West (1986–94). Although political life restricts his musical career, he has appeared with his Kimberley Country Band at festivals in Tamworth, Perth and elsewhere, and recorded albums in traditional country ballad styles, including *The Great Australian Dream* (1990) about his vision for a water pipeline between the Kimberleys and Perth and Adelaide, and *Two Hundred Years Ago* (1993) about the Mabo land rights debate.

FURTHER REFERENCE

Raymond W. Conder, *Ernie Bridge: Biography* (WA: Ernie Bridge Promotions, 1985). See also *LattaA*, 44–5.

Bridges, Doreen née Jacobs (*b* Adelaide, 11 June 1918), music educator and researcher. She studied music at the University of Adelaide and in 1946, as Universities Commission professional officer (music) surveyed Australian tertiary music courses. She taught at all levels of music education, including the NSW Conservatorium and the music department, University of Sydney, 1957–69, and was senior lecturer at Nursery School Teachers' College, Sydney, 1974–1978, then continued teaching pre-school music, private students, graduate music education classes and teachers' inservice courses. Her PhD, the first in music education in Australia (University of Sydney, 1971), considered the universities' role in Australian music education. Subsequently with the Australian Council for Educational Research she developed a test of acquired perceptual-cognitive musical abilities of potential tertiary music students—the Australian Test for Advanced Music Studies.

Bridges served on the International Society for Music Education Research Commission (1974–80). Her research encompasses many music education issues. She collaborated with Deanna Hoemann in rewriting the *Developmental Music Program*, and compiled *Catch a Song*, a popular children's song collection. She held office in ASME, of which she was made an honorary life member (1992); she was made Fellow of the Australian College of Education for services to music education (1982) and honoured with the AM (1984).

FURTHER REFERENCE

M. Comte, ed., *Doreen Bridges: Music Educator* (Melbourne: ASME, 1992).

JANE SOUTHCOTT

Brier, Percy (*b* Petrie, nr Caboolture, Qld, 7 June 1885; *d* Scarborough, Qld, 9 May 1970), pianist, organist, composer. After lessons with Mrs H. Reeve at Brisbane, he won a scholarship to Trinity College London where he studied with G.E. Bambridge, Gordon Saunders, and C.W. Pearce (1902–6). Returning to Brisbane in 1906, he appeared in chamber music with Elizabeth Jefferies (from 1910), in piano recitals, and as organist at City Tabernacle Baptist church (1912–19) and at St James church in Sydney (1926). He formed the Indooroopilly Choral Society, which sang chamber repertoire 1937–42, and was conductor of the Queensland State and Municipal Choir, the Apollo Club and other choirs. He was for many years a popular eisteddfod adjudicator and AMEB examiner, and was founding president of the Music Teachers' Association of Queensland from 1921. An influential teacher with many prominent students, his writings include *The Pioneers of Music in Queensland* (Brisbane: Music Teachers Association of Queensland, 1962), an autobiography and various compositions, including two piano concertos, songs, choral music and organ works (unpublished).

FURTHER REFERENCE
Robert Boughen, *ADB*, 7; Percy Brier, *Autobiography of a Musician: Percy Brier* (Brisbane: E.B. Brier, 1973); *AMN* (Jan. 1926); *GlennonA*, 146.

Bright, Ruth née Ockendon (*b* Melbourne, 1929), music therapist. She studied music at the University of Melbourne (BMus 1953), then became involved in the use of music in medicine, establishing pioneering music therapy services at the Parkside Hospital, SA, then at Rozelle and Lidcombe Hospitals in Sydney. She was the founding president of the Australian Music Therapy Association and president of the World Federation of Music Therapy, as well as president of the NSW division of the Australian Association of Gerontology, president of the National Association for Loss and Grief. Her seven books are major texts in music therapy. A founding figure in this field in Australia, she was honoured with the AM in 1992 for services to music therapy and community health.

FURTHER REFERENCE
Her writings include *Music Therapy and the Dementias* (St Louis, Mo.: MMB, 1988); *Music in Geriatric Care: A Second Look* (Sydney: Music Therapy Enterprises, 1991); *Grief and Powerlessness* (London: Jessica Kingsley, 1996).

DENISE ERDONMEZ GROCKE

Brimer, Michael (*b* 8 Aug. 1933, Cape Town, South Africa), pianist, conductor. He studied piano under Eleanor Bonner (Cape Town), Franz Osborn, Franz Reizenstein (London) and Josef Dichler (Vienna), and organ under Harold Darke (London), obtaining his MA (Cantab., 1963), FRCO (1954), and LRAM (1954). He has held three chairs in music—Ormond professor at the University of Melbourne (1980–88), dean and faculty director at Cape Town University (1974–79), and foundation professor at the University of Natal, South Africa (1971–73). Currently head of performance and musicology at the Australian Institute of Music, as a performer and researcher his interests include the complete piano output of Beethoven, Schubert and Schumann, which he has performed in chronological order at a series of lecture recitals, all of which have been recorded by the ABC.

FURTHER REFERENCE
James May, *GroveD*.

CYRUS MEHER-HOMJI

Brinkman, Alan Ernest (*b* Glen Lusk, Tas, 24 Aug. 1917), jazz reed player. He began clarinet in Hobart at the age of nine, later adding saxophones, playing for church functions and silent films. Introduced to jazz by dance musician Sid Collins, he began playing at dances, graduating to Ron Richards' band in 1936. Moving to Melbourne, he worked with Stan Bourne, then Frank ★Coughlan until 1942. His army service was terminated by illness; he then resumed work in Hobart with dance bands, the ABC Orchestra, and groups co-led by Tom Pickering and Ian Pearce, in which he was a full member, from 1987 until his retirement in the early 1990s. One of Tasmania's most durable and accomplished jazz musicians, he ranges easily from traditional to West Coast styles.

FURTHER REFERENCE
Recordings include *Ian Pearce Quartet with Pam French* (n.d., mid-1960s, W & G Records, WG SL-662); and two tracks on *Tasmanian Jazz Composers vol. 1* (1992, Little Arthur Productions LACD 01). See also *OxfordJ*. BRUCE JOHNSON

Brisbane, pop. (1991) 1 327 000. Capital city of Queensland, set on the Brisbane River, inland from Moreton Bay (a penal colony from 1825 to 1839). Free settlers arrived from 1842 and Queensland separated from NSW in 1859. Queensland was recognised as a state at Federation in 1901, and Brisbane was declared a city in 1902. Immigration records show the vast majority of Queensland's early settlers were of British, Irish or German origin, but the early phase of European music-making in Brisbane was shaped primarily by German and Welsh musicians. Domestic music-making seems to have been popular among the colonists, with steady importation of pianos and harmoniums, and great demand for dance music and arrangements that did not overly tax the drawing-room pianist. That was not to say that the colonists were not interested in quality: in music, as in all other aspects of their lives in a new and harsh country, they had to 'make do'. Touring musical celebrities were enthusiastically received and as early as 1850 the School of Arts in Brisbane was conducting public lectures on music.

1. Heritage. One of Brisbane's early musical patrons was Robert Mackenzie, who became the first colonial treasurer of Queensland. In 1857, he invited 'professor' Andrew ★Seal (originally Siegel) and his wind quartet to give a series of concerts in the Botanic Gardens, and after that he secured employment for them in order to retain their musical expertise in Brisbane. While there had been amateur bands of locals from as early as 1848, their quality was dubious; in 1861, however, Seal formed the Queensland Volunteer Band using the same local resources, but instilling from the outset a previously unknown precision in their playing. This exposure to the German regimental band tradition rapidly broadened the repertoire and the musical expectations of the band and its listeners. German immigrants also made significant impact in orchestral and choral music: the Brisbane Philharmonic Society was founded in 1861, conducted by Otto Linden. Linden apparently managed to have his chorus and orchestra of inadequately trained but enthusiastic amateurs do justice to major repertoire, including excerpts from Handel's *Messiah* and a Mozart Mass. A Deutsche Liedertafel was formed in the early 1860s, and another German immigrant, Carl Neimitz, conducted the Orpheus Glee Club after his arrival in 1865. Welsh immigrants to Brisbane and the nearby mining town of Ipswich brought their own distinctive musical culture to the colony. The first eisteddfod held in Queensland took place in the mining town of Gympie in 1885, and Brisbane hosted its first eisteddfod in 1889 with the grand prize divided between the Blackstone United choir and the Brisbane Cambrian choir. The Queensland Eisteddfod council was established in 1908.

One of the most influential musical immigrants to Brisbane was the violinist and conductor R.T. ★Jefferies. Trained at the Royal Academy of Music, he stamped a certain Englishness on the Brisbane musical scene soon after his arrival in 1872 as conductor of the newly established Brisbane Musical Union and Orchestra. In the union's first four years, Brisbane audiences heard for the first time several Handel and Mendelssohn oratorios. By the end of the 19th century, little distinguished a Brisbane concert program from a London concert program—a comfortable situation for a population who were largely either new immigrants from Britain or descendants of British settlers and who expressed a common view of England as 'home'.

2. Development. (i) Choral. The choral tradition in Brisbane, well established before Federation, flourished with amateur choirs of high standard under a succession of inspirational figures, particularly George ★Sampson and Robert ★Dalley-Scarlett. Sampson arrived in Brisbane in 1898 as the organist to St John's Cathedral, succeeding Jefferies as conductor of the Brisbane Musical Union (in 1929 renamed the Queensland State and Municipal Choir after Sampson managed to get financial backing from the state and city). Sampson retired when the choir amalgamated with the Brisbane Austral Choir in 1936. The Queensland State and Municipal Choir has had a close association with the ABC and over its long history has given Australian premieres of numerous Australian and British choral works and performed with visiting conductors of international calibre.

Dalley-Scarlett came to Brisbane in 1919 as organist at St Andrew's Presbyterian church, and was conductor of the University Musical Society from 1920 to 1930. His major contribution, however, was in his championing of Baroque choral music, founding both the Bach Choir and the Handel Society (1933) and organising the first Australian Bach and Handel Festivals. The Handel Society was disbanded after his death in 1959, but by that time it had performed virtually all the choral works of Handel. Dalley-Scarlett's outstanding service to the cause of Handel's music was internationally acknowledged when he was awarded the Hallé medal in 1940.

The eisteddfod tradition has been strong in Queensland and has continued to foster a spirit of competitiveness among choirs. Following Welsh tradition, the location of eisteddfod competitions has been rotated around major centres of Queensland. The last fifteen years has seen a nationwide decline in choral music-making but the tradition has been a vigorous one: 100 separate choirs contested the 1939 Brisbane Eisteddfod and presented a Bardic Chair to the Welsh National Eisteddfod in 1938.

Relatively new to the Brisbane musical scene is the Australian Voices Youth Choir, conducted by Graeme Morton. Their performances, particularly of Australian contemporary choral compositions, have been internationally acclaimed.

(ii) Instrumental. From Jefferies' first achievement with the amateur orchestra of the Musical Union there has been a history of growth and increasing expertise fostered by far-sighted planning. George Sampson, successor to Jefferies as conductor of the Brisbane Musical Union, was soon confronted with the financial problems of the orchestra. In 1925 it separated from the Brisbane Musical Union and was reformed as the Sampson Orchestra until 1930 when Sampson found a permanent solution to its financial difficulties by securing funding from the Queensland government and the Brisbane City Council. Renamed as the Queensland State and Municipal Orchestra, it became the foundation, along with the ABC studio orchestra set up in 1936, for what is now the Queensland Symphony Orchestra, whose regular concert seasons and celebrity artists are a mainstay of Brisbane culture. Its regional tours since the 1950s have brought classical music of a high standard to Queensland's more isolated communities. Other orchestras of particular note centred in Brisbane are the Queensland Philharmonic Orchestra and the ★Queensland Youth Orchestra; the latter was established in 1976 and has gained an impressive reputation on tours in Australia and overseas under its director John Curro.

Sampson also made a major impact in his capacity as organist at St John's Cathedral and through his recitals as city organist—positions he held until 1947. He oversaw design of the organ for the new cathedral (1910) and the rebuilding of the city hall organ (1927). The present musical director at St John's cathedral, Robert ★Boughen, has, like Sampson, enriched the musical life of Brisbane with his infinitely varied repertoire as city organist. He has continued and broadened Anglican musical tradition at the cathedral over the last 30 years, recently founding separate female voice choirs.

Chamber music has been fostered from the days of the Quartet Society, founded in 1910 by Valda and Mary Jefferies (daughters of R.T. Jefferies) and Percy ★Brier, and the Brisbane Chamber Music Society (formed 1921). Funding from the Queensland government backed the state quartet founded after World War II that also toured northern and central Queensland. The Brisbane branch of Musica Viva was established in the 1950s, and since 1961 subscription seasons have been a feature in Brisbane and regional centres. The formation in 1988 of a contemporary chamber music ensemble has added to variety. ★Perihelion, resident at the University of Queensland, fulfils an important role in performing, commissioning and recording works by Australia's leading contemporary composers.

(iii) Opera. By 1908 the Brisbane Amateur Operatic Society was well established and there has been an unbroken tradition of amateur light opera companies in Brisbane since, purveying a musical fare of Broadway musicals and the ever popular 'G & S'. But while a 'do-it-yourself' attitude prevailed in the domain of choral music and musical comedy, serious opera (probably for a combination of economic and musical reasons) was the province of touring companies and this situation persisted until fairly recently. Brisbane's first serious opera production appears to have been on 6 July 1865, given by Lyster's Royal Italian and English Opera Co., with Donizetti's *Lucrezia Borgia* and *Daughter of the Regiment* on the same billing. This first season consisted of seventeen performances representing fifteen operas. Donizetti, Bellini and Verdi operas figured prominently in the early tours, but the hardships of the journey to Brisbane made tours very infrequent—even the ubiquitous J.C. Williamson company made few appearances in Brisbane.

Attempts to establish an opera touring company made by Brisbane-based composer Colin ★Brumby and Marissa Brumby led to formation of the Queensland Opera Company which gave Brisbane seasons for around 10 years and in 1982 was succeeded by the ★Lyric Opera of Queensland. The Lyric Opera has a permanent home at the Lyric Theatre in the Queensland Performing Arts Complex (opened 1985), also providing venues for tours of the ★Australian Opera and other companies.

(iv) Popular Music. Before World War I, the most popular musical entertainment with Brisbane audiences seems to have been refined vaudeville, such as could be heard at the Cremorne theatre on the south bank of the Brisbane River and at the Empire theatre, where Gladys

Moncrieff sang in 1913. Between the wars, jazz influences in popular music became more prominent with touring bands and the formation of the Brisbane Swing Club in 1936. During World War II, Brisbane hosted a huge contingent of American troops which had a potent effect on local musicians, meeting demands of dance halls and calls from the servicemen for 'hotter' jazz. Jazz concerts during the 1940s and 50s featured such groups as the Canecutters, but the popularity of these waned by the late 1950s. The Brisbane Jazz Club was formed in the late 1960s, with leading figures such as Ray Scribener and Mileham Hayes, and contemporary jazz in Brisbane has been championed by Ted Vining.

Folk music has retained popularity since its revival in the 1960s and folk festivals, particularly the annual festival held at the Sunshine Coast hinterland town of Maleny, are increasingly popular. Rock and country music enjoy a strong following as attested to by radio programming on both AM and FM bands. Multicultural awareness has given rise to ethnic radio programs and a multitude of ethnic musical ensembles, some funded through the Queensland Arts Council. The German-speaking community of Brisbane is musically represented by a Liedertafel, which with ensembles like the Finnish community choir perform a valuable social function and cultural outreach proclaiming ethnic diversity. The Brisbane Ethnic Music and Arts Centre maintains two 'world music' ensembles, Slivanje and Selengi, while some of the needs of Aboriginal musicians are met through the Djurubalak Musicians Co-operative.

(v) Institutions. The diversity of musical opportunities in Brisbane is catered for by a wide variety of educational bodies. Music specialist teachers are employed in both primary and secondary schools in the Queensland state school system and opportunities are available for students to learn orchestral and band instruments through the schools from mid-primary years. Tertiary education in practical and more theoretical aspects of music is provided by the University of Queensland, the Queensland Conservatorium of Music (Griffith University) and the Queensland University of Technology. The University of Queensland established a music department in the 1930s, has had a chair since 1965, and also offers specialist training in music therapy, choral music, and a Kodály program. The Conservatorium has provided a high standard of practical training for musicians for the last 30 years and is particularly noted for its opera program, and with the Queensland University of Technology complements its classical options with tertiary training in jazz.

The Brisbane Warana Festival and Brisbane Biennial Festival (from 1991) provide regular opportunities for the showcasing of local talent and interstate and overseas celebrities.

FURTHER REFERENCE
Austin, C.G., 'Early History of Music in Queensland', *Journal of the Royal Historical Society of Queensland* 6/4 (1961–62), 1052–67.

Bebbington, Warren, 'Music in 19th-Century Brisbane: The German Impact', in *The German Presence in Queensland over the last 150 Years*, ed. M. Jurgensen and A. Corkhill (Brisbane: Department of German, Univ. Queensland, 1988) 267–75.

Boughen, Robert. An Account of the Music of St. John's Cathedral Brisbane from 1843–1887, MMus (Qual), Univ. of Queensland, 1974.

Brier, Percy, One Hundred Years and More of Music in Queensland. TS copy, Brisbane, Univ. Queensland Architecture/Music Library.

Dawson, Jenny, Opera in Colonial Brisbane: The First 25 Years (1859–1884), MMus, Univ. Queensland, 1987.

Erickson, Frederick, Bands and Orchestras of Colonial Brisbane, PhD, Univ. Queensland, 1987.

Hebden, Barbara J., Life and Influence of Mr Robert Thomas Jefferies, MA (Qual), Univ. Queensland, 1974.

Orchard, W. Arundel, *Music in Australia: More than 150 Years of Development* (Melbourne: Georgian House, 1952).

Pixley, Norman Stewart, 'Entertainment in Brisbane: Recollections', *Journal of the Royal Historical Society of Queensland*, 10/2 (1976–77), 10–26.

A.H. FORBES

Brisbane Biennial.

Since its inauguration in 1991, the 12-day Brisbane Biennial has been held in May as an international performing arts festival that includes music, dance, film, cabaret and theatre. An eclectic and diverse program aims to cater for a wide variety of musical tastes from classical and traditional music, through contemporary and world music to jazz. Both Australian and international artists have participated in the festival, for example Victoria de los Angeles, the Hilliard Ensemble and James Morrison. The 1995 festival comprised a total of 118 indoor and outdoor events using 20 performance venues throughout the city. Biennial events have included a fully staged 12th-century musical play (*Daniel and the Lions*) and a concert version of Wagner's *Parsifal* in addition to exhibitions, installations, lectures, forums and workshops.

FURTHER REFERENCE
Brisbane Biennial *Festival Reports*, 1991, 1993, 1995.

KERRY VANN

Brisbane Ladies

[The Drover; Farewell to the Ladies of Brisbane], drover's ballad. By Saul Mendelssohn (*d* 1897) of Nanango, Queensland, it is the jaunty ballad of nomadic Queensland cattlemen who, having sold their herd and caroused at Brisbane, are beginning their trek back to remote Augathella Station. First published in *Boomerang* (28 February 1891), it was set to 'Spanish Ladies', but a minor key version is better known today, collected and recorded by A.L. Lloyd in 1956.

FURTHER REFERENCE
Edition with notes in *ManifoldP*; *RadicS*, 24.

British Music Society of Victoria.

Founded in 1921 by Louise ★Dyer (later Hanson-Dyer) as an overseas chapter of the British Music Society, which had been formed at London three years before. The Victorian society aimed to foster music-making by Melbourne players and composers, who in the interwar years were mostly happy to be identified as British. In its early days it was a forum for concerts of considerable glamour and importance; after the demise of the London parent body in 1933 it became autonomous, benefiting from a substantial endowment by James and Louise Dyer in 1936 and establishing an office in Swanston Street. After Dyer's departure the secretary for more than 40 years (to 1983) was Sibyl Hewitt. Currently with about 60 members, it continues to present monthly recitals at the chapel, Royal Freemasons Homes, Prahran, and for many years has quietly continued to commission and present premieres of works by Melbourne composers for its Dorian Le Gallienne Award.

FURTHER REFERENCE
Jim Davidson, *Lyrebird Rising: Louise Hanson Dyer of L'Oiseau-Lyre 1884–1962* (Melbourne: MUP, 1994), 148–59.

Broadside Ballads.

Verses written for singing, published (until *c*.1860) in broadsides—crudely printed handbills. In late 18th-century Britain newspapers were the subject of heavy taxes and high printing costs, and single news items of popular interest came to be circulated through mass-produced broadsides. In Australia too, broadsides circulated from convict times until the gold-rush years, bringing news of deaths, murders, tragedies, political developments, the activities of prominent people, or sporting events. The broadside collections preserved in Britain, at the Mitchell Library, Sydney, and at the National Library of Australia have proved a significant source for research in folk music and Australian history, and work based on them has been published by various scholars, notably Ron ★Edwards, Hugh ★Anderson and Geoffrey C. Ingleton. See *Folk Music*.

FURTHER REFERENCE
Ron Edwards, *The Convict Maid. Early Broadsides Relating to Australia* (Kuranda, Qld: Rams Skull Press, 1985); Hugh Anderson, *Farewell to Old England. A Broadside History of Early Australia* (Adelaide: Rigby, 1964); Geoffrey C. Ingleton, *True Patriots All* (Vermont, USA: Charles Tuttle, 1988).

Broadstock, Brenton Thomas

(*b* 12 Dec. 1952), composer. Raised playing band instruments in a Salvation Army family, he studied arts at Monash University, Melbourne, then composition with Donald Freund at Memphis State University and Peter Sculthorpe at the University of Sydney. Since 1982 he has been teaching at the University of Melbourne, now as head of composition. His Tuba Concerto (1985) won the 1987 Hambacher Preis, and since being composer-in-residence with the Melbourne Symphony Orchestra in 1988 he has steadily emerged as one of Australia's most widely recorded and performed composers.

A gently expressive voice, richly coloured in his orchestral works by a sure ear for brass and percussion sonority, his music takes flight from themes of personal anguish (as in Symphony No. 1 *Towards the Shining Light*), concern with the environment (*Deserts Bloom . . . Lakes Die*), or vivid literary images (Symphony No. 5 *Born From Good Angels' Tears*), becoming in recent years increasingly lyrical. Played by the BBC Symphony as well as by all orchestras and major chamber ensembles in Australia, his work includes five symphonies, four string quartets, a series of brass band works, four *Aureole* for solo or duo instruments, and a chamber opera *Fahrenheit 451*. He compiled *Sound Ideas: Australian Composers Born Since 1950* (Sydney, 1995).

WORKS (Selective)
Principal publisher: G. Schirmer (Aust.). Most ms works available in facsimile from Australian Music Centre, Sydney.
Orchestral *Festive Overture* (1981; 1993, ABC/Polygram CD 438611–2), *The Mountain*, small orch (1984), Tuba Concerto (1985), *Battlements* (1986), Piano Concerto (1987), Symphony No. 1 *Towards the Shining Light* (1988; 1988, ABC Classics 426807–2), Symphony No. 2 *Stars In A Dark Night* (1989), Symphony No. 3 *Voices From The Fire* (1991), *Away In A Manger* (trad.), arr. for orch (ms, 1993; Tall Poppies TP016 CD), *In A Brilliant Blaze* small orch (ms, 1993), Symphony No. 5 *Born From Good Angels' Tears* (ms, 1995) .
Instrumental String Quartet No. 2 (ms, 1981), *Aureole 1*, fl, pf (ms, 1992; rec 1995, ABC Classics CD 446738–2), *Aureole 2*, bass cl (ms, 1983), *Aureole 3*, ob, pf (ms, 1984; 1995, Move MD 3165), *Aureole 4*, solo pf (ms, 1984), *Beast From Air*, trbn, perc (ms, 1985), *And No Birds Sing*, fl, cl, vn, pf, perc (ms, 1987), *In The Silence of Night*, pf (1989; rec 1992, Move MCD042), *In Chains*, alto fl, gui (1990), String Quartet No. 4, (1990), *Deserts Bloom ... Lakes Die*, 2 ob, 2 cl, 2 hn, 2 bn, db (1990), *Giants In The Land*, org or pf (ms, 1991), *All That Is Solid ...*, fl, bass cl, pf (ms, 1992), *Nearer and Farther*, hn, pf (ms, 1992), *Breath ... In Time*, pf (1993; Melbourne: Red House, 1994), *Pennscapes*, cl, va, pf, vc (ms, 1994; 1994, Perihelion), Symphony No. 4 *Celebration*, fl, cl, pf, str qt (ms, 1995; 1996, Tall Poppies CD), *The Clear Flame Within*, vc, pf (ms, 1995).
Brass Band, Wind Ensemble *Aurora Australis*, trbn ensemble (ms, n.d.; Audio Village [USA] cassette), *Valiant* (ms, 1994; 1994, Triumphonic TRLPS–42), *St. Aelred*, *Rhapsody for Band* (ms, 1981), *Click*, *Festival March* (ms, 1982; Triumphonic Records), *Fantasia* (ms, 1984; Klarion Records LP MWB 011), *Fanfare and Processional* (ms, 1985), *Festival Prelude* (ms, 1986), *My Shepherd* (ms, 1988; CD CR008), *Meditation on Rapture* (ms, 1990; MSB CD RR5866), *Rutherford Variations* (ms, 1990; MSB CD RR5866), *Songs of the Pilgrim* (ms, 1991; MSB CD 9327), Saxophone Concertino, soprano sax, wind ensemble (ms, 1995).
Theatre *Fahrenheit 451*, chamber opera, 5 vv, elecs (ms, 1990, 1, composer, after Ray Bradbury), 22 Oct. 1992, Sydney Metropolitan Opera, Belvoir Street Theatre.
Vocal *Eheu Fugaces*, S, fl, cl, vn, vc, pf, perc (ms, 1981; rec 1995: Vox Australis CD VAST018–2), *Bright Tracks*, S, vn, va, vc (ms, 1994).

FURTHER REFERENCE
His writings include 'Australian Symphonies Today', *Speaking of Music* (Sydney: ABC Books, 1991). See also *Broadstock S*; *Age* 10 Dec. 1988; Rebecca Guymer, The Symphonies of Brenton Broadstock, unpub. BA (Hons), Monash Univ., 1990.

Broken-Down Squatter, The, pastoral ballad. The text was attributed in its first publication (1893) to Dick Stuart, and later to Queensland station-owner Charles Augustus ★Flower. Set to 'The Hunting Day', it is the lament of a defeated squatter of the 1880s, riding his horse away from his drought-ravaged property. It was published by A.B. Paterson in his *Old Bush Songs*, 1905.

FURTHER REFERENCE
Edition and commentary in *Edwards G*.

Brokensha, Jack Joseph (*b* Adelaide, 5 Jan. 1926), jazz drummer, bandleader, arranger. First engaged at the age of six on the xylophone, he later mastered piano and drums. He joined the Adelaide Symphony Orchestra, and was attracted to jazz during his war service in the RAAF. After his discharge in 1946 he came to prominence in the progressive jazz movement, through influential performing, composing and arranging in the leading bands of various cities. With Bryce ★Rohde he moved to Ontario, Canada, to co-found the highly successful Australian Jazz Quartet (later ★Australian Jazz Quintet) in 1953. Following the band's break-up in Australia 1959, he worked briefly in Sydney until returning to Detroit where he now runs his own music production company.

FURTHER REFERENCE
For recordings, see *Australian Jazz Quintet*. See also *Bisset B*; *Grove J*; *Oxford J*; Jim McLeod, *Jazztrack* (ABC Books, Sydney, 1994), 58–73.

BRUCE JOHNSON

Bromley, Sid (Sidney Joseph) (*b* Brisbane, 7 June 1920), jazz drummer, clarinettist, manager. He started playing clarinet in 1940, then drums, and formed the first of many swing clubs. Wartime postings brought him into contact with interstate musicians, and after his discharge in 1946 he focused on the entrepreneurial activity for which his career became most significant. He formed and managed the Canecutters, which until its dissolution (*c*.1952) was Brisbane's best-known jazz band, winning the *Tempo* top group award in 1948. While playing casually with Len ★Barnard and others, he organised numerous jazz clubs, such as the Brisbane Jazz Club in 1957, which operated intermittently into the 1960s. His subsequent jazz activities, for example with the Qld Jazz Action Society, have been mainly organisational.

FURTHER REFERENCE
Bisset B; *Oxford J*.   BRUCE JOHNSON

Bronhill, June [June Mary Gough] (*b*. Broken Hill, NSW, 26 June 1929), soprano. Awarded third prize in the *Sun* Aria Competition in 1949, she used the prize money to travel to England for further study (1952). Her funds were supplemented by a considerable sum raised by the residents of Broken Hill, and in gratitude she changed her surname to a contraction of the town's name. In 1954 she was engaged by Sadler's Wells Opera Co. and in 1959 made her debut at Covent Garden in the title role of *Lucia di Lammermoor*. Her many roles in both England and Australia (with the national and state companies) include Gilda, Norina (*Don Pasquale*), Queen of the Night, Zerbinetta (*Ariadne auf Naxos*, for which she received great critical acclaim in London), the title role in *Maria Stuarda*, Saffi (*The Gypsy Baron*), Adela (*Die Fledermaus*), and *Orpheus in the Underworld*.

Despite her success as a coloratura soprano in grand opera, she is best known for her work in operetta and musical comedy. She enjoyed immense success in the Sadler's Wells production of *The Merry Widow* (1958–60) in London, regional England and subsequently Australia. She performed in an extended Australian season of *The Sound of Music* (1962–64) before returning to England for a 19-month season of *Robert and Elizabeth*, a musical version of *The Barretts of Wimpole Street*, which also toured Australia and South Africa. In recent years she has appeared in an Australian tour of *The Pirates of Penzance* (1984) and as a stage actress. She was awarded the OBE in 1977.

FURTHER REFERENCE
June Bronhill, *The Merry Bronhill* (Methuen: Sydney, 1987); *MackenzieS*, 197–8.   KERRY VANN

Brookes, Herbert and Ivy, music philanthropists. Herbert (*b* Bendigo, Vic., 20 Dec. 1867; *d* 1 Dec. 1963) studied engineering at the University of Melbourne, Ivy (*b* South Yarra, Melbourne, 14 July 1883; *d* 27 Dec. 1970) received the Ormond Scholarship at the University of Melbourne for singing (1904), played first violin in the *Marshall-Hall Orchestra (1903–13), and also attended Marshall-Hall's Melbourne Conservatorium. After their marriage in 1905 their residence, 'Winwick' in South Yarra, was a venue for evening recitals, always open to artists seeking advice, financial or personal support. Herbert became editor and proprietor of *The Liberal*, from 1929 Australian commissioner-general to the USA, and vice-chairman of the ABC, 1932–39. Ivy was vice-president of the ladies' advisory committee of the Melbourne Symphony Orchestra and the Royal Melbourne Philharmonic Society. In 1908 the Brookeses helped create the Lady *Northcote Permanent Orchestra Trust Fund; in 1929 they presented the University of Melbourne Conservatorium with an E. Phillips-Fox portrait of Marshall-Hall, the pair's chief inspiration, and in 1934, despite the Depression, they endowed the Conservatorium with a Marshall-Hall wing at a cost of £4000. At 92 Herbert gave the Conservatorium £2000 to purchase instruments. Dedicated supporters of Melbourne's musical life, they sought to influence the sustenance of high ideals in music through their generous gifts.

FURTHER REFERENCE
Alison Patrick, *ADB*, 7; Rohan Rivett, *Australian Citizen: Herbert Brookes 1867–1963* (Melbourne: MUP, 1965).

KYLIE MOLONEY

Brookes Memorial Fellowship, Dame Mabel. Awarded annually since 1983 by application to a member of the Victorian State Opera Young Artist program, in memory of the late Mabel Brookes, a long-time supporter of opera in Victoria. Winners have included Deborah Riedel and Christine Ferraro. Administered by the Opera Foundation Australia, Sydney, the prize is currently $15 000.

Brophy, Gerard (*b* Sydney, 7 Jan. 1953), composer. He studied at the NSW State Conservatorium 1978–81, and with Franco Donatoni at the Accademia Nazionale di Santa Cecilia in Rome 1982–83. Composer-in-residence for Musica Viva (1984), the Queensland Conservatorium of Music (1987), and the Pittsburg New Music Ensemble (1988), he has been lecturer in composition at the Queensland Conservatorium of Music since 1988 and has selected works published by Ricordi. Recent compositions include *Slang* (1994–95) for alto flute, bass clarinet, piano and ensemble, *Umbigada, obrigado!* (1995) for percussion quartet, *The room of the saints* (1995) for violin and darabuka, *We Bop* (1995) for alto saxophone and vibraphone, *Voile parfumé* (1995) for three trumpets, *Trash* (1995) for junk percussion (four players), *GloVe* (1995) for bass clarinet, cello and piano, *chArm* (1995) for flute, viola and harp, and *The Republic of Dreams* (1995) for solo harp and ensemble.

WORKS (Selective)
Orchestral and Concerto   *Salammbo* (1980), *Nadja*, perc qrt, orch (1981), *Exu*, amplified solo vn, large orch (1982, Ricordi), *Orfeo*, str orch (1982, Ricordi), *Le Reveil de l'Ange*, pf, small orch (1987, Ricordi), *Matho* (1987, Ricordi), *Forbidden colours*, small orch (1988, rec VASTO15–2), *Les roses sanglantes*, solo bass cl, small orch (1990), *Lautreamont*, solo fl, small orch (1992), *Colour red...your mouth...heart*, large orch (1994).
Chamber Instrumental   *Linia*, chamber orch (1980), *Ikhos*, 2 tpt, 3 trbn, 2 pf, harmonium (1981), *Iemenja*, concertante fl, ens (1981), *Senso ... dopo Skin d'Amourdo* fl/pic, cl/bass cl, perc, pf/celeste, vn, vc (1982, Ricordi), *Sofre*, vibraphone, hpd, celeste, 2 vn, va, vc (1983), *Breathless*, 3 fl, pf (1983), *Cries and Whispers*, pic, bass cl, perc, hp, gui, mandolin (1983), *Rondino*, str qrt (1984), *Scintille*, alto fl, cl/bass cl, pf, vn, va, vc (1984, Ricordi), *Chrome*, wind quintet, fl, ob, cl, bn, hn (1984, Editio Musica Budapest), *Lace*, str qrt (1985, Ricordi), *Mercurio*, amplified fl, 2 pf (1985), *Tres doux tremblement de terre*, 2 pf (1983), *Chiarissima*, vc and pf (1987, Ricordi), *Chiarissima*, vc, pf (1988, Ricordi), *Seraphita*, fl, cl, pf, vn, va, vc (1988), *Head*, pic, bass cl, pf (1988), *... pink chair light green*

violet violent FLASH, pic, 4 perc (1990), *Glint*, crotales, 2 glocken-spiel, 2 vibraphones, gongs (1992), *Xanthe*, fl, ob, cl, bn, hn, tpt, 2 perc, 2 pf (1992), *O dolcezz'amarissime*, bass cl, tpt, 2 perc, pf, vn, va, vc (1992), *Chrome d'oro*, S, gongs, vibraphone (1993), *La Domaine Enchantée*, afl, english hn, 2 elec gui, hp, perc, vn, va, vc, db (1993), *Seduire c'est tout!*, cl, bn, hn, vn, db (1993), *Vox Angelica*, perc, 2 vn, va, vc (1993), *A flor da pele*, vn, mar (1993), *Tudo Liq-uido*, 3 cl, 3 trbn, pf, 2 perc (1994), *Bisoux*, english hn, bcl (1994), *Rubber*, alto fl, bass cl, vibraphone, pf (1994), *Slang*, alto fl, bass cl, pf, ens (1994/5), *Umbigada, obrigado!*, 4 perc (1995), *The room of the saints*, vn, darabuka (1995), *We bop*, alto sax, vibraphone (1995), *Voile parfumé*, 3 tpt (1995), *Trash*, 4 perc (1995), *GloVe*, bass cl, vc, pf (1995), *chArm*, fl, va, hp 1995), *The Republic of Dreams*, solo hp, fl, cl, 2 perc, 2 vn, va, vc, db (1995), *Iza*, bass ob, bass cl (1996), *Trip*, 2 fl, ob, 2 cl, 2 bn, 2 hn (1996).

Solo Instrumental   *Gheranos*, pf (1980), *Axé*, solo perc (1982), *Nymph-echo morphologique*, amplified fl (1989, VAST010–2CD), *Pluck it!*, gui (1991), *Tweak*, pic (1991), *Angelicon*, pf (1991, TP040), *Spiked heels*, pf (1992), *Twist*, bass cl (1993, 1.710), *Es*, fl (1994), *November Snow*, music box (1994).

Vocal/Choral   *Flesh*, cantata buffa (1987, Ricordi), *Vorrei bacia-rti …*, Bar, alto fl, english hn, cl, hn, tpt, pf, perc, vn, va, vc (1991).

Theatre   *The Temptation of St Antony*, opera (1985, 1, Martin Buzacott), 1986, Sydney.

FURTHER REFERENCE
Recordings include *Nadja*, Sydney Symphony Orchestra (OZM 1002); *Hydra*, Synergy (Canberra School of Music, CSM 2). See also *BroadstockS*; P. Brown and B. Swain, 'Gerard Brophy's *Axé*: a Critical Analysis', *AMC News* 11 (March 1986), 6–9; C. Dench and I. Shanahan, eds, 'An Emotional Geography of Australian Composition II', *SA* 46 (Winter 1995), 9–31; A. Ford, *Composer to Composer: Conversations About Contemporary Music* (Sydney: Allen & Unwin, 1993).

MICHAEL BARKL

Brown, Brian   (*b* Melbourne, 29 Dec. 1933), jazz flute and reed player, composer. He began playing tenor saxo-phone in 1952, then other reeds and flute, soon playing professionally with Melbourne dance bands led by William Flynn, Mick Walker and others. He studied in London in 1953–54, and on returning to Melbourne he formed groups with Keith Hounslow, Stewie Speer and later Keith Stirling, and became a leading exponent of progressive styles, notably at Jazz Centre 44. Withdrawing from jazz in the early 1960s, he studied architecture and did session work. He resumed jazz activity at the Fat Black Pussycat, 1965–69, playing with Ted Vining, Barry Buckley (bass), Tony ★Gould and others, and following more exploratory lines. Playing sporadically through the early 1970s with David Tolley, Bob Sedergreen, Mike Murphy (drums) and others, he recorded the first of several of his own suites, *Carlton Streets*, in 1974. He opened the Commune, where he played through the late 1970s, with emerging young avant-gardists among others; he also played in Sydney and toured overseas. In the 1980s he became director of the jazz studies program at the Victorian College of the Arts, a

position he still holds. Establishing the independent record label AIJA, he led his Australian Jazz Ensemble which also performed at Sydney in 1985.

Brown has been a pivotal influence in the progressive jazz movement in Melbourne for over 40 years. He has continued to compose and record, sometimes with Aus-tralia Council commissions; his opera *Winged Messenger* was premiered in 1994, and in 1995 he performed in the USA with Tony Gould. He was honoured with the OAM in 1993.

FURTHER REFERENCE
Recordings include *Carlton Streets*, Brian Brown Quintet (1974, 44 Records 6357 700); *The Planets*, Brian Brown (1985, Larrikin LRJ 151); *Winged Messenger*, Brian Brown Quartet with Judy Jacques (1987, AIJA 004); *Spirit of the Rainbow*, Brian Brown and Tony Gould (1990, Move MD 3085). An interview with him is in *WilliamsA*, 106–11. See also *ClareB*; *BissetB*; *GroveJ*; *OxfordJ*; Adrian Jackson, 'Brian Brown, Still A Force', *JA* (March/April 1983), 4–8; Jeff Pressing, ed., *Compositions for Improvisers, An Australian Perspective* (Melbourne: La Trobe University Press, 1994), 5–7.

BRUCE JOHNSON

Brown, Ray   (*b* Hurstville, Sydney), pop singer. He left school at 15 to work as a clerk and joined the Nocturnes in 1964, an instrumental band who as the Whispers adopted a neo-Beatles image and became regulars at Surf City, Sydney. His first single was the Chubby Checker hit *20 Miles*, which reached No. 26 in the charts in 1965; a series of hits followed, including three that year, *Pride*, which reached No. 7, *Fool, Fool, Fool* which reached No. 7 and *In The Midnight Hour* which reached No. 4. *Ten-nessee Waltz* was No. 5 in 1966, but the Whispers dissolved in 1967, and when his attempt at working with a new membership did not last, Brown went to the USA and signed with Capitol Records. Not finding success, he returned to Australia in 1970 with a new bearded, unkempt look, and formed the country-rock group Moonstone, then in 1971 One Ton Gypsy, which worked in Sydney discos. In the 1980s he occasionally re-formed the Whispers for revival concerts.

FURTHER REFERENCE
Recordings include *20 Miles* (1965, Leedon); *Pride* (1965, Lee-don); *Fool, Fool, Fool* (1965, Leedon); *Wait Till The Midnight Hour* (1965, Leedon). For discography, see *SpencerA*. See also *Guin-nessP*, I, 347; *McGrathA*; *SpencerW*.

Browne, Allan Vincent   (*b* Deniliquin, NSW, 28 July 1944), jazz drummer, bandleader. Initially self-taught on the drums, his first major work was with the ★Red Onion Jazz Band, with whom he continues to perform for reunions. By the mid-1970s he was extending his stylistic compass through lessons with Graham Morgan and work with bassist Ray Martin and Bob Sedergreen, trumpeter Peter Gaudion, and trombonist Dave Rankin's fusion group Rankin File. In the early 1980s he formed Onaje, which focused on compositions by its band members, including Dick Miller and Sedergreen, and which performed at the Montreal Jazz Festival in 1992. He has led numerous groups, with bassist Geoff Kluke, pianist Jex Saarelahrt and others, and has also been active as support for visiting musicians, including Milt Jackson, Phil Woods, Plas Johnson, Wild Bill Davidson and Johnny Griffin.

Browne's versatility has found him working across the full spectrum of Melbourne jazz styles, from Frank Traynor, Geoff Kitchen, the group Odwala, and singer Vince Jones to saxophonist Ken Schroder and Paul Grabowsky. Something of his range is represented on the recording *Genre Jumping Jazz*. He currently works with the Paul ★Grabowsky Trio, guitarist Paul Rettke and singer Margie Lou Dyer, and his New Orleans Rascals, which includes the significant emerging multi-instrumentalist Stephen Grant. He also teaches jazz history and has won an ARIA award (with Grabowsky).

FURTHER REFERENCE

Recordings include *Big Band Memories*, Red Onion Jazz Band (1967, W&G Records, WG-25-5065); *Straight As A Briefcase*, Onaje (1981, East EAS 082); *Genre Jumping Jazz*, Allan Browne (1989, Newmarket, DEX CD.206); *Six By Three*, Paul Grabowsky Trio (1989, Spiral Scratch, OOO1); *Crisis*, Red Onion Jazz Band (1993, Newmarket, NEW 1015.2); *Bird Calls*, Allan Browne Quartet (1994, Newmarket, NEW1067.2). See also *ClareB*; *OxfordJ*; Adrian Jackson, 'Allan Browne and Richard Miller, Modernists & Traditionalists', *JA* (Winter/Spring, 1986), 12–18.

BRUCE JOHNSON

Browne, Lindsay ['L.B.'] (*b* Melbourne, 6 Oct. 1915), music critic. After working as a clerk, he joined the Melbourne *Star* as a cadet reporter, then the *Sydney Morning Herald* in 1935. For the latter he wrote music criticism from 1936, and after a period as New York correspondent replaced Neville Cardus as chief arts reviewer (1946–60). He wrote for the *Bulletin*, was co-ordinator of promotion for the Australian Elizabethan Theatre Trust (1963–71), and had a column on music with the *Sydney Morning Herald* (1971–81). Signing articles 'L.B.', he preserved the high standards and constructive tone set by his predecessor Cardus in a clear, incisive style. He also supplied crossword puzzles to newspapers from 1939.

FURTHER REFERENCE

Gavin Souter, *Company of Heralds* (Melbourne: MUP, 1981), 329–30; *ParsonsC*.

Brownlee, John Donald Mackenzie (*b* Geelong, Vic., 1 Jan. 1900; *d* New York, 10 Jan. 1969), baritone. As a child he played cornet in the Geelong Municipal Band under Percy ★Jones Sr, but won the vocal championship at the South Street Eisteddfod, Ballarat, aged 21. He studied with Ivor Boustead at the Albert Street Conservatorium,

Melbourne, where he was heard singing *Messiah* by Melba and advised to study in Europe. He studied with Dinh Gilly in Paris from 1923 and in 1925 began singing French operetta with the Trianon Theatre, Montmartre. Again he was heard by Melba, who invited him to participate in her farewell Covent Garden concert in June 1926. He made his debut (Paris Opéra, 1927) as Athanaël in *Thaïs* and quickly established himself on the international circuit, singing French and Italian opera and Mozart roles (Don Alfonso, Don Giovanni, Papageno, Count Almaviva). He remained with the Paris Opéra until 1936. In the 1930s he was known as an outstanding Mozart interpreter, working at Glyndebourne and Covent Garden. At his New York debut (Metropolitan, 1937) he sang Rigoletto and worked there until 1958. He taught at the Manhattan School of Music from 1953; from 1956 he was appointed director. He established a highly regarded opera workshop and directed many productions.

His first return to Australia was with the Williamson-Melba Grand Opera Co. in 1928, when his voice was described as 'of very beautiful quality, perfectly even throughout the range . . . allied with a dignified bearing and energy of emotional expression' (*The Argus*). He made a concert tour in 1932–33, also singing Rigoletto, Amonasro, Scarpia and Marcello for J.C. Williamsons in Melbourne. Later Australian tours were 1939, 1949 and 1952. A John Brownlee Vocal Scholarship in Melbourne commemorates his distinguished career as singer and teacher.

FURTHER REFERENCE

Obit. in *Opera* 20 (March 1969), 209–16. See also L. Bell, 'John Brownlee as Singing Master', *AJME* 12 (1973), 23; *MackenzieS*, 117–22; Desmond Shawe-Taylor, *GroveD*; Morris S. Williams, *ADB*, 7.

WARREN BOURNE

Bruce, Barry Robert (*b* Perth, WA, 4 Sept. 1938), jazz pianist. He began piano in his teens, starting in dance work and then forming the Westport Jazz Band, which performed at the 1960 Australian Jazz Convention. Apart from the six months he spent in Dubbo, NSW, he was with the Riverside Jazz Group from 1961 until it disbanded in 1963. He then joined Ray ★Price until 1969, then returned to Perth and played in pop music until resuming jazz work with the formation of the Chicago Jazz Band in the late 1970s. He now teaches jazz and has continued to perform.

FURTHER REFERENCE

Recordings include *King Fisher's All Stars* (1965, Jazzology 3–13); *The West Coast Jazz Band* (1978, Tempo, TPB-101). See also *OxfordJ*.

BRUCE JOHNSON

Brumby, Colin James (*b* Melbourne, 18 June 1933), composer. He was organist at St Oswald's, Glen Iris, 1950–53, studied at the University of Melbourne Conservatorium from 1954, where he received encouragement from Verdon ★Williams and Robert ★Hughes, completing a diploma of education in 1957, then taught in schools until becoming head of music at Kelvin Grove Teachers' College, Brisbane. In 1962 he went to Europe, studying in Spain with Philipp Jarnach (composition) and Maestro Ribo (choral conducting), and in London with Alexander Goehr (composition) and John Carewe (conducting). Appointed lecturer (now associate professor) at the University of Queensland in 1964, he was awarded the DMus by the University of Melbourne (1971), and undertook advanced composition studies in Rome in 1972–73 with Franco Evangelisti. His many students have included composers Andrew ★Schultz, Moya ★Henderson, and Stephen ★Cronin. After holding the musical directorship of a number of ensembles, in 1968 he co-founded the Vocal Arts Ensemble, Brisbane, which became the ★Queensland Opera Company (1969), and as its music director until 1971 he conducted the Australian premieres of Bizet's *Le Docteur Miracle* and Haydn's *L'infedeltà delusa*. Between 1968 and 1971 he composed nine operas for this ensemble, including seven operettas for children, the latter playing to 75 000 children at 400 schools throughout Queensland.

Brumby's earliest works are tonal with traditional harmonies. As a student he became attracted to Schoenberg's music, and after study with Goehr he became Australia's most notable serial composer of the late 1960s and early 70s, and also began to explore aleatoricism. During his study in Rome, Brumby began to question these techniques and finally, in *The Phoenix and the Turtle* (1974), rejected them for a tonal style with traditional or late-Romantic harmonies. He has a predilection for canon, especially in choral works. A composer for whom melody is the principal means of expression, he excels in opera, song, and concerto. He is acutely aware of the importance of providing children with serious music tailored to their abilities, and has produced a notable body of pedagogical works for solo and ensemble performance. The influence of the church and its music has also been important, and he has written more than 200 choral works suitable for liturgical performance. Travel, especially in Italy, is also a strong influence, ranging from his choice of texts, such as *Lorenzaccio,* to his emotive responses to landscapes. Two collaborators are of particular importance: Thomas ★Shapcott, as librettist for two of his operas and a majority of the large choral works; and his wife, Jenny Dawson, as performer (soprano) and librettist, and with whom he, as a baritone, has presented many recitals focusing on the Italian operatic repertoire, a number of which have been broadcast.

What is central to his conception of music is clear from his book, *The Art of Prolonging the Musical Tone* (1968): his concern with form is implicit in the title; 'The Concept of Melody' analyses a vocal chant and examines the relationship between text and music; in 'The Concept of Development' he states: 'Fundamentally, to *develop* is to *vary*'; and in the final chapter, 'The Polyphonic Concept',

he discusses the manifold possibilities of polyphony in 20th-century composition. Although his style has changed radically, these concepts have remained constant.

Brumby has received an extraordinarily large number of commissions, including from the ABC, Adelaide Festival, ASME, Brisbane Biennial, Musica Viva, Queensland Ballet, Perth Festival, Jan Sedivka, and the Australian UNESCO Committee for Music. He has won numerous awards, including the Albert Maggs award (1968), Advance Australia award (1981), Don Banks fellowship (1990), and the APRA award for most performed Australasian serious work (1990). His works being loved by performers and audience alike, he is one of Australia's most highly regarded and most frequently performed composers, and one of the few to have firmly established an international reputation.

WORKS (Selective)

Orchestral Suite for Chamber Orchestra (1954), *Mediterranean Suite,* str orch (1956), *Fibonacci Variations* (1963), *Antitheses,* str orch (1964, rev. 1967), *Antipodea* (1965), *Realisations* (1966), *Entradas* (1968), *Litanies of the Sun* (1970), *Threnody,* school orch (1970), *The Phoenix and the Turtle,* str orch, hpd (1974), *Musagettes* (1978), *Festival Overture on Australian Themes* (1981), Symphony No. 1 *The Sun* (1981), *Paean* (1982), *Pacific Overture* (1983), *Australian Overture* (1984), *South Bank Overture* (1984), *God Save the Queen,* arr. str (1985), Symphony No. 2 *Mosaics of Ravenna* (1993), *West End Overture* (1993).

Brass Ensemble/Concert Band *Fanfare,* brass ens, perc (1968, Sydney: Albert, 1973), *Ceremonies* (1969), *ANZAAS Fanfare* [i], 3 tpt (1969), *ANZAAS Fanfare* [ii], 3 tpt, 3 trbn (1980), *Congressional Fanfare,* 3 tpt, 3 hn, 3 trbn (1981), *Fanfare for the Governor-General,* 4 tpt, 3 trbn (1981), *Pacific Fanfare,* brass ens (1981), *Gallery Fanfare,* 3 tpt, 3 trbn (1982), *Librarians' Fanfare,* 2 tpt, hn, trbn (1984), *Fanfare,* tpt, hn, trbn (1989), *Carnival at Viareggio,* concert band (1995).

Solo Instrument with Orchestra *Romance,* ob, str (1956), *Aegean Suite,* fl, str (1957), Concertino for Viola and Strings (1960), *Partite,* cl, str (1961), *Pantos,* fl, str (1962), *Homage à Santiago,* gui, orch (1965), *Diversion,* hn, orch (1966), Violin Concerto No. 1 (1969), Concerto for Horn and Strings (1971), Concerto for Flute and Orchestra (1975), Concerto for Bassoon and Orchestra (1982), Violin Concerto No. 2 (1982), Concerto for Guitar (1983), Piano Concerto No. 1 (1984), Concertino for Oboe and Orchestra (1986), *Scena for Cor Anglais and Strings* (1988), Clarinet Concerto (1988), Viola Concerto *Tre aspetti di Roma* (1990), Trumpet Concerto (1991), Concerto for Organ and Strings *Schifanoia* (1994), Cello Concerto (1995).

Chamber *Air and Movement,* rec, pf (195?), *Four Exotic Pieces,* fl, hp (1961, New York: Lyra, [1988]), Three Little Pieces, 3 cl (1963), Four Miniatures, fl, pf (1964), *Strophe,* vn, cl, pf (1964), Wind Quintet, fl, ob, cl, hn, bn (1964), *Doubles for Woodwind Quartet* (1965), Trio, fl, cl, hn (1965), *Cameo,* fl, pf (1966), *Doriana Suite,* 2 descant rec, 1 treble rec (1966, Sydney: Albert, 1966), *French Suite,* 6 hn (1967), *Declamations,* fl, ob, pf (1969), String Quartet (1968, Sydney: Albert, 1969), *Player Chooses,* 3 insts, kbd (1972), Four Clarinet Duos (Sydney: Albert, 1975), *Suite,* 4 db (1975,

London:Yorke, [1978]),Theme and Variations, fl, gui (1975), Four Simple Duos for Descant Recorders (Sydney: Albert, 1976), *Chiaroscuro*, pf, cl, vc (1977), *Haydn Down Under*, bn, str qt (1980), *Short and Sweet*, treble, bass, chordal inst (Brisbane: ASMUSE, 1981), Wind Quintet No. 2 *The Seven Ages of Man*, fl, ob, cl, hn, bn, optional nar (1981), Clarinet Sonatina (1982, Melbourne: Allans, 1991), *Eine kleine Streichmusik*, str (1983), Wind Quintet No. 3, fl, ob, cl, hn, bn (1983), Bassoon Sonata, bn, pf (1984), Flute Sonatina, fl, pf (1984), Piano Quartet, pf, vn, va, vc (1984), *Fair and Flexi*, melody and bass insts with chords (1984, Brisbane: ASMUSE, 1985), *Four Aphorisms*, cl, pf (1986), *All Together Now: Three Easy String Ensemble Pieces*, vn, vc (1988), *Easy Does It*, vn, vc (1988), *Good Things Come in Threes:Three Easy Ensemble Pieces*, 2 vn, vc (1988), *Mundoolun*, cor anglais, pf (1989), *Borromeo Suite*, fl, gui (1990, Sydney: Classical, 1992), *Aubade*, vn, pf (1991), *Gardens of the Villa Taranto*, fl, guitar (1991), *Dance of the Shepherds*, mandolins, gui (1993), *Berceuse*, tpt, pf (1995), *In memoriam*, tpt, pf (1995), *Song of the Bard*, tpt, pf (1995), *Twilight Hymn*, tpt, pf (1995), *Aria*, vn, pf (1996), *Little Waltz*, vn, pf (1996).

Solo Instrumental *Sicilian Dance*, pf (1961, Sydney: Chappell, 1967), Prelude and Nocturne No. 1, gui (1962), Four Little Piano Pieces (1963),Theme and Variations, pf (1963, Melbourne: Allans, 1963),Three Pieces, cl (1963), Four Antiphons for Organ (1963), *Chance Piece*, pf (1965), *Keyboard Fun*, pf (Melbourne: Allans, [1967]), *Joe the Fisherman: Suite for Piano* (Sydney: Albert, 1967), *Old Fiddle Tune, and Strange Song*, pf (Sydney: Chappell, [1967]), *Ritornelle*, pf (Melbourne: Allans, [1967]), Organ Sonata (1969), *Hesperian Suite*, gui (1971), *Doubles*, pf (1970–71, Sydney: Albert, 1974), *Two Characteristic Pieces for Guitar* (Sydney: Albert, 1974), *Danza*, cl, pf (1975), *Antistrophe*, pf (1976), *Exploring* [originally *Three Little Piano Pieces*] (1976, Sydney: Albert, 1976), The Little Guitar Book (1976), *Mantra*, fl (1976), Prelude and Nocturne No. 2, gui (1976, Sydney: Currency, 1990), Duettino, pf duet (in *Piano Duets Book 2*, Sydney: Albert, [1978]), *Cancion*, pf duet (in *Piano Duets Book 3*, Melbourne: Allans, [1978]), *Demotica*, pf (1980), *Improvisation*, org (1981), *Reverie*, pf (in *Piano Music for one Hand*, Melbourne: Allans, [1984]), *Harlequinade*, pf (1986, Northants, UK: Fentone, 1987), Scherzo, pf (1987, in *Bicentennial Piano Album*, Melbourne:Allans, 1988), *Captain Logan's Fancy*, org (1988, in *Organ australis*, Sydney: Currency, 1991), *Three Christmas Preludes*, org (1992), *Three Easter Preludes*, org (1992), *Capriccio*, bn (1993), *Mists of Islay*, celtic hp (1994), *Twilight Pastoral*, pf (1994), *Encore*, pf (1995), *Intermezzo* (1995),Toccata, org (1995), *Turkish March*, pf (1995).

Operas [*Persephone* (1968, 1), incomplete], *The Seven Deadly Sins* (1970, 2, Thomas Shapcott, vocal score pub. Ipswich, Qld: TW Shapcott in conjunction with the Queensland Opera Co., 1970), 12 Sept. 1970, Brisbane, *The Marriage Machine* (1971, 1, Composer, orchestrated 1985), 28 Jan. 1972, Sydney, orch version 4 Sept. 1985, Sydney, [*Ishtar's Mirror* (1971, 3,Thomas Shapcott), incomplete], [*Goldie* (1971, 3,Thomas Shapcott), incomplete], *La Donna* (1986, 1, David Goddard), 2 July 1988, Sydney [workshop performance], *Lorenzaccio* (1986, 3, Composer after Alfred de Musset), excerpts, 20 Oct. 1986, Sydney [workshop performance], *Fire on the Wind* (1990, 2, Composer after Anthony Coburn), *Summer Carol* (1990, 1, Thomas Shapcott), 10 Aug. 1991, Canberra.

Children's Operettas (all 1 act, libretti by the composer) *The Three Suitors* (1967), premiered by the Adelaide Singers, *Rita and Dita* (1967, after J.L. and W.C. Grimm's *Hänsel und Gretel)*, 13 May 1968, Brisbane, *The Wise Shoemaker* (1967), 13 May 1968, Brisbane, *Rita and Dita and the Pirate* [originally *More Adventures of Rita and Dita*] (1968, Sydney: Albert, 1969), 24 Feb. 1969, Brisbane, *The Prince who Couldn't Laugh* (1968, Sydney:Albert, 1969), 24 Feb. 1969, Brisbane, *Rita and Dita in Toyland* (1969), 23 Feb. 1970, Rockhampton, *The Two Suitors* [adaptation of *The Three Suitors*] (1969), 23 Feb. 1970, Rockhampton, *Rita and Dita and the Jolly Swagman* (1970, after 'Banjo' Paterson's *Waltzing Matilda)*, 15 Feb. 1971, Brisbane.

Ballets *Bunyip* (1966, 1), 1967, ABC Television, Brisbane, *Cataclysm* (tape montage compiled by Charles Lisner from recorded works of Brumby available at the time), 16 Mar. 1971, Brisbane, *Cinderella* (1975, 2), 10 Dec. 1975, Brisbane, *Masques* (1977, 1), 18 Aug. 1980, Brisbane, *Alice* (1987, 2), 30 June 1989, Brisbane.

Choral with Orchestra or Instruments (texts by Thomas Shapcott unless stated otherwise) *Stabat Mater Speciosa: A Christmas Cantata*, S, Mez, T, Bar soli, SATB, str and wind qts, hp, perc (1965, trad text), *Bring Out Your Christmas Masks*, 3S, T, Bar soli, SATB, boys' ch, speakers, orch, tape (1969), *Charlie Bubbles' Book of Hours*, S, Mez, T, Bar soli, SATB, orch, tape (1969, composer), *A Windy Beach*, 3 solo vv, speakers, unison ch, 2 descant rec, pf duet, perc (1970, Sydney: Albert, 1970), *Ballade for St Cecilia*, S, Mez, T, Bar soli, SATB, orch (1971), *Celebrations and Lamentations*, S, Bar soli, 4 SATB, speakers, brass, wind, perc, org (1971), *This is the Vine*, S, Mez, T, Bar soli, SATB, orch (1972), *Flood Valley*, S, Mez soli, SAB, SSA, 3 verse-speaking chs, orch, tape (1976, Kensington Park, SA: Pembroke School, n.d.), *Victimae Paschali: An Easter Cantata*, SATB, str (1977, trad text), *Three Baroque Angels*, SATB, orch (1978), *Orpheus Beach*, S, Bar soli, SATB, 2 speakers, orch (1978), Incidental Music to Euripides' *Hippolytus*, vv, ch, fl, ob, gui, org, harmonium, perc (1979, Euripides), *Where the Pelican Builds Her Nest*, SS, 2 fl, 2 cl, pf duet (1983, Mary Hannay Foote), *Festival Mass* (1984, trad text), *Great is Truth and Mighty Above All Things*, Bar solo, SATB, orch (1984, Apocrypha), *Psalm 148*, SATB, wind ens, perc, org (1984, Biblical), *The Vision and the Gap*, S, A, T, Bar soli, SATB, orch (1984), *The Ballad of Charlie Blow*, SAB, SSA, orc (1988, Jenny Dawson), *The Ballad of Sydney Hospital*, Mez, Bar soli, SATB, orch (1988, Sydney: Sydney Hospitallers, c.1988), *A Special Inheritance*, S, Mez soli, SSA, SA, unison ch, verse-speaking ch, orch (1990), *Gaudeamus*, SATB, orch (1992, trad), *Song of Mary*, SSA, str orch (1995, Biblical).

Musico-Dramatic (texts by Thomas Shapcott) *Gilgamesh*, speaker, SATB, brass, perc (1967), *Five Days Lost*, speaker, orch (1969), *Those who are Compelled*, 2 Bar, 3 speakers, orch, tape (1979).

Sacred Choral *The Cloths of Heaven*, SSA, pf (1958, London: Boosey, [1961]), *Christus resurgens*, SATB (1961), *I Will Lift Up Mine Eyes*, SATB (1961, Sydney: Classical Publications, 1992), *Magnificat and Nunc Dimittis*, unison, org (1961), *Jesu, Who Dost in Mary Dwell*, SATB (1962), *Three Kings in Great Glory*, SATB, optional echo ch (1964), *Ave Maria*, SATB (1965), *Dormi Jesu*, SATB (1965, London: Galliard, [1965]), *How Joyful 'Tis to Sing* (1967), *Tantum Ergo*, SATB (1967), *O Clap Your Hands*, ATB (1968), *Responses*, SATB (1968), *The Virgin and the Child*, SATB

(1968, Sydney: Albert, 1970), *Carol of the Holy Innocents*, SATB (1969), *Richard de Castre's Prayer to Jesus*, SATB, T solo (1969, Sydney: Albert, 1976), *A Virgin Most Pure*, SATB, optional solos (1969, Sydney: Albert, 1970), *Mass*, unison, org (1973, New York: Walton, 1975), *God Be In My Head* [i], SA, org (1973, Carol Stream, Ill: Hope, 1974), *The Carol Book*, SATB, pf: 'Lully, Lullay', 'In Excelsis Gloria', 'Behold a Silly Tender Babe', 'Nowell, Nowell', 'Adam Lay Ybounden', 'Jesu, Son Most Sweet and Dear', 'Lord When the Wise Men' (1975, Dayton, Ohio: Walton, 1977), *Te Deum*, unison, org, optional brass (1975, New York: Walton, 1976), *O sacrum convivium: Motet and Mass*, SATB, pf (1978), *Music for Christmas*, unison, pf (1980), *Virgin's Cradle Song*, SATB (1981), *Oh, Come and Worship*, SATB, org (1982, Minneapolis: Augsburg Fortress, 1990), *Close Thine Eyes*, SATB, pf (1983), *Nine Sacred Canons*, 2vv, org: 'Drop, Drop, Slow Tears', 'He that is Down', 'Who Would True Valour See', 'Litany to the Holy Spirit', 'Lord, We Give Thanks', 'From All That Dwell', 'Bless Us, Lord', 'My Soul, There is a Country', 'God Be In My Head' [ii] (1983), *O Praise the Lord*, SATB, org (1983, Minneapolis: Augsburg Fortress, 1991), *Three Lenten Motets*, SATB: 'Crucifige eum!', 'Priusquam gallus cantet', 'Tu es Christus' (1983), *Eight Anthems*, SATB: 'Jerusalem', 'Lift Up Your Voices', 'The Love of Christ', 'Litany to the Holy Spirit', 'The Greatness of the Lord', 'My Soul, There is a Country', 'This is the Truth', 'Let Christians Rejoice' (1984), *Christmas Bells*, unison, pf: 'Australian Christmas Bells', 'The Christmas Child', 'The Christmas Flower' (1984, Cambridge: Cambridge UP, 1987), *Missa Canonica*, 2 v, org (1985, Dayton, Ohio: Roger Dean, 1991), *Psalm 33*, SATB (1985), *A Service of Rounds*, 3 equal or mixed vv (1985, New York: Walton, 1986), *Three Anthems to Psalm Texts*, SATB, org (1985), *Ecumenical Mass*, unison, kbd (1986), *Six Australian Christmas Carols*, SATB, kbd: [1] 'Carol of the Flowers', [2] 'The Joy of the World', [3] 'Overhead the Stars are Shining', [4] 'Carol of the Birds', [5] ''Neath Southern Skies', [6] 'The White of Sand' ([1], [4]-[6] pub. as *Four Australian Christmas Carols*, Melbourne: Allans, 1986), *A Mass for Our Time*, unison, org (1986), *A Mass for Peace*, unison, org (1986), *Mater ora filium* [i], SATB, optional solos (1986), *Of a Rose, A Lovely Rose*, SATB, optional solos (1986, Ft Lauderdale, Fla.: Walton, 1994), *Pia Maria*, SSMezTBarB (1986), *Adam Lay Y-Bounden*, SATB (1987), *Magnificat and Nunc Dimittis*, SSA, org (1987), *Te Deum*, SSATTB, org (1988), *Mass of St Peter*, SATB, org (1989), *Choral Settings of the Psalms*, SATB, org (Minneapolis: Augsburg Fortress, 1991), *God Be In My Head* [iii], SATB (1991), *Jesu, Son Most Sweet and Dear* (Ft Lauderdale, Fla.: Walton, 1991), *Litany of Praise to Our God*, SATB, org, optional brass, timpani (1991), *Of One that is so Fair and Bright*, SSA (1991), *In Praise of the Virgin*, SATB (Sydney: Classical Publications, 1992), *Lully, Lullay*, SSA (1992), *Mater ora filium* [ii], SATB (1992), *My Soul, There is a Country*, SSA (1992), *Two Latin Motets*, unison, kbd (1992), *God Be In My Head* [iv], 2-part mixed ch, kbd (Minneapolis: Augsburg Fortress, 1993), *How Great the Tale*, SATB, org (1993), *Irish Prayer*, SATB, org (1993), *Lorica of Saint Patrick*, SATB, org (1993), *Mater ora filium* [iii], SATB, org (1993), *A Peal of Carols*, SATB (Minneapolis: Augsburg Fortress, 1993), *Two Carols*, SATB: 'A Virgin Most Pure', 'From All Creatures' (Minneapolis: Augsburg Fortress, 1993), *Advent Carol*, SATB (1994), *Christ Be With Me*, SATB (1994), *God Be In My Head* [v], equal or mixed ch (Min-

neapolis: Augsburg Fortress, 1994), *Let Us Now Praise Famous Men*, SATB, org (1994), *Litany of the Passion*, cantor, congregation, kbd, optional ch (1994), *The Lord My Pasture: Psalm 23* (1994), *Love, Joy, and Peace*, SATB, kbd (1994), *Mater ora filium* [iv], SATB, optional descant, org (1994), *O Christ, Our Light*, SATB, org (Minneapolis: Augsburg Fortress, 1994), *Oh Your Heart is My Heart*, unison, kbd (1994), *Rejoice, Give Praise*, SATB, kbd (1994), *The Tree of Peace*, SATB, kbd (1994), *Four Sacred Rounds*, mixed or equal vv (1994), *Blessed is He*, SATB, org (1995), *Glory to God*, SATB, org (1995), *Great and Mighty Wonder*, SATB (1995), *Holy, Holy, Holy*, SATB, kbd (1995), *Lamb of God*, SATB, kbd (1995), *Lord, Have Mercy*, SATB, kbd (1995), *Those Who Go Down to the Sea in Ships*, unison, kbd (1995), *When Israel Went Out of Egypt*, SATB (1995), *Iustorum animae*, SATB (1996), *Oculus non vidit*, SATB (1996).

Secular Choral *Bonnie George Campbell*, SA, pf (1958, Melbourne: Allans, 1959), *Five Partsongs for Male Voices*, TTBB: 'How Sleep the Brave', 'It's No Go the Merry-go-Round', 'Once I Loved a Maiden Fair', 'Roman Walls Blues', 'Will There Never Come a Season?' (1961), *Songs and Signs I–II*, songs for infants, pf (1961, Sydney: Albert, 1969), *Songs of Sleep*, SATB (1963), *Andy's Gone with the Cattle*, trad, arr. SATB or SA (1965, Melbourne: Allans, 1966), *Four Rounds*, vv (1965), *We Reach Among Bells*, SATB (1968), *The Wind is Rising: Twelve Bagatelles*, SATB, pf (1970, Sydney: Albert, 1970), *I tarocchi*, SATB, pf 6 hands, perc (1975), *The Round Book* [25 rounds] (1975, Dayton, Ohio: Walton, 1977), *Five English Lyrics*, SATB, pf: 'Balow', 'Tune thy Music', 'The Nut-Brown Maid', 'O My Deir Heart', 'Love is Soft' (New York: Walton, 1975), *The Partsong Book*, SATB, pf: 'How Sleep the Brave', 'Come Away, Come Away, Death', 'The Daffodils', 'Peace' (1978), *Wallaby and the Bull-Ant*, children's vv, pf (1980), *Amarilli*, SATB (New Berlin, USA: Jenson, 1981), *Carmen*, SATB (1981), *Fugues are Fun*, SAB (1981), *Gold: A Canon for 4 Voices*, SATB (1981), *A Receipt for Salad*, SAB (1981), *Signs of Rain*, SATB (1981), *Flexi Scores*, SATB, optional descants, accompaniments, perc (1983), *Four Romantic Choruses*, SATB: 'If There were Dreams to Sell', 'Strew on Her Roses', 'Softly, O Midnight Hours', 'So We'll Go No More A'Roving' (1983, Ft Lauderdale, Fla.: Aberdeen, 1983), *Songs of the Sea*, solo v, unison, or 2 part: 'The Sailor's Consolation', 'Ships of Old Renown', 'Sea Fever', 'To Sea! To Sea!', 'A Song of Desire', 'A Wet Sheet and a Flowing Sea', 'Two Chronometers', 'His Heart was True to Poll', 'El Captain-General', 'The Walloping Window Blind', 'The Hag', 'Sea Foam', 'A Grey Day', 'Lost and Given Over', 'Break, Break, Break!', 'The Port o' Heart's Desire' (Melbourne: Allans, 1983), *Folk Songs of Australia* [13 Folk Songs], arr. SAB, kbd (Melbourne: Allans, 1984), *Fourteen Partsongs*, SSA (1986), *Fife Tune*, SA, fl or fifes, side drum (in *A Collection of Contemporary Australian Compositions*, Toowoomba: ASME Queensland Chapter, 1989), *Carol of the Stars*, SATB (1991), *The Springtime it Brings on the Shearing*, trad, arr for SATB or SSATTB (Perth: Matilda, 1991), *Canon 4:2* (in *Sound and Reason*, Brisbane: Dept of Music, Univ. Queensland, 1992, pp. 120–21), *Dream Pedlary: If There were Dreams to Sell*, SATB (1993), *I Made Another Garden*, SATB (1993), *Three Shakespearian Songs*, SSA (1993), *Unwelcome*, SATB (1993), *When I am Dead, My Dearest*, SATB (1993), *Carol of the Star*, SATB, kbd (1994), *Christmas Bells*, SATB (1994), *Hymn to St. Catherine of*

Siena, unison, kbd (1994), *Not as the Song of Other Lands*, unison, kbd (1995), *My Shadow*, 2-part ch, pf (1996).

Songs with Instruments or Orchestra *Three Pastorals*, medium v, fl, hp: 'All Day I Have Slept at the River', 'I Hear the Wild Sounds at Night', 'Upon the Tired Road' (1961), *Three Italian Songs for High Voice and String Quartet*: 'S'i' fosse foco', 'Orfano', 'Di Maggio' (1964, Sydney: Albert 1971), *Bess Songs*, sop, fl, gui, prepared tape (1973), *Mobiles*, S, Bar, fl, hn, tpt, perc, org (before 1983), *Three Songs*, Bar, gui: 'Arabia', 'Tom-a-Bedlam's Song', 'The Music Makers' (1983), *Canti Pisani*, 8 trad Italian texts, med v, orch (1989).

Songs with Piano *Nel mio orto* (1958, London: Ricordi, 1964), *The Knight of the Holy Grail* (1961), *Ein Traum ist unser Leben* (1966), *Amarilli* (1967), *Easter Carol*, monologue with sung refrains (1967), *I did not Know*, arr. (1967), *The English Songs*: 'Goe, and Catche a Falling Starre', 'Threnos', 'The Lark Now Leaves His Wat'ry Nest', 'Come, Come What Doe I Here?', 'The Souldier Going to the Field' (1975), [6] *Songs from the House at Pooh Corner* (1976), *Three Italian Songs*: 'Fresca rosa novella', 'Quel rosignuol', 'Di giugno' (1979), *Mare* (1980), *Three Songs from a Spanish Madrigal*: 'Tell the Rider that's Coming', 'Where Did He Come From?', 'Don't Complain of the Girl, Stranger' (1980), *Twelve Vocalises* (1980), *Pater's Bathe Song* (1981), *Heinz von Stein* (1982), *Jock O'Dreams* (1982), *Liebesliederbüchlein*: 'Wie schon blut uns', 'Eine dunkle Wolk', 'Ich gib mich' (1982), *Music, When Soft Voices Die* (1982), *Chanson de Berberine* (1984), *A Poor Young Shepherd* (1984), *Said Hanrahan* (spoken v, pf, 1989), *Golden Girl in the Golden Sunlight* (from *Summer Carol*, 1990), *The Trenchant Troubadour*, song cycle (1991), *To Fancy* (1994), *Unwelcome* (1994).

Film Scores *Library Music* (1968), *Follow the Leader* (1977), *The Capital Canberra* (1980).

FURTHER REFERENCE

His writings include *The Art of Prolonging the Musical Tone* (Brisbane, UQP, [1968]); 'Touring in the Outback', *Opera News* 34/11 (10 Jan. 1970), 13; 'Music', in *Australia: A Survey*, Schriften des Instituts für Asienkunde in Hamburg 27 (Frankfurt am Main: Metznen, 1970), 557–71; 'Conference', *Musical Times* 114 (Jan 1973): 63–4.

More than 100 works have been recorded, the earliest, the Suite for Chamber Orchestra (1954, Pictorial MA 029), made when the composer was 21. On CD, the principal publisher is Jade, with Brumby included on 11 CDs, notably the Symphony No. 1, five of the concerti, and the *Three Songs from a Spanish Madrigal* with the composer (pf) and Jenny Dawson (S). Other labels include ABC, Grevillea and MBS. A list of recordings to 1972 is in *PlushD*.

See also Jenni Allen, Aspects of Australians Composing Music Drama for Children with Reference to the Works of Colin Brumby and Judith Clingan, BMus, Univ. Melbourne, 1993; *BrisbaneE*; *CallawayA*; *CA*; *ContemporaryC*; *GroveD*; *GroveO*; Ross F. Jutsum, An Examination of Musical-Textual Relationships in the Choral Music of Colin Brumby, DMA, Univ. North Texas, USA, 1995; *McCredieM*; *MonashB*; *MurdochA*; Wendy Penny, Developing Variation in Selected Works by Colin Brumby: An Analytical Study, BA(Hons), Univ. Queensland, 1977; Philippa Roylance, A Discussion of Two Major Choral Works by Colin Brumby Based

on Texts by Thomas Shapcott, MMus(Qual), Univ. Queensland, 1981; Sook Leng Tee, Formative Factors in Colin Brumby's Musical Style, With Special Reference to the *Stabat Mater Speciosa*, BMus(Hons), Univ. Queensland, 1974; Kerry Vann, A History of the Queensland Opera Company 1968–1980, BMus, Univ. Queensland, 1984; John Villaume, 'Building an Audience for Opera: A Queensland Experiment', *AJME* 4 (April 1969), 5–6; Brisbane, *Courier-Mail*, 1 Apr. 1993.

ROYSTON GUSTAVSON

Buchanan, Colin (*b* Dublin, 1964), country music singer-songwriter, broadcaster. His family arrived in Australia when he was six. After working as a teacher and as a rural labourer at Bourke, NSW, his song 'Galahs in the Gidgee' won the ACMA Best New Talent Award in 1992. Currently a radio broadcaster on the Sydney country and roots station Kick-AM, he also appears on ABC TV's *Playschool*. A traditional bush balladist who aims to capture the experience of ordinary rural lives, he has recorded four albums.

FURTHER REFERENCE

Recordings include *Galahs in the Gidgee* (1991, EMI 4796212) and *The Measure of A Man* (1994, EMI 477531).

Buck, Vera (*b* Melbourne, *c*.1908), pianist, composer. After studies with Frederick Mewton she won the Claude Kingston and Fritz Hart Scholarships at the Albert Street Conservatorium and went to London in 1930. There she coached many stars of musical comedy and film, including Jessie Matthews, Robert Naylor and Florence Desmond, and 15 of her songs were published, including *Serenity*, *To My Lady* (sung by Kenneth Ellis at Wigmore Hall), and *This Is My Prayer* for the London Choral Society. Peter *Dawson sang her *Reminiscence* (A.V. Broadhurst, 1936) on the BBC, and Florence *Austral sang her *The Birds* (1932) and *The Shepherdess*. In 1937 she was director of Memphis Recording Studios, London, and in 1938 she returned to Australia, becoming resident pianist with 3AW. She gave many concerts during the war years. A composer of expressive melodies with restrained, straightforward accompaniments, her *Full Sail* is in *Selected Songs by Australian Composers* vol. 2 (Melbourne: Allans Publishing, 1987) and *Marche Orientale* (Allans) is still in print.

FURTHER REFERENCE

SnellA gives a partial list of works. Recordings include *Until the Day I Die* (Columbia DO2947), *The Donkey* (Columbia DO2820), and her own playing of *To My Lady* (Columbia DO3006). Portrait in *Musical Opinion* 61/723 (Dec. 1937), 243. See also *AMN* 18/6 (Jan. 1929), 25; *AMN* 28/8 (Mar. 1938), 22; for various other references to her in *AMN*, 1925–45, see *MarsiI*.

Buckley, Barry (*b* Melbourne, 10 Sept. 1938), jazz bass player. He began playing bass in his teens and joined a trio with Dave Martin at Melbourne in 1955. He was with Brian *Brown (1956–60), Ted Vining's television band, and briefly with Keith Hounslow. After a period in the USA, he returned to Melbourne and studied dentistry 1961–62, freelancing extensively in the progressive movement, resuming and developing his associations with Brown (including at Fat Black Pussycat, mid-60s), and Vining from 1976. He toured Scandinavia with Brown, then withdrew briefly from music before joining the group Odwala, Bob Sedergreen's Blues on the Boil (1985), and more work with Vining.

FURTHER REFERENCE

Recordings include *Brian Brown Quintet* (1958, 44 Records 44 6357 715); *Ted Vining Trio* (1972, Jazznote JNLP-006/S); *Ted Vining Trio* (1977, 44 Records 44 6357 712); *Upward*, The Brian Brown Quartet (1977, 44 Records 44 6357 711); *The Ted Vining Trio, Live at PBS-FM* (1981, Jazznote JNLP 029); *The Planets*, Brian Brown (1985, Larrikin LRJ 151). See also *ClareB*; *BissetB*; *OxfordJ*; Adrian Jackson, 'Barry Buckley,' *JA* (July/August 1983), 10.   BRUCE JOHNSON

Buddle, Errol (*b* Adelaide, 29 Apr. 1928), jazz reed-player, flute player, leader. He began on the banjo and mandolin, changing to saxophone at the age of eight, with his first public performance within a year. In his teens he was working in dance bands. His growing interest in jazz was stimulated by Bob *Limb, and he began tenor saxophone in 1946 (later adding clarinet, oboe, bassoon and flute). With Jack *Brokensha in Melbourne in 1947, he became active in the early bop movement. He moved to Sydney in 1950, playing nightclub and dance work, then to North America in 1952, playing bassoon in the Ontario Symphony Orch, and working in Detroit jazz venues. With other Australians he invited to join him in the USA, he was a founder member of the Australian Jazz Quartet, and stayed until it disbanded in 1959. In Sydney he was primarily active in session work until joining Col *Nolan in 1972, which led to a resumption of wide-ranging jazz activity in clubs, tours, recording sessions, concerts, with his own and others' groups. He performed in Russia, London and the USA, with the Daly Wilson Big Band in 1975, participated in John Sangster's *Lord of the Rings* project, and was a multi-instrumentalist on the over-dubbed *Buddles Doubles* album. In the USA in 1978–79 on an Australia Council grant, he also toured South East Asia with his own group in 1982. He was based in Adelaide, 1985–94, working in various-sized groups and leading a quartet, as well as performing in the Australian Jazz Quintet reunion concerts of 1986 and 1993. Buddle was a pioneer of double reed instruments in jazz, and a virtuoso who was a frequent poll-winner in the postwar progressive movement. He is currently re-settled in Sydney, freelancing and leading.

FURTHER REFERENCE

Recordings include *Jack Brokensha Quartet* (1948, Jazzart JA 3/4); *Australian Jazz Quartet* (1958, Bethlehem BCP-6029); *The Nolan-*

Buddle Quartet (1975, M7 Records MLF-100); *Lord of the Rings vol. 1* John Sangster (1974, EMI EMC.2525/6), *vol. 2* (1976, EMI EMC 2548/9), *vol. 3* (1977, EMI EMC 2580/1); *Buddles Doubles*, Errol Buddle (1977, M7 Records MLF 216); *The Daly Wilson Big Band* (1979, Hammard MAM-027). See also *ClareB*; *BissetB*; *OxfordJ*; Eric Myers, 'Errol Buddle, A New Era', *JA* (August 1982), 4–8; idem., 'Errol Buddle, Some earlier eras', *JA* (Oct. 1982), 20–3; idem, 'Errol Buddle and the AJQ', *JA* (Jan./Feb. 1983), 22–26.

BRUCE JOHNSON

Buesst. Two brothers in the third generation of a family of musicians at Melbourne.

(1) Aylmer Wilhelny Buesst (*b* Melbourne, 28 Jan. 1883; *d* St Albans, London, 25 Jan. 1970), conductor. He studied violin with César Thomson in Brussels and in Leipzig under Nikisch. Coming to England he was conductor with the Moody-Manners Opera Company 1914–16, the Beecham Opera Company 1918–20, the British National Opera Company 1922–28, the Carl Rosa Opera Company 1928–30 and the Old Vic and Sadler's Wells Company 1930–33. He was assistant music director of the British Broadcasting Corporation 1933–36, conductor of the Scottish Orchestra 1939–40 and professor of conducting at the Guildhall School of Music 1946. In 1923 he conducted *Hänsel und Gretel*, the first opera to be broadcast from a theatre in Europe, in 1928 recorded a complete *Cavalleria rusticana*, and also wrote *Richard Wagner, The Nibelungen Ring: An Act By Act Guide* (1932, rev. 1952).

(2) Victor Augustine Buesst (*b* Melbourne, 20 Oct. 1885; *d* Woburn Sands, Buckinghamshire, England, 13 Mar. 1960), pianist, conductor. After lessons with his grandmother and mother from the age of five, he was taken to Europe for studies with A. de Greef at Brussels, then R. Teichmüller at Leipzig, and Busoni and his assistant Egon Petri. He made his debut at London in 1908 at Bechstein Hall, giving the London premiere of Ravel's *Tombeau de Couperin*. He returned to Australia as accompanist for Amy Castles' tour (1909–10), then toured France and Belgium with the singer Renée de Landriene. He married a wealthy Belgian, Antonia de Wouters, in 1913, but on the outbreak of war sought refuge in England. He served in Egypt during the war, afterwards focusing on conducting and composition. His works included chamber music, a triple piano concerto, a quintet and a number of songs, broadcast in London.

FURTHER REFERENCE

Obit. for Aylmer Buesst in *The Times* (London) 27 Jan. 1970. Recordings for Aylmer Buesst include *Cavalleria Rusticana*, British National Opera (1928, Columbia). See also *Who's Who* (London), 1937–69; 12 references in *AMN*, for an index see *MarsiI*. For Victor Buesst see Lyle Wilson, *A Dictionary of Pianists* (London: Robert Gale, 1985); *AMN*, 7 (June 1918), 323–4; Melbourne *Punch* 29 Apr. 1920.

§1 J.L. HOLMES; §2 editor

Buffalo.   Rock band (1970–77) formed in Sydney, the principal members of which were Dave Tice (vocals), John Baxter (guitar), Peter Wells (bass, slide guitar), and Jimmy Economou (drums). They developed a sizeable following in Sydney among heavy rock fans, but their recordings at first sold slowly. Eventually they became as popular abroad (especially in France) as in Australia. Influenced by Black Sabbath and Deep Purple, their sound was notable for Tice's strong vocals and Wells's slide guitar.

FURTHER REFERENCE
Recordings include singles *Suzie Sunshine* (1972, Philips 6037011) and *What's Going On* (1974, Philips 6037041), and the albums *Dead Forever* (1972, Vertigo 6357007) and *Mother's Choice* (1976, Vertigo 6357103). There is a compilation, *Best Of Buffalo* (1980, Vertigo 6479325). For discography, see *SpencerA*. See also *SpencerW*; *GuinnessP*, I, 361.

Buggy, Brian   (*b* Brisbane, 8 Oct. 1939), conductor. After studying violin with Basil Jones at the Queensland Conservatorium, he was principal trumpet with the Borovansky Ballet in 1959, then conductor of musicals for J.C. Williamson from 1960, touring Australia, NZ and South Africa. Since 1975 he has been director of music at Knox Grammar School, Sydney, founding the Knox Abbotsleigh Youth Orchestra while conducting and presenting school and family concerts with the ABC orchestras in most states, as well as appearing with the Christchurch and New Zealand Symphony Orchestras. He has written film music for Film Australia (1968) and published a Trio for brass (Alberts, 1968), an *Adagio* (Alberts, 1969) for violin and piano and a String Trio (Alberts, 1970).

Bukovsky, Miroslav   (*b* Czechoslovakia, 5 Dec. 1944), jazz trumpeter. He began piano at the age of seven, then trumpet at 12. Playing in dance and jazz bands, he studied at the Prague Conservatorium, then moved to Sydney in 1968, becoming active in rhythm and blues and jazz groups, notably Bob Bertles' Moontrane. He studied and later taught at the NSW Conservatorium, playing with Renée Geyer, Marcia Hines and the Daly Wilson Big Band. From 1980, he moved increasingly into contemporary developments with Dale Barlow, Roger Frampton and others, and studied in the USA with Woody Shaw and Randy Brecker. He currently performs, composes and tours with ★Ten Part Invention and (since 1991) with his own band Wanderlust, with which he has won an ARIA award.

FURTHER REFERENCE
Recordings include *Moontrane*, Bob Bertles (1979, Batjazz BAT-2070); *Ten Part Invention* (1987, ABC Records, 846 729–2); *Tall Stories*, Ten Part Invention (1994, Rufus/Polygram RF 006); *Wanderlust* (1993, ABC/Polygram, 518 650–2); *Border Crossing*, Wanderlust (1995, Rufus/Polygram RF018). See also *ClareB*; *OxfordJ*.
                                                                       BRUCE JOHNSON

Bulch, T.E.   (*b* Ballarat, Vic., *fl.* 1900), band music composer. He wrote waltzes and marches, such as the *Bathurst March*, *Newcastle March*, *Florina Valse*, *Pile Arms March*, *Postman's Parade*, *Typhoon March*, *Visions of Love Waltz*, and songs such as *Home Visions* (1904).

FURTHER REFERENCE
A list of his works is in *SnellA*.

Bull, Geoff (Geoffrey Randolph)   (*b* Sydney, 26 May 1942), jazz trumpeter, leader. He began playing trumpet in 1959 and attended Sydney Jazz Club workshops. He was with the ★Melbourne New Orleans Jazz Band, 1961, then returned to Sydney and formed the Olympia Jazz Band in 1962. Making the first of many visits to New Orleans in 1966–67, he played and recorded, and in Sydney he has led groups at various residencies, notably the Captain Cook, the Cat and Fiddle and the Unity Hall Hotels. He ran a Creole restaurant, 1984–85, and organised tours by US musicians Alton Purnell and Sam Price. Bull has been central to Sydney's New Orleans jazz movement.

FURTHER REFERENCE
Recordings include *Geoff Bull's Olympia Jazz Band* (1969, Swaggie S-1261). See also *OxfordJ*; Eric Myers, 'An interview with Geoff Bull', *JA* (Dec. 1981), 18–21.
                                                                       BRUCE JOHNSON

Bullamakanka.   Bush band (1978–) formed at the Gold Coast, Queensland, currently comprised of Mal Clarke (vocals, bass guitar), Dave 'The Bloke' Ovenden (mandolin, harmonica, drums, vocals), Russell Hinton (electric guitar, vocals), Stuart Watson (fiddle), and Terry Gascoigne (drums). Formed as a trio, by 1981 the band had expanded and had a national following; they played at Fort Worth, Texas, in 1983, where they were honoured by the International Country and Western Association. Original banjo player Rex Radonich was killed in a car accident in 1986, but the band returned to performing in 1988, expanding their appeal into the pop market, and appearing before Elizabeth II at the opening of the Stockman's Hall of Fame in 1995. With a blend of original bluegrass and traditional Australian ballads, they have recorded five albums and won six ACMA Golden Guitars.

FURTHER REFERENCE
Recordings include *Bullamakanka* (1981, Mercury), *Bullas Live* (1985, EMI) and *The Best Of Bullamakanka* (1993, Hughes MWCD 306). See also *LattaA*, 100.

Bull-roarer.   Small piece of carved or notched wood tied to a string, swung in circles, creating a sound of considerable eeriness. In Australia it is sometimes sold as a children's toy, but is chiefly found in certain Aboriginal rituals, where its use and significance is secret.

Bundaberg, pop. (1991) 38074. City on Burnett
River, Queensland, founded 1872, centre of the
national sugar and rum industry. A fertile contributor to
Australian musical life, it is the birthplace of tenor Don-
ald Smith, musicals star Gladys Moncrieff, country
music legend Shirley Thoms, pianist and composer
Betty Beath, folklorist Bill Scott, and the rock band
Xanadu (1967–85). The Carandini Opera troupe visited
in 1876, and many visiting artists appeared at the
Queen's Theatre (opened 1888) until the war years.
Choral life has always been rich, with long-lived choirs
formed by the Musical Union (1882), the Lutheran
Church (1884), the Methodist Church (1898), and the
Liedertafel (1899). The Bundaberg Musical Society was
formed in 1939, presenting *Messiah* and other works,
and at its height won the Queensland Eisteddfod in
1954 and 1958; the Orpheus Singers (founded 1966)
have staged many musicals and oratorios. Bands existed
from earliest days, the Burnett Silver Band winning the
Australian championship in 1935 and merging with
City as the Municipal Band, which became Australian A
Grade champion in 1939 and still functions. The Caledonian Pipe Band (founded 1884) still thrives, and
dance bands travelled the local circuit in the 1930s. The
Musical Union formed an orchestra in 1935, performing Mendelssohn oratorios and such works as Stanford's
The Revenge and MacCunn's *The Wreck of the Hesperus,*
and the Bundaberg Youth Orchestra has existed since
1972. The Bundaberg Eisteddfod was founded in 1905
and continues to serve the district. The annual Bundaberg Country Music Festival has an important talent
quest which attracts talent widely.

FURTHER REFERENCE
Dawn Bates, A History of the Performing and Visual Arts in
Bundaberg 1875–1987. Typescript, Bundaberg & District Histor-
ical and Museum Society, 1987.

Bundjalung. Group of Aboriginal people from the
east coast of Australia and also their traditional language.
The territory of the Bundjalung was between the
Logan River, Queensland, and the Clarence River,
NSW, and extended inland as far as the Great Dividing
Range to Tenterfield, Warwick, Ipswich and Toowoomba. Before European contact probably about 20 closely
related dialects were spoken in the Bundjalung area. The
name Bundjalung referred to the dialect that was originally spoken at Bungawalbin Creek, the south arm of
the Richmond River. Because of European contact,
dialect groups today have amalgamated, bringing a
sense of solidarity; within the last 50 years the term
Bundjalung has replaced most local dialect names.
Today, only one group, the Gidabal of Woodenbong,
maintain their own dialect name.

It was not until the 1950s that Bundjalung songs
began to be recorded and documented; by this time
traditional songs and dances were being performed less

often and remembered by only a handful of older
members of communities. Most recordings were made
by linguists, historians, anthropologists, and projects
conducted by the National Parks and Wildlife Service
in relation to documenting land sites. The earliest
recordings were made by the anthropologist Malcolm
Calley, who in 1955 recorded material at Woodenbong.
During the 1960s John Gordon collected songs from
some older Aboriginal people throughout NSW,
including Bundjalung; and during the 1980s Margaret
Gummow recorded a small number of singers who
could still remember the songs. The most detailed
musicological research has been by Gummow; the linguist Margaret Sharpe is an authority on the Bundjalung language, and has also studied song texts. Today
Bundjalung people are beginning to document and
research their own culture, as they are concerned that
younger people are not learning traditional songs and
culture. One recent project was undertaken by Lorraine Mafi-Williams, who in 1988 produced the film
Eelarmarni, which featured a tribal elder explaining
some of the mythology and performing several songs
from the Mount Warning area of northern NSW.
Other research concerning Aboriginal performances of
NSW has been done by the linguist Tamsin Donaldson
and the anthropologist Jeremy Beckett.

FURTHER REFERENCE
Calley, M.J., Bandjalang Social Organisation, PhD, Univ. Sydney,
1959.
Donaldson, T., 'Kids that got lost: Variation in the words of
Ngiyampaa songs', in *Problems and Solutions: occasional Essays
in Musicology presented to Alice M. Moyle*, ed. J. Kassler and J.
Stubington (Sydney: Hale & Iremonger, 1984), 228–53.
——, 'Making a song (and dance) in South-Eastern Australia', in
Songs of Aboriginal Australia, ed. M. Clunies-Ross, T. Donald-
son and S. Wild, Oceania Monograph 32 (Sydney: Univ.
Sydney, 1987), 14–42.
——, 'Mixes of English and Ancestral Language Words in South-
east Australian Aboriginal songs of Traditional and Intro-
duced Origin', in *The Essence of Singing and the Substance of
Song: Recent Responses to the Aboriginal Performing Arts and other
Essays in Honour of Catherine Ellis*, ed. L. Barwick, A. Marett
and G. Tunstill, Oceania Monograph 46 (Sydney: Univ.
Sydney, 1995), 143–58.
Gordon, J., Transcriptions of Songs (Canberra: AIAS MS 548,
Manuscript, 1968).
Gummow, M.J., Aboriginal Songs from the Bundjalung and Gid-
abul Areas of South-Eastern Australia, PhD, Univ. Sydney,
1992.
——, 'The Power of the Past in the Present: Singers and Songs
From Northern New South Wales', *The World of Music: Jour-
nal of the International Institute for Traditional Music* 36 (1994),
42–50.
——, 'Songs and Sites/Moving Mountains: A Study of One Song
From Northern NSW', in *The Essence of Singing and the Sub-
stance of Song: Recent Responses to the Aboriginal Performing Arts*

and other Essays in Honour of Catherine Ellis, ed. L. Barwick, A. Marett and G. Tunstill, Oceania Monograph 46 (Sydney: Univ. Sydney, 1995), 121–31.

Sharpe, M.C. et al., *An Introduction to the Bundjalong Language and its Dialects* (Armidale: College of Advanced Education, 1985).
MARGARET GUMMOW

Bunggurl. Public singing and dancing in north-central and north-east Arnhem Land. See *Corroboree*.

Burarra. Aboriginal language spoken in north-central Arnhem Land on both sides of the Blyth River between Maningrida and Ramingining. Although linguistically it belongs to the western Arnhem Land languages, its speakers are more oriented ceremonially and musically to eastern Arnhem Land. Clan songs exist as *manikay* as in eastern Arnhem Land, and although songs of this area exhibit some distinctive features they are more like songs in eastern Arnhem Land than western. A number of *manikay* are sung and owned by Burarra speakers, perhaps the best known being Djambidj and Goyulan. Each *manikay* consists of a number of song subjects (e.g. 21 Djambidj subjects, about 30 Goyulan subjects), each one representing a totemic Ancestor or *wangarr*. Some Djambidj subjects are White Cockatoo, Porpoise, and Yam, while Goyulan subjects include Ibis, Sawfish, and Sugar Glider. Burarra *manikay* are performed by at least one singer (there may be two or three) who accompanies himself with clapsticks, and a didjeridu accompanist. As he performs, the singer selects from a repertoire of musical and textual phrases appropriate to the subject for each sung item. An item, lasting up to about a minute, usually consists of a sung introduction of burden syllables or one or two phrases from the subject and accompanied by clapsticks, the main part of the verse accompanied by clapsticks and didjeridu, and an optional unaccompanied vocal coda which is non-metrical. Contexts of performance of Burarra *manikay* are primarily initiation ceremonies, mortuary ceremonies, and purely entertainment. See also *Aboriginal Music* §3(iii).   STEPHEN WILD

Burdett, Louis Charles [Lucien Boiteux] (*b* Adelaide, 8 June 1953), experimental jazz composer-performer. He began studying and playing percussion while serving in the navy 1968–72, and later taught himself flute, saxophone, trumpet, cello and violin. Attracted to jazz as well as other styles, he worked with Serge *Ermoll's Free Kata in the late 1970s, and although based in Sydney has also worked in the Melbourne funk band Young At Heart with Doug *Williams. Active in free improvisation with Jon Rose, he plays occasional festivals and concerts, but now performs rarely, concentrating on composing electronic music.

FURTHER REFERENCE
Recordings include *Cul Cullen* (1974, Earth ELF-003); *Existence is Proof*, Lucien Boiteux (n.d., Fringe Benefit Records 20); *Serge*

Ermoll's Free Kata (1976, KATA 002); *Side of Clues*, Nude (1994, Newmarket NEW 1054.2)
BRUCE JOHNSON

Burnard, (David) Alexander (*b* Adelaide, 1900), composer, teacher. After studies in piano at the Elder Conservatorium he went to London in 1923 and studied piano with Herbert Freyer and orchestration with Vaughan Williams at the Royal College of Music. Returning to Australia, he taught composition at the University of Adelaide, was music critic for the Adelaide *Advertiser* 1930–34, and obtained a DMus (University of Adelaide, 1932). From 1935 he taught harmony and composition at the NSW State Conservatorium for more than 30 years. As a composer he first followed modal and folk-song paths akin to those of Vaughan Williams, and later those of the English school of Grainger's generation. His works included three string quartets, over 50 songs, and eight works for chorus, soloists and orchestra, such as his doctoral work *L'Allegro* (1931, Milton), performed in 1937 by the ABC Orchestras and by the BBC Symphony under Adrian Boult.

FURTHER REFERENCE
Archival ABC recordings include *Puck*, G. Watson, pf (ABC RRC 70); *The Answer*, R. Keene, S. H. Penn, pf (ABC O-N40525); and Songs, W. Coombes, Bar, H. Penn, pf (ABC PRX 5615). A list of compositions is in 'Australian Musicians: Alex Burnard', *The Canon* 11/8 (Mar.–Apr. 1958), 283–4. See also *GlennonA*, 149.

Burnie, pop. (1991) 18 479. City on Tasmania's north-west coast, settled 1827. Attractively set on the shores of Emu Bay against rich farmlands, its seaport is the conduit for the city's paper industry, farm produce of the region, and Tasmania's western mining centres. The town has a surprisingly vigorous musical life for its size. The City of Burnie Brass Band was founded in the 1890s, and the Burnie Highland Pipe Band has a long history. A Burnie Glee Club was formed in the 1950s, developing into the Burnie Musical Society which mounts annual productions, and the Burnie City Eisteddfod (founded 1967) is held each May–June. A Civic Centre was opened in 1976, housing the 1100-seat Town Hall and 400-seat Civic Theatre, home to concerts by the City of Burnie Orchestra. There is an annual Burnie Festival and various youth music activities, including a youth choir and a summer string camp. The North West Jazz Action Society and North West Country Music Club are also based at Burnie.

Burns, Ronnie (Ronald Leslie) (*b* Melbourne, 8 Sept. 1946), popular music singer. Burns showed an early interest in singing, joining his first band at the age of 14, and began his career in 1962 as a folk-singer, performing in coffee lounges in Melbourne. In 1963 he joined the Flies, the first Australian group to perform in the style of the Beatles, who were highly successful, performing with overseas acts such as the Rolling Stones and Roy Orbison. In September 1965 he left the Flies to pursue a solo career, and achieved popularity with a series of singles that included *Coalman* and *Exit Stage Right*. He was voted most popular male vocalist in the 1967 *Go-Set* pop poll, and was featured in an ABC documentary called *The Life of Ronnie Burns*. After the release of *Age of Consent*, his theme from the movie of the same name, he reached the peak of his career with *Smiley*, an anti-Vietnam song which sold over 100 000 copies, earning him a gold record in 1970. He ceased work as a recording artist in the early 1970s, but continued to perform in clubs and made many appearances on television as a performer, adjudicator or compère. In 1980, disillusioned with club performing, he set up an interior design company; he worked as a co-host on Network Ten's *Healthy Wealthy and Wise*, and wrote a book about interior design. He has recently returned to club performing, and is presently singing in a trio with Darryl Cotton and Russell Morris.

FURTHER REFERENCE

The Very Last Day (1966, Spin EK-1346); *Coalman* (1967, Spin EK-1578); *Exit Stage Right* (1967, Spin EK-1789); *Age of Consent* (1968, Spin EK-2627); *Smiley* (1969, Spin EK-3380). A discography is in *SpencerA*. See also *McGrathA*; *SpencerW*; Peter Wilmoth, *Glad All Over: The Countdown Years 1974–1987* (Melbourne: McPhee Gribble, 1993).

NATASHA LANGFORD

Burrows, Don (Donald Vernon)   (*b* Sydney, 8 Aug. 1928), jazz reeds and flute player. He learned flute with Victor McMahon, later adding reeds, and becoming captain of the Metropolitan Schools Flute Band, at the age of 12. Wartime provided his early professional opportunities, including five years with the ABC Dance Band in his teens; he was also with Wally Norman and Bob Gibson. In 1950 he won his first *Music Maker* poll, and travelled abroad, returning to Sydney in 1951 and appearing at the Celebrity Club. In the mid-1950s he began his celebrated association with guitarist George Golla, which lasted 40 years. His range of activities broadened to include orchestral settings and leading groups, notably at *El Rocco and with the Australian All Stars at the Sky Lounge. He became nationally known through appearances on Eric Jupp's *Magic of Music* TV program, toured with Oscar Peterson, and helped to initiate the Cell Block concerts (combining his quartet with the *New Sydney Woodwind Quartet).

A lengthy Wentworth Supper Club residency from 1968 with Ed Gaston, Golla, and others consolidated his status as the public embodiment of Australian jazz. He has toured for the ABC, Musica Viva, and the Department of Foreign Affairs, through Australia, the USA, Europe, South East Asia, NZ, India, South America, and the Middle East. He has accompanied Stéphane Grappelli, Dizzy Gillespie, Lee Konitz and others. For six years he presented his own television series, *The Burrows Collection*,

and through the 1980s his main performance base was the supper club named in his honour at the Regent Hotel. He inaugurated the jazz studies program at the NSW Conservatorium in 1973 and was its director from 1980. In 1988 he produced and narrated a multi-media jazz retrospective at the Sydney Opera House.

Burrows' prolific output includes recordings that have won gold records; his jazz course provided a model for other Australian music schools, and has been largely responsible for the new wave of jazz musicians emerging through the 1980s. His contribution to Australian music has been recognised in numerous awards, the MBE (1972), a Creative Arts Fellowship at the Australian National University (1977), the Queen Elizabeth Silver Jubilee Medal (1977), and the AO (1986). Since retiring from the Conservatorium, he has resumed a more active public role, presenting school programs with the support of an Australian artist's creative fellowship (1994) and photography exhibitions on behalf of the Photographic and Imaging Council of Australia.

FURTHER REFERENCE

Recordings include *Don Burrows, The First Fifty Years, vol. 1 1944–1965* (1993, Polygram/ABC 514 296–2), *vol. 2 1967–1976* (1993, Polygram/ABC 514 297–2), *vol. 3 1977–1979* (1993, Polygram/ABC 514 298–2), *vol. 4 1980–1984* (1993, Polygram/ABC 514 299–2), *vol. 5 1985–1992* (1993, Polygram/ABC 514 300–2). An interview with him is in *WilliamsA*, 58–63. See also *ClareB*; *BissetB*; *CA*; *GroveJ*; *OxfordJ*; Eric Myers, 'Don Burrows, Professor of Jazz', *JA* (March/April 1981), 5–8; Bruce Johnson, 'George Golla and Don Burrows', *Journal of Australian Music and Musicians,* 53 (1982), 5–7; idem, 'Don Burrows, the first fifty years', FM Stereo Radio (August 1993), 8–10.

BRUCE JOHNSON

Burt, Warren Arnold   (*b* Baltimore, USA, 10 Oct. 1949), composer. After studies at State University New York, Albany, and University of California, San Diego, his works such as *Aardvarks II* (1971; published by Lingua Press, Iowa, 1975) for piano attracted the attention of Keith Humble, who appointed him to teach at La Trobe University 1975–78. Since then he has worked freelance, winning Australia Council Fellowships in 1979 and 1991 and several composer residencies in Australia and abroad. His music is freshly inventive, using random processes and environmental sounds, often in humorous ways. Aside from several works for piano or chamber ensemble, his music is chiefly for tape, synthesiser, or computer-processed sound, or for home-made or unique resources, such as *Almond Bread Harmonies* (1985) for 41 treble tuning-forks or *Three Inverse Genres* (1989) for tuning-forks. He designed the installations for the Sensus Technological Playground at Expo 88, Brisbane, and has been a prolific commentator on experimental music through *Cantrill's Filmnotes, New Music Newspaper, New Music, ISCM Journal, Australian Micro* and elsewhere.

FURTHER REFERENCE

Recordings include *Three Inverse Genres* (New Albion) and *Remembering Griffes* for fl and computer (1992, Canberra School of Music, CSM18). He wrote *Writings from a Scarlet Aardvark: 15 Articles on Music and Art*, 1981–93 (USA: Frog Peak Music, 1993). See also *JenkinsT*, 33–40.

Bury, Evelyn (*b* Surrey Hills, Melbourne), country music singer-songwriter. At first a teenage jazz-singer in Melbourne, after her marriage ended she resumed singing at Bundaberg Queensland in 1980, joining the local country band Blue Sky in 1984. She won an ACMA Golden Guitar in 1988 singing her song *I'm Stronger Than I Look* (1987, Selection PRC 060), and now appears regularly in the Hervey Bay area and on televsision. She formed the all-female band Buried Treasure in 1995. Her repertoire includes gospel, ballads and New Country, and a number of her songs focus on women's issues. Her work has helped make the Bundaberg Country Music Club and its Easter Round-Up among the country's most significant in country music.

FURTHER REFERENCE

Recordings include *There's No Place Like Home* (1991, Selection PCD 070) and *We Are One* (1994, Selection PCD 080). See also *LattaA*, 176–8; *Sun-Herald* 11 Aug. 1991; *Sun-Herald* 11 Mar. 1990.

Bush Bass. Folk music stringed instrument, popular in bush bands since being introduced by the original *Bushwhackers (1952), but actually not of traditional origin. Made from a tea-chest or 10-gallon drum, it has a tent pole, sapling or broom handle as a neck which supports a single plucked string of rawhide, shark line or cord. Different notes are obtained not by stopping the string but by bending the neck, which tightens or slackens the string. This proved extremely difficult to pitch reliably, and some bands developed a three-string version (tuned I,IV,V) with a fixed neck, tuned by moveable bridges.

FURTHER REFERENCE

Frank Pitt, 'How to Make a Bush Bass', *Australian Tradition* 2/3 (1965) 27; John Manifold, *The Violin, the Banjo and the Bones* (Ferntree Gully,Vic.: Rams Skull Press, 1957), 12.

Bushwackers, The (1). Bush band (1971–84; 1993–) formed in Melbourne, originally comprised of Jan Wositzky (vocals, harmonica, banjo, bush bass), Dave Isom (guitar, mandolin, vocals), Bert Kahanoff (lagerphone), Mick Slocum (vocals, accordion), and Davey Kidd (fiddle), but with many changes since. Growing out of La Trobe University folk club, they gained a pub following and toured NZ in 1973.Their debut album (1974) topped the British folk charts during their tour of Europe. They published popular song-books with dancing instructions, wrote music for films and television, and were resident performers on ABC-FM *Songs and Stories of*

Australia. Bringing new instruments, amplification, and sophisticated song arrangements to the bush band tradition, they revitalised and popularised the genre. By 1984 when they disbanded, they had toured abroad eight times, and presented massed bush dances around Australia.There were then annual reunions, and they re-formed with changed membership in 1993.

FURTHER REFERENCE

Recordings include *Bushwackers Collection* (1982, Avenue AVE 261353), *Bushwackers Dance Album* (EMI TCFAB 240714) and the compilation *Bushwackers* (1994, ABC). See also *LattaA*, 136–37; *SpencerW.*

Bushwhackers, The (2). Bush band formed in 1952 at Sydney, comprised of John Meredith (button accordion, concertina), Brian Loughlin (lagerphone), and Jack Barrie (bush bass).They came to prominence at the New Theatre, Sydney, playing in the musical *Reedy River* in 1953, which started a craze for folk-songs and bush dances, then they played at the Bush Music Club, Sydney, from 1954, leading the audience in singing and dancing. The first of the revival bush bands, they had great influence on the instrumentation of later bands, although their use of lagerphone and bush bass was not traditional. A Melbourne Bushwhackers band (later renamed the Billabong band) was formed for the second Melbourne production of *Reedy River* in 1955. *Note:* This band, the original one, is spelt Bushwhackers. The band formed in 1971, Bushwackers (1), is spelt differently.The various references to these bands in other entries should be distinguished according to spelling.

FURTHER REFERENCE

BrisbaneE, 275.

Butler, Lindsay (*b* Tenterfield, NSW, 4 Mar. 1942), country music guitarist, record producer.After playing guitar in his own country band from the age of 16, he toured nationally with Athol McCoy in 1968, then with Buddy Williams 1971–73, and Slim Dusty from 1973, including in Dusty's 1988 Bicentennial tour. He settled at Tamworth in 1974, joining the Capital Three Ranch Band, appearing annually at the Tamworth Festival, and from 1983 touring NSW venues with his own show. The first Australian country guitarist to record a solo album, he won the ACMA Best Instrumental award in 1977; Maton Guitars released a Lindsay Butler Tamworth Guitar in 1982. He established his LBS record label in 1988, producing and arranging for major country artists and twice winning the ACMA Record Producer of the Year (1991, 1992).

FURTHER REFERENCE

Recordings include *Lindsay Butler Plays Slim Dusty Favourites* (1976, Hadley CASOLLP 503), *Tamworth Guitar* (Hadley CASOLLP 519), and *Country Strings* (Hadley HCS 51296). See also *LattaA*, 46–7; *SmithB*, 246.

Butterley, Nigel (*b* Sydney, 13 May 1935), composer. Having learnt piano and composed privately from age six, Butterley worked for various ABC departments (1952–61, 1963–72), including music and religious affairs, while studying part-time at the NSW Conservatorium with Noël Nickson and Raymond Hanson (1952). In a short but intense and influential period overseas, he studied with Priaulx Rainier (1962–63) and travelled through Europe and the Holy Land. He was lecturer in composition, University of Newcastle, 1973–91. His awards include the Italia Prize (1966) for *In the Head the Fire*, a Cook Bicentenary commission for *Explorations* (1970), an Australia Council fellowship (1985) for *Lawrence Hargrave Flying Alone* (premiered by the Australian Opera, 1988), and an Australian creative artist's fellowship (1991). He was honoured with the AM (1991), a Sounds Australian Award (1992) for *From Sorrowing Earth*, and an honorary DMus from the University of Newcastle (1996). He attracted attention with *Laudes*, premiered at the 1964 Adelaide Festival, and was commissioned by the ABC to write *In the Head the Fire*, which sealed his reputation as a leading young composer. His university post later served as a base for increasing activity as a composer and also as a performer of contemporary music including Cage, Crumb, Messiaen, Rainier, Tippett and Vaughan Williams. He is especially noted for his performances and recording of Cage's *Sonatas and Interludes* (1993, Tall Poppies, TP025).

Early compositional influences were the English sacred and pastoral traditions, especially the music of Vaughan Williams. His most formative influence, however, was Rainier, who helped him to overcome the limitations of his earlier compositional education. His aesthetic was initially strongly shaped by Anglicanism; many of the early works are religious, even liturgical. But he later evolved a more generalised view of spirituality, especially from the late 1970s onwards, having been influenced by writers such as William Blake, Thomas Traherne and Walt Whitman.

Butterley's pre-1963 output is characterised by highly idiomatic vocal and choral works which are predominantly tonal and/or modal and show a preference for transparent linear textures, open chord structures and small ensembles. Post-1963 works tend to more imaginative text-setting and more angular melodic lines, and increasingly incorporate denser textures, larger ensembles, and a wide variety of musical language, according to the individual expressive needs of each work. Harmonic language encompasses the serial, quasi-serial and atonal, a greater range of instrumental techniques is employed, and orchestral writing is more textural, even including aleatoric procedures.

Butterley aims to write music of durable quality, seeking neither easy popularity nor identification with the avant-garde. He has not participated in debates about Australian musical identity, instead maintaining an individualistic approach and existence. Despite having worked mostly part-time until his retirement, Butterley is a prolific composer of considerable and conspicuous originality and maturity.

WORKS (Selective)

(Mss held by composer)

Principal publishers: J. Albert, Australian Music Centre.

Orchestral   Many major works including *The Meditations of Thomas Traherne* (ms, 1968), *Pentad* (ms, 1968), *Interaction I* painter, orch (ms, 1970), Violin Concerto (ms, 1975), *Explorations*, pf, orch (1970), *First Day Covers*, speaker, orch (Barry Humphries; 1972), *Fire in the Heavens*, orch (1985), *From Sorrowing Earth*, orch (ms, 1990).

Chamber   4 str qts (mss, 1965, 1974, 1980, 1995); very large output in variety of media including: Trio, fl, cl, hp (ms, 1957), Prelude, hp (ms, 1957), *Diversions*, brass quintet (ms, 1958), Sonatina, ob, pf (ms, 1959), *Laudes*, fl/alto fl, cl/bass cl, tpt, hn, vn, va, vc, pf (1965), *The White-Throated Warbler*, sopranino rec, hpd (1965), *Music for Sunrise*, 3 recs, fl, 7 perc (1969), *Evanston Song*, fl, pf (ms, 1978), *Conversation Pieces*, fl, pf (1989), *Forest I*, va, pf (ms, 1990), *Poverty*, 2 fl, 2 cl, 4 hn, hp, str qt, db (ms, 1992), *Forest II*, tpt, pf (ms, 1993), *Of Wood*, vc (ms, 1995).

Keyboard (Piano unless otherwise indicated)   *Toccata*, duet (ms, 1955), *Toccata* (1960), *Arioso* (1965), *Comment on a Popular Song* (1965), *Sonorities*, carillon (ms, 1968), *Letter from Hardy's Bay*, prepared pf (1972), *Uttering Joyous Leaves* (1981), *Lawrence Hargrave Flying Alone* (ms, 1981), *Grevillea* (ms, 1985), *Circle-Citadels*, org (ms, 1989); numerous other short works for piano and organ.

Dramatic   *The Tell-Tale Heart*, ballet: 2 pf, perc (ms, 1961), *In the Head the Fire*, radio work: narr, T, Bar, SATB, orch, tapes (1966), *Lawrence Hargrave Flying Alone*, opera (ms, 1985–88, 2, James McDonald), 24 Sept 1988, Sydney; incidental music including *Childermass* (ms, 1968, Thomas Keneally); many film scores (mostly documentaries).

Choral   *The True Samaritan*, SATB (ms, 1958; rev. 1976); *Prayer During Sickness*, SATB (ms, 1960, Herrick; rev. 1989), *Who Build on Hope*, SATB, org (ms, 1960; rev. 1989), *Psalm 100*, SATB (ms, 1961; rev. 1989), *No Man is an Island*, SSAATTBB (ms, 1977), *Flower in the Crannied Wall*, SSAATTBB (ms, 1980), *There Came a Wind Like a Bugle*, SSAATTBB (ms, 1987, Emily Dickinson), *Sleep*, SSATBB (ms, Kathleen Raine); two masses (1962, 1962), large output of short liturgical works including introits, anthems, hymn tunes, arrangements and descants.

Vocal   Large output including *Six Blake Songs*, Bar, pf (ms, 1956), *Child In Nature*, S, pf (ms, 1957, Robin Gurr), *Carmina*, S, pf/woodwind quintet (ms, 1968; rev. 1990), *The Owl*, S, fl, cl, vn, vc, perc, pf; S, pf version (ms, 1983, James McDonald), *Sometimes with One I Love*, S, Bar, fl, cl, hn, 2 vc, pf, narr (ms, 1975, Walt Whitman), *Watershore*, four speakers, fl, perc, 3 vc, prep pf (ms, 1977, Walt Whitman), *The Woven Light*, S, orch (ms, 1994, Kathleen Raine).

FURTHER REFERENCE

Recordings include Violin Concerto, Melbourne Symphony Orchestra, L. Dommett, vn (ABC 426 993); String Quartet No. 3, Petra String Quartet (Canberra School of Music, CSM 10); *Uttering Joyous Leaves*, L. Sitsky, pf (Move MD 3066). A discography to 1972 is in *PlushD*. See also Catherine Flaherty, Nigel Butterley's Vocal Music: A Study of Stylistic Development, BMus(Hons), Univ. New England [Aust.], 1987; Andrew Ford, 'Flying Alone: Nigel Butterley', *Composer to Composer: Conversations about Contemporary Music* (Sydney: Allen & Unwin, 1993), 163–69; Gordon Kerry, 'The Weaving Light: The Music of Nigel Butterley and Tributes by his Friends and Colleagues', *24 Hours* (May 1995), 34–6; *MurdochA*.   PATRICIA SHAW

By A Fire of Gidgee Coal. Country music ballad (*c*.1956) by Stan ★Coster, telling of the hardships of bush life. One of the earliest songs he wrote for Slim ★Dusty, it began a partnership that has produced recordings of over 70 works. Published in *Slim Dusty Songbook* (Melbourne: Anne O'Donovan, 1984), 94–5; recorded by Dusty on *Slim Dusty Sings Stan Coster* (EMI CD 7016802), as well as by Barry Thornton, Lindsay Butler and others.

Byrne, Debbie (Debra Anne) (*b* Melbourne, 30 Mar. 1957), popular music singer, entertainer. Her professional singing career began after a successful audition for the TV program *Young Talent Time* in 1971; four years on the show gave her wide exposure to the public, establishing her as a household name in Australia. At the age of 16,

she entered the charts with her first single, the Crystals' song *He's a Rebel*, for which she received a gold record. Her success mounted as she was voted best TV teenage personality in 1973–74 and Queen of Pop in 1974–75. After drug problems in the early 1980s, she rose to the limelight again in the 1985 Sydney stage production of *Cats*, where she played Grizabella the Glamour Cat, delivering her unforgettable rendition of *Memories*. Another notable performance was her role as Fantine in the musical *Les Misérables* in 1987.

Her powerful, resonant voice and reputation as a multi-talented entertainer has carried her from cabaret to operetta. In 1990 she returned to recording with *Caught in the Act*, featuring a collection of show songs. Her next album marked her debut as a songwriter: *Sleeping Child* (1995) is a reflective album inspired by her family, written in contemporary adult-pop style.

FURTHER REFERENCE
She's a Rebel (1974, L&Y L35362); *The Persuader* (1985, EMI); *Caught in the Act* (1991, Mushroom TVL 93342); *Sleeping Child* (1995, FESCD 31053). For a discography, see *SpencerA*. See also *McGrathA*; *SpencerW*.

                                                        LILLA ITO-HONGO

C

Cadd, Brian [Brian Caine]   (*b* Perth, 29 Nov. 1949), rock singer-songwriter. Caine learned piano from the age of 10, and an appearance in a Perth talent quest led to work in a child band for a local television children's program. Once his family settled in Melbourne he began playing jazz, then played organ in the Castaways (1965), the Jackson Kings (1965–66), The *Groop (1966–69), and *Axiom (1969–71). He was in the UK in 1970, then back in Australia he formed Bootleg Records in 1972, gathering The Bootleg Family Band for sessions and tours. As Brian Cadd his single *Ginger Man* reached No. 6 in the charts in 1972, his albums *Parabrahm* and *Brian Cadd* reached Nos 1 and 2 respectively in the album charts in 1973, and the single *Let Go* No. 14 in 1974. He did not match these chart successes again, although his *White On White* album was acclaimed in the USA in 1976. He played with Max *Merrit in 1989 and 1991, and in numerous sessions. A gifted songwriter, his songs have been recorded by *Masters Apprentices, Ronnie *Burns, Glen Campbell, *Zoot, John *Farnham and others, in the UK by Cilla Black. In the USA *Let Go* (1974) was recorded by Gene Pitney and *Love Is Like A Rolling Stone* was a hit for The Pointer Sisters. He won five *TV Week* King of Pop awards 1973–74.

FURTHER REFERENCE
Recordings include *Ginger Man* (1972, Bootleg); albums *Parabrahm* (1972, Bootleg); *Brian Cadd* (1973, Bootleg); *White On White* (1976, Interfusion); and *No Stone Unturned* (1985, Graffiti). For discography, see *SpencerA*. See also *GuinnessP*; *McGrathA*; *SpencerW*.

Cade, William Richard   (*b* Adelaide, 30 June 1883; *d* Adelaide, 4 Aug. 1957), violinist, conductor. After studying violin with Hermann *Heinicke and piano with Bryceson Trehearne at the Elder Conservatorium, he went to Germany and studied with Jaengerich at the Max Pohl Conservatorium in 1910. In London he played viola in the Beecham Opera Orchestra, then was leader of the Quinlan Opera Orchestra in 1911. He returned to Australia as musical director for J.C. Williamson from 1911 and was musical director at the Theatre Royal, Adelaide, from 1916, working as leader in Harold Davies' symphony concerts and as guest conductor 1920–28. He conducted a 17-piece ensemble for silent films at the Regent Theatre, Melbourne, from 1928 and was conductor of the Victorian Professional Orchestra. In 1935 he became conductor of the ABC Adelaide Orchestra, which was augmented from 18 to 50 players in 1936; he was then resident conductor until he retired in 1948, after which it was renamed the SA Symphony Orchestra. As a violinist he had a pure tone and precise technique, using the *portamento* and *vibrato* popular at the time; as a conductor he was an unruffled, amiable presence on the podium and a lucid technician. He played an important pioneering role in the early years of the ABC Adelaide Orchestra.

FURTHER REFERENCE
Obit. in *Adelaide Advertiser* 5 Aug. 1957. See also Joyce Gibberd, *ADB*, 13; *MoresbyA*, 151–2; *OrchardM*, 59; *GlennonA*, 114–15.

Cairns   pop. (1991) 64 463, city located on Trinity Bay, south of the mouth of the Barron River, northern Queensland. Before European settlement in 1876, the region was home to the peoples of the Djabugay-Yidiny language group, comprised of the Yirrganydji and Gungganydji tribes in the northern and southern regions respectively. European musical activity has generally flourished more in its outlying areas than in Cairns proper. The earliest records describe the musical activities of four Sisters of Mercy in Cooktown in 1888; a later sister mentions a music teacher, a 'German gentleman', in Cooktown before World War I. The Cooktown convent later moved to Herberton, where there were also the Sisters of the Sacred Advent and private tuition offered by the Mears family; the Sisters began teaching in Cairns in 1892.

The Italian population of the sugar-growing Innisfail region produced a strong interest in opera, with support in recent times from visiting musicians such as James

*Christiansen, Ronald *Maconaghie and John *Curro, as well as locals Rod Taylor, Lewis Reid and Alfred Martinuzzi. Productions have included Mozart's *Bastien and Bastienne,* Donizetti's *L'elisir d'amore,* Verdi's *La traviata* and Puccini's *Madame Butterfly.* From 1886 Mrs Theresa Palmerston (née Rooney) taught the piano, and in 1910 Alfred J. Barnard established a minstrel troupe. In 1928 the latter formed the Innisfail Choral and Orchestral Society.

Cairns has particular strengths in choral and brass music; in 1953 the Cairns Junior Choral and Orchestral Society was formed under Jack Daniel, from which grew the Cairns and District Junior Eisteddfod and the Cairns Choral Society. The first brass band was the Cairns Railway Band. The Cairns Combined School Band was formed in 1931 as the training band for the Cairns Municipal Band. The Cairns Citizens' Band achieved outstanding success on a tour of NZ under Jimmy Compton in 1936.

The Cairns Youth Orchestra (established 1970) formed the basis of the North Queensland Symphony Orchestra (1975). Activities of numerous local groups such as the Far Northern Madrigal Singers (1967), the Cairns Classical Music Group and the Cairns Jazz Club have been supplemented by periodic performances of the Queensland Symphony Orchestra, the Elizabethan Theatre Trust and Musica Viva. Cairns has attracted major international visitors such as Vladimir Ashkenazy, Victoria de Los Angeles, Quadro Hotteterre and Boris Berman. The Hibernian Hall was used extensively as a concert venue before the establishment of the Cairns Civic Centre in 1974. More recent developments which have accelerated audience exposure to music include the Cairns Community Broadcasters 4CCR FM, concerts by the department of music from James Cook University, the Encore Concerts, and the Australian Festival of Chamber Music, directed by Theodore Kuchar, formerly conductor of the Queensland Philharmonic Orchestra.

FURTHER REFERENCE

Wendy Favell, *Moments in History from Cairns and District: Being Five Generations of a Northern Pioneer Family* (Cairns: Bolton, 1976); *Historical Background of the Musical Culture in Cairns,* Minutes of James Cook University Fact Finding Meeting 6 Mar. 1996, James Cook University Music Department, 1996; Kathleen Lynch, Cultural Developments in Queensland 1880–1930, BA, Univ. Queensland, 1954; Murdoch Wales, *Sugarcane and 'Prima Donnas',* pamphlet held in Townsville Library Service Local History Collection, n.d.

PETER GORE-SYMES

Cale, Bruce W. (*b* Leura, NSW, 17 Feb. 1939), jazz bass player, composer. He studied violin from the age of nine, and began his professional career in 1959 in sessions, clubs, concerts, television and radio. Active in the modernist movement, notably in association with Bryce Rohde, he left Australia in 1965, working in the UK with Tubby Hayes and others, then was based in the USA for 11 years, leading groups, appearing with Phil Woods,

Toshiko Akiyoshi and others, and also composing. Apart from study with George Russell in the USA in 1981, he was resident in Australia from 1978. From 1988 he was primarily teaching and composing both orchestral concert and jazz works, until resuming playing recently.

FURTHER REFERENCE

Recordings include *More Spring,* Bryce Rohde Quartet, 1962 (1990, MBS FM Jazz 6); *A Century Of Steps,* The Bruce Cale Orchestra (1981, Larrikin LRJ 071); *Live At The Basement: vol. 1, Rolling Thunder, vol. 2, Rain,* The Bruce Cale Orchestra (1987, Modern Records MR 12144 and Vista VRJ 1001). See also *ClareB*; *BissetB*; *OxfordJ*.

BRUCE JOHNSON

Callaway, Sir Frank Adams (*b* Timaru, NZ, 1919), music educator, conductor. After early training as a violinist he played the viola and bassoon in the orchestras of the NZ Broadcasting Service. He studied at Dunedin Teachers' College (1939–40), then the University of Otago, was a member of the Central Band of the Royal NZ Air Force during World War II and was head of the music department of the King Edward Technical College, Dunedin, New Zealand, 1942–53. He studied at the Royal Academy, London 1947–8, winning the Battison Haynes and Cuthbert Nunn Prizes in Composition, and was awarded a Carnegie Travel Grant for study of music education in the USA in 1949. In 1953 he was appointed reader in music at the University of Western Australia, becoming foundation professor of music in 1959. He was prominent as a choral and orchestral conductor in Australia, particularly as a guest conductor of the ABC orchestras in WA and SA. He was a member of the Advisory Board, Commonwealth Assistance to Australian Composers, 1966–72, organising national seminars and workshops for young composers, and became the foundation president of ASME, 1967–71, editing its journal until 1982. A member of ISME since its inception in 1953, he became president (1968–72), treasurer (1972–88), was founding editor of its *International Journal of Music Education,* and in 1988 was elected its honorary president. As a member of the Australian Commission for UNESCO 1958–76, he represented Australia on the International Music Council, serving on the executive committee as vice-president then as international president, 1980–82. In 1985 he was elected a life member of honour. In 1979 and 1984 he was organising chairman of the Indian Ocean Arts Festivals in Perth, and has since become an honorary member of numerous overseas cultural bodies.

In 1995 the UNESCO director-general described Sir Frank as 'one of the great pioneers and ambassadors of music education in our time'. He has written articles and has edited numerous books, journals and reports, including *Studies in Music* (1967–84), *Challenges in Music Education* (1975), *Australian Composition of the 20th Century* (1978, co-edited by David Tunley) and *Essays in Honour of David Evatt Tunley* (1995). On his retirement from the

University of Western Australia in 1984 the university established the Frank Callaway Foundation for Music, which supports the Callaway International Resource Centre for Music Education (CIRCME). His awards include the FRAM, FACE, honorary doctorates from the Universities of Western Australia (1975) and Melbourne (1982); Sir Bernard Heinze Award, 1988; Percy Grainger Medal, 1991; the OBE (1970), CMG (1975), Kt (1981), and AO (1995).

FURTHER REFERENCE
Fred G. Barr, *The Music Makers: The University of Western Australia Choral Society's First Sixty Years* (Perth: Univ. WA, 1991); Martin Comte, ed., *Music Education: International Viewpoints* (Perth: Australian Society for Music Education, 1994); B.K. de Garis, ed., *Campus in the Community: The University of Western Australia, 1963–1987* (Perth: Univ. WA, 1988), 53–9, 242–3; Rupert Thackray, 'Personalities in World Music Education: No.1—Sir Frank Callaway', *International Journal of Music Education* 6 (1988) 33–5.
HELEN STOWASSER

Cameron, John, (*b* NSW, 20 Mar. 1918), baritone. After studying at the NSW State Conservatorium and working in *Calling the Stars*, a radio variety show on the Macquarie network from 1941, he went to London in 1949 and made his debut as Germont at Covent Garden, singing at Glyndebourne 1953–54, as well as in lieder, oratorio and Gilbert and Sullivan. He revisited Australia to sing *Marriage of Figaro* in the inaugural Elizabethan Theatre Trust Opera season and in recitals in 1956, appearing with the Trust until 1974. With fine intelligence and excellent diction, he sang in the premieres of *Billy Budd*, *Pilgrim's Progress*, Arthur Benjamin's *Tale of Two Cities* and various other works by British composers, and his roles included Figaro, Guglielmo and Papageno. Since 1976 he has taught at the Royal Northern College of Music.

FURTHER REFERENCE
Recordings included Berlioz *L'Enfance du Christ* (1994, Decca CD 443461–2DF2); *Beecham Conducts Delius* (reissue 1987, EMI CDS7 47509–8); and *Favourite Gilbert and Sullivan* (Classics for Pleasure CD-CFP 4609). See also *MackenzieS*, 181–3.

Camilleri, Joe ['Jo Jo Zep', 'Joey Vincent']   (*b* Malta, 1948), rock singer. He emigrated from Malta to Australia with his family during childhood. Primarily a lead vocalist, he also plays saxophone, guitar and harmonica. He left school at 13, and at 16 began performing at school dances with local Melbourne rhythm and blues bands. From 1975 to 1982 he achieved some success as a member of *Jo Jo Zep and the Falcons, with whom he made such hits as *Shape I'm In* and *Taxi Mary*. After the split of the band in 1982, Camilleri released the solo album *Cha* under the pseudonym Jo Jo Zep. His most commercially successful period to date was as the front-up man for the *Black Sorrows (1984–94). Working with lyricist Nick Smith, he produced such commer-

cially popular hits as *Harley and Rose* and *Chained To The Wheel*. In 1989 the Black Sorrows won the ARIA best band award. Camilleri has written the music to a number of film and television drama sound-tracks including *Dogs in Space*, *The Fish are Safe*, and *Painter and the Pallet*. In 1986, he wrote the sound-track for an SBS documentary, which he produced, about migrants returning to their homeland. Throughout the 1980s he managed two independent record labels, Mighty and Spirit, and in 1995 created the new label Head Records, distributed by Mushroom.

Camilleri, whose musical style has been described as an eclectic mix of rhythm and blues, country, and zydeco, is a respected and popular artist within the music industry, having done session work with *Skyhooks, *Cold Chisel, Goanna, *Daddy Cool, *Icehouse and Paul *Kelly and the Coloured Girls. In 1993 he was awarded the Australian Music Awards Crystal Trophy for an outstanding contribution to music, and in 1994 he was inducted into the Melbourne Music Festival Hall of Fame.

FURTHER REFERENCE
Recordings with Jo Jo Zep and the Falcons include *Don't Waste It* (1977, Oz); *Whip it Out* (1977, Oz); *Loud and Clear* (1978, Oz); with the Black Sorrows include *Rockin' Zydeco* (1985, Spirit); *Sonol* (1985, Spirit); *Better Times* (1993, Sony). See also *Australian* 8 June 1991; Glenn A. Baker, 'Joe Camilleri's Black Sorrows', *APRAJ* (Oct 1989), 2–4; *GuinnessP*; *SpencerW*; Sunday *Herald-Sun* 12 Nov. 1995.
LEONIE GOODWIN

Campbell, Bessie (Elizabeth)   (*b* Melbourne, 21 July 1870; *d* Burwood, Melbourne, 28 Apr. 1964), banjo player. She learned five-string banjo from Joe Daniels in London and Hosea Easton in Sydney. Walter Stent taught her various American styles of finger-picking; she never used a plectrum. She began appearing in charity concerts in 1891, and by 1897 she had been acclaimed as 'Australia's greatest lady banjoist', receiving many offers for concerts large and small, and becoming the first female member of the American Banjo Club. Dubbed 'the Banjo Queen' in 1907, she is said to have played with so much ability as to render the banjo almost a classical instrument. Her repertoire included Christy-minstrel songs and Negro spirituals. She never married.

FURTHER REFERENCE
Her papers are in the possession of Mr & Mrs T. Ball, Rhodes, Sydney. See also P. Comrie-Thomson, *ADB*, 7.
KAY DREYFUS

Canberra,   pop. (1991) 278 904. Capital of Australia and seat of the federal government, Canberra is a relatively young city (proclaimed 1911), situated in the Australian Capital Territory 300 km south-west of Sydney. The city has retained much of its natural bushland environment and, although often accused of having the sterility and lifelessness of an artificially planned settlement, it has an active artistic community with most forms of music (the notable exception being opera) receiving regular, professional-standard productions. While the Canberra School of Music, Institute of the Arts, now provides the focus for musical activity in the city, the community sustains a symphony orchestra, numerous choirs and many individual performers.

1. 1911–50: Establishment. Before the founding of Canberra, there had been music in the several churches that dotted the pastures—chief among these being St John's Church of England (consecrated 1845)—and in the various homesteads, but the first public musical event recorded was at the Acton Hall in April 1913, featuring the Canberra Glee Club conducted by Les Edwards. A second hall was officially opened on 6 February 1926 at the Causeway, with a concert arranged by E.A. Mowle. Later that month, 62 people attended the first meeting of what was soon called the Canberra Philharmonic Society.

Mowle conducted the Philharmonic's first concert on 15 May 1926, supplemented by the Stromberra Quartet, a rather idiosyncratic ensemble named for the Commonwealth Solar Observatory on Mount Stromlo, comprised of Mrs W.G. Duffield (violin), her husband the founder and director of the Observatory W.G. Duffield (double-bass), the solicitor-general Sir Robert Garran (clarinet), and the secretary to the Federal Capital Commission C.S. Daley (piano). The Philharmonic's second concert was broadcast in Sydney on radio 2FC. In 1927 the society was invited to participate in the ceremony opening Parliament House, where they accompanied Dame Nellie Melba in singing *God Save the King*. In these early years the government strongly promoted musical societies as a means of overcoming the social inadequacies of the new city. These organisations quickly became independent, drawing members from many walks of life and making Canberra one of the most highly participative communities in the country.

In June 1927 the *Canberra Times* reported that a 'project was on foot for the formation of a new orchestra' and that a Mr Flynn was available to conduct. The Canberra Orchestral Society was formed, comprised of 15 violins, three clarinets, two violas, two cellos, three cornets, two trombones, two double-basses and a pianist. Calls for the amalgamation of the two principal musical organisations led to the emergence of the Canberra Musical Society in 1928. A joint meeting of the committees was told that the 'fusion ... was a necessary preliminary to the development of music in Canberra' and that 'the musical ideals of the citizens and the [Federal Capital] Commission could not be fulfilled if the Societies continued to run as separate identities'. The Musical Society was active in promoting concerts and bringing distinguished artists to the region until the 1950s.

The Canberra Band under bandmasters Maginess, Stevenson and then Rowland, was an important early force in Canberra's musical development and remains the longest-lived of the city's musical organisations. From 1926 it was known as the Canberra Vice-Regal Band and later (after a hiatus in the early 1940s) as the Canberra City Band under long-time conductor W.L. Hoffmann. In its early years the Band performed at many official ceremonies including the annual ANZAC Day commemorations. Its membership often included personnel from the Royal Military College, Duntroon, until a permanent military band was established there in April 1954 under the command of warrant officer Bob Rignold.

The Canberra Male Choir led by William Doig was established in 1930, but was supplanted by the Canberra Ladies' Choir with the departure of World War II servicemen in 1939. The Male Choir sought to establish an eisteddfod in Canberra, and in August 1937 the National Eisteddfod Society was formed by representatives of the Male Choir, Musical Society, Society for Arts and Literature, Canberra Band, Canberra Amateur Operatic Society (formed 1934), Repertory Society, Chamber of Commerce, Highland Society and Burns Club, Australian Natives Association and local schools. A Council for the Encouragement of Music and the Arts was established in 1946, changing its name two years later to the present Arts Council of the ACT. At about the same time, the Canberra Recorded Music Society was founded, giving its members the opportunity to hear gramophone recordings of works unlikely to be heard in live concerts.

Though still with a population of only a few thousand, Canberra was included on the itineraries of many foreign artists. The Waiato Maori Choir from NZ gave concerts in the Albert Hall in April 1935, and the Vienna Mozart Boys' Choir visited in July 1939. From 1937 the ABC brought artists to Canberra in association with the Musical Society: Arthur Rubinstein, Gladys Moncrieff, Lotte Lehmann, the Budapest String Quartet, Dino Borgioli, Guilia Bustabo, Alexander Kipnis, Richard Tauber, Artur Schnabel, Ignaz Friedman, Joan Hammond and Elisabeth Schwarzkopf all appeared before 1950.

On 11 December 1947 Canberra heard its first performance with full orchestra of Handel's *Messiah,* when the Combined Churches Choir was accompanied by the Goulburn Liedertafel Orchestra. With this important event, Canberra seemed to have reached maturity, both as a prospering city—for with postwar construction most government departments were committed to moving to the capital—and as a cultural centre having most of the attributes of its larger neighbours.

2. 1950–Present: Expansion. (i) Orchestras, Choirs, Chamber Music. The 1950s saw a substantial increase in the number of musical bodies in the city. On 3 March 1950, the Canberra Orchestral Society was formed with nine players and a former member of the Hallé Orchestra, John Strange, as its first president. The new orchestra and the Male Singers performed at the 1950 Stars of the Mobil Quest concert, where a capacity audience also heard the winner of the Quest, Joan Sutherland. By 1960 the organisation had been renamed the Canberra Symphony Orchestra, and in September that year it appointed the director of music at Canberra Grammar School, Wilfred Holland, conductor.

Orchestral concerts have continued with annual subscription series from the Canberra Symphony Orchestra and Australian Chamber Orchestra, as well as frequent appearances by the School of Music's orchestras and Canberra Youth Orchestral Society, a training organisation which developed from a small school group in the mid-1960s and has since won international awards. Regular visits by the Sydney and Melbourne Symphony Orchestras ceased during the cutbacks of the mid-1980s. With the support of stalwarts from the Recorded Music Society, the Canberra Chamber Music Society was established in 1956 with Professor Robert Parker as its first president. The society contracted with the recently revived Musica Viva to bring its visiting artists to Canberra. This arrangement continued until 1980, when control passed to the national organisation.

During 1952 Ronald Penny became the first conductor of the newly formed Canberra Choral Group (later the Canberra Choral Society). With the appointment of Holland as conductor in 1961, the society began presenting larger-scale works in association with the Orchestral Society, and the Society of Singers was established to continue giving *a cappella* concerts which included the Australian premiere of Malcolm Williamson's *Symphony for Voices* under Hans Westerman. The Society of Singers disbanded in 1974, their niche being filled in 1977 by the Oriana Chorale under Roger Wellman. In 1963 six musically talented students at the Australian National University created the ANU Choral Society (SCUNA). As it grew, a highly skilled ensemble emerged who entertained Canberra regularly as the University Consort.

The city has been well served by children's choirs. In 1967 Judith Clingan established the Canberra Children's Choir, the first non-school-based group. This was followed closely by Don Whitbread's Woden Valley Youth Choir, which was formed in the southern districts of the city in 1969 and has since undertaken several successful overseas tours. The Canberra Boys' Choir was founded in 1981 with Donald Hollier as director, while the multi-art-form Gaudeamus was created by Clingan in 1981.

(ii) Opera, Music Theatre.
With the founding of the Canberra Philharmonic Society in 1951 (with no ties to the 1926 organisation), Canberra has had regular music-theatre performances. Since its first show, a concert version of *The Yeomen of the Guard*, it has presented over 100 productions in the Albert Hall and the Canberra Theatre. The Canberra Theatre Centre, the first multi-purpose cultural centre operating in Australia, comprised of a 1200-seat auditorium, 300-seat Playhouse, gallery and foyer space, was opened in June 1965 with a performance by the Australian Ballet and Queensland Symphony Orchestra. The Canberra Theatre Trust has since been responsible for many large-budget productions.

Opera has had a more chequered existence, with the Canberra Amateur Operatic Society of the 1930s quickly faltering. From 1966 until the late 1970s, the Elizabethan Trust Opera Company (later the Australian Opera) toured to Canberra, as did the Australian Ballet, usually presenting four operas in two seasons. Under the driving force of theatre critic Ken Healey, Canberra Opera was formed in 1970 as The Opera Group. It presented a wide range of grand opera and operetta, most notably under musical director Donald Hollier, culminating in a vast *Aida* in 1981, the first opera simulcast by the ABC. In the late 1970s and early 1980s, Paul Thom directed numerous highly acclaimed productions of Purcell and Handel operas at the Australian National University. After the demise of Canberra Opera in 1984, Opera ACT and David Parker's ANU Opera and Canberra City Opera staged several productions, but no permanent company has emerged.

(iii) The School of Music, Other Organisations.
The establishment of the Canberra School of Music, which began teaching in September 1965, created a new focus for the musical activities of the national capital. Its staff were soon in high demand to conduct and direct local organisations of all types and sizes. The Canberra Symphony Orchestra appointed the founding director of the School, Ernest *Llewellyn, as its conductor in 1967. Other organisations to have made regular appointments to the school's staff include the Youth Orchestra, Opera, Choral Society and the school's own chamber choir and community choir, now renamed the Llewellyn Choir. Staff also formed such diverse ensembles as the Canberra String Quartet, Canberra Wind Soloists and Guitar Trek. While control of the school was transferred to the Australian National University in 1992, its fine 1442-seat auditorium, now Llewellyn Hall, and other facilities remain available to the people of Canberra and visiting artists.

The school has also been a centre of compositional activity. Organist-composer Donald Hollier lectured in theoretical studies 1967–85; Don Banks was head of composition 1974–76 and ran an electronic music studio which was the precursor of the present Australian Centre for Arts and Technology. Appointed to the founding staff as a pianist, Larry Sitsky succeeded Banks as head of composition. Sitsky also founded the Canberra New Music Society to give performances of contemporary compositions. The school offers a degree in jazz under the leadership of flugelhornist Don Johnson, and its big band and jazz vocal group are regular Canberra performers.

Other musical organisations which now play an important role in the diverse Canberra music scene include the National Folk Festival (founded 1966), Harmonie German Choir (1968), Canberra Recorder and Early Music Society (1975), ACT Lieder Society (1976),

Canberra Stereo Public Radio (1982) and Canberra New Music Ensemble (1987). Canberra is also home to several instrument-makers, among them Gillian Alcock (dulcimers) and the luthier Graeme Caldersmith. The ACT Chapter of the Musicological Society of Australia was established in the early 1970s through the efforts of ethnomusicologist Alice Moyle.

FURTHER REFERENCE

G. Benjamin, *Woden Valley Youth Choir: Twenty Years On* (Canberra: Woden Valley Youth Choir, 1988); P.J. Campbell, Limestone Plains-Song: An Historical Survey of Choral Music in Canberra 1913–1993, MMus, ANU, 1996; C.S. Daley, *As I Recall: Reminiscences of Early Canberra*. Ed. Shirley Purchase (Canberra: Mulini Press in association with the Canberra and District Historical Society, 1994); W.L. Hoffmann, *The Canberra School of Music: The First 25 Years 1965–1990* (Canberra: Canberra Institute of the Arts, 1990); M. Webster, *The Philo Story 1951–1989: The Evolution of the Canberra Philharmonic Society* (Canberra: Canberra Philharmonic Society, 1990).   PETER CAMPBELL

Canberra Opera. Part-time opera company (1970–84). Founded by Ken Healey as the Opera Group and for most of its life under the musical directorship of Donald *Hollier, it presented annual seasons of three or four operas at the Canberra Theatre, which combined repertory operas and operettas with Australian premieres of modern works, such as *Dialogue of the Carmelites*, *The Pilgrim's Progress*, and *The Turn of the Screw*. The company used established directors, conductors and designers and a professional pit orchestra, but was affected by the limitations of its singers, who often included local students and amateurs. A particularly ambitious venture was the production of *Aida*, presented in simulcast by the ABC in 1981. After Hollier's departure the repertoire became less adventurous. After the company's demise there were short-lived ventures such as Opera ACT, but Canberra has not had regular opera seasons since.

Canberra School of Music. Founded in 1965, the school has been affiliated with the Australian National University through the Institute of Arts since 1990. It occupies a striking modern building (designed by Daryl Jackson) containing Llewellyn Hall, Canberra's main concert venue, on the edge of the university campus, and offers a chiefly practical degree and diploma. There is also a pre-tertiary program in conjunction with local schools. Directors have been Ernest *Llewellyn 1965–80, John *Winther 1981–85, and John *Painter 1985–95.

Canberra Symphony Orchestra. Semi-professional orchestra, founded as the Canberra Orchestral Society in 1950. The ensemble remained embryonic until 1957, when a scheme to engage professional musicians was begun, soon with government assistance, and the venture was associated with the new Canberra School of Music from 1965, drawing on its director Ernest

*Llewellyn as conductor, its staff as principal players, and a growing number of its students. After Llewellyn retired, Leonard *Dommett was conductor 1981–94. Today the orchestra is firmly established, offers a well-patronised subscription series at Llewellyn Hall under a variety of conductors, and achieves considerable standards.

Canberra Wind Soloists. Formed from resident staff of the Canberra School of Music (1980), the present members are Vernon *Hill (flute), David Nuttall (oboe), Alan *Vivian (clarinet), Dominic Harvey (french horn) and Richard McIntyre (bassoon). From 1983 they have toured regularly for Musica Viva, and for the Department of Foreign Affairs to East Asia. They have focused on the standard woodwind quintet repertoire, interestingly juxtaposed with modern works, including arrangements such as *Suite for Wind Quintet* by Anton Rubinstein, arr. Larry Sitsky (1986) and their wind quintet and piano version of *Petrouchka* by Stravinsky arr. McIntyre (1995).

FURTHER REFERENCE

Recordings include works of R. Edwards, L. Sitsky and G. Dreyfus (Canberra School of Music, CSM 14); and *Canberra Wind Soloists* (1992, ABC/Polygram).

Canberra Youth Orchestral Society. Founded from a school ensemble in the mid-1960s, the Society has over 200 players in a comprehensive array of youth ensembles and maintains the Canberra Youth Orchestra, which has toured internationally and won several awards. With a full-time administrative office, the society draws on staff of the Canberra School of Music for its tutors and conductors, and gives regular concerts at Llewellyn Hall and other public buildings around Canberra.

Canon, The. Monthly music journal published 1947–66 in Sydney and edited by Franz Holford and containing extended articles often of considerable depth. Vol. 17, no. 3 (Spring 1965) was the first issue of *Musicology*, later *Musicology Australia*.

Cantrell, Lana (*b* Dover Heights, Sydney, 1945), popular music singer, show-business attorney. Daughter of a jazz bass player, she appeared with a jazz band at the Sydney Town Hall at the age of 10 as the 'Boogie Baby'. An appearance on television in Mike Walsh's *Teen Time* in 1961 attracted Brian Henderson's attention, and she became a regular on his *Bandstand* 1961–62, then Graham Kennedy's *In Melbourne Tonight* 1963–64. She moved to the USA in 1964, appearing regularly on Johnny Carson's *Tonight* show and 15 times on the *Ed Sullivan Show*. She recorded the singles *I'm All Smiles* and *Two For the Road*; and her *Like A Sunday Morning* was nominated for a Grammy Award in 1967. One of Australia's most successful teenage pop singers of the 1960s, she retired from singing in 1985 and now practises law in New York as a show-business specialist.

FURTHER REFERENCE
Australian 18 Mar 1995.

Capella Corelli.   Baroque trio devoted to historical performance, founded in Canberra in 1977 by Cynthia O'Brien (baroque violin), Ruth Wilkinson (viola da gamba, recorder) and Paul Thom (harpsichord). The ensemble was one of the first high-quality Baroque ensembles to become established in Australia in the wake of the European revival of the 1960s and 70s, concentrating largely on the violin sonata repertoire from Castello, through Biber to Corelli, Handel, Vivaldi and Bach. The group has toured extensively throughout Australia for Musica Viva. Since 1988 O'Brien has been resident in Vienna and the group continues to present annual seasons in Australia and Europe. Thom's position was taken over by Paul Dyer in 1985 and John *O'Donnell since 1987.

FURTHER REFERENCE
Recordings include Handel and Telemann works (Move MD3126).

JOHN GRIFFITHS

Captain Matchbox Whoopee Band.   Popular music band 1969–80, formed at Melbourne, originally comprised of Dave Hubbard (violin, guitar), Peter Inglis (guitar), Peter Scott (bass), Mick Fleming, Jim Niven and Mick Conway, but with many subsequent changes. After winning a talent quest as the Jelly Bean Jug Band in 1969, they played in Melbourne revues, and appeared in the film *Stork* (1971). Their debut single *My Canary Has Circles Under His Eyes* reached No. 35 in the charts in 1972 and their first album *Smoke Dreams* reached No. 20 in the album charts in 1973. After a brief split-up, they released two more singles in 1974 and their album *Wangaratta Wakine* reached No. 4 in 1975. They toured with Soapbox Circus in 1976, released *If I Can't Hav-Anna in Cuba* (1977) and *Love is Like A Rainbow* (1979), and appeared in the film *Dimboola* (1979). With a humorous, eclectic array of instruments, and style ingredients drawn from vaudeville, jug-band, and circus, their music combined standards and originals in various nostalgic styles, most often with a 1930s flavour.

FURTHER REFERENCE
Recordings include My *Canary Has Circles Under His Eyes* (Image), *Smoke Dreams* (Image), *Wangaratta Wakine* (re-released Sony PACD 069). See also *McGrathA*; *SpencerW.*

Carandini.   Family of theatrical performers.
(1) Gerolamo ('Jerome') Carandini   (*b* Modena, Italy, *c*.1814; *d* Italy, 1870), dancer. Son of the ninth Marquis Carandini de Sarzano, duchy of Modena, he had appeared at his father's opera house before his involvement in radical political activities drove him into exile. At the Royal Italian Opera, London, he was recruited for Hobart in

1842 by Anne *Clarke. There he married the gifted young singer Marie Burgess (2) in 1843 and moved to Sydney in 1844, opening a dancing and languages school in Bligh Street, choreographing and dancing Auber's *La Muette de Portici* for the Royal Victoria Theatre that year and making various other appearances. In the coming years he danced in Melbourne and Sydney as the partner of most of the leading dancers of the day, often in programs where his increasingly famous wife was also singing.

He retired in 1857 to teach and manage his wife's career, coaching Fanny Griffiths and many other dancers who went on to theatrical success. He revisited Italy in 1870, when the political climate had changed, but died before he could reclaim his title.

(2) Madame (Marie) Carandini née Mary Burgess (*b* London, 1 Feb. 1826; *d* Richmond Hill nr Bath, England, 13 Apr. 1894), contralto. Her family came to Hobart for her father's health in 1833; there she met and married Gerolamo Carandini (1) in 1843. After singing tenor roles in the *Clarke opera troupe at Hobart, her husband took her to Sydney in 1844, where she studied with Eliza Bushelle, Isaac *Nathan, and later with Sara *Flower, singing in concerts and opera presentations at the Royal Victoria Theatre from that year. She regularly sang principal roles in Sydney from 1849, as well as at the Queen's Theatre, Melbourne (1853), in Catherine Hayes's return season (1855), and with Anna Bishop in *Norma* for George Coppin (1856).

A strong voice, if at times mannered in her style, her repertoire included principal roles in *Fra Diavolo*, *The Daughter of the Regiment*, *Der Freischütz*, *La Sonnambula*, *Don Pasquale*, *The Bohemian Girl*, and *Maritana*. She gave the Australian premieres of *Il Trovatore* at the Princess Theatre, Melbourne, in 1858 and *Luisa Miller* at the Theatre Royal in 1859. A popular artist in concert tours of the goldfields, she formed her own opera troupe with her daughters and others from 1860 and made remarkably extensive tours of the colonies, appearing from Mount Gambier to Bundaberg and being the first to penetrate such remote centres as Cooktown and Darwin. The most intrepid of all the operatic pioneers in Australia, she gave the first serious musical performances in a staggering number of Australian cities and towns. Her troupe also appeared in NZ, India and the USA; she retired to England in 1892. Of her eight children, five daughters were singers: Rosina (3), Emma (Mrs Robert Wilson, Queensland), Fanny, Isabella and Elizabeth.

(3) Rosina Carandini [Mrs Palmer] (*b* Hobart, 27 Aug. 1844; *d* South Yarra, Melbourne, 16 June 1932) soprano. The eldest daughter of Marie, she studied voice with Frank *Packer in Hobart and made her debut as Adalgisa in *Norma* at the age of 14. She sang on tour with her mother's company, and after being praised by visiting singing star Charles Santley she went to the USA to study, but soon returned when her mother took ill. She married a singer, E.H. Palmer (later a banker), in 1860, and was raising a family in Melbourne from 1866, but continued to appear with the Melbourne Philharmonic Society, the Melbourne Liedertafel, and at concerts in various other cities. She toured Australia and NZ with the American vocal quartet of Agatha States in 1872, was a principal singer at W.J. Turner's popular concerts at the Exhibition Buildings, Melbourne and was soloist at Scots Church, Collins Street, 1880–1910.

FURTHER REFERENCE
Osric [Humphrey Hall and Alfred John Cripps], *The Romance of the Sydney Stage* (ms, 1911; pub. Sydney: Currency Press, 1996), 100–18, passim; on Marie Carandini see Ann K. Wentzel, *ADB*, 3; *MackenzieS*, 255; *BrewerD*; on Rosina Carandini see Thérèse Radic, *ADB*, 5. See also Percy Brier, *The Pioneers of Music in Queensland* (Brisbane: Music Teachers' Association of Queensland, 1962).

Carden, Joan   (*b* Melbourne), soprano. She studied at the London Opera Centre and with Vida Harford, and after appearances at Sadler's Wells Theatre and with Nederlands Dans Theatre she returned to Australia and joined the Australian Opera in 1971. As a guest artist she has subsequently appeared in the UK and USA with major companies, including the Royal Opera Covent Garden, Glyndebourne Festival Opera, Miami Opera and the Metropolitan Opera on its USA tour. Her repertoire is wide-ranging, encompassing Handel's *Alcina*, Cherubini's *Medée*, the major Mozart heroines—Countess Almaviva in *The Marriage of Figaro*, Donna Anna and Donna Elvira in *Don Giovanni*, Pamina in *The Magic Flute*, Constanze in *Die Entführung aus dem Serail* and Vitellia in *La clemenza di Tito*—and the Italian repertoire, most notably Violetta in *La traviata,* Gilda in *Rigoletto,* Leonora in *Il trovatore*, Desdemona in *Otello*, Leonora in *La forza del destino, Madama Butterfly, Tosca*, Mimì in *La Bohème*, Liù in *Turandot*, and *Adriana Lecouvreur*. She has also sung Marguerite in *Faust*, Eva in *Die Meistersinger von Nürnberg*, the Marschallin in *Der Rosenkavalier* and Tatyana in *Eugene Onegin*, and she has been particularly admired as Ellen Orford in *Peter Grimes*.

Joan Carden's operatic career began as a very well schooled lyric soprano with a modest stage personality, but her work with major conductors and collaborations with directors such as John Copley and Peter Hall quickly transformed her into a singing actress of considerable power and craft, held in high esteem by Australian operatic audiences. In 1982 she was awarded the OBE, in 1987 the Dame Joan Hammond Award, and in 1988 the AO.

FURTHER REFERENCE
Recordings include *Italian Opera Arias* (ABC 442 368). See also *CA* (1995–96); *WWA* (1996).

MOFFATT OXENBOULD

Cardier, Glenn ['Sydney Hill', 'Riff Raff'] (*b c.*1950) rock singer–songwriter. Playing guitar and keyboards, he was spotted by Festival Records singing his songs in a tal-

ent quest. He made a single *See My Way* in 1971, then his debut album *Days Of Wilderness* in 1972. He lived in England from 1974, formed Glen Cardier and the Cardinals in 1981, then Bel Aires in 1982. His songs have been recorded by Olivia ★Newton-John and ★Ol'55. As Sydney Hill his *Establishment Blues* was released with *C'mon Aussie, C'mon*.

FURTHER REFERENCE
Recordings include *See My Way* (Infinity INK 4121), *Days Of Wilderness* (Festival L36822). For discography, see *SpencerA*. See also *SpencerW*.

Cardus, Sir Neville   (*b* Rusholme, Lancashire England, 3 Apr. 1888; *d* London 28 Feb. 1975), music critic, writer. While working as a clerk in a marine insurance firm he made his own study of literature, philosophy and the arts. He worked as a music critic for the *Daily Citizen* in 1916, then as a reporter for the *Manchester Guardian* from 1917, coming to attention as a cricket reporter (from 1919), and as music critic from 1927. He visited Australia as reporter for the cricket test in 1936, and returned with Beecham in 1940, becoming music critic for the *Sydney Morning Herald*, writing for the *ABC Weekly*, and broadcasting for ABC radio, notably *The Enjoyment of Music* (from 1942). His 20 books include two written in Australia, *Ten Composers* (1945) and *Autobiography* (1947). He lived in London again from 1949, but visited Australia twice more to report cricket tests. An intuitive and personal writer, he introduced to Australian music criticism fine craftsmanship, humour, and an authority which powerfully lifted the standards of writing and influenced all his successors. He was honoured with the CBE in 1964 and knighted in 1967.

FURTHER REFERENCE
Obit. in *SMH* 9 Mar. 1975. A later autobiography is *My Life* (London: Collins, 1965). See also Christopher Brookes, *His Own Man: The Life of Neville Cardus* (Sydney: Allen & Unwin, 1987); Robin Daniels, *Conversations with Cardus* (London: Gollancz, 1976); Sally O'Neill, *ADB*, 13.

Carey, Clive   (*b* Hedingham, Essex, England, 30 May 1883; *d* London, 30 Apr. 1968), baritone, composer. Carey studied at Cambridge University and at the Royal College of Music, taking composition with Stanford and voice with James Ley and later Jean de Reszke. He sang at Sadler's Wells with Melba, Lilian Baylis and others, and came to Australia in 1924 to teach voice and produce opera at the Elder Conservatorium, Adelaide. He returned to London in 1927, composing and producing for Sadler's Wells in the 1930s, and was again in Australia as director of the Albert Street Conservatorium, Melbourne, 1941–44, before returning to London to teach at the Royal College of Music. An active composer as well as tenor, opera producer and teacher, his singing students included Ruth Naylor and Richard ★Watson in Adelaide,

Elsie *Morison in Melbourne, and Arnold *Matters and most notably Joan *Sutherland (in 1951) in London.

FURTHER REFERENCE
MackenzieS, 16–17; *GlennonA*, 46.

Carey, Rick and Thel. See *Rick and Thel*.

Cargher, John (*b* London, 24 Jan. 1919), radio broadcaster, critic. Trained as a toolmaker, he had a successful career managing his own company Three Arts Ballet in London from 1938 before settling in Melbourne in 1951. He became general manager of Thomas' in 1959, then managing director of the National Theatre, Melbourne, in 1969. His weekly radio broadcasts of fine recordings also commenced in 1959, and he was opera and ballet critic for the *Bulletin* 1964–92.

An encyclopaedic knowledge of musical anecdote and an inexhaustible store of rare recordings, particularly of opera-singers, has kept his ABC programs on air for more than 30 years. His criticism has appeared in the *Australian* and *Opera News*, and he has written six books, including the best-selling *How to Enjoy Opera Without Really Trying* (1986). He was honoured with the AM in 1987.

FURTHER REFERENCE
His other books include *Music for Pleasure* (1970), *Opera and Ballet in Australia* (Cassell, 1977), *There's Music in My Madness* (1984), *How to Enjoy Music Without Really Trying* (1987) and *Bravo! 200 Years of Opera in Australia* (Sydney: ABC/Macmillan, 1988). See also *CA* (1995–96); *WWA* (1996).

Carillon. An instrument of at least 23 cast bronze bells, tuned in chromatic order, played by a keyboard and capable of harmony. After great popularity in the 17th century, carillon art fell into decline until the revival, particularly in the USA, in the years of World War I. There was little interest in carillons in Australia, however, and there are only three Australian carillons in existence: at the University of Sydney's Gothic clock tower (54 Taylor bells, 1928); at the Bathurst city centre (35 Taylor bells, 1933); and the dramatically modern carillon tower on the banks of Lake Burley Griffin, Canberra (53 Taylor bells, 1970). Noted carillonists have been John Gordon (Sydney, from 1944) and John Barrett (Canberra, *b* 1916; *d* 29 Jan. 1983).

FURTHER REFERENCE
John D. Keating, *Bells in Australia* (MUP, 1977).

Carlos, Michael (*b* Germany, 1948), film composer. He migrated to Australia in 1967 and formed the rock group Tully, which featured in the Sydney production of *Hair*, and subsequently toured Australia with great success. Carlos was musical director for several LP recordings, including Jon English's *Wine Dark Sea* and Jeannie Lewis's *Free Fall Through Featherless Flight*, and theatre works, including *Jesus Christ Superstar* (1975–76). He was composer-in-residence for the Nimrod Theatre in Sydney in 1981. A leading exponent in electronic music, Carlos has worked as the official consultant on synthesisers for Boosey & Hawkes in Australia, and written several film scores employing electronic music techniques. His film credits include *Storm Boy* (1976), *Blue Fin* (1978), *Dawn!* and *Long Weekend* (1979), and *The Dark Room* (1982). More recently, Carlos has worked as a music arranger.

FURTHER REFERENCE
LimbacherF.   L.THOMPSON

Carmody, Kev (*b* Darling Downs, Qld), Aboriginal singer-songwriter. Many of Carmody's songs are critical of treatment of Aborigines, while others are generally socially focused, exposing such issues as the conditions of street kids. He supported Bob Dylan, Bonnie Raitt, and Billy Bragg on their Australian tours, and regularly performs with many other Aboriginal musicians, including Ruby *Hunter, Roger *Knox, Archie *Roach, *Mixed Relations, *Tiddas, *Warumpi Band and Bart *Willoughby. He is a regular performer at Aboriginal festivals such as Stompen Ground (Broome, 1992) and Survival Day concerts held at La Perouse, NSW, on 26 January each year, in opposition to the Australia Day celebrations. Tours include Canada and Europe, 1995.

FURTHER REFERENCE
Recordings include *Eulogy (For a Black Person)* (1991, Festival D30692); *Street Beat* (1992, Festival D111344); *Kev Carmody: Bloodlines* (1993 Festival, D30954); and *Images and Illusions* (1995, Festival D31380). See also R. Johnson, 'Looking Out: Interview with Kev Carmody', *Perfect Beat* 1/2 (1993), 43–7.
                                             P. DUNBAR-HALL

Carnegie. Firm of piano manufacturers founded by Jabez Carnegie at Melbourne in 1867. After having been apprenticed as a piano-maker at Collard & Collard and at Broadwood in England, Carnegie came to Victoria in search of gold in 1858, but was soon working as a grocer. He began building pianos from local timbers in 1867, making the veneers from Tasmanian rosewood, mahogany and walnut. After his death in 1892 his four sons developed his business, by the postwar years producing local versions of Rönisch and Thalberg instruments under licence (because of the anti-German sentiment they were sold as 'Francis Howard' and 'Henry Randall' pianos). By 1928 the firm had a factory at Richmond, Melbourne, employing 300 people, and had diversified into radio manufacture (using the same style of elaborate wooden veneer for the cases) and other electrical goods. With the Depression of the 1930s and the increasing popularity of radio as a source for music at home, demand for pianos declined, and the firm ceased manufacture in 1947.

FURTHER REFERENCE

A Carnegie piano is held in the National Gallery of Victoria. See *AthertonA*.

Caron, Leon Francis Victor (*b* Boulogne-sur-Mer, France, 13 Jan. 1850; *d* Sydney, 29 May 1915), conductor, composer. A talented violinist, Caron entered the Paris Conservatoire in the late 1860s, having received lessons in violin from Camilla Urso and composition from Alexandre Guilmant. After migrating to Melbourne in December 1876, he joined William Lyster's Opera Co. and by 1879 was a regular conductor. In 1889, after an ill-fated attempt at forming his own opera group, he joined J.C. *Williamson's company as musical director and later went on to conduct many Gilbert and Sullivan seasons. He also orchestrated scores and composed additional music for Williamson's theatrical productions. His most successful compositions for Williamson were the pantomimes *Djin Djin* (1895) and *Matsa* (1896). Other compositions include three string quartets, a choral symphony, a violin concerto, an opera *Mata-Mati* (unperformed), and the prizewinning cantata *Victoria* written for the 1880 Melbourne International Exhibition.

FURTHER REFERENCE

Herald (Melbourne) 21 May 1949; Kenneth Hince, *ADB*, 3; H. Morin Humphreys, *Men of the Time in Australia*, Victorian Series, 2nd edn. (Melbourne: McCarron, Bird & Co., 1882), xxv–xxvi; Kerry Murphy, 'Leon Caron: His Role in the Musical Life of 19th-Century Australia', *Explorations* 2 (1985), 10–13.

JENNIFER ROYLE

Carr, Warren (*b* Newcastle), popular music pianist, arranger. In 1960 he was pianist with The Kaydets, then in 1961 went solo and became a regular on *Bandstand* and *Six O'Clock Rock*. In the genre of American pianist Floyd Cramer, his singles *Li'l Ole Me* (1961) and *Rondo* (1962) reached Nos. 8 and 10 in the charts respectively; he released an album *L'l Ole Me And My Piano* in 1963. From then on he adopted a more middle-of-the-road style and took club and session work, producing *Mexican Bug* (1966) and *Party Time Piano* (1972).

FURTHER REFERENCE

Recordings include *Li'l Ole Me* (1961, Leedon LK100), *Rondo* (1962, Leedon LK220), *Lil Ole Me And My Piano* (1962, Leedon), *Mexican Bug* (1966, Festival FK1564) and *Party Time Piano* (1972, Summit SRA 250119). For discography, see *SpencerA*. See also *McGrathA*; *SpencerW*.

Carr-Boyd, Ann née Wentzel (*b* Sydney, 13 July 1938), composer, pianist, music historian. Born into a family of professional musicians, she was the first music graduate from the University of Sydney in 1960. She undertook pioneering research in Australian music history financed by a Commonwealth Research Grant. As the Sydney Moss Scholar 1963–65 she studied composition in London with Peter Racine Fricker and Alexander Goehr, returning to Australia in 1967. In 1975 she won the Albert H. Maggs Award for composition, and she was a finalist in the 1986 Aliénor International Harpsichord Compositions Award, Washington DC. She is a prolific composer whose work includes scores for film and television, orchestral and chamber groups, and instrumental and vocal combinations, notably *Fandango* for mandolins. In style her music is eclectic, ranging from neo-Baroque to 12-tone and ragtime, and is characterised by a certain lyricism, rhythmic vitality and lush harmonies. From 1993 she has been senior lecturer in composition at the Australian International Conservatorium of Music, Enfield, Sydney, but in 1996 she moved to Bowral, NSW, mainly to find more time to compose.

FURTHER REFERENCE

Recordings include *The Bells of Sydney Harbour*, David Kinsella, org (1979, SCCD 1002); *Fandango* (1992, JAD CD 1022); *Home Thoughts from Abroad* (1987, JAD CD 1028); *Perpetual Motion* (1992, JAD CD 1029); *Suite Veronese* (1985, JAD CD 1023). Her writings include over 20 articles in *GroveD* and The First Hundred Years in Australian Music: 1788–1888, MA Univ. Sydney, 1963. A list of works appears in *CohenI* and *LePageW*. See also *ADMR*.

THÉRÈSE RADIC

Carroll, Pat (*b* Melbourne, *c.*1946), pop singer. After taking singing lessons, she appeared on television from the age of 11 and then in the musical comedy *Bye Bye, Birdie*. She appeared on the television shows *Bandstand* and *Go!!* and her singles included *He's My Guy* (1964), *He's A Rebel* (1966), and the EP *The Many Faces Of Pat Carroll* (1964). She won the *TV Week* Queen of Pop title and went to England, where she formed a duo with Olivia *Newton-John, working on television and in clubs as Pat and Olivia. Then came *All Kinds Of Everything* (1970) and *Now I'm Stuck On You* (1974). She married John Farrar (of the Strangers) and from the late 1970s she has been based in the USA, continuing to perform.

FURTHER REFERENCE

Recordings included *He's My Guy* (1964, W&G S2302), *He's A Rebel* (1966, W&G S8031), *The Many Faces Of Pat Carroll* (1964 W&G E2408), *All Kinds Of Everything* (1970, Fable FB004) and *Now I'm Stuck On You* (1974, Interfusion ITFK 5288). For discography, see *SpencerA*. See also *McGrathA*; *SpencerW*.

Carter. Two brothers, both of whom studied with George Howard in Melbourne and played with the original Sydney Symphony Orchestra from 1908 and the NSW State Orchestra 1919–22.

(1) Bryce Morrow Carter (*b* Melbourne, 17 June 1879; *d* Longueville, Sydney, 5 Jan. 1939), cellist. After studying with Howard he went to Gerard Vollmer, and he taught cello from 1899. He appeared as associate artist with Melba in 1907 and taught at the NSW State Conservatorium from 1916.

(2) Francis Mowat Carter (*b* Melbourne, 15 Feb. 1882; *d* Strathfield, Sydney 24 Mar 1956), violinist. He taught violin from 1904 and toured as associate artist to Clara Butt.

FURTHER REFERENCE
Tony Mills, *ADB*, 7.

Cary, Tristram Ogilvie (*b* Oxford, England, 14 May 1925), composer. After wartime service in the Royal Navy he completed his studies at Christ Church Oxford, then Trinity College London in 1951. While working in a record shop he developed his first electronic music studio, and from 1955 worked freelance, producing music for radio, television and film, winning a BFA award (1959) and the Prix Italia (1962). He founded the electronic music studio at the Royal College of Music in 1967, came to Australia in 1974 and was senior lecturer (later reader) at the Elder Conservatorium 1975–91. His works were among the first heard in Australia to involve synthesiser or tape, which he typically combined with traditional instruments, as in the cantata *Peccata mundi* (1976) or *Divertimento* (1973), but there are also works for more traditional ensembles, such as the quartets or the orchestral work *Contours and Densities at First Hill* (1976). He has published a *Dictionary of Musical Technology* (Westport, Conn.: Greenwood, 1992).

FURTHER REFERENCE
Recordings include *Peccata mundi* (1976, BBC Transcription Service), *Divertimento* (1973, Move MS 3027), and *Continuum* (Canberra School of Music, CSM 5). His writings include 'Adventures and Dangers', *24 Hours* 1/7 (Aug 1976) and 'Moving Pictures From an Exhibition', *Composer* 25 (Autumn 1967) 10–12. See also Hugo Cole, *GroveD*; Kay Fitton, Tristram Cary: Pioneer of Electronic Music in England, unpub. MMus thesis, Univ. Adelaide, 1984.

Cashmere, Joe (Albert Joseph) ['Balgammon'] (*b* Yandumbla Creek nr Booligal, NSW, 17 Nov. 1872; *d* Bankstown, Sydney, 8 May 1959), traditional musician. He was well known in the Hillston area of NSW as a bush singer, fiddler, yarn spinner and hypnotist from *c*.1890. He contributed poems and articles to the *Bulletin*, the *Worker* and the *Albury Banner* as 'Balgammon.' His fiddling and singing, recorded in the 1950s, encapsulate NSW rural popular music from the mid-19th century to the 1930s. During the 1950s he performed at concerts and on radio. His work is preserved on recordings at *CAnl*.

FURTHER REFERENCE
Examples of his work are transcribed in *MeredithF*, I, 77–88.
                                        ALAN MUSGROVE

Caspers, Ella (*b* Albury, NSW, 1887; *d* 1971), contralto. She appeared at the Sydney Town Hall at the age of 13 and studied voice with Sr Christian, a notable oratorio singer in London who had taken religious orders and established the Garcia School for singers at Potts Point, Sydney. After coming to Dame Clara Butt's attention, she went to study at the Royal Academy, London, in 1913 on an exhibition, then returned to Sydney and sang at the opening of the NSW State Conservatorium in 1915. In London she sang at the Boosey Concerts and was a popular oratorio artist at the Albert Hall and Queen's Hall. With silky diction, delicate tone colours, and a wide range, her appearances in *Elijah* and *The Dream of Gerontius* and her Ruth in Sullivan's *Golden Legend* were particularly memorable.

FURTHER REFERENCE
MackenzieS, 87–9.

Castles. Family of singers raised at Bendigo, Victoria.
(1) Amy Eliza Castles (*b* Melbourne, July 1880; *d* Melbourne, Nov. 1951), soprano. At an early age she moved to Bendigo. She was educated at the Convent of the *Sisters of Mercy where she was taught by a lay singing teacher, E. Allan Bindley. With the help of the *Bendigo Independent* she was discovered in 1898, and early in 1899 under the wing of Mrs Ida Doubleday introduced to Melbourne audiences in a series of large concerts conducted with vice-regal patronage. She was given to the public as a young convent girl, and, dressed to create this impression, her small stature supported the ruse. The *Bulletin* soon noted the great interest taken in Amy by the Catholic Church and the Catholic press, especially the *Freeman's Journal* and the *Catholic Press*. The latter first announced that Amy seemed to be the new Melba, gathering substantial support for the new singer. The Catholic Church, having noted the value of cultural successes like those achieved by Melba, determined to create a weapon to dislodge and replace Melba, who was commonly held to be a 'Protestant tart'.

Castles went to Paris and after a brief period of training with Mathilde Marchesi late in 1899 she was coached by Jacques Bouhy. She undertook extensive concert work, especially in the UK where she sang in ubiquitous ballad concert seasons with the firms Boosey, Chappell and Harrison and made a few appearances in oratorio. She returned to Australia in 1902 and 1909 with Peter *Dawson, making her debut in opera in Australia in a J.C. *Williamson production in 1910. In 1912 she accepted a position as solo singer with the Imperial Opera in Vienna, but within three months had applied to abandon her contract. Before the end of 1913 she travelled to Italy where she studied for a while with Roberto *Hazon, and in 1915 she returned home, singing in a number of war-effort concerts in Australia and the USA in 1917. In 1919, claiming that she was passing up a contract with the Metropolitan Opera in New York, she participated in the 1919–20 Williamson Opera Season. This was her last attempt to find a place in opera, and her career slowly declined through a series of concerts and Australasian regional tours, usually with her sister Eileen (4) and sometimes for charity.

Castles' significance as an opera singer was not great. Reviews in Vienna had been generally cool or negative, critics finding her voice very small, often pushed sharp, and her stage presence affected by stage-fright. Less exacting listeners were enthusiastic, but her life became a pawn in the cultural aspirations of Australia's Irish Catholic Church. As a lucrative drawcard for the Taits and the Williamson Opera Co. she remains a performer of great interest, her life being more closely associated than any other singer with the sectarian forces that have shaped Australia.

(2) George Edward Castles (*b* Melbourne, 1881; *d* 1970), tenor. Brother of Amy Castles (1), he appeared briefly in musical theatre in London before World War I. During the war he sang with a 4th Division concert party in France and was the tenor soloist at a special mass given in Amiens Cathedral to celebrate the Armistice in 1918. In Australia after the war he occasionally appeared in concerts, but worked as the manager of the touring concert careers of his sisters Amy and Eileen (4).

(3) Ethel ('Dolly') Margaret Castles (*b* Bendigo, 1884; *d* 1971), soprano. Sister of Amy Castles (1), she had a short career as a light soprano in musical comedy and operetta. In the USA she created the principal soprano role in the *Tic Toc Man of Oz*, and in Australia she was widely known in Gilbert and Sullivan opera, appearing as Princess Zara in the Australian premiere of *Utopia Limited*. She retired from the stage after World War I.

(4) Eileen Anne Castles (*b* Bendigo, Vic., 1886; *d* 1970), soprano. Sister of Amy Castles (1) she sang Siebel (*Faust*) and Micaëla (*Carmen*) in the 1911 Melba-Williamson Opera Season. In later life she toured extensively with her sister Amy (1), giving concerts of opera arias and popular ballads. Two sound recordings made by Columbia in Australia in 1926–27 show that she had a light, flexible but ordinary voice.

FURTHER REFERENCE
For Amy Castles, recordings (1906–07, 1909, 1917 and 1926) are now rare. See also *GlennonA*, 7–8; *MackenzieS*, 101–6; Thérèse Radic, *ADB*, 3.   JEFF BROWNRIGG

Castro, Juan José (*b* Buenos Aires, 1895; *d* 1968), conductor. Born one of four brothers, each an outstanding musician, Castro studied in Paris, conducted at the Teatro Colon 1930–43, became director of the Buenos Aires Philharmonic Orchestra in 1931, was conductor of the Havana Philharmonic Orchestra 1947–48, the National Symphony Orchestra of Buenos Aires 1955–56, and director of the Puerto Rico Conservatory in 1959. Disagreements with the Perón regime forced him to leave Argentina in 1951. After touring Australia for the ABC, he was appointed conductor of the Victorian Symphony

Orchestra 1951–53. Also a prolific composer, his opera *Proserpina y el extranjero* won the Verdi Prize and was performed at La Scala in 1951.

J.L. HOLMES

Caswell, Alan (*b* Chester, England, 9 Mar. 1952), country music songwriter, singer, producer. His family settled in Australia when he was 12. Listening to Tammy Wynette, George Jones and Hank Williams, with his two brothers he began singing and songwriting in his teens as The Castle Brothers. His song *On The Inside* became the theme for the television series *Prisoner* in 1979; it reached No. 3 in the British charts when the series was released there in 1989. A prolific songwriter, especially on themes of humour or love, he has won three ACMA Golden Guitars. With partner Paul Harrison he regularly writes for Nashville, Tennessee, and with Don *Spencer he has written four albums for children. He has also worked as a producer on various albums, including Deniese Morrison's *Unfinished Business*. More than 350 of his songs have been recorded.

FURTHER REFERENCE
Recordings include *Loco Friday Night* (1980), *Handwritten* (1987) and *Heartwritten* (1990). See also *LattaA*, 48–9; *SmithB*, 158.

Cave, Nick (Nicholas Edward) (*b* Warracknabeal, Vic., 22 Sept. 1957), singer-songwriter. He formed the new-wave band Boys Next Door in Melbourne (1976) with Mick Harvey (guitar), Tracy Pew (bass, voice) and Phil Calvert (drums). Guitarist Rowland Howard joined in 1978, and the band independently released *Door Door* and the mini-album *Hee-Haw* (1979). In 1980 the band changed its name to *Birthday Party and relocated to London. Considered to be one of the most important bands of the post-punk era, Birthday Party recorded several independent albums including *Prayers on Fire* (1981) and *Junkyard* (1983), and collaborated with Lydia Lunch and the Berlin-based Einsturzende Neubauten before disbanding in 1983. By now notorious for his intensely provocative and volatile style, Cave formed the Bad Seeds (1984) with multi-instrumentalist Mick Harvey, former Einsturzende Neubauten guitarist Blixa Bargeld and bassist Barry Adamson. Nick Cave and the Bad Seeds have released an impressive collection of inventive independent albums including *From Her to Eternity* (1984), *The First Born is Dead* (1985), *Your Funeral, My Trial* (1986), *Tender Prey* (1988), *The Good Son* (1990), *Henry's Dream* (1992) and *Let Love In* (1994). Their 1986 release *Kicking Against the Pricks* featured *The Singer*, which topped the UK independent chart, and Cave's duet with Kylie *Minogue, *The Wild Rose* from *Murder Ballads* (1995), enjoyed mainstream chart success in Australia and the UK. Cave played a major role in the Australian film *Ghosts … of the Civil Dead* (1989) and collaborated with Harvey and Bargeld on the film's sound-track. Also contributing to Cave's rise to international acclaim are his live performance in Wim

Wenders' film *Wings of Desire* (1988), and his contributions to the sound-tracks of Wim Wenders' *Until the End of the World* (1991) and *Far Away, So Close!* (1993), *Gas Food Lodging* (1992) and *Batman Forever* (1995). His 1993 song *Red Right Hand* inspired and features in *The X-Files* tribute album *Songs in the Key of X* (1996).

FURTHER REFERENCE
Recordings with Boys Next Door include *Door Door* (1979, Mushroom L 36931); *Hee-Haw* (1979, Missing Link MLEP 3); with Birthday Party *Birthday Party* (1980, Missing Link LINK 77); *Prayers on Fire* (1981, Missing Link LINK 14); *Junkyard* (1982, 4AD CAD 207); *The Bad Seed* (1983, 4AD BAD 301); *It's Still Living* (1985, Missing Link ING 009); *The Bad Seed/The 'Mutiny' Sessions* (1989, Mute CAD 301); Nick Cave and the Bad Seeds *From Her to Eternity* (1984, Mute STUMM 17); *The First Born is Dead* (1985, Mute STUMM 21); *Kicking Against the Pricks* (1986, Mute STUMM 28); *Your Funeral, My Trial* (1986, Mute STUMM 34); *Tender Prey* (1988, Mute STUMM 52); *The Good Son* (1990, Mute STUMM 76); *Henry's Dream* (1992, Mute STUMM 92); *Live Seeds* (1993, Mute STUMM 122); *Let Love In* (1994, Mute STUMM 123); *Murder Ballads* (1995, Liberation/Mute TVD 93452); with Mick Harvey and Blixa Bargeld *Ghosts . . . of the Civil Dead* (1989, IONIC 3). Books include *King Ink* (London: Black Spring, 1988); *And the Ass Saw the Angel* (London: Black Spring, 1988). See also *McGrathA*; *SpencerW*; *GuinnessP*; I. Johnston, *Bad Seed: The Biography of Nick Cave* (London: Little, Brown & Co., 1995).

AARON D.S. CORN

Cawthorne, Charles Witto-Witto (*b* Adelaide, 1854; *d* Adelaide, 26 June 1925), music retailer, conductor. He joined his father's newsagency business in Adelaide at the age of 14 and they became music retailers in 1884. From 1887 Charles was sole proprietor of the business and in 1911 the company acquired a building in Rundle Street. Cawthorne stocked sheet music from England, France and Germany as well as instruments, operated a box office for concerts in Adelaide and by 1900 began publishing. He also conducted the Adelaide Amateur Orchestra, and acted as manager to a succession of Adelaide orchestras in the 1890s. In 1910 he was founder and conductor of the Adelaide Orchestral Society. In 1924 he became chairman of a limited company with his sons as directors.

FURTHER REFERENCE
Suzanne Edgar, Joyce Gibberd, *ADB*, 7.

SUZANNE ROBINSON

Ceberano, Kate (*b* Melbourne, 17 Nov. 1966), rock and jazz singer. Ceberano's career began at the age of 13 with an appearance on the television show *Search for a Star*. She left school and formed the band Essendon Airport, later joining the Hoggie Cats to perform jazz. In 1983, with her band ★I'm Talking, she had three Top 10 records and a gold album, and won the best new talent award at the *Countdown* Awards in 1984. In 1987 her

album *You've Always Got The Blues* won a platinum record. She also won the ARIA best female vocalist, and in 1989 her first solo album *Brave* was released and won triple platinum records. In 1992 she played Mary Magdalene in the revival of *Jesus Christ Superstar*. She toured Southeast Asia, Los Angeles and Spain in support of her funk album *Think About It* (1991), and in 1994 she was with the ABC TV show *Kate and Friends*. Ceberano moves with versatility between her two musical interests, pop with her band Ministry of Fun and jazz with her Sextet; her musical influences range from Ella Fitzgerald to Madonna.

FURTHER REFERENCE
Her recordings include singles *Love Dimension* (1989, Regular Records); *Brave* (1989, Regular Records RMD 51026); *That's What I Call Love* (1990, Regular Records); *See Right Through* (1991, Regular Records); *I Don't Know How to Love Him* (1992, Regular Records); her albums include *Think About It* (1991, Regular Records D 91059); with Wendy Mathews: *You've Always Got The Blues* (1988, EMI 479595–2); and with her Septet: *Kate Ceberano and Her Septet Live* (1987, Regular Records RMD 38708). See also the *Australian* 18 Aug. 1990; Tracee Huchinson, *Your Name's on the Door: 10 Years of Australian Music* (Sydney: ABC Enterprises, 1992); *McGrathA*; Eric Myers, ed., *Australian Jazz Directory* (Sydney: Jazz Co-ordination Association of NSW, 1994); *SpencerW.*

LYNDELL KING

Cecchi, Pietro (*b* Rome *c.*1831; *d* Melbourne, 4 Mar. 1897), tenor, singing teacher. After a European career which included singing in the premiere of Raimondi's *Putifar* in 1852, he arrived in Melbourne in 1871 with the vocal quartet of American soprano Agatha States, who gave concerts and pared-down opera performances with piano accompaniment in Sydney and Melbourne until ★Lyster gave them work the following year. After States left, Cecchi remained in Melbourne and taught singing at Allan's music house from 1873. Clearly a seasoned and experienced singer, his pupils included the young Melba, whom he taught at Presbyterian Ladies' College 1879–81, lending her money (which she never repaid) after she left her husband in 1883, and Maggie Stirling, the mezzo-soprano who became a singer of popular ballads and Scottish songs in Europe.

FURTHER REFERENCE
Obit. *Argus* 5 Mar. 1897 and *Australasian* 6 Mar. 1897, 497. His correspondence with Melba is in Thorold Waters, *Much Besides Music* (Melbourne: Georgian House, 1951), 109–19. See also *MackenzieS*, 38–41; Peter Game, *The Music Sellers* (Melbourne: Hawthorn Press, 1976), 71–6; John Hetherington, *Melba: A Biography* (London: Faber, 1973).

Cedar Tree, The. Musical comedy by Varney ★Monk, libretto by Edmund Barclay on an Australian period theme. First performed by the Frank Thring Co. at the Princess Theatre, Melbourne, in 1935. See *Musical Comedy*.

Celibate Rifles.   Rock group formed in 1981 at Sydney when vocalist Damien Lovelock joined with a group of Forest High School students, now Dave Morris [Moras] (guitar), Kent Steedman (guitar), Rudy Morabito (bass), and Phil Jacquet (drums). Naming themselves as a send-up of the Sex Pistols, they developed a frenetic, satirical post-punk style, musically influenced by *Radio Birdman and *Saints.

FURTHER REFERENCE
Recordings include singles *Pretty Pictures* (1983, Hot HOT 704), *Eddie Phantom* (1986, Phree 2) and *Grooving In The Land Of Love* (1991, Festival); albums include *Sideroxylon* (1983, Hot HOT 1001), *Kiss Kiss, Bang Bang* (1986, Hot HOT1029) and *Blind Ear* (1994, Hot HOT1046CD). For discography, see *SpencerA*. See also *SpencerW*; Michael White, 'Celibate Rifles: Exploiting Contradictions'. *The Next Thing,* ed. Clinton Walker (Kenthurst NSW: Kangaroo Press, 1984), 31–6; *Melody Maker* (5 Jan. 1991), 29.

Cellar, The.   Originally a coffee shop called Blinks at Twin Street, Adelaide, the lease was taken in 1961 by John Howell, who established it as a jazz venue under the name The Cellar. With the jazz boom reaching its peak, The Cellar became a significant centre of Australian modern jazz. Apart from nurturing Adelaide's leading musicians—including Billy Ross and Bob Jeffrey—it also drew interstate musicians for lengthy periods, including Keith Barr, Bob Bertles, Keith Stirling and locally born Bob Gebert. In 1964 Howell sold his interest to Alex Innocenti, who gradually shifted musical emphasis until selling in 1972, when it became a restaurant.

FURTHER REFERENCE
OxfordJ.   BRUCE JOHNSON

Central Australian Aboriginal Media Association (CAAMA).   Based at Alice Springs, NT, it includes a radio broadcasting network, a video production company, an arts and crafts business, and a national music label. Begun in 1980 as a grass-roots organisation run by volunteer workers, CAAMA Radio's satellite broadcasting area comprises the middle third of the continent; its programming consists primarily of Aboriginal content. CAAMA Music, as the largest producer of Aboriginal popular music in Australia, has committed itself to aiding and supporting Aboriginal community and cultural development. Its objectives include empowering the Aboriginal community through production of recorded and broadcast music, concerts, festivals and events of local relevance; encouraging use of traditional Aboriginal languages; demonstrating, promoting and applying appropriate cultural behaviour in all music-based activities; and encouraging the use, recording and performance of traditional music. See also *Aboriginal Music*, §4(iii).

FURTHER REFERENCE
Recordings include *Rebel Voices From Black Australia* (M116, 1983); *Light On,* Areyonga Desert Tigers (M121, 1988*); Lightning Strikes,* Ilkari Maru (M125, 1988); *Bushfire Radio Songs* (M202, 1989); *From the Bush* (M214, 1989); *Ulpanyali Band* (M220, 1991); *Lasseter's Highway,* Wild Brumbys (M224, 1992); *Civilised World,* Amunda (M223, 1992); *In Aboriginal* (M240, 1994); *Desert Calling,* Blackstorm (M246, 1995); *Sing Country,* The Bush Kids (M238, 1995); *Our Home Our Land,* Native Title Album (M252, 1995); *Blekbala Mujik* (M245, 1995); and *Too Much Humbug,* Warumpi Band (1996).   KATHLEEN R. OIEN

Centre for Aboriginal Studies in Music (CASM). From the time of its formation in 1975, CASM, which grew out of the research activities of Catherine *Ellis at the University of Adelaide, provided a unique education through music for indigenous Australian students, encompassing both traditional and non-traditional educational systems, the traditional the province of Pitjantjatjara-speaking elders employed as senior lecturers at the University. Since CASM's move out of the University faculty structure in 1996, when it became a part of Wilto Yerlo (Aboriginal and Torres Strait Islander support unit), traditional teaching by Pitjantjatjara-speaking elders no longer features in the program. All students currently enrolled in CASM study for an associate diploma in Aboriginal studies in music. Some successfully complete their studies, others achieve some form of public recognition as performers in bands, or in CASM productions such as *Urban Corroboree* (1987), or as recipients of grants affording them a specialised training in the music industry. In one instance, for example, the Aboriginal and Torres Strait Islander Commission currently funds two former CASM students training in audio engineering. See also *Aboriginal Music*, §4(iii).
                                                HELEN PAYNE

Centre for Studies in Australian Music.   Associated with University of Melbourne, the centre was established in 1992 by Warren *Bebbington to promote the 'scholarly study and understanding of Australian music through seminars, courses, and publications'. Major projects undertaken there include Bebbington's *Oxford Companion to Australian Music*, Brenton Broadstock's *Sound Ideas: Australian Composers Born Since 1950*, and the Historic Australian Opera Project, which produced critical editions of Marshall-Hall's *Stella,* Alfred Hill's *Giovanni,* and Fritz Hart's *Riders to the Sea*. It has also sponsored performances using those editions, issued a newsletter, launched an academic journal, *Australasian Music Research* (1997–), and various bibliographical resources. Primarily through its publications, the centre has rapidly established itself as a leader in research into Australian music.
                                          ROYSTON GUSTAVSON

Chain.   Blues group (1967–74; 1982–), formed in Melbourne, best known in their Brisbane years with Matt Taylor (vocals), Phil Manning (guitar), Barry 'Big Goose'

Sullivan (bass), and Barry 'Little Goose' Harvey (drums), but passing through numerous membership changes. Their lengthy blues improvising is reflected in *Chain ... Live*, which reached No. 3 in the album charts in 1970; *Towards The Blues* reached No. 3 in 1971. In the same year the single *We're Groaning,* once it was re-released as *Black And Blue,* reached No. 11 in the charts and *Judgement* No. 23, but blues has never sustained wide popularity in Australia and the band did not match these successes again. With Taylor's characteristic growl and Manning's exceptional blues work on guitar, they were the foremost blues band in Australia. They re-formed in Perth for the Mushroom Records tenth anniversary concert in 1982, but with later membership changes drifted towards hard rock in their albums *Child In The Street* (1985) and *Australian Rhythm And Blues* (1987).

FURTHER REFERENCE
Recordings include *Chain ... Live* (1970, Festival); *Towards The Blues* (1971, Infinity); *Black And Blue* (1971, Infinity); *Live Again* (1972, Infinity). For discography, see *SpencerA.* See also *GuinnessP,* 1, 448; *McGrathA*; *SpencerW.*

Challender, Stuart (*b* Hobart, 19 Feb. 1947; *d* Sydney, 13 Dec. 1991), conductor. While studying at the University of Melbourne he was chorusmaster then musical director of the Victorian Opera Co. Upon graduation in 1968 he undertook further study in Hamburg and Vienna, and from 1970 to 1974 worked as *répétiteur* then conductor with various German and Swiss opera houses, culminating in his appointment as resident conductor at the Basel Opera House from 1976 to 1980. He returned to Australia as resident conductor of the Australian Opera 1980–85. Foreign debuts included the Netherlands Opera 1982, the San Diego Opera 1986, the Royal Philharmonic Orchestra 1987, the Boston Symphony in Hong Kong 1989, the Chicago Symphony 1990, and the English National Opera 1991. In Australia he was the artistic director of the Seymour Group, conducted at all major arts festivals, worked with youth orchestras and dance companies, and in 1986 became principal guest conductor then chief conductor and artistic director of the Sydney Symphony Orchestra, a position he held until his death from AIDS in 1991. Highlights from this period included his first commercial recording, of *Voss* with the Australian Opera, the Sydney Symphony Orchestra's critically acclaimed 1988 American tour, and his last engagement, *Der Rosenkavalier* for the Australian Opera. Challender embraced Classical, contemporary and Australian compositions and was renowned for his interpretive skills and musical insight. With the Sydney Symphony Orchestra he established the Stuart Challender Trust to secure future conductors and guest artists for the orchestra.

FURTHER REFERENCE
Obit. in *Australian,* 14 Dec. 1991, *Age* 14 Dec. 1991. Recordings include Mahler Symphony No. 2, Sydney Symphony Orchestra

(ABC 434 778–2); R. Strauss overtures, Sydney Symphony Orchestra (ABC 426 480); Carl Vine Symphonies, Sydney Symphony Orchestra (ABC 426 995); *Symphony Under the Stars,* Sydney Symphony Orchestra (ABC 426 289). For discography see *HolmesC.* See also *Australian* 22–23 Aug. 1987; James Murdoch, 'Life in the Fast Lane with Stuart Challender', *This Australia* 6/4 (Spring 1987), 81–4; Sue Tronser, 'Challender Scores the SSO's US Tour', *24 Hours* (Mar. 1989), 16–17.

MARIANNE RIGBY

Chalwin, Vivian (*b* Surrey, England, 1916; *d* Sydney, 14 Oct. 1980), engineer, musical philanthropist. Educated in the UK as an engineer, he worked in various British corporations before becoming managing director of the diesel engine manufacturer J. & H. McLaren of Leeds, and director of 15 other companies. When he came to Australia in 1951, he was a wealthy man, and built a concert auditorium at his Sydney residence in the spirit of the 18th-century aristocratic music patrons. His home thereby became a venue for private concerts of considerable sophistication, often hosting musical societies such as the Mozart and Schubert Societies. He was a major patron and tireless worker for the Australian Opera and Musica Viva until his death.

FURTHER REFERENCE
Obit. in *SMH* 16 Oct. 1980. See also *SMH* 24 July 1965.

Chamber Made Opera. Contemporary music-theatre company formed in Melbourne in 1988 by Douglas Horton. The company focuses exclusively on new work, often using highly innovative venues—*The Cars That Ate Paris* (1991) was presented in a wrecker's yard. With assistance from the Australia Council and the State Government, Horton commissions works, presents productions of them in Melbourne and at festivals around Australia, and from 1992 has appeared at Covent Garden, Edinburgh, Hong Kong, NZ, Munich, San Jose and elsewhere. His company engages first-rate young singing talent and has presented 15 new works, of which 12 are by Australians, including Gordon Kerry's *Medea*, Andree Greenwell's *Sweet Death*, and Robert Ashley's *Improvement (Don Leaves Linda)*. Extending the possibilities of music-theatre, the company's standing as an independent professional company devoted entirely to contemporary opera is unique in Australia. They won the *Age* Performing Arts Award in 1995 and Horton received an Australia Council creative fellowship in 1996.

Chamber Music. Music in the earliest years of European colonisation was dominated at first by military bands and theatre music, and genuine chamber music was at first rarely heard in Australia. In the few middle-class homes whose social and domestic life attempted to conform to English provincial customs and expectations of the time, parlour music for voice, piano and other instruments was cultivated. The 1820s saw the founding in Sydney of Australia's first concert society, and such societies were founded sooner or later in the major settlements of each colony as they reached a similar stage of social development. Chamber music found a place on their publicly performed programs, but was of less interest than vocal and choral music or utilitarian genres. Non-functional instrumental music was most popular in SA, with its proportionally larger middle class and especially its German immigrants.

While duos, trios, and piano solos by late 18th-century composers were favoured, much chamber music was the type found in popular and economical anthologies of sheet music: recent arrangements of operatic melodies, popular song and dance tunes, and narrative-pictorial works, especially of a patriotic nature. Works by locally resident composers and arrangers complemented the vast amount of imported music.

The first chamber music concerts of note were presented by J.P. ★Deane at Hobart (from 1824) and Sydney (from 1836); with his children he formed a chamber ensemble which presented his own String Trio as well as introducing for the first time many chamber works of Haydn, Mozart and Beethoven. Nevertheless, the professional presentation of the more serious works of the chamber music repertoire remained uncommon and irregular in 19th-century Australia.

The gradual decline in domestic music-making in the first half of the twentieth century was paralleled by an increase in the quantity and quality of professional activities, which helped the growth of interest in chamber music. Most notable among the new professional ensembles was the ★Austral String Quartet, formed at Sydney in 1909. This paved the way for the remarkable ★Verbrugghen Quartet, an ensemble of the front international rank, which was based at Sydney and toured Australia 1916–22.

The Verbrugghen Quartet had been ensemble-in-residence at the NSW State Conservatorium, whose director was the quartet's leader. But the typical professional ensemble of the 1930s and 40s was a semi-permanent group of traditional instrumentation, which drew its members from the principals of the ABC orchestras. Clubs and societies, which by then existed throughout Australia, also sponsored the playing of chamber music in private and semi-public concerts by both professionals and amateurs.

Standard repertoire expanded to include the latest Romantic works, while arrangements were considerably less popular than in the 19th century. The Austral and Verbrugghen Quartets introduced numerous recent works from western Europe, and local composers, usually writing in a more old-fashioned style, also found some favour. Alfred ★Hill and G.W.L. ★Marshall-Hall are notable in this period for their string quartets. Virtually all composers wrote large quantities of piano music, especially miniatures. In many cases they also performed the works themselves; the popular duo pianists Lindley ★Evans and Frank ★Hutchens are notable here.

The founding of ★Musica Viva in 1945, important in itself, also indicates a new direction towards even greater professionalism, in which chamber repertoire plays a much greater part than ever before. In addition, it demonstrated the strong influence of central European immigrants, to whom chamber music was an important part of musical life and who considered Australian musical culture to be sorely lacking in this regard.

Since Musica Viva began its national chamber music subscription series in 1955, and particularly from the early 1970s onwards, many chamber ensembles of traditional instrumentation performing standard repertoire from Mozart to Bartók, as well as some contemporary works, have been formed. Notable among these were the second Austral String Quartet (1958–77) and the ★Sydney String Quartet (1966–71, 1974–83). The first wind chamber ensemble of distinction in Australia was the ★University of Adelaide Wind Quintet (1965–77); its work set the pattern for the ★New Sydney Wind Quintet (founded 1965), the ★Canberra Wind Soloists (founded 1978) and the Australian Wind Virtuosi (1979–85). The most internationally travelled chamber ensemble in the past decade has been the ★Australian String Quartet (founded 1985) in Adelaide. The ★Mittagong Trio (1980–91) left Australia for residence in Hong Kong in 1985. Melbourne has had a very intermittent history of chamber ensembles, the Ormond Trio (1959) and the Melbourne Trio (founded 1974) providing satisfying performances, but there were few attempts at establishing a string quartet until the ★Melbourne String Quartet was founded in 1993. While members of such ensembles are still sometimes ABC principals, more are now in residence at Australian music schools, and some are independent performers specialising in chamber and solo recital repertoire. As yet, none has achieved the longevity of the great European ensembles but some appear set to endure beyond two decades.

An important development has been the enormous growth of groups specialising in contemporary music. These include the ★Seymour Group (founded 1976), the ★Petra String Quartet (1977–89), ★Flederman (1979–89), the ★Australia Ensemble (1980), ★Elision (1986) and ★Perihelion (1988). Most such groups have non-traditional and/or heterogeneous instrumentation and bring contemporary music from overseas to Australia, as well as commissioning works from local composers. Composers themselves have often formed the nucleus of such groups. Much experimental music is also written for specific chamber ensembles, although these tend to be more *ad hoc* and much shorter lived. Recordings emanate primarily from groups specialising in contemporary repertoire, which release many new works, especially those commissioned by the group itself. The Canberra School of Music's ongoing *Anthology of Australian Music on Disc* is a major contribution to the recording of chamber music, as are specialist labels such as Move, Vox Australis and Tall Poppies.

Chamber music is now an integral part of all major festivals which include art music, and is also the focus of many more specialist events such as the Australian Festival of Chamber Music and Chamber Music School in Townsville, Melbourne's Music in the Round, and festivals such as the Barossa and Port Fairy. The prestigious biennial Melbourne International Chamber Music Competition is designed to encourage an increase in the quality of younger ensembles and interest in the genre generally, while creativity is also encouraged through the commissioning of several Australian works for compulsory performance. The Australian String Quartet Composers' Forum also aims to encourage the creation of quality works for the medium.

Chamber ensembles are largely supported, directly and indirectly, by Musica Viva and the Australia Council, as well as by educational institutions. Ensembles typically run their own regular concert series in their home city (this is usually an important element in launching new groups), tour to other states through Musica Viva and/or invitations to festivals, and tour outside capital cities, especially for educational performances. Virtually all conservatoriums and music departments run recital and chamber music series featuring their students, staff and visiting professionals. Music clubs and societies comprised of amateurs and music-lovers still play an important role; their chamber music series in the suburbs and regional centres provide a platform for students and young professionals.

The current scene includes a large number of high-profile ensembles including austraLYSIS, Binneas String Quartet, Canberra New Music Ensemble, Contemporary Music Events Company, Coruscations, Elektra String Quartet, Enigma 5, Evos Music, Kakadu Trio, LIBRA, Machine for Making Sense, ★Macquarie Trio, Nexus, Nova Ensemble, Soundstream, Sydney Alpha Ensemble, and Symeron. The number of less well known groups is enormous.

FURTHER REFERENCE

BrisbaneE; Australian Music Centre, *Catalogue of Instrumental and Chamber Music* (Sydney: Australian Music Centre, 1976) [up-to-date catalogue is available on-line]; idem, *Directory of Australian Music Organisations* (Sydney: Australian Music Centre, c.1985) [up-to-date information is available on-line]; Thérèse Radic, Some Historical Aspects of Musical Associations in Melbourne, 1888–1915, PhD, Univ. Melbourne, 1978; Michael Shmith, *Musica Viva Australia: The First 50 Years* (Sydney: Playbill, 1996); Ann Wentzel (Carr-Boyd), The First Hundred Years of Music in Australia, MA, Univ. Sydney, 1963.

PATRICIA SHAW

Chambermaids, The. All-female woodwind quintet, founded in 1990 from graduates of the Sydney Conservatorium, comprised of Amanda Hollins (flute), Anna Rodger (oboe), Jennie Ford (clarinet), Alison Campbell (french horn), and Jennie McLachlan (bassoon). Formed by expanding the Chambermaids Trio, they play a particularly wide repertoire, ranging from Bach to Berio. They have presented their own concert series at Sydney (since 1993) and toured extensively for Musica Viva.

Chambers, Lucy (*b* Sydney, *c.*1840; *d* Melbourne, 8 June 1894), contralto. She received her first vocal training from Sydney teacher Mrs Logan, cousin of W. Vincent ★Wallace. Encouraged by Catherine ★Hayes, she left Australia in January 1862 to study under Garcia in London and Romani in Florence. In April 1864 she made her operatic debut in Florence as Azucena in *Il Trovatore* and had continued success in Vienna, Berlin, Brussels, Bologna and Milan. In 1870 she returned to Australia as the principal contralto of Lyster's Italian Opera Co. Around 1873 she retired from the operatic stage and concentrated on teaching. Based in Melbourne, she was often described as the 'Australian Marchesi' and was the teacher of Alice ★Rees, Amy ★Sherwin, Ida Osborne and Florence ★Young. Suffering financial losses during the Depression, she made a final public concert appearance at the Melbourne Town Hall on 18 Oct 1893, after 20 years in retirement.

FURTHER REFERENCE

Sydney Mail 23 June 1894: 1277; *Weekly Times* 21 Oct. 1893: 6; H. Morin Humphreys, *Men of the Time in Australia*, Victorian Series, 2nd edn (Melbourne: McCarron, Bird & Co., 1882), xxvii–xxviii.

JENNIFER ROYLE

Change Ringing. Traditional English art of ringing a set of tower bells mounted on bell wheels by a team pulling bell ropes in a series of changes (permutations of the ringing sequence, determined according to strict rules). There are 28 bell towers with ringable peals in Australia. The first installed was likely St Mary's Cathedral, Sydney, in 1843 (replaced in 1882), but the oldest still in use are at Holy Trinity, Hobart (eight Whitechapel bells, installed 1847), St Benedict's, Sydney (six Whitechapel bells, 1850), Christ Church St Laurence, Sydney (six Taylor bells, 1852), and All Saint's, Parramatta (six Whitechapel bells, 1860). In other centres, the oldest are St Patrick's Cathedral, Melbourne (eight Murphy bells, 1868), Adelaide Town Hall (eight John Warner & Sons bells, 1866), St Paul's Maryborough, Queensland (nine Whitechapel bells, 1888), and St George's Cathedral, Perth (eight John Warner & Sons, 1902). The largest is at St Paul's Cathedral, Melbourne (12 Whitechapel bells, 1889), where the most important change ringing society was established, the Victorian Society of Ringers, who toured Australia demonstrating the first full peals heard in Australia (the *GrandSire Triples,* with more than 5000 changes) in 1890.

FURTHER REFERENCE

John D. Keating, *Bells in Australia* (Melbourne: MUP, 1977).

Chard, Geoffrey William   (*b* Sydney, 9 Aug. 1930), baritone. After studies at the NSW State Conservatorium, he sang principal roles with the National Opera of Australia from 1951 and the Elizabethan Opera Co. in 1956. After the birth of his son he focused on concert, radio and television work for a time; but he moved to Britain in 1961, joining the English National Opera, making guest appearances with the Welsh National Opera, Glyndebourne and at the Edinburgh and Aldeburgh Festivals. He was at the London Coliseum 1973–83. Returning periodically to Australia, he appeared with the Australian Opera and Victorian State Opera. He has an extraordinarily wide repertoire: as well as such standard roles as Don Giovanni, Scarpia and Escamillo including contemporary operas by Menotti, Shostakovich, Britten, Janáček, and British composers, singing roles in the premieres of Blake's *Toussaint,* Malcolm Williamson's *Lucky Peter's Journey,* Lennox Berkeley's *The Castaway,* Harrison Birtwistle's *Punch and Judy,* Richard Meale's *Voss,* and in the British premieres of Penderecki's *Die Teufel von Loudun,* Ginastera's *Bomarzo,* and Ligeti's *Le grand macabre.*

FURTHER REFERENCE
MackenzieS, 204–5, Roger Covell, *GroveO; WWA* (1996); *CA* (1995/96).

Charteris, Richard   (*b* Chatham Islands, 24 June 1948), musicologist. He graduated from Victoria University of Wellington (BA, 1969); Canterbury University (MA, 1972); and London (PhD, 1975), and worked from 1991 as professor in historical musicology at the University of Sydney; in 1990 he was elected fellow of the Australian Academy of the Humanities. He has published more than 90 books and critical articles on European music, musicians and musical sources of the 16th and 17th centuries, with particular attention to English, German and Italian music (including that of Coprario and the Ferrabosco family). Many of his editions are used extensively throughout the world for concerts and recordings.

MARGARET KARTOMI

Charts.   Hit parades for popular music were a feature of radio in Australia from the years after World War II, but the first formal compilation of a Top 40 chart was by Sydney radio station 2UE in 1958, based on a survey of sales in local retail record stores. Radio broadcasts comprised of a sequential playing of the Top 40 hits from bottom to top became immensely popular in the early 1960s, based on local charts produced by radio stations in Sydney (2UE, 2UW, 2SM), Melbourne (3UZ, 3DB, 3XY), Brisbane (4BC, 4BH), Adelaide (5AD, 5KA), and Perth (6KY, 6PR). There has been a national Top 40 chart since 1966. Most Australian charts used the retail survey method for compilation; the point of distribution method (which assesses wholesale issue by the recording companies) has not been common in Australia.

Although great store can be placed on chart position in judging success in the popular music industry, charts measure only short-term sales volume, and give no sense of which recordings have become perennial favourites or permanent parts of the musical heritage. The widely used retail survey method also tends to mask regional sales differences: a recording with enormous success in one capital may have low sales elsewhere and not appear high in the national charts, while a recording with substantial success in country areas rather than in capital city retail stores may go undetected altogether. Complete Australian charts have been compiled by Jim Barnes et al. to 1977, then David Kent (see below); a concise compilation of national charts is in *McGrathA.*

FURTHER REFERENCE
Jim Barnes, Fred Dyer, and Hank B. Facer *Top 40 Research 1956–1977* (Merrylands, NSW: Top 40 Research, 1979); David Kent, *Australian Chart Book 1970–1992* (Sydney: Australian Chart Book, 1993); Thomas J. Guest, *Thirty Years of Hits 1960–1990: Melbourne Top 40 Research* (Craigieburn, Vic.: J Maloney, 1991); *McGrathA.*

Cherokees, The.   Rock band (1961–68), the name derived from a popular ice-cream. Formed in Melbourne around former Chessmen Billy Dale (guitar) and Barry Windley (drums), it was first an instrumental band backing Johnny Chester and doing Shadows covers, then Beatles numbers. By 1965 the membership had largely changed; the band then became regulars on the television *Go!!* show, made singles such as *Oh Monah* (1966) and the album *Here Come The Cherokees* (1965), and began extensive touring interstate. Another major membership change brought the peak of their popularity in 1967, when they combined pop, jug-band and swing styles, recording such revivals as *Minnie The Moocher.*

FURTHER REFERENCE
Recordings include *Oh Monah* (1966, Go!! 5045), the album *Here Come The Cherokees* (1965, W&G WGB 1973), and *Minnie The Moocher* (Go!! 5051). A compilation is *The Legendary Go!! Sessions* (1990, Canetoad CTLP 013). For discography, see *SpencerA.* See also *McGrathA; SpencerW.*

Chester, Johnny ['Ches']   (*b* Melbourne, 26 Dec. 1941), pop, country music singer. Working as a mechanic at his father's garage, Chester began seriously to pursue a career in music at the age of 17. Making progress at singing, he formed his first band, the Jaywoods, in 1959. The group gained exposure through dances held at the Preston Town Hall, drawing the attention of Ron Tudor from W&G Records. Already having recorded two Melbourne hits with the ★Thunderbirds, Chester formed his own band, the Chessmen, in 1961, producing a string of hits including *Let's Dance* and *Summertime Blues.* Their success established him as one of Melbourne's top pop idols, highlighted by the group's appearance as support act on the Beatles tour in August 1964. In 1964 he moved into television, compering with the nationally broadcast *Teen Scene* on the ABC. But his image as a pop singer waned throughout the mid-1960s, and he dissolved his association with the Chessmen. In 1966 he joined radio 3UZ as an announcer while making a transition to country music as 'Ches' and forming a new band, Jigsaw. Winning a silver record award for the song *Shame and Scandal* in 1971, he went on to record his biggest-selling hit, *The World's Greatest Mum*, in 1973. He has remained a popular country music figure, forming two bands, The Blue Denim Band (1975) and Hotspur (1978), while maintaining his radio career. His latest musical release was in 1994.

FURTHER REFERENCE

Recordings include *The Hokey Pokey* (1961, W&G WG-S-1173); *Shakin' All Over* (1962, W&G WG-S-1336); *World's Greatest Mum* (1973, Image); *Wild and Warm* (1963, W&G WGB 1545). Compilations are *Best of Ches* (1964, W&G WGB 1746); *Johnny Chester's Greatest Hits* (1965, W&G 2S/2340); *Johnny Chester Collection vol. 1* (1994, Sony PCD 10153); and *Portrait* (1994, EMI 7017782). A discography is in *SpencerA*. See also *LattaA*, 188–9; *McGrathA*; David McLean, comp., *Collected Stories on Australian Rock'n'Roll* (Sydney: Cane Toad Publications, 1991), 154–65; *SpencerW*; Michael Sturma, *Australian Rock n'Roll: The First Wave* (Kenthurst, NSW: Kangaroo Press, 1991).

JENNIFER ROYLE

Chesworth, David (*b* Stoke, England, 31 Mar. 1958), composer. He studied at La Trobe University 1976–79 and was co-ordinator of the Clifton Hill Community Music Centre in Melbourne 1978–82, and a member of the band Essendon Airport 1978–83. Artistic director of the David Chesworth Ensemble since 1994, he writes orchestral and electro-acoustic music for opera, ensembles, installation, dance and film. His compositions include *I Only Have Eyes for You* (1979) for harmonium, cameras and TV monitors, *Skippy Knows ...* (1983) album/performance, *Insatiable* (1985) chamber opera, *Stories of Imitation and Corruption* (1986) for orchestra and tape, *On the Line* (1988) music for dance, *Recital* (1989) music-theatre, *Southgate* (1992) soundscape, and *The Two Executioners* (1994) opera.

FURTHER REFERENCE

Recordings include *Tissues for Issues*, elec (Canberra School of Music, CSM 6). His writings include 'Playing Around in Open Spaces', *AMC News* 14 (Jan. 1987), 15–17. See also *BroadstockS*, *JenkinsT*.

MICHAEL BARKL

Chi, Jimmy (*b* Broome, WA, 1948), singer-songwriter of mixed Aboriginal, Chinese, Japanese, and Scottish background. Leader of the Aboriginal band Kuckles, based at Broome, he was writer of the musical *Bran Nue Dae* (1990), considered the first successful Aboriginal musical. Chi and other members of the band attended CASM at the University of Adelaide in the late 1970s and early 80s. A founding member of the Broome Musicians Aboriginal Corporation, a local community-based support agency for young musicians

FURTHER REFERENCE

Recordings include *Bran Nue Dae* (1993, BND Records 002). The score of *Bran Nue Dae* has been published (Sydney: Currency Press, 1991).

P. DUNBAR-HALL

Child, Eric Charles (*b* England, 27 Apr. 1910, *d* Sydney, 23 Apr. 1995), jazz broadcaster. He played dance band drums in Britain before joining the merchant navy. After his troopship was torpedoed while operating out of Singapore, he settled in Australia and joined radio 2GZ in Orange, NSW. Moving to Brisbane, he began a national ABC jazz program, *Rhythm Unlimited* in 1952, which he presented under a succession of titles until February 1983. In Sydney from 1957 he presented additional ABC jazz programs. After his retirement in 1975 and a public outcry against the ABC's threatened cancellation of his programs, he continued broadcasting on the ABC through the 1980s. He was awarded the OAM in 1979.

FURTHER REFERENCE

OxfordJ; Jack Kelly, 'Behind the Mike, Eric Child plays for Judges and Jailbirds', *JA* (Jan./Feb. 1981), 9–12.

BRUCE JOHNSON

Childe, Mary Fairbairn (*b* Brisbane, 17 July 1913), piano teacher. She studied piano with Margery Stuart, Alice May Cadogan, and Percy *Brier. Her early career included solo piano performances and broadcasts for the ABC. She spent 13 years as a school music mistress before commencing her advanced studies in piano in London in 1948, where she studied under John Wills and furthered her experience in accompaniment and chamber music. On her return to Australia she established her teaching studio in Toowoomba, Queensland. She was an early exponent of group tuition as a supplement to individual lessons and a multi-faceted music education program involving voice, ensemble and secondary instruments. Her pedagogic technique has been recorded in a Music Teachers' Association of Queensland and Technical and Further Education video lecture series. One of Queensland's longest serving and foremost piano teachers, in 1993 she was honoured with the OAM.

RACHEL TEW

Children's Music. Australian composers and songwriters have found a large, ready market for music for young instrumental beginners, for class use, or for school-age ensembles. For pre-school children Zoe McHenry produced many songs for the ABC *Kindergarten of the Air*, they have been recorded by singer Fay White on *Did You See the Wind Today* (Move MC 3083). More recently a number of singer-songwriters have used popular styles in action songs or developmental music for children: Franciscus *Henri and Shirley Jacobs in trad jazz, Peter *Combe and Ronnie *Burns in pop styles, Don *Spencer in country music, and the *Wiggles, Australia's most successful pre-school entertainers, in early rock and roll styles.

For school-age music lessons numerous piano miniatures and children's songs appeared in the interwar years by such composers as Alfred *Hill, Alfred Wheeler, J.A. *Steele, William *James, Horace *Keats, Frank *Hutchens and Louis *Lavater. Taking as their subjects birds, flowers, the bush, elves, or ghosts, many of these seem dated today, but having found their way into the syllabus of the AMEB or the set lists of eisteddfods they have remained current ever since. Bernard De Oleveira, Colin *Brumby, Dulcie *Holland and Miriam *Hyde carried the genre into the 1970s. More recently Margaret Brandman has published numerous easy piano pops pieces and arrangements, and Michael *Atherton has introduced exotic instruments to children on *Radum Scadum* (ABC 838980).

For school-age choirs and vocal classes, choral works include Judith *Clingan's *Modal Magic* (1986), Betty *Beath's *The Raga Who Married an Angel* (1983) and numerous settings by Brumby. Children's operas have appeared, including George *Dreyfus's *Adventures of Sebastian the Fox* (1963), Malcolm *Williamson's *The Happy Prince* (1965) and *Julius Caesar Jones* (1966), Gillian *Whitehead's *The Tinker's Curse* (1979), Malcolm *Fox's *Sid the Serpent* (1985), and Michael *Easton's *Beauty and the Beast* (1992). A number of composers have worked extensively with schoolchildren in residencies, including Sarah *Hopkins, Robert *Smallwood, Stephen *Holgate and Stephen *Leek, who published his school's kit *Voiceworks* (1989). Surprisingly little has been written by Australian composers for school-age bands or orchestras: Peter Rankine is one of only a few who have written for youth orchestra. See also *School and Children's Choirs*.

Choirs and Choral Music

1. Choral Societies. 2. Professional Choral Groups.
3. Community and Ethnic Choirs. 4. Choral Events.
5. Decline and Renewal.

Choral music had an important place in Australia's musical development, especially before there were regular orchestral concerts. The easily transportable human voice, coupled with 19th-century sight-singing methods, allowed this very democratic art-form to reach the most distant pioneer settlements. Choral singing became a middle-class pursuit, and was seen as a respectable, and hence desirable, pastime, with social benefits for the community. Mechanics' Institutes and Schools of Arts in the 19th century, Workers Educational Associations in the early 20th century, and tertiary institutions, stimulated choral development. The eisteddfod movement was also a focus for a

great deal of activity. Few singers in Australia make a living solely from choral work, although some small ensembles operate in a professional market either part-time or full-time. Choral music is therefore an amateur pursuit. See also *Church Choirs; Community Singing; Liedertafel; School and Children's Choirs; University Choirs and Choral Societies.*

1. Choral Societies. (i) Sydney. The earliest public choral concert appears to have been given by the choir of St Mary's Cathedral, Sydney, on 20 January 1835. 'Oratorio' performances were given in 1836, 1838 and 1841, comprised of excerpts from *Messiah* and *The Creation,* plus miscellaneous items, and assisted by regimental bandsmen. A St Mary's Choral Society flourished from 1851 to c.1870. A Philharmonic Society was formed as early as 1836, a Sydney Choral Society was active in the 1870s, and a Sydney Musical Union from 1877. The (Royal) Philharmonic Society of Sydney was established in 1886; its conductors included Roberto Hazon, Howard Carr, and Arnold Mote. The Hurlstone Choral Society (1920–64) was the forerunner of the present Sydney Philharmonia Society.

(ii) Melbourne. The Royal Melbourne Philharmonic Society (1853) became the principal concert-giving body in Melbourne. It claimed to be the oldest choral body in the British Commonwealth with a history of continuous performance. Its centenary history records 550 concerts, which included 134 of *Messiah,* 66 of *Elijah,* and 28 of *The Creation,* thus devoting 40 per cent of its concerts to three standard works. Its record of Australian premieres includes the *St Matthew Passion* (1875), *Israel in Egypt* (1859) Elgar's *The Apostles* (1906) and *The Kingdom* (1908), and Walton's *Belshazzar's Feast* (1938). After the 1888 Centennial Exhibition it was involved in a dispute over a proposed government subsidy to form a choir to work with the similarly sponsored Victorian Orchestra. Its opposition here is considered to have been detrimental to the development of professional choral music. In 1937 the choir was reorganised under the auspices of the ABC, and Bernard *Heinze became conductor. The repertoire expanded, and the society stabilised. However, by the 1960s it was suffering declining standards and falling support. It is still active today, although overshadowed by newer groups like the Melbourne Chorale.

(iii) Adelaide. Glee clubs were established early in Adelaide: the South Australian Glee Club (1841), the Adelaide Glee and Madrigal Society (1855), and the South Australian Philharmonic Society (1842) all met at hotels. The first Adelaide Choral Society was established in 1842 with 23 members, and a repertoire of oratorio and biblical-themed cantatas, religious works like Mozart's 12th Mass, and later secular music. The North Adelaide Choral Society (1854) was reconstituted as the Sacred Harmonic Society and in 1862 a Philharmonic

Society was formed. While singers were doubtless in more than one group, this evidences a large body of keen and serious musical amateurs. A new Adelaide Choral Society (1853) presented the first full *Messiah* performance in SA under the direction of Carl *Linger in 1859, with a choir of 70 and orchestra of 20. It merged with the Sacred Harmonic Society to form the Adelaide Harmonic Society (1859). Another Adelaide Choral Society was formed in 1887, and another in 1899. In 1900, 250 voices presented Gounod's *Redemption* with the Adelaide Grand Orchestra. The repertoire, like other oratorio societies, included once popular but now largely forgotten Victorian composers like Horn, Kalliwoda, Loder and Reissiger. It lapsed in 1931 and re-formed in 1935. The Adelaide Philharmonic Choir was formed in 1937 as the ABC's concert choir. Its conductors inluded John Dempster and Norman Chinner. In 1980 it and the Adelaide Choral Society merged as the Adelaide Chorus. The Adelaide Harmony Choir (1946) presented *Messiah* (1948) and *Elijah* (1949), membership reaching 100 voices, and in 1958 presented the first Bach B Minor Mass performance in Adelaide for 28 years. It also participated in competitions at Bendigo and Ballarat between 1954 and 1963—its win over the Postal Institute Choral Society in 1954 was achieved without singing from books. In 1964 it combined with the Festival of Arts choir, the Adelaide Philharmonic and the Adelaide Symphony Orchestra for Britten's *War Requiem*. It has produced a recording, combined with local and interstate choirs, and toured to the USA in 1986. It remains active a decade later.

(iv) WA. Choirs were operating in Perth and Fremantle in the 1850s and the opening of the Perth Town Hall (1870) stimulated concert-giving. Development accelerated in the 1880s. The Perth Musical Union (1880s to *c*.1900) concentrated almost exclusively on oratorio. It presented the first *Messiah* performance in 1886, and later *Elijah* and other works of Handel, Haydn and Mendelssohn. By 1894 it was being criticised for 'not making a reasonable endeavour to introduce new works to the musical public'. Declining membership, low support from audiences, and conflict between the conductor and the committee, led to the final collapse, but the name appears to have survived as a concert identity until at least 1911.

The 1920s saw increased interest in choral singing, spurred on by eisteddfods and the establishment of suburban choral societies in North Perth, Claremont, and Subiaco. Bunbury Choral Society, in 1914, fielded 80 singers, considered very respectable in a state where the population was constantly on the move. The University of Western Australia became the centre of choral activity from the 1950s, with several ensembles on campus and a connection with the ABC orchestra. The Perth Philharmonic Society (1943) joined with the Teachers' Choral Society in 1967, and was still active in the 1980s.

(v) Queensland. Toowoomba's early choral activity indicates the determination with which choral music was pursued, despite difficulties of finances, transport in a rural community, personnel problems, and weather. Between 1875 and 1920 at least 10 groups were established, some not surviving a year. Toowoomba's choral music centred on the Philharmonic Society, several suburban societies and church choirs until 1933, when the Toowoomba Musical Union was formed. Renamed the Toowoomba Choral Society (1940), and still active, it participated in eisteddfods, formed a Junior Choir (1946), and bought several properties over the years as rehearsal premises. The society undertakes musical comedy productions, and enjoys strong community support.

The South Brisbane Philharmonic Society was formed in 1862, an Orpheus Glee Club in 1865, and the South Brisbane Harmonic Society in 1870. R.T. *Jefferies took over the South Brisbane Harmonic Society in 1872, and a successful concert prompted formation of a North Brisbane Harmonic Society the same year. The two groups merged to form the Brisbane Musical Union with Jefferies as conductor, and its first concert (18 December 1872) featured Romberg's *The Lay of the Bell*. Performances of *Elijah* and *Messiah* followed in 1873, and the union was firmly established. By 1882 the major works performed ranged from Handel, Mendelssohn and Haydn, to Costa's *Eli,* Balfe's *Bohemian Girl,* and Rossini's *Stabat Mater,* plus many part-songs. During the 1890s depression support flagged, and Jefferies was reappointed conductor in a successful bid to resuscitate the union. George *Sampson became conductor in 1898.

The Brisbane Musical Union grew, and *The Dream of Gerontius* was presented in 1910. In 1929 it gained state and local government support, and became known as the Queensland State and Municipal Choir. In 1936 it merged with the Brisbane Austral Choir (formed 1906), under its conductor E.R.B. Jordan, and remains active today. The Austral Choir was a highly successful competition choir, but decided to abandon eisteddfods in 1922 and become a subscription choir. It gave the Australian premiere of Holst's *The Hymn of Jesus* (1923), and in addition to oratorio (*Elijah*, 1934; *St Paul,* 1933; Verdi's *Requiem*, 1930), a British Music series was held (1925), an Australian composer concert (1928), and festivals featuring Percy *Grainger as composer and performer (1926 and 1934). In a letter to Jordan (5 October 1926) Grainger described the Austral Choir as 'an absolutely ideal body of music lovers and ... one of the most perfect and sensitively responsive choirs I have encountered'.

The Blackstone-Ipswich Cambrian Choir, formed in 1886, is currently a mixed-voice choir, with an associated male chorus. It was conducted from 1907 to 1947 by Leonard *Francis, winning the Ballarat Competition in 1908 and the Commonwealth Eisteddfod in Sydney in 1910. Many later victories followed. Concerts were so popular that in 1915 the Ipswich–Brisbane train regularly delayed departure to allow audience members to catch it.

It formed a Junior Choir (1947–59, 1965) and a Youth Choir (1970). Illustrating the sort of loyalty that can occur in societies, some families have four and five generations of involvement, and some individuals have over 50 years' membership.

Following two Handel Festivals (1933, 1934), Robert *Dalley-Scarlett formed the Brisbane Handel Society, which from 1935 to 1942 presented condensed versions of all of Handel's oratorios in radio broadcasts. It also initiated an annual 'uncut' *Messiah*, based on his research into Handel performance practice. With his death the society quickly lost focus, standards fell, and it was officially dissolved in 1961.

(vi) Others. The first Hobart Choral Society was formed in 1843, and a later one flourished from 1925 to 1947. Other groups include the Hobart Musical Union (*fl.*1867 to *c.*1891) and at least three Philharmonic Societies, the third from 1924. Canberra had a Philharmonic Society and a Musical Society from the 1920s, and at present possesses the Canberra Choral Society, a large choir attached to the Canberra School of Music, and several chamber choirs. Darwin also had choral activity from the 1920s, and had to redevelop activities after Cyclone Tracy in 1974. Choral groups can be found in most major cities and towns, and many suburban societies flourished.

2. Professional and Other Choral Groups. Some groups, like Jones and Co., the Meistersingers Quartette, and the Leonine Consort, were single-voice ensembles working within a professional vocal market. The Australian Opera Chorus, and some state companies, are the only full-time professional choruses in Australia, but they rarely appear in concert. Currently the *Song Company is Australia's only full-time professional group. Other chamber groups, lacking the substantial sponsorship given to orchestras, work at a very high standard, and in particular repertoires, but for little or no personal remuneration.

Adelaide's Glenlea Singers (1939–87) was formed as an 'undenominational Christian Society', with a membership of 24 and an average age of 14. A repertoire of light music saw it undertake radio and television work and issue a record (*Sweeter than Wine,* Philips 264). It was a featured performer on radio 5DN's variety show *Radio Canteen* from 1949 to 1961. The members were not paid for their efforts, proceeds going to charity. The Ballarat Y Choir was formed in 1946 as the YWCA Singing Group. It won the popular radio contest *Australia's Amateur Hour* in 1948, undertook broadcasts, and released 24 recordings, including a disk of *Christmas Carols of Australia* for World Record Club in 1971. Performances included special events like the 1967 YWCA World Council Conference, and 'Empire Youth Sunday' events in the early 1960s. In 1957 the group was chosen to represent Australia in a world-wide radio hook-up, *Christmas With Bing.* Still active in the 1990s, the group is smaller, with an older average age.

The most extended example of subsidised professional choirs are the ABC Wireless Choruses. The *Australian Broadcasting Commission Act 1932* directed the ABC to establish and utilise 'groups of musicians for the rendition of orchestral, choral and band music of high quality'. The Commission's first annual report in 1933 advised the formation of the Melbourne Wireless Chorus, and in Sydney a Wireless Chorus, Radio Choir, and a vocal quartet. From September 1935 they were part of an ABC broadcast opera series. Three-month seasons in Sydney and Melbourne included condensed versions (in English) of works like *Parsifal, Fidelio, Boris Godunov* and *Hugh the Drover.* The report also stated that the ABC would make available a vocal quartet to improve the quality of a church service that was to be broadcast. By 1938 there were two conductors and two 16-voice choruses (Sydney and Melbourne) on the permanent staff, with two conductors (Adelaide and Perth) and four 16-voice choirs in regular part-time employment (not on a regular salary).

John *Antill conducted the Sydney Wireless Chorus from his appointment in May 1936 until 1956. Founded from 12 members of the Williamson Grand Opera chorus, plus the ABC's Meistersingers Quartette (two tenors, a bass, and a male alto), it rehearsed full-time, giving numerous performances of repertoire ranging from Palestrina to dance music, part-songs, sea shanties, and larger works. Broadcasts in programs like *Over Hill and Dale* and *In Quires and Places Where They Sing* were also made. Many singers were eager to join—there was a waiting list of 300 in a short time. Dalley-Scarlett conducted the ABC Brisbane Singers from 1940 until their disbandment in 1952. Strictly a broadcast choir, they generally performed on minimum rehearsal time. Highlights include condensed versions of Handel's *Julius Caesar* and *Agrippina,* and Rousseau's *Le Devin du Village,* and the world radio premiere of Thomas Wood's *Chanticleer* on 21 July 1948. Published in January 1948 and described as the longest unaccompanied choral work in existence, it was prepared on two rehearsals.

The Adelaide Singers became a full-time group in 1945, and was the best-known small choir in Australia, with a national reputation. Its conductors included William *Cade, Norman Chinner, Patrick *Thomas and James *Christiansen. It was especially known for its commercial recordings of Australian music such as the *Australian Christmas Carols* of William James, Alfred Hill's *Symphony of Life,* and Nigel Butterley's *In the Head the Fire.* The ABC Choruses declined after the war. Most were disbanded by 1953, as what was described as 'a number of economies' necessary because of increased expenses flowing from economic factors such as a rise in the basic wage, and the last group (the Adelaide Singers) in 1976.

3. Community and Ethnic Choirs. Ethnic community choirs seek to preserve their national cultures while still integrating into Australian society. They usually perform at community functions, church services, local ethnic festivals, and occasionally join with related local and interstate groups for larger events. The Silver Jubilee Festival of the German Harmonie Choir of Canberra (1993) involved the Tanunda Liedertafel 1861, the Lorelei Choir (Newcastle, 1974), Liederkranz Tivoli (Melbourne, 1991), the German male-voice choir 'Sanssouci' (Wollongong, 1963), the Chor Alpenfrieden (an Austrian choir from Adelaide, 1980), and the Liedertafel Arion (Melbourne, 1860). Welsh male-voice choirs were common in mining districts such as the NSW coalfields. The preservation of Welsh traditions of singing and eisteddfods was a motivating force.

Melbourne's first Jewish community choir was a short-lived Melbourne Hebrew Choral Society (*fl.* mid-1880s), formed to promote liturgical music. Other choirs were formed in the 1920s and 30s, some specially catering to the Yiddish-speaking community. The Hazomir Choir (1947) was formed for the performance of Yiddish-language music. Initially a men's choir, it was reconstituted in the early 1960s as a mixed choir, and is still active. The Melbourne Jewish Choral Society (1989) performs music in Yiddish, English and other languages—reflecting a membership of predominantly English-speaking origins.

A 1994 ANCA survey revealed over 70 groups which draw their membership and/or repertoire from an ethnic source. In addition to Welsh groups, there are the more established European immigrant communities—Greek, Italian, German (including the Liedertafels still extant)— and recently formed Ukrainian, Pacific Islands and Latin American groups.

The first NSW Festival of Male Choirs (1989), involving over 500 singers, demonstrates continued activity in this field. The Sydney Male Choir (1913) was established from the Petersham Glee Club. Still active, it has presented numerous concerts, participated in eisteddfods (including Llangollen, 1988), made recordings, appeared in vaudeville, radio and television performances, and even backed a rock band. It has sung annually at the Martin Place ANZAC Day Dawn Service since 1930, and provided music for the film *The Silence of Dean Maitland* (1935).

Workplace choirs were common from the late 19th century to the present. Notable past groups include the WA Commercial Travellers' Association Male Choir, the choirs in the NSW and Victorian railways and the Victorian Postal Institute. The International Harvester Male Chorus (Geelong, 1943) was still active in 1977, after approximately 700 performances.

The popularity of choral singing in the 1920s is demonstrated by the choir of department store Foy and Gibson in Melbourne. Seeking to form a 25-voice workplace choir in 1922, over 500 applications were received; eventually a 600-voice choir performed a program of unaccompanied part-songs in the Melbourne Exhibition Hall, reportedly to an audience of nearly 5000. With the motto 'Service in Song', the NSW Police Choir

(1934–88) gave numerous charity performances, and appeared at correctional institutions and in ABC concerts. It also provided music for the film *The Rats of Tobruk* (1944). Lack of numbers and interest forced it to disband. Several trade union choirs have been formed since 1988.

For some years after World War II Services choirs functioned in a number of cities. The Melbourne choir, of about 100 voices, comprised veterans and POWs, performing mainly a light classical repertoire. The SA Country Women's Association ran many choirs from 1949, the CWA of WA maintained a choir committee (conducting its 29th competitive festival in 1979), and choirs were often formed at YWCA and YMCA branches. Several choirs have also formed in the gay community.

4. Choral Events. (i) Broadcasting and Eisteddfods. The ABC has broadcast choral music regularly since its inception. By 1936 broadcasts of local groups had been made from all states, as well as by visiting groups like the Vienna Boys Choir. 'Community Singing' was claimed to be the first type of audience participation broadcast, and to have prepared the way for more advanced developments. Several regular broadcast programs were started, including *In Quires and Places Where They Sing* (from 1937), and *The Family Hymn Book* (from 1939), to which many choral groups have contributed. Short series were also devised, such as *Youth Sings* (1947 Report)—a sacred music program broadcast over several months, involving about 40 school choirs around Australia.

Eisteddfods served as a major focus of efforts for some choirs. Contests normally included a Chief Choral, Madrigal, and Second Choral section, plus sections for male, female, church and various children's groups; other sections covered workplace and suburban choirs. In addition to prize-money, large shields and trophies were awarded, and were often proudly displayed in photographs of groups like the Brisbane Austral Choir. It was a matter of community pride to have a choir win at an eisteddfod—the Toowoomba Musical Union was formed out of a well-attended public meeting, presided over by the Mayor, which decided to form an eisteddfod choir. The Toowoomba Choral Society was particularly successful, winning all four major sections in 1958 (only the second time in 64 years), and a further eight times between 1962 and 1976. These wins should, however, be balanced against the actual numbers of competitors, especially in later years. Minutes of the debate surrounding the Brisbane Austral Choir's withdrawal from eisteddfods indicate a view that the eisteddfod movement, in 1922, was not progressing, and that it was becoming a cut-throat contest between two or three groups. But eisteddfod work was also considered responsible for their high standard.

Declining participation from the 1950s must call into question the value of such competitions as indicators of the quality of participating (and winning) choirs. Nevertheless new competitions have been established and are well attended. They are not without controversy, the Third

Australian National Choral Championship (1992) being won by the Sydney Gay and Lesbian Choir, which successfully resisted attempts to change its name beforehand.

(ii) Festivals, Exhibitions, Special Concerts.
Choirs are often formed for one-off events, festivals (e.g. the various colonial exhibitions), or for special seasons like Christmas. Adelaide retailer David Jones formed a Staff Christmas Choir in 1954 (following a long-established tradition in Sydney) which presented Christmas carols in the store for 25 years. Massed choir performance has been common, notably through the 19th-century exhibitions, wartime patriotic concerts, and major celebrations. Large choirs were also formed for the support of visiting artists, like the 620-voice choir that supported Madame Albani's 1898 Adelaide concerts. The appeal of such events is attested to by popular massed *Messiah* performances.

The first music festival in Australia was held in 1859 to celebrate the opening of the Great Hall of Sydney University, and coincided with the Handel Centenary. For that occasion a choir of 250 and orchestra of 70 presented *Messiah* and *Creation* excerpts. Handel Centenary concerts were also held in Melbourne and Adelaide. An international exhibition was held in Sydney (1879–80), for which a 700-voice choir and orchestra was formed. A Centennial celebration in 1888 included a cantata by Hugo ★Alpen, performed by a choir of 1 500 schoolchildren. Hobart's International Exhibition (1894–95) featured an orchestra of 42 professional musicians (including a harpist) and a 250-voice choir. They performed a festival cantata, *The Land of Beauty*, by Frederick A. ★Packer. Like others of its kind, it incorporated character choruses (e.g. reapers and hunters) and concluded with a chorus, 'Glory! Honour! Praise! and Worship! Amen', clearly showing the Handelian hold on choral composers. Perth's International Exhibition (21 November 1881 to 6 January 1882) featured a festival cantata written by S. Pascal Needham and sung by a 100-voice choir. Incorporating choruses of pearl-divers and shepherds, the now lost score exalted the 'Fair daughter of the sunny West'.

Melbourne's exhibitions also employed large choral bodies in the presentation of standard repertoire and specially commissioned works. These included the opening of the Melbourne Town Hall in 1870, which featured a choir of 200 performing Charles Edward ★Horsley's cantata *Euterpe*, and the 1882 Melbourne Music Festival Association performance of Costa's *Eli*, with a choir of 900 voices. The 1888 Centennial International Exhibition's six-month series of choral and orchestral concerts prompted the formation of a professional government-sponsored orchestral body in Melbourne. The opening concert of the Melbourne Exhibition of Women's Works (1907) featured an ode, *God Guide Australia*, by Florence Donaldson ★Ewart performed by a 1000-voice female choir.

In 1938 a performance of *Hiawatha* was staged arena-style in the Melbourne Exhibition Building. Directed by T.C. Fairbairn, who had presented similar productions in London's Albert Hall, it involved nearly 1000 performers, including 700 costumed choristers. The distance between choir and orchestra (because of the teepees on stage) necessitated the use of microphones and loudspeakers for co-ordination. The event raised £10 000 for the Red Cross.

Choral groups have also provided choral support to large opera productions, presented masques, operettas, and staged presentations of oratorio. The Canberra Choral Society participated in productions of *Aida* (1981) and *The Pilgrim's Progress* (1980). For its 21st anniversary (1967) the Adelaide Harmony Choir produced an operatic version of Mendelssohn's *Elijah*, with acting, costumes, scenery, and memorised music. Various choral groups combined for Isao Tomita's *Sound Cloud over Sydney* for the 1988 Bicentenary. Other recent events include 'A Choral Sea' (Sydney, 1994), a celebration of Pacific music involving over 700 performers, and the Horizons (Sydney, from 1991) and Australian Voices (Brisbane) festivals that focus on contemporary Australian music.

(iii) Visiting Choirs and Individuals.
Despite its geographical isolation Australia has had numerous choral visitors. The New York Ethiopian Serenaders, a group of six entertainers in the 'negro minstrel' vein, were quite popular in the 1850s and 60s. Their Perth visits (1851–52) prompted establishment of (among others) the Minstrels of the West, offering American negro-style ballads and folksongs. The Minstrels dominated the Perth entertainment scene for a decade. The Fisk Jubilee Singers (1887) presented Negro spiritual music. Other groups include the Scarlett Troubadours (1902), the Westminster Abbey Glee Party (1903), the Royal Welsh Choir (1908), the Sistine Soloists (1925), and the Don Cossacks (1926). The 200-voice Sheffield Choir (1912) was considered an example for Australian choirs to emulate—the press contained articles on the 'educative lessons' of the choir.

The Sistine Choir's 1922 tour was particularly influential for the stimulus it gave local Catholic church music reform along the lines of the *Motu Proprio*. Its conductor Msgr Rella admitted that the main reason the Vatican allowed the tour was the hope that local authorities would be inspired into action. The 50-voice group, which included four male sopranos, played to record houses during two-week seasons in Melbourne and Sydney. The repertoire included music for two spatially separated choirs, and a revelatory performance of the *Marcellus Missa Papae*. The visits of the Vienna Boys' Choir in 1935 and the Vienna Mozart Boys' Choir in 1939 inspired the formation of the Australian Boys' Choir.

Postwar activity has increased dramatically. Among many visits have been British collegiate choirs, the Sistine Chapel Choir (1973), and US university choirs. A major drawcard for Australian participants in the World Festival Choir (1994) was the nature of the experience. Individual visitors have included Americans Frank

Pooler and Rodney Eichenberger, Anders Ohrwall, and many others in the last 20 years. In August 1996 Sydney hosted the 4th World Symposium on Choral Music; 25 visiting choirs, hundreds of delegates, and 39 concerts, made this the largest such gathering in the southern hemisphere. Symposium concerts were broadcast nationally on ABC-FM. Some choirs toured interstate after the event.

5. Decline and Renewal.   As in other countries, Australia's choral music was in decline in the interwar years. E.R.B. Jordan claimed as early as 1929 that people were becoming listeners only. The Hurlstone Choral Society is an oft-cited example: by 1964 standards had dropped so low that the ABC was forced to form a new body of about 80 auditioned singers for its Sydney concerts. Similar actions took place elsewhere. The symptoms of decline included falling standards as membership numbers fell while the average age rose, and a consequent loss of subscriber and audience support (particularly for those groups used by the ABC). Choral music became less and less a part of ABC programs, such that new audiences for choral music were not cultivated to the same extent that audiences for chamber and orchestral music were. It has also been argued that the falling numbers of choirs, the attendant fall in participation, and falling audience involvement, represent a decline in the sense of community in Australia.

The Australia Council's Music Board *Medium Range Plan 1985–1989* acknowledged that choral music required attention. In formulating proposals to 'restore and increase public appreciation, support, and participation' it noted that choral traditions were fading, that no 'professional pyramid' existed for non-operatic vocal music in Australia, and that the maintenance of the choral tradition in Australia was being carried by amateur groups. The proposals included improving the training of singers and conductors, encouragement of school choral activity, encouraging tertiary institutions to offer choral conductor training, encouraging commissioning of local choral music, pooling resources and broadening management skills. Since the late 1970s a renewal has gathered pace, focused particularly on schools and generally raising standards. Many of these proposals are being acted on, and there is renewed activity at all levels.

The *Australian National Choral Association (ANCA) was formed in 1990, and a number of Australian conductors, including John Nickson, Margaret Pride and Faye Dumont, are choral specialists and teachers. Australians are undertaking choral conducting studies overseas, and several institutions, such as the University of Queensland, offer specialist choral conducting studies. Increasingly the professional standards of choral conductors are being scrutinised. ANCA and other musical bodies aim to improve professional development in choral conducting.

FURTHER REFERENCE

Papers for Brisbane Austral Choir are at State Library of Qld; for Brisbane Austral Choir, Robert Dalley-Scarlett and Brisbane Handel Society, George Sampson (Brisbane Musical Union) and R.T. Jefferies at Fryer Library, Univ. Queensland; for Queensland State and Municipal Choir, Brisbane Austral Choir, and Brisbane Musical Union, held by Queensland State and Municipal Choir Archivist. See also various articles in *AMN* (index in *MarsiI*), *The Canon, One Voice, Sing Out.*

Abernethy, Helen J. History of the Toowoomba Choral Society: Its First Fifty Years, B.Mus(Hons), Univ. Qld. 1985.

A Brief Retrospect of the Brisbane Musical Union (Brisbane: Warwick and Sapsford, 1882).

A Retrospect and Resumé of the Work done by the Brisbane Musical Union 1872–1906 (Brisbane: Hodgson Press, 1906).

Breen, J.W., The Melbourne Chorale: A Study of Marketing in a non-profit organization, MBA, Univ. Melbourne, 1981.

Buchanan, Robyn, *Blackstone-Ipswich Cambrian Choir: A Centenary History, 1886–1986.* (n.p., n.d.) Copy held in Oxley Library.

Carne, W.A., *A Century of Harmony: The Official Centenary History of the Royal Melbourne Philharmonic Society* (Melbourne: Royal Melbourne Philharmonic Society, 1954).

Jarrott, J.K., Early Music Societies in Toowoomba, Paper read to the Toowoomba Historical Society, 17 May 1982. Typescript, Oxley Library.

Krips, Michael J., A History of Music in South Australia before 1900. BA (Hons), Univ. Adelaide, 1973.

McCredie, Andrew, ed., *From Colonel Light into the Footlights: The Performing Arts in South Australia from 1836 to the Present* (Adelaide: Pagel Books, 1988).

Manning, Geoffrey H., *50 Years of Singing Chorales, Carols and Community Service: A History of the Adelaide Harmony Choir* (Adelaide: The Adelaide Harmony Choir, Inc., 1996).

Masel, Lloyd, 'The Shule Choir', *Australian Jewish Historical Society Journal* 11/5 (1992), 785–91.

Music Board Medium Range Plan 1985–1989: Working Papers, Feb. 1986 (Sydney: Australia Council, 1986).

Peake, George, *Historical Souvenir, Melbourne Philharmonic Society Diamond Jubilee 1853–1913.* (Melbourne, 1913).

Radic, Thérèse. Aspects of Organised Amateur Music in Melbourne 1836–1890. M.Mus, Univ. Melbourne, 1968.

_____, Some Historical Aspects of Musical Associations in Melbourne 1888–1915, PhD, Uni. Melbourne, 1977.

Rühen, Carl, *Sydney Male Choir: Eighty Years of Fine Harmony* (Sydney: Sydney Male Choir, 1992).

Schafer, Stephen, ed., *SA* 42 (1994), 'Choral Music in Australia'.

Schneider, Lorraine, *Saga of the Singers—Glenlea Style* (Glenelg, SA: Lorraine Schneider, 1990).

Segaloff, Benjamin, *Jewish Choral Music in Victoria* (Melbourne: Benjamin Segaloff, 1995).

Valentine, Nina, *Voices from the Golden City: 45 years of singing by the Ballarat 'Y' Choir* (Ballarat: Ballarat 'Y' Choir, 1990).

Wentzel, Ann K., The First Hundred Years of Music in Australia 1788–1888'. MA, Univ. Sydney, 1963.

NOEL WILMOTT

Christiansen, James Desmond (*b* Goomeri, Qld, 26 Nov. 1931), baritone. After studies with Clement Williams at the University of Adelaide, he taught at the Queensland Conservatorium from 1956, appearing in concert for the ABC and in light music on television, then went to London in 1963, taking lessons from Walther Gruner. He taught at Trinity College, sang at Glyndebourne, the Proms, and for the BBC, and became assistant conductor for *Camelot* at Drury Lane. In 1968 he went to the USA as head of the vocal department at Moorhead State University, Minnesota, appearing with the Minneapolis Symphony Orchestra and the St Paul Opera, including roles in the premieres of Lee Holby's *Summer and Smoke*, Carlisle Floyd's *Of Mice and Men*, and Robert Ward's *The Crucible*. He co-founded and conducted the Fargo-Moorhead Civic Opera Co. Returning to Australia in 1971 to teach at the Tasmanian Conservatorium, he was music supervisor for ABC Adelaide from 1976, then lecturer at the University of Adelaide from 1982, appearing as a principal baritone with most state opera companies and as conductor with most ABC orchestras. An authoritative presence on stage and a widely experienced vocal teacher, he returned to Brisbane in 1987, is now chorusmaster for Opera Queensland and teaches at the University of Queensland.

FURTHER REFERENCE

Recordings as a baritone include *Welcome Child of Mary* (1967, EMI); Puccini *Le Villi* with the Adelaide Symphony Orchestra (Chandos); and Nigel Butterley *Sometimes With One I Love* (EMI); as a conductor *Gilbert and Sullivan Highlights* Adelaide Symphony Orchestra (RCA).

Church and Cathedral Choirs.

1. Catholic. 2. Anglican. 3. Methodist. 4. Lutheran and Other.

Early choral performances in Australia, not unexpectedly, were associated with churches. The choir of St Mary's Catholic Cathedral, Sydney, provided Australia's first public choral recitals, and a service for the opening of St George's Church, Perth (23 Jan 1845) was the first public performance of concert music in WA.

1. Catholic. The issues facing Catholic choirs were the style of music performed and the role of women; in some respects the issues remain unresolved. The choir of St Francis' Church, Melbourne, was a mixed-voice group considered the leading church choir in Victoria during the latter 19th century. Organist Paolo *Giorza had his *Messe Solenelle* performed in 1872, and the choir attracted some of the best singers available. The opening of the new sanctuary (1879) featured a 100-voice choir and orchestra performing the Grand Mass in D by Ballarat composer Austin Turner. Soloists who later achieved fame included the then Mrs Armstrong (later Melba), and Amy *Castles (who made her debut in 1899 singing Gounod's *Ave Maria*).

The papal *Motu Proprio* (1903) was directed against the type of music then in favour at churches like St Francis, and local writers attacked the use of masses by Haydn, Mozart and other Classical masters. Adelaide's Archbishop O'Reily, at the 1904 Australasian Catholic Congress, stated, 'Church music, Pius X declares, has grown degenerate. The methods of our choirs need reforming', and the Palestrina school, as the highest form of church music, had to be restored in ecclesiastical functions in the churches. If the cathedrals and large churches set the lead in restoring the Palestrina School, smaller and less musically gifted churches would soon follow. Gregorian Chant in Australia, he declared, was 'an unstudied, an uncomprehended, an unknown, art'. His address, surprisingly, did not touch on the role of women in church music. Music more in the spirit required was introduced, but a decline in numbers and musical standards ensued. For a while after 1908 the music returned to the old format—soloists were paid, young men from the opera company sang in the chorus, and the choir contained both Catholics and non-Catholics.

Despite the pressures St Francis continued in its practice until 1929. New clergy gradually introduced liturgically correct music, and the women choristers were dismissed in 1937. The choir became a surpliced choir of men and boys, until disbanded in 1955 when a suitable conductor could not be found. A directive from the Archbishop in 1961 encouraged lay participation in the music, and while stating that choirs were an essential part of worship, also decreed that women might sing in choirs and small groups, but were not permitted either to sing solos or to enter the sanctuary as part of a liturgical choir. The choir was re-established in 1961 for regular services, and from 1967 has undertaken special concerts and other activities.

The St Mary's Sydney choir dates back to 1818. A Mrs Catherine Fitzpatrick trained a choir to sing at her son's confirmation, and was ready when the first clergy arrived in 1820. She directed it until 1834, and the choir became a mixed-voice group. It presented Sydney's first oratorio concerts in 1836, 1838 and 1841, and performed masses by Haydn, Mozart and Weber. During the 1840s St Mary's was organised as a monastery, and the monks also performed choral services. John Albert *Delaney was director of music from 1872 to 1877 and 1886 to 1907. During that time he performed Allegri's *Miserere* at Easter Tenebrae (1887), and organised the Australian premiere of *The Dream of Gerontius* (21 December 1903), combining with 18 other choirs. The male surpliced choir was restored in 1955, having been out of existence since 1854. Currently the choir numbers about 70 men and boys. It undertakes formal concerts and radio broadcasts, and has toured overseas.

In the early 1940s St Patrick's Cathedral, Melbourne, had as the nucleus of its choir the Vienna Mozart Boys' Choir. Touring Australia when war broke out, they were

taken to Melbourne under the personal charge of Archbishop Mannix. They were lodged in private homes, the
Archbishop paid their expenses, and they attended a
Christian Brothers College. Their conductor, Dr Gruber,
had developed a light tone in the boys, which the men
had to adapt to. His internment because of Nazi connections led to the appointment first of A.W. Martin, and
then Dr Percy *Jones (1942–73), who sought to establish
a real cathedral choir school. Two groups of boys were
trained: the cathedral choristers, and new boys who
needed special attention. St Stephen's Cathedral, Brisbane,
was conducted by the Protestant Leonard *Francis from
1914 to 1951. He was directed to organise the music
along the lines of the *Motu Proprio*, and by 1921 it was well
established. The 40-voice choir was still a mixed group,
but Cecilian music by Tozer, Wiegand and Giorza dominated the morning service. The St Stephen's choir suffered
its demise in the 1960s, and was revived as an all-male
group in the early 1970s.

2. Anglican.   Two traditions of Anglican choral music
coexist: the cathedral, where the choir is paramount and
congregational singing has little place, and the parish,
where the primary function of the choir is to lead the
congregation. Conflict over which tradition should be
followed was a feature of Anglican church music,
although the coexistence is now stable. The first Anglican
bishop of Melbourne, Charles Perry, was in the parish
tradition, and actively forbade sung services. His successor, Bishop Moorhouse (1876) not only called for the
building of the cathedral, but sought a musical foundation. 'The cathedral service was the best possible form of
uplifting the voice of worship to the gate of heaven and
would serve also as a pattern and example of what the
services of all churches should be.' Proposals that the
choir of St Paul's Church might be used were controversial—it had surpliced women.

St Paul's Cathedral, Melbourne, was intentionally
based on British traditions, with a daily sung service to be
given by a choir of men and boys. The choral foundation
was integral from the start, the Chapter declaring that the
Cathedral use should 'conform as far as possible to what is
understood as cathedral in England'. It opened in 1891
with a new organ, an organist and a surpliced choir who
had been appointed before the building was finished.
Despite initial financial and material problems, the choir
flourished under Ernest *Wood, and then A.E. *Floyd
(1915–47), earning tributes from Sir Percy Buck and Sir
Richard Terry for the high standard at which they maintained the English tradition. In addition to services, the
choir undertook oratorio and concert activities, and
under Wood rarely sang an anthem more than three times
a year. Floyd introduced Elizabethan repertoire, and special commemorations for the Byrd/Weelkes tercentenary
and the Gibbons tercentenary (1925). There has been a
tradition of Good Friday performances of Stainer's *Crucifixion* since 1893.

St John's Cathedral, Brisbane, established in 1842 as
the parish church of Brisbane, became the pro-cathedral
in 1860. Before 1860 services were simple: the singing of
psalms, canticles, and some hymns. The first bishop introduced the *Salisbury Hymnal* and other practices considered quite High Church, which created a furore. R.T.
*Jefferies was appointed organist in 1873, and rapidly
improved the standards, seeking to recruit boys and men
(the choir at that time being mixed).

The focus on a cathedral music tradition was not without problems. The next bishop, Dr Hale (1875), was auto-
cratic and Low Church, with a belief in the power of the
congregation. Conflict with Jefferies' High Church view
was inevitable. In a letter to the church wardens of 29
March 1880, Jefferies compared the St John's music
favourably with what he had heard in England. He insisted
on regular attendance at practice, and of the boys he wrote,
'I feel truly thankful that I have, after much labour, succeeded in extending the compass and softening down the
voices of most of them, but the abominable habit of shout-
ing in the colonial boy is hard to overcome'. He also specified daily practices, Wednesday being occasional, and
under his regime the choir regained its former ability. To
encourage and improve congregational singing he formed
a Choral Association (1877) in association with the cathedral choir. Nonetheless, debate continued. In 1881 he
resigned and moved first to St Mary's, Kangaroo Point, and
in 1896 to All Saints, Wickham Terrace. He was asked to
resign from there in 1897 for no apparent reason, but possibly because of another cathedral versus parish music dispute. Bishop Webber (1885) reintroduced a cathedral style,
and insisted on a musical service. A cathedral tradition, supported by the availability of sufficient men and boys, was
certainly established from 1898, and continues to the present day. The 1970s saw a growing involvement by the
congregation, and a lesser choral contribution. Nonetheless the choir remains a male-voice, surpliced, group in the
English tradition. Under sympathetic clergy the cathedral
has established women's choral groups which give occasional services, as do visiting mixed-voice groups.

3. Methodist.   Methodism stressed congregational
involvement in music-making, introducing prohibitions
on solo singing and choral anthems in the 19th century.
The Australasian church issued its first 'Direction' concerning music in 1863. Only Methodist hymn books
were to be used; there were to be no male solo recitatives,
women soloists, or 'fuguing'; no music festivals; no charity
services where 'theatrical singers' are brought into the
chapel ('such a practice is offensive to the Conference');
and no anthems, since they were not joint worship. These
restrictions led to the practice of the mid-week 'sacred
concert' (outside the service environment), which provided an outlet for choristers' musical aspirations.

These restrictions were partly from concern that
such practices would introduce Catholic and Anglican
ritualism, hence diluting Methodist principles. There

were concerns about the choir perceiving itself as some-how separate from the congregation, as well as the physical placement of the choir, and the behaviour of its members. Despite heated debate in the 1870s, the restrictions were loosened by 1900. Choirs could present appropriate anthems, and undertake special services and concerts. The 'service of song', where music replaced the sermon, became common. Choirs were also required to have meetings and keep minutes (which are now a source of information).

For most of the 20th century the Methodist choirs had a stable existence. Some participated in eisteddfods and ABC religious broadcasts and developed large repertoires, comprised mainly of Victorian anthems, the oratorio literature, and works like 'Mozart's 12th Mass'. Auburn Methodist Church, Melbourne, had a strong musical life between 1899 and 1945. The church trustees of the 1890s viewed the choir as a good revenue-raiser, and organised a series of winter concerts. Musical standards rose under J. Sutton Crow (1916–47) and responsibility shifted from the trustees to the musical director. During the Depression (when choirs served as a free means of social bonding) membership reached 50. It undertook concerts at other local churches, and interchanges with Forest Street, Bendigo, and Lydiard Street, Ballarat. There were choral services with truncated oratorios, and special events used orchestras and professional vocalists. The extensive repertoire was suitable for a large church of the time, but also reflected period tastes. Despite a postwar decline the now smaller choir still plays an active part in worship.

4. Lutheran and Other.   The SA Lutheran Church, following notions of cultural preservation and Lutheran purity, was largely German-speaking until the 1920s, and had little contact with other denominations. Influences were the revival of the Reformation chorale tradition, and the tradition of singing folk hymns and devotional songs outside church worship. Choirs (usually 20–30 voices) were a major feature of Lutheran congregations from early times, but the records are incomplete, the first mention usually being at a church dedication. The Langmeil choir, formed in 1885, was still active in 1960. The repertoire varied according to the skill of the choir and choirmaster, and could include motets and anthems. Details of the individual works sung are not easily found, since there were no printed service books. In the tradition of German *Kirchenblasen*, brass instruments often accompanied the hymn-singing.

Bethlehem Church, Adelaide, had a strong musical life under Immanuel Gotthold *Reimann from 1891 to 1932, with a choir of high standard and a vigorous youth group. Youth and male-voice choirs were formed in the 1920s and 30s. Several important anniversaries in the 1930s were celebrated by massed choirs of up to 200 voices. A South Australian Lutheran Choral Union, comprised of member choirs of the Evangelical Lutheran Synod of Australia, was active in the 1930s and 40s. Mis-sionary activity in Aboriginal communities sometimes saw choirs created on Western models. In 1967 the 90th anniversary of the Hermannsburg Lutheran Mission saw a 24-voice Aboriginal choir tour to Adelaide, Mount Gambier and Alice Springs, presenting a program of Schubert, Negro spirituals, English and German hymns sung to Aboriginal texts, and Bach's *Jesu Joy of Man's Desiring*.

Under Robert *Dalley-Scarlett St Andrew's Presbyterian Church, Brisbane, expanded to 70 voices in the 1920s, performing unaccompanied Renaissance music as well as large concert works. The Queensland premiere of Bach's *St Matthew Passion* (1922) initiated annual performances for the next decade.

As early as the 1850s Jewish congregations in Sydney, Melbourne and Ballarat formed choirs, often for a specific service. Male-voice choirs dominated within Orthodox congregations, and the participation of women and non-Jews has been an issue. A mixed choir has existed at the Great Synagogue, Sydney, since 1870; its conductors included Alfred *Hill (1900–02) and Arundel *Orchard (1910–23).

Church choirs depend heavily on the conductor to attain good musical standards, such that singers are attracted and the clergy and congregation provide support. Since the 1960s they have suffered decreased numbers, falling standards, and general loss of interest—so much so that they became the butt of jokes. Reasons for this include secularism and an erosion of church commitment and the importance of religion; less interest from young people in church music; lower musical literacy; materialism; the increased mobility of the population; the greater range of pursuits available to people; and changing community demographics. Cathedral boys' choirs face problems of finance, supply of voices (because of earlier maturation) and pressures for greater female involvement. Nevertheless the role of choral music in worship is still considered important. The better church choirs undertake weddings, funerals, special services and commemorations. Visits to other choirs, concerts, recordings and radio or television broadcasts may also feature. Choristers can also attend workshops or summer schools such as those conducted by the Royal School of Church Music. See *Church Music*.

FURTHER REFERENCE

Boughen, Robert K., An Account of the Music at St. John's Cathedral, Brisbane, from 1843–1887. MMus(Qual), Univ. Queensland, 1974.

Byrne, John, *Echoes of Home: Music at St. Francis' 1845–1995*. (Melbourne: St. Francis' Choir, 1995).

Byrne, Fr Neil J., 'The Music and Musicians of St. Stephen's Cathedral: The First Sixty Years', *Proceedings of the Brisbane Catholic Historical Society* 2 (1990), 15–29.

Harvie, Paul, The First Sixty Years of Music at St. Paul's Cathedral, Melbourne c. 1887–1947. M.Mus., Univ. Melbourne, 1983.

Hastie, Kelvin J., Music-making in the Wesleyan Churches of New South Wales, 1855–1902: Origins, Attitudes and Practices, MPhil, Univ. Sydney, 1991.

O'Farrell, Patrick, ed., *St. Mary's Cathedral Sydney, 1821–1971* (Sydney: Devonshire Press, 1971).

O'Reily, Most Rev John, *Pius X on Church Music: Paper read at the Australasian Catholic Congress, Melbourne October 1904* (Adelaide: Scrymgour & Sons, 1908).

Roennfeldt, Peter, A History of the First Hundred Years of Lutheran Church Music in South Australia, M.Mus, Univ. Adelaide, 1981.

Solomon, Miriam, 'Music and Musicians of the Great Synagogue, Sydney (1878–1974)', *Australian Jewish Historical Society Journal* 11/6 (1993), 896–920.

Wentzel, Ann K., The First Hundred Years of Music in Australia 1788–1888. MA, Univ. Sydney, 1963.

NOEL WILMOTT

Church Music.

1. Anglican. 2. Catholic. 3. Lutheran. 4. Presbyterian, Methodist, Revivalist and Other Denominations. 5. Convergence and Ecumenism.

In Australia church music has developed largely on a denominational basis, and it is only fairly recently that any degree of convergence has developed between the traditions. Several denominations that have been numerically significant have developed a distinctively Australian musical profile, while others have been more dependent on music from their country of origin.

1. Anglican. Although church and state never officially enjoyed the same relationship in Australia as in England, there was an effective Anglican monopoly for the first 30 years in the early penal colony of NSW. Church music was accompanied at first by military bands, and from the 1820s Anglican singing was dominated by metrical psalms, mostly sung 'according to the version of Dr Brady and Mr Tate'. A words-only edition of psalms was published in Sydney as early as 1828, and others followed elsewhere. An edition with music published in Hobart in 1843 was followed in the 1850s by collections of psalm tunes published by William Johnson (*fl.* 1840s–1850s) of Sydney and George Allan (1826–1897) of Melbourne. Allan, the founder of the prominent Melbourne music retailing firm, conducted weekly congregational rehearsals at St Paul's Church for 'instruction and practice on the Rev. J.J. Waite's system'.

Psalm collections generally included hymn texts as well, but separate hymnals also began to be published in Australia for Anglican use. Early examples of locally composed hymn tunes include a collection by J.C. Tapp (probably Anglican) of Hobart Town, published as *Tasmanian sacred melodies* [1855], and isolated examples by James Johnson (1803–60) of Sydney and Frederick A. ★Packer (1839–1902) of Hobart in the 1860s. The most substantial collection before the turn of the century was one titled *78 Australian Hymn Tunes* (London, 1892), compiled by R. Bentley Young, which included tunes by 23 composers spread throughout the country.

Although the introduction of hymnody in Anglicanism had come initially from evangelical influences in the 18th century, there was a revival of hymns in their ancient 'Catholic' form after the Oxford movement. In Brisbane, Bishop Tufnell (*fl.* 1859–75) introduced *The Salisbury Hymnal*, and the introduction of *Chope's Hymnal* in Sydney in 1865 was greeted with loud protests that some of its contents, having been 'borrowed from the Roman Catholic Church', were 'calculated to infuse into the minds of our people notions contrary to the principles of the English Reformation'. Despite such outrage, *Hymns Ancient & Modern* had been introduced in Brisbane before 1880, and at Christ Church St Laurence, Sydney before the end of the century.

Anglican choral music in Australia emerged later than psalmody and hymnody. There had been a choir at St James', Sydney, from at least 1827, and Anglican choirs existed in Melbourne and Perth by at least the 1840s. The earliest Anglican choirs existed to lead congregational singing, and they normally sang from the gallery. The influence of the revived cathedral-style choral service at Leeds Parish Church in England was soon felt in the colonies, however, and robed all-male chancel choirs were introduced in Sydney (Christ Church St Laurence, 1845), Melbourne (St Peter's Eastern Hill, 1865, and St Paul's, 1886), Adelaide (St Paul's, 1869) and Brisbane (St John's, 1872), by which time they had become associated with ritualist tendencies in the wake of the Oxford movement. The repertoire of such choirs tended to exclude congregational singing, favouring the performance of oratorio movements, anthems and service settings, together with the singing of the psalms to Anglican chants.

James Furley (1831–1912) was responsible for introducing new choral music at St James' King Street, Sydney, where he was organist from 1860 to 1875. This included his own *Nunc Dimittis*, published locally in a series entitled *Harmonia Divina*. Other composers who wrote anthems for Anglican choirs in Australia in the late 19th century included Hector MacLean (*fl.* 1880s ?) of Sydney, and Charles ★Horsley (1822–76) and Revd Dr George ★Torrance (1835–1907) of Melbourne. Choral settings of the eucharist were sung as early as 1873 in Brisbane (St John's) and 1876 in Melbourne (St Peter's), but the earliest Australian settings for Anglican use appear to be those written in the 1890s by E. Harold Davies (1867–1948) for St Paul's Church, Adelaide, and E.H. Wallace Packer for Christ Church, North Adelaide, and in 1904 by William Biggs (*c.*1858–1919) for Christ Church St Laurence, Sydney, where he also performed and arranged masses by Mozart and Gounod 'adapted for English use'.

Controversy raged in some places over 'intoning' and the choral domination of services, and there were calls for the reinstatement of congregational singing. In the tradition established by Henry Smart in London in the 1860s, 'chant services' suitable for congregations were published by the Hobart organist J. Finch Thorne in a series of *Hour Services: Chiefly in Chant Form* (Hobart & London, n.d.).

Such services were also introduced by R.T. ★Jefferies (1841–1920) at St John's, Brisbane, by 1880, along with weekly congregational rehearsals.

With the growth of choral singing in Anglican services, editions of Anglican chants began to be published in Australia, for example by Philip Charles Plaisted (1844–1920) in *The Canticles and Hymns of the Church* (Melbourne, 1869), and by Torrance as *Twelve Double Chants* (Melbourne, 1879). English publications followed: *The Cathedral Psalter* (London, 1875) had been introduced in Brisbane by 1880, and *The Cathedral Prayer Book* (London, 1891) at Christ Church St Laurence by around 1899, where the 'Sydney Gregorian Association' sang Evensong on Saturday evenings. By 1903, an express desire in the Diocese of Sydney for 'a new Chant Book adapted to Australian requirements' led to the publication of *The Australian Psalter* (London, c.1904), although this was in reality no more than a reprint of *The Cathedral Psalter*.

Although Anglican chant and 'intoning' appear to have been described by late 19th-century Anglicans as 'Gregorian', it was not until the early years of the 20th century that a more authentic tradition of plainsong was revived, notably in Melbourne at St Peter's, Eastern Hill, from 1902 under the influence of Arthur Nickson, and at Christ Church St Laurence after 1914 under Richard Kay. Anglican plainsong in Australia has generally followed the English/Sarum tradition cultivated by English adapters, although a short-lived Gregorian Society active in Melbourne in the late 1950s was concerned with the adaptation of the Solesmes versions of the chants to English texts.

Anglican composers in Australia during the first half of the 20th century included Arthur E.H. ★Nickson (1876–1964) and Alfred Ernest ★Floyd (1877–1974) of Melbourne, Canon Horace Percy Finnis (1883–1955) of Adelaide, Revd Alfred Wheeler (b 1865) of Geelong, George ★Sampson (1861–1949) of Brisbane and Edgar ★Bainton (1880–1956) of Sydney. Of these, Wheeler and Floyd were able to publish a number of small-scale anthems and service settings through Allans and Evans respectively in Melbourne, while most of Bainton's sacred output and a little of Sampson's was published in England. English influence has remained strong, and from at least 1932, many Anglican choirs in Australia have been affiliated with the Royal School of Church Music in England, which formed branches throughout the country from the 1950s onwards.

For most of the present century, Australian Anglicans have relied upon the use of imported hymnals, but there was an attempt to compile a collection of Australian Anglican hymnody around 1947 when *The Book of Common Praise* from Canada was reissued with an Australian supplement 'approved for use by the General Synod of the Church of England in Australia'. Under the musical editorship of Edgar Bainton, the supplement contained 36 hymn tunes by 14 Australian composers, including a large number by Bishop C. Venn Pilcher (1879–1961), who

acted as secretary to the project committee. Few, if any, of these have since received wider currency.

The Church of England in Australia received its own constitution in 1962, later changing its name to 'Anglican Church of Australia'. Associated with its growing independence, experimental liturgies were produced in 1969 and 1973, leading to the publication of *An Australian Prayer Book* (1978) and *A Prayer Book for Australia* (1995). The appearance of these new liturgical rites has encouraged a modest amount of musical composition, although the changes have been accompanied by little education of either clergy or musicians.

Congregational settings of the eucharist designed for use with the new Anglican rites have been produced by John Barrett (1915–83) of Canberra, Paul Paviour (b 1931) of Bathurst, jointly by Geoffrey Cox (b 1951) with Graeme Skinner (b 1960) of Melbourne (based on plainchant), Rosalie Bonighton (b 1946) of Ballarat, Lawrence Bartlett (b 1933) of Sydney, David Rumsey (b 1939) of Sydney, Michael ★Dudman (1938–94) of Newcastle, William Pierce (1926–96) of Launceston and others. As in other denominations, there has been a broadening of musical styles employed in worship, and collections of 'worship song' for Anglican use have been published in the 1980s and 90s by Ellaine Downie and Hannah Digby, Annie Judd, Revd Jim Minchin (b 1942) and Peter Mangold.

Among the most prolific of Anglican composers in recent decades have been English-born Paul Paviour, now resident in Goulburn, NSW, whose output includes numerous settings of the eucharist, canticles, anthems, carols and hymns, and Rosalie Bonighton of Ballarat, Victoria, who has produced a significant number of service settings and anthems. Bonighton is also one of very few Anglican musicians to have devoted serious attention to the setting of responsorial psalms, which are still not widely used in the Anglican church.

Robert ★Boughen (b 1929), Ian McKinley (b 1929) and Donald Britton (b 1919) of Brisbane, and June Nixon (b 1942) and Lindsay O'Neill (b 1924) of Melbourne have all continued to produce good-quality choral music in the 'cathedral tradition'. Only two of the Anglican cathedrals in Australia (Melbourne and Sydney), however, have followed the English tradition of singing Evensong on weekdays as well as Sundays. The Anglican choral tradition has also been maintained strongly in some collegiate chapels, notably at Trinity College, Melbourne.

2. Catholic. The proportion of Roman Catholics among Australian Christians has always been higher than might be expected given the country's background in British colonialism. Even by the 1850s around a third of the Christian population in the colony of NSW was Catholic. Although predominantly Irish in background, Australian Catholics have long included Germans and Italians, to whom have been added increasing numbers of central Europeans and South-East Asians since World War

II. Catholicism has been the largest Christian denomination in Australia since 1986.

The earliest existence of Catholic church music in Australia pre-dates even the arrival of the first official Catholic chaplains to the colony in 1820. A choir formed by Mrs Catherine Fitzpatrick in 1817–18 eventually became the choir of the first St Mary's Cathedral in Sydney, which was opened in 1833. Masses by Beethoven, Mozart, Haydn, Weber and Gounod were sung regularly by the most prominent Australian Catholic choirs in the 19th century, such as those at St Mary's Cathedral, Sydney, and St Francis' Church, Melbourne, which maintained strong associations with professional operatic singers. The first choral concert given in the colony at St Mary's Cathedral in 1836, conducted by W. Vincent ★Wallace (in Sydney 1836–38), included movements from Handel's *Messiah* and Haydn's *The Creation*, and the St Mary's Choral Society formed in 1851 by Isaac ★Nathan (1790–1864) was similarly concerned with the presentation of sacred concerts described as 'oratorios', comprised of excerpts from orchestral masses and oratorios.

Large-scale masses written by composers in Australia during the later colonial era include works by George O. Rutter of Tasmania (1851), Austin T. Turner of Ballarat (1878), Hugo Alpen of Sydney (late 1880s), John Albert ★Delany of Sydney (1887 and 1892), J. Furlong of Ballarat (1880), Alfred Plumpton of Melbourne (1881), Ernest Truman of Sydney (1898), and Chevalier Auguste ★Weigand of Sydney (1898). Motets, often performed as 'offertories', were written by 19th-century Australian Catholic composers, including Revd Dr Henry Backhaus (1812–82) of Bendigo, Revd Dr D. Carmusci (*fl.* 1870s–1880s) of Brisbane, Charles A. Tracy (*c.*1838–96), Alfred ★Plumpton (*fl.* 1880s-1890s) and Alberto ★Zelman (*d* 1907) of Melbourne, and Delany (1852–1907) and Hugo ★Alpen (1842–1917) of Sydney.

Catholic congregational singing in the colonial era was limited largely to Latin and English hymns at Vespers and Benediction, and the singing at regular children's masses. Catholic schoolchildren in Australia by the latter decades of the 19th century were commonly trained to sing Vespers, and several hymnals (mostly without music) were published to cater for these needs. These included *Catholic Hymns* (Sydney, 1859 and later editions) in which Archbishop Polding called on congregations to join in the singing of popular hymns, and later *The Australian Catholic Hymn Book* (Sydney, 1884), the *St Patrick's Vesperal & Hymn Book* (Melbourne, 1891), and *The Australian Catholic Hymnal* (Sydney, 1916).

Stemming from the Cecilian movement (*Cäcilienverein*) established by Franz Witt in Ratisbon, there was increasing condemnation during the 1870s to 1890s of secular theatrical or operatic excesses in Catholic church music, and growing support for the revival of Gregorian chant, the music of Palestrina and his contemporaries, and the promotion of 'strictly devotional' music in the church.

This was to culminate in the *Motu proprio* of Pius X (1903), in which both the use of orchestras and the use of women singers in the liturgy were banned. Among the strongest proponents for reform before and around the turn of the century were Alfred Plumpton, Revd George Robinson and Frederick Beard (*c.*1866–1912) of Melbourne, and Archbishop John O'Reily of Adelaide, and the subject of reform was prominent on the agenda of both the First Australasian Catholic Congress in Sydney in 1900 and the Second Congress in Melbourne in 1904. Although the instruction of 1903 was reinforced by several other papal documents in the first half of the century, it was a long time before the reforms took effect in many places: liturgical all-male choirs, for instance, were not formed until much later in the Catholic cathedrals of Perth (1938), Melbourne (1939), Sydney (1955) and Brisbane (1971).

Mainstream composers writing choral settings of the mass in Australia during the early to mid-20th century include Fritz ★Hart (1874–1949) of Melbourne, Alfred Hill (1870–1960) of Sydney and C. Edgar Ford (1881–1961) of Perth, but by far the most prominent Catholic composer of this period was the Spanish-born Benedictine priest Dom Stephen ★Moreno (1889 -1953), who had arrived at New Norcia, WA, around 1910. Moreno published about twenty masses and numerous collections of motets and hymns, which were used throughout the country. His music, together with that of the Italian priest-musician Don Mario Pettorelli, was given prominence at the 29th International Eucharistic Congress, held in Sydney in 1928, at which Pettorelli was appointed to direct the music, and after which Pettorelli remained in Sydney from 1930 to 1933. Another influential musician in Sydney was Spanish-born Fr Joseph Muset-Ferrer (*b* 1889), director of music at St Patrick's College, Manly, during World War II, whose volume *Eucharistic Motets: 33 Motets for Three Equal Voices* was published in Sydney by Chappell in 1951.

With the growing desire expressed in papal documents that Gregorian chant should be restored to congregational use along with popular hymns, notable efforts were made by Revd Dr Percy ★Jones (1914–92) of Melbourne, who published *The Australian Hymnal* (Melbourne, 1942), and subsequently *The Hymnal of St Pius X* (Melbourne, 1952; new edition 1966). The latter included a significant number of original tunes by Jones himself as well as his arrangements of Irish traditional and other hymn melodies. The Guild of St Pius X, founded in Sydney in 1953 'to foster good liturgical taste', was influential in encouraging the publication of music through the Living Parish Series. Its most notable production was *The Living Parish Hymn Book*, edited by Anthony Newman (Sydney, 1961 and later editions). The substantial contributions to this hymnal by composer Richard Connolly (*b* 1927), coupled with texts by Professor James McAuley, stand out for their quality and originality, and have been widely reprinted elsewhere.

Further encouragement was given to congregational participation in the Papal Encyclical *Musicae Sacrae Disciplina* of Pope Pius XII (1955), and the liturgical reforms of that decade included a new Easter rite, for which Revd Ronald Harden (*fl.* 1955–70) of Sydney produced the *All Choirs' Booklet for the Restored Rite of Holy Week* (Sydney, 1958). Following the publication by the Second Vatican Council of the *Constitution on the Sacred Liturgy* (1963), a revised order of the eucharist was implemented in Australian Catholic churches in July 1964, and the decades following have witnessed an expansion and reassessment of Catholic musical repertoire on an unprecedented scale. Coupled with a newfound freedom in the deployment of musical styles and the need for congregational settings of liturgical texts in English, this has resulted in an avalanche of local compositional activity of widely varying worth.

Revd Percy ★Jones and his counterpart as diocesan director of music in Perth, Revd Albert Lynch (*fl.* 1938–1970s), were responsible for numerous adaptations of chant to English texts in the 1960s, as well as for original compositions. Other composers who responded to the immediate needs at this time included Michael Mann (*b* 1929) and Richard Connolly of Sydney, Roger Heagney (*b* 1942) of Melbourne, Dom Eladio Ros of the Benedictine Community in New Norcia, WA, and James Govenlock (*d* 1984) of Adelaide. Of these, Heagney has continued to write extensively, and has contributed significantly to the continuance and expansion of the choral repertoire.

A substantial corpus of Australian composition has also been included in the *Catholic Worship Book* (Sydney, 1985), ed. Revd Dr William Jordan of Melbourne, and to a lesser extent in *The New Living Parish Hymn Book* (Sydney, 1987), ed. Revd John de Luca of Sydney, both attempting to establish a core repertoire of congregational service music, hymnody and psalmody drawn from a variety of traditions. Despite such efforts, however, the level of musical participation has remained abysmally low in most Catholic congregations. With the new emphasis on congregational singing there has been a widespread demise of Catholic choirs, and the musical void has been filled for some by 'worship song' in a folk idiom, many written by members of religious communities. The influence of a commercially driven culture of American popular church music has also been evident in compilations such as *As One Voice* (Sydney, 1992) and *Gather Australia* (Melbourne & Chicago, 1995). Among Australian composers of Catholic church music since the early 1970s, Christopher Willcock (*b* 1947) stands out for the quality and quantity of his work, which displays an uncommon combination of technical proficiency with a sound understanding of current liturgical requirements.

3. Lutheran. There were Lutheran settlers in both South Australia and Queensland from 1838, and in Victoria from 1849. The South Australian settlers were Old Lutherans who had left Prussia in protest against the union of Lutheran and Reformed churches, and SA has remained the principal centre of Lutheranism in Australia. From the time of an early schism in 1846 between the two Lutheran pastors in SA (Kavel and Fritzsche), the Lutheran Church in Australia was divided into a number of synods based in South Australia, Victoria and Queensland. Various partial amalgamations led eventually in 1921 to the formation of the United Evangelical Lutheran Church in Australia (UELCA), from which only the Evangelical Lutheran Church of Australia (ELCA) was excluded. These two bodies finally came together in 1966 to form the Lutheran Church of Australia. While there has been some influence from other denominations, especially in recent years, Australian Lutheranism has maintained an independent identity from other denominations.

The Lutheran liturgy was generally conducted in German until around the time of World War I, when English became widely used. The earliest hymn-books were imported from Germany, but Australian editions of German hymns were soon produced. These included the *Christliches Gesangbuch* (1860) edited by Pastor Maschmedt in Adelaide, *Gesangbuch der Deutschen Evangelischen Gemeinde in Sydney* (1866), edited by A.L. Heyde, and the *Gesangbuchlein* (1890), edited by E. Darsow. In Mrs G. Mano's *Lobgesänge in Prosa aus dem Englischen* (Adelaide, 1871), English hymns are translated into German prose. *Lutheran Hymns* (Mount Gambier, 1893) was the first such publication in English.

Liturgical and musical norms in the 19th century were drawn from a variety of sources (Luneburg, Missouri, Wittenburg), but greater uniformity of practice was gradually achieved. An *Agende*, first published in 1890 by the Evangelical Lutheran Synod of Australia (ELSA), was translated into English in 1914 by Immanuel Reimann, and subsequently incorporated into the *Australian Lutheran Hymnal* (words edition 1922; music edition 1925). The latter also included a small number of locally composed hymn tunes by Johannes Paul Löhe (1869–1952), E. Starick, Hilda Schurmann and others.

Following the formation of the UELCA in 1921, the 1928 General Convention adopted the German Church Book and Liturgy published by the Evangelical Lutheran Church of Iowa, USA, and the English 'Liturgy and Agenda' of the Evangelical Lutheran Missouri Synod, USA, as the official liturgical books, and at the same time published a *School Hymnal*.

A joint committee of the UELCA and ELCA met from 1951 and eventually produced the *Lutheran Hymnal* (Adelaide, 1973), authorised by the Lutheran Church of Australia, to which James Thiele (*b* 1930) of Adelaide was a major editorial contributor. The volume also contains a significant number of original hymn tunes and arrangements by Johannes Paul Löhe. A *Supplement to Lutheran Hymnal* (Adelaide, 1987), prepared by the Commission on Worship of the Lutheran Church of Australia, includes a substantial number of hymn tunes by Australian contributors in a more modern idiom, notably those by Robin

Mann (*b* 1949). Other significant Australian Lutheran composers have included Gotthard Daniel Fritzsche (1797–1863) and Adolph Ortenburger (1871–1957), the latter of whom published two books of anthems.

4. Presbyterian, Methodist, Revivalist and Other Denominations. (i) Presbyterian. The Presbyterian presence in Australia can be dated from the arrival of the first minister, Dr John Dunmore Lang, in 1823. Mid-19th-century divisions in the wider Presbyterian Church (represented by the Established Church of Scotland, the Free Church of Scotland, and the United Presbyterian Church) were reflected in various Australian synods, and there were also further local divisions. The separate synods in Australia were united initially on a geographical basis, forming, for example, the Presbyterian Church of Victoria (1859), the Presbyterian Church of Queensland (1863), the Presbyterian Church of New South Wales (1865) and the Presbyterian Church of South Australia (1865). After meetings that stretched back to the first Federal Assembly in Sydney in 1886, the Presbyterian Church of Australia finally came into existence in 1901. It did not include various Free Church groups, who formed the Free Presbyterian Church of Australia in 1913.

The austerity of Presbyterian worship, in which the only musical component had been the unaccompanied singing of metrical psalms and paraphrases led by the precentor, was gradually modified. Musical and liturgical innovations of the 1850s-1870s included the introduction of organs or harmoniums, choirs, hymn-singing, sitting or kneeling (rather than standing) to pray, and standing (rather than sitting) to sing. Although these changes reflected innovations in Scotland, as well as increasing local prosperity, and to some extent perhaps also the influence of other denominations, they were resisted by some congregations of the conservative Free Church Minority (the 'wee Free') as late as the 1890s.

Lang published several collections of hymn and psalm texts, but the earliest Australian Presbyterian music publication was *The psalmody of the Presbyterian Church of New South Wales, being a collection of the standards tunes, for the use of the Union Church of Sydney and the colony* (1865). The Victorian General Assembly in 1863 appointed a committee to work on a collection of hymns, but Australian Presbyterians have largely relied on imported collections. The *Church Praise* book of the Presbyterian Church of England, for example, was adopted by some congregations in the 1880s.

The most widely used collection of Presbyterian psalmody was *The Psalter in Metre and Scripture Paraphrases* (London, 1913, 1925), which was reissued after the union of the Church of Scotland and the United Free Church of Scotland as *The Scottish Psalter 1929 and Scripture Paraphrases*. This volume was used in conjunction with the *Church Hymnary* (1898; revised edition 1927), both being officially authorised for use in public worship by the Presbyterian Church of Australia. After the formation of the

Uniting Church in Australia in 1977, which incorporated many formerly Presbyterian parishes, the continuing Presbyterian Church of Australia produced its own hymnal, *Rejoice! A Collection of Psalms, Hymns and Spiritual Songs* (Sydney, 1987), a largely retrospective collection with little Australian content.

Presbyterian composers of choral works include W.R. Knox (*b* 1861) of Adelaide, who wrote a number of anthems and cantatas, and Robert *Dalley-Scarlett (1890–1959) of Brisbane.

(ii) Methodist. The official presence of the Methodist Church in Australia can be dated back to 1812, when the 'New South Wales District' was established under the British Wesleyan Conference. The early divisions of Methodism in Australia reflected divisions elsewhere. These included, in addition to the Wesleyan Methodists, the Primitive Methodists (especially in Victoria and Tasmania), Bible Christians (initially brought to SA by Cornish miners), and the Wesleyan Methodist Association (which joined the Arminian Methodists in 1857 to form the United Methodist Free Church). The Australasian Conference was constituted in 1855, and in 1902 the Wesleyan Methodists and Primitive Methodists united to form the Methodist Church of Australasia.

Although there was suspicion of hymns and instrumental music in the Calvinist sectors of Methodism, the tradition of hymn-singing was strong from the start with the Wesleyans. Indeed, it was the Wesleyans who were responsible for the publication of the first hymnal in Australia: *An Abridgment of the Wesleyan Hymns, Selected from the Larger Hymn-Book, Published in England, for the Use of the People called Methodists, by the Reverend John Wesley*, which was published in 1821 by George Howe, the government printer at Port Jackson, albeit without music. A few Sunday School hymn-books and collections for individual congregations were published in Australia in the 1860s and 80s, but Methodists came to rely generally on overseas publications.

Both the 1904 and 1933 editions of *The Methodist Hymn-Book* included an 'Australasian Supplement,' although these did not contain any tunes. This shortcoming was redressed by Revd Dr E.W.H. Fowles of Brisbane, who published *The New Methodist Hymn-Book Companion and Supplement for Australasia and New Zealand* (Brisbane, 1935), including tunes by Harald F.V. Bjelke-Petersen of Sydney, Revd Brian Wibberley of Adelaide and H.J. Williams of Brisbane, along with contributions from local Anglican composers George Sampson, Dr C.A. Jarman (of Bathurst) and Canon Alfred Wheeler. Bjelke-Petersen also published hymn tunes monthly in *The Methodist* (Sydney) between 1934 and 1936. The Australian supplement to *The School Hymn-Book of the Methodist Church* [1950] included tunes by two Australian composers, Edwin C. Burchett (1884–1966) of Melbourne and Hugh Jeffrey (*fl.* 1930s-1960s) of Sydney.

Methodist hymn-singing was at first performed by 'lining-out', the system whereby one or two lines at a time were given by the preacher or precentor and sung by the whole congregation in response, but this practice died out as levels of literacy rose through the 1860s-1880s. Gospel hymns deriving from the revivalists came to be used in Methodist churches alongside the authorised hymn-book in the latter part of the 19th century, and the influence of this style of music continued through the 20th century, culminating in the use of anthems and cantatas by American writers such as John W. Petersen in the 1960s and 70s.

The latter decades of the 19th century also saw the multiplication of choirs, soloists and organs in Methodist churches, and the gradual introduction of the choir 'anthem' in spite of zealous resistance. The anthem repertoire of the period was dominated by the popular Victorian works of Barnby, Stainer and Sullivan, and their lesser contemporaries, Caleb Simper and J.H. Maunder, together with tuneful works by continental composers such as Charles Gounod, Friedrich Himmel, Felix Mendelssohn and Louis Spohr.

In imitation of contemporary Anglican practice, a few Methodist churches during the latter part of the century also introduced the chanting of items such as a Gloria and Te Deum, but for the majority the Sunday service was dominated musically by the hearty singing of hymns. Choirs in the major city churches often gave large-scaled performances of oratorios in the 1870s and 80s, and much energy was devoted to music at Sunday school anniversaries, and the performance of cantatas (including J.H. Maunder's popular *Olivet to Calvary*) at 'services of song'. These traditions remained essential ingredients in Methodist worship of the 20th century.

Australian Methodist composers have not been prominent, but isolated examples of their work survive. John Eggleston, a Methodist organist in Melbourne during the 1870s-1890s, published several anthems and sacred songs under the imprint of the Diocesan Book Society, Melbourne. The Lancashire-born James Lord (*b* 1840), who was organist at Albert Street Methodist Church, Brisbane, in the late 1870s-1880s, but apparently living in WA by 1900, was probably the composer of an anthem published in Melbourne in that year. William Bowen Chinner (*b c.*1850), organist of the Pirie Street Wesleyan Church in Adelaide from 1869, wrote a significant number of anthems and cantatas, some published by Novello in London. Methodist composers of carols published in Melbourne have included Edwin Cyril Burchett (1884–1966) of Melbourne, and W.H. Keith Young (*c* 1912–1995) of Ballarat. William G. James (1895–1977), who was organist and choirmaster at Wesley Church, Melbourne from around 1925 until 1938, published three sets of *Five Australian Christmas Carols* (Sydney, 1948, 1954, 1961) which have become widely known.

(iii) *Revivalist and Other Denominations.* Methodists were always strongly associated with evangelism, and the

music associated with the campaigns and missions of visiting revivalists played an important part in Methodist music-making from the late 19th century onwards. Here there are many intersections with other denominations, including the Baptists and the *Salvation Army, as publications of revival hymns and gospel songs were designed to appeal to Christians of all denominations.

The various editions of Ira Sankey's *Sacred Songs and Solos* from 1873 onwards were used in Australia through the 1880s and 90s in association with the campaigns of visiting evangelists, and Charles Alexander's collections of gospel hymns and songs were used in campaigns after 1900. These publications were generally issued as Australian imprints, most of their contents deriving from American and English sources. One notable exception was the inclusion of about 70 items by the Bendigo-born composer Robert Harkness in various editions of Alexander's hymns around 1910. In addition to the Anglican and Lutheran composers already mentioned, more recent composers in the 'gospel' tradition include Ross Langmead (Baptist) and Douglas Simper (Methodist/Uniting Church).

5. *Convergence and Ecumenism.* Although the Second Vatican Council was not constituted as an ecumenical one, its promulgations from 1963 onwards have had considerable influence on the liturgical and musical practices of most denominations. This has occurred not least through the establishment of international committees aimed at finding agreement on common English liturgical texts. The work within the Roman Catholic Church of the International Committee on English in the Liturgy (ICEL) since 1965 has been supplemented by that of the ecumenical International Consultation on English Texts (ICET) since 1969. The latter has been subsumed since 1985 within the broader agenda of the English Language Liturgical Consultation (ELLC). Together, these bodies, all of which have involved Australian representation, have reached consensus on a large number of liturgical texts which are gradually being adopted across the denominations.

The formation of the Uniting Church in Australia in 1977, which incorporated all formerly Methodist and Congregational parishes as well as many formerly Presbyterian ones, coincided with these wider liturgical trends. A large proportion of the texts contained in the official book of services of the Uniting Church, *Uniting in Worship* (1988), are therefore consistent with those used by other denominations. Similarly, growing independence within the Anglican communion coincided with these trends, and the new prayer-books of the Anglican Church of Australia have also drawn heavily on the same sources.

The notion of an Australian ecumenical hymn-book was conceived in the 1960s by representatives of the Anglican, Congregational, Presbyterian and Methodist Churches in Australia. Impetus for the project undoubtedly came from discussions leading to the establishment of the Uniting Church, and an editorial committee was formed in 1967. After the publication of the committee's first report, the Roman Catholic Archdiocese of Sydney also sought involvement, with the result that *The Australian Hymn Book* was finally published in 1977 in two versions, one of which included a 'Catholic Supplement'. The book has also been published internationally under the title *With One Voice*.

Apart from being a remarkable ecumenical achievement, *AHB* was also a significant national one, although it included only around 35 original tunes by Australian composers. Of these the most significant contribution comprises 15 tunes previously published by Richard Connolly (2. above). *Sing Alleluia* (London, 1987), the supplement to *AHB*, included further contributions by Australian composers, as well as settings of the eucharist by Michael Dudman, Canon Lawrence Bartlett (chairman of the editorial committee), John Barrett, Dulcie ★Holland (*b* 1913) and Br Colin Smith. A revised edition of *The Australian Hymn Book* is planned for publication in the late 1990s, and the editorial committee has been broadened to include representatives of the Churches of Christ and the Lutheran Church.

Convergence and ecumenism in church music are also evident on an organisational level with the formation in 1995 of 'RSCM Australia: A National Church Music Association,' which stems from the branches of the English-based Royal School of Church Music that were formed throughout the country from the 1950s onwards. Although Anglican in origin, the RSCM branches have increasingly attracted members from other denominations, and have established a national identity since 1956 through annual Australian summer schools. RSCM Australia is in the process of developing formal links with various church bodies across the denominations at both state and national levels.

Mainstream composers, many holding academic positions, have also contributed significantly to the repertoire of church music in Australia, often as a result of commissions. Undoubtedly the most prolific of these has been Colin ★Brumby (*b* 1933) of Brisbane, whose output includes a remarkable variety of service music, anthems and carols, ranging from simple to festive settings. Others whose stylistic and technical contribution to the repertory has been welcomed include William★ Lovelock (1899 –1986), Nigel ★Butterley (*b* 1935), Donald ★Hollier (*b* 1934), Robert Illing (*b* 1917), Eric★ Gross (*b* 1926), and more recently Stephen ★Cronin (*b* 1960). Like the church music of overseas resident Malcolm ★Williamson (*b* 1931), however, the works of these composers have not been widely performed in Australia.

See also *Church and Cathedral Choirs*; *Hymnody*; *Jewish Music, Greek Music, Salvation Army*.

FURTHER REFERENCE

Allen, Laura Mary, *A History of Christ Church S. Laurence* (Sydney: Finn, 1939), 212–38.

Australian Music Centre, *Catalogue of Australian Religious Choral Works* (Sydney: AMC, 1991).

Bonighton, Rosalie M., Contemporary Liturgical Music and the Composer, MA, La Trobe Univ., 1992.

Boughen, Robert, An Account of the Music at St John's Cathedral, Brisbane, from 1843–1887, MMus (qual), Univ. Queensland, 1974.

Byrne, John, *Echoes of Home: Music at St Francis' [Melbourne] 1845–1995* (Melbourne: Spectrum, 1995).

De Luca, John, The Implementation of the *Motu Proprio* 'Tra Le Sollecitudini' of Pope Pius X in the Sydney Catholic Church, 1903–1963, MMus, Univ. New South Wales, 1994.

Gome, Dianne, 'Australian Hymnody, 1821–1901: an annotated checklist of sources located in Australian libraries', *Continuo* 24 (1995), 1–28.

Hastie, Kelvin, Music-Making in the Wesleyan Churches of New South Wales, 1855–1902, MPhil, Univ. Sydney, 1991.

Lea-Scarlett, Errol, 'Music, Choir and Organ'. In *St Mary's Cathedral, Sydney, 1821–1971*, ed. Patrick O'Farrell (Sydney: Devonshire Press, 1971), 157–81.

McKnight, Judith, Music for *Uniting in Worship* (1988): A Background Investigation of Music for the Services of the Uniting Church in Australia, BMus(Hons), Australian Catholic Univ., 1993.

Mansfield, Joan, 'Music—A Window on Australian Christian Life'. In *Re-Visioning Australian Colonial Christianity: New Essays in the Australian Christian Experience, 1788–1900*, ed. M. Hutchinson & E. Campion. Studies in Australian Christianity, vol. 1 (Sydney: Centre for the Study of Australian Christianity, 1994), 131–52.

___, 'The Music of Australian Revivalism'. In *Reviving Australia: Essays on the History and Experience of Revival and Revivalism in Australian Christianity*, ed. M. Hutchinson, E. Campion & S. Piggin. Studies in Australian Christianity, vol. 3 (Sydney: Centre for the Study of Australian Christianity, 1994), 123–42.

Morton, Graeme, Contemporary Australian Church Music: Styles, Influences and Trends in Recent Choral Settings, BMus(Hons), Univ. Queensland, 1974.

Morton, Ralph, Music in Worship in the Methodist Churches of Brisbane, BMus(Hons), Univ. Queensland, 1970.

Phillips, Beverley, The Impact of Vatican II on Musical Settings for the Mass of the Roman Rite by Australian Composers, published before 1973, BMus(Hons), Australian Catholic Univ., 1992.

Prentis, Malcolm D., 'Changes in Presbyterian Worship in Colonial Australia, 1860–1900', *Church Heritage* 2/1 (March 1981), 46–57.

Roennfeldt, Peter, A History of the First Hundred Years of Lutheran Church Music in South Australia, MMus, Univ. Adelaide, 1981.

Swale, David, 'Liturgical and Choral traditions in South Australia', *From Colonel Light Into The Footlights: The Performing Arts in South Australia From 1836 to the Present*, ed. A. McCredie (Norwood, SA: Pagel, 1988), 193–207.

Taylor, Paul, Twentieth-Century Catholic Hymnody in Australia: A Study of Selected Published Hymnals, 1942–1985, BMus(Hons), Australian Catholic Univ., 1991.   G.COX

Church, The. Rock band formed at Canberra (1980) by Steve Kilbey (bass, vocals) with Peter Koppes (guitar, vocals), Marty Willson-Piper (*b* Sweden; guitar, vocals) and Nick Ward (drums until 1981, then Richard Ploog). Their debut album *Of Skins and Heart* (1981), which was released in Europe as *The Church*, gained some radio and television exposure, and their debut single *The Unguarded Moment* indicated great promise for their future. Their second album, *The Blurred Crusade* (1982), hit No. 10, and included tracks such as *Almost With You* and *When You Were Mine*, which featured 12-stringed guitars that were stylistically reminiscent of the Byrds and other bands of the 1960s. Their following albums, *Sing-Songs* (1982), *Seance* (1983), *Remote Luxury* (1984), *Persia* (1984) and *Heyday* (1986), all charted in Australia with varying success. The Church's 1988 album *Starfish* hit No. 11 and received college radio airplay in the USA. As a result, the extracted single *Under the Milky Way* hit No. 22 and reached the US Top 30.

Although this period also saw the Church's popularity increase in some parts of Europe, the band found themselves playing primarily to a small yet dedicated cult audience. *Gold Afternoon Fix* (1990) charted well in Australia, reaching No. 13, with the single *Metropolis* peaking at No. 15. After the departure of Richard Ploog in 1991, former Patti Smith group drummer Jay Dee Dougherty joined the Church to record *Priest = Aura* (1992) and *Sometime Anywhere* (1994).

In addition to the Church's activities, its members have also been involved in solo and collaborative ventures. Marty Willson-Piper released two solo albums, *In Reflection Chase* (1987) and *Art Attack Survival* (1988), and played guitar part-time with All About Eve (1991). Peter Koppes's EP *When Reason Forbids* was released in 1987, as were Steve Kilbey's solo albums *Unearthed* and *The Slow Crack*. Kilbey also collaborated with Go-Between's guitarist Grant McLennan to record *Jack Frost* (1991).

FURTHER REFERENCE

Recordings include *Of Skins and Heart* (1981, Parlophone PCSO 7583); *The Blurred Crusade* (1982, Parlophone PCSO 7585); *Sing-Songs* (1982, Parlophone BUG 2); *Seance* (1983, Parlophone PCSO 7590); *Remote Luxury* (1984, Parlophone BUG 5); *Persia* (1984, Parlophone BUG 430017); *Heyday* (1986, Parlophone PCSO 430034); *Starfish* (1988, Mushroom RML 53266); *Gold Afternoon Fix* (1990, Mushroom TVL 93321); *Priest = Aura* (1992, Mushroom TVD 93356); *Sometime Anywhere* (1994, White Records TVD 93396). See also *GuinnessP; SpencerW*.

AARON D.S. CORN

Cillario, Carlo Felice (*b* San Rafael, Argentina, 1915), conductor. He studied violin at Buenos Aires, then at the Bologna Conservatory and gave solo recitals in Italy and elsewhere. He taught at the Accademia di Santa Cecilia, Rome, then from 1942 studied conducting with Cerniatinsky and Enesco, making his conducting debut at the Odessa Opera. After conducting the Bucharest Philharmonic Orchestra, he returned to Argentina in 1947, conducting opera and concerts there and increasingly in Europe and the UK. He was joint musical director of the Stockholm Opera, and came to Australia as musical director of the Australian Opera, making his debut with *Tannhäuser* in 1968. He was musical director of the company 1968–71, then made his Metropolitan Opera debut in 1972 and returned frequently to the Australian Opera as guest conductor, conducting a very wide range of repertoire.

An excellent interpreter, he has so florid and flamboyant a style that at his Australian debut in *Tannhäuser* his gestures during the Songfest scene knocked his score to the ground and broke his braces, leading to a memorably long pause while matters were rectified. He produces a shimmering quality to Puccini and Verdi and a luscious sound in Wagner, and his performances of *Aida*, *Simon Boccanegra*, *Parsifal* (1977) and *Die Walküre* (1982) have been particularly memorable. Much loved by singers, who find him unfailingly inspirational, he has conducted more frequently for the Australian Opera than any other conductor save Richard *Bonynge.

FURTHER REFERENCE

For his extensive discography, see *HolmesC*. See also John Cargher, *Bravo! 200 Years of Opera in Australia* (Sydney: ABC/Macmillan, 1988); Neil Warren-Smith *25 Years of Australian Opera*, with F. Salter (Melbourne: OUP, 1983), 139–41.

Clan Songs (Manikay). Specific genre of singing associated with public ceremonial performance at funerals, memorial ceremonies, male circumcisions, and cleansing or purification rites in north-eastern and north-central Arnhem Land. Clan songs are sung by one or more men playing pairs of wood clapsticks, with a single male didjeriduist accompanying; they may be sung both with and without corresponding women's and men's mimetic dances. A performance of clan songs may run for several hours, comprised of hundreds of short verses separated by brief periods of conversation. Most of the verses sung in a given ceremonial performance are regarded as purely ancestral creations, while some 'newsong verses' (*yuta manikay*) are the acknowledged creations of contemporary (or late) Yolngu singers (see *Yolngu*). At certain times during ceremonies women engage in *ngätji* (crying), a form of ritual wailing. Performed without clapsticks or didjeridu accompaniment, *ngätji* allude to the same ancestral spirits and incorporate the same melodic formulae as men's clan songs. Women performing *ngätji* may combine extemporised personal expressions of grief with text pertaining to the ancestral song subject.

The subject matter of clan songs includes many ancestral spirit-beings sung in the form of animals, plants, natural elements, cultural artefacts and anthropomorphic figures. The semi-improvised text of each short verse poetically alludes to certain essential qualities or behaviours of the sung ancestral being; long successions of these brief poetic images allude, in turn, to important events of the ancestral past. There are conventions that partly determine the ordering of ancestral song subjects during performance, but specific song subjects and specific sets of song words alluding to particular ancestral events may be included or excluded in accordance with the immediate performance context, at the lead singer's discretion.

The songs are organised into overlapping repertoires associated with specific clans (patrilineally defined extended families). In the case of Yolngu clan songs, the concept of 'repertoire' may be applied not only to song subject matter (that is, the ancestral spirit beings alluded to) but also to clan-specific melodic characteristics and particular clapstick beating patterns, the use of specific clan-related dialects and/or vocabulary, and certain clan-related dance movements. In Yolngu clan song performance, clan-owned melodic characteristics comprised of variably tuned scales, modes and specific melodic formulae are called *dhambu* (head). The uniqueness of each set of *dhambu* characteristics is significant, for *dhambu* provide the main aural distinctions between the sung performances of various clans. This is not surprising since each clan maintains only one or two *dhambu*, whereas a clan has a relatively large number of clapstick patterns or special song-related vocabularies.

Apart from their use in traditional religious ceremonies, clan songs are also used in secular contexts such as school graduations or building dedications. Yolngu clan songs and dances are regularly incorporated into the repertoires of professional pan-Australian Aboriginal dance companies. The contemporary Yolngu band *Yothu Yindi includes some traditional *manikay* in their work, and also draws upon textual and musical aspects of *manikay* in the creation of some of their pop material.

STEVEN KNOPOFF

Clapton, Richard [Terry Gonk], singer, songwriter and guitarist. His stage-name is derived from those of Keith Richards and Eric Clapton. Richard Clapton started his musical career playing in bands in London and Berlin (1967–72). Returning to Australia, he recorded *The Last Train to Marseille* (1972), and after a brief stint with Sun (1972) released his first solo album *Prussian Blue* (1973). Although this album received little airplay, it sold steadily and displayed Clapton's laconic wailing vocal style and talent for writing strong lyrics and melodies. In 1974 he recruited a backing band and recorded *Girls on the Avenue*; its title single, which he was later reluctant to admit was about prostitution, hit No. 4. After the release of *Main Street Jive* (1976) he toured Europe, and on his return recorded *Capricorn Dancer* (1977) for the soundtrack of the film *Highway One*. With its powerful evocation of sea and surf images, *Capricorn Dancer* became a popular anthem of east-coast Australian beach culture. Aspects of contemporary Australian society such as life in the cities, beach culture and growing up were also perceptively portrayed in the No. 11 hit album *Goodbye Tiger*

(1977). Returning from a 1978–79 tour of Europe and the US, he released *Hearts on the Nightline* (1979) and *Dark Spaces* (1980) which reached No. 17 and No. 23 respectively. His highest charting album, *The Great Escape* (1982), hit No. 8. During 1983 Clapton replaced James Reyne in the Party Boys but continued his solo career with *Solidarity* (1984), *Glory Road* (1987), *Best Years of Our Lives* (1989), *Distant Voices* (1993) and *Angeltown* (1996).

FURTHER REFERENCE

Recordings include *Last Train to Marseille* (1972, Festival); *Prussian Blue* (1973, Infinity); *Girls on the Avenue* (1975, Infinity L 35508); *Main Street Jive* (1976, Infinity L 35963); *Capricorn Dancer* (1977, Infinity K 6681); *Goodbye Tiger* (1977, Infinity L 36352); *Past Hits and Previews* (1978, Infinity L 36691); *Hearts on the Nightline* (1979, Interfusion L 36932); *Dark Spaces* (1980, Infinity L 37331); *Great Escape* (1982, WEA 600106); *The Very Best of Richard Clapton* (1982, Infinity L 37674); *Solidarity* (1984, Mushroom RML 53137); *Glory Road* (1987, WEA 600144–1); *Best Years of Our Lives* (1989, WEA 256582–1); *Distant Thunder* (1993, Sony); *Angeltown* (1995, Roadshow 17982–2). See also *GuinnessP; McGrathA; SpencerW.* AARON D.S. CORN

Clare, John (Lester) ['Gail Brennan'] (*b* Sydney, 15 Jan. 1940), jazz writer. He has written for most major Australian jazz journals, for the English journal *Town*, and in mainstream journalism including as jazz reviewer for the *Sydney Morning Herald*, and on the arts generally. A player of trumpet in dance and rock-based settings, he has also improvised spoken lines with Serge Ermoll's Free Kata, and is a published poet. His interests run through the full range of jazz schools and styles, but in particular he has, since the late 1950s, been the earliest, most steadfast and most energetic proselytiser for Australia's progressive jazz movement.

FURTHER REFERENCE

Recordings include *Free Kata* (1976, Free Kata 003). See also John Clare (Gail Brennan), *Bodgie Dada & The Cult Of Cool* (Sydney: UNSWP, 1995). BRUCE JOHNSON

Clari, or The Maid of Milan. Melodrama (1823) in two acts by John Howard Payne with music by Henry Bishop, best remembered today for the song 'Home, Sweet Home'. One of the earliest music-theatre works to be performed in Australia, it was first played at Hobart by Samson Cameron's troupe in January 1834 with George Peck conducting.

Clark, Alexander (*b* Dundee, Scotland, 10 June 1843; *d* Adelaide, 15 Mar. 1913), music educator. Clark emigrated to Sydney in 1867. In 1876 he was appointed headmaster of Grote Street Model Schools, Adelaide. As a school inspector (1884–1902) he championed the cause of music in state schools, introduced a tonic sol-fa school syllabus and encouraged and trained teachers. In 1890 he co-founded the Public School Decoration Society and inaugurated the annual Thousand Voices Choir concerts which he skilfully conducted until his death. In 1902 he

Traditional song series (*manikay*), often with dance, are performed in important rituals as well as for entertainment. Brolga dance from the Goyulan *manikay*, Kopanga at mouth of Blyth River, Arnhem Land, NT, 1982. (AIATSIS)

The didjeridu, Australia's most recognised indigenous instrument. Player accompanying two singers, Kopanga at mouth of Blyth River, Arnhem Land, NT, 1982. (AIATSIS)

Aboriginal Christian music: an Easter corroboree, women's version, portraying soldiers coming to arrest Jesus at Gethsemane, Warlpiri and Kaytetye women, Ali Curung, NT, 1979. (AIATSIS)

Right: Tjulpurrpa Yinuwurru public ritual, entry of the dancers, Old Balgo Mission, WA, 1982. (Richard Moyle)

AUSTRALIA COUNCIL: Its panels constructed entirely of musicians, it decides grants at 'arm's length' from the Federal Government. Music Committees, 1991.
(Courtesy Australian Music Centre)

BRASS BANDS

St Joseph's Total Abstinence Society Band, Launceston, founded 1845, the longest surviving civilian brass band in the British Commonwealth. (Courtesy St Joseph's Band)

Military and government service bands have a long history. South Australian Police Band at the Adelaide Children's Hospital Fête, c.1898. (Courtesy SA Police Historical Society)

Right: Well-organised civic bands are found in almost every regional centre. Mildura District Brass Band, 1985 National B Grade Champions. (Courtesy Mildura District Brass Band)

Below: One band toured Britain in 1924 to great acclaim. Newcastle Steelworks Band in Aeolian Co. recording studio, London, with conductor Albert H. Baile. (*front, third from left*) (Courtesy Jack Greaves, band historian)

Verbrugghen String Quartet, Sydney, c.1920, led by Henri Verbrugghen with J. Cullen, D. Nichols, J. Messens.
(Sydney Conservatorium Archive)

Original Melbourne String Quartet, led by Alberto Zelman Jr, with J.B. North, J.W. Dawson, Louis Hattenbach.
(Courtesy Don Fairweather)

Goldner String Quartet, Sydney, 1948, led by Richard Goldner, with Edward Cockman, Robert Pikler, Theo Salzman.
(Max Dupain, courtesy Musica Viva Australia)

Austral Quartet, Sydney, *c.*1972, led by Donald Hazelwood, with R. Ryder, R. Cragg, G. Elmaloglou.
(ABC Document Archives, Sydney)

Australian String Quartet, 1995, led by William Hennessy (*right*), with Elinor Lea, Keith Crellin, and Janis Laurs.

The all-male Liedertafels met for smoke nights or gala concerts. Metropolitan Liedertafel at the Melbourne Town Hall, 1879. (Grainger Museum, University of Melbourne)

CHURCH MUSIC

The abbey of Holy Trinity, New Norcia, WA, founded in 1844 by Spanish Benedictine missionary Dom Rosendo Salvado, who composed liturgical music and gave Perth's earliest piano recital to raise money for his mission.
(Alan Gill)

Revd Dr G.W. Torrance, c.1880, organist and composer of numerous anthems. (Trinity College, University of Melbourne)

Ernest Wood, organist of St Paul's Cathedral, Melbourne, c.1900. (St Paul's Cathedral Church, Melbourne)

George Sampson, organist of St John's Cathedral, Brisbane, 1940. (Courtesy Robert Boughen)

Sir William McKie, organist at Westminster Abbey, London. (*One Voice* 7/2 (Advent 1992), courtesy Revd H. Hollis)

Royal Victoria Theatre, Sydney, *c.* 1838, interior. (Joseph Fowles, 'Sydney in 1848', MS, courtesy Mitchell Library, Sydney)

Sidney Myer Music Bowl, Melbourne, with the Victorian Symphony Orchestra in rehearsal under Sir Malcolm Sargent, *c.*1959. (Melbourne Symphony Archive)

CONCERT HALL AND VENUES

Sydney Opera House, on Sydney Harbour, exterior. (Sydney Opera House Trust)

Victorian Arts Centre, Southbank, Melbourne, exterior.
(Victorian Arts Centre Trust)

CHILDREN'S MUSIC

Australia's most successful pre-school entertainers, the Wiggles. (ABC For Kids)

W. Vincent Wallace

Isaac Nathan, c.1820 (National Library of Australia)

Alfred Hill

May Brahe (Courtesy Harold Morgan)

Percy Grainger, *c.*1910 (Grainger Museum, University of Melbourne)

Esther Rofe (Simon Schlüter)

Peggy Glanville-Hicks (Australian Music Centre)

John Antill (Australian Music Centre)

COMPOSERS

Peter Sculthorpe (Perry Andronos)

Richard Meale (Australian Music Centre)

Don Banks (Australian Music Centre)

Colin Brumby (McChesney Clark)

George Dreyfus (Klaus Beuz)

Malcolm Williamson, receiving an honorary DMus degree at the University of Melbourne, 1982.
(Australian Music Centre)

Left: Larry Sitsky at the Bechstein double-piano.
(William Hall)

COMPOSERS

Barry Conyngham

Roger Smalley
(Belinda Webster, courtesy Australian Music Centre)

Brenton Broadstock

Ross Edwards
(Belinda Webster, courtesy Australian Music Centre)

Moya Henderson
(Milan Scepanovic, courtesy Australian Music Centre)

Richard Mills
(Courtesy Arts Management)

Carl Vine (Belinda Webster, courtesy Australian Music Centre)

CONDUCTORS

Sir Bernard Heinze (ABC Document Archives)

Sir Eugene Goossens (Sydney Conservatorium Archive)

Joseph Post (ABC Document Archives)

John Hopkins

Hiroyuki Iwaki (Melbourne Symphony Archive)

Richard Bonynge (Opera Australia)   Sir Charles Mackerras (ABC Document Archives)

Stuart Challender (Tracey Schramm, courtesy Sydney Symphony Orchestra)

CONDUCTORS

Richard Divall (Courtesy Opera Australia)

Patrick Thomas (ABC Document Archives)

Simone Young (Linda Southon, courtesy Arts Management)

Tex Morton, a playbill for his travelling show.
(Courtesy Eric Watson)

Buddy Williams
(Courtesy Eric Watson)

Smoky Dawson (Courtesy Eric Watson)

Reg Poole, on the road. (Courtesy Eric Watson)

Slim Dusty (Courtesy EMI Music Australia)

John Williamson

The Renaissance Players. *Rear, l. to r.:* Lyndon Terracini (nakers), John McLaughlin (vielle), Barbara Stackpool (bells), Wayne Richmond (crumhorn, gaita gallega). *Middle:* Stephen Stewart (portative organ), Winsome Evans (director, cornetto, shawm), Michael Atherton (lute).

La Romanesca. *L.to r.:* John Griffiths (lute), Hartley Newnham (countertenor), Ruth Wilkinson (gamba), Ros Bandt (recorder) (Linda Tanner).

William S. Lyster, Australia's major operatic impresario
for two decades from 1861. (*Weekly Times* 12 Sept. 1874)

Hector Crawford conducts his *Music for the People* concerts. Crawford was one of few classical music promoters on
commercial radio and television to survive against the ABC's domination. (Crawford Productions)

returned to the ranks as a headmaster. A popular figure, he was an inspirational music educator who formed the state school music curriculum in SA. His death was widely mourned.

FURTHER REFERENCE
Jane Southcott, 'The Establishment of the Music Curriculum in South Australia: The Role of Alexander Clark', *Research Studies in Music Education* 5 (Dec. 1995), 1–10..   JANE SOUTHCOTT

Clark, Jacob Richard   (*b* Taunton, England, 1822; *d* Sydney, 1893), music publisher, retailer. Clark arrived in Sydney in 1850 and established a business in George Street, from 1854 in partnership with W.P. Woolcott, and as sole proprietor from 1858 of J.R. Clarke's Music Repository (his name later became Clarke). In 1855 he published an *Australian Presentation Album* and in 1857 and 1863 he published his *Australian Musical Albums* and continued to publish a range of popular dances, songs and piano pieces with titles such as the 'Sydney Herald Polka' and 'Woolloomooloo Schottische'. The composers of these included William Vincent *Wallace, Frederick Ellard and Ernesto Spagnoletti. Clark was considered one of the leading booksellers and music publishers in Sydney, and an expert on architecture and engraving, but the business made substantial losses at the time of the 1879 International Exhibition and Clarke was declared insolvent in 1885.

FURTHER REFERENCE
Death of an Old Citizen: Mr Jacob Richard Clarke (Sydney[?], 1893).
                                                              SUZANNE ROBINSON

Clarke, Mrs Anne Therese née Remans   (*b* England, *c.*1806; *d* ?), singer, entrepreneur. After singing at a London theatre, Remans arrived in Tasmania in 1834, married Michael Clarke and appeared at J.P. *Deane's concerts and in Samson Cameron's Opera Co., as well as in burlesques and plays. She was at the Royal Victoria Theatre, Sydney, 1837–39, then became manager of the Theatre Royal, Hobart, from 1840. On a trip to England in 1841 she recruited Gerolamo *Carandini, the *Howsons and Theodosia *Stirling for her company, all of whom made significant careers in Australia after appearing in her Hobart and Launceston seasons. One of the earliest pioneers of opera and music-theatre in Australia, with a reputation for presenting properly rehearsed and varied programs at modest prices, she appears to have retired from her business in 1847.

FURTHER REFERENCE
Harold Love, ed., *The Australian Stage: A Documentary History* (Sydney UNSWP, 1984), 2ff; *ParsonsC*; *MackenzieS*, 255–7; *Hobart Town Courier*, 29 Aug. 1834.

Clarke, (Alfred) Bruce   (*b* Melbourne, 1 Dec. 1925), jazz composer, arranger, performer. He began guitar at 17, became associated with the early bop movement, notably with Splinter Reeves and Don Banks, then began extensive radio, television and session work through his music production organisation (with Frank Smith). An interest in experimentation emerged through a succession of activities including workshop groups, his record label Cumquat, and in the late 1960s he produced electronic and aleatoric work. He also worked in orchestral settings, and continues to teach (including at the Victorian College of the Arts from 1977). He served on the Music Board of the Australia Council, and was president of the Melbourne Chapter of ISCM in the 1970s.

FURTHER REFERENCE
Recordings include *The Bruce Clarke Quintet* (1949, Jazzart JA-17); *Splinter Reeves and his Splintette* (1949, Jazzart JA-31, JA-32); *Don Banks Orchestra* (1950, Jazzart JA-48); *Stratusphunk*, Bruce Clarke Quintet (1974, Cumquat CQR 12–04); *In Memory of Charlie Christian*, Bruce Clarke (1980, Ode, Pol 056). An interview with him is in *WilliamsA*, 80–7. See also *BissetB*; *OxfordJ*.   BRUCE JOHNSON

Clarke, Marcus   (*b* London, 24 Apr. 1846; *d* Melbourne, 2 Aug. 1881), journalist, novelist. Arriving in Australia alone in his teens, he stayed with an uncle in Ararat, Victoria, then joined the *Argus* and wrote as 'The Peripatetic Philosopher' from 1867. He worked for a succession of Melbourne newspapers, his famous novel *His Natural Life* (1870–72) first appearing as a serial in the *Australian Journal*. He also wrote stage works, most translations or adaptations, but including the extravaganza *Alfred the Great* (1878), set to music by Henry Keiley and Alfred Plumpton and staged successfully at the Academy of Music, Melbourne. Paolo *Giorza set his cantata *Proi* (1881), and Henry *Kowalski set his unfinished comic opera *Queen Venus* to music as *Moustique* (1889). He was one of the best-known writers of colonial times.

FURTHER REFERENCE
ParsonsC; *IrvinD*.

Clarke, Terrence   (*b* Sydney, 10 Feb. 1935), stage director, composer. After studying music and mathematics at the University of Sydney he worked as a schoolteacher, then joined the Nimrod Theatre as an actor and pianist. In 1971 he directed his first music-theatre work, the ballad-opera *Flash Jim Vaux*, then with Nick Enright he wrote the musicals *The Venetian Twins* (1979), *Variations* (1981) and *Summer Rain* (1983/89), the last presented by the Sydney Theatre Co. He wrote incidental music for various plays and directed more than 80 theatrical productions. An effective theatre composer in straightforward pastiche and ballad styles, he was associate director of the National Theatre Co., Perth (1973–75), founding artistic director of the Hunter Valley Theatre Co., and head of directing and new work at NIDA (1991–93).

Clarke, Sir William John (*b* Lovely Banks, Tas., 31 Mar. 1831; *d* Melbourne, 15 May 1897), philanthropist. He was educated in Hobart Town and in England. In 1874, he inherited an estate from his father valued at around £1 500 000 and became a leader in society, including as a member of the Legislative Council 1878–97 and president of the Melbourne Exhibition 1880–81; he was also president of the Melbourne Cricket Club and of the Victorian Football Association. Among his many acts of philanthropy, in 1882 he founded, with 3000 guineas, the first major Australian music scholarship, the Royal College of Music, London, South Province Scholarship, known as the ★Clarke Scholarship. He was created a baronet in 1882.

FURTHER REFERENCE
Sylvia Morrissey, *ADB* 3; *OrchardM*, 166 gives a list of Clarke scholars to 1950.

ROYSTON GUSTAVSON

Clarke Scholarship. Oldest musical travelling scholarship in Australia, awarded annually for a musician from Victoria to study at the Royal College of Music, London. Previous winners have included Sir Bernard ★Heinze, Sir William ★McKie, and many other prominent Australian performers. Pastoralist Sir William ★Clarke established a trust at the then newly founded college for the award in 1882; his grandson Sir Rupert Clarke established a trust at the University of Melbourne in 1996 to enhance the value of the award, which with supplementary grants from the Victorian Government is currently $10 000.

Clarkson, Stanley (*b* Sydney, 1905; *d* 1961), bass. Originally a linotype operator, he took lessons with Rex de Rego and then at the NSW State Conservatorium with Spencer Thomas, and sang solo in choral and orchestral concerts. He turned professional in 1938, at first heard in numerous principal operatic roles in ABC radio broadcasts, although he had scant experience of the stage. Moving to England, he appeared in oratorio at Leeds and York, and after coaching with Arnold ★Matters and Clive ★Carey, joined Sadler's Wells in 1948 as principal baritone. He toured Australia for the Elizabethan Theatre Trust Opera season of 1956. A striking figure on stage with a voice of impressive power, by the time of his sudden death his roles included Mephistopheles, Basilio, Sarastro, Alidoro in *Cinderella,* Mr Gruff in *The School for Fathers*, and appearances in the premieres of *Kát'a Kabanova*, Sutermeister's *Romeo and Juliet*, and Lennox Berkeley's *Nelson*.

FURTHER REFERENCE
MackenzieS, 177–9; *AMN* 39 (Apr. 1949) 16.

Click Go The Shears, folk-song. Set to 'Ring the Bell, Watchman' by Henry Clay Work (1865), it describes the vigorous cycle of the sheep-shearer's nomadic life.

Collected and first published by Percy ★Jones in the *Burl Ives Folio of Australian Folksongs* (1953); other versions have been collected by John Meredith (1954) and Ron Edwards (1969).

FURTHER REFERENCE
Edition and commentary in *EdwardsG*; *RadicS,* 8.

Clifford, May [Mamie] (*b* 22 Nov. 1919), pianist. A pupil of Waldemar Seidel, she won the South Street Eisteddfod, Ballarat (in sight reading) and an AMEB Exhibition in 1937 and entered the University of Melbourne Conservatorium. She won Bernard Heinze's Melbourne Symphony Orchestra Concerto Competition in 1941, then appeared in ABC concerts and broadcasts and established a teaching practice. In 1956 she went to England and studied with Kathleen Long, appearing as a recitalist and accompanist and coaching Australian singers who were studying in London. She returned to Australia in 1960, worked as an accompanist for the ABC, taught at the University of Melbourne Conservatorium, examined for the AMEB, and remains the long-serving president of the Victorian Music Teachers' Association. A sympathetic accompanist and dedicated teacher, she has long been the doyen of studio music teachers in Victoria.

FURTHER REFERENCE
AMN 31 (May 1941), 15; *AMN* 32 (Dec. 1941), 16; *AMN* 50 (Mar. 1960), 16; *AMN* 28 (June 1938), 28.

Clinch, Peter Gladstone (*b* Geraldton, WA, 26 June 1930; *d* Melbourne, 6 June 1995), saxophonist, clarinettist. At 17 he played clarinet with the ABC (Perth) Orchestra, then from 1948 studied clarinet and saxophone in Melbourne, Sydney and abroad. He was clarinettist in the RAAF Central Band from 1953, worked as a composer and arranger for radio 3DB and HSV7, Melbourne (from 1959), then played clarinet with the West Australian Symphony Orchestra from 1966, making three ABC tours as a soloist. After studies in composition and musicology at the University of Western Australia he was appointed lecturer (later reader and head) at the music department of the Melbourne State College in 1974, taking a doctorate in musical acoustics from Monash University in 1980. He played with ACME (1989) and the Peter Clinch Saxophone Quartet from 1991, conducted the Heidelberg Youth Orchestra, and made numerous regional and overseas tours. A tireless and dedicated teacher and performer, he published editions of clarinet music, articles in *The Clarinet*, and a widely used *Clarinet Tutor* (Melbourne: Allans Music, 1975). Saxophone concertos were written for him by William Lovelock and James Penberthy. As a composer his works included numerous commercial arrangements, as well as compositions for saxophone. Despite the encroachment of cancer in 1995 he continued working, giving his last concert just weeks before his death.

FURTHER REFERENCE

Recordings as a soloist include James Penberthy, Saxophone Concerto (Festival); W. Lovelock, Saxophone Concerto, West Australian Symphony Orchestra, cond. V. Williams (1974, ABC 1009); W. Lovelock, Sonata (W&G); and with the Peter Clinch Saxophone Quartet *Journeys* (Move MS 3058). His edition of Franz Tausch, Clarinet Concerto No. 3, is in *SMA*, 8 (1974), supplement; articles include 'The Importance of Vocal Tract Resonance in Clarinet and Saxophone Performance: A Preliminary Account', with G.J. Troupe and L. Harris, *Acustica*, 50/4 (1982), 280–4.

Clingan, Judith Ann (*b* Sydney, 19 Jan. 1945), composer, choral music educator. After graduating in languages from the Australian National University, she founded and directed the Canberra Children's Choir 1967–79 and Young Music Society from 1970. She studied at the Kodaly Pedagogical Institute, Kecskemet, Hungary, in 1982, and then founded and directed Gaudeamus (1983–93), through which she offered a choral training program influenced by Kodaly principles. Her choral work led her into composition for children, for which her steadily growing recognition in the 1980s culminated in a fellowship from the Australia Council in 1991. Since 1994 she has been music director at Mount Barker Waldorf School, SA, and of Voicebox Youth Opera, SA. Many of her works are for SSA chorus, such as the attractive *Modal Magic* (1986); there are also larger sacred settings such as *Lux Mundi* (1985), and several music-theatre works, including the operas *Francis* (1986) and *Marco* (1991).

WORKS (Selective)

Most ms works available in facsimile from Australian Music Centre, Sydney.

Dramatic *Francis*, children's opera, Mez, SSA, children SSA, orch (ms, 3, 1986, composer), *Just Looking*, children's music-theatre (ms, 1988 composer), *Terra Beata, Terra Firma*, children's music-theatre, (ms, 1991 composer), *Marco*, children's music-theatre (ms, 1991, composer), *The Grandfather Clock*, children's music-theatre (ms, 1992, composer).

Choral Various short SSA works published as *The Complete Chorister* (1971), sacred and folk-song settings for SSA in *So Good A Thing* (1981), *Music is for Everyone* (Watson, ACT: Aust. Early Childhood Association, 1984). *A Canticle of Light*, SSAATTBB, SSA, vv, ens (ms, nd), *Lux mundi*, children SSA, SA, v, orch (ms, 1985), *Modal Magic*, SSA (1986), *Missa Donata* SATB octet, SATB, tpts, org (ms, 1986) *Ngambra* multiple chs, ens (ms, 1988), *The Bird's Noel*, SATB, band (ms, 1990), *Kakadu*, SAB, ens (ms, 1990).

Vocal *A Canberra Cycle*, S, Bar, ens (1991), *Songs of Solitude*, S, ens (1991)

Instrumental *Seven Deadly Sins*, rec, perc (1990).

FURTHER REFERENCE

Some of her songs have been recorded on *Pocketful of Rye* (Aust Music Centre, CASS004). See also Marie Fitzpatrick, *GroveW*; *CohenI*; *WWA* (1996).

Clutsam, George H. (*b* Sydney, 26 Nov. 1866; *d* 1951), composer, critic. Born in Sydney but moving to Dunedin, NZ, in childhood, he came to attention with his composition of *La pluie de printemps* for piano at the age of 13. He settled in England in 1889 and worked as a pianist and critic for the London *Observer* 1903–18. Beecham's production of his opera *A Summer Night* began a series of successful works he produced for the stage. His eight published theatre works include the enormously successful musical *Lilac Time* (1922), with adaptations of Schubert's music, and he was composer of *Ma Curly Headed Babby*, made famous by American bass Paul Robeson.

FURTHER REFERENCE

IrvinD.

Clynes, Manfred (*b* Vienna, Austria, 14 Aug. 1925), pianist, neuroscientist, engineer. He emigrated to Australia aged 13, having studied piano at the Liszt Ferenc Academia in Budapest, and became known as a pianist, winning the ABC Concerto Competition three times. As an undergraduate he undertook majors in both music and engineering (BEngSc, University of Melbourne, 1946). He studied piano with Raymond *Lambert, then obtained a graduate fellowship to Juilliard, where he studied with Sascha Gorodnitzki and Olga Samaroff-Stokowski. He also took a masterclass with Edwin Fischer (1953) and gave concerts in London. He took a doctorate in science at the University of Melbourne in 1965, when he was already active as a neuroscientist. From 1958 to 1973 he was chief research scientist at the Rockland State Hospital Research Center in Orangeburg, New York, and later became head of the Research Centre of the NSW State Conservatorium 1978–87 and Sugden Fellow at Queen's College, University of Melbourne 1988–90.

Clynes' research on musical expression was inspired by the profound musicianship of Pablo Casals. He developed an experimentally supported theory that each basic emotion has a specific dynamic shape, genetically and neurophysiologically encoded, which is capable of expression in any motor output including small finger movements. His work also includes a theory of 'composer's pulses', an integral combination of agogic and dynamic stress patterns specific to a composer. On leaving Melbourne in 1991, he moved to the USA and became President of Microsound International (California), in order to develop software implementing his ideas on expressive microstructural interpretation. His program SuperConductor allows users to interpret music by using scores as input, then making fine microstructural adjustments in rhythm and 'predictive note sculpting' according to his guidelines. The output sound is unusually 'lifelike' when compared with other synthesised music.

FURTHER REFERENCE

His writings include *Sentics: The Touch of the Emotions* (New York: Doubleday, 1977; reprinted by Prism Press (Bridport,

Dorset, UK) in 1989); 'Some Guidelines for the Synthesis and Testing of Pulse Microstructure in Relation to Musical Meaning', *Music Perception* 7 (1990), 403–21; and with N. Nettheim, 'The Living Quality of Music: Neurobiologic Basis of Communicating Feeling', in *Music, Mind and Brain: the Neuropsychology of Music*, ed. M. Clynes (New York: Plenum Press, 1982), 47–82. See also William Thompson, 'Composer-Specific Aspects of Musical Performance: An Evaluation of Clynes's Theory of Pulse for Performances of Mozart and Beethoven', *Music Perception* 7 (1989), 15–42.

NAOMI CUMMING

Cobbers, The. Bush-band (1974–89) originally comprised of John Armstrong (fiddle, vocals), Chris Armstrong (guitar, vocals), and Mark 'Blossom' Brown (bass, *d* 1979), then joined by Christy Cooney (banjo, vocals) and Maitland Swallow (accordion). As the Freewheelers then the Longford Street Band, they played at dances from 1968, becoming full-time in 1974. They appeared at the Bushland Dreaming concert, Melbourne, in 1979, toured Australia, the UK and the USA in the early 1980s, appearing on the Louisiana Hayride, at the Reading Rock Festival (UK), the Texas State Fair and for 16 years at the Gum Tree Folk Dances, La Trobe University. They combine Australian folk-song with an image akin to the Dubliners (UK). Although they have disbanded they occasionally reassemble for engagements.

FURTHER REFERENCE
Recordings include their debut album *All For Me Grog* (1980, Festival C37484), *Portraits of Australian Women* (1980 Festival C37595) and a set of dance-teaching tapes, *Bush Dancing Made Easy* (1986). See also *Stringybark and Greenhide* 2/3 (June 1980).

Cockies of Bungaree, The, folk-song. The plaint of a jackeroo worked to exhaustion by the farmers of Bungaree, a settlement near Ballarat, Victoria. Collected and recorded by A.L. Lloyd (1956); other versions have been collected by Percy *Jones in 1957, and Mary Jean Officer and Norm O'Connor in 1963.

FURTHER REFERENCE
Edition and commentary in *EdwardsG*; *ManifoldP*; *RadicS*, 39.

Cockroaches, The. Rock band (1984–92) formed in Sydney, comprised of Paul Field (vocals), John and Anthony Field (guitars), Jeff Fatt (guitar), Phil Carson (bass until 1987, then various others) and Tony Henry (drums). Combining good stage presence with the early rock and roll style, they made over 20 singles, including *See You In Spain* (1984), *Permanently Single* (1988), and *I Must Have Been Blind* (1991), before two members left in 1992 to form the nucleus of the greatly popular children's entertainment band the *Wiggles. Their albums include *The Cockroaches* (1987) and *Positive* (1991).

FURTHER REFERENCE
Recordings include *See You In Spain* (1984, Powderworks POW 0200), *Permanently Single* (1988, Regular K769), and *I Must Have Been Blind* (1991, Regular C10381); albums include *The Cockroaches* (1987, Regular L38709) and *Positive* (1991, Regular L30592). For discography, see *SpencerA*. See also *SpencerW.*

Code, Percy (Edward Percival) (*b* South Melbourne, 3 July 1888; *d* Melbourne, 16 Oct. 1953), conductor, cornettist. He was born into a musical family; his father was a musician and a conductor of brass bands. He learnt cornet from his father and won the South Street Eisteddfod in his teens; this enabled him to play with the Besses o' the Barn band in Australia and England. During his tour of England he studied composition and arranging at the Royal College of Music. He returned to Australia in 1912 to work as a conductor and teacher, mainly with brass bands and choirs. In the early 1920s he played trumpet with the San Francisco Symphony Orchestra and the Grand Opera Orchestra, San Francisco, then returned to Melbourne in 1924 and was appointed principal conductor for the Australian Broadcasting Company in 1929. In 1936 he moved to Sydney to conduct the Sydney Symphony Orchestra, and returned to the Melbourne Symphony Orchestra in 1947. He also helped form the Queensland Symphony Orchestra. Code composed quantities of band music in his early career, much of which is still played today in competition.

FURTHER REFERENCE
H.J. Gibbney, *ADB*, 8; Sigmund Leon Sokolowski, Percy Code and the Band Movement in Australia, MMus(Prelim), Univ. Melbourne, 1989.   BRUCE PETHERICK

Colborne-Veel, John (*b* Melbourne, 21 Feb. 1945), composer, jazz trombonist. He studied composition with Dallas Haslam, and began music professionally in 1963, playing trombone, bass and tuba in Melbourne jazz venues. After military service in Vietnam (1967–69), he settled in Sydney. He was a founder member of Eclipse Alley Five, studied at the NSW Conservatorium, and through the early 1970s was mainly active composing and arranging for club orchestras. With Graeme Bell (1977–79), then Ray Price (1979–80), he was increasingly active as an internationally performed composer-arranger in popular music, classical ballet, opera, and liturgical works as well as jazz. A writer, broadcaster, and president of the Fellowship of Australian Composers since 1992, he has vigorously lobbied for the advancement of Australian music.

FURTHER REFERENCE
Recordings include *Adrian Ford's Big Band* (1977, Hammard HAM-022); *Saint Mary, A Festival Mass with Jazz Soloists* (1986, Chevalier Records MR 12016); *Angelique, Midnight—Media Noche* (1986, Innovation Records INLP 01); *Music From The Fel-*

lowship of Australian Composers (1993, JADCD 1036); *An Anniversary Bouquet* (1995, MBS Records MBS 34). See also *OxfordJ*; Bruce Johnson, 'John Colborne-Veel, the plight of the unknown Australian jazz composer', *APRAJ* (Mar. 1984), 18–19.

BRUCE JOHNSON

Cold Chisel.   Rock band formed at Adelaide 1974 by singer Jimmy ★Barnes (*b* Scotland, 1957, vocals), Ian Moss (guitar, vocals), Don Walker (piano, vocals), Les Kaczmarek (bass) and Steve Prestwich (drums). The band spent the first four years of its career playing the Australian pub circuit, during which time Kaczmarek was replaced by bass-guitarist Phil Small (1976). Following the release of their self-titled debut album in 1978, Cold Chisel's second album, *Breakfast at Sweethearts* (1979), reached No. 4. Many songs on this album were the product of Walker's formidable compositional talent, and showed his keen insight into contemporary Australian social issues. Their third album, *East* (1980), contained songs written by all members of the band and covered a diverse selection of themes ranging from riots to beach parties. *East* peaked at No. 2, while the singles *Choir Girl* and *Cheap Wine* hit No. 14 and No. 8 respectively.

With the release of *Swingshift* in 1981, the group began to consolidate its position as one of Australia's most popular bands. The album topped the chart, while *You Got Nothing I Want* peaked at No. 12. The following year saw the release of their most highly acclaimed album, *Circus Animals* (1982), which provided the band with its second No. 1 hit. This album also contained their most successful single release, *Forever Now*, which reached No. 4. The group announced that it would disband after it had performed the Last Stand concert series in November and December 1983 and recorded its final album. In early 1984 *Twentieth Century* was released and became Cold Chisel's third chart-topping album, but drummer Steve Prestwich played in only three of the songs, with Ray Arnott replacing him on the remaining tracks.

Cold Chisel was undoubtedly one of Australia's most successful bands, and this was largely due to the talents of their foremost songwriters, Walker, Moss and Prestwich. In the latter half of the 1980s Barnes and Moss both moved on to successful solo careers, with Barnes's first five solo albums making their debut at No. 1. Although Walker's post-Chisel ventures have been less successful, he has written Top 5 hits for both Barnes and Moss. In 1994, a new album called *Teenage Love* was released which consisted of out-takes from Cold Chisel recording sessions, dating back as far as 1976, and recordings of live performances. The first single released from this album, *Hands Out of My Pocket*, was recorded in 1980 and hit No. 9 (1994).

FURTHER REFERENCE
Recordings include *Cold Chisel* (1978, Atlantic 600038); *Breakfast at Sweethearts* (1979, Elektra 600042); *East* (1980, WEA 600064);

Swingshift (1981, WEA 800003); *Circus Animals* (1982, WEA 600113); *Twentieth Century* (1984, WEA 250390–1); *Teenage Love* (1994, Warner 4509980552). See also *GuinnessP*; *SpencerW*.

AARON D.S. CORN

Colley, Ada   (*b* Parramatta, NSW, 1873; *d* London, 1946), vaudeville and stage singer. Her father was the superintendent of the Parramatta Hospital for the Insane, and her mother the choirmaster at the Parramatta Catholic Church. After initial training at Rose Bay Convent she appeared professionally in vaudeville. She had an attractive voice of extraordinary range. After her father's death her mother took the family to London to further her career. Saint-Saëns might have written a vocalise, *The Nightingale*, for her, and she had leading roles in *Manon*, *Faust* and *Cosi Fan Tutti* in Berlin, St Petersburg and elsewhere. Early in the century she returned to vaudeville, probably with other members of her family and in 1907, together with English variety artists Marie Lloyd and Albert Chevalier, was a leader of the English actors' strike which resulted in the formation of the Variety Artists' Federation. The strikers' demands were met but retribution followed. She then attempted to create a vaudeville circuit of her own, without success. In Australia, after 1912, stories about a throat ailment circulated and Colley disappeared from the musical scene.

JEFF BROWNRIGG

Collier, Frederick Redmond   (*b* Collingwood, Melbourne, 5 Oct. 1885; *d* South Yarra, Melbourne, 14 Oct. 1964), bass baritone. While a labourer on the railway he was bass soloist at St Patrick's Cathedral, Melbourne and won the South Street Eisteddfod in 1907. He joined the Melbourne office of Chappel & Co. in 1917 and appeared in Melbourne concerts, then with the ★Rigo Opera Co. on tour in 1919. Moving to England in 1921, he joined the British National Opera Co. in 1922, then Carl Rosa Co. on tour from 1928. He returned to Australia in 1934, sang with the Benjamin Fuller Opera Co., ABC radio, and was a senior member of the National Theatre Movement Opera Co. from its outset. He joined the ABC's Melbourne Wireless Chorus (later Melbourne Singers) in 1940 and made his last stage appearance in 1961. His acting was notable, and he was outstanding in the Wagnerian roles Klingsor, Wotan, Hagen and Kurneval as well as in Mephistopheles or the Father in *Hansel and Gretel*. His Amonasro in particular was long remembered.

FURTHER REFERENCE
Recordings include *Götterdämmerung* excerpts (reissued 1995, Pearl GEMMCD 59137) and Vaughan Williams works cond. M. Sargent (Pearl GEMMCD 9468). See also *MonashB*; Sally O'Neill, *ADB*, 8; *MackenzieS*, 126–7; *AMN* 25 (Oct. 1934), 13.

Collier, Marie   (*b* Ballarat, Vic., 16 Apr. 1927; *d* London, 8 Dec. 1971), dramatic soprano. After losing her bursary at the University of Melbourne Conservatorium for singing in the chorus of J.C. Williamson musicals, she studied privately with Katherine Wielaert and Gertrude *Johnson and worked as assistant in a pharmacy. She made her debut as Santuzza in *Cavalleria Rusticana* with Johnson's Australian National Theatre Movement Opera Co. in 1952 and was a stunning Magda Soerl in *The Consul* before going to Milan to study with Ugo Benevenuto-Giusti in 1955. From 1956 she appeared at Covent Garden, replacing Callas in *Tosca* to great acclaim in 1965, and sang at Sadler's Wells, the Metropolitan Opera, throughout Europe and in Latin America. A singer of great dramatic imagination, stamina and virtuosic technique, she tackled many contemporary operas, including *Wozzeck, The Makropulos Affair, The Angel of Fire* (Prokofiev), *Mourning Becomes Electra, Katerina Ismailova, King Priam* (Tippett), *Midsummer Night's Dream* (Britten), as well as Tosca, Musetta, and lead roles in *Butterfly, Turandot, Don Carlos*. At the pinnacle of international fame, she fell from a London window to her death at the age of 44.

FURTHER REFERENCE
Obit. (Stephen Hall) in *Australian Opera Yearbook*, 1972. Recordings include the Solti *Elektra* (1966, Decca 417345–2DHZ); Gerhilde in the Leinsdorf *Die Walküre* (1961, Decca 430 391–2DM3); and Walton *Troilus and Cressida* (1968, EMI CDM7 64199–2). See also *MonashB*; Alan Blyth, *GroveO*; Thérèse Radic, *ADB*, 13; John Cargher, *Bravo! 200 Years of Opera in Australia* (Melbourne: Macmillan, 1988), 47–52; *MackenzieS*, 207–11; *GlennonA*, 9–10.

Collins, Geoffrey (*b* Adelaide, 1955), flautist. While studying piano with Nancy Salas and flute with Victor McMahon at the NSW State Conservatorium, he played contemporary repertoire with AZ Music (world tour 1972). He won the first National Flute Competition in 1976 and played in the Elizabethan Theatre Trust (Sydney) Orchestra, then the Sydney Symphony Orchestra, becoming associate principal flute. His appearances in contemporary ensembles continued with Keith Humble's ACME and the Seymour Group, and he went to Europe on a Churchill fellowship in 1982, studying with William Bennett, Michel Dubost and Peter Lukas-Graf. From 1983 he was with the Australia Ensemble, the Australian Chamber Orchestra, and Flederman (European tour, 1988). With a sparkling, dexterous technique and a wide repertoire, particularly notable in contemporary music, he has been a soloist with most of the ABC orchestras.

FURTHER REFERENCE
Recordings include *Flute Australia*, 2 vols (2MBS); *Spinning: New Australian Flute Music* (1995, Tall Poppies TP O69), and Mozart, *Flute Quartets* (1994, Tall Poppies TP O29).

Collits' Inn. Musical comedy by Varney *Monk and librettist T. Stuart Gurr, completed 1932. After two brief amateur seasons the 'first Australian Historical Romance'

received its hugely successful professional premiere in Melbourne on 23 December 1933 under entrepreneur F.W. Thring, starring Gladys *Moncrieff, George Wallace and Robert Chisholm. The romantic storyline, concerning the beautiful Mary Collits, with a bushranger and army captain as rival lovers, is noteworthy for its use of an Australian historical setting and inclusion of an elaborately costumed 'authentic' aboriginal Corroboree Ballet, both of which were claimed as firsts. Complete orchestral and piano parts are extant in manuscript form.

FURTHER REFERENCE
Bronwen Arthur, Varney Monk and Collits Inn: A landmark in Australian musical history, unpub BMus(Hons), ANU, 1994; idem, 'The Pub with no Peer, or *Collits' Inn:* The First Australian Musical Romance', in *One Hand on the Manuscript: Music in Australian Cultural History 1930–1960*, ed. N. Brown et al. (Canberra: Humanities Research Centre, ANU, 1995), 128–40; Stuart T. Gurr, *Collits' Inn*, ed. and with intro. by John West (Sydney: Currency, 1990).   BRONWEN ARTHUR

Colman, Charles (*b* Inverell, NSW, 1936), choral conductor. While studying at the University of Sydney he conducted the Sydney University Musical Society from 1954. Winning a scholarship, he studied conducting at the Royal College of Music, London, and in Munich and Sienna; he returned to Australia in 1964, taught at the Cranbrook School and became musical director of the Leonine Consort, then, from 1984, the *Song Company. Building the Song Company into Australia's finest small vocal ensemble, as well as its only full-time choral group, he toured extensively for Musica Viva in Australia and South-East Asia, appearing at two Adelaide Festivals and the NZ International Festival (1988). He was also guest conductor with Sydney Philharmonia, the Australian Chamber Orchestra, and Canberra Choral Society, and for nine years taught at the University of New England summer school. Since 1988 he has lived in Italy.

FURTHER REFERENCE
Recordings with the Leonine Consort include *Balmain Collection* (1978, Cherry Pie CPF 104); *Jump Down, Turn Around* (1979, Cherry Pie CPF 1044); and *The Company of Lovers* (1982, Arika AR 002).

Colonial Song. Work for soprano, tenor, harp and orchestra by Percy Grainger, completed 1912. Subsequently arranged by the composer for piano trio (1912), solo piano (1914) and band (1918). First performed in London with the composer conducting the New Symphony Orchestra on 25 February 1913. Scored as a Yule gift for his mother Rose, it was the first of a projected series of 'Sentimentals', and expressed feelings 'aroused by thoughts of the scenery and people of Australia'. It prompted Beecham to exclaim, somewhat unfairly, that it was 'the worst piece of modern times.'

ALESSANDRO SERVADEI

Coloured Stone. One of the most widely recorded and longest-running Aboriginal rock groups, active since 1978. Originally from Koonibba SA, they were later based in Sydney. They toured widely both within Australia and internationally, including tours of Aboriginal communities in the NT, and the 1986–87 Edinburgh Festival. They won an ARIA award for album *Human Love* in 1987. Their songs address Aboriginal, political, and environmental issues.

FURTHER REFERENCE
Recordings include *Island of Greed* (RCA SPCD 1088); *Koonibba Rock* (1986, RCA SPCD 1087); *Black Rock from the Red Centre* (1986, RCA SPCD 1209); *Human Love* (1986, RCA SPCD 1208); *Wild Desert Rose* (RCA, SPCD 1206); and *Crazy Mind* (1989, RCA VPK1 0821); *Inma Juju: Dance Music* (1991, RCA VPCD 0847).

P. DUNBAR-HALL

Colton, Dave David Geoffrey (*b* Gawler, SA, 5 Oct. 1951), jazz guitarist. He began guitar at the age of 17, and worked in pop and jazz settings in Adelaide until moving to Sydney in 1979. He played in sessions, festivals, small groups and big bands including with Daly Wilson Big Band, Errol Buddle, Col Nolan, Joe Lane, Ed Gaston, and more recently with Grace Knight and James Morrison. Backing visitors, he has played with Red Holloway, Richie Cole, Randy Brecker and others. His awards including the 1988 Bicentennial most outstanding jazz guitarist and the Australian Jazz Critics Award, guitar category (1992). He lectured in jazz studies at the University of Wollongong (1990–93) and is currently at the Sydney Conservatorium.

FURTHER REFERENCE
Recordings include *Woman of Mystery*, Maree Montgomery (1986, Larrikin LRJ 189); *Love Dance*, Pamela Knowles (1993, Larrikin CD LRJ 327); *Moving Forward*, Johnny Nicol (1995, JN 001CD); *Live*, Grace Knight (1996, ABC Records 4835822); *James Morrison, Live at the Sydney Opera House* (1996, East West 0630151462).

BRUCE JOHNSON

Combe, Peter, Adelaide-based children's singer-songwriter. Singing and playing piano and guitar, he presents his rock-influenced comic songs such as *Newspaper Mama* and *Spaghetti Bolognaise* to small children, and has been featured on ABC Playschool, on his videos and in his many live appearances for children. His *Songs for Little Kids* has been recorded by the ABC.

Comettant, Oscar (*b* Bordeaux, France, 18 Apr. 1819; *d* Montevilliers, France, 24 Jan. 1898), music critic, writer. After studying at the Paris Conservatoire he appeared as a pianist, toured North America 1852–55, then taught at Paris, becoming music critic for *Le Siècle* in 1856. He came to Australia in 1888 as an art and music

judge at the Melbourne International Centennial Exhibition. On his return to Paris he wrote *Au pays des kangourous et des mines d'or* (Paris, 1890), which as well as its observations of Australian life generally is an important source for Melbourne musical life during his visit.

FURTHER REFERENCE
Obit. in *Argus*, 15 Apr. 1890. His book (reprint, Paris: Fischbacher, 1960) has been translated by Judith Armstrong as *In the Land of Kangaroos and Goldmines* (Adelaide: Rigby, 1980). See also Genevieve Davison, 'Oscar Comettant Visits Brighton', *Explorations; Argus* 11 Sept. 1888.

Community Singing. Participatory entertainment popular after World War I. Introduced from the USA by former editor of the *Australian Musical News* Gibson Young, at Melbourne's Music Week in 1921 a grand choral concert was held at the Exhibition Buildings during which the public was invited to join in the singing. Community singing quickly became widespread in cinemas, where between silent movies the cinema ensemble would lead singing, the words of the songs projected on the screen; it was also common in town halls as lunchtime entertainment. By 1922 the mayor of Perth could say that 'community singing has come to stay, not only in Perth but in every civilised centre in Australia'.

The concept was taken up by radio and was very popular in the Depression years. Programs were broadcast live from town halls, often with the proceeds going to charity. Dick Fair's program on 2BL Sydney was particularly popular; and songs such as *Home Sweet Home*, *Old Folks At Home* and *Ching Chong* were favourites, sung to piano accompaniment, with local instrumental entertainers featured as guests. The ABC published *ABC Community Music Books* and *Community Songsters* for its programs. By 1938, however, the ABC Controller was reporting that the gatherings were mostly female and middle-aged, and the music 'old-time songs of no value whatsoever'. After World War II the practice continued only in sacred broadcasts, such as the ABC's *Community Hymn Singing*, and in the ambitious *Australia's Hour of Song* (1952–55), sponsored by Lever Brothers on Sydney 2UE, in which Gladys *Moncrieff, Peter *Dawson and overseas visitors such as Tommy Trinder and Allan Jones appeared.

With the advent of television, community singing broadcasts survived only in daytime programs for schools. The ABC *Village Glee Club* persisted until 1971, but by this time the live audience had been replaced by a professional chorus, and the community flavour had evaporated.

FURTHER REFERENCE
Jacqueline Kent, *Out of the Bakelite Box: the Heyday of Australian Radio* (Sydney: W: ABC, 1983), 80–1, 199–200; Alan Thomas, *Broadcast and Be Damned: The ABC's First Two Decades* (Melbourne: MUP, 1980), 34; Nancy Bridges, *Wonderful Wireless: Reminiscences of the Stars of Australia's Live Radio* (Sydney: Methuen Aust., 1983), 80, 103, 120.

Competitions and Eisteddfods.

Eisteddfods were, and still are, a venerated Welsh tradition. The word *eisteddfod* (Welsh, 'session') refers to a gathering where music was performed and recitations of the spoken word given. They were the first form of musical competition in the Australian colonies and this strong cultural tradition was an integral part of the 'melting-pot' society which existed in Australia during the middle of the 19th century. The traditional Welsh eisteddfod focused on poetry spoken (and sometimes sung) in the Welsh language and was usually only a few days in duration. The Australian tradition developed from this into a more diverse form of competition with a variety of forms of the performing arts, including individual and group music performance, dance and drama, and were often programmed over a number of weeks.

Public announcements in 1851 of Australian gold discoveries drew thousands of fortune-seekers from all parts of the world, and one of the first cultural manifestations to appear on the goldfields was the Welsh eisteddfod. A contemporary observer recalled that the first Ballarat Eisteddfod was held in 1855; this was almost certainly the first eisteddfod held in Australia. Ballarat was home to a large number of Welsh miners who took pride in preserving their native language and musical traditions, in a community composed chiefly of English-speaking people. Following the success of the first eisteddfod they were encouraged to issue a program inviting participation by all, irrespective of nationality, a gesture later described by a contemporary observer as 'an example to the colony of cosmopolitan liberality in fostering the development of native talent, and which has been happily imitated by many kindred societies'.

These early eisteddfods were generally located in the densely populated mining communities and metropolitan centres including Newcastle (1875), Brisbane (1881), Gympie (1885), Blackstone and Ipswich (1887) and Charters Towers (1888), all of which had significant Welsh and Cornish mining communities. As these communities integrated into the growing Australian population the eisteddfods evolved into more diverse competitions with emphasis on the choral tradition, drawing on the English choral festival model. Queensland had a particularly intense history of choral eisteddfods until World War II, with groups of cities forming the Queensland Eisteddfod Council in 1908 and the North Queensland Eisteddfod Council in 1921.

Many of the early eisteddfods were in a concert format, later developing into a competitive format. Programs for the competitive eisteddfods, usually advertised a few months in advance of the meeting, were in sections of established age groups with appropriately set pieces, divided into particular instrument, voice or ensemble. This format enabled the adjudicator and audience to enjoy the opportunity for comparison, and now provides an insight for the historian into contemporary musical taste and standard.

In Victoria, the internationally famous Royal South Street Eisteddfod held in Ballarat had its origins in the South Street Literary and Debating Society, founded in 1879. The Royal South Street Eisteddfod was first held in 1891 and continues today, the longest-running cultural competition in Australia. The first competition included debating, oratory, instrumental and vocal sections and was held over 10 days. Today the competition has hundreds of sections held over three months, attracting participants from as far away as NZ. Past winners have included Amy Castles, Peter Dawson, Florence Austral, Marjorie Lawrence and Bernard Heinze. For many years the *Herald-Sun Aria* (formerly the *Sun* Aria, introduced in 1924 and run under the auspices of the Royal South Street Society) was the richest vocal prize in Australasia and launched the careers of many singers including New Zealander Kiri Te Kanawa. The tradition continues in Victoria through the prosperous Dandenong Music and Art Festival in Melbourne (established 1947), small suburban eisteddfods and country eisteddfods including Ararat, Bendigo, Mildura and Traralgon.

A short-lived eisteddfod began in Sydney in 1909, but the City of Sydney Eisteddfod commenced in 1933 and attracts thousands of competitors to its numerous instrumental, vocal, choral and dancing sections, including the McDonalds Aria (formerly the *Sun* Aria), begun in 1933. Eisteddfods in country areas of NSW, including Wagga Wagga, Lismore, Bathurst and Cowra, serve their local communities. The National Eisteddfod in Canberra serves the national capital. Communities in Queensland, including Ipswich, Nambour, Dalby, Bundaberg and Gladstone, continue the tradition. Currently the Queensland National Eisteddfod and the North Queensland Eisteddfod are rotated around various host towns. The Mount Gambier Eisteddfod was established in 1905 and the City of Adelaide Competitions have been successfully run since 1955. In Western Australia mining centres including Kalgoorlie-Boulder were host to eisteddfods in the early years of this century. In 1924 the West Australian Grand Eisteddfod was first organised by the WA Music Teachers' Association. In 1928 the title 'eisteddfod' was replaced by 'music festival' and 'branch' festivals were held in country areas including Northam, Bunbury, Geraldton and Albany. The Perth Music Festival still continues today. In Tasmania the Launceston Eisteddfod dates from the early years of the century, but the Hobart, Burnie, and Devonport events date from after World War II. In the NT the annual Darwin eisteddfod has in recent years included Aboriginal song and dance sections, and a Centralian Eisteddfod operates from Alice Springs.

A principal benefit of eisteddfods to Australian musical life has been the criticism and encouragement provided by adjudicators and judges. Of high musical standing in the community, often being noted pedagogues or performers trained in England, the adjudicators created high standards for performers and the teaching profession. Sensing that their duty went beyond mere individual criticism, some adjudicators used the opportunity to offer assistance and encouragement to the local musical community as a whole. For example, London-trained musician George Peake who officiated at the Ballarat South Street Society competitions during the 1890s published a lengthy article in the Ballarat *Courier* (1898) in which, drawing parallels with Bayreuth, he urged local citizens to make Ballarat a musical capital based on traditions of celebrated European musical festivals. He urged the local business community to support competitions as a prudent commercial benefit.

Records of Welsh language sections in eisteddfods exist until the 1940s, but as the Welsh and traditional mining communities lost their strength in the postwar population boom, eisteddfods were often replaced by general arts competitions. Funding for the establishment of these competitions has come from many sources including membership subscriptions, entrance fees, local and state government, commercial sponsorship and bequests. Their success has also relied on the enthusiasm of the local communities interested in the arts and encouragement of young artists.

State competitions have offered many opportunities for young musicians to participate in a number of competitions which operate nationally. The Australian Natives Association ran a concerto competition in the 1920s, and the ABC Young Performers Award (established as the ABC Concerto Competition in 1944), has given numerous talented young musicians the opportunity to be recognised by the country's main employer of professional musicians and to win the opportunity to perform with a state orchestra. Using the medium of radio, the *Australian Amateur Hour* (1937–60) and *Mobil Quest* (1949–55) had great success. Programs such as *New Faces* and the more recent *Quest* have offered opportunities for young performers on the popular medium of television.

Opportunities for singers abound in the richly endowed Australian Singing Competition, which include the Metropolitan Opera Auditions (founded 1963) and German Opera Award, and included a popular section 1983–89. Pianists have the David Paul Landa Competition (established 1987) and the Florence Davey Scholarship (since 1984); violinists have the immensely valuable Dorcas McLean Scholarship (established 1990). The ABC Composition competition flourished for some years from 1933; today composers have the opportunity to participate in the Spivakovsky Award, the Albert Maggs Award and the richest composition prize in Australia, the Paul Lowin Prizes for orchestral works and song cycles.

For popular music performers, the Battle of the Sounds functioned 1966–72; today there is the Yamaha National Organ Competition and the AusMusic Rock Eisteddfod. The development of international competitions including the Sydney International Piano Competition in 1977 and the Melbourne International Chamber Music Competition in 1991 have drawn Australia into the international music competition circuit with the accompanying panels of renowned jurors and critics from overseas contributing to Australia's musical standing.

Eisteddfods and competitions have played a significant role in the development of young musicians in Australia in providing performance opportunities, enhancement of standards, and encouragement of musical patronage in the community. Despite continuing criticism of the value of competition in the arts, new competitions continue to be introduced and supported by government, philanthropic and corporate organisations. In contrast, many of the older and isolated competitions have not been reassessed and continue to be presented with antiquated rules and questionable standards. The value of eisteddfods and competitions should not be denied in the development of an Australian performing tradition. Many distinguished Australian musicians experienced their first opportunities for public performance through the eisteddfods and competitions offered in the country and cities of Australia. (See also entries under individual competitions).

FURTHER REFERENCE

Georgina Binns, Music Eisteddfods in Ballarat to 1900, BMus(Hons), Univ. Melbourne, 1982; Ann Ross, 'Eisteddfods', *Australian Encyclopedia*, 5th edn (Sydney: Australian Geographic Society, 1988); *Royal South Street Society: The First One Hundred Years* (Ballarat: The Society, 1979).

GEORGINA BINNS

Composition in Australia

1. From European Settlement to 1960. 2. 1960 to the Present.

1. From European Settlement to 1960. (i) 1788–1890.

Almost without exception, composers of any significance active in the Australian colonies during the 19th century were either visitors for varying terms or immigrants who arrived in middle or later life, and their significance was on the whole more historical than musical. The styles of these composers were conservative for the time and the music often slight in substance. Many such composers came from Britain, which itself hardly produced composers of more than national significance for most of the century, but there were also a number from Germany.

The earliest music claimed to have been composed or produced by Europeans in Australia was a set of *Five Australian Quadrilles* (1825) attributed to Joseph ★Reichenberg (1790–1851), the bandmaster of the 40th Regiment stationed in Sydney, though possibly the work of William Ellard of Dublin. There were, following contemporary practice, arrangements and/or free adaptations of popular songs and arias from operas. They were 'Australianised' largely by their titles—*La Sydney, La Wooloomooloo* [sic], *La Illawarra, La Bong Bong* and *La Engehurst*. In 1826 another bandmaster, Kavanagh, compiled a set of marches and songs collectively titled 'Original Australian Music'; but the extent to which these pieces—which included the earliest of a long line of patriotic songs, entitled *The Trumpet Sounds Australia's Fame*— were also adaptations of existing pieces or involved some fresh composition on Australian soil is unknown since the original manuscripts have been lost. The first piece reputed to have been written by a composer actually born in Australia was *The Minstrel Waltz* by Thomas Stubbs in 1836, while two years earlier a Polish scientist, John Lhotsky, had published a song for voice and piano claimed to be based upon an Aboriginal women's song from southern NSW and 'humbly inscribed as the first specimen of Australian music'.

The general patterns of musical life, including musical creation, were, not surprisingly, similar in each of the Australian colonies. Each had its share of competent musicians, including those who composed; but the earliest notable figures in the history of Australian composition were, predictably, associated with the first established—and for many years the most developed—of the Australian colonies, NSW. Three of these early musicians deserve mention. The first is John Philip ★Deane (1796–1849) who came to Sydney in 1836 (after 14 years in Hobart) and lived there for the rest of his life. There he was recognised as a composer (his String Trio was probably the first piece of chamber music composed and performed in Australia), performer and teacher, forming, with members of his family, one of the numerous private 'music academies' which sprang up and withered at various times in each of the colonies in the days before the establishment of the larger public schools of music or conservatoriums. The Irish composer William Vincent ★Wallace (1812–65) also lived in Hobart (1835) as well as Sydney (1836–38) and likewise founded a 'music academy', as well as being a noted performer, in the latter city, but none of his major compositions (including the opera *Maritana* of 1846) was created in Australia. Finally, Isaac ★Nathan (1792–1864) arrived in Sydney, after a brief stay in Melbourne, in 1841 and spent the rest of his life there. Nathan had already made a name for himself as a composer in England, his early works including operas and settings of texts by Lord Byron, to whom he had been introduced in 1814. In Australia his most notable achievements were the composition of the first two operas written in the country, *Merry Freaks in Troublous Times* (1843) and *Don John of Austria* (1847) as well as the transcription of Aboriginal melodies (again, like Lhotsky's earlier attempt, adapted to the idiom of 19th-century European music) published in a miscellany titled *The Southern Euphrosyne* in 1849. Other works composed in Australia include patriotic songs and an ode, *Leichhardt's Grave* (1846), mourning the explorer's supposed death.

In the second half of the 19th century, following the discoveries of gold, the rapid increase in migration and the establishment of a solid middle class led to an equally rapid increase in the volume of music composed in Australia. The most favoured genres were the song and piano miniature for domestic performance, and the public forms of oratorio, cantata, ode and choral song, especially on patriotic subjects. Opera flourished to a remarkable extent, although the number of operas by

Australian resident composers remained small. Chamber music flourished only modestly, while the signal lack of symphonic output can be linked to the absence of any permanent symphony orchestras in Australia until well into the 20th century.

During this period there were numerous composers active who were of relatively equal significance, so that the selection of representative names must be somewhat arbitrary. Charles ★Horsley (1822–76) lived in Australia (variously in Sydney and Melbourne) between 1862 and 1870 and wrote an ode, *Euterpe* (1870), to words by Henry Kendall, to mark the opening of the Melbourne Town Hall. Charles ★Packer (1810–83) came to Hobart in 1848 and then lived successively in Brisbane and Sydney; while John ★Delany (1852–1907 and resident in Sydney from 1872) is best known for his cantata *Captain Cook* (1888). Carl ★Linger (1810–62), German-born, came to Adelaide in 1850 as an established composer chiefly of sacred and orchestral music, and is best known in Australia for his composition of the patriotic *Song of Australia* to words by Mrs Caroline Carleton. Dom Rosendo ★Salvado (1814–1900) arrived in WA from Spain in 1846 to establish a Benedictine mission to the Aborigines. He became the first abbot of the monastery at New Norcia, just north of Perth, where he remained (save for brief periodic returns to Europe) for the rest of his life, retiring to Rome only in 1899. Salvado was a musician of substance—a virtuoso pianist as well as a composer of piano and choral music, his piano music reflecting some of the flamboyance of the early Liszt. Others of note trained outside England were Alfred ★Seal (1834–1904) at Brisbane, Moritz ★Heuzenroeder (1849–97) at Adelaide, Henri ★Kowalski (1841–1916) and Stephen Hale ★Marsh (1805–88) at Sydney, G.W. ★Torrance (1835–1907), Julius ★Herz (1841–98) and Julius ★Siede at Melbourne.

(ii) 1890–1918. The years immediately preceding Federation and up to World War I saw a new stage in the development of Australian musical composition. During this period emerged the first group of composers whose work is of more than primarily historical interest: G.W.L. ★Marshall-Hall (1862–1915), Fritz ★Hart (1874–1949), Alfred ★Hill (1870–1960) and Percy ★Grainger (1882–1961). The last two are notable as being Australia's first native-born composers of significance, while Marshall-Hall and Hart were English immigrant composers who wrote in styles rather more progressive than had been heard hitherto in Australia.

Marshall-Hall, who arrived in Melbourne in 1891 to take up the post of foundation professor of music at the university, embraced, as a composer, Wagnerian styles and later those of Puccini, Debussy and Strauss. As Australia's first orchestral conductor of significance, as music educator, writer, free thinker and also associate of Tom Roberts and other members of the Heidelberg School of artists, Marshall-Hall was a representative of the most forward-looking artistic thought of his time in Australia. As with

Hart and Hill, opera occupied an important place in Marshall-Hall's output, the most notable in the Australian context being *Stella* (1909), to the composer's own libretto and set in colonial Australia.

Fritz Hart came to Australia in 1909 as a theatre conductor and subsequently became director of the Albert Street (later Melba) Conservatorium in Melbourne, a post he held for over two decades until he left Australia for Hawaii in 1936. During this time he was immensely influential as a conductor, teacher and composer, his creative style (especially in his large output of operas—about 15 composed in Australia) belonging firmly to that of the English post-Romantic school of Holst, Ireland, Bax and Vaughan Williams, with a strong literary bent towards Celticism as witnessed in his opera *Riders to the Sea* (1915) based on Synge's play.

If Hart's example was to swing Australia's early 20th-century composers strongly towards contemporary British music as their chief stylistic source, Alfred Hill's music—also thus influenced to some extent—nevertheless retained a strong mid-19th-century central European flavour stemming from his studies in Leipzig in the 1880s and 90s. This conservative style, owing much to Schumann, Bruch and Dvořák, remained throughout Hill's career notwithstanding his occasional superficial use of both Maori and Aboriginal melodic and rhythmic materials, for example in the Second String Quartet (1913), subtitled 'Maori Legend', and the *Australia* Symphony (1951). Hill's work during the period from the 1890s till the early 1920s was principally in the fields of opera and cantata: most of his instrumental music—chamber music, symphonies and concertos—came later (see §(iii) below). His 14 operas, composed during his various periods in both NZ and Australia, range from comedies based on the English ballad opera or French *opéra-comique* types (i.e. with spoken dialogue) to more through-composed operas, some making use of Wagnerian leitmotif techniques. The libretti set by Hill varied widely, from European through Oriental and Maori to Australian subjects, examples of the latter including *Auster* (1922, libretto after Emily Congeau) and *The Ship of Heaven* (1923, libretto by Hugh McCrae).

The dramatic works of Hill, together with those of Hart and Marshall-Hall, represent a remarkable efflorescence of Australian operatic composition during this period, the seeds of which were no doubt fertilised by the equally remarkable vigour of operatic activity in Australia during the later 19th century. Its sharp decline after the early 1920s may be linked to the strong growth in orchestral concert activity and the advent of radio broadcasting, each offering strong alternative sources of musical entertainment not hitherto available.

The fourth composer of this early 20th-century group, Percy Grainger, may be sharply contrasted with nearly every composer so far considered, in that he was Australia's first significant expatriate rather than immigrant composer. However, although the Melbourne-born Grainger lived most of his life outside Australia, he always took pains to describe and promote himself as an Australian composer and musician. Furthermore he expressed his conviction that his best works had distinctly Australian qualities—for example the ideal of large, 'monotonous' yet non-repetitive forms as distinct from the sectional structures of European music with their patterns of repetition and contrast which he equated with the small, 'patchwork' appearance of European landscapes as compared to Australia's vast tracts of unbroken terrain.

Regardless of the validity or otherwise of these views, Grainger's work and ideas form an indispensable contribution to the theme of 'Australianism' that ran through the work of many composers since the time of the earliest patriotic songs and the first arrangements of Aboriginal melodies, as noted at the beginning of this entry. The period beginning with the Centenary Exhibition in Melbourne in 1888 and the years leading to and beyond Federation, culminating in Australia's participation in World War I, were identified with a strong surge of nationalist sentiments in all areas of Australian cultural expression. Apart from Grainger, a minor Melbourne composer and writer, Henry ★Tate (1873–1926), is today remembered for his important contribution to the ongoing debate about an Australian identity in music—even if his ideas seem rather naive or quaint in the late 20th century. Tate's conceptions were propagated in a series of newspaper and journal articles published during the later years of, and those immediately following, World War I; a number were republished in a small volume entitled *Australian Musical Possibilities* which appeared in 1924. His ideas are strongly allied with those of the nationalist literary movement of the time centred on Bernard O'Dowd, who wrote a strongly laudatory introduction to Tate's collection of essays. These essays speculate on the nature of a specifically Australian national contribution to the history of European music following the lead of the various folk-based national schools, notably Russia. Here, however, he takes the somewhat illogical step of equating the relationship of the various European national schools to their own folksong, with the possibility of Australian composers finding such an 'undersong' in the music of the Australian Aborigine and the sounds of the bush—notably birdsong, from which Tate extracted a number of melodic and rhythmic patterns which he felt could be translated into a recognisably Australian musical idiom.

Tate's own compositions, including piano pieces, vocal music and even an orchestral rhapsody, *Dawn*, unfortunately fail, through their limited technical and expressive resource, to provide a convincing advocacy of his conceptions. Nevertheless, his and Grainger's ideas have not been without subsequent influence, and have found echoes in the work of such later composers as Douglas, Antill, Penberthy and Sculthorpe.

(iii) 1918–60. The period between the world wars and up to 1960 forms a coherent post-colonial stage in

Australian musical composition. Composers of this period were native-born or else spent all, or virtually all, of their creative careers in Australia. Their style sources range from late 19th-century survivals together with the milder forms of English impressionism—the so-called pastoral style—to more astringent manifestations of early 20th-century or neo-classical idioms represented by such composers as Stravinsky, Bartók, Prokofiev, Hindemith and the French *Six*. The expressionist, atonal and dodecaphonic styles of the Viennese School (Schoenberg, Berg and Webern) were virtually unheard of in Australia until after 1960, reflecting an isolation from the most radical European trends which was (in common with patterns often found in young transplanted cultures) even more pronounced than that prevailing in England during the same period.

The oldest composer active during these years was Alfred Hill. Hill was foundation professor of harmony, theory and composition at the NSW State Conservatorium from 1916 until 1934. During the later years of this period and up till 1938 his major compositional work was in the field of chamber music which included 13 of his 17 string quartets; while from 1941 onwards he concentrated on the production of 12 of his 13 symphonies—these late essays being transcriptions of string quartets and an early piano quintet. These larger instrumental works, together with a number of concertos, show most strongly Hill's links with late 19th-century sources. But he also composed many shorter works for orchestra, smaller ensembles or piano, with or without voices, which generally have a much greater affinity with English pastoralism. Hill's overall stylistic range is also reflected in the work of such composers as Mirrie ★Hill (1892–1986), Frank ★Hutchens (1892–1965), Lindley ★Evans (1895–1982) and Miriam ★Hyde (b 1913), to name no others. The style represented by these composers was, for much of the post-colonial period, the most audible voice of Australian music and was particularly evident in music written for educational purposes—songs, short choral and piano pieces, for example.

The generation following Alfred Hill, however, included composers who, to varying extents, came to grips with more mainstream 20th-century techniques. Chief among these was Margaret ★Sutherland (1897–1984), Adelaide-born but resident in Melbourne for virtually all her life. A student of Fritz Hart, Sutherland subsequently gained first-hand knowledge of contemporary European music through a self-promoted trip to London, Paris and Vienna from 1923 to 1925 during which time she studied with Arnold Bax. The English bias such a pedigree (Hart and Bax) might suggest was complemented, and later largely superseded, by her personal absorption of continental (mainly neo-classical) sources such as those mentioned earlier in this section. Toward the end of her career (mostly after 1960) she ventured towards free atonality, but even here never really embraced the tenets of the Viennese School so much as the possibilities arising from Bartók's

dissonant counterpoint. Sutherland's most prolific instrumental production was in the field of chamber music of which the early Violin Sonata (1925) and her second string quartet titled *Discussion* (1954) are notable among many splendid examples; while her orchestral music was mostly written during the late flowering of her career after 1950 and includes the tone poem *Haunted Hills* (1950) and a violin concerto (1960). She also wrote much piano and vocal music ranging from a large body of short choral pieces and piano music for educational purposes to the complexities of the *Six Songs* to poems of Judith Wright (1951–63; published 1967) and the piano piece *Extension* (1967). Her only opera was a one-act chamber opera, *The Young Kabbarli* (1964), to a libretto by Maie Casey and based upon an episode in the life of Daisy Bates among the Aborigines of north-west Australia.

The Aboriginal subject of the last-named work and Sutherland's use in it of the didjeridu as well as stylised evocations of Aboriginal chants comprised an isolated excursion by her into what has been referred to as musical 'jindyworobakism'. The Aboriginal word *jindyworobak* (to annex or join) was adopted by a group of writers working in the late 1930s and 40s for whom the basis of a truly Australian literary culture lay in the absorption of, and emphasis on, Australia's landscape, history and tradition, especially those of the Aborigines. This can be seen as yet another attempt (related to that of O'Dowd and Tate) to forge an authentic sense of 'Australianism' in the arts; the chief composers associated with such ideals at this time were Clive ★Douglas (1903–77) and John ★Antill (1904–86). Douglas, of Melbourne, devoted the major part of his creative output to the production of stage and programmatic orchestral works such as the operetta *Kaditcha* (1938), the symphonic poems *Carwoola* (1939) and *Sturt* 1829 (1952) and the Symphony No. 2 (*Namatjira*) (1956). His colourful orchestral style derives principally from Debussy, early Stravinsky, Rimsky-Korsakov and the English pastoralists, while seeking to evoke a uniquely Australian flavour via the stylised adaptation of Aboriginal melodies, rhythms and timbres. His achievement in this is rather overshadowed by the suite (later ballet) *Corroboree* (1946) by John Antill of Sydney. Showing considerable affinities with Stravinsky's *The Rite of Spring* (although Antill denied any acquaintance with this work at the time) *Corroboree* made an enormous impact on Australian audiences after its premiere in Sydney under Eugene Goossens and is arguably the most famous piece of Australian orchestral music of the first half of the 20th century. Antill had worked on the score for at least a decade and it is the main product of the composer's fascination with Aboriginal culture which can be traced back to a boyhood experience of performances by Aboriginal dancers and musicians at La Perouse, Botany Bay.

Antill and Douglas, and also the younger James ★Penberthy (b 1917), were the most overtly nationalist figures in Australian composition during the post-colonial period: however, none of these composers' work was limited to musical jindyworobakism. *Corroboree* remained Antill's most vital and also advanced work, his general style otherwise retaining a strongly English flavour and conservatism reflecting his early education at St Andrew's Cathedral School and his composition study with Alfred Hill. Douglas's later music encompassed more neo-classical areas of expression as well as venturing somewhat modestly into a kind of tonally based 12-note technique.

Three other composers make up, with Margaret Sutherland, a significant group whose styles absorbed interwar English and continental neo-classical sources. These are Robert ★Hughes (*b* 1912) and Dorian ★Le Gallienne (1915–63) of Melbourne, and Raymond ★Hanson (1913–76) of Sydney. Each has achieved a distinct musical personality, Hughes almost exclusively in the field of orchestral music and Le Gallienne and Hanson across a wider range of musical genres. A rather more isolated figure of interest is the Sydney composer Roy ★Agnew (1893—1944) whose output (largely for piano) exhibits a densely textured manner owing most to Ireland, Bax and Scriabin.

The most significant Australian composers of this time were thus far from unacquainted with contemporary European trends, even if, following the British example, they knew less of, or declined to follow, the most radical ones. But it is important to note that general audience tastes of this period, reflected by the institutional agencies for the public dissemination of contemporary Australian music, largely ensured that composers of any but the most innocuously conservative styles had great difficulty in gaining performance, publication or recording of their works. The musical isolation which was the lot of the Australian composer during this period would suggest that a host of them might have followed Grainger's example and pursued their careers overseas. There are, however, only two significant expatriate composers whose careers lay in the post-colonial period: Arthur ★Benjamin (1893–1960) and Peggy ★Glanville-Hicks (1912–90). Benjamin, born in Sydney, lived most of his life in London where he taught piano and composition at the Royal College of Music; while the Melbourne-born Glanville-Hicks, after periods of study in London, Vienna and Paris, worked in the USA during the 1940s and 50s.

2. 1961 to the Present. The death of Percy Grainger in 1961 marked the passing of an era in Australian composition. The English-oriented music which he and Hill, Antill, Sutherland and Douglas had written up to the late 1950s gave way to the much more independent music of Peter Sculthorpe, Nigel Butterley and Richard Meale, and then to the multifarious internationalism of Gerard Brophy, Michael Smetanin, Carl Vine, Liza Lim and Mary Finsterer in the 1990s. If a 'national school' of composition ever existed in Australia, it was in the era prior to 1961, for with continuing European immigration, the end of the White Australia policy and the increasing 'Asianisation', the growing accessibility of air travel and the explosion of communications, it has become impossible to identify a single and quintessential Australian 'sound'.

(i) 1961–72: The Tyranny of Distance. The 1960s saw several important changes in the support for Australian composers. The two Australian branches of the ISCM began to play an important role in bringing contemporary music into the mainstream, and the appointment of British conductor John ★Hopkins as federal director of music for the ABC in 1963 brought about the commissioning, programming and performance of the works of many Australian composers (and other contemporary composers) at a level never previously experienced and not matched since.

Hopkins found many composers still clinging to the limiting traditions of Europe, particularly the English 'pastoral' tradition, while younger figures were making a belated discovery of the early 20th-century expressionist movements of Vienna. The prominent composers were either born overseas or felt it necessary to train in Europe. The music of Sutherland continued to display a stark and biting quality; Douglas continued attempting to address the issue of Australianness in his music by using Aboriginal names such as *Kaditcha*, *Carwoola*, *Wangadilla* and *Coolawidgee* and programmatic titles *Blue Billabong*, *Sand Ballads of the Outback*; and very little of Antill's later work, often reflecting Australian images and sentiments (*G'Day Digger*, *Song of a Silver City*, *An Outback Overture* and *Snowy*) matched the vitality of the internationally successful *Corroboree*.

Robert Hughes has not been influenced by the changing compositional fads: his music may have been reminiscent of early 20th-century composers such as Walton, Bartók or Ravel, but it was pervaded by elements of unease and tension which gave works such as *Xanadu*, *The Forbidden Rite* and the *Essays 1* and *2* a distinctive voice. The music of Raymond Hanson (1913–76) was strongly influenced by the philosophy of Hindemith and throughout his life he continued to write impeccably crafted works, strongly contrapuntal and eschewing tonality (such as the Trumpet Concerto, String Quartet, and the Symphony). James ★Penberthy (*b* 1917) became well known for his eclecticism and for a prolific output which included numerous symphonies, ballets and operas. His music was virile and powerful and often influenced by Australian themes (the ballets *Brolga*, *Boomerang*, *Kooree and the Mists*), but it also reflected a passion for experimentalism (in such works as the concertos for saxophone and trombone). Felix ★Werder (*b* Germany, 1922) came to Australia in 1940 and developed a reputation, based on a very large output of works (symphonies, string quartets, operas, concertos and many chamber works), for an atonal complexity of sound and construction.

George ★Dreyfus (*b* Germany, 1928) was 11 when he came to Australia. He became one of Australia's best-known composers, principally for his highly successful film and television music, but his reputation also rests on a number of finely crafted concert works (two symphonies, *Galgenlieder*, the opera *Garni Sands* and much chamber music). Pianist, conductor and composer Keith ★Humble (1927–95) studied in Paris with Leibowitz, and works such as *Arcade* show his interest in serialist methods. Peter ★Sculthorpe (b 1929) is possibly Australia's most successful composer, having developed a musical language, influenced by Aboriginal, Balinese and Japanese music, which attempts to reflect the Australian landscape. Works such as *Sun Music*, *Red Landscape*, *Tabu Tabuhan*, *Mangrove* and *Kakadu* have received wide recognition in Australia and overseas.

Sculthorpe, Don ★Banks (1923–80), Keith ★Humble (1927–95), Malcolm ★Williamson (b 1931) and David ★Lumsdaine (b 1931) left Australia and took up residence in the UK and Europe. Williamson, known for a large output of works of neo-classical style, later became Master of the Queen's Music; Lumsdaine set up the electronic music studio at the University of Durham before returning to Australia in the mid-1980s. The early works of Richard ★Meale (b 1932), such as *Homage to Garcia Lorca*, *Very High Kings*, *Coruscations* and *Images* (showing a variety of influences both Asian and European), established his place as a disciple of the avant-garde. In the mid-1970s with the orchestral work *Viridian*, however, Meale's style became more lush and evocative, an Australian impressionism, and is now established with recent works such as the operas *Voss* and *Mer de Glace* and the First Symphony.

Colin ★Brumby (b 1933) began his compositional career using European serialism in works such as the *Fibonacci Variations* and the Wind Quintet, and, like Meale, underwent a stylistic change in the early 1970s toward works which are now tonal and accessible. Nigel ★Butterley (b 1935) is known for sinewy and incisive music which often draws on issues of mysticism and metaphysics; from the early *Meditations of Thomas Traherne* to the recent *Goldengrove* the quality and consistency of his music has remained constant and highly respected. Other composers of importance were pianist-composer Larry ★Sitsky (b China 1934), Eric ★Gross (b 1926), Peter ★Tahourdin (b 1928), George ★Tibbits (b 1933) and Helen ★Gifford (b 1935).

In 1967 the Advisory Board, Commonwealth Assistance to Australian Composers was created with a budget of $10 000; this rose to $60 000 in 1970–71. A new era of institutionalised patronage for Australian composers had begun, soon to be dramatically enlarged by a visionary new government.

(ii) 1972–80: Rites of Passage. The election of a national Labor government led by Prime Minister Gough Whitlam in 1972, after 23 years of conservative rule, brought a great change in the nature of Australian society. In many ways Australia 'came of age', not only politically and socially, but also culturally. This transformation was brought about by Whitlam who, as Minister for the Arts, spearheaded a veritable cultural revolution, encouraging

the arts in all their forms and providing substantial financial assistance. The 1970s was an era of optimism for the arts and saw the opening of the Sydney Opera House (1973), the establishment of state and regional opera companies, and the establishment of a national ABC 24-hour fine music service (1976).

In 1973 the Australian Council for the Arts was created, consolidating the new patronage system. The Music Board of the Council was chaired by composer Don Banks and started programs of commissioning, residencies and performance which enabled composers to be reasonably compensated for their work and gave some legitimation to their profession. In 1976 the Australian Music Centre was established in Sydney to provide a focal point for composers and the dissemination of their music. In the late 1960s and early 1970s many new music schools were established throughout the country, most of which began to offer composition as a separate discipline and not merely as an adjunct to performance training as was typical of the established conservatoriums. Several ensembles were established, often by composers, specialising in contemporary music; notably the Australian Contemporary Music Ensemble (ACME), Flederman, and the Seymour Group.

Composers began to have the confidence to explore their own languages free of slavish imitation of European models, and they also had the security to do so in depth. Several students of Peter Sculthorpe at the University of Sydney came to prominence, each after further study elsewhere, notably Ross ★Edwards (b 1943), Barry ★Conyngham (b 1944), Anne ★Boyd (b 1946) and Martin ★Wesley-Smith. Edwards went on to study with Peter Maxwell Davies in Britain, and developed a compositional voice of austere beauty; his Piano Concerto and his *Maninyas* cycle, based on nonsense syllables, are works of great gaiety and rhythmic buoyancy. Conyngham came to attention with Japanese-influenced works he wrote after a period of study with Toru Takemitsu in Japan, such as *Water … Footsteps … Time* (1970–71); since then he has produced a series of distinguished works, such as the theatre pieces *Bony Anderson* (1978), the puppet opera *Bennelong* (1988) and the ballet *Vast* (1988) for Australia's Bicentenary. Boyd went to Bernard Rands and Wilfrid Mellers at York University and gained attention in the UK and Hong Kong before returning to Australia; her output of lean, limpid chamber works shows the influence of Asian techniques such as gamelan and *gagaku*. Wesley-Smith also went to York University and now writes humorously for music-theatre and choir, his children's work *Boojum!* (1986, after Lewis Carroll) having considerable success. He has also been an exponent of electronic and computer music.

Among many other composers prominent in these years with strong European pedigrees are Moya ★Henderson (b 1941) and Roger ★Smalley (b England 1943). Henderson studied in Cologne with Kagel and Stockhausen and has mostly written for music-theatre and chamber ensembles; she is currently working on an opera for the Australian Opera based on the Lindy Chamberlain case. Roger ★Smalley (*b* England 1943), a pupil of Goehr, Stockhausen and Boulez, settled in Australia at Perth and came to wide attention, winning the Paris Rostrum with his Piano Concerto, a work of Chopinesque pianism but articulate modernist idiom.

(iii) 1980–96: The New Internationalism.

With the 1980s, Australian composers could feel the benefits of nearly 20 years of grand government sponsorship and public exposure. They could assess the value of previous imitation, innovation, or isolation, and choose their own stylistic position less self-consciously. Their music continued to adopt influences from Europe and the USA, but more easily, comfortably, and with the confidence of artists sure of their home territory. An increasing number of Australian composers have found performances abroad as well as in Australia, moving more frequently between countries; a number continued to opt for European models with some rigour, and there was a renewal of British and European ideas through a number of immigrant composers. Composers such as Richard Mills, Vincent Plush, Ros Bandt, Sarah Hopkins, Gordon Kerry and Carl Vine have been able to survive as freelance artists, while others like Michael Atherton, Brenton Broadstock, Stephen Cronin, Brian Howard, Graeme Koehne and Andrew Schultz have become some of the first non-immigrants appointed to Australian university posts in composition.

Composer, conductor and percussionist Richard ★Mills (*b* 1949) returned from studies with Edmund Rubbra in London to make a major contribution to Australian orchestral repertoire; works such as *Bamaga Diptych* have been frequently played by the ABC orchestras, and his ballet *Snugglepot and Cuddlepie* is a favourite of the Australian Ballet. Adelaide-born Vincent ★Plush (*b* 1950) has broadcast frequently on Australian music and is best known for works which have Australian historical associations, such as the appealing song cycle *Australian Folksongs*, *Bakery Hill Rising*, for french horns, and the orchestral works *Pacifica* and *Concord/Eendracht*. Ros ★Bandt (*b* 1951), emerging from Monash University and Keith Humble's La Trobe University, became an experimental sound artist whose work embraces sound sculpture, interactive installations, and atmospheric music for zithers, gongs, or instruments of her own invention. She has held residencies in Australia and the USA. Composer and pianist Carl ★Vine (*b* 1954) studied with John Exton and Barry Conyngham and has established a secure reputation based on a large and diverse output — six symphonies, numerous dance and theatre works (many for the Sydney Dance Company), much chamber music mostly written for the ensemble Flederman (of which he was a founding member), including *Love Song* and *Miniature 1–4*, three string quartets, and sonatas for flute and piano; he has also written for film and television. Sarah ★Hopkins (*b* NZ 1958) came to Australia in 1964 and studied at

the Victorian College of the Arts School of Music. She has written works—such as *Awakening Earth*, *Sky Song*, *Past Life Melodies*, *Reclaiming the Spirit*—which manifest her interest in the space and energy of the Australian landscape, using the cello, voice, whirly instruments and handbells. She makes extensive use of extended techniques including circular bowing, bowed harmonics and harmonic overtone singing, and has worked in theatre, dance, film and with other collaborative artists.

Among those in universities, Brian ★Howard (*b* 1951), now at the WA Conservatorium in Perth, studied composition with Peter Sculthorpe, Richard Meale, Bernard Rands and Peter Maxwell Davies and came to attention in 1978 with his orchestral work *Il tramonto della luna*. Since this time he has devoted most of his compositional energy to music theatre and operatic works such as *Inner Voices*, *Metamorphosis* (both for the Victoria State Opera), *Whitsunday* (for the Australian Opera) and *Wide Sargasso Sea* (for the State Opera of South Australia). Brenton ★Broadstock (*b* 1952), now at the University of Melbourne, studied with Donald Freund in Memphis, USA, and with Peter Sculthorpe. His works, such as *Toward The Shining Light*, *Stars In a Dark Night*, *And No Birds Sing* and *Celebration*, mostly have an extramusical inspiration of a political, social or personal nature and have been widely played in Australia and overseas, including London, Berlin and Munich; he is also one of the few composers to write extensively for brass band. Graeme ★Koehne (*b* 1956), studied with Richard Meale and has created an accessible style based on popular musics. His early style, typified by the lush orchestral works *Rainforest* and *riverrun …*, has developed into one which uses popular rhythmic and harmonic structures; works such as *Unchained Melody* and *Powerhouse* have been widely played by ABC orchestras. He has also written extensively for the theatre, including four ballets (*Nocturnes* was presented by the Australian Ballet in London) and has produced several fine chamber and solo works, such as *Ricerare and Burletta*, *Gothic Toccata* and *Capriccio*.

European ideas continue to have their stricter adherents, particularly among students of Richard ★Toop at the Sydney Conservatorium. Michael ★Smetanin (*b* 1958) is known for his aggressive, unrelenting and sometimes controversial works such as *Track*, *Ladder of Escape*, *Bellevue II*, *The Skinless Kiss of Angels*, *Strip* and the orchestral work *Black Snow*, which combine elements of minimalism, rock music and modernist extended technique. Gerard ★Brophy (*b* 1953) has studied with Kagel and Donatoni, and works such as *Breathless*, *Flesh*, *Shiver* and *Cries and Whispers* reflect a European complexity tempered by Italianate filigree features. More recently his work, notably the orchestral works *Forbidden Colours* and *Colour red … your mouth … heart*, has become more focused on colour and melody. Other composers of European orientation include Claudio ★Pompili (*b* 1949), Michael ★Whiticker (*b* 1954), Mark ★Pollard (*b* 1957), Michael ★Barkl (*b* 1958) and Stephen ★Cronin (*b* 1960).

The new wave of British immigrants included Michael ★Easton (*b* 1954), Andrew ★Ford (*b* 1957), and Chris ★Dench (*b* 1953). Easton settled in Melbourne and writes in an easily accessible style influenced by his studies with Lennox Berkeley in London; his work includes five piano concertos and several music-theatre works, of which the children's opera *Beauty and the Beast* has been performed by the Victoria State Opera. Ford taught at Wollongong University as well as broadcasting and writing on Australian music with considerable distinction; he was a pupil of Edward Cowie at the University of Lancaster and a productive composer with various commissions, whose works include three operas for young people and eight works for tenor Gerald English. Chris Dench is mostly self-taught and writes music, such as *Afterimages, Funk, Driftglass, planetary allegiances* and *propriocepts*, that is known for its intricacy and complexity. Dench's music has been played at major contemporary music festivals around the world.

Australia has produced a large number of composers who have worked on the fringe of mainstream music, in the areas of electronic and computer music, interdisciplinary arts and experimental music. Some of these include the American-born Warren ★Burt and Jeff Pressing, who (along with Keith Humble and Laurie Whiffen at La Trobe University) have taught and influenced a number of interesting composers, notably David Hirst (*b* 1952), Graeme Gerrard (*b* 1953), Richard ★Vella (*b* 1954), Rainer ★Linz (*b* 1955), Alistair ★Riddell (*b* 1955), David ★Chesworth (*b* England 1958). Other 'non-mainstream' composers include Ross ★Bolleter (*b* 1946), Ron ★Nagorcka (*b* 1948), Chris ★Mann (*b* 1949), Ernie ★Althoff (*b* 1950), David ★Worrall (*b* 1954), and Sherre DeLys (*b* USA 1958).

A younger generation came to attention in the mid-1980s and early 1990s. Nigel ★Westlake (*b* 1958), a composer of attractive minimalist scores, has written copiously for television, radio and film, as well as writing many jazz-influenced chamber works. Of those born in the 1960s, Liza ★Lim (*b* 1966) and Mary ★Finsterer (*b* 1966) may both be mentioned. Lim first studied in Melbourne and has been closely associated with the contemporary ensemble Elision, her terse, eclectic style interweaving often disparate materials in a chamber music texture. Her music-theatre work *The Oresteia* (1993) has been recorded and published by Ricordi. Finsterer has produced a number of short works for ABC orchestras such as *Scat* (1993), and the chamber work *Sentence for Dinner* (1986) has been recorded for the BBC. About these and others even younger it is perhaps too soon to be definitive, but their future seems bright.

FURTHER REFERENCE
(i) Before 1960
Biographical entries may be found in *ADB*; *CallawayA*; *CA*; *CohenI*; *GroveD*; *GroveO*; *GroveW*; *LePageW*; *MonashB*; *MoresbyA*; *MurdochA*. A discography of ABC recordings of Australian

composers to 1972 is *PlushD*. See also Roger Covell, *Australia's Music: Themes of a New Society* (Melbourne: Sun Books, 1967); A. Kornweibel, *Apollo and the Pioneers: The Story of the First Hundred Years of Music in Western Australia* (Perth: The Music Council of Western Australia, 1973); Andrew McCredie, *Musical Composition in Australia* (Canberra: Australian Government Printer, 1969). Idem, *A Catalogue of Forty-Six Australian Composers and Selected Works* (Canberra: Australian Government Printer, 1969); Ann Wentzel, The First Hundred Years of Music in Australia, 1788–1888, unpublished MA thesis, Univ. Sydney, 1963.
(ii) Since 1960
Biographical entries may be found in *BroadstockS*; *CallawayA*; *CA*; *CohenI*; *ContemporaryC*; *GroveO*; *GroveW*; *JenkinsT*; *LePageW*; *MonashB*; *MurdochA*. Articles about many aspects of Australian composition since 1987 are in *SA*. See also Andrew Ford, *Composer to Composer* (Sydney: Allen & Unwin, 1993).

DAVID SYMONS, §1;
BRENTON BROADSTOCK, §2
(§2iii with Editor)

Computers and Music. The first computer music appeared in the USA in 1957; but in Australia significant computer music emerged only from 1975, when the prototype of the ★Fairlight CMI was installed at the Canberra School of Music. Marketed from 1978, this computer musical instrument has made a worldwide impact.

Aside from the developers of the Fairlight, many individuals in Australia have contributed to experimental developments in hardware and software. Leading roles have been played by La Trobe University, the Sydney Conservatorium, the University of Adelaide, the Australian Centre for Arts and Technology at the Canberra School of Music (ACAT, established 1989), and the Australian Computer Music Association (ACMA, established 1989).

In the late 1970s and 80s this work was carried out chiefly in institutional studios, but in the 1990s more has come to depend on the equipment of individuals. Greg ★Schiemer (Sydney Conservatorium) built a specialised MIDI device with associated software for algorithmic composition interacting with a human performer; Alistair ★Riddell (La Trobe University) built a computer-controlled action for grand pianos. Others connected with hardware and software development are Ross Bencina, Warren ★Burt, Barry ★Conyngham, Howard Davidson, Jon Drummond, Stuart Favilla, Malcolm ★Fox, Ian Fredericks, Graeme Gerrard, Rex Harris, David Hirst, Graham Kirner, Gordon Monro, Jeff Pressing, Roger ★Smalley, Jim Sosnin and Thomas Stainsby.

Much of the computer music composed so far is so new that its lasting value cannot yet be judged reliably. Those who have used computers in composition include, in addition to some already mentioned, Ros ★Bandt, Bruce ★Clarke, Tristram ★Cary, John ★Exton, Gerald ★Glynn, Anthony Hood, Stephen Ingham, Chris ★Knowles, Ian ★Shanahan, Martin ★Wesley-Smith, and David ★Worrall. Many composers of notated music use computer typesetting to produce printed scores and parts.

In musicology, the earliest significant work by an Australian using computer methods was carried out by Glyn Marillier (initially at the University of Otago, NZ) from 1971. He encoded on punch-cards the tonal progressions of all 106 Haydn Symphonies and processed the data on a mainframe computer to yield instructive conclusions about large-scale tonality and its temporal proportions. The most prominent work in providing computer-readable musical databases has been carried out by John Stinson at La Trobe University. The program Scribe, written under his direction, allows the user to analyse and print items from Stinson's extensive collection of 14th-century music and to enter new examples. An existing computer database of 6000 German folksongs was analysed by Nigel Nettheim in 1993 for the musical behaviour in the vicinity of the barline; a custom program took into account pitch, rhythm and metre jointly, providing evidence of the means by which the pulse perceived in musical performance is manifested in the score. Pitch directions were studied by Graham Pont in 1990 in an existing database of 14 000 incipits of classical and popular music; a tendency for initial progressions to ascend was confirmed in most repertoires.

Computer library catalogues are now taken for granted in Australia, and specialist music databases, such as that at the National Film and Sound Archive, have been developed. An Australian contribution to the computer encoding of music-related texts was made with the complete letters of Franz Schubert encoded by Nigel Nettheim for the Oxford Text Archive.

Extensive research on algorithmic expression was carried out by Manfred *Clynes at the Sydney Conservatorium of Music in the 1980s. As raw material encoded from a score sounds mechanical if reproduced literally, nuances are needed to provide expression. The nuances modify primarily the length and loudness of the notes: to provide an appropriate beat or pulse each location within the bar receives its own modifications and the bar pattern is reproduced throughout a movement. The pulses of various classical composers were distinguished. The composer's personal pulse corresponds to the groove of popular music.

Sonification, the rendering into sound of statistical data normally viewed as numbers, allows the ear to take part in scientific data analysis, for instance by detecting outlying values. This area has been explored by Stephen Barrass at the CSIRO, Canberra; his preparatory work cleverly related musical timbre to visual colour (see *Synaesthetica '94*).

Several of the larger educational institutions have developed computer-aided instruction since the 1980s. A prominent Australian commercial product in this area is the program Music Master, by Datasonics, an elaborate integrated package used in Australian schools and competing successfully with products abroad. Another commercial program, Auralia, by Rising Software, handles aural training.

Australian documentation of computer work in music includes Philip Drummond's historically valuable compilation (1984) and Tristram Cary's notable compendium (1992). As the balance desirable for music between the computer and the human musician has been slowly worked out over the past twenty years, the computer's contribution has increased; but it is too early to predict the eventual outcome. (See also *Electronic Music, Experimental Music.*)

FURTHER REFERENCE

Cary, Tristram, *Illustrated Compendium of Musical Technology* (London: Faber & Faber, 1992).

Clynes, Manfred, 'Expressive Microstructure in Music, Linked to Living Qualities'. In *Studies of Music Performance,* ed. J. Sundberg. Royal Swedish Academy of Music Publication No. 39 (Stockholm: Royal Swedish Academy of Music, 1983), 76–181.

Drummond, Philip J., Computer Applications to Music: A Survey and Review of the Literature. MEngSci diss., Univ. NSW, 1984.

Hirst, David, ed., *Micropolyphonie* 1 (1995). Papers from the ACMA 1993 Conference.

Jones, Anthony, ed. SA 14/47 (1996). Special edition on 'Technology and Music: Revolution or Development?'

Marillier, Cecil Glyn, 'Computer Assisted Analysis of Tonal Structure in the Classical Symphony', *Haydn Yearbook* 14 (1983), 187–99.

Nettheim, Nigel, 'On the Accuracy of Musical Data, with Examples from Gregorian Chant and German Folksong', *Computers and the Humanities* 27 (1993), 111–20.

——, 'The pulse in German folksong: a statistical investigation', *Musikometrika* 5 (1993), 69–89.

Pont, Graham, 'Geography and Human Song'. *New Scientist* 125 (20 Jan. 1990), 38–41.

Riddell, Alistair, ed., *NMA* 6 (Melbourne: NMA Publications, 1988). Issue on recent developments in music technology in Australia.

Stainsby, Thomas, et al., eds, *Proceedings of the ACMA 1995 Conference.* Melbourne: ACMA, 1995.

Synaesthetica '94: Symposium on Computer Animation and Computer Music. Proceedings 1–3 July 1994.

NIGEL NETTHEIM

Concert Halls and Venues. The earliest public concerts in Australia were given in hotels at Hobart and Sydney, then in theatres, which were built in considerable number from the opening of the Royal Victoria Theatre (1838), Sydney, and the Theatre Royal (1841) and the Queen's (1845), Melbourne. These were gracefully decorated, tiered venues of substantial proportions, the Royal Victoria holding 1800 people and the Queen's over 800; many of the later theatres had the rich acoustics which come from an abundance of ornate pillars, plasterwork, statues and scrollwork.

In the 1850s concerts on the goldfields were at first given in makeshift tent auditoriums, but in many regional towns Schools of Arts and Mechanics' Institutes quickly appeared, with small, flat-floored assembly rooms suited to soirées or chamber music. Band concerts were popular in city parks and gardens from the 1860s, with most towns of any size having band rotundas by the 1880s. With the growth of choral societies as well as civic functions, town halls appeared in many cities, notably Hobart (1864), Adelaide (1866), Melbourne (rebuilt 1870), Perth (1870), and Sydney (1889); these were oblong, flat-floored halls, with a balcony and at one end a raised platform to which in many cases a large pipe organ was soon added. Very large buildings were created for the intercolonial and international exhibitions and their massed choral and orchestral performances, such as the Garden Palace, Sydney (1879) and the Exhibition Buildings, Melbourne (1888); these featured vast, oblong halls of long reverberation time, with side balconies and on the platform steep-tiered choir stalls below an ornate pipe organ.

With the growing popularity of music hall and variety, recital halls appeared such as the Academy of Music, Sydney (1884, later renamed the Alhambra) which seated 600, and the Sydney Music Hall (1895). The opening of the conservatoriums brought more long-lasting recital halls of medium capacity, flat floors and estimable acoustics: Elder Hall (1900) in Adelaide, Melba Hall (1909) in Melbourne and the NSW Conservatorium Hall (1915, later renamed Verbrugghen Hall) in Sydney. The Tait management built the fine three-tiered Auditorium (1913) in Melbourne for its celebrity recitals.

The ABC orchestral concerts began in 1934 in town halls and university auditoriums, but once the orchestras were securely established, by 1950, plans were made for orchestral concert venues. With a major gift from retailer Sidney Myer, the Myer Music Bowl was opened in 1959 to serve the massed outdoor symphony concerts that had thrived in Melbourne since the 1930s; its striking, canopy-like acoustic shell projects the sound across an amphitheatre capable of holding over 20 000. But most of the other orchestral concert venue schemes required public fund-raising that delayed their completion for decades, and it was not until 1973 that the first were to open: the Sydney Opera House, the Adelaide Festival Centre, and Perth Concert Hall. These were followed by the Canberra School of Music Auditorium (1977, later renamed Llewellyn Hall), the Melbourne Concert Hall (1982), the Queensland Performing Arts Centre, Brisbane (1984), and the Darwin Performing Arts Centre (1986). These are all venues of modern tiered design with capacities of over 2000, elaborate amenities, in most cases excellent pipe organs, and various systems of moveable panels, discs, or drapes designed to meet the increased demands of changeable acoustics for period instruments, orchestral repertoire or contemporary ensembles.

The growth of the Arts Council movement was followed by the building of regional civic centres across the country, ranging from the multi-purpose civic halls at Wagga Wagga (1963), Broken Hill (1970) and Albury

(1973) to the spectacular Araluen Arts Centre, Alice Springs (1984). Educational institutions have also increasingly built superior concert halls: a remarkable example of an acoustically tunable small hall is the Callaway Music Auditorium (1975) at the University of Western Australia, and the Concert Hall at the Newcastle Conservatorium (1988) also boasts admirable acoustic architecture.

FURTHER REFERENCE
Noel Ancell, 'The Top Ten Performing Venues', *Sing Out* 13/2 (July 1996), 24–6.

Conductors
1. Symphony Orchestras. 2. Chamber Orchestras. 3. Opera Companies.

The role of the conductor is the most glamorous of all in the musical world; the interpretation of the music being performed is his sole responsibility. Most of the great conductors since the 19th century have been associated for long periods with particular orchestras which achieved exceptional levels of excellence under their direction. The history of conductors and conducting in Australia is essentially bound up with the history of Australian opera companies, choral societies and predominantly symphony orchestras. Almost all the great European orchestras today have been the result of years under one eminent conductor, their standards continuing long afterwards. Australian orchestras have not been so fortunate, their conductors being mostly short-term visitors from Europe, who often have two or three simultaneous appointments and devote a good part of the year to guest-conducting.

Some distinguished conductors visited Australia from colonial times, beginning with Sir Frederick Cowen, a noted British conductor brought out for the Melbourne International Exhibition in 1878. Sir Hamilton Harty, who had been conductor of the Hallé Orchestra at Manchester, made a profound impact when he came in 1934, and after this the ABC began to engage overseas conductors regularly to perform with its orchestras in the capital cities. The first of these were Sir Malcolm Sargent (1936), George Szell (1937 and 1939), Georg Schnéevoigt (1940) and Sir Thomas Beecham (1940). In 1943, during World War II, Eugene Ormandy made a memorable tour of Australia. In the meantime, Australian-born Sir Bernard ★Heinze, who was Ormond professor of music at Melbourne University from 1925 to 1956, was conductor of the Melbourne Symphony Orchestra (from 1933 to 1956); he was appointed conductor-in-chief by the ABC during World War II, and in these and subsequent years contributed much to musical life in Australia, outshining local conductors such as Percy ★Code, Clive ★Douglas and Joseph ★Post, who were also active.

1. Symphony Orchestras. (i) Sydney   In Sydney the pioneer was the Belgian Henri ★Verbrugghen who was the first director of the NSW Conservatorium of Music, and was conductor of the NSW State Orchestra from 1919 to 1922, where he made a profound impression. He was succeeded by W. Arundel ★Orchard (from 1923 to 1933), who was conductor of the original Sydney Symphony Orchestra in 1909.

After World War II, the ABC initiated the formation of professional symphony orchestras in the capital cities of Australia, negotiating funding agreements with the civic authorities and the state governments. The first to be formed was the Sydney Symphony Orchestra, of which Sir Eugene ★Goossens was musical director from 1947 to 1956; his influence was very significant in raising performance standards and in introducing audiences to a comprehensive international repertoire. After Goossens the Sydney Symphony was led by visitors such as Nicolai Malko, Dean Dixon, Moshe Atzmon, Willem van ★Otterloo and Louis Frémaux; the first Australian conductor of the orchestra was Sir Charles ★Mackerras (from 1982 to 1985); later the Tasmanian-born Stuart ★Challender led the orchestra with distinction from 1987 until his death in 1991. Challender had also served as conductor with the Australian Opera. An Australian conductor who has followed an international career as a conductor of opera is Richard ★Bonynge, who was director of the Australian Opera from 1976 to 1984. The principal conductor of the Sydney Symphony since 1994 is the Dutchman Edo de Waart.

(ii) Melbourne.   The pioneer in Melbourne was the first Ormond professor at the University of Melbourne, G.W.L. ★Marshall-Hall, who conducted subscription orchestral concerts from 1891 to 1912. His influence was not matched until Heinze began his university concerts in 1927; he was conductor of the Melbourne Symphony Orchestra from 1933. Once the ABC formed a full-time orchestra in 1950–51, Alceo Galliera was appointed principal conductor, to be followed by Juan José Castro (from 1951 to 1952), Walter Susskind (from 1953 to 1955), Kurt Woess (from 1956 to 1959) and Georges Tzipine (from 1961 to 1964). Later Willem van Otterloo was conductor (from 1967 to 1973), assuming the conductorship of the Sydney Symphony from 1973 until 1978. Hiroyuki ★Iwaki has been the longest-serving principal conductor of the Melbourne Symphony, being appointed in 1974.

(iii) Other Cities.   The conductors of the symphony orchestras in the other capital cities of Australia, which are all under the administration of the ABC, have included John Farnsworth ★Hall (Queensland Symphony 1947–54 and West Australian Symphony 1955–65), Rudolf ★Pekarek (West Australian Symphony 1949–54 and Queensland Symphony 1954–67), Henry ★Krips (Adelaide Symphony 1949–72), Muirson Bourne (Tasmanian Symphony 1942–62), Vanco Cavdarski (Tasmanian Symphony 1973–77 and Queensland Symphony 1978–81), Thomas Mayer (West Australian Symphony 1965–71),

David ★Measham (West Australian Symphony 1973–81), Thomas Matthews (Tasmanian Symphony 1962–68), Patrick ★Thomas (Queensland Symphony 1973–78) and Barry Tuckwell (Tasmanian Symphony 1981–83). To these must be added John ★Hopkins, the musical director of the ABC from 1963 to 1973, who led many concerts throughout Australia, and was associate conductor to Dean Dixon when the Sydney Symphony toured England in 1965. The Hungarian-born Tibor ★Paul was active with many of the ABC's orchestras until his death in 1973; Patrick Thomas has also been the ABC's conductor-in-residence. Some Australian composers have conducted the local orchestras, among them Richard ★Mills.

The ABC has continued to engage guest conductors who have performed with the various orchestras during their tours of Australia. Among those in the immediate postwar decades were Walter Susskind, Paul Kletzki, Rafael Kubelik, Otto Klemperer, Sir Malcolm Sargent, Jean Martinon, André Cluytens, Sir John Barbirolli, Igor Markevitch, Fernando Previtali, Hans Schmidt-Isserstedt, Enrique Jorda, Josef Krips, Efrem Kurtz, Constantin Silvestri, Karel Ancerl and Lorin Maazel. The visits of Otto Klemperer were particularly notable, especially his performances of symphonies by Bruckner and Mahler. But as time went on the most important conductors of the day became too expensive and were reluctant to contract for prolonged tours of Australia, and Australian audiences have consequently been deprived of the opportunity of hearing these great artists unless they travel abroad. Nonetheless, many distinguished overseas musicians have supplemented the regular principal conductors of the Australian orchestras and have added to the variety and interest of local musical activities. Those who have been engaged by the ABC for guest appearances with the Sydney Symphony and other ABC orchestras in recent seasons include Eduardo Mata, Stanislaw Skrowaczewski, Hugh Wolff, Claus Peter Flor, Adam Fischer, Gilbert Vaga, Vladimir Verbitsky, Vernon Handley, Hans Vonk, Mark Elder, Graham Abbott, En Shao, Peter Jablonski, Ion Marin, Jiri Kout, Bruno Weil, Gilbert Varga, Stefan Sanderling, John Nelson, Paul Daniel, Mariss Jansons and Lawrence Foster. At the same time some of the world's leading orchestras and their conductors have visited Australia for short tours: among them have been the Chicago Symphony with Sir Georg Solti, the Czech Philharmonic with Karel Ancerl, the Boston Symphony with Charles Munch, the Cleveland Orchestra with Lorin Maazel and Erich Leinsdorf, the New York Philharmonic with Leonard Bernstein, the USSR State Symphony with Yevgeny Svetlanov, the Royal Philharmonic with Okko Kamu and the London Philharmonic with Sir Malcolm Sargent.

2. Chamber Orchestras.   A chamber orchestra drawn from the Sydney Symphony Orchestra, under the baton of Joseph Post, performed concerts in Sydney in the 1950s. Several chamber orchestras are now giving regular concert series; the main one, the Australian Chamber Orchestra, whose leader is Richard Tognetti, occasionally engages guest conductors, such as Stephen Kovacevich and Richard Hickox.

3. Opera Companies.   The Elizabethan Theatre Trust Opera Co. was founded in 1954, and Joseph Post was its distinguished musical director until 1958. Many conductors have performed with its successor, the Australian Opera, starting with Karl *Rankl who became musical director in 1958. Others have included Georg *Tintner, Charles Rosen, Bonynge, Challender, Sir Charles *Mackerras, Carlo Felice*Cillario, Myer *Fredman (now musical director of the State Opera of South Australia), Edward Downes (who led the first performance at the opening of the Sydney Opera House of Prokofiev's *War and Peace* in 1973), Mark Elder, David Stanhope, Christopher Hogwood, Dobbs Franks, Marco Guidarini, Zdenek Kosler, John Fiore, Richard *Gill, Richard Hickox, Graeme Jenkins, Vladimir Kamirski, Jorge Mester, Patrick Summers, Tom Woods, Roderick Brydon, Michael Collins, Christopher Lyndon Gee, David Porcelijn, Julian Smith, David Agler, Julia de Plater, György Fischer, Johannes Fritsch, Junichi Hirokami, Carlo Rizzi, Heinz Wallberg, and Richard *Divall (founding musical director of the Victoria State Opera). John Lanchbery, conductor of the Royal Ballet, Covent Garden, also has been principal conductor of the Australian Ballet.

Female conductors so far have made little impact on the Australian scene, although Australian orchestras have always included many female instrumentalists. One, Simone *Young, has made a distinct impression in European opera houses, and first appeared with the Australian Opera in the 1995 season.

See also entries under individual conductors.

FURTHER REFERENCE
Many local and visiting conductors with Australian orchestras have been recorded on CD with the ABC Classics label. Two notable examples are Beethoven's *Missa Solemnis* (Sydney Symphony et al. under Sir Charles Mackerras) and Mahler's Symphony No. 2 (Sydney Symphony et al. under Stuart Challender). Others are Omri Hadari, John Hopkins, Jorg Mester, Vernon Handley, Geoffrey Simon, David Measham, Diego Masson, Albert Rosen, Werner Andreas Albert, Richard Mills, Richard Bonynge, Geoffrey Lancaster, Dobbs Franks, Shalom Ronly-Riklis, Hiroyuki Iwaki, Nicolas Braithwaite, Vladimir Verbitsky, and Patrick Thomas.

Two CDs in particular record the first 60 years of the Melbourne and Sydney Symphony Orchestras (ABC 438 895 and ABC 438 896 respectively), with excerpts from performances led by Ormandy, Heinze, Goossens, Klemperer, Otterloo, Sargent, Dommett, Iwaki and Frémaux. In his years with the Sydney Symphony, Goossens also made a series of LP recordings; one of the most substantial contributions with an Australian symphony orchestra in the recording studio on LP was an exemplary series of most of the Beethoven symphonies, and some

other major works, by Otterloo and the Sydney Symphony. See also *HomesC*; Charles Buttrose, *Playing for Australia* (Melbourne: Macmillan, 1982); John Cargher, *Opera and Ballet in Australia* (Sydney: Cassell, 1977).   J.L. HOLMES

Confessions to My Dogs.   Song cycle by Moya *Henderson. Recorded 1982 (Oz Music OZM 1003).

Conservatoriums.   Unlike Europe, where they have usually been independent, the first two schools specialising in practical musical training in Australia were established within universities and offered BMus degrees from the outset, the University of Melbourne Conservatorium (founded 1895) and the Elder Conservatorium at the University of Adelaide (1897). Most others were at first independent, funded directly by their state governments to offer practical diplomas, and managed without university affiliations until reforms to government funding from 1987 forced them into mergers. The largest of these, all publicly funded, are the University of Sydney Conservatorium (formerly NSW State Conservatorium), Sydney (1915), the Queensland Conservatorium (Griffith University, Brisbane) (1956), the Tasmanian Conservatorium (University of Tasmania) (1964), the WA Conservatorium (Edith Cowan University, Perth) (1985), the School of Music, Victorian College of the Arts (University of Melbourne) (1974) and the School of Music, Canberra Institute of the Arts (Australian National University) (1965).

Among the smaller schools, the Melba Memorial Conservatorium, Melbourne (Victorian University of Technology) (1895) has a long tradition of vocal excellence, the Newcastle Conservatorium (Newcastle Univ.) (1952) has one of the finest medium-sized auditoriums in Australia, and Wollongong Conservatorium (1972), the Central Queensland Conservatorium, Mackay (1983), the Music School, University of the Northern Territory, and the Mitchell Conservatorium, Bathurst (Charles Sturt Univ.) (1978) are developing to serve their regional areas. Several others have their origins as regional community music centres, notably the Central Coast Conservatorium, Gosford (1982), the Tamworth Regional Conservatorium (1984), and the Riverina Music Centre, Wagga Wagga (1981). There are also an increasing number of privately owned music schools offering degrees and diplomas, all still on a relatively small scale, such as the Australian International Conservatorium of Music, Sydney, and the Australian Institute of Music, Sydney. See also *University Choirs and Choral Societies*; *Music Education*.

Contemporary music.   (1) In Europe and the USA the term applies to current classical compositions which break new ground rather than adhering to established conventions or schools, or works of the recent past which were revolutionary in their time. See *Composition in Australia*, *Experimental Music*. (2) In Australia a parliamentary report on the music industry, the Leo McLeay Report (1987), applied the term generally to rock music, and this usage has gained widespread currency, causing considerable confusion. See *Popular Music* §2.

Contes Héraldiques. Ballet by Dorian *Le Gallienne (1947), choreography by Laurel Martyn. Telling the story of a sleeping princess, it was first performed by the Victorian Ballet Guild in 1947 and recorded by the Victorian Symphony Orchestra under Clive Douglas (1961, ABC 2XS 1343).

Conway, Deborah (*b* Melbourne), rock singer. She studied arts at the University of Melbourne, supporting herself by modelling work, and sang in the Benders (1980–81). Moving to Sydney, she formed Do Re Mi (1982). In 1988 she was voted *Rolling Stone* (Aust.) best female singer and went to London to a recording deal with Virgin records, recording a solo album that was not released. She played Juno in Peter Greenaway's film *Prospero's Books* (1990), singing music by Michael Nyman. Returning to Melbourne and signing with Mushroom Records, she formed Deborah Conway and the Mothers of Pearl in 1991, her debut album *String of Pearls* reaching No. 21 in the charts. Her session work includes the soundtrack *Sweet and Sour* and work with Peter Townsend. A country-tinged rock artist with vibrant stage presence, she won the ARIA best female performer in 1992.

FURTHER REFERENCE
Recordings include *String of Pearls* (1991, Mushroom D30601); *Today I Am A Daisy* (1994 Mushroom D11719). For discography see *SpencerA*. See also *SpencerW*; *Bulletin* 3 Dec. 1991; *Age* 7 Nov. 1993.

Conway, Lee (*b* Poland, 10 Mar. 1944), country music singer-songwriter. After playing in Adelaide bands as a teenager, he managed the Laurie Allen Revue (1967–69), then was supporting act on the Australian tours of Jerry Lee Lewis (1970), Slim Whitman (1971), Wayne Jennings, Tom T. Hall, Conway Twitty, Loretta Lynn and others. He toured with his own show, appearing at the Royal Command Performance before Elizabeth II at Brisbane in 1982. He compered a television show, *Conway Country*, in the early 1980s, settling at the Gold Coast, Qld, to write advertising jingles with his own music production company. An internationalist in repertoire, he sings Australian country and American mainstream songs with a characteristic growl.

FURTHER REFERENCE
Recordings for EMI include *Lee Conway* (1975), *Conway Country* (1982) and *Lay A Country Song On Me* (1993, EMI 7017862). See also *LattaA*, 180; *SmithB*, 39.

Conyngham, Barry Ernest (*b* Sydney, 27 Aug. 1944), composer. Conyngham learnt piano as a child and was passionately interested in avant-garde jazz, but studied law before deciding to become a composer after

hearing a performance of the Bartók string quartets in 1965. He studied with Peter Sculthorpe at the University of Sydney (1965–69), and along with other Sculthorpe students he attracted attention early, benefiting from the arts boom of the time. His first mature work, *Farben*, premiered at the 1968 Adelaide Festival and was followed by several commissioned works including *Crisis: thoughts in a city* (1969), *Five Windows* (1969) and a sound-track, *Horizon*, for the Australian pavilion at Expo '70 in Osaka. He was lecturer and tutor, University of Sydney and NIDA (1968–70).

Conyngham spent a crucial six months in Japan with Toru Takemitsu (1970), meeting many important avant-garde composers. He was later senior tutor, University of Western Australia (1971), studied at the University of California San Diego (1972–73), was visiting Harkness fellow, Princeton (1973–74) and composer-in-residence, University of Aix-Marseille (1975). He subsequently built a high-profile career in Australia as a composer and university teacher. He was lecturer (later reader) at the University of Melbourne (1974–90), taking a DMus there, and with Rex Harris established the university's Computer Music Research Project (1977); as a Fulbright Senior Fellow, Conyngham was visiting scholar, University of Minnesota, and visiting fellow, Penn State University (1982). He has been involved in arts organisations as a member, Victorian Ministry of Arts Board (1982–85), member (1982–85) and chair (1985–87), Australia Council Music Board, and Deputy Chair, Australian Opera Board since 1994. He became professor, University of Wollongong (1990–94) and has been vice-chancellor, Southern Cross University, since 1994.

Influenced by Sculthorpe, Conyngham developed an aesthetic of 'Australian-ness', first seen in *Crisis* and reflected in dramatic subjects such as convicts (*Apology of Bony Anderson*, 1974–77), bushrangers (*Ned*, 1972–75/76), and explorers (*Edward John Eyre*, 1969–71/73), *Fly*, 1982–84), in landscape imagery (*Vast*, 1987; *Waterways*, 1989–90/91; *Monuments*), in literary borrowings (*Voss*), and even musical material; *Waltzing Matilda* is quoted in *Imaginary Letters*, *Southern Cross* (1981) and *Matilda* (1987–88). This in part accounts for a number of important official commissions including *Fly* (opening of Victorian State Theatre), *Antipodes* (Victorian Sesquicentenary), *Southern Cross* and *Decades* (50th and 60th anniversaries of ABC), and *Matilda* and *Vast* (Bicentenary). The 1970s saw his especial interest in Japanese influences in *Ice Carving* (1970) *Water … Footsteps … Time* (1970–71), *Bashō* (1980), and in dramatic works and electronic media.

From his most important influences, Sculthorpe and Takemitsu, Conyngham derived an 'otherness' from Western tradition, an orchestral style dependent on texture, timbre and 'space', and an interest in extra-musical stimuli. His most characteristic works are dramatic, orchestral and concertos. Since about 1981 he has written increasingly melodic, even contrapuntal, textures, often comprised of contrasting blocks of layered ostinati.

WORKS (Selective)

(Mss held by composer)

Principal publishers: Universal, Australian Music Centre.

Orchestral   *Crisis: Thoughts in a City* (c.1975), *Five Windows* (c.1976), *Water…Footsteps…Time* (c.1977), *Six I & II* (1971, 1971), *Sky* (1981), *Horizons* (c.1981), *Mirages* (1982), *Recurrences* (c.1986), *Decades* (ms, 1991–92).

Concertos   *Ice Carving*, vn, orchestra (c.1977), *Shadows of Nōh*, db, orch (1979), *Southern Cross*, vn, pf, orch (c.1992), Cello Concerto (1990), *Waterways*, va, orch (1990), *Cloudlines I & II*, hp, orch (1990), *Monuments*, kbd, orch (ms, 1988–89).

Chamber   Large output including: *Five*, fl, cl, ob, bn, hn (1971), *Three*, perc, str qrt (c.1977), *Snowflake*, kbd (1980), *Journeys*, cl, tape (1981), *Streams*, fl, va, hp (1988), *Voicings*, fl, trbn, perc, pf, tape (1988), String Quartet (c.1984).

Electronic   Significant output in 1970s incl. *Horizon* (ms, 1970), *Through Clouds: solitude* (ms, 1974), *To be alone* (ms, 1978).

Dramatic   *Edward John Eyre*, music-theatre (1973, 1, Meredith Oakes), 1 May 1971, Sydney, *The Apology of Bony Anderson*, music-theatre (1977, 1 Murray Copland), 1 Sept. 1978, Melbourne, *Fly*, opera (1984, 2, Murray Copland), 25 Aug. 1984, Melbourne, *The Oath of Bad Brown Bill*, children's opera (1985, 2, Murray Copland and Stephen Axelson), 6 Jan 1986, Melbourne, *Bennelong*, puppet opera (1987, 1, Murray Copland), 7 Oct. 1988, Newcastle, *Vast*, ballet (1987, 4), 4 Mar. 1988, Melbourne; several film scores; incidental music.

Choral   *Farben* (ms, 1968), *Imaginary Letters* (c.1981), *Antipodes* (1984–85), *Matilda* (ms, 1987–88).

Vocal   *Bashō* (1984, Matsuo Bashō), *Voss* (1972, no text).

FURTHER REFERENCE

Recordings include *Edward John Eyre*, Univ. NSW Ensemble (EMI OASD 7582), *Ice Carving*, Wilfred Lehmann, vn *Southern Cross*, Wanda Wilkomirska, vn, Roger Woodward, pf (EMI OASD 27 0403), *Fly*, Victoria State Opera (Move MD 3076), *Vast*, Australian Youth Orchestra, cond. John Hopkins (ABC 432 528–2), *Southern Cross*, *Monuments*, Robert Davidovici, vn, kbd Tamás Ungár, kbd (Cala CACD 1008). See also *Callaway.A*; Andrew Ford, *Composer to Composer* (Sydney: Allen & Unwin, 1994), 197–202; *Murdoch.A*; Patricia Shaw, Imagery and music in the string concertos of Barry Conyngham, MMus, Univ. Melbourne, 1993; Graeme Skinner, 'Barry Conyngham', *APRAJ* 3/1 (1983), 11–14.

PATRICIA SHAW

Cooee.   Aboriginal long-distance call (cf. the English *Holla!*), possibly an imitation of phonetically similar bird-calls, such as the eastern whipbird (*Psophodes olivaceus*) and koel (*Eudynamys scolopacea*). It was first recorded by Péron in 1811. Isaac ★Nathan's *Koo-ee* arrangements (1842–49), which include melodic and regional variants, inaugurated a distinctive Anglo-Australian musical genre (see Spagnoletti, 1860) and literary-poetic mode. The fashion extended to many other arts and manufactures, remaining popular until World War II as an expression of national sentiment and cultural identity. *Cooee* songs were sung by volunteers marching to enlist for World War I and *Cooee* competitions are still held annually in NSW.

FURTHER REFERENCE

François Péron, *Voyage de decouvertes aux terres australes. Historique, atlas par MM. Lesueur et Petit* (Paris: Arthus Bertrand, 1811); I. Nathan, *Koorinda Braia* (Sydney: I. Nathan, 1842); idem, *The Southern Euphrosyne* (Sydney: I. Nathan, [1849]); E. Spagnoletti, *Cooey! An Australian Song* (Sydney: John Davis, [1860]). See also G. Pont, *Muse Unruly: The Secret Life of Isaac Nathan* (Sydney: State Library of NSW, 1997).

GRAHAM PONT

Cook, Colin   (*b* Dhaka, Bangladesh), pop singer-songwriter. After learning guitar, clarinet and saxophone he played with the Sapphires (1958) and the ★Thunderbirds (from 1959). He went solo in 1961, producing 21 singles in the coming years. Only two became hits, *It's Up To You* (1962) and *Heart* (1964), which reached No. 8 in the charts. He appeared on TV *Bandstand* and as supporting act to Fabian and other touring groups. His debut album was *Here's Colin Cook* (1964). From the late 1960s he lived in England, writing jingles, working in *Hair* and *Jesus Christ Superstar* (1974–77), and forming Rainer Brothers (1979) and Jealous Guys (1981). He returned to Australia in 1982, and played with Ram Band (1991–92).

FURTHER REFERENCE

Recordings include *It's Up To You* (1962, W&G S1550) and *Heart* (1964 W&G S1809); albums *Here's Colin Cook* (1964, W&G WGB 2573). For discography, see *Spencer.A*. See also *McGrath.A*; *Spencer.W*.

Cook, Jim (James Alfred)   (*b* Perth, 31 Dec. 1943), jazz reed player. He began saxophone in the early 1950s, later adding other reeds, and took dance work with Will Upson (piano), then joined Keith Stirling and Bill Clowes (piano) at the progressive jazz venues, Hole In The Wall and The Shiralee. In the UK 1965–66, he returned to Perth and was active in nightclub work, resuming jazz activity from the mid 70s with the fusion group Collage, Uwe Stengel's Manteca, and the Will Upson Big Band. He continues to be active in session work, but also maintains jazz activity as a performer and educator.

FURTHER REFERENCE

Recordings include *Will Upson Big Band* (1975, Festival L-25183); and *A Tribute to the Embassy Ballroom*, Will Upson Big Band (1982, Embassy Promotions EP1). See also *Oxford.J*.

BRUCE JOHNSON

Cook, Ray   (*b* Adelaide), conductor, composer. Musical director for more than 20 musicals, including his own *Side by Side With Sondheim*. His compositions are chiefly for dance or theatre, including several commissions for Australian Dance Theatre. His recordings include the original

London casts in Sondheim's *A Little Night Music* (1975, RCA) and Loewe's *Gigi* (1985 First Night Records).

Cooke, Max(well) Joseph Lorimer (*b* 14 Feb. 1924), pianist, teacher. After studying piano with Roy ★Shepherd and languages at the University of Melbourne Conservatorium, Max Cook went to Paris in 1949, studying with Alfred Cortot. He returned to Australia in 1951 and taught at the University of Melbourne Conservatorium, appearing as a solo performer and accompanist in ABC concerts. A pioneer of the harpsichord revival in Australia, he also appeared as a harpsichordist on radio and in concert in the 1970s. He was guest professor at the Hochschule für Musik, Freiburg (1968) and at Bremen (1972–73) and dean of the Faculty of Music, University of Melbourne (1975–81). He broadcast on 3AW for 10 years and currently has a weekly radio program on 3MBS. After leading several groups exploring teaching methods for gifted young pianists, he formed the Team of Pianists with nine of his most gifted students in 1983, which tours widely in Victoria, presenting workshops and lecture recitals for young pianists; with them he has toured abroad and made five recordings. He was president of the Victorian Music Teachers' Association (1972–73), president of ASME (1975–77), and founding president of the Australian Musicians' Guild. Deeply immersed in advancing the cause of piano pedagogy, he has written many articles on performance training as well as five books for piano teaching, notably *Tone Touch and Technique* (Melbourne: Allans Music, 1964) and *Bach at the Piano* (Melbourne: Allans Music, 1966). He is currently artist-in-residence and adjunct professor at Monash University.

FURTHER REFERENCE
Recordings as a pianist include Sonatas of Mozart and Handel with Leonard Dommett, vn (W&G, BS 5175); as a harpsichordist works of D. Banks, F. Werder and R. Trumble, with L. Dommett, vn, C. Wojtowicz, vc (1975, ABC 1010); with Team of Pianists *Mozart at Melbourne* (1991, Move MCD 046); and *Peter Sculthorpe Piano Music* (1990, Move MD 3031). His articles include 'The Role of Examinations in Practical Music', part I *AJME* 14 (Apr. 1974), 57–9; part II *AJME* 16 (Apr. 1975), 23–6; and part III *AJME* 18 (Apr. 1976), 32–42; and 'Education of the Professional Musician', *International Journal of Music Education* 17 (1991), 58–9. See also *Age* 4 Dec. 1989; *ADMR*; *WWA* (1996);

Cool Jazz. A term used in the late 1940s to contrast the styles of such players as Miles Davis, the Modern Jazz Quartet, or Lester Young from the 'hot' bebop style of the same period; it was also applied to Gerry Mulligan and his circle on the west coast in the early 1950s. Subtle tone colours, often without vibrato, and group improvisation of understated lines were set against soft drumming (or did without drumming altogether). Its following in Australia came later, with such bands as the US-based ★Australian Jazz Quartet (toured Australia in 1958) and the Australian All Stars from 1962. See *Jazz*.

Coombs, H(erbert) C(ole) ('Nugget') (*b* Kalamunda, WA, 24 Feb. 1906), economist, public figure. A graduate of the University of Western Australia and the London School of Economics, he had a long career with the Commonwealth public service, from Director of Rationing in wartime (1942) and Postwar Reconstruction from 1943 to governor of the Commonwealth Bank from 1949 and of the Reserve Bank of Australia 1960–68. A prominent supporter of the arts, particularly music, he was a board member from 1954 and chairman 1960–68 of the ★Australian Elizabethan Theatre Trust, shepherding the company through its difficult early years before the reorganisation of its Opera Co. as the Australian Opera. His influence helped cement federal and state government support for the company, although he drew some criticism for his board's many changes of artistic policy and consequent mixed artistic results achieved in these years. He was chairman of the Australian Council for the Arts 1968–74, and a significant influence on the shaping of its successor, the Australia Council. He has been awarded three honorary doctorates.

FURTHER REFERENCE
His autobiography is *Trial Balance* (Melbourne: Macmillan, 1981). See also *MonashB*; *ParsonsC*.

Coppin, George (*b* Steyning, Sussex, England, 8 Apr. 1819; *d* Sorrento, 14 Mar. 1906), theatrical entrepreneur. After working as a comic actor in London, he came to Australia in 1843, presenting theatrical seasons at Sydney, Launceston, Melbourne (from 1845), Adelaide (1846), and Geelong. He then settled at Melbourne where he opened a succession of theatres, entered the Victorian Parliament, and from 1856 imported an array of actors, singers and entertainments, including presenting concerts by internationally renowned sopranos Anna Bishop and Catherine Hayes, and the first opera season of W.S. ★Lyster's company in 1861. In 1874 he presented the young American actor J.C. ★Williamson, who by the 1880s had supplanted him as the colony's major theatrical entrepreneur, but he continued to present pantomime and melodrama until shortly before his death. Making and losing a fortune several times, he was an important pioneer of Australian theatrical life.

FURTHER REFERENCE
IrvinD; *MackenzieS*, 259; Sally O'Neill, *ADB*, 3; Alec Bagot, *Coppin the Great* (Melbourne: MUP, 1965).

Copyright and Performing Rights.
1. Extent of Protection. 2. Establishing Copyright.
3. Defining a Breach of Copyright. 4. Performing Rights.
5. Conclusion

Copyright in a musical work is a species of property, and both the publication of a work and its performance can be controlled by the copyright owner. Copyright is the sole right to produce or reproduce in any material form an original literary, dramatic or musical work. A tarter definition is that of Thomas Macaulay, referring to writers: 'A tax on readers for the purpose of giving bounty to writers.' Copyright was first recognised in 1709, although not immediately in connection with music; it was not until 1842 that copyright was extended to music, and even after that date music suffered greatly from international piracy. Largely at the instigation of Richard Strauss, the Berne Convention (1886) was passed and immediately adopted throughout the British Empire, giving international protection to intellectual property. In Australia, the law is now governed by the *Copyright Act 1968*.

1. Extent of Protection.

Copyright protects composers, but not performing artists. Even a highly original solo by a jazz musician is not the subject of copyright; it may, however, qualify for protection if it is recorded on disc, tape, paper or other device on which sounds are embodied. Nor does copyright protect ideas, being only a right in artistic work which finds expression in a material form. The musical quality of the work is a matter of indifference to the law: a jingle is as much entitled to protection as a symphony.

The term 'musical work' is not defined in the 1968 Act, but previous legislation (1905) defined it as 'any combination of melody and harmony or either of them, printed, reduced to writing or otherwise graphically produced or reproduced'. While this definition may be helpful in delineating the scope of the law's protection, it raises problems in particular instances. Surely Larry Sitsky's sonata for solo flute is protected although it contains no harmony, and like much music of contemporary composers has a line not easily defined as melody. For works such as *musique concrète* or aleatoric music, one Australian legal scholar James Lahore has suggested that a more apt definition of 'musical work' would be 'the organisation or combination of sounds as to pitch, duration, intensity and rhythm'; but whether notation is always required remains a moot point. Certainly the work must be 'fixed' in some way.

To be protected a work must be original; that is to say, it must emanate from the composer's unaided skill and labour. For a transcription or arrangement, it would depend on the skill involved in transcribing. In one English case, the piano arrangement of an opera was held to be an independent work of art, entitling the arranger to copyright protection; in another case, the piano arrangement of incidental music to a play was also entitled to protection. In these cases, both the original work and the transcriptions enjoy copyright protection. An anthology of music, such as Radic's *Treasury of Favourite Australian Songs*, is subject to copyright protection for its compilation, for it has required skill in selection.

Folk music, being part of an oral culture, does not enjoy protection. Nevertheless, if it is reduced to notation (such as in George Dreyfus's *Theme from 'Rush'*) it will enjoy separate protection. A thorny question arises, however, where folk-songs are collected by a sound recordist. There seems to be doubt whether there would be sufficient independent skill involved in this exercise to render it a 'musical work'. In opera both the composer and the lyricist have copyright; the same is usually true of a song, though sometimes it is impossible to separate the instrumental backing of a song from its vocal part. In such a case there would be co-ownership of the copyright.

Copyright also applies to mechanical reproduction, sound recordings being specifically made the subject of independent copyright. In this case the copyright vests in the maker of the recording (usually the recording company), whether it be a gramophone record, a perforated roll, a cassette tape, a compact disc, a cartridge, or any other instrument in which sounds are embodied. Copyright dates from the moment the first record was produced, and production of a copy or a master copy will usually suffice to identify this moment. In Australia as elsewhere, there is an organisation that collects fees for mechanical copyright owners, AMCOS.

2. Establishing Copyright.

Copyright does not need to be registered (at least in Australia), and no formality is necessary to protect it, but in order to enjoy protection in Australia, the composer or performer must prove a connecting factor with this country. Either the work must have been published in Australia or the complainant must be an Australian citizen, a habitual resident of Australia or otherwise an Australian protected person. In order to obtain world copyright, the composer or assignee must place © on the score together with the place and date of publication of the work.

A composer must, of nature, be a human person, but an incorporated body, which in law has a separate legal personality from the persons who constitute it, may sue in the case of a sound recording. Copyright may be assigned in writing, and both the composer and his heirs may control publication and performance. Its duration is 50 years after the calendar year in which the composer died.

Breach of copyright is difficult to police. It is possible to breach it innocently as well as deliberately; in either case, damages will be claimable. It may also be possible to seek an injunction preventing a breach of copyright. It is a matter of great difficulty to determine what is and is not the copying of music. Plagiarism is undoubtedly a serious artistic offence, but there are only 12 notes in an octave and the number of permutations of these, though large, is not infinite. Therefore it may easily happen that two composers hit on the same melody or harmony working independently. It is, moreover, possible to breach a copyright by 'subconscious imitation'. In England, such a case actually reached the High Court in 1963, concerning two popular tunes, *In a Little Spanish Town* and *Why*. The melodies of each are printed in the Court Report and they are indeed very similar. The plaintiffs, publishers of *Spanish Town* in 1927, claimed that the composer of *Why* (in 1959) had copied their song. There was some fascinating evidence given by musical experts. In fact the judgment, most unusually, contains notation and some detailed musical terminology. The trial judge found that on the evidence the composer of *Why* had not deliberately copied *Spanish Town*.

This was confirmed on appeal, but the Court of Appeal said that it was possible to have 'unconscious copying'. This may sound like a contradiction, but if a composer has a tune in the back of his mind and reproduces it in substantially the same form, then he is guilty of a breach of copyright. The Court of Appeal decided that there was no unconscious copying in this case because it accepted the evidence that the composer of *Why* had no knowledge of the tune *Spanish Town*. He said he had heard it once when he was a boy and had forgotten it, and this was believed. It must be said that this is an assertion not easy to believe, for *Spanish Town* was a standard tune very frequently played in the 1950s.

3. Defining a Breach of Copyright. In effect, the breach must be substantial to entitle the copyright owner to sue. The law's famous maxim *De minibus non curat lex* (The law does not care about trivial things) applies here. But it is possible to have a partial as well as a total breach: the whole work does not need to be reproduced. Imitation is the sincerest form of flattery, provided it is not blatant, and it is no offence to borrow the chordal or melodic ideas of a master, even without acknowledgment. Similarities of style, phrasing or rhythm are inevitable, if they are common or within the common domain of a musical heritage. Nevertheless, the courts appear to be leaning in favour of protection in cases of doubt. Certainly a note-for-note comparison is not necessary: it may indeed be said that similarity is prima facie evidence of copying.

4. Performing Rights. Since 1911 an important aspect of copyright has been the right of the copyright-holder to regulate public performance. It is possible to obtain fees for granting the right to perform a piece of music, and these rights may be granted only by the composer or his heirs, or by an assignee. Usually, the composer assigns performing rights to his publisher.

Performing rights are even harder to police than copyright. As in many countries, there is a Performing Rights Society in Australia (APRA) which exists to collect fees. In theory, every time a piece is publicly performed the composer (or his assignee) is entitled to a fee, but it is sometimes difficult to decide whether a particular performance is public. A performance has been held to be public even though it takes place in a private club. Nor does an entrance fee need to be charged: a trio playing after-dinner music to guests at a hotel has been held to be giving a public performance. But a rehearsal is not a public performance. Where there is a public performance without permission, the owners of the venue and the organisers will also be liable, on the grounds that they have authorised the performances. Lack of intention is irrelevant.

5. Conclusion. Copyright is a complex area of law, imperfectly policed. It is in effect a species of property, providing protection to the efforts of the skill and labour of artists. In so far as this is an acknowledgment of the artistry of composers and executant musicians—a greatly underrated value in a commercially oriented world—it is to be applauded as an interest worthy of recognition in a civilised community.

FURTHER REFERENCE

For relevant cases, see *GBS Records (Australia) Ltd v Gross* (1969) *Australian Intellectual Property Cases*, 90–627; Francis Day & Hunter Ltd v Bron [1963] Chancery 587; *Australian Performing Rights Association v Canterbury/Bankstown Leagues Club* [1964–65] *NSW Reports* 138; *Performing Rights Society v Hawthorn Hotel* [1933] Chancery 855; and *Australian Performing Rights Society v Miles* [1962] *NSW Reports* 405, a case involving a band at the Dee Why RSL Club in Sydney.   J. NEVILLE TURNER

Coquette, The. Comic operetta in two acts by W. Arundel ★Orchard (1905), libretto by W.J. Curtis and J.I. Hunt. Telling the comic adventures of a suicide club, it was first performed at the Palace Theatre, Sydney, on 28 August 1905. Unpublished.

Corder, Ada Elizabeth (*b* Ararat, Vic., 20 Mar. 1895; *d* Camberwell, Melbourne, 27 Sept. 1987), music educator. At the age of eight she won an under-13 piano championship. Her early musical development was fostered by Sr Mary Agnes, in 1910 she was selected as a solo pianist for a series of concerts in Melbourne with the Australian tenor Walter Kirby, and in 1911 she was awarded an ANA Scholarship and attained her LRSM and LTCL. At 17 she entered the University of Melbourne Conservatorium of Music where she studied piano under Edward ★Goll. In 1930 she took postgraduate study in Berlin and London with Artur Schnabel. As a solo pianist she gave first performances of works by Elgar, Prokofiev and Ravel, and as a teacher she discovered and promoted many young Australians of exceptional talent, among them Stephen ★McIntyre, Geoffrey Saba, Raymond O'Connell and Nancy ★Weir, with whom in 1965 she founded the Australian Musicians Overseas Scholarship. In 1974 she was awarded an MBE for her services to music.

FURTHER REFERENCE

Andrea Lofthouse, *Who's Who of Australian Women* (Sydney: Methuen Australia, 1982); Sr Mary Clare O'Connor, *The Sisters, Faithful Companions of Jesus in Australia* (Melbourne: The Sisters, Faithful Companions of Jesus in Australia, 1982); *Principal Women of the Empire: Australia and New Zealand*, vol. 1 (London: Mitre Press, 1940); Melbourne *Herald* 24 June 1975.

EMMA MATTHEWS

Cordner, William John   (b Dungannon, Tyrone, Ireland, 4 Dec. 1826; d Woolloomooloo, Sydney, 15 June 1870), organist. He was a choirboy at Armagh Cathedral, taking organ lessons with its organist Robert Turle from the age of seven. After years at sea, he arrived in Australia in 1854 and became organist at St Patrick's, Sydney, then at St Mary's Cathedral from 1857, periodically giving organ recitals and conducting or playing in choral concerts. Despite his coarse seaman's manner, he became one of the leading organists in the colony and considerably enhanced the choral standards at the cathedral; he also composed various liturgical settings.

FURTHER REFERENCE
E.J. Lea-Scarlett, *ADB*, 3.

Corroboree (1).   An Australian Aboriginal dance with music, generally one which is performed publicly. The term probably originated in a NSW Aboriginal language, although it now has a wider currency among non-Aboriginal Australians than among Aborigines. The words 'boojery carib-berie' (good dance) appear in John Hunter's *An Historical Journal of Events at Sydney and at Sea, 1787–1792*. Aboriginal words for public singing and dancing vary among different language groups in other parts of Australia, for example *purlapa* (Warlpiri language), *inma* (Pitjantjatjara), *turlku* (Pintupi), *ltarta* (Alyawarra) in the central and western desert; *dyunba* (Wunambal, Worora, Ungarinyin), *nurlu* (Nyigina, Yawuru, Dyugun, Ngumbarl, Dyabirr Dyabirr, Warrwa), *ilma* (Nyul Nyul, Bardi), *maru* (Garadyarri), *dyudyu* (Walmadyarri, Mangarla) in the Kimberleys; *wangga, lirrga* and *gunborrg* in north-western NT; *yoi* (Tiwi) on Bathurst and Melville Islands, NT; *bunggurl* (Yolngu, Burarra, Rembarrnga, Djinang) in north-central and north-eastern Arnhem Land, NT; and *warma* in parts of Cape York, Queensland. These names are sometimes used for particular dances in regions other than those in which they originated, with similar corroborees performed by people hundreds of miles apart, for in some traditions public songs and dances may be traded.

Corroborees are intended for public performance and may be attended by all members of the community. They are usually held after sunset, when large fires are lit for illumination. Even if they frequently have religious connotations, all participants also expect to be entertained. A single corroboree, consisting of a succession of dances, may last for several hours. Each dance is related to a corresponding song performance, and lasts generally for one or two minutes, or less. Only some songs have associated dances, and others are performed unaccompanied by dance movements. The songs and dances of a corroboree are related to each other, both textually and musically, because they belong to the same Dreaming. In some traditions, the same songs and dances may be used in closed rituals which are performed in private and always some distance from the public area.

Styles of singing and dancing in corroborees vary from region to region; in parts of the north there is more freedom of movement and greater opportunity for musical improvisation than in the central and western deserts. Regional variations occur in the size and organisation of the singing and dancing groups: typically, in Arnhem Land singing is performed by a single singer accompanied by a didjeridu player, and dancing is performed by a group of dancers; in central Australia and the western desert singing is usually performed by a group of performers, and dancing is more individualistic. There are also variations in the musical instruments used, the nature of calls made by dancers, and in body decorations and hand-held objects.

The singing in a corroboree is normally led by the senior owner of the songs, who is often also the person who received the corroboree. (Corroborees are often received in dreams, either from spirits of the dead or by spirit familiars. Anyone may receive corroborees, although there is a tendency for receivers to be senior figures in ritual life. Sometimes different parts of a corroboree are received by different individuals over a period of time.) Women participate with men in corroborees to a greater or lesser degree depending on the region. In Arnhem Land, women dance while men sing; in the central and western desert, women sing as well as dance in corroborees. Children are generally allowed greater opportunity to participate in corroboree performance in northern Australian than elsewhere; in central Australia children tend to be more rigidly excluded from serious participation in adult performances. See *Aboriginal Music*.

STEPHEN WILD

Corroboree (2).   Ballet by John ★Antill, choreography by Rex Reid, designed by William Constable, first performed at the Empire Theatre, Sydney by the National Theatre Ballet on 3 July 1950. Although the composer wrote the work with balletic intentions, its first performance in 1946 was as a concert piece. Both the critics and the general public considered the work to be outstanding, and Antill became for a time the musical voice of Australia. With such a reaction it was not long before the Australian ballet enthusiasts pressed choreographers to realise *Corroboree's* theatrical scope. Reid choreographed the ballet with close attention to Antill's detailed scenario. In 1954 Beth Dean choreographed the work anew, and included an array of Aboriginal dance movements. Dean dispensed with Antill's scenario and some of his music and reinterpreted *Corroboree* to illustrate the initiation ceremony of an Aboriginal boy.

FURTHER REFERENCE
Beth Dean and Victor Carell, *Gentle Genius: A Life of John Antill* (Sydney: Akron Press, 1987).   JOEL CROTTY

Cosmic Psychos.   Rock group formed (1985) in Melbourne, originally comprised of Peter Jones (guitar, vocals), Ross Knight (bass, vocals), and Bill Walsh (drums).

The trio began as Spring Plains in 1983, changing their name in 1985. A hard-core thrash band, their stage antics owe something to the Three Stooges, and their power guitar style to Jimi Hendrix.

FURTHER REFERENCE
Recordings include *Down On The Farm* (1985, Mr Spaceman MRSM03); *Cosmic Psychos* (1987, Mr Spaceman MRSM08); *Slave To The Grave* (1991, Rattlesnake RAT 19); and *Palomina Pizza* (1993, Arsloch ARSCH001). See also *SpencerW*.

Costantino, Romola née Enyi   (*b* Sydney, 14 Sept. 1930; *d* Adelaide, Dec. 1988), pianist. After studies with Alexander ★Sverjensky at the NSW State Conservatorium, she went to Italy in 1956, studying at the Academy of St Cecilia, Rome and the Accademia Chigiana, Sienna. Returning to Australia in 1958, she appeared as a soloist and associate artist in ABC concerts, was music critic for the *Sydney Morning Herald* from 1962 and taught at the University of Sydney from 1968. She won a Churchill fellowship in 1971 and gave the first piano recital at the Music Room of the Sydney Opera House in 1973. She was a popular adjudicator and lecturer on music. She joined the staff of the SA College of Advanced Education School of Music, Adelaide and was a busy teacher until her untimely death. She was honoured with the OBE in 1978.

FURTHER REFERENCE
Recordings include two of solo piano works (Cetra MRC-1) and (EMI OASD 7545). See also *ADMR*.

Costello, Gary   (*b* 7 June 1952), jazz bass player. He began electric bass in 1967 and studied acoustic bass in the early 1970s with Marjan Brajsa, with jazz coaching from Murray Wall. Active primarily in contemporary styles from the late 1970s, he joined Allan Browne's Onaje in 1982, also working with saxophonist Ken Schroder, the trombone group McCabe's Bones, and Vince Jones. He has backed numerous touring Australian and international visitors including Mal Waldron, Richie Cole, Bobby Shew, Don Burrows, John Sangster and Kerrie Biddell. He teaches at Victorian College of the Arts and has maintained a lengthy musical association with Paul Grabowsky.

FURTHER REFERENCE
Recordings include *Onaje's Rage*, Onaje (1980, East EAS 080); *Waltz for Stella,* Onaje (1985, Larrikin LRJ174); *Six By Three* (1989, Spiral Scratch 0001); *Ringing The Bell Backwards*, Australian Art Orchestra (1994, Origin OR 008). See also *OxfordJ*; Adrian Jackson, 'Gary Costello', *JA* (Spring 1983), 19, 25.
BRUCE JOHNSON

Coster, Stan   (*b* Casino, NSW, 27 May 1930), country music songwriter. Working in the bush in his early twenties, he began writing songs of his bush experiences in 1956. He sent a folio of 11 songs to Slim ★Dusty in 1964, who at once recorded *By a Fire of Gidgee Coal,* now one of the best-known of all Australian country ballads. This began a long partnership in which Dusty recorded more than 70 of his songs; they were also taken up by Buddy Williams, John Williamson, Rick and Thel and others. In 1979 he recorded the first of his own albums and formed a traditional tent show which has been touring north Australia ever since. One of Australia's greatest traditional country balladeers, he has recorded 11 albums, won two ACMA Golden Guitars, the Tamworth Songwriters' Association Song Maker Award (1982) and in 1990 was honoured in the ACMA Roll of Renown.

FURTHER REFERENCE
Recordings include *My People* (1979, Hadley CASSOLL 509), *Coster Sings Coster* (EMI 7017982), and *This Big Old Land* (1983 EMI 1572062). See also *LattaA*, 54–5; *SmithB*, 252.

Cotton, Daryl   (*b* Adelaide), pop singer-songwriter. From 1964 he played in the Adelaide groups the Mermen and Times Unlimited, joining ★Zoot as lead singer in 1965, through which he built a wide following. After Zoot disbanded in 1970 he worked in Frieze, then in the USA as Cotton, Lloyd and Christian (1973–75), doing session work for Olivia ★Newton-John and writing songs for movies. He returned to Australia in 1978, where he released eight singles, beginning with *Don't Let It Get To You*, and hosted *Summer Rock* on Adelaide television. He formed the Daryl Cotton Band in 1980, his *Same Old Girl* reaching No. 6 in the charts.

FURTHER REFERENCE
Recordings include *Don't Let It Get To You* (Oz Oz11774), *Same Old Girl* (EMI EMI204); albums *Best Seat In The House* (1980, EMI EMX101) and *It's Rockin' Good Fun* (1984, Hammond HAM107). For discography, see *SpencerA*. See also *McGrathA*; *SpencerW*; David Day and Tim Parker, *SA Great: It's Our Music 1956–1986* (Glandore SA: Day and Parker, 1987).

Coughlan, Frank (Francis James)   (*b* Emmaville (Vegetable Creek), NSW, 10 Sept. 1904; *d* Sydney, 6 or 7 Apr. 1979), dance band leader, jazz trumpeter, trombonist. His father was bandmaster of the Glen Innes District Band, in which he played, and his four brothers were also musicians from childhood. In 1922 he moved to Sydney where exposure to the recordings of US jazz trombonist Miff Mole revolutionised his attitudes to music. As a trombonist (and also a trumpeter and singer), Coughlan established himself in the Sydney and Melbourne dance band profession at a time when jazz was a significant innovation. Apart from work with local bands, he was also recruited into a visiting US band, the Californians, under Walter Beban in 1924. He was in England for twelve months from December 1928, where he played with top bands including those led by Jack Hylton and Fred Elizalde. Back in Australia he continued to work under leaders in Sydney, Brisbane, Melbourne, then led his own band at the Bondi Esplanade in 1935.

At the top of his profession, Coughlan was appointed to form a band for the Sydney Trocadero from its opening in April 1936. Coinciding with the advent of swing, this consolidated his reputation nationally, and gave him international exposure though the film *The Flying Doctor*, parts of which were set in the Trocadero. He left the Trocadero in August 1939 and led bands in Sydney (including New Romano's) and at the Melbourne Trocadero before joining the army in June 1943, as bandleader, 9th Division. Discharged in 1945, he returned to work in Sydney, resuming leadership at the Trocadero from October 1946 to July 1951. After leading the band for several months at Christy's nightclub, Sydney, he again took over the Melbourne Trocadero band from January 1952. He returned to the Sydney Trocadero to lead the band from September 1954 until its closure at the end of 1970, after which he retired apart from occasional club engagements.

Coughlan was a focal point for Australian dance music during an era in which it was being radically transformed by American influences. In association with the Sydney Trocadero he came to embody popular dance when it was a major social entertainment. With trombonist Clarrie Collins, who worked with Paul Whiteman, Coughlan was one of the first of many Australian musicians to establish his reputation at the highest professional level overseas. In addition, he was one of the country's first convincing jazz musicians, and continued to be an active proselytiser for the music throughout his lifetime. A powerful interpreter of dixieland and swing, he also encouraged more traditional forms in association with the Sydney Jazz Club. Graeme Bell has referred to him as 'the father of Australian jazz'.

FURTHER REFERENCE
Recordings include *The Great Band Era—Australia*, Frank Coughlan and his Dixielanders (1965, Reader's Digest—RCA SPS-8); *The Troc* (1991, MBS Jazz 8, Linehan Series). See also *BissetB*; *OxfordJ*; *GroveJ*; Graeme Bell & Jack Mitchell, 'Frank Coughlan: An appreciation', *Quarterly Rag* 13 [New Series] (Oct. 1979), 12–18; Joan Ford, *Meet Me at the Trocadero* (Cowra, NSW: Joan Ford, 1995).

BRUCE JOHNSON

Countdown. Weekly rock music program 1974–87 on ABC TV, co-ordinated by Ian 'Molly' *Meldrum. Presenting an array of live performances, concert excerpts, video clips, and interviews with Australian and international rock celebrities, it was hosted each week by a different rock guest artist. With Meldrum's segment, a characteristically impromptu commentary on the recordings and tours of new and rising Australian artists, the show became the most influential in the Australian rock industry. It took over the King of Pop Awards as the *Countdown* Awards from 1979, and had its own magazine.

FURTHER REFERENCE
Peter Wilmoth, *The Countdown Years 1974–1987* (Melbourne: McPhee Gribble, 1993).

Countertenor. The male alto voice, in the English cathedral choir tradition a falsetto rather than a naturally produced high tenor. There is little evidence of cultivation of the voice in Australian cathedral choirs until the arrival of English organist Ernest *Wood at St Paul's Cathedral, Melbourne, in 1890, but with the modern revival of the voice in solo parts, Australia has produced a number of fine countertenors, including Hartley Newnham, John Collis, and best known in Europe, Andrew Dalton.

Country Express. Bluegrass band formed at Adelaide (1973), comprised of Brent Miller, John Munro, Mike O'Callaghan and Mike Smith. It grew from Munro and Miller's the Skillet Lickers, formed in 1967. They have worked together only occasionally, but since 1983 have appeared regularly at the National Folk Festival and Port Fairy Festival.

FURTHER REFERENCE
Recordings include *The Country Express* (1975, Hadley HLP 1227), *A Place In The Choir* (1987, Sandstock SSM 020), *Another Lonesome Morning* (1985, Sandstock SSM 013), and *Bluegrass In The Bulldust* (Nationwide GNLP 7055). See also *LattaA*, 56–7; *SmithB*, 82–3.

Country Gardens. Piano solo by Percy *Grainger, based on an English Morris Dance Tune collected by Cecil *Sharp, 1918. Undoubtedly Grainger's most popular work for piano, it was published by G. Schirmer, New York, and Schott & Co., London, in 1919. By the early 1920s it was breaking all Schirmer's sales records, selling at a rate of about 24 000 copies a year. Half the royalties were paid to Sharp's estate. Various other arrangements were made in subsequent years, many of which have been recorded. Its swinging, ebullient and vigorous style epitomises the best qualities of Grainger's own piano playing—he recorded it three times (Columbia, USA, 1927, Duo-Art, 1919, Vanguard, unreleased, 1957)—but also marked him as a composer of cheerful unseriousness.

FURTHER REFERENCE
Teresa Balough, *A Complete Catalogue of the Works of Percy Grainger* (Perth: Univ. WA, DepMusic, Music Monograph 2, 1975); Malcolm Gillies and David Pear, eds, *The All-Round Man: Selected Letters of Percy Grainger 1914–1961* (Oxford: Clarendon Press, 1994).

KAY DREYFUS

Country Music.
1. From the Beginnings to 1936. 2. Tex Morton and the Classic Era, 1936–50. 3. The 1950s: Country Music Comes to Suburbia. 4. The 1960s: The Travelling Shows, Radio, Clubs and Recording Companies. 5. The 1970s: The Rise of Tamworth. 6. Country Music Today.

If country music means the rurally based music of its origins, then the diminishing of differences between rural and urban lifestyles and mores could be expected to be reflected in the music itself. But the market and media drive to 'broaden the base' of Australian country music and make it more acceptable to a wider range of people has necessarily swept it increasingly towards the general market rather than the specialised areas of its origins. What is termed country music in Australia today has gained many new supporters, particularly among the young, but has alienated many of its traditional devotees. Any attempt to write seriously about country music today will therefore disappoint those at either end of the spectrum; both the inclusions and omissions of certain artists attract debate and even hostility.

1. From the Beginnings to 1936. From the early 19th century, when settlers first left the confines of Sydney Cove or Hobart Town for the bush, rural ballads appeared, usually based on the folk-tunes of the British Isles, but adapted to reflect the struggles, aspirations, discoveries and unique emerging lifestyle of the bush. These reached their fullest development in the years of growing national awareness before World War I (see *Folk Music*).

The advent of sound recording and wireless revolutionised listening habits: now a singer could reach a vast audience well out of earshot. In the USA the songs of western cowboys and the southern hill folk were recorded early, and by the late 1920s Jimmy Rodgers, the Carter Family, Bradley Kincaid and many others singing traditional rural music had become known the world over. This brought an important change in direction for Australia's rural music: until then it had been passed on orally; now through the gramophone and the growing band of radio stations the American hillbillies, as they were coming to be termed, were freely available. The younger generation in the Australian bush took the American music to their hearts. Australian rural music had not been recorded and went into a temporary limbo, not because it was inferior but because the new technology was overseas-owned and it was easier to import the already proven product than to nurture our own. Soon the younger generation was doing with the American hillbilly music what their forebears had done with the British ballads: they began making music in the imported style, but with words drawn from their own experience, usually for a solo voice accompanied by straightforward harmonic accompaniment on a single guitar.

2. Tex Morton and the Classic Era, 1936–50. The first significant exponent of this new genre to record in Australia was the NZ-born Tex *Morton. He migrated to Australia at the age of 16, lived a nomadic life in the Depression years, and made his first recordings in 1936 at the age of 19. At first he recorded mostly cover versions of American hillbilly songs, but his own prolific writing on Australian themes developed rapidly and became the most popular element in his immediate success. With brevity, realism, and none of the sentimentality or flippancy of popular music, he sang of bush heroes and anti-heroes, of the boundless space of the outback, of loneliness and hardship. His name became a household word in Australia, but his importance lies equally in the pattern he set for the emerging artists: in the decade after his work first appeared there was an explosion of talent which, setting texts of Australian bush life to the American country idiom, consolidated the classic Australian country music genre.

From the Northern Rivers dairy belt of NSW, where the new music had established one of its greatest holds, Buddy *Williams was the next to come to wide prominence, making his first recordings in 1939. Williams was an authentic product of Australian country life, and his songs grew squarely from his rural environment, if retaining American influences in their themes, style, and occasionally in their terminology. Like Morton, his output was prolific and his acceptance immediate: before long he was second only to Morton in national popularity and influence.

In the early 1940s, despite the wartime preoccupations and austerities, other artists began to emerge, notably Smoky *Dawson (from 1941) and three teenagers Shirley *Thoms (from 1941, aged 16), June *Holms (from 1942, aged 17), and Gordon *Parsons (from 1946, aged 19). In 1946 a 20-year-old farm lad from Kempsey, NSW, Slim *Dusty, cut his first commercial recordings, beginning a career that was to span half a century and bring the genre to its classic maturity.

Even before his first recordings, Dusty had developed a wide following through radio broadcasts; now commercial success took his music across Australia, and he could soon match Morton and Williams in popularity with the growing mass of country music fans. Although the war was over, Australia was still in the grip of austerity measures, and country recording was scanty throughout the late 1940s. But in the 14 years from Morton's first recording to 1950 these artists, many still teenagers, had created a recognisable Australian country sound; moreover, every regional centre was sprouting guitar-playing, singing and songwriting youngsters in their image.

3. The 1950s: Country Music Comes to Suburbia. The passing of the 1940s saw considerable change in Australian society. Wartime restrictions gave way to an economic boom, country people flocked to the cities in search of new, better-paid work, and those who stayed on their farms found rapidly improving transport, communications and a measure of prosperity relieving their isolation and changing their outlook. Many arrivals in Sydney from the bush settled in the western suburbs and brought with them their taste in music; other capital cities played host to a similar phenomenon.

This created a demand for country music where it had never been previously heard. Suburban country music shows began to appear, and Dusty, Parsons, Tim *McNamara, the *McKean Sisters and many others who had worked in the bush now settled in the city to work the suburban venues. More imitators, many of whom had no experience of the world beyond the cities, joined their ranks, and the once earthy country music scene became urbanised, its songs more often following the love themes heard in American popular music recordings than the mores of the Australian bush. Also following the Americans, the lone guitarist began to be backed by a band, often with steel or amplified guitar and strong dance rhythms influenced by jazz, Cajun, or pop. McNamara, Lily Connors and others were accused of leaning more to American pop than Australian country. Conspicuously exempt from such criticisms were Williams, who had remained in the bush, and Dusty, who had returned to it after two years in the city; but even they were now travellers through the bush rather than its residents. Morton spent the 1950s abroad.

4. The 1960s. (i) The Travelling Shows.

The demise of suburban country music shows came with the arrival of rock and roll from 1957. The film *Rock Around the Clock* and its title tune broke all records; hard on its heels came television, and the audience for live shows of any kind (other than rock and roll) evaporated. The clamour of defections by artists to rock and roll reached the point of hysteria; many on the fringe of country music converted to rock and roll overnight. However, television had not yet reached many country areas, and rock and roll's impact was noticeably less beyond the cities. Williams and Dusty were now touring the outback with their travelling shows, and soon these shows became the mainstay for country music, taking the music to country people directly, in their own territory. By the end of the 1960s there were probably a dozen such shows leapfrogging one another around country halls.

For Dusty and his wife and indispensable partner Joy McKean the touring experience was enriching. Not only did they achieve a heightened portrayal of the Australian country environment and its people, but as they roughed it around the outback they also came into contact with many new songwriting hopefuls, to whom they gave encouragement and incentive. Stan *Coster is a notable example: he has become responsible for over 70 songs recorded by Dusty and later went on to a travelling career himself. Other songwriters who followed included Kelly Dixon and Tom McIvor. For the audiences too, the shows were ennobling. They were seeing a mirror held up to their way of life, and they responded with a devotion they gave to no other form of entertainment. The arrival of the shows became their calendar. The penetration of television into rural areas eventually reduced the shows' impact, and today only a few hardy shows survive.

(ii) The Role of Radio.

Radio had always been the main source of dissemination for country music, but it remained a rather mixed blessing. From its beginnings, Australian country music on radio had been the victim of a musical apartheid, despised and segregated into 'hillbilly sessions' of 15–30 minutes. Yet to the chagrin of their presenters, request programs on rural stations were often dominated by country music, and young people in the bush learned to twiddle their radio dials incessantly, searching for any 'hillbillies' they could pick up.

Some presenters developed a genuine interest in country music and produced informed and constructive programs. The most famous of these was John *Minson's *Hoedown* on 2TM Tamworth from 1965. But in the 1970s country music largely disappeared from commercial radio. In recent years a few stations in the capital cities, among them 2SM in Sydney and 4BC in Brisbane, have tried a country format, but attempting to please both country and more general audiences at the same time, they mixed in rock and pop, ignored traditional country, and pleased no one. In the 1990s Australian country music has settled into community radio stations such as 2SER in Sydney, 3CR in Melbourne, 7LTN in Launceston and Logan FM and 4AAA in Queensland where enthusiasts run some of the best-informed programs in the music's history. CAAMA began broadcasting Aboriginal country artists from Alice Springs, NT, and on the ABC, Ian McNamara's *Australia All Over* carried a variety of country artists to a huge network of stations.

(iii) Country Music Clubs and Festivals.

From 1944 the influential Australian Hillbilly Club and its offspring the Trailblazers had started at Melbourne, and in the 1950s many country radio stations had social clubs built around their hillbilly sessions. The Modern Country Music Association (from 1979 the Australian Country Music Association) was formed at Brisbane in 1960 to co-ordinate existing clubs and open new branches. Today country music clubs thrive throughout regional Australia, providing a social outlet for their members, a focal point for touring artists, and a training ground where young talent can be developed. Very strong clubs include those at Yandina, Bundaberg, Townsville, and Brisbane Northern Suburbs in Queensland; Capital at Tamworth and Central Coast at Wyong in NSW; and Pioneer Village, Perth in WA. Most clubs run an annual talent quest, often with valuable prizes which attract large numbers of competitors from a wide area. Some of these annual talent quests have grown into major festivals, including Wandong and Mildura Festivals in Victoria; the Gympie Muster, Amamoor Creek, Charters Towers and Bundaberg Festivals in Queensland; the Port Pirie Festival in SA; the Boyup Brook awards in WA; and Bungendore and Tamworth in NSW. These combine their talent quests with large professional shows and attract audiences in their thousands. Sadly, some of the festivals lean towards rock music as the organisers and sponsors seek ever bigger crowds.

(iv) Recording Companies. For more than 20 years the Columbia Record Co. was the only recording company in Australia, introducing American artists and later their local counterparts to the public. The Australian Record Co., through its Rodeo label (1949–56), recorded country artists from the Sydney shows circuit; then the arrival of the tape recorder and microgroove record in the 1950s made recording suddenly easier, and independent labels appeared, many of them little more than backyard operations. The recording industry had been concentrated in Sydney, but now Melbourne companies Spotlight, W&G, Planet and Fable appeared using the new technology.

Independent country labels emerged as the presence of foreign labels increased; these have included Beat'n'-Trak, Opal and Enrec in Tamworth, and Kookaburra, Bunyip and True Blue in Sydney. Today the record industry generally is dominated by the Australian subsidiaries of seven major multinational companies which aggressively market their American artists. EMI has issued Slim Dusty's work for 50 years, and others like Sony, Warner and Festival occasionally release a token Australian country artist, but there is little other interest in the genre. Three country independents, Hadley Records (founded 1961), the first label of substance devoted to country music, Selection Records (founded 1978) and LBS Records (founded 1989) have achieved dedicated and lasting operation. ABC Records and Southland also have strong country lists and Imparja records many Aboriginal country artists in central Australia. In Australia today there are virtually two separate recording industries: the Australian industry and the overseas industry entrenched in Australia. Some overlapping tends to cloud the issue, but it is important to recognise the real and conflicting interests. With their financial backing, their influence with the media and their control of the distribution outlets, the multinationals are able to mould public opinion in the direction of the American trends, to the cultural and economic detriment of our own.

(v) Critics and Journals. Among the very few capital city music critics to pay attention to country music have been Stuart Coupe at the *Sydney Morning Herald*, Joan and Feyne Weaver in the Melbourne *Sun* (1974–84), then Susan Jarvis in the *Sun Herald*. A number of country newspapers like the *Weekly Times*, *The Land*, or the *Gold Coast Bulletin* have had regular coverage of country music, while a number of dedicated journals, like *Capital News*, Tamworth, or *Country Beat*, Mildura, document current developments. While some of these writers know their subject, others unfortunately lack any real depth of understanding.

5. The 1970s: the Rise of Tamworth. (i) The Festival. Building on the success of Minson's *Hoedown*, the Tamworth branch of the Country Music Association staged a concert at the Tamworth Town Hall in 1967 which soon grew into an annual festival. Eric Scott moved

Hadley Records to Tamworth and joined 2TM in 1968, and with Minson and the 2TM manger Max Ellis he discussed the possibility of promoting the city as Australia's country music capital. At the Tamworth Festival in 1973, 2TM staged the first Australasian Country Music Awards. Their success was immediate, and they soon became the focal point for the entire event. The festival grew from a weekend to a celebration lasting a fortnight, each year with bigger crowds, more spectacular and diverse shows, increasing community and business participation and wider media coverage. Today Tamworth is firmly established as Australia's national country music centre, a meeting place for artists and the industry, a proving ground for aspiring talent, a haven for buskers, a venue for industry seminars and workshops and a showcase where delighted fans can enjoy whatever branch of the music or its hybrid offshoots interests them. On the other hand, among the concerns that naturally flow from such a complex operation, many believe that in the quest for growth and diversity the music is in danger of losing its rural identity.

(ii) The Country Music Association of Australia. From its inception until 1992, the Tamworth country music capital concept was virtually controlled by the business arm of 2TM, BAL Marketing. BAL owned the awards, provided an umbrella under which the festival could spread, and was always ready to help anyone with a new festival idea to develop. The Tamworth licensed clubs, too, played an important role, providing virtually round-the-clock entertainment during the event on several different stages simultaneously.

In 1992 the Country Music Association of Australia (CMAA), an organisation of artists and industry executives, took control of the awards and their associated activities. Dissatisfied with some aspects of BAL's conduct of the event, CMAA believed artists should have control of the award system rather than a commercial enterprise, however benign. The festival and the awards had always had individuals involved who believed that, in order to gain increased exposure for country music, they needed to 'broaden the base' (usually by tipping the events towards rock music) to make it more acceptable to the young. These pressures, previously felt under BAL, seem to have intensified under CMAA. As the composition of the CMAA leans increasingly towards recording and publishing company executives, radio personnel and media operatives, and away from the artists it was originally designed to represent, the position may move even further in that direction.

6. Country Music Today. Country music in Australia today is a huge, diverse, volatile, controversial and exciting field. Among its leading exponents are survivors from a more predictable era like Slim Dusty, Rex *Dallas, Reg *Poole, and Brian *Young. They rub shoulders with newcomers like Brian Letton, Glenn Jones, Evelyn

*Bury and yodellers like Owen *Blundell. There are huge commercial successes such as John *Williamson and Lee *Kernaghan, crossover acts from jazz, pop and folk like Shanley Del, Graeme Connors, and the *Bushwackers, clones of the latest American quasi-country sensations like Keith Urban, Steve Gibson and Mark O'Shea, Aboriginal artists like Jimmy *Little, Archie *Roach and Troy Cassar-Daly, and an endless array of hybrid combinations of all these like the Wheel, Kev *Carmody or the Sensitive New Age Cowpersons, most claiming to be country artists. There are also many mainstream artists who include a country number in their acts. Instrumental skills have reached new levels and songwriters are increasingly eloquent. Claims that the bush ballad is the only true country music are countered with pronouncements that the genre now has little to do with the bush at all. Defenders of the music's traditional values are accused of inhibiting change, while the innovators are often tagged as saboteurs of the traditional heritage.

Meanwhile, American artists and songs continue to dominate the airwaves and record stores. Radio programmers are bombarded with more material than they can possibly absorb; they therefore continue to act mainly as American chart-readers, and the young artists, both amateur and professional, become American imitators in repertoire, style and accent. A stroll among the buskers at the Tamworth Festival or a visit to a country music club talent quest anywhere in Australia will confirm that, among the present generation, country music is struggling to preserve any distinction from the dominant American pop phenomenon. While there are many artists who sing recognisable Australian songs and sound Australian, the majority affect a contrived and often unconvincing American flavour and accent.

A plethora of diverse and often quite conflicting musical styles, bracketed by the musical establishment as country, is gaining widespread popularity in Australia, and in the light of the commercial and technological pressures and the vested interests involved, it is difficult to see the trend being contained, let alone reversed. The optimists fall back on the comforting thought that 'as long as there are country people there'll be country music', yet one cannot but fear that the genre's special identity is being absorbed into the amorphous mass of international popular music. It may well be that if the Australian country identity is to survive, the music has to regroup elsewhere, away from its present strongholds.

See also *New Country*, *Yodellers*, *Bluegrass*, entries under individual artists.

FURTHER REFERENCE

The principal references are *WatsonC*; *LattaA*; *SmithB*. See also Monika Allan, *The Tamworth Country Music Festival* (Sydney: Horwitz Grahame, 1988); Slim Dusty, *Walk a Country Mile* (Adelaide: Rigby, 1979).

ERIC WATSON

Country Outcasts.   Aboriginal country music group. See *Williams, Harry and Wilga*.

Courtneidge, Dame (Esmeralda) Cicely   (b Sydney, 1 Apr. 1893; d London, 26 Apr. 1980), English musicals actress. Daughter of actor and producer Robert Courtneidge, she was best known for her London appearances in music hall, revues and musicals, famous for her comic routines and for the vitality and exuberance she brought to her roles. Her first stage appearance was in 1901 as Peaseblossom in *A Midsummer Night's Dream* and she appeared regularly on stage from 1909. In 1914 she married actor Jack Hulbert and the pair formed a celebrated stage partnership for many years, including in the very successful *Under Your Hat* (1938). Among the numerous productions in which she performed were *The Arcadians* (1909), *Folly To Be Wise* (1931), Ivor Novello's *Gay's the Word* (1951), and *High Spirits* (1964). From the 1930s she also appeared in 17 films. Born while her parents were on tour in Australia she returned only once, in 1948–49, starring in the musical comedy *Under the Counter* and in variety shows. She continued her stage work until the early 1970s, and was made a DBE in 1973.

FURTHER REFERENCE

Her memoirs are *Cicely* (London: Hutchinson, 1953); Jack Hulbert, *The Little Woman's Always Right* (London: Allen, 1975).

BRONWEN ARTHUR

Courtship of Miles Standish, The.   Opera in four acts, music and libretto by Florence *Ewart, after Longfellow. First performed in concert at the New Conservatorium, Melbourne, in May 1931.

Covell, Roger   (b Sydney, 1 Feb. 1931), musicologist, critic, conductor. He graduated from the University of Queensland (BA) and the University of New South Wales (PhD, 1975). As founding head of the music department at the University of New South Wales since 1966 (professor since 1984), he developed a primarily musicological school of music and music education which now employs 11 full-time lecturers. As musical director of the Grainger Consort and artistic director of the professional University of New South Wales Opera since 1968, he strongly supports Australian composers by presenting many of their stage works. He was elected president of ASME 1978–81 and the Musicological Society of Australia 1983–84, and was a member of the Australia Council 1977–83.

His influence on Australian music has been manifest primarily through his long employment, since 1960, as chief music critic for the *Sydney Morning Herald,* work which earned him the Geraldine Pascall Prize for music criticism in 1993 and gave him enough space to explain his opinions. As a musicologist Covell regards music's social contexts as a basic element of its historical study. Apart from Baroque opera and late 19th-century French opera, his chief area of research is music in Australia. His major publication, *Australia's Music: Themes of a New Society*, became a touchstone for subsequent research into Australian music history. He also co-authored *Folk Songs of Australia* vol. 2, edited and arranged the first Australian musical play, Edward Geoghegan's *The Currency Lass*, and contributed multiple entries to *The New Grove Dictionary of Opera* (1992). He was honoured with the AM (1986) and elected Fellow of the Australian Academy of the Humanities (1983).

FURTHER REFERENCE
His writings include *Australia's Music: Themes of a New Society* (Melbourne: Sun Books, 1967); *Music in Australia: Needs and Prospects* (Sydney: Unisearch Ltd., Univ. NSW, 1970); *The Currency Lass* (Sydney: Currency Press, 1976).
MARGARET KARTOMI

Cowen, Sir Frederick Hymen (*b* Kingston, Jamaica, 29 Jan. 1852; *d* London, 6 Oct. 1935), English conductor. After studies at the Leipzig Conservatorium and the Stern Conservatorium, Berlin, his prominence as a composer and conductor in London led to his invitation to conduct the orchestra of the International Centennial Exhibition, Melbourne, in 1888. Strengthening the local forces with a nucleus of 15 London players, he conducted 244 concerts at the Exhibition Buildings, including most symphonies, concertos and oratorios standard in European programs at the time, as well as some of his own works. His success created the expectation of a standard and regularity of orchestral concerts which, without the government subsidy and concentration of talent he had commanded, did not long survive his departure, despite efforts to form a permanent orchestra.

FURTHER REFERENCE
His autobiography is *My Art and My Friends* (London: E. Arnold, 1913). See also Kenneth Hince, *ADB*, 3; *Musical Times* 39 (1898), 713; J.M. Levien, *DNB*.

Cowen, Marie. See *Waltzing Matilda*.

Cowie, Edward (*b* Birmingham, England, 17 Aug. 1943), composer, painter, conductor, film-maker. Cowie was educated at the University of London, Trinity College of Music, the University of Southampton (DMus, 1979) and the University of Lancaster (PhD, 1983). He married Stephanie McGrath in 1986 and has two sons. After a professional career as a lecturer in Europe he came to Wollongong University as foundation professor of creative arts; he was visiting professor at James Cook University, Townsville, Queensland, and has been artistic director of the Australian Arts Fusion Centre, Brisbane, since 1991. Since 1975 Cowie has also established a reputation as a painter and has been involved in the television productions of *Edward Lear* (Granada, 1978) and *Leonardo da Vinci* (BBC, 1985) and the ABC FM commission in 1988 for the series *Voices of the Land*. Cowie has conducted the

Royal Liverpool Philharmonic Orchestra, Philomusica of London, the BBC singers and the ABC symphony orchestras. He was the recipient of the Radcliffe Prize (1970) and the Chopin Fellowship, Warsaw (1971). Cowie's music is highly colourful and is inspired by nature and the works of painters. He believes the sounds of his music are those of the 'echoes' of the world around us, and is attracted to bird song as well as employing elements of serialism and tonality in his compositions.

FURTHER REFERENCE
Recordings include *Kelly Variations*, Peter Lawson, (1982, EDROO1); Clarinet Concerto No. 2, Op. 5, Royal London Philharmonic Orchestra, cond. H. Williams, (1985, A66120); and Concerto for Orchestra, Op. 19, Royal London Philharmonic Orchestra, cond. H. Williams (1985, A66120). His writings include 'The Shock of the Old', *Composer* 75 (1979–82), 13–15, and 'Kelly Choruses', *Composer* 78 (1982–85), 15. See also: Anthony Burton, 'People, Places and Music', *The Listener* (June 1979); *ContemporaryC*.
SARAH LARKIN

Coyle, Graham Francis (*b* Melbourne, 10 Aug. 1932), jazz pianist. He began piano in his father's dance trio in the late 1940s, moving into jazz settings in the 1950s with Tony Newstead, Frank Traynor and others. In Shepparton, Victoria, as a surveyor 1951–53, he came under the informal tutelage of pianist Rex Green. Back in Melbourne, he was increasingly active in the traditional movement, including with Len Barnard (with whom he recorded the celebrated *Naked Dance* album) and Alan Lee. With Lee his range continued expanding, leading to increasingly broad-based jazz activity with virtually every traditional to mainstream group in Melbourne. He is currently with the Hotter Than Six Jazz Band.

FURTHER REFERENCE
Recordings include *The Naked Dance*, Len Barnard's Jazz Band (1961, Astor ALP-1007); *Jazz From The Pulpit*, Frank Traynor's Jazz Preachers (1963, W & G Records WG-B-1722); *Graham Coyle Plays Piano 1955–1973* (1991, The Bill Haesler Collection H001); *Cooking Up A Storm*, Hotter Than Six Jazz Band (1995, Newmarket NEW 1074.2). See also *BissetB*; *OxfordJ*.
BRUCE JOHNSON

Cran, John (*b* Sydney, 6 Nov. 1927), bassoonist. After studying with Charles Sammul at the NSW State Conservatorium, he became principal bassoon in the West Australian Symphony Orchestra and the Tasmanian Symphony Orchestra, then was principal bassoon in the Sydney Symphony Orchestra from 1957. He has taught at the NSW State Conservatorium since 1968, has had a long association with the National Music Camp Association, and won a Churchill fellowship to observe bassoon teaching methods in the USA and Europe. He has given numerous recitals as a soloist, and played with a succession of woodwind chamber music groups, currently the *Sydney Soloists.

FURTHER REFERENCE
Recordings include Mozart, Bassoon Concerto, Sydney Symphony Orchestra, cond. R. Pikler (RCA).

Crawford, Hector William (*b* Melbourne, 14 Aug. 1913; *d* Melbourne, 11 Mar. 1991), producer, conductor. Born into a musical family, he was a choirboy at St Paul's Cathedral, Melbourne, then studied music at the University of Melbourne. He developed and conducted the long-running *Music For The People* outdoor concerts for radio broadcast from 1938. From 1941 he was music and recording director for Broadcast Exchange of Australia and in 1945, with his sister the radio announcer Dorothy Crawford, he established Hector Crawford Productions, supplying classical music programs to commercial radio in Australia, NZ and Canada. Through his company he conducted *Opera for the People* for radio, and produced the radio music serials *The Melba Story*, *The Amazing Oscar Hammerstein* and *The Blue Danube*. His *Mobil Quest* (1949–56) became an influential radio talent quest. One of Australia's most important radio and TV producers, he was one of the few to successfully popularise classical music through commercial radio and television. From 1956 he produced television programs. He married the coloratura soprano Glenda Raymond in 1950. He won five TV Logie awards and was honoured with the OBE (1968), the CBE, then the AO in 1986.

FURTHER REFERENCE
Obit. in *Age* 12 Mar. 1991, *Australian* 16 Mar. 1991. See also Jacqueline Kent, *Out of the Bakelite Box: the Heyday of Australian Radio* (Sydney: ABC, 1983), 75–9; *MonashB*.

Crichton, Pat (Patrick Stuart) (*b* Palmerston North, NZ, 22 June 1943), jazz trumpeter. He began trumpet at the age of 14, then moved to Sydney in the mid-1960s and joined Ray Price; he also worked in jazz-rock groups. With the Daly Wilson Big Band 1975–77, he was active in session work, and moved to Perth in 1979, joining Will Upson's Big Band. He became director of the WA Youth Jazz Orchestra, and founding head of the jazz studies course at Mount Lawley College of Advanced Education, now Edith Cowan University. In this position Crichton presides over initiatives which, together with his own public performance activity, have considerably increased the program's public recognition.

FURTHER REFERENCE
Recordings include *The Peter Lane Big Band* (1973, Troubadour TCS-036); *The Daly Wilson Big Band* (1975, Reprise 60–0023); *Reflections of Western Australia* (1992, Request Records RQCD 2001); *Jazzwest Big Band, Take The Light* (1995, Request Records RQCD 2002). See also *OxfordJ*.

BRUCE JOHNSON

Criticism.

1. *The Colonial Phase, 1820–1850*. 2. *The Goldrush, 1850–1890*. 3. *Federation, 1890–1914*. 4. *The World Wars, 1914–1945*. 5. *After the War, 1945 to the Present*.

Music criticism, the public expression of an opinion about music, has existed in Australia since the first public concerts in Sydney and Hobart in 1826. Australian music criticism has usually been in the form of reviews in the daily press of performances: the prevalence of reviewing and the absence of a broader critical context in Australian music has been a recurring recent complaint. Similarly, the potential of the electronic media as a form of criticism as opposed to transmission has, with a few distinguished exceptions, been underdeveloped, a situation for which the ABC has received some blame. Indeed, recent evaluations of Australian music criticism have rarely been favourable. An Australian UNESCO forum at the University of Sydney in 1968 concluded that 'current daily press reviews were virtually useless to composers, performers and critics alike', and similar sentiments were echoed at a composers' conference in Sydney in 1988 and elsewhere.

Unlike theatre and literary criticism, music criticism in Australia has yet to be the subject of a comprehensive study. In the absence of such a study, a preliminary division of critical phases into five periods can be made, from the colonial phase to the postwar growth of a national musical establishment. Ranging across these periods, it is possible to identify variations on common concerns: Australianism versus Europeanism and the intermittent search for a national identity; classics (representing 'high' art but also 'elitist' art) versus *vox populi* ('low' art but also egalitarianism); and the encouragement of local talent paired with an almost unquenchable thirst for international artists.

1. The Colonial Phase, 1820–50. At the time of the first public musical performances in Sydney by Barnett Levey in 1826, Sydney's population of about 10 000 was served by three newspapers, the *Australian*, the *Gazette*, and the *Monitor*. Scant on musical detail, and showing no particular evidence of wide musical experience among their writers, the earliest reviews embodied high-minded endorsement of the 'civilising' role of high art combined with moralising disapproval of low art both for its association with the easy virtue of the theatre and the poor behaviour it inspired in the front benches. Thus in 1826 the *Sydney Monitor* wrote:

> Mr Paul and Mr Levey executed two comic songs in such good style as to be received with raptures. In these raptures, however, we could not join. A theatre and a concert are diverse; and we think it scarcely candid to intrinch on the character of the latter by pantomime and farce.

In the *Australian*'s review of *The Currency Lass*, the first Australian ballad opera, the 'Cabbage-tree hats' were castigated for their approval of low dialogue. The pedigree of the 'fashionable audience' was a frequent topic for comment, as were 'the ineffable recollections of European performances' (*Australian*, 1843). Reviews, always anonymous, supported most musical events in the growing colony, with the *Sydney Gazette* commenting in 1839 that 'never at any other previous time have so many concerts taken place during so short a period'. Taken together, these characteristics could be seen as a manifestation of the anxieties of an emerging middle class, where the behaviour of an underclass majority needed continually to be kept in check (free settlers were less than a fifth of population at the beginning of the century, rising to over half in the 1830s).

2. The Goldrush, 1850–90.

The goldrush of the 1850s saw the effective end of the convict colony and brought disposable incomes for leisure, touring opera companies, immigrants with imported tastes, and a new breed of educated writers whose pretensions to European musical experience could be taken seriously. Among these were J.E. ★Neild, the argumentative critic of the *Examiner*, later writing as Jacques in the *Australasian*, James Smith of the *Argus*, both from Melbourne, Mrs Carl Fischer and F.C. ★Brewer in Sydney. Melbourne, however, seems to have assumed the mantle of the cultural capital of Australia. The *Argus* by the 1880s was widely seen as the best daily outside England and by some second only to the London *Times*, and its companion the *Australasian* was the leading opinion-forming paper of the colony. Criticism during this period exerted a considerable influence on musical development. Most of the daily newspapers had a companion weekly often employing the same critics: the *Sydney Morning Herald* published the weekly *Sydney Mail*; the *Argus* (Melbourne) published the *Examiner* and later the *Australasian*; the *Herald* (Melbourne) published *Bell's Life*, and the *Telegraph* (Melbourne) the *Weekly Times*. Since the 1840s there had also been a steady growth in the periodical literature, with Sydney and Hobart producing more periodicals during the 1840s than at any other time during the 19th century. The *Sydney Morning Herald* employed no specialist arts writers between 1830 and 1879, when Mrs Carl Fischer, who remained an influential voice until the 1890s, moved from Melbourne. The *Bulletin* (founded 1880) with its intolerance of middle-class affectation, could be said to embody the better aspects of the anti-elitist and also somewhat anti-intellectual side of late 19th-century Australian criticism. Its first issue set out the following critical credo:

> In this department of our *Bulletin* it will be our aim to supply our readers with candid, impartial, and judicious criticism … We shall studiously avoid hypercritical fault-finding, petty abuse, or insufferable flattery—believing all three to be equally pernicious to improvement in art or to the elevation of the standard of public taste to the height at which we would like to see it in the … Hypercriticism,

with its peculiar scientific phrases, its assumption of learning, is especially to be eschewed.

Adelaide, however, retained many of the moralising characteristics of the pre-goldrush days, with one critic remarking of an 1861 performance of *La Traviata*:

> We ourselves have no squeamishness respecting it, but simply because it is calculated to offend the taste of many and because we think the business of the dramatist is to amuse and instruct, we think such subjects as the story of *La Traviata* should be shunned as much as possible. (Horden 1988: 432)

3. Federation, 1890–1914.

While the economic downturn of the 1890s brought a decline in the number of international touring companies and artists, whether it is true that music criticism responded with the same slackening of critical edge and confidence which has been noted in theatre criticism is arguable. It is difficult to find any impact in the musical press of the pro-British patriotism brought about by Federation and involvement in European wars, and the distinctly Australian identity of the *Bulletin*, manifest in its advocacy of the White Australia policy, has no apparent impact on its music reviews.

The conservative taste of the time is summed up in the writings of Gerald Marr Thompson, chief critic of the *Sydney Morning Herald* 1891–1924, taking over from Neville Barnett. Having broadly approved of the *verismo* novelties, *Cavalleria Rusticana* and *Pagliacci* (staged here within two years of the latter's world premiere) in 1893 he reported general relief at a revival of *Faust*.

> For four or five weeks our audiences have been mentally overtaxed by the successive and continuous presentation of new and advanced operas. The intellectual strain has been felt by the most enthusiastic opera-goers of this music-loving community; and when it was announced that one of the old familiar works would be performed, all flocked at once to the theatre for rest and recreation. (Gyger 1990: 89)

F.C. Brewer's *The Drama and Music in New South Wales*, commissioned by the NSW Government for the Chicago World's Columbia Exposition, marks one of the earliest approaches to an historical overview, although Brewer largely restricted his early research to notices in the *Sydney Morning Herald*. While critical reception of Italian opera was quick and positive, Wagner still inspired populist mistrust. The year of Federation, 1901, saw immediate critical acclaim for Puccini's *La Bohème* and Verdi's *Otello*, while the belated premier of *Tannhäuser*, *Der Fliegende Holländer* and the revival of *Lohengrin* (staged in 1877 by Lyster) drew mixed reviews: 'long-drawn German weariness' according to the *Bulletin*, but 'truly an epoch-making event' according to the *Herald*. However, the period between Federation and World War I is one of the strongest in terms of Wagner reception in Australia's history, with unanimous critical praise for *Tristan und Isolde* in 1912 and *The Ring* cycle the following year, just before war with Germany.

4. The World Wars, 1914–45. Reflecting the distaste for popular culture of a century earlier, the establishment musical press in Australia all but ignored the arrival of jazz and dance clubs in the 1920s in favour of a quest for international standards. Two contradictory themes dominate the critical writing of this period. The first is the establishment of a critical benchmark of world standards by means of the parade of international artists who toured during these years: Melba, Kreisler, Heifetz, Paderewski, Galli-Curci, Tauber, Zimbalist, Grainger and Backhaus to name only the most eminent.

Although comparisons with European performances have been a recurring feature of Australian criticism, it is fair to say that the cultural cringe derided later in the century owes much of its gestation to this period. In 1928 C.N. Baeryertz, passionate arts writer, founder of *Triad* magazine and critic of the *Sunday Times* could still write: 'Last night for the first time in our history we heard an adequate performance of opera … worthy to rank with good European productions.' A particularly harsh example was Griffen ★Foley at the Sydney *Sun* (1910–24). Against this dominant culture of what Katharine Brisbane has called 'middle-class internationalism' is the much less prevalent but arguably equally significant second theme, the assertion of Australian nationalism, manifest in critical musical writings almost exclusively in the writings of Henry Tate and in literature in the work of Bernard O'Dowd. Tate's two books of collected writings, *Australian Musical Resources* (1917) and *Australian Musical Possibilities* (1924), praised Melba's 'innate Australianism' and advocated the use of Australian bush sounds and birdsong in composition. In the writings of Alex ★Burnard (*Adelaide Advertiser*) and H .★Brewster Jones there was a more analytical and scholarly focus. In the *West Australian,* A.H. ★Kornweibel ('Fidelio') presided agreeably for 50 years, from 1916 to 1965, while the tabloid journalism of the Melbourne *Sun* attracted Thorold ★Waters ('Salamander', 1923–48) and the Melbourne *Herald* John ★Sinclair (1947–85).

The aspiration towards international values found its pinnacle in Sir Neville ★Cardus, music critic of the *Manchester Guardian* from 1917, chief critic from 1927 and music critic for the *Sydney Morning Herald* 1939–47, succeeding Kenneth Wilkinson, who himself succeeded Paddy Nolan in 1933. Although Cardus's love of cricket may have endeared him to Australians as much as his international credentials, he set the tone for postwar sophistication allied with a mistrust of modernism, particularly German modernism. Australia also provided Britain with one of its leading critics of the period, Melbourne-born W.J. ★Turner, who wrote for the *New Statesman,* 1915–40.

5. After the War: 1945 to the Present. After World War II, particularly in the 1960s, internationalism gave way to nationalism. In its worst manifestations this became defensive parochialism, but it also served to represent the interests of local performers and the emerging school of pre- and postwar composers. In 1958 Dorian ★Le Gallienne, composer and critic for the *Argus* and the *Age* between 1950 and 1963, wrote:

> We certainly need to hear all the expert performers from overseas that we can, but we also need to know if there is any other place in the world with pretensions to musical culture where the native musician is so firmly and irrevocably classed as second rate. (Thomas 1992: 29)

It is perhaps no coincidence that several of the harshest critics of the cultural cringe were themselves composers, including Felix ★Werder (critic for the *Age* in the 1960s), David ★Ahern (Sydney *Telegraph*), and the expatriate composer Peggy ★Glanville-Hicks, who wrote for the New York *Herald-Tribune* under Virgil Thomson from 1947 to 1954. Following were a generation of writers who defined their role as to encourage Australian creativity and map its culture as much as to report on what was fine, such as Nadine ★Amadio (*Australian Financial Review*), John Carmody (*National Times* and Sydney's *Sun Herald*) and Roger ★Covell, chief critic of the *Sydney Morning Herald* since 1960 (taking over from Lindsay ★Browne ['LB'] 1946–60). Covell's support of the generation of Meale, Butterley and Sculthorpe could be seen as one of the most decisive critical interventions on behalf of Australian composition, and his *Australia's Music: Themes of a New Society* (1967) remains a landmark of Australian critical discussion.

As well as the nationalist backlash, internationalism also bequeathed a national music establishment supported by government patronage through the ABC, the Australian Opera and what became the Australia Council. A parallel critical development was the development of a national daily, the *Australian,* bringing for the first time a regular national coverage of the arts; its music writers have included the opera singer Maria ★Prerauer ('Marietta'), Martin Long and Laurie Strahan. Despite domination by the major organisations, the main capital city dailies have maintained support for local activity, as in the work of Fred ★Blanks (*Sydney Morning Herald* and Australian correspondent for the *Musical Times*), Elizabeth Silsbury (*Adelaide Advertiser*), Patricia Brown (*Sydney Morning Herald*), William ★Lovelock (Brisbane *Courier-Mail*) and Kenneth ★Hince (*Age*). Among the specialist music magazines, the ABC's *24 Hours* and David Gyger's *Opera Australia* have provided a continuity and depth of critical coverage missing in the dailies, while *Music Now, NMA Articles,* and *Sounds Australian* have catered particularly for the growth of discourse in contemporary Australian music.

FURTHER REFERENCE

BrisbaneE; BrewerD.

Australian UNESCO Seminar: Criticism in the Arts (Canberra: Australian National Advisory Committee for UNESCO, 1970).

Covell, Roger, *Australia's Music: Themes of a New Society* (Melbourne: Sun Books, 1967).

Horden, Sam, '…"with one eye on the clock": a review of music criticism in South Australia.' In *From Colonel Light into the*

Footlights: The Performing Arts in South Australia from 1836 to the Present, ed. Andrew McCredie (Adelaide: Pagel Books, 1988).

Gyger, Alison, *Opera for the Antipodes* (Sydney: Currency, 1990).

Irvin, Eric, 'Australia's first public concerts', *SMA* 5 (1971), 77–86.

Love, Harold, *The Golden Age of Australian Opera* (Sydney: Currency, 1981).

McCallum, Peter, and Andrew Schultz, eds, 'To criticise the critic', *SA* 35 (1992).

Skinner, Graeme, *The Composer Speaks* (Sydney: Sounds Australian, 1992).

Smith, Bernard, *The Critic as Advocate: Selected Essays 1948–88* (Melbourne: OUP, 1989).

Souter, Gavin, *A Company of Heralds* (Melbourne: MUP, 1981).

Thomas, Adrian, 'The Composer as Critic and Advocate: Dorian Le Gallienne', *SA* 35 (1992), 24–32.

Waters, Thorold, *Much Besides Music* (Melbourne: Georgian House, 1951).

P. McCALLUM

Cronin, Stephen (*b* Brisbane, 1960), composer. While studying piano and composition at the University of Queensland he wrote chiefly choral settings, instrumental solos and duos. He studied at the University of London in 1985, and has been lecturer at the Queensland Conservatorium since 1986. Writing accessible yet imaginative music, he came to wide attention when he won the Paul Lowin Composition Prize for his song cycle *House Songs* in 1991 and the Albert Maggs Award in 1992. His Piano Concerto (1989) has been recorded, as have *Cries and Whispers* for orchestra (1993), *Carmina Pu!* for vocal sextet (1992), and several chamber works such as *The Snake Pit* (1990).

WORKS (Selective)
Orchestral Suite for Recorder and Strings (*Homage to Vaughan Williams*), treble rec, str orch (1984), *The Drover's Wife*, nar, orch (1987), Concerto for Piano and Orchestra (1989), *Cries and Whispers,* orch (1993).
Chamber *The Snake Pit*, cl, va, vc, pf/hpd (1990), *Eros and Agape*, chamber orch (1990), *Eros Reclaimed*, fl, cl, perc, pf, vn, vc (1993), *Blow*, wind octet (1994).
Vocal/Choral *Requiem*, SATB, hp, 2 pf, perc (1985), *House Songs*, T, ens (1991), *Carmina Pu!*, vocal sextet (1992).

FURTHER REFERENCE
Recordings include the Piano Concerto (Vienna Modern Masters VMM 3011) and *Carmina Pu!* (Vox Australis VAST016–2), and there are ABC tapes of several chamber works, including *Cries and Whispers* and *The Snake Pit*. See also *BroadstockS*.

Crossley, Ada Jemima (*b* Tarraville, Vic., 3 Mar. 1871, *d* Great Missenden, Buckinghamshire, England, 17 Oct. 1929), contralto. She studied with Alberto Zelman Sr and Mme Fanny *Simonsen in Melbourne, with Charles Santley in London and Mme Marchesi in Paris. Her London debut was at the Queen's Hall in May 1895, but her real opportunity came when she substituted for Clara Butt in Manchester. She was noted as a singer of oratorio, sacred songs and ballads. A woman of great style, her voice was admired for its 'luscious richness'. In America, 1902–3, she recorded for the Victor Gramophone Co.'s Red Seal Celebrity Series. Always a generous patron of fellow Australian singers, she toured Australasia twice with Percy *Grainger (1903–4; 1908–9).

FURTHER REFERENCE
Obit. in *AMN* 19 (Nov. 1929), 25. Her clippings and letters are in *PVgm*. See also M. Missen, *ADB*, 8; K. Dreyfus, *The Farthest North of Humanness: Letters of Percy Grainger 1901–14* (Melbourne: Macmillan, 1985).

KAY DREYFUS

Crowded House. Pop-rock group (1985–96) formed in Melbourne, originally comprised of Neil Finn (vocals, guitar; *b* Te Awamutu, NZ, 1958), Paul Hester (drums; *b* Melbourne, 1959), and Nick Seymour (bass; *b* Benalla, Vic., 1958). Finn and Hester formed the group after the break-up of the *Split Enz, with Finn in particular wanting a vehicle to demonstrate his increasing confidence as a quality songwriter. Nick Seymour joined the group and after an initial delay they were signed to Capitol Records in Los Angeles. Their self-titled debut album in 1986 took close to a year to reach the Australian Top 10, but it also yielded two Top 10 hits in the USA in 1987, *Don't Dream It's Over* and *Something So Strong*. Their second album, *Temple of Low Men* (1988), attracted a reasonable critical response but was only a moderate chart success.

Neil's older brother and former Split Enz member Tim *Finn joined the group in 1991, playing keyboards, singing and writing. Now a quartet, they released *Woodface* in the same year to widespread critical acclaim and commercial success. Possibly the album most often associated with the group, it displayed the Finn brothers' gift for vocal harmony and melodic invention, and drew comparisons with the Beatles. Tim Finn's stay was short-lived, however: he left in late 1991 to continue a solo career. He was replaced by American musician Mark Hart who played on *Together Alone* (1993). The group disbanded in 1996, remembered best for its finely crafted, almost perfect pop.

FURTHER REFERENCE
Recordings include *Crowded House* (1986, Capitol 7466932); *Temple of Low Men* (1988, Capitol 7487632); *Woodface* (1991, Capitol 7935592); *Together Alone* (1993, Capitol 7243 8 27048 29); *Recurring Dream: The Very Best Of* (1996, EMI 838396–2). For discography see *SpencerA*. See also *SpencerW*; *McGrathA*.

WILLIAM VAN PINXTEREN

Cruel Sea, The. Rock group formed (1988) at Sydney, comprised of Tex Perkins (vocals), James Cruikshank (guitar), Danny Rumour (guitar), Ken Gormley (bass) and James Elliot (drums). Emerging from Sekret

Sekret (1980–87), they were formed as an instrumental band and at first drew a following in the pub circuit. Adding Perkins from Beasts of Bourbon, they became a popular alternative band, and *The Honeymoon Is Over* reached No. 4 in the charts. In 1994 they toured Europe supporting Nick ★Cave and the Bad Seeds. A compelling live band with an alluring lead singer, their sound melds elements of rhythm and blues and swamp rock. They won the ARIA best group, best album, best single and best song in 1994.

FURTHER REFERENCE
Recordings include *Down Below* (1991, Red Eye RED19); *This Is Not The Way Home* (1992, Red Eye RED 25); *The Honeymoon Is Over* (1993, Red Eye RED 35). See also *Rolling Stone* (Aust) 508 (Apr. 1995), 50–6; *SpencerW*.

Cubbin, David   (*b* Melbourne, 1930, *d* 19 May 1997), flautist, administrator. After studies with Leslie ★Barklamb at the University of Melbourne Conservatorium, he became principal flute of the SA Symphony Orchestra in 1954. He taught flute at the Elder Conservatorium from 1964, was a foundation member of the ★University of Adelaide Wind Quintet, and founded the Flute Society of SA in 1972. He then became head of woodwind at the Canberra School of Music from 1975, taught at the Queensland Conservatorium from 1979, and directed two national flute conventions in 1976 and 1980. He was director of the School of Arts, Northern Rivers CAE, from 1981 and professor and director of the Tasmanian Conservatorium from 1985, then head of the tertiary liaison unit at the NSW ministry of education 1991–95. A seasoned performer and a committed teacher with an intelligent, methodical approach to his instrument, he had a particularly significant influence on flute teaching over a long period. He was president of the Australian Flute Association 1988–95.

Cugley, Ian Robert   (*b* Richmond, Melbourne, 1945), composer. After studies at the University of Sydney with Peter ★Sculthorpe, during which he wrote choral settings and chamber works, he taught in high schools, coming to wide notice in 1967 when his atonal *Prelude* (1965) and his Asian-influenced *Pan the Lake* (H. Bakaitis, 1965) were performed by the Sydney Symphony Orchestra and published by J. Albert. For a few years he received numerous commissions from major Australian ensembles, but did not again attract such intense attention. His subsequent works include *The Six Days of Creation*, written for Marilyn Richardson and Lauris Elms, *Nocturne* (1970) for two guitars, *Pavane* for lute and guitar, a Chamber Symphony for 11 wind instruments (1971), *Aquarelles* for piano (1974), and a violin concerto (1977). He taught briefly at the NSW State Conservatorium, then the University of Tasmania in 1967, and became principal percussionist in the Tasmanian Symphony Orchestra.

FURTHER REFERENCE
Recordings include *Prelude* and *Pan the Lake*, Sydney Symphony Orchestra, cond. J. Post (1969, EMI OASD 7547); *Pavane* is in *Four Centuries of Lute and Guitar* (Candle CFPS 058). For a list of ABC tapes see *PlushD*. His writings include 'The Contemporary Composer in Education', *Music Now* 2/1 (Apr. 1972). See also Thérèse Radic, *GroveD*; Melvyn Cann, *CallawayA*; *MurdochA*.

Cummings, Stephen   (*b* 1954), popular music singer-songwriter. A member of the rock-swing band Pelaco Brothers 1974–75, he joined the rockabilly-rhythm and blues band the ★Sports 1976–81, writing many of their hit songs. He toured the UK with Graham Parker and the Rumour, his *Who Listens To The Radio* charting particularly well; then he was with his Stephen Cummings Band 1983, A Ring Of Truth 1986, and in Acousticus Maximus with James Reyne 1992. He wrote a rock musical, *Love Town* (1988), and has also worked as a writer. A fine voice, at home in various popular styles, his 19 singles include *We All Make Mistakes* (1982), *Your House Is Falling* (1988), and *I've Got A Lot Of Faith In You* (1993). He was voted *Rolling Stone* (Aust.) best male singer in 1989 and won an APRA award in 1989.

FURTHER REFERENCE
Recordings include *We All Make Mistakes* (1982, Phantom RRSP 719), *Your House Is Falling* (1988, True Tone TS2169), and *I've Got A Lot Of Faith In You* (1993, Polydor TLP 791309). His albums include *Senso* (1984, Regular RRLP 1208) *New Kind Of Blue* (1989, True Tone TLP 791309) and *Falling Swinger* (1994, Polydor 523355). For discography, see *SpencerA*. See also *SpencerW*; *Larkin*, I, 605; *Age* 30 Mar. 1996.

Curby, Harry   (*b* Sydney, 28 May 1933), violinist. He studied at the NSW State Conservatorium with Georgina McClean and Florent Hoegstoel and privately with Leopold Cherniavsky, then formed a string quartet in 1955 which appeared in Sydney concerts and broadcast for the ABC. After military service, he taught violin at the King's School, Parramatta, from 1957, and was in the Sydney Symphony Orchestra from 1959, as well as resuming frequent appearances in chamber music. He was in London with the Philharmonia and other orchestras 1961–63, and returned to the Sydney Symphony Orchestra in 1964, forming the ★Sydney String Quartet in 1965, which became resident at the Conservatorium.

From 1968 he was leader of the Dekany (later Haydn) String Quartet, Holland, and taught at the Royal Flemish Conservatoire, Belgium, from 1971. He returned to Australia in 1974 and re-established the Sydney String Quartet, which he led in numerous recordings and broadcasts and in touring North and South America, Canada, the UK, Europe and South-East Asia. After resigning from the quartet in 1980 he continued to teach and appear in chamber music in Sydney; he was visiting professor of violin at Brigham Young University,

Utah, USA, 1989–90, 1995–96, lecturer at the University of Queensland 1991–93, and at the Canberra School of Music from 1996.

Curby has been one of the most distinguished exponents of the traditional chamber repertoire in Australia. Under his leadership the Sydney String Quartet had its most prestigious period: their complete cycle of Beethoven quartets was performed nationally, and they made various recordings. Curby has also performed the complete Beethoven violin sonatas, the Corelli sonatas, the Brandenburg concertos, and over 100 other works. He was honoured with the OAM in 1986.

Currie, Neil (*b* Moose Jaw, Canada, 4 Dec. 1955), composer. He studied in the Faculty of Arts and Sciences, University of Saskatchewan, Canada, 1973–75, and psychology at the University of Alberta, Edmonton, 1975–77, and the University of British Columbia, Vancouver, 1977–79. Studies in composition followed, at the University of British Columbia 1979–82, then with Peter Sculthorpe at the University of Sydney 1985–88, and with Stephen Chatman at the University of British Columbia, from 1995. He lived in Canada until 1982, then Sydney 1982–90 and Adelaide 1990–95, where he was composer-in-residence with the Adelaide Symphony Orchestra 1990–91. Since 1995 he has returned to Canada. His compositions include *Windmill* (1985) for clarinet and percussion ensemble, *Stopping by Woods on a Snowy Evening* (1985) for solo tenor recorder, *Ortigas Avenue* (1986) for mixed chamber ensemble, *Tumbling Strain* (1991) for trombone and orchestra, and *Concerto for Guitar and Small Orchestra* (1990/93).

FURTHER REFERENCE
Recordings include the Trombone Concerto, Adelaide Symphony Orchestra, cond. N. Braithwaite, Warwick Tyrrell, trbn (ABC 438 825). His writings include 'A Home Away from Home', *SA* 27 (Spring 1990), 27–8, and 'Issues in the Appropriation of Sources for Musical Composition', *SA* 30 (Winter 1991), 15–18. See also *BroadstockS*; I. Shanahan and C. Dench, eds, 'An Emotional Geography of Australian Composition', *SA* 34 (Winter 1992), 8–32.

MICHAEL BARKL

Curro, John (*b* Cairns, 6 Dec. 1932), conductor, violinist, violist. He studied with Ezra Rachlin, Jan *Sedivka and Robert *Pikler. He taught at the Queensland Conservatorium, played in various chamber ensembles, and has conduced extensively in Australia and overseas for ABC orchestras, the Queensland and Shanghai Philharmonic Orchestras, the Christchurch Symphony, London Virtuosi, Queensland and Canberra Operas, Queensland Conservatorium Opera School and Queensland Ballet. He established the *Queensland Youth Orchestra in 1966 and the National Youth Concerto Competition, and has toured with the orchestra on eight international tours. Involved in many youth music organisations in Australia, Europe and Asia, he has toured as conductor with the Australian and Bavarian Youth Orchestras and is an executive member of Toyota World Youth Orchestra Conference. Visiting lecturer to Shanghai and Hong Kong Conservatoriums, he has received numerous awards for support of youth music including an Advance Australia Award (1987), an honorary doctorate from the University of Queensland (1989), the MBE (1980) and the AM (1995).

MELINDA J. SAWERS

Curtis, William John (*b* Sydney, 1 Sept. 1881; *d* May 1940), barrister, writer. Educated at the University of Sydney, he worked as a journalist and playwright before admission to the bar, where he eventually became a King's Counsel. He wrote librettos for W. Arundel *Orchard's comic operas *The Coquette* (1905) and *The Emperor* (1906), which were briefly produced at the Palace Theatre, Sydney, and the text for the cantata *Uller, the Bowman* (1912), which was published in London.

FURTHER REFERENCE
WWA (1938).

D

Daddy Cool. Rock band (1970–75) formed in Melbourne, originally comprised of Ross *Wilson (vocals, guitar), Ross Hannaford (lead guitar), Wayne Duncan (bass guitar), and Gary Young (drums). The group achieved success on the Melbourne dance and disco circuit with their mix of 1950s-style doo-wop and rock and roll covers and an outrageous stage act, with costumes such as Mickey Mouse ears and propeller hats. In May 1971 they released their first single, *Eagle Rock*, written by Wilson, which became the highest-selling Australian single of the year and remained at No.1 on the Australian charts for 25 weeks. The group toured the other Australian capitals and in July 1971 released their debut album, *Daddy Who?... Daddy Cool*, which achieved gold status in 11 weeks, and the band was voted best Australian group of 1971. The band toured the USA and returned with new member, Jeremy Noone. Their second album was the controversial *Sex, Dope, Rock'n'Roll — Teenage Heaven,* which remained at No.9 on the Australian charts for seven weeks. After a further US tour in 1972 the band disbanded. They reformed for the Sunbury festival of 1974, but only Wilson and Hannaford continued into 1975, and the band finally disbanded in September 1975.

FURTHER REFERENCE
Recordings include *Daddy Who?... Daddy Cool* (1971, Sparmac), *Sex, Dope and Rock'n'Roll* (1972, Sparmac), *Last Drive in Movie* (1973, Wizard), *Missing Masters* (1980, Wizard), *Daddy's Coolest* (1982, Wizard), *The Daddy Cool Collection* (1984, Axis). See also *McGrathA*; *SpencerW.*

NIKOLA SHARP

Dalgerie. Tragic opera (1958) in five scenes by James *Penberthy, libretto by Mary Durack after her novel *Keep Him My Country* (1955). First performed 22 January 1959, Somerville Auditorium, Perth.

Dallas, Rex [Fred Doble] (*b* Wallerawang, nr Lithgow, NSW, 6 Nov. 1938), country music singer-songwriter. Playing guitar and yodelling from his childhood, he first appeared on local radio at the age of 15, and moved to Sydney in 1954, becoming a regular on Ted Quigg's *On The Trail* on 2SM and in Quigg's hall show. From 1957 he toured with Lee *Gordon's shows, and in the early 1960s with *Rick and Thel. He signed with Festival Records in 1960, worked in Sydney clubs, and settled at Tamworth in 1972, appearing at the Tamworth Festival and touring with his four sons (the Dallas Cowboys) in his own show. One the most successful of the traditional bush ballad artists, and one of the foremost Australian exponents of yodelling, his repertoire ranges from Scottish and Irish ballads to country and rock and roll. He has won four ACMA Golden Guitars and made over 20 albums, including *We Dig Coal* (1991) a tribute to the coalminers of his home town.

FURTHER REFERENCE
Recordings include *Yodelling Mad* (1979), *Duelling Yodellers* with Owen Blundell (1988, Selection PCD 055), and *We Dig Coal* (1991, Hadley ENC 114).

Dalley-Scarlett, Robert (*b* Sydney, 16 Apr. 1887, *d* Brisbane, 31 July 1959), musicologist, conductor, organist. After early musical studies and freelance work in Sydney, he was appointed organist-choirmaster of Christ Church Anglican Cathedral, Grafton, in 1912. During wartime service in England he undertook further study with Sir Frederick Bridge and Richard Terry. After returning to Australia in 1917 he moved to Brisbane as organist of St Andrew's Presbyterian Church 1919–32, then at the Valley Methodist Church 1932–34, and All Saints' Church 1934–41. He obtained the DMus (University of Adelaide, 1934) via external study, majoring in composition.

Throughout his career Dalley-Scarlett was renowned for his knowledge of music of the 16th–18th centuries, and particularly the vocal works of G.F. Handel. In addition to various church choirs, he conducted the South Brisbane City Choir 1920–25 and the University [of Queensland] Musical Society 1920–30 and 1938–41, presenting with the latter a Bach Festival in 1930. But his main choral activity was the Brisbane Handel Society, which he founded in 1932 and conducted until 1959. In addition to broadcasts of Handel oratorios 1934–42, this choir presented annual unabridged performances of *Messiah* during the 1950s. These performances were supported by an extensive personal library numbering about 5000 volumes, including nearly 150 first editions of Handel and other 18th-century scores.

His ideas on 18th-century performance practice and other topics were published in numerous newspaper articles, the *Canon*, the *Australian Musical News*, and his booklet *Handel's 'Messiah': How Can We Realise the Composer's Intentions?* (New York: Carl Fischer, 1955). International recognition was awarded in the form of the Hallé Medal for Handel research, 1940. He was a full-time employee of the ABC in various capacities from 1941 to 1955, producing numerous music documentaries and radio scripts, and many arrangements of 18th-century works for local performing resources. A special project was a program of English coronation music, broadcast worldwide by the BBC in 1953. Further recognition was gained through his articles on Australian music for the fifth edition of *Grove's Dictionary* and *Hinrichsen's Musical Year Book*, 1949–50.

Dalley-Scarlett's work in relatively isolated Brisbane is significant in pre-empting the late 20th-century early music movement, and the pioneering work of conductors like Charles *Mackerras, whom he encouraged. He was a prolific composer of about 300 works, many of which were performed in concert or broadcast. He was founding president of the Queensland Guild of Composers 1940–53, a member of the University of Queensland's music advisory board 1924–37, and a founding member and later president of the Musical Association of Queensland (now Music Teachers' Association of Queensland). A triennial scholarship to his memory exists within the University of Queensland.

FURTHER REFERENCE

The Dalley-Scarlett collection is in the Fisher Library, University of Sydney, and Fryer Library, University of Queensland. See also Patricia Brown, 'Introduction to Robert Dalley-Scarlett and his Collection' and 'Early Published Handel Scores in the Dally-Scarlett Collection, Fisher Library, University of Sydney: A Descriptive Bibliography', *SMA* 5 (1971), 87–89 and supplement; Errol Lea-Scarlett, 'Robert Dalley Scarlett (1887–1959): Musician—Historian—Bibliophile', *Descent* 1/4, 3–17 and 2/1, 3–19 (1963); Peter Roennfeldt, Robert Dalley-Scarlett: His Contribution to Musical Life in Brisbane 1919–59, BMus(Hons), Univ. Queensland, 1978; idem, *ADB*, 8.   PETER ROENNFELDT

Dallwitz, Dave (David Frederick) (*b* Freeling, SA, 25 Oct. 1914), jazz performer, composer. His first exposure to jazz on recordings in the late 1920s led to his tinkering on the piano, but it was exposure to the recordings of Duke Ellington in the 1930s that consolidated his interest. With the addition of trombone to his repertoire

he became active in Adelaide, assuming leadership of the Southern Jazz Group in 1946, transforming its style from swing to a more 'classic' approach. The Southern Jazz Group, minus its pianist, came to national attention at the first *Australian Jazz Convention (1946), and through recordings and live performances with varying personnel, went on to become seminal in the postwar movement in SA. Through his tightly focused leadership of the group, Dallwitz became one of the main architects of what is frequently argued to be the 'Australian jazz style'. Policy differences between Dallwitz and the reed player Bruce Gray led to the group's break-up in 1951, though there have been occasional reunions since.

Although continuing to work in revues, Dallwitz withdrew from jazz, while pursuing his career as a painter and art teacher. The second stage of his jazz career can be dated from the series of recordings he began making from 1972, leading various bands of different sizes. Although he has continued to appear on concert and festival stages, these and his recordings have functioned primarily as vehicles for his prolific compositional output. This corpus has shown a particular fascination with Australian landscape, culture and history, including evocations of the Coorong, chronicles of Ned Kelly and the goldfields, and portraits of prominent Australians. At all stages Dallwitz has chosen to remain within the formal traditions of the 'classic' jazz style of the 1920s. The convergence of style and subject matter earned from Clement Semmler the apt description of Dallwitz as a 'jazz Jindyworobak'. His approach has sometimes produced rather flat and predictable work, but increasingly in the later period of his career the tensions between established jazz conventions and his attempt to articulate aspects of Australian experience in new ways has produced music which is uniquely powerful and expressive, though still largely unappreciated by the musical establishment. A striking example of his work is the *Ern Malley Suite*. Dallwitz's association with radical arts (he was the founding chairman of the Adelaide Contemporary Art Society) informs this suite, emerging as often disturbing exploratory distortions of traditional musical materials, which reflect the complex ironies of the events on which the suite is based. Dallwitz was awarded the AM in 1986.

FURTHER REFERENCE

Recordings include *Southern Jazz Group, 1946–1950, vols 1–4* (Dawn Club DC 12021 to 12024); *Stompology*, Dave Dallwitz Jazzmen (1972, Swaggie S-1321); *The Ern Malley Suite* (1975, Swaggie S-1360); *Riverboat Days, A Jazz Suite by Dave Dallwitz* (1976, Swaggie S-1366). See also *BissetB*; *OxfordJ*; *GroveJ*; Bruce Clunies-Ross, 'An Australian Sound, Jazz in Melbourne and Adelaide 1941–1951', in P. Spearritt and D. Walker, eds, *Australian Popular Culture* (Sydney: Allen & Unwin, 1979), 62–80; Bruce Johnson, 'Traditional Jazz in Adelaide, Dave Dallwitz and the Southern Jazz Group', *JA* Part 1 (Mar./Apr. 1982) 10–13; Part 2 (May/June 1982), 10–13; Part 3 (Aug. 1982), 10–13.

BRUCE JOHNSON

Dalmatians, The. Opera in three acts, music and libretto by Mona *McBurney after Francis Crawford Marietta's *A Maid of Venice*. Set at Venice in the 15th century, it is the story of a family rivalry. First performed in concert on 10 December 1910 and staged at the Melbourne Playhouse on 25 June 1926.

Daly River Songs. The principal public song genres of the coastal and inland peoples in the vicinity of the Daly River and Anson Bay, NT, are *wangga* and *lirrga*. Language groups who own *wangga* include Marrige, Marrisyabin, Marriamu, Marrithiyel, Ngan'gikurunggurr, Marrimananji, Marranunggu, Emmiyangal, Mendheyangal, Wadjiginy (Batjamalh) and Kiyuk. Those that own *lirrga* include Marringarr, Ngan'gimarri, Ngan'giwumirri and Wagiman. Most members of these language groups now live at the settlements of Port Keats (Wadeye), Daly River, Peppimenarti, Nadirri and Belyuen.

Both *wangga* and *lirrga* are performed by one or two male singers accompanied by a male didjeridu-player. Their formal construction—that is, in the way in which the elements of music, text, didjeridu accompaniment and dance are fitted together in performance—displays considerable flexibility. Songs frequently contain a high proportion in everyday language as well as some text that is semantically opaque. Didjeridu style is marked by a rich sonority and the absence of overblown hoots characteristic of songs from further east.

The dancing associated with *wangga* and *lirrga* is famous both for its virtuosity and its ability to accommodate dancers, men, women and children of varying standards. Songs are acquired by individuals either by dreaming them, or by inheriting them from older singers. They form the musical and choreographic core of a number of traditional ceremonies of a social rather than a revelatory nature, including male circumcision and mortuary rites and ceremonies for the disposal of dead people's belongings. Nowadays they also accompany ceremonies such as college graduations, the dedication of new buildings, and Christian ritual and are frequently performed for entertainment. See also *Aboriginal Music* §3.

ALLAN MARETT

Daly-Wilson Big Band. Formed in Sydney by drummer Warren Daly and trombonist Ed Wilson, making its public debut at the Stage Club, August 1969. Dormant from December 1971 to 1973, it was then revived through private sponsorship. Extensive concert, television and film appearances followed, the band toured nationally and internationally, and won gold records, then broke up in 1983 when the leaders parted company, each going on to form his own groups. It was the most commercially successful jazz-based big band in postwar Australia, providing performance opportunities for many young musicians before the advent of the jazz studies program at the NSW Conservatorium offered them institutional experience.

FURTHER REFERENCE
Recordings include *The Daly-Wilson Band on Tour* (1970). An interview with Warren Daly is in *WilliamsA*, 113–17. See also *BissetB*; *OxfordJ*.

BRUCE JOHNSON

Dan Morgan, folk-song. This traditional bushranging song tells the true story of Dan 'Mad Dog' Morgan, who terrorised squatters on the Victoria–NSW border 1863–65. Of unknown origin, it was first published by the Folklore Council of Australia (1967).

FURTHER REFERENCE
Edition and commentary in *EdwardsG*.

D-an-D. See *Percussion instrument makers*.

Danks & Son, John. Firm of bell-makers, casting from 1888, originally in Melbourne. The three Danks brothers were engineers who settled in Melbourne in 1857 and established a sizeable business making building and gardening tools and engineering equipment; their business expanded to branches in Sydney and NZ over the next decade. They cast miniature bells for an orchestral performance at the Melbourne International Centennial Exhibition in 1888, and opened a foundry at Sydney in 1896. They supplied bells to a number of churches across Australia and the Newcastle City Hall, reaching the peak of their production in 1920s, casting a set of eight chime bells for St Bartholomew's, Burnley, in 1929. Their last known bell was for the Stawell Town Hall in 1938.

FURTHER REFERENCE
John D. Keating, *Bells in Australia* (Melbourne: MUP, 1979), 112–15.

Dargie, Horrie (*b* Melbourne, 1917), harmonica player. After playing diatonic mouth-organ with the Yarraville Mouth Organ Band in his teens, then chromatic mouth-organ with the Victorian Mouth Organ Band from 1937, he won *P&A Parade* on 3KZ, toured with the ABC, and made his first single (1938, Columbia). Moving to Sydney, he started his Horrie Dargie Club harmonica school in 1939 and formed the Rocking Reeds (1940–42), making six recordings. After serving in the Australian entertainment unit during the war, he worked as arranger and saxophonist at the Regent Theatre, Melbourne. He toured abroad with the Horrie Dargie Quintet 1952–57, then became a television quiz show compère, continuing to perform and compose music for television and films. The dominant figure in Australian harmonica-playing, his 15 albums show the harmonica as an instrument of unsuspected character and pliancy.

FURTHER REFERENCE
Recordings include *Horrie Dargie Harmonica Spectacular* (1973) and *Harmonica Favourites* (1974). He has published a harmonica

tutor. See also Ray Grieve, *A Band in a Waistcoat Pocket* (Sydney: Currency Press, 1995), 82–90.

Darwin, pop. (1991) 78 401. Capital of the Northern Territory, situated on a peninsula at Clarence Strait. First settled (as Palmerston) in 1869. A fund-raising concert was held just four years later, the Methodist church choir presented concerts from the early years, and the Palmerston Dramatic and Musical Society was formed in 1883. A stopping point *en route* to Asia, opera soon came to be presented by such travelling companies as the ★Carandinis (1881), Pollard's (1884) and Harding's (1889). But it remained a harsh frontier town whose inhabitants soon moved on, and few resident ensembles survived long.

The advent of air travel in the 1930s, and the rebuilding of the town after the Japanese bombings of 1942 and again after the cyclone of 1974 quickened the pace of development, and today Darwin is a rapidly expanding city. With a growing number of resident players, the semi-professional Darwin Symphony Orchestra regularly plays in the fine 1070-seat Playhouse at the Performing Arts Centre and Beaufort Hotel complex (opened 1986), as well as throughout the NT, including outdoors at Kakadu or Katherine Gorge, under its enterprising conductor Martin Jarvis. There is an active Darwin Chorale, the Darwin Youth Orchestra, and the Darwin Eisteddfod (founded 1958), which attracted 150 competitors in its first year. The Northern Territory University music department (also under Jarvis) offers a degree focusing on music education and community work. At Brown's Mart Community Arts, composer Sarah ★Hopkins did notable experimental work 1982–89. Chinese, Greek and an emerging Timorese community retain their traditional musical customs.

Davey Piano Scholarship, Florence. One of the most valuable piano scholarships in Australia. Florence Davey (*d* 1994), a Brisbane piano teacher who believed her own early development had been stunted by the lack of opportunity to study abroad, established a trust at the University of Queensland in 1984 to create a scholarship for a recent piano graduate of a Queensland music school. Awarded biannually after a public competition, the prize is currently $20 000.

Davidson, Jim (James H.) (*b* Sydney, 6 Aug. 1902; *d* Bowral, NSW, 9 Apr. 1982), jazz drummer, bandleader. He began on brass instruments as a child, then switched to drums, *c*.1919. He worked in Sydney pit orchestras and jazz-influenced dance bands, including that of Jimmy Elkins. He was with Jack Woods at the Ambassadors when it was burned out in 1931. He formed a band at Smith's Oriental, which with additional personnel moved to the Palais Royal from May 1933 to 1934, interrupted by a brief season in Melbourne's St Kilda Palais. He ceased work as a drummer from January 1935 upon taking leadership of the Melbourne ABC Dance Band, resumed

leadership at Sydney's Palais in May 1936, then in 1937 began leading the ABC (Sydney) dance band, which toured nationally. Joining the AIF in 1940, he finished his war service in 1946 as lieutenant colonel in charge of all entertainment units. After the war he was with Harry Wren's organisation before taking up a position with the BBC, London, from 1948, achieving considerable influence in English broadcasting. He returned to Australia in 1964, consulting for the ABC until retiring.

An astute observer of popular taste, Davidson sensed a post-Depression shift in mood, with recordings and broadcasts from the Sydney Palais in 1933 which anticipated the swing craze. His ABC Sydney band was extremely influential, especially by virtue of their tours, which gave national exposure to live swing performances. His wartime service also brought him to an unparalleled position of power in the Australian music industry, making him pivotal in harnessing popular music to the war effort.

FURTHER REFERENCE

Recordings include *The Tuneful 20's and 30's*, Jim Davidson With His New Palais Royal Orchestra & His A.B.C. Dance Orchestra (1977, HMV OXLP 7630). See also *BissetB*; *OxfordJ*; Jim Davidson, *A Showman's Story* (Adelaide: Rigby, 1983); Jack Mitchell, 'Jim Davidson', *JA* (May/June 1982), 33.

BRUCE JOHNSON

Davies, Charles Edward [Edwin]   (*b* 1899; *d* 1978), piano manufacturer. After being apprenticed to ★Beale & Co., by 1921 he had started his own business, buying second-hand pianos and reconditioning them for resale. With his three sons he set up as a manufacturer at Surry Hills, Sydney, in 1946, producing his Symphony range of pianos, which he sold under government contract to schools and hospitals. The frames were cast at the company's foundry at Yagoona, and the instruments were hand-made, chiefly using imported materials, the soundboards being of Canadian spruce. One of the last Australian piano-makers to succumb to the demand for cheap imported instruments, at his death Davies had made about 12 000 pianos; his family continues to work in piano-tuning and maintenance.

FURTHER REFERENCE

AthertonA.

Davies, E(dward) Harold (*b* Oswestry, England, 18 July 1867; *d* Adelaide, 1 July 1947), organist, conductor, professor of music. Davies commenced his tertiary studies at the Elder Conservatorium at the University of Adelaide immediately on emigrating to Australia in 1887. In 1902 he established the Adelaide Bach Society, and in 1920 formed the Adelaide Symphony Orchestra. He became the first person to be awarded a doctorate in music at the University of Adelaide in 1902, and in 1919 he was appointed as Elder professor there. Between 1926 and

1929, he travelled to southern and central Australia to observe and record Aboriginal songs. He was an active board member of the AMEB, playing an important part in the introduction of the LMusA and AMusA in the 1920s. Davies was organist at various Adelaide churches until the 1920s. He was awarded an honorary DMus at the University of Western Australia in 1934.

FURTHER REFERENCE
Catherine J. Ellis, *ADB*, 8; *John's Notable Australians*; *Who's Who in Australia* (1909); Victor Edgeloe, *The Language of Human Feeling* (1985); *GlennonA*, 194; Andrew McCredie, ed., *From Colonel Light into the Footlights: The Performing Arts in South Australia from 1836 into the Present* (Adelaide: Pagel, 1988).

ISOBEL McCLENNAN

Davies, Ivor.   See *Icehouse*.

Davies, (Norman) Brian   (*b* Sydney 1945), pop singer. With an almost artless image in the Frankie Avalon mode, he appeared on television's *Bandstand* from 1959 and made seven singles, including two Top 40 hits—a cover for Mark Wynter's *Dream Girl* (1961) which reached No. 1 in the charts, and *Ten Pin Bowling* (1962). By 1962 the *Brian Davies Show* was on national television when he was only 17. He went to England briefly in 1964, adopting the Beatles' image and style; on his return he recorded another 13 singles including *Alberta* (1967) and the album *Together By Myself* (1968). He re-emerged in 1981 with a short-lived television show *Catch Us If You Can*.

FURTHER REFERENCE
Recordings include *Dream Girl* (1961, HMV EA 4425), *Ten Pin Bowling* (1962, HMV EA4466), *Alberta* (1967, HMV EA4845) and the album *Together By Myself* (1968, Columbia OEX 9498). For discography, see *SpencerA*. See also *McGrathA*; *SpencerW.*

Davis, Herbert Nelson   (*b* Melbourne, 21 Apr. 1899; *d* Melbourne, 17 July 1963), organist. Davis was educated at the St Paul's Cathedral Choir School, Melbourne, and sang as a chorister in the cathedral choir under the direction of Ernest ★Wood, who influenced him greatly. He received organ lessons with Claude Kingston at the Baptist Church, Collins Street, and subsequently held the positions of organist at Richmond Presbyterian Church and in the city of Melbourne, the Australian, Wesley, Independent and Scots Churches. He was an accomplished recitalist and teacher and a founder of the Society of Organists (Victoria) in 1939. Davis was conductor of the Zelman Memorial Orchestra, the Malvern Choral Society, the Presbyterian Oratorio Society, and the Box Hill Choral Society and was director of the Melba Conservatorium from 1952 until his death.

FURTHER REFERENCE
Obit. in *Age* 18 July 1963.

JOHN MAIDMENT

Davy, Ruby Claudia Emily   (*b* Salisbury, SA, 22 Nov. 1883; *d* Adelaide, 12 July 1949), piano teacher. After piano lessons from her mother and Ernest Mitchell, she studied at the Elder Conservatorium and worked as a pianist and teacher at Adelaide from 1909. She also studied composition, becoming in 1918 the first woman to obtain the DMus at the University of Adelaide, and in 1921 the first Australian woman to obtain the FTCL. She established a piano-teaching practice at Prospect, SA, in 1920, then moved to Melbourne in 1934, teaching and giving broadcast lectures. She toured Europe in 1939, giving guest lectures in London.

FURTHER REFERENCE
Joyce Gibberd, Silvia O'Toole, *ADB*, 8.

Dawson, Peter Smith   ['J.P. McCall', etc.]   (*b* Adelaide 31, Jan. 1882; *d* Sydney, 9 Sept. 1961), baritone. Apprenticed as a plumber, early successes as a singer in competitions encouraged him to try his luck in London in 1902. He studied for three years with Charles Santley and began his career as a bass, then lessons with Kantorez developed his latent upper register, allowing him to embrace the entire baritone repertoire. As his concert career was beginning, Gaisberg contracted him to the Gramophone Company: 'Within a few weeks I had him making popular, comic and serious ballads, oratorio and opera arias, Gilbert and Sullivan, solos, duets, trios, quartets, choruses, etc. His first record … appeared in the 1904 catalogue.' He recorded ballads and serious songs under his own name, but other genres under many pseudonyms. He reached the zenith of his career *c*.1934, when 212 of his solo titles were in the HMV catalogue and his annual recording contract paid £3500. Based principally in London until 1939 he toured extensively throughout the British Empire, including seven tours of Australia and NZ. From the advent of radio he was a popular broadcaster, and he also appeared in the first British television transmissions and in several films. He made his last extended tour throughout England at the age of 73.

Although his recordings of the standard operatic arias are exemplary, Dawson did not have an operatic voice. 'The velvety quality of his well-produced voice', said Gaisberg, 'his ability to throw pathos, tears, laughter and drama into it, his quickness in reading, musicianship and contagious good humour, made him a recorder's dream come true.' He has been credited with a repertoire of 2500 songs and sales of 13 million records between 1904 and 1954. Though remembered as 'the ballad king', his repertoire covered the entire vocal spectrum; his concert programs began with a Baroque aria, oratorio or operatic arias then groups of foreign and British art-songs. The popular recorded ballads were only sung as encores. He composed about 60 songs, many recorded, written under several pseudonyms, the most famous being J.P. McCall. Despite his fame and the continued publicity Dawson remained true to the Australian character, an excellent raconteur, generous and something of a larrikin.

His robust tone suggested a stalwart figure, but surprised concertgoers found their icon was a rotund 1.7 m. He helped many artists and composers entering the profession and influenced generations of singers and teachers with his impeccable vocal style and technique.

FURTHER REFERENCE

A representative selection of his recordings is *Peter Dawson: Ambassador of Song*, 10 discs (1982, EMI OXLP 7661–70). His memoirs were *Fifty Years of Song* (London: Hutchinson, 1951). His papers are in NFSA, EMI Archives, and BBC Written Archives, among others. See also *BrisbaneE*, 157; F. Gaisberg, *The Voice* 32 (Jan. 1949), 125–6; James Glennon, *ADB*, 8; *GlennonA*, 47; *MackenzieS*, 92ff; Sydney *Daily Telegraph* 23 Aug. 1991.

                                                          RUSSELL SMITH

Dawson, 'Smoky' (Herbert Henry)   (*b* Warrnambool, Vic., 19 Mar. 1913), country music singer–songwriter. With his mother dead and father frequently unwell, he was placed in an orphanage from 1923 and left school at the age of 13. Playing steel guitar in imitation of the fad for Hawaiian music, he formed the Coral Island Boys with his brother Ted, performing on Melbourne's amateur 3JR from 1932. From 1935 he was a regular performer in *P&A Parade* at 3KZ, then to capitalise on the American hillbilly craze he developed the toothpaste-sponsored *Smoky Dawson and the Pepsodent Rangers* in 1937, the first country and western music show on Australian radio. He continued to broadcast with his South Sea Islanders, and in 1941 made his first country music record, *I'm A Happy Go-Lucky Cowhand*.

After war service he toured with Stan Gill's rodeo, singing, buck-jumping, performing farmyard animal mimicry and a knife-throwing act. He went to the USA, appearing on television, in the movie *The Cowboy From Down Under* in 1950 and in the Broadway production of *Kiss Me, Kate* with his whip act, and signing with Hickory Records. From 1952–1962 his Australian radio serial *The Adventures of Smoky Dawson* and its related promotions for Kellogg's Corn Flakes made his name a household word. Settling at his riding school property at Ingleside in 1957 (destroyed by bushfire in 1979), he recorded only intermittently after 1962, but performed and broadcast from Sydney's 2RDT and 2NSB into his 80s, releasing *The Road To Anywhere* in 1990. In 1996 he collaborated with John *Farnham on an album. With his horse Flash, synonymous with his appearances, he led the annual Cavalcade at Tamworth until the horse died at the age of 35 in 1982.

A major conduit for the absorption in Australia of American popular musical fashions of the pre-war years, he was Australian country music's most commercial exponent of the wholesome, sentimentalised cowboy image. He was honoured in the ACMA Roll of Renown in 1978 and with the MBE in 1983, and won two ACMA Golden Guitars (1988, 1989).

FURTHER REFERENCE

Recordings include *I'm A Happy Go-Lucky Cowhand* (reissued 1991, Kingfisher KF-AUS 16), *Good Time Radio* (Broad Music EMD 050) and *Singin' in the Saddle* (Festival D19212). For discography see *WatsonC*, I. His autobiography is Herbert H. Dawson, *Smoky Dawson: A Life* (Sydney: Allen & Unwin, 1985); *MonashB*.

Day, Archie (Archibald John Shepherdson) (*b* Brisbane, 10 Nov. 1901; *d* Brisbane, 25 Feb. 1975), organist, teacher. In 1920 he won a scholarship to Trinity College, London. He was organist and choirmaster at Ann Street Presbyterian Church, Brisbane, 1923–33, and then at Albert Street Methodist Church until his death. During World War II he joined the army education and entertainment unit. Throughout his long career he was highly respected as a teacher, pianist, accompanist, organ recitalist and AMEB examiner. He was also city organist from 1950 to 1975. He wrote three short organ pieces and three small works for choir, none published.

FURTHER REFERENCE

Gordon Spearritt, *ADB*, 13.   ROBERT BOUGHEN

Day, Trevor   (*b* Lorne, Vic., 3 Nov. 1931), country music singer-songwriter. Listening to Tex *Morton and others from an early age, he began playing guitar in 1951 and performed in Sydney in Tim McNamara's shows, on country radio, and on the showboat *Kalang*, then toured with Reg *Lindsay and Judy *Stone. He came to wide attention during three years with Chad *Morgan in the late 1950s; recording for Columbia, his first single, *The Boy Soldier* (1959), and the EP *Take It Back And Change It For A Boy* were long remembered. One of Australia's finest traditional country ballad performers, he settled at Bonville, NSW, but reappeared in 1978, recording for Hadley and touring with *Rick and Thel in 1979.

FURTHER REFERENCE

Recordings include *The Boy Soldier* (1959, Columbia DO 4042), *Take It Back And Change It For A Boy* (Hadley HEP 538), *The Best Of Trevor Day* (Hadley HCSM 3015), *On The Road: Stories Of People And Places* (Hadley HLP 1258), and *Wisdom, Wit And Wiles* (Hadley HCD 1316). For discography see *WatsonC*, II. See also *WatsonC*, II, 197–203.

De Beaupuis, Emmanuele   (*b* Naples, Italy, *c*.1860; *d* Sydney, 27 Mar. 1913), pianist, composer. De Beaupuis studied at the Naples Royal Conservatory with Benjamin Cesi. After six years in Cairo he arrived in Melbourne in 1889. He became well known locally as a virtuoso pianist and toured Australia and South Africa in 1893. From *c*.1896 he taught and performed in Sydney, appearing as pianist for the last time with Jan Kubelik in 1908. He was knighted by the king of Italy in 1912. De Beaupuis composed mostly salon and concert works for piano; his *Ave Maria* for soprano (published by Ricordi) was well known.

FURTHER REFERENCE

Obit. in *SMH* 28 Mar. 1913. A list of some of his works appears in *SnellA*. See also *Australasian* 29 Mar. 1913; *Freeman's Journal* (Sydney) 3 Apr. 1913.

JENNIFER HILL

de Haan, Simone   (*b* Perth, 23 Oct. 1953), trombonist, administrator. After lessons in Perth and playing in the Australian Youth Orchestra, he became principal trombone in the West Australian Symphony Orchestra, then associate principal with the Elizabethan Theatre Trust (Sydney) Orchestra. In 1975 he received a Churchill fellowship and studied with Denis Wick and others in London and Jean Douay at Paris; he also heard concerts by trombonist-composers James Fulkerson and Vinko Globokar which were to have a profound impact on his own development.

From 1978 he specialised in contemporary performance, playing in Keith Humble's ACME, then ★Flederman, through which he commissioned new works for trombone from many Australian composers. He taught at the Queensland Conservatorium, then from 1981 at the Canberra School of Music, and from 1988 at the Victorian College of the Arts. In Melbourne he founded ★Pipeline, whose innovative work has embraced new music, performance art, and the composer–jazz improviser interface. He was professor and director of the Tasmanian Conservatorium (1991–96), where he directed New Music Tasmania, and is now provost and director of the Queensland Conservatorium.

A naturally gifted and highly innovative player, he is among the foremost figures in Australian contemporary music performance. He views the design of performance contexts and improvisation as central to music-making. Although he has composed works for trombone with tape, including *Soil 1* (1980), and with percussion and tape, such as *Shifting Sliding+* (1991), he regards much of his organisational and ensemble work as 'compositional in the broader sense'.

FURTHER REFERENCE

Recordings include *Anthology of Aust. Music on Disc* vol. 13 with C. Vine, G. Leak, G. Schiemer (Canberra School of Music, CSM 13). His writings include 'Credo', *SA*, 23 (Spring 1989), 6–7, and '20th-Century Trombone Works Since 1970', *Aust. Trombone Education Magazine*, 8 (Apr. 1985), 11 (Dec. 1986), 12 (June 1987). See also *BroadstockS*, 110–12; Roger Dean, 'Improvising the Listener: the Listener Improvises', *SA* 32 (Summer 1991–92), 45–50.

de Hugard, Dave   (*b* Stanthorpe, Qld, 1942), folksinger, songwriter. Trained as a pharmacist, he was inspired by Bill Scott's performances at the Brisbane folk centre to study music; he entered Monash University, then graduated in social anthropology from Macquarie University. He collected folk-song and oral history in NSW in the early 1980s, and plays anglo concertina, fiddle, banjo, accordion and jaws harp, appearing at pubs and folk clubs. His songs include *Three Kids On A Horse* and *Magpie In The Wattle*. A writer and performer of the traditional folk ballad style, he played with the Larrikins, and has performed his songs at Maleny Folk Festival and elsewhere.

FURTHER REFERENCE

Recordings include *Freedom On The Wallaby* (1969) and *Magpie Morning* (1994, Sandstock SSM 047CD). See also *StubingtonC*, 46–7.

de Jong, Sarah   (*b* Christchurch, NZ, 30 Nov. 1952), composer. She studied composition with Barry ★Conyngham and Brian ★Howard at the University of Melbourne. Since 1978 she has been active in composing for theatre, dance, radio, television, film and for the concert hall. She has developed into one of Australia's leading composers for theatre with over 50 scores to her credit; many of these are for plays by Louis Nowra. Her music has supported a number of acclaimed productions including two films entitled *Sparks* and *Flirting* which each won an Australian Institute Best Film Award in 1990; while two radio plays entitled *Summer of the Aliens* and *The Lights of Jericho* won Prix Italia Awards in 1990 and 1994 respectively.

FURTHER REFERENCE

Her writings include 'The Roar of the Greasepaint, the Sniff of a Budget', *SA* 25 (Autumn 1990), 27–9; *Weekend Australian*, 16 Sept. 1989, *Weekend Review* supplement, 13, 16.

JOEL CROTTY

De Kroo Brothers.   Pop music duo (1959–65) comprised of Leo [Leendert] and Doug de Kroo (both vocals, guitar). Arriving from Holland after World War II, they settled in Perth, and from 1957 Doug played with local pop bands while Lee was working as a solo artist; they combined in a local rock and roll band, the Roulettes, and won a radio talent quest in 1959. Moving to Sydney in 1960, they released the first of their 10 singles as the De Kroo Brothers, *On The Job Too Long*, touring country centres 1960–62. Their act was modelled on the Everly Brothers but used characteristically over-sized guitars. *(Her Name is) Scarlett* made the Top 40 in 1963, and for a time they appeared frequently on television, but after the arrival of the Beatles changed teenage tastes they opened a guitar school at Bondi from 1965.

FURTHER REFERENCE

Recordings include *On The Job Too Long* (Columbia DO 4126), *(Her Name is) Scarlett* (Festival FK 438). Their work is available in compilation on *Scarlett* (1988, Festival L19005) and *Collectors' Album* (1988, Canetoad CTLP 002). For discography, see *SpencerA*. See also *McGrathA*; *SpencerW*; Paul Hughes in *Collected Stories on Australia Rock'n'Roll*, ed. David McLean (Sydney: Canetoad Publications, 1991).

de Pieri, Sergio (*b* Treviso, Italy, 22 Nov. 1932),
organist. He graduated from the Benedetto Marcello
Conservatorium, Venice, in 1959 after organ studies
with Sandro dalla Libera, followed by postgraduate
study under Fernando Germani and Ferruccio Vig-
nanelli. Arriving in Australia in 1961, he taught organ at
the University of Melbourne Conservatorium from
1962 and was organist at St Patrick's Cathedral, Melbourne from 1963. He was influential during the 1960s
as teacher, broadcaster, recording artist and recitalist,
introducing the Italian and early English keyboard
repertoire. In 1971 he founded the *Melbourne
Autumn Festival of Organ and Harpsichord and
returned to Italy in 1972 where he was organist of the
Frari Church, Venice, chief study organ professor at the
Benedetto Marcello Conservatorium, a government
inspector of historic organs and founder of several
organ festivals. He returned in 1995 to live in Melbourne where he is a teacher and recitalist.

FURTHER REFERENCE
Recordings include *Organ Recital At St Patrick's Cathedral* (W&G
WG-B-2470); *Five Vivaldi-Bach concertos* [Knox Grammar School]
(Concert Recording [Linwood, CA, USA] CR0040); *Sergio de
Pieri Melbourne Town Hall 19 November 1969* (W&G WG-13-S-
5447); *de Pieri at St Patrick's* (Fidelis [Melbourne] TMS177);
Musica Antiqua [St Hilda's College, University of Melbourne]
(Fidelis [Melbourne] TMS173). Further organ recordings were
made at Wilson Hall, University of Melbourne, St Ignatius'
Church, Richmond, Christ Church, Brunswick, and the Uniting
Church, Toorak.

JOHN MAIDMENT

de Pinna, Herb. Composer of waltzes, marches and
songs in the World War I years, as well as the pantomime
Bunyip (*c*.1916). His songs, published chiefly by Palings,
include *I Love You* (*c*.1916), but most deal with wartime
themes, such as *I Would Like a Letter from Home* (*c*.1917),
Off to the Trenches, and *Bill's Enlisted*. His piano works
included *Eight Interesting Pianoforte Solos* (1916).

FURTHER REFERENCE
A list of songs is in *SnellA*. See also *Theatre* (Jan 1917), 23.

De Profundis. Monodrama by Larry *Sitsky, libretto
by Gwen Harwood after Oscar Wilde. First performed in
concert at the Canberra School of Music on 31 October
1982, and staged at the University of New South Wales on
8 April 1987.

Dead Heat, The. Operetta in one act, music and text
by Fritz *Hart. First performed by the Albert Street Conservatorium in 1931.

Dean Emmerson Dean. Trio founded (1990) at
Brisbane, comprised of Paul Dean (clarinet), Stephen
Emmerson (piano) and Brett Dean (viola). Focusing on

trio and duo sonatas, they have appeared on regional tours
for Musica Viva and in Brisbane. They have released a CD,
night window (1993 ABC).

Deane, J(ohn) P(hillip) (*b* London, 1796; *d* Sydney,
19 Dec. 1849), violinist, organist, teacher. After playing
violin in the London Philharmonic Society, he arrived in
Hobart with his family in 1822, and opened a music business and bookshop; he became organist at St David's
Hobart from 1825 and began giving concerts in 1826. He
moved to Sydney in 1836, where as a soloist or with his
children John and Morris (violins), Rosalie (piano) and
Edward (cello) in a chamber ensemble he gave numerous
soirées and chamber music concerts, including first Australian performances of chamber music by Haydn and
Mozart. He also appeared with W. Vincent *Wallace,
George *Sippe and others in *Messiah*, *The Creation* and
other larger presentations. Willing to turn his hand to
almost any branch of music-making, he and his daughter
Rosalie could offer between them tuition in violin, piano,
voice, cello, flute and music theory, as well as a service
tuning pianos. He also composed (his String Trio was
presented in his concerts), and he conducted operas,
including *La Sonnambula* and *Der Freischütz* for Frank
*Howson at the Royal Victoria Theatre in 1847. A com-
mitted and energetic musician, he was among the earliest
pioneers of musical life in Australia. His son Edward carried on the business after his death.

FURTHER REFERENCE
Ann Wentzel, *ADB*, 1; idem, The First 100 Years of Music in Australia, 1788–1888, MA, Univ. Sydney, 1963; Osric [Humphrey
Hall and Alfred John Cripps], *The Romance of the Sydney Stage* (ms,
1911; pub. Sydney: Currency Press, 1996), 39f.; *GlennonA*; *BrewerD*, 56; *OrchardM*, 13–32.

Death of Ben Hall, folk-song. One of a number of
traditional bushranging songs dealing with Ben Hall, the
Murrurundi farmer who was purportedly driven by harsh
government treatment into outlaw life in 1862, and killed
by police on Lachlan Plain, near Forbes, NSW, in 1865.
Collected by John Meredith in 1955.

FURTHER REFERENCE
Published in *MeredithF*, I, 164, and *ManifoldP*; *RadicS*, 3.

Dee-Jays, The. Rock band (1957–65) formed by
Johnny *O'Keefe, comprised of chiefly Dave Owens and
Johnny Greenan (saxophones), Lou Casch (guitar), Keith
Williams (bass), Mike Tseng (piano) and Johnny 'Catfish'
Purser (drums). Formed to play at suburban dances, they
were soon backing O'Keefe, Eddie Cochran and others in
Lee *Gordon's shows. They became the resident band at
O'Keefe's television show *Six O'Clock Rock* in 1959. The
first professional rock band in Australia, they appear in
O'Keefe's recordings, and on their own in singles includ-
ing *Straight Flush* (1960), *Toy Balloons* (1962), *Sunday Patrol*

(1964), the EPs *OffShore* and *Big Daddy*, and the album *Twisting Drums*.

FURTHER REFERENCE

Recordings, now rare, include *Straight Flush* (1960, Lee Gordon LSG 606), *Toy Balloons* (1962, Festival FK 263) *Sunday Patrol* (1964 Leedon LK 555), the EPs *OffShore* (Leedon LX 10640) and *Big Daddy* (LX 10709), and the album *Twisting Drums* (Leedon LL 30761). For discography, see *SpencerA*. See also *McGrathA*; *SpencerW*; Michael Sturma, *Australian Rock'n'Roll: The First Wave* (Kenhurst, NSW: Kangaroo Press, 1991), 18–21, 28, 35–6.

Deirdre in Exile. Opera, music and libretto by Fritz ★Hart (1926) after Yeats, first performed at Melbourne by the Melba–Williamson Opera Co. on 22 June 1928. Ms in *Msl*.

Delany, John Albert (*b* Ratcliffe, London, 6 July 1852; *d* Paddington, Sydney, 11 May. 1907), conductor, organist. Arriving in Australia in infancy, he studied organ with William Cordner at St Mary's Cathedral, Sydney, then played violin in the Royal Victoria Theatre Orchestra. He was organist and choirmaster at St Mary's 1872–74, then in Melbourne as chorusmaster for the Lyster Opera Co. from 1877 and conductor at the Bijou Theatre, Melbourne, from 1884. Returning to Sydney, he became conductor of the Sydney Liedertafel in 1886, but came to regard male-only singing as 'a disastrous regression' and resigned in 1897 when he was not allowed to incorporate women in the choir. He was director of music at St Mary's from 1886 and a founding teacher at the Sydney College of Music in 1894. A choral conductor of considerable ability, he gave the Australian premiere of Elgar's *Dream of Gerontius* in 1903. His compositions include a fluent cantata, *Captain Cook* (1888, libretto by P.E. Quinn), two masses and various motets. His cantata was revived by Alfred Hill in 1919.

FURTHER REFERENCE

BrewerD, 76; E.J. Lea-Scarlett, *ADB*, 4; Elizabeth Wood, *GroveD*; *Daily Telegraph* 12 Feb. 1898.

Delany, Leonard (*b* 1932), baritone. He won the Sun *Aria* in 1955, then sang in Australian companies and studied in Italy. He sang in various German provincial houses, including *Don Giovanni* at the Hanover Opera in 1965. A singer of excellent technique combined with a handsome stature on stage, his roles were the standard baritone parts, as well as Petruchio in Goetz's *Die widerspenstigen Zähmung* and the Husband in Schoenberg's *Von Heute auf Morgen*.

FURTHER REFERENCE

MackenzieS, 203–4; *AMN* 46 (Nov. 55), cover.

Delltones, The. Rock group founded (1959–73; 1981–) by members of Sydney's Bronte Surf Club, Noel Widerberg (lead vocals; *d* 1962, then Colin Loughlan), Warren Lucas (tenor), Brian Perkins (baritone), and Ian 'Pee Wee' Wilson (bass). They became regulars on television's *Six O'Clock Rock* and signed to the Leedon label, recording and backing Johnny ★O'Keefe and Johnny ★Rebb. Their first national hit was *You're The Limit* (1960), which reached No. 4 in the charts, and they rode the wave of the craze for surf music, *Get A Little Dirt On Your Hands* (1962) reaching No. 17 and *Come A Bit Closer* (1963) No. 2. By 1966, however, tastes had changed; their recording contract was not renewed, and they concentrated on club appearances. They worked in Asia and Europe, returning to Australia in 1971, but failing to regain their popularity they disbanded in 1973. In 1981 Wilson revived the band with new members and recorded *Bop Til Ya Drop!*, which was immediately successful; they have since worked in the club circuit. With 30 singles, 10 EPs and 19 albums, they recorded prodigiously and were at the forefront of the early rock and roll scene in Australia. Their close harmonies and a cappella 'doo-wop' style appealed to all ages; later they added instruments for their club work.

FURTHER REFERENCE

Recordings include *Delltones* (1962, Leedon LL30815); *Surf'n'-Stomp* (1963 Leedon LL31188); *Golden Hist of Golden Groups* (1964 Leedon LL31339); *Bop Til Ya Drop!* (KTel NA666); *All These And More* (1987, Chase CHASE 5). For discography, see *SpencerA*. See also David McLean, ed., *Collected Stories on Australian Rock'n'Roll* (Sydney: Canetoad, 1991), 89–93; *GuinnessP*; *McGrathA*; *SpencerW*.

Dempsey, Gregory (*b* Melbourne, 20 July 1931), tenor. After studies with Mavis Kruger as a baritone, he went to Henry and Annie ★Portnoj in Melbourne and made his debut with the Australian National Theatre Opera Co. as a tenor in 1954. He joined the Elizabethan Theatre Trust Opera Co. 1956–62 then was invited to Sadler's Wells in 1962, and was with them until 1976, and made guest appearances at New Opera Co., London, San Francisco Opera, Aldeburgh, Covent Garden, and in Europe. He was regularly with the Australian Opera from 1977. With a natural stage presence and versatile talent, his roles include Don José, Peter Grimes, Tom Rakewell, Wagner's Mime, as well as contemporary works such as the premieres of Richard Rodney Bennett's *The Mines of Sulphur*, Thea Musgrave's *The Decision,* Janáček's *The Makropulos Case*, Laca in *Jenůfa*, and *The Excursions of Mr Brouček*, Drum Major in *Wozzeck,* Dionysus in Hans Werner Henze's *The Bassarids*, and the Shepherd in Szymanowski's *King Roger*.

FURTHER REFERENCE

Recordings include Red Whiskers in *Billy Budd*, London Symphony Orchestra (London, 417428–2LH3)), and Mime in *The Ring of the Nibelungs*, cond. R. Goodall (1973, EMI CMS7 63595–2). See also Elizabeth Forbes, *GroveO*; *MackenzieS*, 201–2.

Dench, Chris (*b* London, 10 June 1953), composer. He lived in London and Brighton until 1987, then Tuscany 1987–88 and West Berlin 1989. He emigrated to Australia in 1990, and became an Australian citizen in 1992. Until 1995 his works concerned themselves with the combination of holographic unity and complex expressivity; in 1996 his investigations centred on ways of achieving the same artistic ends through simpler means, notably in five unorthodox symphonies, the first four being revisions of earlier works. His compositions include *énoncé* (1983/84) for 15 players, *tilt* (1985) for piano, *dé/ployé* (1987) for piccolo, *sulle scale della Fenice* (1986/9) for flute and *driftglass* (1990/1) for percussion and five amplified instruments.

FURTHER REFERENCE
Recordings include *Music for Flute: Works of Chris Dench* (KTC1146). See also *BroadstockS*; R. Toop, 'Four Facets of "The New Complexity"', *Contact* 32 (1988), 4–50; idem, 'sulle scale della Fenice', *Perspectives of New Music* 29/2 (Summer 1991), 72–92 (with postscript by the composer); idem, 'Beyond the "Crisis of Material": Chris Dench's "funk"', *Contemporary Music Review* 13 /1 (1996), 85–115.

MICHAEL BARKL

Dengate, John, folk-singer, songwriter. After meeting Brian ★Mooney in a pub at Menindee, NSW, he became interested in folk music and started writing songs to traditional Irish, American and Australian tunes he learned from Mooney. He joined the Bush Music Club, Sydney, in 1961, and came under the influence of John ★Meredith, 'Duke' ★Tritton and Alan ★Scott, later appearing in the ABC radio series *While the Billy Boils*. A writer of song texts and poetry on Australian themes, often of political satire, who fits his words to traditional Irish tunes, he has published *My Shout*.

FURTHER REFERENCE
Stringybark and Greenhide 4/3 (1983), 9; *RadicS*, 186.

Dennison, Peter John (*b* Wollongong, NSW, 18 Aug. 1942; *d* 21 Aug. 1989), musicologist. He graduated from the University of Sydney (BMus, 1964) and was awarded a DPhil from Oxford University in 1970 for researching the life and work of Pelham Humfrey. Lecturing at Glasgow University 1968–71 and Cambridge University 1971–75, he was appointed professor of music at the University of Melbourne 1975; elected president of the Musicological Society of Victoria 1977. He published editions and critical writings on Restoration church music, especially that of Purcell, and joined the committee of the Purcell Society in 1972. He was also a researcher of late-Romantic music and Elgar.

MARGARET KARTOMI

Denvermen, The. Rock band (1961–66) comprised of players from Paul Denver and the Denvermen and

Digger and the Lonely Ones, comprised at first of Digger ★Revell (vocals), Peter Burbridge (saxophone), Les Green and Tex Ihasz (guitars), Allan Crowe (bass) and Phil Bower (drums). After gaining a following at their own dances they appeared on *Six O'Clock Rock* from 1961. Adopted by Johnny ★Devlin in 1962, they appeared on his recordings and toured extensively with him, as well as with Revell, Tony Weston, and others. Their single *Surfside* reached No. 6 in the charts in 1963. A highly versatile and well-equipped band playing in the surf music genre, they were the first Australian instrumental group to do well in the Top 40. Their decline began in 1964 as Revell increasingly appeared without them and instrumentals lost their hold in the Beatles era.

FURTHER REFERENCE
Recordings include *Surfside* (HMV EA 4506), *Mystery Waves* (1963, RCA 101540), *Can Tell* (1965, HMV EA 4721), the EP *Stomp Fever* (RCA 20313) and the album *Let's Go Surfside* (1963, RCA 101537). A compilation is *Surfside And Other Great Hits* (1989, Canetoad CTLP 008). For discography, see *SpencerA*. See also *McGrathA*; *SpencerW*; Stephen McParland in *Collected Stories on Australian Rock'n'Roll*, ed. David McClean (Sydney: Canetoad Publications, 1991).

Desmond, Lorrae [Sheila Hunt] (*b* Mittagong, NSW, 1931), actress, popular music singer. She left school at 15, trained in hairdressing and worked as a cigarette girl in a Sydney nightclub. Going to London in 1952, she worked in cabaret, pantomime and comedy, and soon had her own BBC TV show, *Sing Along With Lorrae*. She returned regularly to Australia, recording the *Lorrae Desmond Show* for ABC radio in the early 1960s, and writing some of her own material; she co-wrote the libretto for *The Jesus Christ Revolution*, a musical in the *Superstar* vein which had a short run at Adelaide in 1971 (and as *Man of Sorrows* in 1972). She acted in the television series *A Country Practice* 1981–92 and toured nationally with the musical *High Society* 1993–94.

FURTHER REFERENCE
She has recorded with HMV, Decca and Parlophone. See also *DPA*.

Devereux, John (*b* England, 1810; *d* Melbourne, Aug. 1883), violin-maker. After being apprenticed to Bernhard Simon Fendt in London, he arrived in Australia in 1854, establishing a business as a luthier at Marion Street, Fitzroy, Melbourne, and playing double bass in local concerts. Like Fendt, his instruments were based on the Guarnerius contour, but slightly larger and deeper, creating a more sonorous tone. He made an instrument for the Duke of Edinburgh's visit to Melbourne in 1868, after which he signed himself 'Violin and Bass Maker to HRH the Duke of Edinburgh'. One of the first stringed-instrument makers in Australia, his fine craftsmanship found many local admirers, and his apprentice Richard

Gilmore continued the business after his death. Some of his instruments are still in use; two are at the Museum of Applied Arts and Sciences, Sydney.

FURTHER REFERENCE
AthertonA.

Devil Take Her, The. Comic opera in one act with prologue by Arthur *Benjamin (1931), libretto by A. Collard and J.B. Gordon. First performed at the Royal College of Music, London, on 1 December 1931 and in Australia by the National Theatre Movement Opera Co. in 1953. A vocal score was published (London, 1932).

Devlin, Johnny (*b* NZ, 11 May 1938), rock and roll singer-songwriter. Born into a family of entertainers, he sang country and western music with the Devlin Family around NZ, then went to Auckland and sang Elvis Presley numbers, adopting the Presley style. He signed to Prestige Records and with his band the Devils toured NZ, releasing 10 singles, five EPs and an album. They came to Australia in 1959 and appeared at Lee *Gordon's Big Show; after recording for the Leedon label, Devlin formed his own record company Teen Records. Thirty-five singles, 11 EPs and six albums followed, *Doreen* (1959) reaching No. 20 in the charts, *Gigolo* (1960) No. 25 and *Stomp the Tumbarumba* (1963) No. 30, and he was a regular on television's *Bandstand* and *Six O'Clock Rock*. Devlin sang some of his own songs, and also wrote for the *Denvermen and Patsy Ann *Noble. He was supporting act to the Beatles' Australian tour in 1964, then was in the UK 1965–67 but failed to make an impact. After club work in Australia and NZ, he retired from full-time entertaining in 1972, although he appeared in Johnny *O'Keefe's *Good Ole Days of Rock and Roll* in 1974. One of the most successful rock and roll singers in Australia in the early 1960s, as a songwriter his music has been recorded by Eartha Kitt, the Kinks, and many others. For a time an agent for the Denvermen and Digger *Revell and a manager for RCA, he now lives in NZ.

FURTHER REFERENCE
Recordings include *Doreen* (1959, Leedon LS560); *Gigolo* (1960, Teen TC021); *Stomp the Tumbarumba* (1963, Festival FK472); *Real Nervous* (1960, Teen TL8201); compilations include *24 Original Greats* (1980, Music World MALP 536); and *Stag-O-Lee* (1989, Canetoad CTLP 006). For discography, see *SpencerA*. See also C. Duff, J. Phillips and D. Mittelhauser, 'Johnny Devlin', in *Collected Stories on Australian Rock'n'Roll*, ed. D. McLean, 33–41; *GuinnessP*, I, 684; *McGrathA*; *SpencerW.*

Devonport, pop. (1991) 22660. City at the mouth of the Mersey River, northern Tasmania, formed in 1893 by the amalgamation of the villages on its two banks which date from the 1850s. The settlement remained small until after World War I, but the Devonport Eisteddfod, founded in 1929, immediately attracted over 500 entries of good

standard, and was held over nine days before large audiences. The Devonport Light Opera Co. presented such works as *Marrying Marian* (1937) or *Miss Cherry Blossom* (1938). Today there is an operative Devonport Choral Society, the City of Devonport Brass Band, and annual musical events mounted by the energetic Mersey Arts Council and Performance Tasmania. Local music teachers are active in the north-west branch of the Tasmanian Music Teachers' Association.

d'Hage, Ludwig ['Louis D. Hage'] (*b* Schluckenau, Bohemia, 7 May 1863; *d* Mosman, Sydney, 22 Apr. 1960), violinist. After studying piano and violin at the Gesellschaft der Musikfreunde, Vienna, he arrived in Australia in 1880 with Wildner's Strauss Austrian Band and settled. As 'Louis D. Hage' he established a music teaching practice at Rockhampton in 1885, conducting the Rockhampton Philharmonic and the Orpheus Club Orchestra, which he made renowned in the colony. He moved to Sydney in 1912, played in Cyril *Monk's String Quartet, then the *Austral String Quartet and the NSW State Orchestra. One of the most gifted violinists to reside in Australia at the turn of the century, his pupils included John *Lemmone, Alma *Moodie and others who made notable careers.

FURTHER REFERENCE
Lorna L. McDonald *ADB*, 8.

Didjeridu (1). End-blown, trumpet-like aerophone without a mouthpiece. It is played using a circular breathing technique while buzzing the lips. Although basically mono-tonal, the didjeridu is also capable of producing overtones, and when combined with vocalisations, tonguing and guttural shrieks, complex sounds and rhythms can be created. The didjeridu is originally of Aboriginal provenance and can be seen in rock paintings at least 1500 years old. It was historically limited to the northern tropical regions of Australia and made out of bored-out bamboo or termite-hollowed wood. It was used in sacred and secular contexts, mostly by males. It is now also made from plastic pipes, glass and brass, and used in diverse yet interrelated ways in musical and extra-musical contexts. In education it is used by musicians, storytellers and dancers who present Aboriginal culture to students at primary, secondary and tertiary levels; educators have found it to be an effective way to engage students in the broader issues that inform Aboriginal and non-Aboriginal relations.

The didjeridu is used for entertainment by successful Aboriginal recording artists such as Mark Atkins, Kev *Carmody, Alan Dargin, David Hudson and Richard Walley, and non-Aboriginal artists such as Alistair Black, Andrew Langford, and Charlie McMahon. Contemporary Aboriginal groups such as *Yothu Yindi, Blek Bela Mujik and Sunrize Band feature it prominently in their musical arrangements and marketing images. Abroad it has been used in musical genres as diverse as rock, jazz and symphonic. It is also an important and ubiquitous aural and visual signifier of Aboriginality. It is often used in national political events which have an Aboriginal or multicultural focus, and it has come to be regarded as a concrete example of the efflorescence of Aboriginal musical culture and its incorporation into the national iconography.

The didjeridu is also centre of a commercial enterprise, both as a musical instrument heard on recordings and in live performance, and as a tourist artefact. Thousands of didjeridus are manufactured yearly by Aboriginal and non-Aboriginal artisans and sold to retailers, who market them. The didjeridu also figures prominently in theatrical performances designed for tourists. The didjeridu has moved from its origins in Aboriginal culture to occupy a unique position as perhaps Australia's most readily recognisable contribution to the world's music. See also *Aboriginal Music* §3(i).

FURTHER REFERENCE

Alice Moyle, 'The Australian Didgeridoo: A Late Musical Intrusion', *World Archaeology* 12 (1981), 321–31; Karl Neuenfeldt, ed., *The Didjeridu: From Arnhemland to the Internet* (Sydney: John Libbey/Perfect Beat Publications, 1996).

KARL NEUENFELDT

Didjeridu (2).   Sextet (1971) for didjeridu and wind quintet by George *Dreyfus. Recorded by the Adelaide Wind Quintet with George Winunguj, *George Dreyfus: Chamber and Orchestral Music* (1992, Classic SCCD 1024).

Diggles, Sylvester   (*b* Liverpool, England, 24 Jan. 1817; *d* Kangaroo Point, Brisbane, 21 Mar. 1880), naturalist, pianist. Arriving in Australia in 1853, he settled at Brisbane in 1854, mainly working as a naturalist but also teaching piano and tuning and repairing instruments. One of the most gifted musicians in early Brisbane, he appeared as accompanist with visiting virtuoso violinist Miska *Hauser in 1855. Sponsoring the establishment of the Brisbane Choral Union (1859) and the Brisbane Philharmonic Society (1861), he appointed the pianist F.N. Rosentengel as their conductor in 1866 and served as accompanist at their concerts.

FURTHER REFERENCE

E.N. Marks, *ADB*, 4.

Dimple's Lovers.   Operetta in one act by Cecil *Sharp, libretto by Guy Boothby. First performed at Government House, Adelaide, on 2 September 1890.

Director, The.   Opera in one act, music and libretto by Felix *Werder. First performed at the University of Melbourne on 7 June 1980.

Display, The.   Ballet by Malcolm *Williamson, choreographed by Robert Helpmann with costumes and décor by Sidney Nolan (and Adele Weiss for the 1983 production). First performed at Her Majesty's Theatre, Adelaide, by the Australian Ballet on 14 March 1964. The collaborative team of Williamson, Helpmann and Nolan designed a ballet which incorporated not only native flora and fauna and Australian Rules football but also unsavoury aspects of Australian society including binge drinking, fighting and rape. The work divided the ballet community between those who felt that Australian dance had come of age with the presentation of a darker side of society, and those who considered the scenario to be an inappropriate balletic entertainment. Nonetheless, its merit rather than the controversy ensured that it had 322 performances between 1964 and 1983.

JOEL CROTTY

Dithyramb.   Ballet by Margaret *Sutherland (1937), choreographed by Laurel Martyn. First performed with piano in 1937; orchestrated 1941 and performed by the Victorian Ballet Guild in 1946.

Divall, Richard Sydney   (*b* Sydney, 9 Sept. 1945), conductor, musicologist. From 1961 to 1971 he worked as a music producer with the ABC specialising in opera, Asian music, and early Australian music, simultaneously studying part-time at NSW State Conservatorium, and taking conducting with Joseph *Post. In 1972 he was appointed inaugural music director of the Victoria State Opera, holding this position until 1995, when he became principal guest conductor and was also named conductor laureate. He was a Churchill fellow (1975), and during his career he has been able to work and study with Sir Charles *Mackerras, Wolfgang Wagner, Nikolaus Harnoncourt and Sir Reginald Goodall. Since 1990 has been chairman of the *Marshall-Hall Trust.

Divall has conducted over 120 operas, having a particular affinity with 18th-century opera. Internationally, he has worked for the BBC and Netherlands Opera, and has conducted in Germany, Italy, China, NZ, and Hong Kong. In Australia he conducted the opening opera performances at the Victorian Arts Centre; he has conducted operas at four Adelaide Festivals and regularly conducts for the Australian Ballet. Divall has pioneered the first performances of many Australian music-theatre works, and for 30 years has been active editing operas and ballets, as well as organising performances of Australian colonial music. In 1981 he was awarded an OBE and in 1992 he received an honorary DLitt from Monash University.

FURTHER REFERENCE

ADMR; CA (1995–96). For discography see *HolmesC*.

PAULINE PETRUS

Divinyls.   Rock band formed in Sydney (1980) around the songwriting duo of singer Chrissie Amphlett and guitarist Mark McEntee. Other foundation members included Bjame Ohlin (guitar), Paul Jeremy (bass) and

Matthew Hughes (keyboard, bass). The band's debut mini-album was composed for the 1982 film *Monkey Grip* and included the No. 8 hit single *Boys in Town*. After signing with Chrysalis, their first album *Desperate* (1983) reached No. 5. The Divinyls also toured extensively and gained great popularity as a live act, with much attention drawn to Amphlett's hypnotically suggestive persona and appearances on stage in schoolgirl uniform. The Divinyls' second album, *What a Life* (1985), peaked at No. 4 and produced the No. 11 hit single *Pleasure and Pain*. By the mid-1980s the Divinyls' original membership had been reduced to Amphlett and McEntee, who added augmenting musicians to their duo while touring internationally as the need arose. Although *Temperamental* (1988) charted at No. 11, this album failed to match the standard set by the Divinyls' earlier work, and as a result its songs did not chart well as singles. A return to true form was evident in the Divinyls' self-titled album of 1991, which peaked at No. 4 and contained the notoriously risqué *I Touch Myself*. This single not only topped the national charts but also reached the UK Top 10.

FURTHER REFERENCE

Recordings include Music from *Monkey Grip* (1982, WEA MONKEY 1); *Desperate* (1983, Chrysalis RML 53029); *What a Life* (1985, Chrysalis RML 53130); *Temperamental* (1988, Chrysalis RML 53256); *Divinyls* (1991, Virgin VUSLP 30); *Underworld* (1996, BMG 74321355342). See also *GuinnessP*; *SpencerW*.

AARON D.S. CORN

Dixieland. A jazz style originating in New Orleans brought to international attention by the Original Dixieland Jazz Band from 1917. Usually a trumpet and clarinet improvise simultaneously over a walking trombone bass, with a rhythm section of drums, banjo or guitar, piano and plucked string bass. The Original Dixieland's recordings were heard in Australia from 1921, but its local imitators did not yet understand the style, presenting it as comical or crude. The arrival from the USA of Frank Ellis and the Californians in 1923 provided a more polished example for local players, but Dixieland was not their chief preoccupation. On the whole it was the reissue of early Dixieland recordings in the mid-1930s that had most impact in Australia: led by Graeme *Bell and Ade *Monsbourgh from 1935 and stimulated by the presence of American servicemen from 1941, there was an enduring taste for Dixieland revival bands in Australia. The revival continued in the postwar years through bands such as Frank *Johnson and his Fabulous Dixielanders, and was preserved, though increasingly regressive, by such groups as Frank *Traynor and his Jazz Preachers into the 1980s. See *Jazz*.

Djambidj. Aboriginal clan song series in north-central Arnhem Land. It consists of 21 song subjects, the most important being Hollow Log or Wild Honey. Bees make their nests in hollow logs, which are also used to contain the bones of deceased humans, and thus symbolise both life and death, and the eternal cycle of regeneration. *Djambidj* is performed by at least one singer accompanying himself with clapsticks, and a didjeridu accompanist; sometimes two or three singers perform at the same time. It is sung in initiation ceremonies, mortuary ceremonies, and simply for entertainment, and it may accompany dancing.

STEPHEN WILD

Dodd, Josiah Eustace (*b* Richmond, Melbourne, 16 Aug. 1856; *d* Glenelg, SA, 30 Jan. 1952), organ-builder. Apprenticed in 1869 to George *Fincham for seven years, Dodd moved to Adelaide in 1881 to help operate a branch of the Fincham firm, which he managed 1888–94, when he purchased the branch and set up a firm under his own name. Dodd quickly forged a new and progressive organ-building style which was widely sought after by clients in five Australian states and NZ. Using imported pipework and mechanical components, his instruments were of an advanced symphonic style. He was later joined in partnership by his sons and subsequently amalgamated with the Gunstar Organ Works.

FURTHER REFERENCE

Bruce Naylor, 'J.E. Dodd: a Romantic Organbuilder', *OHTA News* 5/3 (Apr. 1981), 4–20; Graeme D. Rushworth, *Historic Organs of New South Wales* (Sydney: Hale & Iremonger, 1988), 188–195.

JOHN MAIDMENT

Dommett, Leonard Bertram (*b* Toowoomba, Qld, 21 Dec. 1928), violinist, conductor. After studying at the University of Melbourne Conservatorium, he went to London, playing in the BBC Symphony, London Symphony and Royal Opera House Orchestras, 1949–53. Returning to Australia he was in the Queensland Symphony Orchestra 1954–59, appearing as leader and assistant conductor for the Ballet Rambert tour of Australasia and Europe 1947–50 and founding the Musica da Camera Society in Brisbane in 1955. He joined the Sydney Symphony Orchestra 1959–61, was concertmaster of the South Australian Symphony Orchestra 1961–65, and then concertmaster of the Melbourne Symphony Orchestra from 1965 (assistant conductor from 1970), building much of the discipline and professionalism that are still the hallmark of that ensemble. After briefly conducting the ABC Sinfonia 1981, he taught at the Canberra School of Music and was music director of Canberra Symphony Orchestra from 1981. One of Australia's most distinguished violinists, he has performed and recorded 56 violin concertos, 12 in first performances, many of which were written for him. Since his retirement from Canberra in 1994 he has taught at the Queensland University of Technology and the Queensland Conservatorium. He was honoured with the OBE in 1977 and the Sir Bernard Heinze Award in 1993.

FURTHER REFERENCE
Recordings as a violinist include *Australian Violin Concertos* (1991, ABC Classics 426993–2); F. Werder, Violin concerto (1976, Festival SFC 80020); works of D. Banks, F. Werder, R. Trumble, with M. Cooke, hpd, C. Wojtowicz, vc (1975, ABC 1010); as a conductor M. Williamson, concertos, London Philharmonic Orchestra (1975, Lyrita). *PlushD* lists various recordings as a conductor and soloist on ABC tapes before 1972. See also *CA* (1995–96); *WWA* (1996); Tony Scott, 'The Canberra Symphony Orchestra and Leonard Dommett', *Image: Australian Theatrical News and Views*, 1/3 (1987), 54–7; Ann Carr-Boyd, *GroveD*; *GlennonA*, 230.

Don John of Austria. Colonial semi-opera, based on Casimir Delavigne's *Don Juan d'Autriche*. Libretto by Jacob Levi Montefiore (1819–85); the music (and evidently the words of one song, 'The Visions of Youth') composed in Sydney *c*.1846 by Isaac *Nathan, who published five numbers (1848–49). First produced under the composer's direction at Sydney's Royal Victoria Theatre on 3 May 1847, it enjoyed a successful run of six performances, ending with a crowded benefit performance on 17 May which also included the composer's third London opera, *The Illustrious Stranger* (1827). Generally considered the first opera to be composed and produced in Australia, though preceded by Nagel's *The Mock Catalani* and Nathan's unperformed *Merry Freaks in Troub'lous Times* (1843).

FURTHER REFERENCE
The ms vocal score (c.1846–7) by unknown copyist, with additions and corrections in the composer's hand, is in *CAnl*. Nathan's *The Southern Euphrosyne* (Sydney: the editor, [1849]) includes the overture and four arias in vocal score. See also G. Pont, *Muse Unruly: The Secret Life of Isaac Nathan* (Sydney: State Library of NSW, 1997).   GRAHAM PONT

Donovan, Jason (*b* Malvern, Vic., 1 June 1968), pop singer, actor. Son of the actor Terence Donovan and newsreader Sue McIntosh, he appeared on television from the age of 11 after studying piano at the Melba Conservatorium. With a lead role in the TV series *Neighbours* from 1987, he followed co-star Kylie *Minogue in using the show to launch a pop career. His debut single *Nothing Can Divide Us Now* reached No. 5 in the UK charts in 1988 and he had seven Top 10 hits there, 1989–90. His debut album *Ten Good Reasons* reached No. 1 in the UK charts in 1989 and No. 5 in Australia. He starred in *Joseph and the Amazing Technicolour Dreamcoat* at the London Palladium (1991). More popular in the UK than Australia, his other hit singles include *Sealed With A Kiss* (1989), which reached No. 8 in Australia, and *Any Dream Will Do*, which reached No. 1 in the UK and No. 5 in Australia.

FURTHER REFERENCE
Recordings include *Nothing Can Divide Us Now* (Mushroom K594), *Ten Good Reasons* (Mushroom TVL 93295), and *Sealed*

With A Kiss (1989 Mushroom K862). A compilation is *Jason Donovan Greatest Hits* (1991). For discography, see *SpencerA*. See also *CA* (1995–96); *DPA*.

Dorcas McClean Violin Scholarship. Largest award for a violinist in Australia (founded 1990). Offered every two years after a national competition involving heats by tape and a live final at Melbourne, competitors must be under 25 and have been resident in Australia for two years. Administered by the University of Melbourne, past winners have included Adele Anthony and Asmira Woodward-Page. The prize is currently $24 000, and the winner is usually offered an appearance as soloist with the Melbourne Symphony Orchestra at the Sidney Myer Free Concerts the following year.

Dorian Gray. Opera by W. Arundel *Orchard, libretto by W.J. Curtis after Oscar Wilde. First performed at the NSW Conservatorium on 11 September 1919.

Dornan, Stephen (*b* Perth, 12 Oct. 1916), pianist. After lessons in Perth and musical work for the armed forces during the war, he went to London in 1946 and studied with Franz Reizenstein. He returned to Australia in 1951, appearing in chamber music and touring for the ABC as an accompanist to Max Rosenthal, Burl Senofsky and others. He established a teaching practice at Perth, later accepting pupils from the University of Western Australia, but despite offers from several of the leading music schools always declined a full-time post. A very gifted artist and an inspiring mentor, particularly in the interpretation of Romantic piano works, he produced over the years such distinguished pupils as Carl *Vine, Victor Sangiorgo and Donald Thornton. He published *Sight Reading for Teachers and Students*, ed. Gordon Spearritt (Melbourne: Allans Music, 1991).

FURTHER REFERENCE
Recordings include Lindley Evans, *Vignette*, WA Symphony Orchestra, W. Pomroy, pf, cond. T. Mayer (ABC RRCS 381).

Dossor, Lance (*b* Weston-Super-Mare, England, 1916), pianist. After studies with Herbert Fryer at the Royal College of Music, London, he won the Liszt Prize, Vienna, in 1937 and made his London debut, appearing as a soloist with the Royal Philharmonic Orchestra and the Hallé Orchestra, teaching at the Royal College of Music from 1946, and touring England and NZ. He came to Australia in 1953, and has since taught piano at the Elder Conservatorium. He visited England as a soloist with the Royal Liverpool Philharmonic Society, London Philharmonic Orchestra, and for other engagements in 1956, then appeared with the Astra Chamber concerts in Melbourne in 1957 and in the Elder Piano Trio 1959–62. He was visiting professor of piano at the Royal College of Music in 1979 and continues to teach in Adelaide. A refined, somewhat reserved interpreter with an intelligent approach to his instrument, with Clemens Leske he has been at the head of a steadfast school of piano teaching in Adelaide for more than 40 years.

FURTHER REFERENCE

Christopher Symons, *John Bishop: A Life for Music* (Melbourne: Hyland House, 1989), 217–28; *AMN*, 47 (Oct. 1956), 26; *AMN* 48 (Aug 1957), 34.

Doubleday, Leila (*fl.* 1902–45), violinist, librettist. A prodigy and the daughter of music teacher and entrepreneur Ida Doubleday, Leila was brought before the public for routine and benefit concerts before 1914 in Melbourne, and was well received. In Europe she enjoyed considerable success, especially in Britain where she was regularly heard at Australia House concerts and where she recorded for Zonophone. In 1925 she premiered the Margaret ★Sutherland *Violin Sonata* with the composer at the piano. She toured in Australasia for many years between the wars, giving concerts with Ernest★ Goll and Australian pianist Max ★Pirani, whom she married. She provided texts for Australian composer Edith ★Harrhy.

JEFF BROWNRIGG

Douglas, Clive Martin (*b* Rushworth, Vic., 27 July 1903, *d* East Brighton, Melbourne, 29 Apr. 1977), composer, conductor. He began piano lessons with his mother at the age of six and later learnt violin from Franz Schieblich and Alberto ★Zelman. He left school at 15 to work for the State Savings Bank. He studied at the University of Melbourne Conservatorium in 1929–34 and, two years after his graduation, with the support of Bernard ★Heinze, joined the then expanding ABC as a staff conductor, remaining there until his retirement in 1966. His postings were to Hobart for five years, then Brisbane for six years, Sydney for six years and finally Melbourne for 13 years. In his unpublished writings he reveals a deep dissatisfaction with his conducting career: he felt that as a native-born conductor he was unfairly treated by the ABC. From 1949 he also held the position of music adviser to the Federal Government Department of the Interior film division (predecessor of Film Australia), composing and conducting music for documentary films. He received many prizes and awards and gained a DMus from the University of Melbourne in 1958.

Douglas was a prolific composer who wrote mostly for symphony orchestra and often with a 'program'. He is significant as one who tried to express nationality through his music: in many works composed from 1937–38 (*Kaditcha*) to 1959 (*Terra Australis*) he used Australian Aboriginal literary and/or musical references as a means to this end. Like many of his contemporaries he was criticised as conservative—he did not experiment with 12-note music until his Symphony No. 3 (1963)—but his works are well crafted and effectively scored.

WORKS (Selective)

Publishers: APRA, Sydney, and Allan & Co, Melbourne

Orchestral   Symphonic Fantasy, opus 20 (1938), *Carwoola*, opus 22 (1939, Sydney, 1954), *Intermezzo*, from opera *Maid Rosamund*, opus 29 (1942), *Meet the Orchestra*, educational suite, opus 36 (1944), Symphony No. 1, *Jubilee*, opus 48a (1950), *Sturt 1829 (Kaiela)*, opus 53 (self-published, c.1952), *Essay for Strings*, opus 55 (Sydney, c.1952), *Wongadilla Suite*, opus 56 (Sydney, c.1954), *Festival in Natal, Rhapsody on Two South African Folksongs*, opus 57 (1954), *Greet the Orchestra*, educational suite, op. 62 (1955), *Olympic Overture*, opus 64 (Sydney, c.1956), *Coolawidgee*, miniature suite for small orch, opus 66 (1957), Symphony No 2, *Namatjira*, opus 67 (1956), *Sinfonietta* for Festival of Perth, opus 79 (1961), *Variations Symphoniques*, opus 80 (1961), *Fanfare Overture*, opus 82 (1961), *Divertimento II* for 2 pianos & small orch, opus 84 (1962 rev. 1967), Symphony no. 3, opus 87 (1963), *Four Light Orchestra Pieces*, opus 89 (1964), *Three Frescos*, opus 90 (1969), *Movement On a Theme of Alfred Hill* in C major, opus 91 (1969), *Pastorale*, opus 92 (1970), *Carnival*, opus 93 (1970), *Discourse* for strings, opus 94 (1971).

Chamber Music   *Pastorale & ritual dance (from Namatjira)*, opus 68, vn, pf (Melbourne, 1957), *Divertimento I*, op 83, woodwind quintet (1962 extended 1965).

Opera and Ballet   *Ashmadai*, opus 12, opera (1935, 1, comp), Wilson Hall, Univ. Melbourne, August 1936, *Kaditcha (A Bush Legend)*, opus 19/48b, operetta (1938 rev. 1956, 1, comp. after two Aboriginal folk stories), ABC studio, Hobart, 22 June 1938, *Corroboree*, ballet (from opera *Kaditcha*), opus 23 (1939), *Eleanor* trilogy: *Eleanor*, opus 26, *Maid Rosamund*, opus 27, *Henry of Anjou*, opus 28, lyric dramas (1941–34, 3, comp), ABC studio, Brisbane (*Eleanor*, opus 26 only), 6 Jan. 1943.

Vocal and Choral   *The Hound of Heaven*, opus 11, Bar solo, ch, orch (text, Francis Thomson, 1933 rev. 1938), Choral fantasia from opera *Ashmadai*, opus 24, mixed ch, B solo, orch (1939), *Blue Billabong*, suite from opera *Kaditcha*, opus 25, ch, orch (1940), *Five pastels*, opus 51, song cycle for S, celeste, str orch (1952), *Lakes of Tasmania*, opus 58, song cycle, voice, orch (1954), *Song Landscape*, opus 60, song cycle for S/T, str orch/pf (1955), *Terra Australis*, op 76, nar, S solo, ch, orch, (1959).

Other Works   Three radio & TV scores (1936–63), 25 documentary films, including five as co-composer (1947–63).

FURTHER REFERENCE

Obit. in *APRAJ* 2/3 (1977). Recordings (now rare) include *Three Frescos*, Sydney Symphony Orchestra, cond. M. Atzmon (1969, Festival SFC 800–19); and *Sturt 1829*, Victorian Symphony Orchestra, cond. C Douglas (1954, HMV OALP 7511). A discography of his work as a conductor is in *HolmesC* and of his compositions to 1972 is in *PlushD*. His mss are in *Msl*. See also: *CallawayA*; Jennifer Hill, 'Clive Douglas and the ABC: Not a Favourite Aunt', in *One Hand On the Manuscript: Music in Australian Cultural History*, ed. Nicholas Brown et al. (Canberra: Humanities Research Centre, ANU, 1995), 229–42; Elizabeth Wood, *GroveD*.

JENNIFER HILL

Dow, William Henry (*b* Tayport, Scotland, 1835; *d* Melbourne, 1927), violin-maker. He arrived in Melbourne in 1854 and set up an instrument workshop, making violins of beautiful workmanship, at first of the Stradivarius contour, but later tending towards the Guarnerius. His instruments had admirable scrolls and purflings and resonant tone, although he varnished them with three thick coats instead of the multiple thin coats of tradition. He made about 250 violins, violas and cellos, and left a diary with his varnish recipes. Regarded as the best violin-maker in Australia in the 19th century, he won prizes for his instruments at the Inter-Colonial Exhibition 1870 and the International Centennial Exhibition of 1880.

FURTHER REFERENCE
AthertonA.

Dowd, (Eric) Ronald (*b* Sydney, 23 Feb. 1914; *d* Sydney, 15 Mar. 1990), tenor. He sang in a church choir as a boy then worked in a bank until his war service. With a civilian entertainment unit in occupied Japan in 1946, he met conductor Henry *Krips, and toured Australia with Krips' concert vocal ensemble. He sang with the National Theatre Movement Opera Co., Melbourne, from 1948, making his debut as Hoffmann, and in ABC concerts and broadcasts in Australia and NZ. He moved to London in 1956, where he was immediately offered roles at Sadler's Wells, appearing also at Covent Garden, with the Hallé Orchestra, the BBC and at major festivals in Europe. With a muscular voice of splendid lyrical line and expressivity, particularly acclaimed as Peter Grimes, his roles included Tannhäuser, Lohengrin, Idomeneo, Oedipus Rex, Herod, Aeneas (*The Trojans*), Canio, Pinkerton, Cavaradossi, as well as Gerontius and numerous concert parts. He was honoured with the AO in 1976.

FURTHER REFERENCE
Recordings include Schubert, *Winterreise,* with John Winther, pf (1991, ABC 426991B). See also Alan Blyth, *GroveO*; *MackenzieS,* 211–14; *AMN* (Jan. 1956), 17.

Doyle, Peter John (*b* Melbourne 18 July 1949), popular music singer. Singing from the age of nine, he was a member of the television child singing troupe *Swallow's Juniors,* but once a teenager changed to rock music and appeared on the *Go!!* show from 1963. He released eight singles, including *Speechless* (1965) and *The Great Pretender* (1966), as well as the EP *Stupidity* (1965) and the album *Peter's First Album* (1966). He formed Grandma's Tonic as a backing group (1967), and was in the trio The Virgil Brothers 1968–70, recording *Temptation's About To Get Me* (1968). In the UK he joined the New Seekers in 1970, but went solo from 1973. Returning to Australia in 1981, he sang with Standing Room Only and Skin Deep, the American band Regis (1982), Split Level (1986), and Ram Band (1991–92).

FURTHER REFERENCE
Recordings include *Speechless* (1965, Sunshine QK 1001) and *The Great Pretender* (1966, Sunshine QK 1207), the EP *Stupidity* (1965, Sunshine QX 11060) and the album *Peter's First Album* (1966, Sunshine); with the trio the Virgil Brothers *Temptation's About To Get Me* (1968, Parlophone A8390). For discography, see *SpencerA.* See also *McGrathA*; *SpencerW.*

Dragon. Rock band formed in NZ (1972) around the brothers Mark and Todd Hunter. Dragon was initially influenced by English hard rock bands and released two albums in NZ, *Universal Radio* (1973) and *Scented Gardens for the Blind* (1974). By the time the band had emigrated to Australia (1975), however, their tendency was to perform softer sentimental songs written by band member Paul Hewson (keyboard). Among their early Australian albums, *Running Free* (1977) and *O Zambezi* (1978) peaked at No. 6 and No. 3 respectively, producing the No. 2 hit single *April Sun in Cuba* and the chart-topping *Are You Old Enough.*

Dragon was well received by teen and mature audiences alike, and despite the drug-related deaths of Hewson and early drummer Neal Storey, and the band's constantly changing membership, they toured extensively and produced some of New Zealand's most inspiring music. After recording *Power Play* (1979), internal friction between the group's members caused the band to dissolve. Mark Hunter released a solo album which included the Top 20 single *Island Nights*, and Todd Hunter collaborated in the bands XL Capris and Scribble with Johanne Piggott. In 1982 Dragon re-formed and with Piggott released several hit songs including *Rain* (1983) which peaked at No. 2, and the Top 20 hits *Cry* (1984), *Speak No Evil* (1985), *Dreams of Ordinary Men* (1986), *Celebration* (1987) and *Young Years* (1989). *Body and the Beat* (1984) hit No. 5, while subsequent albums *Dreams of Ordinary Men* (1986) and *Bondi Road* (1989) both reached No. 18.

FURTHER REFERENCE
Recordings include *Universal Radio* (1973); *Scented Gardens for the Blind* (1974); *Sunshine* (1977, CBS SBP 234946); *Running Free* (1977, Portrait PR 33005); *O Zambezi* (1978, Portrait PR 33010); *Power Play* (1979, CBS SBP 237352); *Body and the Beat* (1984, Polydor 817 874–1); *Live One* (1985, PolyGram 825 860–1); *Dreams of Ordinary Men* (1986, Polydor 829 828–1); *Bondi Road* (1989, RCA/Wheatley SFL1–0170). See also *GuinnessP*; *SpencerW.*   AARON D.S. CORN

Dreaming, The. See *Aboriginal Music* §1.

Dreyfus, George (*b* Wuppetal, Germany, 22 July 1928), composer. He migrated to Australia in 1939 and studied at the University of Melbourne Conservatorium in 1946 with Fred Morgan (bassoon), enrolling in the diploma of music. Then bassoonist at Her Majesty's Theatre 1948–52 and Melbourne Symphony Orchestra 1953–64, he has been a full-time composer since 1965.

Beginning in a neo-Classical style with works in the spirit of *Gebrauchsmusik* (the *Woodwind Trio*, (1956) and the song cycles *Die Galgenlieder* (1957) and *Songs Comic and Curious* (1959)), he moved into a contemporary mode only with *Music in the Air* (1961), *From within looking out* (1962) and *The Seasons* (1963). His full-length opera *Garni Sands* (1966) has been performed in Sydney (1972, 1982), Melbourne (1972) and New York (1975), and his two symphonies (1967, 1976) have been performed throughout Australia.

Significant works of the 1970s include film scores, his landmark *Sextet for Didjeridu and Wind Instruments* (1971) and the ubiquitous theme for the television series *★Rush* (1974). *An Australian Folk Mass* (1979) marks the peak of his many years of composing and performing with community groups throughout Australia. In the 1970s he also began a long involvement with Melbourne's legendary rough-theatre group Pram Factory, writing music for *Mickey's Moomba* (1979), *Smash Hit* (1980) and *Carboni* (1980). Dreyfus regards this experience as a training ground leading to his 1985 setting of C.J. Dennis's *The Sentimental Bloke*, performed by major theatre companies in Melbourne, Perth, Brisbane and Darwin, and to his music for *Manning Clark's History of Australia: The Musical* in 1987.

The pantopera *The Lamentable Reign of Charles the Last* (1975) was commissioned by the South Australian Opera Company for performance at the 1976 Adelaide festival. He has worked extensively with brass bands, with the result that his popular film and stage music includes numerous brass band arrangements; his *Roaring Days* (1981) was composed for and premiered by the Grimethorpe Colliery Band. A unique creative relationship with Methodist Ladies College, Melbourne, has produced testing works for unaccompanied treble voices, including *Lifestyle* (1988), *Auscapes* (1990), and *Praise*, 1993. More recently the focus of Dreyfus's work has shifted to the German operatic stage, a shift motivated by the fate of *The Gilt-Edged Kid* (1970), commissioned by the Australian Opera, and the spirited campaign he subsequently waged against the company's rejection of the work. With Volker Elis Pilgrim as his librettist, he created *Rathenau* (1992) and *Die Marx Sisters* (1995), as well as the parade *Else* (1993).

Dreyfus is the recipient of many awards and prizes, including a travelling scholarship from UNESCO (1966), a creative arts fellowship from the Australian National University (1967), a US State Department travel grant (1969), the Albert H. Maggs award (1973), a Myer Foundation travel grant, (1975), the Prix de Rome (1976), an APRA serious music award (1986), and the Australia Council's Don Banks fellowship (1991). He was honoured with the AM in 1992.

WORKS (Selective)

Orchestral *Music for Music Camp*, student orch (1967), Symphony No. 1 (1967), *Jingles* (1968), *. . . and more Jingles* (1972),

Symphony No. 2 (1976), *Hallelujah for Handel*, brass band or orch (1976), *Symphonie Concertante*, bn, vn, va, vc, str orch (1978), *Mary Gilmore Goes to Paraguay*, str, brass, perc (1979), *Grand Ridge Road*, suite, small orch (1980), *Folk Music with Large Orchestra* (1982), *German Teddy*, mandolin orch (1984), Symphonic Movement (1987), *Sound Sculptures from Rathenau*, solo insts, orch (1991), *Lighthouse*, str orch (1993), *New Gold Mountain*, traditional Chinese instrumental ensemble (1993), *Love Your Animal*, 2 ob, 2 hn, str (1995).

Brass Band/Concert Band *Roaring Days* (1981), *Euroa Hooray!* (1985), *Salutation on Australia Day*, 8 brass, 2 perc (1993).

Chamber Trio, fl, cl, bn (1956), *The Seasons*, fl, va, perc (1963), Quintet for Wind Instruments (1965), Sextet for Didjeridu and Wind Instruments (1971), *Old Melbourne*, bn, gui (1973), *In Memoriam Raoul Wallenberg*, cl, pf (1984), *Song and Dance for Gabor*, cl, taganing, db (1988), *for four bassoons* (1988), Sonata, vn, va (1989), *Larino, Safe Haven*, 2 ob, cor anglais (1990), *Homage à Victor Bruns*, 4 bn (1994).

Solo Instrumental *Stant Litore Puppes*, org (1985), *There is Something of Don Quixote in All of Us*, gui (1990), *Odyssey for a lone bassoon* (1990).

Dramatic *Garni Sands*, opera (1966, 1, Kellaway), 12 Aug. 1972, Sydney, *The Take Over*, school opera (1969, 1, Kellaway), 1969, Canberra, *The Gilt-Edged Kid*, opera (1970, 1, Lynne Strahan), 1976, Montsalvat, Eltham, Vic., *The Illusionist*, mime-drama, solo dancer, orch (1972, Lynne Strahan), 1972, Melbourne, *The Lamentable Reign of King Charles the Last*, pantopera (1975, 1, Tim Robertson), 1976, Adelaide, *Mickey's Moomba*, incidental music and songs (1979, John Romeril), 1979, Melbourne, *Carboni*, incidental music and songs (1980, John Romeril), 1980, Melbourne, *Smash Hit!*, incidental music and songs (1980, 2, Jack Hibberd), *Mourning Becomes Electra*, incidental music to Eugene O'Neill's play (1981), 1981, Melbourne, *The Sentimental Bloke*, musical (1985, 2, C.J. Dennis), 12 Dec. 1985, Melbourne, *Manning Clark's History of Australia: The Musical*, with other composers (1987, 2, John Romeril, D. Watson and T. Robertson), Jan. 1988, Melbourne, *Widartjy*, incidental music and songs to a puppet play for children (1990, Jack Davies), 1990, Melbourne, *Rathenau*, opera (1992, 12 scenes and prologue, Volker Elis Pilgrim), 19 June 1993, Staatstheater Kassel, Germany, *Die Marx Sisters*, opera (1995, 12 scenes, Volker Elis Pilgrim), 20 Apr 1996, Stadttheater Bielefeld, Germany.

Choral *Song of the Maypole*, children's choruses, orch (1968), *Under the Gum Trees at Sunrise* (1968), *Homage to Igor Stravinsky*, 10-part choir (1968), *Reflections in a Glass-house*, speaker, children's chorus, orch (1969), *Terrigal*, 4–part ch, orch (1977), *Ballad of the Drover*, children's vv (1979), *An Australian Folk Mass*, congregation, orch or brass band (1979), *Celebration*, female vv, pf, orch (1981), *Visions*, congregation, orch (1983), *Charles Rasp*, concert band, male ch, children's ch, pop singer (1984), *The Box Hill Gloria*, brass band, concert band, str orch, mixed ch, children's ch, pipe band, pop-singer (1985), *Lifestyle*, unaccompanied treble vv (1988), *The Song of Brother Sun*, treble voices, hp (1988), *Auscapes*, unaccompanied treble vv (1990), *Catch the Joy*, treble ch, orch (1990), *Praise*, unaccompanied treble vv (1993), *Else*, countertenor, boys' and men's choruses (1993).

Vocal   *Galgenlieder*, Bar, fl, cl, vn, bn (1957), *Songs Comic and Curious*, Bar, fl, ob, cl, hn, bn (1959), *Music in the Air*, Bar, fl, va, perc (1961), *From Within Looking Out*, S, fl, va, celeste, vibraphone (1962), *Ned Kelly Ballads*, folk-singer, 4 hn, rhythmic section (1964), *Mo*, Bar, str orch, continuo (1972), *Ein Kaffeekonzert*, S, pf trio (1977), *Four Italian Songs*, S, pf (1983), *Seven Songs* (1987), *Heidelberg 1890*, S, fl (1990).

Film   *The River Murray* (1964), *Wyperfeld* (1964), *Flaking a Forest* (1964), *The Sky's No Limit* (1964), *Geelong's My Name* (1964), *The Dancing Class* (1964), *The Adventure* (1964), *Nullarbor Hideout* (1965), *The Gunpowder Man* (1965), *Australia Now* (1965), *Actually There's Still Someone In There* (1965), *Treasures of the National Gallery* (1965), *Melbourne* (1966), *Geelong* (1966), *Reflections of Vietnam* (1966), *All the Love* (1966), *To Nurse is to Care* (1966), *The Objector* (1966), *Beyond the Pack Ice* (1968), *Canberra* (1968), *Will the Great Barrier Reef Cure Claude Clough* (1968), *Impressions of Australia* (1969), *Sons of the Anzacs* (1969), *The Big Island* (1970), *RAAF Heritage* (1971), *Our Golden Heritage* (1972), *Maybe Tomorrow* (1973), *A Steam Train Passes* (1974), *And Their Ghosts May Be Heard* (1975), *Let the Balloon Go* (1976), *Break of Day* (1976), *Dimboola* (1978), *Tender Mercies* (1982), *The Fringe Dwellers* (1985), *The Clever Country* (1992), *The Final Stage* (1993).

Television   *The Adventures of Sebastian the Fox* (1963), *Australian Painters* (1963), *Delta* (1969), *Marion* (1973), *Rush* (1974), *Power Without Glory* (1976), *Lawson's Mates* (1978), *We Belong* (1979), *All the Green Year* (1980), *Outbreak of Love* (1980), *Descant for Gossips* (1983), *Waterfront* (1983), *Great Expectations* (1986).

FURTHER REFERENCE
Recordings include the two Symphonies (Southern Cross); Film Music, Melbourne and Queensland Symphony Orchestras, cond. G. Dreyfus (Move MD 3098); *The Adventures of Sebastian the Fox, Rush* Trio, Old Melbourne (Move MD 3071); *Quintet After the Notebook of J.G. Noverre*, Canberra Wind Soloists (Canberra School of Music CSM 14); and *The Marvellous World of George Dreyfus* (Move MD3129). A discography to 1972 is in *PlushD*. His memoirs are *The Last Frivolous Book* (Sydney: Hale & Iremonger, 1984). See also R. Brasch, *Australian Jews of Today* (Sydney: Cassell, 1977), 46–52; Kay Lucas, 'The School Music of George Dreyfus', *AJME* 8 (Apr. 1971), 49–51; idem, 'George Dreyfus's Symphony No. 1', *Music Now* 1/2 (1969), 26–9; George McClean, Stylistic Diversity and the 'Zelig' Principle in the Orchestral Works of George Dreyfus from the First to the Second Symphonies: 1967–1976, MA, Monash Univ., 1994; *MurdochA*; Elizabeth Wood, *GroveD*.   THÉRÈSE RADIC

Dreyfus, (Francis) Kay née Lucas   (*b* Ballarat, Vic., 26 May 1942), musicologist. She graduated from the University of Melbourne (BMus, MMus, PhD), and carried out pre-doctoral studies at the University of York, England 1967–68, Temple University, Philadelphia, USA, 1969, and post-doctoral studies at the City University of New York 1973–74. She worked as curator of the Grainger Museum, Melbourne University, 1974–86, and at Monash University 1989–96 on a research fellowship for studying women with career interruptions and on an

Australian Research Council fellowship. She has published extensively on Grainger and is presently writing a book on female composers up to 1931; she acts as associate editor and Australian co-ordinator of *The Universe of Music* (UNESCO).

MARGARET KARTOMI

Drouyn.   See *Percussion instrument makers.*

Drover, The.   See *Brisbane Ladies.*

Drum, Skin.   See *Single-Headed Skin Drum.*

Dudley, Grahame   (*b* Sydney, 4 Aug. 1942), composer. After studies at the NSW State Conservatorium with Raymond ★Hanson and with Peter Maxwell Davies at the Elder Conservatorium, he conducted a new music ensemble, appearing at the Adelaide Festival in 1968, then conducted at the Cockpit Theatre, London, in 1971. He returned to teach in schools in Adelaide and now teaches at the Elder Conservatorium. His works include *The Snow Queen* (libretto by Nick Enright), premiered at Come Out '85 by the SA State Opera Youth Co. He formed Kidney Art in 1988, an experimental music–theatre group, and the ensemble Lights in 1990, with which he has performed many new works by composers from Australia and beyond.

Dudman, Michael Philip   (*b* Sydney, 2 Oct. 1938; *d* Newcastle, NSW, 6 Aug. 1994), organist. Educated at Sydney High School and the NSW Conservatorium, he began organ studies with Norman Johnston and graduated in 1959 with the prize for the most distinguished student. Awarded the Vasanta scholarship, he studied with André Marchal in Paris; afterwards he was assistant organist at Ely Cathedral under Arthur Wills and organist of Grimsby parish church. Returning to Australia in 1968 he was later appointed organist of Christ Church Cathedral, Newcastle, NSW. Appointed principal of Newcastle Conservatorium 1980, he was professor and dean of the faculty of music, University of Newcastle from 1989. The first Australian artist-in-residence at the Sydney Opera House (1985), afterwards he made recital tours of the USA and Canada. Dudman's repertoire exceeded 1000 works, and he made numerous recordings and radio programs on contemporary and historic organs. Possessed of exceptional virtuosity, he achieved pre-eminence among Australian organists of his time. He was awarded an honorary LittB by the University of New England and in 1990 the AM.

FURTHER REFERENCE
His recordings include *Organ Spectacular* (ABC, 2 CDs) and *Historic Organs of Sydney* (Walsingham/ABC, 3 CDs). See also V.H. Dudman, 'Memento on the Departure of a Beloved Brother', *Sydney Organ Journal* 25/5 (1994), 16–27.

GRAEME RUSHWORTH

Duff, Edwin (*b* 4 June 1928, Dundee, Scotland); jazz singer. He migrated to Australia *c*.1938 and became active during the war in Melbourne ballrooms and services concerts, where he first heard jazz performed by Americans. After a period in Sydney, he joined Jack ★Brokensha for work and tours in Melbourne. Then he was with Frank Marcy in Sydney until he left for Canada in 1954, intending to join the Australian Jazz Quartet, but instead engaging in casual work. He returned to Sydney in the mid-1960s and worked with the ★Daly-Wilson band and on television. From the 80s he was with the Lucy Brown group and freelancing. Duff was the first postwar performer to establish a reputation specifically as a jazz singer in Australia.

FURTHER REFERENCE
Recordings include *Jack Brokensha and His Quartet* (1949, Jazzart JA-23), *Jack Brokensha's Big Band* (1949, Esquire 1004/1006). See also *BissetB*; *OxfordJ*.   BRUCE JOHNSON

Duff, Jeff ['Duffo', 'Cyril Trotts', 'Joopiter Jones', 'Ivor Biggin'] (*b* USA), jazz-rock singer. Appearing on stage and television from the age of seven, after early work in local bands he was lead singer in the Chicago-style jazz-rock band Kush 1971–77. Then he presented eccentric solo shows with such groups as Jeff Duff and the Duffers, releasing *Temptation's About To Get Me* in 1977. In 1978 he moved to London and gained an alternative following as the bizarre nightclub operator Duffo, appearing as Spider Children (1986) with a violinist, tapes and drum machine, and releasing 10 singles including *Walk On The Wild Side* (1987), *Give Me My Brain Back* (1979), *John And Betty Go To LA* (1980) and the albums *Duffo* (1979), and *Bob The Birdman* (1983). A quirky artist with a classically trained tenor voice, he returned to Australia in 1988, forming the jazz-funk band Duffhead (1989) and making *Captain Vitmo* (1989) and *Angels And Rascals* (1994).

FURTHER REFERENCE
Recordings include *Temptation's About To Get Me* (1977 Mushroom K6764), *Walk On The Wild Side* (1987, Powderworks POW 0372), *Give Me My Brain Back* (1979 WEA), *John And Betty Go To LA* (1980 PVK), *Duffo* (1979 WEA 600043), and *Bob The Birdman* (1983, Powderworks POW 6050); with Duffhead *Captain Vitmo* (1989, CV002) and *Angels And Rascals* (1994, MDS RAS10). For discography, see *SpencerA*. See also *McGrathA*; *SpencerW*; *Larkin*, I, 742.

Dugites. Pop band (1974–84) formed at Perth, at first comprised of Linda Nutter (vocals), Peter Crosbie and Gunther Berghofer (guitars), Philip Bailey (bass), and Clarence Bailey (drums). They toured Australia in 1979, appeared on television and as support to Hall and Oates, and released six singles in the style of the Phil Spector female group recordings, including *Hit Single* (1979), *In Your Car* (1980) and *Waiting* (1981) and an album, *The*

Dugites (1980). Moving to Melbourne in 1981, they released four more singles; their album *Cut The Talking* (1984) showed considerably improved playing and production, but it was to be their last.

FURTHER REFERENCE
Recordings include *Hit Single* (1979, EMI PRS 2625), *In Your Car* (1980, Deluxe 103588) and *Waiting* (1981 Deluxe 10319), *The Dugites* (1980, Deluxe VPL 16506), and *Cut The Talking* (1984, Mercury 814691–1). For discography, see *SpencerA*. See also *CoupeN*; *GuinnessP*, I, 742; *McGrathA*; *SpencerW*.

Dullo Trust, Walter. A fund established in memory of Walter Andreas Dullo (1902–78), who was a council member of Musica Viva from its inception in 1945. A cultivated and committed lover of chamber music, he wrote program notes for Musica Viva concerts, broadcast for 2MBS-FM, and was active with the Mozart Society and Schubert Society. Administered by Musica Viva, the trust provides funds to further the cause of chamber music in Australia.

FURTHER REFERENCE
Musica Viva Bulletin, 30/4 (Sept.–Oct. 1978), supplement.

Dunbar, Kate (Ruth Kathleen) née Kelly (*b* Manchester, England, 13 May 1923), jazz singer. Arriving in Australia as a child she had formal training at the NSW Conservatorium. She sang jazz publicly from the 1950s with Ray Price, the Paramount Jazz Band, Graeme Bell, Frank Traynor and others. She was in retirement from 1973, but resumed work in the 1980s with Ted Sly's band. She has been editor of ★Sydney Jazz Club's *Quarterly Rag* and the club's president since 1985. She established the record label Kate Dunbar Presents, and since 1988 has run weekly workshops which have produced some of the city's most successful singers in the 1990s. She was awarded the AM in 1994.

FURTHER REFERENCE
Recordings include *The Famous PIX Sessions, Classic Australian Jazz from the Sixties* (1996, Australian Jazz Reissues AJR-001 A&B). See also *OxfordJ*; Jim McLeod, *Jazztrack* (Sydney: ABC Books, 1994), 192–207.   BRUCE JOHNSON

Duncan. Beer-drinking song (1980) by Pat Alexander. An amateur songwriter, Alexander sent a tape of the song to Slim ★Dusty, who recorded it (1980); one of the few country singles to succeed in the pop charts, it was No. 1 for 23 weeks in 1981, and was also recorded by Frankie Davidson and the Selection Singers.

FURTHER REFERENCE
Recorded versions include those by Slim Dusty (1980, Columbia DO 384), Frankie Davidson (Larrikin LRF 296 CD) and the Selection Singers (selection MBC 603). See also *McGrathA*.

Duncan, Cyril (*b* Numinbah Valley, Qld, 1907), traditional ballad singer. Born into a family of bullock drivers, he worked as a carpenter and canecutter around Queensland, and as a semi-professional boxer. He learned a large repertoire of song from his grandfather, including *Cardigan The Brave*, *Young Ned Kelly*, *A Long Time On The Logan*, *Bullock 'O*, *To My Dear Old Home Once More* and *Bullock Bells At Night*. Stan Arthur of the Queensland Folk Federation transcribed songs from him in 1957, now published in the *Queensland Centenary Songbook*, and Warren Fahey recorded his singing in 1973. He has been a unique source of rare British songs, Australian traditional drover ballads and yarns.

FURTHER REFERENCE
His work may be heard in *Bush Traditions* (1976, Larrikin LRF O07). Recordings made by Fahey are in *CAnl*. See also *OxfordF*.

Durack, Mary (*b* Adelaide, 20 Feb. 1913; *d* 1994), author. After schooling at Loreto Covent, Perth, she wrote children's books, novels and stories of outback life for the *West Australian*; in all over 25 publications, chiefly on outback themes. She wrote the libretto for James *Penberthy's opera *Dalgerie* (1959), about an Aboriginal leper who waits to see her former white lover before she dies; the work was performed at the opening of the Sydney Opera House in 1973.

FURTHER REFERENCE
Obit. in *Australian*, 19 Dec. 1994. See also *WWA* (1995); *Antipodes* 3/1 (Spring 1989), 43–6.

Durbin, Alison (*b* Auckland, NZ, 1950), popular music singer. After singing in a children's choir, her single *Lovers Lane* became a hit in NZ when she was 14. Joining the Mike Perjanik Showband, she went to Sydney and worked in clubs and hotels 1966–67, and toured NZ with Gene Pitney. She settled in Melbourne from 1968, releasing 11 singles, including *Games People Play* (1969) and *Put Your Hand In The Hand* (1971), which reached No. 5 in the charts, and the album *Don't Come Any Closer* (1969). She was voted top Australian female artist by *Go-Set* and Queen of Pop by *TV Week* three years running (1969–71). She recorded with Johnny *Farnham in 1971 and, after having a family, changed to country music, recording six albums from 1976, including *Are You Lonesome Tonight* (1977) and more recently *Reckless Girl* (1991).

FURTHER REFERENCE
Recordings include *Lovers Lane* (1964, Zodiac), *Games People Play* (1969, Columbia DO 8717), *Put Your Hand In The Hand* (1971, Columbia DO 9425), *Don't Come Any Closer* (1969, EMI SOX O7898), *Are You Lonesome Tonight* (1977, Hammond HAM 017) and *Reckless Girl* (1991, Raylan 300348–1A). For discography, see *SpencerA*. See also *McGrathA*; *SpencerW*.

Dusty, Slim [David Gordon Kirkpatrick]   (*b* Kempsey, NSW, 13 June 1927), country music singer-songwriter. He wrote his first song, *The Way the Cowboy Dies*, at the age of 10 and made his debut at the local Kempsey radio station 2KM in 1942. He also made the first of his 'process records' in 1942 at own expense, which he sent to various country stations. His first commercial recording was for Regal Zonophone in 1946, in which he included *When the Rain Tumbles Down in July*, the forerunner of his trademark Australian bush ballads. From 1948 to 1954 he appeared intermittently on radio programs, hall shows and tent shows, working with other country singers such as Tim *McNamara, Reg *Lindsay, Gordon *Parsons, and the *McKean Sisters. His full-time show career began in 1954 with the launch of the first travelling Slim Dusty Show, which included his wife, Joy McKean, and lead guitarist Barry *Thornton. His travelling show expanded in 1964 to 10-month-long annual Round Australia tours. His many wider successes began with his recording of Parson's *The Pub with No Beer* in 1957, which became the biggest-selling record by an Australian artist at the time, topping the Sydney charts for six months and winning the only gold 78 rpm record ever presented to an Australian. With his clear voice and characteristically Australian rural accent, Dusty's songs usually portray the Australian bush life. His long and successful career has made him an Australian folk hero. He was honoured with the MBE in 1970 and is in the ACMA Roll of Renown.

FURTHER REFERENCE
Recordings include *The Best of Slim Dusty* (Readers Digest RD CP 4.387–4); *Slim Dusty Sings His Favourite Songs* (WRC R60533–4); *Slim Dusty Vintage Albums*, 4 vols (OEX 10491–4). His autobiographies are *Slim Dusty: Walk a Country Mile* with John Lapsley (Adelaide: Rigby, 1979), which contains a discography to 1979, and *Another Day Another Town* with Joy McKean (Sydney: Macmillan, 1996). See also *CA* (1995–96); *LattaA*; *National Times* 4 Feb. 1979, 14 Oct. 1979; David Parker and Kent Chadwick, *The Slim Dusty Movie: Across Australia* (Dingley: Budget Books, 1984); Peter Phillips, *Slim Dusty Around Australia* (Canberra: P. Phillips, 1984); *WatsonC*, 1.   YA HUI HUNG

Dyabi.   Songs of Aboriginal people in the Kimberleys which comment on contemporary life, accompanied by a *dyabi* stick, or rasp. See *Rasp*.

Dyer, Louise B(erta) M(osson) née Smith   (*b* Melbourne, 19 July 1884; *d* Monaco, 9 Nov. 1962), music publisher. The daughter of parliamentarian and entrepreneur Dr L.L. Smith, Louise attended Presbyterian Ladies' College, Melbourne, and in 1900 won the Associated Board's gold medal for piano-playing. Subsequently she studied under Eduard Scharf at the Albert Street Conservatorium and in Edinburgh. After marrying the wealthy businessman James Dyer, 25 years her senior, Louise decided that her musical interests might be best advanced by acting as patron. Initially working through PLC and the Alliance Française, in 1921 she founded the Melbourne branch of the *British Music Society which, subsidised by Dyer money, embarked on a vigorous program of chamber concerts (many at her home in Toorak) and a performance of Holst's opera *Savitri*. Before leaving permanently for overseas in 1927, Louise and Jimmy Dyer gave £10 000 towards the establishment of a professional orchestra in Melbourne.

After a short period in London, the Dyers moved to Paris. At first Louise was involved in underwriting a complete edition of the works of Lully, but this broke down. Thereupon she decided to found a press of her own—Éditions de l'Oiseau-lyre, or Lyrebird Press. The first objective was the complete works of François Couperin, whose bicentenary occurred in 1933; much of his music had never been published before. The first editions combined scholarship with sumptuousness, and were sold only to major libraries, universities and musicologists. Notable among them were *Polyphonies du treizième siècle* (1935–48), *Polyphonic Music of the Fourteenth Century* (1956, completed posthumously 1992), *Trésor de musique byzantine* (1934) and *Treize livres de motets parus chez Pierre Attaingnant* (1934, completed posthumously 1964). L'Oiseau-lyre publications extended to contemporary music, including works by Peggy *Glanville-Hicks and Margaret *Sutherland. Among the Sutherland pieces were some settings of poems by John Shaw Neilson, to whom Louise had also acted as patron.

In 1938, in order to make some of this music more accessible, the firm moved into recordings. It was this way that it became best known. Increasingly managed by her second husband, J.B. Hanson, about 25 years younger, the recordings soon followed imperatives of their own. In 1950 l'Oiseau-lyre produced the first long-playing records in Europe, and for the next 15 years was one of the most notable labels specialising in Baroque music. Among its triumphs were early and important recordings by Janet Baker, Colin Davis, Neville Marriner and the Academy of St Martin-in-the-Fields, and Joan *Sutherland. Indeed Louise encouraged Australian artists whenever she could. On her death the bulk of her Australian estate was left to the University of Melbourne.

FURTHER REFERENCE
Jim Davidson, *Lyrebird Rising: Louise Hanson-Dyer of L'Oiseau-Lyre 1884–1962* (Melbourne: Miegunyah/MUP, 1994); idem, 'Louise B.M. Dyer', *ADB*, 8.   JIM DAVIDSON

Dyer, Michael George   (b Sydney, 2 May 1930), musician, educator. He graduated BA from the University of Sydney and took out the diploma from the NSW State Conservatorium in 1952. Further studies in the UK were undertaken with Sir John Dykes Bower, Sir William Harris, Martindale Sidwell and Sir Adrian Boult. His principal appointments have included organist of St James' Church, Sydney 1961–65, lecturer at the NSW State Conservatorium 1961–68, lecturer at Alexander Mackie College

1964–68, organist and director of music at St Philip's Church, Sydney, since 1967, and senior lecturer in charge of music at Nepean College of Advanced Education 1967–88. Dyer's ardent interest in history and architecture has led him to promote concerts in many of Sydney's historic buildings, often exploring music of the historical era of the building. He is also devoted to the development of music education in Australia.

FURTHER REFERENCE
ADMR, 53–4.   ALAN L. MOFFAT

Dying Stockman, The,   stockman's ballad. A parody of Charles Coote's 'The Tarpaulin Jacket', by Queensland pastoralist Horace *Flower and Walton Kent (1882), it is often sung to a version of the Irish fiddle tune 'Rosin the Bow', and describes the last wishes of a stockrider struck down in his youth far from home. One of the best known of Australia's pastoral ballads, it was published in *Portland Mirror* (8 July 1885), then by A.B. Paterson in *Old Bush Songs* (1905). At least nine widely dispersed variants have been collected since.

FURTHER REFERENCE
Edition and commentary in *EdwardsG*; *ManifoldP*; *RadicS*, 29.

Dyirbal.   Languages and dialects spoken by six contiguous Aboriginal groups living in the rainforest just to the south of Cairns, Queensland. From north to south these are Ngajan, Mamu, Jirrbal, Jirru, Gulngay and Girramay. The languages of these groups are mutually intelligible, and may all be regarded as dialects of a single language.

R.M.W. Dixon, who has been working on the language and songs since 1963, has identified five song styles in Dyirbal. Except for some introductory vocalisations, all Dyirbal songs articulate one syllable per note. Often the songs include 'nonsense' syllables, usually at the end of a line of text other than the last, which have a purely metrical function. The metrical requirements of the texts define the song genres, but there is much freedom with the melodies. Within four of the genres, singers create 'signature tunes' or personal melodies, and set different texts to these tunes; thus Jimmy Murray sang all of his *Gama* songs to his own tune, all of his *Marrga* to another, and so on. All songs may be sung by men or women.

Dyirbal people divide the song styles into two categories: corroboree songs, which were performed at gatherings of different groups to accompany organised dancing, and love songs, which were sung to convey the singer's feelings about events or other people. Corroboree songs are *Gama* and *Marrga* styles. *Gama*, the most common and wide-reaching of the five styles, is known all over the Dyirbal-speaking area. *Marrga* is a song style of the Mamu tribe. Both styles may be interspersed with dance calls, and both are accompanied by percussion, which may be two boomerangs clapped together or a 'drum', consisting of an animal skin or membrane stretched across a woman's lap.

Love songs are *Jangala, Burran* and *Gaynyil* styles. The first two styles may be referred to as *Gugulu*, which is the main accompaniment stick, made from hardwood, struck with a piece of lawyer cane. *Jangala* songs, the *Gugulu* style of the Jirrbal and Girramay people, are longer in duration than the other styles, have lengthened notes at the end of each line of text, and tend to repeat the last line sung either at the lowest pitch of the song or after a breath is taken. *Burran* style, of the Gulngay people, is said to have been created by two women; it is the one song style which has an identifiable melody; all singers use the same tune. *Gaynyil* is the love song style of the Mamu people. A performer may lie on his or her back while singing a *Gaynyil*. There is no percussion accompaniment.

FURTHER REFERENCE

R.M.W. Dixon and Grace Koch, *Dyirbal Song Poetry: The Oral Literature of an Australian Rainforest People* (Brisbane: UQP, 1996); idem, *Dyirbal Song Poetry: The Oral Literature of an Australian Rainforest People* (1996, Larrikin RF 3786).   GRACE KOCH

Dynamic Hepnotics. Rhythm and blues band (1978–87) formed in Sydney. With many changes, the members from 1980 were chiefly Robert 'Continental' Susz (vocals, harmonica), Andrew Silver (guitar), Bruce Allen (saxophone), Allan Britton (bass) and Robert Souter (drums). In 1981 they released their debut album, an EP *Shakin' All Over* and then the single *Hepnobeat*, which became a dance hit in Europe and the USA. They toured Australia 1981–83, building a considerable live reputation, and their next recording success was *Soul Kind Of Feeling* in 1984, which reached No. 5 in the charts. They followed this with five more singles, and the albums *Dynamic Hepnotics Live* (1984) and *Take You Higher* (1985).

FURTHER REFERENCE

Recordings include *Hepnobeat* (Mambo ZIP 001), *Soul Kind Of Feeling* (White K9470), *Dynamic Hepnotics Live* (1984, White L27147) and *Take You Higher* (1985, White RML 53164). For discography, see *SpencerA*. See also *CoupeN*; *McGrathA*; *SpencerW*; Stuart Coupe and Glenn A. Baker, *Rock: The Year That Was '85* (Sydney: Bay Books, 1985).

E

Early Music Revival. European interest in performance of Medieval and Renaissance music and the related growth of the historical performance movement have inspired from the late 1960s a small but dedicated group of early music exponents in Australia. The nine-member *Renaissance Players (founded 1966) under Winsome Evans in Sydney were among the first to record and perform early repertoire extensively in Australia; they were followed by the four-member *La Romanesca (founded 1978) under John *Griffiths at Melbourne, who explored Medieval repertoire in particular. Baroque performance on period instruments and with attention to authentic styles was presented by several groups, the string trio repertoire by *Capella Corelli (founded 1977) under Cynthia O'Brien at Canberra, works for Baroque flute and recorder by *Elysium Ensemble (founded 1985) under Greg Dikmans at Melbourne, and early keyboard works by John *O'Donnell in Melbourne, who later gave stylish performances of Baroque choral works with the Tudor Choristers and of 16th-century repertoire with his Ensemble Gombert. In the 1980s Nicholas *Routley gave performances of high quality with his Sydney University Chamber Choir, Geoffrey *Lancaster specialised in fortepiano, working extensively with the Tasmanian Chamber players, and the *Brandenburg Orchestra (founded 1990) under Paul Dyer at Sydney has done increasingly impressive work.

The revival has been strengthened by the growth of historic instrument making in Australia, the early keyboard instruments of Marc *Nobel and Bill *Bright, the Baroque recorders and flutes of Fred *Morgan, the Renaissance lutes and guitars of John Hall, and the period violins of Ian *Watchorn featuring in many performances. In the 1980s the summer school at the University of New England, Armidale was a meeting place for early music enthusiasts; since its demise there have been annual national schools of early music in other centres. Fully staged Baroque opera productions using historic instruments and styles have occasionally been attempted, notably operas of Handel under Paul Thom at the Australian

National University, Canberra, and operas of Monteverdi by the Australian Opera and the Victoria State Opera. Several of these have been enriched by the research on Baroque stage gesture of Dene Barnett (Adelaide).

Earth Mother, The. Opera in three acts (1957–58) by James *Penberthy, libretto by D.R. Stuart and Penberthy.

Earth Poem/Sky Poem. Dance work by Richard *Mills (1993) on an Aboriginal subject. Published by Boosey & Hawkes.

Eastern European Traditional Music. Australia has sizeable communities from Eastern Europe, the most populous from Poland (69 000) and Hungary (27 100), then the Czech Republic (17 800) and Romania (11 300), with smaller groups from Latvia, Lithuania, Estonia and Slovakia. Soon after arriving in Australia as World War II refugee immigrants, ethnic communities were formed by each group to cater for the various interests of their members. Prominent music-making activities within the communities were choirs, smaller singing groups, folk-dancing groups, bands and ensembles. By keeping the cultural traditions within each group alive, members felt a sense of identity within the larger, alien culture to which they had been transplanted. As numbers within the groups have decreased, so the music-making has declined; succeeding generations have not needed the music-making for the same reasons, but many of them enjoy participating with others who are linked by the same emotional bond. Visits to Australia by musicians from the homelands also serve to retain some traditional ties. Most members of these ethnic communities view their orally transmitted songs as being representative of their traditional music in Australia. The music is essentially rural-based.

(i) Czech Republic. Although Czechs still sing together informally, there are at present no Czech choirs in Australia. Dance groups exist only in Sydney and Melbourne.

Well known for their brass tradition, Czech brass bands play together when an important occasion arises, but otherwise do not play regularly.

(ii) Estonia. There are Estonian choirs in Sydney and Melbourne, but those in other cities have now disbanded. Folk-dancing groups are still popular, and a small group of young folk instrumentalists play both modern and folksongs in Sydney. There has been renewed interest in the playing of the cithara, an ancient stringed instrument of long history in Estonia. Other instrumentalists occasionally perform, but most musical accompaniment at Estonian functions is from tapes.

(iii) Hungary. Traditional Hungarian music is strongly maintained in Australia through dance groups and instrumental ensembles. Professional instructors are sometimes hired from Hungary for the dancers, and professional musicians play well-researched Hungarian music on a mixture of folk and orchestral instruments. Participants in the Hungarian dance groups are of mixed descent.

(iv) Latvia. Latvians still follow a strong singing tradition, with 10 choirs currently performing around Australia. Latvian folk-dancing is very popular and a Latvian instrumental ensemble exists in Adelaide, where the traditional folk instrument, the kokle, is played. Latvian cultural festivals where music-making is practised are held every two years.

(v) Lithuania. Lithuanian choirs and folk-dancing groups which include non-Lithuanian participants exist in the larger cities. There are two Lithuanian ensembles made up of older women who perform only traditional songs and dances. A small group of young singers and instrumentalists also performs informally in the traditional Lithuanian style; this group includes players of the ancient kankles. Biennial Lithuanian festivals enable members to continue their musical traditions.

(vi) Poland. Music and dance is very strong among the Polish communities, and the Adelaide and Melbourne Polish musical groups have 80–100 members in each. Most singers dance, and dancers sing, with several groups in each of the capital cities performing regularly. Instrumental ensembles vary with the availability of individual performers on a variety of instruments. There have also been a number of new compositions in the Polish folk style which have been introduced into the repertoire.

(vii) Slovakia. Although Slovak communities were at first musically active, because of their small numbers and gradual dispersal, regular activities have almost disappeared. Musical groups have now ceased to function and Slovaks rely on recordings and performers from other ethnic groups to contribute to their regular festivals.

FURTHER REFERENCE
Recordings include, of Bulgarian *The Martenitsa Choir* (Tall Poppies TP026); of Hungarian *The Transylvaniacs* (Tall Poppies TP063).
JENNIFER RAKAUSKAS

Easton, Michael (*b* Hertfordshire, England, 1954), composer. He studied at the Royal Academy of Music, London, with Sir Lennox Berkeley and Christopher Brown, then with Nadia Boulanger and Leighton Lucas. He worked in music publishing for Chester and Novello from 1976, wrote music for BBC radio and television, and filled commissions from the Royal Philharmonic Orchestra and Bournemouth Symphony Orchestra. He moved to Australia in 1982 to join Allans Music, Melbourne, but from 1986 worked as a freelance composer, lecturer and concert manager. A polished writer in an easily accessible style, his works include two symphonies, a number of concertos including five for piano, several works for voice including the *Cabaret Songs* (1991) for Lauris Elms, three children's operas, of which *Beauty and the Beast* was widely performed by the Victoria State Opera, and the musical *Petrov* (1992). He has also worked as an arranger on recordings of such singers as Marina Prior and Anthony Warlow.

FURTHER REFERENCE
He is published by Schirmer (Aust.). There are ABC tapes of his Concerto for Two Pianos, *La Grande Dictionnaire de Cuisine* (1989) and several vocal works. See also *BroadstockS*, 89–91.

Easybeats. Pop group (1964–70) founded in Sydney, comprised of five recently arrived migrant musicians: Stevie Wright (vocals), Harry Vanda (lead guitar), George Young (guitar), Dick Diamonde (bass), and Gordon 'Snowy' Fleet (drums to 1967, then Tony Cahill). Vanda and Young met at a migrant hostel in Sydney, and after playing at dances they were signed to EMI and went to Melbourne in 1965, where they were an immediate success. In six months they had four national hits, *She's So Fine* reaching No. 1, and in 1966 they had six successive chart hits, *Sorry* reaching No. 1, and two successful albums.

Moving to the UK, their *Friday On My Mind* charted well in Europe, the UK and the USA and reached No. 1 in Australia. They toured the USA with Gene Pitney in 1967 and Australia in 1967 and 1969. Their direction began to change in 1969 but their fans did not move with them, and with their popularity waning they disbanded in 1970. Vanda and Young went on to significant success as a songwriting production team (see *Vanda and Young*). They re-formed for an Australian tour in 1986. Dominating the Australian pop scene in the mid-1960s, they had 15 Top 40 singles and epitomised the 'mod' sound. After the Seekers, the most successful Australian group internationally in these years, they were voted *Go-Set* best Australian group in 1966 and 1967.

FURTHER REFERENCE
Recordings include *She's So Fine* (1965, Parlophone A8157); *Sorry* (1966, Parlophone A8224); *Friday On My Mind* (1966, Parlophone A82324); *Easy* (1965, Parlophone PMCO 7527); a compilation is *Absolute Anthology* (1980, EMI APM1–2). For discography, see *SpencerA*. See also *GuinnessP*, I, 764–5; *McGrathA*; *SpencerW*.

Eclipse Alley Five   (Sydney). Jazz band formed by Peter Gallen (bass) in 1969. In 1970 the band began at the Vanity Fair Hotel what at that time became Australia's longest jazz residency (1970–86) and a primary focus for Sydney's jazz scene. Other residencies followed without interruption, and the group is currently at the Evening Star Hotel, Surry Hills, co-led by Bruce ★Johnson (joined 1972), and still including drummer Viv Carter (joined 1971). Through various personnel changes, the long tenure of some members has maintained continuity, with founder member Paul ★Furniss being a defining presence as leader until he departed in 1990, to be replaced by present co-leader Allan English (reeds).

FURTHER REFERENCE
Recordings include *Vanity Fair*, Paul Furniss and the Eclipse Alley Five (1974, Swaggie S1368). See also *OxfordJ*; Bruce Johnson, 'Goodbye Vanity Fair', *JA* (Winter/Spring 1986), 10–11.
                                                      BRUCE JOHNSON

Eddy, Jenifer Edna   (*b* Melbourne, 18 Feb. 1933), coloratura soprano, concert agent. After studies in Melbourne with J.G. Neilson then Henry and Annie ★Portnoj, she won the first Shell Aria in 1955, made her debut as Nedda in *Pagliacci* at Hobart in 1956, and then sang Susanna, Despina and Papagena in the Mozart Festival of the inaugural Elizabethan Theatre Trust Opera season of 1956. She sang solos in ABC concerts and on television until 1959, when she moved to London. She studied with Bertha Nicklauss Kempner, then Roy Henderson, and was immediately engaged at Covent Garden, making her debut as Frasquita (*Carmen*), singing roles such as Titania, the Niece (*Peter Grimes*), Papagena, Lisa (*La sonnambula*) and Xenia (*Boris Godunov*), and appearing at the Leeds, Edinburgh and Schwetzingen Festivals. After leave for the birth of her son in 1962, she resumed her work at Covent Garden in 1963, appearing at Sadler's Wells, the Scottish Opera, and the Welsh National Opera, as well as in major European festivals and in innumerable BBC broadcasts.

A sparkling coloratura and enticing stage presence, her roles also included Blonde (*Il seraglio*), Musetta, and Sophie (*Rosenkavalier*). Contracted for her American debut at the San Francisco Opera in 1969, illness struck, and she was forced to retire from the stage. She returned to Australia in 1975 and established an opera and concert management agency which now represents a large number of significant Australian singers as well as importing major European artists to Australia.

FURTHER REFERENCE
Recordings include *Il Seraglio* cond. Y. Menuhin (EMI); *Hansel and Gretel* (EMI); and *The Gipsy Baron* (EMI). See also *MackenzieS*, 205–7.

Edgecombe, John   (*b* Sydney, 17 Feb. 1925; *d* Sydney, 11 Dec. 1985), jazz performer, composer. His professional career began in 1939 but was interrupted by war service (1943–46). Edgecombe became ubiquitous in every aspect of jazz as a guitarist, bassist, banjo, tuba and trombone player, and vocalist, as well as a composer and arranger, and across an intimidating range of styles. He worked with every major band in Sydney, including those of Bill Weston, Les Welch, Ralph Mallen, Craig Crawford, and Graeme Bell, and he co-founded the Australian Jazz Club in 1954. From the 1980s he concentrated on jazz playing, joining the Dick ★Hughes Famous Five and Lucy Brown Quartet, with whom he played until his death.

FURTHER REFERENCE
Recordings include *Julian Lee Trio* (1958, Columbia SEGO-70021). See also *OxfordJ*.   BRUCE JOHNSON

Éditions de L'Oiseau-lyre.   See *Dyer, Louise*.

Edmonds, Thomas   (*b* Petersborough, SA, 6 Apr. 1934), tenor. While studying with Arnold ★Matters at the University of Adelaide, he sang for ABC radio from 1962, then went to England and joined the English Opera Group, making his debut in Britten's *Death in Venice* at the Aldeburgh Festival in 1973. He sang at Sadler's Wells, for the BBC and in oratorio at major festivals in the UK and Europe. He returned to Australia in 1976 to join the State Opera of South Australia, and toured in Gilbert and Sullivan. He continued to make guest appearances in the UK and Europe, and appeared in more than 50 roles with the Australian Opera and all state companies. With a focused tone and affecting expression, he has made 22 albums, chiefly for RCA (Aust.), winning two gold records. He was honoured with the OAM in 1982 and AM in 1987.

Edward John Eyre.   Opera in one act by Barry ★Conyngham (1971), libretto by M. Oakes after Eyre's journal. Set in 1840–41, it recounts Eyre's exploration of south-west Australia. It comprises five sung poems, with a series of spoken or intoned interludes, which quote from the journal and effectively convey the explorer's loneliness and sense of the vastness of the new country. First performed at the University of New South Wales on 1 May 1971.

Edwards, Ron(ald) George   (*b* Geelong, Vic., 1930), folklorist, publisher. After studying art at Swinburne Institute of Technology, he collaborated with John ★Manifold to produce the seminal *Bandicoot Ballads* (1951–56), compiled the *Overland Song Book* (1956), and established the Rams Skull Press at Ferntree Gully, in outer Melbourne, publishing works on Australian folk-song by Hugh Anderson, John Manifold, Russel Ward, Harry Pearce, and others. He edited *National Folk* (formerly *Northern Folk*) 1966–70, and founded the Australian Folklore Society in 1984. A fine illustrator, he has also published on traditional bush crafts and yarns. One of Australia's most important field collectors of folk-song, especially in Cairns where he has lived since 1959 and far north Australia, his own collections include *Australian Folk Songs*, *Australian Bawdy Ballads*, *Tune Sources for Australian Folksong* and the definitive *Great Australian Folk Songs* (1976, reprint 1991), which also contains his *Australian Folksong Index* (5th edn, 1994), a major reference tool. He was honoured with the OAM in 1992.

FURTHER REFERENCE
Wendy Lowenstein, 'Ron Edwards and the Rams Skull Press', *Australian Academic and Research Libraries* 23/1 (Mar. 1992), 1–10; OxfordF; OxfordL.

Edwards, Ross (*b* Sydney, 23 Dec. 1943), composer. After attending the NSW State Conservatorium, he studied composition with Peter ★Sculthorpe and Richard ★Meale at the University of Sydney, and Peter Maxwell Davies and Sándor Veress at the University of Adelaide. His music was heard at the ISCM festivals at Stockholm (1966) and Basel (1970), and he moved to the UK for further studies with Maxwell Davies in 1970. From 1973 he taught at the University of Sydney, but has chiefly been a freelance composer, filling commissions for the ABC orchestras, the major Australian contemporary ensembles and occasionally ensembles abroad such as the Academy of St Martin-in-the-Fields. He was Australia Council Don Banks fellow in 1989–90, then a creative arts fellow from 1990.

His music has developed a distinctive voice of austere beauty, often based on the arrangement of attractive elements gathered from nature into abstract patterns. At first he wrote chamber music, such as the series of *Monos* for solo instruments (1970–72) or the String Quartet No. 2, commissioned for Musica Viva. The static patterns of Asian music had their influence in contemplative works such as *The Hermit of the Green Light* (1979), and he became fascinated with materials the sounds of insects could provide, which he explored in *The Tower of Remoteness* (1978) and *Yarrageh* (1989). The *Maninyas* (1981–88) series began with a set of nonsense syllables and appealing melodic fragments, from which he produced six works of great gaiety and rhythmic buoyancy. More recently he has come to wide attention with orchestral works, including the widely played Piano Concerto (1982), the *Maninyas* Violin Concerto (1988) and the Symphony *Da Pacem Domine* (1990–91). He has become one of the most convincing voices Australian music has produced. He won an APRA award in 1993 and ARIA award in 1993.

WORKS (Selective)
Orchestral *Mountain Village in a Clearing Mist* (1973, Universal Edition), *Concerto for Piano and Orchestra* (1982, ABC Classics 426483, pub. UE), *Maninyas—Concerto for Violin and Orchestra* (1988, rec. ABC Classics 438610–2, pub. UE), *Yarrageh—Nocturne for Solo Percussion and Orchestra* (1989, rec. ABC Classics 438610, pub. UE), *Aria and Transcendental Dance,* hn, str orch (1990, UE), *Symphony Da Pacem Domine* (1990–91, rec. ABC Classics 438610, pub. Boosey & Hawkes), *Concerto for Guitar and String Orchestra* (1994–95, BH), *Enyato III* (1995, BH).

Ensemble *Shadow D-Zone,* fl, cl, perc, pf, vn, vc (1977, UE), *The Tower of Remoteness,* cl, pf (1978, rec. Tall Poppies TP004/ TP051, pub. UE), *Laikan,* fl, cl, perc, pf, vn, vc (1979, rec. ABC Classics 434901, pub. UE), *Maninya II,* str qrt (1982, UE), *Ten Little Duets,* 2 high insts (1982, BH), *Maninya III,* wind quintet (1985, rec. Canberra School of Music, CSM 14, pub. UE), *Reflections,* pf, 3 perc (1985, rec. ABC Classics 442350, and Canberra School of Music, CSM 2, pub. UE), *Maninya IV,* bass cl, trbn, marimba (1985–86, UE), *Ecstatic Dances,* 2 fl (1990, rec. Tall Poppies TP051, pub. BH), *Ecstatic Dance II,* va, vc; or 2 vn (1990, rec. Tall Poppies TP051/TP043, pub. BH), *Prelude and Dragonfly Dance,* perc qrt (1991, rec. Tall Poppies TP051/TP030, pub. BH), *Black Mountain Duos,* 2 vc (1992, BH), *Enyato I,* str qrt (1993, BH), *Four Bagatelles,* ob, cl (1994, BH), *Enyato IV,* bass cl, perc (1995, BH).

Solo Instrumental *Monos I,* vc (1970, UE), *Marimba Dances* (1982, rec. Tall Poppies TP051, RCA Victor RD60557 and Celestial Harmonies 13085, pub. UE), *Ulpirra,* rec (1993, rec. Tall Poppies TP051, pub. BH), *Enyato II,* va (1994, BH), *Guitar Dances* (1994, BH).

Keyboard *Monos II* (1970, Albert Publishing), *Five Little Piano Pieces* (1976, UE), *Kumari* (1980–81, rec. Tall Poppies TP051, pub. UE), *Etymalong* (1984, rec. Tall Popies TP051, pub. UE), *Three Children's Pieces:* Fipsis (UE), Gamelan (Currency Press), Emily's Song (BH) (1986–7), *Pond Light Mantras,* 2 pf (1991, BH), *Three Little Piano Duets* (1992, UE/BH), *Sanctuary,* 2 pf, gongs (1995, BH).

Stage *Christina's World,* chamber opera (1983 rev. 1989, 1, Dorothy Hewett, pub. UE), *Sensing,* dance (1992–93, BH).

Choral *Five Carols from Quem Quæritis,* SSAA (1967, UE), *Antifon,* SATB, brass sextet, org, 2 perc (1973, AP), *Ab Estasis Foribus,* SATB (1980, UE), *Flower Songs,* SATB, 2 perc (1986–87, rec. Tall Poppies TP051, pub. UE), *Dance Mantras,* 6 vv, drum (1992, BH).

Vocal *The Hermit of Green Light,* Ct /Mez, pf (1979, rec. MBS 21CD, and MBS 19CD/CSM 15, pub. UE), *Maninya I,* Ct/Mez, vc (1981, rec. MBS 21CD, pub. UE), *Maninya V,* Ct/Mez, pf (1986, rec. MBS 21CD, pub. UE), *Nos Qui Vivimus,* T, vc (1995, BH).

FURTHER REFERENCE
Recordings include the Piano Concerto (ABC 426483), *Maninyas,* Violin Concerto (ABC 438610–2), Symphony *Da Pacem Domine* (ABC 438610); *Mountain In A Clearing Mist* (Oz Music, OZM 2005); *The Hermit of the Green Light* (1991, 2MBS MBS21CD); *The Tower of Remoteness* (1991, 2MBS), *Etymalong* (Canberra School of Music, CSM 3), *Marimba Dances* (Southern Cross SCCD 1021) and *Ecstatic Dance No.2* (1978/90) va,vc (1994, Tall Poppies TP043); *Monos II* (1971, EMI OASD 7567). His writings include 'Credo', *SA* 23 (Spring 1989), 8. See also

CA (1995/96); Jenny Dawson, *ContemporaryC*; *MurdochA*; Michael Hannan, 'Ross Edwards: A Unique Sound World', *APRAJ* (Mar. 1986); Meredith Oakes, 'Ross Edwards and Roger Woodward in London', *Music Now* 2/1 (Apr. 1972).

Egan, Ted, (*b* Melbourne, 6 July 1932), country music singer-songwriter, outback folklorist. After growing up in Melbourne, he left home at 15 and settled in the NT. He began writing songs by ear of his outback experiences, making his first recording, *Outback Australia*, in 1969. He studied arts by correspondence through the Australian National University (1975) and worked for the Department of Aboriginal Affairs for over 20 years. Performing solo, accompanying himself with an empty Fosters beer carton (the 'Fosterphone') he has performed throughout Australia, toured the USA (1985) and released his five-album series *Faces of Australia* (1989). He presented a program *This Land Australia*, featured in the television series *The Great Outdoors*, and has written three books. Writing in Irish traditional ballad style on themes of the working class, the Aborigines, or the outback, his best-known song is *The Drinkers of the Territory*; his 23 albums include *Outback Australia* and *Bangtail Muster*. He was honoured with the AM in 1993, in the ACMA Roll of Renown and an Australian Folk Trust Lifetime Achievement Award in 1995.

FURTHER REFERENCE
Recordings include *Faces of Australia* (1989, EMI TCT ELP 1001–5) and *Bangtail Muster* (RCA). He has written an account of his wartime childhood, *The Paperboy's War* (Sydney: Kerr, 1993). His other books include *Outback Holiday* (1978) and *Would I Lie to You* (1993). See also *Australian* 27 Oct. 1990.

Ekkehard. Opera in four acts, music and libretto by Florence ★Ewart after V. von Sheffel. Excerpt performed at Queen's Hall, Melbourne, on 23 Nov. 1923.

El Rocco. Opened in 1955 as a coffee lounge at Brougham Street, Kings Cross, Sydney, under the management of Arthur James. Drummer Ralph Stock suggested Sunday night jazz be held there, and led the first band from October 1957, with Ken Morrow (piano and piano accordion), Wally Ledwidge (guitar) and Jack Craber (bass). The policy was gradually extended to other nights, with established nightclub musicians such as Don Burrows, Frank Smith, Terry Wilkinson and Dutch-born bassist Freddy Logan, all eager to play unfettered jazz. In time the expanded policy drew in men of a younger generation like Bernie McGann and John Pochée. It attracted the eclectic John Sangster, who took an apartment in the same building to be close to the venue. Newcomers to Australia also established their reputations in El Rocco, such as Londoner Keith Barr (saxophone), and arrivals from NZ included pianists Judy Bailey, Mike Nock, Dave MacRae, drummer Barry Woods, bassists Andy Brown and Irish-born Rick Laird. There can be few progressive

jazz musicians emerging in the postwar period who did not play at El Rocco.

Apart from the established mainstream, El Rocco saw early experiments in free form, and poetry-and-jazz performances in which Dave Levy and American Bob Gillette (saxophone) were conspicuous. In the 1960s its reputation emerged from the underground, with coverage on television, newspapers and leisure magazines. Word-of-mouth reports from visiting musicians such as Lou Rawls, Nancy Wilson and Dizzy Gillespie, and an enthusiastic review in the USA journal *Downbeat*, increased the venue's celebrity internationally. Although James unsuccessfully applied several times for a liquor licence, it was generally felt that the absence of alcohol focused attention more closely on the jazz policy. James travelled overseas in 1968 and on his return he sensed a change in Sydney's entertainment ambience, with the expansion of sporting and RSL clubs providing regular work for musicians. Planned renovations were not implemented, and he closed the venue in 1969. An attempt to revive the name at another venue in the 1980s was short-lived.

El Rocco nurtured Sydney's modern jazz movement for 12 decisive years. Established club musicians confirmed their jazz credentials there, and younger musicians served apprenticeships in an environment which imposed few restrictions on experimentation. The venue became a 'field' workshop through which affinities could be developed, ideas exchanged, and the benefits of experience transmitted between generations. It was Australia's major incubator of the postwar progressive jazz movement; in the 1980s the conservatorium jazz courses were largely taught by El Rocco alumni.

FURTHER REFERENCE
'The Wailing Waltz' and 'Waltz for Adelaide' on *Don Burrows, The First 50 Years, vol. 1* (1992, ABC Polygram 514 296–2) were recorded in El Rocco. See also *BissetB*; *OxfordJ*; *ClareB*; Bruce Johnson, 'The El Rocco, an era in Sydney jazz', *JA* Part 1 (Jan./Feb. 1983), 12–15; Part 2 (Mar./Apr. 1983), 12–15; Part 3 (May/June 1983), 14–23.

BRUCE JOHNSON

Elder Conservatorium. Founded at the University of Adelaide in 1897, it is one of the two oldest music schools in Australia. It was created by absorbing the Adelaide College of Music, after an endowment by pastoralist and mining magnate Sir Thomas Elder established a chair in music at the university (from 1883). Offering a degree with various specialisations, it is housed on the campus in the 1900 Elder Conservatorium building, with its fine Elder Hall. Directors (many also occupants of the Elder chair) have been Joshua ★Ives (1897–1902), Matthew Ennis (1903–17), E. Harold ★Davies (1918–48), John ★Bishop (1949–64), David Galliver (1965–84) and Patrick Brislan (1986–91). The present director is David ★Shephard.

FURTHER REFERENCE

D. Bridges, 'Music in the University of Adelaide: a Retrospective View', *MMA* 8 (1975),1; V.A. Edgeloe, *The Language of Human Feeling: A Brief History of Music in the University of Adelaide* (Univ. Adelaide, 1985).

Elder Overseas Scholarship.   Music scholarship (first awarded 1901) at the University of Adelaide, established by pastoral and mining magnate Sir Thomas Elder to send an Adelaide student to study at the Royal College of Music, London. Former winners include Miriam *Hyde, John *Bishop and Harold Parsons.

Elder Trio.   Piano trio formed (1959) by three staff at the Elder Conservatorium, comprised of Ladislav *Jasek (violin), Lance *Dossor (piano) and James *Whitehead (cello). Named for the benefactor of the university conservatorium, Thomas Elder, its existence was opposed by John Bishop, the conservatorium director, because it interfered with the resident string quartet the Elder Quartet, for which Jasek was also leader. But the Trio soon bettered the standards of the Quartet, toured for Musica Viva and the ABC, and made numerous broadcasts until Jasek went back to Europe in 1962.

Eleanor of Aquitaine.   Opera by Gillian *Whitehead, libretto by Fleur Adcock. Two acts are complete; an excerpt was performed at the Sydney Opera Centre in October 1987.

Electronic Music.   If the term refers to any music produced with the aid of electricity, then most of the world's music today is electronic music. The technology used to record a symphony is the same as that used to make a collage of environmental sounds. For music where the primary production as well as the reproduction is based on electronic equipment or processes of some sort, the history in Australia is shared between art music and more popular and commercial genres, between academia, private studios and commercial facilities. No one genre, style, or venue can claim sole ownership or 'legitimacy' in the medium.

1. Early Days.   The first electronic music made by an Australian occurred in the USA, with the 'free music' experiments of Percy Grainger and Burnett Cross from 1945. The *Free Music machines they built produced a small amount of music, recorded on acetate discs. These examples, made exclusively with sine waves, were the world's first pieces made with these materials. The machines are on display at the Grainger Museum, University of Melbourne.

Visits by overseas composers were an impetus to the development of electronic music in Australia proper. Dutch composer Henk Badings visited the University of Adelaide in 1962, and Keith *Humble organised a five-day electronic music seminar at the University of Mel-

bourne at which American composer Milton Babbitt was the guest in 1971. Many Australian composers trace their first contacts with electronic music to these events. The earliest electronic music studios in Australia were the studios at the University of Adelaide, set up in 1969 by Peter *Tahourdin, and the Melbourne University studio, founded in 1972 by Keith Humble. The earliest private electronic music studio in Australia seems to have belonged to Val Stephen, a physician who produced a number of compositions as a hobby in the late 1960s and early 1970s. The earliest commercial studio, and perhaps the first electronic music studio in Australia, was Bruce *Clarke's Recording Workshop, established in 1962. By 1965 Clarke was producing both jingles and art music such as *Shapes* (1965) in his studio.

Analogue synthesisers produced overseas were prominent in these early days. By 1969 a Moog synthesiser featured in Bruce Clarke's studio, and by 1971 a Moog was installed in the University of Adelaide studios as well. The English VCS3, an inexpensive portable instrument appeared in a number of academic studios and pop bands by the early 1970s. By 1973 the Synthi 100, a much larger machine made by the same firm, was installed at the University of Melbourne, and a similar machine was installed later at the University of Queensland. In the early 1970s public access electronic arts facilities also began to be set up, one of which was the short-lived studio set up by the Melbourne New Music Centre (1972–74).

The most significant academic studios in Australia in the 1970s were the studios at La Trobe University of Melbourne (founded 1975 by Humble, Jim Sosnin and Warren *Burt), and the NSW State Conservatorium studio (founded 1974 by Martin *Wesley-Smith). By the late 1970s almost every academic music institution, and some visual arts schools, had an electronic music studio of some description. By this time as well, many commercial studios and pop bands were regularly using synthesisers and electronic techniques in their work. Parallel with this was the group of composers associated with the Clifton Hill Community Music Centre, where composers Ron *Nagorcka and Burt were developing techniques which used consumer-quality electronic equipment, such as portable monaural cassette recorders, as serious performance instruments.

2. New Instruments.   A number of new electronic musical instruments have been developed in Australia. By far the most commercially successful was the *Fairlight CMI, which was first designed as the *Qasar I by engineer Anthony Furse, with advice from composer Don Banks, who had founded the Canberra School of Music studio in 1972. Later the CMI project was taken over and commercially developed by engineers Peter Vogel and Kim Ryrie. This was the world's first sampler, a device which manipulates digital recordings of real-world sounds. Among the first buyers were the American pop star Stevie Wonder and the NSW Conservatorium.

In addition to the commercial work of Fairlight Instruments, which in the mid-1980s produced a state-of-the-art video synthesiser as well, a number of Australian composers and designers produced their own unique instruments. A by no means exhaustive list of these includes the analogue synthesisers of engineer Julian Driscoll, the UFOs and MIDI Tool Kit of composer Greg ★Schiemer, composer Carl Vine's Patent Little Marvel, composer Rainer Linz's 'discontinuous music' and his more recent computer-controlled analogue system which extends Grainger's free-music principles, the Chromophone, a microtonal MIDI keyboard instrument developed for composer Bill Coates, and Burt's *Aardvarks* series, digital instruments for exploring microtonality and algorithmic composition. Additionally, inventor Simon Veitch's 3DIS system was originally designed and extensively used as an extremely sophisticated motion-detecting control system for electronic music; more recently, however, its advanced design has meant that it has been used almost exclusively as a surveillance and security system.

3. More Recent Studio Developments.   With the advent of expensive but available digital technology in the late 1970s, a number of studios acquired these instruments. Fairlight CMIs were installed at the NSW Conservatorium, the Canberra School of Music and the Victorian College of the Arts, as well as in a number of commercial and private studios. The New England Digital Synclavier was installed at the University of Adelaide Studios by Tristram ★Cary, and a substantial research project involving the use of a PDP-11 mainframe computer was initiated at La Trobe University by Graham ★Hair, while Rex Harris, Barry Conyngham and David ★Worrall at the University of Melbourne pursued a similar project using mainframe computers. With the advent of MIDI (Musical Instrument Digital Interface) synthesisers and desktop computers in the mid-1980s, just about every academic institution or commercial facility was able to acquire a studio. By the late 1980s some undergraduates entering Australian academic institutions had better-equipped studios than the institutions at which they were studying. By the mid-1990s computing power had increased to the point where for less than the price of a new car, an individual could own enough computing and synthesising equipment to do serious research in sound production outside the academic studios. Nonetheless, several institutions had studios capable of producing world-class research and composition, among them La Trobe University, the Australian Centre for the Arts and Technology of the Australian National University, Canberra, the Universities of Sydney and Melbourne, and the NSW Conservatorium.

4. Composer-Performers.   Many composers have worked with electronics in Australia, some exclusively, some in combination with acoustic performers. Some of the high points of art-music electronic music composition in Australia include Conyngham's *Through Clouds* for tape (1974); Humble's *Statico I* for organ and 2 synthesisers (1971); John Exton's *Breathing Space* for tape (1972); Nagorcka's *Atom Bomb* for two singer-instrumentalists and live electronics (1977); Wesley-Smith's *Beta-Globin DNA* for tape and variable instrumentation (1987); Schiemer's *Monophonic Variations* for percussion and live electronics (1985); David Worrall's *'...with fish scales scattered'* for tape (1982); Cary's *Nonette: Computer Music in 4 tracks* for tape (1979); Rik Rue's *Onomatopoeia* for tape (1991); and Burt's *Some Kind of Seasoning,* a 16-hour cycle of live computer music installation/performances from 1990 to 1991.

A number of composer-performers also led or were involved in groups that performed live electronic music. Among these were Peter Mumme, Clarke and Felix ★Werder in Australia Felix; Wesley-Smith and Ian ★Fredericks in Watt; Jeff Pressing with OZDIMO; Nagorcka, Ernie ★Althoff and Graeme Davis in IDA; Worrall, Stuart Ramsden and others in Floating Exceptions; Nagorcka and Burt with Plastic Platypus; and Rue, Mann, Jim Denley, Stevie Wishart and Amanda Stewart in the Machine for Making Sense. Composer-performers who specialised in live electronic music related more closely to the worlds of jazz and pop in the mid-1970s and 1980s included David Tolley, Stephen Dunstan and David Mow. The most internationally successful Australian electronic music pop group of the 1980s was Severed Heads, led by composer Tom Ellard and video artist Stephen Jones. The late 1980s also saw the rise of several pop genres, such as industrial, ambient, techno and rap, all of which had many Australian proponents, and all of which mainly used electronic instruments.

In the mid-1990s many Australian composers are producing world-class work in the field, some touring and performing internationally. A selective list of these would include Worrall, Mann, Schiemer, Graeme Gerrard, Ros ★Bandt, Cindy John, Martin Wesley-Smith, Alistair ★Riddell, Amelia Barden, Paul Schutze, Gordon Monro, David ★Chesworth, Jon Rose, Rainer ★Linz, Rue, Alan ★Lamb and Burt.

A number of Australian visual and performance artists have successfully integrated music technology into their works, and these have been exhibited both nationally and internationally. Among these artists who work simultaneously in both the visual and sonic arts are Joan Brassil, Joyce Hinterding, Rodney Berry, Althoff, and Stelarc. In this category the multimedia installation works by composers and video-film artists Chris Knowles and Tim Gruchy should also be included.

5. Social Context.   Despite a wealth of compositional activity, performing outlets for electronic music have sometimes been hard to find. Large-scale events, such as the 1981 International Music and Technology Conference held at the University of Melbourne, and the annual conferences of the Australian Computer Music Association (since 1992) have proved fertile opportunities for the dissemination of electronic work. Artist-run performing venues and organisations such as the Clifton Hill Community Music Centre (1975–82), Linden Gallery in St Kilda, the Performance Space, Sydney, the Experimental Art Foundation in Adelaide and Evos Music in Perth have provided exposure as have a number of dance companies and venues, such as Danceworks, Dance Exchange, Sydney Dance Company, One Extra Dance Company and Melbourne's Dancehouse.

Radio has also provided a home for this work. On the ABC, programs such as *The Listening Room* and *New Music Australia* regularly broadcast electronic works and commission composers. In the area of public broadcasting, 2MBS-Sydney has been very active, and in 1983 and 1986 the Public Broadcasting Association of Australia commissioned 14 composers to make original electronic works for radio. Recording has been a major form of distributing this work. Record and publishing companies such as Tall Poppies, Move, NMA and Extreme have been active, while a number of historically significant pieces have appeared on the Canberra School of Music's *Anthology of Australian Music on Disk*, and the Australian Computer Music Association has produced two CDs of recent works from the 1990s. But electronic sound itself at present reaches most people in Australia via television and radio. By the mid-1990s it would be hard to find the sounds, apart from speaking voices, in Australian commercials that were not produced electronically, and in the commercial field the use of electronic musical instruments is definitely the status quo.

(See also *Computer Music, Experimental Music*, entries under individual composers.)

FURTHER REFERENCE
Select Discography, 1978–96
Percy Grainger, Tristram Cary, Warren Burt, Darius Clynes and Barry Conyngham, *Australian Digital Music* (1978, Move MS3027); Gary Wright, Chris Wyatt, Paul Turner, Greg Riddell, Ken Guntar and Peter Tahourdin, *Electronic Music, University of Melbourne* (1979, MUMS S001); Ernie Althoff, David Chesworth, John Crawford, the Dave and Phil Duo, Graeme Davis, Essendon Airport, IDA, Ron Nagorcka, Plastic Platypus, David Tolley, Paul Turner, Chris Wyatt, Tsk Tsk Tsk, *New Music 1978–79* (1980, Innocent NON-007); Ad Hoc, Warren Burt, David Chesworth, the Dave and Phil Duo, Essendon Airport, KGB, Laughing Hands, LIME, The Lunatic Fringe, Mark Pollard, the Threeo, Chris Wyatt, Tsk Tsk Tsk, *New Music 1980* (1980, Innocent NON-008); Warren Burt, *Studies (1982) for Synthesizer* (1982, Scarlet Aardvark 000.20); David Hirst, Alistair Riddell, Dan Senn, Warren Burt, Martin Wesley-Smith, David Worrall, Graeme Gerrard, Brian Parish, *Computer Music* (1984, NMA tapes unnumbered); Peter Mumme, Peter Schaefer, Robert Douglas, Jon Rose, Michael Hannan, *Radiophonic Tape Compositions* (1985, 2MBS-FM MBS9); Greg Schiemer, David Hirst, Alistair Riddell, Warren Burt, Mark Rudolf, Cindy John, Amanda Baker, Graeme Gerrard, *NMAtapes 6* (1989, NMAtapes 6); Tristram Cary, Graeme Gerrard, Brian Parish, David Worrall, Claudio

Pompili, Alistair Riddell, *Anthology of Australian Music on Disc, Vol. 4* (1989, Canberra School of Music, CSM 4); David Worrall, Peter Tahourdin, John Exton, Ian Fredericks, Tristram Cary, *Anthology of Australian Music on Disc, vol. 5* (1989, Canberra School of Music, CSM 5); Warren Burt, Peter Milsom, Ernie Althoff, Chris Mann, Peter Mumme, David Chesworth, *Anthology of Australian Music on Disc, vol. 6* (1989, Canberra School of Music, CSM 6); Simone de Haan, Greg Schiemer, Martin Wesley-Smith, *Anthology of Australian Music on Disc, vol. 13* (1989, Canberra School of Music, CSM 13); Jon Rose, *Paganini's Last Testimony* (1989, Konnex KCD5021); Paul Schutze, *Deus Ex Machina: The Soundtrack* (1989, Extreme unnumbered); Alan Lamb, Alistair Riddell, Ros Bandt, Jeff Pressing, *Austral Voices* (1990, New Albion NA028); Chris Mann and Warren Burt, *of course and Anyway* (1990, NMA tapes unnumbered); Warren Burt, *Chaotic Research Music (1989–90)* (1990, Scarlet Aardvark 000.34); Warren Burt, *Some Kind of Seasoning (The Demo Tape)* (1991, Scarlet Aardvark 000.35); Rik Rue, *Onomatopoeia* (1991, Pedestrian PX51); Graeme Gerrard, Warren Burt, Chris Knowles, David Chesworth, Linda Ceff, Jeff Pressing, Cindy John, David Hirst, Felix Werder, OHM *Machine Messages* (1992, Australian Computer Music Association, ACMA 1); Jeff Pressing, Graeme Gerrard, Tristram Cary, Kimmo Vennonen, Warren Burt, David Worrall, *Anthology of Australian Music on Disc, vol. 20* (1994, Canberra School of Music, CSM 20); Chris Mann, Amanda Stewart, Rik Rue, Jim Denley, Stevie Wishart, Kimmo Vennonen, *Machine For Making Sense: On Second Thoughts* (1994, Tall Poppies TP034); Rik Rue, Shane Fahey, Julian Knowles, *Social Interiors: The World Behind You* (1994, Extreme XCD029); Tim Kreger, Andrew Brown, Lawrence Harvey, John Statter, David Boyle, Roger Dean, Rainer Linz/Brigid Burke, Gordon Monro, Ian Fredericks, *Assembly* (1995, Australian Computer Music Association, ACMA 2); Ros Bandt, *Glass and Clay* (1995, Move MD3045); Tim Kreger, Jim Franklin, Steve Adam, David Worrall, Ross Bencina, Ian Fredericks, *Anthology of Australian Music on Disc, vol. 26* (1996, Canberra School of Music, CSM 26).
Select Bibliography
Atherton A; Jenkins T. Dieter Bechtloff, ed., *Kunstforum International* 103 (1989); Warren Burt, and Les Gilbert, *The New Music Newspaper*, 3 issues (1977–78); Warren Burt, ed., *Music and Technology*, *SA* 19 (1988); idem, 'Experimental Music in Australia using Live Electronics', *Contemporary Music Review* 6/1 (1991), 159–172; idem, 'Australian Experimental Music 1963–90', *Leonardo Music Journal* 1/1 (1991), 5–10, also published as 'Some Musical and Sociological Aspects of Australian Experimental Music 1963–93', *SA* 37 (1993), 38–47, 68; Anthony Jones, ed., 'Technology and Music', *SA* 47 (1996); Rainer Linz, ed. 'Computer Music', *NMA* 6 (1989); Nicholas Zurbrugg, ed., 'Electronic Arts in Australia', *Continuum* 8/1 (1994).   WARREN BURT

Elhay, Sylvan ('Schmoe') (b Cairo, Egypt, 13 Jan. 1942), jazz reed player. He began clarinet as a schoolboy, then flute and tenor saxophone. Co-founding the Bottom of the Garden Goblins in 1963, he was later central to the Adelaide progressive movement, leading Schmoe & Co. (formed 1968) and playing in other groups. He also played clarinet in the SA Symphony Orchestra 1964–74.

Active in television, session and festival work, he has performed and workshopped nationally and in the USA, with George Cables among others. He was a member of the Australia Council Music Board (1986–89, 1992), the National Jazz Alliance, and the Music Council of Australia (1993–96), and is currently on the Music Fund, Australia Council. He teaches mathematics and computer science at the University of Adelaide.

FURTHER REFERENCE

Recordings include *Sue Barker* (1977, Crest CRT-036); *Jazz in South Australia*, Southern Spectrum (1987, Larrikin Records LRJ 231). An interview with him is in *WilliamsA*, 118–21. See also *OxfordJ*.   BRUCE JOHNSON

Elision. Contemporary music ensemble, formed 1986 at Melbourne by Darryl Buckley and currently resident at the University of Queensland. An ensemble of up to a dozen contrasting solo instruments, the core comprises violin, viola, clarinet, guitar, mandolin, percussion, double bass, to which are frequently added flute, voice, harp and harpsichord. With a changing (casual) membership, they have worked with various conductors, including Christopher Lyndon-Gee, Sandro Gorli, Denis Cohen and Mark Foster. Their activities have focused on collaboration with a select group of composers whose work they have performed almost exclusively, notably Franco Donatoni, Aldo Clementi and Volker Heyn in Europe, and Lisa ★Lim, Chris ★Dench and Michael ★Smetanin in Australia. At first offering an annual concert series in Melbourne, they toured Australia in 1991, Europe (especially Italy) in 1994, and appeared at the Festival of Perth in 1995.

FURTHER REFERENCE

Recordings include Lim's *Garden of Earthly Desires* (1989, Dischi Ricordi CRMS1020), Dench's *Driftglass* (oneMore 1M 1CD 1018); *Elision Ensemble* (RCA CCD 3011), and Smetanin's *Skinless Kiss of Angels* (1995, ABC/Polygram).

Elkins, Margreta (Margaret Anne Enid) [Geater] (*b* Brisbane, 16 Oct. 1930), mezzo soprano. At 17 she won a Queensland Government scholarship to study dramatic art and musical theory. She later studied in Melbourne with Pauline Bindley and at the Sydney Conservatorium with Harold ★Williams. A finalist in the *Sun Aria* in 1952, she was awarded second place in the Mobil Quest in 1955. She made her debut in Brisbane singing *Carmen* in 1953 with the National Opera of Australia as Margreta Elkins. She toured Australia and NZ with the National Opera 1954–55. Using the Mobil Quest prize-money she travelled to England in 1956 and was engaged immediately by the Grand Opera Society of Dublin. She then toured England and Scotland for three seasons with the Carl Rosa Opera Co. In 1958 she joined the Royal Opera Co., Covent Garden, where she was a resident principal artist until 1968. Covent Garden sent her to study in Milan (1959) and she later created the role of

Helen of Troy in Tippett's *King Priam* (1962). She also appeared for Sadler's Wells and the Welsh National Opera, gave concerts at the Albert Hall, and performed throughout Europe, the USA and Canada. She visited Australia to participate in the Sutherland-Williamson season (1965), later returning permanently in 1976 to join the Australian Opera. She now lectures in vocal studies at the Queensland Conservatorium (since 1982) and was head of vocal studies at the Hong Kong Academy of Performing Arts 1991–94. Elkins' roles include Azucena in *Il trovatore*, Maddelena in *Rigoletto*, Octavian in *Der Rosenkavalier*, Rosina in *The Barber of Seville* and Dalila in *Samson et Dalila*. In 1984 she was awarded an AM and subsequently an honorary DMus by the University of Queensland.

FURTHER REFERENCE

Recordings include Donizetti, *Lucia di Lammermoor*, Royal Opera House, cond. T. Serafin (GDS 21017); Gounod, *Faust*, Ambrosian Opera Chorus, London Symphony Orchestra, cond. R. Bonynge (Decca 421402). See also *MackenzieS*, 222–26.

KERRY VANN

Elliott, Madge (*b* London, 12 May 1898; *d* Los Angeles, 8 Aug. 1955), dancer, actress. While attending school at Toowoomba, she made her stage debut as a dancer at the age of 13 in the 1911 Melba-Williamson opera season. She danced solo roles in the operettas *High Jinks*, *So Long Letty* and *Canary Cottage*, and her partner from 1919 was Cyril Ritchard, whom she married in 1935. In 1925 she went to England, becoming a star of London's West End. She returned to Australia for *Blue Roses* and *Hold My Hand* in 1932, then went back to the UK in 1936, spent three years touring the Middle East and Europe during World War II with *The Merry Widow*, and in 1946 toured Australia in Noël Coward plays, then again for Fuller in 1951. Although her vocal quality was not remarkable, she was a charming and graceful stage presence, one of the best show dancers Australia has produced, and a favourite with audiences. She continued dancing with her husband until the 1950s.

FURTHER REFERENCE

Obit. in *Age* 10 Aug. 1955. See also *ParsonsC*; *PorterS*, 177–8; 248–9.

Ellis, Catherine J. (*b* Birregurra, Vic., 1935; *d* 30 May 1996), Aboriginalist musicologist. After graduating from the University of Melbourne (MusBac, 1956), she worked as a research assistant to T.G.H. Strehlow, University of Adelaide. In 1961 she was awarded a PhD from the University of Glasgow for her work on Strehlow's recordings of Central Australian Aboriginal songs. Between 1964 and 1984 she worked variously as a postdoctoral fellow, lecturer, senior lecturer and reader at Elder Conservatorium of Music, University of Adelaide. She was co-founder, with traditional leaders from

Indulkana, northern SA, of CASM at the University of Adelaide in 1975. She held the inaugural chair of music at the University of New England from 1985 to 1995, after which she retired to Adelaide.

Ellis was elected to the Council of the International Society for Ethnomusicology 1968–71, served as a member of the Aboriginal Arts Advisory Committee, Australian Council for the Arts 1970–73, and was elected president of the Musicological Society of Australia 1988–89. She contributed over 120 publications, including numerous analyses of central and southern traditional tribal music and detribalised Aboriginal music forms. Towards the end of her career she collaborated with Udo Will to analyse frequency performance in Australian Aboriginal vocal music. She was honoured with the AM for service to music education and ethnomusicology, particularly Aboriginal music (1991), and an honorary DLitt, University of New England, for services to community music, ethnomusicological studies and Australian Aboriginal music research (1995).

FURTHER REFERENCE
Her writings include 'Aboriginal Music and Dance in Southern Australia' in S. Sadie, ed., *The New Grove Dictionary of Music and Musicians*, vol. 1 (London: Macmillan, 1980); 'Time Consciousness of Aboriginal Perfromers', in J.C. Kassler and J. Stubington, eds, *Problems and Solutions: Occasional Essays in Musicology presented to Alice M. Moyle* (Sydney: Hale & Iremonger, 1984); *Aboriginal Music: Education for Living. Cross-Cultural Experiences from South Australia* (Brisbane, UQP, 1985); 'Connections and Disconnections of Elements of the Rhythmic Hierarchy in an Aranda Song', *MA* 15 (1992), 44–6; 'Music' in D. Horton, ed., *The Encyclopaedia of Aboriginal Australia* (Canberra: Aboriginal Studies Press, 1994). See also *The Essence of Singing and the Substance of Song: Recent Response to the Aboriginal Performing Arts and Other Essays in Honour of Catherine Ellis*, ed. Linda Barwick, Allan Marett and Guy Tunstill, Oceania Monograph 46 (Sydney: Univ. Sydney, 1995).   MARGARET KARTOMI

Elms, Lauris   (*b* Melbourne, 20 Oct. 1931), contralto. Growing up a violinist, she took singing lessons from Katherine Wielaert and sang folk-songs and ballads with an ABC radio program, as well as with the National Theatre Movement Opera Co. She was a finalist in the *Sun Aria* in 1954, and Dominique Modesti invited her to Paris for lessons. After appearing as a guest in a Covent Garden regional tour in 1957, Rafael Kubelik invited her to join the company, and she sang mezzo-soprano roles in *Elektra*, *The Trojans*, *Tales of Hoffmann* and *Dialogue of the Carmelites*, and played Mrs Sedley in the Covent Garden *Peter Grimes* (conducted by the composer), as well as appearing in concert at the Leeds Centenary Festival and the Israel Tenth Anniversary celebrations. Her husband's work took her back to Australia in 1959, and since then she has appeared frequently with the Australian Opera and in lieder recitals, including as principal contralto in the Sutherland–Williamson season 1965. An intelligent

and musical performer, her roles have included works from Mozart to Bartók's *Bluebeard's Castle* and Honegger's *Joan of Arc*. She was honoured with the OBE in 1974 and the AM in 1982.

FURTHER REFERENCE
Recordings include the Covent Garden *Peter Grimes* cond. B. Britten (Decca 414 577–2DH3). See also *WWA* (1996); Roger Covell, *GroveO*; *MackenzieS*, 226–8; *AMN* 50 (Oct. 1959), 11–12.

Elphick, Steve (Steven James)   (*b* Sydney, 22 Oct. 1955), jazz bass player. He played trumpet in childhood, changing to bass as his main instrument at the age of 18. Most of his career has been in contemporary music with groups performing original compositions, mainly in the jazz idiom but also music based in Eastern European folk traditions. These include Keys Music Association 1982, Sandy Evans' Women and Children First 1983–85, Clarion Fracture Zone 1989–92. He also played in groups led by Phil Treloar, Mark Simmonds 1982–95, Roger Frampton 1983–85 and Bruce Cale 1986–88. At present he is performing, touring and recording with Ten Part Invention (from 1986), Michelle Morgan (from 1993), and the Umbrellas (from 1995).

FURTHER REFERENCE
Recordings include *The March of the Five Limbs*, Keys Music Association (*c*.1980, KMA LP 8301–2); *The Bruce Cale Orchestra, Live At The Basement;* vol. 1, *Rolling Thunder*, vol. 2, *Rain* (1987, Modern Records MR 12144 and Vista VRJ 1001); *Zones on Parade*, Clarion Fracture Zone (1993, Rufus/Polygram RF 001); *Tall Stories*, Ten Part Invention (1993, Rufus/Polygram RF 006); *Fire*, Mark Simmonds Freeboppers (1994, Birdland BL 002); *Ruino Vino*, Mara (1995, Rufus Records RFO 13).
                                                                    BRUCE JOHNSON

Elsasser, Carl Gottlieb   (*b* Hofingen, nr Stuttgart, Germany, 7 June 1817; *d* Hawthorn, Melbourne, 5 Jan. 1885), conductor, composer. After initial musical training in Stuttgart, he completed his studies under the composer and organist Johann Schneider in Dresden. In 1853 he migrated to Melbourne, establishing himself as a conductor, composer and teacher of keyboard and voice. In 1861 he was elected conductor of the Melbourne Philharmonic Society and in 1862 conducted the festival concerts of the German Turn-Verein. An honorary member of the Melbourne Philharmonic Society, the German Turn-Verein and the Metropolitan Liedertafel, his vocal compositions often received performances, particularly his part-songs. He also composed several cantatas including *Praise the Lord* (1860), *Wedding Cantata* (1863), *Peace Festival Cantata* (1871), and *Victoria's Dream* (1880). Although retiring in temperament, Elsasser was well respected in the Melbourne musical community and a monument was erected in his memory by the Metropolitan Liedertafel in 1887.

FURTHER REFERENCE
Argus 6, 8 Jan. 1885, 8 Aug. 1887: 5; Kenneth Hince, *ADB* 4; H.
Morin Humphreys, *Men of the Time in Australia*, Victorian Series,
2nd edn. (Melbourne: McCarron, Bird & Co., 1882), xliv.
                                        JENNIFER ROYLE

Elysium Ensemble.   Baroque performing ensemble
formed in Melbourne by Baroque flute and recorder
player Greg Dikmans. Since its inception in 1985, the
ensemble has presented an annual concert series in Melbourne and has performed at festivals and in concert halls
throughout Australia. Based on a stable core of players, the
group varies in size according to repertoire and thus has
the flexibility to alternate between chamber music and
works of orchestral proportion. Repertoire includes
works of the 17th and 18th centuries, including early
17th-century Italian sonatas, French Baroque suites and
cantatas, as well as larger works such as concertos, opera,
and cantatas by J.S. Bach, Handel and Vivaldi.
                                        JOHN GRIFFITHS

Emmanuel, Tommy   (*b* Gunnedah, NSW, 1955), rock
guitarist. Self-taught, Emmanuel was exposed to music
and touring from an early age, playing with his brothers
and sisters in a family band in the 1960s. In high demand
as a session musician, he has played with national and
international acts, including Stevie Wonder, John ★Farn-
ham and ★Air Supply. During the 1980s he played regularly with the group ★Dragon. Since then his profile has
been that of a virtuosic and versatile soloist, demonstrated
in a succession of recordings in the early 1990s, some with
his brother Phil; and he made numerous television
appearances. Emmanuel is also an accomplished drummer, bass player, arranger and producer.

FURTHER REFERENCE
Recordings include *Determination* (1991, distributed Sony
469132–2), *The Journey* (1993, distributed Sony 474489–2), *Classical Gas* (1995, distributed Sony 481340–2). For discography, see
SpencerA. See also *SpencerW*; *Australian* 8 Feb. 1992.
                                        WILLIAM VAN PINXTEREN

Emperor, The.   Comic operetta in two acts by W.
Arundel ★Orchard (1906), libretto by W. J. Curtis.
Intended as a sequel to *The Coquette,* which Orchard and
Curtis had presented the previous year, it was not as suc-
cessful. First performed at Sydney on 7 November 1906.
Unpublished.

Endymion.   Opera in one act with prologue, music and
libretto by John ★Antill (*c.*1920) after the Keats poem.
First performed by the National Opera of Australia at the
Sydney Tivoli in 1953.

England, Buddy [Ian Douglas Kilgower]   (*b* Surrey,
England, 1946), pop singer. Arriving in Australia in 1954,
he appeared on the television *Go!!* show from 1964,

releasing 11 singles, including *If I Never Get To Love You*
which reached No. 17 on the charts in 1966, and his
biggest seller *Movin' Man* in 1967. He worked in England
1967–69 and was briefly with the ★Mixtures 1969–70
and the Vibrants 1972. After working as an A&R manager
for Astor Records, he replaced Bruce Woodley in the
Seekers (1977).

FURTHER REFERENCE
Recordings include *If I Never Get To Love You* (HMV EA 4756)
and *Movin' Man* (HMV EA 4836), and the EP *Movin' Man*
(HMV 7EG O70074). For discography, see *SpencerA*. See also
McGrathA.

English Eccentrics.   Chamber opera in two acts by
Malcolm ★Williamson, libretto by G. Dunn after Edith
Sitwell's book. Commissioned by the English Opera
Group and first performed at the Aldeburgh Festival on
11 June 1964. Published by Chappell. There is an orches-
tral suite (1964) published by Chappell.

English, George Philip John   (*b* 1882; *d* 1972),
choral conductor, composer. He conducted in William
McKie's Melbourne Bach festival in 1932, and was later
director' of the Brisbane Opera Society.

FURTHER REFERENCE
See also Robert Dalley-Scarlett, 'Art in a Garret', *Canon* 2/3
(Oct. 1948), 100–2.

English, George Selwyn   (*b* 1912; *d* Sydney, Sept.
1980), composer. He worked as a music critic in London
in the 1930s, and after the war composed music for films,
documentaries and radio. He won the ABC Composition
prize for a symphonic work (1952) and his music for the
radio feature *Death of a Wombat* (Southern Music, 1959)
won the Prix Italia (1959). A firmly traditional melodist
and fluent orchestrator, his works include, aside from
many film scores, the orchestral works *Music for a Royal
Occasion* (1952) and *Botany Bay, 1770* (1960), chamber
works such as the string trio *Chiaroscuro* (Southern Music,
1966) and *Quintet for Wind* (Chappell, 1969), songs such
as *Cypress Tree* and various short works for dance band or
light concert ensemble, such as *Myuna Moon*, *Ski Trails* and
Yulunga. He was foundation president of the Fellowship of
Australian Composers.

FURTHER REFERENCE
Obit. in *APRAJ*, 8 (Jan. 1981). Recordings include *Death of a
Wombat*, Sydney Symphony Orchestra (1959, RCA LI6233);
Quintet for Wind, New Sydney Wind Quintet (RCA SL 16374);
Chiaroscuro Hazelwood String Trio (1967, ABC RRCS 129); and
Myuna Moon Light Concert Orchestra, cond. K. Herweg (HMV
OCLP 7132). Discography in *PlushD*.

English, Gerald   (*b* Hull, England, 6 Nov. 1925), lyric
tenor. After studies at the Royal College of Music, Lon-

don and war service, he appeared at Sadler's Wells, Covent Garden and Glyndebourne, as well as in Europe and the USA. He taught at the Royal College of Music from 1960, and then came to Australia as director of the opera studio, Victorian College of the Arts, 1977–91. A singer of a highly distinctive voice, projected with great intensity, his repertoire has been unusually wide, ranging from operas of Monteverdi and Mozart to concert works of Stravinsky, Fauré, Orff and Dallapiccola. He was awarded an honorary DMus by the University of Sydney in 1989.

FURTHER REFERENCE
Recordings include Pandarus in Covent Garden's *Troilus and Cressida* (1976, EMI CM55 65550–2); Mr By-Ends in the London Philharmonic Orchestra *Pilgrim's Progress* (EMI CMS7 64212–2); Bach Cantatas 211 and 212 (Deutsche Harmonia Mundi GD77151); and the André Previn *Carmina Burana* (1974, EMI CDC7 47411–2). See also *CA* (1995–96); David Scott, *GroveD*.

English, Jon (*b* London, 1949), pop singer, actor, composer. He lived in Hampstead, London, until the age of 13 when he moved to Liverpool, near Sydney. His father was an excellent (though not professional) musician who taught him to play the guitar. A trainee teacher at the University of NSW, he left the course before finishing, joining the Sebastian Hardie Blues Band, which performed rock and roll around Sydney's suburbs, and spent six months backing Johnny *O'Keefe on a national tour. In 1972 he got the role of Judas in *Jesus Christ Superstar*, after first auditioning only for a chorus part; this was followed by his role as the Pirate King in the *Pirates of Penzance* (1983–84, then again 10 years later). His first record album *Wine Dark Sea* was launched in 1972. He played Jonathan Garrett in the award-winning television series *Against the Wind*, and in 1979 he won a major Australian award for composing the sound-track for this series. He was awarded Entertainer of the Year in 1984, 1985 and 1986.

FURTHER REFERENCE
His recordings include *Wine Dark Sea* (1973, Warm & Genuine 2079 006); *Six Ribbons* (1978, Polydor 2079 125); *Hold Back the Night* (1981, Mercury 6038 021); *Against the Wind* [Sound-track] (1979, Polydor 2907 048); *Calm Before the Storm* (1980, Mercury 6357 067); *Dark Horses* (1987, Chase/Midnight 450599 1). See also *Australian,* 30 June 1979; Melbourne *Herald* 14 Mar. 1973; *Australian* 2 May 1987; *Herald* 14 Jan. *Age,* 8 Apr. 1982; *CA* (1995–96); *McGrathA*; *SpencerW.*

AMANDA CUMMINS

Ensemble I. Chamber ensemble founded in Vienna which soon came to Australia as ensemble-in-residence at the Victorian College of the Arts 1976–78. Comprised of Spiros *Rantos (violin), Thomas Pinschof (flute), Dawn Hannay (viola), Tanya Hunt (cello), Richard Runnels (horn) and Brachi Tilles (piano), its members all settled in

Australia and have gone on to make a considerable impact individually as teachers and performers.

FURTHER REFERENCE
Recordings include works of Mahler, Hummel and Mozart (Adelcord).

Ensemble of the Classic Era. Trio comprised of Paul Wright (classical violin), Geoffrey Lancaster (fortepiano), and Susan Blake (classical cello). They have focused on works of the Classical era, performed on period instruments and with attention to the authentic performance practice of the time. One of very few ensembles to explore techniques of this period in Australia, they tour regularly for Musica Viva.

Entrepreneurs. The function of entrepreneurs in Australian music has been to contribute money and taste, the first of which allows them to bet on the keenness of the second. In practice the odds have always been against them. In early times, abilities were hard to assess across the wide seas that separated Australia from London and New York, and that added months of unearning time to the expenses of entrepreneurship. Even today, fleeting reputations built through the electronic media do not always prove transferable to live, local performance.

Moreover, at all periods until the last few decades, the second-rate imported talent has always had a stronger box-office pull than the first-rate native one. That careers such as those of Nellie *Stewart and Gladys *Moncrieff overcame this prejudice owed a lot to entrepreneurs, in one case George Musgrove and in the other the Tait brothers (though they are also to be blamed for endlessly milking Moncrieff's appeal in old favourites such as *The Desert Song* at the expense of new roles that would have required new sets and costumes). In the face of these difficulties, it was usually safest to go either for the long-familiar name or for budding, and therefore cheaper, talent. As a result the great musical artists of the 19th and early 20th centuries were mostly heard by Australian audiences either in immature youth or mellow decline.

1. History. The history of entrepreneurship in Australian music begins with the theatrical giants of the goldboom era, William Saurin *Lyster and George Selth *Coppin. Before that time secular music performances generally took place in hotels and their attached halls, or in the theatres, which maintained the only significant professional orchestras and included pantomimes, burlesques and cut-down versions of popular operas among their regular offerings. In this they followed the tradition of the London 'minors', which had been led to accentuate the musical aspects of stage performance in order to circumvent the monopoly rights over spoken drama of the two 'patent' theatres. As early as 1841 a woman entrepreneur, Anne *Clarke, visited England to collect a group of musically trained actors for her theatre at Hobart. In the concert life of the 1830s and 1840s the risk-taker was not the entrepreneur but the artist: William Vincent *Wallace, who arrived in Sydney in 1836, and Isaac *Nathan, who followed him in 1841, usually promoted their own concerts. In the mid-1850s a violinist of some international distinction, Miska *Hauser, was still travelling from town to town, performing with an accompanist when he could find one and solo when he could not, using whatever venue he could hire at short notice.

The gold discoveries changed everything. From the mid-1850s Australian managements were able to offer overseas musical stars terms that they could hardly refuse, to confront flies, dust, incessant travel and the danger of shipwreck, but also audiences who were known to shower their favourites with nuggets. The Australian tours of the sopranos Catherine *Hayes and Anna Bishop amply rewarded their enterprise, with only Bishop being actually shipwrecked. (She also once crossed the Andes on a mule.) Hayes in 1855 became a counter in an entrepreneurial war between Coppin and John Black, the builder of Melbourne's enormous Theatre Royal. Meanwhile, a bassoonist-turned-entrepreneur named Winterbottom had brought together Australia's first large concert orchestras for promenade seasons in Melbourne and Sydney. Modelled on Jullien's band in London, they specialised in quadrilles.

Coppin, as Australia's first intercolonial theatre manager, was responsible during the 1850s and 60s for several musical imports but was primarily a spoken-drama entrepreneur. Lyster, on the other hand, was from the start an opera manager. His decision to cross from California in 1861 may well have been inspired by a realisation that the imminent civil war was likely to bisect his company's regular touring route up and down the Mississippi valley. However, the Pacific route was a popular one for musicians and theatricals, who were not at that date able to return to New York by rail. Like most earlier visitors he seems to have arrived 'on spec', without any prior commitment from a local entrepreneur. Throughout the 1860s his role was that of the owner-manager of a touring opera company, occasionally taking theatres in Melbourne or Sydney on long leases which could be padded out with other attractions. Verdi and Meyerbeer were his major drawcards, along with *Faust*, first performed in March 1864.

From 1870, however, after a brief return to the United States, he became an entrepreneur in the fullest sense, touring not only his own indigenous 'English' opera (later *opéra bouffe*) company, but a series of imported Italian companies of some distinction. He also brought in concert artists such as the pianist Henry Ketten and the cornettist Jules Levy for extensive intercolonial tours. In 1877 he drew on the profits of his Offenbach productions to mount an astonishing Melbourne opera season which saw the Australian premieres of *Lohengrin* and *Aida*. In 1879, returning from an overseas talent-spotting trip, he gave Australia its first *Carmen*. Martin and Fanny *Simonsen,

who had performed with him in the 1860s and 70s, became opera entrepreneurs in their own right in Australia and NZ.

On Lyster's death in 1880 his mantle descended upon his talented but erratic nephew, George *Musgrove. By this time the character actor J.C. *Williamson was also aspiring to intercolonial management along the lines pioneered by Lyster. He and Musgrove, sometimes in partnership and sometimes out of it, were to dominate musical theatre for the next 30 years. The 'firm' which they founded in 1881 with Arthur Garner, and which by Federation had become an entrenched national chain with theatres under its control in all colonial capitals, provided Australian audiences with a steady diet of Gilbert and Sullivan and, later, musical comedy, interspersed with grand opera seasons which were more widely spaced than Lyster's but as a rule better capitalised. It was during a Musgrove season of *Faust* in 1888 with Nellie Stewart as Marguerite that the basso Federici died, giving Australian theatre its most famous ghost story. Melba toured as a concert artist for Musgrove in 1902–3 and in opera for Williamsons in 1911, 1924 and 1928 (Williamson himself died in 1913).

The interwar phase of Australian musical entrepreneurship was dominated by the five *Tait brothers, who from successful beginnings in concert promotion were able to stage a managerial takeover of the Williamson organisation in 1920. Their period as concert managers had been responsible for attractions which ranged from brass bands and a Welsh male-voice choir to musicians as distinguished as Emma Calvé, Clara Butt, John McCormack, Jascha Heifetz and Benno Moiseiwitsch. Ensconced at J.C.W.'s, they continued the second tradition with tours by Galli-Curci, Chaliapin, Pavlova, Lawrence Tibbett, Richard Crooks, Kirsten Flagstad, Jan Kubelik and the young Yehudi Menuhin, to look no further. But not Fritz Kreisler, who was snatched from under their noses by a rival entrepreneur, E.J. Carroll. Claude Kingston, who managed many of these tours for the Taits, gives a lively anecdotal account of them in his *It don't seem a Day too Much,* with Viola Tait's *A Family of Brothers* covering the boardroom side. Tours by popular artists and jazz and swing bands were still largely the preserve of the two major vaudeville chains, the Tivoli and the NZ-based *Fuller network.

The role of the private sector entrepreneur, however, diminished steadily in the face of state-subsidised competition. By the 1940s the major share of the concert action was already in the hands of a national bureaucracy, the Australian Broadcasting Commission, whose successive managing directors and concert directors worked as musical bureaucrats, not entrepreneurs. It was for the ABC not the Taits that Artur Schnabel, Arthur Rubinstein, Eileen Joyce, Alexander Kipnis, Richard Tauber and Lotte Lehmann toured in the years just before World War II. And Musica Viva, the national chamber music touring organisation which began in 1946 as a small society of enthusiasts, has for many years been Australia's main impresario for both chamber music and national tours by small orchestras and specialist vocal ensembles. Nor should we forget a brief but lively period during World War II when the US Army functioned in Australia as a musical promoter.

J.C.W.'s enjoyed a final Indian summer in the 1960s under the direction of Sir Frank Tait's chosen successor, John McCallum, before succumbing to a new order of things in which the permanent state and national opera companies took over the more prestigious side of musical theatre, and stage musical and rock theatre promotion passed into the hands of younger entrepreneurs who were unencumbered with bricks and mortar. Of these the flamboyant New Zealander Harry M. *Miller made the strongest impression on public consciousness with his productions of *Hair* in 1969 and *Jesus Christ Superstar* in 1972. But by the 1980s the emphasis was passing from the local impresario to the international owners of hot properties, most notably the successive musical confections of Andrew Lloyd Webber. The ability of these pieces to bring huge numbers of tourists into favoured cities meant that state governments became active partners in negotiations to secure them, further minimising the role of the entrepreneur.

From the 1950s, moreover, a new group of salaried promoters had emerged whose role, although it involved no risk to their own capital, was still recognisably entrepreneurial. These were the directors of the various metropolitan arts festivals, charged with the preparation of all-embracing cultural events which have always had a strong musical content. Taste and contacts were clearly at a premium, but so was a willingness to take risks, since the success or failure of a festival, together with the degree of flair displayed in its compilation, would determine whether they were ever to be asked back. David Blenkinsop's long association with the Perth Festival (Australia's earliest) marks him as the most successful of these impresarios, though it also suggests a certain degree of conservatism. To have outraged a festival trust to the degree of provoking dismissal is not always a sign of artistic failure—or fatal to a career. Anthony *Steele and Jim Sharman were among the more memorable directors of the Adelaide Festival, the nation's most celebrated. The controversy surrounding the appointment of the Sydney resident, Leo Schofield, to plan and direct the 1994 Melbourne festival made him a major public figure in his new city.

2. *Entrepreneurship Today.* Entrepreneurship, considered so far in terms of live performance, is also fundamental to other media, most notably the sheet music and recording industries. A fuller account than this would consider the history of the three firms which dominated the publication of printed music in Australia, *Palings, *Allans and *Alberts, and the history of the small number of local recording companies which were not offshoots of

the internationals. It would also survey the career of Louise *Hanson-Dyer of the Paris- and later Monaco-based Lyrebird publishing and recording companies. While often described as a patron, the role in which she was most visible in her native country, Dyer was in fact the first major entrepreneur of the international early music revival.

The mid-19th-century entrepreneurs conducted their activities as free financial agents, pocketing all the profits and bearing the full brunt of loss. Coppin's career was one which led him several times to bankruptcy, only to bounce him back to prosperity again as the result of some lucky speculation. But there were times when even he had the need of backers to which he then became responsible, while Lyster was from 1874 the managing director of a public company, which required him to consider the interests of his shareholders as well as following his personal star. In so far as such figures have their successors today, it is mainly in the field of pop and rock entrepreneurship, where huge sums are wagered against the fickleness of public taste, where the demands of top artists are close to extortionate, and where illness or bad publicity of the kind that afflicted Michael Jackson in 1994 can bring enormous loss. It is nonetheless still a field in which fortunes can be made, as Kenn Brodziak showed when he signed the Beatles for an Australian tour just before their sudden rise to mega-stardom.

Neither should we overlook the individuals who are not professional entrepreneurs but who will from time to time invest in the visit of some favourite overseas country singer, jazz soloist or ethnic performer. At a grass-roots level, to which a summary of this kind cannot hope to penetrate, the 19th-century spirit is still alive.

FURTHER REFERENCE

ParsonsC; *ADB*; *IrvinD*; *BrisbaneE*.

Bagot, Alec, *Coppin the Great* (Melbourne: MUP, 1965).

Dicker, Ian G., *JCW: A Short Biography of James Cassius Williamson* (Sydney: Elizabeth Tudor Press, 1974).

Irvin, Eric, *Gentleman George, The King of Melodrama* (Brisbane: UQP, 1980).

Love, Harold, *The Golden Age of Australian Opera* (Sydney: Currency Press, 1981).

_____. *The Australian Stage: A Documentary History* (Sydney: UNSWP, 1984).

Kingston, Claude, *It Don't Seem a Day Too Much* (Adelaide: Rigby, 1971).

Miller, Harry M., *My Story*, with Denis O'Brien (Melbourne: Macmillan, 1983).

Tait, Viola, *A Family of Brothers* (Melbourne: Heinemann, 1971).

HAROLD LOVE

Epstein, June Sadie   (*b* Perth, 29 June, 1918), music educator, writer. At 17, Epstein won the coveted Trinity College Overseas Scholarship. In London she completed the Trinity College diploma of teaching and the LRAM, and was awarded the Silver Medal for the most outstanding student over three years. Epstein studied piano with Elizabeth Carey in Perth, Henry Geehl in London and Jascha Spivakovsky in Melbourne. Long associated with the ABC as pianist, scriptwriter, composer and broadcaster for radio and television, she created such programs as *Singing and Listening* (1967–75). She began teaching at the Kindergarten Training College (later the Institute of Early Childhood Development), Melbourne, in 1946, and 30 years later retired as senior lecturer. Epstein has written many books, including a music education text and a history of the National Music Camp Association; she has composed numerous songs for children and compiled song collections. In 1986 she was awarded the OAM.

FURTHER REFERENCE

Her memoirs are *Woman with Two Hats: An Autobiography* (Melbourne: Hyland House, 1988). Her other writings include *Enjoying Music with Young Children* (Melbourne: Allans, 1973); *Concert Pitch: The Story of the National Music Camp Association and the National Youth Orchestra* (Melbourne: Hyland House, 1984); *A Swag of Songs* (Melbourne: OUP, 1984); *A Second Swag of Songs* (Melbourne: OUP, 1986).   JANE SOUTHCOTT

Erby, Nick   (*b* Parramatta, NSW, 23 Mar. 1945), country music broadcaster, advocate. At the age of 18 he became a part-time compere for *Serill's Ranch Club* at 2VM Moree, and then hosted country programs for 4GR from 1966 and 2UE Sydney from 1971. He became a professional broadcaster in 1977 as host of the *Country Music Jamboree*, today carried by 40 radio stations; he had a television show, *Country Close-Up*, in 1980. Settling at Tamworth in 1987, he broadcasts for 2TM, is executive producer of *Hoedown*, and plays a vital role as talent co-ordinator and judge for the annual ACMA awards. Since 1992 he has made the monthly *Boomerang Cafe*, a Federal Government promotional program broadcast to 30 countries. He was awarded an ACMA Golden Guitar in 1979.

FURTHER REFERENCE

LattaA, 74–5; *SmithB*, 176–8; *Herald-Sun* 22 Jan. 1992.

Ermoll, Serge   (*b* Shanghai, China, 16 Aug. 1943), jazz pianist. He studied piano before arriving in Australia at the age of nine, then switched to trumpet, returning to piano at 17. His teachers included Chuck Yates and Dave Levy. He led a trio at *El Rocco 1963–69, apart from 1964–66 when he was in the UK; in London 1970–74 he worked in major venues such as Ronnie Scott's. In the late 1970s he formed Free Kata, an influential group in free improvisation that included saxophonist Eddie Bronson and drummer Louis Burdett. Subsequently he has worked in more conventionally structured bands in a range of styles, including recording with Sonny Stitt, Herb Ellis, Richie Cole, and Ray Brown, and is currently composing orchestral music.

FURTHER REFERENCE

Recordings include *Free Kata* (1974, Philips 6357 021); *Free Kata* (1976, Free Kata 002 and 003); *Dedication to Horst Liepolt,* Serge Ermoll Concert Ensemble (1980, Janda Jazz JJ 1002); *Clouds,* Serge Ermoll with Richie Cole & George Golla (1987, Aim Records, AIM 1009); *Jungle Juice,* Serge Ermoll (1985, Larrikin LRJ 193); *The Jazz Masters* (1996, Aim Records AIM 1039). See also *ClareB*; *OxfordJ*; Eric Myers, 'Serge Ermoll', *APRAJ* 4 (August, 1987), 52–3.   BRUCE JOHNSON

Estrella.   Comic opera in three acts by Luscombe *Searelle (1883), libretto by Walter Parke, first performed at Prince's Theatre, Manchester, England, on 14 May 1883, then at London on 24 May 1883. It had 18 performances at Sydney in 1884. Unpublished.

Eumerella Shore, The   [Numerella Shore, New Marilla Shore], political ballad. Sung in one version to 'Darling Nelly Gray', it satirises the lawless free selector, running his bullocks on a squatter's land and branding the squatter's cattle under cover of darkness. Probably set at the Umaralla River, near Cooma, NSW (or the town Numeralla, on its banks), it dates from the angry Sydney rallies over land legislation in 1860; Sir John Robertson (mentioned in the chorus) was premier of NSW from that year. First published in the *Launceston Examiner* (7 Mar. 1861) as 'The Numerella Shore'; another version, 'The New Marilla Shore', is in the Hurd Collection (1894–97); another was published by A.B. Paterson in *Old Bush Songs* (1905) and later collected with at least three variants; another version was collected by Ron Edwards (1969).

FURTHER REFERENCE

Edition and commentary in *EdwardsG*; *ManifoldP*.

Eurogliders.   Pop group formed 1980 in Perth, originally as Living Single, comprised of principally Bernie Lynch (guitar, vocals, songwriter), Grace Knight (vocals), Crispin Akerman (lead guitar), Amanda Vincent (keyboards), Jeff Rosenberg (bass), and John Bennetts (drums), although the line-up changed over the years. The band's fourth single, *Heaven (Must Be There)* from their second album *This Island*, was the most successful, reaching No. 1 on the Australian charts and the Top 50 in the USA. The film-clip for *Heaven* received the silver award for the best rock video at the New York International Film and Television Awards. In 1986 the band signed a sponsorship deal with the Faberge jeans manufacturer, and a television commercial for jeans featured all the band members and the music of their single *Absolutely!* (March 1986).

Eurogliders had a reputation as hard-working and they appeared extensively. They produced four albums, 12 singles and a video, mainly of dance music; they made appearances at local Bluelight discos, played in the huge Rockalong Concert at Yarrawonga on the 1986 Australia Day Weekend and were involved in the Incredible Penguins (a group of musicians who recorded John Lennon's *Merry Christmas: War Is Over* as a fund-raiser for research into Phillip Island's fairy penguins). They also toured the USA and Japan successfully.

FURTHER REFERENCE

Recordings include the singles *Without You* (1982, Mercury 6038 057); *Heaven (Must Be There)* (1984, CBS BA 223178); *We Will Together* (1985, CBS BA 3277); *The City of Soul* (1985, CBS BA 3339); *Can't Wait to See You* (1985, CBS BA 3375); *Absolutely!* (CBS BA 3397); *Groove* (1988, CBS 651236 7); and the albums *Pink Suit Blue Day* (1982, Mercury 6437 154); *This Island* (1984, CBS SBP 237994); *Absolutely!* (1985, CBS SBP 8106); *Groove* (1988, CBS 460864 1). See also *McGrathA; SpencerW.*

NATASCHA SCHMIDT

Euterpe. See *William Horatio Wilson.*

Euterpe, An Ode to Music. Ode by Charles *Horsley (1870), libretto by Henry Kendall, for soloists (SATB), chorus and orchestra, performed by the Melbourne Philharmonic Society at the opening of the rebuilt Melbourne Town Hall on 9 August 1870. Unpublished.

Evans, Ken (*b* Geelong, Vic., 28 Oct. 1926), jazz brass player. He began on clarinet, switching to trombone and later trumpet, french horn and tuba. After jazz and symphonic work in Geelong, he joined Frank Johnson on trumpet in 1949, and he was active in dance and jazz bands, notably with John *Sangster. He withdrew from music in 1958, then resumed performing in 1975 with Alan Leake and others, as well as teaching, arranging and composing with Australia Council commissions. Increased activity after his move to Noosa, Queensland, in 1988 included work with the Jazz Noosa Trio and the 16 piece Chorale. At present he is composing, directing workshops and the Brisbane Jazz Youth Band, and performing with orchestral and choral groups.

FURTHER REFERENCE

Recordings include *Frank Johnson's Fabulous Dixielanders* (1949, Swaggie JCS-33768); *Ken Evans' Jazz Men* (1976, Astor ALPS-1050); *Jazz Foundations* (1977, Swaggie S-1385). See also *BissetB; OxfordJ.*

BRUCE JOHNSON

Evans, Lindley (*b* Cape Town, South Africa, 18 Nov. 1895; *d* Sydney, 2 Dec. 1982), pianist. After singing in the Cape Town cathedral choir as a boy, he played organ for silent films at Cape Town in 1911, and his family moved to Australia in 1912. He studied with Frank *Hutchens at the NSW State Conservatorium from 1915, and from 1919 he taught classes in a girls' school and piano at Palings, Sydney. In 1922 he went to England as Melba's accompanist, taking lessons with Tobias Matthay. Returning to Australia the following year he joined the NSW State Conservatorium staff, continued touring with Melba (1924, 1927–28), and was organist and choirmaster

at the Presbyterian church, Randwick. He formed a duo with Hutchens, his former teacher, which gave two-piano recitals and broadcasts for over 40 years. He broadcast *Adventures in Music* for the ABC (1932–39), and was 'Mr Melody Man' on the ABC children's hour (1941–69).

A tall, brilliantly musical pianist and energetic teacher, his students included Richard *Bonynge, Winsome Evans and many others who made notable careers. He also composed, his works including choral, vocal, chamber music, an *Idyll* for two pianos and music for the films *40,000 Horsemen* (1940) and *Rats of Tobruk* (1944), and he was involved with the national music camps from 1953. He was honoured with the OBE in 1963.

FURTHER REFERENCE

Obit. in *SMH* 3 Dec 1982, *APRAJ* 3/1 (Jul 1983). His autobiography is *Hello Mr Melody Man: Lindley Evans Remembers* (London: Angus & Robertson, 1983). Recordings of his works include *Vignette,* M. Barton, pf (Brolga CTX 1122) and *Idyll,* WA Symphony Orchestra, W. Pomroy, S Dornan, pfs, cond. T. Mayer (ABC RRCS 381). See also *GlennonA,* 71; For an index to references in *AMN,* see *MarsiI.*

Evans, Sandra Janette (*b* Manly, Sydney, 29 June 1960), jazz performer, composer. She began piano at the age of four, later flute, and from her late teens tenor saxophone. Associated with the Northside Big Band, she entered the NSW Conservatorium jazz program in 1982, and co-founded Women and Children First, taking them on an Australian tour in 1985. She was with Ten Part Invention from 1986, then overseas for study and performances, returning in 1988. Co-founding the Clarion Fracture Zone, which won the ARIA jazz award, she tours Australia and internationally. Currently she is also performing, composing and recording with The catholics and the Australian Art Orchestra; she has also performed and composed for the *Seymour Group and the *Australian Chamber Orchestra. She was awarded a Young Australian creative fellowship in 1995.

FURTHER REFERENCE

Recordings include *The March of the Five Limbs* (Keys Music Association, *c.*1980, KMA LP 8301–2); *Women and Children First* (1984, Hot Records); *Blue Shift,* Clarion Fracture Zone (1990, ABC Records 846 221–1–4–2); *Zones on Parade,* Clarion Fracture Zone (1993, Rufus/Polygram RF001); *The catholics* (1993, Spiral Scratch 0011); *Tall Stories,* Ten Part Invention (1993, Rufus/Polygram RF006); *Simple,* The catholics (1994, Rufus Polygram RF009); *What This Love Can Do,* Clarion Fracture Zone (1994, Rufus/Polygram RF010). See also *ClareB;* Bruce Johnson, 'Sandy Evans, Portrait of the Artist as a Young Woman,' *2MBS-FM, Stereo FM Radio* (Feb. 1991), 3–6.

BRUCE JOHNSON

Even Unto Bethlehem. Nativity music-theatre in four scenes, music and libretto by Fritz *Hart (1943). Excerpt performed by the Melbourne Conservatorium, but first complete performance at the Academy of Arts, Honolulu, 20 December 1943. Revived in 1973. MS in *Msl*.

Ewart, Florence Maud Donaldson (*b* London, 16 Nov. 1864; *d* Melbourne, 8 Nov. 1949), composer. Ewart received musical diplomas from the National Training School for Musicians, London (1882) and the Hochschule für Musik, Leipzig (1885). From 1906, she lived in Melbourne where she was known as a conductor, performer and composer until the early 1930s, and participated in a large range of musical and cultural activities. She composed over 60 works in a broad range of genres. Most of her smaller works were performed for musical and literary clubs and societies and occasionally for cultural events. Her longer works included operas, a symphonic poem, a string quartet and several works for voice and orchestra, though she enjoyed limited success in getting performances for these works. Excerpts of two operas, ★*Ekkehard* (1910) and *The Courtship of Miles Standish* (1930), and several performances of the String Quartet in D Minor (1930) were reviewed. Two works were published: *Ode to Australia* (Allans, Australia, 1911) and *Irish Lullaby* (Stainer & Bell, London, 1936).

FURTHER REFERENCE

Her mss works and papers are in *PVgm*. See also Faye E. Patton, 'Rediscovering our Musical Past: The Works of Mona McBurney and Florence Donaldson Ewart', *SA* 21 (Autumn 1988–89), 10–12; idem, *GroveD*; idem, *GroveW*; idem, 'Florence Donaldson Ewart: A Critique of a Compositional Method', in T. Radic, ed., *Repercussions: Australian Composing Women's Festival and Conference, 1994* (Melbourne: National Centre for Australian Studies, Monash University, 1995), 57–61; idem, 'Lofty ode captures early national spirit?', *Sing Out* 12/1 (1995), 20–21.   FAYE PATTON

Executives, The. Pop band (1966–69, 1974–) formed in Sydney, comprised at first of Keith Leslie (vocals, saxophone), Carole King (vocals), Dudley Hood (guitar), Brian King (keyboards), Dennis Allgood (vocals, bass) and Rhys Clarke (drums). A sophisticated group skilled at numerous instruments, they quickly became very popular singing covers, and gradually introduced their own music, including *You're Bad* (1967), *My Aim Is To Please You* (1967) which reached No. 26 in the charts, the EP *It's A Happening World* (1968) and the album *The Executives*. They visited the USA in 1968, then released *Parenthesis* (1969). Moving to the USA in 1969, they changed their name to Inner Sense, but were not a success and disbanded. Reformed by Carole and Brian King with different members in 1974, they released *Tinker Taylor* (1976) but did not regain their earlier popularity.

FURTHER REFERENCE

Recordings include *You're Bad* (1967 Festival, FK 1583), *My Aim Is To Please You* (1967, Festival; FK 1776), *It's A Happening World*

(1968, Festival FX 11487), *The Executives* (Festival FL 32813), *Parenthesis* (1969, Festival FK 3283); reformed in 1974 *Tinker Taylor* (1976, Polydor 2079092). For discography, see *SpencerA*. See also *McGrathA*; *SpencerW*; *GuinnessP*, I, 814.

Experimental Music.
1. Context. 2. Sound Sources. 3. Technology. 4. Groups. 5. History. 6. Documentation.

Experimental music may be defined as any aural creation devoted to the process of exploration. The nature of the experiment is very often more important than the musical outcome. The word experiment is derived from the Latin verb *experior*, 'to try'. It is probably also related to Greek *peira*, the noun for 'attempt'. The process of trial is a generous one; it allows diverse phenomena to be legitimised as music. Experimental processes can occur at any stage in the entire music-making event, from the conceptual idea of the work to its final presentation, and may include reshaping the context of the music, the invention of new instruments, or innovations in tuning, pitch, form and content, notation, performance practice, documentation and audience relationships.

1. Context.   In Australia as elsewhere, most experimental composers work outside the musical mainstream. Locations for experimental performance are diverse: lakes, concert halls, warehouses, homes, factories, the street, the desert, art galleries, rivers, schools, gardens, computer screens, or anywhere else can be its habitat. Sometimes contexts are created anew, as with David ★Worrall's portable geodesic dome, an attempt to define a new multimedia public listening space, equipped with moving surround sound and multiple screens. The exploratory process of experimental music has meant that all boundaries can collapse and anything or everything can or may be considered to be possible in the audible world. But contexts are critical to the experiments, as their acoustic, geographic, social and physical characteristics are bound to condition and modify the musical event, and are chosen carefully. A cult of rugged individualism is central to the spirit of Australian experimental music, and nowhere is this seen more clearly than in the performances of Syd Clayton or the vocal utterances of composer-performer Chris ★Mann in his 'compositional linguistics'.

2. Sound Sources.   The inclusion of all sound as potential musical material has meant that the sound sources of experimental music events are infinitely varied. The microphone has allowed the transference of sound from place to place, and the presence of environmental sound in experimental compositions has been common since the invention of the tape recorder in 1950. Composers like Ron Nagorcka, Peter Mumme and Les Gilbert have sensitively redefined the musical possibilities of the soundscape. Alan ★Lamb and Ros ★Bandt have designed and built aeolian harps to bridle the wind as performer, while

Joyce Hinterding and Joan Brassil have worked with translating the phenomenology of nature into exhibited audible sound. The ease of recording means that multi-media artists have happily incorporated 'found sound' from any source, often subjecting it to experimental modification in studio, tape, performance and theatrical applications.

The spatial positioning of sound has been of the greatest importance for many artists. Jo Truman's didjeridu-playing in drainage pipes, Leigh Hobba's work in wells in Turkey and Bandt's investigations of the sonic properties of wheat silos, cement water tanks, and subterranean car-park cylinders are live exploratory performances in resonant spaces, but the extreme difficulty of creating in these spaces has meant the musical process can often only be shared on tape at a different listening location. The American Bill Fontana worked in Australia in the 1970s at dispersing sounds from one location to another: microphones inside strategically placed resonating chambers transmitted sounds to other locations remote from the sound source. One could stand in the one town and listen to the sounds of water from Kirribilli Wharf, Sydney, Gundagai Bridge, NSW, or Flinders Street Station, Melbourne. Gilbert's Australian and international installations in aquariums, museums and public spaces have also used multi-track sounds designed to be triggered by people and the environment through sophisticated computer interfaces. Multi-track pieces which moved sound through the listening space were pioneered much earlier by Ian Fredericks and Greg Schiemer. A large body of experimental music embraced the idea of music as three-dimensional space through time, and site-specific work became popular as a result.

The excitement of discovering what happens when a sound experiment has been set up has been enough to drive many Australians to devise extremely inventive work. The search for new timbres and sonorities has sparked an interest in building original instruments and machines—electronic installations as well as mechanical contraptions using found objects. The juxtaposition of new and old is often visually and technically apparent, as in Grainger's *Free Music machines. Many original instruments are designed so that the instrument and its musical practice become a form unique to its composer-performer, as in the case of Jon Rose's adapted string instruments, Colin Offord's Great Island Mouthbow, Ion Pearce's playable Strange Machine, Bandt's glass & clay music, and Gonghouse's original Gamelan. The interest in devising original sound sources extends beyond the concept of playable instruments to automata, play sculptures, sound sculptures, installations and environmental events which position sounds in space in a unique way. Ernie *Althoff's sound machines are self-generating experimental compositions in their own right.

In 1981 Bandt's two-storey, playable Sound Playground took musical experiment to the public in the open air, while the same year Warren *Burt curated the first Australian show of sound sculpture for the International Music and Technology Conference at the University of Melbourne. This field has burgeoned to include many new interdisciplinary artists whose work defies classification. Sound, technology and visual stimuli are being combined in new hybrid audio-visual art-forms challenging all customary forms of expression.

3. Technology. Experimental music has always been interested in new technology for its possibilities, its restrictions and its politics. Many musical experiments deal with technology alone. Old technologies have continually undergone new applications. The theremin, which had so excited Grainger in the 1930s and led to the revision of his *Free Music 1* for four theremins in 1937, has been applied to quite different ends in the works of Burt, Dan Senn, Gilbert and Lamb. Alistair ★Riddell's computerised pianos, Ross ★Bolleter's ruined pianos and the plethora of PVC extensions for wind instruments, have changed the face and function of their traditional components. Electrical means have provided new musical outcomes in Gilbert's early use of sensor technology and Schiemer's home-made electronic installations such as the Tupperware Gamelan. Bill Coates' interest in new microtonal tunings led him to make a variety of original electronic instruments in order to effect his tuning ratios accurately. In association with the CSIRO, Burt built a unique set of micro-tonally-tuned aluminium tuning-forks. Australia's landmark invention of the ★Fairlight CMI by Anthony Furse in 1975 was the result of years of experimentation. Don ★Banks, Ian ★Bonighton, Tristram ★Cary (with his Synklavier), Barry ★Conyngham and Martin ★Wesley-Smith in their experimental phases have all made important contributions to the development of synthesisers, electronic and computer music.

In the 1990s the electronic art revolution and the widening of the global cyberspace through internets have broadened the communication base in ways never available before. Interactive surveillance systems such as Simon Veitch's three-dimensional interactive space, 3 DIS, allow composers, dancers or an audience to program sound through space with a clever four-channel video to MIDI computer conversion. Video, film and interactive computer systems have been developed by Chris ★Knowles, Burt, Phil Brophy, Garth Paine and many others to create audio-visual experimental music of many types. Satellite ensembles are no longer figments of the imagination. Much experimental music now happens on the personal computer screen. The commercially available machines and systems have been integrated in new ways and often subjected to intense scrutiny by experimental composers. David ★Chesworth and Brophy's satirical deconstruction of techno-pop in the 1970s wittily transferred values from the popular culture and marketplace to the foreground of musical ideas for exposure and re-examination.

4. Groups. Experimental music groups have included Plastic Platypus, NIAGGRA, Tsk Tsk Tsk, LIME, the Dave

& Phil Duo, Pipeline, the Relative Band, Mind/Body Split, Kiva, Gonghouse, the Machine for Making Sense and many others. Many of these were collaborative, favouring group composition over the earlier style of composer-directed ensembles such as those of Humble and Werder. The Melbourne Improvisers' Association (MIA), an offshoot of the Victorian College of the Arts improvisation program, has held regular series of performances in alternative venues such as pubs and small theatrical houses, and artists from different disciplines, writers, sculptors, actors, poets, dancers and computer engineers have often collaborated. Improvisation, realtime composition and indeterminacy have been continually integrated in the form of these works. Recently, experimental music has started to reflect Australia's demographic mix. Some Aboriginal fusion bands and multicultural ensembles are creating new musical genres based on their intercultural exchanges. Instruments from other cultures, sampled sounds and indigenous influences have always been part of experimental music when required. It is a nomadic and eclectic art-form. Experimental music has rarely stayed within the discipline of music, as the large multi-media groups Synchronos and Floating Exceptions can testify.

5. History. As a child in the early 1890s, Percy Grainger conceived of 'Free Music', and his experimental machines for tuning oscillators to create 'hills and dales' of microtonal music, built from 1945, were remarkable forerunners of the synthesiser. In the late 1960s the Nuniques of Keith ★Humble and Jean Charles François brought the spirit of 'happenings' to Monash University in Melbourne in performances which involved bicycles, parachute tents, whistles, graphic scores, and simultaneous events. Early electronic experiments were carried out at the Grainger museum and through the ISCM, and then the first public access sound studio, the New Music Centre, Flemington, was founded under the guidance of Mumme. There were organised regular performances. An experimental tradition was forming in Melbourne which identified venues to cater for musical experiments. The experiments spread to the alternative theatre La Mama and to radio sessions at the ABC Waverley studios organised by Felix ★Werder. Humble introduced the new minimalist process music of Steve Reich to Australia, and his formation of the La Trobe University music department in 1974 for a time legitimised all kinds of musical experiments, improvisation, process music and group composition. Ron ★Nagorcka set up the Clifton Hill Community Music Centre (1976–83), a proving ground for many artists, complete with its own newspaper and a full diary of cross-media events including video and film. A free, non-selective venue where anyone could perform whatever they liked, it allowed musical experiment to flourish in extremely diverse ways. With works by so many composer-performers and groups, this period could be seen as the watershed of experimental music in Australia.

Meanwhile in Sydney, David ★Ahern's exploratory A-Z Music at the NSW Conservatorium was an *ad hoc* orchestra which included Robert Irving, Greg ★Schiemer, Roger Frampton, the dancer Philippa Cullen and others who were inclined towards a range of anarchic and free activities. A splinter group, Teletopea, the spatial live electronics of Ian Fredericks and the multi-media events of Wesley-Smith with George Gittoes in their cross-art ensemble WATT yielded other important experimental performances. Various small festivals, such as Adelaide's Fringe (from 1974), became important venues for showcasing these events.

In the 1980s in Perth the entrepreneurial group Evos, instigated by Tos Mahoney, hosted many sound-artist/composer residencies, concerts, events and seminars which investigate music, the soundscape, exhibitions, instrument-building and telecommunication music. Australian experimental music was represented at the Paris Autumn Festival of 1983, Ars Electronica, Linz, 1989, the ISCM World Music Days 1992 and other international festivals.

In the 1990s sonic experiments have been welcomed in the art schools of Sydney under the umbrella of 'sound art'. A program in acoustic design, yielding fascinating studies in sound sculpture and architectural models, has begun in the department of environmental studies at the Royal Melbourne Institute of Technology. Australia has embraced the new sonic forms more readily in non-musical contexts than in musical ones, through festivals such as Sound Culture (1991), TISEA electronic art symposium (1992), the Experimenta festivals in Melbourne, and the ICA sound symposium, Sound in Space (1995) in Sydney. Today four major host venues for experimental music are the Linden Gallery, St Kilda, Melbourne, the Australian Computer Music Association, the MIA, and most recently Theatreworks.

6. Documentation. Experimental sound events are rarely documented for many reasons: the complexity of the medium, the inaccessibility or remoteness of the venue, a lack of finance, a general resistance to documenting ephemeral work by some artists, or a lack of interest and knowledge of the area on the part of the established journalists. The sonic works themselves are often very difficult to record. Andrew McLennan and Jaroslav Kovaricek have regularly recorded and played new experimental music of all types on ABC radio, while Warren Burt, John Campbell and others have run their own radio shows on public and community radio stations.

Apart from a few radio commissions and the occasional grant from the Australia Council, the production, funding, and distribution of recordings or discussions of experimental music has been left largely up to the artists themselves. A few artists have been released by Move Records, Melbourne, and Tall Poppies, Sydney, but mostly composers have issued their own recordings. Evos circulated a very fine new music newspaper for several years; artists rotated the editorship of the *New Music* paper, and a dedicated publishing house New

Music Articles was run by composers Rainer Linz and Richard Vella. Jenkins's seminal *22 Australian Composers* is still the definitive text in the area, along with Warren Burt's excellent 1993 article. Much remains which needs documentation.

FURTHER REFERENCE
Select Discography
Ernie Althoff, *Music for Seven Metal Machines* (1990, Pedestrian Tapes, Sydney, PX037); Ian Andrews, Joan Brassil, Densil Cabrera, Richard Vella, Frances Dyson, Douglas Kahn, Ashley Scott, Sherre DeLys, *NMA 8* (1991, NMA Publications [Brunswick] NMA TAPES 8); Ros Bandt/LIME, *Soft & Fragile: Music in Glass & Clay* (1995, Move Records CD 3045); Ros Bandt, *Stargazer* (1989, Move Records MD 3075 and Vox Australis VAST 004–2); *Best Seats in the House!* [Anthology of improvisation] (1991, NMA Publications); Ross Bolleter, *The Country of Here Below* (1994, Tall Poppies TP045); Ross Bolleter and Ryszard Ratajczak, Stephen Benfall, Nathan Crotty, Stuart Davies-Slate, Zac Laskewica, Lindsay Vickery, Jonathan Mustard, Rowan Hammond, *NMA 9* (1991, NMA Publications (Brunswick) NMA TAPES 9); Warren Burt, *Chaotic Research Music* (1992, Scarlett Aardvark); Warren Burt, Linda Ceff, David Chesworth, Graeme Gerrard, Geoff Pressing, David Hirst, Felix Werder and OHM, *Machine Messages* (1992, Australian Computer Music Association vol. 1); Bill Coates, *31 Note Music*, 3 cassettes (1991, Bill Coates [Blackheath]); Jim Denley, *Dark Matter* (1992, Tall Poppies TP008); Jim Denley and Kimmo Vennonen, *Time of Non Duration* (1989, Split Records [Sydney] 002); Les Gilbert, *Kakadu Billabong* (1991, Natural Symphonies [Camden] NS131); Percy Grainger, Free Music I & II realised by Barry Conyngham, *Australian Digital Music* (1978, Move Records MS 3027); Sarah Hopkins and Alan Lamb, *Sky Song* (1990, ABC Records 838–503–4); Alan Lamb 'Wire Music', Ross Bolleter 'Ruined Pianos', Warren Burt 'Tuning Forks', *Austral Voices* (1990, New Albion Records NA028CD); *The Listening Room: Alpha, Beta, Gamma, Delta* (1994, ABC Records, EMI, 4 compact discs 479758–2, 479759–2, 479760–2, 479761–2); Colin Offord, *Pacific Sound* (1990, Move Records MD 3105 and 1992, Vox Australis VAST 002–2); Rick Rue, *Ocean Flows* (1993, Tall Poppies TP036).
Bibliography
AthertonA; JenkinsT.
Archee, Ray, 'Art, Culture, Communication & Virtual Reality: A review of the Tisea Symposia', *Media Information Australia* 68 (May 1993), 93–8.
Burt, Warren, 'Instrumental Composition', *SA* 9 (1985), 3–15.
——, 'Some Musical and Sociological Aspects of Australian Experimental Music 1963–1993', *SA* 37 (Autumn 1993), 38–47. (The fullest overview to date. Excellent bibliography and discography.)

Brophy, Phil, 'Subculture: The meaning of style', *Art & Text* 1 (1981), 69–74.
——, 'A face without a place', *Art & Text* 16 (1984), 68–80.
Carter, Paul, *The Sound In Between* (Sydney: UNSWP, 1992).
Grainger, Percy, Free Music—6 Dec. 1938. Legend held in Grainger Museum Collections, Univ. Melbourne.
Harrison, Martin, 'Three works from memory', *Continuum* 6:1 (1992), 148–61.
Hopkins, Sarah, 'Whirly Instruments', *Experimental Musical Instruments* 6/3 (1990), 11–13.
Jordan, Teresa, 'Arts to Ashes', *Artlink* 11/4 (1991/2), 90–1.
Miller, Toby, ed., *Continuum: The Australian Journal of Media & Culture* 6/1 (1992).
Nyman, Michael, *Experimental Music: Cage and Beyond* (London: Dutton, 1975).
Stewart, Amanda, 'About =', *Leonardo Music Journal* 3 (1993), 75–6.
Whiteoak, John, Australian Approaches to Improvisatory Musical Practice, 1836–1970: A Melbourne Perspective. PhD, La Trobe Univ., 1993.
Zurbrugg, Nicolas, 'Electronic Art in Australia', *Continuum* 11/4 (1994).

ROS BANDT

Exton, John (*b* Wolverton, England, 1933), composer. A gifted violinist, he was leader of the National Youth Orchestra in Britain. After studies with Robin Orr and Matyas Seiber, then with Dallapiccola, he took a doctorate in music theory from Cambridge University and taught at Bedales school, Hampshire, from 1963. His *Partita* (1957) for string quartet was played by the Amici Quartet at the 1962 ISCM London Festival and published by Chester. He moved to Australia as senior lecturer (later associate professor) at the University of Western Australia in 1966, where he had charge of developing the electronic music studios, and has since produced a number of tape pieces for electronic means, as well as continuing with acoustic composition. He has published articles in *Studies in Music*, *Critic* and elsewhere.

FURTHER REFERENCE
Recordings include String Quartet No. 3 (1969), Oriel String Quartet (1971, Festival SFC 800–25). String Quartet No. 5, Petra String Quartet (Canberra School of Music CSM 10); *Movements for Orchestra* (1963) WA Symphony Orchestra, cond. T. Mayer (1969, ABC RRCS 381). His articles include 'Forward to First Principles', *SMA* 1 (1967), 89–97, and 'The *I Ching* and Structure: A Note on the Composition of my String Quartet,' *SMA* 7 (1963), 77. See also Roger Smalley, *CallawayA,* 182–9.

F

Fahey, Warren. See *Larrikins, the*.

Fairlight CMI. Computer music instrument manufactured (from 1979) by Fairlight Instruments, founded in Sydney by Peter Vogel and Kim Ryrie. It consists of a velocity-sensitive keyboard, VDU, light-pen, two disc drives, and a printer.

Working for an electronics magazine, Ryrie had published a popular do-it-yourself synthesiser design, and in 1975 he combined with Vogel to explore ways in which microchip technology could improve its control. With computer technician Anthony Furse they developed a prototype, named for a hydrofoil on Sydney Harbour, installed at the Canberra School of Music. After nearly four years of work, they had a version ready for sale in 1979, which pioneered sampling (the gathering of real sounds and their manipulation at specific pitch by a musical keyboard), allowed the user to create a sound from scratch, to create or modify a waveform using a pen on an interactive screen, and to create music from realtime at a keyboard, which it could then store or print out in musical notation.

The international interest in the instrument was immediate, and within five years almost all sales were to buyers abroad, including pop musicians such as Stevie Wonder and Kate Bush, film composer Peter Best and director Stanley Kubrick, university and radio electronic laboratories as well as Robert Moog himself, designer of the original synthesiser. Fierce competition in the late 1980s, however, sent the company into financial difficulty, but it remains a greatly popular digital synthesiser in both classical and popular fields. See *Computer Music*; *Electronic Music*.

FURTHER REFERENCE
AthertonA; Hugh Davies, *GroveI*.

Fall of the House of Usher. Opera (1965) in one act by Larry *Sitsky, libretto by Gwen Harwood after the story by Edgar Allan Poe. Commissioned for the Hobart Festival of Contemporary Opera and Music, and first performed 18 August 1965, Theatre Royal, Hobart. The first opera to be staged at the Sydney Opera House, 25 July 1973.

Falson, Ron (Ronald Albert) (*b* Sydney, 2 Jan. 1928), jazz trumpeter. He began trumpet at the age of 15, joining a schoolboy group, led by Les Welch, which played in wartime Red Cross shows. At first a Dixieland player, he evolved into one of Sydney's foremost exponents of bop in the postwar decade, prominent with his own band, the Beboppers, and with others including Ralph Mallen's and Wally Norman's. Active in nightclubs, dance circuits and jazz concerts, he joined Bob Gibson in 1956, touring and backing visitors such as Frank Sinatra and Buddy Rich. Later he concentrated on radio and television session work, playing french horn, composing and arranging.

FURTHER REFERENCE
Recordings include *Ron Falson's Beboppers* (1948, Jazz At The Town Hall, unnumbered); *Don Burrows, The First 50 Years, vol. 1, 1944–1965* (1993, ABC Polygram 514 296–2; *For Leon Bismark*, John Sangster (1977 Swaggie S-1379). See also *BissetB*; *OxfordJ*; *ClareB*.   BRUCE JOHNSON

Farbach, Kent (*b* Southport, Qld, 2 Aug. 1961), composer. He studied at the Queensland Conservatorium 1984–89 and 1991–95, and with Philip Bracanin at the University of Queensland, from 1996. His works include *Beneath the Forest Canopy* (1989) for flute ensemble, *Life Stratum* (1990) for orchestra, *Time Remembered* (1990) for harp and cello, *1845: an Irish Elegy* (1992) for orchestra, *From Quiet Places* (1993) for six instruments, *Into the Landscape* (1994) for orchestra, and *Sneaking* (1995) for mixed children's choir. Farbach's works often reflect the presence and inspiration of the natural environment of Queensland.

FURTHER REFERENCE

His writings include 'Music Technology: A Question of Aesthetics', *SA* 25 (Autumn 1990), 24–5. See also *BroadstockS*.

MICHAEL BARKL

Farnham, John Peter (*b* Dagenham, Essex, England, 1 July 1949), rock singer. Farnham moved to Melbourne with his family in 1959 and attended local primary and secondary schools in the outer south-eastern suburbs. He signed on as an apprentice plumber, but his singing in local bands had already attracted the attention of Darryl Sambell, who became his manager and guided his early years of stardom. In 1967 the single *Sadie (The Cleaning Lady)* reached the top of the Australian charts, as did *Raindrops Keep Falling on My Head* in 1969. Firmly established as a pop identity, he went on to become King of Pop for five years in succession, 1969–73. The early 1970s were busy years, and apart from recording and concert engagements he starred in the stage productions *Charlie Girl* (1971) and *Pippin* (1974). He was crowned King of Melbourne's Moomba Festival in 1972, and won the most outstanding performance of a composition award at the World Popular Song Festival in Tokyo with his version of Brian Cadd's *Don't You Know It's Magic*. During the second half of the 1970s however, his career lost momentum.

It was not until 1980 that Farnham, now managed by Glenn Wheatley, was back in the Australian charts when his distinctive version of the Beatles' *Help* reached No. 8. In 1982 he was asked to join the ★Little River Band, and although this act was in its declining years, Farnham's work as frontman was committed and enthusiastic. More importantly it persuaded the Australian public, which still associated him with stage musicals and catchy but light-weight material, that he could sing mainstream pop and rock very well. Leaving the Little River Band in 1984, Farnham resumed his solo career, eventually releasing the *Whispering Jack* album in October 1986; it contained the memorable hit *You're The Voice,* which reached the No. 1 position on the charts. Successful beyond all expectations, the album became the best-selling album in Australian recording history. With his pop-rock credentials now secured, Farnham embarked on sell-out national tours backed by a strong band and his own considerable performing experience. In 1988 he released the *Age of Reason* album, another commercial success, and was named Australian of the Year in the country's Bicentennial celebrations. In the same year he toured nationally with the Melbourne Symphony Orchestra.

In a career spanning three decades, Farnham has been one of Australia's most enduring and high-profile pop stars. In the 1990s he has continued regularly releasing albums and touring. In 1992 he sang the role of Jesus in a national tour of *Jesus Christ Superstar.* While the exceptional chart success of the 1980s has been hard to recapture, his concerts remain hugely popular and he routinely sells out stadium venues.

FURTHER REFERENCE

Recordings include *The Classic Gold Collection (1967–85)* (EMI 814580–2); *The Farnham Years (LRB)* (EMI CDMID 166189); *Whispering Jack* (1986, BMG SFCD 0149); *Age of Reason* (1988, BMG SFCD 0168); *Chain Reaction* (1990, BMG VPCD 0830); *Full House (Live)* (1991, BMG VPCD 0843); *Romeo's Heart* (1996, BMG 74321373002). For discography see *SpencerA*. See also *McGrath A*; *SpencerW*.

WILLIAM VAN PINXTEREN

Farr, Ian (*b* Hamley Bridge, SA, 10 May 1941), composer, pianist. After studies in piano, double bass and composition (with Raymond ★Hanson) at the NSW State Conservatorium, he played double bass with the Sydney Symphony Orchestra 1961–65, then worked in the ABC Music Department from 1966, taking private lessons with Richard ★Meale. He appeared as a pianist in contemporary music concerts at Sydney from 1967, and from 1972 working freelance in theater, film and clubs, and as an accompanist for Jeannie ★Lewis, Margret ★RoadKnight and others. His work includes incidental music for over 30 productions for the State Theatre Co. of SA, the Junction Theatre Co., and other companies, as well as concert works, including the piano works *Baby Under the Bridge* (1990) and *Girl with the Dancing Air* (1991).

FURTHER REFERENCE

His Cello Sonata (1969, J. Albert & Son) was recorded by Gregory Elmaloglou (Festival SFC 800–22). See also *MurdochA*.

Farren-Price, Ronald William (*b* Brisbane, 2 July 1930), pianist, teacher. He studied at the University of Melbourne Conservatorium, winning the ABC Concerto Competition in 1950. This was followed by three years of intensive training with Claudio Arrau on a personal scholarship donated by Arrau himself. In 1955 he joined the staff of the University of Melbourne, an institution he has been closely associated with ever since, serving as dean for five years and then as head of keyboard and associate professor. His concert career has been consistently intense, performing in about 50 countries in the world's major concert halls, including 12 tours of Russia. He has appeared with a number of the world's leading conductors, Willem van Otterloo, Antal Dorati and Sir Charles Groves among them. He has released a number of recordings and has a distinguished broadcast career.

Farren-Price has also had an illustrious and influential teaching career over several decades for which the faculty of music, University of Melbourne, has been his base. He has taught many of the younger generation of Australian musicians, and a number of overseas students have come to Australia to study with him. He has also been active in masterclasses and adjudication for many years and has served as a jury member for various national and international awards and competitions. His approach to performance is very much in the grand tradition of his great mentor, Arrau. He was awarded an AM for his services to music in 1990.

FURTHER REFERENCE
Recordings include *Reflections* (1992, Move MD 3117); *Farren-Price Plays Chopin* (1995, Move MD 3147).

IAN HOLTHAM

Faust and Gretchen. Operetta in four acts by Moritz *Heuzenroeder, libretto by R. Jaentsch. First performed at the Albert Hall, Adelaide, on 19 March 1883.

Featherstone, Bennie (Geoffrey Benjamin) (*b* Brown's Creek, Tas., 30 July 1912; *d* Melbourne, 6 Apr. 1977), jazz trumpeter. In his childhood Featherstone moved to Melbourne where he played in school orchestras. He was inspired to take up jazz by the visiting American band of Ray Tellier in 1925. He became proficient on virtually every dance band instrument, notably trumpet, trombone, and drums, and joined Joe Watson at 17. Becoming prominent, he was often billed as 'Australia's Louis Armstrong'; in 1933 he travelled to England, where he met and played with Armstrong and Duke Ellington. Back in Melbourne in 1934, he joined Art Chapman, freelanced as an instrumentalist, singer and conductor, and formed a band (the first of many) which including Frank Coughlan. At Faulkner Park and the 3AW Swing Club he was significant in the late 1930s jazz resurgence. Apart from service in the Merchant Marine he continued to be active, leading his Dixielanders (including Roger Bell, Don Banks, and Charlie Blott), playing American service clubs in Queensland, and in 1945 visiting the USA where he sat in with Jimmie Lunceford. There is little evidence of his postwar musical activity; he became a shipping clerk in 1958, retiring in 1975.

Featherstone was regarded in the profession as the greatest jazz musician of his milieu, although relatively obscure because of his wayward temperament, inadequate recording opportunities, and a jazz historiography which has difficulty accommodating a progressive swing player who was neither wholly traditionalist nor modernist. Nonetheless Featherstone remains one of the influential musicians of pre-war Australian jazz.

FURTHER REFERENCE
Recordings include *Joe Watson and His Green Mill Orchestra* (1929, Embassy 8036); *The Beachcombers* (1930, Broadcast, unnumbered). See also *ClareB*; *BissetB*; *OxfordJ*; Ernst Grossmann, articles, photographs, and discography in *Jazzline* (March 1980), 24–33; (June 1980), 16–21; (June 1981), 9–18.

BRUCE JOHNSON

Fellowship of Australian Composers. Established in 1959 as the representative voice of Australian composers. Since that time it has constantly drawn the attention of the government and the music industry to the importance of Australian music to the national image, and the needs of those who write it. Persistent representations by the fellowship over a number of years led to the establishment of the Advisory Board for Commonwealth Assistance to Australian Composers in 1967, and the Australian Music Centre in 1975. The fellowship has been an active member of the Asian Composers' League since 1974.

JOHN COLBORNE-VEEL

Festival of Perth. The oldest of Australia's major festivals. Founded in 1953, it began as a summer program at the University of Western Australia, but spread to city venues in 1956 and achieved national attention from 1976. With funds from the state and municipal governments and significant private sponsorship, the festival features an array of international artists as well as outstanding Australians and has a strong musical component.

Festivals. In Australia arts festivals flourish in almost every city and regional centre; there is scarcely a week in the year when a festival of some kind is not offered. Usually annual and spanning anything from a weekend to three weeks, these events rarely have the origins in commemoration or religious ritual common among festivals elsewhere, but simply set out to give meaning and cohesiveness to their communities through artistic experience.

In the 19th century expressions of civic pride and nationalism played their part in such massed events as the festival for the opening of the Great Hall, University of Sydney (1859), the Melbourne Intercolonial Exhibition (1866), the Metropolitan and Intercolonial Exhibition, Sydney (1870), the Sydney International Exhibition (1879), and the International Centennial Exhibition, Melbourne (1888). As at international exhibitions in Europe, large-scale choral and orchestral presentations and exhibitions of instruments were characteristic of these events.

Today there is a major government-sponsored festival in most capital cities, usually a broadly based showcase of arts and popular culture for people of all ages, social and ethnic backgrounds. All of these have strong musical components of both visiting international artists and outstanding Australians. The oldest is the *Festival of Perth (founded 1953). The Melbourne Moomba Festival (founded 1955) has been overshadowed by the *Melbourne International Festival (founded 1986). The largest and best known abroad is the *Adelaide Festival (founded 1960), but the *Sydney Festival (founded 1976), and the *Brisbane Biennial (founded 1990) are also well patronised. The Adelaide Fringe Festival, the biennial Come Out Youth Festival, Adelaide, the International *Barossa Music Festival, the Warana Festival, Brisbane, and the Fremantle Festival are more local in character.

Since the 1970s many special-interest music festivals have also come to be established, especially jazz and country music festivals in regional centres, where their role in attracting tourism was soon recognised. These focus on local and nationally known Australian artists. The Australasian Country Music Festival at *Tamworth (founded 1973) is the largest. The *Australian Jazz Convention (founded at Melbourne, 1944) has emphasised traditional jazz. The National Folk Festival organised by the ★Australian Folk Trust rotates between cities and has a strong musical component. The ★Melbourne Autumn Festival of Organ and Harpsichord Music (founded 1971), the Australian Festival of Chamber Music at Townsville, the Darwin International Guitar Festival, and the ★Newcastle Conservatorium Keyboard Festival (founded 1989) all feature artists from abroad as well as Australians, and there are a number of folk festivals presented by Australian ethnic communities with strong dance or music components. However, opera festivals, contemporary music festivals, choral festivals, and early music festivals have been much less prevalent than in Europe, and the tradition of commissioning new works, so integral to festivals abroad, has not taken root. (See also entries under individual ethnic community and city names.)

Fiancées, The.   Operetta in one act, music and text by Fritz ★Hart (1931). First performed by the Albert Street Conservatorium in 1931.

Fidelio.   Pen-name; see *Kornweibel, Albert H.*

Field, Billy   (*b* Urbana, NSW, 1954), popular music singer-songwriter. After learning violin and piano as a child, at school in 1969 he joined the band King Fox which released two singles, notably *Unforgotten Dreams* (1969, Du Monde). He operated a recording studio in Sydney, then released four jazz-pop singles, including *Bad Habits*, which reached No. 4 in the charts in 1981, and *You Weren't In Love With Me* (1981), which reached No. 1. He appeared on television and toured Australia, presenting his jazz big band to pop audiences, then moved to the USA and Europe in 1983, where he has appeared at Las Vegas. His albums included *Try Biology* (1982) and *Western Light* (1992). He won the Tokyo Song Festival Gold Award in 1983.

FURTHER REFERENCE
Recordings include Western *Light* (1992, Jade JADCD 103393) and a compilation *The Best Of Billy Field* (Warner 2551372). Early singles were on WEA. For discography, see *SpencerA*. See also *McGrathA*; *SpencerW*; *APRAJ* 2/9 (Dec. 1981), 2–3.

Fields, Venetta   (*b* Buffalo, New York), pop music session singer, coach. After singing in gospel choirs in the American South, she became one of the original Ikettes, the backing group for Ike and Tina Turner, in the 1960s. In the 1970s she was with Blackberries, then toured with many of the world's star performers, including Diana Ross, Neil Diamond, the Rolling Stones, and Boz Scaggs, and did session work for nearly 80 leading pop artists in the UK and the USA. She came to Australia in 1981 and sang with the Richard ★Clapton Band (1983–84), her own Venetta's Taxi (1984), and Yu-en (1986), as well as taking session work with numerous prominent Australian rock artists. She presented a show, *Gospel Jubilee* (1986),

tracing the development of gospel music, then was in the musical *The Big River* (1989) and with the John ★Farnham Band (1990). One of the most sought after session singers in Australia, as a voice coach she taught Jason ★Donovan, James Reyne, and Neil and Tim Finn. Her one single is *Only One* (1987).

FURTHER REFERENCE
Recording *Only One* (1987, Fenner FEN 001). See also *SpencerW*; *Age* 11 July 1986; *Age* 21 Apr. 1989.

Fiery Tales.   Opera in one act by Larry ★Sitsky, libretto by Gwen Harwood after Chaucer and Boccaccio. First performed at Adelaide on 23 March 1976.

Film and Television Music.   After a vast number of musicians who made live music for silent films disappeared with the arrival of sound in 1929, Australian film music had a sporadic existence until the rebirth of the Australian film industry from 1975. Today more than a dozen Australian composers have made their careers in film, and a large and very diverse group of musicians contribute music to television.

1. Music for Film. (i) Earliest Examples. Melbourne audiences first experienced the confluence of image, sound and music as public entertainment in 1890 when British showman E. Douglas Archibald demonstrated Edison's wax cylinder phonograph. He made recordings of members of the audience, presented a lantern slide tour of the Edison laboratory and played recordings of local artists including Nellie Stewart and members of the Victorian Orchestra. Then, in 1894, an amusement parlour in Sydney introduced five Edison kinetoscopes, in which patrons viewed through an eyepiece a continuous film loop lasting 30 seconds. Music was provided by a wax cylinder phonograph, or at times by the orchestra from the nearby Lyceum Theatre. In 1895, Charters Towers, Queensland, had three Edison kinetophones, kinetoscopes with internal phonographs which supplied, through stethoscope tubes plugged to viewers' ears, two and a half minutes of music on wax cylinders, unsynchronised with the film. Each shipment of films was accompanied by a playlist of popular pieces, and the exhibitor selected a sequence to accompany the films from the Edison catalogue.

(ii) The Silent Era.   Until 1910 the Salvation Army was Australia's largest producer of film, exhibiting over 300 documentary films, slides and sound recordings as lecture presentations, always with musical accompaniment. On lecture tours throughout Australia to promote its social work, the Army's Limelight Department travelled with its own orchestras, the Biorama Bands, comprised of as many as 20 players. The first documentary film to be given an original score was *Pearls and Savages* (1921), with music compiled by cinema organist Emanuel (Manny) Aarons

from field recordings the cinematographer Frank Hurley had made in New Guinea.

Of the 250 silent feature films made in Australia between 1906 and 1930, about 30 survive in whole or in part today. These include (silent) scenes of bush dances, soirées, and (from the 1920s) the latest dance craze, jazz. In the picture theatres, which began operating from 1905 and soon appeared in every city and town, the actual musical sound was supplied by orchestras, small ensembles, a pianist, or (infrequently) a player-piano operator. Professional cinema musicians appeared in great number, and to fit the films with illustrative music, film music libraries appeared. Their collections included concert music, Edwardian 'popular classics', salon pieces, dance styles from the waltz to the charleston, tin pan alley, and later 'hot' jazz arrangements, all available with as many orchestral parts as required. Accompanying the scores were cue sheets prepared by parent motion picture companies, itemising the duration, tempo and title of the music and action for each sequence in the film. Clearly, musicians in the cinema pits played an extensive repertoire across a wide spectrum of styles.

The first contributions from local composers were in the run-of-the-mill genre familiar from pantomime and melodrama, neither innovative nor troublesome. Surviving Australian scores from publishers such as Cawthorne & Co. in Adelaide and Allan & Co. in Melbourne are short, episodic pieces of sentimental charm, or standard illustrative music such as the *Hurries* or *Misterioso* to augment the appropriate emotional moments in the film. Although written as piano pieces, they were easily embellished (and sometimes marked with cues) for ensemble or small orchestra. But these Australian scores were few, almost buried in film music libraries beneath the weight of music from abroad. Many popular songwriters composed songs to promote Australian and imported films and, after 1956, television productions. Jack *O'Hagan claimed he was the first with his *Anatol* (1921), featured with Paramount's *The Affairs of Anatol*. Another 12 O'Hagan theme songs for films followed, including those he performed in Efftee Production's *Jack O'Hagan—Vocalist Composer* (1931).

Live music was also presented in the cinema as a diversion. Australian exhibitors vied for foreign musicians to promote their programs, and audiences were beguiled by their performances. Wurlitzer organs were imported to furnish new picture palaces in the capital cities. Costing anything up to £25 000 and with import duty of £2000, these elaborate consoles were played with dazzling showmanship by visiting American organists, who became 'essential' to realise their full potential. Orchestra leaders from Europe were engaged for their Continental manners and exotic flair, which they demonstrated in a repertoire of mid-European gypsy music and virtuoso violin pieces.

By 1928 imported pit musicians engaged at below-award wages had displaced an estimated 3000 local players, and the Federal Government agreed to the Musicians'

Union demands for an embargo. But the embargo did not extend to orchestra conductors, theatre organists, concert virtuosi or contract vaudevillians. In the same year, a downturn in business encouraged exhibitors to consider mechanical music with a single operator. In 1929 the Depression caused economic hardship everywhere; 2000 musicians were dismissed in 164 cinemas in Sydney and Melbourne alone. By 1930 a third of Australia's cinemas were wired for sound, accelerating the dismissal of the last cinema musicians. 'Talked Out By The Talkies!' became their catch-cry.

(iii) The Sound Era. The first sound film was made by De Forest Phonofilm (Australia) in 1927. But after 1930, feature film production became sporadic in Australia and restricted opportunities available for composers in film. For 40 years most Australian composers lacked local experience, and as a consequence had little chance of success in the international film music industry. With limited financial resources, music was the lowest priority in Australian film production, and to keep within budget, works by composers of the past, Beethoven, Mendelssohn, Tchaikovsky, Wagner and Elgar often functioned as background music.

In 1929 sound engineers Arthur Smith (1902–93) and Clive Cross (*b* 1912) produced the Smith and Cross Recording Equipment used to record sound (and music) in the sixteen feature films produced by Cinesound Productions, 1932–40. Directed by Ken Hall (1900–94), all these films save *Strike Me Lucky* (1932) were a commercial success. Cinesound feature films made increasing use of film music as Hall's musical directors became more practised at delivering what was required. The first time Wagner's *Leitmotiven* were heard in an Australian production was in Cinesound's *The Silence of Dean Maitland* (1934), where Hamilton Webber employed themes from Wagner's *Träume* to depict Alma, the seductress of a willing clergyman. A particularly outstanding production was the 1938 musical drama *The Broken Melody*, with an operetta climax composed by Alfred *Hill, conducted by Hamilton Webber; it involved tenor Lionello Cecil, the Richard McLelland Choir and members of the ABC Sydney Symphony Orchestra. In Melbourne in the 1930s Efftee Productions made shorts using a diversity of musical talent including singer Kathleen Goodall (accompanying herself at the piano), instrumentalists, vocal ensembles, vaudevillian George Wallace, the Melbourne Chinese Orchestra and Melbourne's Regent Theatre Orchestra. In 1939 Australia's first all-coloured animated cartoon, *Willie The Wombat*, was released with the theme song *Waste Not, Want Not* composed by Lance Watkinson, featuring the Dudley Cantrell Orchestra and the voice of Bert Cantrell.

The largest employer of composers after World War II was the Department of the Interior's film unit (later, the Commonwealth Film Unit, now Film Australia) which, to the present, has commissioned nearly 400 scores from more than 100 composers. One of the earliest was composed by the young Charles *Mackerras for *Namatjira* (1947).

Foreign production companies used Australia for their location from the 1950s, but scores for their films were commissioned from composers abroad: Ernest Gold's score for *On the Beach* (1959) and Dimitri Tiomkin's score for *The Sundowners* (1960) achieved international acclaim. Australian composers were hurt and bewildered by their exclusion from such projects; some, notably John *Antill, Esther *Rofe, Robert *Hughes and Dulcie *Holland, had been composing documentary film scores since the mid-1940s and their success in mastering the medium was acknowledged by innovative producers at the time as an enormous step forward for film music in this country. Others had contributed film scores for Australian feature films and documentaries, including Willy Redstone, Mackerras, Hill, Sydney John Kay, Lindley *Evans, Raymond *Hanson, Dorian *Le Gallienne, Peter *Sculthorpe and Don *Burrows. Only three composers were engaged for international projects, Hill and Henry Krips for Columbia Pictures' *Smithy* (1946) and Sydney John Kay for the Rank Organisation's *Bush Christmas* (1947). Sculthorpe wrote a score for Michael Powell's production *Age of Consent* (1969), but after technical problems in the recording session it was replaced with a score by the English composer Stanley Myers.

Where Australia's indigenous people were a film's subject, composers showed little interest in referring musically to Aboriginal chants and rhythms in films, although Isador *Goodman achieved some success in his score for *Jedda* (1955), as did Mirrie *Hill (1892–1986) in her documentary film score, *Aborigines of the Sea Coast* (1951). During the 1960s few feature films and fewer film scores were produced.

(iv) From 1975 to the Present. After 1975 the so-called New Wave in the film industry offered greater opportunities for Australian composers, which encouraged unique and creative approaches. Bruce *Smeaton in *Picnic at Hanging Rock* (1975), Peter *Best in *Picture Show Man* (1977), Michael *Carlos, in *Storm Boy* and Brian *May in *Mad Max* (1979) were all influential. Yet many Australian producers continued to approach overseas composers, and to offer them better remuneration. Government guidelines for film tax incentives were amended to address this issue in the 1980s, to ensure commissions came to Australian composers. The establishment of the Australian Guild of Screen Composers in 1984 promoted awareness of the importance for music in film and television, representing composers' interests and lobbying to extend the AFI, APRA and Logie Awards to include most categories of film and television composition.

Today most composers for film tend to specialise in the medium, crafting anything from symphonic drama to popular music in all its styles. Composers Bruce *Rowland in *The Man From Snowy River* (1982), William

*Motzing in *Young Einstein* (1986), Martin Armiger in *Sweetie* (1988), Sarah de Jong in *Flirting* (1990), David Hirschfelder in *Strictly Ballroom* (1991) and *Shine* (1996), Chris *Neal, in *The Nostradamus Kid* (1992) and Nigel *Westlake in *The Edge* (1996) and *Babe* (1996) are representatives of musical talent to emerge in the last decades. Two composers for the concert hall who have made notable contributions to film are Sculthorpe in *They Found A Cave* (1962), *Manganinnie* (1974) and *Burke and Wills* (1985) and George *Dreyfus (*b*.1929), whose work includes *Let The Balloon Go* (1976) and a score for the ABC tele-series *Rush*, which entered the pop charts.

2. Music for Television. Early television featured variety shows with such artists as pianist Isador *Goodman and entertainers Bobby Limb and Dawn Lake, and many other artists who transferred from radio or the popular theatre, accompanied by a studio orchestra. For composers television provided new opportunities, for commercial jingles, scores and signature themes for television series. A large number of composers, performer-composers, jazz musicians, and songwriters have written music for television, from figures such as saxophonist Peter *Clinch and harmonica player Horrie *Dargie in its early days to jazz pianist Paul *Grabovsky, songwriters *Vanda and Young, Jacki *Trent and Tony Hatch, today. A particularly distinguished figure for a long period has been Tommy *Tycho, conductor of the ATN7 Orchestra, Sydney, 1958–73, and writer and arranger for many programs since. Eric *Jupp's familiar music for *Skippy* has been heard in 130 countries; he also conducted the ABC's *Magic of Music* for six years. Current composers of theme music for television series include Mark Isaacs for *GP* (1989), David Cheshire for *Embassy* (series, 1993), Felicity Foxx for *Under the Skin* (1993) and Gary Hardman for *Police Rescue* (1993).

FURTHER REFERENCE.
Many early films are in the National Film and Sound Archive, Canberra and film scores in *CAnl*; *BrisbaneE*; Diane Napthali, Music and the Australian Film Industry, 1894–1969: A Seventy-Five Year Consideration, PhD, Univ. NSW, 1997; Andrew Pike, and Ross Cooper, *Australian Film 1900–1977: A Guide to Feature Film Production* (Melbourne: OUP, 1980); Peter Pinne, *Australian Performers: A Discography from Film TV, Theatre, Radio & Concert* (Melbourne: Performing Arts Museum, 1987).

DIANE NAPTHALI

Fincham, George (*b* London, 20 Aug. 1828; *d* Hawthorn, Melbourne, 21 Dec. 1910), organ-builder. Fincham was apprenticed to the leading London organ-builder Henry Bevington in 1842 and later worked as a foreman with J.C. Bishop in London before emigrating to Melbourne in 1852. Building and equipping a new factory in Richmond, his first instrument was completed in 1862. From small beginnings, the firm prospered, and by the end of the century had built almost 150 new organs for churches and public halls in four Australian states and

NZ. Initially adopting mechanical action, the firm developed a new system of tubular-pneumatic action which was used for many instruments from the late 1880s onwards. Fincham's workers were fully occupied in 1880 building the grand organ for the Melbourne International Exhibition of that year, a four-manual instrument of 70 stops, one of the largest in the world at the time. Fincham placed instruments in many exhibitions, winning prize medals for their excellence of construction. The firm had a subsidiary branch in Adelaide 1881–94, initially under the direction of Arthur Hobday (1851–1911), who was in partnership with Fincham until 1896 when he departed for NZ. During the boom period of the 1880s the firm built no less than 57 instruments, but only 26 were built in the following decade owing to the Depression. These were characterised by the use of spotted metal pipework, low wind pressures, generally complete choruses and multi-towered cases. Prominent instruments from the later 19th century included the Melbourne Exhibition organ (1880), Freemasons Hall, Melbourne (1888), the Australian Church, Melbourne (1890), St Kilda Town Hall (1892), St Joseph's, Warrnambool (1892) and St Mary's Star-of-the-Sea, West Melbourne (1898–1900).

Fincham took his son Leslie (1879–1955) into partnership in 1901 and in 1904 opened a branch in Sydney. Upon his father's death in 1910, Leslie assumed control of the firm, which became a limited company in 1920. During the 1920s and 30s competition with other firms for the limited work often available resulted in fewer contracts, but 41 organs were built at this time, all with tubular-pneumatic action and a tonal palette emphasising unison sounds rather than upperwork. Prominent organs of this period included the Anglican and Catholic cathedral organs in Ballarat and St John's, Clifton Hill, together with a rebuilding of the Hobart Town Hall organ. After World War II, the firm responded to the demand for new and rebuilt organs under the direction of George B. Fincham (b 1917), adopting almost exclusively electropneumatic actions, well-engineered mechanisms and an expanding tonal palette, including upperwork. Many standardised organs were produced on the extension principle at an affordable cost. The firm's major work at this time was the four-manual organ in St Patrick's Cathedral, Melbourne (opened 1964). Later, many instruments were built with mechanical action, total encasement and classical voicing under the supervision of David G. Fincham (b 1944), these including organs for NSW, Victoria and SA.

The firm still remains at its original site in Richmond and has been responsible for building more than 300 new organs together with many rebuildings and restorations through its 130-year history.

FURTHER REFERENCE
E.N. Matthews, *Colonial Organs and Organbuilders* (Melbourne: MUP, 1969); Graeme Rushworth, 'A Century Plus of Fincham Organs', *OHTA News* 19/2 (Apr. 1995), 10–21.

JOHN MAIDMENT

Finn, Tim (Brian Timothy)   (*b* Te Awamutu, NZ, 25 June 1952), singer, pianist, songwriter. Founder of the successful NZ band Split Enz, with whom he recorded eight albums including the chart topper *True Colours* (1980). Finn's debut solo album *Escapade* (1983) and single *Fraction Too Much Friction* both hit No. 8 in Australia, and in 1984 he left Split Enz to pursue a solo career. He joined his brother Neil's band, ★Crowded House, to record its third album *Woodface* (1990), but in 1992 returned to solo recording. He recorded *Attitude* (1995) with Liam O'Mainlai and Andy White under the name ALT, and later collaborated with brother Neil to record *FINN* (1995).

FURTHER REFERENCE
Recordings with Split Enz include *Mental Notes* (1975, Mushroom L 35588); *True Colours* (1980, Mushroom L 37167); *Corroboree* (1982, Mushroom RML 53001); *Anniversary* (1993, Mushroom D 98010); solo albums *Escapade* (1983, Mushroom RML 53104); *Big Canoe* (1986, Virgin V 2369); *Tim Finn* (1989, Capitol ST 748735); *Before & After* (1993, EMI 0777 7 94904 2 4); *The Magnificent Nose* (1994, BMG); with Crowded House *Woodface* (1990, Capitol 793559–2); with ALT *Attitude* (1995, EMI 8324472); and with the Finn Brothers *FINN* (1995, EMI 7243 8 35632 2 7). See also M. Chunn, *Stranger than Fiction: The Life and Times of Split Enz* (Wellington: GP Publications, 1992); *CA* (1995–96); *GuinnessP*; D. Rees and L. Crampton, eds, *Rock Movers and Shakers* (Santa Barbara, CA: ABC-CLIO, 1991); *SpencerW*.

AARON D.S. CORN

Finsterer, Mary   (*b* 25 Aug. 1962), composer. She studied with Brenton Broadstock at the University of Melbourne, then as an Australia Council fellow at Amsterdam in 1993. She has won the Dorian Le Gallienne, Ian Potter, Albert Maggs, and Alfred Bequest awards for composition. Rapid and early success with works, frequently using an aggressive, confrontational style, gave her performances by the Melbourne, Sydney, Queensland and Tasmanian Symphony Orchestras, as well as by Elision, Le Nouvel Ensemble Moderne, the Pittsburgh New Music Ensemble, the Sydney Metropolitan Opera, Paris Rostrum (prize 1992), CBC Radio Canada, and the BBC. In 1992–3 she was composer-in-residence with the Sydney Symphony Orchestra. She has written for opera, large and small orchestral forces, ensembles, electronic combinations, cabaret-theatre and film.

WORKS
Principal publisher: Ricordi.

Orchestral   *Atlas* (1988), *Continuum* (1991), *Nextwave Fanfare* (1992, Ricordi), *Scat*, chromatic harmonica, Orchestra (1993, Ricordi), *Cor* (1994, Ricordi).

Chamber Instrumental   *Sentence for Dinner*, S, fl (1986) *Cyme*, gui, perc (1988), *Madam He*, S, ob, vc, pf (1988), *Ruisselant*, chamber orch (1991, Ricordi), *Triplice*, soprano sax, bass cl, pf (1992, Ricordi), *Catch*, soprano sax, bass cl, pf (1992, Ricordi), *Scimmia*, 17 str (1994, Ricordi).

Solo Instrumental   *Tract,* vc (1993, Red House Editions).
Vocal   *Omaggio alla Pieta,* 6 vv, db (optional), perc (1993, Ricordi).

FURTHER REFERENCE
Recordings include *Tract,* D. Pereira, vc (Tall Poppies TP075). There are ABC, Le Nem, and CBC Canada tapes of her works. See also *BroadstockS.*

THÉRÈSE RADIC

Fire At Ross's Farm.   Ballet by James *Penberthy (1961) after the Henry Lawson story. First performed at Perth in 1961.

Fire on the Wind.   Opera in two acts, music and libretto by Colin *Brumby, after the play by Anthony Coburn. Excerpt performed in workshop by the Lyric Opera of Queensland on 25 September 1991.

First Christmas, The.   Christmas opera in one act by John *Antill, libretto by Pat Flower. First heard on ABC radio on Christmas Day 1969.

Fisenden, Owen Hunt   (*b* Sandringham, Vic., 12 Nov. 1927; *d* 4 Mar. 1984), flautist. After studying with Leslie *Barklamb at the University Conservatorium, Melbourne, he played principal flute for J.C. Williamson's productions and the Victorian Ballet, then in the West Australian Orchestra, 1950–83. He developed a large teaching practice, teaching flute at Perth Modern School and the University of Western Australia, and became founding president of the WA Flute Society in 1972. He made a study tour of Europe and Japan on a Churchill fellowship in 1975, and published *Formula for Fluting* (Albert, 1976). The premier flute teacher in WA and one of the longest serving players in any ABC orchestra, after his untimely death from cancer his son Owen succeeded him as principal flute in the West Australian Symphony Orchestra.

Fisher, James Churchill   (*b* Portsmouth, England, 1826; *d* Parramatta, NSW, 22 Mar. 1891), music educator. He emigrated to NSW in 1852 and was conductor of the Sydney Choral Society. He introduced the tonic sol-fa teaching method to NSW through adult singing classes and, after various positions as a schoolmaster, was appointed as singing master to Sydney schools and teacher training colleges. He initiated tonic sol-fa teaching in public schools in 1863; it was adopted as the official music teaching method in 1867. He composed school songs and cantatas, and published several tonic sol-fa song-books and a textbook.

FURTHER REFERENCE
R.S. Stevens, Music in State-Supported Education in New South Wales and Victoria, 1848–1920, PhD, Univ. Melbourne, 1978.

R. S. STEVENS

Fisher, Sylvia Gwendoline Victoria   (*b* Melbourne, 18 Apr. 1910; *d* Melbourne, 25 Aug. 1996), soprano. Fisher studied singing at the Albert Street Conservatorium with Mary Campbell, then for 11 years with Adolf Spivakovsky, winning the Melbourne *Sun* Aria (1936), and singing on ABC radio in concert and opera. In 1947 she went to England, which became the almost exclusive focus of her career. Her debut in a complete operatic role was at Covent Garden as Leonora *(Fidelio)* on 9 December 1948, the first of 326 peformances in 19 roles there; she was the house's leading dramatic soprano of the 1950s. Fisher returned to Australia for an ABC concert and recital tour in 1955 and for the Australian Elizabethan Theatre Trust in 1958.

Although distinguished as a Wagnerian, especially as Isolde, the *Walküre* Brünnhilde, and Sieglinde (the last generally regarded as the finest heard in Britain in the postwar period), and as Strauss's Marschallin, as the 1950s progressed she began increasingly to concentrate on 20th-century repertoire. She triumphed in British premieres as Mother Marie (*Dialogues des Carmélites*) and as Kostelnička *(Jenůfa).* Most important, however, was her association with Benjamin Britten, especially 1963–71 as part of the English Opera Group. She was notable as Ellen Orford (*Peter Grimes*), the Female Chorus (*The Rape of Lucretia*), Lady Billows (*Albert Herring*), Queen Elizabeth (*Gloriana*), Mrs Grose (*Turn of the Screw*), and Miss Wingrave (*Owen Wingrave*), a role written for her and which she created.

She made no commercial recordings in her prime; unpublished live recordings, including Isolde's narration and Act III of *Die Walküre,* reveal sensitivity in interpretation, and a dramatic soprano voice of great warmth and beauty. She was honoured with the AM in 1994.

FURTHER REFERENCE
Obits in London *Times,* 30 Aug. 1996 and *Age,* 18 Sept. 1996. Recordings were *Albert Herring,* cond. B. Britten (1964, Decca 421 849–2LH2); *Owen Wingrave,* cond. B. Britten (1971, Decca 430 200–2LH02); Nielsen's *Saul and David* (1972, Unicorn RHS343–5). Her writings include 'Creating a Role', *Opera* 8 (1957), 275–8. See also: *Australian,* 30 June 1995; 19 articles in *AMN* (Index in *MarsiI*); *MackenzieS;* Harold Rosenthal, *Great Singers of Today* (London: Calder & Boyars, 1966), 62–4; idem, *GroveD.*

ROYSTON GUSTAVSON

Fitzgibbon, 'Smacka' (Graham Francis)   (*b* Melbourne, 12 Feb. 1930; *d* Melbourne, 15 Dec. 1979); jazz performer, restaurateur. He began ukulele as a child, later switching to banjo. Forming the Steamboat Stompers, he freelanced in the traditional jazz scene, including with Frank Johnson. After a period in rural Victoria he resumed activity in Melbourne in the 1960s, leading bands and managing hotels and restaurants as jazz venues. In addition to playing and singing, he became prominent beyond the jazz community through entrepreneurial work, on television, and as composer of the theme for the film *The Adventures of Barry McKenzie.*

FURTHER REFERENCE
Recordings include *Len Barnard And His South City Stompers* (1949, Jazzart JA-34); *Frisco Joe's Goodtime Boys* (1953, Swaggie 1209); *Smacka* (1979, SPT 01). See also *ADB*, 14.

                                BRUCE JOHNSON

Flannery, Ken (Kenneth John) (*b* Sydney, 15 May 1927), jazz trumpeter. He began trumpet in his teens, becoming founder member and sometimes leader of the *Port Jackson Jazz Band, with which he continues to perform for reunion concerts. This association was interrupted for several periods, among them military service and travel overseas. He freelanced extensively in nightclubs, and played in jazz concerts and gave performances with Frank Coughlan. From late 50s he was also active in television orchestras and as a member of the NSW Police Concert Band until retiring in 1992. He was with drummer John Fearnley's Pacific Coast Jazzmen, which included an appearance at the Bix Beiderbecke Festival, USA, in 1992, and is currently freelancing.

FURTHER REFERENCE
For recordings, see Port Jackson Jazz Band. See also *BissetB*; *OxfordJ*.

                                BRUCE JOHNSON

Flash and the Pan. Name used (from 1976) by former Easybeats Harry *Vanda and George Young for their occasional pop recordings. Preferring songwriting and producing, they have rejected offers to tour, despite the success of their recordings in Europe. Their singles include *Hey St Peter* (1977) which reached No. 3 in the charts, *Down Among The Dead* (1978), which reached No. 4, and *Waiting For A Train* (1982). They have also recorded under at least seven other names (Marcus Hook Roll Band, Paintbox, Moondance, etc.).

FURTHER REFERENCE
Recordings include *Hey St Peter* (1977, Albert AP 11224), *Down Among The Dead* (1978, Albert AP 11755), *Waiting For A Train* (1982, Albert AP 927), *Tell It To The Moon* (1988, Albert); albums *Flash And The Pan* (1978, Albert APLP 035) and *The Flash And The Pan Collection* (1993, Albert 4674932). For discography, see *SpencerA*. See also *McGrathA*; *SpencerW*.

Flash Jack From Gundagai, folk-song. The boast by a nomadic shearer of his travels, coloured by his nostalgia for a property at One-Tree Plain, near Hay, NSW. Published by A.B. Paterson in *Old Bush Songs* (1905); the tune based on 'The Son of a Gambolier' collected and recorded by A.L. Lloyd (1957).

FURTHER REFERENCE
Edition and commentary in *EdwardsG*; *RadicS*, 13.

Flederman. Contemporary music ensemble (1979–89) formed to replace the Australian Contemporary Music Ensemble, Keith Humble's ensemble which had focused on new work by Australian composers. At first a duo comprised of Carl *Vine (piano) and Simone *de Haan (trombone), from 1980 it was resident at the Queensland Conservatorium as a trio, and then a sextet, adding Geoffrey *Collins (flute), Christian *Wojtowitz (cello), Graham Leake (percussion) and David Miller (piano). The group commissioned nearly 80 new Australian works, which it played on tour in all capital cities, as well as in NZ, the USA, Europe and the UK. A group whose challenging repertoire was played with flamboyance and virtuosity, it began winding down its activities after Australia Council support was reduced in 1987. They won an ARIA award in 1988.

FURTHER REFERENCE
Recordings include *Flederman 1* (LRF156) and *Flederman 2* (1988, MBS14CD). See also Simone de Haan, 'Flederman: A Retrospective Assessment', *NMA* 7 (1989), 27–29.

Flower. Songwriting brothers in Queensland, the sons of a wealthy pastoralist.

(1) Horace Flower (*b* Port Fairy, Vic., 28 Apr. 1854; *d* Brisbane, 29 June 1916), bank manager, songwriter. After schooling in England he joined the Bank of Australasia at Warrnambool in 1873, and later transferred to Brisbane, then from 1878 was with the Queensland National Bank, managing various branches until his retirement from ill health in 1901. With Walton Kent at Gatton, Queensland, in 1882 he wrote *The Dying Stockman* as a parody of a stockman's song; it was published in the *Portland Mirror* (8 July 1885) and became greatly popular.

(2) Charles Flower (*b* Port Fairy, Vic., 13 June 1856; *d* Brisbane, June 1948), station owner, songwriter. After schooling in England he worked as a jackeroo in the Riverina, in 1881 became overseer at Blythdale, east of Roma, Queensland, and from 1884 owned Durham Downs Station, which he left after the 1902 drought. He purchased Garraburra, Queensland, in 1906, a property which still remains in his family. He wrote many verses which became widely popular, including *The Broken Down Squatter, The Cabbage Tree Hat* and *1,000 Miles Away*.

FURTHER REFERENCE
Charles Flower's verses are preserved in ms, now in the Oxley Library, Brisbane. See also *Australian Tradition* 2/1 (May 1965), 3; Peter Hay, ed. *Meeting of Sighs: The Folk Verse of Victoria's Western District* (Warrnambool, Vic.: Warrnambool Institute Press, 1981); Alexander Henderson, *Henderson's Australian Families* (Melbourne: A. Henderson, 1941).

Flowers. See *Icehouse*.

Floyd, A(lfred) E(rnest) (*b* Birmingham, England, 5 Jan. 1877; *d* Armadale, Vic., 13 Jan. 1974), organist, broadcaster. In 1890 his family moved to Cambridge, where Floyd attended the Leys School and was accepted as an organ pupil by A.H. Mann, organist of King's College in the University of Cambridge. After leaving school he took up the position of assistant organist to G.B. Arnold (a favourite pupil of Samuel Sebastian Wesley) at Winchester Cathedral. Here he conceived his lifelong enthusiasm for Wesley's music. In February 1915 Floyd arrived in Melbourne to take up the position of organist and choirmaster of St Paul's Cathedral; he had been appointed from a field of 200 applicants. His success at the cathedral was immediate. In September 1917 the degree of MusDoc was conferred on him by the Archbishop of Canterbury on the recommendation of a group of leading English church musicians who had visited Melbourne.

During Floyd's 32 years at the cathedral, his influence permeated its musical life. The superb standard maintained by the choir in daily and Sunday services was recognised as equal to that of the best of the English cathedrals. His specialities were the extemporisations before the service, much in the Mann–Wesley style, his accompaniments of the psalms, which paralleled the light and shade of the words, and his vital accompaniment of canticles and anthems. From his early days he was from time to time an examiner for the University of Melbourne Conservatorium, and for many years he lectured on music for the Workers' Educational Association and until 1963 for the Council of Adult Education. In 1933–34 he made a brief foray into music journalism as music critic for the *Argus*, enjoying the spate of concertgoing despite its excessive demands, and for many years he broadcast a weekly program, *Music Lover's Hour*, on ABC radio. He resigned his cathedral post, still at the peak of his powers, in May 1947.

Floyd's influence on music in Australia cannot be overrated. When one considers the numerous organists he taught, the successive choirs he influenced, his empathy with schools such as Methodist Ladies' College, one is confronted by a powerful figure indeed. Precise, but with an impish sense of humour, he quickly won over his audiences in lectures, and on radio his genius lay in bringing good music, carefully selected, to ordinary people. There was a sense of national loss when his usual radio farewell, 'Goodbye till next time', had to be 'Goodbye'. He was awarded the OBE in 1948, and in 1971 an honorary DLitt from Monash University.

FURTHER REFERENCE
His writings include 'In Search of Australian Organ Music', *Canon* 6/11 (June 1953), 475–7. See also W.F. Chappell, *ADB*, 8; idem, 'A.E. Floyd', *AJME* 13 (Oct. 1973), 15–19.   W. F. CHAPPELL

Fly. Opera (1984) by Barry ★Conyngham, libretto by Murray Copland. Tells of the achievements of explorer and aviation pioneer Lawrence Hargrave (1850–1915) and his search for recognition. First performed 25 August 1984, Victorian State Opera, State Theatre, Melbourne. Recorded by Move Records; published by Universal, 1984.

Flying Circus. Country-rock band (1969–74) formed in Sydney, comprised chiefly Greg Grace (vocals), James Wynne and Doug Rowe (guitars), Warren Ward (bass), and Colin Walker (drums). In 1969 they released their first single, *Hayride*, then *La La*, which reached No. 9 in the charts, and their debut album *Flying Circus*. They won the Battle of the Sounds in 1970, then worked in Canada, recording *Finding My Way* (1971) and revisiting Australia twice. After touring as support for Lighthouse, two of the members joined that band, and Flying Circus disbanded. Despite pressure to aim its singles at the pop market, it remained largely a country-rock band in its sound.

FURTHER REFERENCE
Recordings include *Hayride* (Columbia DO 8617), *La La* (Columbia DO 8775), *Flying Circus* (Columbia SCX O7907), and *Finding My Way* (1971, HMV EA 9608). A compilation is *Steam Trains And Country Lanes* (1977 EMI EMA 326). For discography, see *SpencerA*. See also *McGrathA*; *SpencerW*; *GuinnessP,* I, 883–4.

Flying Emus, The. New country band (1984–90), originally comprised of Genni Kane (acoustic guitar, vocals), her brother John Kane (acoustic guitar, mandolin, vocals), Michael Kerin (fiddle, mandolin, vocals) Ian Simpson (acoustic and electric guitars, banjo, vocals), Michael Vidale (bass), and Hanuman Dass (drums). As the acoustic band Stage Fright, they played Hank Williams and Patsy Cline covers, then went full-time and pioneered the new country sound in Australia, incorporating the bluegrass skill of Simpson and Kerin with western swing, rockabilly and pop. Their works were chiefly written by the Kanes, including *Emu Strut* (1987), *Jackeroo* (1988) and *Dixie Breakdown* (1991). A spontaneous, amusing stage act, they recorded four albums and won two ACMA Golden Guitars.

FURTHER REFERENCE
Recordings included their debut *Look Out Below* (1985, Larrikin), and *Thankyou And Goodnight* (1990, Festival D30471). See also *LattaA,* 106–7; *APRAJ* 6/1 (Jan. 1988), 18–19.

FMusA. Fellowship in Music, Australia. Established in 1992, it is now the highest diploma awarded by the AMEB. Quite unlike the British FRSM or FTCL, the diploma is awarded after a full evening public recital, at which the standards of a professional concert soloist must be demonstrated. So far, fewer than 20 have been awarded each year. The AMEB also occasionally makes honorary awards of the diploma to distinguished musicians who have made an outstanding contribution to its work.

Fogg, Anthony (*b* Sydney), pianist, administrator. He was tutor at the University of NSW and artistic director of the Seymour Group, as well as a piano soloist chiefly in contemporary works in broadcast and concert with the ABC. From 1986 he was head of orchestral programming for the ABC in Sydney, greatly influencing the direction and character of repertoire and bringing an expansion in the audience base to the orchestras. In 1994 he became artistic administrator of the Boston Symphony Orchestra, where he continues to make occasional appearances as a pianist.

FURTHER REFERENCE
Recordings include Sculthorpe, Piano Concerto, Melbourne Symphony Orchestra (ABC 426 483). See also *CA* (1995–96).

Folded Leaf. See *Gumleaf.*

Foley, A(llan) J(ames) [Signor Foli] (*b* Cahir, Tipperary, 7 Aug. 1835; *d* Southport, Lancashire, England, 20 Oct. 1899), bass. After working as a carpenter Foley studied with Bisaccia at Naples and sang in Italian houses, joining Mapelson's Opera Co. in London in 1865 and appearing at Covent Garden and in Europe. His roles included Bertram (*Robert le diable*), Daland, Saint-Bris (*Les Huguenots*) and the title role in Rossini's *Mosé,* and he made many concert appearances in the UK. After his retirement from the stage in London, he came to Australia in 1892 as 'Signor Foli' in a concert tour with English tenor Orlando Harley and pianist Edouard Scharff, and sang with Fanny *Simonsen's Opera Co. (under Williamson's management).

FURTHER REFERENCE
Harold Rosenthal, *GroveD.*

Foley, Griffen James Joseph (*b* Hyderabad, Pakistan, 1872; *d* Chatswood, Sydney, 12 May 1924), bass, music critic of Irish parents. After studying singing in Italy for four years, he went to London, singing in cathedral choirs and appearing as Leporello in *Don Giovanni,* and came to Australia *c.*1900. He settled first at Dubbo, then at Sydney, singing in Philip Newbury's popular concerts at the Town Hall, working as choirmaster at All Saints, Woollahra, teaching and giving concerts with his pupils as the Griffen Foley Choristers and the Euterpean Society. He became music critic for the Sydney *Star* (1909), then retired from singing and was music and theatre critic for *The Sun* (from 1910), also writing for the *Australian Musical News,* the *Musical Times* (UK) and the *Musical Courier* (USA). A perceptive critic of vocal performance, his scathing style had developed for him a long list of enemies by the time of his death from cancer.

FURTHER REFERENCE
Obit. in *SMH* 14 May 1924; Sydney *Sun* 14 May 1924; *AMN,* 2 June 1924. See also John Carmody, *ADB,* 9.

Folk Music.
1. 19th-Century Vernacular Songs. 2. 19th-Century Social Dance Music. 3. Other Cultures and Traditions. 4. The 20th Century. 5. Sources and Collections.

In Australia, the term usually refers to styles of 19th-century vernacular song and social dance music, as well as to more recent musical genres which assert an affinity with traditional oral/aural genres through relatively unmediated performance, or a tacit or explicit assertion of the importance of musical community. Although many commentators are uncomfortable with the term, it is widely used.

1. 19th-Century Vernacular Songs. (i) Genres and History. White colonial Australia was founded on the convict transportations to the colonies of eastern Australia and convicts and their descendants formed the majority of the white population until the massive immigration of the goldrush of 1853 to 1860. Both convicts and free settlers came from diverse areas and social backgrounds, and many of them brought to Australia the song cultures of Britain and Ireland of the 19th century, which included street ballads, popular theatrical songs, local, regional and ceremonial songs, and other forms of narrative vocal music. Among lower-class groups, and especially itinerant rural workers, some of this music continued to be performed, and it became the basis of the composition of songs in a similar style. Many narrative broadside ballads current in the British Isles remained popular, but songs which were closely associated with specific regions or social groups quickly dropped out of currency. Singers of anonymous traditional ballads typically also performed popular songs deriving from published sources and public entertainment. From the 1850s onwards, minstrel shows and popular theatre became the major sources not only of songs for informal performance but also of tunes to which the popular localised verses would be set.

Local composition of vernacular songs began in the convict era. In 1820 the composition of narrative ballads celebrating the desperate exploits of escaped convicts was noted in the journal of a ship's surgeon. Bushranger ballads, almost always sympathetic accounts of social banditry and heroic defiance, continued throughout the 19th century. Of particular popularity were several compositions by the convict poet Frank *MacNamara, 1830–50. His verse, widely disseminated among convicts and others, both orally and in manuscript form, includes the lyrical Irish-style song *Moreton Bay,* which details the cruelties of a convict's life set to a melody from a widely used Irish tune family.

Several songs preserved by oral transmission into the 20th century come from the goldrush, 1853–63. Some depict the persona of the roving labourer, and are set to traditional tunes. Working in a discernibly different idiom—theatrical popular song rather than traditional balladry—the prolific goldfields entertainer Charles *Thatcher composed and performed topical narratives and commentaries. Many of these were localised parodies of popular songs. Judging by reports of his contemporary reception and the success of his published song-books, his work was widely known, but its topicality was ephemeral; few of his songs outlasted the memory of his own performance. However, his work typifies one style of 19th-century popular song-making: based, often as parody, on *volkstümlich* ('folksy'), minstrel show and popular theatrical tunes, and on well-known verse forms and themes.

Most of the occupational songs of itinerant workers (shearers, drovers, bullock drivers and the like), which make up the best-known part of the Australian folk-song canon, come from the period 1860–90, though 19th-century commentators suggest that localised songs were being composed even before the goldrush period. The creative impulse was generally poetic and literary as much as musical, and songs were conceived as verse set to well-known traditional, minstrel show or even parlour ballad airs. Such verse is to be found in newspapers, union journals, personal manuscript collections, and songsters of the period.

The bush ballad verse style was widely practised by the popular writers of the 1880s and 1890s, particularly Henry *Lawson and Banjo *Paterson, and some of their published poems became part of a song repertoire used by the rural workers, whom they heroised. In 1898 Paterson began to collect Australian vernacular ballads, and in 1905 his *Old Bush Songs* appeared, which brought together many texts from other publications and correspondents. After a lull in the first 30 years of the 20th century, a related musical tradition re-emerged in a new form in the newly available musical style of hillbilly music, and Australian country music continues to produce bush ballads for rural audiences (see *Country Music*).

(ii) Musical Structure, Performance Style and Performance Context.   The musical evidence from the 19th century is scant and elusive. We can draw guarded conclusions from the titles of popular tunes cited as airs to which published poetic texts might be sung, as well as from 20th-century sound recording collections. Therefore the descriptions of style given here refer both to presumed 19th-century practice, and to 20th-century performance practice, of singers who appear to have continued a style.

The strophic narrative song was the dominant form of Australian vernacular song, with two or four balanced musical phrases. Unaccompanied singing seems to have been the norm in domestic and other small-group contexts of performance. Musical phrase lengths can be subject to extension or contraction to fit a text, a practice which may sometimes give rise to asymmetric rhythmic patterns. Tunes using major diatonic scales predominate, but there are some modal tunes, sometimes with a tendency towards flexible or indefinite pitch levels at the third and seventh degrees of the scale, creating a fluctuating or indefinite modality. Many of these songs use the prosodic and melodic model of the *Come All Ye* ballad, with a 6/8 pattern, gapped scales and an ABBA melodic phrase structure. Sometimes these tunes are truncated to a simple AB form.

Many commentators, associated with radical-nationalist historiography, have identified a strong Irish influence in Australian traditional song. But as Waters points out, it is scarcely possible to isolate distinct Irish, English, and Scottish provenances for traditional songs from the 18th century onwards. Although some songs can easily be traced to Irish models, the English and Scottish origins of other traditional songs, song makers and song performers may well be equally important. Popular song tunes from theatrical and popular entertainments were usually simplified to a four–line structure with modulations eliminated. Typical tune provenances of a selection of Australian traditional and popular songs are given in Radic's *A Treasury of Favourite Australian Folk Songs* and *Songs of Australian Working Life*. Nineteenth-century accounts of the socio-musical context and performance style locate this music in informal entertainments of itinerant rural workers and contractors such as shearers, bullock drivers and the like. Henry Lawson's short story 'The songs they used to sing' is a fictional account of such an informal musical gathering which indicates aspects of repertoire, performance style, and social significance of traditional and popular songs in the 1850s.

Contemporary accounts of singing style suggest a general similarity to performance idioms in Britain and America. Writers make observations such as 'the bushman drones the melody through his nose', 'is accompanied by a rattling chorus', 'invariably finishes the song with the last three words spoken', and always appears 'to sing without instrumental accompaniment'. This clearly is describing a musical style close to that practised by traditional rural singers of Britain and Ireland, and recordings made in the 1950s of older performers, born from about 1880 onwards, show similar musical styles. The pace of textual delivery is often quite slow, with relatively little melodic variation or ornamentation. The recordings *Traditional Singers of Victoria* (1960) and *A Garland for Sally* (1983) illustrate this stylistic approach well.

2. 19th-Century Social Dance Music. (i) Genres and History.   During the 19th century there was a great expansion of public dancing, especially of closed couples dances and of quadrille styles, and an enormous volume of dance music was composed and published. In many urban dance venues, literate musicians performed from published scores, but rural and traditional musicians were usually not music readers, and tended to play traditional tunes or modified versions of published music which were orally learnt. In these the modulation and thematic development found in literate composed dance music was modified to the simpler alternating binary structures of traditional dance music. The dances favoured in the 19th century were waltzes, polkas, polka mazurkas, varsoviennes, various versions of quadrilles (especially the lancers and the alberts), as well as group dances such as the haymaker's jig, Sir Roger de Coverley, the scotch reel, and others.

Tunes to accompany these dances are the most common legacy of 19th-century instrumental music found among some older Australian rural players today. Polka tunes were popular, both for closed couples dances and for parts of quadrilles. Waltzes were often derived from popular songs or published dance tunes, often simplified. Schottisches, varsoviennes and polka mazurkas all have distinctive rhythmic and phrasing structures.

As well as group and couples dances, solo step dancing was common for display and competitions, and the tunes usually called for were of the hornpipe or clog-dance type. These tunes were usually in the familiar 16- or 32-bar duple time pattern, usually played with a characteristic dotted inequality between the constituent quaver notes. Many Irish and Scottish settlers continued stepdancing and with it the required musical genres. Among Irish immigrants there were skilful players of dance music, some of whom are documented by the turn-of-the-century historian of Irish dance music, Francis O'Neill. Manuscript tune-books from the 19th century give evidence of literate violin players who played a traditional dance tune repertoire as well as a functional group dance repertoire. Highland bagpipe playing was particularly widespread, and, to this day, piping flourishes in Australia.

(ii) Dance Music Instruments. The most popular instruments were, overwhelmingly, the single-action free-reed instruments: the button accordion, the mouth-organ, and the Anglo-German concertina. These have similar tuning systems, and many performers played all of them. Their single diatonic scale eliminated accidentals and modulations. Twentieth-century players almost always use the tonic and dominant bass buttons in a vamping style, and frequently double the melodic notes in octaves. Playing is relatively unornamented, but well measured with great attention paid to a clear and consistent dance rhythm. It is likely that 19th-century players used similar styles. Concertinas almost always were of the Anglo-German system. Players probably tended to use octave doubling to reinforce a single melody line, and, to a greater extent than accordion players, developed playing styles which made good use of a variety of alternative fingering and phrasing patterns.

All of these free-reed instruments were imported in great numbers during the second half of the 19th century, and some concertinas were manufactured in Australia. Penny whistles and jaws harps were also popular. These latter instruments, along with *gumleaf playing, which uses a folded leaf as a free double reed aerophone, tended to be used for personal entertainment rather than to provide practical dance accompaniment.

Fiddle players were also common. They almost invariably used the instrument in the first position, open string style of British and American traditional fiddlers, playing in the keys of D, G and A major and occasionally in related modal minor keys. Tone was often thin and light, and ornamentation limited to a few upper grace notes. This style can be heard on the recordings of Harry Cotter and Charlie *Batchelor listed below in the discography. (See also *Folk instrument making.*)

3. Other Cultures and Traditions. Almost all of the non-Aboriginal population of 19th-century Australia came from Britain and Ireland. German settlers were the next most populous group, comprising between 5 and 10 per cent of the population, although unevenly distributed. However, the social dance practice of the 19th century was pan-European, and current researchers are suggesting that European migrants may have had a more active influence on traditional dance music in Australia than has previously been recognised.

Other cultural groups prominent in the 19th century, such as the Chinese and the Pacific Islander indentured labourers, may have practised traditional informal musical genres, but these have gone unnoted except for some items collected by Edwards in North Queensland. Australian Aborigines, of course, had a socio-musical culture so distinct from that of European immigrants that virtually no musical syncretism occurred, except possibly for transmission of the techniques of gumleaf playing. However, Aborigines, Melanesians, and Islanders in conditions of cultural contact have been knowledgable users of European traditional musical forms, and the most highly skilled players of traditional dance music in recent years have been Aborigines.

Other traditional music genres such as children's play songs, or male bawdy and obscene songs flourish in 20th-century Australia, and no doubt equivalent music existed in the 19th century.

4. The 20th Century. Folk genres diminished in popularity during this century. Although collectors in the 1950s were able to locate a number of performers of narrative ballads typical of 19th-century vernacular performance, by the 1970s there were few performers whose repertoire and style had been maintained through the types of face-to-face interaction and performance described above. But the folk revival movements of the 1950s and 1960s gave a new public currency to this material.

(i) Revivals. By the late 19th century, songs associated with earlier periods had begun to be accorded a national significance, in particular among the urban-based mythologisers of the *Bulletin* writers and poets. In this atmosphere Paterson set about collecting the texts which were to make up his *Old Bush Songs.* Publication of poems and song texts in newspapers continued, and one column edited by Alexander *Vennard ('Ben Bowyang') in the *North Queensland Register* published many songs and recitations, often contributed by readers. These were issued in a series of reciters in the 1920s and 30s. But none of these solicitations and publications included tunes. In the early 1940s in the Melbourne *Sun,* a column, 'The Songs of Yesteryear', appeared which stimulated the atten-

tion of musicologist Dr Percy *Jones, who contacted a small number of contributors and notated their tunes. These songs were given public prominence by the American folk-singer Burl Ives, who performed them in his Australian tour, and they were published in 1953 in *The Burl Ives Folio of Australian Songs*.

In the late 1940s and early 50s, the left intelligentsia and the labour movement were vigorously promoting a radical nationalism based on the promotion of Australian culture, and stressing the concept of folk. With the success of the folk-musical *Reedy River* in 1953, the small group of writers, performers, and general enthusiasts began to constitute the core of a socio-musical movement. From this period a number of collectors started to work and the vast majority of the material which we know as Australian folk music was collected, edited or assembled in this period. Organisations such as the Sydney Bush Music Club and the *Victorian Folk Music Club were formed. This movement was greatly inspired by the public folk revivals of the USA and UK, and in general public performance involved the use of accompaniment. The performers in *Reedy River* had used an assemblage of popular instruments including button accordion and *lagerphone, and this became the model of a 'bush band', an entirely fabricated but popular instrumental model for accompaniment, which developed further in the 1970s.

From about 1963, the international folk boom struck Australia. Folk clubs and coffee shops appeared where the individual singer-guitarist could perform. Australian folksongs, as collected during the decade before, became part of the public repertoire, and performers such as Gary *Shearston, Lionel Long and Lenore *Somerset became popular figures singing Australian songs. Material from other British, Irish, Anglo-American and Afro-American sources were just as commonly performed. In this early period the powerful British folk club movement was extremely influential on performers. One of these, Martyn Wyndam Reed was a well-known performer of Australian traditional song strongly influenced by the English singer and scholar A.L. *Lloyd, who had lived in outback New South Wales in the 1930s, and had influential views on Australian rural balladry. Many British and Irish immigrants became the conduit of the British folk-club movement's organisational styles and performance practices, and the authoritative and somewhat elitist posture of the performer which it fostered.

By the late 1960s performers were generally thought of as either 'traditional' or 'contemporary'. The 'traditional' category contained a few imitators of oral performance sources, but many were singer-guitarists with distinctive personal styles and a conscious attempt to place their performance with respect to traditional vocal and instrumental genres. Important performers were Declan *Affley, Michael *O'Rourke, Peter *Parkhill and Margret *RoadKnight. The 'contemporary' category was at this stage relatively less important in folk-clubs and festivals. Folk-song had become an adjunct to the popular

music movement, the audience tended to be lower middle class, tertiary students and professionals, and maintained a left-liberal or radical stance. Even when the first flush of fashion of the mid-1960s evaporated, the folk movement continued until around 1980 to attract young audiences and performers. In the early 1970s folk-clubs situated in pubs began to emerge, parallel to the development of pub-rock. Electrified groups, the new bush bands, became a standard mode of presentation of Australian material. Instrumental musical styles became more widely practised and competently played, and Irish dance music, bluegrass, and 'Old timey' American music were the most influential of these.

By the late 1970s, although bush bands such as the *Bushwackers and the *Cobbers had gained a new public following, and the explicitly radical folk/rock group *Redgum was popular beyond the insular folk-club movement, the audience attracted to folk music had began to age significantly. This led to a gradual demise of the importance of folk-clubs, but there was a corresponding growth in folk festivals as performance venues and centres of the organisation of the folk music scene. National folk festivals had been held in capital cities since the late 1960s, and various regional festivals grew up during the 1970s. In the 1980s some developed into massive popular music festivals which staged a great diversity of musical genres.

In the early 1980s the domination of the Anglo-Celtic repertoire was challenged by a number of groups inspired by other musical styles. Latin-American performers and groups associated with the new song movement and Andean music movement of Chile were often seen in folk-clubs and festivals. Also a number of poly-ethnic fusion groups such as *Sirocco and Tansey's Fancy became well known, and with them a repertoire which made reference to traditions from *Eastern Europe and the Middle East. In almost all cases, the performers were Anglo-Australians, although they were often thought of as representative of the new Australian spirit of multicultural pluralism. As a popular music cluster outside the commercial mainstream, this movement has gained considerable support from the ABC as its major promoter and sponsor.

With the diversification of genres performed, the folk movement's idea of folk music has increasingly become associated with live performance, relatively unmediated by the music industry and supported by some ideal of a musical community. Those outside the movement itself may be more likely to think of these genres as world music and acoustic performance. Such categorisations, like that of folk music, often disclose other commentators' ideas of the place of music in society.

(ii) Non-Anglophone Traditions and Movements. Within the communities of postwar migrants to Australia, various musical styles flourished in informal social performance, in officially sponsored ethnic and community organisations, and in popular entertainment contexts. Some of these have attracted the attention of broader community audiences seeking new genres to imagine as 'authentic' folk genres, as representations of a new multicultural Australia, or as stylistic alternatives to established popular music styles. For example, among *Greek immigrants a range of narrative ballads, romances, and dance songs are known to the older generation of rural immigrants. These might be performed in domestic, relatively private circumstances. Traditional folk dance ensembles have been vigorously promoted among second-generation immigrants as a vehicle for ethnic cultural preservation and the public presentation of ethnicity and regional identification. A number of performers of traditional dance music on such instruments as the lyras of Pontis and Crete, and the widespread clarino and santouri, have found audiences to sustain their skill in Australia. Similarly, the urban popular style of rebetika music has had some public prominence in the folk revival, particularly as promoted by second-generation performers inspired by a revival in Greece, whose performance aesthetics and self-presentation are consonant with the Anglo-Australian folk movement.

Similar ranges of social uses of traditional music styles, from private domestic use through to ethnic community entertainment and ritual contexts, have also been seen in other European and Middle-Eastern ethnic communities in the postwar period. A few groups and performers from these backgrounds have gained a public stage in the Anglo-Australian folk revival movement, particularly those whose style of presentation has been shaped by other revivalist movements. Various Hungarian, Bulgarian and Balkan groups, as well as almost totally naturalised Irish traditional musicians, have offered music from their own cultural bases in styles of presentation which anglophone audiences find easy to accept.

In the mid-1990s, the redefinitions offered by world music challenge some of the ideologies of the folk revival movement and offer other positions from which to hear and understand non-mainstream musical styles. This will no doubt contribute to a further weakening of the category of folk music, particularly as the idealised non-commercial yet socially sanctioned music genre of informal oral traditions becomes harder to locate socially or to fantasise into being.

5. Sources and Collections. Many songs from the 19th century, usually reconstructed from text-only sources, appear in Australian folk-song collections, particularly Hugh *Anderson's *The Story of Australian Folk Song*. The two volumes of John *Meredith's *Folk Songs of Australia and the Men and Women who Sang Them* are a good sample of what remains of this repertoire among older performers in the second half of the 20th century. His field tapes, and those of several other folk-song collectors, are housed in the Australian National Library, Canberra. Many other song-books aimed at a popular market have been published since 1960. One of these, Ron *Edwards' *200 Years of Australian Folk Song*, contains an invaluable listing of

almost all publication of material identified as Australian folk-song, linked to a comprehensive bibliography. Several researchers, particularly Chris *Sullivan, have documented strong traditions of performance of European vernacular material in Aboriginal communities in the 1980s and 1990s. John *Manifold's *Who Wrote the Ballads* is a highly personal, Marxist, but nonetheless perceptive reading of Australian song-making. Edgar *Waters' article 'Folk Song' in the *Oxford Companion to Australian Folklore* is a more balanced overview of the subject. Some research into ethnic community traditional forms has taken place, notably by Peter Parkhill, whose extensive collections are housed in the National Library.

Although many recordings of revivalist reinterpretations of these musical styles have been released, only a handful of recordings of older traditional singers are of value in reconstructing 19th-century performance style. These are listed in the discography, but unfortunately the historic *Wattle recordings are no longer commercially available.

FURTHER REFERENCE
Discography
Bush Traditions, various performers, collected by and notes by Warren Fahey (LP. Larrikin records 007 [1976]); *Charlie Batchelor and his Horton River Band*. Performed by Charlie Batchelor (1897–1984) and others. Notes by Chris Sullivan. Aural Repossessions Collective ARC 002 [1985]); *A Garland for Sally*, performed by Sally Sloane (1894–1982), notes by Warren Fahey (Larrikin LRF 136 [1983]); *Harry Cotter of Binalong, N.S.W.* performed by Harry Cotter, notes by Peter Parkhill (Victorian Folk Song and Dance Society SF 276 [1975]); *Traditional Singers and Musicians in Victoria*, various performers, notes by Edgar Waters (Wattle D4, Archive series no 2. [1960]); *Australian Traditional Singers and Musicians*, various performers (Wattle D3, Archive series no. 1 [1957]).

Bibliography
EdwardsG; *ManifoldP*; *MeredithF*; *RadicT*; *RadicS*; *OxfordF*; *WatsonC*.

Anderson, Hugh, *The Story of Australian Folk Song* (Melbourne: Hill of Content, 1970).

Davey, Gwenda B., and Graham Seal, *The Oxford Companion to Australian Folklore* (Melbourne: OUP 1993).

Manifold, John, *Who Wrote the Ballads* (Sydney: Australasian Book Society, 1964).

Smith, Graeme, 'Making Folk Music', *Meanjin* 44 (1985), 477–90.

——, 'Irish Meets Folk: The Genesis of the Bush Band'. In *Music-Cultures in Contact: Convergences and Collisions*, ed. Margaret Kartomi and Stephen Blum (Sydney: Currency, 1993).

Waters, Edgar 'Folk Song', 1992. In Davey and Seal 1993, 153–66.

GRAEME SMITH

Folk Music Venues. The modern settings for folk music performance are usually found in urban centres. After the musical *Reedy River* attracted wide popular interest in Australian folk-song, folk music clubs appeared, at which folk-dancing and singing was presented; the most successful were the Bush Music Club, Sydney (from 1954) and the Victorian Bush Music Club (from 1959). After the tour of American folk-singer Pete Seeger in 1963, coffee lounges and (from the mid-1960s) pubs also began featuring local folk performers in all capital cities, such as Troubadour, Sydney and Traynors, Melbourne. The longest lived was the Folk Centre, Brisbane (founded 1964), which was active into the 1970s.

In the 1960s bush dances were also a popular platform for folk performers, as well as such television programs as *Jazz Meets Folks* in Melbourne and Gary *Shearston's *Just Folk* in Sydney. In the 1970s folk festivals became the most important outlet for folk music performance, and from the 1980s there has been a variety of annual national and regional festivals around Australia throughout the year. See individual city entries; *Australian Folk Trust*.

Ford, Adrian de Brabander   (*b* Sydney, 26 Apr. 1940), jazz pianist. He began piano at the age of eight, later adding trombone and clarinet. Joining his first band in 1963, he was then with Geoff Bull (1965–67), York Gospel Singers and rock groups; he joined Maurie Garbutt for his overseas tour 1969–71 and the Australian tour with Alvin Alcorn, 1973. He returned to Sydney and worked in numerous groups including with Bill Haesler and trumpeter Nick Boston. Forming a big band which also presented his own compositions, he has written for film and won composition awards at the Australian Jazz Conventions.

FURTHER REFERENCE

Alvin Alcorn with the Yarra Yarra Jazz Band (1973, Emulation EMU-001); *Bill Haesler's Washboard Band* (1973, Picture Records PRF-1004); *The Unity Jazz Ensemble* (1973, Picture Records PRF-1002); *Adrian Ford Big Band* (1976, Endrust Records, ER-1); *The Adrian Ford Orchestra* (1976, 44 Records 44 9288 02). See also *OxfordJ*.

BRUCE JOHNSON

Ford, Andrew   (*b* Liverpool, England, 1957), composer. He studied composition with Edward *Cowie and John Butler at the University of Lancaster, and was fellow in music, University of Bradford (1978–82), where he gained considerable experience conducting campus choirs and orchestras. His *Portraits* for piano won the 1982 Yorkshire Young Arts Composers' Award. He then followed Cowie to Australia in 1983 as lecturer in creative arts, University of Wollongong, and since then his works have been heard both in Australia and at the Salzburg Festival (1984) and Aspen (1988). He has been composer in residence for Evos, WA (1991) and the Australian Chamber Orchestra (1993–94).

A productive composer who writes in most genres, his music includes three operas for young people, five orchestral works, several works commissioned by leading Aus-

tralian chamber groups, such as the String Quartet (1986), eight works for tenor Gerald *English and five for pianist Lisa *Moore. He has appeared as conductor of various contemporary ensembles and is a frequent writer for *24 Hours* and broadcaster on music, for which he has won two Sounds Australian Awards (1989, 1990).

FURTHER REFERENCE

Recordings include his String Quartet, Sydney String Quartet (1986, ABC CD 426992); *A Cumquat for John Keats,* Lisa Moore pf (Tall Poppies, TO040); *The Art of Puffing: 17 Elegies for Thomas Chatterton,* Duo Contemporain (Tall Poppies, TP069); *The Laughter of Mermaids,* The Song Company (Vox Australis, VAST016–2); and *Whispers* Gerald English (T), Griffith University Ensemble (Tall Poppies TP069). His writings include *Composer to Composer: Conversations About Contemporary Music* (Sydney: Allen & Unwin, 1993). See also *BroadstockS*, 96–100; Margaret Drake, 'Andrew Ford', *2MBS-FM Program Guide* 16/3 (Mar. 1990). 74.

Ford, C(harles) Edgar   (*b* Upper Penn, Staffordshire, England, 26 Nov. 1881; *d* Perth, 19 July 1961), English organist, composer. He studied organ with (Alfred) Madeley Richardson at Southwark Cathedral, and composition with Charles Herbert Kitson. He took the DMus (Oxon) in 1913, and in 1920 was appointed an examiner for Trinity College of Music, London. Having first visited Australia in 1917, he settled permanently in Perth in 1941, where he became associated as organist with St Mary's Roman Catholic Cathedral. He continued to tour as an examiner in Asia, Africa and NZ, and performed widely as an organist, being admired especially for his improvisatory skills. Ford's major orchestral works include *Bushland Magic, Strange Nullarbor, Springtime in Puppet Land, Tawarri,* and an incomplete Symphony. He wrote several cantatas, including *Zuleika* and *The River,* motets and masses (two with orchestra), part-songs, piano and organ works.

FURTHER REFERENCE

Recordings of his compositions include *Australian Summer,* WA Symphony Orchestra, cond. J. Farnsworth-Hall (HMV OCLP 7632). For a list of ABC tape recordings to 1972, see *PlushD.* See also *GlennonA*, 153.

G. COX (with F. Callaway)

Forde, Florrie   [Florence Flanagan]   (*b* Fitzroy, Melbourne, 14 Aug. 1876; *d* Aberdeen, Scotland, 18 Apr. 1940), music hall singer. After running away to Sydney, Forde made her debut at the Polytechnic Music Hall in Pitt Street on 1 February 1893 singing *See Me Dance the Polka.* She also played dramatic roles in Sydney but returned to vaudeville with a long run at the Melbourne Alhambra singing the tin pan alley hit *After the Ball.* She came to prominence as principal boy in George Rignold's 1894–95 pantomime *The House that Jack Built* at Her Majesty's, Sydney. After a period working Harry *Rickards' Tivoli circuit, the offer from the British comedian G.H. Chirgwin of a three-year British contract which she refused, and a profitable benefit concert at Her Majesty's, she left for Britain in 1897.

Forde first appeared in London on 2 August that year at three venues in one night, and quickly established herself as one of British music hall's great entertainers. Not a songwriter herself, she consistently chose catchy material which she delivered in a strong voice, drilling the audience until it could join in the chorus. Songs particularly associated with her include *Has Anybody Here Seen Kelly?*, *Down at the Old Bull and Bush*, *Hold Your Hand Out*, *Naughty Boy*, *Pack up your Troubles*, and *It's a Long Way to Tipperary*. She began recording in 1903 and made about 700 records during her career. She also produced and played principal boy in pantomime annually. She died suddenly after entertaining patients in a naval hospital.

FURTHER REFERENCE

Frank Van Straten, 'Fabulous Florrie Forde', *Victorian Arts Centre Magazine* (May 1987), 21.

JENNIFER HILL

Formosa, Riccardo (*b* Rome, 1 Sept. 1954), composer. He studied at the NSW State Conservatorium, 1979–80, and with Franco Donatoni at the Accademia Nazionale di Santa Cecilia in Rome 1982–83. He has worked in Australia since 1974 as guitarist, arranger, orchestrator, conductor, producer and composer. Formosa's career has spanned both popular music, including recording credits on more than 40 LPs, and art music. His compositions include *Abacus* (1980) for harpsichord, *Sospiri* (1981) for orchestra, *Dedica* (1982) for concertante oboe and orchestra, *Tableaux (1982)* for five instruments, *Domino* (1983) for piccolo clarinet, *Pour les vingt doigts* (1983) for two pianos, *Durchfuehrung* (1984) for piano quartet, *Iter* (1985) for cello, *Silhouette* (1986) for alto flute, *Cinq variations pour Monsieur T* (1986) for piano, and *Vertigo* (1986) for four instruments. His works are significant for their concentration on a rigorous but elegant composition technique.

FURTHER REFERENCE

Recordings include *Dedica*, ob, orch (1982, VAST 015–2); *Silhouette*, alto fl, (1986 VAST007–2). See also M. Barkl, 'Riccardo Formosa's "Vertigo"', *SA* 31 (1991), 18–19, 48; *SA* 32 (1991–92), 11–19, 65; idem, Vertigo: Riccardo Formosa's Composition Technique, PhD Deakin Univ., 1994; *BroadstockS*; J. Wilkinson, 'Riccardo Formosa's "Domino"', *Ossia*. 1 (1989), 10–16.

MICHAEL BARKL

Fortified Few. Jazz band formed at Canberra by trumpeter Neil Steeper, 1966, and resident at the Hotel Dickson until disbanding in 1968. It re-formed in 1969 under the joint leadership of Steeper and trombonist John Sharpe and resumed the Dickson residency in 1970, in addition to other engagements, until disbanding in 1983,

one of the longest residencies in Australian jazz history. The band came to represent traditional jazz in Canberra for nearly two decades when the music was not always sustained elsewhere, employing mostly traditional and mainstream musicians in Canberra and the surrounding area and building a national reputation through recordings, tours and festival appearances.

FURTHER REFERENCE

Recordings include *Caught in the ACT*, The Fortified Few (1980, Jazznote JNLP 027). See also *OxfordJ*.

BRUCE JOHNSON

Foster, Roland (*b* Dundalk, Ireland, 12 July 1879; *d* Hunters Hill, Sydney, 1 Nov. 1966), singing teacher. After working as a clerk and studies with Eugène Goossens Sr and Frederick Austin at Hampstead Conservatorium and the Guildhall School, London, he came to Australia in 1913 as secretary-manager to Clara Butt and Kennerley Rumford, and joined the NSW State Conservatorium staff in 1916, becoming director of the newly formed opera department in 1934. He was founding president of the City of Sydney Eisteddfod in 1933, and adjudicated in the *Sun Aria*. An articulate and resourceful teacher, his students included Geoffrey ★Chard, Ethel ★Osborn, Raymond ★Beatty and others who went on to international careers. His success as a teacher lent authority to his various articles in *Australian Musical News* and his books *Vocal Success and How to Achieve It* (Sydney: Palings & Co, 1934) and *Competitive Singing* (Sydney: Chappell, 1955). He was honoured with the OBE in 1954.

FURTHER REFERENCE

His autobiography is *Come Listen to My Song* (Sydney: Collins, 1949); for an index to his numerous articles in *AMN* see *MarsiI*. See also H.J. Gibbney, *ADB*, 8; *GlennonA*, 241.

Fowler, Jennifer (*b* Bunbury, WA, 14 Apr. 1939), composer. After training as a teacher at the University of Western Australia, she undertook composition studies with John ★Exton and in the university electronic music studio. She taught in schools from 1962, then studied at Utrecht University electronic studio (1968), settled in London in 1969 and since 1972 has worked as a freelance composer. Her *Hours of the Day* (1968) won first prize at the Berlin Academy of the Arts in 1970, *Revelation* (1971) shared a Radcliffe Trust Award in 1971, and she won first prize for chamber music in the Mannheim International Contest for Women Composers in 1974. Since then she has also worked with choreographers in dance and with folk ensembles. Sacred subjects run through some of her works, such as *Invocation to the Veiled Mysteries* (1982). Using unpretentious ideas which she develops with wit and grace, textures involving the voice and carefully coloured ensembles of solo woodwind and strings are typical of her work, as in *Echoes From an Antique Land* (1983/6) or *And Ever Shall Be* (1989) for the BBC.

WORKS
Publisher: Universal Edition

FURTHER REFERENCE
Recordings include *Sculpture in Four Dimensions,* WA Symphony
Orchestra, cond. J. Hopkins (1970, ABC RRCS 385) and *Chimes
Fractured,* Sydney Symphony Orchestra, cond. J. Hopkins (1972,
Festival SFC 800–27). See also Thérèse Radic and Toni Calam,
GroveW; *CohenI*; *CallawayA,* 237–8.

Fowles, Glenys   (*b* Perth, 4 Nov. 1946), soprano. After
studying with Margarita Mayer at Sydney and winning
the Metropolitan Opera Auditions (Aust.), she appeared
with the WA Opera in 1968, then joined the Australian
Opera, making her debut as Octavian in *Der Rosenkavalier*
in 1969. She went to New York in 1974, studying with
Kurt Adler and singing with the New York City Opera,
then to London, studying with Jani Strasser and singing at
Glyndebourne, the Scottish Opera, and in Europe. Since
1981 she has sung with the Australian Opera, notably in
Turandot (1991) and as the Marschallin (1992). With a
vivid tone and excellent technique, combined with strik-
ing looks, her roles have included Juliet, Zerlina, Pamina,
Mélisande, Marguerite, Gilda, Poppea, Susanna, Mimi,
Sophie, Lauretta, Nanetta, and Anne Truelove.

FURTHER REFERENCE
Roger Covell, *GroveO*; Melbourne *Herald* 23 Nov 1976; *Age* 11
Aug. 1987.

Fox, Malcolm   (*b* Windsor, England, 13 Oct. 1946),
composer. After studies at the Royal College of Music
and the University of London with Alexander Goehr,
Gordon Jacob and Humphrey Searle, he became music
director of the Cockpit Theatre, London in 1972, then
settled in Australia as lecturer (later senior lecturer) at the
University of Adelaide in 1974. While his output includes
works for electronic tape and miniatures for solo instruments or chamber ensembles, it is his children's music that
is most widely known, notably the operas ★*Sid the Serpent*
(1985) and *The Iron Man* (Sue Rider and Jim Vile, after a
Ted Hughes short story, 1985), and the choral work *From
Adelaide to Alice* (1978/89).

Frampton, Roger Donald   (*b* Portsmouth, England,
20 May 1948), jazz reeds player. He changed from tuba to
saxophone and piano at secondary school in Portsmouth,
forming his first quintet at the age of 15. He emigrated to
Adelaide in 1967, becoming active in nightclubs and jazz
venues, including at the Cellar with Billy Ross, saxophonist Bob Jeffrey, Ted Nettelbeck and others, and with
Neville Dunn's big band at the 1968 Adelaide Festival of
Arts. He moved to Sydney in 1968, and was at El Rocco
with Bruce Cale, also working with bassist Dieter Vogt.
Increasingly active in experimental improvisation, he
toured Europe with David Ahern's Teletopa in 1972,
establishing the group Jazz Co-op, later joined by saxo-

phonist Howie Smith, then director of the new jazz studies program at the NSW Conservatorium.

He also began teaching at the NSW Conservatorium
in 1974, including as director in 1979. He has played support for visiting musicians including Dave Liebman, Lee
Konitz (1985 and 1995), Steve Lacey, and has performed
with expatriate American trumpeter Don Rader (1994–
95). He has composed extensively for various groups, film
and radio, and has won the NSW Jazz Action Society's
composition award. His compositions have been performed at the Sydney Opera House and the NSW Conservatorium and he has frequently toured nationally and
internationally both as a soloist and as member of Galapagos Duck, his own group Intersections, formed 1982, and
John Pochée's Ten Part Invention and its rhythm section,
the Engine Room, with which he is currently most active
as a composer and performer.

FURTHER REFERENCE
Recordings include *Jazz Co-op* (1974, Philips 6641 225); *Out To
Lunch* (1976, 44 Records 44 6357 707); *Roger Frampton* (1978,
Cherry Pie CPF-1039); *Pure Piano,* Roger Frampton, (1993, Tall
Poppies TPO19). An interview with him is in *WilliamsA,* 126–9.
See also *ClareB*; *OxfordJ*; John Clare, 'Roger Frampton And The
Resurgence Of Creative Music', *JA* (Winter/Spring 1984), 4–7;
Omar Williams, 'The Pori Jazz Festival, 1984, *JA* (Winter/Spring
1984), 7; Frampton, Roger, 'Australian Jazz', *SA* (1992); Tony
Wellington, 'Roger Frampton, A Black Sheep in Australian Jazz',
JA (Jan./Feb. 1983), 8–9.

BRUCE JOHNSON

Francis, Howard.   Brand name for a German piano
made under Australian licence. See *Carnegie.*

Francis, Leonard   (*b* Exeter, England, 1 Apr. 1866; *d*
Brisbane, 6 Apr. 1947), conductor, baritone. A choirboy
at Exeter Cathedral then a student of Pasey, Keith Con-
with and Isador de Solla, he settled in Australia, teaching at Sydney from 1903 then at Brisbane from 1905.
He conducted the largely Welsh Blackstone-Ipswich
Cambrian Choir for 20 years (from 1906), through
many competitions making it pre-eminent in Queensland choirs, winning the South Street Eisteddfod in
1908 and various other competitions. He was associated
with various other choirs as patron or president. An
outstanding choral conductor who achieved great deli-
cacy of expression, he was a warm, gregarious personality, and contributed greatly to building choral music in
Queensland to the national pre-eminence it enjoyed at
that time.

FURTHER REFERENCE
John Villaume, *ADB,* 8; *OrchardA,* 190.

Frank the Poet [Francis MacNamara]   (*b* Cashell,
Tipperary, Ireland, 1811; *d* ?Melbourne), convict balladist. Transported to Sydney for stealing a piece of cloth

at Kilkenny in 1832, his 'insolent' versifying and indomitable spirit (as well as a partiality for alcohol) brought him exceptionally frequent doses of flogging, solitary, and tours in iron gangs or on the treadmill. His seven-year sentence was repeatedly extended, and in all he was confined for 17 years. At Port Arthur, allowed to entertain his comrades on Christmas Day, he would routinely introduce himself as 'sworn to be a tyrants foe, and while I live I'll crow'. After his release he seems to have survived from singing his ballads in low-life pubs, perhaps chiefly in Melbourne, if Marcus Clarke's encounter with him (in *His Natural Life*) can be accepted as fact. In his witty recitations we can glimpse knowledge of the Bible and the classics, as well as a passionate spirit; ballads attributed to him through the scholarship of John Meredith and Rex Whalan include several which passed into folk-song, *A Dialogue Between Two Hibernians in Botany Bay*, *Labouring With the Hoe*, *The Cyprus Brig*, and best known of all, *Moreton Bay*.

FURTHER REFERENCE

John Meredith and R. Whalan, *Frank the Poet: The Life and Works of Francis MacNamara* (Ascot Vale, Vic.: Red Rooster Press, 1979); James Lester Burke, *The Adventures of Martin Cash* (1870, reprinted as *The Bushranger of Van Diemen's Land* 5th edn, Hobart: Walch, 1929); *OxfordF.*

Frankston, pop. (1991) 83 819. City on south-eastern Port Phillip Bay, now an outer suburb of Melbourne. Although established as a settlement in 1830, Frankston's popularity as a seaside resort from 1882 stimulated musical activity. Early musical performances, mainly revues and musical theatre, were held in the Mechanics' Institute, established in 1875. In 1890 the Frankston Town Band was formed, backed by a committee led by Mark W. Young; previous efforts at bands in the town, the Temperance Band and the Frankston Brass Band, had been short-lived. Led by bandmaster Dave Hannah, the group of 32 brass musicians gave regular performances in a rotunda near Frankston Pier. During the 1920s and 30s Jack Nolan's orchestra and Graeme ★Bell's Jazz Gang travelled from Melbourne to perform in Frankston dance halls. During this time the Frankston Music School, led by director Leo Collins, offered lessons in piano, violin, singing and theory of music, and the Dorothea MacMaster Pianoforte School opened its studio.

Since the late 1940s the musical life of Frankston has become increasingly active. In 1948 the Frankston Silver Band (later the Frankston City Band, 1966) was formed under the direction of Methodist minister Revd Freeman. The Peninsula Light Operatic Society began in 1962, staging musical comedy and light operetta. Its twice annual performances have included *My Fair Lady*, *The Mikado* and *Annie Get Your Gun*. In 1967 pianist Vera ★Bradford helped local music teachers form the Frankston Music Society, the administrative body for the Frankston Symphony Orchestra, which gave its first subscription concert in 1968. The Continuing Choir was founded in 1979 to accompany the orchestra in its annual oratorio. The orchestra has made regular appearances with guest artists from Melbourne. The Frankston City Highland Band, later the RSL Pipes and Drums Band (1986), was formed in 1975, and the Frankston Ladies Choir under the direction of Ted Prosser began in the same year. The Peninsula Youth Music Society was initiated in 1980 as part of a special government-sponsored enterprise, comprised of the Peninsula Orchestra, the Nemet Orchestra and the Youth Wind Ensemble. The George Jenkins Theatre at Monash University Frankston and the Frankston Cultural Centre (opened 1995) are venues for many of the local musical performances.

Frankston has an extensive history of amateur music-making. From the early brass bands to a present diversity of musical groups, music plays an important part in the life of the local community.

FURTHER REFERENCE

M.A. Jones, *Frankston: Resort to City* (Sydney: Allen & Unwin, 1989); *Parish of St. Francis Xavier, Frankston 1889–1989 Centenary Commemorative Edition* (Melbourne: Whitehorse Press, 1989); Dawne Pickup, *Changing Tides: A History of Wesley Uniting Church, Frankston 1860–1990* (Scoresby, Vic.: Magenta Press, 1990); E.C. Rowland, *Some Frankston Portraits 1909–1980* (Frankston: Frankston Secretarial Group, 1977); idem, *Further Frankston Portraits 1909–1980* (Frankston: Frankston Secretarial Group, 1984); Gwenyth Steel, *Frankston: An Outline of the District's Early History* (Melbourne: Standard Commercial Printers, 1977).

JESSICA SPICCIA

Fraser, Simon Alexander (*b* Port Arthur, Tas. 13 Feb. 1845; *d* Mansfield, Vic., 17 Apr. 1934), bagpiper of Scottish descent. A stockrider and whipmaker, he played violin, flute, accordion, concertina, and the bagpipes. He took lessons from Peter Bruce at Benalla in the pipes. From his mother, a MacCrimmons (traditional hereditary pipers to the clan MacLeod), he learned the pibroch vocables (*piobaireachd*), and the *canntaireachd* notation, and became in later years a primary source for Scottish folklorists of tunes and folklore from the lost bagpipe traditions of Scotland.

FURTHER REFERENCE

His ms letters are now in the National Library of Scotland, Edinburgh. See Joan Gillison, *ADB*, 8.

Fredman, Myer (*b* Plymouth, England, 29 Jan. 1932), conductor. After studies at the London Opera School, army service and regional work, he joined Glyndebourne in 1959, rising from *répétiteur* to chorusmaster, then music director of the Touring Company 1969–74. He appeared with the Australian Opera from 1974, was music director of the State Opera of South Australia from 1975, and was head of the opera department, NSW State Conservatorium 1981–92. A conductor of very broad repertoire, he has made guest appearances conducting opera in various European and American centres and in concert with several ABC orchestras.

FURTHER REFERENCE
Recordings include Bax Symphonies 1 and 2, H. Brian Symphonies 16 and 22, London Philharmonic Orchestra; Delius *Paradise Garden,* Royal Philharmonic Orchestra (Lyrita); Bax Symphony No. 3 and works of Respighi, Sydney Symphony Orchestra (HK). See also *GroveO*; Arthur Jacobs, *GroveD; WWA* (1996).

Free Jazz. The improvisation practices of Americans Cecil Taylor, Ornette Coleman, John Coltrane and others, which spread during the early 1960s and became a major stream in jazz. The improvisations do not adhere to the metric pattern or the harmonic progression of the chart being played, and the results at times border on atonality. In Australia the approach came to be heard in the 1970s through Jon Rose, Serge *Ermoll and others.

Free Music Machine. An early precursor of the synthesiser, designed to perform Percy *Grainger's *Free Music.* Three working prototypes were constructed by Grainger and scientist Burnett Cross during the 1950s and early 1960s, now preserved at the Grainger Museum, University of Melbourne. The *Reed-Box Tone-Tool* (1951) consisted of a vacuum cleaner blowing through a modified piano-roll mechanism and a set of accordion reeds tuned in sixth tones. The *Kangaroo-Pouch Machine* (1952) used oscillators and has moving rolls of cardboard whose 'hills and dales' are read by pitch/volume wheels. The *Electric-Eye Tone-Tool* (1960) again employed oscillators and works by shining lights through photocells, via graphs drawn on a moving plastic sheet.   ALESSANDRO SERVADEI

Fregon. Fregon, a former outstation of Ernabella Aboriginal Mission established in 1961 on the banks of the Officer Creek, supports a community (known as Aparawatatja) of about 300 Aborigines. The community holds rights in ceremonial items comprised of song, dance, body and object markings that link them with other communities situated in Anangu Pitjantjatjaraku lands. Both men and women hold these rights for their respective ceremonies, which 'name' sites located around Fregon, and these in turn are linked with other sites on ancestral paths which criss-cross Anangu Pitjantjatjaraku lands. In ceremonially 'singing sites' men and women from Fregon are usually joined by their counterparts from other Anangu Pitjantjatjaraku communities, but there is acknowledgment that certain ceremonial sections belong to Aparawatatja as opposed to other community groups.

FURTHER REFERENCE
See F. Myers, To Have and To Hold: A Study of Persistence and Change in Pintupi Social Life, PhD, Bryn Mawr College, Bryn Mawr, Pa, 1976; H. Payne, Singing a Sister's Sites: Women's Land Rites in the Australian Musgrave Ranges, PhD, Univ. Qld, 1988.
                                                                   HELEN PAYNE

Fremantle, pop. (1991) 28 387, city and main port of WA, situated at the mouth of the Swan River. Founded in 1829, its early cultural life mimicked that of England, and with the introduction of convicts in 1850, bands (particularly brass) became fashionable, providing popular entertainment and music for social and ceremonial occasions. By the end of the century the Fremantle Orchestral Society (1887–1937), the first orchestra in WA, had been established by Charles L. Clifton (his cousin Robert C. Clifton made the first organ in WA). The formation of the Western Liedertafel was indicative of the interest in choral singing and Fremantle had two Music Societies. Today Fremantle boasts the City of Fremantle Symphony Orchestra, the Fremantle Choir, the Fremantle Musical and Dramatic Club, and Highland and Brass bands. The Fremantle Music School, founded privately in 1955, established the Fremantle (now WA) Mandolin Orchestra, the Fremantle Youth Orchestra, and the Fremantle Eisteddfod. Over the last two decades, jazz, folk, Aboriginal, experimental, ethnic and popular music have flourished. Fremantle has hosted national folk and jazz festivals, fostered Nansing and the Jam Tarts, and is home to the Italian women's choir the Joys of the Women. The Fremantle Festival is an established feature of the city's cultural life. The Fremantle Town Hall, Fremantle Arts Centre and Fly by Night Club—the latter established to provide entertainment during the America's Cup (1986–87)—are important venues for the diverse range of present-day music-making. Sponsorship comes from private and public sources, with the City of Fremantle playing a vital role.

FURTHER REFERENCE
Papers of the Fremantle Orchestral Society are in the State Archives of WA. See also A.H. Kornweibel, *Apollo and the Pioneers* (Perth: Music Council of WA, 1973).
                                                              PATRICIA THORPE

Fretwell, Betty (Elizabeth Drina) (*b* Glenhuntly, Melbourne, 13 Aug. 1920), soprano. She began her career in 1950 with the National Theatre Movement Opera Co. in Melbourne where her roles included Tosca, Madame Butterfly, and Antonia in *The Tales of Hoffmann* which she sang at the 1954 Royal Gala Performance. She joined Sadler's Wells Opera, London, in 1956 where she excelled in *La traviata, Ariadne auf Naxos, Fidelio,* as Minnie in *La fanciulla del west* and Ellen Orford in *Peter Grimes.* She returned to Australia in 1970 to join the Australian Opera where her many roles included Aida, Amelia in *Un ballo in maschera*, Lady Macbeth in *Macbeth* and Kostelnička in *Jenůfa*. She was awarded the OBE in 1977.

FURTHER REFERENCE

MackenzieS, 214–16; *WWA* (1996). For an index to references in *AMN* see *MarsiI*.

MOFFATT OXENBOULD

Friedman, Ignaz   (*b* nr Cracow, Poland, 13 Feb. 1882; *d* Sydney, 26 Jan. 1948), pianist. Friedman was one of the greatest pianists of his age, and a prolific composer of piano pieces, chamber music, and songs. He studied piano with Leschetizky and also briefly with Busoni in Vienna, and theory with Riemann and Adler. In nearly 40 years he played over 3000 concerts, and was famous as a Chopin interpreter. He toured Australia in 1927 and in 1941 found refuge from the war in Sydney, settling there until his death. His many Australian pupils included Manfred *Clynes, Muriel Cohen, Lawrence Davis, Arthur Denereaz, Joseph Gurt, Bruce *Hungerford, Mack Jost, and Rachel Valler.   NEIL McKELVIE, ALLAN EVANS

Fringe of Leaves, A.   Opera by Brian *Howard after Patrick White's novel. The text employs a stream of nonsense vowel sounds inspired by the novel; the music is for double SATB with no soloists. Commissioned by the Australian Chamber Orchestra and first performed at the Opera Centre in October 1987.

Frost, Lilian   (*b* Launceston, Tas., 4 Sept. 1870; *d* Launceston, Tas., 22 Dec. 1953), organist. As she displayed exceptional musical talent as a child, she was taken to London to study piano and theory and attended the Guildhall School of Music. On returning to Launceston she studied organ with W.W. Thornthwaite and at age 15 was appointed organist at Christ Church Congregational. She gave a series of organ recitals at the Albert Hall, Launceston, 1891–92 and in 1895 moved to Sydney to become organist to the Congregational Church, Pitt Street, a position she occupied for 52 years. In 1912 she visited England and France to study with W.G. Alcock and Charles-Marie Widor. Her weekly midday recitals, inaugurated in 1913, became an institution among musicians and the public. Through 1927 she gave recitals in England and North America. With impeccable organ technique and musical taste, Frost was one of the most influential Sydney organists and teachers in the first half of this century.

FURTHER REFERENCE

Graeme D. Rushworth, *Historic Organs of New South Wales* (Sydney: Hale & Iremonger, 1988), 384–6.

GRAEME RUSHWORTH

Fry, Stanley   (*b* Melbourne, 1930), french horn player. After playing in a brass band at primary school, he worked in dance bands, then studied french horn in Melbourne

and Sydney and joined the Sydney Symphony Orchestra in 1953. He became principal horn in the Adelaide Symphony Orchestra from 1954, a position he held for 41 years, save for 1963, which he spent in London as a freelance player, and 1965–70, when he taught horn at the University of Adelaide and played in the Adelaide Brass Quintet. A stalwart of horn playing and teaching in Adelaide over a very long period, he was honoured with the AM in 1988.

Fuller, Sir Benjamin   (*b* London, 20 Mar. 1875; *d* 10 Mar. 1952), theatrical entrepreneur. After singing on stage from the age of nine, he went to NZ in 1894, working with his father's minstrel and vaudeville show. With his father he built a theatre circuit that promoted vaudeville throughout Australia and NZ, and went into films from 1907. From 1914 with his brother John he was based in Sydney, presenting pantomime, melodrama and, in 1916, a season of Italian opera. From 1923 he was in partnership with Hugh Ward, and expanded into musical comedy, including *No, No, Nanette* with Gladys *Moncrieff in 1928 and a tour by the *Gonzalez Opera Co. He purchased cinemas from 1930, and with his Royal Grand Opera Co. in 1934 attempted to establish a permanent Australian opera company to sing in English. He presented opera seasons in Melbourne, Sydney and Newcastle, but failed to gain government support and lost money heavily. A presenter of music-theatre of routinely excellent quality, his contribution to opera in Australia was an important one in the years before the *National Theatre Movement was established. He was in partnership with Garnet Carroll from 1946 and merged with Hoyts Theatres Ltd in 1950.

FURTHER REFERENCE

Martha Ruthledge, *ADB*, 8; *ParsonsC*; *Theatre*, 1 Aug. 1912.

Funston, Grace Theresa   (*b* Paddington, Sydney, 30 Jan. 1900; *d* Melbourne, 7 May 1984), cornettist, bandleader. The seventh of 10 children, Funston's musical education took place within her family. Choosing cornet in emulation of her brothers, she entered the profession through Mme Cecilia Summerhayes's Magpies Ladies Orchestra (1913). Launched in 1917 as a vaudeville and theatre musician, she was first trumpet in J.C. Williamsons' No. 2 Musical Comedy Co. (1927–39). Between tours she worked casually in and sometimes led various all-girls dance bands, touring India with Evelyn Goold (1932–33) and joining Harry Jacobs' women's orchestra at the Palais Picture Theatre, St Kilda (1942–49). She never married. Her will provided an annual scholarship at the University of Melbourne.

FURTHER REFERENCE

The Funston Collection is at the Performing Arts Museum, Victorian Arts Centre, Melbourne. See also B. May, *Amazing Grace: The Story of a Unique Australian Musician, Grace Funston* (Adelaide:

B. May, 1995); K. Dreyfus, 'Sweethearts of Rhythm', *Stages (Magazine of the Victorian Arts Centre Trust)* (Mar. 1995), 34–5.

                                                          KAY DREYFUS

Furniss, Paul Anthony   (*b* Sydney, 27 Nov. 1944), jazz reeds player. He began recorder and flute at the age of seven, later adding clarinet (at age 11) and other reeds, with lessons from Don Burrows and others. Studying at the NSW Conservatorium, he then taught in its jazz program. Growing interest in jazz led to attendance at Sydney Jazz Club workshops and work with trombonist Bob Learmonth. He joined Geoff Bull in 1965, then had nine years with Graeme Bell from 1969. A founder member then leader of the Eclipse Alley Five, he was increasingly prominent in a wide range of groups from the 1970s, playing with Adrian Ford, Tom Baker (from whom he assumed leadership of the San Francisco Jazz Band), the saxophone quartet Saxafari, and post-bop musicians such as Bernie McGann and Miroslav Bukowsky. He has worked with orchestra, including as soloist in *Concerto for Orchestra and Improvising Soprano Saxophone*, written specifically for him by John Colborne-Veel. He has played support for numerous visiting musicians, and toured in Australia and beyond with his own groups for Musica Viva and imported shows including One Mo' Time and Bill Dillard.

   Among musicians emerging from the traditional movement, Furniss's technical and theoretical authority and his stylistic range are unsurpassed. His current activity includes work with Baker, the Café Society Orchestra, and his trio with Gary Holgate (bass) and Chuck Morgan (guitar). In the 1990s he is increasingly in demand as a soloist at festivals in Australia and abroad, including Edinburgh, Ascona, Breda, Osaka and the USA. He also composes, winning awards at the Australian Jazz Conventions.

FURTHER REFERENCE
Recordings include *Graeme Bell All Stars* (1973, Festival L-25079); *Vanity Fair,* The Eclipse Alley Five (1974, Swaggie S-1368); *The Adrian Ford Orchestra* (1976, 44 Records 44 9288 002); *Nancy, Nancy Stewart* (1977, 44 Records 44 6357 717); *Tom Baker's San Francisco Jazz Band* (1976, Jazz & Jazz J&J-001); *The Original Tunes* (1980, Jazznote JNLP-026); *Requiem for a Loved One,* John Sangster (1980, Rain Forest RFLP 005); *Jazz 'n' Blues* (1992, Disctronics ACD-6492). See also *OxfordJ*; Bruce Johnson 'Paul Furniss, More Than A Trad Player', *JA* (Winter/Spring 1986), 8–10.

                                                          BRUCE JOHNSON

Furse, Anthony.   See *Qasar I.*

Future Life.   Oratorio by Henri *Kowalski (1895), text by A.B. Wood. First performed in Sydney in 1895. Libretto published by W.A. Pepperday, Sydney, 1896.

G

Gagaku. Japanese court music of ancient origin, including types involving ensemble music with or without dance, court song, and ritual Shinto music. The ensembles have various traditional wind, stringed instruments, and drums, and involve embellished melodies set against a complex texture of cluster-chords and repeating percussion patterns. At the University of Sydney in the late 1960s through Donald *Peart's interest in music outside the West, a number of young Australian composers became interested in aspects of *gagaku*, and its influence may be found in certain works of Peter *Sculthorpe, Richard *Meale, Anne *Boyd and others. Musicological research in the origins of *gagaku* has been done by Noël *Nickson.

Galapagos Duck. Jazz band formed at Sydney from a group of musicians playing at the Snowy Mountains resorts c.1970, then at the Old Push. Galapagos Duck opened at the *Basement, August 1973, with Tom Hare (saxophones, trumpet), Marty Mooney, Chris (bass, brass, keyboard), Willie Qua (drums, saxophones) and Doug Robson (piano). Their versatility and eclecticism produced a striking stylistic and textural range. Through the Basement residency, national and international tours, recordings and concerts, they became Australia's best-known jazz-based band. Various personnel changes have embraced an extensive cross-section of Sydney's jazz musicians; since Hare's departure for Queensland the band has been led by Greg Foster (trombone, harmonica).

FURTHER REFERENCE
Recordings include *Ebony Quill* (1973, Philips 6357 015); *Habitat* (1989, WEA 256904–1). See also *OxfordJ*.

BRUCE JOHNSON

Gallaher, Simon (*b* Brisbane, 24 Oct. 1958), popular music singer. After studying voice, piano and cello at the Queensland Conservatorium, he worked in the chorus of the Queensland Opera Co. and the Queensland Light Opera Co. He was successful in the television talent quest

Showcase in 1978 and became a regular on the *Mike Walsh Show*, touring as supporting act for Debbie Reynolds in 1979. After working in the USA 1979–80, he presented *The Simon Gallaher Show* on ABC TV (from 1981), his single *My Friend* reaching the Top 10, then starred in the modernised *Pirates of Penzance* (1984). With his company Essgee Melodies he has presented a modernised *Mikado* (1995). Combining a polished natural voice with a handsome stage presence, he won three Mo awards, three gold albums, and a TV Logie in 1981.

FURTHER REFERENCE
Sunday Age 10 Sept. 1995.

Gamelan. In Australia, gamelan of several Indonesian cultures are currently played by both Indonesian and other Australians, with varying degrees of expertise. These include, among others: Central Javanese, Balinese, East Javanese, and Sundanese. Most of these instrumental ensembles in Australia are located in or associated with universities and museums and Indonesian Consulates. In some Australian high schools where Indonesian language is taught, compatible ensemble programs have been developed in music and other departments. Gamelan Digul was the first gamelan brought to Australia: it was made by Indonesian prisoners in a Dutch detention camp, Tanah Merah (now in Irian Jaya). After the Japanese deposed the Dutch in 1942, these instruments were brought to Melbourne, where they were played by the ex-prisoners and then donated to Monash University. Other ensembles have been commissioned from a particular maker by the buying organisation or purchased ready-made.

Indonesian musics have intermittently been part of several university music curricula since the late 1960s, notably the University of Sydney and Monash University. Ensembles also exist at, among others, the University of New England (Armidale), Flinders University, University of Melbourne, University of Southern Queensland, University of Western Sydney, museums in Sydney, Darwin and Brisbane, the Indonesian Embassy in Canberra, and most of the Consulates around Australia. There are several community-based ensembles, notably in Fremantle and Sydney. Some of these groups perform music from classical repertoires, others perform new music written by both Australian and Indonesian composers. Since 1987 there have been frequent performances of traditional shadow puppet theatre from Bali and Java with live accompaniment from Australian-based gamelan groups. Perth has seen the rise of an Australian shadow puppet theatre tradition based on the Ned Kelly stories with accompaniment derived from East and Central Javanese gamelan traditions mixed with that of the Australian bush band.

Over the last 10 years the University of Sydney has sponsored several visiting performing artists who have travelled around Australia teaching and participating in performances, and Australian students now frequently travel to study music traditions in Indonesia funded both by the Indonesian Government's Dharma Siswa program and their own universities as well as independently. Professional Indonesian musicians are currently employed at Monash University and in the Information Section at the Indonesian Embassy in Canberra.

FURTHER REFERENCE

Margaret Kartomi, 'Indonesian Music in Australia's Tertiary Institutions', *Indonesia Circle* 35 (1984), 3–10; idem, 'The *Gamelan Digul*', *Canang* 1 (1990), 19–24.

SARAH WEISS

Gamley, Douglas   (*b* Melbourne 1924), composer, arranger, conductor. First appearing as a pianist at the age of six, after studies at the University of Melbourne Conservatorium he went to a Salzburg composition school in 1949, then studied with Franz Reizenstein and Walter Goehr in London. He began composing film music as assistant to the director Hollingsworth, and worked on more than 40 films, including *The Admirable Crichton* (1957), *Tarzan's Greatest Adventure* (1959), *Spring and Port Wine* (1970), *Sunday, Bloody Sunday* and *The Little Prince*, which was nominated for an Academy Award. From 1965 he also worked as an arranger with such singers as Joan Sutherland, Renata Tebaldi, Victoria de los Angeles and Luciano Pavarotti, and on *Pavarotti in Concert* all but two of the 16 arias are his arrangements. His version (with Richard Bonynge) of *The Beggar's Opera* has been recorded (1981). As a conductor he has recorded light music with the London Philharmonic Orchestra, and from 1982 he has been artistic director of the Australian Pops Orchestra. He is one of the most successful film composers Australia has produced.

FURTHER REFERENCE

For a list of his film music, see *LimbacherF*. Recordings as a conductor include opera overtures, Royal Philharmonic Orchestra (EMI); popular overtures, New Philharmonic Orchestra (Readers Digest); see *HomesC* for a full list. As an arranger, *The Beggar's Opera,* New Philharmonia Orchestra (1981, Decca D252D2);

The Power of the Symphony, London Philharmonic Orchestra (1976, Rainbow J124); *Pops Concert in Vienna,* London Philharmonic Orchestra (Rainbow RGA7819), *Australian Pops Orchestra* (Warner 450990485–2); *Overture on Australian Themes,* Australian Youth Orchestra (ABC 834 740–2); and his ballet suite *Bal de Vienne* for *Die Fledermaus,* arranged from music by the Strauss family, National Philharmonic Orchestra (Decca). See also *AMN* 41/1 (July 1950), 9–10; *Age* 30 Dec. 1982.

GANGgajang.   Rock band (1984–) formed in Sydney from already seasoned players, chiefly Kayellen Bee and Marilyn Delaney (vocals), Mark Callaghan and Gordon Sullivan (guitars), James Black (keyboards), Chris Bailey (bass) and Graham Bidstrup (drums). Their debut single was *Gimme Some Loving* in 1984, and the eight that followed included *Giver Of Life* (1985) and *American Money* (1987). Their debut album *GANGgajang* (1985) reached No.27 in the charts.

FURTHER REFERENCE

Recordings include *Gimme Some Loving* (Mercury 880351–7), *Giver Of Life* (1985 Truetone 880935–7), *American Money* (1987 Polygram 888749), *GANGgajang* (1985 Truetone 8263491), *Gangagain* (1987 Mercury 832586–1), *True To The Tone* (1990 Phonogram 846704–2) and *Lingo* (1994 rooArt 4509955452). For discography, see *SpencerA*. See also *SpencerW*; *CoupeN*.

Garbutt, Maurie   (*b* Melbourne, 29 May 1941), jazz trumpeter. He joined the Port Melbourne Brass Band in 1954, then began attending jazz functions including those of the *Melbourne New Orleans Jazz Band with bassist Bob Brown, with whom he formed his first band in 1958. Since taking the name Yarra Yarra Jazz Band for a dance residency at Dantes Inferno, 1959, Garbutt's career has been coeval with bands bearing that name. Most New Orleans musicians emerging from Melbourne are alumni of this band, but its reputation was established during the early 1960s when additional personnel including trombonist Les Fithall, drummer Don Hall, clarinettists Eddie Robbins, Denis Ball and Nick Polites, banjoists Lee Treanor and John Brown, singers Judy Jacques, Pat Purchase and Kerrie Male. During this time numerous residencies followed, including Jazz Centre 44, the Yarra Yarra Centre, and filling gaps left by the departure of the Melbourne New Orleans Jazz Band for its overseas tour from 1961.

From the mid-60s, work diminished with the abatement of the jazz boom. With fluctuating personnel the band toured successfully overseas from March 1969 to October 1971, including England, Europe and the USA. The band has remained continuously in existence under Garbutt's leadership, playing residencies (notably at Bells Hotel, 1984–95), and reunion concerts and tours (including with American trumpeter Alvin Alcorn 1973). Activity through the 1980s included the Wangaratta and Montsalvat Festivals, and Japan's Kobe, Tokyo and Osaka Festivals. It has been the most durable rallying point for the Melbourne New Orleans movement, and with Frank

Turville, Garbutt has been the most significant and authoritative trumpeter that Australia has produced in the New Orleans style.

FURTHER REFERENCE

Recordings include *The Yarra Yarra New Orleans Jazz Band* (1962, Crest CRT-7-EP-006 and -008); *The Yarra Yarra Jazz Band* (1971, GHB Records GHB 78 and 79); *Alvin Alcorn with the Yarra Yarra Jazz Band* (1973, Emulation EMU-001); *The Yarra Yarra Reunion Band Featuring Judy Jacques* (1994, Newmarket NEW1041.2). See also *ClareB*; *OxfordJ*; Eric Brown, *15 Years of the Yarra Yarra Jazz Band* (Melbourne: The Australian Jazz Archives, 1974); idem, '25 Years of the Yarra Yarra Jazz Band—1958–84', *Jazzline*, Part 1 17/3 (Spring 1984), 21–2, Part 2 [Mis-headed 'Part 1'], 18/1 (Autumn 1985), 24–7.

BRUCE JOHNSON

Gard, Robert Joseph (*b* Padstow, Cornwall, England, 7 Mar. 1927), tenor. After studies with Dino Borgioli and Walter Hyde at the Guildhall School of Music, then Kaiser Breme at Bayreuth, he made his debut with the English National Opera in Lennox Berkeley's *Ruth* in 1957, singing at the Welsh National Opera and the Aldeburgh festival. He came to Australia in 1960 and joined the Australian Opera in 1963, appearing in numerous roles as well as in concert and as a guest for the state companies. With a rich, pliant voice and an excellent actor, he has sung roles ranging from Don Basilio, Tamino, Don Ottavio, Peter Grimes and Tom Rakewell to Aschenbach in *Death in Venice* (on television film), Loge, Siegmund, Herod, and Le Mesurier in *Voss*. He was honoured with the OBE in 1981.

FURTHER REFERENCE

Recordings include Eisenstein in the Australian Opera *Die Fledermaus* (Virgin Vision Video VVD781). See also *CA* (1995/96); Roger Covell, *GroveO*.

Garni Sands. Opera (1965) in two acts by George *Dreyfus, libretto by Frank Kellaway. It tells of a colonial squatter's family, their relations with the convicts they employ, and the hardships which carry them towards catastrophe. First performed 12 August 1972, University of New South Wales Opera. Vocal score published by Allans, Melbourne.

Garood, Roger William (*b* London, 20 Aug. 1937), jazz saxophonist. He studied piano from the age of four, then saxophone from the age of 15. Adding other reeds while in his National Service 1955–58, he worked in cabaret and show bands with occasional jazz work in England and Europe until 1965. Following a brief retirement from music, he began working on cruise ships, then settled at Perth in 1971. He played in pop music radio and television, until the expansion of Perth's jazz opportunities provided work as a sideman and leader; he now teaches in the jazz program at the WA Conservatorium.

FURTHER REFERENCE

Recordings include *Will Upson Big Band* (1975, Festival L-25183); *A Tribute to the Embassy Ballroom,* Will Upson Big Band (1982, EP 1); *Reflections of Western Australia* (1992, Request Records RQCD 2001); *I Mean You,* Garry Lee (1992, Request Records RQCD 1502). See also *OxfordJ*.   BRUCE JOHNSON

Gaston, Ed (Edwin Porter) (*b* Granite Falls, North Carolina, USA, 9 Jan. 1929), jazz bass player. He began clarinet at the age of 13, later switching to bass and joining the touring Australian Jazz Quartet in 1957, until it disbanded in Australia in 1959. He joined the Bryce *Rohde Quartet until it disbanded in the USA, where he freelanced with Shelly Manne, June Christie and others. Returning to Australia in 1963, he joined Don Burrows, his freelance work including a tour with Stephane Grappelli in 1975. In the USA again with Barney Kessel, Terry Gibbs and others 1977–80, since returning to Australia he continues to be in high demand as freelancer and backing visitors such as Sonny Stitt and Milt Jackson.

FURTHER REFERENCE

Recordings include *The Australian Jazz Quintet* (1957, Bethlehem BCP-6022); *The Bryce Rohde Quartet In Concert* (1960, Coronet KLP-909); *My Favourite Things,* The Judy Bailey Quintet (1965, CBS BP-233263); *Don Burrows Quartet* (1966, Columbia Co 330SX-7781); *The Daly Wilson Big Band* (1971, Festival SFL-934453); *Bob Barnard All Star Jazz Group* (1971, Axis 6014); *The Stephane Grappelli Quartet* (1975, Philips 9286 893). See also *BissetB*; *OxfordJ*; Carl Witty in 'The Great Australian Bassists: An Australia-Wide Survey, Part 1', *JA* (July/August 1983), 11.

BRUCE JOHNSON

Gaudion, Peter Graham (*b* Melbourne, 19 Oct. 1947), jazz trumpeter, venue owner. He began trumpet in 1963 and worked in traditional groups from the mid-1960s, freelancing and forming the Kansas City Six in 1967. With Frank Traynor in the 1970s, he left in 1978 to form his own band, Blues Express, and also invested in the first of several jazz venues at which he presented his band and overseas visitors including Herb Ellis and Jimmy Witherspoon. His band became dormant in 1984, and he joined Chris Ludowyk's Society Syncopators, remaining with them following the revival of Blues Express and the opening of his venue Jazz Lane.

FURTHER REFERENCE

Recordings include *Jimmy Witherspoon Sings the Blues* (1980, AIM Records AIM 1005). See also *OxfordJ*; Mike Williams, 'Blues Express, greater than the sum of the parts', *JA* (Jan./Feb. 1981), 17–18.   BRUCE JOHNSON

Gautrot French Opera Company. A six-member opera and vaudeville touring company, perhaps the first to visit Australia, directed by violinist Henri Gautrot (*b* c.1775; *d* 1850), and his wife, a gifted singer. The couple arrived in Sydney in 1839 and settled, giving concerts and bowdlerised operatic presentations at the Royal Victoria Theatre, Sydney, and in Melbourne; but meeting with less and less success they left for Calcutta in 1846.

FURTHER REFERENCE
Osric [Humphrey Hall and Alfred John Cripps], *The Romance of the Sydney Stage* (ms, 1911; pub. Sydney: Currency Press, 1996), 50–2, passim; *BrisbaneE,* 35–40.

Gebert, Bobby (John Robert)   (*b* Adelaide 1 Apr. 1944), jazz pianist. He took classical and popular piano lessons in Adelaide, some of them through the London College of Music. At 17 he led a trio at the Embers, Melbourne, then returned to Adelaide and became influential in the modern jazz movement, notably at the Cellar. He moved to Sydney in 1966, and played at ★El Rocco, with John ★Sangster among others. Throughout the 1970s he was active in session and theatre work, for example with Jeannie Lewis and *Hair*, and television and film work including *Crystal Voyager.* He studied in the USA, 1980–81, and is now receiving increasing recognition as a performer-composer through festivals and concerts, including as a support for such visitors as Junior Cook, Richie Cole Jimmy Witherspoon.

FURTHER REFERENCE
Recordings include *Bobby Gebert* (1961, Driftwood DJ-003 and DJ-004); *Jazz Australia* (1967, CBS BP-233450); *Kindred Spirits,* Bernie McGann Quartet (1987, Emanem 3602); *The Sculptor,* Bobby Gebert (1994, ABC Records 4797572/4). See also *ClareB; OxfordJ;* John Shand, 'Bobby Gebert, Sculpting a Career', *Australian Jazz and Blues,* 1/5 (1994), 23–4.
                                                    BRUCE JOHNSON

Geddes, Alan   (*b* Lithgow, NSW, 24 May 1927), jazz drummer. He began playing drums in 1944, building a reputation in nightclub, dance and concert settings in and around Sydney such as Ciros, Bondi Esplanade, and Romanos. Active as a freelancer, he was a member of numerous jazz groups including Frank Smith at the Embers (Melbourne 1960), the Port Jackson Jazz Band, Ray Price, Graeme Bell, Dick Hughes, Bob Barnard, John McCarthy, Roger Janes and American bassist Jack Lesberg. He led his own groups, with a residency at Bondi Icebergers 1982–86. Highly respected as a mainstream drummer, Geddes has also been a significant influence on younger percussionists in all styles.

FURTHER REFERENCE
Recordings include *The Jack Lesberg Quartet* (1973 ATA ATAL-34782); *Bob Barnard's Jazz Band* (1974, ATA L-25187); *Dick Hughes Looks Back and Around* (1977, 44 6357 716). See also *OxfordJ.*   BRUCE JOHNSON

Geelong,   pop. (1991) 126 306, second largest city in Victoria, situated on Corio Bay 75 km south-west of Melbourne. Music has played and continues to play an important role in Geelong's history. Early in its development many community musical groups were established, the band movement being one of the earliest. The Geelong Brass Band may have been the earliest Geelong band, followed by similar groups from the military, the Geelong Harbour Trust and councils. The most successful pre-war bands were the Geelong West Harmonica Band and Geelong Harbour Trust Band, which amalgamated with the Geelong Municipal Band in 1915 and today exists as the Geelong City Band. Choral societies have also played an important role since the 1850s, successful early groups including the Geelong Musical Society Choir (formed *c.*1901) continuing until the late 1920s. St Paul's Anglican Church choir also existed in the early 1900s, but became more renowned after 1945 under the direction of John Brockman, its achievements including performances with the Melbourne Symphony Orchestra.

The Geelong Association of Music and Art (GAMA) was formed in the mid-1940s, today contributing another accomplished choir, the GAMA Singers, to Geelong's musical scene, and incorporating the Geelong Musical Association. Various community orchestras existed, including that of the Philharmonic Society (mid to late 19th century), the GAMA Orchestra (intermittent until its end *c.*1980) and most recently the Geelong Community Orchestra (since *c.*1986). The Geelong Opera Society was formed in the 1920s. It had a strong following until World War II, when it was in recess, re-forming in 1946 as the Geelong Society of Operatic and Dramatic Art. This group (including the Geelong Musical Comedy Co. and the Junior Players) and the Lyric Opera Society still exist, both producing local musical comedy, with the Lyric performing Gilbert and Sullivan shows at regular intervals. Opera singers Peter Wright and Cheryl Barker spent time in these companies before beginning their professional training.

The concert life has always been strong, with regular public concerts given by amateur groups and professional artists. Several Geelong groups held prestigious musical (singing) and speech competitions, including the Geelong Musical Society and the Commun na Feine, where the Wagnerian soprano Marjorie ★Lawrence made her debut. The competition tradition is carried on today by the Geelong Eisteddfod, run by the Welsh Society of Geelong, and by other groups which offer the youth of Geelong and wider Victoria various prizes. The local paper, the *Geelong Advertiser*, sponsors an annual Australia-wide competition for instrumentalists. Since 1980 Geelong's musical activity has continued to thrive, with new groups forming, especially in youth music. These include the Geelong Children's Choir and the Bay City Strings Inc. (both formed 1988), catering for string players aged 5–19 years.

While few truly professional performers earned their living performing in Geelong in the past, 1995 saw the debut of Geelong's first modern professional group, the Geelong Chamber Orchestra. Geelong has also been home to Australian musical personalities such as John

*Brownlee, Keith *Humble, Percy and Basil *Jones, A.J. *Leckie, Ros *Bandt, pianist Janine Sowden and choral composer Malcolm John.   LYNDELL KING

Gell, Heather Doris   (*b* Glenelg, SA, 19 May 1896; *d* Christies Beach, SA, 23 Oct. 1988), music educator. A kindergarten teacher, she became an expert Dalcroze Eurhythmics teacher, completing a teacher's certificate at the London School of Dalcroze Eurhythmics in 1923. On her return to Adelaide she established a Dalcroze Eurhythmics studio, and completed the LRAM (1930). A driving force in the South Australian Women's Centenary Council, Gell co-produced a celebrated *Heritage Pageant* (1936). She moved to Sydney, and in 1940 began broadcasting the ABC national educational programs *Music and Movement*. Gell was the first Australian to gain a diploma at the Institut Jaques-Dalcroze, Geneva (1953–54). She founded the Dalcroze Society of Australia (1970), and was honoured with the MBE (1977) for services to music and education.

FURTHER REFERENCE
Her publications include *Music Movement and the Young Child* (Sydney: Australasian Publishing Company, 1949).
     JANE SOUTHCOTT

Geminiani Orchestra. Founded at Melbourne (1985) by Marco van Pagee as the student chamber orchestra of the Victorian College of the Arts, it soon became an independent youth orchestra, receiving assistance from the Australia Council, the State Government and other local sources. Comprising more than 70 high school and college players, it aims to provide ensemble training of high standard to student performers. It offers an annual subscription series of four concerts, usually conducted by van Pagee and often with soloists drawn from the orchestra. It has achieved consistently excellent standards, seldom bettered anywhere in Australia.

George, Linda   (*b* England, 1949), popular music singer. Raised singing in harmony at home, she arrived in Australia in 1964 and settled at Adelaide. Moving to Melbourne, she was in Nova Express (1968–70), and toured Vietnam with the ABC Showband (1970). Success came in 1973 with *Neither One Of Us*, which reached No. 12 in the charts; seven more singles followed, including *Mama's Little Girl* (1974) which reached No. 9 and her albums *Linda* (1974) and *Step By Step* (1975). She won the ARIA best female vocal single in 1973. After this she sang television commercials, formed the Linda George Band (1975–76), was in Souled Out (1976–77), then concentrated on session work with Brian *Cadd, Tina *Arena, Alex Pertout and others. Possessing a voice of limpid pensiveness, she also sang jazz with WJAZ 1986–92.

FURTHER REFERENCE
Recordings include *Neither One Of Us* (Image 15132), *Mama's Little Girl* (1974, Image 15152), *Linda* (1974, Image ILP 741) and *Step By Step* (1975, Image ILP 750). For discography, see *SpencerA*. See also *McGrathA*; *SpencerW*; David Day and Tim Parker, *SA Great: It's Our Music 1956–1986* (Glandore SA: Day and Parker, 1987), 144–7.

Geraldton,   pop. (1991) 24 361, city and Indian Ocean port on Champion Bay, 400 km north of Perth, WA. Gazetted as a town site in 1850, in the 1890s it became the centre for the Murchison goldfields; current industries include fishing, wheat, wool and market gardening. Early cultural activities were the Geraldton Amateur Dramatic and Music Club (1880), the Geraldton Variety Troupe (1882), the Temperance Crusade Concerts (1883), the Geraldton Musical Union (founder Francis Hart, 1885), the Geraldton Orchestral Society (1890) and the Volunteer Town Band. Concerts were held in the Masonic Hall.

In the first half of the 20th century significant events included the arrival of Irish piper John Wayland (1913) and a performance of *The Mikado* (1917). Linda Marsh established the Lyric Orchestra for string students in the 1930s; the Xaverian Orchestra was founded and conducted by James O'Dea in the 1940s; the Geraldton Music Lovers Glee Club (1948) evolved out of the pre-war Music Lovers Club and the Geraldton Catholic Diocese instituted an ambitious choir program in 1949. In 1986 a community music program was implemented, partially funded by the Australia Council and the State Government, with co-operation from the WA Academy of Performing Arts. Highlights have included a regional tour by Aboriginal bands (1989) and workshops in composition, recording and film scoring (1990). Current musical organisations include the Geraldton Choral Society, the Geraldton City Band, the Buskers Music Club, the Geraldton Music School, and the Geraldton Country Music Club. Private teachers and the Catholic school system continue their long and successful traditions of instrumental teaching, while state schools also implement a music program.

FURTHER REFERENCE
Bill Coackley and Janda Gooding, *Ring Up the Curtain: A Short History of Gilbert and Sullivan in Western Australia 1879–1892* (Perth: The Gilbert and Sullivan/A.N. Bullock Memorial Trust, n.d.), 27–32. Papers on musical history are in the Geraldton City Library Local Studies Collection.   PATRICIA THORPE

German Operatic Award. Awarded annually (since 1988) after a national competition for a singer under 33 who has been resident in Australia for at least six months and has a working knowledge of German. The winner becomes a member of the Cologne State Opera studio for two years. Administered by Opera Foundation Australia, the prize is currently valued at $30 000.

Geyer, Renee   (*b* Melbourne, 11 Sept. 1953), blues and soul singer. She sang with the dance band Dry Red from the age of 16, then the jazz-blues group Sun in

1972, the blues group Mother Earth in 1973 and Sanctuary in 1974. She went solo from 1973, signing with RCA and having her first hits with the James Brown standard *It's a Man's Man's World*, which reached No. 33 in the singles charts in 1974, and the album of the same name, which reached No. 16. She formed the Renee Geyer Band from 1975; *Heading in the Right Direction* reached No. 15 and the album *Ready to Deal*, which includes some of her own songs, reached No. 12 and a gold record. Making her first trip to the USA in 1976, she recorded the album *Moving Along* there, which reached No. 10 in 1977, and she toured Australia in 1976–77, and the single *Stares and Whispers* reached No. 12. She lived in Los Angeles 1977–81, her album *So Lucky* (1981) being highly acclaimed and the single *Say I Love You* reaching No. 1 in Australia. She appeared in the film *My First Wife*, worked with Easy Pieces (from 1988), continued to produce a succession of albums, including *Sing to Me* (1985) and *Live in the Basement* (1988), appeared extensively in Australia and has toured abroad regularly, and has done regular session work.

First influenced by Aretha Franklin, Thelma Houston and others, she has become a very versatile artist, spanning styles from soul and rhythm and blues to jazz-rock and reggae. One of Australia's finest blues and soul singers, she is also one of the most prolific of Australian women recording artists, having made more than 26 singles as a solo artist, as well as others with Jon *English and Glen *Shorrock, and 20 albums.

FURTHER REFERENCE
Early recordings include *It's a Man's Man's World* (1974, RCA); *Ready to Deal* (1975, RCA), *Moving Along* (1977, RCA); more recent work is with Mushroom Records. For a discography, see *SpencerA*. See also *McGrathB*; *SpencerW*; *AthertonA*.

Ghandar, Anne (*b* Adelaide, 1 Nov. 1943), composer, pianist. She studied composition and piano with Richard *Meale and Lance *Dossor at Adelaide University, with Larry *Sitsky at the Canberra School of Music, and with Jonathan Harvey at Southampton University. She also studied English at the Australian National University (MA, 1970). Since 1974 she has taught at the University of New England, and she was a visiting lecturer in the USA at the University of California (Los Angeles) and elsewhere in 1987. As a pianist she has given first Australian performances of works by Ives and Messiaen, and has appeared abroad, notably in Cairo (1992). Her compositions include works for brass band, piano solo, and chamber groups. She writes in a spare, rhythmically restless atonal idiom, in some ways resonant of Sitsky; but she has also been influenced by her study of the Middle Eastern 'ud and quanum, the piano work *Eshelgharam* (1978), for example, taking its title from the Arabic. Her works have been heard at new music festivals and conferences in Australia and abroad.

WORKS
Most available in facsimile from the Australian Music Centre, Sydney.
Orchestral, Band   *Serein*, orch (1974), *Music for the Prince*, brass band (1982).
Chamber, Solo   Sonata, fl, pf (1973), *Recollections Of a Latvian Song*, fl, ob, cl, pf (1973), *The Earth Sings Mi-Fa-Mi*, pf (1973), *Paraselene*, pf (1973), *… uncertain comets chance-drifting…*, pf (1973), *Haloes*, pf qrt (1975), *Six Pieces*, str trio (1975), *The Prisoners*, S, fl, vc,pf (1975), *Eshelgharam*, pf (1978; in *Contemporary Australian Piano*, [Bundoora: La Trobe University Press, 1985]), *Lentus in Umbra*, fl, vc pf (1984), *Sydney Sounds*, ens (1986).

FURTHER REFERENCE
Recordings include *Eshelgharam*, Larry Sitsky, pf (Move MD3066). See also *CohenI*.

Gibb, Barry, Robin, and Maurice.   See *Bee Gees*.

Gibbons, Denis   (*b* Port Elliot, SA, 1932), folksinger, broadcaster. Singing in a band from the age of 17, he joined 3UL at Warragul, Victoria, in 1952. After hearing Burl Ives's recordings from Percy *Jones's collection in 1952, he started a folk music program on 3SR Shepparton. He made the first of his many recordings as a folk-singer in 1954, appearing in a regular television spot for some years. With the Macquarie network as announcer, writer and producer for 20 years, he also broadcast *Understanding Australian Folksong* on Radio Australia, using materials he collected in northern Australia 1975–79.

FURTHER REFERENCE
Albums include *Australian Folksong* vols 1–3 (W&G WG5361, 5504, 5556), and *The Fair Dinkum Matilda* (1995, Move MD 3175). See also *WatsonC*, II, 190–2; *Age* 28 June 1995; *Herald* 21 Mar 1979.

Gibson, Greg (Gregory Edmund Campion)   (*b* Stawell, Vic., 23 Jan. 1930), jazz reeds player. After trying various instruments, he settled on clarinet in 1949, later adding saxophones. Following work with groups in Melbourne, including Smacka *Fitzgibbon and Frank *Traynor, he joined the Cootamundra Jazz Band until moving to Canberra in 1957. As a member of the diplomatic service his career has since alternated between Canberra and overseas postings in South-East Asia and Europe, where he has worked in various bands, including his own Jazz Australia UK Incorporated in England. When based in Canberra he has led groups, freelanced, and played as a member of the Fortified Few.

FURTHER REFERENCE
Recordings include *The Cootamundra Jazz Band* (1956, Parlophone PMDO-7513); *The Trouper*, Len Barnard's Famous Jazz Band (1972, Swaggie S 1302); *Mood Indigo* (1972, Jazznote JNLP-

005/S); *The Fortified Few* (1980, Jazznote JNLP-027). An interview with him is in *WilliamsA*, 34–9. See also *BissetB*; *OxfordJ*; *WWA*.   BRUCE JOHNSON

Gibson, Bob (Robert Alan Franklin) (*b* Perth, 23 May 1912), jazz/dance musician. A violinist in the Harold Newton Symphony Orchestra at 14, he subsequently added reeds, piano, and cornet to his repertoire. He worked in dance bands, including Ron Moyle's, then moved to Melbourne in 1936, joining Ern Pettifer, followed by other bands. His Palm Grove band (formed 1940) became nationally known through concerts and broadcasts. He worked in England, 1948–50, then was based in Sydney leading big bands for dances, concerts, and radio. In the 1960s he was involved in the television program *The Sound of Music*; from 1972 he was musical director for the Eastern Suburbs Leagues Club. He ran a music production agency with Bob Limb in the 1980s.

FURTHER REFERENCE
Recordings include *Bob Gibson at the Surreyville* (1957, Columbia 330S-7569). See also *BissetB*; *OxfordJ*.
                                  BRUCE JOHNSON

Gifford, Helen Margaret (*b* Melbourne, 5 Sept. 1935), composer. She studied at the University of Melbourne with Dorian *Le Gallienne. In 1958 her second work, *Fantasy* for flute and piano, had its first performance in Holland and was broadcast by Radio Hilversum II. In 1964 her *Phantasma* for string orchestra was chosen by the Australian jury for submission to the ISCM Festival, Copenhagen, and in 1965 she won the Dorian Le Gallienne Award for composition, producing her String Quartet (1965), first performed at the 1966 Adelaide Festival. In 1974 she held a senior composer's fellowship from the Australian Council for the Arts and was composer-in-residence to the Australian Opera. She has been continually commissioned since 1965. Recent commissions include those from Elision, Sydney Alpha Centauri Ensemble, Sally May and Astra.

She was attached to the Melbourne Theatre Co. as a composer of incidental music from 1970, and in 1980 she was appointed to the Australia Council's artists-in-schools program.

A sensitive and highly individual composer, Gifford was at first influenced by the music of the French impressionists. A year of travel in Europe in 1962 brought her into direct contact with contemporary idioms, and she has remained indebted to Lutoslawski and the Polish school in general. Her Indian travels in 1967 and a visit to Indonesia in 1971 brought the increasing influence of Asian music into her work. In her theatre scores she has been able to explore new creative fields through workshopping. Her most substantial work to date is the recent *Point of Ignition*, written with the assistance of an Australia Council Fellowship awarded in 1995. Her highly inter-nalised writing displays a rare clarity of form and integrity of approach, with a subtle use of percussive effect central to most of the work.

WORKS (selective list)
Principal publishers: Albert & Son; Australian Music Centre, Sydney; Red House Editions.
Orchestral *Phantasma*, str (1963), *Chimaera* (1967), *Imperium* (1969), *Point of Ignition*, Mez, orch (1996).
Chamber and Instrumental *Fantasy*, fl, pf (1958), Septet, fl, ob, bn, hpd, str trio (1962), *Fable*, hp (1967), *Canzone*, 9 wind, celeste (1968), *Myriad*, 3 fl, pf, celeste, 4 perc (1968), *Sonnet*, fl, gui, hpd (1969), *Military Overture*, cl, bn, cornet, bass trbn, perc, vn, db (1970, [withdrawn]), *Of Old Angkor*, hn, marimba (1970), *Company of Brass*, 9 brass (1972), *Going South*, 5 brass (1987).
Piano Sonata (1960), *Catalysis* (1964), Waltz (1966), *The Spell* (1966), *Cantillation* (1966), *Souvenance* (1973 [withdrawn]), *Toccata Attacco* (1990).
Stage *Jo Being*, opera (1974 [withdrawn], 1, Peter Murphy), *Regarding Faustus*, music-theatre (1983, 1, composer after Christopher Marlowe), *Iphigenia in Exile*, music-theatre (1985, 1, Richard Meredith), *Music for the Adonia*, music theatre (1992), Incidental Music: Shakespeare, Brecht, Congreve, Fry, Shaffer, Stoppard, Tourneur.
Vocal *As Dew in Aprille*, S, pf, hp, gui (1955), *The Wanderer*, male speaker, fl, english hn, va, perc (1963), *Red Autumn in Valvins*, Mez, pf (1964) *The Glass Castle*, S, 5-v ch (1968), *Bird Calls from an Old Land,* 5S, 5-v female ch, perc (1971).

FURTHER REFERENCE
Recordings include *Cantillation* and *The Spell* (1988, Move MD3066); *Catalysis* (1989, Canberra School of Music CSM 3); *Fable* (1996, Tall Poppies TP071); *Fantasie for Flute and Piano* (1996, ABC 446738–2); *Music of the Spheres* and *Willow Song* (1994, New 1042.2). See also *CohenI*; *ContemporaryC*; *GroveW*; James Murdoch, 'Regarding Faustus', *Arts National* 3/2 (1985).
                                  THÉRÈSE RADIC

Gill, Richard James (*b* Sydney, 4 Nov. 1941), conductor, music educator. After studies at the NSW State Conservatorium and Sydney Teachers' College, he taught in schools 1963–69, gaining a reputation as a passionate and energetic conductor of choirs and youth ensembles. A vivid, magnetic teacher, he wrote teaching materials and music for children, made broadcasts, and published articles on music education. He attended classes at the Orff Institut and Mozarteum, Salzburg, in 1972, and became lecturer at the NSW State Conservatorium 1974–86. He was a guest conductor with ABC orchestras from 1976, as well as working in theatre and ballet conducting, and became dean of music at the WA Conservatorium in 1986, then chorusmaster and conductor for the Australian Opera in 1992.

Gillies, Malcolm George William (*b* Brisbane, 23 Dec. 1954), musicologist. He is an authority on Bartók and Grainger, having published books and articles on each. He graduated from the Australian National University (BA 1977), then Cambridge University (BA 1980; MA 1984) and the University of London (MMus 1981; PhD 1986). Lecturing at the Victorian College of the Arts 1983–86 and the University of Melbourne 1986–91, he has been professor of music at the University of Queensland since 1992, president of the Musicological Society of Australia 1992–94, fellow of the Australian Academy of the Humanities 1992, and chair of the Arts Electoral Section of the Academy 1994, as well as chair of Tertiary Education Panel, Music Council of Australia 1994.

MARGARET KARTOMI

Gilt-Edged Kid, The. Opera (1970) in one act by George *Dreyfus, libretto by Lynne Strahan. A black satire of an Australian political leadership contest. Commissioned by the Australian Opera but not accepted for performance; first performed 15 May 1976 by a scratch company at Montsalvat, Eltham, Victoria. Vocal score published (Melbourne, 1976).

Giorza, Paolo (*b* Milan, Italy, 11 Nov. 1832; *d* Seattle, USA, 4 May 1914), composer, conductor, organist. He arrived from America with Agatha States Opera troupe (and tenor Pietro *Cecchi), first performing at Sydney on 27 December 1871. There he conducted and arranged for the Italian Opera companies of Lyster, Cagli, and Pompei, and for J.C. Williamson's first performances of Gilbert and Sullivan. He was organist and choirmaster St Francis' Melbourne, 1872–74, then conducted and stage-directed for touring artistes Adelaide Ristori and Ilma de Murska at Sydney in 1875. He had returned to Milan by 1884 and was composing an opera at the time of his death.

Giorza was the most significant 19th-century Italian composer to visit Australia. His Australian compositions included *Souvenir de La Juive d'Halevy, Faust, a Transcrizione libera per Piano* and the songs *I am Alone, Forget me Not,* and *Near My Heart.* He presented his *Messe Solennelle* No. 3 (publ. Milan 1870) with a choir of 100 at the Melbourne Town Hall in December 1872, his *Cantata in Honor of the Centenary Celebration of Daniel O'Connell* (words by Charles Badham) was presented at Sydney on 6 August 1875, and his Mass No. 4 was first heard at the Masonic Hall, 30 September 1876. As musical director of the Sydney International Exhibition, Giorza's *Cantata* (words by Henry Kendall) was performed at the opening ceremony on 17 Sep 1879, and his exhibition album includes *Belles of Australia Waltzes, Australia March, Manly Beach Polka,* and *Italian Quadrille.*

FURTHER REFERENCE
His mss are in *CAnl* and *Msl.* See also: *SMH* 27–31 Dec. 1871; Melbourne *Advocate* 17 Aug. 1872, 7 Dec. 1872; *Seattle Post Intelligencer,* 5 May 1914; Alison Guyger, *Opera for the Antipodes* (Sydney: Currency & Pellinor, 1990); Harold Love, *The Golden Age of Australian Opera* (Sydney: Currency, 1981); D'Amico Silvio, *Enciclopedia dello Spettacolo,* ed. C. Sartori (Rome: Casa Editrice le Maschere, 1954–62).   ROSLYN MAGUIRE

Giovanni. Opera in three short acts by Alfred *Hill (1913), text by Harriet Callan. It tells of a provincial Italian sculptor who, jilted by his royal patroness and lover in Florence, returns to his first sweetheart. First performed by the Australian Opera League at Sydney on 3 August 1914, then at Melbourne. A modern edition has been published, edited by Haydn Reeder, Kerry Murphy and Jennifer Hill (Melbourne: Centre for Studies in Australian Music, University of Melbourne, 1994), and the opera was revived by the University of Melbourne in 1996.

Glanville-Hicks, Peggy (*b* Melbourne, 29 Dec. 1912; *d* Sydney, 25 June 1990), critic, composer. At the age of 15 she began composition studies with Fritz *Hart at the Albert Street Conservatorium in Melbourne. In 1932 she travelled to London and the Royal College of Music, London, where she studied composition with Vaughan Williams and was the recipient of the Carlotta Rowe Scholarship. With the Octavia Travelling Scholarship in 1936 she undertook further study in Vienna with Egon Wellesz, and afterwards in Milan, Florence and Paris, where she studied with Nadia Boulanger. In 1938 she returned to Australia briefly but was in London in June when her *Choral Suite* was performed at the ISCM festival and several songs were published by L'Oiseau-lyre. In November 1938 she married the English composer Stanley Bate, and when war was declared they travelled to Australia. Despite several performances they were disappointed with the lack of opportunities in Australia and in 1941 departed for the United States, settling in New York.

In 1948 Virgil Thomson offered her a position as a 'stringer' on the New York *Herald Tribune;* Thomson was to remain her greatest friend and benefactor. Between 1948 and 1955 she worked from October to April for the *Tribune* and then spent the summer in Europe or Australia, visiting festivals, holidaying and composing. In 1953 she was offered a commission for an opera by the Louisville Philharmonic Society, the first such offer made to a woman. Based on a novel by Thomas Mann, *The Transposed Heads* borrows from Hindu legend and the rhythmic and percussive characteristics of Indian music; it was performed in 1954 and again in New York in 1958. In 1954 she was invited to contribute 98 articles to the fifth edition of *Grove's Dictionary.* Throughout the 1950s she was also director of the Composers' Forum in New York, arranging the performance of new music and the introduction of new composers. She resigned this position on moving to Athens in 1959, and soon after became involved in preparations for the performance of her opera *Nausicaa,* based on a libretto by Robert Graves, which took place in the amphitheatre of Herodus Atticus in 1961, receiving international attention. Her association with the choreographer John Butler led to several ballet commissions in New York.

On her return to New York in 1967 it was found that she was suffering from a brain tumour, requiring major surgery. Despite completing her opera *Sappho* while recuperating, the illness effectively destroyed her ability to compose. She continued to live in Greece until the early 1970s when she returned to Sydney. At her death in 1990 she bequeathed her house as a residence for young composers. Although familiar with the avant-garde, Glanville-Hicks always retained a romantic and impressionistic quality in her music while being inspired by the sounds of Asian music. She regarded her five operas as her greatest achievement.

WORKS (Selective)

Principal publishers: Associated, Colfrank, Hargail, Peters, Schott, Weintraub.

Orchestral *Meditation* (by 1933), *Sinfonietta No. 1* (1934), *Concerto no. 1 for Piano and Orchestra* (1936), *Concerto for Flute and Orchestra* (1937), *Prelude and Scherzo* (1937), *Sinfonietta No. 2* (by 1938), *Sinfonia da Pacifica* (1953), *Etruscan Concerto,* pf, chamber orch (1956), *Concerto romantico,* va, orch (1957), *Tapestry for Orchestra* (1958), *Drama for Orchestra* (1959).

Instrumental Trio for Pipes, I and II (1934), String Quartet (1937), Sonatina, treble rec/fl, pf (1939), Sonatina, pf (1939), *Concertino da camera,* fl, cl, bn, pf (1945), Sonata, hp, fl, hn (1950), Sonata, hp (1951), Sonata, pf, 5 perc (1951), *Three Gymnopédies,* I for ob, hp, str; II for hp, celeste, str; III for hp, str (1953), *Concertino Antico,* hp, str qrt (1955), *Musica Antiqua No. 1,* 2 fl, hp, marimba, perc (1957), *Prelude and Presto for Ancient American Instruments* (1957), *Prelude for a Pensive Pupil* (1958), *Girondelle for Giraffes,* fl/pic, trbn, db, perc (1978).

Film scores *The Robot* (1936), *Clouds* (1938), *Glacier* (1938), *Tulsa* (1949), *Tel* (1950), *The African Story* (1956), *A Scary Time* (1958).

Operas *Caedmon* (1933, 3 scenes, P. Glanville-Hicks), *The Transposed Heads* (1953, 6 scenes, Glanville-Hicks, after T. Mann's *Die vertauschten Köpfe*), 3 Apr. 1954, Louisville, KY, USA, *The Glittering Gate* (1956, 1, Glanville-Hicks after Lord Dunsany), 14 May 1959, New York, *Nausicaa* (1960, prol, 3, R. Graves and A. Reid, after Graves' *Homer's Daughter*), 19 Aug 1961 Athens, Greece, *Carlos among the Candles* (1962), *Sappho* (1963, 3, L. Durrell, after his play).

Ballets *Hylas and the Nymphs* (1935), *Postman's Knock* (1938), *Killer-of-Enemies* (1946), *The Masque of the Wild Man* (1958), 10 June 1958, Spoleto, Italy, *Triad* (1958), 10 June 1958, Spoleto, Italy, *Saul and the Witch of Endor* (1959), 7 June 1959, CBS TV, *A Season in Hell* (1965), 15 Nov. 1967, New York, *Tragic Celebration (Jephtha's Daughter)* (1966), 6 Nov. 1966, CBS TV.

Vocal *Choral Suite,* female ch, ob, str orch (1937), *Last Poems,* 5 songs, 1v, pf (1945), *Profiles from China,* 5 songs, T, pf, chamber orch (1945), *Ballade,* 3 songs, 1v, pf (1945), *13 Ways of Looking at a Blackbird,* S, pf (1947), *Thomsoniana,* S, T, fl, hn, str quartet, pf (1949), *Letters from Morocco,* 6 songs, T, chamber orch (1952).

FURTHER REFERENCE

Recordings include *The Transposed Heads,* West Australian Symphony Orchestra, cond. D. Measham, soloists (ABC 434 139);

Three Gymnopédies, ABC orchs (ABC 442 374). A discography to 1972 is in *PlushD.* See also Deborah Hayes, *Peggy Glanville-Hicks: A Bio-Bibliography* (New York: Greenwood Press, 1990); *MurdochA*; Elizabeth Wood, *GroveD.*

SUZANNE ROBINSON

Glass, Dudley (*b* Adelaide, 24 Sept. 1899; *d* Melbourne, Nov. 1981), composer, author. After studying arts at the University of Melbourne Conservatorium and composition with Fritz *Hart at the Albert Street Conservatorium, he wrote *Australia Land of Ours* in 1925, which was adopted in Victoria and NSW as an anthem for schoolchildren. He visited New York, then settled in London, his *The Beloved Vagabond* (1927, Adrian Ross) having a huge success there in 1927, and being staged in Australia with Gladys *Moncrieff in 1934. From 1929 he wrote revues, including *This and That, Colour Blind, Eldorado* and *The Toymaker of Nurnberg* (1930). He set 100 songs, particularly songs for children, including Hilaire Belloc's *Bad Child's Book of Beasts,* Edward Lear's *Nonsense Songs* (London: F. Warne, 1933) and Beatrix Potter's *The Songs of Peter Rabbit* (London: F. Warne, 1951).

In the war years he gave lecture-recitals to the troops stationed in the USA; after the war he made a lecture tour of the USA (1946) and broadcast on art and music for the BBC and (from 1947) for the ABC. His *Drake of England* (1954) was broadcast on the BBC and the ABC, but his style of music-theatre had become passé, and he turned to lecturing and writing for London papers.

FURTHER REFERENCE

Manuscripts in *CAnl.* Partial list of works in *SnellA.* Eric Irvin, 'Around the World with Music: The Itinerant Career of Dudley Glass, Australian Composer and Author', *Journal, Australian Jewish Historical Society* 10, (1986) 399–408.

Glass, Keith (*b* St Kilda, Melbourne), country music singer-songwriter, broadcaster. After playing in his own blues band while at high school, he worked in pop bands until being cast as Berger in the original Australian production of *Hair* (1969–71). In 1970 he formed the short-lived band Sundown, whose innovative mix of country and rock proved still ahead of the urban audience's taste; in the following years he worked as a manager and promoter, establishing Missing Link Records, Melbourne. From 1983 he formed a succession of New Country bands, leading to Keith Glass and the Tumblers (from 1986) with which he has toured extensively, appearing at the Tamworth and Port Fairy festivals (1990–91), his song *Outback (In Our Backyard)* (1991) becoming widely known. A leading exponent of New Country, his music combines country, blues, rock and rockabilly, and takes country music to new, often urban audiences. He co-hosted the New Country program *High In The Saddle* for 3RRR for seven years, now hosts *Across The Borderline* for Sydney Kick-AM, and writes for country music magazines.

FURTHER REFERENCE

Recordings include *Going Over Old Ground* (1989,Virgin), *Living Down My Past* (1991,Virgin), and *Rocking Cowboy* with Gary Young and Mick Hamilton (Larrikin LRF 287 CD). See also *LattaA*, 78–9; *Capital News* Aug. 1993; *Sun-Herald* 10 Sept. 1993.

Gleeson, Horace (*b* Williamstown, Melbourne, 1878; *d* ?), song composer, accompanist. He studied piano and composition with G.W. ★Torrance and had violin lessons for a time, then concentrated on the piano and twice won the South Street Eisteddfod, Ballarat. He joined Pollard's Opera Co. in NZ as an accompanist in 1899, writing his first song, *Speak To Me*, which was sung by Charles Carter in *The Belle of New York*. Back in Melbourne, he won the composition prize at the ANA Competitions in 1903 and became one of Melbourne's leading accompanists. He produced a steady stream of songs, which were sung by Ada Crossley, John McCormack, Horace Stevens, Peter Dawson, and Paul Althouse. In all he produced over 150 songs, including *Bells and Hobbles* (1931), *A Bush Bird in a Gum Tree*, *The Merry Minstrels* (1940); one of the last was *Three Shamrock Leaves* (1950).

FURTHER REFERENCE

A partial list of works is in *SnellA*. Recordings include *Bells and Hobbles* (1931, HMV EA1093), *A Bush Bird in a Gum Tree* (Columbia DO3390), *The Merry Minstrels* (1940, Parlophone A7620) and *Three Shamrock Leaves* (1950, Columbia, DO3324). Portrait in *Weekly Times* 14 Mar. 1903, and *AMN* 39/3 (Sept. 1948), 7. See also *MoresbyA*, 132–3; *AMN* 38 (July 1947), 7.

Glittering Gate, The. Opera in one act, music and libretto by Peggy ★Glanville-Hicks (1957) after Lord Dunsany. First performed at New York on 15 May 1959 and in Australia in 1972 Adelaide Festival. Published by Colfrank, New York, 1957.

Glynn, Gerald (*b* Brisbane, 3 Sept. 1943), composer. After studying music, literature and languages at the Universities of Queensland and Sydney, he was awarded a French Government Scholarship in 1967, and went to the Paris Conservatoire to study with Olivier Messiaen. He settled in Paris, and worked for two years in the electronic music studios of French radio. In the coming years he travelled to Africa, Asia and Latin America in search of sources for his composition. In 1981 he was visiting lecturer in composition at the NSW State Conservatorium, and his music has been performed in Britain, Europe and North America. His works are chiefly for solo instruments, such as *Whirligig* (1983) and *Gorlywhorl* 1984) for solo clarinet, as well as chamber works such as his Chamber Concerto (1982).

FURTHER REFERENCE

Recordings include *Love's Coming* (1990, 2MBS-FM MBS 21). See also Belinda Webster, 'Gerald Glynn: An Australian in Paris', *SA* 27 (Spring 1990), 15–18.

Go Betweens, The. Folk-rock band (1977–89) formed in Brisbane. At first Robert Foster and Grant McLennan (both vocals, guitar) played as a duo; their debut single *Lee Remick* (1978) showed the influence of the folk-rock style of Bob Dylan, Talking Heads and Velvet Underground. They expanded to a trio, then to six members, recording four more singles, including *I Need Two Heads* (1980) and their album *Before Hollywood* (1983). They were in the UK from 1983, where they built a large following, recording seven singles and four albums. Returning to Australia in 1987, their last works included *Was There Anything I Could Do* (1988) and the albums *16 Lovers Lane* (1988). They were a folk-rock group with fine harmonic sound, good vocals, and polished songs.

FURTHER REFERENCE

Recordings include *Lee Remick* (1978 Abel AB 001), *I Need Two Heads* (1980 Missing Link, Miss 23), *Before Hollywood* (1983 Stunn STUN 508), *Was There Anything I Could Do* (1988, Mushroom K698) and *16 Lovers Lane* (1988, Mushroom L38950). A compilation is *Go Betweens 1978–1990* (1990, Beggars Banquet BEG 104). For discography, see *SpencerA*. See also *McGrathA*; *SpencerW.*

Goerke, Annette Maureen (*b* Perth, 8 Sept. 1938), organist, church musician. She studied organ initially with Albert Lynch at St Mary's Cathedral, Perth, where she was appointed organist in 1956 and director of music in 1974. After graduating in composition from the University of Western Australia in 1971, she was awarded a Churchill fellowship, enabling her to undertake advanced organ studies in Europe in 1972, chiefly with Marie-Claire Alain in Paris. She has presented numerous broadcast organ recitals for the ABC, and has appeared both as soloist and as orchestral organist with the West Australian Symphony Orchestra on many occasions. As a regular recitalist at the University of Western Australia since 1973 she has introduced audiences to many large-scale 20th-century works by Charles Camilleri, Petr Eben and, in particular, Olivier Messiaen.   G. COX

Golden Guitar. Australasian Country Music Awards in the shape of miniature guitars, made annually since 1973 for various categories of country music song-writing and performance by the Country Music Association of Australia during their annual festival at Tamworth each January. A catalogue of winners appears in the *Directory of Australian Country Music* No. 1 (Tamworth, NSW: Max Ellis Marketing/Country Music Association of Australia, 1996).

Goldner, Richard (*b* Romania, 1918; *d* Sydney, 1994), violist, teacher. Playing viola in a string quartet from the age of 10, he entered the Technische Hochschule, Vienna, to study architecture but abandoned it to play viola in the Vienna State Opera Orchestra and to study with Simon Pullman at the Vienna Hochschule. From 1930 he played in the Vienna Chamber Orchestra and did session work for films, from 1933 playing in Hermann Scherchen's Vienna Concert Orchestra (later renamed the Musica Viva Orchestra). With the worsening persecutions of Jews in Vienna and the war, he came to Australia in 1939. He worked in a Sydney leathergoods firm (having been prevented by the Musicians Union from taking a post in the Sydney Symphony Orchestra because he was not Australian).

In 1945 he formed the Sydney Musica Viva, a 17-member string orchestra using Pullman's method of playing string quartets in a string choir, first rehearsed as four separate quartets. From 1947, with a smaller group, renamed the *Musica Viva Society, he toured Australia until he retired from playing in 1951. In 1955 the Musica Viva Society re-formed as an entrepreneur, and he gradually became alienated from it; from 1961 he taught at the NSW State Conservatorium, producing a stream of notable violinists. Marrying a student, Charmian Gadd, he moved to the USA in 1966, teaching at Pittsburgh, then Washington State. He returned to Sydney in 1981.

At times an irascible personality but a teacher and player with a profound enthusiasm for Viennese chamber music style and standards in the postwar years, he was an important pioneer of fine chamber music concerts in Australia.

FURTHER REFERENCE
His memoirs are unpublished. See Michael Shmith, 'Richard Goldner—the Musical Moses', *Musica Viva Australia: The First Fifty Years,* ed. Michael Shmith (Sydney: Playbill, 1996), 4–7; *BrisbaneE,* 260.

Goldner String Quartet. See *Australia Ensemble.*

Golem, The. Opera by Larry *Sitsky(1980), libretto by Gwen Harwood. Commissioned by the Australian Opera but as yet unperformed.

Goll, Edward (*b* Kadam, Bohemia, 4 Feb. 1884; *d* Melbourne, 11 Jan. 1949), pianist. After lessons in violin with Otakar Ševčík and in piano he gave his first concert at the age of nine. He studied with Dvořák at the Prague Conservatorium from the age of 13 (winning the Anton Rubinstein Prize), then with Emil Sauer at Vienna. In 1904 he appeared as a soloist in the piano concertos of Liszt, Mendelssohn and Arensky at Paris under Arthur Nikisch and at London under Henry Wood. He toured Europe and Russia with the violinist Jan Kubelik and cellist Ludwig Schwab, and settled in England in 1907. Visiting Australia on tour with the singer Benjamin Davis in 1911, he married an Australian, who returned to Europe with him for a honeymoon in 1912 but brought him back to settle at Melbourne in 1914. Appearing in recitals around Australia, he gave many memorable performances of the Beethoven violin and piano sonatas with Henri *Verbrugghen (1915–22), with whom he also toured the

USA and Canada. He was in Europe for refresher lessons 1922–23 and continued to give numerous recitals until 1938, when illness curtailed his activities. He had joined the staff of the Albert Street Conservatorium, then the University of Melbourne Conservatorium in 1915, where he taught until 1948.

One of the most outstanding pianists to settle in Australia, his repertoire was remarkably wide, covering over 30 composers, including many works unknown in Australia by Arnold Bax, Max Reger, Cyril Scott and others. As a teacher he emphasised technique, sight reading and practice; his pupils included Nancy *Weir, Margaret *Sutherland, and others who went on to notable careers.

FURTHER REFERENCE
He made early cylinder recordings with Phonotikia Italiana and Brunswick Records, now rare. See Peter Tregear, *The Conservatorium of Music, University of Melbourne: An Historical Essay* (Melbourne: Univ. Melbourne Faculty of Music, 1997), 57–61; H.J. Gibbney and Mimi Colligan, *ADB,* 9.

Gondwanaland. Rock band formed in Sydney (1983) by Charlie 'Hook' McMahon (didjeridu), Peter Carolan (synthesiser) and Eddie Duquemin (percussion). They combined the didjeridu and synthesisers in pop-inspired extended instrumental works. Gondwanaland's members found inspiration for their compositions in the diverse fauna and environments of the Australian continent, and their experiences in the Australian outback. McMahon learnt to play didjeridu as a child, and later lived among Aboriginal communities in Australia's Western Desert and Arnhem Land. Recordings, live performances and occasional television appearances earned Gondwanaland's members a reputation as composers of innovative, uniquely Australian music. After the release of *Wide Skies* (1992) Gondwanaland disbanded, and McMahon later recorded *Travelling* (1994) with a different band called Gondwana and *Tjilatjila* (1996).

FURTHER REFERENCE
Recordings by Gondwanaland include *Terra Incognita* (1984, WEA 255411–1); *Let the Dog Out* (1986, WEA 255412–1); *Gondwanaland* (1987, WEA 255135–1); *Wildlife* (1989, WEA 256415–1); *Wide Skies* (1992, Oceanic DIN9007D); by Gondwana *Travelling* (1994, Oceanic OM8998D); by Charlie McMahon *Tjilatjila* (1996, Oceanic OM9011D). See also C. McMahon, *Didjeridu* video produced by Jeni Kendell and Paul Tait (One World Films, 1992); *SpencerW*.

AARON D.S. CORN

Gonzalez Italian Opera Company. Giuseppe Gonzalez was a Spanish impresario who with his extended family presented pared-down productions of operatic standards on a tour circuit he developed through Egypt, Russia and Asia Minor before World War I. Of his four brothers, Giovanni and Ernesto were the conductors, Rodolfo the director, and Arturo a double bass player, while of his children, Ernestina was a soprano, Giovanni the first flute, and Rodolfo a manager; several husbands and wives were also in the company. When the outbreak of World War I prevented him returning north from Vladivostok in 1914, he toured South East Asia, then Australia 1916–17. After the tour the company moved on, but some of his artists stayed in Australia as the Italian-Australian Opera Co. or with the ★Rigo Grand Opera Co. in 1919. The company visited Australia again in 1928. In both visits the singers were of uneven quality and the productions rather threadbare, but the company was well received, for at that time operatic works were seldom seen in Australia.

FURTHER REFERENCE
Alison Gyger, *Opera in the Antipodes: Opera in Australia 1881–1939* (Sydney: Currency Press and Pellinor, 1980), 202–16, 251–8; *BrisbaneE,* 79, 209.

Goodchild, Geoff (*b* NSW), tuba player. He was principal tuba with ABC Military Band from 1936 and the Sydney Symphony Orchestra 1951–87. During his three decades with the ABC he appeared several times as soloist in the Vaughan Williams tuba concerto, formed the Sydney Brass Ensemble from the orchestra, and since the 1960s has directed Sydney Brass. Deeply involved in the brass band movement, he was secretary of the National Band Council of Australia and president of the Band Association of NSW. His son Paul Goodchild has succeeded him in the Sydney Symphony Orchestra.

Goodman, (Moses) Isador [Tsidore Goodman] (*b* Cape Town, South Africa, 27 May 1909; *d* Sydney, Dec. 1982), pianist. He gave his first public performance at the age of six with the Cape Town Symphony Orchestra playing Mozart's D Minor Piano Concerto. He studied at the Royal College of Music, London, from 1919, giving his debut in 1926, and was appointed a piano professor in 1927. In 1928 he won the Chappell and Challen Gold Medals. In 1930 he came to Australia to join the staff of the NSW State Conservatorium. He taught there for 50 years, as well as sustaining a career as a concert pianist, composer and conductor. He broadcast on radio extensively; for the 1935 film *The Burgomeister* he wrote, directed and conducted the orchestral score; he was also very active formulating and conducting theatre orchestras at Melbourne's Capitol Theatre, and for radio shows such as *Sunday Night at Eight*. His career was marred by three nervous breakdowns. A pianist of crystal-clear technique and great interpretive authority, the Goodman trademarks were an unusually flat hand position on the piano, and a distinctive profile. His recordings primarily featured music by the Romantics Chopin, Liszt, Schumann and Rachmaninov. He was awarded the AM in 1981.

FURTHER REFERENCE
Obit. in *Variety* 15 Dec. 1982. Recordings include Chopin works (ABC 432 137); *The Isador Goodman Legacy* (ABC 432 207);

Works of Debussy, Paganini, etc (ABC 432 208). See also Rudolf Brasch, *Australian Jews of Today* (Sydney: Cassell, 1977), 53–9; Ann Carr-Boyd, *GroveD*; Virginia Goodman, *Isador Goodman: A Life in Music* (Sydney: William Collins, 1983), which contains a complete discography; Wilson Lyle, *A Dictionary of Pianists* (London: Robert Hale, 1985).

THOMAS JUDE SAMMUT

Goossens, Sir Eugene (*b* London, 26 May 1893; *d* Hillingdon, England, 13 June 1962), conductor, composer. Born into a family of musicians of Belgian origin, Goossens was educated at the Bruges Conservatoire, the Liverpool College of Music and the Royal College of Music, was a violinist in the Queen's Hall Orchestra (1912–15) and in a string quartet, and then became an assistant conductor with the Beecham Opera Co. In 1921, with his own orchestra, he presented a series of subscription concerts in London, the programs including the first British performance of Stravinsky's *Le Sacre du printemps*. This led to engagements with the major British orchestras, Diaghilev's Ballets Russes, the Carl Rosa and British National Opera Cos and with European orchestras. In 1923 he moved to the USA to become director of the Eastman Rochester Orchestra, and in 1931 he succeeded Reiner as conductor of the Cincinnati Symphony Orchestra. After touring Australia for the ABC in 1946, he was invited to be the principal conductor of the newly constituted Sydney Symphony Orchestra, and at the same time director of the NSW State Conservatorium, starting in 1947.

In the Australian summer months he returned to the USA and Europe for conducting engagements. He was knighted in 1955 for his services to Australian music, but his appointments in Sydney came to an abrupt end in 1956 after he was convicted of a customs offence when returning from Europe. He resided for the remaining years of his life in London, and was active as a conductor. His compositions include two symphonies, an oboe concerto written for his brother, the oboist Leon Goossens, music for string orchestra, chamber works, the operas *Judith* and *Don Juan de Mañara*, and the oratorio *The Apocalypse*, which was much acclaimed at its premiere in Sydney in 1954. He also arranged for modern orchestra Handel's *Messiah* for Sir Thomas Beecham, who recorded this version. He recorded extensively with London orchestras and the Cincinnati Symphony Orchestra, and made a series of 78 rpm recordings with the Sydney Symphony Orchestra, the first the orchestra had released.

Goossens' seven years in Australia were quite significant in the development of both standards of orchestral performance and the audience's musical sophistication. His natural taste and strengths as a conductor were essentially in the late 19th and early 20th-century Romantic repertoire, and in French composers such as Debussy and Ravel, but he brought to his programs a wide variety of music from all eras except the Viennese atonal school, with which he had no sympathy. His concerts introduced major compositions of Mahler, Rachmaninov, Strauss, Glière, Prokofiev, Nielsen, and other works new to the Australian musical public, in consistently high levels of performance. In addition, with the limited resources available to him he staged operas at the Conservatorium, including *Die Walküre*. His advocacy for an opera house in Sydney was the origin of the move that eventually led to the construction of the Sydney Opera House at Circular Quay. The circumstances of his departure in 1956 tended to leave his reputation in neglect, but in recent times his contribution to musical life, particularly in Sydney, has become more readily appreciated.

FURTHER REFERENCE
Recordings as a conductor include Beethoven, Symphony No. 2 and Mendelssohn, Symphony No. 5, Sydney Symphony Orchestra (EMI). As a composer, recordings include Symphony No. 2, *Concertino, Fantasy*, Sydney Symphony Orchestra, cond. V. Handley (ABC 442 364). A discography is in *HolmesC*. See also Stephen Banfield, *GroveD*; Ava Hubble, *The Strange Case of Eugene Goossens and Other Tales from the Sydney Opera House* (Sydney: Collins, 1988); Carole Rosen, *The Goossens: A Musical Century* (London: Andre Deutsch, 1993).

J.L. HOLMES

Gordon, Adam Lindsay   (*b* Faiol, Azores, Portugal, 19 Oct. 1833; *d* Brighton, Melbourne, 24 June 1870), poet. A horsebreaker and steeplechase rider, he wrote sporting verse for Victorian newspapers, and his volumes of poetry include *Bush Ballads and Galloping Rhymes* (1870), which laid the ground for the stockman's ballad idiom. Suffering from riding injuries and depression, he shot himself at the age of 36.

FURTHER REFERENCE
OxfordL.

Gordon, Lee   (*b* Coral Gables, Florida, USA, 1920; *d* London, 7 Nov. 1963), rock and roll entrepreneur. After trying various business ventures, he emigrated to Australia in 1953 and worked as a furniture merchant. In 1957 he came to national attention by bringing Bill Haley and the Comets to Australia, presenting them first at Newcastle, then in the Sydney Stadium; from then on his Big Shows at the Stadium featured American stars from Little Richard to Frank Sinatra. He used local rock and roll artists as supporting acts in his shows and recorded their work on his own label. In this way he brought Johnny *O'Keefe, Lonnie *Lee, Col *Joye and many other Australian pop artists to attention in the next few years, making him the leading promoter of early rock and roll in Australia. But he also had alcohol, drug and serious gambling problems; a bankrupt by 1963, he went abroad to escape his debts, dying of a heart attack in a London hotel at the age of 43.

Go-Set.   Weekly newspaper based in Melbourne (1966–74) aimed at teenagers and young adults. At first covering local pop artists, fashion, sport and musical events, within a year the coverage had expanded to national music news and features of teenage interest, adding jazz and folk columns in 1968. From 1969 *Go-Set* awards for the best bands, solo artists and albums were made, and by 1971 the focus was almost exclusively musical, including reports from the Los Angeles and London popular music scenes. There was still a central focus on Melbourne, which was maintained until the newspaper's demise in 1974.

Gosford,   pop. (1991) 51 178. City on Broken Bay, north of Sydney, established 1839. Located on scenic Brisbane Waters, it is a suburb of Sydney and centre for farm produce and building materials. The Gosford City Band was active by World War I, and there is also the Gosford City Orchestra and the Gosford Philharmonia (founded 1962), which presents choral, orchestral works and operettas. The Central Coast Conservatorium, affiliated with the University of Newcastle, offers BMus and DipMus degrees, tuition on an array of instruments, and maintains an orchestra. There are also several pipe bands and the Central Coast Harmony Chorus.

Gospel Music.   Black American music derived from church services in the 1930s, its sources in spirituals and the blues. The style involves choirs in antiphonal counterpoint with an improvising soloist, pianos, organs and an array of other instruments. In Australia there is a small number of pentecostal and fundamentalist churches where the music has been cultivated, but in general Australian gospel musicians have sought their own genres, and a mood which differs from the unrestrained exuberance of the American style. The best-known Australian gospel singer, for example, is Jim *Muir, who sings in country style.

Goulburn,   pop. (1991) 21 459. City on tablelands of south-eastern NSW, established 1833 as a convict settlement. By the time virtuoso violinist Miska *Hauser toured in 1854 it had become a sheep and cattle trading centre, but Hauser found only a rudimentary wooden shed to play in. The post office clock tower bells chimed the quarter hours from 1877; the large St Saviour's Cathedral imported a three-manual organ from England in 1884, rebuilt in 1908; the Cathedral of Saints Peter and Paul also imported a large instrument from London in 1890. A group of eight tubular bells rang attractively from the Passionist Monastery from 1892, and the Goulburn Liedertafel presented concerts and such musicals as *The Cingalee* (1926). The Goulburn Eisteddfod was founded 1927 and by 1935 had 180 sections, with the winners appearing on local radio. A prominent musical figure in the city for many years has been the organist, British-born composer Paul Paviour, who has conducted many concerts and taught at the former Goulburn College of Advanced Education.

Gould, Tony (Anthony James)
(*b* Melbourne, 2 Feb. 1940), jazz pianist. He studied classical piano at the University of Melbourne with Max Cooke. He has had wide-ranging activity as a pianist and composer, including in studio and concert work with particular emphasis on acoustic music. A frequent support for visitors such as Dave Brubeck, the Chicago Art Ensemble, and Sarah Vaughan, he played accompaniment for Clark Terry, Ernestine Anderson and Mark Murphy. He toured Asia (1982) with Keith *Hounslow as the duo McJad. His other appearances include sessions with John Sangster and Brian *Brown, and the *Geminiani Chamber Orchestra. His film and full orchestral compositions include concerti for saxophone, piano, percussion and strings. He holds graduate degrees in musicology (La Trobe University PhD, 1990), has been active in music journalism, and is head of postgraduate studies at the Victorian College of the Arts.

FURTHER REFERENCE
Recordings include *Len Barnard* (1969, W & G Records WG-25S-5455); *Tony Gould Orchestra* (1978, Move 3021); *Introducing McJad* (1978, AIJA Recording 001); *Requiem for a Loved One,* John Sangster (1980, Rain Forest Records RFLP 005); *Lirik* (1993, Newmarket NEW 1035.2); *Gateway* (1996, Newmarket NEW 202.2). An interview with him is in *WilliamsA*, 68–73. See also *ClareB*; *BissetB*; *OxfordJ*.   BRUCE JOHNSON

Govenlock, James Cockburn
(*b* Adelaide, 1 June 1918; *d* Adelaide, 9 Nov. 1974), organist, choral conductor. His talent became evident early. He was a convert to Catholicism and became organist and choirmaster of St Francis Xavier's Cathedral, Adelaide, in 1945 in succession to his teacher, Harold Wylde, who had already established a good musical tradition there. His cathedral work was interrupted by a period in England on an Elder Overseas Scholarship, during which he won the Limpus Prize in the FRCO examinations. He subsequently taught organ and theory at the Elder Conservatorium, Adelaide. Govenlock excelled as a liturgical organist and set high standards in choral music. The Corinthian Singers, which have retained a respected position in Adelaide's musical life, were founded by him in 1963, and he was their first director. His services to Catholic church music were rewarded with a papal knighthood (Order of St Gregory) in 1977.

FURTHER REFERENCE
Helen Harrison, *Laudate Dominum: Music at Adelaide's Catholic Cathedral (1845–1995)* (Adelaide, in progress); Andrew McCredie, ed., *From Colonel Light into the Footlights: The Performing Arts in South Australia from 1836 to the present* (Adelaide: Pagel, 1988).   DAVID SWALE

Goyulan
(Morning Star). Aboriginal clan song series from north-central Arnhem Land, NT. The songs form the backbone of a religious ritual, and are owned by several clans of the Arbarra people. They are sung at important rituals such as circumcision, funerals and *rom* ceremonies between song owners and distant but friendly tribes, as well as outside the ritual context around the campfire. Goyulan is one of the most important of about 30 song subjects in the series. Women may not be public singers of Goyulan and only a few men of each generation are recognised as singers. The songs are accompanied on clapsticks with didjeridu and a group of dancers. See *Aboriginal Music.*

FURTHER REFERENCE
Margaret Clunies Ross and Johnny Mundrugmundrug, *Goyulan, the Morning Star: An Aboriginal Clan Song Series from North East Arnhem Land* (Canberra: Aboriginal Studies Press, 1988); also recording (1982, Australian Institute of Aboriginal Studies AIAS 18); Stephen Wild, ed., *Rom: An Aboriginal Ritual of Diplomacy* (Canberra: AIAS, 1986).

Grabowsky [Grabowski], Paul
(*b* Lae, New Guinea, 1958), jazz pianist, composer. He settled in Melbourne and began classical piano training at the age of five, later taking lessons from Mack Jost (1965–79). Forming fusion and bop groups, he worked in theatre and cabaret, and began studies at the University of Melbourne Conservatorium. Withdrawing in 1980 he travelled abroad, including five years in Munich, working and touring with saxophonist Gunther Klatt; he also worked with Chet Baker, Johnny Griffin and Art Farmer. Returning to Melbourne in 1985, he became active in progressive jazz, including as co-founder with Dale *Barlow of the award-winning Wizards of Oz in 1986, and pianist with Australian Jazz Orchestra, both of which toured locally and internationally (1988).

He has also written prolifically for television, including the series *Phoenix* and *Janus*, and for films, including *Last Days Of Chez Nous*. He has been musical director for television series including *Tonight Live*, and also for singer Vince Jones. In New York he has worked and recorded with Dewey Redman and Paul Motian (1988), and was voted *Rolling Stone* (Aust.) jazz artist of the year (1989). He gives frequent performances as a leader of small groups, including with Allan Browne and Gary Costello, and critically acclaimed Melbourne saxophonist Ian Chaplin. In 1993 his suite *Ringing The Bell Backwards* was premiered in Melbourne by his Australian Art Orchestra, the development of which has been catalysed by both his high public profile and the interest in big band music generated by such groups as John Pochée's Ten Part Invention.

FURTHER REFERENCE
Recordings include *Soundtrack,* Wizards of Oz (1988, Polygram 834 531–2); *Six By Three* (1989, Spiral Scratch 0001); *Ringing The*

Bell Backwards (1995, Origin OR 008); *When Words Fail,* Paul Grabowsky Trio (1995, Origin OR 010). See also *ClareB; Bulletin* 14 Sept. 1993, 93–5; Adrian Jackson, 'Paul Grabowsky', *APRAJ* (November 1991), 7–9; Jim McLeod, *Jazztrack* (Sydney: ABC Books, 1994), 178–91.

BRUCE JOHNSON

Grainger, Percy Aldridge [George Percy Grainger] (*b* Brighton, Melbourne, 8 July 1882; *d* White Plains, NY, 20 Feb. 1961), pianist, composer, ethnologist and 'all-round man'.
1. *Early years (1882–1914). 2. United States (1914–61). 3. Grainger and Australia.*

1. Early Years. (i) Australia, 1882–95. Grainger was born into comfortable middle-class circumstances in a Melbourne still primed by the affluence of the 1850s goldrushes. His general and musical education was mainly undertaken at home, under the guidance of his mother, Rose. She early instilled into the young Grainger a love of the arts and that freedom-loving, heroic outlook which would so characterise his mature attitudes. The reading of classical legends and Icelandic sagas left particularly strong impressions upon him. Private tutorials were occasionally also arranged in language studies, art (Frederick McCubbin), drama and elocution (Thomas A. Sisley) and, from *c*.1892, piano (Louis Pabst). In 1894 Grainger first appeared as a pianist before the Melbourne public; the acclaim led to the formation of a benefit committee to support musical studies in Germany.

(ii) Germany, 1895–1901. Grainger studied at the Hoch Conservatory in Frankfurt am Main from 1895. He had initially hoped to study with Clara Schumann, but his main teachers in Frankfurt were James Kwast (piano) and Ivan Knorr (composition, theory). His artistic development there was, however, strongly influenced by a retired lithographer, Karl Klimsch, several English students (Cyril Scott, Balfour Gardiner and Roger Quilter, who were, with Grainger, the key members of the so-called 'Frankfurt Group'), the Danish cellist and composer Herman Sandby, and his mother. In 1897–98 Grainger first came in contact with the writings of Rudyard Kipling, which inspired his many Kipling settings, notably the *Kipling 'Jungle Book' Cycle* (1898–1956), and Walt Whitman, in 'loving adoration' of whom he wrote his *Marching Song of Democracy* (1901–15).

(iii) Britain, 1901–14. In 1901 Grainger moved to London, where he slowly established a career as a concert pianist, in earlier years finding most engagements in 'society' concerts as an assistant artist and sometimes accompanist, but from 1910 strengthening his reputation as a recitalist and orchestral soloist in Britain and northern Europe. He twice undertook lengthy tours of Australasia, in 1903–4 and 1908–9, in collaboration with the Australian contralto Ada *Crossley. Early champions of

Grainger's pianistic talents were Stanford, Grieg (whose Piano Concerto Grainger promoted), Delius, Henry Wood and the critic Robin Legge. From 1905 Grainger took to collecting and transcribing English folk-songs, where he was one of the earlier users of the phonograph. By 1910 his collection numbered about 435 songs, many of which he set imaginatively for a wide range of vocal and instrumental ensembles. Although during his first decade in London he composed major works, such as *Hillsong* No. 1 (1901–2), *Hillsong* No. 2 (1901–7) and *English Dance* (1899–1909), and tried out many of his compositions in private circles, Grainger did not 'launch' himself as a composer until his reputation as a pianist was secure. In 1911 Schott (London) started regularly to publish his compositions; in 1912 the first public concert devoted solely to his own works took place in London, and in 1912–13 he gained high exposure as a composer and performer in the Balfour Gardiner series of 'new music' concerts. Highly popular compositions in the immediate pre-war years included *Shepherd's Hey* (1908–13), Grainger's arrangement of an English Morris dance tune, and *Handel in the Strand* (1911–12), a clog dance. In 1913, with Stravinsky's recent ballet music in mind, Grainger began one of his few larger-scale compositions, his 'music to an imaginary ballet', *The Warriors,* which he completed in 1916.

2. United States, 1914–61. Shortly after the outbreak of World War I Grainger sailed to the USA, ostensibly for a few months in the interest of his mother's health. He would, however, settle in New York, where his reputation, both as pianist and composer, rapidly surpassed his London status. He signed lucrative contracts for piano rolls (Duo-Art Company) and gramophone recordings (Columbia), and settled on G. Schirmer as the publisher of his music in the USA. In 1916 his orchestral suite *In a Nutshell* (1905–16) was premiered at the Norfolk Festival in Connecticut, where his *Warriors* also came to first performance in 1917. Following accusations of cowardice in both the British and American presses, Grainger did eventually enlist in the US Army, shortly after American entry into the war in 1917. He first played oboe and soprano saxophone in an army band and was later appointed a band instructor. In 1918 he took out American citizenship. In that year he also completed his most popular composition, *Country Gardens,* a setting for piano of a Morris dance tune collected by Cecil J. Sharp.

Grainger's hectic career of performing, occasional composition and summer-school teaching suddenly came to a halt in April 1922, when his mother committed suicide by leaping from a New York skyscraper while he was on tour. Her death caused him, over the following few years, to review many aspects of his life. He rejected many of his recent American friends and reverted more to the friends of his youth, became a vegetarian, developed his ideas of 'blue-eyed' English, became more extreme in his racial views (partly under the influence of Houston Stewart Chamberlain's writings), became less inhibited in sexual matters (particularly, flagellation and sexual fantasy), and even more zealously crusaded for performances of contemporary music, not least his own works and those of his friends. He revived his interest in collecting folk music, on four occasions during the 1920s visiting Denmark to collect folk-songs with the ethnologist Evald Tang Kristensen, to whom he dedicated his *Danish Folk-music Suite* (1922–30). Grainger also visited Australia for concert tours and to see relatives in 1924 and 1926. While returning from the latter tour he met the Swede Ella Ström, whom two years later he married during a concert in the Hollywood Bowl which featured the premiere of his *To a Nordic Princess* (1927–28). In his attempt to expand the possibilities of band and orchestral performances of his own music and arrangements of the music of others, he developed during the 1920s the principles of 'elastic scoring', whereby music was written for 'tone strands' rather than for inflexible combinations of instruments. It was the conductor's role to assign the available instruments to the various strands, so as to ensure an appropriate overall balance of sound.

In the 1930s Grainger's educational and promotional enthusiasms came to overshadow his performing and compositional activities. He attended the Haslemere Festival in 1931, and became a keen promoter of Arnold Dolmetsch's pioneering work with early music repertory and performance. During 1932–33 he assumed the position of head of the department of music at New York University, where his lecture course on 'The Manifold Nature of Music' became the basis of the twelve radio lectures on 'Music: A Commonsense View of All Types', which he presented over the ABC in 1934–35, when he undertook his most extensive Australasian tour. It was during this visit, too, that he supervised the building of the first stage of the Grainger Museum at the University of Melbourne, which he envisaged as a diverse music museum as well as a more personal archive and display of his own interests and passions. He visited Melbourne again in 1938 for the building of the museum's second stage. Grainger's frequent work with bands led to his 'bunch of musical wildflowers', *Lincolnshire Posy* (1937), a setting of six English folk-songs which remains today a cornerstone of the repertory of American bands.

World War II provided Grainger with opportunities to revitalise his concert career, and further promote performances of his own music. From his wartime base in Springfield, Missouri, he toured with a frequency not seen since the 1910s. Many of these performances were benefit concerts for troops. He also continued to teach each summer at the National Music Camp, Interlochen, until 1944. After the war Grainger thought of moving back to Australia, but could never find sufficient incentive for doing so. Even after his last formal American concert tour in 1948 he continued to perform frequently in schools and colleges until 1960. Although he composed little new music, he did work with the physicist Burnett

Cross during 1945–60 on various ★Free Music machines, designed to 'introduce Hogarth's curve of beauty into music' with their gliding intervals and freedoms of rhythm and harmony. These experimental machines advanced ideas about a 'free music' which Grainger had nurtured since his childhood, and which had found occasional earlier expression in his *Train Music (Charging Irishry)* (1900–1), his sketch for *Sea-song* (1907) and his early example of *Free Music No. 1*, for string quartet (1935). Grainger's final decade was, however, one of increasing frustration as he saw the havoc which age and cancer were wreaking upon his multitude of plans. His only postwar visit to Australia was in 1955–56, when he and his wife spent several months arranging the exhibits of his museum. The old Grainger was, however, undiminished in his prophetic gifts, and provided early warnings of the dangers of uncontrolled population growth, wood-pulping, pollution and meat-eating: 'Nature will have to teach man a cruel lesson', he warned in 1950.

3. Grainger and Australia.   Grainger was never technically an Australian. During his childhood he was a citizen of the self-governing British colony of Victoria, and remained British until he took American citizenship in 1918. Despite this change in citizenship, he rarely attempted an American style in his music, but proudly remained closest to his German-educated English peers. To Gardiner he wrote in 1941 of their common Englishness: 'You (Hardy-in-tones), I (Kipling-in-tones), you for rural England & I for the yeoman Colonies . . .' Grainger saw no contradiction in claiming to be Australia's 'only famous' composer, and unashamedly used the argument of self-preservation in Australia's artistic interest as one reason for avoiding military service during 1914–17.

Although Grainger recognised the need for a distinctively Australian music, with a vastness and monotony to match the national landscape, he did not systematically attempt such a music himself. Rather, he sought, within a normally small-scale British folk-influenced style, to express his own memories of, or nostalgia for, Australia. In his program note to *Colonial Song* (1905–12), the first of a planned series of 'Sentimentals', he explained: 'I have wished to express feelings aroused by thoughts of the scenery and people of my native land, Australia.' Even in this work, as in the 'Gumsuckers March' from *In a Nutshell* and *Australian Up-Country Song* (1928)—all three of which share some common thematic materials— Grainger did not use Australian tunes (which he showed little interest in collecting), but rather attempted 'a melody typical of Australia, as Stephen Foster's songs are typical of America'. Many other of his works he saw as Australian in intention or appeal. His *Marching Song of Democracy*, despite its thoroughly American inspiration, applied 'no less to Australia and the other younger democracies', he explained.

Grainger's Australianness needs to be seen against his strident espousal of Nordic racialism in music and his interest in Asian–Pacific cultures. Certainly from the 1920s onward, he maintained that his music expressed the unity of the far-flung, individualistic Nordic (blue-eyed) race, as found in Scandinavia, the British Isles, North America and Australasia. At other times, however, he saw his music as reflecting the 'soft & yielding Pacific Ocean attitude towards life', in contrast to the harsher 'Atlantic' view common to Europeans and Americans.

It is in personality and body image that Grainger approached most closely to something quintessentially Australian. He embodied the resourceful, golden-haired, muscular Australian youth, and battled to preserve this image into his fifties through careful attention to food and exercise, well-publicised feats of physical endurance and athletic antics even while on stage. He juxtaposed this Antipodean Nordic 'all-roundedness' with the growing specialisation in European and American societies, which he believed enfeebled the human spirit and threatened the well-springs of artistic inspiration. Among 'all-rounded' icons posed by him was the Australian Norman Lindsay.

Grainger's influence upon Australian music and culture has been more conceptual than stylistic. His vision of a distinctively Australian music, analogous to the national landscape and true to the country's Asian–Pacific location, was persuasive to many composers prominent since the 1960s, in particular Peter ★Sculthorpe and Barry ★Conyngham. His avant-garde experiments with 'free music', so painstakingly carried out in the pre-electronic era, however, quickly became dated by the massive technological advances of the late 1950s and 1960s. Grainger's skill as a setter of folk-songs proved most influential upon the next generation of British composers, especially Benjamin Britten, who recognised Grainger in this regard as his 'master', while Grainger's innovations in scoring and balancing of instrumental timbres have a vibrant legacy in the music of subsequent generations of American composers of band music.

WORKS

(Many mss in Grainger Museum, Univ. Melbourne; Grainger Library, White Plains, NY, USA)

A definitive listing, by genre, of Grainger's extensive output is impossible, because of his constant revision and rescoring of works, as well as the frequent use of 'elastic scoring' in his later decades. Dates of composition, revision and rescoring so often span several decades that a meaningful chronological listing is also not possible. The list below presents the more significant of Grainger's published and unpublished original works, in alphabetical order, followed by date(s) of initial or substantial composition. A summary listing of Grainger's numerous collections of folk music settings and the more prominent of the individual folk music settings then follows. For a more comprehensive listing of works, including dates of first editions, see Josephson (1986). For detailed catalogues of Grainger's works, including his transcriptions, arrangements, paraphrases and editions of the music of other composers, see Balough (1975) and Dreyfus (1978, 1995).

Grainger's main publishers were Schott (London/Mainz), from 1911, and G. Schirmer (New York), from 1915.

Major original works: instrumental, vocal, choral
Arrival Platform Humlet (1908–12, 1916); *Australian Up-country Song* (1905, 1928); *The Bride's Tragedy* (Swinburne, 1908–13); *Children's March 'Over the Hills and Far Away'* (1916–18); *Colonial Song* (1905–12); *Eastern Intermezzo* (1898–99, 1922); *English Dance* (1899–1909); *English Waltz* (1899–1901); *Free Music No. 1*, sample for str qrt (1907, 1935); *Free Music*, for 6 theremins, (?1935–36, unpub.); *Gay But Wistful* (1912–16); *Gumsuckers March* (1905–11); *Handel in the Strand* (1911–12); *Harvest Hymn* (1905–6, 1932); *Hillsong No. 1* (1901–2); *Hillsong No. 2* (1901–7); *The Immovable Do* (1933–40); *In Dahomey* (1903–9); *'In a Nutshell' Suite*, orchestral suite comprised of *Arrival Platform Humlet, Gay but Wistful, Pastoral, Gumsuckers March*; *Kipling 'Jungle Book' Cycle* (11 settings, 1898–1956); *Kipling settings* (at least 24 settings additional to the *'Jungle Book' Cycle*, 1898–1948; pub. from 1911, and unpub.); *The Lads of Wamphray* (1904–5); *The Lonely Desert-man Sees the Tents of the Happy Tribes* (1911–14); *Love Verses from 'The Song of Solomon'* (1899–1901, 1911); *Lullaby from 'Tribute to Foster'* (1915); *Marching Song of Democracy* (1901–15); *Mock Morris* (1910); *Pastoral* (1915–16); *The Power of Rome and the Christian Heart* (1918–43); *Random Round* (1912–14); *A Reiver's Neck-verse* (Swinburne, 1908); *Sailor's Song* (1900–54); *Sea-song* (1907, unpub.); *A Song of Autumn* (A.L. Gordon, 1899); *To a Nordic Princess* (1927–28); *Train Music (Charging Irishry)* (1900–1, unpub.); *Tribute to Foster* (1913–16); *Walking Tune* (1900–12); *The Warriors* (1913–16); *The Wraith of Odin* (1903); *Youthful Rapture* (1901); *Youthful Suite* (1899–1945); *Zanzibar Boat Song* (1902).

Settings of folk music

Grainger's collections of folk music settings are *American Folk-music Settings, British Folk-music Settings, Danish Folk-music Settings, Sea Chanty Settings, Settings of Songs and Tunes from William Chappell's 'Old English Popular Music', Settings of Dance-folksongs from the Faeroe Islands, Two Welsh Fighting Songs.*

Significant among his folk music settings are *Bold William Taylor* (1908); *Brigg Fair* (1906); *Country Gardens* (1908–18); *Danish Folk-music Suite*, orchestral suite comprised of *The Power of Love, Lord Peter's Stable Boy, The Nightingale and the Two Sisters, Jutish Medley; Father and Daughter* (1908–9); *Green Bushes* (1905–6); *I'm Seventeen Come Sunday* (1905–12); *Irish Tune from County Derry* (1902; also *County Derry Air*, 1919–20); *Jutish Medley* (1923–27); *Let's Dance Gay in Green Meadow* (1905); *Lincolnshire Posy* (1937); *Lord Peter's Stable Boy* (1922–27); *Molly on the Shore* (1907); *My Robin is to the Greenwood Gone* (1904–12); *The Nightingale and the Two Sisters* (1923–30); *The Power of Love* (1922); *La Scandinavie (Scandinavian Suite)* (1902); *Scotch Strathspey and Reel* (1901–2); *Shallow Brown* (1910); *Shepherd's Hey* (1908–13); *Spoon River* (1919–22); *The Sussex Mummers' Christmas Carol* (1905–11); *There was a Pig Went Out to Dig* (1905); *Ye Banks and Braes o'Bonnie Doon* (1901).

FURTHER REFERENCE
Balogh, T. *A Complete Catalogue of the Works of Percy Grainger* (Perth: Univ. WA, 1975).

Bird, J., *Percy Grainger* (London: Elek Books, 1976).

Dreyfus, K., *Music by Percy Aldridge Grainger,* 2 vols (Melbourne: Univ. Melbourne, 1978, 1995).

——, ed., *The Farthest North of Humanness: Letters of Percy Grainger, 1901–14* (Melbourne: Macmillan, 1985).

Gillies, M., and D. Pear, eds, *The All-Round Man: Selected Letters of Percy Grainger, 1914–1961* (Oxford: Clarendon Press, 1994).

Josephson, D., 'Grainger, (George) Percy (Aldridge)', in *The New Grove Dictionary of American Music,* ed. H. Wiley Hitchcock and Stanley Sadie vol. 2 (London: Macmillan, 1986).

Mellers, W., *Percy Grainger* (Oxford: OUP, 1992).

MALCOLM GILLIES

Grandi, Marghareta [Margaret Garde] *b* Hobart, 4 Oct. 1894; *d* 1972), soprano. After showing startling talent in Hobart as a child, she went to London to study as a mezzo-soprano at the Royal College of Music at the age of 16, then to Paris for lessons with Emma Calvé. She made her debut in Massenet's *Werther* and as Carmen at the Opéra Comique in 1914, then sang in the premiere of Massenet's *Amadis* at Monte Carlo in 1915. Seeking further study with Gianina Russ in Milan, she was detained for the rest of World War I; marrying the set designer Giovanni Grandi she made her debut as a soprano as Aida at Teatro Carcano, Milan, in 1932, and eventually achieved wide fame as Elena in Boito's *Mefistofele* at La Scala in 1933. Thereafter she sang in major Italian houses, as well as at Vienna, made her Glyndebourne debut in 1939, and sang at the Edinburgh Festival. Prevented from public appearance in Italy during World War II, she resumed her career in 1946, singing in many European houses and touring South America and Egypt. She never returned to appear in Australia.

A striking actress with a voice of thrilling power, her roles included Lady Macbeth, Donna Anna, Leonora (*ll trovatore*), Tosca, Amelia (*Simon Boccanegra*), Norma, Leonora (*Force of Destiny*), the premieres of Bliss's *The Olympians,* and Gomez's *La schiano,* and the Italian premiere of Strauss's *Friedenstag.*

FURTHER REFERENCE

Recordings included the Beecham *Tales of Hoffmann* with the Royal Philharmonic Orchestra (1950, not current); *Record of Singing vol. 4—Italian School* (reissue, EMI CH57 69741–2). See also *MonashB*; *MackenzieS,* 144–46; Harold Rosenthal, *GroveO*; K.J. Kutsch and Leo Riemann *Grosses Sängerlexikon* (Bern: Francke Verlag, 1987).

Graney, Dave (*b* Mount Gambier, SA, 1959), rock singer. He began performing rock music while a teenager, joining the Moodists in 1980 and going with them to the UK in 1984. He returned in 1988 with a new band, the Coral Snakes, then from 1989 formed the White Buffaloes. Based in Melbourne, he has appeared in the alternative venues in St Kilda and Fitzroy under various aliases, including the Golden Wolverine, Son of the Morning Star, and the Salvage Sportsman. Singing in a half-spoken, characteristic low grumble, he delivers monologues between his songs, which are unconfined and multifarious.

FURTHER REFERENCE

Recordings include *My Life On The Plains* with White Buffaloes (1990, Blaze 45T); *The Lure Of The Tropics* with Coral Snakes (1992, Torn & Frayed TORN 1); *Night Of The Wolverine* (1993, Id ID00152); *You Wanna Be There* (1994, Id 522381–2). See also *SpencerW*; *Age* 23 Apr. 1994.

Grant, Clifford Scantlebury (*b* Randwick, Sydney, 11 Sept. 1930), bass. After studies at the NSW State Conservatorium with Isador Hill, then at Melbourne with Henry and Annie ★Portnoj, he made his debut with the National Opera Co. of NSW as Raimondo in *Lucia di Lammermoor* in 1952. He took other Australian engagements, then moved to London and studied with Otakar Kraus. From 1966 he sang with the English National Opera and San Francisco Opera, making guest appearances at Glyndebourne, Covent Garden, the Welsh National Opera, and in Europe. He made his Metropolitan Opera debut in 1977 in *Esclarmonde* and appeared with the Australian Opera 1976–90, from 1993 returning to the stage at Opera North, UK. With an authoritative voice and a noble presence on the stage, his repertoire was very wide, extending from Nettuno in *Il ritorno d'Ulisse* and *The Coronation of Poppea* through powerful appearances in Wagnerian roles to *Oedipus Rex* and Meale's *Voss*. He recorded very extensively.

FURTHER REFERENCE

Recordings include Fafner and Hunding in *The Ring of the Nibelungs* cond. Reginald Goodall (EMI CMS 763595–2); Monterone in *Rigoletto,* London Symphony Orchestra (Decca 4144269–2DH2); Phorocas in *Esclarmonde,* National Philharmonic Orchestra (Decca 425651–2DM3); Bartolo in *Nozze di Figaro,* BBC Symphony (Philips 422540–2PME3); Giovanni in *Il Corsaro,* New Philharmonia (Philips 426118–2PM2); Angelotti in *Tosca,* New Philharmonia (RCA RD 80105); Maurevert and Monk III in *Huguenots,* New Philharmonic Orchestra (Decca); Oroviso in *Norma,* Australian Opera (Vision Video VVD 1138); Raimondo in *Lucia di Lammermoor,* Australian Opera (VVD 779); and bass *The Apostles,* cond. A. Boult (EMI CMS 764206–2). See also Alan Blythe, *GroveD;* Roger Covell, *GroveO*.

Gratton, Frances Lymer (*b* Halifax, England, 5 Dec. 1871; *d* Seacliff, SA, 26 Nov. 1946), music educator, musician, conductor. A product of the SA state school system, in which she trained and taught apart from a six-year sojourn as first assistant at Charles Street School, Launceston, Tasmania, Gratton demonstrated musical aptitude in the prevailing tonic sol-fa pedagogy, eventually becoming an Associate of the Tonic Sol-fa College, London (1906). In 1914 she was appointed inspector of music at the Training College in Adelaide, and between 1920 and his retirement in 1936 he was the supervisor of music in the SA education department. Gratton was also the acclaimed conductor of the massed children's Thousand Voices Concerts, 1920–37.   JANE SOUTHCOTT

Gray, Bruce (Athol)   (b Adelaide, 18 Aug. 1926), jazz reeds player. He began on fife and violin before playing clarinet (later, saxophones, flute) and joining the military band of the Adelaide College of Music. Forming a quartet in secondary school with Bill Munro and Bob Wright, he worked with Mal Badenoch, then Malcolm Bills until 1946. A founder member of the Southern Jazz Group, after its disbandment he went on to lead various more mainstream bands. He is also active in dance and session work, including the ABC orchestras, and has resumed occasional association with Dave Dallwitz. Gray is a central figure in Adelaide traditional mainstream jazz.

FURTHER REFERENCE
Recordings include *Southern Jazz Group, 1946–1950, Vols 1–4* (Dawn Club DC 12021 to 12024) *Bruce Gray's Vintage Jazz Band, 1973* (1988, Swaggie S-1418); Southern Spectrum, Jazz South Australia (1987, Larrikin LRJ 231); *The Adelaide Sound,* The Bruce Gray and Bill Munro Bands (1990, Swaggie Cassette 1). See also *BissetB*; *OxfordJ*.   BRUCE JOHNSON

Greek Music.   There are 136 300 Greeks in Australia, but including those Australian-born there are over 300 000. The largest communities are in Melbourne, Sydney and Adelaide, and they are creators and participants in a sacred and lively secular music-making culture. The regular services of the Greek Orthodox church (first established at Surry Hills, Sydney, in 1898; a Metropolis from 1924) provide an arena for the chanting of ritual monodic Byzantine ecclesiastical hymns, and the Greek community also supports amateur choirs which perform ecclesiastical, traditional, contemporary and local Greek music. Local ensembles include the Byzantine Chanters, Sydney; the Australian Greek Choir, Melbourne; and the Hellenic Symphonia, the Choir of Byzantine Ecclesiastical Music and the Sirens, Adelaide. In addition, each week Greek-Australians attend celebrations such as engagement parties, wedding receptions (see Tsounis 1986) and baptisms, as well as *choroesperides* (social-civic and regional fraternity dances), restaurants and festivals where they participate in spontaneous and collective Greek dancing.

(i) Traditional and Popular Music.   Greek-Australian musicians are accomplished performers of a variety of Greek musical styles and genres. Much of their repertoire consists of traditional folk and urban music genres that accompany dancing, the *nisiotika* (island music), *dimotika* (demotic regional folk music) and *rebetika* (traditional-popular urban music). Peculiar to the Australian context is the recurring performance of at least nine Greek dance forms: the *chasapikos* (butcher's dance, a slow Anatolian line dance in duple meter), *chasaposervikos* (Serbian butcher's dance, an accelerating Anatolian line dance in duple

meter), *kalamatianos* (dance of Kalamata, an open circle dance in a seven-beat meter), *kotsari* (a Pontian line dance in duple meter), *syrtos* (dragging dance, an open circle dance in duple meter), *tik* (a Pontian line dance in duple meter), *tsamikos* (an open circle dance in triple meter), *tsifteteli* (double-strings dance, a solo Anatolian dance in duple or quadruple meter), and *zeïbekikos* (dance of the Zeïbeks, a solo Anatolian dance in nine-beat meter). This core group is ever expanding to include new requests from Greek dancing patrons, who continue to maintain a strong regional identity. The dance culture is also sustained by the activities of numerous Greek dance troupes around Australia, such as the Aristotelion Academy of Greek Traditional Dances, Sydney, or the Hellenic Youth Dancers, Adelaide which specialise in researching, performing and teaching choreographies of traditional dances.

Greek-Australian musicians retain considerable national musical detail in their performances of traditional and popular Greek music genres, including the rhythmic complexity, modality, ornamentation, and improvisation. There are times when musical compromises are reached, such as the modal harmonisation of diatonic and modal melodies with triadic chords derived from the modal series rather than from functional harmony. Some first-generation immigrants perform demotic music associated with their specific regions of origin using traditional instruments: the Pontian or Cretan lyra (upright fiddle), the violin, the clarinet, the santouri (hammer dulcimer) and the lagouto (long-necked lute). Since the 1980s, the *rebetika* has enjoyed considerable popularity among music lovers at concerts, nightclubs, folk festivals, multicultural carnivals and art exhibitions, with the Arabic-Persian-Turkish style of music and its songs of love, sorrow and hashish. The music is often performed on acoustic instruments, such as long-necked lutes (bouzouki, tzouras, baglamas), violin, outi (short-necked lute), banjo, piano, piano accordion, guitar, double bass, toumberleki (hourglass drum), zilia (finger cymbals) and castanets. *Rebetika* music was featured at the international 1995 World of Music and Dance festival performed by the Adelaide ensemble the Rockin' Rembets.

By far the largest component of the repertoire of Greek bands is Greek urban popular music—*laïka* (popular) and *elafro-laïka* (light-popular)—which ranges in style from Western to traditional Greek to Arabic popular. Greek urban popular music is played on instruments of the typical all-male Greek band: vocals in the Greek language, the bouzouki, electric guitar, electric bass guitar and drum kit. Women are gradually joining the public ranks of Greek musicians, usually as vocalists or keyboard-players. Outside the typical Greek band they play violin, toumberleki and baglamas. Despite the variety of instrumentation found in the Greek music-making scene, the occurrence of songs in the Greek language accompanied by bouzouki perseveres as musical symbols of 'Greekness' in Australia. Greek-Australian music-making also features the performance of special concerts dedicated to particular composers such as Manos Loizos or Vasilis Tsitsanis, to particular eras such as the *laïka* of the 1930s–50s or *entechna* of the 1950s–80s, and to particular themes such as migration or the seaside culture.

(ii) Greek–Australian Composition. Greek-Australian musicians who have performed and recorded their own compositions inspired by contemporary experiences of Australian life and a pride in a Greek heritage include Costas Tsikaderis, Stelios Tsiolas, Christos Ioannides and Tassos Ioannides in Melbourne; Themos Mexis in Sydney; Constantine Koukias in Hobart, and John Kourbelis, Steve Papadopoulos, Nick Arabatsis, Demeter Tsounis, and Ilias Arhontoulis in Adelaide. These composers write for theatre, cinema, dance, orchestras and ensembles, drawing upon a heterogeneous set of traditional and contemporary raw materials available to them in Greek, Western and other musical styles. Beyond the Greek community, Greek-Australian musicians play a variety of styles and genres, from Western classical to rock, blues and jazz.

A striking feature of Greek-Australian music is the way in which it has adapted to the diverse regional origins, migration, settlement histories and musical tastes of Greek people developing unique music repertoires and music-making events. Greek music has become a significant Hellenic icon for the Greek diaspora in Australia, and the music-making activities of Greek-Australians are integral to the dynamic processes of the celebration of life, community formation and self-identification. Nurtured and patronised by the Greek community since the first arrival of Greek migrants in the 19th century, Greek music is now an important feature of Australian mainstream society, especially of multicultural events.

FURTHER REFERENCE
Anna Chatzinikolaou and Stathis Gauntlett, 'Greek-Australian folk song', *OxfordF*; Demeter Tsounis, Multicultural Music-Making and Dancing at Wedding Receptions: A Study of the Music-Making and Dancing Activities of Greek People in Adelaide, BMus(Hons), Univ. Adelaide, 1986; idem, 'Transnationalism and Music: Australia: Greeks', *Garland Encyclopedia of World Music, Oceania,* ed. A.L. Kaeppler and J. Wainwright Love (Washington: Smithsonian Institute, in press); idem, 'Metaphors of Centre and Periphery in the Symbolic-Ideological Narratives of *Rebetika* Music-Making in Adelaide, South Australia', *Modern Greek Studies* 3 (1995), 151–74.   DEMETER TSOUNIS

Griffin, Guy Aubrey   (*b* Birmingham, England, 1878; *d* Sydney, 1965), violin-maker. Arriving in Australia in 1907, he was apprenticed to A.E. *Smith in Sydney from 1915, becoming his chief repairer and making his own instruments. In the violins he produced, the sound holes and middle bouts were based on the Guarnerius, the bodies coated with a fine reddish-orange varnish of his own preparation, and the tone was full and rich. An excellent maker, he made 173 violins, five violas and one cello before his death.

FURTHER REFERENCE
AthertonA.

Griffiths, John Anthony   (*b* Melbourne, 2 Dec. 1952), musicologist, performer of lute, vihuela, theorbo and baroque guitar. He graduated from Monash University (BA Hons 1975, PhD 1984), then studied at the Catedrático de Guitarra at the Conservatorio Municipal de Música, Spain, and the Schola Cantorum Basiliensis, Switzerland. He has worked at the University of Melbourne since 1980, having been appointed deputy dean of the faculty of music and professor of music in 1994. Awarded the Officer of the Order of Isabella the Catholic for contribution to Spanish music and culture (1993), his research is widely published in Europe, America and Australia. His solo CD *Echo of Orpheus* was released in 1995.
MARGARET KARTOMI

Groop, The.   Rock band (1964–69; 1988–89) formed in Melbourne when a schoolboy group comprised of Peter McKeddie (vocals), Max Ross (bass) and Richard Wright (drums) added Peter Bruce (guitar). Seeking a distinctive sound by mixing folk, rhythm and blues, and rock style elements, they released five singles, including *Ol' Hound Dog* (1965), which reached No. 7 in the charts, four EPs, and the album *The Groop* (1965). Adding Brian Caine [Brian *Cadd] (organ) and Ronnie Charles (vocals) in 1966, their sound became richer and they recorded five more singles, including *Woman You're Breaking Me* (1967). They won the Battle of the Sounds (1967), and went to England in 1968. Finding little success there, they returned to Australia and had another hit with *Such A Lovely Way* (1969), but they disbanded soon after. With a significantly changed membership they re-formed in 1988–89.

FURTHER REFERENCE
Recordings include *Ol' Hound Dog* (1965, CBS BA 221234), *The Groop* (1965, CBS BP 233305), *Woman You're Breaking Me* (1967, CBS BA 221406), *Such A Lovely Way* (1969, CBS BA 221583). A compilation is *Great Hits From The Groop* (Music for Pleasure MFP 8132). For discography, see *SpencerA.* See also *McGrathA; SpencerW.*

Gross, Eric   (*b* Vienna, 16 Sept. 1926), composer. Taking refuge from Hitler in England as a child in 1938, after the war he studied at Trinity College London, and worked as a pianist in dance orchestras 1945–49 and for Radio Ceylon 1950–53. He studied at the University of Aberdeen 1953–57, came to Australia to work as a light music arranger in 1958, then taught at the NSW State Conservatorium 1959–60, joining the University of Sydney as lecturer (now associate professor) in 1960. As a composer he has been prolific, following a path independent of the avant garde. His works include numerous scores for film and television in the British light music mould, as well as contemplative yet tersely conceived choral and orchestral works, and music for a wide variety of chamber ensembles, from saxophone or recorder quartet to mandolin duet. He won the Albert Maggs Award in 1976.

FURTHER REFERENCE
Recordings of his concert works include the Trio Op. 10, fl, ob, cl (1971, HMV ASD 77565); Quintet for Alto Saxophone and String Quartet (2MBS MS 3058); *Klavierstücke* I–II, Sally Mays, pf (Canberra School of Music CSM 3); *Geburtstagsgruss* and *Prelude to Paradise* (Jade JADE1013); and *Antubconseas*, orch (1973, Jade JADCD1038). A list of ABC tapes to 1971 is in *PlushD*. See also *CA* (1995/96); Ian Shanahan, *ContemporaryC*; *MurdochA*, 108–11; *ADMR*; *APRAJ* 5 (1971), 25; *Canon* 17/4 (1965), 22–3.

Gross, Guy (*b* Tel Aviv, Israel, 18 Aug. 1966), film composer, music producer. He emigrated to Australia in 1968 and studied composition with Edwin Carr. His early achievements include successes at the Roland International Tape Competition in 1981, and the 1985 Commercial Music competition. Gross's career as a film composer was launched in 1985 with the production of *Epic*. Since then he has worked extensively on children's animated feature film in particular, television series, documentaries, and commercials. Gross was awarded Best Music for a Children's Television Series by the Australian Guild of Screen Composers in 1994 for *Blinky Bill*, and nominated by both the Australian Guild of Screen Composers and the British Academy Awards for best original music score for *The Adventures of Priscilla, Queen of the Desert*. He lives in Sydney, NSW.

FURTHER REFERENCE
His film credits include *Blinky Bill* (1992), *Dot and the Ketto* (1985), *Dot and the Whale* (1986), *Dot and the Smugglers* and *Dot Goes to Hollywood* (1987), *The Adventures of Priscilla, Queen of the Desert* and *Frauds* (1994), the mini-series *Bordertown* (1995), and the ABC drama series *Fallen Angels* (1996).

L. THOMPSON

Growing Castle, The. Chamber opera in two acts, music and libretto by Malcolm *Williamson after Strindberg's *A Dream Play*. First performed at Dynevor Castle, Wales on 13 August 1968.

Guided Imagery and Music (GIM). A specialised area of music therapy in which clients listen to classical music in a deeply relaxed state and in which visual imagery, changes in mood and physiological effects in the body are experienced. GIM was developed by Dr Helen Bonny, a music therapist at the Baltimore Psychiatric Institute, USA, in 1970. It has been practised in Australia since 1985. The method is based on the principles of music psychotherapy, where unresolved psychological issues in the client are brought to the surface by the dynamic shifts in the music selections. The clients' issues are represented in symbolic form in the visual images,

feeling states and body responses. The therapist engages the client in a dialogue to enhance the experience of the imagery. Each of the music programs (of 40 minutes) incorporates selections from the standard classical music repertoire. A movement of a larger work may be programmed alongside a work of another composer or another stylistic period. Each music program is designed to have a beginning piece which stimulates imagery, a middle selection to deepen the experience emotionally, and a final selection which returns the client to a normal emotional state. The choice of music for each program is made according to the potential for inducing imagery and deepening emotion. Research in GIM has focused on clinical applications of the method in depression (Holligan), the terminally ill (Erdonmez) and in physical illness (Short). A quantitative study has shown increased brain wave activity while clients are engaged in visual imagery, which is heightened during particularly soft passages of music (Lem). See *Music Therapy*.

FURTHER REFERENCE
D. Erdonmez, 'Clinical Applications of Guided Imagery and Music', *Australian Journal of Music Therapy* 3 (1992), 37–44; idem, 'Guided Imagery and Music: A Case Study', in *Music Therapy Collection*, ed. A. Lem (Canberra: Ausdance, 1985), 11–16; F. Holligan, 'Case study in Guided Imagery and Music', *Australian Journal of Music Therapy* 3 (1992), 45–51; A. Lem, An Integrated Profile of Brain-wave activity and structural variability of music in the study of music and imagery experiences in vivo, MMus, Univ. Melbourne, 1995; A. Short, 'Physical Illness in the Process of Guided Imagery and Music', *Australian Journal of Music Therapy* 1 (1990), 9–14.

DENISE ERDONMEZ GROCKE

Guitar-making. Australian guitar-making is a recent development; few instruments were built prior to *c*.1960. Among the first instruments were the steel-stringed instruments made from *c*.1946 and classical guitars from the early 1960s built by the *Maton Co. in Melbourne. Cheaper Asian guitars now dominate the market, but makers have emerged to fill the niche for hand-made concert instruments. Andries de Jaeger was the first to build such instruments in his Perth workshop from the late 1950s. Within a decade, other makers commenced work, principally self-trained craftsmen. Peter van Ree and John Hall started work in Sydney in the 1960s. Hall later changed direction towards early instrument reproductions, while van Ree established a workshop in Melbourne and produced excellent classical and flamenco guitars. During the 1970s and 80s, numerous guitar-makers established themselves throughout Australia, including Lindsay Churchland (Sydney), Richard Howell (Melbourne), Gunar Jakobson (Adelaide), Eugene Philip (Glen Innes, NSW) and Paul Sheridan (Perth).

Australian makers have generally adopted European construction traditions. There is no particular identity to Australian guitars nor any school of guitar-makers;

makers themselves often work in relative isolation, fashioning their instruments initially after leading imported styles, particularly after Spanish makers such as Ramirez and Fleta, and few train apprentices. In recent years, however, some makers have experimented with new designs and materials. Greg *Smallman (Glen Innes, NSW) has achieved notoriety for his unorthodox barring of the soundboard in lattice configuration and use of materials such as carbon fibre, and has produced guitars of exceptional volume and quality that are highly acclaimed internationally.   JOHN GRIFFITHS

Gumleaf.   Reed instrument, its use in Australasia confined by the distribution of eucalypt trees relative to the climate and seasons. Players select gumleaves, as well as various non-native leaves, according to their morphology, age, flexibility and pitch range, and they perform an eclectic repertoire using varied methods and ornamental techniques. As an Aboriginal instrument the gumleaf was used in signalling (Moyle 1974; 1978), juvenile amusement (Haagen 1994), ancient ceremony, hunting and ghost sounds (Ryan and Patten 1995). Some Aborigines conceived of the bird calls and other sounds mimicked on native leaves as sources of individual, clan or regional identification. In the early 20th century gumleaf bands appeared and mushroomed on south-eastern Australia mission stations. A gumleaf ensemble of Aborigines marched for the opening of the Sydney Harbour Bridge (1932), and the Lake Tyers, Vic., gumleaf band stirred troops to World War II. Herbert Patten (*b.* 1943) is a renowned soloist.

As a folk instrument the non-Aboriginal gumleaf tradition emerged from the mid-19th-century central Victorian goldrush, and at the turn of the century Salvation Army captain Tom 'Mudgee' Robertson then perpetuated the tradition. Evidence also exists that various 20th-century players were taught by Aborigines. The national Golden Gumleaf Award, founded by Fred Treble in Maryborough Vic., is a unique, characteristically Australian competition which has produced seven (all non-Aboriginal) champions since its inception in 1977. Considerable media exposure has led to commercial engagements for jazz-blues exponent Virgil Reutens (six times champion) and busker Philip Elwood.

FURTHER REFERENCE
C. Haagen, *Bush Toys. Aboriginal Children at Play* (Canberra: Aboriginal Studies Press, 1994); A.M. Moyle, North Australian Music, PhD, Monash Univ., 1974; R. Ryan and H. Patten, 'Eukalyptusblattmusik', in *Die Musik in Geschichte und Gegenwart*, 2nd edn, ed. Ludwig Finscher (Kassel: Bärenreiter, 1995), vol. 3, columns 208–11.

ROBIN RYAN

Gum-Suckers March, The.   Orchestral work by Percy *Grainger, completed 1914. Subsequently arranged by the composer for solo piano and piano duet (1916), and band (1942). First performed in Norfolk, Connecticut, with Arthur Mees conducting the Norfolk Festival Orchestra, on 8 June 1916. Originally entitled 'The Cornstalks March', although often played separately, it is the final movement of Grainger's *In a Nutshell* Suite (1905–16). The 'Gum-Sucker' of the title is, according to the composer, a nickname for those coming from Victoria, Australia. Apparently the leaves of the 'gum' (eucalyptus) trees are 'very refreshing to suck in the parching summer weather'.

ALESSANDRO SERVADEI

Gunborg.   Public singing and dancing in north-western NT. See *Corroboree*; *Aboriginal Music* §3(iii).

Gyger, Elliot   (*b* Sydney 1968), composer. After studies with Stephen *Leek and Ross *Edwards, and then at the University of Sydney with Eric *Gross and Peter *Sculthorpe, his vocal music began to be heard in Sydney and elsewhere, and he was musician-in-residence with the Song Company 1993. His works include piano, vocal and choral settings, and a music-theatre work *The Hammer That Shapes* (1989). He is artistic director of the Contemporary Singers.

FURTHER REFERENCE
BroadstockS.

H

Haesler, Bill (William John) (*b* Melbourne, 20 Apr. 1931), jazz broadcaster, writer. He was briefly involved in jazz on trombone in Melbourne, but most of his playing has been since moving to Sydney in 1966, leading groups on washboard for concerts, broadcasts and residencies; he played at Soup Plus, where he inaugurated the jazz policy in 1975. Prominent as a jazz administrator, writer and broadcaster, he was co-founder and president of Melbourne Jazz Club, served terms as president of the Sydney Jazz Club, was editor of the *Australian Jazz Quarterly* (1954–57), *Matrix* (1954–57), and *Quarterly Rag* (1976–77), and an office-holder and trustee for numerous Australian Jazz Conventions. Since 1982 he has presented a regular jazz program on 2MBS-FM.

FURTHER REFERENCE
Recordings include *Bill Haesler's Washboard Band* (1973, Festival, Harlequin Series, L25065); *Bill Haesler's Washboard Band* (1973, Picture Records PRF-1004). See also *OxfordJ*; Norman Linehan, ed., *Bob Barnard, Graeme Bell, Bill Haesler, John Sangster on the Australian Jazz Convention* (Sydney: Australian Jazz Convention Trust Fund, 1981). BRUCE JOHNSON

Hair, Graham (*b* Geelong, 27 Feb. 1943), composer, conductor. He studied initially as a pianist at the University of Melbourne to 1964, then studied analysis of 20th-century music (DPhil, University of Sheffield, 1973), becoming senior lecturer at La Trobe University, Melbourne, 1976–79, head of composition at the NSW State Conservatorium 1980–90, visiting professor at Princeton University 1985, and currently Gardiner professor of music at the University of Glasgow. He has been associated with important Australian ensembles including Australia Contemporary Music Ensemble (1970s), ★Flederman and the Australian Ensemble (1980s). In 1988 he formed his own ensemble, Voiceworks, and more recently in Glasgow, Scottish Voices. Both comprise three or more predominantly women's voices plus a variable chamber

ensemble, an instrumentation that forms the basis of much of his music.

An interest in Renaissance, Baroque and 20th-century North American music informs Hair's compositional thinking. His musical language is typified by a heterogeneous approach to general continuities, pitch and rhythmic materials, the latter characterised by polyrhythms and polymetres. The harmonic concepts in his music, especially that of harmonic succession, are an area of his significant originality. His earlier music has its basis in atonality, while many of his more recent pieces employ the notions of 'unpicking tonality' (interweaving consonance with dissonance, diatonicism with chromaticism, continuity with discontinuity) and 'centricity' (focusing upon a sequence of single pitch-classes). Since 1990 he has written many paraphrases of popular 20th-century music.

WORKS (Selective)
Publisher: Southern Voices

Instrumental *Ganymede/Prometheus,* fl/pic/alto-fl, tenor trbn/alto trbn, perc, pf (1982), *Under Aldebaran,* pf (1984) Concertino for Three Soloists, tenor trbn, bass gui, perc (1979/1995), *Seven Fleeting Glimpses,* pf (1987).

Vocal *In Ecclesiis,* motet, SATB, SATB soli, fl, tenor tbn, 2 kbd, perc (1981), *The Setting of the Moon,* cantata, S, fl/alto fl/pic, cl/bass cl, tpt, tenor trbn, vn, vc, hp, pf, celeste, chamber org, 2 perc (1978/1986, 1, Giacomo Leopardi), 12 Sep 1984, Sydney, *Songs of the Sibyls,* oratorio S, Mez, A, fl, cor anglais, tenor trbn, vc, 2 kbd, perc (1983–89, 4 parts, text from the motet cycle *Prophetiae Sibyllarum* by Orlando Lassus), 12 Sept. 1989, Sydney, *Serenissima,* S, S, Mez, Alto, hp (1994).

Vernacular Paraphrases Variations on items from American popular song, and Latin-American, Gospel and Jazz-rock originals; *c.*50 items, mostly women's voices and ensemble: *Gershwin Encores,* SSA, pf (1990), *Gershwin Paraphrases,* SSA, fl, cl, 2 vn, vla, vc, pf (1992); *Arlen Trios,* SSA, pf (1993), *Cole Porter Paraphrases,* 16-part str orch (1994), *Gospel Paraphrases,* SSAA, bass gui (1994); *Weather Report Studies,* pf, cl, va (1994), *Salsa Paraphrases,* SSAA, perc, bass gui (1995), *Latin-American Carols,* SSAA, perc, bass gui (1995), *Dancing on the Ceiling,* va, vc (1996).

FURTHER REFERENCE

His recordings include *Ganymede/Prometheus,* Flederman (Canberra School of Music, CSM 1); *Colours of Rain and Iron,* S. de Haan et al. (Canberra School of Music, CSM 13); Concertino for Three Soloists, Flederman (Larrikin, LRF 156); *Seven Fleeting Glimpses* and *Under Aldebaran,* Daniel Herscovitch, pf (Tall Poppies TP020).   TOM HALL

Hale, Una (*b* Adelaide, 1925), soprano. After lessons with Hilda Gill at Adelaide University, she won the state finals of the ABC Concerto and Vocal Competition in 1946. Her father moved the family to London and she studied at the Royal College of Music, making her debut as Marguerite in the Carl Rosa Opera Co. in 1948. She sang in *Carmen* at Covent Garden in 1949, joining the company in 1953 as well as making guest appearances at the Aldeburgh Festival, and the Gulbenkian Festival, Portugal. She returned to Australia for the Elizabethan Theatre Trust Opera Co. in 1962 as Ariadne (*Ariadne auf Naxos*) and was a guest artist at Brussels in 1963. With a voice of flexibility, power and fine lyrical line, her roles included Musetta, Mimi, the Countess, Eva, Ellen Orford (*Peter Grimes*) and Cressida (*Troilus and Cressida*). She married the stage director of the Royal Ballet, Martin Carr, in 1960 and now lives at Bath, England.

FURTHER REFERENCE

MackenzieS 191–3; *AMN* 40 (Apr. 1950) 19.

Hall, Elsie Maud Stanley (*b* Toowoomba, Qld, 22 June 1877; *d* Wynberg, South Africa, 27 June 1976), pianist. A child prodigy, she studied with violinist Josef Kretschmann and was giving concerts in Queensland by the age of seven. Her family moved to Sydney in 1882 and she appeared as a concerto soloist at the age of nine. She went to the Stuttgart Conservatorium in 1888, appearing at the 1889 Paris Exposition, studied with John Farmer at the Harrow Music School, then Ernst Rudorff and Rudolf Joachim at the Berlin Hochschule, and appeared with the Berlin Symphony Orchestra in 1897 and at a recital with the Australian violinist Johann *Kruse at London. Returning to Australia in 1897, she performed in regional centres and taught at the Elder Conservatorium for six years, but then established herself in England, appearing at the Coliseum and Hippodrome (1908) and teaching the composer Constant Lambert among others. In 1913 she married and settled in South Africa. After giving concerts for allied troops in England and France during the war, in the postwar years she appeared with the Cape Town Symphony Orchestra, made periodic trips to Europe, and occasionally visited Australia. An outstanding interpreter of the 19th-century repertoire with an extraordinarily long-running career, she continued to give concerts until she was 93.

FURTHER REFERENCE

Obit. in London *Times* 28 July 1976. Her autobiography is *The Good Die Young* (1969). She made cylinder recordings (1910, Pathé), and 78s (1930s, HMV and Decca), all now rare. See also Peter Burgis, *ADB,* 9; Caroline Mears, *GroveD*; *BrewerD,* 87; *Leader* 12 Apr. 1890; *Illustrated News and Musical Times,* 1 May 1890; *Weekly Times,* 26 Mar. 1898; *Theatre,* 1 May 1912.

Hall, Fred(erick) Fifield ['Gabriel Morel', 'Georges Brand', etc.] (*b* Carlton, Melbourne, 1878; *d* Mitcham, Melbourne, 27 Sept. 1956), popular music composer. Hall studied piano with his father and worked as a pianist and conductor while still in his teens. He conducted for Harry *Rickards at the Melbourne Opera House (later the Tivoli Theatre). He was Melbourne publisher Allan & Co.'s music editor 1914–38, then came out of retirement to work for them again during World War II. He also spent 18 months as musical director of 3LO *c.*1928. Hall was enormously prolific; most of his estimated 600 compositions were published by Allans under one of his 30-odd *noms de plume* which included Gabriel Morel, Georges Brand and Anthony Dare. He wrote songs such as the hit *Goodbye Melbourne Town* (Allans, 1908), piano music such as the 'tone poem' *Omar,* children's music and incidental orchestral music for numerous J.C. Williamson productions.

FURTHER REFERENCE

A list of some of his works appears in *SnellA.*

                                                                    JENNIFER HILL

Hall, John, lute-maker. An amateur guitar player, he began making guitars in his early twenties, then lutes, vihuelas, mandolins and viols. After teaching architecture at University of Sydney, he went to London to study lute-making with Thomas Gough, and returned to Australia as a full-time maker. He went to Europe with an Australia Council grant to examine original lutes in 1974, considerably changing his models thereafter. One of the finest of the first generation of early instrument-makers in Australia, more recently he has also made violins and cellos.

FURTHER REFERENCE

AthertonA, 170–1.

Hall, John Farnsworth (*b* Sydney, 1899), conductor, violinist. Hall studied under Cyril *Monk and Henri *Verbrugghen at the NSW State Conservatorium of Music, and became deputy leader of the NSW State Orchestra in 1919. He went to England in 1925 and studied with Albert Sammons, then played in the London Symphony Orchestra and other London orchestras under Beecham, Weingartner and Sir Hamilton Harty, and in the Three Choirs Festival under Elgar. Returning to Australia he was a violinist then deputy conductor with the Sydney Symphony Orchestra, then was appointed conductor of the Queensland Symphony Orchestra 1947–54 and the

West Australian Symphony Orchestra 1955–65, and also was at one time assistant conductor of the Melbourne and Sydney Symphony Orchestras and guest conductor with the Elizabethan Theatre Trust Opera Co. Tall, athletic, courteous in rehearsal and with a graceful beat, he was warmly regarded by his players and audiences, and did much to establish two of Australia's ABC orchestras on a firm foundation.

FURTHER REFERENCE
GlennonA, 121; *MoresbyA*, 154–6; clipping file *Msl*.   J.L. HOLMES

Hall, Rodney   (*b* Solihull, Warwickshire, England, 18 Nov. 1935), writer, musician. He studied at the University of Queensland and worked as a freelance writer and actor, aided by an Australia Council fellowship 1974–80. While best known as the award-winning author of over 500 poems and 27 books, notably *Just Relations* (1982) and *The Second Bridegroom* (1991), he is also an accomplished Baroque recorder player, and taught recorder ensemble periodically at the University of New England Summer School from 1967 and at the Canberra School of Music 1979–83. He was chairman of the Australia Council 1991–94 and was honoured with the AM in 1990.

FURTHER REFERENCE
OxfordL; *CA* (1995–96); *WWA* (1996).

Hames, Richard David   (*b* Chelwood Gate, England, 2 Sept. 1945), composer. He studied with Gordon Jacob, Ralph Downes and Adrian Boult at the Royal College of Music, London, then with Olivier Messiaen and Nadia Boulanger in Paris, and analysis and semiology of new music with Benjamin Boretz. He moved to Australia in 1976 and founded the chamber music ensemble Victorian Time Machine, for which most of his compositions of the late 1970s and early 80s were written. The majority of his works use electro-acoustic instrumentation, and comprise aspects of music-theatre. His music is mostly dramatic and virtuosic, with complex multi-layers and highly detailed rhythmic structures. Although known and performed in Australia, his works receive the majority of their performances in Europe.

WORKS (Selective)
Principal publishers: Scarecrow, Edition Modern
Orchestral   *Melancolia* (1979–80), *Djara*, chamber orch (1981–83).
Chamber   *Danseries*, amplified renaissance ens (1967–79), *Planh super carmen gregorianum ex membrana veteri et semilacera*, chamber ens (1968), *A bell ringing in the empty sky*, 3 players, pre-recorded tape (1976), *Natalis invicti solis*, 6 perc (1977), *Nuper rosarum flores*, chamber ens, early music consort (1980), *Reliquary I*, chamber ens (1983), *The tragic passion of old Dame Dorrity*, 6 perc (1983), *Tsunami after Hokusai*, shakuhachi, 2 hp, str octet (1983–84), *Archivi*, str qrt (1984), *Tya*, fl, ob, cl, bn, hn, trbn, pf (1984), *Autefons*, brass quintet (1984).

Solo Instrumental   *Monody for St Michael*, org (1967), *A solis ortus cardine*, pf, bass trbn (1975), *Alba after Guiraut de Borneth*, fl, perc ens (1977), *Primsang I-II*, amplified trbn (I) vc (II), electronic tape, tape delay system (1978–79), *Ite missa est*, amplified prepared pf, pre-recorded tape (1979), *As I crossed a bridge of dreams*, amplified str instrument, pre-recorded tape (1980), *Orgelwerk*, org (1980), *Entr'actes*, bass cl (1980–1982), *Zurna*, amplified soprano sax (1982), *Finisterre*, pf (1983–84), *Memorabilia*, cl (1984), *Darabukka*, amplified db (1984), *Karvai*, perc (1984), *Djurunga*, bass cl, marimba (1985), *In the flickering dust of sunlight*, str qrt (1988), *Dreamings*, vn, pf (1989), *Finnian's rant*, amplified contrabass, perc (1993).
Music-Theatre   *The Hours of Hieronymous Bosch*, opera (1976–1986, 3, Colin Ryan), *Ku*, wind instrument, multiple tape delay system, dancer (1979), Amsterdam, 8 Sept. 1980, . . . *quasi somnolentum Amanita Muscaria*, amplified microsounds, choreographed actions (1979), Melbourne 28 Oct. 1979, *Quête*, perambulatory percussionist (1984), *Kshayavriddhi*, dancer, alto fl, perc (1985), *Raison d'être* (*Hommage à Jean Tinguely*) dancer, amplified prepared pf, pre-recorded tape (1986), *Danses Gothiques* (*Nine ceremonies after Erik Satie*) S, puppets, ens (1987), *Fiddler's crus*, dancer, electric vn, perc (1988).
Choral   *Carols*, boys' vv (1965–72), *Sangbec I*, 6 vv (1968–70), *Glossae*, 8 amp. vv (1978), *From the Book of Thel*, 16 vv (1982).
Voice and Instruments   *Sangbec II*, S, cl (1978–79), *Basho I-III*, T, insts (1979–83), *Caoineadh*, Mez, vc (1987).

FURTHER REFERENCE
Recordings include *Nuper Rosarum Flores*, Victorian Time Machine (Move MS 3028). His writings include *Richard David Hames* (Melbourne: Scarecrow, 1984).   MELINDA J. SAWERS

Hammond, Dame Joan Hood   (*b* Christchurch, NZ, 24 May 1912; *d* Bowral, NSW, 26 Nov. 1996), soprano. Her family moved from New Zealand to Sydney when she was a child. When an injury to her left wrist prevented her pursuing obvious talent as a violinist, she studied voice at the NSW State Conservatorium, and sang minor roles with J.C. Williamson's Italian Grand Opera Co. in Australia and NZ in 1934. An outstanding swimmer, three times Women's Golfing Champion of NSW and for a time Australian Women's Golfing Champion, her golfing friends raised funds for her to study abroad from 1935, first at the Vienna Choir Training School then with Dino Norgioli in Italy. She made her London debut in *Messiah* in 1938. Engaged as principal soprano at the Vienna State Opera in 1939, when war broke out she was in London for the Sir Henry Wood Proms, and became an ambulance driver in the Women's Voluntary Service, as well as giving numerous concerts for the troops in the coming years. She was with the Carl Rosa Co. 1942–45, toured Australia for the ABC in 1946, and returned to the Vienna State Opera in 1947. Her debuts at Covent Garden (1948) and Sadler's Wells (1950) led to numerous appearances in principal roles in London, as well as in major European houses, in Russia, in New York, and in Australia for the Elizabethan Theatre Trust Opera Co (1957, 1960).

With a dazzling voice of great stamina and versatility and a commanding presence on stage, her title roles included Salome, Desdemona, Aida, wonderfully warm portrayals of Tosca and Butterfly, as well as the principal soprano parts in *Il trovatore, Fidelio, Don Carlos, Eugene Onegin*. Greatly loved by the British and Australian public for her combination of artistic brilliance and vigorous sporting prowess, for her many BBC broadcasts, and for her selfless work in wartime, such recordings as 'O My Beloved Father' (Puccini) became immensely popular, winning a gold record in 1969, and her *Turandot* was the first classical album to sell more than a million copies.

A heart ailment brought her early farewell to the stage in 1965, after which she settled at Airey's Inlet, Victoria. She was artistic director to the fledgling Victorian Opera Co. 1971–76 and head of vocal studies at the Victorian College of the Arts from its founding in 1975 until 1992, then taught at the University of Melbourne Conservatorium until her health finally failed in 1995. She was honoured with the CBE in 1963 and the CMG in 1972, and created Dame of the British Empire in 1974.

FURTHER REFERENCE
Reissues of her recordings include Dame *Joan Hammond—A Celebration* (Testament SBT 1013); *Great Voices of the Century Sing Puccini* (Memoir Records CDMOIR 412); Puccini arias and songs of Gounod, Dvořák, Tchaikovsky (1991, 166284); and *Record of Singing Vol. 4* (EMI CHS7 69741–2). Her memoirs are *A Voice, A Life: the Autobiography of Joan Hammond* (London: Gollancz, 1970). See also *CA* (1995/96); *MonashB*; Alan Blyth, *GroveO*; *MackenzieS*, 167–70; *MoresbyA*, 116–18; William Mann, 'Joan Hammond', *Opera* 10/2 (Feb. 1959), 82–5.

Hannan, Eilene (*b* Melbourne, 4 Nov. 1946), soprano. After studies in Australia and in London, she appeared with the Australian Opera from 1971 as Barbarina in *Figaro*, as a guest at Glyndebourne and Wexford, with the English National Opera from 1978, then at Covent Garden. She lives in London, and in Australia her roles have included Natasha in *War and Peace* at the opening of the Sydney Opera House 1973, *Jenůfa* 1992 and Pat Nixon in *Nixon in China* for the SA Opera Co. 1992. Her roles have shown a versatile talent, and include Mozart's Zerlina, Cherubino, Pamina and Susanna, Janáček's Vixen and Mila (*Osud*), the Duchess of Parma in Busoni's *Doktor Faustus*, Salomé in Massenet's *Hérodiade*, Leila in *The Pearl Fishers*, Santuzza, Poppea, Mélisande, Kát'á Kabanová, the British premiere of Sallinen's *The King Goes Forth to France*, but also the Marschallin and Wagner's Venus. She was honoured with the AM.

FURTHER REFERENCE
Recordings include *Rusalka*, English National Opera (MCEG VVD 392) and *Eugene Onegin* (excerpts) London Philharmonic Orchestra (EMI Eminence CDEMX 2187). See also *CA* (1995/96); Elizabeth Forbes, *GroveO*.

Hansford, Brian (*b* 1934), baritone. First trained as an accountant, he won the *Sun* Aria in 1956 and went to Germany to study with Hans Hotter and at the Munich Hochschule with Gerhard Husch. After competition successes there and in Vienna he sang roles with the Munich State Opera in 1960. Returning to Australia in 1961, he specialised in German lieder while appearing frequently in opera and oratorio. He sang the premiere of Larry Sitsky's *The Fall of the House of Usher* in 1971, which was also recorded for television. Establishing an influential teaching practice, he was lecturer at the University of Melbourne Conservatorium from 1964, and has been lecturer then senior lecturer at the Victorian College of the Arts since 1976.

FURTHER REFERENCE
Recordings include Larry Sitsky's *The Fall of the House of Usher* (excerpt) West Australian Symphony Orchestra (1971, Festival SFC 800–24). See also *MackenzieS*, 202–3; *AMN* 48 (Nov. 1957), 8–9; *AMN* 49 (Aug. 1958), 23–4.

Hanson, Raymond Charles (*b* Burwood, Sydney, 23 Nov. 1913; *d* Sydney, 6 Dec. 1976), composer. Hanson's importance to Australian music lies in his activity as composer, teacher and administrator. The apprentice years of the 1930s and early 1940s included piano pieces, vocal settings of poems by Rabindranath Tagore, sonatas for piano, for flute and for violin, and a set of six *Preludes* (op. 11) for piano solo. Two public concerts of his works in 1941 led to critical acclaim from Neville Cardus, and the Gordon Vickers scholarship for study at the NSW State Conservatorium.

After army service he studied briefly with Dr Alex Burnard from 1947, discovered the theories of Paul Hindemith, was awarded the Conservatorium Fellowship, and joined the Conservatorium staff as temporary piano teacher. Despite miserable pay and working conditions he eventually taught aural training, harmony and counterpoint, and composition, and helped raise the educational standard of the institution by a complete overhaul of the available coursework and the introduction of the BMusEd course. As a teacher in the 1950s, he was able to help some of today's outstanding musicians, including Don *Burrows, Roger *Woodward, Nigel *Butterley, Richard *Meale and Larry *Sitsky, to develop their own personal and original style.

The postwar period also saw the maturing of his own compositional craft, with a string quartet, a symphony, concertos for flute, trumpet, piano, trombone and violin, several chamber works, an opera based on the Rum Rebellion (*Jane Greer*), film music, and an oratorio, *The Immortal Touch*, based on texts of Tagore.

WORKS (selective)
A full catalogue of his works by Graham Hardie is in Sydney Conservatorium Library. Most ms works available in facsimile from Sydney Conservatorium library.

Orchestral   *Dhoogor*, op. 18, ballet music (1945), Violin Concerto, op. 21 (1946), *Novelette*, op. 22 (1947), Trumpet Concerto, op. 27 (1948), Symphony, op. 28 (1952), Trombone Concerto, op. 31 (1955), *Three in One*, op. 35, film music (1956), *Portrait of Australia*, op. 46, film music (1960), *Gula* (1967), Piano Concerto (1972).

Instrumental   *On Holidays*, op. 1, pf (1933), Sonata, op. 5, vn, pf (1940), Sonata, op. 12, pf (1940; rev. 1963), Sonata, op. 10, fl, pf (1941), *Preludes*, op. 11, pf (1941), *Idylle in D major*, op. 15, pf (1942), Quintet, op. 17, pf, 2 vn, va, vc (1944), *Three Fancies*, op. 19, vn, pf (1946), *Legende*, op. 20, vn, pf (1947), *Five Portraits*, op. 23, pf (1948), *Episodes on 'Tarry Trousers'*, op. 24, pf (1948), *Sonatina for Piano*, op. 26, pf (1949), *Sonata for Organ*, op. 29, org (1952), *Seascape*, op. 32, vn, pf (1953), *Sonatina for Viola and Piano*, op. 34, va, pf (1956), *Still Winds*, fl, vibraphone, gui, db (1956), *Three Preludes for Organ*, solo org (1963), String Quartet (1967), *Romance for E flat Tuba and Piano*, tba, pf (1975)

Brass Band, Wind Ensemble   *Divertimento for Woodwind Quintet*, fl, ob, cl, sax, bn (1972), *Van Diemen's Land*, brass band (1972), *Dedication*, 2 fl, cl (1973), *Fanfare for Graduation Ceremony*, brass ensemble (1975)

Theatre   *The Lost Child*, opera, vv, narrator, ch, orch (1956), *Jane Greer*, opera, vv, ch, orch (1974)

Vocal   *I dreamt that she sat by my head*, op. 3, Mez or Bar, pf (1935), *Fallen Veils*, op. 6, S, pf (1938), *Three Songs*, op. 16: *The Cliff; Mirage; Spindrift*, Mez or Bar, pf (1946), *Two Songs*, op. 30: *I am restless; Do not keep to yourself*, T, pf (1953), *Simple as a song*, op. 36, 3 S, org (1956), *The Cyclone*, v, pf (1960), *The Web Is Wove*, ch, pf (1968), *Fern Hill*, S, Orchestra (1969), *The Lord Reigneth*, cantata, A, org, strs (1969), *The Immortal Touch*, oratorio, S, Bar, ch, orch (1952–76).

FURTHER REFERENCE
Obit. in *APRAJ* 2/3. Recordings include Trumpet Concerto, Sydney Symphony Orchestra, cond. J. Post, J. Robertson, tr (1968, RCA 16371); *Fern Hill*, West Australian Symphony Orchestra, cond. B. Heinze, (1970, Festival SFC 800–21); and *Six Preludes*, Murray Sharp, pf (Move MS 3043). A discography to 1972 is in *PlushD*. An interview with him by Mrs Hazel de Berg (31 Aug. 1973) is in Oral History section, *CAnl*. See also *MurdochA*, 112–15.
                                                GRAHAM HARDIE

Hanson-Dyer, Louise.   See *Dyer, Louise*

Happy Prince, The.   Children's opera in one act, music and libretto by Malcolm ★Williamson (1965) after Oscar Wilde, commissioned for the Farnham Festival, UK. First performed at Farnham parish church on 22 May 1965 and published by Joseph Weinberger, 1965.

Hardy, Col   (*b* Brewarrina, NSW, 19 July 1940), Aboriginal country music performer. He listened to Slim ★Dusty on radio and taught himself guitar. After showing promise performing in rural NSW talent quests, he toured country areas with the Willy Fennell show and then moved to Sydney, appearing in Sydney clubs. He was in Ted Quigg's *All Coloured Show*, and was signed by Opal Records in 1972. His first EP was *Protest, Protest*, he won a

Golden Guitar at the first ACMA awards in 1973, and then his band was for some years resident at the Ramsgate RSL Club, Sydney, as well as working with Auriel Andrew and on tour with Brian Young.

FURTHER REFERENCE
Recordings include *Black Gold* (1973, Opal), *Black And White Tangle* (Larrikin OLLP 523 TC), and *Remember Me* (Larrikin OLLP 536 TC).

Hardy, Lance (Lancelot Arthur)   (*b* Derby, England, 17 Dec. 1907; *d* Melbourne, 4 July 1993), organist, church musician. He studied at the University of Melbourne under A.E.H. Nickson and at the Royal College of Music under George Thalben-Ball and Henry Ley. Awarded the FRCO with the Harding Prize in 1931, he received his BMus from London University, and was organist at St Augustine's Kilburn 1931–36. Returning to Australia in 1938, he was director of music at Geelong Grammar School, then saw war service in Europe. He was organist and master of choristers at St Paul's Cathedral, Melbourne (1951–73), giving more than 500 lunchtime recitals which included a wide repertoire. Under his direction, the choir maintained and developed the traditions established by his predecessor, A.E. Floyd. He was organist to the Melbourne Symphony Orchestra and teacher at the University of Melbourne Conservatorium.

FURTHER REFERENCE
Obit. in *OHTA News* 17/3 (July 1993), 4–5. See also John Maidment, 'Profiles of People and Places: Lance Hardy', *One Voice* 8/2 (Advent 1993), 16–20.
                                                JOHN MAIDMENT

Harman, Harry (Henry Ernest)   (*b* Melbourne, 19 Dec. 1927), jazz bass player. He began guitar in 1946, later adding banjo, bass and tuba to his repertoire. He attended his first Australian Jazz Convention in 1948, and settled in Sydney in 1949. Starting to rehearse what became the Paramount Jazz Band, he made a public debut at the inaugural function of the ★Sydney Jazz Club, which Harman founded in 1953 to create a venue for the band. The Paramount remained the club's house band into the 1960s, though Harman was absent from the band during the late 1950s while working with the Port Jackson Jazz Band. He moved to Graeme Bell's All Stars in 1962, remaining with them until moving to Newcastle in 1976, where he was musically inactive. On his return to Sydney in 1981 he joined the Eclipse Alley Five, and later the New Wolverine Orchestra, with whom he toured internationally in 1993 and 1996; he is currently a member of both bands. In addition he has resumed working locally with Graeme Bell as well as freelancing in other groups. Harman's musical and organisational activities have made him central to major episodes in Sydney's postwar traditional jazz movement. In the early 1990s he was made a patron of the Sydney Jazz Club, and in 1994 he became involved as a jazz broadcaster with Radio 2CCC FM north of Sydney.

FURTHER REFERENCE

Recordings include *The Sydney Jazz Club 1953–1993* (1993, MBS Jazz 9, Linehan Series); *The Famous PIX Sessions, Classic Australian Jazz from the Sixties* (1996, Australian Jazz Reissues AJR-001 A&B); *The New Wolverine Jazz Orchestra, vol. 4, Friends With Pleasure* (1996, NWJO 196). See also *OxfordJ*.

BRUCE JOHNSON

Harpsichord-making. The history of plucked-string keyboard instrument-making in Australia dates from the second half of the 20th century. The small number of original harpsichords, spinets, virginals, and indeed Viennese-action fortepianos variously held by museums, universities, or in private ownership were all imported into the country from the 1930s onwards (see *Instrument Collections*). In the early days of the revival of interest in early keyboard instruments, the large music houses imported small numbers of English, American and Continental harpsichords, spinets and virginals in competition with a growing number of local makers. Essentially, the thrust of current production philosophies is the close copying of originals of all types, with the work of the best makers equalling the best available from abroad. A small number of instruments have been exported by such makers as William Bright, Alastair McAllister, Mars McMillan and Marc Nobel, with others such as Cary Beebe, Richard Schaumloffel, Alan Todd and Peter Watchorn making an equal contribution to an awareness of the importance of these instruments in music-making.

Surviving original instruments were not the products of a rationalised standardisation and it is pleasing to note that Australia's makers offer broad aesthetics in the detailing of an instrument. In this context the successful employment of Australian timbers continues to receive ongoing consideration by a number of makers which to some degree hints at a desire to achieve a more nationalistic approach to the building of instruments that had already fallen from favour before the country had been settled by Europeans. See *Instrument-making*.

FURTHER REFERENCE

AthertonA.   ALASTAIR MCALLISTER

Harrell, Bev (*b* Adelaide), popular music singer. After winning a radio talent quest at the age of six, she appeared with the Vibrants at dances in the Adelaide suburbs, then from 1960 on the television shows *Bandstand, Kommotion* and *Uptight*, and as supporting act for Herb Alpert and the Tijuana Brass, Roy Orbison, the Rolling Stones and other touring artists. Among her 14 singles, *What Am I Doing Here* reached No. 13 in the charts in 1967 and *One In A Million* reached No. 29 in 1968; she won the *Go-Set* popularity poll in the same year. Later recordings included *The Looking Glass* (1970), *Mon Pere*

(1974) and the album *I Believe In Music* (1974). She won the Tokyo Song Festival in 1971 and now divides her time between Australia and touring abroad, doing club and cabaret work.

FURTHER REFERENCE

Recordings include *What Am I Doing Here* (HMV EA 4820), *One In A Million* (Columbia DO 5058), *The Looking Glass* (1970, Columbia DO 9081), *Mon Pere* (1974, RCA 102510), and *I Believe In Music* (1974, RCA MVLP 10017). For discography, see *SpencerA*. See also *McGrathA*; *SpencerW*; David Day and Tim Parker, *SA Great: It's Our Music 1956–1986* (Glandore, SA: Day and Parker, 1987), 53–7.

Harrhy, Edith (Mary) (*b* London, 19 Dec., 1893; *d* Oxley, Brisbane, 24 Feb. 1969), composer, entertainer. Educated at Shenley House School, London, and at the Guildhall School of Music, she first visited Australia with violinist Mary Law in 1915. She settled in Melbourne after her marriage in 1919, adapting her career as a recitalist and broadcaster to her husband's work as a commercial traveller. Her concerts centred on performances of her own compositions, with her singing, playing piano and accompanying other musicians. Her works include two light operas, *Alaya* and *The Jolly Friar*, and many songs, including *What the Red Haired Bosun Said* recorded by John Brownlee, and songs for children. The Music Theatre Guild's Edith Harrhy Award commemorates her long association as composer and musical director with many amateur and semi-professional musical theatre groups, including Gertrude Johnson's National Theatre Movement from its inception in 1935.

FURTHER REFERENCE

Her papers are in *CAnl* and held privately by Mrs Honor Coutts, Bermagui, NSW. See also *ADB*, 14; *CohenI*; *SnellA*; Peter Townsend and David Simmons, eds, *Who's Who in Music* (London, 1962).

KAY DREYFUS

Harris, Rolf (*b* Perth, 30 Mar. 1930), variety entertainer. He came to attention at the age of 17, winning a record number of listeners' votes on the national radio show *Australia's Amateur Hour*. After graduating from the University of Western Australia as a primary school teacher, he went to London with a repertoire of Danny Kaye impersonations, and appeared on British television from 1954. He appeared in films, including *You Lucky People* (1955) and *Web of Suspicion* (1959), then had a major international hit in the UK, USA and Australia with *Tie Me Kangaroo Down Sport* in 1960. This was followed by five more hit singles, including *Jake The Peg* (1966) and *Two Little Boys* (1969). He then had a succession of British television shows, beginning with *Hey Presto It's Rolf* (1966) and *The Rolf Harris Show* (1969), presenting a melange of his singing, quick painting, and musical novelties, most notably on his 'wobble board', a thin wooden sheet which he oscillates between his hands to produce a rhythmic accompaniment. A sunny, sentimental comic and an entertainer of many talents, he has become a great favourite of British television audiences. He has written 12 books, including *Write Your Own Pop Song* (1968). He was honoured with the MBE (1968), OBE (1978) and AM (1989). He currently compères *Animal Hospital*, and has caused comment singing adaptations of Led Zeppelin and Rolling Stones hits.

FURTHER REFERENCE

Recordings include *Definitive Rolf Harris* (EMI 8144792), *Rolf Rules OK!* (Polygram 5148502) and *Rolf's Country Stories* (EMI 7017952). See also *McGrathA*.

Hart, Fritz Bennicke (*b* Brockley, England, 11 Feb. 1874; *d* Honolulu 1949), composer, conductor, teacher. The eldest of five children, Hart was a chorister at Westminster Abbey, later studying piano and organ at the Royal College of Music. After graduation Hart worked in London as a music-theatre conductor. In 1909 he took up a contract with J.C. Williamson to conduct touring companies in Australia, then in 1913, with the prolonged absence of Marshall-Hall from Australia, he obtained the directorship of Marshall-Hall's Conservatorium in Albert Street, East Melbourne.

Attracting the patronage of Dame Nellie Melba, the Conservatorium developed under Hart's directorship as a formidable singing school. In 1927, after the death of Alberto Zelman Jr, Hart accepted the conductorship of the Melbourne Symphony Orchestra. The Depression and strong competition from the University of Melbourne Conservatorium and its professor Bernard Heinze saw both the Albert Street Conservatorium and the orchestra in decline by the early 1930s; in 1936 he accepted the conductorship of the Honolulu Symphony Orchestra and was appointed foundation professor of music at the University of Hawaii. The bombing of Pearl Harbor in 1941 ended his academic post, and he retired from the conductorship in 1949, dying later that year at the age of 75.

Hart was a highly regarded teacher, especially of composition; his pupils included Peggy ★Glanville-Hicks and Margaret ★Sutherland. A prolific composer himself, his works reveal a predilection for English folk-song, empirical harmony, and evocative tone colouring. Later in life, he was influenced by Celticism, which he believed could be used to express a unique response to the Australian landscape.

WORKS (Selective)

(Mss in *Msl*)

Orchestral *The Bush*, symphonic suite, op. 59 (1923), Symphony, op. 107 (1934), *Symphonic Rhapsody*, vn, orch, op. 131 (1939), 12 other works.

Instrumental Works for str and str qrt, 3 sonatas for vn, pf, numerous pieces and arrangements for pf.

Stage Operas: *Pierrette*, op. 13 (1913), *Malvolio*, op. 14 (1913), *The Land of Heart's Desire*, op. 18 (1914), *Riders to the Sea*, op. 19 (1915), *Deirdre of the Sorrows*, op. 21 (1916), *Ruth and Naomi*, op. 24 (1917), *The Fantastics*, op. 35 (1918), *The Travelling Man*, op. 41 (1920), *The King*, op. 43 (1921), *Esther*, op. 57 (1923), *The Woman who Laughed at Faery*, op. 58 (1924), *Deirdre in Exile*, op. 66 (1926), *The Forced Marriage*, op. 79 (1928), *St George and the Dragon*, op. 99 (1930), *The Nativity*, op. 105 (1931), *Isolt of the White Hands*, op. 106 (1933), *St Francis of Assisi*, op. 117 (1937), *Even unto Bethlehem*, op. 155 (1943), *The Swineherd, The Toad and the Princess*, op. 156 (1944), *The Vengeance of Faery*, op. 164 (1947).

Operettas *The Dead Heat* (1931), *The Fiancées* (1931).

Choral *3 Australian Ballads*, op. 5 (1909), *Mass Vexilla Regis* (1912), *The Song of Mary*, op. 55 (1922), *New Year's Eve*, op. 60 (1924), *Salve Caput Cruentatum*, op. 62 (1924), *Ode on a Grecian Urn*, op. 65 (1925), *Gods*, op. 78 (1927), *Joll's Credo*, op. 98 (1930), numerous accompanied and unaccompanied part-songs, anthems, and other smaller pieces.

Songs 495 extant, including settings of poems by Robert Herrick (127), William Sharp/Fiona Macleod (60), and A.E. (George Russell) (49). One song cycle, *The Gilly of Christ*, op. 49 (1922), to words by Joseph Campbell.

FURTHER REFERENCE

Hubert Clifford, *GroveD*; Anne-Marie Forbes, 'The Songs of F. B. Hart: A Contribution to Literature on Twentieth Century English Solo Song', *MMA* 15 (1988), 172–86; Thérèse Radic, *ADB*, 9; Peter Tregear, Fritz Hart: An Introduction to his Life and Music, M.Mus, Univ. Melbourne, 1993; idem, ed., *Fritz Bennicke Hart: 10 Songs Op. 64 and Op. 124* (Melbourne: Marshall-Hall Trust, 1996).   PETER TREGEAR

Harvey, Michael Kieran (*b* Sydney, 7 July 1961), pianist. He studied at the NSW State Conservatorium, then under Sandor Falvoi at the Liszt Academy, Hungary. Winning the Debussy Medal in Paris (1985), he returned to Australia to teach at the Victorian College of the Arts. In 1993 he won the prestigious Ivo Pogorelich International Solo Piano Competition in Pasadena, California, and now resides in Sydney, giving recitals in Europe and the USA as well as in Australia, and appearing as soloist with the ABC orchestras. A lively presence on the concert platform with a crystalline technique, he has been particularly noted for his interpretations of contemporary and Australian works, he has appeared with Synergy, Pipeline, and other new music ensembles, and with Sydney Dance Co., and has given the first performances of a number of commissioned works.

Harwood, Gwen(doline) Nessie née Foster (*b* Brisbane, 8 June 1920; *d* Hobart, 1995), poet, librettist. She studied and taught music at Brisbane, where she first collaborated with the composer Larry ★Sitsky, then moved to Tasmania after her marriage in 1945. She published her first collection of poems in 1963, and is particularly noted for *The Lion's Bride* (1981) and *Bone Scan* (1988). She wrote numerous librettos, notably for Larry Sitsky's operas

Fall of the House of Usher (1965) after Edgar Allan Poe, *Lenz* (1973) after Georg Büchner, *Fiery Tales* (1976), *De Profundis* (1985) and *Golem* (1993), but also for Ian Cugley's *Sea Changes* (1974) and the libretto for Don Kay's *The Golden Crane* (1985).

FURTHER REFERENCE
Stephanie Trigg, *Gwen Harwood* (Melbourne: OUP, 1994); *MonashB*; *OxfordL*; Gwen Harwood, 'Words and Music', *Southerly* 4 (Dec. 1986), 367–76.

Hatch, Tony. See *Trent, Jackie*.

Hauser, Miska (*b* Pozsony, Hungary, 1822; *d* Vienna, 9 Dec. 1887), violinist. After studies with Josef Matalay then at Vienna with Joseph Mayseder, he toured Germany giving recitals in 1840. From then on he toured most of Europe, and went to the USA with Jenny Lind. He visited Australia in 1854–56, playing in Sydney, Brisbane, Melbourne, Hobart and Adelaide and touring extensively through the regional centres. His reception was tumultuous, although he played chiefly transcriptions of operatic melodies, facile showpieces and trifles of his own, such as *The Bird in a Tree*, and appeared with local accompanists Charles ★Packer, Sylvester ★Diggles and others. The first European instrumental virtuoso to make an extended visit to Australia, his lengthy letters are a somewhat florid but nevertheless useful account of musical life in the colonies at the time.

FURTHER REFERENCE
His correspondence *Aus dem Handerbuche eines osterreichischen Virtuosen* has been translated (excerpts) by Colin Roderick as *Miska Hauser's Letters to Australia 1854–1858* (Ascot Vale, Vic.: Red Rooster Press, 1988) pub. 1988. See also *BrisbaneE*, 52.

Hawking Brothers, The. Country music group comprised of singer-songwriters Russell Hawking (*b* Mooroopna, Vic., 1 July 1931; *d* Melbourne, 2 Nov. 1976) and Alan Hawking (*b* Melbourne, 7 July 1933; *d* Melbourne, 19 Sept. 1988). Separated in early childhood after the death of their mother, the brothers were brought up by separate grandparents. Russell grew up in Mooroopna, a Buddy ★Williams fan; he moved to Melbourne after he left school to look for work. Alan was brought up by their maternal grandparents in Melbourne.

The brothers joined the Trailblazers in the early 1950s, an early Melbourne country music group at the Australian Hillbilly Club. In the early years they performed both as a duo and as soloists on the 3XY Saturday morning shows. Coming a disappointing second on *Australia's Amateur Hour* in 1953, they approached EMI in 1955 and made their first recording on the Regal-Zonophone label (78 rpm). Throughout their career they recorded numerous albums and singles, and among these recordings were several hits, including *Catfish John*, *The Melbourne Cup*, and *One Day At A Time*. They also provided vocal and instrumental backing for other artists during the 1950s and 60s. Their early repertoire was mainly American, and their style influenced by the Carter Family. By 1974, however, elements of Australian folk-song were adapted into their country music style, the outcome of a television commercial they did which focused around Australian folk-songs. Their album, *Australian Heritage* (1975), demonstrated this synthesis of styles.

Established as a successful duo by the 1960s, they formed a five-man band, incorporating three other musicians, retaining the name the Hawking Brothers to identify the group. By 1970, when the brothers decided to launch a full-time career in music, the band membership was composed of the brothers as the nucleus, George Xanthos, Gary Newton and Peter Cohen. The band performed as backing for other artists, in their own right, and as support for Johnny Cash and Buck Owen's tours of Australia in 1973 and 1974 respectively. The Cash and Owen tours were considered by the Hawking Brothers as invaluable experiences. Their first visit to America in 1975 was a marked height in their career. They were the first Australian band accepted to perform on the Grand Ole Opry; and 12 songs by Alan and his wife Diane were recorded on an album at the prestigious RCA Nashville Sound Studio. However, Russell's death from a heart attack late in 1976 saw the decline of the band; it only continued to exist until 1981, when Alan decided to pursue a solo career. Pioneers of country music in Melbourne, the Hawking Brothers did much during their lives to open doors for country music in hotels and clubs around Melbourne. They were elected to the Tamworth Country Music Roll of Renown in 1989, and they had also won many country music awards.

FURTHER REFERENCE
Recordings include *Portrait Of The Folksy Hawking Brothers* (1950s, W&G B1745); *The Hawking Brothers And The Wildwoods* (1960s, Parlophone PCSO 7559); *Australian Heritage* (1975, Fable FBSA 006); *Australian Heritage* vol. 2 (1970s, Fable FBSA 048); *The Hawking Brothers in Nashville* (1970s, Fable FBSA 051); *21 Years With The Hawking Brothers* (1970s, Fable FBSA 065); *Country Travellin'* (1977, RCA VLPI 0155); *One Day At A Time* (1978, RCA VLPI 0188); *The Hawks* (*c*.1979, RCA VLPI 0250); *Flying High In Concert* (*c*.1979, RCA VLPI 0294). See also Ian B. Allen, 'The Trailblazers', *Across Country: Australia's National Country Music Magazine* No. 10 (June 1979), 9; The Hawking Brothers, 'Flying into the 80's: The Hawking Bros.', *Across Country: Australia's National Country Music Magazine* 13 (Sept. 1979), 15–18; *LattaA*; 'Jazzer' James Smith, 'Alan Hawking Tells of Times Past, People Known, of the Trials and Tribulations of Being a Hawking Brother', *Across Country: Australia's National Country Music Magazine* 5 (Dec. 1978–Jan. 1979), 14; *SmithB*; *WatsonC*, 2.   YA HUI HUNG

Hayes, Catherine (*b* Limerick, Ireland, 25 Oct. 1828; *d* Sydenham, London, 11 Aug. 1861), Irish soprano. Star of Covent Garden and La Scala, Milan, and fresh from an enormously successful tour of the USA, in 1854–56 she was the first internationally famous singer to tour Australia, attracting large adoring crowds wherever she went. She made various concert appearances and sang opera in Sydney and in the 1856 Coppin season at Melbourne. Her success in Australia attracted other leading European performers to follow, beginning with Anna *Bishop. She had studied under Giorgio Ronconi at Milan, and also Manuel Garcia at Paris, and likely following her example, several young Australians were later to seek tuition with Garcia's disciple Mathilde Marchesi, including Melba and Frances Alda.

FURTHER REFERENCE
Dennis Shoesmith, *ADB*, 4; George Grove/ E.D. Mackerness, *GroveD*; Osric [Humphrey Hall and Alfred John Cripps], *The Romance of the Sydney Stage* (ms, 1911; pub. Sydney: Currency Press, 1996), 155–63.

Hayes, Evie (Evelyn Vina) (*b* Seattle, Washington, USA, 1 June 1911; *d* Elsternwick, Melbourne, 26 Dec. 1988), theatrical singer, actress of American birth. She appeared on stage from the age of six, tried her luck as a starlet at 20th Century Fox studios, then went into radio, having her own show in New York. She came to Australia in 1938 with her husband Will *Mahoney, and in World War II presented variety shows for the American troops at the Cremorne Theatre, Brisbane. She made her Australian reputation with *Annie Get Your Gun* for J.C. Williamsons in 1947, then had numerous leading roles in musicals and as principal boy in Tivoli pantomimes, including *Call Me Madam, Kiss Me, Kate, Oklahoma!* and *Funny Girl* (1966). One of the most successful singers in postwar musicals in Australia, she was a regular on television from 1956, but contracted multiple sclerosis in 1974 and spent her later years training and encouraging young talent.

FURTHER REFERENCE
John Crampton, *Evie Hayes: And I Loves Ya Back!* (Sydney: Angus & Robertson, 1992); *ParsonsC*.

Hayes, Mileham Geoffrey (*b* Brisbane, 27 Nov. 1940), jazz broadcaster, entrepreneur. He began on clarinet, later adding banjo, and was a founder member of the Varsity Five. Musically inactive while pursuing a medical career 1964–74, he began presenting the ABC radio program *Stomp Off! Let's Go!* and led bands for residencies, touring, and for his television series *Dr Jazz*. Increasingly active as an entrepreneur and lobbyist, he was president of the 1976 Australian Jazz Convention (Brisbane), which played a significant role in the revitalisation of Brisbane's jazz activity. He also established the Queensland Jazz Club (1980) and several jazz venues, organised jazz festivals and a national conference on jazz.

FURTHER REFERENCE
Recordings include *The Varsity Five* (1962, Philips PD-39); *The Band of the Vintage Jazz Society of Brisbane* (1975, VJS-1); *The Band of Dr. Jazz* (1976, EMI EMC-2590); *The World's Hottest Jazz Band*

(1976, EMI EMC-2635). See also *OxfordJ*; Sallie Gardner, 'Mileham Hayes, Player & Visionary', *JA* (Dec. 1982), 8–9.

BRUCE JOHNSON

Hazelwood, Donald Leslie Grant (*b* Sydney, 1 Mar. 1930), violinist. After studying at the NSW State Conservatorium, he played in the Sydney Symphony Orchestra from 1952 and went to France in 1955, studying at the Paris Conservatoire. After this he returned to the Sydney Symphony Orchestra, becoming joint concertmaster in 1965 then concertmaster from 1966. He was also active in chamber music as leader of the highly successful *Austral String Quartet, the *Hazelwood String Quartet and Hazelwood Trio. He had a long association with the National Music Camps, serving as director of the camps, 1989–91. A gracious and invariably thoughtful concertmaster and a committed teacher, his contribution to symphonic music and chamber music has been considerable over a very long period. He was honoured with the OBE (1977) and AO (1988).

FURTHER REFERENCE
Recordings include *Album Leaves*, works of E. Gross, A. Carr-Boyd et al. (1991, Jade JADECD 1023). See also *CA* (1995–96); *WWA* (1996); *Image: Australian Theatrical News and Views*, 1/3 (1987), 92.

Hazelwood String Quartet. Currently comprised of current or former members of the Sydney Symphony Orchestra, Donald *Hazelwood and Georges Lentz (violins), Peter Pfuhl (viola) and Catherine Hewgill (cello). They have focused on the Classical string quartet repertoire, as well as presenting works by Australian composers. They tour regularly for Musica Viva and broadcast on the ABC.

Hazon, Roberto (*b* Borgotaro di Parma, Italy, 25 Sept. 1854; *d* Milan, 9 Sept. 1920), conductor. Educated in Parma and Milan, Hazon became conductor at the Teatro Dal Verme in Milan before becoming musical director for *Simonsen's New Royal Italian Opera Co., arriving in Melbourne in 1886. He toured Australia with the company and settled in Sydney. He became conductor of the Sydney Philharmonic and the Metropolitan Liedertafel, in 1889 conducting an orchestra of 57 and choir of 575 at the opening of the Sydney Town Hall. By then the leading conductor in Sydney, in 1891 he founded the Sydney Amateur Orchestral Society. He returned to Milan in ill health in 1907.

FURTHER REFERENCE
Martha Rutledge, *ADB*, 9; *BrewerD*, 86–7.

SUZANNE ROBINSON

Heinicke, (August Moritz) Hermann (*b* Dresden, Germany, 21 July 1863; *d* 11 July 1949), violinist and leading conductor of choral and orchestral music in Adelaide. He was educated at the Royal Saxon Conservatorium in Dresden, studying violin with Eduard Rappoldi. After acting as concertmaster and conductor of German orchestras, a dispute precipitated his emigration, and he became teacher of violin at the *Adelaide College of Music. He arrived in Adelaide in 1890, where he began a German male voice choir, which later merged with the Adelaide Liedertafel, and from 1891 conducted Heinicke's Grand Orchestra. When the Elder Conservatorium was established in 1898 he became a string teacher and conductor of the orchestra, which merged with his Grand Orchestra. He resigned from the Conservatorium in 1916.   SUZANNE ROBINSON

Heinze, Sir Bernard Thomas (*b* Shepparton, Vic., 1 July 1894; *d* Melbourne, 10 June 1982), conductor, administrator. Heinze studied at the University of Melbourne, won a scholarship to attend the Royal College of Music, London, and after five years' service in the Royal Artillery in World War I studied under d'Indy at the Schola Cantorum in Paris and with Hess in Berlin, also performing as a violinist in the Lejeune Quartet. Returning to Australia in 1924, he joined the staff of the University of Melbourne Conservatorium, and was Ormond professor there (1925–56). He formed the Melbourne String Quartet, and his career as a conductor began in 1924 when he formed the Melbourne University Symphony Orchestra, which he led for 10 years. He was director-general of music for the *ABC 1929–32, then striving to have full symphony orchestras formed in each state; in 1933 he became conductor of the *Melbourne Symphony Orchestra (later, from 1949, the Victorian Symphony Orchestra), which he led until 1953 when Walter Susskind was appointed principal conductor. He was also conductor of the Royal Philharmonic Society in Melbourne 1927–53, toured Europe in the 1930s and Canada in 1947, and in 1956 succeeded *Goossens as director of the NSW State Conservatorium of Music. In 1967 he was appointed chairman of Commonwealth Assistance to Australian Composers, and in 1968 of the music advisory committee of the Australian Council of the Arts.

Heinze's contribution to musical life in Australia was inestimable. He was a vital force in establishing fully professional symphony orchestras and developing standards of musical performance, and his influence was felt throughout the country. He visited Europe and the USA in 1938 to investigate the role of radio in promoting music, was a judge at the Ysaÿe Competition in Brussels, and conducted in London, Paris, Berlin, Budapest and Helsinki. During World War II he was particularly active in Australia, leading festivals of the music of Beethoven and Russian composers in Sydney, and was the major Australian conductor keeping alive the orchestral tradition and maintaining performance standards at that time. When the ABC in collaboration with state and municipal authorities set up orchestras in the Australian capital cities after the war he was very supportive, appearing as a guest conductor with all of them.

One of his lasting achievements was the promotion of music among younger audiences through school and youth concerts at which he lectured about the music performed, giving the first public concert for schools in Australia in 1924, and in 1947 he was responsible for establishing the ABC's series of Youth Orchestral Concerts which introduced vast numbers of young people to orchestral music. His strength as a conductor lay more in Romantic music than in earlier periods, composers such as Elgar, Richard Strauss and Mahler receiving committed performances. He was knighted in 1949, received the UNESCO award in 1979, and was appointed AC in 1975.

FURTHER REFERENCE
For discography, see *HolmesC*. An interview by Doreen Bridges is in *AJME* 12 (Apr. 1973), 21–2. See also Thérèse Radic, *Bernard Heinze: A Biography* (Melbourne: Macmillan, 1986); idem, *GroveD*; Desmond O'Shaughnessy, 'Professor Bernard Heinze', *Canon* 1/11 (June 1948), 28–31.   J.L. HOLMES

Helfgott, David (*b* Melbourne, 19 May 1947), pianist. Born of Polish parents, he moved to Perth in 1953, where he studied with Frank Arndt and Alice Carrard, a pupil of Bela Bartók's. Winner of the State finals of the ABC Concerto and Vocal Competition four times, in 1966 he went to study with Cyril Smith at the Royal College of Music, London. He appeared at the Royal Albert Hall as soloist in the Liszt Piano Concerto in 1970, but illness precipitated his return to Australia, and although he worked as a *répétiteur* with the WA Opera Company and gave several local recitals, he lived in obscurity. With the support of Gillian Helfgott, whom he married in 1984, he began touring Australia and Europe, particularly Denmark and Germany, and making recordings. The 1995 film *Shine*, based on the story of his life, brought him worldwide acclaim.

FURTHER REFERENCE
Recordings include *Rachmaninov: The Last Great Romantic* (1966, RCA Victor); *Shine* (1996, Phillips); *David Helfgott Plays Liszt* (1995 RAP); *David Helfgott* (1990, EMI). See also Gillian Helfgott and Alissa Tanskaya, *Love You To Bits And Pieces: Life With David Helfgott* (Ringwood, Vic., Penguin, 1996).
                      ALISSA TANSKAYA

Helmrich, Dorothy Jane Adele (*b* Sydney, 25 July 1889; *d* Sydney, 1 Sept. 1984), mezzo-soprano. Piano lessons as a child were followed by amateur singing with the Mosman Musical Society and studies first with William Beattie, then Stefan Mavrogordato at the Sydney Conservatorium. In 1921 she studied at the Royal College of Music, London, with Plunket Green, George Henschel and Hugh Allen. Her debut at the Wigmore Hall in 1926 was followed by regular engagements with Henry Wood's Promenade Concerts and touring in Britain and Europe: one of her early accompanists was Gerald Moore. In 1936 she was invited by the ABC to inaugurate the new celebrity concert series, performing French, German and English lieder. In the early years of World War II she toured for the British Council for the Encouragement of Music and the Arts. Back in Australia in 1941 for another tour, she was invited to remain as a singing teacher at the NSW State Conservatorium, from which she retired in 1975.

Alfred Einstein in Berlin described Helmrich as 'a singer of distinction, knowledge and charm of presentation', and a Warsaw critic wrote that her 'voice is clear and voluminous, the quality as velvet, and the colour very warm'. She specialised in lieder recitals, giving an important place to English folk-songs and repertoire from Purcell to Britten, and was especially noted for her interpretation of song cycles of Schubert, Schumann and Mahler. She initiated plans for an Australian equivalent of the British Council, renamed in 1945 the ★Arts Council of Australia, in which she played a leading role. She was particularly concerned to develop relatively autonomous rural branches of the Council to ensure that country towns and schools received regular performing arts events, touring into communities that had rarely been visited by professional singers, instrumentalists and dancers.

FURTHER REFERENCE
Victor Carell and Beth Dean, *On Wings of Song: Dorothy Helmrich and the Arts Council* (Sydney: Alternative Publishing Co-op, 1982); *MackenzieS*, 136.   WARREN BOURNE

Henderson, Bob (Robert James)   (*b* Sydney, 2 Nov. 1941), jazz trumpeter. He began cornet in 1951 (later also a vocalist), trained with the Glen Innes Municipal Band and later took classical lessons. Playing in dance band work in the Hunter Valley area, he was based at Newcastle in the 1960s and 70s, appearing with the Harbourside Six (1962–68) and in club, television, cabaret, theatre and touring shows including *Moscow Circus on Ice* and *Disney on Parade*. Joining the ★Daly-Wilson Big Band in 1985, he also worked with other big bands, including Bob Gibson's. He played in the pit orchestras of *Anything Goes* (1989) and *42nd Street* (1990), and has been with Graeme ★Bell's All Stars since 1979 as well as freelancing and leading.

FURTHER REFERENCE
Recordings include *Graeme Bell in Holland with the Graeme Bell All Stars* (1981, Sea Horse Records SHL 004). See also *OxfordJ*.
BRUCE JOHNSON

Henderson, Don   (*b* Melbourne, 17 Jan. 1937; *d* Brisbane, 20 Aug. 1991), protest song singer, songwriter. After studying violin as a child, he began playing mandolin, guitar and banjo, and in 1957 was one of the original ★Thunderbirds rock and roll band. He moved to Sydney in 1958 and worked as a guitar-maker, becoming well known performing in folk-clubs and pubs, and writing *Put A Light In Every Country Window* (1960) about the Snowy Mountains Electricity Scheme. From 1961 he worked as an itinerant musician, playing in the Union Singers at trade union events. He was in England from 1971 with his guitar business as well as performing, then from 1979 settled in Brisbane and helped revitalise the Queensland Folk Federation, performing and exhibiting his instruments in the coming years. Writing in folk, hillbilly and blues styles of themes of wage justice and the labour movement, he was one of the first in the 1960s to write protest songs in Australia.

FURTHER REFERENCE
Recordings include *Ballad of Women* (1964, Union), *Flames Of Discontent* (1979) for the Seamen's Union of Aust., *In My Time* (1986, Hot to Trot TCHTT 001), and *Basic Wage Dream* for the Aust. Council of Salaried and Professional Associations. See also *Australian Tradition* 2/2 (July 1965), 2; *Australian Tradition* 7 (Sept. 1970), 7; *RadicS*, 185–6; Don Henderson, *A Quiet Century: 100 Songs and Poems* (Nambour, Qld: Qld Folk Federation, 1994), vi-vii.

Henderson, Moya   (*b* Quirindi, NSW, 2 Aug. 1941), composer. Recognition came early for Henderson as, immediately upon graduating from the University of Queensland (with first class honours), she was appointed resident composer with the Australian Opera during its inaugural season at the Sydney Opera House in 1973. In 1974 she accepted a German Academic Exchange Scholarship to study music-theatre with Mauricio Kagel and composition with Karlheinz Stockhausen at the Cologne Musikhochschule, where she produced the prize-winning work *Clearing the Air* (Darmstadt, 1974), *Marxisms* (1974) and *Stubble* (1976). In 1976 she returned to Australia and based herself in Sydney, where she has been working as a freelance composer ever since.

She has composed a substantial catalogue of works encompassing all significant genres (orchestral, chamber, vocal, piano, organ, opera, music-theatre, incidental music, radiophonic works and music which uses electronic and computerised technology) in which she exhibits a highly distinctive and original musical voice. Moya Henderson's music is of interest both for its idiosyncratic musical style and for the concerns it raises through extra-musical references about the Australian environment, feminism and women's issues, the Aboriginal people and their plight since colonisation, and other related political themes. Significant among works which pick up in these themes are *The Dreaming* (1985), *Cross Hatching* (1984), *Kudikynah Cave* (1987), *Pellucid Days* (1989) and *Wild Card* (1991). Her music is accessible, passionate and often challenging and difficult to perform. Some of her works are satirical and humorous while others are profoundly moving and spiritual. A major project begun in 1992 has been her opera *Lindy* to a libretto by poet Judith Rodriguez on the Azaria Chamberlain affair, which was commissioned by the Australian Opera. Moya Henderson was made a member of the Order of Australia (AM) in the 1996 Australia Day honours list.

WORKS (Selective)

Mss in Australian Music Centre

Orchestral *The Dreaming,* str orch (1985), *Celebration 40,000,* pf, orch (1988).

Ensemble *Alanbiq,* tuned triangles, perc (6 players) (1977), *Min Min Light,* cl, vn, va, vc (1982), *Larrikins Lot,* fl, trbn, perc, pf (1982), *Kudikynah Cave,* str qrt (1987), *G'day Africa,* cl, pf, va, vc (1990), *Waking up the Flies,* pf trio (1990), *G'day Africa II & III,* cl, pf, va, vc (1995).

Keyboard *Sacred Site,* grand org, tape (1983), *Cross-Hatching (Rarrk),* pf (1984), *Reef,* org (1988).

Music–Theatre *Marxisms,* vc (1973), Sydney Opera House, 1973, *Clearing the Air,* db, 4 wind and/or brass (1974), Darmstadt, Germany, 1974; *Stubble,* S, talking table (male voice) (1976), Cologne, Germany, 1976.

Voice and Orchestra *Six Urban Songs,* Mez, Orchestra (1983), *Confessions to my Dogs,* cabaret song-cycle, Mez profundo, pf (1986; arr. 1987), *Pellucid Days,* S, Mez, hn, str orch (1989), *Wild Card,* S, vc, pf (1991), *Anzac Fanfare,* S, orch (1995).

Choral *Songs about Music* (1987).

Radio Plays *Currawong: A symphony of bird sounds* (1988), 6 Aug. 1988, ABC FM, *Meditations and Distractions on the Theme of the Singing Nun* (1990), 19 Feb. 1990, ABC FM.

FURTHER REFERENCE

Recordings include *Sacred Site,* (1989, 5th Continent Music SCCD1002); *Confessions To My Dogs* (1989, Oz Music OZM1003); *I wonder as I wander* (1992, Tall Poppies TP 016); *O Joyous Child of Poverty* (1993, Tall Poppies TP 046); *Waltzing Matilda* (1994, New Market Music NEW1042.2); *G'day Africa* (1994, Tall Poppies TP 043); *Cross-Hatching* (1994, Tall Poppies TP 037); and *Currawong* (1994, Alpha ABC 4797582).

Her writings include 'Assorted Influences', *SA* 26 (Winter 1990), 17–18; 'The Tosca Alemba: Ringing the changes', *Acoustics Australia* 22/1 (Apr. 1994), 11–14, reprinted in *Journal of the Australian Association of Musical Instrument Makers (JAAMIM)* 13/3 (1994), 30–40.

See also *GroveW;* A. Ford, 'The unlevel playing field', *Composer to Composer: Conversations about Contemporary Music* (Sydney: Allen & Unwin, 1993), 101–6; S. Macarthur, 'Moya Henderson'. In *Annäherung V—an sieben Komponistinnen,* ed. B. Sonntag and R. Matthei (Kassel: Furore-Verlag, 1988), 43–52; idem, 'Moya Henderson in Profile', *2MBS FM Programme Guide* (January 1990), 7–9; idem, 'Ripping the Beard off Analysis: Writing Moya Henderson and Gillian Whitehead into the Discourse', *SA* 31 (Spring 1991), 29–34; P. McCallum, 'Variations on a theme for Survivors: Moya Henderson talks to Peter McCallum about influences on her work', *SMH* 10 Oct 1992.

SALLY MACARTHUR

Hennig, Dennis (*b* Melbourne, 1951; *d* Sydney, 17 Jan. 1993), pianist. He studied piano with Roy Shepherd (University of Melbourne), Mme Bascourret de Queraldi (Paris) and Sidney Harrison (London). A lecturer in music history at the Canberra School of Music, then (from 1981) the NSW State Conservatorium, he broadcast for the ABC, and commissioned and was dedicatee of Ross

Edwards' Piano Concerto. A pianist of wide tastes, his repertoire ranged from concertos, virtuoso 19th-century solo piano works (transcriptions, in particular) to cabaret and theatre performances.

FURTHER REFERENCE

His recordings include: Ross Edwards, Piano Concerto, Queensland Symphony Orchestra (ABC 426 483); *Pianistic Peccadilloes,* works of Grainger, Eileen Joyce and others (ABC 426 997); works by Martinu (Conifer); Cyril Scott (Etcetera); Tausig transcriptions of works by Schubert, Liszt and Wagner (Etcetera).

CYRUS MEHER-HOMJI

Henri, Franciscus (*b* The Hague, The Netherlands, 7 Aug. 1947), children's entertainer. He came to Australia at the age of nine, and after training as a high school teacher, released singles and albums of modern religious songs (from 1970) before turning to children's music. He was artist-in-residence in Victorian schools, wrote and presented children's theatre works for the arts councils in all eastern states, and presented *Storyworld* for ABC radio (1980–85) and *Launching Pad* for commercial television. He has written over 200 songs for small children, many in styles influenced by trad jazz. His three books include *Franciscus Henri Song Book vol. 1* (1987), and his 12 children's albums include *Dancing In the Kitchen* (1991, ABC Video 8143932/4) and *My Favourite Nursery Rhymes* (1993, ABC Video 8143552/4).

Henslowe, Francis Hartwell (*b* Fulham, London, 1811; *d* Lee, Kent, 10 May 1878), composer. A civil servant at the British Embassy at Turin 1830–33, he emigrated to Australia in 1841 and became private secretary to the governor at Hobart. A composer of dances and light pieces, he also wrote a set of sacred works, *Songs of Zion.*

FURTHER REFERENCE

A list of his compositions is in C. Craig, *The Engravers of Van Diemen's Land* (Hobart, 1861). See also G.T. Stilwell, *ADB,* 1.

Herald-Sun Aria. See *Sun Aria.*

Herbert, William (*b* Melbourne, 6 Dec. 1920), tenor. Trained as a choirboy under A.E. *Floyd at St Paul's Cathedral, Melbourne, after singing tenor solo in *Messiah* with the Victorian Symphony Orchestra at the age of 18, he was engaged for numerous ABC oratorio performances throughout Australia. He went to England in 1947, at once appearing in the Albert Hall Proms; after this he was soon in demand throughout Britain and Europe, appearing frequently at the Three Choirs and Edinburgh Festivals, as well as at the opening of the Royal Festival Hall and the Coronation of Elizabeth II in 1952. His repertoire included the standard concert works of Handel, Elgar, Bach, Mozart, as well as the Beethoven Ninth Symphony and Monteverdi *Vespers.* He returned to Australia as a visiting concert artist periodically after

1950, taught voice at the University of WA from 1963 and at Canberra School of Music from 1965.

FURTHER REFERENCE
Recordings included *Messiah* (Nixa), Bach Cantatas (Decca) and various recordings for L'Oiseau-lyre. See also *MackenzieS* 185–7; K.J.Kutsch and Leo Riemann, *Grosses Sängerlexikon* (Bern: Francke Verlag, 1987); *GlennonA*, 222; *AMN* 41 (Mar. 1951), 3; *AMN* 46 (June 1956), 27.

Hermannsburg. See *Arandic Music.*

Hero. Rock opera (1976) by Craig McGregor. A rock music version of the Orpheus legend, it was first performed by the Australian Opera at the Seymour Centre in 1976 and abandoned mid-season, with the worst attendances the company had ever had.

Herron, Ted (Edwin Martin) (*b* Queenstown, Tas., 16 June 1923; *d* Launceston, Tas., 21 Jan. 1986), jazz trumpeter. Living in Launceston from 1934, he settled on the guitar, and later trumpet and bass. Conscripted for war service in 1941 and posted to the mainland, he gained experience from other jazz musicians. After his discharge he resumed dance work in Launceston with a group which became the Jazzmanians, including drummer Bill Browne and later the Gourlay brothers Max (violin, clarinet) and Bruce (piano). Apart from periods of dormancy, for example while he was in Hobart in the early 1960s, his band became the local focus of jazz activity in Launceston.

FURTHER REFERENCE
Recordings include *Bryan Street Blues,* Ted Herron's Jazzmanians (1946, Ampersand 8). See also *OxfordJ.*
BRUCE JOHNSON

Herz, Julius (*b* Mecklenburg-Schwerin, Germany, 13 Mar. 1841; *d* Mordialloc, Melbourne, 23 Aug. 1898), conductor, organist. After study at the Berlin Conservatorium with Julius Stern, he joined the Conservatorium staff. He came to Australia in 1865, becoming organist at Christ Church Hawthorn, then St James' Cathedral, Melbourne, as well as a teacher of voice and instruments, and an examiner for the Musical Association of Victoria. Conductor of the Melbourne Liedertafel 1870–92, he toured with it to Sydney in 1881 and Adelaide in 1888. He was manager of the Victorian Orchestra in 1890 and in 1892 went to WA, assisting the governor, Sir William *Robinson, with his compositions, and returned to Melbourne in 1894. One of the growing number of German-trained professional musicians in Australia at the close of the colonial era, he was also a composer of songs and miniatures.

FURTHER REFERENCE
Thérèse Radic, *ADB,* 4.

Hesse, Marjorie Anne (*b* Brisbane, 13 Nov, 1911; *d* Sydney, 24 Feb. 1986), pianist, composer. Educated in Brisbane, Hesse began her musical studies at the age of 13 with Sydney May, one of Brisbane's leading teachers. At 15 she won the national prize for piano and harmony, presented by Trinity College, London, to the best contestant chosen from the British Commonwealth. The following year she began her studies with Frank Hutchens at the NSW Conservatorium high school. She went on to the NSW Conservatorium at 17, and continued her studies with Frank Hutchens, but also with Alfred Hill and Mirrie Hill. She graduated in 1931 with a Teacher and Performer diploma. In 1932 she gave her first recital at the Conservatorium, and included *All Suddenly the Wind Comes Soft* in the program, one of her own compositions. It was at this time that she developed an interest in composition, especially for the piano. She later became a composer of pedagogical music, well known to Australian students. During the early 1930s Hesse performed frequently for the ABC radio programs, and she was appointed lecturer in music at the NSW Conservatorium in 1936. In her career as a concert pianist, she toured Australia and other countries both as a concerto soloist, a solo performer, and as an accompanist. During her life, she was also an active music educator and adjudicator, and a prominent examiner for the AMEB. In 1975 she was honoured with the MBE.

WORKS (Selective)
Chamber *An Irish Croon,* vn, pf (London: Augener, 1939).
Piano solo *Growing Up* (Sydney: Paling, 1936), *The Skipping Suite* (Sydney: Paling, 1937), *All Suddenly the Wind Comes Soft* (London: Augener, 1939), *The Piper* (London: Augener, 1939), *Romance* (Syndey: Nicholson's, 1947), *Jollity* (Melbourne: Allan, 1948), *Valse Gracieuse* (Melbourne: Allan, 1950), *Country Jig* (Melbourne: Allan, 1957), *Rustic Dance* (Melbourne: Allan, 1957), *Ten Busy Fingers*: Tin Whistle March, March of the Brownies, Cinderella at the Ball, Follow My Leader, Soldier's Chanty, Come and Play, Scout's March, Snow White Dances (Melbourne: Allan, 1959), *The Ballerina* (Sydney: Leeds, 1961), *La Pastourelle* (Sydney: Leeds, 1961), *Playtime* (Sydney: Leeds, 1961), *Curious* (Melbourne: Allans, 1973), *Discord* (Melbourne: Allans, 1973), Gaiety (Melbourne: Allans, 1973), *Hopscotch* (Melbourne: Allans, 1973), *Leapfrog* (Melbourne: Allans, 1973), *Melancholy* (Melbourne: Allans, 1973), *Siciliana* (Melbourne: Allans, 1973), *Soldiers on Parade* (Melbourne: Allans, 1973), *This and That: 10 Piano Pieces of Medium Difficulty*: I wish, Oranges and Lemons, Hustle, Bustle, The Wee Scottie, Resting, The Happy Yodeller, Toy Band, Merry-go-round, Let's play at Home, The Chinese Mandarin's Song (Sydney: Castle Music, 1982). Undated: *At Play, Curious Piano, Suite for Children, Twilight, When We are Very Young.*
Piano Duet *Asian Waif* (Sydney: Albert & Son, 1976), *Jazzin' down to Rio* (Sydney: Albert & Son, 1976), *With Love from Vienna* (Sydney: Albert & Son, 1978), *Oranges and Lemons* (Melbourne: Allans, 1978), *Hush-a-bye-baby* (Melbourne: Allans, 1978).
Vocal *Seven Songs for Children:* The New Puppy, A Frog's Life, Tortoises, The Kangaroo, Kookaburra, The Koala, The Beetle, vv,

vn, pf (Sydney: Leeds, 1962), *Two Australian songs,* In Early Green Summer, O Singer in Brown (n.d.).

Teaching Pieces   *Sight-reading Excursion,* 8 vols (Sydney: Castle Music)

FURTHER REFERENCE

Obit. in *APRAJ* (Dec. 1986), 41. Recordings include *Curious Piano, A Recital of 33 Modern Piano Pieces,* Max Cooke, pf (1972, W&G BS 5589). See also 7 articles in *AMN* (index in *MarsiI*); 'Australian Musicians: Marjorie Hesse', *Canon* 13 (May–June 1960), 247–8; *CohenI*; *McCredieM.*

YA HUI HUNG

Heuzenroeder, Moritz   (*b* Ottersburg, Germany, 15 July 1849; *d* Tanunda, SA, 9 Nov. 1897), composer, conductor. After visiting Australia as a teenager, he studied composition with Sebert at the Stuttgart Royal Academy of Music. He settled in SA in 1872, teaching singing and piano, giving recitals in the Barossa Valley, and writing operettas in German for the SA German Club 1882–83. He established the Adelaide Harmonic Society and performed several of his works with them. One of the most important musical pioneers of the Barossa, his compositions include songs, patriotic odes and piano works, as well as the operettas *Singvogelchen, Onkel Beckers Geschichte* (1882), *Faust and Gretchen* (1883) and *The Windmill* (1891). His two-act *Immomeena* (1893) has a realistic local setting.

FURTHER REFERENCE

IrvinD; Elizabeth Wood, 'Moritz Heuzenroeder: a Musical Pioneer', *Linguistics in Northern Queensland* 3/1 (1974) 40–8; idem, *GroveD.*

Hewett, Colleen   (Bendigo, Vic., 16 Apr. 1950), popular music singer. After singing at local dances in Bendigo from the age of 12, she joined the Esquires in 1964, then the vocal trio The Creations (from 1967) with whom she toured Australia, the Laurie Allan Revue and Ian Saxon And The Sound. She went solo in 1970, making the first of seven singles, *Superstar* in 1971. An able actor as well as a fine soft-rock vocalist, she starred in the musical *Godspell* 1971–72, her single from the show *Day by Day* (1971) reaching No. 1 in the charts. She released her debut album *Colleen Hewett* in 1972, and appeared in *Tommy* 1973, then *Pippin* 1974. After attempting with little success to establish herself in the USA from 1975, she returned to Australia in 1977, doing session work, appearing in clubs, acting on television, and recording another six singles, including *Dreaming My Dreams With You* in 1979. One of the most successful artists on singles in the years when they were giving way to albums, at her height she won *Bandstand* awards four times (1970–74) and was *TV Week* Queen of Pop.

FURTHER REFERENCE

Recordings include *Superstar* (1971, Festival FK 4542), *Day by Day* (1971, Festival FK 4491), *Colleen Hewett* (Festival SFL

934633), and *Dreaming My Dreams With You* (Wizard ZS319). For discography, see *SpencerA*. See also *McGrathA*; *SpencerW.*

Highwayman, The.   Musical comedy, music and book by Edmond Samuels. Set in colonial Bendigo, it recounts the antics of the police trying to capture a bushranger. First performed by the Frank Thring Co. at the King's Theatre, Melbourne, in 1950. See *Musical Comedy.*

Hill, Alfred Francis   (*b* Melbourne, 16 Nov. 1870, *d* Sydney, 30 Oct. 1960), composer, pedagogue, conductor, violinist. Alfred Hill gained his earliest musical experiences as a violinist and cornet player with the small theatre orchestras associated with the itinerant theatre troupes that flourished on an Australian–NZ touring circuit in the years up to 1886. From 1887 to 1891 he was a student of the Royal Conservatory at Leipzig where his mentors and teachers included Carl Reinecke, Hans Sitt, Gustav Schreck (a later renowned musical director of St Thomas' Church), Oskar Paul, Hermann Bollard and Reckendorf. Already during his student days, Hill had gained orchestral experience as a rank-and-file violinist of the Gewandhaus Orchestra, which also fulfilled theatre duties, at the city's opera house. In this capacity he experienced at first hand working under Reinecke, Nikisch, Brahms, Tchaikovsky, Max Bruch and others.

Hill graduated from the Leipzig Conservatory in July 1891, gaining the Hellbig Prize for outstanding all-round performance, his reputation at this stage enhanced through the publication of six major compositions, including the *Scotch* Sonata for Violin and Piano, and *Air Varié* for Violin and Orchestra. Arriving in NZ on 29 December 1891, he presented himself as soloist, composer, conductor of the Wellington Society and as pedagogue. In the quarter-century between his arrival at Wellington and his appointment in 1915 as professor of composition, harmony and counterpoint at the NSW State Conservatorium, his career was one of peripatetic movement to and fro across the Tasman, between Sydney and the smaller NZ cities. It was at this stage of his career that he attained his most public exposure, as conductor of touring opera and operetta troupes, as conductor of such orchestras as those for the Professional Orchestral Association Sydney 1897–99, Christchurch International Exhibition 1906, the Sydney Liedertafel 1897–1902 and as violinist/violist participant in several string quartets, and as principal of the Austral Orchestral College 1911–14. In this period he was occasionally active as a cultural and musical polemicist in the championship of the concept of Australian opera. As professor at the NSW State Conservatorium 1916–34, he served under its first two directors, Henri Verbrugghen and W. Arundel Orchard, training, in a conservative tradition, a subsequent generation of Australian composers and conductors, among them John Antill and Joseph Post, and was also associated as an associate conductor with Verbrugghen's shortlived NSW State Orchestra. In the quarter century (1935–60) following his retirement, he continued to exert a public seminal influence on Australian and NZ music, championing numerous causes such as the establishment of permanent orchestras in Australia and NZ, and the investigation, conservation and documentation of the indigenous musics of the Maoris and Australian Aborigines.

Hill left a very large corpus of compositions encompassing all genres: 10 operas, three cantatas or oratorio works, 13 symphonies, five concertos, numerous small-scale orchestral works, as well as string quartets and other works for mixed chamber ensembles, and vocal and choral music. This volume is greatly expanded through his numerous other works for small chamber combinations and sonatas, as well as the numerous adaptations and miniatures he made for specific occasions or ensembles such as Clive Amadio's Quintet. His production can be periodised according to the predominance of a particular genre, the first phase (1891–1923) emphasising the operas, cantatas and other music dramatic works, the second phase (1924–41) emphasising the concerted music and the string quartets of which no less than 10 were produced 1934–38, the third and final phase (1941–60) emphasising the 13 symphonies, 12 of them adaptations and reworkings of the already existing string quartets. One work to deviate from this pattern is the *Australia* Symphony, for which he composed a new scherzo, based on the sound-track he had provided for a film sound-track on Arnhem Land in association with C.P. Mountford.

WORKS (Selective)

Dramatic   Hill's operatic and cantata settings were fashioned after libretti based on conventional European topics, Exotic Afro-Oriental Settings, Maori lore and mythology, and Australian literary materials, and included such titles as *Lady Dolly* (1898), *Don Quixote de la Mancha* (1904), *Giovanni the Sculptor* (1913), *A Moorish Maid* (1905), *Rajah of Shivapore* (1913), *Tawhaki* (1897), *Hinemoa* (1895), *Tapu the Tale of a Maori Pahli* (1903), *Terra—the Weird Flute* (1933), *Auster* (1932) and *The Ship of Heaven* (1923). Among his librettists are numbered Arthur Adams, Hugh McCrae, Emily Cogean and A. Dommett.

Orchestral   *Maori Symphony* (1896), *Life Symphony* (1941), the remaining eleven symphonies dating between 1951 and 1959. Concertos for trumpet (1926), horn (n.d.), violin (1932), piano (1936), *Overture Welcome* (1949), and numerous short tone poems and lyric pieces, e.g. *The Lost Hunter*, *The Moon's God Horn* (after Hugh McCrae), *Waiata Poi* and many more.

Chamber, Choral   17 String Quartets (*c*.1905–41), Septet for Wind Instruments, numerous smaller works, including sonatas (e.g. the *Scotch Sonata*, 1891) and miniatures. There survive numerous vocal and choral settings of modest dimensions, including also a Mass in E flat.

FURTHER REFERENCE

Recordings include Symphony No. 2 *Joy of Life* (1971, Festival 800–18); Symphony No. 3, Sydney Symphony Orchestra, cond. H. Krips (1959, HMV ALP 7524); String Quartet No. 2, Austral

String Quartet (1967, Festival FL 30802). A discography to 1972 is in *PlushD*. His mss, papers and documents are located in various libraries, among them the ABC Federal Music Library (Sydney), the State Library of NSW (Sydney), and *CAnl*. See also Jeremy Commons, 'The Operas of Alfred Hill', in *Opera in New Zealand: Aspects of History and Performance,* ed. Adrienne Simpson (Wellington: Witham Press, 1990), 61–74; Roger Covell, *Australia's Music: Themes of a New Society* (Melbourne: Sun Books, 1967); Andrew D. McCredie, 'Alfred Hill (1870–1960): Some backgrounds and perspectives for an Historical Edition', MMA 3 (1968), 181–258; idem, 'Alfred Hill', *CallawayA*, 7–18; idem, 'Alfred Hill (1870–1960): Leipzig Backgrounds and Models and this Significance for his Later Instrumental Music (1920–1960)', in *One Hand on the Manuscript: Music in Australian Cultural History 1930–1960,* ed. Nicholas Brown et al. (Canberra: Humanities Research Centre, ANU, 1995), 18–33; James M. Thomson, 'The Role of the Pioneer Composer: Some Reflections on Alfred Hill (1870–1960)', SMA 4 (1970), 52–61; idem, *A Distant Music: The Life and Times of Alfred Hill* (Auckland: OUP, 1980); idem., *The Oxford History of New Zealand Music 1840–1890* (Auckland: OUP, 1991).   ANDREW D. McCREDIE

Hill, Mirrie Irma née Solomon   (*b* Sydney, 1 Dec. 1892; *d* 1 May 1986), composer, pianist, teacher. She received her first piano lessons from an aunt when she was five and at 13 she became a pupil of Joseph Kretschman. During this time she became interested in composition and commenced harmony lessons with Ernest Truman. Laurence Godfrey Smith, her next piano teacher, introduced her to Alfred ★Hill who gave her composition lessons; she married Hill in 1921. She was the recipient of a scholarship for composition, chamber music and piano at the NSW State Conservatorium; this began a long association, in which she taught harmony and aural studies at the Conservatorium and examined for the AMEB. She travelled with her husband to Europe and America during 1926–27, and in 1939 they visited NZ.

Hill wrote music in many genres, including chamber, piano, and vocal. Her favourite, however, was orchestral music, and she considered perhaps her most ambitious work the *Arnhemland* Symphony, which took its inspiration from the themes and rhythms of the Aborigines. Another work that uses Aboriginal ideas is *Aboriginal Themes*, which uses poems by Dame Mary Gilmore as its basis; while *Avinu Malkeinu*, for solo violin and orchestra, is based on an ancient Ashkenazi Pentecost melody. She also wrote a book, *Aural Culture*. She was made an honorary member of Musica Viva and the Fellowship of Australian Composers.

WORKS

Most music available from Australian Music Centre, Sydney.

Orchestral   *Rhapsody For Piano and Full Orchestra* (1918; APRA), *Cinderella* Suite, str (1925), *The Little Dream* (1930; APRA), *Three Aboriginal Dances,* pf, orch (1950; Southern Music), *Arnhemland* Symphony (1954; rec. 1968, ABC RRCS/145; APRA), *Avinu Malkeinu*, vn, orch (1971; rec 1975, ABC AC 1013 and WRC, R03154; J. Albert and Son, *c*.1977), *Carnival Night* (1971; rec. 1975, ABC AC 1013; APRA), *Andante*, woodwind, hp, str (1975; rec. 1975, ABC AC 1013; APRA), *Fantasia*, (1977).

Instrumental *Garden Sketches*, pf (Allan, *c*.1934), *Child Fancies* vol. 1, pf (Allans, *c*.1935), *Sketches at the Zoo*, pf (Allan & Co., *c*.1936), *Dreams*, pf (Boosey and Hawkes, *c*.1942), *Minuet*, pf (rec. Columbia DO 3091; Boosey & Hawkes, 1942), *Waltz*, pf (rec. 1995, Tall Poppies TP049 and 1996 Tall Poppies TP049 CSM 27; Boosey & Hawkes, *c*.1942), *Incidental Music for Three Shepherds*, 2vn, va, vc (1945), *Dancing Slippers*, pf (W.H. Paling, *c*.1948), *Happy Swaggie*, pf (W.H. Paling, *c*.1948), *Mr Roo*, pf (W.H. Paling, *c*.1948), *Advertisements*, pf (Southern Music, *c*.1949), *In a Moonlit Garden*, pf, vn (Allan, *c*.1949), *All in a Day*, pf (1950; Allan, *c*.1950), *Brolga (The Dancer)*, pf (Southern Music, 1950), *Dancing Feet*, pf (Allan, *c*.1950), *Leafy Lanes of Kent*, (W.H. Paling, *c*.1950), *The Kunkarunkara Women*, (Southern Music, 1950) *Three Aboriginal Dances*, pf (Southern Music, *c*.1950), *Bell Birds*, pf (W.H. Paling, 1952), *Blue Tongue Lizard*, pf (1952; W.H. Paling, *c*.1952), *Goblins' Dance*, pf (Allan, *c*.1953), *Moonlight Dance* pf (Allan, *c*.1953), *Sea Magic*, pf (Allan, *c*.1957), *Jolly Jack Tar*, vn, pf (W.H. Paling, 1959), *Come Summer*, cl, pf (1969; Boosey & Hawkes, *c*.1969), *Dancing Faun*, fl, pf (1969; Boosey & Hawkes, *c*.1969), *Pipe Reel and All Through the Night*, pf 4 hands (Albert & Son, *c*.1970), *Three Nice Mice and Summer Shower*, pf 4 hands (Albert & Son, *c*.1970), *Bourree*, fl, pf (Castle Music, *c*.1971), *Fun in the Sun* and *The Worm that Wriggled* and *Possum Scampers* and *Dancing in the Sand*, pf (Castle Music, *c*.1971), *Jolly Wallaby*, pf (Castle Music, *c*.1971), *Sarabande*, fl, pf (Castle Music, *c*.1971), *Simple Melodies for Recorder: Stage 1*, descant rec, treble rec (Albert & son, *c*.1971), *Simple Melodies for Recorder: Stage 2*, 2 descant rec, 2 treble rec (Albert & son, *c*.1971), *Three Highland Tunes*, pf (Castle Music, *c*.1971), *Bonny Oh!*, pf (1973; Castle Music, *c*.1973), *Dance of the Cunning Mouse*, pf (Castle Music, *c*.1973), *March of a Robot*, pf (Castle Music, *c*.1973), *Merry Romp*, pf (Castle Music, *c*.1973), *My Bird Sings*, pf (Castle Music, *c*.1973), *Saturday*, pf (Castle Music, *c*.1973), *The Two Frogs*, pf (Castle Music, *c*.1973), *Up and Down*, pf (Castle Music, *c*.1973), *Willow Wind*, pf (Albert & Son, *c*.1973), *Avinu Malkeinu*, vn, pf (rec. MBS 27 CD; Albert and Son, *c*.1974), *Meditation*, pf (Southern Music, *c*.1954), *Merry Imp*, pf (Albert & Son, *c*.1976), *Child Fancies* vol. 2, pf (Allans, *c*.1978), *Birthday Bouquet*, pf, 4 hands (Schaum Publications), *Bourree, Sarabande, Pan Plucked a Reed*, ob, pf, *Eleven Short Pieces*, str qrt, *Improvisations*, vn, pf, *Melody Corner*, pf, 4 hands (Allans), *Natalicic Feliz*, pf (Irmacs Vitale Cia), *Petite Waltz*, pf (Century Music Publising Co.), Piano Trio in B minor, *Pow Wow*, pf (Century Music Publishing Company), Prelude for Solo Oboe (1974; rec. ABC AC 1049B), String Quartet in D major, String Quartet in A major.

Vocal *Gum Trees: Seven Australian Songs*, v, pf (Allan & Co., *c*.1925), *An Autumn Day*, v, pf (Allan, *c*.1935), *Old Mr Sundown in Fairyland*, children's ch, pf (Allan, *c*.1935), *I Heard a Sound of Singing*, v, pf (rec. Columbia DO 2508; Chappell, *c*.1936), *Down in the Sunlit Glades*, v, pf (Chappell, *c*.1937), *The White Ship*, v, pf (Chappell, *c*.1943), *In Spite of All*, v, pf (rec. Columbia DO 3330; Chappell, *c*.1947), *Dream Cloud*, v, pf (Allans, *c*.1949), *And Everyone Will Love Me*, v, pf (rec. M7 MLX 147 and Columbia DO 3325; Chappell, *c*.1950), *Caprice*, v, pf (Chappell, *c*.1950), *God be in my Head (Sarum Primer 1559)*, vv, pf (rec.

Columbia DO 3325; Chappell, *c*.1950), *My Bird Singing*, v, pf (Chappell, *c*.1952), *Little Babe of Arnhem Land* v, pf (Chappell, *c*.1954), *Four songs for medium voice*, v, pf (Nicholson's, 1954), *Mothers Day*, v, pf (Nicholson's, *c*.1957), *A Garden is a Lovesome Thing*, S, A, pf (Allan, *c*.1963), *If I Were a Little Brown Elf*, 2vv, pf (Southern Music, *c*.1963), *Pan Plucked a Reed*, 2vv, pf (Southern Music, *c*.1963), *Come Early Morn (Mt Wilson)*, S, A, pf (Chappell, 1969), *In This Land*, children's vv, pf (Albert & Son, *c*.1970) *Three Children's Songs*, v, pf (Albert & Son, *c*.1970), *Aboriginal Themes*, Mez, Bar, fl, ob, hp, str (1971; rec. 1975, ABC AC 1013 and WRC, R03154; APRA), *My Heart Singing*, v, pf (Allans, *c*.1987), *Five songs for voice and string quartet, Grace for a Child*, v, pf, *Let Your Song Be Delicate*, S, pf (rec. ABC O/N40525), *My Little Dove*, v, pf.

FURTHER REFERENCE
Recordings include *Aboriginal Themes*, Adelaide Symphony Orchestra, cond. H. Krips. (WRC, R03154); *Aboriginal Themes*, Adelaide Symphony Orchestra, cond. H. Krips, soloists N. Hunter, A. McKie (1975, ABC AC 1013); *Avinu Malkeinu*, Adelaide Symphony Orchestra, cond. H. Krips, soloist R. Cooper (1975, ABC AC 1013). A list of ABC tapes to 1972 is in *PlushD*. Her writings include 'Some Autobiographical Notes', *Canon* 13/11 (July 1960), 277–8. See also *CallawayA; CohenI;* 'Introducing Australian Composer, Mirrie Hill', *Federation of Australian Music Teachers Association Quarterly* (May 1980), 27–8; 'Mirrie Hill' *APRAJ* 5 (July 1971), 24; *MurdochA*.

FIONA SHADE

Hill, Sydney. See *Cardier, Glenn.*

Hill, Vernon Kingsley (*b* Melbourne, 25 Aug. 1944), flautist. After attending school at Brisbane, he obtained his AMusA and LTCL and joined the Australian Ballet Orchestra while in his teens. He was principal piccolo with the Queensland Symphony Orchestra from 1964, then principal flute with the Melbourne Symphony Orchestra 1967–80, and guest principal flute with the BBC Symphony Orchestra and London Symphony Orchestra 1974. He has been head of woodwind at the Canberra School of Music since 1980 and guest principal flute with the Sydney Symphony Orchestra 1984–95. As a soloist he has appeared with all ABC orchestras on tour in NZ, Europe and Israel, and with the ★Canberra Wind Soloists. A naturally gifted and innately musical player, he is the best known of Australia's flautists; he is also a committed and exuberant teacher who has given masterclasses very widely. He has published *The Flute Player's Book* (1995).

FURTHER REFERENCE
Recordings include Bach, Complete Flute Sonatas (Move MD 3118). See also *CA* (1995–96).

Hince, Kenneth (*b* Melbourne, 1924) music critic, writer. After war service with the RAAF, he resumed studies at the University of Melbourne, eventually abandoning medicine in favour of music and English. He became music librarian at the University of Melbourne 1949–52, writing music criticism for *Canon*, *Bulletin* and other magazines, and articles on music for many literary journals. He established a noted antiquarian bookselling business in Melbourne and amassed a substantial collection of historical musical materials, especially from the 19th century, now at the National Library of Australia. He was critic for the *Australian* from 1964, then the *Age* 1979–94. A graceful and accomplished writer in the Neville Cardus mould, he could be eloquent in praise of performers who showed respect for the text of the traditional masters; he was a conservative, whose taste contrasted strongly with the freewheeling enthusiasms of his predecessor at the *Age*, Felix ★Werder, and heralded the sober, less adventurous repertoire which settled on Melbourne's music with the passing of the 1970s.

FURTHER REFERENCE
Age 26 Aug. 1994.

Hine Mundy, Clytie May (*b* Adelaide, 8 May 1887; *d* New York, 27 June 1983), soprano. She studied with Frederick Bevan at the Elder Conservatorium, Adelaide, and with Medora Henson at the Royal College of Music, London. She made her Covent Garden debut in 1911 and later sang with the opera companies of Ernst Denhof, Thomas Beecham and, in the USA, William Wade Hinshaw. After her retirement from performing in the late 1920s, Hine Mundy became an important voice teacher in New York; Peter Pears and Kathleen Ferrier were among her many distinguished pupils. She taught at the Academy of Vocal Arts, Philadelphia, and was musical adviser to the American Theatre Wing, New York.

WAYNE HANCOCK (with M. Elphinstone)

Hines, Marcia (*b* Boston, USA, 20 July 1953), popular music singer of American birth. Growing up singing in church, she was recruited at the age of 16 for the Australian production of the musical *Hair* (1969). She stayed to star in *Jesus Christ Superstar*, sang with the Daly-Wilson Big Band, and made the first of 17 singles *Fire And Rain*, which reached No. 9 in the charts in 1975. *I Just Don't Know What to Do With Myself* reached No. 3 in 1976 and *You* reached No. 1 in 1977. Her debut album was *Marcia Hines* (1975), and *Shining* (1976) won a triple platinum record; in all she has had 12 hit singles and seven multiple platinum albums. She was supporting act to Gene Pitney (1976) then toured Australia, Europe, the USA and Asia with her own band in the following years. A passionate singer of soul and middle-of-the-road repertoire, she had her own TV show, *Marcia Hines Music* (1978–79), and recorded with Jon English (1982).

FURTHER REFERENCE
Recordings include *Fire And Rain* (Wizard ZS124), *I Just Don't Know What to Do With Myself* (Wizard ZS1253), *You* (Miracle MS 508, *Marcia Hines* (1975, Wizard ZL 209), *Shining* (1976 Wizard ML 701), *Marcia Hines Collection* (1984, Axis AX 260314) and more recently *Right Here And Now* (1994, WEA 450981122). For discography, see *SpencerA*. See also *McGrathA*; *SpencerW*; *GuinnessP*, II,1152.

History of European Music in Australia.
1. Early Years, 1788–1825. 2. Beginning of Public Concerts and Theatre Music, 1826–50. 3. Visiting Celebrities, Musical Societies, 1851–87. 4. Exhibitions, Orchestras, Conservatories, 1888–1922. 5. The ABC, Chamber Music and Resident Opera Companies, 1923–73. 6. Composers and the Australia Council 1974– .

1. Early Years, 1788–1825. From its first settlement in 1788, Australia was a British penal colony, and its earliest European music was therefore limited to the rudimentary fife-and-drum routines of a garrison. The earliest governors, battle-hardened naval or army commanders, had no time for music; in any event, short supplies, disease, rebellious troops, hostile Aborigines, and the failure of the few free settlers to develop a staple industry made survival their central preoccupation for the first 20 years. Some marine officers and settlers at Sydney, Hobart and Launceston (from 1804), and Bathurst (1815) had brought instruments (a few had violins, oboes, flutes, even pianos), but these were for their private amusement. By 1800 regimental bands were stationed at Sydney, playing outdoors in the barracks square, giving weekly evening concerts at Macquarie Place, and playing at the occasional balls given by the Governor or dances on board ships. But there were no other outlets for public music-making save in the hotels, where the playing was of the crudest kind.

The convicts, of course, had not arrived with instruments, and they fell back on singing vigorously among themselves. Their singing was tolerated, but convict poets composing original ballads, especially any like Francis Macnamara (★Frank the Poet) who sang lines critical of their captors, were flogged. The situation was little different at Newcastle (settled 1804), Goulburn (1833), Moreton Bay (1824) or the garrison at Albany, WA (1826). Remarkably, at Norfolk Island Captain Alexander Maconochie established a sizeable convict brass band when he was commandant 1840–44, regarding music as the linchpin of the reforms he sought to make to the correctional system.

2. Beginning of Public Concerts and Theatre Music, 1826–50. At Sydney civilian musical life dates from the arrival of the more urbane governor Ralph Darling in 1825, by which time a measure of stability had been achieved. Public concerts appeared, and some of the more enterprising military bandsmen began offering newly composed dances and marches for sale. The earliest concerts were given in 1826 at Sydney hotels by amateur societies; they consisted of vocal and instrumental trifles played by bandsmen (often George ★Sippe, Thomas Stubbs, Joseph ★Reichenberg, or Robert Mackintosh), or the few local music teachers and their pupils. Although generally unpopular as a governor, Darling supported the musicians by his presence at their concerts, and one bandmaster (Kavanagh) repaid his favour with the composition of *General Ralph Darling's Australian Slow March*. Performance standards were indifferent: at one concert in Darling's presence the highlight was a comic song sung by actor-entrepreneur Barnett ★Levey. But the *Sydney Monitor* was full of praise for 'the only public recreation we have', and audiences quickly grew from 120 at the first concert in June 1826 to 400 people at one at the Schoolroom, Castlereagh Street, a month later. 'Professor' John Edwards established his music warehouse in 1825, and formed a choir at St James' Church (where an organ was installed in 1827). In Tasmania too, where some semblance of order had finally been achieved under regional governor Arthur and pastoralists had been prospering rapidly, J.P. ★Deane and Reichenberg gave concerts from the same year in similar circumstances; Deane launched a music lessons and instrument repair business, and at St David's Church, where J. Livingstone had conducted a wind band from 1821, Deane became organist.

By 1833 the 'Theatre Royal' of Levey's Royal Hotel, Sydney, included a tiny 'orchestra' for its concerts, directed by Edwards, with Sippe as cello solo. Societies came and went: the Caecilian Society, for example, was founded by Joseph ★Cavendish, stage manager of several of the Royal Hotel concerts, also with Edwards as conductor. Within a few years this society had its own concert room in Phillip Street, where in 1840 it could perform the Overture to Rossini's *Italian Girl in Algiers*. The Australian Harmonic Society, founded in 1834, also gave concerts until at least 1841.

By the time Melbourne was settled in mid-1834, the wool trade had begun to bring significant growth to the colony, and ambitions for a more cultivated society started to occupy the settlers' attention. There were a handful of music teachers and music shops and in Sydney Edwards was selling pianos in some quantity. More churches installed organs and appointed music teachers to their schools; Mechanics' Institutes were built; the number of music teachers multiplied. Two families of thoroughly professional musicians arrived—the violinist-composer W. Vincent ★Wallace with his sister soprano Eliza Wallace and brother violinist Spencer W. Wallace (at Sydney from 1836), and the violinist J.P. Deane and his children, who formed a string trio (at Hobart from 1824, then Sydney from 1836). Wallace was a fine performer, and gave concerts of his own compositions at which the Deanes and others assisted; Deane was an able musician ready to turn his hand to performing, teaching, music selling, or tuning. After Wallace fled the country and his debts in 1838, Eliza Wallace (soon to be Mrs John Bushelle) gave further concerts at the Royal Hotel, then with her husband at the Victoria Theatre in 1841 with Spencer Wallace leading the orchestra and Thomas Leggatt conducting. In 1841 another gifted professional and noted writer on music,

Isaac ★Nathan, arrived in Sydney, became organist at St Mary's and began giving concerts. The first complete *Messiah* was given in 1842.

Governor Darling had opposed the licensing of a theatre in Sydney, and music-theatre presentations were thus inhibited until his departure in 1831. His successor, Sir Richard Bourke, encouraged music more liberally. The earliest attempt at opera in Sydney was Sir Henry Bishop's butchered version of *Don Giovanni*, given under Levey's management in 1833. In Hobart Samson Cameron's troupe gave Bishop's entertainment *Clari; or the Maid of Milan* in 1834, a work of similar idiom to *Don Giovanni* in which the popular 'Home Sweet Home' was sung, with George Peck conducting. Makeshift theatres opened in Hobart and Launceston in the following year; in Sydney the permanent Victoria Theatre opened in 1838, and the plays presented there were complemented with musical items, often with Deane leading the orchestra.

Attempts at more serious opera came more slowly. The four-member ★Gautrot Opera troupe arrived at Sydney in 1838, giving their pared-down performances to piano accompaniment; they found only modest support and finally left in 1846. Some of the resident professionals mounted fragmentary presentations as the Foreign Opera Co. at the Royal Hotel. But fully staged operatic productions were at first unknown: *Rosina* (William Shield), given in Hobart in 1835, *Guy Mannering* (Bishop), performed at the Victoria in 1842, or *Rob Roy* (J. Davy) in 1844 scarcely qualify as opera, while *Figaro*, *The Barber of Seville* and *La sonnambula*, given in 1843, were brutally abridged, translated and arranged with music by others more easily at hand. Rossini's *Cenerentola* followed a year later, probably in a similarly unsatisfactory state. The City Theatre, rival to the Victoria, opened in 1843, with Spencer Wallace leading the band and Leggatt conducting, but the fare was no more ambitious.

Opera performances in Sydney became more frequent and considerably more satisfactory in 1844 with the arrival from Hobart of another two professional musical families, the ★Carandinis and the ★Howsons; they sustained 26 performances of *The Bohemian Girl* (Balfe) in 1846. But still in 1847 the *Australian* could write that the Victoria Theatre orchestra:

> … might be able to rasp through the 'Highland Fling' or 'Rory O'More,' or similar tap-room staves, but to grapple with the elaborate instrumentations of Weber, Auber, Bellini, Rossini, etc, is a flight far beyond their puny skill. A well-trained orchestra will aid and support a singer and cover his defects, but at the Victoria we have too frequently the singers supporting the orchestra.

The first operas written in Australia, Charles ★Nagel's *The Mock Catalani* and Nathan's *Don John of Austria*, were premiered. These and other early compositions were frankly British, their subjects exhibiting no taste for the new country's life nor an ear for its sounds; for them

Australia was an empty and silent void. Nor was there any influence of Aboriginal music, for which the first attempt at arrangement, by John Lhotsky (1834), had more in common with English ballad than its ancient materials. *Maritana*, the work that finally made Wallace's fortune in London after he had fled the country, was heard at Sydney in 1849, and subsequently became the most popular opera in the colony. Presumably its first Sydney performance also suffered from the defective orchestral resources other works had endured.

Elsewhere, similar developments followed more slowly. Adelaide was settled from 1836, but as parts of the state proved arid it languished until the discovery of copper in the region in 1845. Governor Hindmarsh's wife acquired a piano, and a 'Royal Theatre' opened in 1838, then violinist George Bennett organised concerts in hotels in the 1840s. The first season of opera came with George *Coppin's company in 1856. In Queensland, cattle and pastoral expansion occupied the vastly scattered settlers. The Moreton Bay penal colony was eventually supplanted by a free community at Brisbane in 1850, and regular concerts were heard there from 1857 with the arrival of the bandsman Alfred *Seal and his brother Auguste.

Perth had been enthusiastically settled in 1829, some settlers bringing pianos, but less than half of its disillusioned pioneers remained three years later, and they began a long struggle for survival. A sacred concerto was heard at St George's Church in 1845, but over the next 30 years the piano recital by Dom Rosendo *Salvado, abbot of the Spanish Benedictine monastery at New Norcia, provided almost the only music of quality. The West continued to lag in its development until the 1880s, when the discovery of the Kimberley pastoral lands and gold changed its fortunes. A 'Theatre Royal' was at last opened in a Perth hotel in 1897, and Her Majesty's Theatre was built in 1904; the *Rigo Opera Co. brought opera performances in 1924–25. The tiny frontier settlement at Palmerston (later Darwin) was more fortunate in having music presented by various troupes passing through on their way to Asia, notably opera by the Carandinis in 1881.

3. Visiting Celebrities, Musical Societies, 1851–87. The discovery of gold in NSW and then in Victoria in 1851 brought dramatic population growth and a new spirit of optimism to Australia. Victoria in particular was quickly transformed into the most celebrated colony of the British Empire, and despite a miners' revolt in 1854, the impetus of the gold boom sustained its capital, Melbourne, for a generation, stimulating the development of a vigorous cultural life.

The enlarged and newly wealthy public in Sydney and Melbourne attracted Catherine *Hayes, the star of La Scala and Covent Garden, to tour in 1854–55; she was the first musician of front international rank to visit Australia, and she was mobbed by adoring crowds wherever she went. News of the reception now awaiting real talent in Australia soon reached Europe, and it was partly because of her success, as well the swifter passage available with the advent of steamships, that a succession of outstanding artists began to visit, from the virtuoso violinist Miska *Hauser (1854–58) and soprano Anna *Bishop (1856–57) to Paderewski (1904) and Jan Kubelik (1908). These visitors made a profound impression on musicians and the public alike: when the young Melba went to Europe she sought lessons in the tradition that had taught Hayes.

The national strength of the musicians of the combined colonies was exhibited in 1859, when the finest were brought together for the opening of the Great Hall, University of Sydney, in *Messiah* and *Creation* under L.H. *Lavenu; later similarly splendid festivals were held at the Melbourne Intercolonial Exhibition (1866), the Metropolitan and Intercolonial Exhibition, Sydney (1870), and the Sydney International Exhibition (1879). Yet there was no ambition to create a national musical life; the pattern of separate states which were to constitute Australia already existed (if it had not yet everywhere been proclaimed), and each capital focused solely on building its own urban institutions and identity. Choirs, the central vehicle of British music at the time, were formed in all capital cities, as well as in many regional centres: the Adelaide Choral Society (1842), the Melbourne Philharmonic Society (1853) under John Russel, the Sydney Philharmonic Society, the Adelaide Liedertafel under Carl *Linger in 1857, the Brisbane Philharmonic (1862), the Musical Society of Victoria (1861), and the Hobart Philharmonic (1867). See *Choirs and Choral Music*.

An opera company of considerable strength was now ready to make the voyage from the USA. W.S. *Lyster's Opera Co., resident in Australia 1861–68 and 1870–80, brought two dazzling decades of fine talent, surprisingly well staged productions and a startling array of operas. Inspired by Lyster's example, Australian entrepreneurs developed ambitious opera seasons of their own: J.C. *Williamson took up the mantle of principal opera impresario after Lyster's death in 1880, as well as bringing new Gilbert and Sullivan operettas and musicals from Britain; George *Musgrove began a similar business in 1881, for a time in partnership with Williamson but later offering him vigorous competition. Williamson arranged Melba's opera season of 1911, and after his death his firm under Hugh Ward and E.J. *Tait organised Melba's tours of 1924 and 1928; the firm was much later to arrange the Sutherland-Williamson season of 1965. Other visiting companies in later years were the enormous *Quinlan Opera Co. which brought Wagner's works to Australia (1912, 1913), including *Ring of the Nibelungs*, and Sir Benjamin *Fuller's Opera Co. (1928). See *Opera and Opera Companies; Entrepreneurs*.

4. Exhibitions, Orchestras, Conservatories, 1888–1922. The centenary of Australia's settlement in 1888 was the occasion for large commemorations. A *Centenary Cantata* by Hugo ★Alpen was performed by a choir of 1500 in Sydney, and an International Centennial Exhibition was held in Melbourne. Large cathedral and town hall organs were built, and distinguished players arrived to give recitals, most notably T.H. Best in 1890 and Edwin Lemare in 1903 at the five-manual Sydney Town Hall organ, then the largest organ in the world.

Several capital cities also opened permanent ★conservatoriums: the University Conservatorium in Melbourne (1895), the Elder Conservatorium in Adelaide (1897) and the Sydney Conservatorium (1914). The Queensland Conservatorium was not established until 1956, the music department at the University of Western Australia (1959) and the Tasmanian Conservatorium later still (1964). Following the popular Welsh pattern, musical ★eisteddfods sprang up in every city and town, the most important being the ★Royal South Street Eisteddfod, Ballarat (founded 1891). In many of these the music prescribed for competition was trivial, but for numerous Australian musicians of note eisteddfods became early performing opportunities and their first public recognition. A public music examination authority was established by the Universities of Adelaide and Melbourne to supplant the British systems in 1911; this became the ★AMEB in 1918, insinuating its influence into music teaching everywhere and profoundly affecting the shape of practical music education.

Symphony orchestras began to be formed in the eastern capitals, but were yet to attract attention away from the long-established choirs and were often short-lived. Frederick ★Cowen had been brought from London to conduct a dazzling season with the exhibition orchestra at the Melbourne International Exhibition in 1888, and after the intervening loss of momentum following his departure, the first music professor of the University of Melbourne, G.W.L. ★Marshall-Hall, formed an orchestra in 1892 which was to provide fine subscription concerts at Melbourne for nearly 20 years. An equally long-lived series, if less notable musically, was the Grand Orchestra, Adelaide (1893–1910) under August ★Heinecke formed after the Adelaide Orchestral Society (1879–80) had collapsed a decade before. Roberto ★Hazon's Amateur Orchestral Society in Sydney (from 1888) grew into the semi-professional Sydney Symphony Orchestra in 1908, but it was not until the NSW State Orchestra was established (1919–21) under the Conservatorium's director Henri ★Verbrugghen that concerts of high quality were to be heard in Sydney. The Brisbane Musical Union (1880) under R.T. ★Jefferies and later George ★Sampson, the Fremantle Orchestral Society (1887) and the Perth Musical Union (1880) were all valiantly supported by their audiences, but most suffered from their mix of amateur and professional players.

Australian composition continued to be prescribed by British models. Luscombe ★Searelle's comic opera *Estrella* had numerous performances in Sydney and Melbourne

in 1880, and G.W. ★Torrance's oratorio *The Revelation* was given in Melbourne in 1882. There were songs of stilted enthusiasm for the innocence and clear sunny skies of the new country, hymned in the English art-song idiom. In the years before World War I, full-scale symphonies and dramatic works by Marshall-Hall, Alfred ★Hill and Fritz ★Hart were performed. While still more derivative than original, these were at least full-length works of fluency and coherence, and one (Marshall-Hall's *Stella*, 1910) had an Australian subject.

The states federated as a nation in 1901. Vast distances within the new country, not to mention the jealous rivalries between the states, militated against the establishment of national musical institutions: even the AMEB, despite its national syllabus, was to retain a sovereign separation among its state branches. But Australians could rejoice that their country had now made its place on the worldwide musical map through the success of a number of its own musicians who had recently become international celebrities: Nellie ★Melba, Percy ★Grainger, Ada ★Crossley, Amy ★Castles, Johann S. ★Kruse, Ernest ★Hutcheson and Amy ★Sherwin. They were soon to be joined by Peter ★Dawson, John ★McCormack, Una ★Bourne, John ★Brownlee and Browning ★Mummery.

5. The ABC, Chamber Music, and Resident Opera Companies, 1923–73.
The first Australian radio concert was broadcast in 1921 and regular radio broadcasts began in 1923. Several commercial stations at first maintained ensembles for light music, and the national government network, the ★ABC, was no exception, at its formation in 1932 establishing wireless choruses and concert orchestras. But from 1936, with University of Melbourne professor Bernard ★Heinze as its adviser, the ABC began a much grander project, to create a nucleus of Australian full-time players in each state around which permanent symphony orchestras could eventually be built. ABC Celebrity Concerts were begun, sold by subscription and each broadcast on ABC radio. Each year a distinguished conductor was brought out to conduct some of the concerts, beginning with Sir Hamilton Harty in 1934, and following with figures of the calibre of Sir Thomas Beecham, Eugene Ormandy, Otto Klemperer, and on several occasions Malcolm Sargent. Important soloists were also featured in the pre-war years, including Arthur Rubinstein, Artur Schnabel, Lotte Lehmann and Richard Tauber.

In the face of such overwhelming resources and the ABC's new dominance of concert venues, Williamsons and other entrepreneurs were forced to withdraw from concert promotion and confine themselves to musicals and shows. The great choral societies, too, began slowly to wither as their loyal audiences deserted them. After the war, its monopoly secure, the ABC moved quickly to complete its plan, establishing the Sydney Symphony Orchestra (1946) with the magnetic and exceptionally gifted Eugene ★Goossens as conductor (from 1948), followed by the Queensland Symphony Orchestra (1947) under John Farnsworth *Hall, the Adelaide Symphony Orchestra (1949) under William *Cade, the Tasmania Symphony Orchestra (1948) under Clive *Douglas, the Melbourne Symphony Orchestra (1949), and the West Australian Symphony Orchestra (1950) under Rudolf *Pekarek. The ABC and Heinze had created one of the largest radio-orchestral networks in the world, 20 years before most other countries had attempted it.

The dynamic Heinze's remarkable schools concerts around the country had immeasurably enlarged the audience for the new orchestras. In the 1950s the ABC's roster of visiting conductors continued for a time to include those of the front rank, while visiting soloists included Arrau, Gieseking, Isaac Stern, Elisabeth Schwarzkopf and Hans Hotter. Many Australians successful abroad were brought back for tours, including Eileen *Joyce, Laurie *Kennedy, Harold *Williams, William *Herbert and Marjorie *Lawrence. Rapid European immigration in the postwar years brought an audience for first-class chamber music, and *Musica Viva pioneered subscription chamber music concerts and began importing ensembles from 1955, developing into a remarkable national concert network for fine chamber music, perhaps the largest of its kind in the world.

These years were seminal for national operatic life. A remarkable harvest of outstanding voices appeared in the postwar years: Lawrence, Joan *Hammond, Donald *Smith, and Joan *Sutherland to name some. In 1936 the soprano Gertrude *Johnson had returned from Covent Garden to create her *National Theatre Movement, which staged opera in Melbourne 1938–54, introducing many of these young singers to their first stage experience. In 1951 Clarice Lorenz created a somewhat similar *National Opera Co. from students of the NSW State Conservatorium; the two were then eclipsed by the *Australian Elizabethan Theatre Trust in 1954, which gave opera on a more professional basis from 1956. With mixed production standards and ever-changing policies, the Trust's progress was unsteady, but it eventually evolved in 1970 into a national full-time company, the Australian Opera. State opera companies were founded, each building on earlier semi-professional groups: the Victorian Opera Co. (1962), the New Opera of South Australia (1973), the Queensland Opera (1975) and the West Australia Opera.

The visionary University of Adelaide professor John *Bishop started his annual National Music Camps and the Australian youth orchestra movement in the 1950s, which thereafter became a central training ground for the ABC orchestras. But elsewhere, directors of the conservatoriums were no longer the pioneering figures of the past. William *Lovelock in Queensland, Edgar *Bainton in Sydney, and George *Loughlin in Melbourne were all English organist-composers, and the conservatism of English pastoralism which coloured their own music became reflected in the music of the Australian composers of the period. Significant amounts of neo-British piano music, songs and choral miniatures were published by Australians in these years: Hill, Alfred Wheeler, William *James, Horace *Keats, Frank *Hutchens and Louis *Lavater were all popular. They wrote religious choruses, patriotic anthems, love songs, and children's pieces on themes of birds, the Australian wattle, elves or ghosts. Some significant Australian poets were treated, but Aboriginal themes were extremely rare. Arthur Steadman Loam was the sole vocal arranger of Aboriginal music for choirs, and his arrangements were quite anglicised. Henry *Tate believed the native birdcalls of the Australian bush could produce a national music, but as late as 1948 Bainton was emphatic that Australian music would have to be based on British musical models.

Only a few escaped the British influence to be more original: the bitonality of Dorian *Le Gallienne, the Aboriginal-inspired primitivism of John *Antill's *Corroboree* in 1946, or the athletic linear voice of Margaret *Sutherland ensured their individuality. Sutherland alone sought in her folk-song arrangements to escape the English style and in *Haunted Hills* to capture the physical uniqueness of the land. With the conservatism of the conservatoriums, the younger composers of the 1950s obtained their real education from the gramophone. Schoenberg, Bartók and Stravinsky, and presently the European avant-garde of Messiaen, Boulez and Stockhausen were becoming available on the new LP records, and in their image Richard *Meale, Peter *Sculthorpe and Nigel *Butterley adopted a neo-European structuralism which marked, from about 1963, the beginning of much more significant musical composition in Australia. Finding a distinctive voice independent of Europe proved more difficult. Sculthorpe first turned to Asia, using Balinese rice-pounding patterns in his String Quartet No. 8 (1969), elsewhere Japanese *gagaku*. The landscape at last became a significant theme in Australian composition: Sculthorpe soon found a voice for the desert in the *Sun Music* series, and was followed by David *Lumsdaine and others. In Sculthorpe Australia found it possessed a major expressionist whose inspiration by the Australian landscape, from the desert heat or rainforest cool, was highly evocative. He absorbed Aboriginal melody only much later in *Port Essington* and *Kakadu* (1992). His pupil Barry *Conyngham studied with Takemitsu in Japan from 1969, producing *Ice Carving* and *Water...Footsteps...Time*.

6. Composers and the Australia Council, 1974– . The number of Australian composers successful internationally had been small: Grainger, Arthur *Benjamin, Peggy *Glanville-Hicks, and few others. The ABC had professed an interest in Australian composition, but had preferred the genteel niceties of songs by William James or Horace Keats; nothing serious was done until John *Hopkins became its music director, 1963–73. Suddenly the voices already versed in Viennese serialism and even more recent developments came to be heard. New works not just by Sculthorpe, Meale and Butterley, but also Keith *Humble, Larry *Sitsky, Don *Banks, Malcolm *Williamson and others were commissioned, old works (notably by Grainger and Alfred Hill) were revived, and all were performed and recorded by the ABC orchestras in considerable quantity, often under Hopkins' personal, highly sympathetic baton. There was discussion of the European avant-garde, and a new climate that directed attention away from the previous preoccupations with nationalism or British music towards international aesthetic issues. Severe European structuralism, electronic music, the aleatoric ideas of Cage, and the post-serialism of Stockhausen all developed their adherents.

Then the grand ambitions of E.G. Whitlam's reforming government, elected in 1972, brought Australian composition rapidly to maturity. Hopkins' extraordinary decade with the ABC had laid the groundwork on which Whitlam's Australia Council (founded 1974) could build: the talented composers Hopkins had brought before the public, together with others younger who now felt able to write with some confidence of performance, were called upon to compete for the largest government-supported commissioning program ever mounted in a Western country. The works of Martin *Wesley-Smith, Ross *Edwards, Roger *Smalley, Richard *Mills, Carl *Vine and others were published and recorded, ensembles were enticed to perform them, and an Australian Music Centre was established to advance their cause. An astonishing plurality of influences became audible, ranging not just from the American experimental tradition to European new Romanticism, but including a continuing vein of South-East Asian and Japanese ideas and sonorities as well.

In the late 1970s many major Australian composers rejected the terse European serialism they had previously espoused and rediscovered lyricism: Meale's *Viridian* surprised audiences with its evocation of the rainforest (1979). Edwards turned from the dense complexity of *Monos II* (1970) to the meditative, static, Asian-influenced *Mountain Village in a Clearing Mist* (1973), and then busy, diatonic repeating motives in the Piano Concerto (1982) and *Maninyas* series. Butterley's *From Sorrowing Earth* (1991) was another newly lyrical work. Even Brophy, strict European modernist, moved towards melody from *Seraphita* (1988). They were followed by Brenton *Broadstock, Andrew *Schultz, Moya *Henderson, Graeme *Koehne, Michael *Smetanin, Gerard *Brophy, and a growing number of women, including Gillian *Whitehead, Sarah *Hopkins, Ros *Bandt and Liza *Lim. The minimalism of Reich, the European new complexity, or the postmodernist quotation of popular culture were all employed towards Australian ends.

Today Australian composers have been astonishingly increased in their number and greatly strengthened by the exposure the Australia Council has brought them. The tersely abstract and stridently political voices have moderated or disappeared, and there has been a real awakening to the possibilities of the cultures of the region, although the use of Aboriginal music continues to be marginal in their idioms. Australian composers still have the same values as their counterparts abroad, although changes in their music are less a result of direct foreign influence. Sadly, this has coincided with a great increase of conservatism among audiences, and in the late 1990s the opportunities and funds of the last 20 years seem to be diminishing. Nevertheless, the Australia Council remains the richest and most interesting patron of music in Australia.

See also *Bands, Composition in Australia, Conductors, Church Music, Dance and Music, Musical Comedy, Radio and Music, Popular Music, Music Education, Orchestras*, and entries under individual cities or composers.

FURTHER REFERENCE
Roger Covell, *Australia's Music: Themes of a New Society* (Melbourne: Sun Books, 1967); J.W.C. Cumes, *Their Chastity Was Not Too Rigid: Leisure Times in Early Australia* (Melbourne: Longman Cheshire/A.H. & A.W. Reed, 1979); Eric Irvin, 'Australia's First Public Concerts', *SMA* 5 (1971), 77–86; *BrisbaneE*; *OrchardM*. A major history of Australian music by Thérèse Radic is in preparation.

Hit Parades in Australia.   See *Charts*.

Hitmen, The.   Hard-rock band (1977–84) formed in Sydney from several *Radio Birdman members, the core comprised chiefly of Johnny Kannis and Chris Masuak (vocals), Charlie Georges (guitar), Warwick Gilbert (bass) and Mark Kingsmill (drums). With sharp-edged melodies and infectiously energetic rock playing, they built a dedicated live following and released *Didn't Tell The Man* (1979), then were supporting act to the Tom Petty and the Heartbreakers tour in 1980. With the advent of disco, however, taste for hard rock was at low ebb, and they made little headway. Their fine debut album *The Hitmen* (1981) and the single *Bwana Devil* (1982) are among their relatively few recordings; several members left to join the Hoodoo Gurus and the Screaming Tribesmen, and the band dissolved. They re-formed with a significantly different membership, 1989–92.

FURTHER REFERENCE
Recordings include *Didn't Tell The Man* (1979 WEA 100095), *The Hitmen* (1981 WEA 600097), *Bwana Devil* (1982, WEA 104097). There is a compilation *The Hitmen 1978–82* (1988, Survival SRLP 04). See also Peter Wise, 'The Hitmen. Solid as a Rock!' *Prehistoric Sounds* I/3 (1995), 48–51; *CoupeN*; *SpencerW.*

Hmelnitsky.   Family of musicians.
(1) Alexander Hmelnitsky   (*b* Kiev, Ukraine, 16 Apr. 1891; *d* Katoomba, NSW, 15 Jan. 1965), pianist, teacher. He graduated from the Moscow Conservatorium under Constantine Igumnov and Alexander Scriabin. He made a world tour as musical director to the famous Russian ballerina Anna Pavlova. He emigrated to Australia 1925, becoming musical director of radio station 2FC Sydney

and touring Australia with his cellist wife Ludmilla. He moved to Java in 1930, returning to Sydney in 1942 where he taught for many years at Palings building. He brought the severe training methods of the Moscow school to his studio. His pupils included Joy Cross, Laurence Davis, William Fraser, Igor Hmelnitsky (2), Marie van Hove, Elizabeth Hunt, Maureen Jones, Robert Kolben, Rachel Valler and Norma Williams.

(2) Igor Hmelnitsky (*b* Java, 27 Dec. 1920; *d* Sydney, 27 Sept. 1987), pianist, teacher. His piano teachers included Simon Barere, Ignaz ★Friedman, and his father Alexander (1). He signed a recording contract with Columbia at the age of nine. Settling in Australia in 1938, he served with the Royal Dutch Air Force in the war. His premiere performances include Malcolm Williamson's Piano Concerto No. 1 with the Sydney Symphony Orchestra under Nicolai Malko (1959); he gave many ABC recitals, playing in the 'grand' manner. He taught at the NSW State Conservatorium 1972–85, using closed-circuit television in his teaching, with cameras left, right and overhead. He undertook extensive medical studies to assist in his teaching. His pupils include Roy Howat and Gabriella Pusner; with the latter he recorded works of Raymond ★Hanson.

FURTHER REFERENCE
Igor Hmelnitsky and Nigel Nettheim, 'Weight-bearing Manipulation: A Neglected Area of Medical Science Relevant to Piano Playing and Overuse Syndrome', *Medical Hypotheses* 23 (1987), 209–17.   NIGEL NETTHEIM

Hmong Music. Australia is now home for just over 1500 Hmong people from Laos, most of whom have arrived as refugees since 1975. They live in the main cities on the east coast of Australia. Cultural activities in their new environment are restricted by the small size of the community, its relative youthfulness and the absence of traditional kinship networks. In 1978 the Hmong–Australia Society was established to assist Hmong refugees in their resettlement in Australia in various ways, including the maintenance of culture and religion. Hmong now have enough confidence to perform traditional rituals such as soul calling (*hu plig*), shamanic trance, and wrist stringing (*khi tes*). Simplified versions of the funeral ceremony (*Kab Ke Pam Tuag*) and New Year celebrations use the khaen or *qeej,* a set of six bamboo pipes with free reeds. Cultural expression in the public domain, outside the home or the community, usually features a pipe player in full traditional dress as well as displays of the handicrafts for which the Hmong are famous. Other instrumental music forms, including the use of soft-sounding instruments such as the jaws harp (*nja*) and the single free reed pipe (*cha mblay*) in courtship, have largely been replaced by the use of the telephone.

Traditional vocal forms include various genres of extemporised solo singing, which now belongs mainly to the elderly of the Hmong community. Expressions of loneliness and estrangement from the traditional natural and social environment are recorded on cassette and sent to relatives who have resettled in Canada, the United States and France or who were still awaiting resettlement in the refugee camps in Thailand. Young Hmong are keen consumers of Laotian popular music both from Laos and from Hmong and Laotian rock bands in the USA and France. The songs on these cassettes are almost entirely about love. Hmong rock bands, such as *Dejavu* (formerly the Boomerang Band) and *Neej Tshiab Band* (New Life Band) in Melbourne, perform at Hmong wedding receptions, fund-raising activities and New Year festivities alongside the traditional singing and pipe playing.

FURTHER REFERENCE
Catherine Falk, 'The Music of the Hmong in Australia', *The Garland Encyclopedia of World Music* (Washington: Smithsonian Institution, 1995).   CATHERINE FALK

Hobart, pop. (1991) 181 832. Capital of Tasmania. Situated in south-eastern Tasmania on the banks of the Derwent River estuary, amongst the foothills of Mount Wellington, it is the southernmost capital city in Australia.

1. The Colonial Era. Settled as Hobart Town in 1804, conditions were often difficult in the early years, and music was initially limited to the activities of regimental bands stationed there for the early lieutenant governors, and the church. The first organ imported into Australia was installed at St David's church in 1825, and relocated to St Matthew's in 1858; it is still in use. The first significant musician to settle in Hobart was John Phillip ★Deane, performer, teacher and composer, who arrived in the brig *Deveron* in 1822. He carried on a business as a general storekeeper, but had brought with him many musical instruments and taught piano and violin, inspired and conducted the colony's first public concerts in 1826, and became first organist at St David's. These concerts provided, according to the *Hobart Town Gazette,* 'a pleasant forgetfulness of the cares, the fatigues and the troubles of the previous day'. Together with other local musicians, including Joseph ★Reichenberg, William Russell, Sam Marshall and George Peck, Deane and his family contributed to Hobart's musical life for another 10 years before moving to Sydney.

The foundation stone of a theatre was laid at Campbell Street in 1834, and the Royal Victoria (later, Theatre Royal) opened in 1836; this beautiful building has been extensively used since for theatrical entertainments, concerts and opera. Irish composer W. Vincent ★Wallace visited Tasmania in 1838 and stayed at the Bush Inn, New Norfolk. It is claimed he wrote much of the music for his opera *Maritana* at that time, and its performance at the Bush Inn in 1932 revived this story. John Williams, a piano-maker trained by Broadwood, London, established a business in the 1840s, making pianos 'better adapted for the colony, by means of metal string plates and other ironwork, than any imported'. After his death in 1865, two other London piano-makers, Stanley and Winter, took over his plant, carrying on similar business.

A Choral Society and Orchestra led by Russell began activities in the 1840s. Much of the music they performed was of arrangements of European works, but there were also new compositions, and among local composers John *Howson and Henry Mundy were advertising the availability of their 'Tasmanian Waltzes' and quadrilles. A musical periodical, the *Tasmanian Musical Miscellany*, was established in 1844.

By mid-century, Hobart was the third largest city in Australia, and glowed with self-confidence in the arts. It was a confidence born of the direct, if time-consuming, importation of musicians from London; but indigenous talent also began to appear, and the 'Tasmanian Nightingale' Amy *Sherwin (b 1858) later won worldwide fame as a singer. Frederick *Packer came to Hobart in 1852 and was appointed organist at St David's; one of his sons, F.A. Packer, figured prominently as organist, composer and conductor in the latter decades of the century. Another arrival in the 1850s, Camille Del Sarte taught voice production and became conductor of the Hobart City Band and New Town Philharmonic Society; he built a music hall at Harrington Street at his own expense in 1860.

The vigorous Hobart Musical Union was formed in 1867; conducted first by Tapfield, then later by J.A. Schott, G.B. Allen and Maughan Barnett, it achieved much in the choral and orchestral field and survived into the 1890s. The first performance of *Elijah*, conducted by F.A. Packer, was presented as a benefit for the organ fund in the new town hall in 1868; the organ itself was installed in 1870, and Packer became the first city organist. Later city organists have included T.J. Heywood, J. Scott-Power and John Nicholls. Tasmania's longest-running musical society, the male voice Orpheus Club was founded as a black-face minstrel group in 1877, and survives to this day.

J.R. McCann established a music shop (later McCann Bros) in 1881, and fathered seven sons and a daughter, all musicians. Frank McCann's versatility was exceptional; he played string, woodwind, brass and keyboard instruments, and had compositions to his credit. The Hobart City Band acquired the services of T.W. Hopkins as bandmaster in 1891, and it could soon claim to be the 'finest in Australia'. Hopkins later went on to conduct the Derwent Concert Band until his retirement in 1935. Bradshaw Major settled in Hobart in the early 1890s and became active as pianist, organist and composer. Trained at the Leipzig Conservatorium, he was appointed conductor of the newly formed Hobart Operatic Society, whose first production, *Martha*, was pronounced a 'phenomenal success' in 1894.

In the aftermath of the 1890s Depression, Hobart staged an ambitious Tasmanian International Exhibition in 1894–95. Packer's cantata *The Land of Beauty* was performed at the opening by a choir numbering 400 and an orchestra of 40. A new Fincham organ, later installed in St Mary's Cathedral, was a central feature of the Exhibition, with Stanley Chipperfield as organist. Inspired by the entrepreneurial singing teacher Lucy *Benson, a Philharmonic Society was founded in 1896, with the Durham-educated Arundel *Orchard as conductor. When Orchard moved to Sydney at the turn of the century, Major took his place.

2. 1900 to the Present: (i) New Organisations. Orchestral resources gathered around string teacher J. Glanville Bishop in the early 1900s, and the Mendelssohn centenary concert of 1909 featured Bishop's orchestra in the Masonic Hall. The cavernous City Hall, built in 1915, was soon resounding with band and orchestral entertainment, and Bishop became conductor of the Hobart Orchestral Society when it was established in 1923. Silent movies had long provided employment to local pianists and small orchestras, but with the advent of 'talkies' from 1924 many musicians became redundant. T.W. Hopkins and Ted *McCann worked hard to reverse this trend, persuading theatre managements to include musical items in the film intermissions. Then, as a counter to the Depression, McCann and music critic Robert Atkinson organised elaborate week-long annual music festivals, 1932–34. When commercial radio station 7ZL was licensed in 1925, McCann had established a small radio orchestra; the ABC, founded in 1932, subsequently took over 7ZL and transformed the radio orchestra into the ABC Studio Orchestra under Clive Douglas in 1936.

Orchard returned to Hobart 1934–38, initiating a short-lived BMus course at the University of Tasmania, and taking over as conductor of the Hobart Orchestral Society when Bishop retired in 1935. After Orchard left again, the Orchestral Society was reorganised with the ABC's studio players as the Hobart Symphony Orchestra, giving its first concert in 1939 with conductor Douglas and pianist Jessie Wakefield. From this grouping, the Tasmanian Symphony Orchestra was then established, giving its first concert in 1948 with conductor Joseph Post and Tasmanian-born pianist Eileen Joyce.

Other organisations founded at the time included the Arts Club (1948); the National Theatre and Fine Arts Society (1949), guided in its early operatic endeavours by Walter Stiasny; the Hobart City Eisteddfod (1951); the Tasmanian Music Teachers' Association (by Helen George, 1956); and the Friends of Music (by Daniel Koletz, 1957), founded to promote chamber music and soon linked with Musica Viva, becoming a branch of that organisation in the mid-1970s.

Thomas Matthews became conductor of the Tasmanian Symphony in 1962. A modern pioneer 'making do' with small numbers (*Symphonie Fantastique* with four First Violins), he held the view that 'practically anything could be performed if you had a piano and a few orchestral players' (ABC music arranger, Felix Gethen). As violinist, he often gave recitals with his pianist wife, Eileen Ralf, a teacher of great distinction.

Both the Tasmanian Youth Orchestra and the Australian Rosny Children's Choir (as it was later called) were founded in 1965. Under director Jennifer Filby, the Australian Rosny Children's Choir has brought music to audiences in many parts of the world and represented Australia officially in first cultural exchanges with the People's Republic of China. The semi-professional Derwent Symphony Orchestra was founded in 1979.

(ii) The Tasmanian Conservatorium.   Picking up threads where Orchard had left off, the university established a lectureship in music in 1961, with Rex ★Hobcroft as first appointee. It was Hobcroft who inspired two seminal events that had a profound effect on the future of composition in Australia: the first ever Australian Composers' Seminar (1963) and its sequel, a Festival of Contemporary Opera and Music (1965). The long-awaited Tasmanian School of Music was established by the state education department, with Hobcroft as honorary director in 1964, becoming the Tasmanian Conservatorium of Music in 1965. Early staff appointments included Barrie de Jersey (keyboard), Jan ★Sedivka (violin, chamber music), Graeme Buchanan (accompaniment, administration) and Don ★Kay (composition), while composer Ian ★Cugley was appointed tutor in music for the university's arts degree.

Sedivka's appointment was particularly significant, not only because of the European heritage and teaching traditions he represented (he had studied with Ševčik, Thibaud and Rostal), but also because of the chamber music he brought to Tasmania, in recital with his wife, pianist Beryl Sedivka (a pupil of Ciampi and Solomon) and with cellist Sela Trau (a pupil of Feuermann) as the Tasmanian Conservatorium Trio. The influence of these three European-trained musicians on the musical life of Tasmania has been incalculable. When Hobcroft moved to Sydney in 1971, Sedivka became director, and over the next decade the Conservatorium brought new strength to musical life in Hobart, apparent to the public in an expanded range of concert activities, with major orchestral, choral and operatic presentations. Staff identified with these included Keith Crellin, Gwyn Roberts and Joanne Roose, Edward Talbot, founder of the Conservatorium Chorale, and Russell Smith.

In the 1970s, musical activities at the university were carried on by the Tasmania University Musical Society, or were managed by an entrepreneurial music committee. The Conservatorium was administered by the Tasmanian College of Advanced Education, but was transferred to the university umbrella in 1980. The Conservatorium established an annual string summer school (1971–88), organised by Lyndal Edmiston, which became a powerful magnet for attracting young string students to Hobart. Chamber music burgeoned in the new institution and the Rialannah String Quartet and the ★Petra String Quartet were established; the Petra later focused attention on Aus-

tralian composition, commissioning works extensively until its termination in 1985.

When Sedivka retired as Conservatorium director in 1982, Graeme Buchanan took over, but died tragically soon afterwards, and distinguished flautist David ★Cubbin became foundation professor in 1984. While the Conservatorium had flourished in the previous 20 years, it had also made do with temporary premises, occupying a small house in View Street and sharing accommodation with a school on Mount Nelson. Cubbin now began concerted action with the government and university to achieve a suitable single building, but his efforts were thwarted and he resigned in 1989. The accommodation barrier was only finally overcome in 1993, when the Conservatorium moved into the ABC's former television building in Sandy Bay Road, appropriately refurbished and with a new recital hall. In tandem with this major event, eminent trombonist Simone ★de Haan was appointed professor and the staffing profile soon underwent significant changes. De Haan saw the Conservatorium as both an educational institution and a readily accessible community resource, and a new phase in Hobart's musical life was signalled.

The pioneering spirit of Tasmania's early years, revealed in its capacity to 'make do', to achieve in spite of all odds, together with a frequent ambition to excel, is still apparent in Hobart today. The smallest capital city in Australia, it has the highest per capita attendance at ABC orchestral concerts in the country, a measure of the priority its citizens give to music. In the words of Hobcroft, 'Tasmania is a paradise… Hobart could easily be the Salzburg of Australia'.

FURTHER REFERENCE
OrchardM; Peter Bolger, 'Hobart Town', (ANU, 1973); B.A. Clark and J.M.S. Johnson, *Pipe Organs of Tasmania* (Hobart: Hobart Guild of Organists, 1981); Lyndal Edmiston, *Beginning the Journey: The First 25 Years* (Hobart: Tasmanian Conservatorium of Music, 1990); David Hansen, ed. *The Exhibition Exhibition: A Centenary Celebration of the Tasmanian International Exhibition, 1894–95* (Hobart: Tasmanian Museum and Art Gallery, 1994); Dudley Madden, *A History of Hobart's Brass Bands* (Devonport: C.L. Richmond & Sons, 1986); Jennifer Stops, A Century of Music in Hobart 1804–1904, unpublished special study, Univ. of Melbourne, 1965; *The Cyclopaedia of Tasmania* (Hobart: Maitland & Krone, 1900).   LEON STEMLER

Hobbit Suite, The.   Jazz composition by John Sangster (1973) after Tolkien. See *Sangster, John*.

Hobcroft, Rex Kelvin   (*b* Renmark, SA, 1925), pianist, administrator, composer. He studied at the University of Melbourne with Raymond Lambert and the École Normale de Musique, Paris with Madame Bascovsret. His appointments included foundation head of piano at the Queensland Conservatorium 1957-61, foundation head of the music department at the University of Tasmania 1961–70 and foundation director of the Tasmanian Conservatorium 1963–71. During his directorship of the NSW State Conservatorium, 1972–82, he co-founded the Sydney International Piano Competition (1976). He was awarded a Churchill fellowship in 1967 and a Japan Foundation fellowship in 1975 and was made an honorary Fellow of the Sydney Conservatorium. He was honoured with the AM in 1990.

FURTHER REFERENCE
WWA (1996).   PHILIPPA ROYLANCE

Hoermann, Deanna (*b* Sydney), music educator. Founder of the Kodaly Education Institute of Australia, she was the pioneer in the introduction of Zoltan Kodaly's methods to music education in NSW schools, and one of the key figures in the Australian Kodaly movement. Her numerous recordings, song-books and manuals for school music programs, including *Kodaly for Kindergarten* (1976), *A Developmental Music Program* (1977–84), and *Catch A Little Song* (1985), are used widely in Australia, and she has been international president of the Kodaly Institute.

Holgate, Stephen (*b* Luton, England, 12 May 1953), composer, teacher. After training as a schoolteacher, he studied composition at the University of Melbourne with Barry ★Conyngham and Peter ★Tahourdin from 1975, and attended the Darmstadt Summer School in 1980. He travelled widely in South-East Asia, and in 1981 was in residence at Wangaratta as part of a government community project. He was coordinator of the Bendigo musician/teacher project 1984–87 and currently teaches at Kyneton Secondary College, central Victoria. Deeply influenced by the traditions of the Catholic Church, his music includes hymns, psalms and masses, and school music for concert band or children's choir, such as *Song of the North-East* (1981) and *Earth Dream* (1984/85), or for school orchestra, such as *Return to the Centre* (1993).

FURTHER REFERENCE
Recordings include *Moments from Return* (1992), Michael Kieran Harvey, pf (Red House RED9401). See also *BroadstockS,* 121–22.

Holland, Dulcie Sybil (*b* Sydney, 5 Jan. 1913) composer, pianist, teacher. She studied piano with Grace Middenway and Frank Hutchens, cello with Gladstone Bell, and composition with Alfred Hill and Roy Agnew at the NSW State Conservatorium 1929–33, then in England she studied composition with John Ireland at the Royal College of Music, London, 1936–1939, and won the Cobbett Prize and Blumenthal Composition Scholarship, and later studied with Matyas Seiber. A prolific composer of educational, film, song, chamber, orchestral, piano and

various instrumental works, she is also author of several music theory textbooks for beginners, and from 1967 a popular AMEB examiner for 16 years. She was honoured with the AM in 1977 and an honorary DLitt from Macquarie University in 1994.

FURTHER REFERENCE
Recordings include *Ballad*, C. Amadio, cl, O. Krasnik, pf (Columbia 33 OS 7560); *A Scattering of Leaves: Australian Piano Music,* pf, played by Dulcie Holland and Tessa Birnie (1993, SC 1028); selected piano miniatures, instrumental and chamber works on various JAD recordings. A discography to 1972 is in *PlushD.* Her *Master Your Theory* series is published by EMI. See also *CohenI*; Rita Crews, An Analytical Study of the Piano Works of Roy Agnew, Margaret Sutherland and Dulcie Holland, including Biographical Material, PhD, Univ. of New England, 1994; *GlennonA.*
                                                           RITA CREWS

Hollier, Donald Russell (*b* Sydney, 7 May 1934), composer, conductor. After studies in piano (with L. Godfrey-Smith) and organ at the NSW State Conservatorium, the Royal Academy of Music, London, and at the University of London, he was director of music at Newington College, Sydney, 1962–63. As head of academic studies at the Canberra School of Music 1967–85 and musical director of the Canberra Choral Society and ★Canberra Opera, he conducted Australian premieres of works by Poulenc, Britten, Walton, Vaughan Williams and others. Freelance since then, he was composer-in-residence with the Tasmanian Symphony Orchestra 1990–91.

A flamboyant and naturally gifted composer, his works seem spontaneously atonal and happily discursive, with instrumental parts always well crafted. Some of his works are for extremely large forces: *The Revelation of St John the Divine* (1975), for example, requires soloist, three choirs, string orchestra, three organs, pre-recorded tape, as well as numerous brass and percussion instruments. He has also written solo works for organ, piano or voice, and a series of concertos for highly individual combinations—*Concerto 6* (1983) is for 25 trombones and pre-recorded tape. His opera *The Heiress* (1975) was produced in Melbourne to critical acclaim.

FURTHER REFERENCE
Recordings include *Musick's Empire* (1965), B, orch, Sydney Symphony Orchestra, cond. D. Franks (1970, Festival SFC 800–24); *Variations on a Theme of Larry Sitsky* (1969), vn, pf (1970 Festival SFC 800–22); Sonatina, Robert Zocchi, pf (1971, Canberra School of Music, CSM12); and some of the *12 Preludes,* gui (1979, Canberra School of Music, CSM11). *PlushD* lists other works to 1972 on ABC tape. See also Elizabeth Wood, *GroveD.*

Hollow Log (or canoe). A hollow log sitting on the ground which is struck by a piece of wood, such as a stump. These resonant beats, either at a slow or fast tempo, accompany Aboriginal singing for the *Ubar* (hollow log) ceremony of northern Arnhem Land. In north Queensland, two sticks struck against either a hollow log or a canoe provide an accompaniment for Aboriginal singing. More recently, the canoe has been replaced by an empty metal kerosene tin or oil drum. 'Island dance', or songs originating from Tonga, Samoa and other Pacific islands, is often accompanied by these metal drums. See *Aboriginal Music* §3(i), §4(i).   GRACE KOCH

Holm, June (*b* Brisbane, 14 June 1925; *d* Brisbane, 31 Dec. 1966), country music singer. She made her first appearance yodelling and playing steel guitar at the age of 10. She then worked for the Brisbane entrepreneur Frank Tozer in a duo with steel bassist Beverly Thorne, joining the Tivoli circuit in 1939 and doing live shows with Vince Axleby, as well as yodelling on the *Kookaburra* show on 4BH. During the war she toured Australia with the Red Cross entertainment unit, and her six singles for Regal Zonophone in 1942, the only recordings she made, secured her reputation as a yodeller of unusual clarity and force. After the war she toured with Harry Wren's Stage Spectaculars; she married in 1948 but was still occasionally heard on 4BK until 1958. She retired from entertaining in 1960.

FURTHER REFERENCE
Recordings for Regal Zonophone have been reissued as *Songs To Be Remembered* (1981, Country Style). See also *SmithB*, 111–12 *WatsonC*, 77–9.

Holyoak, Alf (*b* Adelaide, 26 Dec. 1913; *d* Adelaide, 27 Mar. 1985), jazz reeds player. He was introduced to jazz by his reed teacher Frank McMahon, and began dance band work at the Palais Royale in 1932. He was active in pit work and broadcasting until entering the RAAF in 1941, where he served in entertainment units and earned a national reputation. Following his discharge in 1945, he resumed work in Adelaide as a performer, arranger and teacher, ending his career as the city's most respected 'society band' leader. Most of Adelaide's progressive jazz musicians were his protégés, including Maurie *Le Doeuff, Bob *Limb, Bryce *Rohde, Errol *Buddle, Clare Bail, and Bob Young.

FURTHER REFERENCE
BissetB; *OxfordJ*.   BRUCE JOHNSON

Homage to Garcia Lorca. Work for two string orchestras by Richard *Meale (1962–63) first performed by the Sydney Symphony Orchestra in 1964. Published by Boosey & Hawkes (Aust.). Recorded by the WA Symphony Orchestra (Festival SFC 80021).

Home, Sweet Home. Song (1823) by Henry Bishop, words by J.R. Planché, originally for his *Who Wants a Wife* (1816) but better known from J.H. Payne's melodrama *Clari, or The Maid of Milan*, first performed at

Covent Garden 8 May 1823. One of the earliest theatre works performed in Australia, it was heard at Hobart from 1834 and Sydney from 1835, but has long since vanished from the stage. Only the song survives, a sentimental artsong that became greatly identified with Nellie Melba, who recorded it and sang it as the encore at her various farewells in Europe and Australia.

Hoodoo Gurus, The. Rock band formed (1981) in Sydney, originally named Le Hoodoo Gurus, comprised of Dave Faulkner (guitar, vocals), Kimble Rendall (guitar), Brad Shepherd (lead guitar), and James Baker (drums). The band first featured three guitars and drums, without bass guitar. It added Clyde Bramley (bass) and evolved into a standard four-piece by 1982 and has enjoyed enduring success in Australasia, America and Europe through recording and live tours. Their first single, *Leilani*, was released in 1982. The band developed a wider following with the release of the landmark first album *Stoneage Romeos* in 1983, voted debut album of the year in Australia, and No. 1 on the American College Radio charts. Since 1983 the band has released seven albums: *Mars Needs Guitars* (1985), *Blow Your Cool* (1986), *Magnum Cum Louder* (1989), *Kinky* (1991), compilation album *Electric Soup* (1992), *Crank* (1994). The albums have been commercially successful; most have achieved gold and platinum status within weeks of their release. *Electric Soup* won the ARIA biggest-selling domestic album of the year. Their seventh album, *Blue Cave*, was released in June 1996.

FURTHER REFERENCE
For discography see *SpencerA*. See also *McGrathA*; *SpencerW*.
                    HELEN GAGLIANO

Hopkins, John Raymond (*b* Preston nr Hull, England, 19 July 1927), conductor, music administrator. After training as a cellist with Haydn Rogerson at the Royal Manchester College of Music, he studied conducting with Joseph Lewis at the Guildhall School, London, and Carlo Zecchi at the Mozarteum, Salzburg. He became assistant conductor of the BBC Glasgow Orchestra 1949, then conductor of the BBC Northern Orchestra 1952, at the age of 25 the youngest conductor of a major orchestra in Britain. He moved to NZ as conductor of the National Orchestra and musical director of the New Zealand Opera Co. in 1957, his great vitality and musicianship making a reputation that has regularly taken him back to that country ever since.

He moved to Australia as federal director of music for the ABC in 1963, and under his leadership, Australia had perhaps the most important decade of its orchestral development. With overall responsibility for the national network of orchestras, he at once set about varying the traditional subscription concerts with contemporary series and youth events modelled on the London Proms. He immeasurably enlarged the repertoire of the orchestras, introducing many contemporary European scores to the programs, including works by Tippett, Menotti, Maxwell Davies, Davidovsky and Babbitt. He championed Australian composers, initiating many ABC orchestral commissions and commercial recordings, and personally conducting innumerable premieres of Australian works. He developed a passion for Percy Grainger, leading a revival of interest in that artist's larger compositions; he introduced the young Conyngham to the public and brought such composers as Brumby, Butterley, Meale, and Sculthorpe a much wider audience. He arranged and directed international tours for the Melbourne Symphony Orchestra to NZ in 1964 and for the Sydney Symphony Orchestra to Asia and Britain in 1965.

Recognising the importance of training young players, he took a deep interest in the National Music Camp Association, directing camps, conducting the Australian Youth Orchestra at the Adelaide Festival in 1964 and on several international tours. In 1973 he became founding dean of music, Victorian College of the Arts, then director of the NSW State Conservatorium and artistic adviser to the Sydney Symphony Orchestra 1986–92. He remains principal conductor of the Auckland Philharmonic Orchestra and continues to make guest appearances around Australia and in Europe. He has been heard in Belgium, Holland, Sweden, Canada, the USA, three times in the USSR, and elsewhere.

FURTHER REFERENCE
Recordings include many Australian works for the World Record Club (WRC), such as Grainger, *Tribute to Foster and other works*, Sydney Symphony Orchestra (WRC); Sculthorpe, *Sun Music*, Melbourne Symphony Orchestra (WRC); Le Gallienne, *Sinfonietta*, Melbourne Symphony Orchestra (WRC). With the Australian Youth Orchestra: Dvořák, Symphony No. 8 (Music for Pleasure) and Britten, *Young Person's Guide To The Orchestra* (EMI). With other orchestras: Tchaikovsky Symphony No. 5, Sydney Symphony Orchestra (EMI); Britten and Copland, Melbourne Symphony Orchestra (Chandos); works of Delius, Slovak Philharmonic Orchestra (Records Int.); Conyngham's *Fly*, Victoria State Opera (Move). For discography, see *HomesC*. See also Meredith Oakes, *Music Now* 1/2 (1969); *GroveD*; *WWA* (1996).

Hopkins, Sarah (*b* Lower Hutt, NZ, 13 Aug. 1958), composer, performance artist. After training as a cellist at the Victorian College of the Arts, she was musician-in-residence at a series of colleges and regional centres in Victoria 1978–82, at Browns Mart, Darwin and other Northern Territory groups 1982–89, then in Queensland since 1990. She was resident at the Exploration, San Francisco, in 1988. Her work combines acoustic instruments with non-musical objects in ways demonstrating a rare imagination and individuality. Revealing a profound sense of musical sensitivity, she has explored timbres made by tuned whirly instruments (in *Interweave*, 1984, and later

works), recorded telegraph wires (in *Sky Song*, 1985, with Alan ★Lamb), wind chimes, voices singing harmonic overtones (as in *Awakening Earth*, 1990), or extended cello techniques. Her work focuses on performance art, often with community participation, and creates textures often of astonishing beauty.

WORKS (Selective)
Ensemble *Interweave*, 6 players using tuned whirly insts (1984), *Eclipse*, 14 players using tuned whirly insts, handbells (1986), *Transformation*, 6 players with handbells (1989), *Celestial Song*, 12 players of tuned whirly instruments, handbells, voices, wind chimes (1990), *Spirit of Gaia*, 6 players with chime bars, whirly insts, with harmonic singing, *Past Life Melodies*, 12 vc (1992), *Reclaiming the Spirit*, cl, va (or vn), vc, v (or fl), whirly insts (1993).
Solo instrumental *Seasons II*, amplified vc, tape delay (1978), *Cello Chi*, vc, v (1986), *Flight of the Wild Goose*, vc (1987), *Awakening Earth*, vc, v (1990), *Reclaiming the Spirit*, vc, v (1994).
Choral *Past Life Melodies*, mixed vv (1991), *Two Kyries from the Winds of Heaven*, treble vv or mixed vv (1992–93).
Collaborative *Sky Song* (with Alan Lamb), recorded wire music, vc, v (1985), *New Journey* (with Alan Lamb), recorded wire music, vc, vv, whirly insts, wind chimes (1988), *First Light* (with Peter Carolan), wind chimes, bells, synthesiser, v, vc (1990).

FURTHER REFERENCE
Recordings include Sky Song (1985, ABC 838503B); *Cello Chi*, v, vc (1986, New Albion NA028); *New Journey*, vv, vc, telephone wires, whirlies, wind chimes (1988, Vox Australis VAST012–2); *Awakening Earth*, vc, v (1990, Fortuna Records, NWCD 777); and *Reclaiming the Spirit* (1993), cl, va, vc, v, whirly (1994, Tall Poppies TP043). Her writings include 'Sounds From the Top End', *AMCN* 4 (1984) and 9; 'Manifesto', *SA* 22 (1989), 7–9. See also Graham Hair and Greta Mary Hair, *GroveW*; *BroadstockS*, 123–6, 303–5; *JenkinsT*, 75–84.

Horn, Margory Walker (*b* 1918; *d* Brisbane, 20 Jan. 1984), organist. Her early education was in Brisbane then at Trinity College, London, where she took organ lessons from George ★Thalben-Ball, obtaining her FTCL and ARCM. Here she broadcast for the BBC and in Australia she made organ broadcasts for the ABC and other concert appearances. She advertised in Brisbane as teaching piano, violin, organ and theory, examined for the AMEB and was intermittently organist for Brisbane First Christian Scientist Church. Shortly before her death, she endowed an annual organ scholarship in her name at the Queensland Conservatorium.   ROBERT BOUGHEN

Horne, Richard Hengist [Richard Henry] (*b* Edmonton, London, 31 Dec. 1802; *d* Margate, England, 13 Mar. 1884), novelist, librettist. After attending military college he embarked on a literary career in London, publishing books from 1833 and editing the *Monthly Repository* 1836–37. He came to wide attention with his epic poem *Orion* (1843). Arriving in Victoria in search of gold in 1852, he held a succession of short-lived civil service posts, and did not write seriously until 1863, when he became warden of the Blue Mountain goldfield near Trentham. There he wrote the lyric drama *Prometheus the Fire-Bringer* (1864), the libretto for Charles *Horsley's masque *The South Seas Sisters* (1866), which contained a representation of an Aboriginal corroboree, and the text for Joseph Summers' cantata *Galatea Secunda* (1867). His middle name, Henry, was replaced with 'Hengist' from then on. His libretto for C. Schmitt's operetta *Cazille* was produced (in excerpt) in Sydney in 1872. Nevertheless, having produced little in Australia to match his early books, he returned disillusioned to London in 1869, writing new works but not repeating his earlier success.

FURTHER REFERENCE
A. Blainey, *The Farthing Poet: A Biography of Richard Hengist Horne 1802–1884* (London: Longmans, 1968); *ADB*, 4.

Horsley, Charles Edward (*b* London, 16 Dec. 1822; *d* New York, 28 Feb. 1876), organist. The son of composer William Horsley, whose family was closely associated with Mendelssohn, he studied in Germany and was an organist and composer in England before his arrival in Melbourne in 1861. He was successively organist at Christ Church South Yarra, St Stephen's Richmond and St Francis' Melbourne. In Melbourne he acted as a music critic, composed several cantatas and conducted the Melbourne Philharmonic Society choir. In 1871 he returned to England, but in 1873 moved to New York where he was organist to St John's Chapel and conductor to the Church Music Association.

FURTHER REFERENCE
E.N. Matthews, *Colonial Organs and Organbuilders* (Melbourne: MUP, 1969), 77–8; M.T. Radic, *ADB*, 4; Nicholas Temperley, *GroveD*.   JOHN MAIDMENT

Hort, Harold (*b* Sydney, 12 Aug. 1920), music broadcasting administrator. After studying anthropology at the University of Sydney and organ and piano at the Sydney Conservatorium, he joined the ABC as a cadet in 1941. He rose from music assistant to music supervisor for Tasmania in 1950, and after working in the television division became assistant director of music in 1966 under John *Hopkins, planning the programs *Musica Australia* (1969–71), which broadcast many Australian works for the first time. He followed Hopkins as ABC federal director of music 1974–85 and published articles on Australian music in *24 Hours*.

FURTHER REFERENCE
His unpub. MA thesis is The Development of Australian Music 1788–1850, Macquarie Univ., 1977. See also *ADMR*.

Hounslow, Keith (*b* Perth, 19 Sept. 1928), jazz trumpeter. He began cornet in the late 1940s, in 1947 joining the West Side Jazz Group and attending the Australian Jazz Convention. Accompanying the Rex Stewart tour as a baggage boy, he was then briefly in Adelaide with the Southern Jazz Group. Settling in Melbourne in the early 1950s, he freelanced with Frank *Coughlan, Brian *Brown and others. From 1962 to the early 1970s he was musically dormant while active in film and television production, returning to music through casual work, and with Tony *Gould and Frank Traynor. Subsequently based in Sydney, he was freelancing and leading his own groups. At present he is living near Kiama, NSW.

FURTHER REFERENCE
Recordings include *Winners!* The Datsun Dixielanders (1977, Jazznote JNLP 017/S); *Introducing McJad* (1978, AIJA 001); *At Last,* Keith Hounslow's Jazzmakers (1988 Emanem 3605). See also *ClareB*; *BissetB*; *OxfordJ*; Gail Brennan, 'Keith Hounslow, A New Career Phase', *JA* (Winter/Spring 1986), 4–7, 63.
BRUCE JOHNSON

Howard, Brian Robert (*b* Sydney, 3 Jan. 1951), composer. He was a choirboy at St Andrew's Cathedral, Sydney. After studies with Peter *Sculthorpe at the University of Sydney and Richard *Meale at the University of Adelaide, he was at Darmstadt and with Peter Maxwell Davies, and studied conducting at Basle. He became a *répétiteur* with the Australian Opera, conducting in various centres, then taught at the University of Melbourne 1977–79, obtaining the DMus. He was music director of the WA Ballet 1983–85, taught at the WA Conservatorium from 1985 (dean 1991–95), and is now President of Lasalle College, Singapore. He has had two composition fellowships from the Australia Council, has been resident at the Cité Internationale des Arts, Paris, and with the Royal Danish Ballet, and his *Il Tramonto della Luna* (1976) received the highest award at the 1978 Trieste International Competition for Symphonic Composition. A composer of rigorous method and sure dramatic sense, he was widely acclaimed after the success of his operas *Inner Voices* (1977) and *Metamorphosis* (1983), the latter performed by both the Victoria State Opera and the Australian Opera. He subsequently received commissions from major Australian ensembles, although his meticulousness has meant some works have been slow coming to fruition, while others he has withdrawn.

WORKS (Selective)
Principal publisher: Boosey & Hawkes
Orchestral *Il Tramonto Della Luna* (1976), *Temple of the Golden Pavilion* (1978), *Sun and Steel* (1986), *Wildbird Dreaming* (1988).
Chamber *Chanson De La Plus Haute Tour*, fl, cl, trbn, 2 perc, hp, db (1980), *The Rainbow Serpent*, fl/pic, cl/bass cl, tpt, trbn, perc, vn, vc (1984), *Fly Away Peter*, wind quintet (1984).
Theatre *Inner Voices*, chamber opera (1979 rev. 1980, 10 scenes, Louis Nowra), Melbourne, 2 Oct. 1979; *Metamorphosis*, chamber opera (1983, six scenes, Steven Berkoff), Melbourne, 30 Sept. 1983, *Whitsunday* (1988).
Choral *A Fringe of Leaves*, chamber ch, str (1988).

FURTHER REFERENCE

Recordings include *Sun and Steel* (1986) for 12 solo insts (Move MD 3066). See also *CA* (1995/96); *BroadstockS*, 128–9; *West Australian* 17 Oct. 1992; Julie Barnes, Brian Howard's *Metamorphosis*, BMus, Univ. Melbourne, 1984.

Howard, Jenny [Daisy Evelyn Louise Blose] (*b* London, England, 1904), pantomime singer, entertainer. Entering a talent quest at London's East End at the age of 10, she worked as an actress in the Yachtsmen troupe from 1926. She appeared at the London Palladium and came to Australia in 1928 to appear in the Tivoli circuit. Back in London, she worked with Gladys ★Moncrieff and Bud Flanagan, and returned to Australia and the Tivoli to star in *Crazy Show* with Bob Dyer and George Wallace in 1940. During the war she gave many concerts for Australian troops, and continued to star in variety shows, including *Aladdin*, *Thanks For The Memory* (1955) and *Many Happy Returns* (1959). She made her operetta debut in *Pippin* (1974). One of Australia's leading pantomime stars and an outstanding principal boy for more than 30 years, she was an adaptable talent, as at home in farce as in love ballads. She retired to the Gold Coast after the death of her husband, the theatrical manager Percy King, in 1984.

FURTHER REFERENCE

ParsonsC; Nancye Bridges, *Curtain Call* (Sydney: Cassell,1980), 92–6.

Howard, Leslie John   (*b* Melbourne, 29 Apr. 1948), pianist, composer. Educated at Monash University, Howard later studied with Guido Agosti in Italy and Noretta Conci in London. Named the 'Klemperer of the piano' by the *Guardian*, his most important achievement is the recording of the complete piano works by Liszt for the Hyperion label, a projected total of 70 discs. In 1986 he was awarded the Ferenc Liszt Medal of Honour. Resident in London since 1972, he has also recorded the complete keyboard works of Grainger and has been a member of staff of the Guildhall School of Music since 1987.

FURTHER REFERENCE

Recordings include Liszt, Complete Music for Solo Piano, vols. 1–70 (Hyperion, in progress); Grainger, Piano Works (ABC 432 247); Grainger, *Molly On The Shore* (ABC 442 380–2). See also *CA* (1995–96).   SUZANNE ROBINSON

Howson.   Family of two brothers and two sisters and their children, all singers. One sister, Emma Albertazzi, née Howson (*b* 1814; *d* 1847) also created the ballet role Giselle at the London premiere of Loder's *The Night Dancers,* and died soon after when her dress caught fire. The two brothers Frank (1) and John (2) settled in Australia.

(1) Frank Howson   (*b* 1817; *d* Omaha, USA, 16 Sept. 1869), baritone, entrepreneur. He fought in Spain with the British Legion *c.*1835, and after singing in the Drury Lane Co., with his brother was brought to Hobart in 1842 by singer-entrepreneur Anne Clarke for her concerts in the Argyle Rooms and her opera in Hobart theatres. Beginning with Dibdin's *The Quaker*, the Howson brothers' appearances included *Fra Diavolo, The Beggar's Opera* and Boieldieu's *Jean de Paris.* They moved to Sydney in 1844, and in the following years presented an extensive repertoire of operas as well as concerts at the Royal Victoria Theatre from 1845 and at the Prince of Wales Theatre from 1855, including Auber's *Gustavus III, La muette de Portici*, 26 performances of *The Bohemian Girl* in 1846, and 28 performances of *Norma* in 1852.

No stranger to new works, he appeared in the premiere of Nathan's *Don John of Austria* (1847), sang Don José in the Australian premiere of *Maritana* (1849), which he also directed, sang Figaro in *The Marriage of Figaro* (Bishop), and produced Loder's *The Night Dancers.* Beyond Sydney he sang for George Coppin in *Norma* at the Theatre Royal, Melbourne, in 1856, and managed Andrew and Louise Torning's troupe, touring the colonies with a full array of principals, chorus and orchestra, and presenting such works as *Barber of Seville, Martha, Ernani, Don Pasquale, The Beggar's Opera* and (from 1859) *Il Trovatore.*

A baritone of rich quality if limited range and volume, and an able director, Howson continued to present opera after the W.S. ★Lyster Opera Co. arrived in 1861, notably a season at the Melbourne Haymarket (January–March 1864), but his work was soon outclassed by the newcomers. He then toured the USA from 1866 with Howson's English and Italian Opera Troupe, which included his daughters Emma (3) and Clelia and his sons Frank Alfred Jr and J. Jerome, until his death from cancer.

Both Emma and Frank Jr found notable careers; Frank became director of music for Henry Irving at the Lyceum, London, and then as Francis A. Howson IV worked as a conductor and composer in New York with John Philip Sousa and others.

(2) John Howson   (*b c.*1819; *d* 16 Feb. 1888), tenor, composer. After singing in Drury Lane, he appeared in numerous opera and concert performances with his brother Frank (1) at Hobart 1842–43, then at Sydney from 1843. He sang numerous operatic roles, arranged the music for the Australian premiere of *Maritana* in 1849, for which he also sang Don Caesar, and although a tenor essayed the bass role of Almaviva in Bishop's *Marriage of Figaro.* With his brother he presented his own opera, *The Corsair,* at Sydney in 1848, the libretto based on the Byron poem which had been the source for Verdi's *Il Corsaro* not long before. Beyond Sydney he toured the colonies with his brother's troupe. He had a serviceable, flexible tone and was a good actor, but his work became overshadowed by the talents of the W.S. ★Lyster Opera Co. in the 1860s, and he retired from the stage.

(3) Emma Howson,   (*b c.*1845; *d* 1890), contralto. Daughter of Frank Howson (1). She studied with Sara

*Flower, made her debut in Sydney in 1859 and sang the title role in *La Cenerentola* in Melbourne in 1863. Her father took her to the USA in 1866, and after his death in 1869 she toured the country with her brother Frank Alfred Howson Jr. They went to London in 1873. She took lessons with Lamperti in Milan, appearing in opera at Leghorn, Malta, England and Ireland. Her appearances at Florence in 1876 in *Figaro, La sonnambula* and *Martha* attracted high praise, and she became a popular figure in Britain, creating the role of Josephine in *HMS Pinafore* in 1878. After this she returned to the USA to teach.

FURTHER REFERENCE
Obit. for John Howson, *Theatrical Courier* 18 Feb. 1888. The diaries of Frank A. Howson Jr are in the possession of his grandson Howson H. Hartley, Worcester, New York, USA. See also Alison Jones, 'Our Forgotten Singers No. 2 The Howson Family', *Opera Australia* 206 (Feb. 1995), 7–10; Osric [Humphrey Hall and Alfred John Cripps], *The Romance of the Sydney Stage* (ms, 1911; pub. Sydney: Currency Press, 1996), 100–14, passim; *IrvinD; idem, Theatre Comes to Australia* (Brisbane: UQP, 1971); Ann Wenzel, The First 100 Years of Music in Australia, MA, Univ. Sydney, 1963; *OrchardM*, 164–65; *BrewerD*.

Hudson, Bob, popular singer-songwriter. After working as a schoolteacher in the Riverina from 1968, he appeared in *The Rocky Horror Show* (1972) and the ABC series *Sit Yourself Down*. From his album *The Newcastle Song Recorded Live* (1975, RCA MLF 083), the title track was edited and released as a single, *The Newcastle Song*, reaching No. 1 in the charts in 1975 and remaining there for 20 weeks. His other compositions include *Rak Off Normie* and *Girls In Our Town* (1973). A writer of humorous, topical songs in the folk-ballad style, he toured with Margret RoadKnight in 1979, worked on ABC radio from 1983 and wrote on music for the *National Times*.

FURTHER REFERENCE
Recordings include the single *After Me Cat Left Home* (1975), *The Newcastle Song Recorded Live* (RCA MLF 083), and the album *Party Pieces* (1980 Larrikin, LRF 058). See also *McGrathA*.

Hughes, Dick (*b* Melbourne, 8 July 1931), jazz pianist, journalist. Pianist Will McIntyre was his early inspiration, leading him to jazz playing as a pianist, singer, and as president of the Melbourne University Rhythm Club 1950–51. Based in England 1952–55, he worked with Cy Laurie, and took lessons from Mary Lou Williams, who was also one of many musicians, including Billie Holiday and Sidney Bechet, whom he interviewed for the ABC. He settled in Sydney from 1955, and became prominent in the traditional jazz community as a musician and journalist.

Working with the *Port Jackson Jazz Band and the Ray *Price groups, he began leading his own groups, with residencies at the Macquarie Hotel, Windsor Castle Hotel, Adams Hotel and French's Tavern into the 1970s. He played support (and toured as baggage boy) for Eddie

Condon's touring group in Australia in 1964, toured with Alvin Ailey's American Dance Theatre in 1965, and attended the Newport Jazz Festival as a journalist in 1972. He was the first solo pianist to perform in the Sydney Opera House (1973). From the early 1970s he led a trio at the Journalists' Club, and in 1977 began leading his Famous Five at the Soup Plus restaurant in a residency that continued through most of the 1980s. This band also played broadcasts and support for visiting musicians including Stan Getz, Kenny Ball and Chris Barber. In the 1990s Hughes has been less active as a leader, playing solo performances, Port Jackson Jazz Band reunion concerts, and playing with his daughter, singer-guitarist Christa.

FURTHER REFERENCE
Recordings include *The Famous PIX Sessions, Classic Australian Jazz from the Sixties* (1996, Australian Jazz Reissues AJR-001 A&B); *Dick Hughes Looks Back And Around* (1977, 44 Records 6357 716); *The Last Train Leaves For Casablanca Once In A Blue Moon* (1986, Larrikin LRJ 176). His memoirs are *Daddy's Practising Again* (Melbourne: Marlin Books, 1977). An interview with him is in *WilliamsA*, 40–45. See also *BissetB; CA; ClareB; OxfordJ*; Roger Frampton, 'Australian Jaz', *SA* (1992), 37–41.

BRUCE JOHNSON

Hughes, Robert Watson (*b* Leven, Scotland, 27 Mar. 1912), composer. A largely self-taught composer who maintained a career as a music editor, arranger and orchestrator with the ABC between 1946 and 1976. In his capacity as chairman of APRA he promoted Australian composition in national and overseas forums. Hughes is one of his generation's most brilliant orchestrators, with the consequence that almost his entire acknowledged output is for orchestra. Although his approach to composition errs on the side of conservatism, his work displays fine craftsmanship. He was honoured with the MBE in 1978.

WORKS (Selective)
Orchestral *Diversions on a Dance Tune* (1947), *Festival Overture* (1948), Fantasia for Strings (1948 rev. 1953), *Farrago* (1949 rev. 1965), Symphony (1951 rev. 1971), *Serenade* (1952); *Essay for Orchestra* (1953), *Linn o' Dee: A Highland Fancy for Orchestra* (1954), *Xanadu*, ballet suite (1954), *Elegy*, str (1955), *Masquerade*, overture (1956), *Sinfonietta* (1957), Fantasia (1963 rev. 1967–68), *Synthesis* (1969), *Ballade* (1969), *The Forbidden Rite*, ballet suite (1961 rev. 1971), *Sea Spell* (1973), *Essay II* (1982).
Choral *Five Indian Poems*, SATB, winds, perc (1971), *A Song For Exiles*, SATB, ob/Eng hn, org, pf (1991).

FURTHER REFERENCE
Recordings include *Sinfonietta*, Sydney Symphony Orchestra, cond. N. Malko (RCA L6233); *Xanadu* Suite, Sydney Symphony Orchestra, cond. J. Post (HMV OALP 7511); Symphony No. 1, Sydney Symphony Orchestra, cond. J Post (1971, Festival SFC 800–23). A discography to 1972 is in *PlushD*. See also *CallawayA, MurdochA*; Matthew Orlovich, The Music of Robert Hughes, MMus, Univ. of Sydney, 1994; Elizabeth Wood, *GroveD*.

JOEL CROTTY

Humble, (Leslie) Keith (*b* Geelong, 6 Sept., 1927; *d* Geelong, 23 May 1995), composer, pianist, educator. A child prodigy, he studied piano under Roy Shepherd at the University of Melbourne Conservatorium and won many awards, including a coveted scholarship to study at the Royal Academy of Music, London. During the same years, 1947–49, he gained a reputation as a swing band pianist in Melbourne, which subtly influenced his later approaches to composition and performance. Formal studies in Paris 1952–54 led to a more profound influence: René Leibowitz, and the tightly disciplined sonic world of serialism. In the 1950s he toured Europe as accompanist to Ethel Semser, Robert Gartside and others, was musical assistant to Leibowitz, and composed various chamber, vocal and piano works. By 1960 he was the founding director of the Centre de Musique, Paris, a locus for creative collaboration and experimentation that rivalled Pierre Boulez's famous Domaine Musical.

Returning to the University of Melbourne as lecturer in 1966 with a vast knowledge of contemporary repertoire, concepts and techniques, he worked tirelessly to raise the profile of contemporary music in Australia though his teaching, performing, composing, experimenting and organising activities. Among other things he formed the progressive Society for the Private Performance of New Music, promoted electronic music studies, convened a national seminar on electronic music in 1971, held creative music workshops for children, and produced various music-theatre works, including his own *Nunique* (music for now) series (from 1968), and the multi-media work *La Legende* (1970). In the early 1970s, he became involved in the establishment and activities of the celebrated Centre for Music Experiment, University of California, San Diego, and in 1974 became founding professor of the department of music, La Trobe University, creating a major Australian platform for contemporary music creation and research. His co-founding and direction of the Australian Contemporary Music Ensemble 1975–78 provided the prototype and impulse for later contemporary ensembles such as *Flederman and Pipeline.

Humble's impact on Australian contemporary music was profound and continues through the many current leaders in Australian music whom he influenced, his distinctive ideas about music education, performance and composition, and his own musical works. His career was a complex, interactive multi-layering of often contrasting activities which defies brief description. A lifetime association with improvisation found ultimate freedom of expression though his collaboration in the international touring ensemble KIVA (1982–90); yet paradoxically his abiding passion was for a personal musical language in which deep expressivity is mediated though an extraordinarily precise syntax. His achievement in this respect is heard in, for example, *Eight Bagatelles* (1992) and *Symphony of Sorrows* (1993). In 1996 the Humble Research Collection Project was established at the department of music, La Trobe University, as an international site for the ongoing projection and study of Humble's music and ideas.

WORKS (Selective)
Principal publisher: Australian Music Centre [AMC].
Orchestral *Arcade V* (1969, rec. 198?, Vox Australis VAST 006–2, pub. Universal), *Statico III* (1973, MS is part of Humble Estate, Geelong), *Symphony of Sorrows* (1994, AMC).
Chamber String Trio (1954, AMC), Sonata for Flute and Piano (1991; rec. 1992, Canberra School of Music, CSM 18; and 1995, Tall Poppies TP069, pub. New York: John Wion, 1994), *A Music for Baroque Ensemble,* hpd, fl, ob, db (1971, [1975]?, ABC AC1011, Universal), *Molly's Lament,* fl, cl, vn, vc, tpt, perc, pf (1978, AMC), *Ways, By-Ways,* fl, vc, trbn, celeste, perc, pf (1985; rec. 1985, Larrikin Records LRF 156, pub. AMC), *Four All Seasons,* 1–4 str qrts or str orchs (1989, AMC).
Piano Three Piano Pieces, pp. 3 (1959, AMC), Piano Sonata I (1959, La Trobe University Press), *Arcade 11: A Folio for Piano Solo* (1969; rec. 1993, Tall Poppies TPO37, pub. Universal), Piano Sonata II (1977, rev. 1980, La Trobe University Press), Piano Sonata III (1985; rec. 1992, Tall Poppies TP058, pub. AMC), Piano Sonata IV (1990; rec. 1992, Tall Poppies TP058, pub. AMC), 8 Bagatelles (1992; rec. Tall Poppies TP808 and ASTRA CD1, pub AMC).
Theatre *L'Entreprise* (1962, ms is part of Humble Estate, Geelong), *Le Printemps* (1963, MS is part of Humble Estate, Geelong).
Music-Theatre *Nunique* I–IX (1968–?, ms is part of Humble Estate, Geelong).
Choral *3 Nocturnes,* ch, chamber orch (1990, AMC), *Trois Poèmes a Crier et a Danser* (1968, Universal), *The Seasons,* a setting of seven haiku, 4 mixed chs (1971, Universal), *In Pace,* a set of introits, chorales, and chorale preludes, ch, hp, perc (1990, AMC).
Songs *A Book of Songs of Love and Death,* T, pf (1966, AMC), *8 Cabaret Songs,* S, pf (1989, AMC), *Trois Poemes D'Amour,* T, pf (1970, AMC).

FURTHER REFERENCE
His recordings as a conductor include *Australian Contemporary Music Ensemble* vol. 1, dir. Keith Humble ([1976]?, Cherry Pie, CPF 1029). See also: N. Delanoë, *Le Raspail Vert, L'American Center à Paris 1934–1994, Une Histoire des Avant-Gardes Franco-Américaines* (Paris: Seghers, 1994), 69–109; L. Harris, *CallawayA;* J.C. Françoise, 'In Memoriam: Keith Humble', *Perspectives of New Music* 33 (Winter 1985); 108–15; *MurdochA;* J. Whiteoak, *Improvisatory Music-Making in Australia, 1836–1970* (Sydney: Currency Press, in press) ch.7; idem, 'Interview with Keith Humble', *New Music Articles* (NMA) 7 (1989); 21–6; idem, 'Keith Humble, the Music-Maker with a Message: A Tribute, *Context* 10 (Summer 1995); 5–9.
JOHN WHITEOAK

Hungerford, Bruce [Leonard Hungerford] (*b* Korumburra, Vic., 1922; *d* New York, 27 Jan. 1977), pianist. After studying with Roy *Shepherd at the University of Melbourne Conservatorium and Ignaz Friedman, he went to New York, taking lessons with Ernst *Hutcheson at the Juilliard School and later Karl Friedberg. He made his debut as Leonard Hungerford at New York in 1951. He was pianist-in-residence at the Bayreuth Festival 1959–66, recording the complete piano works of Wagner from 1960. He toured extensively and gave masterclasses, visiting Australia in the 1970s, and was on the staff at the

Mannes School of Music, New York, when he was killed in a car accident. Particularly noted for his interpretations of Beethoven, Schubert and Wagner, he was better known in the USA than in Australia at the time of his death.

FURTHER REFERENCE
Obit. in *Australian* 28 Jan. 1977; *Key Vivre* (Autumn 1977), 13–14. Recordings include works of Beethoven (1967, Vanguard VSD 71174).

Hunt, Kevin (*b* Sydney, 22 Jan. 1961), jazz pianist. He began piano in 1979 under Chuck ★Yates and Dave ★Levy, and later through NSW Conservatorium jazz program. With the Northside and Daly-Wilson Big Bands, from 1983 he played in clubs and jazz venues, including a 10-year residency at the Regent Hotel, and toured with Judy Bailey, Bob Bertles, James Morrison and others. Also active in television and session work, he formed the Commuters in 1985, then joined Kinetic Energy Theatre Co. in 1989. He began BMus studies at the Sydney Conservatorium in 1992, interrupting his course to study and perform in Europe. Playing as support for visitors including Herb Ellis and Billy Cobham, he is currently performing and touring with Don Burrows.

FURTHER REFERENCE,
Recordings include *James Morrison, Live at the Winery* (1992, ABC Records 479232; first issued 1985); *Visa*, Steve Hunter (1986, Streamline Records SL 8601); *Carl Orr* (1990, rooArt Jazz 846 309–2); *Free Spirits* (1990, rooArt Jazz 846307–2); *Tim Hopkins' Good Heavens!* (1993, Larrikin, LRJ 299). See also Jill Morris, 'Kevin Hunt', *Australian Jazz and Blues* 1/2 (Summer 1993–94), 19.   BRUCE JOHNSON

Hunter, Marc.   See *Dragon*.

Hunter, Ruby (*b* Adelaide, 1955), Ngarrindjeri–Pitjantjatjara singer-songwriter. Her performances include numerous Aboriginal events and festivals such as Building Bridges, Sydney, the Survival Day Concerts (each 26 January in Sydney), and the Brunswick Koori Arts Festival, Victoria. She toured to the USA with Archie ★Roach in 1992, supporting Joan Armatrading and Bob Dylan; other tours followed to America and the UK (1993), the UK (1994), and to Canada with Kev Carmody, Archie Roach and Tiddas (1995). Active in Aboriginal cultural politics, she writes songs about Aborigines, gender and socially committed issues.

FURTHER REFERENCE
Recordings include *Koorie* (1988, Victorian Aboriginal Cultural Heritage Trust); and *Thoughts Within* (1994, White Records, D31108).   P. DUNBAR-HALL

Hunter Symphony Orchestra. Part-time professional orchestra based at Newcastle, NSW, the most successful orchestra outside the Australian capital cities. Founded as the Hunter Orchestra, it gave well-patronised

subscription concert seasons under Ulrich Bernstein from 1985; after his death from illness in 1989 it was placed on a more professional basis and conducted by Roland Peelman.

Hunters and Collectors. Alternative rock group formed (1981) in Melbourne, revolving around Mark Seymour (lead vocals, guitar), Jack Howard (trumpet/keyboards), Martin Lubran (guitar to 1984), Barry Palmer (guitar from 1988), Jeremy Smith (keyboards, french horn, guitar), Michael Waters (trombone, keyboards), Robert Miles (sound design), John Archer (bass), and Doug Falconer (drums). Their early sound owed much to English punk and funk, but with successive albums came further refinements, and a more straightforward brand of rock emerged. Nevertheless the group always retained some of its characteristic raw sound, led by Seymour's powerful vocals and coloured with distinctive brass and instrumental arrangements. Some of the group's material has focused on the Australian experience, most notably in the song *Ghost Nation*.

FURTHER REFERENCE
Recordings include *The Way to Go Out* (1985, White L27148); *What's a Few Men* (1987, White L53253); *Ghost Nation* (1989, White TVD 93314 [D533143]); *Collected Works* (1990, White distributed Festival D24523); *Denim Flower* (1994, White TVD 93401/RMD 53401). For discography see *SpencerA.* See also *McGrathA*; *SpencerW*   WILLIAM VAN PINXTEREN

Hush. Commercial pop-rock group (1973–78), its members Les Gock (guitar), Keith Lamb (vocals), Rick Lum (bass) and Chris 'Smiley' Palinthorpe (drums). At its peak the group was surpassed only by ★Skyhooks and ★Sherbet in popularity, and had become well known through recordings, extensive touring and numerous appearances on television's *Countdown*. Hush had an exotic image due largely to the presence of their two Chinese guitarists, and also their liking for English glam rock with contrived stage and costume decoration. Hits include *Bony Moronie* and *Glad All Over*, both from 1975. Jacques de Jongh joined the group in 1976 to take over some bass and guitar duties, but the group dissolved by 1978. Gock then became a successful writer of advertising jingles, and co-wrote the 1988 Australian Bicentennial theme, *Celebration of A Nation*.

FURTHER REFERENCE
Recordings include *The Best of Hush* (BMG PCD 10211). For discography see *SpencerA.* See also *McGrathA*; *SpencerW.*
     WILLIAM VAN PINXTEREN

Hutchence, Michael.   See *INXS*.

Hutchens, Frank (*b* Christchurch, NZ, 15 Jan. 1892; *d* 18 Oct. 1965), pianist, composer. He went to London at the age of 13, studying with Tobias Matthay and Frederick Corder at the Royal Academy of Music, and winning the Chappell Gold Medal for piano. Returning to NZ in 1911 he found few opportunities, and came to Sydney in 1913. He was a founding member of the NSW State Conservatorium staff from 1915, and a teacher and AMEB examiner of wide influence for a long period. After the visit of the Guy Maier-Lee Pattison duo to Sydney in 1924, he formed a piano duo with his former student Lindley *Evans, which gave numerous concerts, broadcasts and recordings for over 40 years, including performances of their own works. He visited London and gave concerts at the Aeolian Hall in 1933 and was made a Fellow of the Royal Academy of Music in 1939. He appeared as a concerto soloist with all the ABC orchestras.

With an elegant technique and poetic sense, he was one of the most influential pianists in Australia for half a century. As a composer, he wrote *Air Mail Palestine* for baritone and orchestra, songs, music for violin, cello, and over 60 works for the piano, including *Concerto Symphonique*, a concerto for piano and strings, and a quintet for piano and string quartet. He performed his Fantasy Concerto with the Sydney Symphony Orchestra in 1943. He was honoured with the OBE in 1962, three years before his death in a car accident.

FURTHER REFERENCE

Recordings include Quintet for Piano and Strings, Austral String Quartet, J. Hutchinson, pf (1971, Festival SFC 800–25). ABC tapes of other works are listed in *PlushD*. See also Sandra Jobson, ed., *Frank Hutchens: Notes on an Australian Musician* (Sydney: Wentworth Books, 1971); Helen Bainton, *ADB*, 9; Wych Elm, 'Frank Hutchens: Pianist-Composer', *The Canon* 13/2 (Sept. 1959), 22–30; Elizabeth Ogilvie, 'Frank Hutchens: A Tribute', *The Canon*, 17/6 (1963), 75–78; Elizabeth Wood, *GroveD*; *Victorian Historical Magazine* 36/4 (Nov. 1965), 134–5.

Hutcheson, Ernest   (*b* Melbourne, 20 July 1871; *d* New York, USA, 9 Feb. 1951), Australian-born pianist, composer, teacher. Promoted as an 'infant Mozart', Hutcheson was taken on tour throughout the Australian colonies in 1877. In 1878 G.W. *Torrance sought to guide his development and formed a committee to administer funds subscribed for his welfare. As a teenager he left Australia permanently to undertake studies at the Leipzig Conservatory, graduating in 1890. He toured Australia in the following year, as well as England, Europe and the USA. From 1898 to 1900 he taught at the Stern Conservatory, Berlin, and then became a teacher at the Peabody Conservatory, Baltimore, USA, until 1912. In 1924 he joined the staff of the Juilliard Graduate School of Music and was dean 1927–37, then president 1937–45. His compositions include a two-piano concerto, a symphonic poem, a symphony, a violin concerto, and many piano pieces. He also wrote several books including *A Musical Guide to the Ring of the Nibelungs* (1940) and *The Literature of the Piano; a Guide for Amateur and Student* (1950).

FURTHER REFERENCE

Obit. in *New York Times* 10 Feb. 1951. See also *Australasian Sketcher* (14 Apr. 1877), 10; Hariette Brower, *Piano Mastery 2: Talks with Master Pianists and Teachers* (New York: Frederick A. Stokes, *c.*1917), 100–13; *Who's Who in Australia*, 1938–50.

JENNIFER ROYLE

Hyde, Miriam Beatrice   (*b* Adelaide, 15 Jan. 1913), composer, teacher, performer. She studied piano until the age of 12 with her mother Muriel, a professional pianist and teacher. In 1925 she won a three-year AMEB scholarship to study at the Elder Conservatorium, University of Adelaide, then won the Elder Overseas Scholarship in 1932 for study in England at the Royal Academy of Music 1932–35. Her teachers at the Academy were Howard Hadley, Arthur Benjamin and Kendall Taylor for piano; and R.O. Morris and Gordon Jacob for composition, and she won the Farrar, Sullivan and Cobbett composition prizes. She was soloist with the London Philharmonic Orchestra in her Piano Concerto No. 1 under Leslie Heward and with the London Symphony Orchestra in her Piano Concerto No. 2 under Constant Lambert.

Returning to Australia in 1936, she lived in Sydney and had opportunities there for performing many of her piano and chamber works. She wrote the orchestral work *Adelaide* Overture as a tribute to her home state, SA. Marrying a soldier, Marcus Edwards, in 1939, she returned alone to Adelaide to wait out the war years, and wrote her Piano Sonata in G minor, the most significant of her solo piano works. Teaching piano at the Elder Conservatorium, she pursued a growing career as a public performer and composer. After the war she returned to Sydney to be reunited with her husband and from 1945 was a popular examiner with the AMEB for nearly 40 years.

Early influences on her include the music of Brahms, Rachmaninov, Debussy and Scriabin. Her compositional style reflects Romantic-Impressionist tendencies, and her exposure to the English pastoral tradition became a further influence on her compositional language. Her prolific output includes orchestral, choral, song, chamber and instrumental works, including numerous piano solos and educational works for students. She has also written poetry, some used for her songs, and is author of textbooks for students and numerous articles for music teachers. She is a well-respected and distinguished teacher and performer, regularly giving lectures and master classes. She was honoured with the OBE in 1981, the AO in 1991, and an honorary DLitt by Macquarie University in 1993.

WORKS (Selective)

Principal publishers: Allans Chappell EMI. MS works available in facsimile from Australian Music Centre, Sydney

Orchestral   Piano Concerto No. 1 in E-flat minor (1932–33), Piano Concerto No. 2 in Cs minor (1934–35), *Adelaide* Overture (1935), Incidental music for *Heritage* (1936), Fantasy-Romantic pf, orch (1938–39), *Village Fair* (1943), tone-poem, *The Symbolic Gate* (1945), *Happy Occasion* Overture (1957), *Kelso* Overture (1957), Six Variations on a Theme of Alfred Hill (1970).

Instrumental *Dryad's Dance*, vn (1936), Sonata in B minor, va (1937), *Passing Thoughts* va (1946), *Serenade* vn (1954), *Nightfall and Merrymaking*, ob (1955), Sonata in G minor, fl (1962), *Sea Shell Fantasy*, fl (1975), *Legend* cl (1982), *Autumn in Princes Gardens*, fl (1983), *Sunlit Waterfall,* hp (1993).

Chamber Sonata in F minor cl, pf (1949, rec. Tall Poppies TP 004), Fantasy-Trio in B minor, vn, vc, pf (1932–33), Trio in G, fl, cl, pf (1948), Trio, Prelude and Scherzo, fl, ob, pf (1952), String Quartet in G minor (1952), *Sailing Boats* fl, ob, cl, pf (1969).

Vocal *c.*40 songs, *The Wind in the Sedges* (1937), *Sunrise by the Sea* (1954), *Winter Willow Music* (1955), *The Illawarra Flame* (1955), *Nightfall by the River* (1955), *Sea Shells*, women's vv, pf (1956) *Elfin Fantasy* (1958), *Green Year* (1988), *Tone Poems of the Sea*, song cycle (1995).

Keyboard *c.*90 works for piano, *The Fountain* (1928), *Forest Echoes* (1928–36), Chorale in D minor, org (1929), Variations and Fugue in C minor (1931), *Rhapsody* in Fs minor (1933), *Concert Study* in Fs major (1935), *The Poplar Avenue* (1936), *Waltz-Fantasia* 2 pf, (1936), *Brownhill Creek in Spring* (1942), *The Forest Stream* (1942), Sonata in G minor (1941–44), *Susan Bray's Album* for left hand (1945), *Magpies at Sunrise* (1946), *Reflected Reeds* (1956), *Grey Foreshore* (1961), *Woodland Sketch* (1966), *Study in Blue, White and Gold* (1969), *Ear Rings from Spain* (1970), *Toccata for Two* pf duet (1973), *Autumn Stream* pf duet (1973), *Water Nymph* (1986), *Scherzo Fantastico* (1986), *Valley of Rocks* (1988), *The Vision of Mary MacKillop* (1992), teaching materials, notably *Miriam Hyde's Graded Piano Series*, 6 vols (Chappell, 1986–87).

FURTHER REFERENCE

Recordings include *Kathryn Selby Plays*, pf (ABC 432 700); *AMEB Compositions*, pf (Cherry Pie 015); *Brownhill Creek in Spring: Australian Piano Music*, pf, includes Sonata in G minor and selected miniatures played by Miriam Hyde (1993, SC 1027); selected piano miniatures, instrumental and chamber works on various JAD recordings; forthcoming anthology of chamber works to be released by Walsingham (1996). Her memoirs are *Complete Accord* (Sydney: Currency Press, 1991). A discography to 1972 is in *PlushD*. See also *CallawayA*; R. Crews, Miriam Hyde and the European Heritage of Australian Music, BA(Hons), Univ. New England, 1987; *CohenI*; *GlennonA*.   RITA CREWS

Hymn. A song sung by the congregation in Christian worship, characterised by a metrical, strophic text and austere four-part harmonic setting. Hymnody spread in English churches following the publication of *Hymns Ancient and Modern* in 1861, which soon became used in Australia; the works of Australian hymn composers appeared in *78 Australian Hymn Tunes* (1892) and the widely used ★*Australian Hymn Book* (1977). See *Church Music*.

Hymnody. The hymnody of Australian churches has always been dominated by overseas repertoire and publications. Nevertheless a strong tradition of Australian hymnody has been evident since 1821, when the first of many local publications of hymns was produced to meet the shortage of hymn books in the colony. Australian

hymnals dating from the latter part of the 19th century reflect a growing perceived need for hymn collections (of non-Australian content) designed to suit the needs and tastes of particular congregations and dioceses. By the end of the century there was also an emerging body of locally composed hymns, often stimulated by important anniversaries or events (which could be of a civic nature). A landmark of Australian hymnody is *Seventy-Eight Australian Hymn Tunes* (1892), which features music by 25 composers from five colonies.

Australian hymnals of the present century include a number of Catholic publications which have aimed to serve changing liturgical needs. The *Catholic Worship Book* (1984) comprises a fine example of hymnody and service music for the post-Vatican II era. Undoubtedly the best-known modern Australian hymnal is the ecumenical *Australian Hymn Book* (1977), along with its companion *Sing Alleluia* (1987). Other Australian denominations to publish hymnals in recent times are the Lutheran (1995), Presbyterian (1987) and the Seventh-day Adventist (1985). There is also a vast body of collections composed or compiled by individuals and serving more general needs, as for example those by Mann (1991), Simper (1988) and Willcock (1995).

Distinguished composers of Australian hymnody include George ★Torrance (1835–1907), A.E. ★Floyd (1877–1974), Dom Stephen ★Moreno (1889–1953), Richard Connolly (*b* 1927), Lawrence Bartlett (*b* 1933), Roger Heagney (*b* 1942), and Christopher ★Willcock SJ (*b* 1947). See *Church Music*.

FURTHER REFERENCE

Current hymn-books are *Australian Hymn Book* (Blackburn: Collins Liturgical, 1977); *Catholic Worship Book* (London: Collins Liturgical, 1984); *Lutheran Hymnal*, 3rd edn (Adelaide: Open Book, 1995); R. Mann, *All Together Now* (Adelaide: Lutheran Publishing, 1991); *Rejoice! A Collection of Psalms, Hymns and Spiritual Songs* (Sydney: Presbyterian Church of Australia, 1987); *Seventh-day Adventist Hymnal* (Warburton: Review and Herald Publishing Association, 1985); D. Simper, ed., *Songs from the Still Strange Land* (Melbourne: Joint Board of Christian Education, 1988); *Sing Alleluia* (Blackburn: Collins Liturgical, 1987); C. Willcock, *God Here Among Us* (Portland, Oregon: OCP, 1995); J. Wood, ed., *Gather Australia* (Ashburton: NLMC Publications, 1995); Young, R.B.

See also D. Gome, 'Australian hymnody 1821–1901: An annotated checklist of sources located in Australian libraries', *Continuo* 24 (1995), 1–28; idem, 'Hymnody in the Australian colonies, 1788–1901: A preliminary investigation of sources and functions of hymns', *Australasian Music Research 1* (1996); W. Milgate, *Songs of the People of God: A Companion to the* Australian Hymn Book/With One Voice (London: Collins Liturgical, 1982); P. Taylor, Twentieth-century Catholic hymnody in Australia: A study of selected published hymnals, 1942–1981, BMus(Hons). Australian Catholic University, 1991; D'A Wood, '*AHB* moves into the next century', *One Voice* 8/1 (1993); 10–12.

        D. GOME

I

I Dips Me Lid.   Popular song by Albert ★Arlen from his musical version of C.J. Dennis' *The Sentimental Bloke*, first performed at Canberra in 1961, then in the J.C. Williamson production of the following years.

I Love Aeroplane Jelly.   Advertising jingle (1930) by Frank Leonard [Albert Francis Lenertz] (*b* 1889; *d* 1943), composed when he was managing director of the Aeroplane Jelly Company, originally as a song in praise of the prime minister, Billy Hughes. When Hughes ignored it Leonard adapted it for advertising, and, recorded by five-year-old Joy Kelly, it was presented on Sydney's 2KY in 1932. The country's first singing commercial, it became immensely popular with a craze at the time for aviation. The manuscript is in the National Library of Australia.

FURTHER REFERENCE
Dale Coulthard, ed., *Australia's Heritage in Song* (Moorooka Qld: Music Store Books, 1988), 82–83; John Bryden-Brown *Ads that Made Australia* (Lane Cove, NSW: Doubleday, 1981), 71

I Passed By Your Window.   Song by May ★Brahe (1916), lyrics by Helen Taylor. Originally published as part of the album *Song Pictures*, by 1919 it was selling at the rate of 200 000 copies per year. It was eventually to sell more than a million copies, having become 'violently epidemic' all over the British Empire. Twenty-seven recordings have been traced for the decade 1917–27, marking the peak of the song's popularity which, unlike ★*Bless This House*, did not survive the advent of the long-playing record. The key phrase of the song's lyrics has inspired cartoons and parodies of all descriptions, including an advertisement for Guinness Stout, while the music appeals through a simple directness.

FURTHER REFERENCE
Percy Scholes, 'Melody', *Oxford Companion to Music*, 4th ed (London: Oxford University Press, 1942), p. 560; Thorold Waters, 'Hysteria about our Musical Taste: Danger of Letting Wrong Impressions go Far Afield', *AMN* (Oct 1927): 1–2; P. Burgis and

Kay Dreyfus, 'May Brahe Composition Discography: A Prototype for Australian Composition Discographies', *Australasian Music Research* 1 (1997).

KAY DREYFUS

I Still Call Australia Home.   Popular song, words and music by Peter ★Allen (1980). Written in the intermission of a concert during Allen's Up In One national tour in 1980, it was presented at his last Melbourne show to enthusiastic response, and became No. 1 in the charts in Australia. Filled with nostalgia for the Australian countryside and its customs, it has come to rival ★*Waltzing Matilda* for recognition as a national Australian song. Published by Rondor Music (Aust.), Sydney 1980.

FURTHER REFERENCE
David Smith and Neal Petrus, *Peter Allen: 'I Still Call Australia Home'* (Adelaide: Souvenir Press, 1983), 125.

I Was Only 19.   Anti-war ballad by the folk-rock band ★Redgum (1983), which tells of a young soldier's experience of the Vietnam War. Recorded by Redgum (CBS 463241), it was No. 1 in the charts for 16 weeks in 1983 and won an ACMA Golden Guitar in 1984. Published Tombola Publishing, 1983.

Icehouse.   Rock band formed in Melbourne (1980) by Iva (formerly Ivor) Davies (*b* 22 May 1955, vocals, guitar, oboe) with John Lloyd (drums), Keith Welsh (bass) and Anthony Smith (keyboard). Under its original name Flowers, the band's debut single *Can't Help Myself* hit No. 10. Their debut album *Icehouse* hit No. 4, and displayed the influence of Brian Ferry and David Bowie on Davies' early songwriting. After signing worldwide with Chrysalis Records in 1981, the band was renamed Icehouse to avoid conflict with the Scottish group the Flowers, and embarked on tours of the UK, USA and Canada. The band's original line-up split in 1982, and Davies recorded *Primitive Man* (1982) alone under Icehouse's name. With the return of drummer John Lloyd and new recruits Guy

Pratt (bass), Andy Quinta (keyboards), Michael Hoste (keyboards) and Bob Kretschmer (guitar), Icehouse played an extensive Australian tour later that year. After supporting David Bowie's tour of the UK and Davies' work on the sound-track of Russell Malcahy's film *Razorback* (1983), Icehouse recorded *Sidewalk* (1984) and *Measure for Measure* (1986) in addition to Davies and Kretschmer's collaboration in writing music for Graeme Murphy's ballet *Boxes* (1985). Icehouse's popularity peaked with *Man of Colours* (1988), which topped the national charts and reached No. 7 in the USA. Singles from this album included *Crazy* which reached No. 4 and *Electric Blue* which was co-written by John Hall and made No. 1. *Man of Colours* was followed by No. 2 hit *Great Southern Land* (1989) and No. 5 hit *Code Blue* (1990). In 1995, Iva Davies and Icehouse composed music for a second Graeme Murphy ballet *Berlin* (1995).

FURTHER REFERENCE

Recordings as Flowers include *Icehouse* (1980, Regular L 37436); as Icehouse *Primitive Man* (1982, Regular RRLP 1204); *Sidewalk* (1984, Regular RRLP 1206); *Measure for Measure* (1986, Regular RML 53180); *Man of Colours* (1987, Regular RML 53239); *Great Southern Land* (1989, Regular TVL 93315/6); *Code Blue* (1990, Regular TVL 93330); *Masterfile* (1992, Massive 780807–0), *Big Wheel* (1993, EMI); *The Berlin Tapes* (1995, Massive 731069–2). See also *GuinnessP*; D. Rees and L. Crampton, eds, *Rock Movers and Shakers* (Santa Barbara, CA: ABC-CLIO, 1991); *SpencerW*.

AARON D.S. CORN

Illing, Rosamund Elizabeth Anne   (*b* UK, 23 Mar. 1953), soprano. Daughter of the musicologist Robert Illing, her family arrived in Australia in her childhood and she studied at the University of Adelaide. She made her debut as the Governess in *Turn of the Screw* at the Barbican, London, then sang with the Welsh National Opera from 1981, the Australian Opera from 1983, the Victoria State Opera, the English National Opera and Covent Garden from 1987, and has also had extensive concert work. With a rich and commanding tone, her roles have included Zerlina, Butterfly, Musetta, Valencienne, Despina, Donna Anna. She has won an Emmy award.

FURTHER REFERENCE

Recordings include Beethoven *Missa Solemnis*, Sydney Philharmonia, Sydney Symphony Orchestra, cond. C. Mackerras (ABC 434 722); Mahler, Symphony No. 2, Sydney Symphony Orchestra, cond. S. Challender (ABC 434 778–4); and *Romantic Concert Arias*, Melbourne Symphony Orchestra, cond. H. Esser (ABC 434 898). See also *CA* (1995/96); *MonashB*.

Ilma.   Public singing and dancing in the Kimberleys. See *Corroboree*.

I'm Talking.   Pop-funk band (1983–87) formed in Melbourne from the electronic experimental dance band Essendon Airport (1978–83). It was comprised of Kate

★Ceberano and Zan (vocals), Ian Cox (guitar, saxophone), Stephen Charlesworth (keyboards), Kevin Wiltshire (keyboards), Robert Goodge (guitar), Barbara Hogarth (bass), and Warren McLean (drums). They toured with the Models in 1985, releasing the single *Trust Me*, which reached No. 10 in the charts and won a Countdown award. A disco band, combining funk dance rhythms, a rock back beat and the charged vocals of Ceberano, they also had hits with *Love Don't Live Here Anymore* (1985), *Holy Word* (1986) which reached No. 9, and their albums *Bear Witness* (1986) and *Dance* (1988).

FURTHER REFERENCE

Recordings include *Trust Me* (Regular RRSP 744), *Love Don't Live Here Anymore* (1985, Regular K9817), *Holy Word* (1986, Regular K39), *Bear Witness* (1986, Regular RML 53202) and *Dance* (1988, Regular L18009). For discography, see *SpencerA*. See also *SpencerW*; *BakerA*, 40–5; Wendy Milsom and Helen Thomas, *Pay to Play* (Ringwood, Vic.: Penguin, 1986); *Melody Maker* 27 Sept 1986, 21.

Immomeena.   Opera in two acts by Moritz ★Heuzenroeder, libretto by H. Congreve Evans. Set in contemporary SA, it was first performed by the Adelaide Harmonie Society in 1893.

In The Head The Fire.   Radio tableaux (1966) by Nigel ★Butterley, with texts from traditional sources (Dead Sea Scrolls, the Latin Mass, Irish). Requiring narrator, soloists, chorus, 23 players (double woodwind, brass, 4 recorders, piano, portative organ, percussion), and tape, it is performed by compilation of 100 separately recorded excepts. Commissioned by the ABC, it was first performed by the Adelaide Singers and members of the Sydney and South Australian Symphony Orchestras, conducted by John Hopkins (1968, World Record Club S2495). It won the Italia Prize for a radio work in 1966.

Incidental Music.   Music written to accompany or intersperse dramatic performances on stage, film, radio or television has as long a history in Australia as elsewhere. Given the focus in such performances on the drama, a great deal of incidental music has been composed without posterity in mind, and has passed into oblivion with little public notice.

Incidental music is known to have illustrated theatre productions in Australia from William Shield's *The Poor Soldier* at Sydney in 1796. The Sydney theatres maintained small orchestras from the late 1830s, with scores provided or embellished by local bandmasters. A great quantity of such music was created for silent film in Australia, and J.C. ★Williamsons, ★Fuller and other early cinema chains maintained cinema ensembles in their cinemas, often of substantial size. Horace ★Keats, Percy ★Code, and William ★Cade were among many to provide music for these venues. The cinema ensembles passed into radio work in the late 1920s. For the theatre Helen ★Gifford and Mara ★Kiek are among the many specialists.

For television and film Eric ★Gross, Peter ★Clinch, George ★Dreyfus, Bruce ★Smeaton, Peter ★Best, Brian May and Paul ★Grabowsky are among those who have provided notable incidental music. Some concert works have been adapted to incidental purposes for radio or television programs, such as Margaret Sutherland's *Haunted Hills.* See *Film Music; Musical Theatre.*

Indian Music. There are over 61 600 Indians in Australia. Indian music in Australia is grounded within the social and cultural interaction that exists between and connects India with its diaspora. On one hand there is traditional and popular music whose source is clearly located within the subcontinent but which in its practice can often vary depending on local circumstances. On the other hand there are genres not specifically centred in India but produced by and consumed within the Indian diaspora and its host communities including Australia, but which are also patronised in India.

The most commonly heard traditional music within the broader Australian community is one of the two distinct systems of classical Indian music. Performers and institutions representing both Hindustani (North India) and Karnatic music (South India) classical traditions in Australia regularly present concerts. The Australian Institute of Eastern Music, Sydney, is the principal teaching and concert organising institute of Hindustani music, while the Academy of Indian Music, Melbourne, is the largest body for the teaching and concert promotion of Karnatic music, and there are also smaller bodies promoting classical music in these and other major cities. Additionally, Indian classical music is periodically taught as part of music programs in universities and schools. Regular tours of visiting classical Indian musicians date from the late 1950s, there is an annual Indian music festival in Bendigo, Vic. (inaugurated 1983), there are broadcasts by ABC and FM subscription radio, and musical accompaniment for the steadily increasing number of Indian classical dance companies in Australia.

Nonetheless, there is a far greater diversity of Indian musical activity in Australia than the twofold system represents. Less known but more active is the devotional and regional music-making of the Indian population, representing six religions, 15 separate languages and a far greater number of distinct cultural groups. Devotional music such as Hindu *bhajans* and Sikh *kirtans* is regularly performed in temples and homes as part of the religious and life rituals of the community. A strong and growing tradition of community music-making, which presents something of the regional music of most of the 27 states of India, has been transplanted to Australia. Additionally, the local and touring performances of *ghazal*, poetic texts in Urdu based on themes of love, and Indian film song genres are highly popular and commercially lucrative.

Over the last 10 years popular commercial genres distilled within the Indian diaspora have also become prominent among the affluent westernised Indian community at nightclubs and formal social occasions. This music, which is generating a growing number of internationally recognised local performers such as Pupinder Mintu, is loosely drawn from folk, religious and film song sources, sometimes combined with Western popular influences. This musical activity is supported by weekly Indian programs on regional radio and the Indian-Australian press.

ADRIAN MCNEIL

Indulkana. Situated in ★Pitjantjatjara land in northern SA, a centre for Pitjantjatjara, Antakarinya and Yankunytjatjara peoples. Much fieldwork and recording has been completed there: the *Talku* (kangaroo rat) songline was performed by Antakarinya men and women and recorded by Catherine ★Ellis in 1968, while the *Langka* (blue-tongue lizard) songline performed by Pitjantjatjara and Antakarinya singers was recorded at Indulkana during 1969, 1970 and 1977. A number of the singers involved at CAAMA come from Indulkana. See *Aboriginal Music.*

Ingram, Lance. See *Lance, Albert.*

Inma (Pitjantjatjara), new Aboriginal songs. See *Aboriginal Music*, §2(i).

Inner Voices. Chamber opera in one act by Brian ★Howard, libretto by Louis Nowra. First performed at Nimrod Theatre, Sydney, on 25 Feb. 1977 and by the Victoria State Opera at the Grant Street Theatre in 1979.

Instrument Collections. Of 225 Australian museums and collecting institutions known to hold musical instruments, fewer than 20 could be regarded as dedicated collections of musical instruments or as having a substantial emphasis on musical instruments in their collections. These include the Powerhouse Museum, Sydney; Darnum Musical Village, Vic.; Grainger Museum, University of Melbourne; Museum, Australian Defence Forces School of Music, Watsonia, Vic.; and collections associated with a significant number of university music faculties, departments, and conservatoriums (Howard, 1997).

Australia's history of museums and collecting institutions is relatively short, dating from the late 19th century with the creation of small natural history museums in the various colonies. These developed in time into the state museums and collections now found throughout Australia. At first, these general collections were conceived as scientific in nature, often with a strong natural history focus, but also with an interest in the extraordinary, the curious, and the mundane. The earliest collection in the Queensland Museum, for example, consisted of 'Curios, Machinery, Weapons, and Furniture'. In this respect, early Australian museums reflected a much older tradition of collecting, the focus of which, in Francis Bacon's words, was to preserve 'whatsoever singularity, chance, and the shuffle of things hath produced'. However in this collecting agenda, musical instruments had only an incidental and peripheral place, along with socio-historical artefacts in general.

The situation for musical instruments has not significantly changed. Today they form the central focus of only a small number of specialist collections, and for the most part musical instruments are only incidentally and marginally represented in more general collections, even if sometimes in significant numbers. Some of the largest holdings of musical instruments are to be found in state museums and collections, but are seldom discrete and separately identified elements within those institutions. Rather, musical instruments are usually to be found distributed through various general collections where they reflect collecting policies and priorities which may have little to do with their identities as musical instruments. For example, the Queensland Museum and the South Australian Museum each hold in excess of 500 instruments, while the Museum of Victoria, the Museum of Tropical Queensland at James Cook University, and the Anthropology Museum, University of Queensland each hold in excess of 200 instruments, the majority in the context of collections of Australian Aboriginal, Oceanic, and Melanesian materials. This reflects the historical development of the large Australian museums, with their strong emphasis on natural history, anthropology, and ethnology.

(i) Aboriginal, Pacific and Melanesian Instruments.
There is a strong representation of musical instruments from Aboriginal, Pacific and Melanesian sources in the dispersed national collection, although the reasons for their collection are often unrelated to their functions as musical instruments. For example, the Queensland Museum holds some 207 long cylindrical and waisted drums, 193 of them from Papua New Guinea, although it appears never to have designed their acquisition for musicological purposes. Generally, musical instruments have been subject to passive collection practices in the past, collected not because they are musical instruments but for other reasons, and have not been recognised as contributing in any special way to the construction of Australian cultural histories. Slowly, however, this is changing, with many institutional collections seeking to explore new ways of presenting and interpreting the diverse cultural meanings of social artefacts (including musical instruments) in their collections.

Although Australian collections are for the most part the result of relatively unsystematic collection practices, they include many instruments which speak profoundly and eloquently of this nation's short cultural history and of the long history of its traditional owners. This is evident in the rich collections of Aboriginal material in institutions including the state collections, as well as collections in educational institutions (notably the Anthropology Museum, University of Queensland, the Berndt Museum of Anthro-

pology, University of Western Australia, and the Museum of Tropical Queensland, James Cook University). Indeed, collectively, this material may constitute the most coherent and significant single part of the national collection.

(ii) Parlour and Anglo-European Instruments.
A great many small collections developed as a result of a major expansion of interest in local and regional historical collections, heritage sites and historical societies over the past 20 years. While this development is admirable for preserving artefacts which might otherwise disappear from the historical record, such collections are often ill equipped to appropriately select, document, conserve and manage musical instruments as a meaningful part of their collections. On the other hand, it is evident that these collections, often situated in regional and rural areas, preserve a somewhat distinctive range of instruments indicative of the musical interests and practices of their historical communities. Strongly represented among them are typical parlour instruments (pianos, pianolas and harmoniums), brass band instruments reflecting the importance of this musical genre in regional towns, and instruments associated with bush bands and private music-making (including a significantly large representation of accordions and related instruments).

(iii) Instruments of Other Immigrant Communities.
As a nation with a long history of diverse migrant settlement, it might be expected that the national instrument resource would reflect that musical diversity. The record here is rather more sketchy and difficult to interpret. Probably the earliest musical records of European contact with the Australian continent consist of parts of a Conrad Drochl (Nuremberg) trumpet dated to 1618 as well as some other musical items retrieved from the wrecks of the *Batavia* and *Vergulde Draek* off the coast of WA by the WA Maritime Museum. Later European settlement is reflected chiefly in the regional and rural collections noted above and in instruments largely from traditions of home and community music-making.

In many ways early urban musical culture appears to differ little from rural culture except for a greater representation of quality keyboard instruments held in various collections (for example, Darnum Musical Village). Nineteenth-century Chinese immigration is represented in a few collections, notably the Golden Dragon Museum, Bendigo, which holds a significant collection of musical instruments, costumes and accessories dating back to 1882 and brought to Australia from China for use by the local Chinese population in Bendigo in its annual processions and celebrations. This community museum is an important example of a small museum which has achieved high standards of museum practice.

More recent immigrant populations are at present poorly represented in Australian collections, although some institutions like the Powerhouse Museum are paying attention to instruments produced by contemporary

Australian instrument-makers from diverse cultural traditions. Interesting examples of instruments of Australian provenance in Australian collections include a chamber tracker action pipe organ dating from 1877 held by the Darnum Musical Village, two *shakuhachis* by Melbourne maker David Brown in the Monash University Japanese Music Archive, a violin and bow from local timbers made around 1900 in Noosa Shire, Queensland, by a local resident and held by the Cooroora Historical Society, an otherwise unidentified instrument described as 'an Australian stringed instrument made from a cigar box' in the Colonial Inn Museum, Mudgee, Queensland, and instruments produced and improvised by Australian prisoners of war in Japanese camps during World War II in the collection of the Australian War Memorial.

(iv) Care, Documentation. An important factor in good collection practices is the work of specialist curators. Only three Australian institutions with significant musical instrument collections appear to have professional curatorial staff with expertise in working with musical instruments (the Powerhouse Museum, Grainger Museum, and Darnum Musical Village). A number of other collections, particularly those in universities, draw on the expertise of academic staff, postgraduate students or community volunteers in honorary or partly paid curatorial roles. But in many cases, they do not have the time or resources to house the collection adequately or maintain it efficiently. The quality of much of the national dispersed collection, however, deserves the professional attention of curators, musicologists and conservators to a greater extent than it receives.

So far, little attention has been given to the study of this national collection. A study of musical instruments in the Queensland Museum by Corn (1995) is one of the first detailed studies and is a model for future work. The *National Survey of Musical Instruments in Australian Collections*, conducted 1993–96, and *Directory of Australian Collections Holding Musical Instruments* (1996) are the first comprehensive attempt at a listing of collections and their holdings.

INSTITUTIONAL COLLECTIONS
(i) Over 500 Instruments
Faculty and Conservatorium of Music, Univ. Newcastle
Powerhouse Museum, Sydney
Queensland Museum, Brisbane
South Australian Museum, Adelaide
(ii) 201–500 Instruments
Anthropology Museum, Univ. Queensland, Brisbane
Darnum Musical Village, Darnum, Vic.
Grainger Museum, Univ. Melbourne, Parkville, Vic
Museum of Victoria, Melbourne
Music Department, Monash Univ., Clayton, Vic
Music Program, Queensland Univ. Technology, Brisbane
Museum of Tropical Queensland, James Cook Univ., Townsville, Qld

(iii) 101–200 Instruments
Australian War Memorial, Canberra
Charles Sturt Univ.—Mitchell, Bathurst, NSW
Faculty of Music, Univ. Melbourne, Parkville
Mitchell Conservatorium, Bathurst, NSW
Museum of Victoria—Scienceworks, Melbourne
National Museum of Australia, Canberra
Northern Territory Museum of Arts and Sciences, Darwin, NT
School of Music, Univ. Western Australia, Perth
Tineriba Tribal Gallery and Museum, Hahndorf, SA
(iv) 51–100 Instruments
Berndt Museum of Anthropology, Univ. Western Australia, Perth
Elder Conservatorium, Univ. Adelaide
Faculty of Education, Central Queensland Univ., Rockhampton, Qld
Gilfedder, Francis, Brisbane
Golden Dragon Museum, Bendigo Chinese Association Catalogue Collection, Bendigo, Vic.
Macleay Museum, Univ. Sydney
Music Department, Univ. Sydney
Penrhos College, Como, WA.
Queensland Conservatorium of Music, Griffith Univ., Brisbane
Sturt Buildings, Flinders Univ. (formerly SA College of Advanced Education), Adelaide
Tasmanian Museum and Art Gallery, Hobart
School of Music, Institute of the Arts, ANU, Canberra
(v) 21–50 Instruments
Army Museum Society, Sydney
Boyd's Antiquatorium, Bundaberg, Qld
Caboolture Historical Village, Caboolture, Qld
Deakin Univ., Burwood, Vic.
Gulgong Historical Society, Gulgong, NSW
James Cook Historical Museum, Cooktown, Qld
Monarch Historical Museum, Williamstown, NSW
Museum, Australian Defence Force School of Music, Watsonia, Vic.
National Gallery of Victoria, Melbourne
Queen Victoria Museum and Art Gallery, Launceston, Tas.
Redland Museum, Cleveland, Qld
Tenterfield and District Historical Society, Tenterfield, NSW
Univ. Western Sydney, Sydney
Western Australian Museum, Perth
Wimmera Mallee Pioneer Museum, Jeparit, Vic.
Yankalilla District Historical Museum, Yankalilla, SA

FURTHER REFERENCE

Arnold-Forster, Kate, and Hélène La Rue, *Museums of Music: A Review of Musical Collections in the United Kingdom* (London: HMSO and Museums and Galleries Commission, 1993).

Australian National Committee for ICOM, *Australian Museums Directory* (Canberra: AGPS, 1972).

Barclay, Robert, *Recommendations for the Conservation of Musical Instruments: An Annotated Bibliography* (CIMCIM Publications No.1. Edinburgh: CIMCIM, 1993).

Corn, Aaron, Musical Instruments in Cultural Heritage Collections: A Case Study of the Queensland Museum. MPhil, Queensland Conservatorium of Music, Griffith Univ., 1995.

Dournon, Geneviève, *Guide for the Collection of Traditional Musical Instruments* (Protection of Cultural Heritage: Technical Handbooks for Museums and Monuments 5. Paris: UNESCO, 1981).

Eliason, Robert E., and Friedemann Hellwig, eds, *Musical Instrument Exhibitions in Scandinavia: A Study of the Basic Concepts, Educational Objectives, and Conservational Techniques of Three Recently Installed Exhibitions*. By the International Committee of Musical Instrument Collections (CIMCIM) of the International Council of Museums (ICOM). *CIMCIM Newsletter.* Special issue, 1986.

Howard, Gregg, 'An Introduction to the *National Survey of Musical Instruments in Australian Collections* and the *Directory of Australian Collections Holding Musical Instruments*', *Australasian Music Research* 1 (1997).

——, and Bradley Young, comps. 'Directory of Australian Collections Holding Musical Instruments', *Australasian Music Research* 1 (1997).

ICOM Asia–Pacific Organisation, *Directory of Museums of the Asia-Pacific Countries*, (ICOM, 1993).

Jenkins, Jean, and International Committee of Musical Instruments in Museums and Collections, eds, *Ethnic Musical Instruments: Identification, Conservation* (London: H. Evelyn for ICOM, 1970).

——, ed. *International Directory of Musical Instrument Collections* (Buren, Netherlands: Frits Knuf for ICOM, 1977).

GREGG HOWARD

Instrument-making

1. Indigenous Instruments. 2. Pianos. 3. Violin Family.
4. Guitars. 5. Orchestral Instruments. 6. Pipe Organ Builders.
7. Folk and Non-Western Instruments 8. Early Music
Instruments 9. Sound Alternatives, Electronic Instruments.

In Australia there is no manufacturing industry for instruments. Making is carried out by a small number of individuals, and instruments from the didjeridu to digital sound producers are hand-made in ateliers. This dynamic, pluralistic musical environment has produced instruments which range from the European folk traditions, the orchestra and the early music revival to the instruments of post-World War II immigrants from around the world.

Australian makers are multi-skilled, idealistic, even reclusive. Their philosophies range from a conservative adherence to tradition to iconoclastic methods and daring innovations. Many began as musicians and came to making either through repairing or improving upon their own instruments. Many were immigrants from an increasingly diverse range of musical backgrounds, with ability and a wish to make the most out of their new environment. In the 19th-century goldrushes and post-goldrush boom, a few immigrants turned to making musical instruments, the life of the goldfields and the new country making inventiveness a necessity. Remoteness from European suppliers brought its own problems, the solutions to which required resourcefulness and ingenuity.

Instrument-makers tend to be self-starters, for formal training for them has never existed in Australia. The Australian maker has usually begun at home, turning the kitchen table into a workbench, converting the garden shed or garage, and possibly later sharing space in a small warehouse. Some have had the opportunity to work as apprentices, formally or informally with established makers. A handful have studied overseas, supported by government grants, and others have gone to Europe to undertake their own research in museums.

Recurrent and juxtaposed themes in Australian musical instrument-making are imitation and emulation, together with innovation and experimentation in meeting the challenge of local conditions. The making of instruments with a long European tradition, such as the violin family and the instruments of early music, while exhibiting some examples of real creativity, has tended to be shaped by the force of their histories. But away from these instruments enthusiastic experimentation can be seen in the invention of new instruments or the development of new technologies or strategies for making old ones.

Until 1940 most instrument-making activity in Australia centred on the piano, the violin and occasionally the guitar. Today, after successive waves of post-war immigration, the emergence of early music as a discipline, the development of cross-cultural music activity, and more recently the pursuit of sound art and world music, the situation has changed considerably.

1. Indigenous Instruments. Instrument-making in Australia began with the activities of the Aborigines. Their musical instruments were mostly idiophones—paired boomerangs (rhythm clappers), paired sticks, rasps, seed pods, and aerophones—the bull-roarer and *didjeridu. See *Instruments, Aboriginal.*

The didjeridu is a natural trumpet, unique among musical instruments in its playing technique. The first stage of its construction is undertaken by white ants, which hatch from eggs under the tree bark; as they grow they eat their way through the hard timber to the core of the tree and turn its branches into pipes. The didjeridu-maker selects a piped branch and works it into an instrument: the bark is removed, the surface smoothed and the inside bore cleaned with a pointed stick and water. Any cracks are sealed with mud or with sugarbag (beeswax). Traditionally, didjeridus were handcrafted for a particular ceremony. Instruments made by Larrtjannga (Melville Bay, NT), George Jangawanga (Maningrida, NT) and David Blanatji (Arnhem Land, NT) are considered to be among the best playing instruments available, but there is a tendency today to produce many heavily decorated instruments for the tourist market. The didjeridu has been the subject of a number of experiments. Mark Atkins plays a diatonic didjeridu with adapted bassoon key mechanisms which permits a range of fundamentals and overtones. There are also players who have experimented with telescopic slide instruments made from PVC, fitted with radio microphones.

2. Pianos.   Piano-making in Australia was a natural outcome of the 19th-century settlers' enthusiasm for their European musical heritage. A flourishing local industry developed in Victoria, built on foundations established by the firms of Wilkie-Kilner & Co., Jabez ★Carnegie (Melbourne), W.R. Blazey (Richmond, Melbourne), Andrew Anderson (Geelong, Vic.) and William Matthew (Emerald Hill, Vic.), all prize-winners at inter-colonial exhibitions. This tradition continued in the early 20th century with a second generation of piano makers, until its decline in the face of the popularity of the wireless and the economic conditions of the Great Depression, coupled with the unpopularity of German products after World War I.

Joseph Kilner and Jabez Carnegie both arrived in Australia in the middle of the 19th century. Kilner had come from England to the Victorian goldfields in 1854 but he turned his earlier apprenticeship with the London firm Broadwood to good use when he began making pianos in Melbourne in 1856. Carnegie, trained with the English firms of Collard & Collard and Broadwood, began making pianos in Melbourne in 1867. The second generation of piano-makers is represented by the sons of Kilner and Carnegie; by Hugo ★Wertheim and his son Herbert; and a former Wertheim employee, Paul Zenker, who teamed up with Carl Schultes in the 1920s. The ascendancy of piano-making also affected NSW, where Octavius Beale, the founder of ★Beale and Co., began making pianos in 1893. The high point of piano-making was the late 1920s, when the Carnegie and the Wertheim businesses and the Beale factory employed around 300 people each.

While all of these piano-makers followed European traditions and styles, especially the German iron-framed pianos, they also responded in different ways to the challenges of Australian conditions. Wertheim was keen to use Australian timbers and floral motifs; Carnegie used Australian timbers in the casework—using veneers from Tasmania of rosewood, mahogany and walnut; the Beale company became renowned for its research and development in the use of Australian timbers which led to the growth of an independent plywood and veneer industry. Beale also invented and patented an all-iron tuning system in 1902, which involved a locking principle to prevent the piano slipping out of tune in sudden weather changes.

Although these businesses did not survive much past the 1930s, fine instruments remain as testimony to the sophistication of the craft in its high period: Beale grand pianos are in both prime-ministerial residences, The Lodge in Canberra and Kirribilli House in Sydney. However, there are instances of renewed interest in making Australian pianos, albeit on an individual level. Maurice Power in Victoria and Tony Caught (NT) are two examples.

3. Violin Family.   The challenges for all violin-makers have been the same: how to accommodate the European tradition within the knowledge, skills and resources available in Australia. The practical problems have also been constant: how to examine the great European violins, how to obtain the timbers, how to develop the varnishes, and how to obtain good tools. Gaining entry into European violin-making schools is seen as a considerable advantage in developing the craft. Apprenticeship with makers like Arthur ★Smith, who made his last violin in 1970 at the age of 89, has provided the nearest local approximation of the training of the European schools.

Smith was the most famous of the emulators, by the late 1920s Australia's best-known maker. He earned his title 'father of Australian violin-makers' not only through his reputation as a maker but also through his training of and associations with a number who went on to independent careers in violin-making—his daughter Kitty Smith, grandson Roderick Smith, apprentices Phillip Burgess and Harry ★Vatiliotis, Charles H. Clarke who worked with him from 1918, Guy A ★Griffin, who worked with him from 1915, Gerard W. Paszek who worked with him after moving to Sydney from Poland via Perth in 1915, then set up his own business in Sydney in 1918, and Arthur H. Patton who joined him in 1923, eventually branching out on his own.

Other makers of the period included John Anderson (Melbourne), William Auchterlonie (Sydney) and Revd William M. Holliday, a champion of Australian timbers. Emulators active today include Mark Pengilley (Blackburn, Vic) and Norman Miller (Toowoomba, Queensland). Those who have sought to take a different approach, emphasising experimentation and innovation, notably through experiments with local timbers, include Kevin Williams (Wooragee, Vic.) and Warren Nolan Fordham (Eltham, Vic.). An important adjunct to the craft of violin-making is that of bow-making; Australia's notable contributor is Jeffrey Ellis (Stanmore, Sydney).

4. Guitars.   The outstanding figure in the history of guitar-making in Australia is Bill May of ★Maton guitars, who began in a garage in 1944 and developed a firm which has produced a wide range of guitars, acoustic, semi-acoustic and electric. The Maton company has always been innovative in its approach: in 1946 May patented the double thrust truss rod, a device which enabled guitar-makers and repairers to ensure a true instrument neck at all times. During the 1980s the company began researching and producing guitar-synthesiser instruments as well as experimenting with rapid wood seasoning techniques.

Australia has many fine acoustic guitar-makers. Greg ★Smallman, for example is the preferred maker of guitarist John Williams. Smallman is an innovator, using carbon fibre lattice bracing in the construction of the guitar belly, a significant breakthrough in world evolution of the Spanish guitar. Smallman guitars have greater projection. Gerard Gilet (Botany, Sydney) makes uniquely Australian slide-guitars, combining local timber and a resonant membrane as part of the soundboard. Other prominent makers of acoustic guitars include Jim Williams (Newcastle, NSW), Robin Moyes (Nowra, NSW), and Scott Wise (Perth). There are two specialist Flamenco guitar-makers, Lindsay Churchland (Surry Hills, Sydney) and Eugene Philp (Armidale, NSW). Guitar-making continues to invite scientific research. In addition to the work of May, the Maton company and Smallman, others like Simon Marty have focused on guitar acoustics, using laser holographic studies of guitar plate vibrations.

5. Orchestral Instruments. Aside from violins there has been little orchestral instrument-making in Australia. Success in the orchestral field has been difficult to achieve while the worldwide market in these instruments is dominated by the European manufacturers. But Ray Holliday and John Lehner (Lilyfield, Sydney) enjoy a worldwide reputation for their flute headjoints; Bill White made some oboes early in the 20th century and his example is being followed today by makers Jack Garraty (Wollongong, NSW), and Tom Sparkes (Sydney), the latter specialising in using both synthetic materials and Australian timbers. Among the percussion instruments the *Drouyn family (South Brisbane) are drum-makers, while Jim Bailey and John White (Adelaide) are makers of marimbas and vibraphones.

6. Pipe Organ Builders. Australia has not had many pipe organ builders, but those who have succeeded are notable for the fine quality of their work, which has won them an international reputation. Ron *Sharp (Sydney) is renowned for his building of the Sydney Opera House instrument, which took 10 years to complete. Other contemporary makers include Knud *Smenge (Melbourne), who brought his Danish experience in organ-building to Australia in 1979, and Roger *Pogson (Orange, NSW), who had been apprenticed to the postwar organ-builder and engineer S.T. Noad.

Organ-building in Australia is not a recent phenomenon. The first pipe organ built in Australia was built by the firm of William Johnson and John Kinloch in 1840. The most enduring business was begun by the prolific George *Fincham, who began building organs in 1865, and is continued by his great-grandson. Smenge worked with the Fincham firm before going out on his own as an independent maker. Innovative responses to the problems of making instruments in Australia can be seen also in the field of organ-building. For example, Fincham stocked Tasmanian blackwood and Sydney cedar, which he considered to be excellent substitutes for Honduras mahogany. Sharpe included in the design of the Opera House organ microprocessors, which enable combinations of stops to be recorded and reloaded from cassette in a few seconds. Coupled with this facility is a recording facility so that the organist can hear back his or her own actual playing. Smenge has vigorously pursued the use of Australian material—native timbers such as blackwood

and myrtle have been consistently employed. Most of his mechanical components have been manufactured locally and the pipework of his organs is made in Melbourne.

7. Folk and Non-Western Instruments. The folk instrument makers of Australia are a diverse group. The term *folk* itself has many meanings, from the bush music tradition and its revival in the 1960s to the multicultural folk music and the folk revival (in particular immigrant communities) of the 1980s and 90s. The making of folk musical instruments is largely free of the prescriptive approach of some of the traditions of orchestral instrument-making: makers are clearly responding to the need of performers in a marketplace defined by the shifting ground of Australian musical activity and the growth and nurturing of the music of ethnic minorities and the emergence of a strong hybrid arts subculture.

(i) Bagpipes and Free Reeds. Bagpipe-making began in Australia during the 19th century with the work of George J. Sherar (*fl.* 1840–80), whose highland bagpipes received numerous accolades at international exhibitions. James Center (Brunswick, Melbourne) came from Edinburgh in 1908 and set up a workshop, making over 50 sets of highland pipes during his career as a champion piper as well as maker. The main focus of pipe-making since Center has been *uilleann* pipes, and Geoff Wooff (Mailor's Flat, Vic.) has become successful in both Australia and Ireland as a maker of a variety of British and Irish pipes. Other pipe-makers include Ian McKenzie (Blackheath, NSW); and Jim Martin (Dee Why, Sydney). Bagpipes of other traditions have also attracted the interest of Australian pipe-makers. Makers of instruments like the Macedonian and Bulgarian *gaida*, the Galician-Spanish *gaita gallega* and the French *chabretta* include Risto Todoroski (Seven Hills, NSW, originally from Skopje); Linsey Pollak (Brisbane); Ian McKenzie and Bill O'Toole (Bondi, Sydney).

The British folk music tradition was reflected in the work of makers such as John Stanley, the 'concertina doctor', who came to the Australian goldfields in 1853. Stanley's Bathurst business is reputed to have made about 500 concertinas. A tradition of concertina and accordion-making has continued into this century with the work of Peter Hyde (Aldgate, SA) and Richard Evans (Bell, NSW). Both have incorporated Australian materials in their instruments. Hyde uses kangaroo leather for the bellows and has developed his own version of the button accordion, the Mallee Grand Organ, a development of a German instrument. Evans uses Australian timber on all the visible parts of his concertinas.

(ii) Stringed Instruments. There is a great range of stringed instruments being made, and numerous examples of ingenuity and application. For example, the *Australele was a simple three-chord zither or autoharp made in the 1930s for amateur music-making. The range of instruments includes folk fiddles, mandolins, the

Melbourne Lithuanian Choir (Melbourno Dainos Samburis), conducted by Albertas Celna, 1976. (Courtesy Birute Prasmutas)

Greek community groups include instrumental ensembles, such as Meraki Ensemble, 1991. (Courtesy Multicultural Arts Trust of SA)

Greek choral groups include Sirens Women's Choir, Adelaide, 1994. Director, Demeter Tsounis (*back, second from left*). (Linda Young)

Irish folk music at the Normandy Hotel, Melbourne, 1996. (Bohdan Ferens)

Dang Kim Hien (moon lute) and Le Tuan Hung (zither) play *nhac Hue*, from central Vietnam. (Courtesy Australia Asia Foundation Archive)

Pipeline Contemporary Music Project (formed 1987), explored the composer–performer interface in live improvisatory collaborations. *R. to l.*: Simone de Haan (director), with Daryl Pratt, Mardi McSullea, Michael Kieren Harvey, and Geoff Dodds. (Australian Music Centre)

Sarah Hopkins performs with her whirly instruments, 1984–. (Paul Guy, courtesy Australian Music Centre)

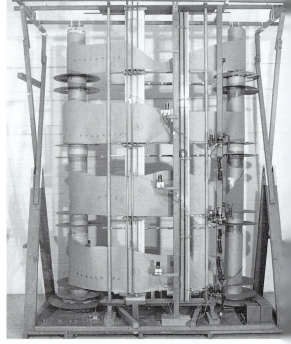

Above: Percy Grainger, Kangaroo Pouch Machine, Free Music Machine, 1952, displayed in the Grainger Museum, University of Melbourne.
(Grainger Museum, University of Melbourne)

Left: Ros Bandt, *Altars of Power and Desire*, 1993, interactive sound installation at Ball State University, Indiana, USA. (Ball State *Daily News,* Oct. 1993)

1888 International Centennial Exhibition
Choir and Orchestra, conducted by
Frederick Cowen, Exhibition Buildings,
Melbourne.
(Grainger Museum, University of Melbourne)

Right: Festival of Perth, established 1953,
presents music in outdoor and indoor
settings. WA Symphony Orchestra plays
in Abbeyvale Vineyard, Yallingup, WA.
(Festival of Perth)

FILM MUSIC

Silent films brought cinema orchestras to every city and town. Lyceum Pictures Orchestra,
Deniliquin, NSW, 1905. (Bicentennial Copying Project, State Library of NSW)

Charles Thatcher, whose songs of the goldfields
(from 1852) entered the traditional heritage.
(Redrawn by Ron Edwards, courtesy Hugh Anderson)

Sally Sloan, Teralba, NSW, from whom more than 150
traditional songs and bush dances were collected by
John Meredith, 1954–61.
(John Meredith Collection, National Library of Australia)

Joe Cashmere, Sylvania, NSW, shearer and bullock teamster,
source of many traditional bush songs and fiddle tunes,
1955–. (John Meredith Collection, National Library of Australia)

Gary Shearston, host of TV's *Just Folk* (1966), one
of the few artists of the folk music revival to achieve
Top 40 success.

Margret RoadKnight, a favourite of the folk movement since the mid 1960s. (Nadège Lamy)

The Bushwackers, 1971. Their songbooks and new (amplified) instrumentation helped popularise folk music in the 1970s. (From *The Bushwackers Australian Song Book*, ed. Dobe Newton and Ian Wositzky. Pub. Anne O'Donovan, 1978)

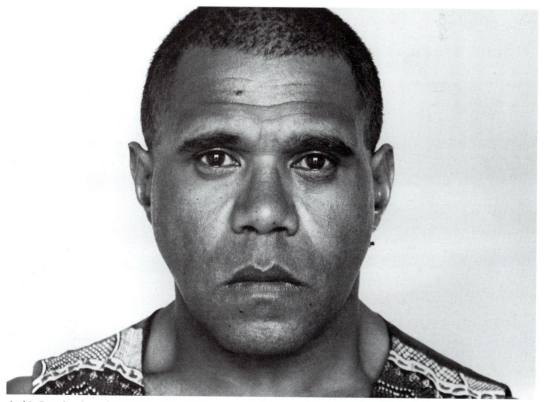

Archie Roach, whose folk ballads of the 1990s mourn the injustice of Australia's treatment of the Aborigines.

George Fincham, one of the oldest of several fine organ-building firms in Australia. Fincham built this two-manual, twenty-stop instrument in 1874 for St Ignatius, Richmond, in Melbourne. (Robert Tobin)

Above & right: Pianos were manufactured using production line techniques in the boom years before radio replaced them as the pillar of home entertainment. At the Beale Piano Factory, Annandale, Sydney, separate teams fixed backs and assembled keyboards.
(Courtesy Michael Atherton)

Below: A.E. Smith, Sydney, who retired at 90 (1970), the most outstanding of Australia's violin-makers.

Fred Morgan, Daylesford, Vic., whose recorders have a worldwide reputation. (Michael Atherton)

William Bright, Barraba, NSW, one of a small number of harpsichord-makers whose instruments have found international admirers.

Bush bass, mainstay of bush bands, although not a traditional bush instrument. (Michael Atherton)

Gum leaf, played by Herbert Patten. (Robin Ryan, Monash University)

Bell carillon at Lake Burley Griffin, Canberra, one of only three in Australia. (Australian Information Service)

Frank Coughlan and the Trocadero Orchestra, *c.* 1936–37. *L. to r.*: Don Baker, Dick Freeman, Reg Robinson, Reg Lewis, Frank Scott, Jack Baines, Bunny Austin, Frank Coughlan, Ted McMinn, Frank Ellery, Colin Bergeson, Jack Crotty, Dave Price, Stan Holland, Billy Miller. (Courtesy Bruce Johnson)

Frank Johnson Fabulous Dixielanders, 1958. Johnson is second from the left. (Courtesy Mike Sutcliffe)

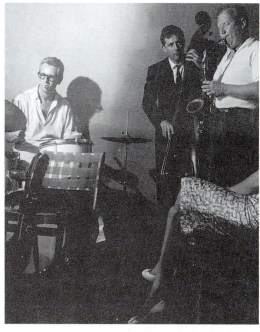

Graeme Bell, 1988 (Jane March, courtesy Eric Myers)

El Rocco, 1958. *L. to r.* Ralph Stock, Cliff Barnett, and Frank Smith. (Courtesy Bruce Johnson)

Frank Traynor's Jazz Preachers, *c.*1978. Traynor is second from the right. (Courtesy Bruce Johnson)

Don Burrows, 1982 (Vicki Skarratt, courtesy Eric Myers)

Ten Part Invention. *L to r.* Ken James, James Greening, Steve Elphick, Sandy Evans, Mivoslav Bukovsky, John Pochée, Bernie McGann, Warwick Alder, Bob Bertles, Roger Frampton. (Courtesy Eric Myers)

John Sangster (Peter Sinclair, courtesy Eric Myers).

Mike Nock (Courtesy Eric Myers)

Several universities have significant archives or collections for music research. The Grainger Museum, University of Melbourne (established 1934), houses manuscripts, correspondence and artefacts of Percy Grainger and his circle. (Garth Kendall, courtesy Grainger Museum, University of Melbourne)

Doyen of Australian musicologists, Professor Andrew McCredie (*second from left*) with colleagues. *L. to r.*, Jan Stockigt, Thérèse Radic and Professor Margaret Kartomi, Monash University (also theatre critic Leonard Radic, *rear*). (Courtesy Margaret Kartomi)

J.P. Deane, a violinist who established his music teaching business at Hobart (from 1822), then Sydney (from 1836).

A.J. Leckie, organist and choral conductor, founded WA Music Teachers' Association in 1910 and was a major influence on music education in WA for thirty years.

John Bishop, founder of the National Music Camps (now Youth Music Australia), conducts the orchestra on the beach at Point Lonsdale, Vic., at the second camp, 1948. (Youth Music Australia)

Sir Frank Callaway, founder of ASME, with colleagues in the Callaway International Resource Centre for Music Education (CIRCME), University of WA. (CIRCME)

Jan Sedivka, at the Tasmanian Conservatorium, a profound influence on national string teaching for thirty years, with his Conservatorium Trio, Beryl Sedivka (piano) and Sela Trau (cello), 1966. (*Mercury*, Hobart)

Greek *bouzouki,* the flat-iron or Irish bouzouki, Turkish *baglama* and *tanbur,* Irish harp, hammer dulcimer, Appalachian dulcimer, bandura, banjo, cittern, African *cora* and the hurdy-gurdy.

Of the plucked stringed instruments, Stephen Gilchrist (Warrnambool, Vic.) has a fine reputation in making carved-top mandolins, which are mostly exported to Nashville, USA. Banjo-making is a speciality of Pat Doole (Geelong, Vic.). Where Gilchrist uses the traditional timbers of spruce and maple, Doole prefers to use local timbers. Other makers of mandolins and banjos include Geoff Bridgland (SA), Taffy Evans (NT), Jakob Stiefel (Vic.), Bernard Besasparis (Qld) and Alan Tomlinson (NSW). Appalachian dulcimer-making was popularised in the 1960s folk revival. Makers include Kevin Johnson (Bellingen, NSW), Geoff Bridgland, Pete McMahon (Balmain, Sydney) and Morgan McKay (Vic.).

In Australia the bouzouki is understandably made for and played by the large Greek community. Bob Meadows is adept at making the bouzouki and the mandolin as well as a range of early music instruments. A popular hybrid instrument has emerged called the Irish bouzouki; this instrument is played in traditional Irish music, bush bands, multicultural ensembles and folk-rock bands. It symbolises the cross-fertilisation of musical styles that is taking place in Australian music. Makers include Graham McDonald (Canberra) and Arnold Black (Hobart).

Irish harps are made by Frank O'Gallagher (Carlingford, Sydney); George Callaghan (Huonville, Tas.); Sean McMullen (Vic.); Bernie Farrow (SA) and Andy Rigby (Melbourne). There are two known hurdy-gurdy makers, Charles Moller (Marrickville, Sydney) and Bob Meadows (Newtown, Sydney). Like the pipe organ, the intricacies of construction attract only the hardiest of instrument-makers. Interest in the hurdy-gurdy in Australia stemmed from its revival in several European countries in the 1970s. Other unusual stringed instruments made in Australia include the Hardanger fiddle (Geoff Bridgland) and the Ukrainian *bandura* (Fedir Deriashnyj).

(iii) Flutes and Reeds.   A similar diversity is evident in the field of folk flutes: from the Italian *zufulo* to the South American clay ocarina and the *shakuhachi.* Included in this group are the folk reed instruments (those without bellows and bags)—the Macedonian *zurla,* Turkish *zurna* and Hungarian *tarogato* made by Linsey Pollak. A variety of folk flutes from local timbers are made by Terry McGee (Farrer, Canberra) and Mark Binns (Perth). McGee makes Irish flutes; and Binns makes wooden whistles, double fipple flutes and the Bulgarian *kaval.*

(iv) Percussion Instruments.   The making of drums and other percussive instruments is flourishing: from the *bodhrans* of Irish tradition to the side drums of Macedonia and Turkey, the *djembe* of West Africa, and the Jamaican steel drum. Other instruments include the African *mbira* and slit drums modelled on those of the Cook Islands and

African-styled marimbas and *balofons.* An early example of local ingenuity was the production of the ★lagerphone or Murrumbidgee River Rattler. The fosterphone, a novel instrument invented by folklorist Ted ★Egan (Alice Springs NT), uses an empty Fosters' beer carton as a percussive accompaniment to singing, reflecting the same qualities of imagination and adaptiveness that have characterised much of Australia's musical instrument-making history and traditions.

8. Early Music Instruments.   The making of early music instruments in Australia is an extension of the European revival of interest in early music from the 1960s. While the approach to the making of these instruments has principally been to emulate the instruments of European history, elements of adaptability and ingenuity are evident. The success of one individual can lead to a wave of enthusiasm in making. From the 1970s John 'Ben' ★Hall inspired several others to develop their interest and nurture their craft through seeking out instrument collections in Europe and studying in instrument-making schools overseas.

(i) Keyboard Instruments.   Harpsichord-making has developed rapidly since 1970, when a group of harpsichord-makers living in and around Clifton Hill, Melbourne, shared ideas and engendered a healthy rivalry. Mars McMillan, Marc Nobel and Alastair McAllister have become highly successful makers and suppliers to individuals and institutions. Whereas the Clifton Hill group are well supported in Australia, Bill Bright (Barraba, NSW) has become Australia's internationally renowned maker, providing instruments for such doyens of European harpsichord playing as Gustav Leonhardt.

(ii) Stringed Instruments.   Undoubtedly, it has been lutes and guitars and the combinations of solo and continuo requirements in early music performance which have provided, until recently, the steadiest market for local makers. As scholarship and performance practice in early music moved its ambit ever closer to the present century, the demand for plucked strings has waned, but during the years 1970–85 all kinds of lutes, ranging from the medieval *ud* through the renaissance types to the chitarrone and theorbo, were being made and played around the country. Classical guitarists, who had until then played only transcriptions, started to explore the lute repertoire on appropriate instruments. As lute-making activity declined, a handful of makers began producing renaissance and baroque viols including Geoff Wills (Lota, Qld) and John Dale (Eltham, Vic.).

(iii) Flutes and Recorders.   There are few makers of recorders in Australia, but Fred ★Morgan (Daylesford, Vic.) and Michael Grinter (Chewton, Vic.) have become internationally successful in this field. Morgan's work has been inspirational to a number of followers such as Joanne

Saunders (Daylesford, Vic.) and Howard Oberg (Belrose, Sydney). Morgan prefers using European timbers to satisfy professional players who demand facsimiles of museum originals.

9. Sound Alternatives, Electronic Instruments. The imagination of Australia's instrument-makers is seen most vividly in the inventiveness with which some have pursued new ideas in sound production and instrument design. Since the 1960s the making of new musical instruments has expressed a combination of inquisitiveness, a search for the new, and in many cases a sense of humour. Behind creations with captivating names from the *Bambooda* to the *Great Jacaranda Mouth Bow*, from *Wind Organs* and *Pot Lid Gamelans*, from the *B-Flat Army Boot* to the *Flagong* lies a talent for creating wizardry from recycled materials. Jon Rose has deconstructed and constructed the violin many times as an essential component of his improvised music.

Australians have also proved to be pioneers in developing the technology of synthesised music. The ★Fairlight CMI was the first commercially available sampling instrument in the world, the 'must have' of contemporary popular music in the late 1980s. It became the first major production instrument in Australia since the piano, but like the piano also suffered a demise. Other notable developments in electronic instruments include the Sentient-6, a guitar synthesiser developed by the now defunct PAS-SAC company, *c.*1987. (See also *Bells in Australia, Organbuilding, Harpsichord-making, Guitars, Recorders.*)

FURTHER REFERENCE

AthertonA; R. Bandt, *Sounds in Space* (Melbourne: Victorian Arts Council, 1985); V. Braden, *Handcrafted Musical Instrument Making in Australia: A Survey for the Crafts Board and the Music Board* (Sydney: The Australia Council, 1982); E.N. Matthews, *Colonial Organs and Organ Builders* (MUP, 1969); B. Ottley, Piano Building in Victoria, unpub., Preston Institute of Technology, 1987.

MICHAEL ATHERTON

Instruments, Aboriginal. Relatively few instruments are found in the indigenous musics of Australia, and in their traditional use are chiefly confined to specific regions. Most are percussion instruments, such as the ★bark pad played by women in eastern and south-eastern Australia, the ★boomerang clapsticks in north Queensland, NT and WA, the ★single-headed skin drum in Cape York and the Torres Strait, the ★hollow log in Arnhem Land and north Queensland, the ★rasp in the Kimberleys, and the ★rattle of seeds or shell found in Cape York. The few pitched instruments are mostly wind, including the blown ★reed or bone pipe of Cape York, the ★didjeridu, and the ★gum leaf. The last was traditionally confined to regions where eucalypts grew but, like the didjeridu, now appears very widely in folk music and non-traditional settings. The ★bull-roarer is of secret significance in Aboriginal ritual. See *Aboriginal Music.*

International Society for Contemporary Music (ISCM). Founded in Europe (1922) by a group including Bartók, Hindemith, Webern and others to further the cause of contemporary music. An Australian chapter appeared briefly in 1928, presenting concerts under the auspices of the ★British Music Society, but had little influence until it was re-established by Donald ★Peart at University of Sydney in 1956. A Melbourne branch followed in 1965, initiated by George ★Dreyfus, James ★Murdoch and others. The two branches presented performances of new works by Australian composers, and selected representatives and scores to send to the annual ISCM festivals in Europe.

In Australia the society's membership was small and the performances were often of a workshop character, although frequently involving the substantial pianistic talents of Richard ★Meale in Sydney and Keith ★Humble in Melbourne. Yet almost all significant Australian composers of the period had works performed at the meetings, and at its height in the late 1960s the society presented featured concerts at the Adelaide Festival and in conjunction with the ABC by the Sydney Symphony Orchestra. By the mid-1970s, however, an increasing number of composers were following mainstream paths they felt were not welcomed by the ISCM; they withdrew from its activities, and the society gradually became marginal. Activities eventually ceased and in 1993 the Australian Music Centre assumed the role of the Australian chapter, nominating works for the ISCM World Music Days.

FURTHER REFERENCE

BrisbaneE, 302.

International Society for Music Education (ISME). Established 1953 in Brussels at an international conference on 'The Role and Place of Music in Education', organised by the International Music Council under the auspices of UNESCO. Bernard ★Heinze was a member of the inaugural board of directors, and Frank ★Callaway, a director from 1958, was president 1968–72, treasurer 1972–88, and succeeded Kabalevsky as honorary president in 1988. ISME holds a biennial International Conference, which has been hosted twice by Australia (Perth 1974, Canberra 1988), and its specialist commissions organise seminars. It has published *The International Music Educator* (1960–72), the *International Music Education Yearbook* (1973–87), its *Conference Proceedings* (1990–94), and *The International Journal of Music Education* (1983–). Australians who have served on commissions include Doreen ★Bridges (Research), Martin Comte (Music in Schools and Teacher Education), William Hawkey, Graham ★Bartle and Max ★Cooke (Education of the Professional Musician), Shirley Harris (Music Therapy) and Olive McMahon (Early Childhood). The latter was elected to the ISME board in 1992.

DOREEN BRIDGES

INXS. Rock band formed in Sydney in 1977 by Michael Hutchence (*b* Sydney, 22 Jan. 1960, vocals), Kirk Pengilly (*b* 4 July 1958, guitar, saxophone, vocals), Garry Beers (*b* 22 June 1957, bass, vocals), and brothers Tim (*b* 16 Aug. 1957, guitar, bass), Andrew (*b* 27 Mar. 1959, keyboard, guitar) and Jon Farris (*b* 18 Aug. 1961, drums, vocals). Originally called the Farris Brothers, the band spent 1978 in Perth developing their songwriting and performance before their debut as INXS at the Oceanview Hotel in Toukley, NSW (1979). Between 1979 and 1983 they played over 200 pub and club gigs a year and built a large following of Australian fans. After releasing four albums throughout the early 1980s, including the No. 3 hit *Shabooh Shoobah* (1982), their fifth album, *The Swing* (1984), topped the national charts. Songs from this album included the No. 1 hit *Original Sin*, and the No. 3 hits *I Send a Message* and *Burn for You*. Later in 1984 they played a three-month tour of the USA, and enjoyed wide television exposure on American MTV. In July 1985 their performance at the Australian venue of the Live Aid concert was beamed worldwide, and their next album *Listen Like Thieves* (1985) topped the national charts. *Need You Tonight* hit No. 1 in the USA, No. 2 in the UK and No. 3 in Australia, while its parent album *Kick* (1987) hit No. 1 in Australia, No. 3 in the USA and No. 9 in the UK. *X* (1990) also hit No. 1 in Australia, No. 2 in the UK and No. 5 in the USA, and was followed by the No. 3 hit *Welcome to Wherever You Are* (1992) and *Full Moon, Dirty Hearts* (1993).

FURTHER REFERENCE
Recordings include *INXS* (1980, DeLuxe VPL1–6529); *Underneath the Colours* (1981, DeLuxe VPL1–6601); *Shabooh Shoobah* (1982, WEA 600133); *INXSive* (1983, DeLuxe SP 245); *The Swing* (1984, WEA 250389–1); *Dekadance* (1985, WEA XS 4); *Listen Like Thieves* (1985, WEA 252362–1); *Kick* (1987, WEA 255080–1); *X* (1990, WEA 903172497–1); *Live Baby Live* (1991, East West 903175630–2); *Welcome to Wherever You Are* (1992, East West 450990493–2), *Full Moon, Dirty Hearts* (1993, East West 450994218–2). See also *GuinnessP*; D. Rees and L. Crampton, eds, *Rock Movers and Shakers* (Santa Barbara, CA: ABC-CLIO, 1991); *SpencerW*.

AARON D.S. CORN

Ipswich, pop. (1991) 71 861, regional city 40 km south-west of Brisbane, Queensland. Free settlement commenced in 1843, with the Municipality of Ipswich being proclaimed on 2 March 1860 and the City of Ipswich on 22 November 1904. The coalmining industry attracted numerous immigrants of Welsh descent who have since the 1880s figured prominently in the city's musical life. The Welsh community of nearby Blackstone was closely involved in the establishment of the annual Queensland Eisteddfod in the mid-1880s, as well as the Blackstone-Ipswich Cambrian Choir, which has enjoyed an uninterrupted history since then. Among its early conductors was Leonard *Francis who led the choir to Eisteddfod successes throughout Queensland and beyond,

including at Ballarat (1908) and Sydney (1910). Later performances included oratorios and operettas and, from 1927, broadcasts for the ABC. Other choral societies active at various times this century include the Welsh Community Choir, Silkstone-Booval Choral Union, Silkstone Apollo Club, and more recently the Junior Cambrian Choir, Ipswich Choral Society and the Ipswich Orpheus Chorale. In addition to hosting the Queensland Eisteddfod numerous times, Ipswich boasts a Juvenile Eisteddfod founded in 1946.

Instrumental music is less well presented by Ipswich institutions of long standing, though the years before World War II saw the existence of the Ipswich Civic Concert Orchestra and several bands including the Vice-Regal Band. Church music in Ipswich has benefited from the significant contribution of people such as F.E. Willesden and Henderson Johnston. The oldest extant organ installed in the state is the Walker instrument (1859) in St Paul's Anglican church. Notable music teachers include Sydney *May (one of the first organisers for the AMEB in Queensland, 1927–53), Ida Ponti, Nancy Jones (née White), and Lyla McGuire, the first visiting music specialist in Ipswich schools for the state education department, c.1940–70.

FURTHER REFERENCE
Percy Brier, *The Pioneers of Music in Queensland* (Brisbane: Musical Association of Queensland, 1962); Robyn Buchanan, ed., *Blackstone-Ipswich Cambrian Choir: A Centenary History 1886–1986* (Ipswich: Cambrian, 1986); Geo. Harrison, ed., *Jubilee History of Ipswich: A Record of Municipal, Industrial and Social Progress* (Brisbane: Diddams, 1910); Leslie Edgar Slaughter, *Ipswich Municipal Centenary* (Brisbane: Slaughter, 1960).

PETER ROENNFELDT

Irish Music. In 19th-century Australia, different social contexts used different genres of Irish ethnic music. Genteel Irish drawing-room songs, especially the songs of Thomas Moore, were favourites at public concerts identifying with Ireland, particularly St Patrick's Day celebrations. Step-dancing to traditional dance music was more frequently performed as physical competition at St Patrick's Day celebrations, and Irish comic songs were part of the popular theatre, often performed by racial-stereotypic characters. Some pipers and fiddlers also toured through popular theatres. Irish-style come-all-ye ballads were important in informal vernacular song creation and performance (see *Folk Music*).

In the late 19th century in Australia, Irish pipe bands formed, inspired by the growth of Irish cultural nationalism. These, and linked Irish language and cultural groups, promoted Irish social dancing, solo step-dancing and music. Incorporating and supporting these cultural enthusiasts, the Catholic Church fostered Irish-Australian identity to establish and defend its role in Australian society. Throughout the first half of the 20th century, as fewer of its laity had direct ties with Ireland, this association with Ireland became increasingly diffuse. The small groups of cultural enthusiasts playing Irish dance music served to maintain a public emblematic Irish cultural presence through performances at concerts and through organised dancing classes.

The new wave of Irish immigrants in the 1950s and 60s included relatively skilled dance music players. The ethnic immigrant community set up sports and social clubs, which used these musicians at social dances, and immigrants encouraged their children to learn Irish step-dancing. Following the revival of traditional music in Ireland in the 1960s, branches of Comhaltas Ceolteóiri Eireann (Irish Musicians' Association) were established in Melbourne and Sydney in the early 1970s.

Active contact between the Australian folk revival and the Irish immigrant community developed in the early 1970s, which led to the use of Irish traditional dance music in the Australian bush bands such as the ★Wild Colonial Boys, and to the prominence of the open social playing contexts known as 'sessions' at folk festivals and venues, featuring such musicians as Declan ★Affley. A movement of dedicated Irish traditional dance music players has developed, mainly Australian-born, but also including immigrant players, who perform with each other at sessions in pubs, and sometimes in organised groups. In the mid-1980s, in response to a new wave of immigrants, many 'ballad bands' were formed, performing in Irish pubs, usually playing popular Irish traditional ballads in the style of the Dubliners, recent Irish popular songs and occasional traditional dance tunes.

In the 1990s, for the general popular listening public Celtic music is a sound in the 'world music' movement and there is an enhanced interest in unaccompanied Irish traditional song. Australian Irish music now includes genres ranging from roistering convivial music in the pubs to ethereal modal vocal melodic music.

FURTHER REFERENCE
Graeme Smith, 'Irish Music in Melbourne, 1950–1980', in *Papers from the Sixth Irish-Australian Conference, 1990,* ed. Phillip Bull (Bundoora, Melbourne: Department of History, La Trobe University, 1992), pp. 217–27; idem, 'Irish meets Folk: The Genesis of the Bush Band', in *Music-Cultures in Contact: Convergences and Collisions,* ed. Margaret Kartomi and Stephen Blum (Sydney: Currency, 1994), 186–203.

GRAEME SMITH

Iron Man, The. Children's opera by Malcolm ★Fox (1986). Staged by State Opera of SA in 1986.

Isaacs, Mark (*b* London, 22 June 1958), jazz pianist, composer. He began piano at the age of six. Composition training with Peter Sculthorpe followed his immigration to Sydney, and he joined Kerrie ★Biddell in 1978, then studied in New York 1979 and Jerusalem 1980. He was with Errol ★Buddle 1981–82, also composing for television and theatre. With the Don Banks Fellowship (1984) he took further study in the USA, where he recorded an

album of his own compositions with Dave Holland and Roy Haynes. His compositions include orchestral and chamber music settings, and his piano concerto was premiered with the St Petersburg Symphony Orchestra during his 1994 Russian tour.

FURTHER REFERENCE,
Recordings include *Originals* (1980, Batjazz BAT-2071); *Preludes* (1987, Jarra Hill JHR 2003); *Encounters* (1988, ABC 846 220–1); *Fire* (1995, ABC Records 4798232); *Air* (1995, ABC Records 4798242); *Water* (1995, ABC Records 4798252); *Earth* (1995, ABC Records 4798262). See also *OxfordJ*; John Shand, 'Mark Isaacs, Between Two Worlds', *APRAJp* 4/2 (Sept. 1994).

BRUCE JOHNSON

Isadora. Light opera in three acts by Luscombe ★Searelle of a melodramatic *Flying Dutchman*-like plot. Retitled *The Black Rover* for the season at Melbourne commencing 7 July 1885.

Island Dance. Group singing and dancing of the Torres Strait Islands peoples. See *Aboriginal Music* § 4(i).

Italian Music. There are 254 700 Italians in Australia, and with their descendants they constitute the largest immigrant group of non-English-speaking background in Australia—approximately 4 per cent of the population. The vast majority arrived between 1952 and 1963. Between the wars northern Italian immigrants predominated, while after 1945 most immigrants were agricultural workers from the poor southern regions of Campania, Calabria and Puglie. By the 1970s immigration had slowed to a trickle, and in the 1990s returnees outnumber new immigrants. A process of chain migration, in which immigrants were sponsored by relatives or friends from the same village, has led to the establishment of distinct Italian neighbourhoods.

Since Italy has an extremely diversified regional culture, immigrants from different parts of the country had little in common, and their regional dialects were often mutually incomprehensible. In Australia second-generation Italians have frequently failed to learn the dialects or the rich vocal traditions of their parents' region, so that the ballads of northern Italy and the *stornelli* of the centre and south are rarely transmitted except in educational contexts. By contrast, Italian dance music brought by itinerant musicians to the Victorian goldfields in the 19th century has sometimes survived in family tradition.

With the adoption of the policy of multiculturalism in the 1970s, pan-Italian identification was encouraged, the Italian language was taught in secondary and tertiary institutions, and a number of Italian-identified performance groups flourished. In the 1970s and 80s in Adelaide a number of groups—including the Italian Folk Ensemble (founded by Antonio Comin), Terra Mia, Compagnia Folk and La Lega—performed traditional Italian songs at Italian community venues as part of theatrical productions, and at multicultural events including National Folk Festivals. Doppio Teatro, an Adelaide Italian theatre group directed by Teresa Crea, has also incorporated traditional song into its bilingual productions. Italian–Australian composer Claudio ★Pompili's suite *La Madonna Emigrante* (1987) was used to accompany a Doppio Teatro production recounting the voyage of a religious statue from a village in Italy to its new home in Australia.

Since most Italians are Roman Catholic, religious occasions such as the blessing of the fishing fleet (which takes place annually in Italian fishing communities from Balmain in Sydney to Fremantle, WA) have provided the occasion for some community music-making, although religious songs are more likely to be in official Italian rather than in regional dialects. Secular choral traditions from northern Italy may be continued by such groups as the Italian Community Choir from Griffith, NSW, while other groups have tried to include repertoire of traditional folk-songs from throughout Italy. Such is the case for Perth's Joys of the Women (*Le Gioie delle Donne*), an amateur singing group founded by Kavisha Mazzella, which was the subject of a successful film of the same name directed by Franco di Chiera (released in 1993).

FURTHER REFERENCE
Linda Barwick, 'Italian Traditional Music in Adelaide', *Australian Folklore* 1 (1987), 44–67; idem, 'Same Tunes, Different Voices: Contemporary use of Traditional Models in the Italian Folk Ensemble's *Ballata grande per Francesco Fantin* (Adelaide, 1990)', *MA* 14 (1991), 47–67; idem, 'Performance Spaces / Imaginary Places of the Tuscan Maggio (sung popular theatre) in Italy and Australia'. Paper presented to the World Congress of the International Council for Traditional Music, Berlin, June 1993; Antonio Comin with Linda Barwick, '*Ballata grande per Francesco Fantin*/Ballad for Francesco Fantin: Text and musical transcriptions as performed in Adelaide 1990', *MA* 14 (1991), 68–84; Andrea Faulkner, 'The Italian Contribution to South Australian Music-Making', in A. McCredie, ed., *From Colonel Light into the Footlights: The Performing Arts in South Australia from 1836 to the Present* (Adelaide: Pagel Books, 1988), 354–69.
LINDA BARWICK

Ives, Joshua (*b* London Hyde, Cheshire, England, 2 May 1854; *d* Kew, Melbourne, 16 June 1931) organist, teacher. After studying with Frederick Bridge and Henry Hiles, he became organist and choirmaster at Anderston church, Glasgow, teaching at the Glasgow Athenaeum from 1879. He took a BMus from Cambridge University (1884) and came to Australia as the first Elder professor of music at the University of Adelaide and jointly as Adelaide city organist in 1885.

In Adelaide he instigated an academic course of the type familiar to him from Cambridge, teaching most subjects himself, and established public music examinations with the University of Melbourne (1887) which became widely popular, later developing into the AMEB. He

appeared as organist and conductor, conducting the featured concert for the South Australian Intercolonial and Jubilee Exhibition in 1887. He absorbed the ★Adelaide College of Music as the Elder Conservatorium in 1897, putting up a conservatorium building (completed in 1900) on the university campus. Difficulties over this and complaints from local teachers over his conduct of the public examinations, exacerbated by his continuing arguments with the University over an array of matters, led to the termination of his appointment in 1901. He settled in Melbourne and taught privately.

An excellent teacher of harmony and counterpoint and a pioneer of the music examinations system, he had an argumentative style which was mourned by few when he left Adelaide. He composed various songs and organ pieces (unpublished).

FURTHER REFERENCE
Doreen Bridges, *ADB*, 9; portrait. in *OrchardM*.

Iwaki, Hiroyuki (*b* Tokyo, 6 Sept. 1932), conductor. He studied at the instrumental music department of the Tokyo University of Fine Arts. In September 1956 he made his conducting debut with the NHK Symphony Orchestra, and in 1963 he assumed the post of conductor of that orchestra; he has toured worldwide with them, now chief conductor for life. In 1988 he founded the Orchestra Ensemble Kanazawa, Japan's only permanent professional chamber orchestra. Iwaki has made an enormous contribution to the Melbourne Symphony Orchestra, making his first appearance as guest conductor in 1972 and assuming the post of chief conductor in 1974, then becoming the orchestra's first conductor laureate in 1987, a title granted for life. He has been instrumental in enhancing the orchestra's profile by raising its standard and initiating the 1987 and 1994 tours of Japan. Iwaki has been very successful in Europe, conducting many of its principal orchestras. In 1978 at the Hessischen Rundfunk in Germany he employed his training as a percussionist and performed in Bartók's *Sonata for two Pianos and Percussion* along with his wife, concert pianist Kaori Kimura.

Iwaki specialises in the late Romantic style and has also conducted many premieres, a symbol of his support of contemporary music. Iwaki is also an accomplished author and in 1991 won the Japan Essayist Club Award. In 1993 he was presented with the NHK Broadcasting Culture Award by the Japanese Broadcasting Co., and in 1985 he was awarded the AM.

FURTHER REFERENCE
For discography see *HolmesC*. See also *Herald-Sun,* 11 Mar. 1995; Manfred Karallus, 'Wettstreit am Schlagzeug: Rundfunkkonzert in der Alten Oper mit Hiroyuki Iwaki', *Das Orchester* 32 (June 1984), 553–4.
NATASCHA SCHMIDT

J

Jackson, Ronal (*b* Bathurst, NSW), baritone. After working as a real estate agent, his singing at army concerts and with the ABC Military and Dance Bands during World War II led him to postwar study at the NSW State Conservatorium. He won the ABC Concerto and Vocal Competition in 1948 and the first Mobil Quest in 1949. After lessons in London he toured with the Carl Rosa Opera Co. for two years, then went to Vienna on the Richard Tauber Scholarship. Despite guest appearances at Covent Garden and with the Welsh National Opera, he preferred work in the various German centres, notably the Kiel Opera and Wuppertal Opera. He returned to Australia in 1960 for the Elizabethan Theatre Trust Opera, and after many appearances in opera, concerts and television he became head of the opera school at the NSW State Conservatorium until 1980.

FURTHER REFERENCE
MackenzieS, 190–1; *AMN* 46 (Feb. 1956), 12.

Jacques. See *Neild, James Edward*.

Jacques, Judy (*b* Melbourne, 17 May 1944), jazz singer. She was with the Yarra Yarra Jazz Band 1960–63, and for their subsequent reunion concerts. From television and club work she broadened her work into experimental music at La Mama and the Clifton Hill music centre, Melbourne, performing increasingly experimental work with Barry Veith from 1977, and teaching at the Victorian College of the Arts. Elected to the Montsalvat Jazz Festival Roll of Honour in 1992, she has composed and performed her own and currently leads the Wild Dog Ensemble, working with Bob ★Sedergreen, Brian ★Brown and others, and developing multi-media improvisational projects.

FURTHER REFERENCE
Recordings include *Winged Messenger*, Brian Brown Quartet with Judy Jacques (1987, AIJA 004); *The Yarra Yarra Reunion Band Featuring Judy Jacques* (1994, Newmarket NEW1041.2). See also

OxfordJ; Thérèse Radic, ed., *Repercussions, Australian Composing Women's Festival and Conference, 1994* (Melbourne: National Centre for Australian Studies, Monash Univ., 1994), 173.

BRUCE JOHNSON

Jamaican Rumba. Two-piano work for four hands, best-known piece of Arthur ★Benjamin (1938).

James, Ken (Kenneth Ian) (*b* Sydney, 4 Jan. 1944), jazz reeds player. He freelanced as a reeds and flute player in early 1970s, then joined Judy Bailey 1974–77 and played with Bernie ★McGann in the Last Straw 1975–78. He lead several groups, then formed his Reunion band with John ★Pochée in 1982. The band played concerts, broadcasts, and festivals, and supported visitors such as Eddie Daniels, Herb Ellis, and Monty Alexander. He has also appeared with Herbie Mann and Stephane Grappelli, and is a founder member of Pochée's Ten Part Invention. His primary activity is in studio and session work, and he also teaches jazz privately and in jazz clinics.

FURTHER REFERENCE
Recordings include *One Moment*, The Judy Bailey Quartet (1974, Philips 6357 018); *Colours*, Judy Bailey Quartet (1976, Eureka E-103); *Ten Part Invention* (1987, ABC/Phonogram 846 729–2); *The Last Straw* (1990, Spiral Scratch 0005); *Tall Stories*, Ten Part Invention (1993, Rufus/Polygram RF006). See also *OxfordJ*.

BRUCE JOHNSON

James, W(illiam) G(arnet) (*b* Ballarat, Vic., 1895; *d* Sydney, 10 Mar. 1977), pianist, composer. He studied piano at the University of Melbourne Conservatorium, graduating with honours, and in 1914 went to London and studied with Arthur de Greef. He performed with the Queen's Hall Orchestra, conducted by Sir Henry Wood, and toured the UK with artists such as Tettrazini, Kubelik, Kreisler, Edna Thornton, and Australians ★Florence Austral, Peter ★Dawson, and Marie Hall. His career was cut short when he had to cancel his first

European tour to return to Australia for family reasons. From 1935 to 1957 he was the first federal director of music for the ABC.

As a composer he is mainly remembered for two works, *Fifteen Australian Christmas Carols*, to texts by John Wheeler, and a ballet suite, *By Candlelight*. James began composing while in London and wrote a musical fantasy called *The Golden Girl*, some ballet music, and *Six Australian Bush Songs*. He was also under contract to Ricordi publishers to provide each year a number of original vocal works. When he returned to Australia he wrote orchestral suites, song settings and several keyboard miniatures. His songs are considered his most successful compositions, often displaying a direct, unforced quality and memorable tunefulness, and his *Christmas Carols* are unique in the way they present the Christmas story in an Australian context. James can be regarded as one of the pioneers of broadcasting, bringing to Australia many of the ABC's early international performers, but being a product of his time and conservative in his tastes, he tended not to actively encourage them to present any significant 20th-century repertoire.

FURTHER REFERENCE
Obit. in *APRAJ* 2/3 (June 1977). Recordings include *15 Christmas Carols* Adelaide Singers, SA Symphony Orchestra, cond. P. Thomas (1969, HMV OCSD 7672); other recordings (now rare) are listed in *PlushD*. See also *GlennonA*, 163.

PAULINE PETRUS

Janes, (Colin) Roger   (*b* Bristol, England, 24 May 1942), jazz trombonist. He began trombone at the age of 19 while living in Colac, Victoria. Moving to Melbourne, he worked in traditional groups, among others with Maurie ★Garbutt. He went to Sydney then to England in 1967, where he toured with Graeme ★Bell then with Garbutt, with whom he returned to Melbourne and later performed for reunion work. In Sydney again, he joined Geoff ★Bull in the mid-1970s. He began leading his own groups in 1978, with residencies including Unity Hall Hotel, Balmain, and he has also performed in Japan, the USA and Africa. An eclectic player and singer, he is active in Sydney leading, freelancing and working with Tom ★Baker's groups.

FURTHER REFERENCE
Recordings include *Alvin Alcorn with the Yarra Yarra Jazz Band* (1973, Emulation EMU-001); *The Roger Janes Band* (1981, Jazznote JNLP 028); *The Yarra Yarra Reunion Band Featuring Judy Jacques* (1994, Newmarket NEW1041.2). See also *OxfordJ*.

BRUCE JOHNSON

Jasek, Ladislav   (*b* Monna, Czechoslovakia, 1929), violinist. After attending the Prague Academy of Music he won a government grant for three years of advanced study in 1952, during which he gave concert performances throughout Czechoslovakia. He played as a guest with a number of European and British orchestras, and after tortuous negotiations with the (Communist) Czech Government, John Bishop was able to bring him to Australia in 1959 to teach at the Elder Conservatorium. There he featured in a Czech festival of music, became leader of the Elder Quartet and founded the ★Elder Trio, the latter making tours and broadcasts for the ABC and Musica Viva. In 1962 he was obliged to returned to Prague; there he was resident soloist with the Czech Philharmonic Orchestra and toured Europe. In 1966 he taught at the University of Auckland, NZ, and then was guest concertmaster with the Royal Philharmonic Orchestra and London Mozart Players. A profoundly gifted player and chamber musician of the first rank, he eventually settled in Australia as concertmaster of the Elizabethan Theatre Trust (Sydney) Orchestra and from 1983 with the Adelaide Symphony Orchestra.

FURTHER REFERENCE
Recordings include Bach violin concertos, with Josef Suk (1966, Supraphon SUAST 56672). See also Murray Bramwell, 'Adelaide's Amadeus, the Salzburg of the South?' *Symphony Australia* (1991), 14–16; Christopher Symons, *John Bishop: A Life for Music* (Melbourne: Hyland House, 1989), 219–21, 236–37.

Jazz

1. History. 2. Audience, Institutions, Events. 3. Styles and Characteristics.

1. History. (i) Beginnings to 1929.   The emergence of jazz in Australia as a clearly identifiable genre can be placed in the years immediately after World War I. Johnson (1987) calls this period 'the first wave', and historians cite several performances which can be regarded as significant markers, among them those by Belle Sylvia and Her Jazz Band in Sydney in 1918, publicised as 'Australia's first jazz band', and those by Frank Ellis and His Californians, who visited from the USA in 1923. Such events, with their impact on the broader community, together with the social interaction between Americans and the impressionable Australians during and after the war, and the increasing exposure to the new world of American entertainment generally, resulted in jazz soon becoming the principal popular music in the nation.

Although no recordings exist of the earliest attempts by Australians to play the 'hot' new music (which at first often included comic costumes and theatrical antics), it is likely that they were crude imitations of the American models. Historians suggest that the distinguishing features of jazz in Australia in the 1920s were its rhythmic aggressiveness and lack of subtlety, paralleling the new American dance crazes which quickly overtook the more refined styles from the old world. With only spasmodic visits by overseas performers and limited exposure to the music on recordings (from 1927 for a time a tariff on imported recordings limited their availability), the enthusiasm of musicians wanting to learn was, understandably, not yet matched by skill or knowledge of the idiom. Nonetheless early small-group jazz was infectious in its novelty and vitality and ideally suited the Australian tendency to 'have a go'.

The late 1920s were times of great change. With broadcast radio well established and the arrival of the 'talkies', the novelty and vitality of jazz was soon in competition with other new forms of entertainment, and the Great Depression which followed radically changed the character of popular music. The early 1930s was no time for joyous and raucous music; the majority turned to quieter, more calming forms. Sentimentality was the order of the day, and with it came the era of the American popular song. Again, what became fashionable in America quickly became so in Australia. In terms of popularity, jazz suffered a setback from which it never fully recovered.

(ii) The Swing Era, 1930–45. As the effects of the Depression diminished, the 1930s saw the emergence of swing, a term given to the dance music of the day but one which, like jazz itself, defies precise definition. It may best be described as a more refined, more widely appealing jazz idiom which contrasted with the earlier style of extrovert, collective improvisation: the label 'swing' suggested a new, modern genre to which the younger generation could relate. Despite arguments that it commercialised and sanitised the earlier Black American styles, the rise in popularity of the swing band did much to renew public interest in the essential character of jazz, the antithesis of the sentimental, saccharine popular song which had satisfied the needs of those who had lived through the Depression. Among the most notable Australian bands which fall comfortably into the category of swing were those led in the 1930s by Frank ★Coughlan and Jim ★Davidson. Such bands enjoyed immense popularity in the major dance venues of Melbourne and Sydney and through live radio broadcasts. Bisset (1979) writes colourfully of the period, describing the high energy and unfettered willingness of Australians to play both the earlier and the newer styles.

Another milestone in the changing face of jazz in Australia was a concert in 1941 of 'hot jazz' presented by the Contemporary Art Society in Melbourne featuring Graeme ★Bell's Band, Don ★Banks, and others in a jam session. The intention was to highlight the essence of jazz improvisation, and thus draw a clear distinction between jazz and other forms of popular, commercial music, including swing. Bell and Banks would become major figures in Australian music, the former in jazz and the latter in the classical music world; Banks's *Nexus* (1971) for jazz quintet and symphony orchestra remains one of the few major Australian works in the concert repertoire which successfully fuses the classical and jazz idioms. The World War II years saw the general public look mainly to sentimental music, as it had in the time of the Depression. At the same time, the American armed forces visiting Australia wanted to hear the dance music and jazz sounds

of their homeland. They had a strong influence, especially amongst musicians, and many local musicians sat in with visiting American bands, resulting in a revitalisation of jazz and an improvement in the quality of performance.

(iii) After the War, 1945 to 1960. It was not long however before the schism between jazz and popular dance music widened. After the war, when the swing bands became less fashionable, those interested in music for its own sake rather than for its attachment to other forms of entertainment pursued jazz with a greater focus on its real essence, spontaneous improvisation. It is in this period that Australia produced its first outstanding jazz musicians: alongside Bell and Banks were such names as Benny ★Featherstone, Ade ★Monsbourgh, Roger ★Bell, Tom ★Pickering and Jack ★Brokensha. Both the traditionalists and modernists among them helped to establish the country's future directions and identity in the idiom.

The two main streams, traditional and modern, moved further away from the notion of popular music and into a more defined jazz environment. Traditional jazz in the late 1940s coexisted with the new bebop movement, whose musicians were driven by a desire to reject any hint of commercialism. There was a defiance in bebop which can be traced to black American musicians and its leading exponent Charlie Parker, who made a distinctive musical and social comment on the times. The music, with its generally fast, non-danceable tempos and new language, was an ideal way for contemporary jazz players in Australia to distance themselves from both traditional jazz and popular music. Musicians at the forefront of the new jazz included Wally ★Norman (and his Be-Boppers), Splinter ★Reeves (and the Splintets), Banks (and his Boptet), Bruce ★Clarke and Charlie ★Blott.

A good indication of the state and variety of jazz in Australia in the late 1940s and early 50s is the programs put together for what might be called the Era of the Jazz Concert. It was an era brought on mainly by the gradual decline of older-style large dance venues, where bands and repertoire had not kept pace with the times. These concerts, often held in town halls, featured both traditional and modern groups: it was not uncommon to hear on the same program Frank ★Johnson and his Fabulous Dixielanders and a quartet led by Alan ★Lee which played in the style of America's Modern Jazz Quartet. It was an era which did not survive beyond the mid-1950s; its demise can be attributed to the nature of the musical content—short, predictable formal structures, a repertoire in the older styles which barely changed, and a musical language and format which was losing its broad appeal. The new sounds of modern jazz alone could not attract large audiences.

The music now began to be heard in more intimate surroundings—jazz clubs and small dance venues which promoted either traditional or modern jazz, the latter by now made up of combinations resembling the Benny Goodman/Lionel Hampton small ensembles falling loosely under the title swing, and more radical-sounding groups which took their inspiration from bebop. The large venue concerts became the domain of visiting jazz greats from abroad. These cannot be underestimated for their effect on the local scene: Louis Armstrong, Ella Fitzgerald, Gene Krupa, Stan Kenton, Buddy Rich, Dave Brubeck, followed later by names such as Dizzy Gillespie, Thelonious Monk, Oscar Peterson. All were an inspiration to the local musicians, many of whom played as supporting acts in the concerts, at a time when the rest of the world was being swamped by the new force in popular music, rock and roll.

Notwithstanding the occasional, short-lived crossover musics like fusion, and jazz's learning from rock's use of amplification and technology, it was rock and roll and the more commercially packaged pop which drove the most profound wedge between jazz and other non-classical genres. Jazz retreated into a world where there was less need for compromise. In this sense rock was a blessing in disguise for the creative, improvising musician, and may be one of the catalysts in the development of new styles and languages in jazz in the future. One consequence was the opening of several important jazz clubs, the El Rocco in Sydney, Jazz Centre 44 in Melbourne, the Cellar in Adelaide, where musicians such as Don *Burrows, Frank *Smith, John *Sangster, Judy *Bailey, Brian *Brown and Stewie *Speer presented the new jazz music of the time on a regular basis. It was in these and similar venues that the modern tradition born of the bebop movement moved into newer and more diverse areas.

(iv) 1960 to the Present. From the time these clubs began to promote more personal, modern styles of jazz there can be no simple outline of developments. The 1960s saw several changes occurring in the direction of contemporary jazz, the first in repertoire generally, brought about by jazz musicians' gradual disinclination to continue drawing so heavily on the standards of the 1930s, the music of Gershwin, Kern, Porter and others. A small but dedicated group were inspired by the new ideas and sounds of Miles Davis and John Coltrane. Modal jazz and extended forms, which for some would eventually lead to free jazz, were breaks from the stylised language of bebop. Others were taken with the music and styles of Dave Brubeck, Paul Desmond, George Shearing and the excursions of Stan Getz into bossa nova. Thus the 1960s was a period of great activity, with a new breed, among them Dave *Levy, Bruce *Cale, Roger *Frampton and Bernie *McGann, together with some of the older-generation modernists like Charlie *Munro exploring new pathways.

Since the 1970s the various streams of jazz and improvised music have broadened further to embrace musical elements of many countries. Multicultural Australia has been an ideal artistic environment for the continuous injection of new elements into the improvised world of jazz. The younger generation of musicians are now embracing the musical sounds and concepts of many countries, including those of Greek, Indian and Asian origin, well beyond the sambas and bossa novas of South America which musicians such as Burrows and George Golla have brought to jazz in Australia. This has inspired further the tendency since the 1960s for musicians to write and play their own compositions.

Australian jazz is an excellent window through which to view a country which, while still paying excessive homage to overseas genres, is now looking more to the creative output of its own people. While history is not ignored—jazz in Australia still acknowledges the traditional and contemporary concepts of its African-American source—the influence of the country's multiculturalism makes the idiom an ideal medium for the pursuit of an individual voice and style in music. At the same time it reflects the character and identity of the Australian culture.

2. Audience, Institutions, Events: (i) Jazz in Australian Society. Jazz is an essentially urban music, and consequently exists mainly in the capital cities of each state, in Sydney, Melbourne, Adelaide, and to a lesser extent in Brisbane, Perth and Hobart. To varying degrees most of the styles which have existed throughout the history of jazz are still played and listened to today. Some traditional players and audiences cling feverishly to the glorious past, others uphold the African-American traditions of the modern varieties, still others choose to pay less attention to the past and pursue the notion of improvisation without the safety net of history or a heavy reliance on external influences.

The place of jazz in society can be identified by bodies of ardent fans who have as their main source recordings, the listening experience of which is enhanced by an ever-increasing number of festivals around the country, and a small number of jazz venues which cater for traditional or contemporary jazz. Few venues, especially those catering for contemporary styles, could be said to be secure in their dedication to the well-being of the music, for there is inevitably financial risk in presenting this type of music. Consequently there is a tendency, with few exceptions, for the music to 'move around' as the availability of performing spaces changes.

Jazz has a small public following in Australia compared to the popular music genres. It is less clear how it fares against classical music in terms of live performance, for some varieties of jazz can be heard live in the capital cities most nights, although in venues that are small compared to those used for concerts of established symphony orchestras and chamber music groups. Most musicians who play jazz are, by necessity, involved in other activities. They come from all walks of life, and especially in traditional jazz circles they indulge in their art on a casual, part-time basis. Jazz has the nature of a minority music which has now taken its place in society. Many of those involved in the contemporary idiom supplement their income by teaching. The two main styles of jazz, traditional and modern, are separated not only by musical language and time but also by their respective devotees, a division not dissimilar to that which can be found in the classical world between lovers of the traditional repertoire and those whose interest lies in contemporary music.

(ii) Radio, Journals, Conferences. Jazz broadcasts on radio are limited to the ABC and several smaller community radio stations which run by subscription. Jazz on television is limited to 'one off' events and occurs infrequently. Retail outlets for recorded music focus largely on popular and classical music, but usually have a jazz section, sometimes quite extensive. Outlets which cater for jazz exclusively are rare, Sydney's store Birdland and Melbourne's Mainly Jazz being among the few that are well established. The print media pay comparatively little attention to jazz save for reviews of selected performances and recordings by casual contributors. Journals and periodicals on jazz have had a tenuous existence, although in more recent times small periodic publications and newsletters such as *Jazzchord,* produced in the government-funded offices of the national jazz co-ordinator have some permanency, as does the *Jazz Educators Journal* which emanates from America but includes occasional articles on Australian jazz.

An annual conference on jazz, Jazz Australia takes place in Perth at Edith Cowan University's Academy of Performing Arts, bringing together musicians from around the country and overseas and is important as an ongoing source of information and in raising the profile and status of the idiom. The place of jazz in society and education is acknowledged by government bodies, state and federal. The latter's Australia Council disperses funds for the promotion of concerts, touring nationally and internationally, composition, recording projects and festivals. The Australian Music Centre in Sydney ensures that the works of Australian jazz musicians are well documented in print and on recordings.

(iii) Courses, Funding. Since Don Burrows instigated the first jazz studies course in Sydney's Conservatorium in the early 1970s, jazz studies programs have been established in many tertiary institutions around Australia. This has helped to create a new breed of musician who has either embraced the jazz idiom wholeheartedly or has taken some of the ingredients from the genre and set out on his/her own creative journey. Mainly through the development of these programs in an 'academic' environment, the number of women in jazz continues to grow, in what has long been a male-dominated world. Significant, too, is the increasing number of postgraduate theses on aspects of Australian jazz and related improvisatory musics being written in Australia's leading universities.

Several important large groups have emerged in the last two decades which confirm the trend towards a more home-grown form of jazz and a more established place for it in society. Among them are the Sydney-based group Ten Part Invention led by John ★Pochée and Roger ★Frampton, the Australian Art Orchestra led by Paul ★Grabowsky and with a personnel drawn from various parts of the country, and various groups led by Melbourne's Brian ★Brown. With few exceptions all the music played by these groups is composed by the performers. One of the best examples of this increased profile can be seen in the activities of the government-funded Australian Art Orchestra with its ongoing charter and commitment to produce Australian jazz and take it into new artistic territories, including dance and theatre. Although jazz remains firmly in the shadow of popular music, and is less well treated than classical music in terms of financial support, its place in Australian society is assured as long as the creative process in the arts continues to be regarded as fundamental to education and to the well-being and development of the culture.

3. Styles and Characteristics. By its very nature, traditional jazz has not changed significantly over the years. However, despite the close ties with the early American models in terms of instrumentation, formal structures and general mood, perceptive listeners may hear in Australian performers and groups qualities which reflect characteristics of the Australian culture, suggesting that Australians assimilate rather than imitate when embracing ideas and styles from elsewhere. It seems logical and reasonable to suspect that a borrowed musical genre, especially one so open to manipulation as jazz, will take on some of the unique qualities of its new home. It is not a flight of the imagination to suggest that Australian traditional jazz bands have a certain humour to them, and a freshness of approach, down-to-earth to be sure, but not weighted down by convention or history.

If these characteristics are difficult to perceive aurally, then the writings of Graeme Bell (1988), Dick ★Hughes (1977) and John Sangster (1988) will help to alleviate any doubts about the unique qualities of Australian jazz musicians. The music of Dave ★Dallwitz, the Bells, Monsbourgh, Pickering, Bob and Len ★Barnard, while firmly entrenched in the traditional idioms of Dixieland, New Orleans and Chicago jazz, has not only personal idiosyncrasies but also characteristics suggestive of the culture in which it was born. They can best be described as having a somewhat carefree, open approach to performance and materials, tinged with a hint of friendly defiance of the original, 'authentic' style. This is true also in the music of John ★Sangster, and such newer groups as Clarion Fracture Zone, The catholics and Musiikki-Oy. All have moved away to varying degrees from the African-American models of jazz. They also have a freshness and vitality not always apparent in the music of countries with longer artistic traditions. If one hears in this music aspects which suggest the flaunting of conventions from elsewhere, they should be seen above any other considerations as products of the culture.

The group Art Attack, formed by Bob ★Sedergreen in the 1980s, exemplifies in the most obvious way the multicultural make-up of Australia, with musicians from many different cultures, including one from Australia's indigenous Aboriginal culture. The musical content, although jazz-based, allows for each member of the group to infuse performances with musical elements of their own particular culture. The music and concepts of Brian ★Brown represent perhaps the most decisive move away from the American notions of jazz. While his music is still based on improvisatory and rhythmic elements traceable to the jazz tradition, his chord structures show a distinct departure from those of jazz and his melodies are gestural rather than tied to a pulse. In these respects it reflects more his Anglo-Saxon background than the influences of African-American jazz. Other important contributors to the myriad of styles include Grabowsky, John Rodgers, and David Jones, who in language, formal structures, concepts, and technique in the broadest sense of the term, connect elements of African-American music with those of European classical music, European jazz and the music of non-Western cultures.

At the same time the trend towards original music in preference to jazz standards has not dulled enthusiasm for the post-1960s harmonic language. As evidenced in Pressing (1994), tonal and pan-tonal melodies and harmonic movements still abound, as does a predilection for short formal structures in keeping with the tradition. However, within these confines there often exists a freer, more asymmetrical approach to phrase structures and overall design. Such characteristics can be seen in the works of Mike ★Nock, Roger ★Frampton and Dale ★Barlow. While some of the works of Judy Bailey hark back to an earlier 1960s language, with their tonal, functional harmonic movement, the music of Sandy ★Evans, although maintaining the spirit and rhythmic energy of jazz seems to look with more complex time-signatures and absence of chord movements beyond the jazz tradition and into the music of other cultures. To varying degrees the young, emerging jazz-based musicians are embracing these styles and ideas, promoting constant change and diversification and at the same time, somewhat paradoxically, defining more clearly the character and identity of Australian jazz and its offshoots.

FURTHER REFERENCE
Select Discography
(i) Anthologies
Australian Jazz 1947–1950 (1947–50, BMG 74321105302); *Bonfa, Burrows, Brazil* (1978, Cherry Pie Records, SPCD 1084); *Jim McLeod's Jazz Tracks* (1981, ABC 838 832–2); *Tasmanian Jazz Composers Vol 1* (c.1992 Little Arthur Productions 01); *Wangaratta Jazz vol. 1* (1991, Subaru Jazz, SJ001).
(ii) Individual Artists
Judy Bailey & Friends, *Sundial* (1993, ABC 5149718–2); Dale Barlow, *Horn* (1990, Spiral Scratch 003); Graeme Bell *The EMI Australian Recordings* (1947–52, EMI CDAX 701583); Brian Brown, *Spirit of the Rainbow* (1989, Move Records MD3085); *Don Burrows vol. 1, 1944–1965* (ABC 4796712); *Don Burrows vol. 2, 1967–1976* (ABC 4796702); *Don Burrows vol. 3, 1977–1979* (ABC 4796732); *Don Burrows Vol 4, 1980–1984* (ABC 4796742); *Don Burrows, vol. 5, 1985–1992* (ABC 4796752); *The catholics* (1991, Spiral Scratch, Sydney, 0011); Clarion Fracture Zone, *Blue Shift* (1990, ABC 846221–2); Bruce Clarke, *Soft Winds* (1979, ABC 846224–2); Crossfire, *Tension Release* (c.1991, East West 903174300–2); Paul Grabowsky, *The Moon and You* (c.1990, WEA 171142–2); Paul Grabowsky, *Ring The Bell Backwards* (1994, Origin OR008); David Jones, *Atmosphere Flying* (1993, Tall Poppies TP038); James Morrison, *Two the Max* (1991, East West 903177125–2); Musikkii-Oy, *Without Warning* (1992, unlabelled); Mike Nock, *Touch* (1993, Birdland Records BL001); Bernie McGann, *Ugly Beauty* (c.1991, Spiral Scratch 0010); John Pochée, Roger Frampton, *Ten Part Invention* (1987, ABC 846729–2); Ren Walters, *Start* (c.1992, Newmarket 1016); *Yarra Yarra Reunion Band* (1994, Newmarket 1041–2).

Bibliography
Australian Compositions: Jazz (Sydney: Australian Music Centre, 1978).

Bell, Graeme, *Australian Jazzman* (Sydney: Child & Associates, 1988).

Bisset, Andrew, *Black Roots, White Flowers* (Sydney: Golden Press, 1979).

Hughes, Dick, *Daddy's Practising Again* (Sydney: Marlin Books, 1977).

Jazzchord (Sydney).

Jazz Educators Journal.

Johnson, Bruce, *The Oxford Companion to Australian Jazz* (Melbourne: OUP, 1987).

Linehan, Norm, *Norm Linehan's Australian Jazz Picture Book* (Sydney: Child & Henry, 1978).

McLeod, Jim, *Jim McLeod's Jazztrack*. Sydney: ABC Books, 1994.

McMillan, Ros, 'A Terrible Honesty': The Development of a Personal Voice in Musical Improvisation, PhD, Univ. Melbourne, 1996.

Mitchell, Jack, *Australian Jazz on Record 1925–1980* (Canberra: AGPS Press, 1988).

Pressing, Jeff, *Compositions for Improvisers: An Australian Perspective* (Melbourne: La Trobe Univ., 1994).

Sangster, John, *Seeing the Rafters* (Ringwood, Vic: Penguin Books, 1988).

Whiteoak, John, Australian Approaches to Improvisatory Musical Practice 1836–1970: A Melbourne Perspective, PhD, La Trobe Univ., 1993.

Williams, Mike, *The Australian Jazz Explosion* (Sydney: Angus & Robertson, 1981).

TONY GOULD

Jazz Action Societies. Although jazz societies date from the 1930s in Australia, the Jazz Action Society movement differs in several respects, not the least of which is its lobbying for funding from government agencies. The first Jazz Action Society was established at Sydney in 1974, publishing a journal and presenting monthly concerts for which recordings were sometimes made. It was followed by the establishment of similar bodies throughout the country, reflecting the spread of jazz activity to regional centres. Many of the societies bear the same name although they have no formal affiliation.

FURTHER REFERENCE
Recordings from the NSW society include *The Jazz Action Sessions vol. 1* (1983, 2MBS-FM Jazz-2/3). See also *BissetB*; *OxfordJ*.
BRUCE JOHNSON

Jazz Centre 44. Founded in Melbourne by Horst Liepolt in 1957, with the Graham Morgan Quintet. Brian Brown later became central in the venue's progressive jazz programs, which included poetry and jazz presentations from 1960. Liepolt moved to Sydney in 1960, where he made a major entrepreneurial contribution, before settling in New York in 1981. After his departure from Melbourne traditional jazz gradually predominated, taking over completely from 1963. Until that time Jazz Centre 44 was the main centre for Melbourne's progressive jazz movement, nurturing the musicians who led the movement until the 1980s. By 1966 the venue was moribund.

FURTHER REFERENCE
BissetB; *OxfordJ*.   BRUCE JOHNSON

Jazz Co-ordination Programs. First established with Australia Council funds in 1983, a jazz co-ordinator was appointed in each Australian state to provide information and services which might help local jazz musicians and organisations to achieve their objectives. Eric Myers has held the NSW position since its inception, receiving supplementary state funding since 1984 and editing *Jazzchord*, and in 1986 he took on the additional position of national jazz co-ordinator, publishing the *Australian Jazz Directory*. With proliferating jazz education courses, these programs have stimulated increased institutional recognition of jazz in Australia.

FURTHER REFERENCE
BissetB.   BRUCE JOHNSON

Jazz Spectrum. Ballet by television band leader Les Patching (1963), choreography by Betty Pounder. Commissioned by the Australian Ballet and first performed at the Adelaide Festival in 1964.

Jazz Venues. Despite its abundance of fine jazz musicians, Australia has not had a history of enduring interest in jazz performance by its cabarets, coffee houses and nightclubs. An important early outlet was the Fawkner Park Kiosk, Melbourne (1936–41); the Stage Door cabaret supported jam sessions by the small Hobart jazz community in the 1930s; and the Story Bridge Hotel, Brisbane, presented its 'Storyville' traditional jazz most weeknights 1955–59. But ★El Rocco, Sydney

(1955–69), pioneered the club format as a setting for new jazz developments in Australia, featuring many innovative visiting artists and launching the careers of several significant experimenters. The Tivoli Theatre, Adelaide, hosted traditional and mainstream jazz in the same period, then from 1962 The Cellar and a succession of venues called the ★Tavern catered to traditional jazz in Adelaide until 1968. Modern jazz was presented in the Shiralee and similar coffee lounges at Perth in the early 1960s. In Melbourne, ★Jazz Centre 44 (1957–66) soon became a leading venue, notable for embracing a very wide range of styles, and as its tastes narrowed to traditional jazz the Fat Black Pussycat (1963–66) became a centre for contemporary jazz. More recently, the Vanity Fair Hotel, Sydney (1970–86), home of the long-running Eclipse Alley Five, presented both traditional and modern jazz. The most significant venue today is the ★Basement, Sydney (founded 1973), home of ★Galapagos Duck and chiefly a forum for contemporary jazz.

Jazz-Rock (Fusion). A style beginning in the 1970s in the playing of Americans Herbie Hancock, Chick Corea, John McLaughlin and others, in which jazz solo improvisations are accompanied by the electric and electronic instruments and rhythms of rock music. In Australia there were many hard-edged bands including jazz-rock in their work in the 1970s; ★Galapagos Duck have created a more soft-edged and enduring jazz-rock style.

Jefferies, R(ichard) T(homas) (*b* Middlesex, England, 2 Nov. 1841, *d* Brisbane, 4 Aug. 1920), conductor, violinist, organist. Established professionally in London as a violinist, violist, conductor and organist of distinction, he arrived in Brisbane on 11 September 1871, destined to be referred to as 'the father of music in Brisbane'. He introduced public recitals to the city in 1872, formed Brisbane's first permanent string quartet in 1876, and conducted the debut performance of Brisbane Musical Union in 1872. The union was the direct progenitor of the Queensland State and Municipal Choir, and its orchestra became the Sampson Orchestra, of which the Queensland Symphony Orchestra is the immediate descendant. In 1873 he was appointed organist and choirmaster at St John's Church (the Pro-Cathedral), where he laid the foundations of future liturgical excellence. As a composer, an early work was chosen as 'Australian National Anthem' at the laying of the foundation stone at the Academy of Music, Melbourne on 24 May 1876.

FURTHER REFERENCE
Robert Boughen, *ADB*, 9.   BARBARA HEBDEN

Jeffery, Bob (*b* Adelaide, 28 Dec. 1941), jazz reeds player. He began alto saxophone at the age of nine (later adding bass). Drawn to jazz but with few opportunities presenting themselves, he worked in rock groups including Penny Rockets and Hi Marks, and toured with

Johnny O'Keefe. The Cellar provided a progressive jazz forum to which he became central. From the late 1960s he was more active in pop music, but a renewal of public interest in jazz again gave him a lengthy residency at the Gateway Hotel and numerous local Jazz Action Society Concerts, including backing Milt Jackson, Georgie Fame, and on bass with Ruby Braff.

FURTHER REFERENCE

Recordings include *Sue Barker* (1977, Crest CRT-036); *Jazz in South Australia,* Southern Spectrum (1987, Larrikin Records LRJ 231).   BRUCE JOHNSON

Jennings, Herb (Herbert Vincent)   (*b* Melbourne, 21 July 1942), jazz trombonist. He began serious trombone study in 1969, and that year gave the first of his many performances at the ★Australian Jazz Convention, where he has also won composition awards. Adding saxophone, singing, composition and arrangement to his repertoire, he formed the Golden City Six in 1970, and with variations of this band has led jazz activity in Victoria's central highlands, where he is based. He has led the band at residencies, television appearances and festivals in Australia and overseas. He has recorded Australian jazz compositions and compiled a chord book.

FURTHER REFERENCE

Recordings include *The Golden City Seven* (1980, Anteater 001 and 004); *Winners—Australian Jazz Convention Original Tune Competition,* Golden City Jazz Band (vol. 1 1992, Eureka Jazz, EJCD 1, and vol. 2, 1993, Eureka Jazz EJCD 2); *We're Unplugged Too* (1995, Eureka Jazz EJCD 3). See also *OxfordJ.*
                                        BRUCE JOHNSON

Jewish Music in Australia.   Jewish religious observance in Australia ranges from the ultra-Orthodox to the Progressive. Australian Jews are predominantly Ashkenazi, of Central and East European ancestry, and mostly concentrated in the urban centres, the two largest communities being in Melbourne and Sydney. In Melbourne especially, ultra-Orthodox and some Orthodox congregations closely retain their East European roots by using Yiddish-influenced pronunciation and tunes, many of which are generations old and orally transmitted. More recently, American and Israeli influences have also been filtering into services.

Australia's oldest synagogues are Anglo-Jewish and moderately Orthodox. Musically, they follow the British model of the German Ashkenazi tradition, with male choirs usually being an integral part of the service. For these congregations *The Voice of Prayer and Praise*, the so-called 'Blue Book', provides the basis of the choral repertoire for every congregational occasion throughout the Jewish year. Originally compiled in 1887 by Rabbi Francis Cohen, chief minister of the Great Synagogue, Sydney, the book consists of a selection of compositions by Lewandowski, Sulzer, Mombach, Naumberg and others as well as traditional melodies arranged in four-part vocal style. Progressive congregations have a repertoire comparable to the British model for their mixed choirs. The first Ashkenazi synagogues were established in 1844 in Sydney and in 1845 in Hobart; the latter still stands and is the oldest synagogue in Australia. Public prayer service can also be held in a *shtibl* (room set aside for that purpose) in any private premises, as long as there is a *minyan* (quorum of 10 males over the age of 13) available to take part.

The few Sephardi groups, of Mediterranean ancestry, at first had the choice of forming their own *shtibl minyans* or attending Ashkenazi synagogue services and risking loss of their own traditions. In 1962, however, the first Sephardi synagogue was established in Sydney, with another in Melbourne some years later. Although the Sephardis may be relatively small in number, many are strongly committed to maintaining their ancient Hebrew melodies and rituals.

In both types of congregation cantors lead the services, which include call and response patterns, congregational singing, and on Mondays, Thursdays, Saturdays and festivals, reading from the *Torah* using prescribed incantations. Australian synagogues without a professional cantor usually have one or more congregants who are confident about their vocal ability and thoroughly conversant with the melodic nuances of Jewish liturgy to assume the cantorial role. In some synagogues the rabbi is the cantor. Ashkenazi cantors sing with an almost operatic tone quality, range and use of virtuosic melodic embellishment; Sephardi cantors sing with a more constricted throat, their melodies often having the nasal quality, narrow range and types of scale associated with Arabic music. Traditionally, a cantor has always been male, but since the 1960s Progressive congregations in Australia have accepted female cantors. Progressive services also include instrumental accompaniment, usually on the organ; men and women may sit together during services and choirs are mixed. For all Orthodox congregations, however, the *shofar* (ram's horn) is the extent of instrumental usage in religious services, blown during the month leading up to and including the Jewish New Year; men and women are segregated, and choirs, where they exist, are usually all male.

FURTHER REFERENCE

Cohen, Rabbi Francis L., and David M. Davis. *The Voice of Prayer and Praise: A Handbook of Synagogue Music for Congregational Singing*, 3rd edn (London: Office of the United Synagogue, 1958).

Gallou, Laura, ed., 'A Bibliography of Australian Judaica. Second Revised Edition', in *Studies in Judaica*, 4, The Mandelbaum Trust and the University of Sydney Library, Sydney 1991.

Rubinstein, Hilary L., *The Jews in Australia: A Thematic History,* vol. 1 (Melbourne: Heinemann, 1991), Chs 4 & 5.

Rubinstein, W.D., *The Jews in Australia: A Thematic History,* vol. 2 (Melbourne: Heinemann, 1991), Ch. 3.

Segaloff, Benjamin, *Jewish Choral Music in Victoria* (Southland, Vic.: Benjamin Segaloff, 1993).

Solomon, Miriam, 'Music and Musicians of the Great Synagogue, Sydney (1878–1974)', *Journal of the Australian Jewish
Historical Society* 11/6 (1993), 896–920.

BRONIA KORNHAUSER

Jigsaw. Pop group (1968–78) formed in Melbourne
by Johnny ★Chester as his backing band, comprised originally of Ray Eames and Ron Gilby (guitars), Dennis
Tucker (bass), and Ollie Fenton (drums). They gained a
following in their own right, their *Yellow River* reaching
No. 1 in the charts in 1970, *How Do You Do?* reaching No.
11 in 1972, and *A Rose Has To Die* reaching No. 9 in 1974.
With a style combining rock and roll with country music,
their later singles were less successful; they then played in
Melbourne pubs and disbanded in 1978.

FURTHER REFERENCE
Recordings include *Yellow River* (Fable FB 018), *How Do You Do?*
(Fable FB 105), *A Rose Has To Die* (Fable FB 218). A compilation
is *Best Of Jigsaw* (Fable). For discography, see *SpencerA*. See also
McGrathA; *SpencerW*.

Jim Jones (of Botany Bay), folk-song. Set to a version of 'Irish Molly-O', a convict transported to NSW
vows revenge against the cruelty of his captors. Collected
by Goulburn squatter Charles MacAlister and published
in his *Old Pioneering Days in the Sunny South* (1907); a
fuller text was published by John Meredith in *Bushwacker
Broadsides* (1954).

FURTHER REFERENCE
Edition and commentary in *EdwardsG*; *ManifoldP*.

Jimmy and the Boys. Rock group (1975–82)
formed in Sydney, comprised of Ignatius Jones [Juan
Ignacio Esteban] (vocals), William O'Riordan (keyboards), Steven Hall and Rick Sutton ['Joe P. Rick']
(guitars), Danny Damjanovic (saxophone, flute), Michael
Parks (bass, vocals), Michael Vidale (bass) and Scott Johnson and Barry Lytten (drums). At first a jazz-rock band,
with Jones playing the drag queen 'Joylene Hairmouth',
they pioneered camp theatrical antics for pop bands in
Australia. Their single *They Won't Let My Girlfriend Talk To
Me* reached No. 8 in the charts in 1981. A deliberately
jarring mix of styles, their albums included *Not Like
Everyone Else* (1979) and *In Hell With Your Mother* (1982).
They toured Australia in 1980, and went into abeyance
while Jones appeared in *Rocky Horror Show* (1981–82).

FURTHER REFERENCE
Recordings include *They Won't Let My Girlfriend Talk To Me*
(Avenue K8271), *Not Like Everyone Else* (1979, Avenue L37141)
and *In Hell With Your Mother* (1982, Avenue SBP 237865). For
discography, see *SpencerA*. See also *McGrathA*; *SpencerW*.

Jo Jo Zep and the Falcons. Rhythm and blues-
reggae band (1976–82) formed in Melbourne, originally

comprised of Joe Camilleri (vocals, saxophone, guitar),
Robert Price (vocals), Jeff Burstin (guitar), Wayne Burt
(guitar, vocals), John Power (bass, vocals), and Gary Young
(drums). The first of their 12 singles, *Beating Around The
Bush* (1976), and their album *Don't Waste It* were released
in Europe and Australia. *So Young* reached No. 29 in the
charts in 1978, *Hit And Run* reached No. 12 in 1979, and
All I Wanna Do No. 34 in 1980. Their album *Screaming Tar-
gets* reached No. 13 in the album charts in 1979. They
toured Europe and the USA in 1980, their membership
and sound changing significantly in 1981. At first a
rhythm and blues band, they absorbed reggae and latin
influences; they disbanded once Camilleri appeared with
his own band from 1982.

FURTHER REFERENCE
Recordings include *Beating Around The Bush* (1976, Oz OZ 001),
Don't Waste It (Oz, OZS 1003), *So Young* (Oz OZ 11794), *Hit And
Run* (Mushroom K7525), and *All I Wanna Do* (Mushroom
K7897). A compilation is *The Sound Of Jo Jo Zep And The Falcons*
(1983, Mushroom RML 53117). For discography, see *SpencerA*.
See also *McGrathA*; *SpencerW*; *GuinnessP*, II, 1287.

Johnnys, The. Rock band (1982–88) formed in Sydney by Roddy Radalj (vocals), Paul Doherty (guitar),
Spencer Jones (piano, guitar, vocals), Graham Hood (bass,
vocals) and Billy Pommer (drums). At first a punk trio
who dressed as cowboys, they transformed their style into
the goodtime rock typical of the period. They have made
11 singles.

FURTHER REFERENCE
Recordings include singles *I Think You're Cute* (1983, Regular
RRSP 728), *Showdown* (1986, Mushroom K9940), and *Anything
Could Happen* (1988 Mushroom K671); albums *Highlights Of A
Dangerous Life* (1986, Mushroom L42004) and *Grown Up Wrong*
(1988, Mushroom L38917). For discography, see *SpencerA*. See
also *SpencerW*.

Johnson, (Anthony John) Bruce (*b* Adelaide 30
September 1943), jazz trumpeter, scholar. After studies at
the University of Adelaide and University of London he
taught in schools from 1965, and became lecturer (later
senior lecturer) in English at the University of New South
Wales from 1972 (head of the school 1984–86). A sensitive trumpet and flugelhorn player, largely self taught, he
appeared in local bands at Adelaide dances from 1965, at
the Velvet Tavern, then in Sydney at the Vanity Fair Hotel
(for 14 years) and Soup Plus (for 12 years), as well as in
Britain during his visiting lectureships and fellowships. He
has worked with Graeme ★Bell's All Stars, Dick ★Hughes's
Famous Five, and other groups, and appeared as support in
tours by Stan Getz, Chris Barber and Turk Murphy.

A prolific jazz scholar, he edited the Sydney Jazz
Club *Quarterly Rag* (1978–85), wrote *The Oxford Companion to Australian Jazz* (Melbourne: OUP, 1987) and
has contributed numerous articles to *New Grove Dictio-*

nary of *Jazz*, *Jazzline*, *Contemporary Music and Popular Culture*, *Meanjin*, and other journals. He has arranged jazz broadcasts on 2MBS-FM since 1978. Chairman of the National Jazz Alliance since 1993 and chairman of the NSW Jazz Co-ordination Committee since 1989, he is currently resident at the Evening Star Hotel, Surry Hills, with Eclipse Alley Five, and can be heard on their recordings.

Johnson, Frank (Francis Walter) (*b* Melbourne, 22 May 1927), jazz trumpeter. He began cornet in 1944, and inspired by Graeme *Bell founded his Fabulous Dix-ielanders with Geoff *Kitchen in 1945, playing its debut at the Eureka Hot Jazz Society. In 1947 the band began a dance residency at the Collingwood Town Hall which lasted until its dissolution. Other significant engagements were the Maison de Luxe in Elwood, and numerous other town hall jazz concerts, in which they were frequently poll winners. Through its lifetime Johnson's band included Doc Willis, Nick Polites, Ken Evans, and the exuberant trombonist, pianist and vocalist 'Wocka' Dyer, who was killed in a road accident returning from a rural engagement in 1955. Although he was replaced by Frank *Traynor, Dyer's death led to the band's break-up the following year. Johnson went on to form a succession of groups, then joined a dance band 1959–61, after which he returned to jazz, playing in casual work, concerts and occasional recordings.

During its lifetime Johnson's Fabulous Dixielanders was among the most celebrated bands in Melbourne, taking over from Graeme Bell's groups to lead the second generation of the revivalist movement. In the late 1980s Johnson moved to Noosa, Queensland, where he continues to work casually and to organise jazz performances and local festivals. He has also been closely connected with the Australian Jazz Conventions and occasionally active as a jazz writer.

FURTHER REFERENCE
Recordings include *Frank Johnson's Fabulous Dixielanders 1951–55* (1982, Swaggie S-1319); *Dixieland Jazz, Frank Johnson's Fabulous Dixielanders 1954–56* (Swaggie S-1325); *Frank Johnson Takes Off With Triad* (1963, Astor ALP-1015). An interview with him is in *WilliamsA*, 8–13. See also *BissetB*; *OxfordJ*.
                                                    BRUCE JOHNSON

Johnson, Gertrude Emily (*b* Hawksburn, Melbourne, 1894; *d* Melbourne, 28 Mar. 1973), coloratura soprano, opera school director. After studies at the Albert Street Conservatorium with Ann Williams and Melba, she appeared with the *Gonzalez Opera Co. on tour in Australia (1917) and the *Rigo Grand Opera Co. (1919), in principal parts including Gilda, Violetta and Nedda. She went to London in 1921 and was soon engaged for the new British National Opera Co., appearing in opera throughout Britain in the following years as well as in concert at the Albert Hall, Queens Hall, and the

Salzburg Festival. With a sparkling voice of purity and charm, she was especially noted in Mozart as Queen of the Night or Constanza, but was also a Marguerite (*Faust*) or Micaela (*Carmen*).

She returned to Melbourne in 1935 with a scheme for a national theatre, which would offer seasons of full-scale opera, ballet and theatre productions so that young artists would not need to go abroad for their formative stage experience. Her *National Theatre Movement opera seasons began in 1938 and by 1949 could boast substantial government assistance as well as a large public following. Her venture provided debuts to a host of Australian singers who later had international careers and directly influenced the formation of the *Australian Elizabethan Theatre Trust in 1954, the opera company which became the Australian Opera.

Despite invitations to join with the Trust, Johnson pressed on with her own venture to the end of her life, and a permanent National Theatre at St Kilda was finally finished and opened in 1974, a few months after her death. By this time her schools had lost their position at the centre of the national theatrical life.

FURTHER REFERENCE
Roger Covell, *GroveD*; John Cargher, *Opera and Ballet in Australia* (Melbourne: Cassell, 1978), 21–7; Thérèse Radic, 'The Australian National Theatre Movement as the Catalyst for The Australian Opera: Tug-Boat to Flagship', in *One Hand On the Manuscript: Music in Australian Cultural History 1930–1960*, ed. Nicholas Brown et al. (Canberra: Humanities Research Centre, ANU, 1995), 201–16; Frank van Straten, *Stages* 1993; Katerina Persic, Gertrude Johnson: A Portrait, BMus, Univ. Melbourne 1993; *MackenzieS*, 122–6.

Johnson, Kevin, popular music singer–songwriter. Writing rock and roll songs from the early 1960s for Col *Joye and other *Bandstand* regulars, he released his own album, *In Quiet Corners Of My Mind*, in 1969 and produced 19 singles, including *Bonnie Please Don't Go*, which reached No. 15 in the charts in 1971. *Rock And Roll (I Gave You All The Best years Of My Life)* reached No. 4 in the charts in 1973 and was recorded very widely by other artists. Becoming more middle-of-the-road, he toured Europe extensively 1975–82, making *Spirit Of Time* in 1985. He received an APRA award in 1976.

FURTHER REFERENCE
Recordings include *In Quiet Corners Of My Mind* (Sweet Peach), *Bonnie Please Don't Go* (Sweet Peach SP 108), *Rock And Roll (I Gave You All The Best years Of My Life)* (Good Thyme GTR 1001), and *Spirit Of Time* (Festival). A compilation is *Best Of Kevin Johnson* (1979, Infinity L36945). For discography, see *SpencerA*. See also *McGrathA*; *SpencerW*; *GuinnessP*, II, 1298.

Johnston, Cynthia Anne (*b* Launceston, Tas., 8 May 1932), soprano. She studied at the NSW State Conservatorium and in London and made her debut with the Elizabethan Trust Opera Company in 1962 as Violetta in *La traviata*. From 1965 she sang in the UK, principally with Sadler's Wells Opera, and in 1971 returned to the Australian Opera where her many roles included Susanna in *The Marriage of Figaro*, Despina in *Così fan tutte*, Papagena and Pamina in *The Magic Flute* and Golde in *Fiddler on the Roof*. In 1984 she became adviser to the Australian Opera's young artists development program and was awarded the AO in 1992.   MOFFATT OXENBOULD

Jones. Family of musicians at Geelong, Vic.

(1) Percy Jones [Senior] (*b* Melbourne, 1 Jun 1885; *d* Geelong, Vic., 8 Oct. 1948), cornettist, bandmaster. As a child he played cornet and appeared as conductor of St Augustine's Boys' Band, Geelong, winning the band championships at the South Street Eisteddfod, Ballarat. With funds raised by public subscription he went to Vienna in 1908, studying at the Leschetiszky school. He returned to Australia in 1911, teaching piano and wind instruments in Geelong and Melbourne. He conducted the Geelong Citizens' Band and various school bands, and was music master at Geelong Grammar School (from 1932), then taught at Geelong College. Two of his sons became musicians, Percy (2) and Basil (3).

(2) Fr Percy Jones (*b* Geelong, Vic., 14 Jan. 1914; *d* Geelong, 11 Dec. 1992), musicologist, church musician. Educated by Christian Brothers, Geelong, he had his music education at the hands of his father (1). At the age of 16 he was sent by Archbishop Mannix to study for the priesthood in Rome and to prepare himself to undertake in the Melbourne archdiocese the application of the norms for sacred music propagated by Pius X in the decree *Tra le Sollecitudini*. He studied at Propaganda College, Rome, where he took the then existing course work Doctorate in Philosophy. Theological studies at All Hallows' Dublin followed, and he returned to Australia in 1939 after gaining the SacMusDott from the Istituto di Musica Sacra, Rome, for a thesis on the *Glosses de Musica* of John Scotus Erigena.

With a nucleus of boys from the Mozart Vienna Boys' Choir, stranded in Australia at the outbreak of World War II, he developed Saint Patrick's Cathedral choir, which he directed 1942–73. For parish and school use, he published two hymn-books, *The Australian Catholic Hymnal* (1942) and the *Pius X Hymnal* (1950), and he also composed *A Parish Mass* (1959), *A Mass in Honour of Pope Paul VI* (1971) and several songs, published by Allan & Co. From 1940 he directed the radio program *The Catholic Hour*, through which he attempted to raise the level of appreciation of liturgical music, and in 1948 he founded the Catholic Philharmonic Society. Both preceding and following the Second Vatican Council he was a member of the commissions for music in the liturgy and for the Englishing of the liturgical texts.

From 1943 he was involved with John ★Bishop and Ruth ★Alexander in the inception of the National Music Camps Association (now Youth Music Australia) and the Australian Youth Orchestra, and remained a stalwart of the organisation until his retirement. In 1950 he became vice-director (later reader) of the University of Melbourne Conservatorium, where he taught at all levels, supervising the first higher degrees within the faculty, encouraging the institution of a music education degree, and establishing the study of music therapy. For some time he directed the University Choral Society, and he produced choral productions within the faculty, including the Monteverdi *Vespers* in 1967. He pioneered the collecting of Australian folk-songs, publishing in 1952 the first modern arrangement of *Click Go The Shears* and other traditional works, recorded and popularised in his version by American singer Burl Ives. He was honoured with the MBE (1967), the OBE, and from the University of Melbourne an honorary MA and DMus.

(3) Basil Jones (*b* Geelong, Vic., 6 Oct. 1915), violinist, administrator. After studying violin with Benjamin Heselev and Edouard Lambert at the University of Melbourne Conservatorium, he was awarded his AMusA at the age of 14 and LRSM at 17, and appeared as a soloist with the Melbourne Symphony Orchestra, winning the first Victorian Music Teachers' Association violin championship (1933). With funds from a benefit concert in Geelong he went to Switzerland in 1937 and studied with Adolf Busch, recording with the Busch Chamber Players. During the war he served with the AIF, and from 1946 taught at the University of Melbourne Conservatorium, conducting the Melbourne Junior Symphony Orchestra from 1948 and founding the Victorian Chamber Players in 1951. He was appointed to the staff of the new Queensland Conservatorium in 1957, becoming acting director in 1959, then director from 1960. An intuitive, unaffected musician of great warmth and musicality, he oversaw the steady growth of the Queensland institution in its first two decades, and also became a principal force in the AMEB, continuing for many years after his retirement as a popular examiner and adjudicator.

FURTHER REFERENCE

For Percy Jones Sr, see *Signature* [Melbourne] (Apr./May) 1973; *St Augustine's Geelong 1857–1957* (Geelong, Vic.: St Augustine's School, 1957). For Fr Percy Jones, his folksong edition is *Burl Ives Folio of Australian Folksongs* (Southern Music Publishing, 1953). His publications include *Glosses de Musica of John Scotus Erigena* (Rome, 1957); *English and the Liturgy: An Analysis of the Underlying Aesthetics of The Constitution of the Liturgy of the Vatican Council II* (London: Geoffrey Chapman, 1964). See also Donald Cave, *Percy Jones, Priest, Musician, Teacher* (Melbourne: MUP, 1988); *ADMR*. For Basil Jones, see *WWA* (1996); *GlennonA*, 203.

DONALD CAVE, §2; editor §1,3

Jones, H(ooper Josse) Brewster. See *Brewster-Jones, H*.

Jones, Ignatius. See *Jimmy and the Boys*.

Jones, Marcie (*b* 26 June 1945), popular music singer. She sang with the ★Thunderbirds from 1962, then Normie ★Rowe's Playboys, and after releasing the first of five singles, *I Wanna Know*, in 1965 she was regularly seen on television. After *You Can't Bypass Love* (1967) she formed Marcie Jones and the Cookies with Beverley and Wendy Cook, building a strong following at Brisbane and touring England with Cliff Richard. Returning to Australia in 1970, she made four more singles as a soloist, her *Gonna Get Married* reaching No. 31 in the charts in 1974. Her albums include *That Jones Girl* (1973) and with the Allstars *Still Rocking On* (1993).

FURTHER REFERENCE
Recordings include *I Wanna Know* (Sunshine QK 985), *You Can't Bypass Love* (1967, Sunshine QK 1718), *Gonna Get Married* (Atlantic 10030), *That Jones Girl* (1973 Atlantic SD 60001) and with the Allstars *Still Rocking On* (1993, MDS ASR 5000). For discography, see *SpencerA*. See also *McGrathA*; *SpencerW*.

Jones, Trevor Alan (*b* Sydney, 18 Dec. 1932), musicologist. He studied at Sydney and Oxford Universities, and his MA thesis (University of Sydney, 1959) was on the music of Arnhem Land. Founding professor of music at Monash University, he appointed the first team of ethnomusicologists to any Australian university. He published widely on the didjeridu, dealing especially with its detailed comparative organology and musical functions. The pioneer of serious and lasting studies of ethnomusicology in Australia, he was also a strong advocate of the efficacy of the ethnomusicological approach to general education.
MARGARET KARTOMI

Jones, Vince (*b* Scotland, 24 Mar. 1954), jazz performer. Arriving in Australia as a child, he learned trumpet and from 1975 played in Melbourne rock and soul bands as well as singing and playing jazz. With his own band he was supporting act to Oscar Peterson and The Pointer Sisters (1981) and in 1982 released his debut album *Watch What Happens*. By 1984 he was touring nationally, and he visited Europe and the USA several times in 1991–94. His soundtrack for the television series *Come In Spinner* sold well. A soft-voiced, evocative performer with a repertoire encompassing jazz, blues and original songs, he has achieved success with the mainstream audience. He received an APRA award in 1986 for his song *For All Colours*.

FURTHER REFERENCE
Recordings include *Watch What Happens* (EMI CDP 7921012), *For All Colours* (EMI 4320072), and *On The Brink Of It* (EMI 7461992). For discography, see *SpencerA*. See also *SpencerW*; Adrian Jackson, *APRAJ* 4/2 (Dec. 1986), 2–5; *Stilleto* 44 (Dec. 1987), 28–30.

Jorgensen, Bertha (*b* Castlemaine, Vic., 1904), violinist. Jorgensen began violin tuition at the age of six with Alberto ★Zelman Jr at his private studio in Melbourne and

was with him for nine years. In 1919 she entered the amateur Melbourne Symphony Orchestra under Zelman's directorship. By 1924 she had ascended from the back desks to become principal player and participated regularly throughout the 1920s and 30s in radio ensemble performances for the ABC. In 1948 she was officially nominated concertmaster of the Victorian Symphony Orchestra, becoming the first Australian woman to acquire such a position. She remained with the orchestra until her retirement in 1969. She was honoured with the MBE in 1961.

FURTHER REFERENCE
Charles Buttrose, *Playing for Australia* (Sydney: ABC/Macmillan, 1982); Christopher Symons, *The Melbourne Symphony Orchestra* (Melbourne: Melbourne Symphony Orchestra, 1987).
MONIQUE GEITENBEEK

Journals and Magazines.
1. Early Music Magazines, 1840–88. 2. Magazines, Newsletters, General and Specialist, 1888–1945. 3. Journals, Magazines, National Newsletters, 1945 to the Present.

In Australia the periodical literature has included music journals and magazines of all types and qualities, ranging from short-lived newsletters of ephemeral interest to long-running periodicals of great importance for their record of music history.

1. Early Music Magazines, 1840–88. Periodical literature presumes a bourgeois culture which is both self-aware and reflective, and the conscious development of such a culture followed the growth of free settlement. By the 1830s free settlers in Sydney had established the basis of a free economy, independent government, and a modest cultural life which already supported a small class of professional teacher-musicians. Reference to the quality of local bands appeared sporadically in Sydney newspapers from 1800, and musical notices from 1826, but the first literary journal to include articles on music was the *New South Wales Magazine* (from 1843).

Urbanisation increased after the discovery of gold in the early 1850s, leading to a growing demand for the refinements of civilised life in Melbourne, Sydney and Adelaide. From this time, articles on music appeared in some of the literary journals of all three cities—although with little consistency over the next 40 years. Daily theatrical broadsheets included notices of operatic performances, and some, like the Melbourne *Entr'acte,* included reviews. By the 1890s at least two literary journals, the *Australasian Critic* and the *Tatler*, were publishing musical material. A NZ journal, the *Triad,* also enjoyed wide circulation. It included reviews of music in Australia, although after its move to Sydney in 1915, little of greater musical consequence was published.

The earliest magazines regarded by their publishers as primarily musical appeared in Adelaide and Melbourne in the 1860s, and were small-scale and local in interest. The first of these was the *Adelaide Musical Herald and Journal of Literature, Etc.* (1862–63), which was published by the Adelaide music retailer Charles Platts. Significantly, it closely followed on the death of Carl Linger, who had directed Adelaide's first performance of *Messiah* in 1859, and coincided with a second performance in 1862. Its contents were a pot-pourri of news, fashion, printed music, rudimentary music theory and a musical biography in the style of Burney. Its theoretical articles and the musical biography were substantially repeated and extended by the *Adelaide Miscellany: A Journal of News, Literature, Music, Etc.* (1868–69). If anything, the *Adelaide Miscellany* was more concerned with the publication of original music, which was the main interest of its printer-publishers, Walter Sims and Joseph Elliott. In the same decade, the Melbourne music retailer W.H. Glen published the *Australian Musical and Dramatic Review* (1866), the first Victorian magazine to acknowledge music in its title. Its combination of music and drama reflects the close relationship which developed in Melbourne between music and the theatre.

No other independent music magazines were published in Australia in the 1870s or 80s. The composite content of theatrical and literary magazines which included music indicates that, for most of the 19th century, music was not considered as an autonomous element of Australian cultural life. It was inextricably linked with the theatre, while concert life—mainly amateur and choral—embraced a network of social relationships which tended to heighten its social and obscure its aesthetic character. It was not felt to require the critical reflection of a periodical; colonial society agreed with Burney that music was an 'innocent luxury.'

2. Magazines, Newsletters, General and Specialist, 1888–1945. (i) State, National, Educational.

Consistent publication of music magazines awaited the development of a musical culture increasingly dominated by instrumental music, performed by professional musicians for audiences which embraced an aesthetic assuming the 'intelligibility' of wordless music. It is significant that Cowan's spectacular season with the Exhibition Orchestra in 1888 was soon followed by David Syme's publication of the *Musical Times* (1889–90) as a supplement to the *Illustrated Australian News*. While the *Musical Times* was not an independent journal it shared the local and critical character of later music magazines.

Until 1910 the gradual development of Australian music around the orchestras, conservatoriums and professional associations encouraged an intermittent series of independent publications. Far from the centres of culture, *The Musical Times of Queensland* (1890) probably finished after its first issue. In Adelaide, on the other hand, the strong development of Heinicke's orchestra and the secure establishment of the Elder Conservatorium created an ideal environment for the publication of the *South Australian Musical Journal* (1895–96) and *Music* (1896–1900). With the *Register*'s music critic W.J. Sanders as its editor

and Charles Cawthorne as its publisher, *Music* was a successful journal with high journalistic standards and strong sympathy with orchestral music.

In Sydney and Melbourne music magazines were not as successful. While Sydney's music was no less active than Adelaide's, the *Australian Musical Times and Magazine of Art* (1897–98) appeared in the face of apathy from the University of Sydney, which would not give music the same institutional support as the Universities of Melbourne and Adelaide, and in the face also of a disturbing drift of musicians to Melbourne. This malaise adversely affected the publication of music magazines in Sydney for almost 20 years.

Despite Melbourne's thriving musical culture in the 1890s, the first music magazines in Melbourne appeared only after 1900. The *Australian Musical Times* (1903), the *Australian Musical Monthly* (1905–6) and the *Encore* (1908–9) were short-lived, but reflected Melbourne's increasingly confident and professional musical culture. This is especially evident in the *Encore*, a sumptuous publication which embraced an adventurous musical canon extending to Richard Strauss and Debussy.

The publication of the ★*Australian Musical News* (1911–63) reflected a new level of maturity in a national magazine based almost exclusively on local musical news. Albert Maucum, its first publisher, had been one of the owners of the *Encore*. He clearly conceived the new magazine as the *Encore*'s successor. But the *Australian Musical News* was owned by Allan's Music, and from the beginning its immediacy, relevance and modest appearance were the natural outcome of their commercial interest. Thorold ★Waters' vigorous editorship (1923–46) also shaped the style of the magazine. As Waters observed in his autobiography:

No policy of music had ever shaped itself in my brain, and none shaped itself now, except the general one that a critic should be fair minded, deal directly with performance, [and] take for granted that people wished to hear about last night rather than about the lives and birth-pains of Bach and Beethoven. (*Much Besides Music*, 211–12)

At the same time more music magazines were published with a specific tendency towards regional and specialist interests. Where the *Australian Musical News* provided a national overview, these magazines concentrated on education, recorded music, local professional and trade news, or popular music.

Among educational journals, the *Conservatorium Magazine* (1916–20) and its successor, *Musical Australia* (1920–25), were the most important. They were the product of the new and self-confident Conservatorium in Sydney, and of the stimulation to musical and educational thought provided by its director, Henri Verbrugghen. Preconditions for an educational journal were not favourable. Whereas local news could only be provided by local magazines, good educational material was available in such British and American journals as the *Music Student*, *Musical America* and *Musical Opinion*, all of which circulated in

Australia. The *Conservatorium Magazine* and *Musical Australia* prospered in a developing professional environment which encouraged a practical and rational pedagogy strongly influenced by Conservatorium staff members such as Frank Hutchens, Mary Cochran and Roland Foster. In later magazines, until the *Australian Journal of Music Education* (1967–82), educational material was largely mixed with more general content or, as with a children's magazine like the *'Treble Clef' Magazine* (1932–c.37), directed at a very particular market.

(ii). Radio, Record, Regional.

Broadcasting and phonographic magazines also appeared in the 1920s. While broadcasting journals like the *Radio Weekly* contained musical reviews, their emphasis was technological. Phonographic magazines, on the other hand, specialised in reviews of recorded music for an increasingly isolated and critical audience of amateurs. The *Australasian Phonograph Monthly* (1925–28) and The *Australian Phonograph News* (1929–c.31) were the most outstanding of these, mainly for the exceptional reviews of L. de Noskowski who, with Thorold Waters and C.N. Bayertz, was among the most prominent music critics in Australia before World War II.

Periodicals based on regional interests were the product of professional and community organisations within each state. The earliest known of these was the *Musician*, a weekly paper of the Sydney branch of the Professional Musicians' Union in 1913 which was published at a time of considerable controversy over the status of amateur players. Most, however, were issued by the state musical (or music teachers') associations which, after about 1910, were increasingly influential in the co-ordination of the profession for tuition and music-making, specifically at a local level. As tools for publicity, the regional music magazines were an important extension of this role. Langley Simmons's *Queensland Musical and Dramatic Times and Cinema Record* (1920–c.1921) coincided with the foundation of the Music Teachers' Association of Queensland and acted as its official organ. Five years later, on behalf of the same association, W. Preston Day published the *Queensland Musical Review* (1926–31) as a supplement to the *Steering Wheel*. From the mid-1920s, all of the state musical associations with the exception of Tasmania began the periodical publication of teaching registers, yearbooks and conference papers.

The late 1920s saw the development of music weeks, many eisteddfods and local music clubs, each supported by at least one magazine as its 'official organ'. Keith Barry's *Music in Australia* (1928–31) was the first of these; although it was a continuation of the *Australasian Phonograph Monthly*, its phonographic content dwindled with the onset of the Depression, and its function as an intermediary between the profession and the community increased with its representation of Oliver King's Association of Music Clubs of Australia and Barry's Music Advancement Guild of NSW. In spite of its title, *Music in Australia* was

strongly regional. This combination of community and regional interests also characterised the two most successful and more serious publications of the 1930s: *Music and the Drama* (1933–39), a West Australian magazine edited chiefly by Edward Black on behalf of the music clubs and dramatic societies of Perth, and *Harmony* (1933–36), a women's music magazine published by Emily Marks and later by Florence Taylor for Sydney's music clubs.

(iii) Popular Music, Bands, Jazz.

Popular music was initially represented by a few successful brass band journals. The earliest of these were also Australia's first regional music magazines; namely the *Australasian Bandsman* (originally Bathurst, NSW; 1898–1926), and the *Australian Band News* (originally Bairnsdale, Vic., [1909]-25). In 1925 the *Australian Band News* was taken over by Allan's, which published it as the *Australian Band and Orchestra News*, incorporating the *Australasian Bandsman* in 1926. For more than 10 years the magazine was edited by Thorold Waters as a companion publication to the *Australian Musical News*. The Salvation Army continues to publish a music magazine, primarily for bands, which was first issued as the *Local Officer and Bandsman* (1910–47) and later as the *Musician of the Salvation Army in Australia* (1947–).

Commercial influences in the 1930s led to the replacement of brass band journals with magazines for jazz enthusiasts. The *Australian Dance Band News* (1932–40), published in Sydney by Eric Sheldon, was the first magazine of this type. At an early stage its title was changed to the *Australian Music Maker and Dance Band News*, and by 1936 Nicholson's took over publication. In 1937 Allan's revamped the *Australian Band and Orchestra News*, changing its title to the *Australasian Band and Dance Band News* and replacing Waters as editor. In 1940 Nicholson's incorporated both publications in a popular magazine called *Music Maker* (1940–73). *Tempo* (later *Tempo and Television*, 1937–60), published by Frank Johnson, was a more serious jazz publication. Revivalist trends in the 1940s and 1950s were represented by *Jazz Notes and Blue Rhythm* (1941–50 and 1960–62) and the *Australian Jazz Quarterly* (1946–57).

3. Journals, Magazines, National Newsletters, 1945 to the Present.

In contrast with about 50 music magazines published between 1862 and 1945, more than 700 periodicals and newsletters have been published since the war. This development reflects the increasing concentration of musical activity according to locality and specialised interests. The decline of the *Australian Musical News* and *Tempo* in the late 1950s and of *Music Maker* in the 1960s was symptomatic of a culture which was increasingly decentralised and less able to sustain national music magazines; among their successors *Canon* (1947–66) was the most important, reflecting a growing critical and musicological sophistication. In 1965 one issue of *Canon* was also the first issue of *Musicology* (founded 1964, from 1985 *★Musicology Australia*), the earliest of a number of musicological magazines and newsletters, including *Miscellanea Musicologica* (1966–) and *Studies in Music* (1967–92).

The trend towards specialisation continues with some national magazines also emerging. *Cadenza* (1983–85) was a short-lived attempt at an independent musical review in the style of *Canon*. A more natural market for a national publication was created with the advent of ABC-FM radio in the mid-1970s, which has produced essentially popular magazines like *24 Hours* (1976). Growth in the same market is also reflected in the more recent success of *Soundscapes* (1993–), which represents a return to the more concentrated critique found in the phonographic reviews of the 1920s.

Numerous associations and institutions issue newsletters, ranging from the most ephemeral fan-club news sheets to important archival and scholarly publications like *Continuo: Newsletter of the International Association of Music Libraries. Australian and New Zealand* (1971–1993; now called *Intermezzo*). Magazines have also continued to specialise; some, like the *Australian Jazz Quarterly* and the *Australian Journal of Music Education*, have become internationally significant, while others, like *APRA Journal* (1969–), are more localised. Although some rock magazines like *The Big Beat of the 50's* (1977–) have been issued by small interest groups, popular music has been dominated by glossy magazines, published for the international industry, and by Australian editions of American magazines like *Rolling Stone* (1969–). By contrast, jazz magazines like the *Quarterly Rag* (1955–66 and 1976–) and *Jazzline* (1968–), as well as folk publications like *Northern Folk* (1966–71) and the *Cornstalk Gazette* (1985–), reveal a lively culture with very strong regional support.

FURTHER REFERENCE
Mary O'Mara, ed., *Union Catalogue of Music Serials in Australian Libraries* (Brisbane: International Association of Music Libraries, Archives and Documentation Centres [Australian Branch]), 1992; *Serials in Australian Libraries: NUCOS on Disc.* CD ROM. ([Melbourne]: Royal Melbourne Institute of Technology, INFORMIT, in association with the National Library of Australia, 1993–).   PETER DART

Joy Boys. Rock and roll band formed in 1957 in Sydney, originally comprised of Kevin Jacobson (piano), Keith Jacobson (bass guitar), Dave Bridge (guitar), Laurie Erwin (saxophone) and John Bogie (drums), with Colin Jacobson (later known as Col *Joye) as vocalist. At first known as the KJ Quintet, the band secured a regular place at a hotel in Maroubra. When entrepreneur Bill McColl asked the KJ Quintet to play in his 1957 Jazzorama concert the band changed their name to Col Joye and the Joy Boys; this debut marked the start of their rise to fame. In 1958 the Joy Boys became the second Australian band to be signed by Festival Records. Their first big hit was *Bye Bye Baby* and they regularly backed Col Joye on Channel 9's *Bandstand*. The band recorded successfully in its own right for

many years, releasing singles, EPs and albums. Their biggest hit was *Southern 'Rora* which remained at No. 5 in the charts for 16 weeks in 1962. The Joy Boys owned their own music publishing company (Joye Music), recording company (ATA) and booking agency, managing artists such as Judy *Stone, *Little Pattie and the *Allen Brothers. Their last release was the 1976 single *Slow Dancin'*.

FURTHER REFERENCE
Recordings include the albums *Col Joye's Joy Boys* (1960, Festival), *New Old Time* (1962, Festival), *Cookin' up a Party* (1963, Festival), *Fabulous Hits* (1963, Festival), *Surfin' Stompin' Joys* (1964, Festival), *On Top of the World* (1974, Festival), *Instrumental Yours* (1976, Festival). For discography, see *SpencerA*. See also *GuinnessP*; *McGrathA*; *SpencerW*; Michael Sturma, *Australian Rock'n'Roll: The First Wave* (Kenhurst, NSW: Kangaroo Press, 1991).
                    CATHERINE STEVENS

Joyce, Eileen (*b* Zeehan, Tas., 21 Nov. 1908; *d* Limpsfield, England, 25 Mar. 1991), pianist. She grew up in Boulder City, WA. Showing remarkable adeptness for the piano at an early age, she was sent to the Loreto Convent, Perth, for further study, and performed for Percy Grainger and Wilhelm Backhaus. At Backhaus's instigation she studied at the Leipzig Conservatory with Max Pauer and Robert Teichmuller; later in London with Adelina de Lara, Tobias Matthay, attending Schnabel's masterclasses, and made her London debut with Sir Henry Wood playing Prokofiev's Piano Concerto No. 3 (1930). She was renowned for the precision and clarity of her playing as well as its strength and stamina, sometimes performing three or four concertos at a single concert, and developed a fashion for changing her concert dress to suit the atmosphere of specific works during a performance. She retired from public performance after a recital in Aberdeen in 1960.

A woman of arresting physical beauty, she appeared in films, playing the sound-track to *Brief Encounter* on screen. She recorded concertos and concertante works by Ireland, Shostakovich, Grieg, Franck, Bliss (including the premiere recording of *Barazza*) and piano trios by Arensky and Haydn. Later in her career she took up the harpsichord. The facts of her life have been largely distorted by the appearance of the children's book *Prelude* (1949) by Clare Hoskyns-Abbahall and the film *Wherever She Goes* (1951). First patron of the Sydney International Piano Competition, she was awarded two honorary doctorates (Cantab, 1971; University of Western Australia, 1979), and made benefactions to the music department of the University of Western Australia, including, notably, the Eileen Joyce Studio.

FURTHER REFERENCE
Recordings for Parlophone, Columbia, Decca and Saga; several of her most stylish virtuoso recordings are the études by Paul de Schlozer and Liszt (1930s, Parlophone).
                    CYRUS MEHER-HOMJI

Joye, Col [Colin Frederick Jacobson] (*b* Sydney, 13 Apr. 1937), rock and roll singer. At first a jewellery salesman, he began playing rock and roll with his brothers at local dances and at cinemas in 1957, later that year appearing as Col Joy and the ★Joy Boys at Bill McColl's Jazzorama at Manly, Sydney. Becoming a regular on television's *Bandstand*, in 1959 his single *Oh Yeah, Uh Uh* reached No. 1 in the charts, *Rockin' Rollin' Clementine* No. 2 and *Bye, Bye Baby* No. 3. With his brothers he established a publishing company, Joye Music, in 1960. Seven more hits followed over the next five years, in 1960 *Bad Man* (written for him by Conway Twitty) reaching No. 17, *Yes Sir, She's My Baby* No. 13 and *Teenage Baby* No. 11, then *Starlight Of Love* (written for him by Barry Gibb) reaching the Top 40 in 1963. He was also a regular duet artist on *Bandstand* with ★Little Pattie. From 1964, with tastes changing, he adopted a country style and middle-of-the-road ballads, but lost his hold on the charts. He established a record label ATA in 1966, on which numerous Sydney artists recorded, and entered artist management. His single *Heaven Is My Woman's Love* reached No. 1 in 1973. With good looks and a happy-go-lucky manner, Joye attracted a huge following and, despite an unremarkable voice, vied with Johnny ★O'Keefe as foremost Australian artist in the early rock and roll years. He released over 50 singles between 1958 and 1965, and is still active on the revival circuit.

FURTHER REFERENCE
Recordings include *Oh Yeah, Uh Uh* (1959, Festival); *Bye Bye, Baby* (1959, Festival); compilations are *Very Best 22 Golden Hits* (1980, J&B); *Boxed Set,* 5 LPs (1989, ATA). For discography, see *SpencerA*. See also *GuinnessP*, II, 1328–29. *SpencerW*; *McGrathA*.

Juke. National weekly newspaper for rock music, published in Melbourne 1975–94. It was cut back to a monthly in its last 12 months.

Julius Caesar Jones. Children's opera in two acts (1966) by Malcolm ★Williamson, libretto by G. Dunn,

commissioned for the Finchley Children's Music Group, UK. First performed by Jeannetta Cochrane at London on 4 January 1966 and published by Joseph Weinberger, 1966.

Jupp, Eric (*b* England, 1922), popular music composer, arranger. A well-known dance band leader on radio and television, he hosted the ABC variety show *The Magic of Music* 1961–67, employing in his studio orchestra such outstanding jazz players as George Golla and Jimmy Shaw, and bringing a personality of quiet grace to the program. He married his co-host Shirley McDonald in 1969. He wrote the words and music for the television theme *Skippy the Bush Kangaroo* (Castle Music, 1968), and was then conductor and arranger for the ABC Showband until it disbanded in 1976.

FURTHER REFERENCE
Herald 11 Feb 1976.

Justin, Jay (*b* Sydney, 1 May 1940), popular music singer-songwriter. After studies at the NSW State Conservatorium, he became a singer in the Sinatra style in 1960, releasing the first of 23 singles, *Nobody's Darling But Mine*, in the same year. In 1961 he was a regular on *Bandstand* and the *Johnny O'Keefe Show*, his *Why Don't You Try* reaching No. 21 in the charts, and in 1962 he made No. 1 with *Proud Of You*. He released his debut album *Just Jay* and then wrote songs for Bryan ★Davies, Patsy Ann ★Noble and ★Little Pattie, working in Sydney clubs and reappearing with *Old Story Teller* in 1981. He was one of the most polished of the singers in Australia's early rock and roll era.

FURTHER REFERENCE
Recordings include *Nobody's Darling But Mine* (HMV EA 4389), *Why Don't You Try* (HMV EA 4428), *Proud Of You* (HMV EA 4553), *Just Jay* (HMV 1963), *Old Story Teller* (1981, EMI). A compilation is *Jay Justin Greatest Hits* (EMI 1982). For discography, see *SpencerA*. See also *McGrathA*; *SpencerW*.

K

Kain, Timothy (*b* Braidwood, NSW, 25 Jan. 1951), classical guitarist. After playing flamenco and popular guitar, he studied with Sadie Bishop at the Canberra School of Music, then with Jose Tomas in Spain and Gordon Crosskey in Manchester. He has toured widely in Europe, the Middle East and the USA, with John Williams in Attacca (1992) and as a duo (1994). Since 1982 he has taught at the Canberra School of Music. He has toured and recorded with an ensemble of his former students, Guitar Trek.

FURTHER REFERENCE
Recordings with Guitar Trek include *Music for A Guitar Family* (1991, ABC 432698B); with John Williams, *The Mantis And The Moon* (11996).

Kaine, Carmel (*b* Wagga Wagga, NSW, 1937), violinist. After studying at the NSW State Conservatorium, she went to London in 1956, studying with Frederick Grinke at the Royal Academy of Music, then to the Juilliard School, New York. She made her Wigmore Hall debut in 1964 and returned to Australia to play at the Adelaide Festival in 1966. Winning the Vienna International Violin Competition in 1967, for a decade she played in the Academy of St Martin-in-the-Fields, winning international awards for her recordings of Vivaldi's *La Stravaganza* and the Mozart *Concertante*. She gave recitals for the BBC, appeared as a soloist at festivals in England and Europe, was guest leader of the Melos Ensemble, the Virtuosi of London and played in the Quartet of London. She taught at the Menuhin School and the Royal Academy of Music. Since 1990 she has been senior lecturer at the Queensland Conservatorium.

One of the most seasoned and abundantly talented violinists teaching in Australia, she was made a Fellow of the Royal Academy of Music in 1982.

FURTHER REFERENCE
Recordings as soloist with the Academy of St Martin-in-the-Fields include Vivaldi, *Cimento dell'armonia e dell' inventione* (1975, Philips 420 482–2).

Kalgoorlie-Boulder pop. (1991) 25 016, inland town on the western edge of the Nullarbor Plain 600 km east of Perth, regional centre for the eastern goldfields. Founded in 1893, by 1910 the position of regional centre having been wrested from nearby Coolgardie (1892) and following the area's most vigorous growth, musical activities included the Boulder Band, the Boulder Liedertafel, the Kalgoorlie Operatic Society, the Welsh Choir, the Salter's Lyric Orchestra, church choirs, touring companies, street entertainment and concert parties. The Tivoli Gardens (1897) was Kalgoorlie's first purpose-built entertainment centre; the Kalgoorlie and Boulder Town Halls (1908) are still used.

Several music schools had been established by the early 1900s, and local pianist, O.C. Campbell Egan, became the first superintendent for music, speech and drama in the WA education department. The opening of St Joseph's Convent, Boulder, (1897) began a history of music education by local convents, producing some talented pianists including Eileen ★Joyce (1912–92). Stanley Brown, MBE, formed the Goldfields Boys Choir (1969–77) and in 1979 launched the idea of a trust-funded music school; this came under the auspices of the Kalgoorlie College in 1984 and subsequently affiliated with the WA Academy of Performing Arts. Organisations currently associated with the Kalgoorlie College are the Goldfields Choral Society and Orchestra, chamber and vocal ensembles, and a stage band. Community groups include the Goldfields Blues Band, the Boulder Brass Band, the Folk Music Club and the Jazz Appreciation Society. The Goldfields Arts Centre was opened in 1993.

FURTHER REFERENCE
Margaret Bull, 'The History of Music on the Goldfields, Kalgoorlie, 1985' (collection of newspaper cuttings and interviews), State Archives of WA; Jean Farrant, The History of Music in Coolgardie, Kalgoorlie and Boulder 1892 to 1908, MA, Univ. of WA, 1992.   PATRICIA THORPE

Kamahl [Kandiah Kamalesvaran] (*b* Kamalsvaran, Malaysia, 1940), popular music singer. His father was a founding member of the Indian Music Academy, Kuala Lumpur, and they came to Australia in 1954. He began singing publicly in his late teens, winning a television talent quest and appearing at Adelaide nightclubs, then he recorded his first album, *A Voice To Remember*, in 1967. His single *Sounds Of Goodbye* reached No. 11 in the charts in 1969, then *You've Got To Learn* (1970) and *One Hundred Children* (1971) each entered the Top 40; his charity album *Peace On Earth* (1970) became enormously popular, and by 1973 he had 20 gold records. His *The Elephant Song* reached No. 1 in the charts in NZ and Holland, and he appeared at the London Palladium and Talk of the Town in the 1970s. A singer of sentimental love songs appealing chiefly to the older audience, he continues to be a perennial favourite in Australian variety shows and clubs. He has recorded 33 albums and was honoured with the AM in 1994.

FURTHER REFERENCE

Recordings include *Sounds of Kamahl* (1970, Philips), *Journeys* (1978), *Somebody Loves You* (1981) and *The Platinum Collection* (1994). See also Christopher Day *Kamahl: An Impossible Dream* (Sydney: Random House, 1995); *McGrathA*; *Sunday Age* 21 Aug. 1994.

Kartomi, Margaret Joy   (*b* Adelaide, 24 Nov. 1940), musicologist. She studied at the University of Adelaide 1959–64, graduating BA and BMus, with a diploma for piano, and gaining recognition as composer and performer. From 1964 to 1968 she was a student in the musicological institute at the Humboldt University in Berlin, receiving her doctorate for a study on the Matjapat songs of Central and West Java (ANU Press, 1973). Returning to Australia in 1968, she was appointed to Monash University as research fellow (later reader) then professor and head of the department of music from 1989, as well as fulfilling visiting professorships, for example in 1986 at Berkeley, USA. She is widely travelled as visiting lecturer and research scholar.

Kartomi is a scholar, pedagogue and organiser of wide-ranging experience and catholicity of interests. While the central corpus of her research and publication (over 100 titles) focuses upon Indonesian and South-East Asian musics, she has embraced other fields of Australian (e.g. Pitjantjatjara children's music), Asian, Judaic and European studies. As contributor for the *New Grove History of Musical Instruments* and in her study *On Concepts and Classification of Musical Instruments* (1990) she has emerged as a systematic musicologist in the fields of palaeo- and comparative organography. This range has also identified her as a scholar of powerful epistemological orientation within the total discipline of musicology. In 1988 she organised the Symposium of the International Musicological Society at Melbourne as part of the Australian Bicentenary Celebrations. She has served twice as president of the Musicological Society of Australia (1979–80, 1984–86), and has fulfilled major editorial advisory duties

for *Acta Musicologica* and Chicago University Press. She was elected a Fellow of the Australian Academy of the Humanities (1982), was a recipient of the German Record Critics' Award (1983) for the best ethnographic record of the year, and in 1992 was honoured with the AM.

FURTHER REFERENCE

Her writings include *Matjapat Songs of Central and West Java* (Canberra: ANU Press, 1973); 'The Processes and Results of Musical Culture Contact: A Discussion of Terminology and Concepts', *Ethnomusicology* 25 (1981), 227–50; 262 signed and unsigned entries in *The New Grove Dictionary of Musical Instruments,* ed. Stanley Sadie (London: Macmillan, 1984); *Musical Instruments of Indonesia* (Melbourne: Indonesian Arts Society, 1985); *On Concepts and Classification of Musical Instruments* (Chicago: Univ. Chicago Press, 1991); 'Comparative Musicology and Music Aesthetics: What has become of those subdivisions of Adler's "Systematic Musicology" and "Historical Musicology" of 1885?', *Systematische Musikwissenschaft* 1/2 (Bratislava 1993), 257–82.

ANDREW D. McCREDIE

Kassler, Jamie Croy   (*b* Neenah, Wisconsin, USA, 10 Nov. 1938), musicologist. Awarded first prize (1960) in the State of Wisconsin for String Quartet No. 1, she studied at the University of Wisconsin (BMus 1964), then was faculty scholar at Columbia University, New York, 1966–67 (MA 1967; PhD 1971). She taught at Barnard College and the Columbia-Princeton Electronic Music Center, New York, editing *Current Musicology* (1965–66), and was post-doctoral research fellow, department of music, University of Sydney (1975–77). She held various part-time ARC research fellow positions at the University of New South Wales in the schools of History and Philosophy of Science (1980–84), English (1982–87), and Science and Technology Studies (1988–89; 1991–92), lectured part-time at the NSW Conservatorium (1980–84) and the University of NSW (European Studies), and was visiting Fellow at the School of Science and Technology Studies, University of NSW.

Her publications have focused on the history of ideas of English music between the 17th and 20th centuries. In *The Science of Music in Britain* she related technical doctrines of music performance and composition to contemporary thought, including the mathematical (e.g. doctrines of tuning and scale), the critical (doctrines of musical excellence), and the physical (doctrines of sound production and reception). She researched Thomas Britton on music as a model in early science; co-authored a work on Robert Hooke's music-theoretical and cosmological ideas; co-edited the writings on music of Roger North; and published a book on the role of music in the transformation of knowledge. She was elected fellow of the Australian Academy of the Humanities for contributions to musicological theory (1991).

FURTHER REFERENCE

Her writings include *The Science of Music in Britain, 1714–1830: A Catalogue of Writings, Lectures and Inventions*, 2 vols (New York: Garland, 1979); with M. Chan, *Roger North's The Musicall Grammarian 1728* (Cambridge: CUP, 1990); 'Man à la Mode: or, Interpreting the Universe from a Musical Point of View', in *Metaphor—A Musical Dimension*, ed. J.C. Kassler, Australian Studies in the History, Philosophy and Social Studies of Music, vol. 1 (Sydney: Currency Press, 1991), 160–76; *Inner Music: Hobbes, Hooke and North on Internal Character* (London: Athlone, 1995).

MARGARET KARTOMI

Kay, Don Henry (*b* Smithton, Tas., 25 Jan. 1933), composer. In 1955 Kay graduated from the University of Melbourne Conservatorium, then studied with Malcolm Williamson privately in London 1959–64. He has worked at the Tasmanian Conservatorium since 1967 as head of composition. His most notable compositions include *The Golden Crane* (1985) an opera for young people's theatre; *The Legend of Moinee* (1989) for cello and orchestra for the Tasmanian Symphony Orchestra; and *Dance Concertante* (1990) for string orchestra. His work is strongly influenced by the Tasmanian environment. In 1991 he was honoured with the AM.

FURTHER REFERENCE

Recordings include Three *Canzonas*, D. Cubbin, fl, R. Bolton, va (Canberra School of Music, CSM 7); *Hastings Triptych*, fl (AMC 002); *Songs of Come and Gone* (Move MS 3040). See also *ADMR*, *GlennonA*, 164.   KERRI-ANN SHEPPARD

Kaytetye. Aboriginal tribe whose country stretches from near Central Mount Stuart in the south to the Devils Marbles in the north of the central Australian desert. They have been enshrined in history by the 'Barrow Creek Massacre', where, in 1874, three telegraph station staff were speared. In reality, the retribution wreaked upon the Kaytetye and neighbouring tribes far outweighed the original event, and Kaytetye people today remember stories told to them by their ancestors about that frightening time.

Kaytetye people today have intermarried with the neighbouring Alyawarr, Anmatjera, Warlpiri and Warumungu, and many of their songs contain texts in those languages. There are 'countries' or Dreaming groups within the Kaytetye area. Recordings have been made from Etwerrpe, Akalperre, Warlekerlange, Jarra Jarra, Waake, Akwerlpe, Arnerre and Karlantyarenge. As well as linguistic and anthropological studies, land claim research along the northern and eastern parts of Kaytetye land have produced recordings of ceremonial activity, which is still vital to Kaytetye culture.

Songs encapsulate the spirits of the Dreamtime ancestors, thus providing the energy for ceremonies and for important life events. Clan groups own songs and regulate when and by whom they may be sung. Research has identified songs for initiation, rainmaking, easing birth and love magic. As in most Centralian singing, songs trace the travels of a Dreamtime ancestor who sang as it created topographical features of the land. These song series consist of melodies starting on a high note with a series of descents to the final pitch, which is sung for at least one repetition of the entire text.

FURTHER REFERENCE

D. Bell, *Daughters of the Dreaming*, 2nd edn (Sydney: Allen & Unwin, 1993); G. Koch, *Kaytetye Country: An Aboriginal history of the Barrow Creek area* (Alice Springs: Institute for Aboriginal Development, 1993); R.M. Moyle and Slippery Morton, *Alyawarr music: songs and society in a central Australian Community: with the help of Slippery Morton, Alyawarr interpreter* (Canberra: AIAS, 1986).   GRACE KOCH

Keats, Horace (*b* Mitcham, Surrey, England, 20 July 1895; *d* Sydney, 21 Aug. 1945), composer, accompanist. A boy soprano at the Brompton Road Oratory, Kensington, he ran away to sea at the age of 13. He was accompanist to variety singer Nella Webb on her tour of the USA and the Pacific in 1914, and arrived in Australia in 1915. He worked as accompanist to Peter ★Dawson and Ella ★Caspers, played music for silent films for J.C. Williamson 1916–20, then led a popular music trio 1920–23, which he took into radio from 1923. By 1929 he was conducting a 29-piece radio orchestra. He was briefly in London working for the BBC in 1930, then in Perth for the ABC in 1932, and resumed his work as a freelance accompanist in Sydney from 1934. He published *Three Spanish Dances* in 1922, but most of his music is for voice and dates from the last 12 years of his life. Writing attractive melodies with economical accompaniments, he focused on settings of the Australian poets Christopher Brennan, Hugh McCrae and Kenneth Mackenzie. He wrote at least 115 songs, two choral works, incidental music for radio and film, and a musical *Atsomari* (1935). His songs were recorded by Dawson, Harold ★Williams, and others; the best known were *She Walks in Beauty* and *Road Beside the Sea*. Thirty were published by W.H. Paling & Co.

FURTHER REFERENCE

Recordings include *The Constant Lover*, B, pf (1956, ABC PR 2644); *Columbine*, S, pf (ABC O N40525); and *Three Piano Pieces*, Gordon Watson, pf (ABC PRX 5433). See also Warren Bebbington, *ADB*, 9; idem, 'Horace Keats', *APRAJ*, 2/9 (Dec. 1981), 16–18; *MoresbyA*, 141–3.

Kellaway, Frank (*b* London, 19 Apr. 1922), novelist, poet. After studies at the University of Melbourne he taught at the Preston Institute of Technology from 1948. He published fiction, including *A Straight Furrow* (1960) and *The Quest for Golden Dan* (1962), and later volumes of poetry, including *Beanstalk* (1973) and *Mare's Nest* (1978). He wrote libretti for a number of George

*Dreyfus's works, notably the opera *Garni Sands* (1969), *Song of the Maypole* (1970) and the children's opera *The Takeover* (1969).

FURTHER REFERENCE
OxfordL; Kay Lucas, 'George Dreyfus's *Garni Sands*', *SMA* 7 (1973), 78–87.

Kelly, Jan   (*b* Heyfield, Vic., 23 Apr. 1948), country music singer. She began her career at the age of 15 with a Melbourne party club performing for the elderly, and in 1968 moved to Sydney to work in the club circuit, becoming resident vocalist with Nev Nicholls' Country Playboys at the Texas Tavern in 1970. She was with Kevin King and the Country Sounds at the Crystal Palace Hotel, Sydney (in which her husband Terry Smith was bass guitarist), 1973–77, toured with Don Gibson and Slim Whitman in 1975, then played at the Transport Club from 1977. Her Kelly Express (1980–86) had a major tyre company as sponsor and appeared at country music festivals and on major country television shows. Her recordings include *I'm A Woman, Sorry* and *Without Reason;* her album reached No. 1 in the country charts in 1995. She was honoured in the ACMA Hands of Fame in 1985.

FURTHER REFERENCE
SmithB, 293.

Kelly, Norma   (*b* Ireland, 18 Mar. 1944), country music singer. After working with the country band Summer Wine in England from 1972, she arrived in Australia in 1981 and settled at Perth. She joined Nashville, then formed her own bands Tennessee Rain and (from 1991) Fresco, becoming the leading female country vocalist in WA. A strong, soulful and very expressive vocalist with a crossover repertoire, she has recorded five albums, was twice voted Queen of Country by the WA Country Music Club and has won three Boyup Brook Country Music Awards.

FURTHER REFERENCE
Recordings include *Together Again, Live At The White Stetson Club* and *My Kind Of Country*. See also *LattaA*, 179–80; *SmithB*, 292.

Kelly, Paul   (*b* Adelaide, 13 Jan. 1955), popular music singer, songwriter. The sixth of nine children, Kelly attended a Christian Brothers school where he played trumpet, captained the cricket team and was dux of his final year. He came from a musical family; his grandmother was the Contessa Fillippini, an opera singer and the first woman to have conducted a symphony orchestra in Australia. He formed his first band, Paul Kelly and the Dots, at Melbourne in 1976 and began to gather together a small but loyal following. Critical and commercial success came for his 1984 album *Post,* recorded in Sydney with a new band, the Coloured Girls (later the Messengers), and he was awarded the *Rolling Stone*

(Aust.) best album of the year. In 1989 he won two Mo awards for best male performer and best band as well as the *Rolling Stone*'s readers' and critics' choice as songwriter of the year. He has co-written many songs such as *Treaty* for *Yothu Yindi and had many songs covered, such as *Beggar on the Street of Love* performed by Jenny Morris. He has written for and performed in theatre, notably *Funerals and Circuses* at the 1992 Adelaide and Melbourne Festivals, and produced a film score, *Everynight, Everynight*, in 1994.

Kelly's songs are catchy melodies set to a simple rock and roll accompaniment of rhythm and lead guitar, keyboards, bass and drums. He is influenced by country and blues styles and has achieved particular recognition for his sensitive and evocative lyrics, a book of which was published in 1993. His economical wording, owing much to the writings of American writer Raymond Carver, conjures up Melbourne (*Leaps and Bounds, Gossip*), drug addiction (*Post*), and ordinary people and their lives (*To Her Door, Under the Sun*). He has been hailed as one of Australia's 'two or three essential poets' and as 'one of the best songwriters in the English language'.

FURTHER REFERENCE
Recordings include *Talk* (1981, Mushroom); *Leaps and Bounds* (1987, Mushroom); *Wanted Man* (1994, Mushroom); with Coloured Girls, *To Her Door* (1987, Mushroom); *Gossip* (1986 White); *Post* (1985, White); with Messengers, *Under the Sun* (1987, White); *Love Never Runs on Time* (1994, Mushroom). His song lyrics are published as *Lyrics* (Sydney: Angus & Robertson, 1993). See also 'Paul Kelly Performance Poet', *Rolling Stone* 653 (24 Apr. 1993); *Age*, 24 Sept. 1993; *Australian*, 18 June 1994; Glenn A. Baker, 'Paul Kelly', *APRAJ* (Aug. 1987), 55–6; John O'Donnell, 'Paul Kelly Interview', *Rolling Stone Australia* (Oct. 1989), 51–5; *SpencerW*; *Time*, 28 Feb. 1994.

JENNIFER OLDFIELD

Kennedy.   Anglo-Australian family of three generations of musicians.
(1) Daisy Fowler Kennedy (*b* Kooringa, SA, 16 Jan. 1893; *d* London, 30 July 1981), violinist. She studied with Hermann *Heinicke at the Elder Conservatorium (1906–8), then with Ottakar Ševčík in Prague and Vienna (1908–12). A woman of dramatic beauty, she made her debuts in London (16 December 1911) and New York (29 November 1920). In 1919–20 she toured Australia with her husband Benno Moiseiwitsch; divorced in 1924, she married John Drinkwater. She appeared less frequently in public after the birth of her third daughter in 1928, until the sudden death of her husband in 1937 left her impecunious. She then became leader and conductor of the orchestra at London's Regent Palace Hotel until her retirement in 1950.
(2) Laurie Kennedy (*b* Sydney 1898; *d* Sacramento, Calif., USA, 1985), cellist. Son of S.R. Kennedy (*d* New York, 6 Jan. 1926), and cousin of Daisy Kennedy (1), he studied in Vienna and London with his brothers violin-

ist Keith and flautist Lance before they toured extensively as the Kennedy Concert Co. (South Africa, 1923; Malaya, Java, NZ and Australia). Later he was principal cellist of the BBC Symphony Orchestra 1929–35, of the London Philharmonic Orchestra and Covent Garden Orchestra under Sir Thomas Beecham 1935–37, and of the NBC Orchestra under Arturo Toscanini from 1938. Also a recitalist and chamber music player, he toured Australia with his pianist wife Dorothy (née McBride) for the ABC in 1938. Noted as a splendid technician and master of tone, he was 'good to look at for the sheer ease of his bowing style'. His son was the cellist John Kennedy (3).

(3) John Kennedy (*b* London, 1923; *d* Melbourne, 1978), cellist. Son of Laurie Kennedy (2), he moved between England and Australia, playing as principal cellist in the Liverpool Symphony Orchestra under Sir Malcolm Sargent, then in the Sydney Symphony Orchestra, then returning to England in 1951 to join the orchestra at Covent Garden. In 1960 he took up an appointment at the University of Melbourne Conservatorium, where with other staff he formed the Ormond Trio, and later toured widely with the Melbourne Trio. His students included Philip Green, but his heavy schedule of outside engagements attracted controversy, and with failing health he had few students by 1975. He was married three times, and his children include violinist Nigel Kennedy (4).

(4) Nigel Paul Kennedy (*b* Brighton, England, 28 Dec. 1956), violinist. Son of cellist John Kennedy (3), his considerable reputation is enhanced by the ease with which he has broken down the barriers between classical and popular music, in repertoire, performance and personal style.

FURTHER REFERENCE

For Daisy Kennedy, see *Biographical R*; J. Creighton, *Discopaedia of the Violin 1889–1971* (Toronto: University of Toronto Press, 1974); *GlennonA*, 101; *MoresbyA*, 77–80; W. Hancock, *Daisy Kennedy and her Adelaide Concerts* (Adelaide: W. Hancock, 1995). Her papers are in the Performing Arts Collection, Adelaide Festival Centre Trust, Adelaide. For Laurie Kennedy, see Ann Carr-Boyd *GroveD*; *GlennonA*, 105; *MoresbyA*, 95–8. His recordings included *Kol Nidrei* (Edison 80580). For Nigel Kennedy, see *Baker's Biographical Dictionary of Musicians*, 8th edn., ed. Nicholas Slonimsky (New York: Schirmer, 1992). For an index to references to the family in *AMN* see *MarsiI*.

KAY DREYFUS

Kennedy, John, rock singer. Lead singer with the punk hybrid band JFK and the Cuban Crisis in Brisbane, he moved to Sydney in 1982, acquiring a dedicated following. He formed the country-rock band Love Gone Wrong in 1984, releasing singles including *Singing City* (1987) and *Out Of Town* (1989) and the albums *From Go To Woe* (1986) and *Have Songs Will Travel* (1990). His music is a crossbreed of styles ranging from gospel music and blues to punk-rock.

FURTHER REFERENCE

Recordings include *Singing City* (1987, Mighty Boys MB 20037), *Out Of Town* (1989, Mighty Boys MB 20217), *From Go To Woe* (1986, Red Eye RED 11) and *Have Songs Will Travel* (1990, Red Eye REDCD 20). For discography, see *SpencerA*. See also *SpencerW.*

Kenny, Yvonne (*b* Sydney, 25 Nov. 1950), soprano. After studies at the NSW State Conservatorium and the Opera School of La Scala, Milan, she made her London concert debut in 1975, and appeared at Covent Garden from 1976, the English National Opera from 1977, and major houses throughout Europe. She has made numerous concert appearances under major conductors, frequent opera appearances in Australia, and has recorded extensively. An intelligent interpreter with excellent technique and a deep interest in little-heard Baroque or new repertoire, her roles have ranged from Handel's Semele, Alcina (at Covent Garden in 1992), Deborah (at the Proms in 1993), and Romilda (*Xerxes*) and Purcell's *Faery Queen* (at the Coliseum in 1995) to the premieres of Hans Werner Henze's *We Come to the River* and Gavin Bryars' *Medea*. She was honoured with the AM in 1989 and the Sir Bernard Heinze Award in 1995.

FURTHER REFERENCE

Recordings include Barbarina in *Figaro*, London Philharmonic Orchestra (Decca 410 150–2DH3); Constanze in *Die Entführung*, cond. N. Harnoncourt (Teldec 2292–42643–2); Aspasia in *Mitridate*, cond. N. Harnoncourt (Decca 071 407–1DH2); Adelia in Donizetti's *Ugo Conte di Parigi*, New Philharmonia (Opera Rara OR C001); Emilia in *Emilia di Liverpool* (Opera Rara OR C008); Britten, *Folk Songs* (Etcetera KTC 1046); soprano in Elgar, *The Kingdom* (RCA); Mozart, *Requiem*, St John's College Cambridge (Chandos CHAN 8574); Vaughan Williams, *Sea* Symphony and Symphony No. 3 (Chandos CHAN 9087/91); Mendelssohn *Elijah* (Philips 432984–2PH2); Stravinsky, *Pulcinella* (Sony SK 45965); Beethoven, Symphony No. 9 (EMI CMS 565184–2); Bach Cantata 208 (Teldec); and Mozart, *Coronation Mass* (RCA/BMG). See also *CA* (1995/96); *Opera Magazine* (Dec. 1992), 1385–93; Elizabeth Forbes, *GroveO*.

Kernaghan. Family of country music performers.

(1) Ray Kernaghan (*b* Corowa, NSW, *c.*1943), country music singer, producer. He played the guitar from the age of 14, appearing in local talent quests and charity shows. From the early 1960s he toured with *Rick and Thel, then with his own show, making his first album, *Me And Louie On The Road*, in 1977, which won four gold and one platinum records. He formed an independent label, KCR, in 1977 to develop production and distribution methods tailored to country performers. Continuing his tours, now with his trademark jet-powered truck 'Waltzing Matilda', he released *Family Tradition* in 1986. The same year he appeared with his son Lee at the International Fan Fair, Nashville, Tennessee. His children, Tania-

Maree (singer), Greg (drummer), Lee (2), and Fiona (singer), are all country performers.

(2) Lee Kernaghan (b Albury, NSW, 1964), country music singer-songwriter. Born into a family of singers, he first sang on Albury radio 2AY at the age of five, and formed his first band, the Blue Devils, with his brother and sister. With his father Ray (1) he toured with ★Rick and Thel in 1978 and wrote his first song at the age of 13. In 1982 he toured with his father's Cavalcade of Stars show and wrote songs for Castle Music, but sufficient work was hard to find and he played in rock and roll bands until 1992, when the release of his album *The Outback Club*, won him wider popularity. A frenetic, entertaining vocalist who plays New Country honky-tonk piano on stage, his *Three Chain Road* (1993) entered the pop charts. Since 1993 he has won a succession of ACMA Golden Guitars.

FURTHER REFERENCE
For Ray Kernaghan, see *LattaA*, 153; *SmithB*, 91. For Lee Kernaghan, recordings include *The Outback Club* (EMI 4795842) and *Three Chain Road* (1993 EMI 4797672). See also *LattaA*, 153; *SmithB*, 293; *Sunday Age* 16 Jan. 1994.

Kerry, Gordon (b Melbourne, 1961), composer. After studying composition with Barry ★Conyngham at the University of Melbourne, he settled at Sydney in 1986. He was composer-in-residence with the Sydney Philharmonia (1990), a fellow of the Centre for Creative Arts, Virginia, USA (1991), and a resident with Musica Viva in Schools, the Peggy Glanville-Hicks House (1994), and the Youth Music Australia Summer Academy (1994–95). His *Harvesting the Solstice Thunders* (1993) has been performed by most ABC orchestras, he has written for most of Australia's leading contemporary music ensembles, and his chamber opera, *Medea* (1992), has been heard in three states. A composer of complex rhythms but attractive colours and evocative harmonic textures, his song cycle *Obsessions* for mezzo-soprano (1985, Melbourne: Allans, 1987) and *Siderus Nuncius* (UMP, 1985) have been published.

FURTHER REFERENCE
Recordings include Sonatas 3 and 4 in *A Patchwork of Shadows*, Ian Munro, pf (1994, Tall Poppies TP058); *Canticles for Evening Prayer*, SATB (1986, Move MS3064); *Torquing Points*, Melbourne String Quartet (Move MD 3143) *Ongaku* (1991, Jade JADCD1025); and *Winter Through Glass*, hpd (1994, Tall Poppies TP058). See also *BroadstockS*, 147–8, 310–12; *Opera Australia* 191 (Nov. 1993), 5; *SA* 42 (Winter 1994), 36–7.

Kiek, Mara, composer-performer. Playing a variety of Eastern European instruments, she has worked extensively in theatre and dance, including with the One Extra Dance Co. and Meryl Tankard Australian Dance Theatre. She founded Mesane Selata at Sydney in 1983, perform-

ing music of the Balkans, then Girls In Your Town in 1986. She toured Australia and Europe with her folk-jazz ensemble MARA!. She is also an early music performer, having played with the Renaissance Players from 1982, and toured Australia, the UK and Europe with Sinfonye 1986–89. With an Australia Council grant she went to Bulgaria in 1988, on her return forming the Martenitsa Choir, which uses *a cappella* Bulgarian vocal techniques. With the choir she appeared at the Adelaide Festival in 1992 and toured Australia. She has combined Australian folk music, traditional European techniques and jazz styles in a unique blend.

FURTHER REFERENCE
Recordings include *Songs With Mara* (Tall Poppies TP082); *The Martenitsa Choir* (Tall Poppies TP026).

Kilner, Joseph. See *Piano-makers.*

Kimber, Beryl (b Perth), violinist. Born to a musical family in Perth, she made her debut as a soloist with the Melbourne Symphony Orchestra at the age of 13, won the ABC Instrumental and Vocal Competition, and studied at the Royal Academy of Music, London, on a British Council Scholarship, then with Georges Enesco in Paris. She made her London debut at Wigmore Hall in 1950. Winning First Distinction at the 1958 Tchaikovsky Competition in Moscow, she studied with David Oistrakh and toured the Soviet Union. Appearing as a soloist with several London orchestras in 1962, she returned to Australia in 1963 as lecturer (later senior lecturer) at the Elder Conservatorium, Adelaide, and appeared in concert for the ABC, as well as with every ABC orchestra. She continued to appear abroad, making five tours of Russia, and in 1982 served on the jury of the Tchaikovsky Competition. For more than 30 years she has been the doyen of string teachers in SA, producing a number of distinguished pupils. She married pianist Clemens ★Leske, and their son Clemens Leske Jr is also a gifted pianist. She was honoured with the OBE.

King of Pop. Rock music awards (1967–79), begun by the Channel 0–10 television network, but with changing sponsors known as the *Go-Set* King of Pop, then the *TV Week* King of Pop, from 1971. Based on popular voting, in 1969 a female artist award was added, which became Queen of Pop in 1972, and in 1971 other awards were added for instrumentalists, groups and songwriting. Winners included Normie ★Rowe, John ★Farnham, Colleen ★Hewitt, Marcia ★Hines and Daryl ★Braithwaite. In 1979 the sponsor withdrew and the prizes became the ★ABC Countdown Awards.

King Of The Other Country, The. Opera by Gillian ★Whitehead, first performed at the NSW State Conservatorium on 5 Jun 1984.

Kirkpatrick, Anne (*b* Sydney, 4 July 1952), country music singer, guitarist. Daughter of Slim *Dusty and Joy *McKean, she was on the road with her parents from infancy, and began performing in their show at the age of 11. She studied biological sciences at the University of Sydney, and performed in Sydney clubs, absorbing blue-grass and other styles. She sang with the Hamilton Blue-grass Band, releasing her first solo album, *Down Here*, in 1971, and formed the Anne Kirkpatrick Band in 1976. After having a family, she returned to the limelight with the album *Come Back Again* in 1987, and continues to per-form both solo and with the Slim Dusty Show. A pro-foundly soulful vocalist, her crossover combination of traditional, folk, bluegrass and country-rock has won her an unusually wide following, and she has won four ACMA Golden Guitars.

FURTHER REFERENCE
Recordings include *Out Of The Blue (*1991, EMI 4796122) and *Anne Kirkpatrick And Friends Live* (1995, ABC 4798102/4) recorded with her parents at the Tamworth 21st anniversary con-cert. See also *LattaA*, 108–9. *SmithB*, 295.

Kisses for a Quid. Opera in one act by Felix *Werder (1960), libretto by Alan Marshall. A pastiche of the 1920s, it was first performed at Melbourne at the Queen's Theatre on 23 Mar. 1961.

Kitchen, Geoff (Geoffrey William) (*b* Mel-bourne, 23 Oct. 1929; *d* Melbourne, 26 Jan. 1986), jazz reeds player, arranger. Shifting from guitar to clarinet in 1944, he later added other reeds, played with Frank *Johnson 1945–51, and also freelanced and led groups including for the film *Night Club* (1952). He was in Syd-ney 1957–59, with Bob Gibson, then in Melbourne as GTV-9 arranger until 1965, in commercial music produc-tion until 1976, then formed the Jazz Foundations, which recorded his compositions. In the 1980s he ran a music production company, performed with Bruce *Clarke (guitar) and served as president of the Music Arrangers Guild of Australia.

FURTHER REFERENCE
Recordings include *Geoff Kitchen's Quintet* (1953, Spotlight Vari-eties SV-25); *Dixieland Jazz*, Frank Johnson And Friends 1954–56 (1973, Swaggie S1325); *Jazz Foundations* (1977, Swag-gie S-1385); *Dick Tattam's Jazz Ensemble* (1980, Jazznote JNLP-025). See also *BissetB*; *OxfordJ*.   BRUCE JOHNSON

Knehans, Douglas (*b* St Louis, Miss., USA, 3 Apr. 1957), composer. He studied flute and composition at the Canberra School of Music, then with Thea Mus-grave at Queen's College, New York, and for his doctor-ate with Jacob Druckman at Yale University. His terse scores, often portraying themes of darkness or solitude, attracted numerous commissions from Australian ensembles from 1985, a composition fellowship of the

Victorian Council for the Arts in 1987, and from several American soloists since 1991. His works include *In Light* for orchestra (1987) and a chamber opera, *The Ascension of Robert Flau* (1990). Since 1993 he has taught at the University of Alabama, and he is published by Armadillo Edition, New Haven.

FURTHER REFERENCE
BroadstockS, 149–50.

Knowles, Chris (*b* Melbourne, 1955), composer, teacher. After childhood lessons in piano, he studied art and design at the Preston Institute of Technology and formed Ad Hoc, an electronic improvisation group, in 1978, performing at La Mama and Clifton Hill Commu-nity Music Centre. From 1979 he began combining film, synthesisers and tape in works such as *Doctor Dark* (1984). He performed in Signals (1980–83), recording his works *Death of a Hero* (1982) and *Gimme Some Lovin'* (1983), and worked on sound-tracks for experimental films, including *Corpse* (Ronin Films, 1982), *The Hour Before My Brother Dies* (ABC, 1986), *Oblique* (1987, Aust. Film Commis-sion), and *Myself When 14* (1989). Working almost exclu-sively with electronic instruments, his work has explored the connection between musical structure and the general sonic environment.

FURTHER REFERENCE
Recordings include *Death of a Hero* (1982, Rash R004); and *Gimme Some Lovin'* (1983 Rash R008). See also *JenkinsT*, 93–9.

Knox, Roger (*b* 1948, Moree, NSW), Aboriginal country singer. Based at Tamworth, he is leader of the group Euraba, which also includes his son Buddy Knox. Recording extensively through Enrec Studios, his 1983 album *Give it a Go* is considered the first commercially released album with strong Aboriginal content. He made a national tour of Australia in 1981, of the NT and to Canada and the USA in 1988. He won a NADOC award as Aboriginal artist of the year in 1993.

FURTHER REFERENCE
Recordings include *Roger Knox: Give It A Go* (1983, Enrec ENC 001); *Roger Knox: The Gospel Album* (1986, Enrec ENC 020); *War-rior in Chains* (1993, Enrec EN 160CD); and *Koori Classic* series, vols 1, 2, 4, 7 (Enrec). See also A. Rutherford, *Aboriginal Culture Today* (Kenthurst, NSW: Kangaroo Press, 1988).

P. DUNBAR-HALL

Koehne, Graeme (*b* Adelaide, 3 Aug. 1956), com-poser, pianist. He studied at the University of Adelaide, and later at Yale University on a Harkness fellowship (1985–87). Throughout the 1980s and 90s Koehne has been composing across the genres and honing a con-servative approach to his craft. The lush, Ravel-influenced *Rain Forest* (1981) for orchestra with its antithesis in the neo-Baroque *To His Servant Bach, God*

Grants *A Final Glimpse: The Morning Star* (1989) for string orchestra or quartet through to the rumba-based *Powerhouse* (1993) for orchestra, represent the range of his stylistic palate. He has won numerous awards and scholarships for his music, the most important being the ABC Peter Stuyvesant young composers award in 1982 for *Rain Forest.*

WORKS (Selective)
Orchestral *The Iridian Plateau* (1977), *First Blue Hours* (1979), *Rain Forest* (1981, rec. ABC Classics 426478 CD), *riverrun....* (1982), *Unchained Melody* (1990), *Powerhouse* (1993).
Chamber Instrumental Guitar Quartet, gui, va, pf, perc (1974), String Quartet No. 1, *Divertissement:Trois Pieces Bourgeoises* (1983), *Ricercare and Burletta*, str trio (1984), *Miniature*, fl, cl, 2 vn, va, vc (1985), *Capriccio*, pf, str (1987), *Fanfare*, brass, perc (1988), *Aria Da Lonto*, S, pf (1988), *To His Servant Bach, God Grants A Final Glimpse: The Morning Star*, str qrt or str orch (1989), String Quartet No. 2 *Shaker Dances* (1995).
Solo Instrumental *Piano Sonata* (1976), *Twilight Rain*, pf (1979), *Gothic Toccata* (aka *Toccata Aurora*), org (1983, rec. Fifth Continent SCCD 1022 CD), *Aphorisms*, pf (1989).
Theatre *Palm Court Suite* (aka *Old Friends, New Friends*) (1984), *Love Burns* (1991–92, 2, Louis Nowra), 28 Feb. 1992, Adelaide.
Ballet *The Selfish Giant* (1982, 7 scenes, choreog. Graeme Murphy), 12 Jan. 1982, Sydney, *Nearly Beloved* (1986, 3, choreog. Graeme Murphy), 23 Aug 1986, Sydney, *Nocturnes* (aka *Gallery*) (1987, 4 scenes, choreog. Graeme Murphy), 7 Oct. 1987, Melbourne, *Rhythmic Birds of the Antipodes* (aka *Voyage Within*) (1988, 4 scenes, choreog. Garth Welch), 8 July 1988, Perth, *The Summer of Our Memories* (aka *Once Around The Sun*) (1988, 1, choreog. Pamela Buckman and Harold Collins), 7 July 1988, Brisbane.
Vocal/Choral *Dreamer of Dreams*, large ch, orch, org (1986).
Film *The Kid Stakes*, orch, to accompany the 1927 silent film by Tal Ordell (1994), *The Sentimental Bloke*, orch, to accompany the 1919 silent film by Raymond Longford (1995).

FURTHER REFERENCE
Recordings include String Quartet, Australian String Quartet (ABC 442 347); *Gothic Toccata*, D. Kinsela, org (ABC 432 527); *Rain Forest,* Australian Youth Orchestra, cond. C. Eschenbach (CD 42678–2). His writings include 'Art—Capital A, entertainment—small e?' *SA* 22 (Winter 1989), 22, and various letters to the editor in *SA*. See also *BroadstockS.*   JOEL CROTTY

Kooree and the Mists. Ballet by James ★Penberthy (1958), based on an Aboriginal story. First performed at Perth in 1960. As a suite it was recorded by the Sydney Symphony Orchestra under Patrick Thomas (ABC RRC 28).

Kornweibel, Albert H. ('Korny') ['Fidelio'] (*b* London, 22 Dec. 1892; *d* Perth, 7 Mar. 1980), music critic. He had piano lessons as a child and came to Australia in 1912, briefly working on a farm at Wooroloo, WA, then becoming a cadet reporter for the *West Australian,* rising to columnist and subeditor. As 'Fidelio' he

was music critic for the newspaper for nearly 50 years, 1916–65. As a critic he was benign, rarely writing harshly or negatively, and encouraging both professionals and amateurs alike. With hearing failing in his later years he carried a large hearing apparatus into concerts in a box. In his last years he wrote *Apollo and the Pioneers*, the first history of music in WA.

FURTHER REFERENCE
Obit. in *West Australian* 10 Mar. 1980. His book is *Apollo and the Pioneers: The Story of the First 100 Years of Music in WA* (Perth: Music Council of WA, 1973).

Kos, Bozidar (*b* Novo Mesto, Slovenia, 3 May 1934), composer. After studying and teaching cello and theory in Novo Mesto State Music School, Slovenia, he settled in Australia, studying composition with Richard ★Meale at the Elder Conservatorium. He taught at Torrens College of Advanced Education 1975, the Elder Conservatorium 1976–83, and has been lecturer (later senior lecturer) at the NSW State Conservatorium since 1984. His early works include the two-orchestra *Meditations* (1974) and electronic music such as *Modulations* (1974); more recently he has written a violin concerto (1986) and focused on chamber ensembles such as *Ludus ex Nominum* (1989) or *Quaser* (1987). He won the Maggs Award (1983), third prize in the Premio musicale, Città di Trieste (1987), and a Sounds Australian Award in 1991.

FURTHER REFERENCE
Recordings include Violin Concerto (1986, VAST O15–2); *Quasar*, perc qrt (1987, VAST 001–2); and Sonata for pf (1981, Tall Poppies).

Kowalski, Henri (*b* Paris, 1841; *d* Bordeaux, France, 8 July 1916), pianist, composer. After studying piano with Antoine Marmontel, Anatole Petit and composition with Michelle Carofa and Samuel David at the Paris Conservatoire, he became a chorister in the Imperial Chapel, then pianist at the Paris Opéra. He toured France (1864) and Europe (1868) and worked as a music critic for *L'Europe*. He was in the USA 1870–79, then came to Melbourne to give piano recitals at the 1880 Melbourne International Exhibition, and stayed to give promenade concerts in 1881–82. He went to Brussels 1883, then was in Sydney 1885–96, teaching, conducting the Sydney Philharmonic Society and helping form the Orpheus Club (from 1887), with which he gave numerous chamber music concerts.

A fine pianist and widely performed composer, he wrote three operas, songs, and over 100 piano pieces, among which the *Marche Hongroise* (1864) sold a vast number of copies. Excerpts from his opera *Moustique* (1881) with a libretto by Marcus Clarke were performed under his direction at Sydney in 1889, his *Vercingétorix* (1881) was performed at Sydney and Melbourne, and his oratorio *The Future Life* (Sydney: W.A. Pepperday, 1896) was given at Sydney in 1895.

FURTHER REFERENCE

His writing may be sampled in *A travers l'Amerique: impressions d'un musicien* (Paris: E. Lachaud, 1872). See also E. Wood, *GroveD*; *Irvin D*; Eric Irvin, *Australian Melodrama: 80 Years of Popular Theatre* (Sydney: Hale & Iremonger, 1981); Viola Tait, *A Family of Brothers* (Melbourne: Heinemann, 1971), 23; Oscar Comettant, *Kangaroos and Goldmines* (Adelaide: Rigby, 1980).

Krape, Evelyn   (*b* Melbourne, 2 Aug. 1949), musical comedy actress, singer. After studying voice at the University of Melbourne and drama at the Melbourne State College, she became a founding member of the Australian Performing Group at the Pram Factory, Melbourne, and later married its resident dramatist Jack Hibberd in 1978. As well as appearing in plays such as *Don's Party* and *Female Parts*, she has appeared in the musicals *A Toast To Melba* (1976) and the revues *Back to Bourke Street*, *Betty Can Jump*, and *Sonia's Knee and Thigh Show*, winning a Green Room Award for her performance in the musical *Ginger* (1992). An adaptable performer, she thrives in the more provocative and stimulating fringes of musical comedy.

FURTHER REFERENCE

Kevin Childs, *A Month of Lunches: 28 Lives Celebrate Melbourne* (Melbourne: OUP, 1984), 77–80; *ParsonsC*; *Age* 6 June 1991.

Krasnik, William   (*b* Sydney, *c*. 1911; *d* London, 1981), viola player. After studying at the NSW State Conservatorium he played in the ABC (Sydney) string quartet formed in 1932 for radio broadcast, was a founding member of the Sydney String Quartet in 1945, and replaced Richard ★Goldner in the Musica Viva Society ensemble in 1950. He went to London and joined the Royal Opera House Orchestra, and was with the London Symphony Orchestra for 15 years, making recordings for the BBC, and some with his sister, the pianist Olga Krasnik. He toured Australia shortly before his death in 1981.

Kriol.   Language developed from pidgin with an estimated 20 000 speakers in NT, parts of WA and Queensland. The name was originally given to the creole of the Roper River and Barunga areas, northern NT, but now commonly applies to any related varieties used throughout the area. Much of Kriol derives from English, and some Aboriginal people consider it has been a factor in the decline in the use of ancestral languages. The Aboriginal band Blekbala Mujik sings in Kriol and performs traditional material; they may be heard on *Midnait Mujik* (1990, CAAMA Music 213). See *Aboriginal Music*.

Krips, Henry   (*b* Vienna, 1912; *d* Adelaide, 1987), conductor. The brother of Josef Krips, he studied at the Vienna University and Conservatory. After an appointment as conductor at Innsbruck, he migrated to Australia in 1938, conducted opera and ballet, became resident conductor of the ABC Perth Symphony Orchestra (1946–49), and then for 23 years was conductor of the South Australian Symphony Orchestra (1949–72), making a remarkable impact on musical life in Adelaide. During annual visits to Europe he conducted orchestras in London and on the Continent, and conducted at Sadler's Wells Opera and the English National Opera. His compositions include operas, ballets, songs and piano works.

FURTHER REFERENCE

He recorded for EMI, RCA, Festival and the World Record Club; for discography see *HolmesC*. See also Noël Goodwin, *GroveD*; *GlennonA*, 126.

J.L. HOLMES

Kruse, Johann(es) Secundus   (*b* Melbourne, 1859; *d* Nov. 1927), violinist. Born of German parents, he was a child prodigy, playing at the front desk of the Philharmonic Society concerts at Melbourne at the age of nine, then as a soloist at the Metropolitan Liedertafel concerts. With funds raised through the Liedertafel, he went to Berlin in 1875 and studied with Joseph Joachim. He was principal violin in the Berlin Philharmonic Society from 1880, then a member of the Joachim Quartet from 1892. Settling in London in 1897, he gave concerts and had his own quartet. He visited Australia for concerts in 1884 and 1895. A player with gifts of the front international rank, he was the first Australian instrumentalist to find success in Europe.

FURTHER REFERENCE

Sally O'Neill *ADB*, 5; W. Cobbett, *GroveD*; *BrewerD*, 84; Viola Tait, *A Family of Brothers* (Melbourne: Heinemann, 1971), 10–11.

Kuckles.   Broome-based Aboriginal band led by Jimmy Chi; some members were also in the band ★Scrap Metal. See *Chi, Jimmy*.

Kuepper, Ed(mund)   (*b* Germany, 20 Dec. 1955), rock guitarist-songwriter. He founded the ★Saints at Brisbane (1975–77), then the jazz-rock band the Laughing Clowns (1979–85). His album *Electrical Storm* (1986), on which he plays most instruments, was acclaimed by rock critics, and he formed The Yard Goes On Forever as a backing band (1986–), touring and releasing the single *Nothing Changes In My House* (1987) and the album *Everybody's Got To* (1988). He played with the Apartments (1989–90), the hard-rock, jazz-influenced The Aints (1991–), Mephisto Waltz (1991), and recorded as Today Wonder (1990), releasing *Way I Made You Feel* (1992) and the album *Character Assassination* (1994). An important individualist among rock musicians and a guitarist of strong harmonic imagination, he was voted *Rolling Stone* (Aust.) Best Guitarist in 1988 and won an ARIA award for *Black Ticket Day* in 1992.

FURTHER REFERENCE

Recordings include *Electrical Storm* (1986, Hot HOTLP 1020), *Nothing Changes In My House* (1987, Truetone TS 2025), *Every-*

body's *Got To* (1988, Truetone TLP 790513), *Way I Made You Feel* (1992, Hot HIT 1), *Character Assassination* (1994, Hot HOT 1049CD), and *Black Ticket Day* (Hot HOT 1040). For discography, see *SpencerA*. See also *CA* (1995–96); Larkin, II, 1409; *SpencerW*.

Kukatja. People of the desert region around Balgo, central-eastern WA, among the last desert nomads to experience Western influence. Although family groups of Kukatja live at several north-western settlements, the greatest concentration live at Balgo and its southern outstations. Despite Balgo's existence for 40 years as a Roman Catholic mission, ritual life has continued largely uninterrupted, and the region is recognised and widely revered as a 'Law' place. Particularly during the early 1980s, ritual life for men, women, and integrated groups flourished to an extent unreported elsewhere, with rehearsals, preparations and enactments occurring almost daily.

Centrally located in the north-western desert, the Kukatja have long operated an active trade network among much of the Walmatjarri, Warlpiri and Pitjantjat-jara-speaking regions, exchanging not only material goods and marriage partners but also rituals. Indeed, more than half the rituals in the Balgo repertoire are of non-Kukatja origin. Those of local origin fall into the same segregated and integrated categories found throughout the desert region. Road (and, since the 1970s, air) mobility allows residents to travel several hundred kilometres to participate in large multi-tribal ceremonies or smaller, subsection-based rites; the recent establishment of Pintupi outstations to the south and the blazing of new cross-country routes have further widened the contact network.

Acquisition of the *tjuluru* ritual in the mid-1970s and subsequent administration of its sanctioned physical control over the inhabitants of neighbouring settlements resulted in it being commonly called 'Balgo Business' and even repulsed in individual locations.

In general, songs in the Kukatja repertoire exhibit the same stylistic characteristics as those of their desert neighbours. Of particular interest is the use of an analytical vocabulary centring on the term *tjarra* (fork, division) to refer both to individual isorhythms within a song and to the rhythmic make-up of complete songs. Unusually in the region, and as a result of extended pre-European contact with the Warlpiri, Kukatja fathers are able to choose between their own and the Warlpiri forms of male initiation ritual for their sons. See also *Aboriginal Music* §2.

FURTHER REFERENCE
Richard M. Moyle, *Balgo: The Music Life of a Desert Community* (Perth: Univ. WA Press, in press).

RICHARD MOYLE

L

La De Das. Rock group (1964–75) founded in NZ, originally comprised of Kevin ★Borich (guitar, vocals), Bruce Howard (organ), Phil Key (vocals), Trevor Wilson (bass to 1970, then Peter Roberts), and Brett Neilson (drums, vocals to 1967, then Keith Barber). Initially formed as the Mergers in 1964 and influenced by the Rolling Stones and mod fashion, after local success in NZ their *How Is The Air Up There?* topped the Sydney charts in 1966 and they moved to Sydney in 1967. Changing to an experimental, psychedelic image with unusual instrumentation involving organ, flute, sitar, mandolin and cello, by 1968 they were at the forefront of the 'flower power' fashion and were voted *Go-Set* best Australian act. Their *Happy Prince* (1969), based on the Oscar Wilde story, was Australia's first concept album. In 1969 they went to the UK, but the fashion was already in decline, and they returned to Australia in 1970. After internal friction the band was reduced to a trio, with a further change of style to hard-rock boogie, featuring Borich's guitar work. In 1971 they were at the forefront of Australian popularity and a favourite at major festivals, *Gonna See My Baby Tonight* reaching No. 12 in the charts; they toured NZ in 1972.

With strong individual musicianship, they had sustained success through three substantial style changes, producing 11 successful singles. Despite continuing success, with *Too Pooped To Pop* reaching No. 26 in 1974, they disbanded in 1975 amid internal animosity, loss of momentum and the sense that their current style was again passing out of favour.

FURTHER REFERENCE
Recordings include *Other Love* (1967, Philips BF315); *Gonna See My Baby Tonight* (1971, HMV EA 9638); *Too Pooped To Pop* (1974, EMI EMI 10464); *Happy Prince* (1969, HMV SCX6 7899); *Rock-'n'Roll Sandwich* (1973, EMI EMC 2504); a compilation is *Rock N Roll Decade 1969–74* (1981, EMI EMY 508–9). For discography, see *SpencerA*. See also *GuinnessP*, II, 1417; John Dix, 'The Ten Year Saga of the La De Das', in *Stranded in Paradise* (NZ: Paradise Publications, 1988), 67–75. *McGrathA*; *SpencerW.*

La Donna. Opera in one act by Colin ★Brumby, libretto by David Goddard. Workshop performance at the Sydney Opera Centre on 2 July 1988.

La Romanesca. Early music group specialising in the Medieval, Renaissance and early Baroque periods. Founded in Melbourne in 1978 by Ruth Wilkinson (recorder, viola da gamba), Ros ★Bandt (recorder, psaltery), Hartley Newnham (countertenor), and John ★Griffiths (lutes), the ensemble maintains its original membership but frequently expands its resources for specific projects. La Romanesca has played a decisive role in the flowering of early music in Australia, and was the first Australian early music ensemble to achieve international prominence in tours to Europe, Asia, and the USA (1982–87). The ensemble has made numerous recordings for Move Records of music from the Iberian Peninsula, France and Italy.

FURTHER REFERENCE
Recordings include *Medieval Monodies* (Move MD 3044); *Iberian Triangle* (Move MD 3114).   JOHN GRIFFITHS

Lagerphone [Murrumbidgee River Rattler]. Folk music percussion instrument popular with bush bands since being introduced by the original ★Bushwhackers (1952), who had observed its use at Holbrook, NSW. Essentially a rattle, perhaps related to the Turkish crescent, it is not of traditional bush band origin. It is constructed of a shoulder-height pole, often with transverse boards, to which larger bottletops are loosely nailed. It is stamped on the ground or struck or bowed with a serrated stick.

FURTHER REFERENCE
Merle Lamb, 'Make Yourself a Lagerphone', *Australian Tradition* 3/1 (Mar. 1966), 25–6; John Manifold, *The Violin, the Banjo and the Bones* (Ferntree Gully, Vic.: Rams Skull Press, 1957), 13–14.

Lamb, Alan (*b* Edinburgh, Scotland, 1944), physiologist, sound experimenter. He studied medicine at the University of Western Australia, then physiology at the

University of Edinburgh. From 1971 he began to experiment with recording and processing the sounds inherent in catgut, nylon thread and later telephone wires suspended in natural environments. Beginning with *Primal Image* (1982), he has produced various works exploring these materials, and from 1984 he collaborated with Sarah *Hopkins, producing the striking *Sky Song* (1985), choreographed for dances by Danceworks.

FURTHER REFERENCE
Recordings include *Sky Song* (1985, ABC 838503) and *Journeys On the Winds of Time I* (1987, New Albion NA028). See also *Jenkins T*, 107–14.

Lambert, Raymond Edouard (*b* Ostend, Belgium, 13 June 1908; *d* Melbourne, 17 Jan. 1966), pianist, teacher.
He studied at the Liège and Brussels Conservatoriums and later received lessons from Arthur deGreef. He arrived in Australia in 1926 with his father Edouard Lambert, an eminent violinist who became leader of the Melbourne Symphony Orchestra. The Lamberts were well received in Australia, Raymond being praised for his polished performances and natural technique. In 1932 he was appointed a chief study teacher at the University of Melbourne Conservatorium, a position he held until his death. A regular soloist for the ABC, he gave Australian premiere performances of several concertos including Gershwin's *Rhapsody in Blue*. Well known for his involvement in chamber music, he was official accompanist for the ABC and toured Australia and overseas with musicians such as Joan *Hammond, Clara Butt, John *Brownlee, Florence *Austral, Alexander Kipnis, Michael Rabin, Ruggiero Ricci, and Marjorie *Lawrence. A frequent radio broadcaster, he gave a series of recital broadcasts called *The Evolution of French Piano Music* in 1963.

FURTHER REFERENCE
Obit. in *Age* 18 Jan. 1966. Recordings include two solo albums (1958, 1961, W&G) now not current. For references in *AMN*, see *Marsi I*. See also theatre programs collection, *Msl*; Raymond Lambert papers, MS 95/88, *Msl*.   JENNIFER ROYLE

Lamentable Reign of King Charles the Last, The. Pantomime opera in one act by George *Dreyfus (1976), libretto by Tim Robertson. It is a satire of the British royalty. First performed at the Adelaide Festival on 25 March 1976.

Lamond, Toni [Patricia Lamond Lawman] (*b* Sydney, 29 Mar. 1932), theatrical singer, actress. Daughter of the comedian Joe Lawman and variety actress Stella Lamond, she first appeared on stage as a child, and made a career in stage musicals for the Tivoli circuit from 1952, notably in *Pyjama Game* (1957), *Wildcat* (1963) and *Oliver* (1966). While raising a family from 1956 she appeared in television variety programs; the suicide of her ex-husband, the producer Frank Sheldon, in 1966 adversely affected her

for several years, but she was working again from 1969. In 1976 she moved to Los Angeles, returning to Australia for the television series *The Last Frontier* (1986), the musical *42nd Street* (1989–92) and the film *Spotswood* (1991). A very successful stage personality in Australia since the 1950s, she has won two Logies for her television work. Her son is the actor Tony Sheldon.

FURTHER REFERENCE
Australian 8 Feb. 1992; *DPA*; *Parsons C*.

Lancaster, Geoffrey, harpsichordist, fortepianist.
After piano study with Larry *Sitsky at the Canberra School of Music and Beryl *Sedivka at the Tasmanian Conservatorium, he studied fortepiano at the Royal Conservatorium, The Hague, on an Australia Council international study grant, winning the 23rd Festival of Flanders International Mozart Fortepiano Competition. He has performed in early music concerts in Europe, the USA and NZ, as well as for the ABC and at early music festivals in Australia. Teaching at the Tasmanian Conservatorium, from 1987 he directed Baroque works from the harpsichord with the Tasmanian Symphony Chamber Players. He was at the Queensland Conservatorium and director of the Queensland Philharmonic Orchestra from 1989. Curator of musical instruments at the Powerhouse Museum, Sydney, from 1990, he worked as an Australia Council creative arts fellow 1993–95. Australia's most successful fortepianist and one of its leading exponents of Baroque and early Classical authentic performance practice, he won an ARIA award with the Tasmanian Symphony Chamber Players in 1990.

FURTHER REFERENCE
Recordings include Vivaldi, *Four Seasons*, Tasmanian Symphony Chamber Players (ABC); *Geoffrey Lancaster: Fortepiano* (1990, ABC 432248–2); and Mozart, *Eine kleine Nachtmusik*/ Telemann and Bach, Tasmanian Symphony Orchestra (1992, ABC 434899–2).

Lance, Albert [Lance(lot) Albert Ingram] (*b* Menindie, NSW, 12 July 1925), tenor. After lessons with Greta Callow in Adelaide, Ingram sang in vaudeville and on radio in Melbourne from 1946 as 'The Voice in a Million'; his operatic career began with the National Theatre Opera Co. in 1951 and as Cavaradossi at Sydney in 1952. Dominique Modesti heard him and invited him to Paris for lessons 1954–55, and having changed his name to Lance to avoid *ungram* (Fr. light weight), he gave a stunning debut and became principal tenor at the Paris Opéra and Opéra-Comique from 1956. He sang at Covent Garden from 1958, the Bolshoi Theatre 1965–66, and Strasbourg 1972–76, making guest appearances in French-speaking, Soviet and American houses. Highly regarded in France, at his height he was one of the finest tenors in Europe. Roles in which he was unsurpassable included Cavaradossi, Don José, Pinkerton,

Hoffmann, and the Duke of Mantua; he sang the British premiere of Roussel's *Padmâvati*. From 1974 he taught at Nice Conservatory.

FURTHER REFERENCE
Recordings (most now rare) include *Werther* (Adès DES 140083–2); *Madame Butterfly, Tosca* and Massenet *Hérodiade* (Pathé); and a solo recital *Albert Lance* (Columbia). Two reissues are *Callas at the Paris Opéra* (EMI LDB 91258–1) and *Les Contes d'Hoffmann* (excerpts) (Adès 13208–2). See also Roger Covell, *GroveO*; *MackenzieS*, 194–6.

Land of Beauty, The. Ode by Frederick A. *Packer (1894) for choir, organ and orchestra, performed at the opening of the Hobart International Exhibition by the Exhibition Choir and Orchestra on 15 November 1894. Unpublished.

Land of Heart's Desire, The. Opera in one act, music and text by Fritz *Hart, after the Yeats poem, first performed by the Melbourne Conservatorium in 1914.

Landa, Albert (*b* Sydney, 21 Apr. 1937), pianist. He played the Mozart concerto in D K.466 at the Sydney Town Hall at the age of 10 and completed his AMusA at the record age of 11. Also studying french horn, he played in the Sydney Symphony Orchestra 1959–63 and formed the short-lived Sydney Chamber Orchestra for which he was conductor and soloist. He then went to the Royal Academy of Music, London, and studied with Clifford Curzon in 1966, giving concerts in England and Europe, and returned to Australia in 1971 to teach at the NSW State Conservatorium. Appearing with all major Australian orchestras, he has also occasionally composed, and his Symphony has been broadcast by the ABC. He retired from the Conservatorium in 1995, but continues to be associated with the David Paul Landa Scholarship, established in memory of his brother, former attorney-general of NSW.

FURTHER REFERENCE
Recordings include *Piano Classics for Pleasure* (1972, EMI/Axis AXIS 7004) and *16 Popular Piano Encores* (EMI/Axis AXIS 7012). See also *Australian* 4 Apr. 1992.

Lane, Joe (Keith Joseph) (*b* Sydney, 21 Mar. 1927); jazz singer. He began on drums, but later became more notable as a singer, working in nightclubs and coffee lounges in the postwar period, alternating between Melbourne and Sydney. A proselytiser for bop, he was especially influential among the younger generation of modernists. He was in Sydney from 1963, but with little visibility owing to the dormancy of jazz; the late 1970s jazz resurgence has given him new prominence, when he generally led his own groups, including Killer Joe. He is Australia's most individual and intense bop singer.

FURTHER REFERENCE
His recording is *The Arrival,* Joe Bebop Lane (1996, Spiral Scratch 0012). See also *ClareB*; *BissetB*; *OxfordJ*. BRUCE JOHNSON

Lane, Piers (*b* London 1958), pianist. He moved to Australia at a very early age, and studied piano with Nancy Weir (Queensland Conservatorium), Bela Siki (Seattle), Kendall Taylor and Yonty Solomon (London) and participated in masterclasses with Jorge Bolet. He has performed widely with all the major UK orchestras and at their major recital venues. Based in London, he regularly tours Australia and has also played in the USA, Latin America, Asia, the Middle East and Europe. Especially sought after for his brilliant performances of rarer virtuoso 19th-century repertoire, both solo piano and concertante, he has performed the Bliss piano concerto at a Promenade concert in London's Royal Albert Hall for the composer's centenary celebrations. In 1995 he gave the first performance in 101 years of the Parry piano concerto and has recorded extensively. He is professor of music at the Royal Academy of Music, London.

FURTHER REFERENCE
His recordings include Parry Concerto, Stanford, Piano Concerto No. 1 (Hyperion); Moszkowski Concerto op. 59, Paderewski Concerto, d'Albert Concertos Nos 1 and 2 (Hyperion); Delius Concerto, Vaughan Williams Concerto (EMI); William Busch Piano Concerto (Lyrita); Scriabin *Études* (Hyperion); Brahms Piano Quintet (Hyperion); and transcriptions of works by Johann Strauss II (Hyperion).

CYRUS MEHER-HOMJI

Larrikins, The. Folk music band formed in Sydney, comprised of Ned Alexander (fiddle), Tony Sutter (button accordion, anglo concertina), Jack Fallis (mandolin, guitar), Paddy McLaughlin (banjo), and Liora Claff (guitar, whistle). Formed by Sydney folklorist Warren Fahey to present authentic Australian folk music and promote the traditional folk heritage, they provided music for the ABC radio series *While the Billy Boils,* devised by Fahey to trace Australia's history through songs.

FURTHER REFERENCE
Their recordings include *Limejuice and Vinegar* (Larrikin LRF 159), *The Larrikin Sessions* (EMI CD 4796472) and *Australia's Awake* (Larrikin LRE 043). See also Warren Fahey, *The Balls of Bob Menzies: Australian Political Songs 1900–1980* (Sydney: Angus & Robertson, 1989).

Las Alboradas. Work for flute, violin, horn, and piano by Richard *Meale (1963) featured at the Adelaide Festival in 1964. Published by Boosey & Hawkes, and recorded with the composer directing (World Record Club S/2472).

Laudes. Chamber work (1963) by Nigel *Butterley. The four movements are meditations in praise (Latin, *laudes)* of four churches: Sant'Apollinare Nuovo at Ravenna, Norwich Cathedral, King's College Chapel at Cambridge, and the Church of the Resurrection of the Taizé community, Burgundy. First performed at the Adelaide Festival, 1964; Recorded 1965 (World Record Club A602).

Laughing Clowns, The. Rock group (1979–83) formed in Sydney and comprised of players from a mixture of jazz, soul and rock backgrounds under Ed ★Kuepper, formerly of the ★Saints. They made their debut appearance only after Kuepper rehearsed them for six months, but his fans at first found the complex mixture of styles opaque. Their mini-LP *Laughing Clowns* was released in 1980; after that Kuepper set up Prince Melon Records to control later records, such as *Laughing Clowns 3*. With an expanded membership they were supporting act to the UK band Magazine in 1980. After releasing their debut album *Mr Uddich-Schmuddich Goes To Town* (1981) they toured Australia and the UK 1982–83, their innovative mixture of hard rock and modern jazz ideas gradually winning considerable influence. But Kuepper's numerous membership changes to the band led to acrimony, and after *Ghosts Of An Ideal Wife* tensions led to their disbanding.

FURTHER REFERENCE
Recordings include *Laughing Clowns* (Missing Link ING 001), *Laughing Clowns 3* (1980 PM 05LP), *Mr Uddich-Schmuddich Goes To Town* (1981, Prince Melon PM 5000), and *Ghosts Of An Ideal Wife* (reissued 1993, Hot HOT 1013). For discography, see *SpencerA*. See also *McGrathA*; *SpencerW*; *GuinnessP*, II, 1434; Ian McFarlane, 'Laughing Clowns, Eternally Yours', *Prehistoric Sounds* 1/2 (1995), 40–4.

Launceston, pop. (1991) 66 747. Second largest city in Tasmania, settled from 1804. Set on the Tamar River, it is the chief port of northern Tasmania. Musical life began early: by 1826 an English organ had been imported for the new St John's Church, and by 1834 Hobart artists such as singer Anne ★Clarke were visiting to perform; by 1836 a theatre had opened, and Clarke brought her own opera troupe for seasons from 1842. St Joseph's Total Abstinence Society Band, the first civilian brass band in Australia, was formed by 1845 and still survives today, having the longest history of any such band in Commonwealth countries outside Britain. Virtuoso violinist Miska ★Hauser toured in 1855 and was followed by a succession of others. A Mechanics' Institute was built and installed a three-manual English organ *c*.1859, which in 1891 was moved to the Albert Hall and extended for the Tasmanian International Exhibition. The Launceston Competitions Association was formed in 1901, and celebrated its jubilee in 1927 by bringing Fritz ★Hart from Melbourne as adjudicator and offering prizes of £500. The Launceston Studio Music Society (formed in 1932) held Chopin soirées,

the Launceston Choral Union gave oratorio performances such as *Elijah* (1936), bringing soloists from Melbourne.

Today there are at least six brass bands operating in the city, a pipe band, the Launceston Jazz Club, the Old Novitiate Folk Club, the Northern Tasmanian Country Music Club, a Light Opera Society and an Orchestral Society. The Tasmanian Symphony and mainland opera and ballet perform at the Civic Centre.

Lavater, Louis Isador   (*b* St Kilda, Melbourne, 2 Mar. 1867; *d* St Kilda, Melbourne, 22 May 1953), composer, poet. Abandoning medical studies at the University of Melbourne, he worked in a bank from 1885 while pursuing his musical interests, then settled at Colac, Vic., in 1892 to teach music and conduct local choirs. He taught piano at the University of Melbourne Conservatorium from 1894, was a popular adjudicator of eisteddfods, and also wrote poetry under various pseudonyms. He published orchestral works, motets, part songs and a piano sonata, and his ballet suite *Nina* was performed in Australia and London. He was secretary of the British Music Society, president of the Association of Music Teachers of Victoria and, to promote music by Australians, founded the Guild of Australian Composers in 1935.

FURTHER REFERENCE
Valerie Kent, *ADB* 10; B. Nettie Palmer, 'Louis Lavater', *Meanjin* 10 (1951), 352, 364–7; Allen and F.T. Macartney, 'Louis Lavater', *Meanjin* 12 (1953), 319–24.

Lavenu, Louis Henry   (*b* London, 1818; *d* Sydney, 1 Aug. 1859), conductor, cellist. Son of a flautist and music-seller, then after his father's death stepson of the violinist Nicholas Mori, he sang in the choir of Westminster Abbey as a boy and studied composition with Bochsa and Potter at the Royal Academy of Music. He worked as a cellist at the Drury Lane Opera, and after Mori's death in 1839 continued the family music-selling business, publishing his own songs and piano works. His opera *Loretta, A Tale of Seville* was performed at Drury Lane in 1846, and he toured England as associate artist with the singers Giulia Grisi and Giovanni Mario. He toured abroad with Catherine Hayes, visiting Australia with her in 1853–54. The tour with Hayes took him next to India, but he soon returned to Australia to settle, conducting for the Torning Opera troupe from 1856 at Sydney and Melbourne. His conducting appearances included the Melbourne premiere of *Il trovatore* (1858, for which he also arranged the music). A musician of excellent talent who set about raising the standards of theatre music in Australia, his work was soon cut short by epilepsy. Suffering from the stress of conducting the festival at the opening of the University of Sydney Great Hall in 1859, he died of an epileptic fit a few days afterwards.

FURTHER REFERENCE
Obit. in Melbourne *Examiner* 6 Aug. 1859; *SMH* 13 Aug. 1859.
See also: George Grove, *A Dictionary of Music and Musicians* [1st
edn.], 4 vols (London: Macmillan, 1889), II; *OrchardM*, 168–9;
Illustrated Sydney News 1 Oct. 1854.

Laver, W(illiam) A(dolphus) (*b* Castlemaine, Vic.,
20 Aug. 1866; *d* Kinglake,Vic., 2 July 1940), music professor. A child prodigy on the violin, Laver studied at the
Hoch Conservatorium in Frankfurt. Upon his return to
Australia in 1889, he drew up plans for a National Academy of Music, which were substantially realised in the
creation of the Conservatorium of Music for the University of Melbourne in 1895. He served on the staff of the
Conservatorium, teaching piano and theory from its
inception, and was Ormond professor from 1915 to his
retirement in 1925. A musician of multifarious talents,
Laver was by all accounts an inspirational teacher. An
overture was composed by him for the jubilee celebrations of the university in 1906.

FURTHER REFERENCE
Thérèse Radic, *ADB*, 10.   PETER TREGEAR

Lawrance, Alf(red) J. (*fl.* 1905–50), English songwriter. Composer of thousands of songs, some performed
by English music hall stars including Ada Reeve, Vesta
Tilley and Marie Lloyd. He spent at least 1914–15 in Australia and NZ, touring the Fuller vaudeville circuit as
pianist for his singer and monologuist wife Violet Carmen. He wrote many songs on NZ and Australian subjects and published some with prominent Sydney and
Melbourne firms and in Britain. His songs featured here
in vaudeville, musical comedy, revue and pantomine: it
was his *Babes in the Wood* that George Willoughby
imported and localised for the 1914–15 season, and nearly
12 of Lawrance's songs were included. His *And the Kookaburra Laughed* and *Night in the Bush* were both recorded
by Columbia.

FURTHER REFERENCE
A list of some of his works appears in *SnellA*. See also *Theatre* 1
Apr. 1914, 31; *Theatre* 1 Apr. 1915, 1–2.   JENNIFER HILL

Lawrence, Marjorie Florence (*b* Dean's Marsh, nr
Melbourne, 17 Feb. 1907 [not 1909], *d* Little Rock,
Arkansas, USA, 13 Jan. 1979), soprano. She studied singing
from 1925 with Ivor Boustead in Melbourne and, after
winning the Geelong *Sun* Aria in 1928, with Cécile Gilly
in Paris. Her operatic debut, as Elisabeth in Wagner's
Tannhäuser, was at Monte Carlo on 21 January 1932. Aged
only 26, she made her debut at the Paris Opéra as Ortrud
in Wagner's *Lohengrin* on 25 February 1933, and gave a
further 32 performances there that year, as Brünnhilde in
Wagner's *Walküre* and *Götterdämmerung,* Salomé in
Massenet's *Hérodiade,* Rachel in Halévy's *La juive,* Verdi's
Aida, and created the role of Keltis in Canteloube's *Verc-*

ingétorix. By the time she left Paris in 1936, she had added,
among others, Strauss's Salome, and Brunehild in Reyer's
Sigurd. She made her debut with the Metropolitan Opera,
New York, on 18 December 1935 as Brünnhilde in *Die
Walküre;* three weeks later, instead of leading her horse,
she boldly leapt onto him and rode him into the flames in
Götterdämmerung, an event which has passed into legend.

The rest of her operatic career was centred at the 'Met'
with which, until 1944, she sang 12 roles in 74 performances, concentrating on Strauss's Salome (seven performances) and the Wagnerian roles of Ortrud (13), Venus in
Tannhäuser (11) and, above all, Brünnhilde in *Die Walküre*
(18), *Siegfried* (six) and *Götterdämmerung* (six); other roles
included Puccini's Tosca, Massenet's Thaïs, Gluck's Alceste,
and Sieglinde in *Die Walküre*. By the beginning of 1941 it
appeared that she would become one of the century's
greatest dramatic sopranos, but in Mexico City she caught
polio and was partially paralysed; at the age of 34 her
career was effectively over. Through an extraordinary
effort, she recovered enough to continue a limited career,
in concert on a wheeled platform, and, from 1942, in
special operatic productions designed so that she could
remain seated throughout the performance. The latter
included her Amneris in *Aida* for the (Australian)
National Theatre Opera Co., as part of her fourth Australian tour (1951), her earlier Australian tours being in
1939, 1944 and 1949. She was noted for her war effort,
undertaking tours to entertain troops in the south-west
Pacific in 1944, and in occupied Europe in 1945 and
1948. She retired from performance in 1952, teaching at
Tulane (New Orleans) and Southern Illinois Universities.

Her studio recordings, made in her mid-twenties,
show a dramatic soprano voice of great richness and
intensity, Lawrence infusing her roles with a youthful *joie
de vivre*. In a career of effectively only nine years, she established herself as one of the two finest dramatic sopranos
Australia has produced. She was awarded the Légion
d'honneur in 1946, and the CBE in 1976.

FURTHER REFERENCE
Studio recordings include highlights of her Ortrud, Brünnhilde,
Salome, and Brunehild (Paris 1933–34, Lebendige Vergangenheit
89011); live recordings include her Senta in *Der fliegende Holländer* (1936, Pearl GEMM CDS9910); *Götterdämmerung* Brünnhilde
(1936, Walhall WHL24); Ortrud (1936, Melodram MEL 310);
Carmen in Bizet's *Carmen* (1940, EJS 266); *Walküre* Brünnhilde
(1940, EJS 178), and Sieglinde (1940, UORC 186). Her autobiography, *Interrupted Melody* (Sydney: Invincible, 1949), was
released as a movie in 1955. Her papers (1938–68) are in *CAnl*,
MS 7225. See also: more than 100 articles in *AMN* (index in
MarsiI); *BrisbaneE*; Helga Griffin, *ADB* 10; *MackenzieS*.
                                        ROYSTON GUSTAVSON

Lawrence, (Raymond) Douglas (*b* Melbourne, 17
Aug. 1943), organist, choral conductor. Educated at the
University of Melbourne where he studied organ with
Lance *Hardy and Sergio *de Pieri, he later spent two

years at the Vienna Academy under Anton Heiller and returned to Melbourne in 1971. In 1972 he was appointed the artistic director of the *Melbourne Autumn (International) Festival of Organ and Harpsichord, a position he occupied until 1985. An organ teacher at the University of Melbourne, he has undertaken many recital tours locally and overseas and made numerous recordings. He also holds two church appointments: master of the Chapel Music at Ormond College and director of music at the Scots Church, Melbourne. He was awarded the OAM in 1992.

FURTHER REFERENCE

Recordings as an organist include *Pachelbel, His Canon and More* (Move MD 3013); *Festival of Organ Masterpieces* (Move MD 3020); as conductor of the Choir of Ormond College, *I Heard the Owl Call My Name* (Move MD 3130); *I Can Tell The World* (Move MD 3109).   JOHN MAIDMENT

Lawson, Henry Archibald (*b* Grenfell, NSW, 17 June 1867; *d* Abbotsford, Sydney, 22 Sept. 1922), balladist, short story writer. Sent to the bush by the *Bulletin* in 1892, he returned to write tales of country life whose blend of endurance and hopelessness are among the masterpieces of Australian storytelling. A number of his ballads passed into folk-song, including 'Andy's Gone With Cattle', 'Ballad of the Drover', 'Freedom on the Wallaby', 'Reedy River', 'The Shearer's Dream', and 'Taking His Chance [Jack Dean]'. His works have a traditional ring to them, and it is not always clear where he has edited existing material rather than written the verses he presents. His talent expired early, and his later years were melancholy: separated from his wife, he had periods in jail and a mental hospital, and died of alcoholism at the age of 54.

FURTHER REFERENCE

Songs From Lawson ed. John Meredith (Sydney: Scott, 1956); Chris Kempster, *The Songs of Henry Lawson* (Ringwood, Vic.: Viking O'Neill, 1989). See also *OxfordL*; *OxfordF*.

Lazar, Samuel (*b* Nov. 1838; *d* Sydney, Nov. 1883), theatre manager, musical entrepreneur. Son of the theatrical entrepreneur John Lazar, he made his stage debut at the age of five in Fielding's burlesque *Tom Thumb* at the Royal Victoria Theatre, Sydney, in 1843. As an adult he worked in a stock and station agency until 1868, when he helped build and then managed the Theatre Royal, Adelaide. He managed the Queens Theatre, Sydney, then built and managed the new Theatre Royal (1875–82), where J.C. Williamson acted in his first Australian season. His most notable musical achievement was to bring to Australia an excellent season of Italian opera in 1876, with a large company he had imported for the purpose, lavish productions, and a first-rate cast, including Pietro Favas, Carlo Orlandini, the dancer Emilia Pasta, and conductor Paolo Giorza. The company toured Sydney, Brisbane and Melbourne, its

repertoire including *Don Giovanni, Faust, Il trovatore* and the Australian premieres of *Ruy Blas* (Marchetti), *Tutti in maschera* (Pedrotti), and *La vestale* (Mercadante).

FURTHER REFERENCE

Obit. in *Australasian* 17 Nov. 1883. See also *ParsonsC*; *IrvinD*.

L.B. See *Lindsay Browne*.

Le Doeuff, Maurie (Maurice Alan) (*b* Adelaide, 27 Aug. 1918), jazz reeds player. He began professional work in 1938, and with coaching on reeds from Alf *Holyoak became professionally prominent with Mark Ollington and involved with the Adelaide Jazz Lovers Society in 1941. Following war service in entertainment units, he resumed civilian dance work and formed concert and broadcast groups in the West Coast style. He was in Sydney and Melbourne 1948–49, with progressive bands such as Ralph *Mallen and Wally *Norman. Back in Adelaide he led the Palais Royale orchestra until 1957, proceeding to television work 1959–70. He lectured in music at the Adelaide College of Advanced Education until retiring in 1983.

FURTHER REFERENCE

Recordings include *Charlie Munro's Music* (1944, Prestophone X-1/X-2); *The ABC Big Band* (1967, WG-BS-5177). See also *BissetB*; *OxfordJ*.   BRUCE JOHNSON

Le Gallienne, Dorian Leon Marlois (*b* Melbourne, 19 Apr. 1915; *d* Melbourne, 27 July 1963), composer. Of a cultured family, Le Gallienne was educated at Melbourne Grammar school and obtained a diploma of music from the University of Melbourne Conservatorium. In 1938 he studied at the Royal College of Music, London, travelling in Europe before his return to Australia in 1938. During World War II he worked for the Department of Information and for the ABC, prevented from active service by diabetes. In 1951 he was awarded a British Council Commonwealth Jubilee Scholarship and returned to England, studying with Gordon Jacob and composing the sombre Concert Overture, the *Sinfonietta*, and the suave Symphony in E. On his return to Australia in 1954 he became music critic for the *Age* and from 1955 taught harmony at the University of Melbourne Conservatorium, where composition was not taught at the time.

In 1960 he took up residence in Greece at Kifissia. Back in Australia in 1961 he completed the first movement of a second symphony but died of heart problems and neglect of his diabetic state. Le Gallienne was impatient of the new direction composition was taking, preferring to write in an outmoded tonal idiom. His music, particularly the vocal music, is refined and sparse. For long discarded as a lone figure left behind by the tide of contemporary developments, his music is now undergoing reconsideration, not least for its fine use of language and its control of form.

The Dorian Le Gallienne Award was founded to commemorate his life in music in 1963 and though the prize-money is small, to win the award is seen as particularly prestigious.

WORKS

Orchestral *Contes Héraldiques* (The Sleepy Princess) (1947), *Little Plays of St Francis,* incidental music (1947), *Peer Gynt,* incidental music (1948), Overture in E Flat (1952), Symphony No.1 (1953), *Voyageur,* ballet (1954), *Sinfonietta* (1956), Symphony No. 2 (Symphonic Study) (1963).

Chamber *Sonata,* fl, pf (1943), *Sonata,* vn, pf (1945), *Othello,* stage music for ob, gui (1947), *Hamlet,* mime scene incidental music, 3 recorders, 2 tpt, bass drum (1947), *Duo,* vn, va (1956, MUP), *Trio,* ob, vn, va (1957), *Two Pieces,* vn, vc, cl, perc, hp; 2 cl, str qrt (1959).

Piano *Nocturne* (1937), *Symphonic Study* (1940), *Sonatina for Piano Duet* (1941), *Sonatina for Two Pianos,* 3 movements (1941), *Three Piano Pieces* (1947), *Macbeth,* incidental music, 2 pf (1947), *The Rivals* incidental music, 2 pf (1947), *Lento* (1951), *Sonata* (1951), *Sonatina* (unfinished).

Choral *Go Heart,* unison (1956), *O, Rose Thou Art Sick,* SSATB (1956), *Matthew, Mark, Luke, and John,* SATB (1956), *Most Blessed of Mornings,* SATB (1956).

Voice and Instrument(s) *Fear No More the Heat of the Sun* (1943), *Four Nursery Rhymes* (1945), *Three Sonnets of Shakespeare* (1946), *Solveig's Song* from 'Peer Gynt' (1946), *Twelfth Night,* incidental music, fl, pf, str (1947), *Three Psalms:* Psalm 93, Psalm 142, Psalm 47 (1948), *I Bind unto Myself Today* (1948), *Moonlight* (1948), *Four Divine Poems of John Donne* (1950, Kurrajong Press), *The Apparition* (1956), *The Cactus of the Moon,* v, str quartet (1956), *Three Songs:* The Ghost, Winter, Cranes Earp (1957).

Film Music (Eltham Films) *Sebastian and the Sausages* (1961), *The Dance of the Angels* (1962), *The Stations of the Cross* (1962).

FURTHER REFERENCE
Recordings are now rare; see *PlushD* for a list to 1972. See also *CallawayA*; JD Garretty, Three Australian Composers, MA, Univ. Melbourne, 1963; *MurdochA*; Noël Nickson, *GroveD*; idem, 'Dorian Le Gallienne: Two Instrumental Works', *SMA* 10 (1976), 25–36, with musical supplement.   THÉRÈSE RADIC

Leaf Playing. See *Gumleaf.*

Leake, Allan Bruce (*b* Melbourne, 16 Aug. 1935), jazz drummer. He began drums in 1954 and became active in the traditional movement. Forming the first of his Storyville bands in 1968, he founded the Storyville Club in 1970, which ran for over 12 years. His activities included touring, recording (including the formation of Jazznote Records), and the organisation of annual Jazz Parties (1976–80), involving musicians from all over the country. He founded Perdido Musical Enterprises (1979), reactivated the Storyville Club (1983) and produced jazz shows through his Melbourne Jazz Repertory Co. Moving to Queensland in 1990, he continues to perform and organise jazz functions.

FURTHER REFERENCE
Recordings include *Storyville And All That Jazz,* The Storyville Jazzmen with Penny Eames and Dutch Tilders (1974, World Record Club, WRC-R 02168/9); *The Storyville Jazztet* (1993, Newmarket NEW1018.2). An interview with him is in *WilliamsA,* 74–9. See also *OxfordJ.*   BRUCE JOHNSON

Leckie, Alexander Joseph (*b* Newtown, Geelong, Vic., 31 Aug. 1881; *d* Perth, 17 Sept. 1966), organist, choral conductor. Working as a clerk at Geelong, he took organ lessons with R.J. Shanks in Melbourne, and went to London in 1904 to study at the Royal College of Music and for his FRCO. He returned to Australia in 1907 and became organist at St John's, Camberwell, Melbourne, then settled at Perth as organist and choirmaster at St George's Cathedral (1908–17). He gave recitals and lessons, becoming foundation president of the WA Music Teachers' Association from 1910 and conductor of the Metropolitan Liedertafel 1913–23. After leaving the cathedral, he established the Perth Ladies Choir (from 1932 the Oriana Ladies Choir) which he conducted for 28 years until 1946. He was music director for radio 6WF from its earliest days, and from 1931 lectured at the University of Western Australia, founding and for 14 years conducting the University Choral Society. An important figure in music teaching and choral music in Perth for more than 30 years, he was honoured with the MBE in 1963.

FURTHER REFERENCE
Brian Pope, *ADB,* 10; A.H. Kornweibel, *Apollo and the Pioneers* (Perth: Music Council of WA, 1973), 94; *OrchardM,* 85–6; portrait, 206.

Lee, Alan Whitely (*b* Melbourne, 29 July 1936), jazz vibraphone player. He began piano, later guitar, then vibraphone in the 1950s. Active over a broad stylistic range, his work included Jazz Centre 44 and appearances with saxophonist Kenn Jones (1959–61). He moved to Sydney in 1963, working in modern and traditional venues such as ★El Rocco. Returning to Melbourne, he continued eclectic work (*Hair,* 1970), playing in classical groups and Brazilian percussion, and he was also active as a journalist. Apart from a period in Sydney, and playing while engaged in seminarian study in Kansas City 1987–89, he remained based in Melbourne until moving to Perth where he currently resides.

FURTHER REFERENCE
Recordings include *Jazzways With Len Barnard* (1961, World Record Club JS 2); *The Alan Lee Quartet* (1961, Swaggie S-4531); *The Alan Lee Jazz Quartet And Friends* (1973, Cumquat CQR-03); *Carlton Streets,* Brian Brown Quintet (1975, 44 Records, 44 6357 700); *The Alan Lee Jazz Quintet* (1976, 44 Records, 44 6357 708); *Hobbit Double Vibes,* John Sangster (1977, Swaggie S-1376); *Alan Lee and Friends* (1995, Request Records RQCD 1511). An interview with him appears in *WilliamsA,* 92–7. See also *ClareB*; *BissetB*; *OxfordJ.*   BRUCE JOHNSON

Lee, David (*b* Armagh, Ireland, 20 Mar. 1837; *d* South Yarra, Melbourne, 12 May 1897), organist. A chorister and deputy organist at Armagh Cathedral, Lee arrived in Melbourne in 1864, where he was soon appointed organist of St Luke's, Emerald Hill. He held a succession of church appointments in various city and suburban churches and was widely sought after as a recitalist, opening many new organs. He was both organist and conductor to the Melbourne Philharmonic Society and for a time was in partnership in a music and organ-building business. In 1872 he was appointed Melbourne city organist, giving twice-weekly recitals for many years.

FURTHER REFERENCE
E.N. Matthews, *Colonial Organs and Organbuilders* (Melbourne: MUP, 1969), 78–9; Sally O'Neill and M.T. Radic, *ADB*, 5.
JOHN MAIDMENT

Lee, Dinah [Dianne Marie Jacobs] (*b* Waimate, NZ, 19 Aug. 1946), popular music singer. After studying piano and music theory, she sang at her father's nightclub from the age of 15 and in Auckland coffee lounges. She came to Australia in 1964 to appear on Johnny O'Keefe's television show *Sing Sing Sing,* and toured with the Searchers, Del Shannon and Eden Kane. A regular on *Bandstand,* her singles *Don't You Know Yockomo* reached No. 1 on the charts in 1964, *Reet Petite* reached No. 6 in the same year, then *I'll Forgive You Then Forget You* reached No. 17 in 1965. Known as 'Miss Mod' for her faddish outfits, she had a natural, rhythmic and at times strident style; she released the albums *Introducing Dinah Lee* (1964) and *The Mod World Of Dinah Lee* (1966), toured the USA and the UK in 1965, settling finally in Sydney and appearing in the club circuit. She toured with Johnny O'Keefe's *Good Old Days of Rock and Roll* show in 1974.

FURTHER REFERENCE
Recordings include *Don't You Know Yockomo* (HMV EA 4639, *Reet Petite* (HMV EA 4648), *I'll Forgive You Then Forget You* (1965, HMV), *Introducing Dinah Lee* (1964, HMV) and *The Mod World Of Dinah Lee* (1966, Viking). For discography, see *SpencerA*. See also *McGrathA*; *SpencerW*; *Collected Stories on Australia Rock'n'Roll,* ed. David McLean (Sydney: Canetoad Publications, 1991), 168–83.

Lee, Garry (*b* Rochford, Essex, England, 27 Dec. 1951), jazz vibraphone player. Migrating to Sydney in 1957, he began guitar in 1967, later taking lessons from George Golla and Johnny Nicol. From 1975 he attended clinics and courses at the NSW Conservatorium, including on vibraphone with Dave Samuels, with whom he later studied in New York. Settling in Perth in 1983, he became active in teaching, for example at the WA Conservatorium from 1984. He was WA jazz co-ordinator 1985–92, and WA representative for National Jazz Alliance. He has played in festivals, on television, and as

support for visitors including Wynton Marsalis; he won the *Australian* jazz award (1993). His compositions include a number of commissions.

FURTHER REFERENCE
Recordings include *I Mean You* (1992, Request Records RQCD 1502); *West Coast Blues* (1995, Request Records RQCD 1510). See also *ClareB*; Geary Larrick, 'Garry Lee,' *Biographical Essays on Twentieth-Century Percussionists* (New York: Edwin Mellen Press, 1992).
BRUCE JOHNSON

Lee, Jack ('Hoop Iron') (*b* Booligal, NSW, 1876; *d* Auburn, Sydney, 1953), shearer, traditional singer. Working as a shearer he learned songs in the shearing sheds, and knew Joe ★Cashmere, and Bill Tully (composer of *The Backblock Shearer*). He was discovered, elderly and blind, by Hilda Lane, and his repertoire was recorded by John ★Meredith and Chris Kempster shortly before his death. The first singer to be recorded by Meredith, he was an important source of rare traditional songs from the turn of the century.

FURTHER REFERENCE
Examples of his work are in *MeredithF*, I, 37–46.

Lee, Julian (*b* Dunedin, NZ, 11 Nov. 1923), jazz pianist. Blind at birth, he began piano at the age of six. He studied music at university and worked in broadcasting in Auckland. Moving to Sydney in 1956, he was active in clubs, studios and music production. He was in the USA 1963–68, performing and arranging, including for Frank Sinatra, Gerry Mulligan and Peggy Lee. Back in Sydney 1968–72, he worked as performer and arranger, at ★El Rocco and other venues. Then he went to the USA again in 1972–74, NZ in 1974–78, then Sydney for television studio work and live performances, some with the Sydney Symphony Orchestra. He arranged and produced records, backed visitors including Lee Konitz and Red Rodney, and worked as a radio announcer.

FURTHER REFERENCE
Recordings include *Don Burrows Presents The Tasman Connection* (1976, Cherry Pie CPF-1026); *Julian Lee Orchestra* (1980, Battyman Records, YPRX 1802); *Just Foolin' Around, A Tribute to Louis Armstrong,* Ricky May and Bob Barnard with the Julian Lee Orchestra (1987, ABC Records, L 60027/8). See also *CA*; *BissetB*; *OxfordJ*; Joya Jenson, 'Three of a (very special) kind', *JA* (May/June 1981), 14–16.
BRUCE JOHNSON

Lee, Lonnie [David Laurence Rix] (*b* Rowena, NSW, 18 Sept. 1940; *d* Feb. 1992), popular music singer. Singing and playing guitar from an early age, he sang in the Johnnie Ray mould on the 2UW Amateur Hour in 1956 then worked in clubs. He won an Elvis Presley contest at the Trocadero, Sydney, in 1957; the compère was Johnny ★O'Keefe, who arranged for him to work for Lee ★Gordon. With his own band the Leemen, Lee appeared on television's *Bandstand* and *Six O'Clock Rock* and toured with the Fabian Show (1959). His debut single, a rock and roll number *Ain't It So*, reached No. 4 in the charts in 1959, then *Starlight, Starbright* reached No. 1 in 1960. Another 11 singles followed, including *I Found A New Love* (1960) and *When The Bells Stop Ringing* (1962). His debut album was *A Night Out With Lonnie Lee* (1961). After tastes changed with Beatlemania in 1964, he switched to country music and released *A Country Boy At Heart* (1965), but could not sustain his earlier success; his record contract was cancelled and he suffered a nervous collapse in 1967. On his recovery he sang in cabaret in Asia and Europe, and from 1973 worked in country music chiefly at Nashville, Tennessee. He returned to Australia for O'Keefe's touring show in 1974, then established his Starbright recording company.

One of Australia's best early rock and roll artists, his style a transparent imitation of Presley, at his height he was surpassed in popularity only by O'Keefe himself.

FURTHER REFERENCE

Recordings include *Ain't It So* (Lee Gordon LS573), *Starlight, Starbright* (Lee Gordon LS587), *I Found A New Love* (1960, Lee Gordon LS601), *When The Bells Stop Ringing* (1962, Leedon K171), *A Night Out With Lonnie Lee* (1961, Leedon LP 203), and *A Country Boy At Heart* (1965, Leedon). A compilation is *Lonnie Lee Greatest Hits* (Calendar SP 669943). For discography, see *SpencerA*. See also *McGrathA*; *SpencerW*; Colin Duff in *Collected Stories on Australia Rock'n'Roll*, ed. David McLean (Sydney: Canetoad Publications, 1991), 53–6.

Lee, Riley Kelly   (*b* Plainview, Texas, USA, 19 July 1951), shakuhachi player. He first studied shakuhachi in Japan 1970–77, in 1980 became its first non-Japanese Dai Shihan (grand master), and in 1993 completed a PhD in ethnomusicology at the University of Sydney. He has toured in many countries and released over 25 recordings, performing traditional and modern Japanese music, both solo and with other Japanese musical instruments; he also composes, performs and records his own music. His Australian-based collaborators include didjeridu player Matthew Doyle, composer-performers Michael ★Atherton and Jim Franklin, ★Synergy's Michael Askill, and harpist Andy Rigby. In January 1996 he became the first musician artist-in-residence at painter Arthur Boyd's Bundanon Estate, NSW. He gave the first performances of David Lumsdaine's *Curlew in the Mist* (1994) and Ross Edwards' *Raftsong at Sunrise* (1996), and he has taught shakuhachi since 1979. Made an honorary fellow of the faculty of visual and performing arts of the University of Western Sydney, Nepean, in 1994, he has resided in the Blue Mountains, NSW, since 1985.

FURTHER REFERENCE

Recordings include *Breath-Sight* (1992, Tall Poppies TP015); *Wild Honey Dreaming* (1993, New World Productions NWCD 710); *Shoalhaven Rise* (1996, Celestial Harmonies BFN 15019).

CATHERINE INGRAM

Leek, Stephen   (*b* Canberra, 1959), composer. After studies in cello and composition (with Larry ★Sitsky) at the Canberra School of Music, he became composer-in-residence with the Tasmanian Dance Co. (1984–87), and since then has had residencies with the Sydney Children's Choir, St Peter's Lutheran College, Brisbane, and various other youth music, theatre, or dance groups, as well as working with his vocal group vOiCeArT and workshop agency ArtsNow Australia. He won two Sounds Australian Awards (1991) and had an Australia Council composer fellowship (1992). With its attractive, accessible style, particularly successful in creative workshops for young people, his music includes numerous works for youth choir and for classroom workshop as well as four music-theatre pieces. His *VoiceWorks* (1989) is a resource kit introducing vocal creativity to the classroom.

WORKS (Selective)

Principal publisher: Morton Music

Orchestral   *Waverock* (1989), *Tall Trees,* 2 tpt, small orch (1990), *Ra—Five Songs of the Sun* (1991).

Chamber   *Plateau,* vc, pf (1988), *Twelve Apostles,* fl, cl, vn, vc, pf, perc (1991).

Solo Instrumental   *At times, stillness … ,* org (1985), *Sights and Settings,* vc, tape (1986), *Seashells,* cl (1986), *Collections 1–5,* vc (1986).

Theatre   *Stroke,* music-theatre (1989, 1), *Xerxes,* music-theatre (1992).

Choral   *Drought,* SSAA, fl, pf (1988, Morton), *Once on a Mountain,* SATB (1988, Morton), *Songs of Space, Sea and Sky,* SATB (1989), *Voyage,* SATB (1990, Morton), *Breakers,* SATB (1990), *Songs of the Earth,* S, str orch/pf (1991), *Voices of a Land,* S, pf or SSA, pf or SAB, pf or SATB, pf, orch (1991, Morton), *Daintree,* SATB, orch (1992, Morton), *Great Southern Spirits,* SSATBB/SATB ch (1993, Morton), *Island Songs,* SATB or SSA or S, pf (1994, Morton).

Children/Amateur   *Sometimes,* unbroken vv (1987), *A Study in Silence,* perc (1988), *Time and Place,* orch (1988), *Kondalill,* orch (1989), *VoiceWorks,* 71 starter pieces for the classroom (1989, Morton), *In Flight,* orch (1990), *Killcallow Catch,* music-theatre (1990, 2), *Ulysses,* orch (1990), *Yarra Yarra,* orch (1990), *Akama* (Whale), orch (1990), *The Devil Himself,* music-theatre (1991), *Kumbargung,* workshop piece (1991, Morton), *Black Children,* workshop piece (1992, Morton), *Nullarbor,* SATB, orch (1993, Morton), *Riawanna,* workshop piece (1994, Morton).

FURTHER REFERENCE

His educational works are published by Morton Music, Brisbane. Recordings include *At times, stillness…,* org (1985, Canberra School of Music, CSM8) and *Seashells,* cl (1986, NMA). See also *BroadstockS*, 156–60.

Lees, Charlie (Charles Anton)   (*b* Sydney 1913; *d* at sea, Mar. 1981), jazz guitarist. After settling in NZ at the age of 15, he moved to Sydney in 1931. He joined Frank ★Coughlan for the opening of the Trocadero in 1936, playing the first Gibson Super 400 guitar imported into

Australia. Active in nightclubs, pit orchestras, jam sessions, teaching, and film music, he was regarded as the outstanding guitarist of his generation, regularly winning annual polls. After war service he settled in Queensland in 1945, playing at Gold Coast cabarets into the 1960s, interrupted by a period in Sydney. He moved to Townsville, and ceased playing full-time to teach in the 1970s until his disappearance at sea.

FURTHER REFERENCE
Recordings include *The Troc* (1991, MBS Jazz 8, Linehan Series). See also *BissetB*; *OxfordJ*; Bruce Clarke, 'Charlie Lees, Australian Guitar Legend', *Journal of Australian Music and Musicians* 30 (Feb./Mar. 1980), 14–16, 24.   BRUCE JOHNSON

LeGarde Twins, The. Country music duo comprised of identical twins Tom and Ted LeGarde (*b* Mackay, Qld, 15 Mar. 1931). They toured Australia with Buddy Williams and Tex Morton, recording first with Rodeo, then in 1952–57 with Regal Zonophone. They left for North America in late 1957, where they worked first in Canada then settled in the USA. A commercial country music venture pursued in Sydney from 1963–65 failed, and they are now based permanently in Nashville, Tennessee. They visit Australia frequently, however, and promote its country music with their work on US television, including a chat-music show premiered in 1991 on Nashville's WXMT-Channel 30 *Down Home/Down Under.*

FURTHER REFERENCE
Recordings include *Ballads of the Bushland* (OEX 7506); *Twincerely Yours* (OSX 7671); *Songs of Slim and Buddy* (1964); *Brothers* (1990/91). For discography, see *WatsonC*, 2. See also Ray Brown, 'Country Style', *Music Maker* (Feb. 1964) 12–13; *LattaA*.
                                                                    JENNIFER HILL

Legend of King O'Malley, The. Musical comedy by Robert Ellis and Michael Boddy. Produced during the anti-Vietnam war protests, it tells of the life of the Australian politician King O'Malley and his opposition to Prime Minister Billy Hughes's conscription proposal of 1916. First performed at the Jane Street Theatre, Sydney, directed by John Bell, in 1970.

Lehmann, Wilfred (*b* Melbourne 1929), violinist, conductor. After studies at the University of Melbourne Conservatorium, he went to London in 1952 and joined the Philharmonia. He won the prestigious Carl Flesch International Violin Competition in 1958 and toured Europe, Japan, the USSR and Australia. He was resident in Japan from 1962, conducting the Tokyo Philharmonic and Tokyo Metropolitan Symphony Orchestras, and regularly returning to Australia to perform. He was concertmaster and assistant conductor of the Queensland Symphony Orchestra 1972–76, guest conductor for ABC orchestras from 1973, musical director of the Nashville Chamber Orchestra 1979–80,

then conductor of the ABC Sinfonia 1982–85. A spirited, enormously gifted violinist and an instinctive, musical conductor, he became interested in composition in his fifties, and has written several orchestral works, including *Cradle Song I* (1974) and *Bacchanals* (1987), as well as two string quartets and chamber works such as *Polish Variations* for violin (1986).

FURTHER REFERENCE
Recordings as conductor include Beethoven, *Choral* Symphony, Sydney Symphony Orchestra (1984, ABC), also recorded for television; recordings of his compositions include String Quartet No. 2, Sydney String Quartet (1990, ABC/Polygram 426992–2) and *Bacchanals,* Queensland Symphony Orchestra (OZM 2002). See also Charles Buttrose, *Playing for Australia: A Story About ABC Orchestras and Music in Australia* (Sydney: ABC/Macmillan, 1982), 71–2.

Lemmone, John (*b* Ballarat, Vic., 22 June 1861; *d* Darlinghurst, Sydney, 16 Aug. 1949), flautist, composer. Although having received some musical training in Ballarat, Lemmone claimed to be largely self-taught. In the 1870s he was principal flautist of Lyster's Royal Italian Opera Co and later made his solo debut, along with Mrs Armstrong (Nellie Melba), in a benefit concert for the conductor Carl ★Elsasser on 17 May 1884. After touring Australia and Asia with soprano Amy ★Sherwin, he spent a period in London where he renewed his acquaintance with Melba. Developing skills in concert management, he organised Melba's 1902 concert tour of Australia, becoming her personal and business manager in addition to performing as associate artist. Always calm and resourceful, he remained Melba's manager and friend, a role that somewhat overshadowed his work as a composer of many flute pieces. Although retiring from professional life in 1927, he continued to give occasional concerts and in 1938 performed on radio for the ABC.

FURTHER REFERENCE
Obit. in *SMH* 17 Aug. 1949. See also James Duff Brown, *British Musical Biography* (Birmingham: S.S. Stratton, 1897), 244; Mimi Colligan, *ADB*, 10; *GlennonA*, 107; *MoresbyA*, 60–3.
                                                                    JENNIFER ROYLE

Lenz. Opera (1972) in one act by Larry ★Sitsky, libretto by Gwen Harwood after the novella of Georg Büchner, telling of episodes in the disintegrating life of a demented 18th-century poet, Jakob Lenze. First performed 12 March 1974, Sydney Opera House.

Leske, Clemens (*b* Rainbow, Vic., 24 Sept. 1923), pianist. While still at primary school in the Mallee, he attracted the notice of Lindsay ★Biggins who brought him to Melbourne on a school scholarship. He entered the University of Melbourne Conservatorium with an exhibition and the Sidney Myer Scholarship to study with Biggins in 1940. After war service he resumed his studies at the Conservatorium, then went to the Paris Conservatoire in 1947 where he studied with Marcel Ciampoi. He returned to Australia in 1949 and became Biggins's assistant, then taught at the Elder Conservatorium from 1950. He founded and directed the Lutheran Singers (1952–60), toured the USA and Europe in 1958, and was dean (from 1974) and director of the Elder Conservatorium 1977–83. He has had a long involvement with the AMEB, as state chairman (1977–87) and editor of the *AMEB Pianoforte Grade Books Series 13* (Melbourne: Allans Music, 1993). The doyen of pianists in Adelaide for over 40 years and one of the leading piano teachers in Australia, he married violinist Beryl ★Kimber in 1969; their son, Clemens Leske Jr, has also made a successful concert career as a pianist.

FURTHER REFERENCE
MonashB; *GlennonA*; *AMN* 40 (Jan. 1950), 13.

Letts, Richard   (*b* Sydney, 3 Aug. 1935), music advocate, administrator. After music studies at the Universities of NSW and Sydney and a doctorate from the University of California (Berkeley), he became director of the East Bay Center for Performing Arts, Berkeley, in 1972 and then of the MacPhail Center for the Arts, University of Minnesota, in 1981. He returned to Australia in 1982 as director of the ★Australia Council Music Board. Resigning over a council restructure in 1987, he became chief executive of the ★Australia Music Centre, and founded the Music Council of Australia in 1994.

A passionate advocate for Australia's composers and thoughtful commentator on national musical culture, his *Music Board Medium Range Plan* (1985) had a profound influence in reshaping the pattern of government support for music in Australia. At the Australia Music Centre he immeasurably enhanced promotion of Australian composers by developing its Australian works publication and recording series, creating the Sounds Australian Awards, and founding and editing the often controversial journal *Sounds Australian*. He was honoured with the AM in 1995.

FURTHER REFERENCE
His publications include *Your Career As A Composer* (Sydney: Allen & Unwin, 1994), See also *WWA* (1996).

Levey, Barnett   (*b* London, *c*.1798; *d* Sydney, 2 Oct. 1837), theatrical entrepreneur. Arriving in Australia as the first free Jewish male settler in 1821, he established himself as a merchant, then as an auctioneer, and, to the governor's dismay, supplied illicit alcohol and offered unlicensed theatrical productions at his premises from 1826. After a long dispute he obtained a theatrical licence in 1832 and opened the Theatre Royal behind his hotel in 1833. There in partnership with Joseph Simmons he presented the first full-scale music-theatre production in Australia, Bishop's *Don Giovanni in London* in 1834.

Levey's theatre was a rough-hewn affair, with numerous complaints from the press of the lack of rehearsal, crude stage production and raucous audiences. With a worsening alcohol problem and increasing legal disputes with actors and critics, he died in 1837.

FURTHER REFERENCE
George F.J. Bergman, *ADB*, 2; *ParsonsC*, *IrvinD*.

Levy, Dave (David Michael)   (*b* Hobart, 13 Apr. 1936), jazz pianist. He grew up in Sydney from 1938 and began classical piano, then became active in the modern jazz movement of the mid-1950s, including involvement in free-form experiments at ★El Rocco. In Europe and the UK 1964–67, he toured with Jimmie Witherspoon in 1965. Returning to Sydney, he became active in a wide range of performance, including ★Galapagos Duck and the Last Straw, and composed for jazz, ballet and film. He taught in the jazz studies program at the NSW Conservatorium, and has worked as musical director in pop music for club acts and with numerous visiting American performers.

FURTHER REFERENCE
Recordings include *The Removalists,* Galapagos Duck (1975, Philips 6354 020); *The Jazz Action Sessions vol. 1* (1983, 2MBS-FM Jazz-2/3); *Rhythm of the Heart,* The Bob Bertles Quintet (1995, Rufus Polygram RF 017). See also *ClareB*; *BissetB*; *OxfordJ*; Barry Morris, 'This Time The Dream's On Me!', *Australian Jazz and Blues* 1/1 (Aug./Sept. 1993), 20–1.

BRUCE JOHNSON

Lewis, Jeannie (Jean)   (*b* Sydney 1945), popular music singer. While studying French and history at the University of Sydney she performed in Sydney folk clubs and bars. She studied voice at the NSW State Conservatorium in 1969 and came to national attention singing in Peter Sculthorpe's *Love 200* (1972). She formed the Jeannie Lewis Gipsy Train in 1970, sang in the Ray Price Quartet, appeared in the original production of *Hair*, and was supporting artist for John McLaughlan, Buddy Guy, Junior Wells, Jean Luc Ponty and others. She went on a study tour of Europe and the Americas in 1978–79, bringing back material for the show *From Maroubra to Mexico: A Multi-National Stomp*. She had lead roles in *Krazy for You* (1980), *Piaf* (1981), *So You Want Blood* (1983) and *Viva Diva* (1995). A voice of very wide range and versatility, she is equally at home in cabaret, folk-song or pop music.

FURTHER REFERENCE
Her albums include her debut *Free Fall Through Featherless Flight* (1973, EMI 7017792), *Piaf, The Songs And The Story* (1982, WEA) and *So You Want Blood* (1983, Larrikin). See also *McGrathA*; *Age* 6 Jan. 1995.

Libraries and Archives

1. National Music Collections. 2. State Library Music Collections. 3. Other Significant Collections. 4. University Music Collections.

Music resources in Australia are housed in a diverse range of libraries and archives: both government and private, national and state, academic and public, comprehensive and specialist, the diversity being matched by the holdings themselves. The foresight of librarians, archivists, private collectors, researchers and donors since the early 19th century has provided a depth of resources in Western and non-Western music traditions in our libraries and archives which forms the basis for users of today and collection builders of the future. Collections are both historical and contemporary; they consist of printed and manuscript resources, music scores and sound recordings, books and serials, ephemera and realia. The performer, musicologist, researcher and a wide musical audience have access to an extensive range of collections and services around the country.

Access to the principal public collections has in the past been limited to compilations and catalogues on cards or a few inadequate directories. With the development of computer databases and data transfer since the 1980s, access to libraries and repositories has been enhanced. Potential users can now access databases through national networks and the internet to ascertain holdings. A well-developed national and international document delivery network is now enhanced by these databases and directories to provide information on a national basis.

1. National Music Collections. There are a number of national bodies which take responsibility for the conservation of our printed and recorded musical heritage. Music is included in the collecting policies of the major public institutions to varying extents, and these combine to provide extensive coverage of most areas of musical life in Australia.

(i) The National Library of Australia has important collections of music with supporting books and serials to meet research needs and resources for performance. The collections began at Federation in 1901, when the Commonwealth Parliamentary Library became the legal deposit library for all Australian publications (until the formation of the National Library in 1923). Over time collections of approximately 170 000 items have been accumulated and include major strengths in Australian sheet music from the 19th and 20th centuries. These collections exemplify the depth in Australian composition and performance research materials in the library.

The Manuscript Collection contains collections relating to Australian musicians as well as the Australian performing arts industry, including Australian theatre companies and stage entrepreneurs. They include papers and manuscripts of composers Don Banks, John Antill, Margaret Sutherland, George Dreyfus, Miriam Hyde; performers Dame Nellie Melba, June Bronhill and Robin Archer; critics Kenneth Hince and Roger Covell and organisations including the J.C. Williamson Theatre Company, the Royal Philharmonic Society of Sydney, the Australian Opera, and the Musicological Society of Australia. It also holds significant early music manuscripts in the Nan Kivell Collection. Overseas strength in the collections includes Western art-music, especially of the 19th century, reflecting the transplanted European musical culture in Australia. The Music Collection is supported by 12 500 books and serials on many aspects of music, including music theory, history, and biographies of musicians, composers and performers.

The Oral History Collection contains recorded interviews relating to music. Collecting policies of the National Library will ensure the continuing growth of the music collections in focusing on Australia and the Pacific, including the acquisition of original materials and published resources, with retrospective as well as current publications.

(ii) The ABC Print Music Library, Sydney (founded in 1933) contains strong collections of orchestral materials with particular strengths in Australian material including original manuscripts and performing sets for commissioned and non-commissioned works. The ABC also supports its orchestras, and radio and television stations with a number of other resources housed in a number of music and sound libraries situated around the country. The ABC Sound Libraries located in all capital cities house significant collections of sound recordings which are used by ABC staff in programming for radio. The state ABC orchestras situated in each capital city (except Darwin and Canberra) also have small libraries of orchestral performing sets.

(iii) The Australian Music Centre, Sydney (founded in 1973) maintains an active role in collecting music of contemporary Australian composers and promoting the performance and study of Australian music. These activities include a library which actively collects materials relating to the work of Australian composers including chamber, orchestral, jazz and electronic music. Materials include scores (manuscript, facsimile and published), performing parts, sound recordings (commercial and unpublished), books and serials.

(iv) The Australian Institute of Aboriginal and Torres Strait Islanders Studies, Canberra, holds the central resources for Aboriginal music. The Institute library is the major information resource collection on Aborigines and Torres Strait Islanders, with major holdings in music. Collections relating to music include books, pamphlets and journals, film and video, and over 22 000 hours of recorded sound.

(v) The National Film and Sound Archive, Canberra, was established in 1984, as a national institution for the collection and preservation of Australia's screen and recorded sound heritage. Its collections comprise film, television, video and recorded sound materials, providing resources in film music and the history of recorded music in Australia.

2. State Library Music Collections.   In contrast with the comparatively recent establishment of national collecting institutions, many of the state music collections in this country had their origins with the early colonial lending libraries in the 19th century. The early introduction of legal and copyright deposit acts has provided the state and territory libraries with rich collections of published materials (including music), and this system continues to this day. The State Library of New South Wales began in 1826 with legalised copyright deposit commencing in 1879. This was followed by the Melbourne Public Library, now the State Library of Victoria (founded 1853, legal deposit 1869); the John Oxley Library of the State Library of Queensland (founded 1926, legal deposit 1949); the State Library of South Australia (founded 1884, legal deposit 1939); the State Library of Tasmania (founded 1826, legal deposit 1943); and the State Library of Western Australia (legal deposit 1895).

(i) The Mitchell Library, State Library of New South Wales, houses a number of music collections including many relating to Australian musicians and organisations as well as ethnomusicology. Highlights include the private papers of Alfred Hill, Peggy Glanville-Hicks, Isaac Nathan, Sir Eugene Goossens, Dame Nellie Melba and papers relating to Musica Viva and J.C. Williamson Theatres Ltd. An important collection of printed music dating from the early colonial days is held, along with substantial collections of books and journals.

(ii) The State Library of Victoria, in its Arts, Music and Performing Arts and La Trobe Collections, also has important collections including manuscript materials relating to Peggy Glanville Hicks, Fritz Hart, Clive Douglas, Louise Hanson-Dyer, Dorian Le Gallienne and Sir Bernard Heinze. An extensive general collection of music scores, collected editions and sound recordings complement these manuscripts.

(iii) The State Library of South Australia has general holdings of music scores, books, serials and sound recordings. It has an important collection of South Australian published music and the Holyoak jazz collection.

(iv) The State Library of Western Australia has printed and manuscript music in the Battye Collection and a lending collection of music scores and sound recordings in the Central Music Library. A recent development is the collection of sound recordings produced in WA.

(v) The State Library of Queensland has music collections in the John Oxley Library (printed music and manuscripts, programs and archives relating to Queensland musical societies) and the Music Library (general collections of music, books, journals, sound recordings and videos). Special collections include the Palmer collection of 7000 sound recordings (with strength in opera and ballet music) and the Cable collection of hymnology consisting of 4000 hymnals and companion volumes.

3. Other Significant Collections.   A number of local public libraries also have music collections developed for public borrowing including Nunawading Public Library, Melbourne, and the Rockdale Public Library, Sydney. Music-related collections are also housed in the various performing arts museums situated in Brisbane, Melbourne, Adelaide and Sydney. In addition, there are several collections of special significance.

(i) The Denis Wolanski Library, Sydney Opera House, was founded in 1973 and has collections relating to the performing arts and archival materials relating to the history and performances of the Sydney Opera House. The collections include books, serials, press clippings, photographs, sound recordings, posters, technical drawings, realia and a small collection of opera and musical comedy scores. The library is also responsible for the Sydney Opera House oral history project, which holds approximately 50 recorded interviews and transcripts. The library is currently under review and closed.

(ii) The Victorian Performing Arts Museum, Victorian Art Centre, Melbourne, houses a collection of music, sound recordings, costumes and ephemeral materials. Strengths in Victorian-related performing arts activities include a large archive of J.C. Williamson material.

(iii) Other Resources. Many of the national performing bodies including Opera Australia and the Australian Ballet, as well as the major state opera companies, operate libraries with music, books, journals and archival collections of programs, cuttings, set and costume designs, relating to their activities. The various national and state museums also hold small collections of music-related materials. The Powerhouse Museum in Sydney has collections of instruments including keyboard instruments, violins and flutes. The Museums of Victoria and Tasmania also have collections of sound recordings including early cylinder recordings of Aboriginal music.

Music societies, which include the many choral and orchestral organisations in the community, are an often forgotten source of music. Some have been in existence for over a century and have built up collections of performing sets as well as important archival collections which document the social history of music in Australia. Access to these collections is often only available by directly approaching the organisation.

4. University Music Collections. Libraries in academic institutions provide comprehensive collections of performing scores, collected editions and monuments of music in Western music, monographs, serials and sound recordings. The Universities of Sydney (incorporating the Sydney Conservatorium of Music), Melbourne, Adelaide, Western Australia, Tasmania (incorporating the Tasmanian Conservatorium of Music), Newcastle (incorporating the Newcastle Conservatorium of Music) and the Australian National (incorporating the Canberra School of Music), Griffith (incorporating the Queensland Conservatorium of Music), Monash, La Trobe, Curtin (incorporating the Western Australian Academy of the Arts), and Southern Cross Universities, and the Victorian College of the Arts, among many other tertiary institutions, all have comprehensive music collections to support the teaching and research requirements of their institutions. In line with the research emphasis in these institutions many important special collections have been developed.

(i) *The Grainger Museum, University of Melbourne,* is a unique institution in Australia. Founded in 1934 by Percy Grainger, the Australian composer and performer, the museum houses an extensive archive of music manuscripts and published music, correspondence, photographs, instruments, costumes, and other realia relating to his life and career. He also deposited extensive collections of materials by contemporary musicians whom he came to know when living in Europe and America, including music by Frederick Delius, Edvard Grieg and Cyril Scott. Other collections which have been lodged at the Grainger Museum include those of composers G.W.L. Marshall-Hall and Florence Ewart and the Royal Victorian Liedertafel.

(ii) *The Fisher Library of the University of Sydney* houses the Robert Dalley-Scarlett Collection of Handel including early published editions of music and books, and the smaller but complementary Richardson collection of Handeliana, which includes scores, programs and periodicals.

(iii) *The Stuart Challender Collection, University of Tasmania,* includes scores, books and ephemera relating to this distinguished conductor's career.

(iv) *The Keith Humble Archive, La Trobe University,* includes manuscripts and papers relating to this distinguished composer and academic.

(v) *The Callaway International Resource Centre for Music Education, University Of Western Australia,* is a comprehensive and unique collection of music education materials. These include correspondence, publications and other materials relating to the professional life of emeritus professor Sir Frank Callaway, the Verdon Williams Collection of orchestral materials, the Dalcroze Collection and the Westrup Collection relating to music education research.

(vi) *The Gordon Anderson Collection, University of New England, Armidale, NSW,* includes the research materials and publications of this world-renowned Medieval music specialist.

(vii) *The Centre for Studies in Australian Music Research, University of Melbourne,* has a collection which includes books, dissertations, periodicals, music, sound recordings and videos relating to Australian music.

(viii) *The Percy Jones Collection, Australian Catholic University, Mercy Campus, Melbourne,* named after Revd Dr Percy Jones (1914–92), a monumental figure in the history of Australian church music, has a collection focus on church music, particularly in Australia, which includes manuscripts and published editions of Australian hymnals and psalters, dissertations and periodicals.

(ix) *Monash University Music Library* houses an extensive ethnomusicology sound archive with strengths in South-East Asian music and a developing Jewish Music Archive, and is located in the university's music department.

The variety of Australian libraries and archives with music resources provides a substantial and wide-ranging source for public and professional users. To continue to build on this diversity, the libraries and archives will need to actively engage in establishing high profiles among the community as the preservers of our musical heritage. Access to this musical heritage is also a key issue and needs to be a consideration in the development of information and document delivery systems. The large distances between Australian libraries and archives, and beyond to the libraries and archives overseas, will continue to be broken down by computer technology to provide easier and quicker access to music resources.

See also *Instrument Collections.*

FURTHER REFERENCE

Georgina Binns, comp, 'Australian Music Resources in Selected Libraries, Archives and Museums', *Continuo: Journal of the International Association of Music Libraries (Australia)* 24 (1995), 37–54; Alan Bundy and Judith Bundy, comps, *ALED3: Australian Libraries: The Essential Directory,* 3rd edn (Adelaide: Auslib Press, 1995); Michele Potter, *A Full House: The ESSO Guide to the Performing Arts Collections of the National Library of Australia* (Canberra: National Library of Australia, 1991). GEORGINA BINNS

Liedertafel. Originating in Germany around 1809 as private men-only social singing clubs, the liedertafel also aimed to foster German nationalism and culture. This nationalistic focus distinguished them from the English glee clubs. Smoking and drinking were features of their gatherings, which came to be known as 'smoke nights'. A press report of November 1896 referred to an Adelaide liedertafel smoke concert as an event where members meet to 'discuss "things in general" over the convivial glass, and smoke once more the pipe of peace, while they listen to the sweet sounds that are conjured up by chorus or soloist'. In addition to these gatherings, the Australian groups presented public concerts, and formed associated ladies' choirs and orchestras. Originally brought to Adelaide by German immigrants, the 1848 European revolutions and the 1850s goldrush spurred immigration and spread the concept to Melbourne and beyond. They were usually aligned with local German community organisations, but in the later 19th century became more anglicised, and the concept was adopted by non-Germans.

Nash records 19 liedertafels in Victoria, six in NSW, three each in WA and Queensland, and two each in SA and Tasmania, mostly founded between 1880 and 1900. Liedertafels were found in many regional centres, including Broken Hill, Cairns, Charters Towers, Coolgardie and Kalgoorlie. Goulburn Liedertafel (1891) celebrated its 100th concert in 1912 with a 73-voice male choir and a well-balanced 42-piece orchestra; it had vice-regal patronage and owned its own premises. An associated Ladies' Chorus was introduced in 1897. Comprised of 50 voices, this group enabled the performance of operas and mixed-voice works. The Adelaider Liedertafel (1858) originally performed to German-speaking audiences, promoting German culture and causes. In 1870 it participated in a fund-raising performance of Carl Puttmann's comic opera *Mordgrundbruck (Murder Valley Bridge)* in aid of the German Imperial Franco–Prussian War Relief Fund. A reconstitution of the society followed a period under an English conductor who spoke no German, and which saw membership and standards fall. The 1891 Rules, printed in German, specified that active members had to speak German. Hermann ★Heinicke was appointed conductor and re-formed the choir with 64 members auditioned from 158 applicants. Its focus had shifted by March 1900, when it presented a concert to show loyalty to Great Britain and 'our troops in the Transvaal'. Proceeds went to a Boer War Patriotic Fund, and the repertoire (mostly sung in English) included *Soldiers of the Queen* and *Dear Mother England*.

The Sydney Liedertafel was founded in 1881, inspired by a visit from the Melbourne liedertafels. John ★Delaney conducted it in the 1880s, and wrote his cantata *Captain Cook* for the 1888 joint Sydney and Melbourne centennial liedertafel concert. But he resigned in 1898 because the society insisted that a ladies' choir he formed in 1897 be removed. 'The return to the old style of male singing only is, in my opinion, from an art point of view, a disastrous retrogression', he wrote in his resignation letter (*Daily Telegraph* 12 Feb. 1898). He was succeeded by Alfred ★Hill, whose comic opera *Lady Dolly* was sponsored by the society in 1899.

Arundel ★Orchard was brought to Australia in 1903 by the Sydney Liedertafel as its next conductor. He served

for 13 years, writing his cantata, *Ulla the Bowman* (1909) for its 150th concert. In 1911, augmented by 130 ladies, it presented the Australian premiere of Granville Bantock's *Omar Khayyam*. Delaney's *Captain Cook* was revived for the 1938 Australian sesquicentennial celebrations, with the combined Royal Victorian Liedertafel and Royal Sydney Apollo Club.

The main Melbourne societies were the Melbourne Deutscher Liedertafel (established 1868 as a German-speaking society) and the Metropolitan Liedertafel (1870). The Deutscher Liedertafel split in 1878 over the use of English, re-forming in 1879 as an English-speaking society—the Melbourne Liedertafel. It and the (by then) Royal Metropolitan Liedertafel merged in 1905 to become the Royal Victorian Liedertafel. The Melbourne liedertafels led an active social life, especially in the late 19th century: annual picnic excursions, boat cruises, train trips interstate, and moonlight family picnics and singing at the beach (a scene depicted in G.W.L. ★Marshall-Hall's *Stella*). They practised the German serenade tradition, ranging from a formal musical greeting to a newly arrived governor, to less sober greetings delivered from the street outside a visiting singer's hotel. Extensive charity work was undertaken, members could 'network' socially and professionally, and there were no class barriers—a membership list of the Melbourne Deutscher Liedertafel (1868–78) showed occupations as diverse as clerk, gardener, engineer, 'squatter', 'gentleman', and private detective. Their concerts combined light music—absurd part-songs like 'The Bachelor's Galop', and 'Old Daddy Long Legs'—with serious works (opera excerpts, cantatas, and new music), plus solo and instrumental items.

The anti-German paranoia of World War I led some societies to change their names. Despite receiving a Royal Charter in 1911, Royal Sydney Liedertafel changed to Royal Sydney Apollo Club, the Brisbane Liedertafel (1885) became the Brisbane Apollo Club, the Goulburn Liedertafel became the Leader Choral Society, and the Perth Metropolitan Liedertafel (originally founded as 'Herr Hartmann's Liedertafel') became the Metropolitan Gleemen of Western Australia. Other groups faded away, while the Gisborne, Tanunda, Adelaide and the Royal Victorian liedertafels chose to retain their names. The justification was that after 50 years the word was thoroughly anglicised. The Adelaide groups, probably the strongest in German sentiments, simply suspended activity during the wars.

In the postwar period the liedertafels declined and are now nearly forgotten. An attempted solution in the early 1960s were 'Royal Victorian Liedertafel Scholarships for Male Voices', which offered no fee but gave free vocal tuition with the group's conductor, and required a 12-month membership of the Liedertafel. But results were not encouraging. The Royal Victorian Liedertafel changed its name in 1980 to Royal Victorian Choir, finding the term *liedertafel* a hindrance in recruiting (since many people were now unaware of its meaning). Nevertheless, by 1981 only 10 members were attending, and after further internal dispute the group dissolved.

A number of liedertafel groups are still active, and represent some of the oldest established choral groups in the country. The Tanunda Liedertafel (1861) was still active in 1993. Continually active as a male-voice choir (apart from the two world wars) the Adelaide Liedertafel added '1858' to its name in 1968, and was awarded the Zelter Plaque by the German Federal Republic in 1978, the first Australian German choir so honoured. It is the oldest German choir in Australia. The Liedertafel Arion (Melbourne), which traces its ancestry back to 1856, adopted its present name in 1860. Currently affiliated with Germany's Federal Association of German Choirs, most of the members are of German descent, and members are required to speak German. It participated in German choral festivals in 1970, 1972 and 1975, the last, Sängerfest 75, involving 12 participating choirs (with about 370 voices) from all over Australia.

FURTHER REFERENCE
Royal Victorian Liedertafel papers are at *PVgm*. See also William P. Nash, *Music in the Cabbage Garden: Pioneers of Music in Victoria.* (Melbourne: Innisfallen Press, 1983); Thérèse Radic, Aspects of Organised Amateur Music in Melbourne 1836–1890, MMus, Univ. Melbourne, 1968; idem, Some Historical Aspects of Musical Associations in Melbourne 1888–1915, PhD, Univ. Melbourne, 1977; idem, The Liedertafels of Melbourne, unpub. typescript, *PVgm*. NOEL WILMOTT

Light, Alan (*b* Sydney, 15 July 1916), bass, singing teacher. After study with Marianne Mathy at Sydney from 1938, he sang as a baritone in the National Opera of Australia from 1949, then as a bass/baritone with the Elizabethan Theatre Trust Opera Co. (later the Australian Opera) from 1958, as well as on radio and television. He directed student operas at the University of Melbourne Conservatorium from 1963, and with Australia Council grants made two study tours of the UK, Europe and the USA (1980, 1986). He retired from singing in 1989 and now conducts workshops and masterclasses in Australia and NZ. A gifted actor in sinister characters, with a dark, rich-toned voice, his roles included Mephistopheles, Pizarro, the four evil roles in *Tales of Hoffmann,* Basilio and Bartolo in *Barber of Seville,* as well as principal parts in Gilbert and Sullivan operettas and musicals.

FURTHER REFERENCE
Recordings include *Alan Light Sings Bass Ballads* (Move MD 3029); *Artisans of Australia* (Jade CD 1054); and *Songs of Robert Burns* (RCA VRL1–0124). See also John Cargher, *Bravo! 200 Years of Opera in Australia* (Melbourne: Macmillan, 1988).

Lim, Liza (*b* Perth, 30 Aug. 1966), composer. As well as attending the Victorian College of the Arts then the University of Melbourne, she studied composition with

Richard David ★Hames, Riccardo ★Formosa and at the Sweelinck Conservatorium with Ton de Leeuw. Her *Garden of Earthly Desires* (1988–89) in which an electric guitar is cleverly dovetailed among 10 classical instruments, was recorded by ★Elision Ensemble, with whom she has chiefly been associated. On an Australia Council composer fellowship she wrote a music-theatre work, *The Oresteia* (Tony Harrison, 1993); it has a complex, tersely linear score using non-traditional vocal techniques, and was produced in Melbourne in 1993. With artist Domenico de Clario she produced *Bar-do'i-thos-grol (The Tibetan Book of the Dead)*, a seven-night installation-performance cycle at a demolition yard in Lismore in 1994. An eclectic in her materials and choice of styles, she has a fine, detailed understanding of sound and has worked at interweaving and disguising often quite disparate materials. She won a Young Australian Creative Fellowship in 1995.

WORKS (Selective)
Principal publisher: Ricordi
Orchestral *Cathedral* (1994, Ricordi).
Chamber *Garden Of Earthly Desire,* 11 insts (1988/89, rec. Dischi Ricordi CRMCD 1020, pub. Ricordi), *Voodoo Child,* S, chamber ens (1989), *Diabolical Birds,* pic, bass cl, pf, vn, vc, vibraphone (1990), *HELL,* str qrt (1992, Ricordi), *Li Shang Yin,* S, 15 insts (1993, Ricordi), *KOTO,* fl/pic, ob d'amore, flugel hn, koto, va, 2 vc, perc (1993, Ricordi).
Solo instrumental *Amulet,* va (1992, Ricordi).
Music-theatre *The Oresteia* (1991–93, rec. Dischi Ricordi CRMCD 1030, pub. Ricordi).
Installation *Bar-do'i-thos-grol (The Tibetan Book of the Dead),* collaborative works with Domenico de Clario and 7 musicians of Elision (1994).

FURTHER REFERENCE
Her works are published by Ricordi. Recordings, all with Elision, include *Garden of Earthly Desires* (Dischi Ricordi CRMCD 1020); *Driftglass* (1992, One More IMICD 1018; *Voodoo Child* (1990, Pro Musica Nova) and The *Oresteia* (Dischi Ricordi CRMCD 1030). See also Andrew Ford, *Composer to Composer* (Sydney: Allen & Unwin, 1993), 157–62; *BroadstockS,* 161–2; *Age* 3 Nov. 1995; *Weekend Australian* 5 June 1993.

Limb, Bobby (*b* Adelaide, 10 Oct 1924), jazz saxophonist. He settled on saxophone at the age of nine, taking a scholarship at the Adelaide College of Music. In 1942 he participated in the Adelaide Jazz Lovers Society sessions, joining Maurie ★Le Doeuff, then Harry Boake-Smith. Moving to Melbourne in 1947 to join Bob Gibson, he became active in the bop movement, and led his own band, including Don ★Banks, Charlie ★Blott, and Jack ★Brokensha, playing concerts for the Modern Music Society of Victoria at the New Theatre. He moved to Sydney in 1950, playing in nightclubs, broadcasts and concerts. After a period in the UK, 1953–57, he was active in television variety and as an entrepreneur. He was awarded the OBE in 1967.

FURTHER REFERENCE
Recordings include *Alan Nash And His Orchestra* (1950, Jazzart JA-53). See also *BissetB*; *OxfordJ*: *WWA*; Judy Judd, *Life & Limb* (Sydney: Horwitz Grahame, 1987).   BRUCE JOHNSON

Lime Spiders. Rock group (1979–86; 1987–) formed in Sydney. Developed by Mick Blood (vocals) and Daryl Mather (guitar) under the influence of *Radio Birdman, at first its members were a changing array of musicians. Their double EP *25th Hour* (1983) won a local band contest and in 1985 they released a mini-LP *Slavegirl* in Europe and the USA. They recorded for the film *Young Einstein* (1985), and after a hiatus while Blood appeared in Europe, their single *Weirdo Libido* (1987) entered the charts, their debut album *The Cave Comes Alive* (1987) reached No. 1 on the USA college charts and they toured the USA. They played with a straightforward, crudely energetic style reminiscent of early rock and roll.

FURTHER REFERENCE
Recordings include *25th Hour* (1983, Green BTS 972), *Slavegirl* (1985, Bigtime), *Weirdo Libido* (1987, Virgin VOZ 012, *The Cave Comes Alive* (1987, Virgin VOZ 2006), *My Favourite Room* (1987, Virgin VOZ 016), *Volatile* (1988 Virgin VOZ 2015), and *Blood Sugar Sex Lawson* (1992, Virgin). For discography, see *SpencerA*. See also *SpencerW*; J.J. Adams, 'Lime Spiders', *APRAJ* 6/1 (Jan. 1988), 22–3.

Lindsay, Reg (*b* Sydney, 7 July 1930), country music singer-songwriter. The radio was one of the major sources of entertainment in Lindsay's rural childhood, from which his love for country music originated. His musical training began at the age of two on a harmonica his father gave him, and later he also mastered the banjo, mandolin, guitar and fiddle. His first taste of success, on *Australia's Amateur Hour* in 1950, persuaded him to pursue a singing career. In 1951 he won the historic talent quest on *Tim McNamara's Show*, singing Wilf Carter's *Streamline Yodel*, which led to his first recording contract with Rodeo Records. This achievement marked the beginning of his long and successful career, which has spanned over 40 years and two continents. His rich and mellow voice is his trademark.

Throughout his active career Lindsay produced and compèred shows on many major Australian radio stations, including 2CH, 2SM and 2KY. In 1964 he expanded into the television industry; and his top-rating show, *Reg Lindsay's Country Homestead*, won the best Queensland television production in 1978. Besides his radio and television commitments, he also appeared regularly on live shows around Sydney, performing alongside other major Australian country music artists such as Slim Dusty, the McKean Sisters and Les Partell. The first of the Reg Lindsay Show road tours was launched in 1954; a tour that began as Wilf Carter's Australian tour, which he was forced to abandon after a week because of laryngitis. In addition to his success in Australia, he was the first Australian solo artist to perform on the prestigious Saturday night show of Grand Ole Opry at the Ryman Auditorium in 1968. Constantly in demand in America, he divided his time between the two countries for about 20 years, and operated almost entirely from USA until he returned to Australia in 1986.

A prolific songwriter and recording artist, Lindsay wrote over 500 songs, recorded over 60 albums and 250 singles. His repertoire embraces all country music styles, from bluegrass to ballads. An innovator, he is probably the first Australian country singer to use an electric lead guitar, and even a didjeridu on one occasion—in *Walkabout Rock 'n' Roll*. Four of his biggest hits were *Armstrong* (1971), *July, You're A Woman* (1974), *Silence On The Line* (1978), and *The Empty Arms Hotel* (1980). A recipient of many awards, among them major broadcasting network awards and ACMA Gold Guitars, he was inducted to the Tamworth Country Music Roll of Renown in 1984 and was awarded an OAM in 1989. Recuperating from cerebral haemorrhage and a heart attack he suffered in 1995, Lindsay now leads a quiet life, with a much reduced performance schedule.

FURTHER REFERENCE
Recordings include *Country Music Comes To Town* (1961, Columbia OSX 7647); *Songs For Country Folk* (1964, Columbia OSX 7741); *Reg Lindsay's National Country & Western Hour* (1965, Festival); *Country Duets From Reg And Heather* (1968, Festival); *She Taught Me to Yodel* (1970, Festival L33375); *Armstrong* (1970, Festival L34197); *Country And Western Greats* (1972, Calendar SR 66 9820); *Country Music Jamboree* (1973, Summit SRA 250004); *Australia's King Of The Road* (1973, Festival); *21st Anniversary Album* (1973, Festival); *Reg Lindsay* (1974, Festival FL 34760); *Reg Lindsay In Nashville* (1975, Festival L35451); *Silence On The Line* (1977, EMI EMA 324); *The World Of Rodeo* (1978, EMI EMC 2680); *Ten Ten Two And A Quarter* (1980, Brook); *If You Could See Me Now* (1981, Telmak); *Will The Real Reg Lindsay* (1982, Powderworks); *I've Always Wanted To Do That* (1985, RCA); *Lifetime Of Country Music* (1987, Hammard); *40th Anniversary Album* (1992, Dino); *Reasons To Rise* (1993, Larrikin); *No Slowin' Down* (1994, Festival LRF 355).

See also Monika Allan, *The Tamworth Country Music Festival* (Sydney: Horwitz Grahame, 1988); *LattaA*; James 'Jazzer' Smith, 'Why is Reg Lindsay's "Country Homestead" being ignored by Sydney and Melbourne TV?', *Across Country: Australia's National Country Music Magazine* 1 (Aug. 1978), 4; *SmithB*; *WatsonC*, 2.
                                    YA HUI HUNG

Linger, Carl Ferdinand August (*b* Berlin, 15 Mar. 1810; *d* Adelaide, 16 Feb. 1862), composer, conductor. He studied composition with Reissiger and Klein in Berlin, where he wrote a considerable quantity of music including symphonies, motets, songs and two operas. He migrated to SA in 1849 and soon established himself as the colony's leading musician. His work as a teacher and as conductor of both the Adelaide Choral Society and Adelaider Liedertafel was to have a decisive impact on the early musical development of SA. His few surviving works include *Sechs Deutsche Lieder* and *Sechs Zwischenspiele*; he is best remembered for his *Song of Australia* (1859), a patriotic song that achieved remarkable popularity.

FURTHER REFERENCE
ADB, 5; Elizabeth Wood, *GroveD*; *GlennonA*; L.A. Triebel, 'A Carl Linger Letter', *South Australiana* 2/1 (Adelaide, Mar. 1963), 6–14.
WAYNE HANCOCK with M. Elphinstone

Linz, Rainer (*b* Essen, Germany, 3 Feb. 1955), composer. He studied at the University of Sydney 1974, the University of Adelaide 1975–76, with Mauricio Kagel at the Cologne Musikhochschule 1978, and at La Trobe University 1979–82. Active at the Clifton Hill Community Music Centre in Melbourne 1979–83, he was co-founder and publisher of *New Music Articles,* 1982 to the present. His compositions, which are often concerned with collaboration and the investigation of the processes of performance, include *Saturn Winds* (1981) for orchestra; the opera *Crossed Purposes* (1986), a radiophonic work; *October 88* (1988) for trombone and percussion; *…Cassenoisette…* (1989) for variable speed tape recorders, *Volcano and Vision* (1987/90), a chamber opera; *The Encounter* (1993), a music-theatre work; and *The Rehearsal* (1995), a radiophonic work. Linz's innovative and entrepreneurial work in Melbourne has been a significant factor in the city's prominence in experimental music.

FURTHER REFERENCE
Recordings include *No Consolation,* pf 1994, (Red House RH 9401); *(Dis)Continuous Music,* elec (1982, NMA Tapes 2); *Crossed Purposes,* excerpts (AMC 018). His writings include: 'The Opera, *Crossed Purposes*', *SA* 15 (Oct. 1987): 34–35; '3 Pieces for Radio', *SA* 45 (Autumn 1995): 32–3. See also: *BroadstockS*; *JenkinsT.*
MICHAEL BARKL

Lirrga. Public singing and dancing in north-western NT. See *Corroboree.*

Lismore, pop. (1991) 27 246. The district where the pioneer of Australian country music Buddy ★Williams grew up, it is set in the fertile Richmond River valley, inland from Ballina, north-east NSW. Settled in 1858, it became chiefly a rural centre for processing farm products. The Star Court Theatre was opened in 1921 to stage opera and vaudeville and the Lismore Philharmonic Society presented oratorios with over 100 members in 1925. The Lismore Eisteddfod, held each September, was established to serve local needs, for many years vying in the same month with the Lismore Music Festival Society, which by 1926 ran for seven days and had a choral prize of £100. The Lismore Music Lovers' Club was active in the postwar years. Since the 1960s the district has been a centre for folk arts, and the Lismore Folk Festival is held each October. Southern Cross University (founded as Northern Rivers College of Advanced Education, 1970) has a music department focusing on rock and commercial music.

Little Boy Lost. Country music song (1960) by Johnny ★Ashcroft with Tony Withers. A swift response to the true story of a four-year-old who disappeared in the rugged New England Ranges, NSW, in February 1960 and was found alive after nearly four days, it was recorded by Ashcroft two weeks later and reached No. 1 in the pop charts, only to be withdrawn from radio airplay three months later when another boy was kidnapped and later found dead. One of Australia's most inspired country music songs, it made Ashcroft a household name.

FURTHER REFERENCE
Ashcroft's recording is (Columbia DO 4128). See also *SmithB*, 40–1; *WatsonC*, II, 59–60.

Little Heroes, (The). Pop band (1980–84) formed in Melbourne comprised originally of Roger Hart (vocals, guitar), David Crosbie (keyboard), former Secret Police member John Taylor [Fred(die) Franks] (bass), and Alan 'Clutch' Robertson (drums). They won the National Battle of the Bands in 1980 and released the first of 11 singles, *She Says.* They toured nationally in 1982, their *One Perfect Day* reaching No. 12 in the charts and *Modern Times* (1983) also doing well. Their success drew strongly on Hart as a songwriter.

FURTHER REFERENCE
Recordings include *She Says* (L'il SOPL 0001), *One Perfect Day* (EMI EMI679), *Modern Times* (1983, EMI EMI1237), *The Little Heroes* (1981, Giant GIANT 02), *Watch The World* and *Play By Numbers* (reissued together 1994, EMI 2504262). For discography, see *SpencerA*. See also *McGrathA*; *SpencerW.*

Little, Jimmy (*b* Cumeragunja Mission, Vic.), Aboriginal country music and gospel singer. Before the advent of groups such as Yothu Yindi in the late 1980s, Little was arguably the best-known Aboriginal musician in Australia. He made his first recording in 1956 and continues to record to the present. His fame was secured in the early 1960s with the release of his recording of the gospel-country song *Royal Telephone.* Little's recorded output exceeds 30, 45rpm singles and 35 albums. He has appeared in films and documentaries, among them the Billy Graham *Shadow of the Boomerang* and Wim Wenders' *Until the End of the World.* In 1989 he was selected as Aboriginal of the Year.

FURTHER REFERENCE
Recordings include *An Evening with Jimmy Little* (1978, Festival L45825/6); *Jimmy Little by Request* (1973, Calendar L15035); *Twenty Golden Country Greats* (1979, Festival L25324); *Winterwood* (1972, Festival FL34721); *I Can't Stop Loving You* (1974, Universal Summit). A discography is in P. Dunbar-Hall, *Discography of Aboriginal and Torres Strait Islander Performers* (Sydney: Australian Music Centre, 1996). See also *LattaA*; *SmithB*. P. DUNBAR-HALL

Little Pattie [Patricia Thelma Amplett] (*b* Sydney, 1949), pop singer. Singing at Sydney surf clubs from the age of 14, her debut single *He's My Blond Headed Stompie Wompie Real Gone Surfer Boy* (1963) reached No. 25 in the charts, then she had other hits, *Dance, Puppet, Dance* (1965) reaching No. 27. By 1964 she was appearing regularly on television's *Saturday Date* and *Sing, Sing, Sing*, but by 1966 she was on the club circuit, the surf craze having passed. She sang before the Queen Mother at the Adelaide Festival and had her last hit, *I'll Eat My Hat*, in 1967, but she went on to make 12 more singles, moving towards country music in numbers such as *What Am I Gonna Do* (1977). A meteoric rise with the Sydney surf music fad of the early 1960s, by the time she was 17 she had released eight singles, two EPs and two albums.

FURTHER REFERENCE
Recordings include *He's My Blond Headed Stompie Wompie Real Gone Surfer Boy* (1963, HMV EA 4604), *Dance, Puppet, Dance* (1965, HMV EA 4703), *I'll Eat My Hat* (1967, HMV EA 4846), *What Am I Gonna Do* (1977, ATA), and *The Many Moods of Little Pattie* (HMV). A compilation is *20 Stompy Wompy Hits* (1981, EMI EMV 504). For discography, see *SpencerA*. See also *McGrathA*; *SpencerW*; Michael Sturma, *Australian Rock'n'Roll: The First Wave* (Kenhurst, NSW: Kangaroo Press, 1991), 67–9.

Little River Band. Rock band (1975–86, reappeared 1988–89), formed when Glenn ★Shorrock (vocals, formerly of The ★Twilights and ★Axiom) joined forces with Graham Goble and Beeb Birtles (guitars, vocals) from the band Mississippi; subsequent members included Derek Pellici, Rick Formosa, Roger McLachlan, Stephen Housden, George McArdle, David Briggs, Mal Logan, Steven Preswitch, Wayne Nelson and David Hirschfelder. The band's name was inspired by a road sign the members saw while driving to their first engagement at Geelong, Vic. The tight, intricate harmonies of their debut single *Curiosity Killed the Cat* (1975) became their trademark. In 1977 they took soft rock to its source in Los Angeles, achieving three Top 30 hits on the American charts and becoming the first Australian group to earn gold record status in the USA for their third album *Diamantina Cocktail*, also Australia's biggest-selling album of 1977. The band was achieving success in South America and most European countries by 1978, when Shorrock recorded versions of their hit song *Reminiscing* in Spanish and French. When Shorrock resigned in February 1982 manager Glen Wheatley recruited John ★Farnham as lead vocalist; in October the band toured the USA to promote their new image. The band toured Japan, Alaska, the USA and Canada in 1983 and released *The Net*, followed by *Playing to Win* in 1984. It won the 1985 Mo award for the best rock group, and in 1987 their version of Cold Chisel's *When the War is Over* became a theme for the mini-series *Sword of Honor*. When their 1986 album *No Reins* did not sell well Farnham left the band, his experience having groomed him for his successful *Whispering*

Jack album. Internal anxieties, tension and competitiveness contributed to the gradual demise of the band, detracting from their creativity.

Australia's first guitar-based band to achieve an international reputation, Little River Band had considerable success in the USA after Wheatley clinched a deal with Capitol, and Shorrock remains one of the most distinguished voices to have emerged from Australian rock. Their earlier country-rock material was artistically superior to the more heavily orchestrated but less original middle-of-the-road pop ballads of their later records. In nearly nine years they underwent nine line-up changes, Goble being the only original member left at the end.

FURTHER REFERENCE
LP records include *Little River Band* and *After Hours* (1976, EMI); *Diamantina Cocktail* (1977, EMI); *Beginnings*, *It's a Long Way There* and *Sleeper Catcher* (1978, EMI); *First Under the Wire* (1979, EMI); *Backstage Pass* and *Live in America* (1980, EMI); *Time Exposure* (1981, EMI); *The Net* (1983, Capitol); *Playing to Win* (1984, Capitol); *No Reins* (1985, Capitol); *Monsoon* (1988, WEA); *Too Late to Load* and *The Farnham Years* (1989, EMI); *Get Lucky* (1993, MCA Records); *Live Exposure* (EMI video, E6015). Reissues on CD include *Diamantina Cocktail* (1989, EMI 98313932); *The Classic Collection* (1992, EMI 8140752); *Most of the Little River Band* vol. I (1993, EMI 4380312) and vol. 2 (1993, EMI 4380342); *Live Classics* (1992, EMI 7808482); *Reminiscing: The 20th Anniversary Album* (1995, EMI 8319602). See also Clark Forbes, *Whispering Jack: The John Farnham Story* (Sydney: Hutchinson Australia, 1989); Valerie Krantz & Diana Chase, *John Farnham: The Voice* (Melbourne: Macmillan, 1993); *McGregorA*; *SpencerW*.

ROBIN RYAN

Livermore, Reg (*b* Parramatta, 11 Dec. 1938), actor, theatrical singer. After training in classical acting with John Alden at the Independent Theatre School, Sydney, he was a founding member of the Ensemble Theatre Co., Melbourne, in 1957, then the Union Theatre Repertory Co. from 1961. He was a notable presence in the comedy *A Cup of Tea, A Bex and A Good Lie Down* at the Philip Street Theatre, Sydney, in 1965, and came to national prominence as the lead in *Hair!* from 1970, then in *The Rocky Horror Show* and *Jesus Christ Superstar*. He then developed a solo show, *Betty Blockbuster Follies* (1975), appeared as a female impersonator in *Wonder Woman* (1976), and with his own music in *Ned Kelly: The Electric Music Show* (1978). He withdrew from the limelight in 1980, re-emerging for the modernised *Pirates of Penzance* in 1992 and more recently in the pantomime *Mother Goose* (1993) and *Wish You Were Here* (1994). One of the most successful of Australia's theatrical performers, he has developed a loyal following for his more innovative solo work.

FURTHER REFERENCE
MonashB; *Age* 28 Aug 1991; *DPA*, 172.

Llewellyn, Ernest Victor (*b* Kurri Kurri, NSW, 21 June 1915; *d* Sydney, 12 July 1982), violinist. As a child Llewellyn was known as the 'boy wonder violinist', studying with Jascha Gopinko from the age of seven. At 13 he played before Szigeti, who urged him to abandon formal schooling. He attended the NSW State Conservatorium for six months and money was raised for him to study overseas, but in the Depression it was rescinded. In 1939 he married the daughter of the Sydney violin-maker, A.E. *Smith, and was to use one of Smith's violins for the rest of his life. He joined the Sydney String Quartet as violist and later became violist in the Sydney Symphony Orchestra. At this time he was considered the best violinist in the country. Georg Szell offered him the leadership of the Scottish National and The Hague Orchestras but Llewellyn refused. *Goossens invited him to become concertmaster of the Sydney Symphony Orchestra, which position he held from 1949 until 1965. In 1955 he won the William Kapell Memorial and Fulbright scholarships to study in New York, but refused all invitations to work overseas. After his retirement from the Sydney Symphony Orchestra he initiated the foundation of the Canberra School of Music, becoming the first director in 1965. In 1978 he was the first Australian to adjudicate at the Tchaikovsky Competition in Moscow. After his retirement from the Canberra School of Music he continued to teach and to perform in chamber music concerts. He was awarded the MBE, OBE and CBE.

FURTHER REFERENCE
Ruth Llewellyn, 'A Short History of Ernest Llewellyn CBE', *2MBS-FM Programme Guide* (June 1990), 5–7; J.V. Yates, ed., *Who's Who in Music and Musicians International Directory,* 6th edn (London: Burke's Peerage, 1972).   SUZANNE ROBINSON

Lloyd, A(lbert) L(ancaster) (*b* London, 29 Feb. 1908; *d* London, 29 Sept. 1982), English folklorist, folk performer. Compiler of *The Penguin Book of English Folk Songs* (1959, with Ralph Vaughan Williams) and *Folk Songs of England* (1967), he worked as a jackeroo in NSW 1925–33, collecting Australian folk-songs which he later performed in a series of recordings (Wattle, 1956–58) issued with extended booklets containing the texts. His work was the only significant folk-song collecting done in Australia between A.B. *Paterson (1905) and the revival of the 1950s, but the published examples he gave were atypical of Australia in their polish. The extent to which he may have revised them or adapted them from the collections of others remains controversial. He visited Australia again in the 1970s to lecture and perform.

FURTHER REFERENCE
Obit. in *Folkmusic Journal* 4/4 (1983). A compilation of his work is *Classic A.L. Lloyd* (Sandstock SSM FE 098CD). See also *Stringybark and Greenhide* 4/3 (1983), 13–15; *OxfordF.*

LMusA. Licentiate in Music, Australia. Diploma awarded by the AMEB. Originally modelled on the British LRSM, the award is based on an advanced examination in an instrument or music theory, taken after completion of practical and theoretical prerequisites in the Board's higher-grade examinations. Often taken after the completion of an *AMusA, it was the highest diploma awarded by the Board until the creation of the *FMusA in 1992. A quite demanding examination, about 70 candidates are successful each year, mostly young adults but also a few unusually gifted teenagers.

Loam, Arthur Steadman (*b* Weymouth, England, *c*.1896; *d* ?), composer, teacher. Playing piano, organ and violin from childhood, he was a boy soloist in Salisbury Cathedral Choir. Arriving in Australia in 1914, he soon joined the AIF; after the war he conducted cinema ensembles at Bendigo, Victoria, until 1924, then Melbourne until 1930. He wrote numerous songs and children's pieces such as *Playhouse Pieces* (1951) and *Songs for Movement and Action*, and his *My Country* (after the poem *I Love a Sunburnt Country*) became immensely popular in schools. A composer in the English art-song genre of the day, his choral settings of Aboriginal themes was one of the rare attempts to use Aboriginal materials at that time. He taught piano and became active as an adjudicator and examiner for the AMEB, writing articles for *Australian Musical News* and publishing *Grade 2 Test Papers* (1951).

FURTHER REFERENCE
AMN 30 (Aug. 1939), 27. Clipping file, *Msl.*

Lobl, Phyl (*b* Ballarat, Vic., 1937), folk-singer, songwriter. Working as a primary school teacher, she performed as a folk-singer from 1962, playing guitar and banjo. She toured Australia, NZ, the UK and the USA, representing Australia at the Cologne Song Festival in 1982. As a member of the Australia Council Music Board (1984–87) she contributed to the establishment of a federal funding policy for folk music. She has given workshops and frequently performed at folk festivals.

FURTHER REFERENCE
Recordings include *Bass Strait Crossing, Broadmeadow Thistle* (Larrikin LRF 051) and *Bullockies Bushwackers and Booze* (Score). A collection of 35 of her songs is published as *Songs of a Bronzelwing* (Connells Point, NSW: Tully Publishing, 1991). See also *OxfordF.*

Lola Montez. Musical comedy by Peter Stannard, lyrics by Peter Benjamin and book by Alan Burke. It tells of an Irish miner's infatuation with Lola Montez. First performed by the Elizabethan Theatre Trust with the Union Repertory Co. at the Union Theatre, University of Melbourne, in February 1958, then in an enlarged production at the Elizabethan Theatre, Newtown, Sydney.

Long, Kenneth R. (*b* UK, *c.*1925), organist. After studies and early appointments in England he arrived in Australia in 1953 and became organist and choirmaster at St Andrew's Cathedral, Sydney. A learned and very able player in traditional repertoire, he was also an orchestral and choral conductor, and presented major oratorios at the cathedral with the combined choirs and Sydney Symphony Orchestra.

FURTHER REFERENCE
AMN 47 (Oct. 1956) 22; *AMN* 44 (Sept. 1953) 22, 31.

Lord Of The Rings. Extended jazz composition in six sections (1974–77) by John Sangster after Tolkien, recorded in six albums. See *Sangster, John.*

Lorenzaccio. Opera in three acts, music and libretto by Colin ★Brumby (1986), after the play by Alfred de Musset. Set in the Medici torture chambers of 16th-century Florence, an excerpt was first performed in workshop by the Australian Opera at the Broadwalk Studio, Sydney Opera House, on 29 October 1986. Score from Australian Music Centre.

Loughlin, George Frederick (*b* Liverpool, England, 1914; *d* Melbourne, 12 June 1984), composer, professor of music. After studies in piano with Arthur ★Benjamin, in composition with Sir Edward Bairstow and Gordon Jacob at the Royal College of Music, London, and in organ with Denys Pouncey at Wells Cathedral, he was a schoolteacher in England, then taught at the University of Toronto, Canada 1950–53 and the University of Glasgow 1954–57 before succeeding Sir Bernard Heinze as Ormond professor and director of the Conservatorium at the University of Melbourne in 1958, where he remained until his retirement in 1979. A sensitive accompanist and gifted teacher, his book *Diatonic Harmony* (Melbourne: Allans, 1966) was widely used as a text in Australia. He wrote well-crafted compositions in traditional idioms, mostly unpublished and unheard in Australia.

FURTHER REFERENCE
His memoir *Cities of Departure: An Autobiography* (Melbourne, 1984) was privately published after his death. See *GlennonA*, 208.

Loughnan, Col (Colin John) (*b* Sydney, 26 Oct. 1942), jazz reeds player. After playing in rock groups he moved into jazz, playing reeds with Col Nolan 1968–69, the ★Daly-Wilson Big Band 1969–72 and session work 1970–72. He was based overseas 1970–73, then returned to Australia and played with ★Ayers Rock (1974), in session work, as musical director for Marcia ★Hines and the John ★Farnham-Debbie Byrne ABC television series, and made further tours overseas. He worked in jazz with Judy ★Bailey and others, and as support for visitors including Don Rader and Toshiko Akiyoshi. He taught in the jazz

program at the NSW Conservatorium from 1984, and is currently resident in Queensland.

FURTHER REFERENCE
Recordings include *Col Nolan and the Soul Syndicate* (1968, CBS SBP-233612); *The Exciting Daly Wilson Big Band* (1971, Festival SFL-934453); *The Julian Lee Orchestra* (1980, Batjazz BAT-2072); *Feel the Breeze* (1981, Seaside Records YRPX 1862). See also *OxfordJ*.   BRUCE JOHNSON

Loved Ones, The Rock band (1965–67; 1988) formed in Melbourne by combining Gerry Humphreys (vocals), Ian Clyne (piano) and Kim Lynch (bass) from the trad jazz ★Red Onions Jazz Band with Rob Lovett (guitar) and Gavin Anderson (drums) from the ★Wild Cherries. In 1966 Clyne wrote the first two of their seven singles to Humphreys' lyrics, *The Loved One*, which reached No. 15 in the charts and *Ever Lovin' Man*, which reached No. 2; they released the EP *Blueberry Hill* in the same year. After membership changes they toured with the Animals and the Hollies (1967) and worked in Melbourne discos, releasing an album that has become a minor classic, *Magic Box*. In one of the finest pop bands of the 1960s, Humphreys' powerful rhythm and blues vocals combined with the seasoned rock and jazz skills of the others to produce an uncommon individuality, which they presented in untamed style on stage. They reformed for a tour in 1987, releasing *Live On Blueberry Hill* (1988).

FURTHER REFERENCE
Recordings include *The Loved One* (In records INS 2610), *Ever Lovin' Man* (In records INS 8007), *Blueberry Hill* (W&G GE 271), *Magic Box* (reissued 1990, Raven RVCD 02), *and Live On Blueberry Hill* (1988, Mushroom L38882). For discography, see *SpencerA*. See also *McGrathA*; *SpencerW*; *GuinnessP*, III, 15–24.

Lovelock, William (*b* London, 13 Mar. 1899; *d* London, 26 June 1986), composer, writer on music. After studies with C.W. Pearce and Henry Geehl at Trinity College, London, and service in World War I, he taught at Trinity College from 1919. He was private organist to the Viscountess Cowdray 1923–26, organist at St Clement's Eastcheap, London, and took a doctorate in composition at the University of London in 1932. He served in the Far East in World War II, and was an established teacher, author of music theory textbooks, and music examiner in London before he came to Australia in 1956 as founding director of the Queensland Conservatorium. His traditional approach to the new school brought difficulties, and he resigned in 1959, after which he was for many years music critic for the Brisbane *Courier-Mail* as well as a popular adjudicator and examiner for the AMEB and Trinity College.

His compositions, all peerlessly written in frankly Romantic idioms, range from teaching pieces for children to full-scale orchestral, choral, brass, and military band works, including 14 concertos. He produced more than 20 books, including *A Concise History of Music* (1953), *Rudiments of Music, Test Your Theory, General Knowledge, Transposition at the Keyboard*, which remain universally used in Australia as well as in many other countries.

FURTHER REFERENCE
Recordings include the Symphony in C-Sharp Minor, Sydney Symphony Orchestra, cond. J. Post (ABC PRX 6514); Flute Concerto, Vernon Hill, fl, Melbourne Symphony Orchestra, cond. L. Dommett (Festival SFC 800–26); and the Trumpet Concerto, John Robertson, tr, Sydney Symphony Orchestra, cond. J Post (RCA SL 16371) or with Geoffrey Payne, Melbourne Symphony Orchestra, cond. J. Hopkins (1991, ABC 426990). *PlushD* lists other works on ABC tapes to 1971. Most of his books are published by Allans Music, Melbourne. See also *MonashB*; *CallawayA*, 228–31; *AJME* 19 (Oct. 1976); *GlennonA*, 167.

Lowe, Robert [Viscount Sherbrooke] (*b* Bingham, Nottinghamshire, England, 4 Dec. 1811; *d* Warlingham, Surrey, England, 27 July 1892), parliamentarian, folksong writer. Educated at Oxford in law he practised as a barrister, but came to Australia in 1842 to ward off his supposedly impending blindness (he was an albino). In 1843 he became a member of the NSW Legislative Council, but disillusioned he resigned in 1844 and worked as editor of *Atlas,* publishing many anti-government poems in *Songs of the Squatters*. He rejoined the Legislative Council in 1845, and returned to England in 1850 where he was in the House of Commons (from 1852) then the House of Lords (from 1880). His songs, *The Commissioner, The Squatter To His Bride* and others, became well known in Australia.

FURTHER REFERENCE
His verse is in *Poems of a Life,* 2nd edn (London: Kegan, Paul, Trench & Co., 1885). See also *ADB*, 2; *OxfordL*; *OxfordF*; Royal Australian Historical Society *Journal and Proceedings* 12 (1926), 51–9.

Lowenstein, Wendy née Robertson (*b* 25 June 1927), folklorist. After raising a family she trained as a teacher-librarian and worked in schools. She was one of the founders of the Folk Lore Society of Victoria in 1955, and then editor of its journal *Australian Tradition* 1961–75. She contributed to a collection of schoolyard rhymes and songs, *Cinderella Dressed in Yella* (1969), and with a government grant made a national field trip in 1969. One of Australia's foremost collectors of oral history and folklore, she compiled *Shocking, Shocking, Shocking: The Improper Play Rhymes of Australian Children* (1974), as well as other collections on popular culture.

FURTHER REFERENCE
The folklore recollections and material she collected now are at *CAnl*. See also *OxfordF*; *OxfordL*; Gloria Frydman, *Protesters* (Melbourne: Collins Dove, 1987), 109–17.

Lowin Composition Prizes, Paul. Awarded every two years in June (since 1991), there are two prizes, one for an orchestral work and one for a song cycle. Based on submission of scores, applicants must be at least 18 and Australian citizens or resident in Australia for three years. Previous winners have included Julian *Yu, Stephen *Cronin, and Brenton *Broadstock. Administered by Perpetual Trustees from the estate of the late Paul Lowin, a Sydney music-lover, they are Australia's most valuable composition prizes; currently the orchestral award is $25 000 and the song cycle award is $15 000.

Loyau, George Etienne [George Chanson; Remos] (*b* London, 15 Apr. 1835; *d* Bundaberg, Qld, 23 Apr. 1898), journalist, folk-song writer. Arriving in Australia at the age of 18, he went to the goldfields, then worked in the eastern states as a stockman, cook and tutor. He began writing verse and novels, and from 1861 worked in a succession of newspapers in Queensland, Sydney, Melbourne and Adelaide, from the *Maryborough Chronicle* (1861–62) to the *Illustrated Adelaide News* (1880–81), before returning to Queensland in 1895. Using his mother's maiden name Chanson, he published bush ballads and music hall songs in the *Sydney Songster* (*c*.1865), and the *Queensland New Colonial Camp Fire Song Book* (Sydney, *c*.1869). He published three volumes of verse including *Colonial Lyrics* (1872). He also wrote two volumes of biographical studies. Through Hugh Anderson's scholarship, he has come to be recognised as author and compiler of the earliest sources of some of the oldest and best-known Australian bush ballads.

FURTHER REFERENCE
His autobiography is *The Personal Adventures of George E. Loyau* (1883). See also *ADB*, 5; Hugh Anderson, *George Loyau: The Man Who Wrote Bush Ballads* (Melbourne: Red Rooster Press, 1991); *OxfordL*.

Loyde, Lobby [John Baslington (Barry) Lyde], rock guitarist-songwriter. At first in a local Brisbane band, the Stilettos, he came to national attention in the hard-rock rhythm and blues band Purple Hearts 1963–67, then played with the *Wild Cherries 1967–68 and Billy *Thorpe and the Aztecs 1969–71, releasing a solo album, *Lobby Loyde Plays George Guitar* (1971). He formed the raucous skinhead band The Coloured Balls (1972–74), then worked with the Joy Band and the Southern Electric Band 1974–76. He was in England 1977–79 in new-wave bands, then played in the heavy metal band Rose Tattoo 1979–80, releasing *Live With Dubs* (1979). The leading Australian guitarist of loud, hard rock of the late 1960s, he explored the reaches of the idiom from rhythm and blues styles to heavy metal and experimental rock. From 1980 he produced alternative rock recordings, played session work and appeared with Dirt (1987, 1990).

FURTHER REFERENCE
Recordings include *Lobby Loyde Plays George Guitar* (1971, Infinity SIN L93426), and *Live With Dubs* (1979, Mushroom L37399). For discography, see *SpencerA*. See also 'Coloured Balls' and 'Wild Cherries' in *McGrathA* and SpencerW.

Ltarta (Alyawarra), public singing and dancing in the central desert. See *Corroboree*.

Lucky-Peter's Journey. Fairy-tale opera in three acts by Malcolm *Williamson, libretto by E. Tracey after Strindberg. First performed at the London Coliseum on 18 December 1969.

Ludowyk, Chris (Christopher John) (*b* Sri Lanka, 6 Mar. 1944), jazz trombonist. He emigrated to Geelong, Vic., in 1962, becoming involved in the traditional movement on bass and trombone, playing in the Crescent City, Green Horse and Baton Rouge jazz bands. Moving to Melbourne in 1968, he joined the New Harlem Band, taking over its leadership in 1979–82. After a period in England where he worked with Cuff Billett, he returned to Melbourne and formed the Society Syncopators (1984) which he has continued to lead, playing local residencies, festivals, and international tours. He is also a workshop director for the Victorian Jazz Club.

FURTHER REFERENCE
Recordings include *Never Swat a Fly,* The New Harlem Jazz Band, (1977, Jazz & Jazz 6357 902); *Les Copains D'abord,* Chris Ludowyk's Society Syncopators (1992, SSCD 920); *Movin' Up,* Society Syncopators (1994, Newmarket New 1077–2); *Revolutionary Blues,* Society Syncopators (1996, Newmarket New 2022–2). See also *OxfordJ*.   BRUCE JOHNSON

Lumsdaine, David (*b* Sydney, 31 Oct. 1931), composer. He studied at the NSW Conservatorium and the University of Sydney, then under Matyas Seiber at the Royal Academy of Music in London, and again under Lennox Berkeley from 1961. He was lecturer at the University of Durham from 1970, then at King's College, London from 1981, then honorary visiting professor at the University of York from 1995. He has been visiting professor at the University of Adelaide, visiting composer at the University of Sydney and Canberra School of Music (1976), joint composer-in-residence at the NSW Conservatorium (1979), and chair for the Australian National Composers' School (1985, 1987).

A composer of great originality, Lumsdaine's methods nevertheless embrace a series of mainstream 20th-century techniques and influences including serialism, the Orient, electro-acoustic systems, and the use of birdsong as a source and inspiration. He composes mostly to commission, writing for a range of ensembles and organisations including the Pierrot Players, Gemini, the London Sinfonietta, the Huddersfield Contemporary Music Festival, the BBC and the ABC. Australian themes are a major

inspiration for his compositions. *Salvation Creek with Eagle* (a vision of Australian nature), *A Dance and a Hymn for Alexander Maconochie* (a tribute to the commandant of the Norfolk Island penal colony who let the prisoners out for the day to 'rediscover their dignity'), *Kelly Ground* (focusing on the death of the Australian bushranger Ned Kelly) and *Aria for Edward John Eyre* (the Yorkshire explorer diverted to Albany by the great salt lake) are among those that have their roots in, if not their stories from, the Australian continent. Lumsdaine considers his imagination is still caught up in the country of his childhood: 'It's as if I had to get away from it in order to find it.'

Before leaving Australia, his main influences were Stravinsky and Britten; added to these on arrival in London were those of Varèse, Messiaen and Webern. Compositions from this early period followed a rigorous serialism, one of the most accomplished works being *Kelly Ground*, which uses a basic rhythmic cycle of two bells in a ratio of 4:5, bells which could be interpreted as Kelly's death knell. This sound dominates the piece, which becomes ever more complex, functioning in a manner which has been likened to an isorhythmic motet. The later and more relaxed *Aria for Edward John Eyre* is, in essence, a piece of psychological music-theatre with narrators (one narrator is given extracts from Eyre's diary, a second Eyre's inner thoughts) and a soprano solo (who sings the aria that is deep inside the explorer), against an amplified bass, pre-recorded tape, live electronics, and an instrumental ensemble. Lumsdaine is also capable of the lighter touch as shown in *What Shall I Sing?* a glorious song cycle for soprano and two clarinets, of 13 nonsensical songs; these are no less skilful than the more serious compositions, and are as carefully wrought as any other.

Lumsdaine's philosophy is best summed up by his remark: 'Too often we think of music as a score that a composer presents to a player, saying "Here's my music. Take it [the music] away, learn it [the music] and play it [the music]." But music is an activity, not a piece of paper.' In essence, the activity for Lumsdaine is listening: listening as the activity of the composer, and as the business of the players, and of the audience, without the traditional distinction between the three. He subscribes to the Lévi-Straussian view that 'music becomes actual … through and by the listener', and modifies Lévi-Strauss's 'Music has its being in me, and I listen to myself,' to 'Music has its being in me. I compose myself through it.'

WORKS (Selective)
Principal publishers: Universal; University of York Music Press (UYMP)
Orchestral *Salvation Creek with Eagle* (1974, UYMP), *Hagoromo* (1977, UYMP), *Mandala 5* (1988, UYMP).
Vocal *Annotations of Auschwitz,* S, fl, hn, tr, pf, vn, vc (1964, after Peter Porter and the Bible), London, 3 Nov. 1965 (London, 1975), *Aria for Edward John Eyre,* S and db soloists, 2 nar, chamber ens, tapes, live electronics (1973, after E.J. Eyre, pub. UYMP), Liv-

erpool, 23 Jan. 1965, *What shall I sing?*, sp, 2 cl (1982, traditional, pub. UYMP), Helmsley, 3 Aug. 1983.

Ensemble *Mandala 1,* wind quintet (1967, UYMP), *Mandala 2,* fl, cl, perc, va, vc (1969, UYMP), *Mandala 3,* pf (solo), fl, cl, chinese bell, va, vc, (1978, UYMP), *Manadla 4,* str qrt (1983, UYMP), *A Dance and a Hymn for Alexander Maconochie,* fl, cl, perc, mandolin, gui, vn, db (1988, UYMP).

Instrumental *Kelly Ground,* pf (1966, London 1967), *Kangaroo Hunt,* perc, pf (1971, Oxford, 1971).

Electro-accoustic *Four Soundscapes: Lake Emu, Meunga Creek, River Red Gums & Black Box, Pied Butcher Birds of Spirey Creek,* (1990), *Soundscape 5: Cambewarra* (1991), *Soundscape 6: Mutawinji* (1995).

FURTHER REFERENCE
Recordings include *Hagoromo, Salvation Creek, Shoalhaven, Mandala 5* (1990, 1991, ABC Classics 426 994–2), *What shall I sing?, Aria for Edward John Eyre* (1991, NMC D007), *Cambewarra: Australian Soundscapes,* vol. 1 (1995, Tall Poppies TP083), *Pied Butcher Birds of Spirey Creek, Mutawinji: Australian Soundscapes,* vol. 2 (1996, Tall Poppies TP092), *Lake Emu, River Red Gums & Black Box: Australian Soundscapes,* vol. 3 (1996, Tall Poppies TP092). See also Andrew Ford, 'David Lumsdaine', in *Composer to Composer: Conversations about Contemporary Music* (London: Quartet, 1993), 69–77; A. Gilbert, *Contemporary C;* M. Hall, 'The Country of my Childhood', *Musical Times* 133 (1992), 329–31; N. Lefanu, 'David Lumsdaine's "Sunflower"', *Musical Times* 117 (1976), 25–7; A. Schultz, 'Identity and Memory Temporality in the Music of David Lumsdaine', *SMA* 25 (1991), 95–101.

MICHAEL BURDEN

Lumsdaine, Jack (John Sinclair) (*b* 18 Nov. 1895; *d* 28 Aug. 1948), popular music songwriter. He was a choirboy at St Andrew's Cathedral, Sydney, then toured with the All Blacks Vaudeville Co. from 1911. After war service he worked for Allans Music, Melbourne, and as an accompanist in vaudeville and silent movies. From 1923 he was a popular songwriter on Sydney radio. He wrote hundreds of songs in the nostalgic English popular song style of the day, setting sentimental, comic, or sporting themes, such as *Our Eleven* (*c.*1930), *Phar Lap: Farewell To You* (*c.*1932), *Aussie Rose, Since Ma's Gone Mad On Community Singing* (*c.*1930), or his greatest success *Guiding Star* (Chappell & Co. 1933). At least 24 of his songs were published by Alberts, Allans, Chappell & Co. and others, and 16 were recorded by Regal Zonophone.

FURTHER REFERENCE
Murray Goot, *ADB,* 10.

Luritja. People of the Central Australian desert west of Palmer River and around Mount Leibig, NT, neighbours of ★Warlpiri, ★Antakarinja, ★Pitjantjatjara, ★Pintupi and others. After White contact in the 1930s, the Luritja settled at Haasts Bluff and Papunya. The rock band Areyonga

Desert Tigers are Luritja, their *Light On* released by Imparja Records. See *Aboriginal Music.*

Lyall, Graeme William (*b* Melbourne, 25 Jan. 1942), jazz reeds player. He studied reeds with Frank Smith, then trained at the NSW Conservatorium from 1961. With TCN-9 Orchestra 1963–71, he was also active at ★El Rocco. He was with Don Burrows in 1970, returning to Melbourne in 1971, and in television orchestras through the 1970s. Musical director for Olivia ★Newton-John in 1981, he taught at Victorian College of the Arts until 1986. Moving to north-east Victoria, he directed school and community music programs, then returned to Melbourne in 1991 as musical director for the television series *Hey Hey, It's Saturday.* From 1992 he has been assistant head of jazz studies at the Sydney Conservatorium, then lecturer at the WA Conservatorium from 1995.

FURTHER REFERENCE
Recordings include *My Favourite Things,* the Judy Bailey Quartet (1965, CBS BP-233263); *The Don Burrows Octet* (1967, CBS BP-233450); *The Graeme Lyall Orchestra* (1968, Columbia Co SXCO-7897); *Charlie Munro's Jazz Orchestra* (1969, Columbia Co SCXO-7911); *Lord of the Rings vol. 1,* John Sangster (1974, EMI EMC 2525/6), vol. 2 (1976, EMI EMC 2548/9), vol. 3 (1977, EMI EMC 2580/1). See also *ClareB; BissetB; OxfordJ.*

BRUCE JOHNSON

Lyric Opera of Queensland. See *Opera Queensland.*

Lyster, W(illiam) S(aurin) (*b* Dublin, 21 Mar. 1827; *d* Melbourne, 27 Nov. 1880), opera impresario of Irish birth. After seeing combat as a soldier in the Cape Frontier and Nicaragua and managing his brother's touring opera company in New Orleans, he recruited his own company for seasons in California, which became resident in Australia 1861–68. Bringing Lucy ★Escott and Henry ★Squires as his principals, he staged over 40 operas by Donizetti, Verdi, Auber, Rossini, Meyerbeer and many others, and gave an extraordinary number of performances throughout the colonial settlements, often under very adverse conditions. He returned to Australia in 1870, presenting in the decade before his death full-scale productions of the latest Verdi and Wagner works, several Italian touring companies, concerts and numerous *opéras bouffe.* An entrepreneur of astonishing courage, resourcefulness and business acumen, he was unquestionably the principal pioneer of regular operatic life in Australia.

FURTHER REFERENCE
Harold Love, *The Golden Age of Australian Opera* (Sydney: Currency Press, 1981); idem, 'Lyster's 1862 *Huguenots:* A Milestone of Musical Theatre in Australia', *SMA* 11 (1977); Sally O'Neill and Thérèse Radic, *ADB,* 5; *IrvinD; BrewerD,* 66ff.

M

Ma Curly Headed Babby. Popular song with music and text by expatriate Australian composer George H. *Clutsam (1866–1951), written in London in 1897 and first published in the *Strand Musical Magazine,* then by Edwin Ashdown as sheet music in 1900. This 'plantation' lullaby was Clutsam's most successful song; it had sold 200 000 copies by 1914. The song was recorded a number of times in the early 1920s and very successfully revived in 1932 by American bass-baritone Paul Robeson (1898–1976) for HMV in London. Richard Tauber recorded a German language version in 1933.

FURTHER REFERENCE
W.M., 'Notable Australians: G.H. Clutsam', *Lone Hand* (1 May 1914), 412.   JENNIFER HILL

McBurney, Mona Margaret (*b* Isle of Man, 29 July 1862; *d* Melbourne, 4 Dec. 1932), composer. McBurney received her early musical training from Alexander Mackenzie in Edinburgh. She went to the University of Melbourne in 1881, and in 1896 was the first woman BMus graduate in Australia. As a composer she received considerable recognition. Her *Ode to Dante* (1902) received an honourable mention by the Società Dante Alighieri in Rome, and was performed throughout Australia and NZ, and her opera *The Dalmatian* (1905, Francis Marion Crawford) was recognised by the selection committee of the Ricordi Prize in London. It was performed at the Albert Street Conservatorium in 1910, and a performance in 1926 at the Playhouse, Melbourne, was the first performance of an opera by a woman composer in Australia. An instrumental work *A Northern Ballad* (a Nordic myth) was performed at the Exhibition of Women's Works in 1907 and by the Marshall-Hall Orchestra in 1908. Several songs were published in London, Paris and Australia, and were frequently performed in Melbourne, and two songs, *Persian Song of Spring* and *Song on May Morning*, published by Allan & Co. were in print until the 1950s. Her early piano students included the composers May *Brahe and

Margaret *Sutherland, and from 1918 to 1931 she was a tutor in Italian and French at the University Conservatorium of Music, Melbourne.

FURTHER REFERENCE
Her works and papers are in *PVgm*. See also Faye Patton, *ADB*, 10; idem, 'Rediscovering Our Musical Past: The Works of Mona McBurney and Florence Ewart', *SA* (1988/89), 10–12; idem, *GroveO*.   FAYE PATTON

McBurney, Samuel (*b* Glasgow, Scotland, 30 Apr. 1847; *d* Melbourne, 5 July 1909), music educator, tonic sol-fa advocate. His early training was in tonic sol-fa, then he took MusBac and MusDoc degrees from Trinity College Dublin (1890). He emigrated to Victoria in 1870 and after teaching in public schools became principal of Geelong Ladies' College. As part of a lifelong dissemination of the tonic sol-fa music-teaching method, he published numerous school textbooks, song-books, choral works and articles. In 1887 he toured eastern Australia, NZ, the USA and the UK promoting tonic sol-fa. Returning to Victoria, he gained approval for tonic sol-fa in state schools and was appointed as inspector of music, Victorian department of education (1891); he was then principal of a ladies' college in St Kilda and taught at the University of Melbourne Conservatorium of Music (MusDoc *ad eundem* 1901).

FURTHER REFERENCE
R.S. Stevens, 'Samuel McBurney: The Stanley of Sol-fa', *Journal of Research in Music Education* 34/ 2 (Summer 1986), 77–87.
                          R. S. STEVENS

McCann, Ted (Edward John) (*b* Hobart, 18 Apr. 1888; *d* Lenah Valley, Tas., 18 July 1973), musician, radio executive. Born into a musical family, while a jeweller's apprentice he was choirmaster of St Mary's Cathedral, Hobart, 1915–22 and played violin in his brother Arthur's silent film ensemble. He then formed an ensemble of his own, conducting it for film screenings at the Prince of

Wales Theatre, Hobart, and on radio 7ZL's *Golden Hour.* Moving into the business side of radio, from 1931 he managed 7ZL, then became controller of programs for the Tasmanian Broadcasting Company. He was a prime mover in organising Tasmanian eisteddfods and the annual music weeks in the same years, and manager of ABC Tasmania 1946–53. An important figure in the early days of music broadcasting in Tasmania, he was president of the Musical Association of Tasmania 1945–50.

FURTHER REFERENCE
Obit. in Hobart *Mercury* 20 July 1973. See also Tom Pickering, *ADB*, 10.

McCarthy, John Grant　(*b* Sydney, 6 Jan. 1930), jazz reeds player. He began clarinet at the age of 13, later adding other reeds. With the Riverside Jazz Band from 1947 to the early 1950s, he was then with the *Port Jackson Jazz Band full-time by 1955 and the Ray *Price Quartet from 1958. He joined Dick *Hughes in 1962, and was with Graeme *Bell in the mid-1960s. He also played session work and in clubs, including as leader at Paddington-Woollahra RSL until 1978. A foundation member of Bob Barnard's band, he led his own group at Rocks Push, 1978. He joined Hughes's Famous Five at Soup Plus in 1985, where he later co-led the band with Bruce *Johnson. He continues leading and as a freelancer.

FURTHER REFERENCE
Recordings include *The Famous PIX Sessions, Classic Australian Jazz from the Sixties* (1996, Australian Jazz Reissues (AJR–001 A&B); *The Hobbit Suite,* John Sangster (1973, Swaggie S–1340); *Lord of the Rings Vol 1,* John Sangster (1974, EMI EMC 2525/6), vol. 2 (1976, EMI EMC 2548/9), vol. 3 (1977, EMI EMC 2580/1); *Bud Freeman With Bob Barnard's Jazz Band* (1976, Swaggie S–1367); *Ned Kelly Jazz Suite,* Bob Barnard and Friends (1977, Swaggie S–1374). See also *ClareB*; *BissetB*; *OxfordJ*.
BRUCE JOHNSON

McClellan, Mike　(*b* Melbourne, 24 Aug. 1945), popular music singer-songwriter, guitarist. He trained as a teacher and became involved in the folk music revival, first appearing at the Troubadour, Sydney, then moved towards blues and country, influenced by Chet Atkins, B.B. King and others. After winning a television talent quest he left the teaching service and sang with the Claire Poole Singers on the television series *Sound of Music,* and in 1972 formed the Currency Blues Company. His *Song And Dance Man* reached No. 33 on the charts in 1974, and was followed by *Rock'n'Roll Lady* (1975) and *Rock'n'Roll Man* (1980). He formed the Star Suite in 1975, toured Australia with Melanie (1976), Pentangle, the Hollies and others, and toured country areas in 1978. He had a television show, *Mike McClellan's Country Music* on the ABC (1981) and toured Europe and the USA in 1982, then produced film scores and commercials and played session work. His songs have been recorded by Rick Nelson, Melanie and others. As a player he is equally at home on six-string, 12-string, bottleneck, acoustic, and electric guitars. He was honoured in the Tamworth Hands of Fame in 1984.

FURTHER REFERENCE
Albums include *Mike McClellan* (1972, ATA), *Laughing at The Dark* (1980, EMI), and *Heartland* (1989, EMI). See also *McGrathA*; *SpencerW*; *SmithB*; *Age* 4 Nov. 1981.

McCredie, Andrew D.　(*b* Sydney, 3 Sept. 1930), musicologist. He studied at the University of Sydney 1948–54 (BA, MA) and the University of Hamburg (DPhil 1963). From 1965 he was senior research fellow (later professor) at the University of Adelaide, during which time he initiated the teaching and research of musicology at the university, established and edited the Adelaide-based journal *Miscellanea Musicologica* and the *Paperbacks in Musicology* series of Heinrichshofens Verlag, served as Australian area editor to the *New Grove Dictionary of Music and Musicians* and other music lexica, and organised national and international musicology conferences.

Australia's pioneering musicologist, McCredie was elected president of the Musicological Society of Australia from 1981–82 to 1991–92. His publications deal mainly with North German Baroque music-theatre and instrumental forms *c.*1830, Australian music (especially composer Alfred Hill), Byzantine-Slavic chant, and German composers from the Renaissance and mannerist to the contemporary, especially Hartmann, Frankenstein, Thuike, Egk, Stephen and Klebe. He made important contributions to musicological theory via several interdisciplinary areas, especially comparative literature, style, topos and reception theory; he produced performing editions of Monteverdi's shorter dramatic works and the *Vespers,* and issued five of Hartmann's posthumous symphonic works. He received numerous international awards, including the Edward J. Dent medal from the International Musicological Society and the Royal Musical Association of Great Britain (1974), and the Ignaz Paderewski Medallion of the Musica Antiqua Europae Orientalis Philharmonia in Bydgozez (1982). Elected first fellow of the Australian Academy of the Humanities in the discipline of musicology (1975), he was honoured with the AM (1984).

FURTHER REFERENCE
His writings include *Catalogue of 46 Australian Composers and Selected Works; Musical Composition in Australia, Including Select Bibliography and Discography* (Canberra: Advisory Board, Commonwealth Assistance to Australian Composers, 1969); *Karl Amadeus Hartmann: Sein Leben und Werk,* Taschenbücher zur Musikwissenschaft 74 (Wilhelmshaven: Heinrichshofen, 1980); *Musicological Studies in Australia from the Beginnings to the Present* (Sydney: Sydney University Press for the Australian Academy of the Humanities, 1979; 2nd edn, 1983). A *Festschrift for Andrew D. McCredie,* ed. David Swale, is to be published in 1997 by Heinrichshofen.
MARGARET KARTOMI

McDermott, Paul (*b* Melbourne, 1916; *d* 5 Sept. 1985), violinist. After studying violin at the University of Melbourne Conservatorium, he played with the Melbourne Symphony Orchestra from 1937, then went to London and joined the Royal Philharmonic Orchestra in 1946, touring the UK, Europe and the USA under Sir Thomas Beecham. He returned to Australia in 1951 and rejoined the Melbourne Symphony Orchestra, where he played until his retirement. A deep interest in chamber music led him to form the Paul McDermott String Quartet and later the Philharmonia of Melbourne, which gave popular subscription concerts in the 1970s. He was co-founder of the Australian Musicians' Guild in 1969, and to further public interest in chamber music conceived the annual Music in the Round festival, which attracted great public interest from its inception in 1972. A sympathetic, gentle personality and a dedicated performer, he did much to enrich Melbourne's musical life over a long period.

FURTHER REFERENCE
Obit. in *Age* 16 Sept. 1985; clipping file *Msl*.

McDonald, Donald Benjamin (*b* Sydney, 1 Sept. 1938), administrator. After studies in commerce at the University of NSW and work as director of finance for Vogue Publications (1965–68) and for the Australian Opera (1968–72), he became general manager of Musica Viva in 1972, AGC-Paradine in 1978 and the Sydney Theatre Co. in 1980. Probably Australia's most outstanding arts manager, he was appointed general manager of the Australian Opera in 1987, and steered the company away from periodic financial crisis through a decade of relative security and prosperity. Since 1996 he has been chairman of the ABC. He was honoured with the AO in 1991.

FURTHER REFERENCE
CA (1995–96); *WWA* (1996).

McDonald, Hector (*b* Toowoomba, Qld, 16 Mar. 1953), french horn player. He played brass band instruments from the age of nine, becoming NSW junior champion on tenor horn in 1965 and Australian open champion on euphonium in 1969. While in the RAAF band (from 1971) he studied french horn with Alan Mann at the NSW State Conservatorium, and in 1973 joined the ABC Training Orchestra, then the Elizabethan Theatre Trust (Sydney) Orchestra. He went to West Germany in 1975, studying with Hermann Baumann and soon joined the Wuppertal Opera Orchestra, then in 1976 the Berlin Philharmonic and the Berlin Radio Orchestra as solo horn (1977–80). He returned to Australia as head of brass at the Canberra School of Music from 1980, touring and recording with the ★Canberra Wind Soloists. Perhaps the finest horn player Australia has produced, he has a distinctively full, round tone and great technical agility. He has lived in Vienna since 1988.

FURTHER REFERENCE
CA (1995–96).

McDonald, Simon (*b* Springmount, nr Creswick, Vic., 22 Nov. 1907; *d* ?Creswick, 31 May 1968), folk musician. McDonald came from a family that has lived in and around the old goldmining town of Creswick since the time of the goldrushes. His father was also a bush musician who played the fiddle at local highland dances. As a child he played the tin whistle in his family band and taught himself to play his father's violin. From his father he learned many songs, which included not only Australian bush songs but also sailors' songs and British ballads passed down from his father's grandfather, who was an Irish sailor. With the exception of a brief period spent near Mildura as a fruit picker, McDonald spent practically all his life working in the area around Crewsick as a farm labourer, woodcutter and a gold fossicker. He entertained in local pubs with his piano playing and became well known in the district as a singer of traditional songs. He also took over his father's role as fiddler at local dances. Recordings of his singing were made in 1957 and 1960 by the folk-song collectors Norm O'Connor and Maryjean Officer, and his memoirs were recorded on tape during 1967. He died after suffering a stroke while riding his bicycle.

FURTHER REFERENCE
Recordings include *Traditional Singers and Musicians in Victoria* (1963, Wattle Archive Series 2). See also Hugh Anderson, *Time Out of Mind: The Story of Simon McDonald* (1974; reprint Melbourne: Red Rooster Press, 1987).   FLINDER HIEW

McEachern, (Walter) Malcolm Neil (*b* Albury, NSW, 1 Apr. 1883; *d* London, 17 Jan. 1945), singer, entertainer. He had his early tuition from Howard Tracey, then moved to Sydney in 1904, working as a biscuit salesman. He made his Sydney debut on 15 August 1908 in Ella ★Caspers' farewell grand matinee. In 1916 he married pianist Hazel Doyle with whom he appeared in many wartime charity concerts, and he appeared with the Melba Concert Co. in 1915 and the Tivoli theatres in 1917. Touring South Africa, Asia and the USA, he settled permanently in London in 1920, appearing in concert and increasingly in music hall. He formed the popular Flotsam and Jetsam duo with B.C. Hilliam in 1925, making many early BBC broadcasts, and recorded 187 tracks for Vocalion and Columbia 1921–41, including the famous *Is He An Aussie, Lizzie?* He appeared in the 1934 film musical *Chu Chin Chow* and the 1943 West End production of *Show Boat*. He was noted for his very deep, resonant voice, his wide range and his jovial personality.

FURTHER REFERENCE
Peter Burgis, *ADB*, 10; *GlennonA*, 54; *MackenzieS*, 95–7.
                                        PETER CAMPBELL

McGann, Bernie (Bernard Francis) (*b* Sydney 22 June 1937), jazz saxophonist. His early exposure to jazz was through his father, a drummer for whom he occasionally deputised. He began alto saxophone in 1955, and was soon performing at the Mocambo, Newtown, a centre of activity for young progressive musicians such as Dave *Levy and John *Pochée. He was in Melbourne in 1962 for a fortnight season with the American Ballet, with Barry McKimm and recently arrived New Zealanders Barry Woods (drums) and Dave MacRae (piano), with the latter of whom he visited NZ in 1962–63; there he freelanced, with pianist Claude Papish and others, and toured with singer Bobby Vinton. Returning to Sydney, then to Melbourne (1964–65) he played a residency at the Fat Black Pussycat with the Heads (Pochée, MacRae, bassist Andy Brown). In Sydney he worked in jazz-rock groups and played at *El Rocco, the closure of which in 1969 reduced his performance opportunities.

He worked as a postman until performance opportunities began to re-emerge with the late 1970s resurgence of jazz interest. Then he played concerts with Kindred Spirits (Chuck Yates, Phil Treloar percussion, Ron Philpott, Ned Sutherland guitar), and from 1975 to 1978 with the Last Straw at the *Basement, and at nearby Pinball Wizz with singer Wendy Saddington. Resident at Morgan's Feedwell, Glebe, 1979–80, he then had seasons at Soup Plus from the mid-1980s, and was increasingly engaged as support and accompaniment for visitors, including the Art Ensemble of Chicago, Lester Bowie, Freddie Hubbard, Sonny Stitt and Dewey Redman.

The Last Straw was reconstituted for recordings and live performances at venues such as Jenny's Wine Bar (1982–83) and for the *Sydney Improvised Music Association, the formation of which, with its performance forum at the Strawberry Hills Hotel, expanded the compass of McGann's activity and growing influence. Visiting the USA on a performance fellowship from the Australia Council in 1983, he has subsequently toured extensively, nationally and internationally, with groups that include the Australian Jazz Orchestra (USA), the Last Straw (NZ, USSR), and Ten Part Invention (South-East Asia). He regularly performs at festivals, notably Wangaratta and Manly, both as a member of groups and as featured soloist.

After years of obscurity McGann has emerged as a dominant voice among the generation of progressive jazz musicians who appeared from the late 1950s. Originally inspired by Paul Desmond, his assimilation of the work of Ornette Colemen and Albert Ayler has produced perhaps the most strikingly distinctive style in Australia since that of Ade Monsbourgh, both as an alto saxophonist and composer. He is one of the few (though increasingly numerous) Australian jazz composers whose work has entered the performance canon, and his stylistic influence is becoming audible in the work of a number of younger musicians. He has won numerous awards, including a Mo award and an ARIA award.

FURTHER REFERENCE
Recordings include *Jazz Australia* (1967, CBS SBP 233450), *At Long Last,* Bernie McGann Trio (recorded 1983, released 1987, Emanem 3601); *Bernie McGann with the Ted Vining Trio* (1984, Anteater Cassette 108); *Kindred Spirits,* Bernie McGann Quartet, (1987, Emanem 3602); *The Last Straw* (1990, Spiral Scratch 0005); *Ugly Beauty,* Bernie McGann (1991, Spiral Scratch 0010); *Tall Stories,* Ten Part Invention, (1993, Rufus/Polygram RF006); *McGann McGann,* Bernie McGann (1995, Rufus/Polygram RF011). There is an interview with him in Adrian Jackson, 'Bernie McGann, Interview', *JA* (July/Aug. 1983), 14–16. See also *ClareB*; *BissetB*; *OxfordJ*; John Clare, 'Focus on The Last Straw', *Jazz Down Under* (Sept. 1975), 8–10; Bruce Johnson, 'Bernie McGann', *2MBS-FM Stereo FM Radio* (June 1985), 3; Roger Frampton, *Australian Jazz* (Sydney: Sounds Australian, 1992), 113–17.
                                                                    BRUCE JOHNSON

McGregor, Jennifer, soprano. After studying at the NSW State Conservatorium, she worked as a buyer for a Sydney department store, then as an actress. She was with the Australian Opera 1982–86, then made her debut as Queen of the Night at the Heidelberg Opera in 1988. Her roles have included Sophie, Yum-Yum, Rosina, Ophelia, Cleopatra, Gilda, Donna Anna, Leila, Lucia, and Lulu.

FURTHER REFERENCE
Recordings include arias, West Australian Symphony Orchestra (1989, CBS). See also *CA* (1995/96).

Machinations. Disco band (1980–89) formed in Sydney, originally from Fred Loneragan (vocals), Tim Doyle (guitar), Nick 'Nero' Swan (bass), and Tony Starr (drum machine, keyboards, vocals). At first a trio of high school friends, they soon expanded to four, adding backing vocalists in later years. Playing at suburban dances in Sydney, they released the single *Average Inadequacy* (1980) and the mini-LP *The Machinations* (1980). Twelve more singles followed, including *Pressure Sway*, which reached No. 21 in the charts, and they produced the albums *Esteem* (1983), *Big Beat* (1986) and *Uptown* (1988). An accessible blend of attractive melody and disco dance rhythms, their last single was *Cars & Planes* (1989).

FURTHER REFERENCE
Recordings include *Average Inadequacy* (1980, Phantom PH 12), *The Machinations* (1980, Phantom PH 13), *Pressure Sway* (White K9074), *Esteem* (1983, White L37946), *Big Beat* (1986, White L20051) and *Uptown* (1988, White L38925), and *Cars & Planes* (1989, White K708). For discography, see *SpencerA*. See also *McGrathA*; *SpencerW*; *CoupeN*; Stuart Coupe, 'Machinations: From the North Shore to the Plains of the West', in *The Next Thing,* ed. Clinton Walker (Kenthurst, NSW: Kangaroo Press, 1984).

McIntyre, Gordon (*b* Glasgow, Scotland, 1941), folksinger of Scottish birth. He started playing folk music in the UK in 1962, performing at folk clubs and festivals, and came to Australia in 1965. He sang with the *Larrikins, then at Traynor's, Melbourne, for many years, with Danny *Spooner recording *Soldiers and Sailors,* and *A Wench And A Whale And A Pint of Ale.* He moved to Sydney in 1975, performing solo and then in a duo with Kate Delaney (vocals, tin whistle, concertina, fiddle), touring schools and regional centres for the Arts Council. He toured NZ and the UK, and has frequently been heard at folk festivals and clubs.

FURTHER REFERENCE

Recordings include *Caledonia Dreaming* with Kaye Delaney (Sandstock BR 002C), *Prickly Pear* (Larrikin LRF 016) and *Revived Relieved* (Larrikin LR F 016). See also *Stringybark and Greenhide* 3/4 (1981) 20–1.

McIntyre, Stephen (*b* Melbourne, 25 May 1942), pianist. He began piano lessons at the age of eight with Ada *Corder. In 1962 he won an Italian Government Scholarship and went to Italy, studying with Arturo Benedetti Michelangeli and Guido Agosti. While in Rome under the tutelage of Agosti, he was awarded a scholarship to study in France, and in 1965 he became the first Australian resident at the Cité Internationale des Arts. He studied with Nadia Boulanger and Pierre Sancon, and from 1968 to 1974 was based in London. He was solo accompanist for the BBC and also played in recitals in England, France, Germany, Holland, Belgium, Malta, India and Japan. He returned to Australia in 1974 and was appointed head of piano at the Victorian College of the Arts. Since then he has performed frequently with all the principal ABC orchestras, and in 1982 toured Italy, France, Germany and Holland for six months. Since 1989 he has directed and co-ordinated the Melbourne International Festival's chamber music program and is also a founding member of the Australian Chamber Soloists. A pianist of crystalline touch and great polish, his readings of late 19th-century repertoire such as Ravel and Debussy have been particularly notable, and he is a highly sympathetic chamber player. Since 1995 he has been artistic adviser to Musica Viva.

FURTHER REFERENCE

See also *Age* 28 Oct. 1967, 9 Sept. 1989; *Australian* 21 Oct. 1995; *SMH* 6 Dec. 1986.   ROSE PETERSON

Mackay, pop. (1991) 40 250, city and deepwater port at the mouth of the Pioneer River, eastern coast of Queensland. First settled in 1862, it became a city only in 1918. The Community Music Centre of Mackay was established in October 1983, with the Pioneer Shire Council employing a community music co-ordinator, and began offering lessons and classes in 1984 under the direction of voice teacher Lorraine Smith. In 1992 the centre closed and formed Opera North in 1993, which presents at least three productions each year. The Lyrebird Ensemble, a professional orchestra, was formed in 1991; supported by the Conservatorium and the State Government, it has 12 full-time players. In 1989 the first regional campus of the Queensland Conservatorium was established in the city, under the direction of Helen Lancaster; this campus was renamed Central Queensland Conservatorium in 1996, when it became part of Central Queensland University The Conservatorium is the focus of music training from early childhood to adult and tertiary education. It also draws upon other strengths of the city in drama and dance, with a full-time course in music-theatre.

The Mackay Entertainment Centre is an excellent facility, and other notable performance spaces are the Paul Hopkins Theatre at the Conservatorium and the Pansy Wood Music Centre at Whitsunday Anglican School. The city also boasts the Mackay Big Band, the Mackay City Band, the Mackay Youth Orchestra, the Mackay Musical Comedy Players, the Mackay Choral Society and the Con Jazz! combos.   HELEN LANCASTER

McKean Sisters. Country music duo, Joy (1) and Heather (2). Their father played guitar in the traditional country style of the Carter Family, their mother played piano. They first appeared as a child duo on radio 2GB, then in schools concerts and charity shows for the war effort from 1940, and on Dick Fair's *Australia's Amateur Hour* (1942). After the war they appeared in Bill Ferrier's All-Country shows, then with Tim McNamara, Ted Quigg and Reg Lindsay. Their radio show *The Melody Trail* on 2KY (1949–56) became an institution, featuring all the country artists of the day. In 1951 they signed to Rodeo Records and then toured with Shorty Ranger, Gordon *Parsons, again with Reg *Lindsay, and Slim *Dusty (Joy's husband from 1951) until 1953. Traditional country ballad singers and yodellers, their nine singles always featured a newly composed country number on one side, usually by Joy. They were honoured in the ACMA Roll of Renown in 1983 and have occasionally reappeared together since.

(1) Joy McKean (*b* NSW, 1930), country music singer-songwriter. She learned to play (piano, steel guitar, ukulele and piano accordion) from the age of nine, singing with her sister as the McKean Sisters 1940–53. After her marriage to Slim *Dusty and the birth of her daughter (noted country singer Anne *Kirkpatrick) in 1952, she settled in Sydney for a short time, but from 1953 was performing again in the Slim Dusty touring show. She had previously written songs for the McKean Sisters, and now became a major songwriter for Dusty; as his business manager she also contributed significantly to his commercial success. One of the most important writers in the traditional Australian country ballad style, over 90 of her songs have been recorded by Dusty, Kirkpatrick and many others. She has won an ACMA Golden Guitar (1973) and Tamworth Songwriters' Association award.

(2) Heather McKean (*b* Gresford, NSW, 1932), country music singer, businesswoman. Learning the ukulele from the age of seven, she sang with her sister in the McKean Sisters 1940–53. She married Reg *Lindsay in

1954, becoming his business partner and co-producer of his television and radio shows. She became involved in the industry side of country music, representing Australia at the International Fan Fair, Nashville, in 1973, working for the Country Music Association and in Slim Dusty's business. She won an ACMA Golden Guitar for *I Can Feel Love* (1976).

FURTHER REFERENCE
The McKean Sisters singles have been reissued as *McKean Sisters Collection* (1983). Joy McKean's albums include *Lights On The Hill* (1973, EMI), *Biggest Disappointment* (1978, EMI), *Indian Pacific* (1979, EMI), and *Beat Of The Government Stroke*. Heather McKean's singles include *I Can Feel Love* (1976, Festival). For discography see *WatsonC*, II. See also *SmithB*, 304; *WatsonC*, II, 40–3; Monika Allan, *The Tamworth County Music Festival* (Sydney: Horwitz, Grahame, 1988), 70–1.

Mackerras, Sir (Alan) Charles MacLaurin (*b* Schenectady, New York, 17 Nov. 1925), conductor. A descendant of Isaac *Nathan, he studied at the NSW State Conservatorium, then joined the Sydney Symphony Orchestra as principal oboe 1944–46, during which time he began to compose and conduct. He went to Britain in 1947, then studied with Václav Talich in Prague, learning Czech and studying the music of Janáček, of which he was to become a lifelong advocate. A staff conductor at Sadler's Wells 1948–51, he conducted *Kat'á Kabanová*, the first Janáček opera to be performed in Britain. He conducted the English Opera Group and made his debut at the Royal Opera House, Covent Garden, in 1963. He was the first conductor at the Hamburg State Opera 1966–69, music director of Sadler's Wells Opera (now English National Opera) 1970–77, and music director of the Welsh National Opera 1987–92, as well as chief conductor of the Sydney Symphony Orchestra 1982–85, chief guest conductor of the BBC Symphony Orchestra 1976–79, and guest conductor of the Czech Philharmonic Orchestra from 1995.

One of Australia's finest musical exports, Mackerras has spent most of his professional life in Europe; based in London, he has been an active part of the international conducting scene for more than four decades. He has a large repertoire of operas and concert works, and his interests range from Handel and Mozart to Janáček, Gilbert and Sullivan, and Britten. He has enjoyed an active, if sporadic, relationship with Australia: he conducted the Sydney Symphony Orchestra in the opening performance in the Concert Hall of the Sydney Opera House, and also conducted *Die Zauberflöte* in the Australian Opera's inaugural Opera House season. He returns regularly, as well as conducting the Sydney Symphony and Australian Chamber Orchestras on some of their overseas tours. From 1993 he has been principal guest conductor at the San Francisco Opera, the Royal Philharmonic Orchestra, and from 1997 the Czech Philharmonic Orchestra.

His compositions include a fugue based on *Waltzing Matilda* and various arrangements for the ballets *Pineapple Poll* (Sullivan) and *The Lady and the Fool* (Verdi). He has been honoured with honorary membership of the Royal Academy of Music, six honorary DMus degrees and the CBE (1974), and he was knighted in 1979. In 1997 he was awarded the AC.

FURTHER REFERENCE
Recordings include Beethoven, Missa Solemnis, Sydney Symphony Orchestra (ABC 434 722); operas by Janáček, Mozart, Handel and Verdi, and symphonic cycles by Dvořák and Mozart. See also Nancy Phelan, *Charles Mackerras: A Musician's Musician* (Melbourne: OUP, 1987), which includes four appendices by Mackerras on Janáček, the *appoggiatura*, and Handel and Mozart. See also *HolmesC*; Stanley Sadie, *GroveD*.
MICHAEL SHMITH

McKie, Sir William N(eil) (*b* Collingwood, Melbourne, 22 May 1901; *d* Ottawa, Canada, 1 Dec. 1984), organist. He studied organ with A.E.H. *Nickson at Melbourne Grammar School, and was Clarke Scholar for 1919. From the Royal College of Music he went to Worcester College, Oxford, for his MA and MusBac, and became director of music at Clifton College, Bristol, 1926–30. McKie returned to Melbourne as city organist in 1931, to an important decade of musical development. In his Town Hall recitals he made known the established works of the organ's own repertoire to an increasing public, with sensitive artistry, introducing those of Franck, Widor and Vierne. With his flair for administration he was able to enlist the whole of Melbourne's musical resources in a large-scale Bach Festival in 1932, with like success in his promotion of the Bach–Elgar Festival in 1934 for the Victorian Centenary celebrations. At Geelong Grammar School where, from 1934, he was also director of music, the art was given fresh impetus, and he was responsible for a fine new Music School building.

Always staunchly Australian, McKie never lost touch with the music of his homeland when he left for Magdalen College Oxford in 1938. There and at Westminster Abbey, where he planned and directed the music of the Coronation of Elizabeth II in 1953, he welcomed a stream of fellow-countrymen, offering valued help to many students. His last task in London was to assist Richard *Bonynge, Joan *Sutherland and Charles *Mackerras in planning the Grainger Festival of 1970. He gave the inaugural address. Oxford University conferred on him its honorary DMus in 1944; he was knighted in 1953.

FURTHER REFERENCE
Howard Hollis, *The Best of Both Worlds: A Life of Sir William McKie* (Melbourne: Sir William McKie Memorial Trust, 1991).
HOWARD HOLLIS

McKirdy, Arch, jazz broadcaster. He had jazz radio programs on Sydney 2UW and later 2GB, then from 1965 began the long-running *Relax With Me* on ABC late-night radio, which became Australia's leading jazz radio program. Interspersing recordings of American artists with Australians, his program included a wide range of styles, though with a bent towards modern jazz. He worked in ABC management from 1972. With a velvet voice and characteristically tranquil approach, he was Australia's leading jazz broadcaster.

FURTHER REFERENCE
OxfordJ, 116.

McLeod, Jim (James Anthony) (b Sydney, 19 Sept. 1939), jazz broadcaster. Introduced to jazz in the 1940s through radio, his involvement increased through school contacts and attendance at Sydney Jazz Club functions. He joined the ABC in 1956 and was drawn into a broader stylistic range by jazz producer Joe Cramey. Particularly active in promoting Australian jazz, through regular broadcasting activities, notably *Jim McLeod's Jazztrack,* since 1976, he has also worked in record production, written for the ABC's *24 Hours* and *Australian HiFi*, and has acted as a guest compère for jazz festivals in Australia and overseas, including at India's Jazz Yatra and with Radio KJAZ for the Monterey Jazz Festival.

FURTHER REFERENCE
Jim McLeod, *Jim McLeod's Jazztrack* (Sydney: ABC Books, 1994).
BRUCE JOHNSON

McManus, Louis (b Paisley, Scotland, Apr. 1956), folk-rock instrumentalist of Irish descent. The son of a fiddle player who taught him many traditional Irish tunes, he played mandolin from the age of four and took violin lessons for eight years. His family came to Australia when he was nine, and in his teens he played in Irish clubs. With his father he formed the Ramblers; the band toured Ireland (1975), and after it disbanded he and his father toured pubs and festivals. He joined the Irish band Dalriada, then the Bushwackers for their UK tour in 1977; back in Australia he appeared with other bands including Captain Matchbox, Weddings Parties Anything, and No Fixed Address (for their UK tour in 1984). He appeared at folk festivals with Robyn Archer at Cambridge, UK, and with the Bushwackers in Rotterdam, and worked as a session musician for Eric Bogle, Paul Wookey and others. An accomplished musician in traditional Irish music as well as in more hard-edged styles, he plays violin, guitar, mandolin, banjo and bouzouki.

FURTHER REFERENCE
SpencerW; *Stringybark and Greenhide* 5/2 (May 1984).

MacNamara, Frank. See *Frank the Poet.*

McNamara, Ian ('Macca') (b 1948), country music broadcaster. After studying economics at the University of

Sydney he joined the ABC finance department. In 1979 he became a reporter and producer for the ABC TV program *Australia All Over,* and in 1981 became its presenter, developing it into the leading national program of Australian rural and outback heritage. Featuring singers ranging from traditionalist country artists to exponents of New Country, he has compiled four recorded volumes of *Australia All Over* of songs featured in the program and two books, all of which have proved popular.

FURTHER REFERENCE
Recordings include *Australia All Over* (EMI 4796222, 4796382, 4796202, 4796112). See also *LattaA,* 20; *Australian* 18 May 1991.

McNamara, Paul John (b Sydney, 1 Feb. 1945), jazz pianist. After formal piano study he turned to jazz, taking piano lessons from Chuck Yates and becoming active in the modern jazz movement. He was with Galapagos *Duck 1974–76, Bruce *Cale 1978, and Bob Bertles' Moontrane, then studied in New York in 1982, and continues freelancing and leading. Involved as a musical director in pop music, he has also played support for numerous visiting musicians including Buddy Rich, Ella Fitzgerald, Milt Jackson, Woody Shaw and Mark Murphy. He toured with the Daly-Wilson Big Band, Joe Henderson and Don Burrows. Active as a composer, he also gives clinics and has taught at the NSW Conservatorium since 1979.

FURTHER REFERENCE
Recordings include *Galapagos Duck* (1975, 44 Records 44 6357 704); *Bruce Cale Quartet* (1978, 44 Records 44 6357 724); *Moontrane* (1979, Batjazz BAT-2070); *David Baker String Ensemble* (1980, Larrikin LRJ.066); *Point of No Return: Paul McNamara* (1994, Rufus Polygram RF008). He has published *A Twelve Tone Concept For Contemporary Jazz* (Weeamara Productions, 1977). See also *BissetB*; *OxfordJ*.
BRUCE JOHNSON

McNamara, Tim (Timothy Edmund) (b Lucknow, NSW, 10 Oct. 1922; d Sydney, 16 Apr. 1983), country music singer-songwriter. The youngest of 11 children, McNamara left school at the age of 13. Encouraged by his wife Daphne Ford to pursue a singing career in 1940, he was the winner on *Australia's Amateur Hour* in 1941. His singing career was interrupted by World War II, in which he served with the RAAF. He returned to singing in 1945 and appeared often on *Australia's Amateur Hour* as a duo with his brother Tommy Mack. He also started to write his own songs, stylistically influenced by American country music. In 1948 he played a part in the film *Into The Straight*, and sang two of his own songs, *Riding Along* and *We're Going to the Rodeo Today*, both of which were later recorded on his first recording for EMI. He joined 2SM Sydney in 1949 as a country show presenter, in a show in which he helped many country music stars such as Slim *Dusty and Gordon *Parsons to start their careers. One of his greatest contributions to country music was the giant talent quest he persuaded 2SM and Rodeo Records to sponsor in 1950, which was eventually won by Reg *Lindsay. He was an entrepreneur of live shows around Sydney, and many new artists achieved a breakthrough after appearances on his shows.

As a pioneer of Australian country music, he was active throughout his life in promoting shows, and was noted for his encouragement and support of fellow artists. In recognition of his commitment to Australian country music, he was elevated to Tamworth's Country Music Roll of Renown in 1981.

FURTHER REFERENCE
Recordings include *We're Going to the Rodeo Today* (1948, Regal Zonophone G 2526); Riding Along (1948, Regal Zonophone G 25260); *Relaxin'* (EMI 1971); *Campfire of Dreams* (Picture 1974). See also *LattaA*; *SmithB*; *WatsonC*, 1.   YA HUI HUNG

Maconaghie, Ronald Derek Armstrong (*b* Auckland, NZ, 18 Nov. 1931), baritone. After winning the NZ vocal championship in 1951 he won a government scholarship and the Joan Hammond scholarship and went to London, studying at the London Opera School. He was with the English Opera Group and Sadler's Wells from 1956, and returned to NZ, singing with the New Zealand Opera Co. from 1961. He came to Australia to join the Elizabethan Theatre Trust Opera Co. (later the Australian Opera) in 1963 and sang in the Sutherland-Williamson tour (1965). With a liquid tone, a warmth of stage presence and superb sense for comic acting, his Falstaff, Papageno, Figaro, Don Pasquale and Giani Schicchi became classics that were a staple of the Australian Opera until 1986, and he sang in the Australian premieres of Walton's *Troilus and Cressida* and Orff's *The Wise Woman*. He taught at the Canberra School of Music from 1979, was head of vocal studies and deputy dean at the Victorian College of the Arts 1991–95, and currently coaches privately in Sydney. He was honoured with the AM in 1987.

Macquarie Trio. Piano trio founded (1993) as the resident ensemble of Macquarie University, Sydney, and James Cook University, Townsville, comprised of Charmian Gadd (violin), Kathryn *Selby (piano), and Michael Goldschlager (cello), all with previous solo careers. One of very few piano trios current in Australia, their concerts have been highly praised by Australian critics.

McSweeney, John (*b* Brisbane), country music entertainer, producer. Working in a bank, he performed part-time as a country music singer, instrumentalist and comic impersonator from 1962, as support act for Charley Pride, Slim Whitman and Don Gibson, producing *Daisy A Day* in 1972. A committed advocate for country music, he created the independent label Mac Records in 1981 and produces *Country Clipz* for regional television.

FURTHER REFERENCE
His albums include *Mr Country Entertainer* (1979, Larrikin OLLP 510 TC), *Just For You* (1987, Mac), and *The Best Of John McSweeney* (EMI AX 701 386C). See also *LattaA*, 185.

Mageau, Mary (*b* Milwaukee, Wisconsin, USA, 4 Sept. 1934), composer. After studies in harpsichord and composition with Leon Stein at De Paul University, Chicago, and with Ross Lee Finey and Leslie Bassett at the University of Michigan (Ann Arbor), she won a fellowship to study with George Crumb at Tanglewood in 1970, and studied electronic music at the Catholic University, Washington DC. In 1974 she came to Australia as guest lecturer for the Brisbane College of Advanced Education, and settled. She formed the Brisbane Baroque Trio in 1979, which combined Baroque works with new commissions, and currently teaches at the Queensland Conservatorium. An active advocate for women composers in Australia, she broadcasts *Notable Women* on 4MBS-FM. Her works include symphonic, choral, and numerous piano works, as well as chamber works for recorder and wind groups, and she has received various commissions, notably *An Early Autumn's Dreaming* for the Queensland Philharmonic Orchestra (1993). Her harpsichord concerto won the Alienor Harpsichord Contest in 1994.

FURTHER REFERENCE
Recordings include *Sonata Concertante*, Brisbane Baroque Trio (1980, Grevillea GRV1080); *Contrasts*, Gary Williams, vc (Grevillea GRV 1070); Suite for Strings: *Postcards from Czechoslovakia*, Camerata of St Johns (1993, CSJ 1001); *Elite Syncopations*, Larry Sitsky, pf (1988, Move MD3066); and the Triple Concerto (1990, Vienna Modern Masters). *Elite Syncopations* has been published in *Contemporary Australian Piano* (La Trobe Univ. Press, 1985). See also Graham Hair and Greta Mary Hair, *GroveW*; Jenny Dawson, *ContemporaryC*; *CohenI*; *LePageW*; *SA* 27 (Spring 1990), 28–9; *Weekend Australian* 5 June 1993.

Maggie May, sailor's ballad. British traditional song of a Liverpool sailor robbed of his pay and clothes by a streetwalker, Maggie May, who is then transported for the theft to Australia. Collected by John Meredith and published in *Singabout* (1957), but well known among sailors beyond Australia.

FURTHER REFERENCE
Edition with commentary in *ManifoldP.*

Maggs Composition Prize, Albert H. One of Australia's oldest and most coveted composition prizes. Albert H. Maggs (*d* 1995), an unassuming Melbourne bookmaker with several philanthropic interests, established a trust at the University of Melbourne in 1966 to 'encourage composers … who might otherwise abandon their efforts for want of means'. Previous winners include Nigel *Butterley, Colin *Brumby, Larry *Sitsky, Barry

*Conyngham, Andrew *Schultz and many other prominent composers. Awarded annually after national advertisement, the prize is a commission for a work by the winning composer, currently $6000.

Mahony, Will (William James Fitzpatrick) (*b* Montana, USA, 5 Feb. 1894; *d* Melbourne, 8 Feb. 1967), vaudeville comedian, variety manager. He performed in vaudeville from the age of eight, visiting Australia and appearing at the Bijou Theatre, Melbourne, in 1914. A player of six instruments, in his solo show *Why Be Serious* (1924) he danced on an outsize xylophone, the mallets on his feet. He starred in the film *Ants in his Pants* (1938), came to Australia that year with his wife Evie *Hayes and partner Bob Geraghty and played the Tivoli circuit. He ran the Cremorne Theatre in Brisbane from 1942, and continued to appear in musicals, including *A Funny Thing Happened On the Way To The Forum* (1964). A successful variety artist and novelty musical performer, he collapsed in a performance of *Funny Girl* (1966) and died shortly afterwards.

FURTHER REFERENCE
John Crampton, *Evie Hayes: And I Loves Ya Back!* (Sydney: Angus & Robertson, 1992), 32–43; *PotersS*, 199, 238; Anthony Slide, *Encyclopaedia of Vaudeville* (Westport, Conn.: Greenwood Press, 1994).

Majestic Fanfares. Brief orchestral fanfare by Charles Williams, widley known through its use (in both the original form and reorchestrated by Richard *Mills) as the news theme on national ABC radio since 1952.

Malko, Nicolai (*b* Russia, 1888; *d* Sydney 1961), conductor. Malko studied in St Petersburg and Munich, taught conducting at the Moscow (1922) and the Leningrad (1925) Conservatories, and conducted the premiere of Shostakovich's Symphony No. 1 in 1926. He left Russia to become the conductor of the Danish State Radio Symphony Orchestra 1928–32, returning frequently to the orchestra in the next 22 years. During World War II he was in the USA, conducted the Yorkshire Symphony Orchestra, UK, 1954–56, then in 1956 until his death in 1961 was conductor of the Sydney Symphony Orchestra, succeeding *Goossens. He was a distinguished conductor, especially of Russian composers, and also of Haydn and Brahms, and recorded for EMI.

FURTHER REFERENCE
For discography, see *HolmesC*. See also Arthur Jacobs, *GroveD*.
J.L. HOLMES

Mallen, Ralph (*b* Sydney, 21 Jan. 1926; *d* Sydney, 14 Dec. 1956), jazz trombone. He played civilian dance work while in the armed services and upon discharge took lessons at the NSW Conservatorium. In 1946 he joined Ike Holborough, later taking over the band's leadership and building it into the first of Sydney's progressive jazz

concert big bands, also presenting it at the Gaiety auditorium, Bondi Esplanade, and for broadcasts. Following a period of relative inactivity, 1949–53, he returned to the jazz concert stage and the Gaiety, virtually retiring from music when the latter was destroyed by fire in 1954. He was killed in a road accident.

FURTHER REFERENCE
Recordings include *Ralph Mallen And His Orchestra* (1947, Prestophone, unnumbered). See also *BissetB*; *OxfordJ*.
BRUCE JOHNSON

Malouf, David (*b* Brisbane, 20 Mar. 1934), poet, novelist. After teaching at the University of Queensland 1955–57, he lived in Europe 1958–68, then taught at the University of Sydney 1968–77. A freelance writer since then, he has published poetry and novels, often focusing on Australian mythology and the dualities of human nature. His works include *Bicycle and Other poems* (1970), *Fly Away Peter* (1982) and *Remembering Babylon* (1995). He wrote the librettos for Richard *Meale's operas *Voss* (1986), after Patrick White's novel, and *Mer de Glace* (1991), and Michael Berkeley's *Baa Baa Black Sheep: A Jungle Tale* (1993).

FURTHER REFERENCE
Annie Patrick, 'David Malouf the Librettist', *Provisional Maps: Critical Essays on David Malouf*, ed. Amanda Nettlebeck (Perth: Univ. WA, 1994), 133–48; *MonashB*; *OxfordL*.

Malvolio. Light opera in three acts, music and libretto by Fritz *Hart (1913), after Shakespeare's *Twelfth Night*. First act performed by the students of the Melbourne Conservatorium at the Melbourne Playhouse on 5 December 1919. MS in *Msl*.

Mañana. Opera in one act by Arthur *Benjamin, libretto by C. Brahms and G. Foa after Brahms's *Under the Juniper Tree*. The first opera commissioned for BBC TV, it was first performed on 1 February 1956.

Mandrake. Country music ballad (1941) by Tex *Morton. The song tells of a horse who throws any rodeo champion attempting to ride her. Best known of the classics of rough-riding, the song's subject was probably a horse in Morton's rodeo show.

FURTHER REFERENCE
Recorded by Morton on Regal Zonophone (now reissued EMI CD 8142052). Edition with commentary in *RadicS*, 88; see also *Watson C*, I, 9ff.

Manifold, John Streeter (*b* Melbourne, 21 Apr. 1915; *d* Brisbane, 19 Apr. 1985), musicologist, folklorist. Son of a wealthy Victorian pastoralist family from the Western District, Manifold discovered an interest in music, particularly in early music and the music of the Australian bush, during his time at Cambridge University.

Despite little formal training in music, he established a name for himself as a performer and scholar in both areas. His first musical interest was in early music. He became a capable player of the recorder, for which he wrote a tutor, *The Amorous Flute,* in 1948. He made arrangements of much early music, including pieces from Morley's *Plain and Easie Introduction;* he also published a series of articles focusing on various aspects of early music (including an important set on recorder playing) in *Canon.* Perhaps his most lasting contribution in this field was *The Music in English Drama* (1956), which remains a landmark in the scholarship of early English theatrical music and its use.

His interest in Australian folklore derived primarily from the role he saw the poet playing in the ongoing regeneration of tradition. His research led to the discovery of the music for *Freedom on the Wallaby, The Convict Maid,* and the Queensland version of *Waltzing Matilda.* His ballad collecting began in earnest in the late 1950s: he released his findings in three sets of *Bandicoot Ballads* broadsheets. He was the foundation president of the Queensland Federation of Bush Music Clubs. Manifold's most significant musicological contributions to this field are *Who Wrote the Ballads?* (1964) and *The Violin, the Banjo and the Bones: An Essay on the Instruments of Bush Music* (1957), and he compiled the *Queensland Centenary Songbook* and *The Penguin Australian Songbook.*

FURTHER REFERENCE

His publications include *Who Wrote the Ballads?* (Sydney: Australian Book Society, 1964); *Bandicoot Ballads* (Melbourne: Rams Skull Press, 1953); *The Music in English Drama* (London: Rockliff, 1956); *The Amorous Flute* (London: Schott, 1948); *The Violin, the Banjo and the Bones: An Essay on the Instruments of Bush Music* (Melbourne: Rams Skull Press, 1957). His numerous articles include 'Haydn', *Canon* 7 (1953–54), 452–5; 'Matthew Locke', *Canon* 5 (1951–52), 338–44; 'The Recorder' parts 1–5, *Canon* 3 (1950); and 'Volksorchester and Bush Orchestra', *Australian Journal of Music Education* v (1969), 35–9. See also *MonashB*; Rodney Hall, *J.S. Manifold: An Introduction to the Man and his Work* (Brisbane: UQP, 1978).   JOHN WERETKA

Manikay.   Arnhem Land song series. See *Clan Songs*; *Aboriginal Music* §3 (iii).

Maninyas.   Chamber works (1981–86) by Ross *Edwards. A group of works composed over five years, drawing on the same materials; *Maninya I* is for voice and cello, the last, *Maninya V,* is for voice and piano. The title is a nonsense word conceived arbitrarily in writing the text for one of the vocal works in the series. The music is characterised by pentatonic fragments of melody, drone-like harmonies and effervescent rhythms. The *Maninyas* Concerto for Violin has been recorded by Dene Olding with the Sydney Symphony Orchestra (1993, ABC/Polydor 638610–2).

Mann, Chris   (b Melbourne, 9 Mar. 1949), sound artist. While studying Chinese and political science at the

University of Melbourne he was already composing. He worked in music-theatre from 1970, helping to establish the Clifton Hill Community Centre from 1972, collaborating with Peter Mummé and Warren *Burt, and teaching at the Institute of Catholic Education from 1975. He was artist-in-residence at Yallambie and St Margaret's primary schools (1980), at the Shire of Healesville (1984) and for the ABC staff union (1985). He has had commissions from Radio France, Composers' Forum USA, Foundation for Contemporary Performance Arts USA, Danceworks, Dance Exchange, and ABC radio. He toured the USA with Machine for Making Sense in 1993. His music combines linguistics, semiotics, information theory and music, and focuses on electronic manipulation of a voice, usually his own, reading dense texts exploring the textures and cadence of Australian speech. His works include *Scratch, Scratch—a History of Grammar* (1979), *Of Course* (1988), *On Second Thoughts* (1993) and *La De Da* (1991).

FURTHER REFERENCE

Recordings include *doin 2s* (1982, Phon'm Tapes, Melbourne); *Subjective Beats Metaphor* (1983, NMA Tapes 2); *The Rationales* (1987, NMA Tapes 5) and *Snodger (the Mirror)* (1989, Canberra School of Music, CSM 6). See also *Jenkins T*, 125–31; Lyn Gallacher, 'Of Course: A Grammatical Tech Check', *Continuum* 8/1 (1994), 128–31, 181–91, 311–13.

Mann, Peter   (b Germany, c.1918; d London, 7 June 1983), record producer, retailer. With his wife Ruth he launched the record label Score in the mid-1950s. They recorded jazz, Aboriginal music, classical music and spoken word, but also some of the earliest recordings of Australian folk-songs by such artists as Martin Wyndham-Read, Brian *Mooney, Declan *Affley and the *Bushwhackers. He imported Folkways and Bluenote recordings from the USA and in the early 1960s opened Discurio in Melbourne, which was for many years Australia's most important outlet for rare recordings (since 1982 the business has been managed by his son, now merged with Fine Music). He promoted concerts in the mid-1960s, arranging the tours of Peter, Paul and Mary, Sonny Terry and Brownie McGee and others.

FURTHER REFERENCE

See also *OxfordF*; *Age* 9 June 1983.

Manning Clark's History of Australia: The Musical.   Created by a team of five including George Dreyfus and Don Watson, this musical centres on historian Manning Clark and the left-wing political ideas he embraced. First performed at Sydney in 1988. See *Musical Comedy.*

Manning, Phil   (b Tasmania, c.1948), blues guitarist. Learning classical guitar in childhood, he played electric guitar with a high school band from 1964, then joined Cocaine Spell (1965) and Tony Worsley and the Blue Jays

(1966), playing rock covers. He became seriously involved with rhythm and blues in Bay City Union (1967–68) and then came to wide attention in the blues band *Chain (1969–74, which appeared as Pilgrimage in 1971). After this he did session work, played rock in Levi Smith's Clefs (1972) and John Paul *Young and the All Stars (1977), toured with Margret *RoadKnight (1988) and Doc Span's Blues Band (1990), and formed his own bands. A technically very able guitarist, his deeply felt blues-playing with Chain was influential in the early 1970s.

FURTHER REFERENCE
Recordings include *Love Is A Mender* (1974, Mushroom K5730) and the albums *Manning* (1978, Indigo INL 001), *Phil Manning Live* (1979, Polydor PMB 008) and *Can't Stop* (1992, Tamborine TM 103CD). For discography, see *SpencerA*. See also *McGrathA*; *SpencerW*; *GuinnessP*, II, 16–19.

Mara.   See *Kiek, Mara.*

Marcie and the Cookies.   See *Jones, Marcie.*

Marietta.   See *Prerauer, Maria.*

Marks, Herbie   (*b* Rooty Hill, Sydney, 1923), accordion player, composer. Born into a showbusiness family, he played mandolin for Harry Clay's Vaudeville, Sydney, from the age of six. He taught himself the accordion at the age of nine, then had lessons from the American Arbie Hartmann, from 1938 playing with Sam Babicci's band at Rose's Restaurant, Sydney. After the war he became increasingly prominent, working as a magician, instrumentalist and showman; he went to London in 1952, appearing on the BBC TV show *In Town Tonight*, touring Europe and appearing at the London Palladium. He composed for commercials and films, including music for the documentary *Toe Hold in History,* and made many arrangements of music for school use. A showman of many talents, in his hands the accordion was a virtuosic instrument; he has recorded over 20 LPs.

FURTHER REFERENCE
R. Brasch, *Australian Jews of Today* (Sydney: Cassell Aust., 1977), 60–6.

Marriage Machine, The.   Children's comic opera in one act, music and libretto by Colin *Brumby (1971). About a computer that breaks down while engaged in a dating service. First performed with piano at Sydney Teachers' College on 28 January 1972; orchestrated in 1985 and this version first performed at the Cell Block Theatre, Sydney, on 4 September 1985. Score from Australian Music Centre.

Marsh, Stephen Hale Alonzo   (*b* Kensington, London, 4 June 1805; *d* San Francisco, USA, 21 Jan. 1888), harpist, composer. A harp pupil of Nicolas-Charles

Bochsa, he toured Europe and the Middle East, and arrived in Sydney in 1842, establishing a teaching practice and performing frequently at the Royal Victoria Theatre. His *Hail to Thee, O Mighty One* for chorus, orchestra and band (1845) and *Advance Australia* (1845) were both performed at Sydney under his direction. A rival of Isaac *Nathan, he claimed his opera *The Gentleman in Black* (*c.*1847, after James Dalton) was the first written in Australia; it was not, however, the first Australian work staged, not being produced until 1861 when it was given by W.S. Lyster at Melbourne. He left Australia in 1872, spent two years in Japan, and settled at San Francisco as a teacher.

FURTHER REFERENCE
Catherine Mackerras, *ADB,* 5; Elizabeth Wood, *GroveD*.

Marshall-Hall, G(eorge) W(illiam) L(ouis)   (*b* London, 28 Mar. 1862; *d* Melbourne, 18 July 1915), composer, conductor and professor of music. Born into a family of eminent but controversial scientists, Marshall-Hall was disowned by his father as a 'damned fiddler'. Although largely self-taught, he wrote his first opera *Dido and Aeneas* at 15 and published a book of songs at 16. He became a professional organist, choirmaster, teacher and journalist, and in 1888 the prologue to his opera *Harold* was performed in London. On the recommendation of Sir George Grove he was appointed founding Ormond professor of music at the University of Melbourne, arriving in 1891. A 'splendid specimen of a Wagnerian hero', he established the Marshall-Hall Orchestra in 1892, the University of Melbourne Conservatorium in 1895 and, after failing to be reappointed in 1900, the Albert Street Conservatorium. The orchestra performed 111 concerts between 1892 and 1912, mostly Beethoven, Brahms and Wagner, and in the later years contemporary French music.

His compositions in Australia included a Symphony in C (1892), Symphony in E flat (1903) and the operas *Aristodemus* (1902), *Stella* (1910) and *Romeo and Juliet* (1912). *Stella* was performed in Melbourne in 1912 and, subsequently, in a 'mutilated' version in a London music hall. War destroyed hopes of a performance in Germany and in 1914 Marshall-Hall was reinstated to the University of Melbourne. He died of complications from appendicitis soon after his return. An exceptional conductor, Marshall-Hall's orchestral works suggest the high romanticism of Brahms and Wagner; *Stella* has an attractive score and Australian setting.

WORKS
(Mss in *PVgm*)
Dramatic   *Leonard*, opera (*c.*1883, lost); *Dido*, opera (*c.*1884, 5, composer after Virgil) excerpt 11 Oct. 1899, Melbourne; *Harold*, opera (*c.*1887, 4, composer after Lytton), excerpt 2 Feb. 1888, London; *Alcestis*, music-theatre (1898, 3, Euripides), 22 June 1898, Melbourne; *Aristodemus*, music-theatre (1902, 25 scenes, composer), 29 July 1901, Melbourne; *Stella*, opera (1910, 1, com-

poser; critical edn by S. Robinson, Melbourne: Centre for Studies in Australian Music, Univ. Melbourne, 1992), 4 May 1912, Melbourne; *Romeo and Juliet*, opera (1912, 4, composer after Shakespeare; full score pub. London: Paris & Co, 1914), excerpt 14 Dec. 1912, Melbourne.

Orchestral   *Harold* Overture (1888); *Long After: A Study on Tennyson's Maud*, T, orch (*c*.1889); Overture *Giordano Bruno [Dramatic Study;* Overture in G Minor] (1891); Symphony in C (1892); *Idyll* (*c*.1893); *Melody* (*c*.1892); *La belle dame sans merci*, ballade, T, orch (1898–1902); *Caprice*, vn, orch (1898–1902); Symphony in E-flat (1903, duet arrangement pub. Breitkopf und Härtel, 1905); *Phantasy*, hn, orch (1905).

Chamber   *Die Blumen* v, 2 vn, va, vc, db (1896); String Quartet in C (*c*.1894); *Allegro con Brio*, bn, pf (1898–1902); *In the Orchard, Charetsville*, bn, pf (1898–1902); *Deux Fantasies*, vn, pf (*c*.1906; pub. London: Schott & Co, 1907); Quartet, hn, vn, va, pf (*c*.1910); String Quartet in F (*c*. 1910); String Quartet in D Minor [lost].

Vocal, Other   28 early songs, unpub.; 3 early anthems, unpub; 7 pf works, most early; *Song Cycle of Life and Love* (London: Joseph Williams, 1890); *Choral Ode to the 'Helena' of Goethe*, SATB, orch (1898); *An Australian National Song*, SATB, orch (1898–1902); 2 arrangements of Mozart arias for orchestra.

FURTHER REFERENCE
Recordings include Symphony in E-flat, Queensland Theatre Orchestra, cond. W. Bebbington (1987, Move MD 3081). See also Warren Bebbington, *The Operas of GWL Marshall-Hall*, MMus, Univ. Melbourne, 1978; Thérèse Radic, *ADB*, 9; idem, *Portrait of a Lost Crusader: GWL Marshall-Hall* (Perth: Univ. WA, 1982); *IrvinD*; Joseph Rich, *His Thumb Unto His Nose: The Removal of G. W. L. Marshall-Hall from the Ormond Chair of Music*, PhD, Univ. Melbourne, 1986; Julja Szuster, *GroveD*.

SUZANNE ROBINSON

Martin, Bruce   (*b* Northam, WA, 25 Oct. 1941), baritone. After studies at the University of Western Australia, he worked as a schoolteacher and appeared in oratorio and lieder recitals for the ABC in Perth in the 1960s, then sang at Covent Garden 1970–71. He taught at the University of Natal, South Africa, 1972–78. He made his debut with the Australian Opera as Fasolt in *Das Rheingold* in 1979, where he subsequently sang Assur in *Semiramide* with Joan Sutherland, and principal Wagnerian roles, including Wotan in *Rheingold* and *Die Walküre*, Hagen, King Mark and most notably Hans Sachs. His repertoire includes numerous art-songs and over 40 oratorio parts, notably Raimondo, Sarastro, Escamillo, Don Giovanni, Padre Guardiano, Zaccaria (*Nabucco*), Ramfis (*Aida*), and Varlaam (*Boris Godunov*).

FURTHER REFERENCE
CA (1995/96).

Martyn, Laurel   (*b* Toowoomba, Qld, 23 July 1916), choreographer, dancer. She studied ballet with Marjorie Hollingshed in Brisbane and Phyllis Bedells in London. While in England she won the Adeline Genée Gold

Medal (the first Australian to do so), was runner-up in the Pavlova Casket choreographic competition, and secured a choreographic scholarship for the Royal Academy of Dance. Between 1940 and 1946, she was first principal dancer and a choreographer with the ★Borovansky troupe in Melbourne. In 1946 she established the Ballet Guild of Victoria, later known as ★Ballet Victoria. Her commitment to working with Australian composers and artists was immediately evident. Within 10 years she had commissioned scores to choreographically interpret from Margaret ★Sutherland, Esther ★Rofe, John Tallis and Dorian ★Le Gallienne. Over a more extended period Martyn also used pre-existing music from John ★Antill, Harold ★Badger, Arthur ★Benjamin, Clive ★Douglas and Robert ★Hughes. Her company ceased operation in 1976 after a financially crippling season. Since then Martyn has devoted herself to teaching. She was honoured with the OBE in 1976.

FURTHER REFERENCE
Joel Crotty, 'From Balletic Binge to Cultural Cringe: Choreographic Music in Australia, 1936–1956', in Nicholas Brown et al., eds, *One Hand on the Manuscript: Music in Australian Culture 1930–1960* (Canberra: Humanities Research Council, ANU, 1995), 217–28; Edward H. Pask, *Ballet in Australia: The Second Act, 1940–1980* (Melbourne: OUP, 1982).   JOEL CROTTY

Maru   (Garadyarri), public singing and dancing in the Kimberleys. See *Corroboree*.

Maryborough,   pop. (1991) 20 790. City at the mouth of the Mary River, south-east Queensland, settled 1843. At first a wool-shipping point, it has now become a rural marketing centre. It hosted the rotating Blackstone Eisteddfod from the 1890s, which stimulated strong rivalry between city choirs in Queensland. A Maryborough Musical Society, conducted by R.P. Moore, and a Junior Eisteddfod for schools was founded in the 1940s; the Maryborough Eisteddfod still functions. Bands flourishing include the Maryborough Caledonian Pipe Band, Maryborough Excelsior City Band and the Walkers Engineering Works Band; there is a fine Band Rotunda at Queens Park. The Maryborough Choral Society and the Wide Bay Country Music Association are both active.

Mass.   Polyphonic settings of the Ordinary of the eucharist liturgy have been most common in Australia among Roman Catholic composers, but there are also numerous Anglican communion settings. Mass composers in the colonial era included Hugo ★Alpen, John ★Delany, Alfred ★Plumpton and August ★Weigand; in the post-colonial days they included Fritz ★Hart, Alfred ★Hill, and most notably Stephen ★Moreno (New Norcia, WA), who wrote more than 20 masses. Among a sizeable number of more recent masses are those by Ian ★Cugley, John Gordon, Robert Keane, Malcolm ★Williamson, Christopher Willcock and Stephen ★Holgate. Anglican communion settings for the new rites have been produced, among others, by John Barrett, David Rumsey, Michael *Dudman, and most notably Paul Paviour. See *Church Music.*

Masters Apprentices, The. Rock band formed (1965) at Adelaide, evolving from the instrumental surf-music band the Mustangs. The founding members were Mick Bower (guitar), Gavin Webb (bass), Rick Morisson (guitar) and Brian Vaughton (drums). The songs were initially written by Bower, and after adding Jim Keays as lead vocalist, they presented a unique and energetic blend of rhythm and blues, remaining uninfluenced by the mass of American and British music dominating the Australian charts. The band moved to Melbourne in early 1967 with their debut hit *Undecided* and their debut album. Bower left the band soon afterwards, however, and in 1968 Doug Ford joined and created a strong songwriting team with Keays. Shortly afterwards Webb was replaced by Glen Wheatley. After an unsuccessful tour of the UK in 1970, the band released the album *Short Cuts,* which ironically sold extremely well in the UK but had lost its popularity by the time the band had returned to London, and another disappointing tour followed, even with the release of *Toast to Panama Red* in the UK. Keays and Wheatley left in 1972 and the band fell apart, not to be reunited until 1979, after which it produced four new albums. Keays went on to a solo career and Wheatley became one of Australia's most respected rock entrepreneurs, managing the *Little River Band, John *Farnham, and his own record label, with interests in radio stations and music venues in Australia.

The Masters Apprentices, and the long list of members over the band's lengthy existence, are best known for their varied and unique repertoire 'ranging from raw R & B to psychedelic pop and full blown head music with lashings of heavy rock' (I. McFarlane).

FURTHER REFERENCE
Recordings include *Undecided* (1966, Astor); *Master Apprentices* (1967, Astor); *Toast To Panama Red* (1972, Columbia); *Do What You Wanna Do* (1988, Virgin); *The Very Best Of Masters Apprentices* (1988, Virgin). For discography see *SpencerA.* See also *McGrathA*; *SpencerW.*   TOM LIOLIOS

Mathy Scholarship, Marianne. See *Australian Singing Competition.*

Maton. Guitar-makers. Founded in 1944 by Bill May with his wife Vera at Canterbury, Melbourne, the name is a contraction of 'May-tone'. Trained as a technical teacher of furniture design and similar trades, he set up a home workshop. In 1946, joined by his brother Reg, he patented the double-thrust truss-rod (used to keep the neck of a guitar perfectly straight during manufacture or repair) and in 1948 he established a factory at Canterbury, Melbourne. Using Queensland rock maple and other timbers, seasoned by his own microwave process, his firm produces about 300 instruments a year, including Hawaiian slide guitars, solid-body electric guitars, semi-acoustic electric guitars, six- and 12-string steel guitars, classical guitars and an acoustic four-string bass guitar. The best-known guitar-maker in Australia, Maton's instruments have been purchased by George Harrison, Cliff Richard, the *Seekers, George Golla and others.

FURTHER REFERENCE
AthertonA, 83–6.

Matters, Arnold (*b* Adelaide, 11 Apr. 1904; *d* Adelaide, 21 Sept. 1990), baritone. Originally trained as an accountant, after taking lessons from Frederick Bevan at the University of Adelaide he won prizes at the South Street Eisteddfod, Ballarat, in 1926. Encouraged by Melba, he moved to London in 1929, taking lessons with Clive *Carey and W. Johnstone-Douglas at the Royal College of Music, singing for the BBC and in the choir of Westminster Abbey, then becoming principal baritone at Sadler's Wells in 1932. He was in Australia for war service from 1941; after the war he returned to Sadler's Wells and Covent Garden until 1954. With a strong, pure tone and effective dramatic acting, he appeared in more than 100 operas, including the premieres of Britten's *Gloriana* and Vaughan Williams's *Pilgrims' Progress,* and the British premieres of *The Bartered Bride, Simon Boccanegra,* and Lennox Berkeley's *Nelson.* Meanwhile he produced operas for Sadler's Wells, broadcast for the BBC, and taught at the Royal College of Music. He returned to Australia to teach at the Elder Conservatorium 1954–66.

FURTHER REFERENCE
Recordings include Micha in *The Bartered Bride*, cond. T. Beecham (1939, Lyric SR O830). See also Harold Rosenthal, *GroveO; MackenzieS,* 152–4; *AMN* 49 (June 1959), 19.

Matthews, Julia (*b* London, 14 Dec. 1842; *d* St Louis, Missouri, USA, 19 May 1876), dancer, theatrical singer. After dancing lessons with M. Capino at the Theatre Royal, Drury Lane, and singing lessons with Mlle Louise of the Royal Italian Opera, London, she made her debut at the age of eight dancing in *The Bohemian Girl* at the Surrey Theatre, then at Sadler's Wells and throughout the UK. She came to Australia in 1854 and appeared in *Spoiled Child* at Sydney as 'the celebrated infant prodigy', continuing her studies in dancing with Gerolamo *Carandini and in singing with her mother. She appeared for George Coppin at Melbourne in 1855, then joined a touring light opera troupe, becoming a favourite of the goldfields audiences. She toured Australia and NZ, then went to England in 1867, appearing at Covent Garden, where she was more admired for her acting than for her singing.

A precociously gifted singer, actress and dancer, she toured Europe and America in *opéra bouffe* roles until her untimely death from yellow fever.

FURTHER REFERENCE

Obit. in *Argus* 21 June 1876. See also *ADB*, 5; Alec Bagot, *Coppin the Great* (Melbourne: MUP, 1965), 323–4.

May, Brian   (*b* Adelaide, 1934; *d* 1997), film composer. He studied at the Elder Conservatorium, University of Adelaide. Unarguably one of Australia's most prolific and sought-after film composers, May has composed the scores for over 40 features films and mini-series since *The True Story of Eskimo Nell* in 1975. He is the recipient of numerous awards for best music score, including the 1977 Australian TV Society award for *Nowhere to Run*, the 1979 Australian Film Institute award for *Mad Max*, the 1980 Asian Film Festival award for *Harlequin*, the 1981 Paris International Film Festival award for *The Survivor*, and the 1984 APRA Golden Award for *Mad Max*. In 1983 he became the first Australian composer to work in Hollywood for a major film studio, Universal Pictures. May worked as the musical director and conductor of the ABC Melbourne Show Band 1968–82, and in 1988 was the musical director and conductor for the highly acclaimed NSW Royal Bicentennial Concert. He is also active in music education, frequently lecturing at the University of Southern California and many Australian universities and music institutions.

FURTHER REFERENCE

His film credits include: *Patrick* (1978), *Mad Max*, *Snapshot* and *Thirst* (1979), *Harlequin* and *Nightmares* (1980), *Gallipoli, The Killing of Angel Street, Mad Max II, Race for the Yankee Zephyr, Roadgames*, and *The Survivor* (1981), *Breakfast in Paris* and *Turkey Shoot* (1982), *Frog Dreaming* and *Sky Pirates* (1986), television mini-series *A Dangerous Life* (1988), television series *Dark Justice* (1989), *Bloodmoon* (1990), *Freddy's Dead: The Final Nightmare, Dead Sleep*, and *Hurricane Smith* (1991), *Dr Giggles* (1992), and *Blind Side* (1993). See also *LimbacherF.*   L. THOMPSON

May, Sydney Lionel   (*b* Tent Hill, NSW, 30 May 1882; *d* Ipswich, Qld, 21 Nov. 1968), music examiner. He studied piano as a child, was organist and choirmaster at the Central Congregational Church, Ipswich, 1905–20 and organist at Brisbane City Tabernacle Baptist Church 1920–35. Appointed part-time organiser of the AMEB by the University of Queensland in 1928, he was full-time organiser and lecturer from 1934 until his retirement in 1952. After World War II he promoted several annual summer schools in music, attended by hundreds of teachers and students. May built up the numbers of AMEB candidates submitting annually in Queensland from 700 in 1927 to 11 000 in 1952. He maintained music-teaching standards in the 1930s and 40s under difficult wartime conditions, at a time when the university itself was impoverished.

FURTHER REFERENCE

His writings include *The Story of Waltzing Matilda* (1944; rev. Brisbane: Smith & Patterson, 1955). See also G.D. Spearritt, *ADB*, 10;

N. Wilmott, *A History of the Music Department, University of Queensland, 1912–1970*, MA(Qual), Univ. Queensland, 1986; Brisbane *Telegraph*, 27 Nov. 1968.   GORDON SPEARRITT

Mazzella, Kavisha,   folk-singer, songwriter. Studying classical piano and playing folk music since childhood, she began performing American, Celtic and Italian folk music, then her own songs written in traditional ethnic styles. She has worked as a community musician, and performs in the folk trio Journey on tour for Musica Viva. She won two WA Music Industry Association awards in 1993.

Mead, Sister Janet.   See *Sister Janet*.

Meale, Richard   (*b* Sydney, 24 Aug. 1932), composer. Meale attended the NSW State Conservatorium for nine years until 1955, developing as a virtuoso pianist, but he did not study composition and did not graduate. He studied ethnomusicology at the University of California, Los Angeles, with the assistance of a Ford Foundation Grant in 1960–61 and was later an observer at the Julliard School of Music, New York, at the San Francisco Conservatorium and at Berkeley. At UCLA his encounter with non-Western musics was absorbed as compositional influences expressed in the formalism of the orchestral works *Clouds now and then* and *Soon it must die* (1969). For two years he worked as a record buyer for a Sydney department store. He was federal planning and program officer for orchestral music with the ABC, 1962–69, then was appointed as a lecturer (later reader) at the Elder Conservatorium, University of Adelaide, from 1969, speaking on contemporary music to a wide variety of institutions and nationally on radio. Meale was awarded the SA Government's senior fellowship in composition (1974–77). He was awarded the MBE in 1971 and the AM in 1985.

Adopting serialism in the wake of his European and American interludes, Meale developed an unyielding individualism beginning with *Las Alboradas* (1963) and running on through *Homage to García Lorca* (1964), *Nocturnes* (1967) *Incredible Floridas* (1971) and *Evocations* (1974). With *Viridian* (1979) a new linear style made its first appearance. For long the acknowledged pace-setter in Australian composition, Meale made a public declaration of independence from the modern music establishment in 1980 at the time of the premiere of his Second String Quartet at the Adelaide Festival and the commission of his first opera, *Voss* by the Australian Opera. The libretto is by David ★Malouf and is based on the Patrick White novel. Once before, in 1960, he had retreated into silence and reappraisal, withdrawing all former compositions and disowning the influence of Bax, Bartók and Stravinsky in favour of Boulez and Stockhausen. For 20 years he built a formidable reputation with music based on the structural premises of the very modernists he declared outmoded in 1980; with *Voss* he does a complete about-face, espousing melodic shapes, rhythmic structures and forms reminiscent of the romantics. A highly accessible opera on a complex theme, which speaks to the Australian experience — man against the elements which prove to be as much internal as external—*Voss* has entered the repertoire of the Australian Opera, a very rare distinction. His second opera, *Mer de Glace* (1991), again with a libretto by Malouf, received a mixed press. After the success of *Voss,* Meale took early retirement from the University of Adelaide and shifted to the solitude of a farmlet at Mullumbimby, NSW, in order to compose full-time.

WORKS (Selective)

Principal publisher: Universal Edition.

Orchestral   *Homage to García Lorca,* double str orch (1964), *Images (Nagauta)* (1966), *Nocturnes* (1967), *Very High Kings* (1968), *Clouds Now and Then* (1969), *Soon it will Die* (1969), Variations (1970), *Evocations,* ob, chamber orch, vn obbligato (1973), *Viridian* (1979).

Concerto   Concerto, fl, orch (1959).

Chamber and Instrumental   *Orenda,* pf (1959), Sonata, fl, pf (1960), *Las Alboradas,* fl, vn, hn, pf (1963), *Interiors/Exteriors,* 2 pf, 3 perc (1970), Quintet for Winds (1970), *Incredible Floridas,* fl, cl, vn, vc, pf, perc (1971), *Coruscations,* pf (1971), *Plateau,* wind quintet (1971), String Quartet No. 1 (1975), String Quartet No. 2 (1980).

Opera   *Voss* (1986, 2, David Malouf after Patrick White), Adelaide, 1 Mar. 1986; *Mer de Glace* (1991, prologue and 7 scenes, David Malouf), Sydney, 3 Oct. 1991.

Vocal   *Through Gilded Trellises Like the Sun,* S, pf (1949).

FURTHER REFERENCE

Recordings include *Voss*, Australian Opera, cond. S. Challender (1987, Philips 420 928–1); String Quartet No. 2, Petra String Quartet (1990, Canberra School of Music, CSM 10); and *Incredible Floridas,* Seymour Group (ABC 434 901). See also *CallawayA*; Andrew McCredie, *GroveD*; *MurdochA*.   THÉRÈSE RADIC

Measham, David   (*b* Nottingham, England, 1937), conductor. Measham studied at the Guildhall School of Music, was a violinist with several British orchestras, and assisted Stokowski and Bernstein in preparing for concerts and recordings. He conducted in the UK, NZ, Norway, the USA, and toured the USA and Japan with Wakeman's symphonic rock work *Journey to the Centre of the Earth.* In 1974 he was appointed principal conductor of the West Australian Symphony Orchestra, where he made a considerable impact. Measham also recorded with British orchestras and the West Australian Symphony Orchestra for Unicorn and World Record Club.

FURTHER REFERENCE

For discography, see *HolmesC.*   J.L. HOLMES

Mechanical Clocks.   The installation in public buildings of clocks which could mark the hours and quarter-hours with bells, often in elaborate chimes, was very popular in Australia from the 1880s. The operation was at first mechanical in most places and later converted to electrical means. Four city town halls and many regional town halls have clock towers with quarter chimes, but there are also a startling array of towers with mechanically operated bells in court houses and post offices. The Perth Town Hall clock dates from 1870 and the Brisbane General Post Office (GPO) clock from 1872 (removed 1909). These were followed by Adelaide GPO (five bells, 1875), Sydney Town Hall (Gillet & Johnson, five bells, 1885), Fremantle Town Hall (1887), Hobart GPO (1904), Launceston GPO (1909), and many others. The most elaborate chimes are heard at the Melbourne GPO (12 bells, Wilson & Co., 1890), but perhaps the finest is at the Sydney GPO (1891). The largest bells are at the Brisbane Town Hall (1930).

FURTHER REFERENCE

John D. Keating, *Bells in Australia* (Melbourne: MUP, 1977).

Medea (1).   Opera in one act, music and libretto by Felix ★Werder after Euripides. First performed at Melbourne Institute of Advanced Education on 17 September 1985.

Medea (2).   Chamber opera by Gordon ★Kerry (1992), libretto by Justin Macdonnell after Seneca. Scored for four voices, flute, percussion and keyboard, it was first performed by Chamber Made Opera in Melbourne in 1992.

Melba Memorial Conservatorium.   Founded in 1895 as the University of Melbourne Conservatorium, it has been affiliated with the Victorian University of Technology since 1995. It was personally funded by its first director, G.W.L. ★Marshall-Hall; when he was dismissed by the University of Melbourne in a controversy over his bohemian poetry in 1900, he simply continued the enterprise privately as the Melbourne Conservatorium. It took its present name in 1956 and offers a chiefly practical diploma. For many years housed at Albert Street (and thus often known as the Albert Street Conservatorium), then in Abbotsford, it now has premises at Richmond. Directors since Marshall-Hall have included Fritz ★Hart (1912–35), Harold Elvins (1936–43), Herbert Davis (1952–63), Harold ★Badger (1963–74) and Joan Arnold (1975–86). Its present director is Lynette Casey Brereton.

Melba, Dame Nellie   [Helen Porter Mitchell] (*b* Richmond, Melbourne, 19 May 1861, *d* Sydney, 23 Feb. 1931), soprano. She studied with Pietro ★Cecchi (Melbourne, 1879–86) and Mathilde Marchesi (Paris, 1886–87), using her stage name for the first time in a concert at the École Marchesi on 10 April 1887. Her operatic debut was as Gilda in Verdi's *Rigoletto* at the Théâtre de la Monnaie, Brussels, on 13 October 1887; other important debuts were in Donizetti's *Lucia di Lammermoor* at Covent Garden, London (24 May 1888), La Scala, Milan (16

March 1893), and the Metropolitan, New York (4 December 1893), and as Ophélie in Thomas's *Hamlet* at the Paris Opéra (8 May 1889). She toured Australia in 1902 and 1909, and with the Melba-Williamson opera tours of 1911, 1924, and, although not in a complete operatic role, 1928. From 1915 she taught at the Albert Street Conservatorium (now the *Melba Memorial Conservatorium). Noted for her charity work, during World War I she raised as much as £100 000.

Melba's 'artistic home' was Covent Garden where, between 1888 and 1923, the *Times* advertised on 355 occasions her appearance that day in a complete opera; her 19 roles there were: Lucia (1888–1900, 1907; 17 performances); Gilda (1888–1914; 40); Juliette in Gounod's *Roméo et Juliette* (1889–1919; 69); Marguerite in Gounod's *Faust* (1889–1923; 53); Elsa in Wagner's *Lohengrin* (1890–94; 15), Desdemona in Verdi's *Otello* (1892; 1908–14; 9), Nedda in Leoncavallo's *Pagliacci* (1893–94; 11), Violetta in Verdi's *La traviata* (1898–1913; 21), Mimì in Puccini's *La bohème* (1899–1923; 92), and a further 10 roles in 28 performances (1890–1904). Her official farewell performance was at Covent Garden on 8 June 1926, in *Roméo et Juliette* (Act II), *Otello* (Act IV), and *La bohème* (Acts III–IV); the evening was extensively recorded. With the Metropolitan Opera, New York, she took part in 207 performances of complete operas between 1893 and 1910; her 17 roles focused on Marguerite in *Faust* (44), Juliette (33), Lucia (31), Marguerite de Valois in Meyerbeer's *Les Huguenots* (29), Gilda (19) and Mimì (16).

Of her 25 operatic roles, the most important, except Lucia, were studied with their composer: Marguerite, Juliette, Ophélie, Mimì and Gilda. She also studied Manon with Massenet and Lakmé with Delibes. Although Saint-Saëns' *Hélène* and Bemberg's *Elaine* were written for her, they both remained on the periphery of her repertoire, as did Nedda which, at the composer's request, she created in London and New York. Throughout her career Melba was aware of the importance of carefully choosing her repertoire. She sang Brünnhilde in Wagner's *Siegfried* only once; although well received, it was a strain on her voice and was wisely abandoned. As her vocal and dramatic abilities changed with age and experience, she continually modified her repertoire: for example, she dropped Elsa and Lucia, and added Mimì and Desdemona. She added no new roles after 1904. Her recitals included many songs, notably Bishop's *Home, Sweet Home,* Arditi's *Se saran rose* (the 'Melba Waltz'), and *Good-bye* and *Mattinata* by Tosti, who, like Hermann Bemberg, wrote numerous songs for her.

Melba was criticised, mainly earlier in her career, for superficiality of interpretation, although she was often inspired when singing with Jean de Reszke, her great partner in the French repertoire as Caruso was in the Italian. Of her voice there was near-unanimous praise. The great critic W.J. Henderson wrote that it

> … had splendour. The tones glowed with a starlike brilliance. They flamed with a white flame. And they possessed

a remarkable force which the famous singer always used with continence.… [Her voice] extended from B flat below the clef to the high F. The scale was beautifully equalized throughout and there was not the slightest change in the quality from bottom to top. All the tones were forward; there was never even a suspicion of throatiness. The full, flowing and facile emission of the tones has never been surpassed, if matched, by any other singer of our time. The intonation was preëminent in its correctness.… The Melba attack was little short of marvelous … Her trill was ravishing … Her staccati were as firm, as well placed, and as musical as if they had been played on a piano. Her cantilena was flawless in smoothness and purity.

From 1904, when she was 42 and vocally past her prime, she made numerous commercial recordings; although the primitive technology was incapable of preserving adequately the quality of her voice, these recordings are important in preserving some idea of her interpretation. One of the most outstanding singers of opera's 'Golden Age', and one of the two most famous musicians produced by Australia, she was created DBE in 1918, and in 1927 became one of only eight Australians ever to be created GBE; she appears on the Australian $100 bank note.

FURTHER REFERENCE

Melba's recorded legacy runs to 159 items; an additional 46 items which can be identified by name were not issued and are apparently not extant. Non-commercial recordings were made by Bettini (before 1896, New York) and Mapleson (1901, New York), and commercial recordings by the Gramophone Company (1904–26, in London, Hayes, 1 item in Paris) and Victor (1907–16, New York and Camden, NJ). Of the 85 extant recordings made by the Gramophone Company, 83 were reissued in 1976 on five LP discs (HMV RLS 719); the 63 extant recordings made by Victor were reissued in 1994 on three CDs (Romophone 81011–2). The best of the discographies is in Moran (see below), 447–72.

Melba's writings include her autobiography, *Melodies and Memories* (1925), reset with introduction by John Cargher (Melbourne: Thomas Nelson, 1980), and *The Melba Method* (Sydney: Chappell, 1926). See also the anthology of writings compiled by William R. Moran as *Nellie Melba: A Contemporary Review* (Westport, Conn.: Greenwood, 1985); it has an extensive bibliography. Of the biographies, see John Hetherington, *Melba* (London: Faber, 1967; reprinted Melbourne: MUP, 1995); Thérèse Radic, *Melba: The Voice of Australia* (Melbourne: Macmillan, 1986) and Pamela Vestey, *Melba: A Family Memoir* (Melbourne: Phoebe, 1996).

ROYSTON GUSTAVSON

Melbourne,   pop. (1991) 2 948 800. Capital of Victoria, situated on Port Philip Bay around the mouth of the Yarra River. Incorporated as a town in 1842 on land originally inhabited by the Woiworung tribe, and proclaimed a city in 1847, Melbourne today has a greater metropolitan area stretching over 6000 square km, home to nearly three-quarters of the population of the state. The city has traditionally been the headquarters of Australian financial institutions and manufacturing companies, and in recent years has developed and promoted an image of itself as the Australian capital of the arts.

1. Early Colonial Era. 2. 'Marvellous Melbourne'. 3. From Federation to World War II. 4. After 1945. 5. Distinguishing Characteristics Today.

1. Early Colonial Era. The first to settle in the Melbourne area were intending pastoralists from Tasmania who began arriving in 1835. Melbourne, which was established near a source of fresh water upstream from the estuary where ships anchored, thereby did not have Sydney's convict and military origins. Music was soon sought as a source of entertainment and symbol of respectability. The first pianos were imported to the new colony in 1838, and by 1839 the colony could boast several music teachers and frequent balls and quadrille parties. By 1840 the settlement had become a fast-growing shipping, supply and banking centre with a population of more than 4000.

The 1840s was a period of consolidation for the settlement, with the construction of public buildings and churches for the main Christian denominations. These churches, along with a new Jewish synagogue, encouraged a culture of amateur music-making well known in Britain whence the majority of new arrivals came. Choral and organ music became popular, and a philharmonic society was formed to promote orchestral music but was frustrated by the difficulties in procuring not only players of some standard but also instruments. By the end of the decade, however, regular brass band performances had begun on Flagstaff Hill. The first substantial theatre house, the Queen's, was erected in 1845 and there Melbourne saw its first opera production, Auber's *Gustavus III,* in May 1850.

In November 1851 the Colony of Victoria was proclaimed. Within a year, however, its capital had lost many of its workers to the newly discovered goldfields at Ballarat and Bendigo. By 1852 the town had been transformed into a sprawling transit camp. While Melbourne's population was a little more than half that of Sydney's in 1851, by 1861 it was significantly larger and remained so until the late 1890s. The goldrush attracted waves of free immigrants and although they preferred the music hall to the concert hall, the city began to attract the attention of overseas artists. Melbourne became an important port of call for an increasing number of musicians venturing from Europe to tour Australia, such as the singing stars Catherine *Hayes and Anna Bishop or violinist Miska *Hauser.

With a burgeoning population, the range of services provided by and for local musicians increased rapidly. Allans, the pioneer music house of Melbourne, was founded on 1 May 1850 by Joseph Wilkie, George L. *Allan becoming a partner of the firm in 1863. Piano manufacturers appeared, notably Joseph *Kilner from 1856 and Jabez *Carnegie from 1867. In 1853 the longest-running choral organisation in Australia, the (Royal) Melbourne Philharmonic Society, was founded,

giving its first performance of Handel's *Messiah* in December that year. The first season of grand opera opened in 1856 under the management of George *Coppin. Concurrently, an extensive private and Catholic education system developed, within which music education held an important place as a purveyor of respectability and symbol of social mobility.

Opera production had occurred throughout the 1850s in Melbourne with increasing frequency, thanks to the *Howsons, the *Carandinis, the *Gautrots, and other performer-entrepreneurs. Then there was resident opera for nearly 20 years (1861–80) under the impresario William Saurin *Lyster and his companies. Other large-scale ensemble music-making of the time was, by and large, limited to amateur choirs. Through the influence of its German community, Melbourne could boast two liedertafels, the Royal Victorian Liedertafel (which began as a German society, 1868) and the Royal Metropolitan Liedertafel (founded 1870), which merged in 1905. The Musical Association of Victoria was founded in 1861 by the conductor and pianist Charles E. *Horsley; it conducted, as one of its many activities, an examination for a diploma of music, and was reconstituted as the Musical Society of Victoria in 1892. In 1864, in an effort to impose some standards upon music teachers, the Victorian board of education constituted a board of examiners in music which could award a licence to teach and a higher award, the certificate of competency.

2. 'Marvellous Melbourne'. By 1880 the wealth brought from gold made Melbourne one of the richest and most dazzling colonies in the British Empire. A first-rate, sumptuous theatrical life of operettas, pantomimes and musicals was brought by entrepreneurs George *Musgrove and J.C. *Williamson, although opera became less frequent after Lyster's death, the somewhat threadbare productions of the *Simenson Co. proving most interesting. Aspiring musical talent received a boost in 1882, when Sir William Clarke gave £3000 for a perpetual scholarship for a Victorian to the Royal College of Music, London. There was growing public pressure for the creation of a permanent professional orchestra for the city. The international exhibition mounted in Melbourne in 1888 had as a major attraction a series of about 250 orchestral concerts featuring a first-class ensemble conducted by Frederick Cowen.

The first Ormond professor of music at the University of Melbourne was G.W.L. *Marshall-Hall; in 1895, he and William Adolphus *Laver founded a Conservatorium allied to the chair which, in providing a course of practical tuition leading towards a university qualification, was the first institution of its kind in the British Empire. Upon his arrival, Marshall-Hall had also formed a highly competent orchestra from the remnants of the Cowen orchestra of 1888, which had continued for a time as the Victorian Orchestra; Marshall-Hall's orchestra gave well over 100 concerts of a hitherto unheard-of quality in Australia, 1891–1912.

3. From Federation to World War II. Melbourne lost some of its lustre during the economic Depression of the 1890s, but when the six separate colonies federated as Australia in January 1901, Melbourne served as the new nation's capital 1901–27, regaining in these years much of its dented prestige. The theatrical life provided by Musgrove and Williamson now included excellent opera seasons and was further enriched by the vaudevilles and variety of the *Fuller and *Tivoli circuits; major Wagner works, including the first complete *Ring of the Nibelungen*, arrived with the *Quinlan Co. 1912–13. Australian works by Alfred Hill and Fritz Hart were presented by the *National Opera League in 1914.

The Melbourne Symphony Orchestra was founded in 1906 as an amateur organisation by Alberto *Zelman Jr, who continued to conduct it until his death in 1927. Zelman's successor, the English-born composer Fritz Bennicke *Hart, then introduced a series of successful concerts at 'popular' prices and it was Hart's enthusiasm for making orchestral music more generally accessible to the public which in 1929 attracted the wealthy Melbourne businessman Sidney *Myer to fund a series of free outdoor concerts given by the orchestra. These concerts were to capture the patronage of Melbourne audiences from their inception and were welcome relief from the ensuing economic gloom of the Great Depression. Most orchestral concerts were held in the town hall, which remained for a long time the major venue for large-scale concerts and major recitals in the city. In 1925 the hall and its organ were destroyed by fire; the replacement instrument, built by Hill & Son and Norman & Beard of London in 1926, is one of most impressive symphonic organs in existence.

From 1909 Dame Nellie *Melba lived partly in Europe and partly in Melbourne, the place of her birth. Her influence upon musical life in Melbourne was shared by an increasing number of distinguished overseas artists who, with ever-improving forms of transport and more enterprising artistic managements, included Melbourne on their tour itineraries. The outbreak of World War I, however, brought such touring to a temporary end and also brought with it strong patriotic sentiments reflected in a surge of interest in British music. In 1921 the Melbourne-born patron of music Louise Dyer (later *Hanson-Dyer) formed the British Music Society, but the renaissance of popularity of British music did not last in any significant form beyond the decade.

The University of Melbourne Conservatorium gained greatly in stature after the war with the appointment of Bernard *Heinze in 1926 to the Ormond chair. Heinze's impressive early concerts with the University Symphony Orchestra, combined with the effects of the Depression, saw the Melbourne Symphony Orchestra in 1932 faced with financial failure; a merger between the two was made possible through a gift to the university by Sidney Myer, designed not only to put orchestral music in Melbourne on a sure footing but also to ensure that the free open-air concerts would continue indefinitely. The university's controlling interest in the orchestra combined with Heinze's growing interests in the musical operations of the new ABC, also created in 1932, gave the Ormond professor and his Conservatorium a powerful influence, not just over the musical life of the city but also over many developments in musical life across the whole nation. This was the apex of Melbourne's leadership of musical affairs; when Heinze left for the NSW State Conservatorium in 1957 undoubtedly a significant portion of the national prestige of the University of Melbourne Conservatorium went with him.

4. After 1945. During the war, soprano Gertrude *Johnson had brought to fruition her ambitious scheme for a *National Theatre Movement in Melbourne. For the first time since Fuller's last opera season a decade before, the city played host to an opera company which gave ambitious performances featuring some of the finest native talents of the day. Johnson's royal command performances in 1954 were the inspiration for the Elizabethan Theatre Trust, established that year, which led ultimately to the establishment of the Australian Opera. Meanwhile, Heinze's plans for a permanent orchestra were finally brought to fruition in 1950, when the ABC expanded the Melbourne Symphony Orchestra to full-scale symphony size as the Victorian Symphony Orchestra.

With the gradual transfer of federal government functions to Canberra after 1927, Melbourne's rate of growth declined, so that by the end of World War II Sydney was the larger city by a substantial margin. However, when during 1947–66 Australia embarked upon a policy of substantially increasing levels of immigration, the impact of Greek, Italian and Jewish people from Eastern Europe was greater in Melbourne than in any other Australian city because it had more substantial pre-war migration connections. During the 1970s southern European immigration slowed considerably and since then the trend has been towards an increase in immigration from Asian countries and Latin America. Non-British ethnic groups have added considerably to the diversity of musical styles in the city. In Melbourne's inner northern suburbs there exists today a lively café music scene, noted particularly for South American music, showcased through annual festivals such as the Next Wave Festival and La Boite. European immigration, in particular, helped found and support a branch of the Sydney-based Musica Viva organisation in Melbourne in 1954 which continues today to mount highly successful seasons of chamber music.

Jazz first made its influence felt in Melbourne during the 1920s. By the late 1930s Melbourne boasted the popular 3AW Swing Club and the Melbourne University Rhythm Club and witnessed the growth of a number of cafés and coffee lounges providing venues for jazz performance, particularly in the St Kilda area. World War II not only increased the demand for the entertainment provided by jazz bands but also accelerated the importation of American jazz and popular music styles. After the war, Melbourne's popular musical culture became only more cosmopolitan and in the late 1960s rock and electric pop replaced jazz as predominantly the music of the younger generation. Melbourne has since become a stronghold for traditional jazz, reflected and celebrated in the character of the annual Montsalvat Jazz Festival, held in late January in the outer north-east of the city.

The growth of the outer suburbs of Melbourne after the war encouraged the creation and expansion of additional tertiary training courses for music beyond the University of Melbourne. The department of music at Monash University was established in 1965 and specialised in the theory and practice of ethnomusicology. Prompted by changes in federal funding arrangements for tertiary education, 1974 saw the creation of the Victorian College of the Arts. Its music school, founded by John *Hopkins, developed diploma, degree and postgraduate qualifications in music performance and has run an opera school since 1978. The department of music at La Trobe University was founded by professor Keith *Humble in 1974 and through his guidance developed an emphasis on contemporary music and music technology. The Albert Street Conservatorium, renamed Melba Memorial Conservatorium, continued to award diplomas in music, and since 1995 has been affiliated with the Victoria University of Technology. Today Melbourne boasts the largest concentration of musical training courses anywhere in Australia.

5. Distinguishing Characteristics Today. Like most major Australian cities, Melbourne plays host to a number of festivals specifically for music or for the performing arts where music activity plays an important part. The most significant such festival is the Melbourne International Festival of the Arts, first held in 1986. The Melbourne International Festival of Organ and Harpsichord began in 1970 and soon established itself as an important festival, not just for organ and harpsichord but also for early music. The festivals and other major musical bodies and events rely to varying degrees on government funding. The State Government funds a wide range of musical activities. The Melbourne Youth Music Council, an arm of the state education department, administers a Saturday music school and the January music camp for young players. The Victorian Rock Foundation (founded 1990) mounts the Melbourne Music Festival, a showcase of local popular music.

In 1946 the State Government reserved an area immediately south of the Yarra River where in the early 1970s it started developing an arts precinct. The Victorian Arts Centre was built, encompassing the Melbourne Concert Hall (opened November 1982) which seats 2677, and the State Theatre (opened October 1984), which seats 2000. Both venues are situated amid a complex of theatres, galleries, other concert venues, and music, visual and performing art schools. The Victoria State Opera found a

home at the Arts Centre. It emerged from a succession of amateur opera companies in 1976, and under the guidance of conductor Richard *Divall developed a fine reputation in opera production, complementing the superb facilities of the State Theatre. It mounted yearly seasons of opera, operetta and musicals timetabled to complement the season of the Australian Opera, until the two companies merged as Opera Australia in 1996. In 1969 the Elizabethan Trust Melbourne Orchestra was formed to provide orchestral support to the Australian Opera and the Australian Ballet; in 1987 it was renamed the State Orchestra of Victoria, taken over by the Arts Centre, and continues to support opera and ballet performances in the State Theatre.

The Sidney Myer Music Bowl was opened in 1959 and provides an acoustic canopy for outdoor performances unique in Australia. The fixed seating and surrounding lawns provide seating room for about 14 000 people. In recent years the refurbished Princess Theatre has become the premier venue in the country for the staging by theatrical entrepreneurs of seasons of internationally successful musicals which have in their turn attracted national and international audiences. Melbourne also boasts a healthy suburban and amateur musical scene. The Musical Society of Victoria, which today has a number of suburban and country district centres, provides performance opportunities in a non-competitive atmosphere for young musicians. The Astra Society (founded 1951) has been prominent in promoting the works of contemporary international and Australian composers. Melbourne also has its own public classical music broadcasting service, 3MBS-FM (founded 1975). Locally produced popular music is supported by numerous live venues and though the existence of small and innovative recording companies.

The demographic centre of Melbourne is steadily drifting south-east, suggesting that greater decentralisation of music activity from the city centre is likely; Monash University has recently opened a new performing arts centre on its campus in Clayton. The city's ethnic mix is likewise continuing to widen, adding to the diversity of musical tastes and forms presently available. In national terms, however, Melbourne is continuing to expand at a slower rate than the more northern state capitals, and Sydney undoubtedly has a higher international profile. Whether the city's self-proclaimed status as the nation's arts capital can be justified in the future remains to be seen. Without a doubt, however, the city continues to benefit from a lengthy and ongoing tradition of musical endeavour.

FURTHER REFERENCE

W.A. Carne, *A Century of Harmony: The Official Centenary History of the Royal Melbourne Philharmonic Society* (Melbourne, 1954); M.T. Radic, Some Historical Aspects of Musical Organisations in Melbourne, 1888–1915, PhD, Univ. Melbourne, 1978. Peter Tregear, *The Conservatorium of Music, University of Melbourne: An*

Historical Essay to Mark Its Centenary, 1895–1995 (Melbourne: Faculty of Music, Univ. Melbourne, 1997).   PETER TREGEAR

Melbourne Brass Ensemble. Brass quintet founded (1979) from members of the Melbourne Symphony Orchestra, comprised of William Evans and David Farrands (trumpets), Russell Davis (french horn), Kenneth McClimont (trombone), and Fabian Russell (tuba). They have regularly toured regional centres in the eastern states for Musica Viva and broadcast for ABC radio and television.

FURTHER REFERENCE
Recordings include works by R. Simms, P. Grainger et al. (1985, Move MS 3056), and *Fable Fantasy and Folksong* (1988, Move ABW MD 4001).

Melbourne Chamber Orchestra. See *Rantos, Spiros.*

Melbourne Conservatorium. The name is used confusingly for two institutions with the same origin. It properly refers to the school now named the ★Melba Memorial Conservatorium; but there was also a University of Melbourne Conservatorium, now named the ★University of Melbourne Music Faculty.

Melbourne Cup. Ballet by Harold ★Badger (1962), choreography by Rex Reid. The first ballet by an Australian performed by the new Australian Ballet, it relates the first running of the famous horse-race in 1861, for which Badger made a medley of period melodies by Offenbach, Suppé and others. It was first performed in 1962.

Melbourne International Chamber Music Competition. Held every four years in Melbourne from 1991, it has become one of the world's leading chamber music competitions, attracting ensembles from many countries. Administered with assistance from Musica Viva (Victoria) and with substantial government and commercial sponsorship, it is open to string quartets and piano trios whose players are (on average) under 30. Heats are conducted by tape and finalists selected for the week of live finals in Melbourne before a jury of internationally renowned players. In 1995 the first prize was $30 000 for the string quartet and $22 500 for the piano trio, but there are various other awards, the total prize-money being $100 000.

Melbourne International Festival. Founded in 1986, it began as the Spoleto Melbourne Festival under Gian Carlo Menotti, and has since been directed by John Truscott, Richard Wherrett and Leo Schofield. Held over 17 days in October–November, the event is subsidised by the State and municipal governments and includes performing and visual arts, street theatre, river and Botanic Garden events, and a significant number of free events. At times less adventurous than its counterparts in other cities, under Schofield the event appears to have made spectacular gains both artistically and financially.

Melbourne International Festival of Organ and Harpsichord (MIFOH). Founded in May 1971 by Sergio ★de Pieri as the Melbourne Autumn Festival of Organ and Harpsichord, the artistic direction was taken over in 1972 by Douglas ★Lawrence who continued until 1985. With a formula of recitals by many of the world's leading performers, lectures and masterclasses, competitions, exhibitions, heritage tours and social events, the festival soon attracted large audiences from throughout Australia and beyond, including many students. The festival succeeded strongly in promoting the organ and harpsichord and encouraging the manufacture of finely crafted instruments. From 1987 it has been managed by David Agg and the Festival Committee.

FURTHER REFERENCE
John Maidment, 'A Decade of Achievement', *Organists' Review* 66/4 (1981), 38–40.   JOHN MAIDMENT

Melbourne Liedertafel. See *Liedertafel.*

Melbourne New Orleans Jazz Band. Founded by trombonist Llew Hird in 1957 as the New Orleans Jazz Band, the name Melbourne was added after Hird's departure in 1958. Engagements included a residency at the Blue Heaven restaurant until, led by Kevin Shannon, they departed for England in 1961, playing in concerts, radio and television, and on tours. Personnel changes brought other Australian musicians to England until the band dissolved in 1963, with some members returning to Australia to pursue careers in other groups, and others, including trombonist Max Collie, remaining in England. The band pioneered the New Orleans revival in Australia, with trumpeter Frank Turville (*b* 13 Mar. 1935; *d* 30 Nov. 1985) a notable presence.

FURTHER REFERENCE
Recordings include *Australian Jazz of the 60's* (1984, EMI YPRX-2166). See also *OxfordJ*; Eric Brown, 'The Melbourne New Orleans Jazz Band', *Jazzline* 6/3 (Sept. 1973), 3–7, and 6/4 (Dec. 1973), 9–12.   BRUCE JOHNSON

Melbourne String Quartet. Founded in 1993 for the Port Fairy Festival, it is comprised of four players from the Melbourne Symphony Orchestra: Carl ★Pini and Gerard van der Weide (violins), Jane Hazelwood (viola) and Arturs Erzegailis (cello). The only professional string quartet to have been resident in Melbourne for many years, it offers a subscription series at Monash University and has performed the complete Beethoven quartet cycle at the Athenaeum Theatre, Melbourne.

FURTHER REFERENCE
They have released a CD, *Torquing Points* (1994, Move MD 3143).

Melbourne Symphony Orchestra (1). Semi-professional orchestra, founded (1906) by Alberto ★Zelman Jr, which gave concerts and accompanied the Philharmonic Society under his direction. After Zelman's death it was conducted (from 1927) by Fritz ★Hart. With severe financial troubles, its future looked grim until the appearance of retailer Sidney ★Myer in 1932, who paid its debts as part of its merger with the University of Melbourne Orchestra to create the new Melbourne Symphony Orchestra (2).

Melbourne Symphony Orchestra (2). One of the six state orchestras formed under the aegis of the ABC. Its history has been traced, rather tenuously, to the series of 159 daily orchestral concerts given at the Melbourne International Centennial Exhibition (August 1888 to January 1889). But the orchestra as it now exists gave its first public concert under Bernard ★Heinze on 6 November 1934, the program including the First Symphony of Sibelius. Under a plan devised largely by Heinze, the orchestra was formed essentially by fusing the University [of Melbourne] Symphony Orchestra with an existing Melbourne Symphony Orchestra (1) conducted, until his death in 1927, by Alberto ★Zelman Jr. Since 1934 its concert seasons have become increasingly important. Its 1996 season contained 73 programs (123 performances) including 14 different series in Melbourne and Geelong, given by an orchestra of 104 permanent members regularly augmented to a playing strength of 110. Between 1949 and 1965 it played under the title Victorian Symphony Orchestra, and when the original name was resumed the University of Melbourne ceded its copyright in the title Melbourne Symphony Orchestra. The orchestra had in its first 40 years a series of short-term 'permanent' conductors, and never enjoyed the benefit of a training regimen under a first-rate conductor (by contrast with the Sydney Symphony Orchestra, which found its voice and style under Eugene Goossens, 1947–56): Alceo Galliera (1950–51), Juan José Castro (1952–53), Walter Susskind (1953–55), Kurt Wöss (1956–59), Georges Tzipine (1961–65), Willem van Otterloo (1967–70), and the ailing Fritz Rieger (1971–72). However, the inherent standard of performance of the orchestra has risen consistently since the 1950s, and the orchestra is now widely spoken of as the finest in Australia. Its conductor laureate is Hiroyuki ★Iwaki, previously chief conductor since 1974. Markus Stenz became chief conductor designate in 1997, and will formally take the role of chief conductor and music director in 1998.

FURTHER REFERENCE
Recordings include Bruckner, *Romantic* Symphony (ABC 426425); B. Broadstock, *Toward the Shining Light* (1990, ABC 426807–2); A. Hill, Symphony No. 4, cond. W. Lehmann (1983, Marco Polo 8.220345); P. Grainger, orchestral works, cond. J. Hopkins (1980, EMI OASD 430000). See also Christopher Symons, *The Melbourne Symphony Orchestra : An Introduction and Appreciation* (Melbourne: The Orchestra, [1987]); Charles Buttrose, *Playing for Australia: A Story about ABC Orchestras and Music in Australia* (Sydney: ABC/Macmillan, 1982); Kenneth Hince, *The Melbourne Symphony Orchestra: An Appreciation* (Melbourne: ABC, c. 1966).   KENNETH HINCE

Melbourne Youth Music Council. Founded by the Victorian education department as the Secondary Schools Concert Committee in 1967, it seeks to provide school students with the opportunity to perform in ensembles. It established the Secondary Schools Orchestra in 1970, renamed the Melbourne Youth Orchestra in 1972. An annual January music camp began in the same year and a training ensemble and symphonic band were added in 1974.

At its inception, the venture was largely the vision of the tireless education department music inspector Alexandra Cameron, and since her retirement it has been chaired by her long-serving successor Bruce Worland. The Melbourne Youth Orchestra established high standards and enjoyed a central position in musical life under John ★Hopkins, its conductor for a decade from 1974, but has more recently had to compete for players with a growing number of other local youth ensembles. Nevertheless, it remains the largest youth music body in Melbourne; at its Saturday Music School, held at the Victorian College of the Arts and Melbourne High School, the council now offers an array of nine orchestras, bands, string groups and training ensembles, and its annual music camp is attended by over 600 young players.

Meldrum, Ian Alexander ('Molly') (b 29 Jan. 1946), pop and rock music journalist. Meldrum wrote for the music magazine *Go-Set* and produced Russell ★Morris's hit single *The Real Thing* (1969). He came to national prominence as talent co-ordinator for the television program ★*Countdown*, where he presented the weekly 'Humdrum' segment of news from the music industry. His efforts in promoting Australian talent both locally and overseas have been a hallmark of his career, and he has been pivotal in bringing overseas acts to the notice of the Australian public. One of the best-known faces in the Australian music industry, during the 1990s he has had a regular guest spot on commercial television's *Hey! Hey! It's Saturday.*   WILLIAM VAN PINXTEREN

Men At Work. Rock band (1979–85) formed in Melbourne by Colin Hay (vocals) and Ron Strykert (guitar), originally as an acoustic duo, to which they added Greg Ham (keyboards, vocals, winds), John Rees (bass) and Jerry Speiser (drums). They played in suburban pubs, gaining a very strong following, until they were discovered by CBS executive Peter Karpin. The first two of their 10

CBS singles, *Who Can It Be Now* and *Down Under*, reached Nos 2 and 1 respectively in the charts in 1981, and their first albums *Business As Usual* and *Cargo* both reached No. 1 in the album charts in the same year; released internationally, the former remained on the US *Billboard* album charts for 18 months and eventually sold 15 million copies worldwide. They toured the USA as supporting act for Fleetwood Mac in 1982. By 1983 their work had also topped charts in the USA, the UK and Europe, and they embarked on a world tour, their next album winning an American gold record. But by 1985 the membership had almost entirely changed, and they disbanded amid acrimony. Their straightforward, hearty pub band style and meteoric rise greatly enlarged international interest in Australian rock music, especially in the USA. They won three Countdown awards, a Grammy, and a *Rolling Stone* (USA) award.

FURTHER REFERENCE
Recordings include *Who Can It Be Now* (CBS BA 222827) and *Down Under* (CBS BA 222891), *Business As Usual* (CBS SBP 237700) and *Cargo* (CBS SBP 237833). A compilation is *The Works Greatest Hits* (1992, Columbia 450349–2). For discography, see *SpencerA*. See also *McGrathA*; *SpencerW*; *GuinnessP*, II, 1661; *CoupeN*.

Mental As Anything.
Rock group formed (1976) in Sydney comprised of Reg Mombasa ([Chris O'Doherty] guitar, vocals), Martin Plaza ([Martin Murphy] vocals, guitar), Greedy Smith ([Andrew Smith] keyboards, vocals, harmonica), Peter O'Doherty (bass) and Wayne Delisle (drums). On the group's debut album *Get Wet*, the title track, became one of the band's best-known singles. Numerous national Top 40 successes followed, from *The Nips are Getting Bigger* (1979) to *Don't Tell Me Now* (1987), but in Australia the group failed to attain a No.1 in the charts. In 1987 their newly released single *Live It Up* achieved some success on the UK charts, spending 13 weeks at No. 3, but failed to chart as well in Australia. Their style was influenced by rock, rhythm and blues, and rockabilly.

FURTHER REFERENCE
Recordings include *Get Wet* (1979, Regular L37125); *Mouth To Mouth* (1987, CBS 450361 1); and *Cyclone Raymond* (1980, CBS 465645 1). See also *GuinnessP*; J Lacey, *Rock Australia* (Sydney: Magazine Promotions, 1982); *McGrathA*; *SpencerW*.
KATRINA WATSON

Menuhin, Hephzibah
(*b* San Francisco, 20 May 1920; *d* London, 1 Jan. 1981), pianist. She began studying the piano at the age of four and gave her first solo piano recital in San Francisco at the age of eight. During her adolescence, while studying piano in Italy under Marcel Ciampi, she achieved wide fame, performing solo or more often accompanying her older brother, violinist Yehudi Menuhin, in many of the major cities of Europe and America. In 1938, at the age of 18, she married an Australian and moved to Australia, where she remained for the next 19 years. She appeared in concerts and concertos with the Sydney Symphony Orchestra, introducing many of the works of Bloch and Bartók to Australia. She also conducted music therapy sessions at the Callan Park Mental Hospital and lectured to the Bartók Society, which she helped form. In 1957 she moved to London where, with her second husband, she formed the Centre for Human Rights and Responsibilities. During this time, in order to raise money for their work, she continued to perform regularly. In 1977 she was elected president of the Women's International League for Peace and Freedom; she was also a judge of the Sydney International Piano Competition. A Hephzibah Menuhin Memorial Scholarship honours her memory.

FURTHER REFERENCE
Obit. in *National Times,* 28 Feb. 1981; *Age,* 5 Jan. 1981. See also *Age,* 27 Apr. 1985.
LEONIE GOODWIN

Menuhin Memorial Scholarship, Hephzibah.
Awarded biannually (since 1982) after a national piano competition, this scholarship is funded from funds raised by friends and former students of the pianist Hephzibah *Menuhin (sister of violinist Yehudi Menuhin), who had settled to play and teach in Australia. Open to pianists 18–28 years, past winners have included Duncan Gifford, Benjamin Martin and Justin Williams. Administered alternately by the Sydney Conservatorium and the University of Melbourne, the prize is currently $8000.

Mer de Glace.
Opera (1991) in two acts by Richard *Meale, libretto by David Malouf, after Mary Shelley's *Frankenstein* and the historical record of her life. It conflates two narratives: Frankenstein's creation of a monster, and Mary Shelley's antagonism towards her stepsister and absorption of the influence of her husband Percy Shelley and Byron. First performed by the Australian Opera, Sydney, 1991.

Meredith, John
(*b* Holbrook, NSW, 1920), folk-song collector. After teaching himself his father's accordion and learning tunes from a neighbour, he worked in Melbourne from 1944, then went fruit picking in 1947, settling in Sydney. He formed the original *Bushwhackers band in 1952, was a founding member of the Bush Music Club (1954) and early editor of its magazine *Singabout*. Beginning to collect folk-song and dance in search of material for his band, his collecting became more serious, taking him across rural NSW and northern Victoria 1954–60. With a government fellowship in 1960 he collected material for *Folksongs of Australia* vol. 1 (1967, with Hugh Anderson), one of the exemplary collections of Australian folk-song, particularly noted for its placing of the songs collected in the context of the lives of their singers. He wrote more than 12 books, including studies

of ★Frank the Poet, Jack Donahue, 'Duke' ★Tritton and Frank Bourne, and with a National Library of Australia grant returned to the field in 1980, publishing *Folksongs of Australia* vol. 2 (1987, with Roger Covell and Patricia Brown). He wrote two ballad operas *The Wild Colonial Boy* (with Joan Clarke) and *How Many Miles From Gundagai*. One of Australia's most significant collectors of traditional song and bush-dance music, he was honoured with the OAM in 1988, the AM in 1992, and an Australian Folk Trust Lifetime Achievement Award in 1995.

FURTHER REFERENCE

His collections of recordings, yarns, photographs and films are now in the National Film and Sound Archive. Meredith's account of his work is in *Real Folk* (Canberra: National Library of Australia, 1995), v–xiii, and 'John Meredith Speaks for Himself', *Stringybark and Greenhide* 6/2 (1986), 4–9. See also 'Folklore, the National Library of Australia and Gathering Social History', *Voices* 2/1 (1992), 5–15; *OxfordF.*

Merewether, Richard (*b* Merewether, Newcastle, NSW, 17 Sept. 1926; *d* London, 5 Dec. 1986), french horn player, instrument designer. After studying horn with Alan Mann at the NSW State Conservatorium he played horn at the Theatre Royal, Sydney, in 1943, in the Sydney Symphony Orchestra from 1944 and then settled in the UK. He was in the Birmingham Symphony Orchestra in 1950, the Bournemouth Symphony Orchestra 1951–54, then freelanced in London; but after an eye operation in 1971 he had to cease performing. Intrigued with the limits of knowledge of horn acoustics, he designed a double horn in F and F-alto in 1959 and then with Paxman Musical Instruments he began producing other designs, including a double descant horn, triple horn, double Wagner tuba, and others. Paxman's 'RM' horns became greatly sought after; he was full-time with Paxman from 1980 until his accidental death. He wrote articles on the horn for Paxmans, for the *New Grove Dictionary of Music,* and other publications.

FURTHER REFERENCE

2MBS-FM Programme Guide (Nov. 1990).

Merritt, Max and The Meteors. Rock-soul group, comprised of Max Merritt (guitar, vocals), Peter Williams (guitar), Johnny Dick (drums) and Teddy Toi (bass guitar). Max Merritt (*b* Christchurch, NZ 30 Apr. 1941) became involved in rock bands in 1956. In 1964 he and the Meteors came to Australia for a four-week residency at the Rex Hotel in Sydney. The group remained in Sydney and became the Viking label's house band. Over the next four years they released five singles and experienced many line-up changes; a serious car accident in which Merritt lost the sight of one eye took the band out of action for much of 1967–68. On their return to the pub and disco scene their brand of soul music became increasingly popular. A self-titled album

released in 1970 was the biggest-selling Australian album for that year; by that time the band consisted of Max Merritt, Bob Bertles (sax), 'Yuk' Harrison (bass guitar) and Stewart (Stewie) Speer (drums). Speer continued to be associated with the band until his death in 1986. The group spent long periods on the pub circuit in England 1970–76, moving away from a strictly soul sound. Keyboards and slide guitar featured, and rock and country-rock styles became more prominent. Despite its absences abroad the band maintained its popularity in Australia until the late 1970s. In 1978 Merritt made his base in the USA, occasionally returning to Australia to tour with various personnel.

FURTHER REFERENCE

Recordings include *Max Merritt and the Meteors* (1970, RCA SL 101891), *Stray Cats* (1971, RCA SL 101906), *A Little Easier* (1975, Arista ARTY 108), *Out of the Blue* (1976, Arista ARTY 134), *Back Home Live* (1977, Arista ARTY 149), *Keeping in Touch* (1978, Polydor 2383514), *Black Plastic Max* (1980, Polydor 2383558), *17 Trax of Max* (1986, Raven RVLP 24). For discography see *SpencerA.* See also *McGrathA*; *SpencerW.*

CAROLYN MUNTZ

Meryl Tankard Australian Dance Theatre. Founded as the Australian Dance Theatre in 1965 by Elizabeth Cameron Dalman. One of the first full-time professional modern dance companies in Australia, since Dalman's retirement in 1975 the Adelaide-based troupe has had a number of artistic directors, namely Jonathan Taylor (1977–85), Anthony Steel (acting artistic director 1986), Leigh Warren (1987–92), and Meryl Tankard (since 1993). Each of them in their own way maintained Dalman's original aim of experimentation and innovation in dance-theatre. To this end a number of composers have been commissioned to write scores for the troupe, including Peter Crosbie, Blair Greenberg, Sarah ★de Jong, Nicholas Lyon, George Mitchell and Carl ★Vine.

FURTHER REFERENCE

Edward H. Pask, *Ballet in Australia* (Melbourne: OUP, 1982).

JOEL CROTTY

Metamorphosis. Opera in two acts by Brian ★Howard (1983), libretto by Steven Berkoff and Howard after Franz Kafka. First performed by the Victoria State Opera at St Martin's Theatre on 1 October 1983.

Metropolitan Opera Auditions. Scholarship awarded annually (from 1963) after a national competition for singers under 33 resident in Australia for at least six months. Administered by the Opera Foundation Australia, Sydney, the winners receive travel and accommodation to work with staff of the Metropolitan Opera, New York, and compete in the US national finals of the Metropolitan Opera Stage. Previous winners have included

Donald *Shanks, Glenys *Fowles, John *Pringle, Jennifer *McGregor, and Deborah *Riedel. The prize is currently valued at $25 000.

Mewton-Wood, Noel (*b* Melbourne, 20 Nov. 1922; *d* London, 5 Dec. 1953), pianist. He studied with Waldemar Seidel at the University of Melbourne Conservatorium 1931–36, Harold Craxton at Royal Academy of Music, London, 1937, and Artur Schnabel in Italy 1938. He played Beethoven's Concerto No. 3 at his London debut with the London Philharmonic Orchestra under Sir Thomas Beecham. Highly regarded for his performances of Weber and of contemporary works, he premiered Britten's Piano Concerto, was Hindemith's preferred interpreter of *Ludus Tonalis,* and was the dedicatee of piano sonatas by Bliss and Anthony Hopkins. He was also a composer, notably of music for the film *Tawny Pippit* (1944).

FURTHER REFERENCE
Recordings include works by Weber, Schumann (Decca); Chopin, Bliss, Tchaikovsky (Nixa). See also *GlennonA*; Corliss Gustavson, Pianists of Australia, MMus, Univ. Queensland, 1977, 178–82.   LYLE CHAN

Michel, Philip (*b* 8 Mar. 1941), clarinettist. Born into a musical family, he began learning the saxophone then changed to clarinet, and after studies at the University of Melbourne Conservatorium joined the Adelaide Symphony Orchestra and won the ABC Instrumental and Vocal Competition in 1963. He became principal clarinet in the Melbourne Symphony Orchestra in 1964 and studied with Jost Michaels at Detmold, West Germany, on a Churchill Fellowship in 1967. He toured the UK and the USA as a recitalist in 1977 and toured Australia as a concerto soloist for the ABC in 1985, as well as extensively for Musica Viva. A profoundly musical player and a highly sympathetic chamber musician, he teaches at the Victorian College of the Arts and the University of Melbourne.

Midnight Oil. Rock band formed (1975) in Sydney, originally comprised of Peter Garrett (vocals), Robert Hirst (drums), Andrew James (bass), James Moginie (guitar, keyboards) and Martin Rotsey (guitar). The group originated when Hirst, Moginie and Rotsey formed a trio named Farm. Soon after they added Garrett and James and became known as Midnight Oil. From the outset the group refused to conform to the regular machinations of the music industry, going as far as organising their own tours, setting up an independent label, Powderworks, and refusing to appear on television's *Countdown*. As such, the group's profile was initially that of alternative rock, but when their second album *Head Injuries* (1979) achieved gold, it showed that the band also had mainstream marketability. In 1980 James was replaced on bass by Peter Gifford, and their 1982 album *10, 9, 8, 7, 6, 5, 4, 3, 2, 1* upheld their earlier promise, staying in the national charts

for over two years, displaying their approach to rock with persistent but understated guitar riffs, driving bass and rhythm, and Garrett's forceful interpretations of politically and socially laden lyrics evidenced in songs such as *US Forces* and *Short Memory*. Their concerts at this time made wider audiences aware of their potency as a live act, symbolised by the energy of Garrett, instantly recognisable with his shaven head.

Garrett, who holds a law degree, made an unsuccessful bid for the Senate of the Australian Parliament in 1984 as a candidate for the Nuclear Disarmament Party. Midnight Oil's next two albums, *Red Sails in The Sunset* (1984) and *Diesel and Dust* (1987), reflected the group's concerns with nuclear disarmament and Aboriginal land rights. The latter album gave the group its first significant international success, when it charted in the Top 20 in both the USA and the UK. It was three years before they released another album, during which time Dwayne 'Bones' Hillman replaced Gifford on bass. *Blue Sky Mining* (1990) was another high-profile success, with environmental issues prominent in its content. In the same year the group performed outside the offices of Exxon in New York, a protest over the Exxon Valdez oil spill in Alaska. The video of the performance, *Black Rain Falls,* was used to raise money for Greenpeace. For many years the group directed proceeds from some of their performances and recordings to projects of particular interest, including homeless children, Aboriginal communities, nuclear disarmament and environmental groups.

Passionately dedicated to a mixture of music and politics, Midnight Oil became the dominant Australian group of the 1980s, enjoying chart success at home and abroad. The release of *Earth and Sun and Moon* (1993), while not as commercially successful as previous albums, nevertheless showed the group's continuing commitment to issues affecting Australians in the 1990s.

FURTHER REFERENCE
Recordings include *Head Injuries* (1979, Powderworks, distributed by Sony 450903 2); *Place Without A Postcard* (1981, CBS SBP 237704); *10, 9, 8, 7, 6, 5, 4, 3, 2, 1* (1982, CBS SBP 237868); *Red Sails in the Sunset* (1984, CBS SBP 238027) *Diesel and Dust* (1987, CBS 460005); *Blue Sky Mining* (1990, CBS 465653 2); *Earth and Sun and Moon* (1993, Columbia 473605 2).
                                                          WILLIAM VAN PINXTEREN

Migrant Music in Australia
1. Performance Contexts. 2. Performers. 3. Functions.
4. Migrant Arts and Public Policy. 5. Dissemination. 6. Education and Research.

Australia's population is one of great and relatively tension-free cultural and—by extension musical—diversity. Excluding Aboriginal languages, there are over 100 languages other than English in use in Australian households, and about 15 per cent of the total population speaks a language other than English at home.

Although Baluchistani, Sind, Chinese, German, Italian and Kanak peoples had resettled in Australia before World War II as a result of various economic and political forces, the first major influx of immigrants occurred immediately after World War II and consisted mainly of people from western, central and southern Europe. After 1975 the profile of immigrants changed to include a significant number of people born in East Asia.

According to country of birthplace and language spoken at home, Australia's population (1991) includes, from *Melanesia:* Papua New Guinea 23 700; *Polynesia:* Fiji 30 500; Western Samoa 5700; Tonga 6100; *Southern Europe:* Cyprus 22 200; Greece 136 300; Italy 254 700; Portugal 18 000; Spain 14 700; the former Yugoslavia 161 000; *Eastern Europe:* Czechoslovakia 17 800; Hungary 27 100; Poland 69 000; Romania 11 300; *The Middle East:* Iran 13 000; Lebanon 69 000; Syria 5300; Turkey 27 900; Egypt 33 200; *South-East Asia:* Cambodia 17 700; Indonesia 33 300; Laos 9700; Malaysia 72 600; the Philippines 73 700; Singapore 24 600; Thailand 14 000; Vietnam 122 300; *North-East Asia:* China 78 900; Japan 26 000; Republic of Korea 21 000; Taiwan 13 000; *Southern Asia:* India 61 600; Sri Lanka 37 300; *Central America:* El Salvador 8700; and *South America:* Argentina 10 700; Chile 24 200; Uruguay 9700. These figures show groups of people from a common ethnic background of a size large enough to form viable communities and maintain traditional languages and cultures, and are indicative of Australia's place in the many diasporas which characterise population movement in the late 20th century.

1. Performance Contexts. The performance of migrant music in Australia ranges from the private to the very public. Private performances usually occur within and for the community in social situations such as weddings or seasonal celebrations, for religious purposes, in private homes for entertainment or instruction, in community-based Saturday morning cultural maintenance schools, at sporting clubs and restaurants, and at fund-raising events. The *Greek, *Vietnamese and *Hmong communities provide examples of this sort of musical activity. These events are not advertised in the mainstream press, are not part of the press review system, and usually do not take place in the major concert venues of any city. They are sponsored, presented and promoted from within the community itself. An example of 'private' performance is the celebration of the Laotian-Hmong New Year, which usually takes place in a local town hall or community centre and includes speeches in Laotian, Hmong and English, a fashion parade of traditional dress, presentations of Laotian traditional dancing by young girls to music on cassette, a performance by a player of the Hmong multiple reed pipe, the *qeej* or *khaen* followed by a Hmong pop band, such as the Boomerang Band, a group of young self-taught Hmong musicians performing Laotian popular Western-style music with a repertoire consisting mainly of love songs. The extent to which this endemic music-making changes in response to the cultural, physical, psychological and even legal ecology of the Australian environment is a subject much in need of greater scholarly attention than it has received so far (see §6).

Public performances, on the other hand, are usually sponsored, promoted and organised by people from outside the communities themselves, including enthusiastic individuals, entrepreneurial organisations and local and city councils. Such presentations are frequently referred to as 'multicultural', occasionally receive financial support from local, state or federal funding bodies, and often take place with the performers on a stage. This can have implications for the relationship between the performers and the audience, especially with regard to the extent of audience participation and the musicians' response. Such events include, first, showcase productions, such as the former Shell Folkloric in which the glamorous presentation of exotic sound, colour and movement by musicians and dancers from a variety of backgrounds who have resettled in Australia took precedence over considerations of the original context and performance processes of the product.

Second, suburban street festivals featuring multicultural performances are now common in the main cities of Australia where local councils and broadly (ethnically) based community organisations are proud to celebrate the multicultural nature of their constituents. An annual example of this is the celebration of the Chinese and Vietnamese New Year each February; in 1995 an estimated 150 000 people attended this event in Melbourne. In 1996 these festivities in the inner city suburb of Richmond in Melbourne included performances by the Yorta Yorta Koori Dancers, Drums of Polynesia, the University of Melbourne Community Gamelan Group with a Javanese puppet play, and the Hoa Tinh Thuong Vietnamese Opera Company, as well as the Chinese Lion Dance procession and a Vietnamese karaoke competition.

Third, multicultural festivals, workshops, concerts, World Music Cafes and more recently masterclasses are also now quite common in the larger cities (see §5). These events are usually advertised in the mainstream press and nowadays might attract a feature article in the arts pages; sometimes they receive reviews as well as coverage from the electronic media. Their audiences frequently consist of people not from the ethnic communities represented by the musicians themselves.

A program for the Boite's World Music Cafe in Melbourne (September 1995) is a representative sample of the diversity of styles and combinations of genres in migrant and other forms of music making currently taking place in the public domain in Australia. On the first night, the World Music Cafe presented Alfie Massoud and Conga Pa Gozar, playing 'exciting rhythms from Africa, Latin America and the Middle East—cha cha cha, rumba, samba, juju and more'. Subsequent evenings saw 'Africa Beat—Siyo and Aba Baku play the Oromo rhythms of East Africa'; Klezmer Music and Tales, with 'Klezmania—an evening of European Jewish music and songs'; Andean Flutes with Almo y Canto—Rosamel and Orietta Burgos playing *zampona, quena* and *charango*; a 'Koori Kafe'; a night of Middle Eastern Percussion with Ta' esh Fa' esh; a Singers' Night with the Lithuanian Folk Ensemble and contemporary English songwriter Jay Turner; an evening of the music of China with the Australian Chinese Music Ensemble; and finally, a concert titled 'People of the Book—Music of three Spanish cultures' and described as 'instrumental music and songs from Jewish, Muslim and Christian cultures of Spain, with Papua New Guinean women'.

Lastly, the cycles of religious calendars can bring together people either from many ethnic backgrounds—for example, ceremonies held at Buddhist temples such as the Lindh Son Buddhist Congregation in Reservoir, Victoria, or the major Buddhist temple at Wollongong, NSW—or people from ethnically specific religious backgrounds such as the Sikh temple near Coffs Harbour, NSW, and the Tibetan Buddhist Society at Yuroke, Victoria. In Melbourne alone there are about 26 Greek Orthodox and four Russian Orthodox congregations as well as four synagogues and eight Islamic centres.

2. Performers. Migrant communities are not necessarily homogeneous musical entities (see Ryan 1988); in fact proximity to a migrant community frequently reveals a cultural fragmentation which belies the bird's eye view of a unified and shared cultural heritage. Broad social categories including age and generational position, class and gender yield a variety of forms of music-making and musical preferences not only within sections of migrant communities but also among individual members of them. A bottom-up and individual-oriented view of music-making rather than an all-embracing top-down critical perspective is now increasingly used in discussions of the multitudinous forms of urban musics, particularly in the West. A leader in this discourse is Charles Keil, whose comments on ethnic music in the United States can reasonably be extrapolated to describe the Australian musical context:

> I suspect that just about every person you or I meet in the street is less mono-ethnic and much more complicated musically, historically, culturally than we think. Who has four grandparents from one tribe any more? Who listens to fewer than a dozen styles of music? (Keil 1994: 176).

The diversity of musical practices in any one community may include, for example, performers of different regional or dialect styles, or of (indigenously classified) folk, classical or popular music of their countries of origin; performers who have brought with them to Australia knowledge of repertoire and instrumental and vocal traditions acquired in their country of origin; performers who are self-taught in Australia by listening to and copying from recordings from the country of origin; performers trained in Western classical music in Western-style conservatoriums in their country of origin; performers from different schools of musical training from the same musical heritage, particularly in the classical traditions of Asia; performers of Western-style popular music using a combination of non-Western instrumental traditions and languages; and performers interested in experimenting with combinations of styles of music from different heritages.

Examples of the diversity of musical and socio-economic circumstances of some musicians and groups which a bird's eye view would label as migrant but which on closer inspection have in common only the fact that they are making music other than Western classical music include, first, some musicians who are now able to support themselves through teaching and performing, for example the Japanese koto player Satsuki *Odamura, the Javanese musician, dancer and puppeteer *Poedijono and the Indian sarod player Ashok *Roy. Second, in some communities young people from the third, fourth or later generations of immigrants have taught themselves styles of music from their forebears' cultural heritage in revivalist movements. Examples include the Greek *rebetika* ensemble Apodimia Compania, the Chilean ensemble Haravicu and the Chao Feng Chinese Orchestra. Third, there is a growing number of musicians who have undertaken musical training in styles and genres other than that of their heritage by birth and education. These musicians are recognised as skilled practitioners of these other styles and include Riley *Lee (Japanese bamboo flute); Chris Lesser (Ghanaian drum ensembles); Linsey *Pollak (Macedonian bagpipes); Alan *Posselt (Indian sitar) and Adrian McNeil (Indian sarod), to name but a few.

Fourth, many secondary and tertiary educational institutions provide tuition in Indonesian music (in particular, Javanese) to non-Indonesian students. The popularity of Indonesian music as a pedagogical tool in Australian educational settings does not reflect either a large expatriate Indonesian community in Australia or the geographical proximity of the two countries. Rather, it is probably a product of the nature of Javanese *gamelan* or orchestra: the instruments are of fixed pitch and provide an intensely communal or group form of music-making which can quickly elicit an elementary musical product from students with no previous training in any sort of music. In this situation, a musical technology and structure have migrated alone and separate from their human exponents, leaving at home in Java the collective memory of the relevance of this music both to musicians and audiences in its original context.

Fifth, multicultural ensembles which use ethnic musical ideas in the creation of new sounds, such as a pentatonic scale or additive rhythms, or ethnic instruments such as the Andean pipes, the didjeridu or the Indian tabla, flourished during the 1980s. This phenomenon has been seen to be 'largely the result of the federal government's promotion of multiculturalism as an official state ideology' (Dunbar 1990). Such ensembles include *Sirocco, *Southern Crossings and Blindman's Holiday. Finally, in the 1990s ensembles appeared which combine musicians from different musical heritages, for example, the group Slivanje, whose 1995 CD *Where Waters Meet* presents the musicians Pollak, Hernan Flores, Blair Greenberg, Dorinda Hafner, Odamura and Roy in 'creating new Australian music based on the traditions each of the musicians brings into the group, ranging from Indian, Japanese and Latin American to African and Macedonian folk and classical traditions … The resulting sound is a unique cross-cultural style.'

With musicians who visit Australia in order to perform music other than Western classical or popular genres, there is once again a differentiation in terms of performance venue, publicity, press review and audience constitution between those brought by the communities themselves and those who are brought by large entrepreneurs. For example major stars of the Vietnamese popular music industry visit Australia frequently. Their presence goes almost unnoticed beyond the Vietnamese community itself. They perform to huge crowds in school assembly halls or large public parks. On the other hand, ★Chinese Opera troupes, ★Irish Folk groups, South American groups and stars of the ★Indian classical music world circuit are presented quite regularly to predominantly Anglo-Australian audiences at the major Western classical music concert venues with accompanying publicity in the mainstream press and other media.

In this category too are the performers brought from overseas for the major arts festivals held in the main capital cities. The Adelaide Festival, for example, presented a free outdoor series titled 'The Singing Map' for 16 nights in March 1996 with singers from Tibet, West Bengal, Sardinia, Tuva, Cameroon, Mongolia and North India, only one of whom (Tibetan-born Yungchen Lhamo) is an Australian resident. Such displays of world music as they are often called presumably have some impact on Australian musical sensibilities. The showcasing of visiting musicians, going hand in hand as it does with the rapidly growing market for recordings of world music, is regarded here as a form of migrant music, although in these instances it is the musical sounds themselves rather than the transient appearance of the people who make them that are transplanted to countries beyond their origin and context. Perhaps a more educative function is realised by bringing non-Western musicians to Australia to conduct masterclasses. In 1996 for example, the Festival of Perth brought among others the Cuban *sonero* band *Sierra Maestra* to Western Australia for a masterclass in Cuban rhythms and the Cameroon-born composer and guitarist Francis Bebey for a masterclass in the African idiophone *mbira*, the African flute *ndewoo* and guitar.

3. Functions of Migrant Music.

For most people migration to Australia and the adoption of Australian citizenship does not mean the rejection or abandonment of musical practices which they have brought with them either as participant or as audience. However, very many factors may contribute to the extent to which those practices are maintained, including the reasons for migration, the nature of the journey itself (including, for many Indo-Chinese people, years spent in a state of pseudo-migration in refugee camps) and the extent of feelings of belonging to the new country as opposed to feelings of loss and homesickness.

People in the first generation of resettlement may undergo a loss of musical energy (a term used by Bruno Nettl, 1978:129–30) when they face the difficulties of finding housing and employment and learning a new language and new cultural norms; on the other hand they may experience a renewed and vigorous interest in their cultural heritage when confronting the new and the unknown. The degree of language retention and the acceptance or otherwise of intermarriage in second and later generations also contribute to levels of cultural maintenance or dispersal. It may be presumed that people make music in culturally specific forms for a reason.

Far more research is needed to tell the emic or insider story of the functions of music in migrant life, but a very useful and interesting account of the experiences of six resettled musicians in their own words can be found in Russell (1986). The Australia Council (1987) also provides an interesting record of interviews with a number of migrant musicians. Peter Parkhill's account of song texts and musical structures is still one of the most comprehensive and scholarly published contributions to the study of migrant music in Australia. It is worth quoting at some length from his introductory remarks:

> it would be difficult to imagine someone attempting to give an accurate account of traditional music in Australia without referring to the rich and diverse forms which have come to this country through post-war migration. It is clear also that in some respects these musical traditions behave in much the same way as they have always done: they continue to serve certain functions within the community and they change according to a changing environment. The process of change is the life-blood of a tradition, for without it the musical and poetic styles, the dances, instruments and songs would lose their relevance to people's lives, and, for those who live in a new country, forfeit their strong symbolic value. (Parkhill 1983:126)

An example of song text providing insight into the functions of migrant music can be found in this translation of a Greek song, *Redfern*, by Taso Nerandzis:

> As I pass through Redfern station
> Every morning off to work,
> I start cursing the Australian skies
> My heart feels a deadly murmur
> When I see my fellow workers
> All waiting in a line
> With a tired and bored expression.
>
> The Yugoslavs, the Greeks
> the Turks, the English

the Lebanese and Italians
Await the speeding train
To cart them quickly off to work.

Redfern Redfern
Until when will they speed past
Redfern Redfern
Until when will they age
Seeking better days
Until when?

(The Boite, *The Music of Migration, c.*1979)

When music is played in social settings outside the public domain for entertainment it is no more than one factor contributing to feelings of a shared experience of migration and a shared aesthetic, along with verbal and body language, food and norms of social behaviour. It can serve as an icon and an affirmation of identity, whether it be ethnic, religious or political. In small communities in particular, music can signal a pan-ethnic identity which transcends traditional boundaries such as those of clan, tribe, dialect or region. For the musicians themselves, the creative or re-creative impulse can fulfil important psychological and social roles at both personal and community levels. Some musicians may be concerned with the preservation and maintenance of musical repertoires for posterity, especially when they are needed for moments of crisis in the community, such as death (for the Hmong). In some cases preservation of a tradition may lead to a time-warp in traditions, where music being performed in Australia is 30 or more years out of date when compared to contemporary musical practices in the country of origin (for the Lithuanians; see *Eastern European Music*). Finally, music-making is rarely regarded as an opportunity for financial reward, nor does it necessarily enhance the personal prestige or reputation of the musician.

4. Migrant Arts and Public Policy.

Strict assimilationist policies followed the postwar intake of immigrants from Europe. In these years ethnic music-making either remained hidden from the public domain in community-based activities, or became obsolete. It was not officially encouraged. From the mid-1960s ethnic community organisations became more active, vocal and public, with a corresponding increase in the visibility of ethnic cultural activities within the mainstream community. At this time too the Saturday morning cultural maintenance schools started, and continue to operate to this day in the transmission of language, music, dance and other culturally specific skills. In the early 1970s the first notions of multiculturalism appeared and ethnic radio stations commenced broadcasting; the ethnic press also became more visible. A government policy of cultural pluralism rather than cultural assimilation was first articulated in the Galbally Report (*Migrant Services and Programs,* 1978). This report defined four broad principles, the second of which is relevant to this discussion. It stated that 'every person

should be able to maintain their culture without prejudice or disadvantage and should be encouraged to understand and embrace other cultures'.

Funding specifically directed at the ethnic arts by the Federal Government through the Australia Council had already begun at a very minimal level. For example, $88 000 was given to the ethnic arts throughout Australia by the Australia Council in 1975–76. The council has attempted to address issues concerning multicultural art-forms through its various agencies, including the Community Arts Board (established 1977) and then the Multicultural Advisory Committee (subsumed into the Community Cultural Development Unit, 1987). The history of the often difficult relationship between the boards of the Australia Council, its arts and funding policies, and multicultural art-forms is described clearly in that organisation's own publication (Australia Council 1992). The council's terminology for describing migrant art-forms reflects the changes in its arts policy thinking. At first migrant art-forms were described by the council as 'ethnic arts'; later they were 'multicultural arts'; nowadays the expression used is 'arts for a multicultural Australia'.

Not surprisingly, there has been and still is much dissatisfaction among the migrant communities and those who work with them about the council's overall levels of funding for migrant art-forms, the criteria for assessing applications, and the membership of assessing panels. Not the least of the problems is navigating through the application forms: some organisations, such as Multicultural Arts Victoria, regard the provision of assistance in filling out these forms as one of their most important tasks. Further difficulties in applying for assistance arise where the project is multi-art-form and requires assessment from more than one panel. The council acknowledges that there is a tension between its policies of community access and equity on the one hand and the promotion of a standard of excellence and professionalism in the arts on the other. As it says, 'the "ethnic" arts communities were challenging the notion of a universal aesthetic and demanding a renegotiation of what constitutes "Australian" art, "ethnic" art or indeed the very use of the designation "ethnic"' (Australia Council 1992:3).

The most recent statement of federal cultural policy (*Creative Nation* 1994) emphasises the perceived role of federal policy in shaping Australian culture, which it refers to as 'now an exotic hybrid'. This has been achieved through 'enlightened government support for the arts [and] an equally enlightened migration policy', among other factors. Further, it is claimed that 'in fact the meeting of imported and home-grown cultures has massively enriched us. Relatively few manifestations of the old xenophobia and insecurity remain. Multicultural Australia—a society which is both diverse and tolerant of diversity, which actively encourages diversity—is one of our great national achievements' (p. 6). A more detailed and rather less optimistic perspective of the history of immigration and the reception of notions of cultural diversity in Australia can be found in Jamrozik et al. (1995), while multiculturalism, the arts and arts policy are discussed at length in Gunew and Rizvi (1994).

5. Dissemination. Since the late 1970s organisations devoted to the promotion of migrant music have emerged in most capital cities in Australia. Most receive financial assistance from State and Federal Governments. In Melbourne, the Boite (founded 1979) continues to play a pro-active role in presenting migrant and other music to the mainstream community. In its earliest days the Boite perceived its role as one of encouraging the survival and development of oral tradition by organising performances and exhibitions, co-ordinating research activities and resources for schools and the community, presenting workshops and encouraging and supporting artists. The organisation found that it could not sustain its educational role financially. Nowadays it presents a weekly World Music Cafe, and annual major events: the A Cappella Festival, the Big Beat Percussion Festival, the Singers' and Children's Festival and the World Music and Dance Festival. Also in Melbourne, the Footscray Community Arts Centre and the annual Brunswick Music Festival are dedicated to presenting migrant music to a wide public.

Similarly, the Multicultural Arts Centre of Western Australia (MACWA, established 1983 by Pollak) and the Brisbane Ethnic Music and Arts Centre (BEMAC, established 1986) present a weekly Cafe Folklorico as well as festivals, workshops and classes, and a regular world music program on local radio stations, and publish newsletters concerned with local and visiting multicultural arts forms and artists. They also produce occasional publications and recordings. The early days of MACWA are described by the Australia Council (1987). Migrant musical forms are also disseminated to the wider public at major festivals such as Womad and the Adelaide Festival, the Warana Festival in Brisbane and the Brisbane Biennial, and the now defunct Piccolo Spoleto (1986–90) in Melbourne. ABC radio also presents *Music Deli,* a weekly two–hour program which usually includes music by non–Anglo–Australians. It first went to air in July 1986 and retains one of its original producers and presenters, Paul Petran. Finally, some groups of musicians have organised their own mechanisms for the promotion and dissemination of their music, for example the Chao Feng Chinese Music Ensemble in Melbourne and the Academy of Indian Music, Australia.

6. Education and Research. The musical manifestations of Australia's much acclaimed cultural diversity are not well represented in the music curricula of the country's primary, secondary and tertiary educational institutions. Apart from token efforts to include multicultural or non-Western music in some school music activities and curricula such as the organisation of an International Day or reference to publications such as Fong (1994), the music curriculum remains fundamentally committed to the enculturation of all young Australians into the Western musical system of diatonic tunings, functional harmony and divisive rhythm in both classical and popular forms. This situation is entrenched by the absence of preparation in musics outside the Western tradition in most primary and secondary music teacher-training courses and the under-utilisation in educational situations of skilled practitioners of other musical traditions (who may lack a recognised teaching qualification). Almost without exception across the country, access to higher education in the practice of music is restricted to students who are already proficient in Western classical music, regardless of their ethnicity.

Musicological and other scholarly research into migrant music in Australia is still in its infancy, although there are a number of unpublished dissertations by honours and postgraduate students, mainly from Monash University and the University of Adelaide. The published corpus includes the case studies by Barwick of ★Italian music (1987, 1991); Falk of the music of the Hmong (1993, 1994a,b and i.p.); Marett of Turkish music (1987) and Parkhill of Cretan and Lebanese music (1983). The academic discourses about the oral transmission of music, notions of authenticity in oral traditions, and the nature of culture contact and musical change do not seem yet to impinge on any of the popular perceptions or labellings of migrant music. See, for example, *Music-cultures in contact. Convergences and collisions,* edited by Margaret Kartomi and Stephen Blum (1994). As Parkhill has observed, a true account of music in Australia cannot ignore the artistically rich and diverse but still socially and economically marginal forms of music made by people who have resettled in Australia from all over the world. Deeper scholarly understanding of these musics is urgently needed. See also *African Music; Eastern European Music; Folk Music; Irish Music; Italian Music; Jewish Music; Scottish Folk Music; Vietnamese Music; World Music.*

FURTHER REFERENCE

Discography

From the ABC: *Music Deli in the can.* CD, 16 ensembles (1992, ABC/Phonogram).

From The Boite: *Ashok Roy—Sarod. Classical music of North India.* Cassette, (1983, The Boite); *Highly Strung. Traditional stringed instruments of South America, Europe and the Middle East.* Cassette, 12 musicians (1984, The Boite); *Australian A Cappella.* 24 a cappella ensembles (1994, Sandstock SSM 050).

From Brisbane Ethnic Music and Arts Centre: *Echoes under the bridge. New world music from BEMAC,* 11 ensembles (1994, BEMAC 001); *Where waters meet,* Slivanje (1995, BEMAC 002); *Samba Down Under,* Jaider de Oliveira (1995, BEMAC).

From Brunswick Recordings: *The music of migration,* 7 ensembles (1986, BR01); *Rebetika,* Apodimi Compania (1987, BR03); *Papalote … Live in Sydney* (1987, BR07); *Homeland,* Apodimi Compania (1990, BR10); *Melisma,* Apodimi Compania (1992, BR17).

From Klezmania Records: *Oystralia,* Klezmania (1995, Ozklez 001).

From Larrikin Records: *Music Deli—off the air,* 15 ensembles (1988, LRF 227); *Ashok Roy: Master of the Sarod* (1994, LRF 333).

From Move Records: *Quivering String: Back To Back Zithers,* Kari, Le Thi Kim, Le Tuan Hung, Ros Bandt (1992, MD 3141); *Musical Transfiguration: A Journey Across Vietnamese Soundscapes,* Le Tuan Hung and Le Thi Kim (1993, MD3128).

From Tall Poppies: *The Eagle And The Ocean,* Riley Lee and Geoff Ween-Vermazen (1992, TP014); *Yearning For The Bell (vol. 1)—Breath-Sight,* Riley Lee (1992, TP015); *The Martenitsa choir,* Bulgarian Choir (1993, TP026); *Like a bird,* Satsuki Odamura with Ian Cleworth, Riley Lee, Cleis Pearce and Kazue Sawai (1992, TP044); *On our way,* The Transylvaniacs (1994, TP063).

From Tradition Australia: *Cretan traditional music in Australia,* Kostas and George Tsourdalakis; booklet in English (40 pp.) by Peter Parkhill (1984, TAR 010).

Bibliography

Australia Council, *Multiculturalism and the Arts* (Sydney: Australia Council, 1986).

——, *Hidden Music, Silent Voices: The Ethnic Music Centre of Western Australia* (Sydney: Australia Council, 1987).

——, *Profiles of Musicians and Music Making in Adelaide, Brisbane, Melbourne, Sydney* (Sydney: Australia Council, 1987).

——, *Arts for a Multicultural Australia 1973–1991: An Account of Australia Council Policies* (Sydney: Australia Council, 1992).

——, *Policy on Arts for a Multicultural Australia* (Sydney: Australia Council, 1993).

Barwick, Linda, 'Italian traditional music in Adelaide', *The Possum Stirs*. Proceedings of the 2nd National Folklore Conference (Sydney: Australian Folk Trust and the Centre for Leisure and Tourism Studies, Kuring-Gai CAE, 1987), 377–89.

——, 'Same tunes, different voices', *MA* 14 (1991), 47–85.

Creative Nation: Commonwealth Cultural Policy October 1994 (Canberra: AGPS, 1994).

The Boite, *Music of Migration* (Melbourne: The Boite, n.d.).

——, *Three Leaflets on Greek Music* (Melbourne: The Boite, n.d.).

——, *Musical Instruments of the Middle East* (Melbourne: The Boite, n.d.).

——, *Music of South America* (Melbourne: The Boite, n.d.).

——, *Highly Strung.* With cassette (Melbourne The Boite, n.d.).

——, *China: A Social History in Music and Song* (Melbourne: The Boite, 1984).

——, *Hindustani Classical Music of North India* (Melbourne: The Boite, 1984).

——, *Latin American Music: An Introduction to the Music of Brazil, Cuba and the Andes* (Melbourne: The Boite, 1984).

Dunbar, Mark. 'All take, take, take…': Migrant Musicians, The Australia Council, Multiculturalism and Music-Making in Australia, MA, Monash Univ., 1990.

Falk, Catherine, 'The Hmong in Melbourne', *Tirra Lirra* 4/2 (1993), 3–6, 43.

——, 'The Hmong: Music and Ritual', *Tirra Lirra* 4/3 (1994a), 9–13.

——, 'Roots and crowns. The Hmong Funeral Ceremony: From Laos to Australia', *Tirra Lirra* 4/4 (1994b), 19–24.

——, 'Meeting the Ancestors', in *Aflame with Music* (Faculty of Music, Univ. of Melbourne. In press).

——, 'The Music of the Hmong in Australia', *Garland Encyclopedia of World Music* (In press).

Fong, Francis, ed., *World Music in Australia* (Sydney: Australian Music Centre, 1994 [with accompanying CD]).

Gunew, Sneja, and Fazal Rizvi, eds, *Culture, Difference and the Arts* (Sydney: Allen & Unwin, 1994).

Holst, Gail, *A Survey of the Funding of 'Ethnic Arts' in Australia* (Sydney: Community Arts Program, Australia Council, 1976).

Jamrozik, Adam, Cathy Boland and Robert Urquhart, *Social Change and Cultural Transformation in Australia* (Cambridge: CUP, 1995).

Kartomi, Margaret, and Stephen Blum, eds, *Music-Cultures in Contact: Convergences and Collisions* (Sydney: Currency Press, 1994).

Keil, Charles, '"Ethnic" Music Traditions in the USA (Black Music; Country Music; Others; All)', *Popular Music* 13/2 (1994), 175–8.

Marett, Allan, 'Turkish Folk Music in Sydney: A Preliminary Investigation', *MMA* 12 (1987), 80–9.

Nettl, Bruno, 'Some Aspects of the Theory of World Music in the Twentieth Century: Questions, Problems and Concepts', *Ethnomusicology* 22 (1978), 123–36.

Parkhill, Peter, 'Two Folk Epics from Melbourne', *Meanjin* 42/1 (1983), 120–39.

Migrant Services and Programs: Review of Post-Arrival Programs and Services for Migrants (Canberra: AGPS, 1978).

Ryan, Michael, 'Australian Ethnic Music: A Reflection of Divergence', *MA* 11–12 (1988/89), 14–23.

Russell, Heather, *Investigating the Needs and Aspirations of Ethnic Musicians in Melbourne.* Working paper 8, Community Arts Resource Centre, Victorian Ministry for the Arts, 1986.

CATHERINE FALK

Mildura, pop. (1991) 23 176. City on the Murray River in the northern plains of Victoria. A sheeprun from the 1840s, it was settled by two Californians contracted to develop an irrigation system in 1886, and is now a fruit-processing and packing centre for the region.

With its great distance from the capital cities, it has developed a largely self-contained musical life. The Langtree Avenue Hall (opened 1889) was used as a concert hall and theatre from the 1890s; today the Mildura Arts Centre offers a fully equipped theatre for major events. The first of several brass bands was formed in 1890; they were merged into the Mildura District Brass Band in 1909, playing in the Desailly Memorial Band Rotunda, near the shire hall, from 1914. The band still thrives, having had two long-serving bandmasters, Andrew Steedman (1953–65) with whom it won the Australian championships in 1957, and Len Krause (since 1966).

The Mildura Choral Society performed such works as Coleridge Taylor's *The Tale of Old Japan* with a chorus of 45 and orchestra of 15 in 1914, and the Mildura Musical Society had an 80-voice choir which gave its first concert in 1928; today there is a Red Cliffs Musical Society, and major choral works are regularly heard. A Mildura Eisteddfod was founded in 1936 by the Australian Natives Association as a centre for the Wimmera; the present

Eisteddfod Society was formed in 1979 and holds its event each June, attracting about 3000 competitors over nearly two weeks. The Mildura Concert Orchestra was founded in 1943, becoming the Mildura Orchestral Society in 1946 with 450 subscribers; it presented three concerts each year with celebrity visiting artists, augmented by students from the University Conservatorium, Melbourne, which had established a branch in Mildura.

A Mildura Arts Festival commenced in March 1995, presenting major visiting artists at the Mildura Arts Centre. The Mildura Country Music Festival, held each September since 1986, is the third largest in Australia, and the Jazz and Wine Festival organised each November since 1979 by the River City Jazz Club attracts major jazz artists.

Miller, Bill (William Henry) (*b* Melbourne, 22 Feb. 1914), jazz writer, broadcaster. He began playing washboard in 1947, then formed the Portsea Trio, which played in the early 1950s. Subsequently he played informally and gave occasional concerts; his main significance is as a focal point for jazz during the early postwar years. He read law at Oxford University, returning in 1938 with a record collection that became a significant resource for the emergent Melbourne traditional jazz movement, to which his broadcasts on 3UZ also contributed. Founding editor of the influential specialist jazz journals *Jazz Notes* and *Australian Jazz Quarterly*, he founded Ampersand Records, which documented important early bands of the traditionalist revival.

FURTHER REFERENCE
Recordings include *The McIntyre-Hounslow Trio* (1948, Ampersand 21); *Lazy Ade's Late Hour Boys* (1970, Swaggie S-1273). See also *BissetB*; *OxfordJ*; *Jazz Notes, Australian Jazz Quarterly.*
BRUCE JOHNSON

Miller, Dick (*b* Melbourne, 4 Dec. 1944), jazz reeds player. He was with the ★Red Onion Jazz Band as reed player from 1965 until its disbandment. Contact with Roland Kirk during the band's Polish tour led him to investigate post-traditional and more experimental styles, especially in association with Bob ★Sedergreen. At ease over a wide range of styles as a musician and composer, since the 1980s he has been active with Peter Gaudion's Blues Express and Chris Ludowyk's Society Syncopators (with whom he has toured extensively nationally and internationally), Onaje, and has performed and recorded for Red Onion reunions.

FURTHER REFERENCE
Recordings include *Big Band Memories*, Red Onion Jazz Band (1967, W & G Records, WG-25-5065); *Straight As A Briefcase*, Onaje (1981, East EAS 082); *Waltz for Stella*, Onaje (1985, Larrikin LRJ 174); *Genre Jumping Jazz*, Allan Browne (1989, Newmarket, DEX CD.206); *Les Copains D'abord*, Chris Ludowyk's Society Syncopators in Noumea (1992, SSCD 920 52CD 024); *Crisis*, Red Onion Jazz Band (1993, Newmarket, NEW1015.2).

See also *OxfordJ*; Adrian Jackson, 'Allan Browne And Richard Miller, Modernists & Traditionalists', *JA* (Winter/Spring 1986), 12–18
BRUCE JOHNSON

Miller, Harry M. (*b* Auckland, NZ, 6 Jan. 1934), show business entrepreneur. Raised in an orphanage after his father died, he worked in NZ on a dairy farm, then as a concert promoter before coming to Australia in 1963. Within a year he had come to prominence as promoter of tours by Judy Garland, then Arthur Rubenstein; he also toured Louis Armstrong, Ella Fitzgerald, Shirley Bassey and the Rolling Stones. He was consultant to the Australian Opera 1967–70, then produced the hit musicals *Hair* (1969), *Jesus Christ Superstar* (1970), *Grease* (1972), and *The Rocky Horror Show* (1973). With a sure sense for his audience's taste, he was frequently the conduit for major imported shows in Australia throughout the 1960s and 70s. His ticket agency Computicket collapsed in 1979 and he was subsequently jailed for 10 months; after this he developed his artist management interests, staging a revival of *Superstar* (1992) and with Melbourne Theatre Company the Broadway success *M. Butterfly* (1993).

FURTHER REFERENCE
His autobiography is *My Story: Harry M. Miller*, with Denis O'Brien (Melbourne: Macmillan, 1983). See also *MonashB*; *Age* 1 Sept. 1990.

Mills, Richard John (*b* Toowoomba, Qld, 14 Nov. 1949), composer, conductor. After studying arts at the University of Queensland and taking his AMusA and LMusA in piano and theory, he studied at the Guildhall School, London, with Edmund Rubbra (composition) and Gilbert Webster (percussion) and worked as a percussionist in London orchestras. He returned to Australia as percussionist with the ABC orchestras, taught at the Northern Rivers College of Advanced Education 1981–83, then the Queensland Conservatorium 1984–87; during this period he appeared as a composer or guest conductor with all the ABC orchestras. He was artist-in-residence with the Australian Ballet 1987–88, then the ABC 1989–94, and his music has been played by the BBC Scottish Symphony Orchestra and City of Birmingham Symphony. He has been artistic director of the Adelaide Chamber Orchestra since 1991 and the WA Opera since 1996.

Since his early jubilant *Overture with Fanfares* (1981) he has written more than 20 works for large orchestra, making particularly eloquent use of wind and percussion. His Trumpet Concerto (1982), *Soundscapes* (1983) for percussion and orchestra, then *Bamaga Diptych* (1986), a work redolent of far north Queensland, reveal a composer of a rich harmonic palette, superb instrumental craft, and energetic rhythmic imagination. *Snugglepot and Cuddlepie* (1987), his ballet for the Australian Ballet, has been widely performed, and his two-act opera *Summer of the Seventeenth Doll* (1996), after the Ray

Lawler play, was commissioned for the Victoria State Opera. He has also produced chamber works and choral settings which are less well known, although no less polished: the Sonata for Brass Quintet (1985) and the String Quartet (1990) for the Australian String Quartet are very fine works. One of the most frequently performed and commissioned of Australia's composers, he has won the Albert Maggs Composition Award and two Sounds Australian awards (1988, 1991).

WORKS (Selective)

Principal publisher: Boosey & Hawkes

Orchestral   *Toccata for Orchestra* (1976), *Music for Strings* (1977), *Fanfares for Percussion and Orchestra* (1980), *Fantasia on a Rondel* (1981), *Overture with Fanfares* (1981), *March—Australia Victorious* (1983), *Castlemaine Antiphons* (1984), *Bamaga Diptych* (1986, rec. OZM 1002), *Sequenzas Concertante* (1986), *Aeolian Caprices* (1988, rec. ABC Classics 432 251), *Fanfare* (1988), *Seaside Dances* (1989, rec. ABC Classics 432 251), *Snugglepot and Cuddlepie Suite* (1989), *Tenebrae* (1992).

Solo Instrument/s and Orchestra   Trumpet Concerto (1982, rec. ABC Classics 426 990), *Soundscapes for Percussion and Orchestra* (1983, rec. ABC Classics 432 251), *Fantastic Pantomimes* (1987, rec. ABC Classics 432 251), Cello Concerto (1990), Flute Concerto (1990), Violin Concerto (1992), Concerto for Violin and Viola (1993).

Chamber   Sonata for Brass Quintet, 2 tpt, hn, 2 trbn (1985, rec. MC 4001), String Quartet No.1 (1990, rec. ABC Classics 442 347), *Four Miniatures*, vn, cl, pf (1992), *Fragments from the Secret Journal of Monostotos*, fl, cl, pf, str qrt (1995), *Oboe Quintet* (1995).

Solo Instrumental   *Epithalamium*, org (1985), *Four Preludes*, ob (1991).

Stage   *Earth Poem/Sky Poem*, music-theatre (1993), *Snugglepot and Cuddlepie*, ballet (1987, rec. ABC Classics 422 933), *Summer of the Seventeenth Doll*, opera (1994–96, 2, Peter Goldsworthy after Ray Lawler).

Vocal and Choral   *Festival Folksongs*, Mez, T, boy S, ch, children's ch, 2 brass ch, orch (1985), *Festival Folksongs—Concert Band*, Mez, T, boy S, ch, children's ch, concert band (1985–88), *Voyages and Visions*, S, Mez, T, B, boy S, ch, 3 brass bands, perc qrt, tape, orch (1987), *Five Meditations*, S, Bar, ch, orch (1988), *Sappho Monologues*, S, orch (1991).

Educational   *Little Suite for Orchestra*, student orch (1983), *Miniatures and Refrains*, student str qrt (1986), *Sonatina for String Quartet*, student str qrt (1986).

FURTHER REFERENCE

Recordings include *Aeolian Caprices, Fantastic Pantomimes,* and *Seaside Dances* and other works, Queensland Symphony Orchestra, cond. W.A. Albert and R. Mills (1991, ABC 432 251); *Overture with Fanfares* (Festival 4238547); *Bamaga Dyptich,* Australian Chamber Orchestra (AMC OZM 1002); Brass Quintet (Larrikin ABWMC 4001); *Snugglepot and Cuddlepie* (ANC 422 9332); Trumpet Concerto (ABC); and Sonata for Brass Quintet (ABC); *Music for Strings* (1977, EMI ASD 430003). See also *CA* (1995–96); Jenny Dawson, *ContemporaryC*; *APRAJ* 6/1 (1988); *APRAJ* 9/1 (1991).

Minogue, Kylie   (*b* Melbourne, 28 May 1968), pop singer. Having acted in television soaps including *Neighbours* since 1979, Minogue's singing career started with her performance of *Locomotion* at a national league football match in Sydney (1987). Recorded by Mushroom, *Locomotion* topped the national charts and attracted the attention of UK songwriting and production team Stock, Aitken and Waterman. A string of UK No. 1 and 2 hits ensued, including *I Should Be So Lucky* (1988), *Hand on Your Heart* (1989) and *Better the Devil You Know* (1990). In 1991 Minogue forsook her 'girl-next-door' soapie image to embrace the more suggestive, adult-oriented persona of later songs such as *Confide in Me* (1995) and *Put Yourself in My Place* (1995).

FURTHER REFERENCE

Recordings include *Kylie* (1988, Mushroom TVL 93277); *Enjoy Yourself* (1989, Mushroom TVL 93294); *Rhythm of Love* (1990, Mushroom TVL 93340); *Let's Get to It* (1991, Mushroom TVD 93355); *Greatest Hits* (1992, Mushroom TVD 93366); *Kylie Minogue* (1994, Mushroom TVD 93415). See also *CA* (1995–96); *GuinnessP*; D. Rees and L. Crampton, eds, *Rock Movers and Shakers* (Santa Barbara, CA: ABC-CLIO, 1991); *SpencerW*.

AARON D.S. CORN

Minson, John   (*b* England, 5 June 1927), country music broadcaster. Living in Australia from childhood, in 1967 he developed 2TM Tamworth's local country music program into *Hoedown*, which became country music's main means of dissemination in Australia and was seminal in developing Tamworth as the national country music centre. Deeply involved in the Tamworth festival since its inception, he was a key figure in the development of the ACMA awards and the Hands of Fame. For his work he was honoured in the ACMA Roll of Renown in 1988.

FURTHER REFERENCE

Recordings include an album, *The Best of John Minson* (Hadley HCSM 3005). See also *LattaA*, 30–2; *SmithB*, 308–9.

Minton, Yvonne Fay   (*b* Sydney, 4 Dec. 1938), mezzo-soprano. A recipient of the Elsa Stralia Scholarship 1956–59 which enabled her to study at the NSW State Conservatorium, after winning the Shell Aria at Canberra in 1960 she studied in Europe and was awarded the Kathleen Ferrier Prize at the Holland Internale Competition in 1961. She then studied at the Joan Cross Opera School in London. Her career in England commenced in oratorio performances, broadcasts and recordings for Decca until her operatic debut in the title role of Britten's *Rape of Lucretia* for the City Literary Institute (1964). In 1965 she made her Covent Garden debut as Lola in *Cavalleria Rusticana* and remained with the Royal Opera as a principal mezzo-soprano, 1965–71. From 1971 she appeared as a guest principal soprano with numerous companies including Cologne Opera, Hamburg State Opera and Bayreuth Festival, and in Munich, Paris, Salzburg, Metropolitan Opera, San Francisco and Chicago. Her roles include Octavian in *Der Rosenkavalier*, Marina in *Boris Godunov*, Orpheus in *Orpheus and Eurydice*, Ascanio in *Benvenuto Cellini*, Dorabella in *Cosi Fan Tutte*, Sextus in *La clemenza di Tito*, Brangäne in *Tristan und Isolde*, Kundry in *Parsifal*, Waltraute and Frika in *Der Ring des Nibelungen* and Thea in the first performance of Tippett's *The Knot Garden* (Covent Garden, 1970). She also has a wide concert repertoire including Bach, Mahler, Schönberg and Boulez. Minton has made many recordings of complete operas including *Der Rosenkavalier* and *La clemenza di Tito* as well as symphonic items with international orchestras. In 1980 she was awarded a CBE and honorary membership of the Royal Academy of Music.

FURTHER REFERENCE
Recordings include Debussy *Pelléas et Mélisande,* Royal Opera House Orchestra, cond. P. Boulez (Sony SM3K47265); Wagner *Tristan und Isolde*, Bavarian Radio Chorus and Orchestra cond. L. Bernstein (Philips 411036–2); Berg *Lulu*, Paris Opera, cond. P. Boulez (Deutsche Grammophon DG 415892); Bellini *Norma*, London Symphony Orchestra, cond. R. Bonynge (Decca 4254882). See also *CA* (1995–96); Alan Blythe, *GroveD*.

KERRY VANN

Miracle, The. Television opera in one act, music and libretto by James *Penberthy, first performed at Winthrop Hall, Perth, on 28 May 1964.

Miranda. Family of singers.
(1) David Myers Miranda (*b* London, 9 Nov. 1834; *d* Melbourne 1900), tenor. A boy soprano at St Julius Monbach, he took lessons from Howard Glover, making his solo debut at Glasgow under Glover's management at the age of 17. He studied voice with Frederic Shrivall, then in Milan, and sang at Drury Lane from 1854, as well as at Exeter Hall and as soloist at St George's Cathedral, Southwark. He toured the USA with Lucy Escott in 1858–59 and was at Covent Garden from 1866. He went to South Africa in 1869, then settled in Melbourne *c*.1873 and taught singing in Nicholson Street, Carlton; his pupils included Nellie Stewart. His wife, Annetta Hirst, had been a favourite soprano of Queen Victoria, and his daughters Lalla (2) and Beatrice (3) both became singers.
(2) Lalla Miranda (*b* Melbourne, 1871; *d* Edinburgh, Scotland, 1940), soprano. Her first lessons as a vocalist were from her mother, the noted Scottish soprano Annetta Hirst, and from her father, Scottish tenor David Miranda (1). Lessons followed with Mme Richard and Mme De Garretti in Paris. Her career commenced as a pianist and she played at Centennial Exhibition concerts in 1888. She began singing seriously in 1890, performing with the Turner Operatic Co. before leaving for Europe in 1894. She made her debut at the Royal Court Theatre, The Hague, and was well received at La Monnaie, Brussels, where she created the role of the Fairy Queen in Massenet's *Le cendrillon*. A star at the Paris Opera, she often

appeared at Covent Garden and in the USA. In 1912 she returned to Australia with the Quinlan Opera Co. where she was Olympia in the Australian premiere of the *Tales of Hoffmann*. She was enthusiastically reviewed in this and other operas sung in English. In Paris in 1913 she was awarded a Légion d'honneur. She continued to sing infrequently on the continent and in the UK until the 1930s.
(3) Beatrice Miranda (*b* Melbourne, 3 Jan. 1881; *d* Buffalo, New York, USA, 1964), dramatic soprano. Trained as a pianist, after she sang in a Una Bourne concert at Glen's Music Rooms in 1903 she joined the Turner Concert and Operatic Co. and toured Victoria 1904–6. She went to London in 1906, took lessons with Minna Fischer and appeared in the Boosey concerts, Queen's Hall, 1907–8. She made her debut in *Pagliacci* and *Rigoletto* with the Carl Rosa Co. in 1909, singing with them and the Beecham Co. until 1922, the British National Opera Co. 1922–24 and then (until 1939) the Edinburgh Grand Opera Co., which she helped her husband Hebden Foster develop. With her rich dramatic tone she was commanding in Wagner roles both on stage and in the concert hall. She was revered as Isolde, excellent as Brünnhilde, Sieglinde, Elisabeth and Elsa. She also sang roles in *Aida, Tosca,* and the Marquise in the *pasticcio Goldsmith of Toledo*. After the war she founded the Scottish National Opera Co., for which she produced and also conducted until her retirement.

FURTHER REFERENCE
For David Miranda, H. Morin Humphreys, *Men of the Time in Australia* (Victorian Series), 2nd edn (Melbourne, 1882); *MackenzieS*, 280. For Lalla Miranda, *Australasian* 25 May 1912, 1189; *MackenzieS*, 80–2. For Beatrice Miranda, Roger Covell, *GroveO*; *Australasian* 22 Oct. 1921, 814; *MackenzieS,* 140–2; *AMN* 5 (1916), 218.

JEFF BROWNRIGG §2; Editor §1, §3

Miscellanea Musicologica. Annual journal founded (1966) by Andrew *McCredie, published by the Libraries Board of SA in association with the music department of the University of Adelaide. Subtitled 'Adelaide Studies in Musicology', it contains musicological articles chiefly by Australians or scholars who have visited Australia.

Mi-Sex. Rock group (1977–84) formed in NZ, comprised of cabaret singer Steve Gilpin (*d* 1991) and former Fragments of Time members Kevin Stanton (guitar), Murray Burns (keyboards), Don Martin (bass), and Richard Hodgkinson (drums). At first playing new-wave covers, they moved to Sydney in 1978, changing their sound to the synthesiser-pop style of the Angels. In 1979 they toured NZ and were a glossy, polished supporting act to the Talking Heads Australian tour, releasing the first of their 16 Australian singles, *But You Don't Care* (1979), which reached No. 25 in the charts and their debut album *Graffiti Crimes* (1979), which reached No. 16 in the album charts. Their single *Computer Games* reached the Top 10 in Europe in 1980, the album *Space Race* (1980) reached No. 5 and they toured North America. Developing more pulse-driven rock, they released the single *Fallin' In And Out* (1981), which reached No. 20, and the album *Where Do They Go* (1983), but as taste for heavily produced acts declined their following dropped and they disbanded in 1984.

At their peak greatly popular in Australia, they were a sophisticated live band, with a lavishly choreographed act and disciplined, polished material. They won two Countdown awards in 1979 and a Johnny O'Keefe Memorial Award.

FURTHER REFERENCE
Recordings include *But You Don't Care* (1979, CBS BA 222542), *Graffiti Crimes* (1979, CBS SBP 7329), *Computer Games* (1979, CBS BA 222563), *Space Race* (1980, CBS SBP 237442), *Fallin' In And Out* (1981, CBS BA 222809), and *Where Do They Go* (1983 CBS SBP 237954). A compilation is *Caught In The Act* (1992, Rainbow 2RCD 103/104). For discography, see *SpencerA*. See also *McGrathA*; *SpencerW*; *GuinnessP*, II, 1709.

Missing Links, The. Rock band (1964–66) formed in Sydney, originally comprised of Bob Brady (vocals), Peter Anson and Dave Boyne (guitars), Ron Peel (bass), and Danny Cox (bass), but changing membership completely by the end of 1965. Their debut single was *We 2 Should Live* in 1965. They were the first Australian group to adopt the rough-hewn appearance, heavy rhythm and blues sound, and guitar-smashing stage practices of the emerging Rolling Stones and similar British bands of the mid-1960s.

FURTHER REFERENCE
Recordings include *We 2 Should Live* (1965, Parlophone A8145), *Wild About You* (1966, Philips BF 224), the EPs *Links Unchained* (Philips PE31) and *Wild About You* (Raven RV 04) and the album *The Missing Links* (reissued 1984, Raven RVLP 19). For discography, see *SpencerA*. See also *SpencerW.*

Mission Hymn Singing. The hymns, sacred songs and choruses learned at Christian missions became an integral part of Aboriginal and Torres Strait Islander community life. They presented a way of expressing feelings towards local events and rites of passage, such as sorrow at death and joy at celebrations. Mission singing varies between the strict reproduction of hymns as sung by Whites and the use of traditional Aboriginal melodies. The Lutherans taught their chorales, training Aboriginal choirs to sing in three or more parts; the Aboriginal Evangelical Fellowship hymns, based upon *Sankey's Sacred Songs*, *Alexander's Hymns* No. 3 or Billy Graham Crusade songs, were sung fervently by massed congregations along with organ or piano accompaniment. In contrast, the Baptist Warlpiri people of Yuendumu, NT, sing 'Law songs' in octaves to their own melodies along with paired

boomerangs clapped together, and the Anglicans of Lockhart River Mission, Queensland, and Thursday Island Cathedral use Islander melodies accompanied by a drum.

Gospel singing and choruses, which are often repeated many times, are sung by all denominations. They may be borrowed from existing sources or composed by the singers, often in the indigenous languages. The 1979 revival at Elcho Island, where people sang late into the night, provided inspiration for many original choruses which were sung throughout Australia during the resulting mission activity. Whenever Aboriginal language texts were used, the metre would vary in order to accommodate the resulting lengthy strings of syllables. The instrumental interludes between phrases also tend to be much longer than with non-Aboriginal singing. See also *Aboriginal Music* §4 (ii). GRACE KOCH

Mittagong Trio. Piano trio (1980–91) first formed for an appearance at the Musica Viva Mittagong Festival, comprised of John Harding (violin), John *Winther (piano) and Nathan *Waks (cello). The trio focused on the traditional piano trio repertoire, and appeared at the Adelaide Festival and toured regularly for Musica Viva. When they left Australia to become artists-in-residence at the Hong Kong Academy of the Performing Arts in 1985, they were the finest piano trio in the country.

Mixed Relations. Sydney-based Aboriginal/non-Aboriginal rock band, active since 1988 when they appeared at the first NT Aboriginal Rock Festival. The lead singer-songwriter is Bart *Willoughby of *No Fixed Address, and the line-up has included artists well known for their solo careers: Alice Haines, Leroy Cummins, Brenda Gifford, Vanessa Lucas and Rachel Perkins (see *Amunda*). Songs are about Aboriginality, and confront listeners with sentiments such as pleas for justice. They may be heard on the sound-tracks of Wim Wenders' film *To the End of the World*, and of *Jindalee Lady*. Their performances have included the Big Day Out and Survival Day, and besides Australia their tours have included the South Pacific region, Europe, America (1993) and Hong Kong (1994).

FURTHER REFERENCE
Recordings include *Take It or Leave It* (1992, Red Eye Records 865 731–2); *Aboriginal Woman* (1993, Red Eye Records 861 419–2); and *Love* (1993, Redeye/Polydor 5190862).
P. DUNBAR-HALL

Mixtures, The. Pop group (1965–74) formed in Melbourne. Originally a trio comprised of Laurie Arthur (vocals, guitar), Rod Declerck (vocals, bass) and John Creek (vocals, drums), in 1967 they added Fred Wieland (guitar), Dennis Garcia (organ) and Mick Flynn (vocals, bass); among various later changes Buddy *England sang with them 1969–70. Playing at suburban dances, pubs and discos, they built a strong following in Melbourne and recorded the first of their 12 singles, *Koko Joe*, in 1965. Their cover of Mungo Jerry's *In The Summertime* and *Pushbike Song* both reached No. 1 in the charts in 1970, the latter also reaching No. 2 in the UK. They worked in England from 1971, returning to tour and record *Captain Zero* (1971) and an album, *In The Summertime* (1972). Unable to repeat their brief hit success of 1970, they resumed work in Australia 1974, releasing their last single, *Slow Train*, that year.

FURTHER REFERENCE
Recordings include *Koko Joe* (1965, HMV EA 4796), *In The Summertime* (Fable FB 017), *Pushbike Song* (Fable FB 039), *Captain Zero* (1971, Fable FB 088), *In The Summertime* (1972, Fable FBSA 003). A compilation is *Best Of The Mixtures* (1972, Fable FBSA 017). For discography, see *SpencerA*. See also *McGrathA*; *SpencerW*.

Mobil Quest. Short-lived but prestigious radio singing competition held nine times (1949–57) in Sydney. It grew from Hector *Crawford's radio program *Opera for the People* (founded 1946) sponsored by the Vacuum Oil Company. It was an aria competition (except in 1956, when ballads were required). Winners, who received a cash prize and national tour, included Ronal *Jackson, Joan *Sutherland, Donald *Smith, Nance *Grant, but the competition was also an important catalyst to the careers of several of its finalists, Heather *Begg, Neil *Warren-Smith, Robert *Allman and John *Shaw.

Models, The. New-wave rock band that emerged from the punk period in 1978. Original member Sean Kelly (guitar, vocals) and 1982 recruit James Freud (bass) wrote most of the band's music. Other members in a fluctuating line-up included Andrew Duffield (keyboards) who was replaced in 1983 by Roger Mason, drummers Janis ('Johnny Crash') Friedenfields and Barton Price, Mark Ferrie (bass, vocals) and James Valentine (saxophone, keyboards). In the early 1980s the band did well on the Australian alternative charts, and in 1985 their No. 2 hit *Barbados* and chart-topping single *Out of Mind, Out of Sight* brought mainstream success. The Models disbanded in 1987 and are remembered as one of Australia's most interesting and consistently innovative bands.

FURTHER REFERENCE
Recordings include *Alphabetacharliedeltaechofoxtrot* (1980, Mushroom L 37495); *Cut Lunch* (1981, Mushroom L 20001); *Local and/or General* (1981, Mushroom L 37637); *Pleasure of Your Company* (1983, Mushroom L 38065); *Out of Mind, Out of Sight* (1985, Mushroom RML 53166); *Models' Media* (1986, Mushroom RML 53216). See also *GuinnessP*; *SpencerW*. AARON D. S. CORN

Moncrieff, Gladys Lillian (*b* Bundaberg, Qld, 13 Apr. 1892; *d* Southport, Qld, 9 Feb. 1976), soprano.

Gilbert and Sullivan performances at high school in Townsville were followed by touring Queensland with a small family road show, performing popular songs and ballads. In 1912 she auditioned for J.C. Williamsons and studied with Grace Millar. Her debut was in *HMS Pinafore* at Sydney in 1914. Her reputation was consolidated when she appeared in the title role of *Maid of the Mountains* on 22 January 1921 for Williamsons in Melbourne, in an Australia-wide run that lasted two years, plus many subsequent revivals. Her repertoire included *The Merry Widow, The Chocolate Soldier, Floradora, The Gipsy Princess, Lady of the Rose, Rio Rita* and seven G&S operas. In 1926 she established herself in London musical comedy where, despite the failure of *Riki-Tiki,* she received good notices: 'Miss Moncrieff, a new star from Australia, has a beautifully clear and sympathetic voice which she uses with great skill.' Success followed with *The Blue Mazurka,* and her first series of recordings.

In 1928 she returned to Australia and re-established herself as the leading performer of musical comedy. Around 1935 she began to be referred to as 'Our Glad' and gained widespread popular success in *The Merry Widow.* A serious car accident in 1938 interrupted her career, but by 1940 she was singing again and began to give concerts to army personnel around Australia and in New Guinea. Within 18 months she was back in the theatre touring Australia and overseas. In 1951 she again entertained troops in Japan and Korea during the Korean War. She retired from singing while on tour in Hamilton, NZ, in 1959 and settled in Surfers Paradise.

FURTHER REFERENCE
Her recordings for Vocalian (1925–27) and Columbia (1928–35) are not current. Her memoirs are *My Life of Song* (Adelaide: Rigby, 1971), which contains a discography. See also Peter Burgis, *ADB*, 10; Ann Carr-Boyd, *GroveD*; *GlennonA*, 24; *MoresbyA*, 98–101. WARREN BOURNE

Mondo Rock. Pop-rock group formed (1978) in Melbourne by former *Daddy Cool vocalist Ross Wilson. The group went through three separate phases of activity, 1978–80, 1980–88 and 1990–91, each with a variety of members but always fronted by Wilson. The Mondo Rock of the 1980s is probably the best remembered, when Wilson was joined by Eric McCusker (guitar), James Black (keyboards), John James Hackett (drums), and Paul Christie (bass to 1982, then James Gillard). Chart successes included the songs *State of The Heart, No Time,* and *Come Said The Boy,* all written by McCusker.

FURTHER REFERENCE
For discography, see *SpencerA*. See also *McGrathA*; *SpencerW*. WILLIAM VAN PINXTEREN

Monk, Cyril Farnsworth (*b* Surry Hills, Sydney, 9 Mar. 1882; *d* Sydney, 7 Mar. 1970), violinist. After taking piano lessons from the age of four, he studied violin with Samuel Chudleigh, then Josef Kretschmann and theory with Alfred *Hill. He won the Sydney Eisteddfod Gold Medal in 1894 and played in J.C. Williamson's Italian Opera Orchestra 1901–2 and the Sydney Philharmonic Society 1901–3. With funds raised at a benefit concert, he went to London in 1904, studying with Guido Papini at the College of Violinists. Returning to Australia in 1906, he appeared in concerts and was soloist with the New Zealand Orchestra. He settled in Sydney in 1908 and established a teaching practice, forming the *Austral String Quartet in 1910, which presented numerous new works to the public. He taught at the NSW State Conservatorium from its inception in 1916 and was leader of the NSW State Orchestra 1919–23. After his last recital in 1927, he continued to teach until 1955 and was president of the Musical Association of NSW. The leading violinist and teacher in NSW in the first half of the 20th century, he made a very significant contribution to the development of string playing in Sydney. His wife was Varney *Monk.

FURTHER REFERENCE

Obit. *SMH,* 11 Mar. 1970. Helen Bainton, *ADB,* 10; *Lone Hand* (July 1914), 94; *Lone Hand* (Sept. 1914), 244.

Monk, Varney [Isabel Varney Desmond]   née Peterson (*b* Bacchus Marsh, Vic., 18 Jan. 1892; *d* 7 Feb. 1976), composer. She was predominantly self-taught, and came to sensational attention with the musical *Collits' Inn,* presented in Australia starring Gladys *Moncrieff, and she had a successful sequel, *The Cedar Tree.* She also wrote 160 songs and instrumental pieces. Monk strove to make her music identifiably 'Australian' through its text and plot associations. The musicals employ Australian historical settings, and her songs are rich in Australian imagery, both through her own lyrics and her settings of several Australian poets, including Henry Lawson and Henry Kendall. She composed little after the 1940s, instead putting her energy into promoting recognition for Australian musical talent.

WORKS (Selective)

(Mss held National Film and Sound Archive, Canberra, and *CAnl*)

Stage   *Collits' Inn,* musical (1932, 2, Gurr), Melbourne, 23 Dec. 1933, *The Cedar Tree,* musical (1934, 2, Barclay) Melbourne, 22 Dec. 1934.

Vocal and Instrumental   33 published works, including *Names Upon a Stone* (Sydney, 1930), *The Cedar Tree* (Sydney, 1946), *Australia* (Sydney, 1951). 127 unpublished mss, including *Murrumbidgee River Waltz,* pf, str, sax, tpt (n.d.), *On the Night Train* (n.d.), *The Sliprails and the Spur* (n.d.), *We'll Bring You Cobbers Back* (n.d.).

FURTHER REFERENCE

A complete list of compositions and discography is in Bronwen Arthur, Varney Monk and *Collits' Inn: A landmark in Australian

musical history, BMus(Hons), ANU, 1994. *Collits' Inn* is published, ed. by T. Stuart Gurr, with an introduction by John West (Sydney: Currency, 1990). See also Helen Bainton, 'Cyril Monk', *ADB,* 10.   BRONWEN ARTHUR

Monsbourgh, Ade (Adrian Herbert) (*b* Melbourne, 17 Feb. 1917), jazz performer. He took piano lessons from the age of eight, and became interested in jazz with classmate Roger *Bell in the early 1930s. He formed the Shop Swingers in 1935 and over the next few years began playing mainly banjo with the Bell brothers. Starting trombone and trumpet while studying science in 1937, he co-founded the Melbourne University Rhythm Club. He joined the Bell band for their Heidelberg Town Hall residency in 1943, recorded with visiting cornet player Max Kaminsky, and released the first records under his own leadership in 1944, the year he joined the RAAF.

Having rejoined the Bells after his discharge in 1945, he travelled with them on their tours of Europe, where he made a particular impact, leading to the offer of a place in Humphrey Lyttelton's band. Following the break-up of the Bell band in 1952 he established a recorder-manufacturing company with ex-Bell reed player Don 'Pixie' Roberts, and in 1956 recorded ragtime and jazz sessions on recorder, which he had added to a repertoire that now included vocals and all standard jazz instruments. He played alto saxophone with Len *Barnard's band in 1953–55, and in 1954 made a multi-tracked recording on which he played all the instruments. He freelanced through the late 1950s and became resident guest for the Melbourne Jazz Club in 1961, working frequently with Frank *Traynor's band. He has continued to compose, teach, perform and record prolifically with several generations of Australian jazz musicians.

Monsbourgh is one of the most original of jazz stylists, and in his long career the most influential Australia has produced; he is a central voice in producing the 'Australian' jazz sound. He has inspired more imitators than any other Australian jazz musician, and has established musical authority in every group he has worked with. He is among the most prolifically recorded jazz musicians and composers, and one of the most performed of any Australian. Since the late 1930s he has been regarded as a father-figure to several generations of musicians as a consequence of his writings, discussions and his mentoring of individuals and bands, including the *Red Onions. Decades before the advent of formal jazz studies programs, Monsbourgh evolved teaching methods and taxonomies. In Melbourne there can hardly be a jazz musician he has not played with or influenced. Monsbourgh has been pivotal to Australian jazz history and was honoured with the AM in 1992.

FURTHER REFERENCE

Recordings include *Lazy Ade Monsbourgh, Recorder in Ragtime* (1984, Swaggie S-1405); *Lazy Ade Monsbourgh and his late hour boys, A Vintage Selection* (1975, Swaggie S-1344); *Lazy Ade Mons-*

bourgh and his late hour boys (1971, Swaggie S-1283); *Graeme Bell and his Australian Jazz Band, 1948–49* (1982, Swaggie S-1396); *Graeme Bell and his Dixieland Jazz Band, Melbourne 1949* (1970, Swaggie S-1268); *Graeme Bell and his Australian Jazz Band, 1949–52* (1982, Swaggie S-1397); *Roger Bell and his Pagan Pipers* (1968, Swaggie S-1244).

See also *ClareB*; *BissetB*; *OxfordJ*; *GroveJ*; Alan Lee, 'Spotlight on ... Ade Monsbourgh', *Music Maker* (August 1961), 9, 41; Ray Scribner, 'Lazy Ade's Late Hour Boys', *Music Maker* (March, 1970), 23; Diane [*sic*] Allen, 'The Father of Australian Jazz, Lazy Ade', *Australian Jazz and Blues* 1/4 (1994), 20–1; Bruce Johnson, 'Orality and jazz education', *New Music Articles* 10 (1993), 39–46.
BRUCE JOHNSON

Montague-Turner Opera Company. Hawaiian-born soprano Annis Montague and her husband American tenor Charles Turner came to Melbourne for the W.S. *Lyster company in 1880. After Lyster's death they presented opera in English, touring widely in Australia (1881–84, 1891–94), interspersed with spells of concert appearances, teaching and work in the USA (1885–90). They presented popular repertory operas with themselves as principals, supported by Leonora Fabris, Elsa Sherwin and other local singers, with Leon *Caron and later Alberto *Zelman as conductors. Although frequently criticised for their lack of front-rank talent and somewhat tattered stage presentations, they helped fill the need for regular operatic seasons in Australia during the years after Lyster's death.

FURTHER REFERENCE
Alison Gyger, *Opera for the Antipodes* (Sydney: Currency Press, 1990), 6–21; *BrisbaneE*, 101; *BrewerD*, 80.

Moodie, Alma Templeton [Alma Spengler] (*b* Mount Morgan, Qld, 12 Sept. 1898; *d* Frankfurt am Main, Germany, 7 Mar. 1943), violinist. As a child prodigy, Moodie's career path was set in 1907 when Louis (Ludwig) *D'Hage, a Bohemian violinist resident in Rockhampton and her first teacher, sent her to César Thomson and Oscar Back at the Brussels Conservatoire de Musique. An indifferent German debut in 1911 brought her under the patronage of Max Reger, but this promising collaboration was cut short by the outbreak of war. In January 1919 she resumed study with Carl Flesch, making a sensational Berlin debut in November. She toured extensively throughout the 1920s, playing with most of the major orchestras of Europe and in London. Her friendship with the Swiss businessman Werner Reinhart put her in touch with the leading personalities and developments of contemporary music. She premiered concertos written for her by Hans Pfitzner, Ernst Krenek and others and gave the first performance of Stravinsky's *Pulcinella* Suite. Her duo (1921–43) with Eduard Erdmann, with whom she gave her last performance, was renowned. Her marriage in 1927 to Alexander Balthasar Alfred Spengler did not at once affect her career, but the births of her two children (1928 and 1932) sapped her strength. Profoundly affected by the harsh realities of the Nazi regime and the Allied bombing raids, she began to suffer from a bouncing bow. Nonetheless, in 1939 Hermann Reutter appointed her as a teacher at the Staatliche Hochschule für Musik in Frankfurt. Though acclaimed as the greatest female violinist of her generation, she made no recordings. Her death was thought by many to be suicide.

FURTHER REFERENCE
P. Borer, Aspects of European Influence on Australian Violin Playing and Teaching, MMus, Univ. Tasmania, 1988; F. Bridge, 'Alma Moodie', *Grove's Dictionary of Music and Musicians*, 5th edn, ed. E. Blom (London: Macmillan, 1954); C.F. Flesch, *And Do You Also Play the Violin?* (London: Toccata Press, 1990); L. McDonald: *Rockhampton, A History of City and District* (Brisbane: UQP, 1981); P. Sulzer, *Zehn Komponisten um Werner Reinhart*, 3 vols (Winterthur: Stadtbibliothek Winterthur, 1979, 1980 and 1983).
KAY DREYFUS

Mooney, Brian (*b* NSW, 1923), folk-singer. Working as a labourer, he began singing traditional Irish songs in Sydney in the late 1950s, accompanying himself on guitar, mandolin or accordion. He became a full-time artist in 1961, moving to Melbourne and singing at Frank Traynor's folk club 1961–65. He went to Ireland in 1966 and performed with his wife Phyllis in regional pubs, recording *My Country Folk,* then worked as a solo artist. He was in Melbourne again in 1973. One of the earliest exponents of Irish traditional music in Australia, he had significant influence on such singers as Declan *Affley and John *Dengate, and helped promote the folk-song revival of the early 1960s.

FURTHER REFERENCE
His recordings were for Score. See also *Age* 4 Nov. 1978.

Mooney, Marty (*b* Brisbane, 18 Sept. 1943), jazz reeds player. He began playing professionally in 1963 and joined trumpeter Nick Boston in 1964, remaining with him after their move to Sydney in 1966. A founder member of *Galapagos Duck, where the broadening of his style became apparent, he left to join Dick *Hughes in 1977, and from there went to the band led by Roger Janes in 1980, with whom he remains active. He has led his own groups, and been in high demand as a freelancer, with John *Sangster, Eclipse Alley Five and Tom *Baker among others. He has also toured and played support for visiting performers such as Spike Milligan and American pianist Dave Paquette.

FURTHER REFERENCE
Recordings include *Ebony Quill*, Galapagos Duck (1973, Philips 6357 015); *The Removalists,* Galapagos Duck, (1974, Philips 6357 020); *The Roger Janes Band* (1981, Jazznote JNLP 028). See also *OxfordJ*.
BRUCE JOHNSON

Moore, Lisa (*b* Canberra 1960), pianist. After studying with Albert *Landa in Sydney she won the silver medal in the International American Music Competition at Carnegie Hall in 1981, and studied at Paris in 1983 under an Alliance Française (Aust.) award. She won an Australian Music Foundation of London award (1984) and moved to New York in 1985, participating at the Tanglewood Festival on a Bernstein fellowship. She has performed with the New York City Ballet, Philharmonia Virtuosi, the Twentieth Century Music Group and a number of other New York contemporary ensembles, and is resident pianist for the Bang On A Can Festival. Frequently returning to Australia, she has appeared as soloist with several ABC orchestras as well as with the Queensland Philharmonic Orchestra. She has won two Australia Council fellowships and has been musician-in-residence at the University of Wollongong and NSW State Conservatorium (1992–93). One of Australia's most dedicated performers of new piano music, she has premiered works by Lukas Foss, Milton Babbitt, Australians Gerard *Brophy and Michael *Smetanin. Andrew *Ford's concerto *Imaginings* was written for her. She won an ARIA award in 1992 and a *Sounds Australian* Award in 1994.

FURTHER REFERENCE
Recordings include *The Wild Russians,* Shostakovich and Schnittke (1992, Tall Poppies TPO 018); and Michael Smetanin *Stroke* (1994, Tall Poppies TPO 040). See also *Age* 4 June 1992.

Moore, Maggie [Margaret Virginia Sullivan] (*b* San Francisco, USA, 10 Apr. 1851; *d* San Francisco, USA, 16 Mar. 1926), actress, theatrical singer. On stage from an early age, she met J.C. *Williamson when she was 20; they formed a theatrical duo and were married in 1873. They toured Australia with their *Struck Oil* for George *Coppin in 1874–75, then returned to settle in 1879. Beginning with Mabel in *Pirates of Penzance* in 1880, she appeared as lead in a number of Williamson's operetta productions until she divorced him in 1899. After this she went back to the USA, appearing to somewhat mixed success. She returned to Australia in 1908, making further appearances in *Struck Oil* (and in a film version in 1918) and other works, until retiring to California in 1925.

FURTHER REFERENCE
Obit. in *New York Times* 17 Mar. 1926; *SMH* 17 Mar. 1926.

Moorish Maid, A. Comic opera in two acts by Alfred *Hill (1905), libretto by J. Youlin Birch. It sets a story of romance against an exotic comic background of Arabs, Nubian slaves and rogues. First performed at His Majesty's Theatre, Auckland, NZ on 26 June 1905, it had seven performances at Sydney in a modified version by George Stephenson's English Musical Comedy Co. in 1906.

Morel, Gabriel. See *Hall, Fred*.

Moreno, Dom Stephen Anthony (*b* Corella, Navarre, Spain, 17 Jan. 1889; *d* Marseilles, 5 Feb. 1953), Spanish composer. He showed an interest in music from an early age, his first teachers being his father and the local church organist and choirmaster. Accepted into the Benedictine community to train for the priesthood, his musical talent was recognised and he received lessons in harmony and counterpoint from Professor Boezzi in Rome. While there he met Dom Lorenzo Perosi, the musical director of the Sistine Chapel. He spent two years in Munich from 1920 studying with Walter Braunfels, whose late-Romantic style of writing was an important influence.

Moreno was sent to the monastery at New Norcia, WA, in 1908. From the outset his output as a composer was prolific (about 20 masses, 60 motets, offertories, and other settings), as he had considerable resources at his disposal—several choirs, an orchestra and later a Moser pipe organ, purchased while he was in Germany. His choral works, the greater part of his compositions, were based on plainchant and dedicated to the purpose of restoring Gregorian chant as the basis of liturgical worship in accordance with the tenets of *Moto Proprio* as decreed by Pope Pius X. The *Hymni Eucharesties* (1927), *Corona Mariae* (1929), *Missa Nona* (1930) and *Missa Undecima* (1932) were written to redress the problem of a lack of appropriate music for the mass and benediction which was relatively simple to perform and readily accessible. As Chenna, his Italian publishers, were not considered equal to the task of printing English words, he devised his own printing press for *The Little Flower Hymnal* (1937) and the *Gregorian Manual* (1941, re-edited with supplement in 1951).

A specialist in the performance of Gregorian chant, Moreno was a brilliant teacher. He was also a fine pianist and competent organist with a gift for improvisation. During his lifetime his compositions were widely used in educational institutions throughout Australia.

FURTHER REFERENCE
Recordings (now rare) include *Missa Nona* (1930, Parlophone). His mss are held in the New Norcia archives, WA. See also *McCredieM*; Geoffrey Revell, A Biography of Dom Stephen Moreno, O.S.B., with a Complete Catalogue of His Works, MA, Univ. WA, 1990.   JEAN FARRANT

Moresby, Isabelle ('Millie') née Hunt (*b* Williamstown, Melbourne, 1886; *d* Sorrento, Vic., 1956), writer, violinist. Born into a musical family and learning violin and viola at home, she played with the Melbourne Symphony Orchestra from its inception under Alberto *Zelman Jr. She wrote children's stories for the *Argus* and a work on Australia's war effort in New Guinea, *New Guinea: The Sentinel* (1943), but is best remembered for her book *Australia Makes Music* (Melbourne: Longmans, Green & Co, 1948), a pioneering study of Australian musical history, animated with first-hand knowledge of many of its protagonists.

Moreton Bay (Convict's Lament on the Death of Captain Logan), folk-song. Usually set to a variant of the Irish 'Youghal Harbour', this powerful convict ballad tells of the exceptional cruelty that reigned in the Moreton Bay penal colony under Captain Patrick Logan, commandant from 1826 until his murder, apparently by Aborigines, in 1830. Quoted by Ned Kelly in his Jerilderie Letter (1879), Kelly probably learned it from his father, who had been imprisoned with *Frank the Poet (Francis MacNamara), its author. It was not published until Jack Bradshaw's *The True History of Australian Bushrangers, c.*1911.

FURTHER REFERENCE
Edition with commentary in *ManifoldP*; *RadicS*, 1.

Morgan, Chad(wick) William (*b* Wondai, nr Kingaroy, Qld, 12 Feb. 1933), country music singer-song-writer. The eldest of 14 children, Morgan left school at 13 and wrote *The Sheik of Scrubby Creek,* his best-known song, at the age of 16. Success singing *The Sheik in Australia's Amateur Hour* in 1952 led to an offer from EMI to record the song on the Regal Zonophone label (78rpm). His career took off in late 1955 and he toured with country musicians including Slim Dusty, Gordon Parsons and Reg Lindsay, and as a member of the All Star Western Show. From 1959 he toured as star of his own road show. His career was blighted from the mid-1960s by chronic drinking, a nervous breakdown in 1973 and several serious car accidents, one resulting in memory loss. He had some extraordinary successes, however, including a standing ovation at a concert with the Slim Dusty Show at the Sydney Opera House in 1977 and an appearance in the feature film *Newsfront*. Since 1986 he has given up drinking and has been back on the road touring clubs and other venues.

Musically, Morgan's simple, narrative ballads owe most to the style of pre-World War II American country musicians such as Jimmie Rodgers. His recurrent textual themes are womanising, drinking and gambling, and he usually performs solo, accompanying himself on guitar, or with a small band including pedal steel. He is one of Australia's best-known country musicians; memorable for his rural stage character with trademark upturned hat, buck teeth, silly facial expressions and comic songs celebrating Australian larrikinism.

FURTHER REFERENCE
Recordings include *The Sheik of Scrubby Creek* (1952, Regal Zonophone G 25343); *Shotgun Wedding* (1955, Regal Zonophone G 25424); *Duckinwilla Dance* (1955, Regal Zonophone G 25425); *Oh So Nice in the Nuthouse* (Columbia); for discography, see *WatsonC*, 2. See also *Age* 25 Jan. 1992; *LattaA*; *SmithB*.
                                                    JENNIFER HILL

Morgan, Frederick (*b* 1940, Melbourne), recorder-maker. After initial training as a commercial illustrator, Morgan became interested in the possibilities of the recorder while working for the now defunct Pan Recorder Co. in Melbourne. In 1970 he travelled to Europe on a Churchill fellowship to study original instruments and in 1981 published detailed drawings of the original recorders in the private collection of Dutch recorder virtuoso Frans Brüggen. Morgan was a pioneer in the quest to develop a recorder that would play with the fingerings outlined in Silvestro Ganassi's *Opera intitulata Fontegara* (1535). He has an international reputation as a writer and researcher into the reconstruction of recorders based on historical models, and his instruments can be heard on numerous commercial recordings.

FURTHER REFERENCE
His writings include 'Making Recorders Based on Historical Models', *Early Music* 10 (1982), 14–21; and with Frans Brüggen, *The Recorder Collection of Frans Brüggen* (Tokyo: Zen-On Music, 1981). Recordings using his instruments include *Recorder Concertos,* Laurin rec, Drottingholm Baroque Ens (BIS CD 635); *Early Italian Baroque,* Vicki Boeckman rec, Finn Hansen viol, Lars Ulrik Mortensen hpd (Kontra Punkt 32059); and *Telemann, J.S. Bach, C.P.E. Bach,* Laurin rec, fl (BIS CD 675).   PETER NUSSEY

Morison, Elsie Jean (*b* Ballarat, Vic., 15 Aug. 1924), soprano. After studies at the Albert Street Conservatorium with Clive *Carey and a debut in *Messiah* at Melbourne in 1944, she went to London to study at the Royal College of Music. After her appearance in *Acis and Galatea* at the Albert Hall in 1948, she sang with Sadler's Wells until 1954, then at Covent Garden and (from 1953) at Glyndebourne. Projecting great beauty of tone and an endearing warmth of personality, her roles included Fiordiligi, Lauretta, Nanetta, Susanna, Anne Trulove in *The Rake's Progress,* Zerlina, and Marcellina in *Fidelio;* she sang Blanche in the British premiere of *Dialogues des Carmélites* and created the title role in Hughes's *Menna.* The concert platform continually attracted her, and drew her away from the stage almost entirely after her marriage to Rafael Kubelik in 1963.

FURTHER REFERENCE
Recordings include Handel, *Solomon* (now rare); Handel, *Messiah* (Classics for Pleasure CD-CFPD 4718); a series of Gilbert and Sullivan operas with Glyndebourne (EMI CMS7 64394–2, 643397–2, 64409–2); Haydn, *The Seasons* (HMV); Purcell, *The Faery Queen* (L'Oiseau-lyre); Purcell *King Arthur* (Decca 433166–2DM2); and Mahler, Symphony No. 4 (Deutsche Gramophon 435162–2GX13). See also Harold Rosenthal, *GroveO*; *MackenzieS*, 183–5.

Morris, Jenny (*b* Hamilton, NZ), rock singer-songwriter. A schoolteacher in Wellington, NZ, she sang with the all-female Wide Mouthed Frogs from 1978 and joined the new-wave band the Crocodiles in 1980, with whom she arrived in Australia in 1981. After they disbanded she joined QED and worked as a backing singer, touring with INXS in 1985. She formed the Jenny Morris Band in 1989, *She Has To Be Loved* reaching No. 5 in the charts, while her album *Shiver* (1989) reached No. 5 and charted for a year. In 1990 she toured as support for Prince. *Break In The Weather* reached No. 3 in 1991, and then she received airplay as a solo artist, singing her own songs. With a strong voice and songs of homelessness, land rights, the environment and a range of other issues, she won the ARIA best female performer in 1987 and 1988.

FURTHER REFERENCE

Recordings include *She Has To Be Loved* (1989, WEA 7–257487); *Break In The Weather* (1991, EastWest 903175/67–0); *Body And Soul* (1987, WEA 0–258458); *Shiver* (1989, WEA 256462–1); a compilation is *The Story So Far: Best Of Jenny Morris* (1992, East West 4509912112). For discography, see *SpencerA*. See also *McGrathA; SpencerW.*

Morris, Russell   rock singer-songwriter. Morris first came to notice as the lead singer of the group Somebody's Image, managed by Ian 'Molly' ★Meldrum. With his popularity and profile increasing, he launched his solo career in 1968, achieving immediate success with the release of his most significant work, *The Real Thing*, which was No. 1 in the charts for 23 weeks. Written by Johnny ★Young and produced by Meldrum, this work was innovative in its use of choral accompaniment, spoken word and a variety of sound effects. It was almost twice the length of most singles of the period and captured the flavour of the psychedelic movement. He followed this with the double-sided success of *The Girl That I Love / Part Three Into Paper Walls,* which also made No. 1, and he was voted most popular male vocalist in the pop magazine *Go-Set* poll. He toured the UK, then released *Rachel* with only moderate success, but after a national tour his own song *Mr America* reached No. 9 on the charts. His first album, *Bloodstone*, and the single derived from it, *Sweet Sweet Love,* was successful, as was *Live with Friends*, co-written with Brian ★Cadd in 1972.

In 1973 Morris moved to England and, being unable to secure a contract, went to the USA. While he subsequently released a number of songs he has never regained his initial commercial success either overseas or in Australia. After returning from the USA in 1976 he formed a number of bands including the Russell Morris Band (1978–84), the Rubes (1980–81), Russell Morris and the Lonely Boys 1986–89, and most recently Russell Morris and the Word. He has continued to record, including a remake of *The Real Thing* and, in 1991, the CD *A Thousand Suns.*

FURTHER REFERENCE

Recordings include *Real Thing* (1969, Colombia 8710); *Sweet Sweet Love* (1971, HMV 9539); *Bloodstone* (1971, Columbia); *Wings of an Eagle* (1973, EMI 7702). For discography, see *SpencerA*. See also *McGrathA; SpencerW.*   MICHAEL McNAB

Morrison, Deniese   (*b* Tamworth, NSW, 21 Apr. 1956), country music singer. Learning guitar and first appearing at a Johnny ★Ashcroft concert in Kootingal, NSW, at the age of 10, she sang in the first ACMA festival with the Teenage Country Style show, touring from her teenage years with Lee ★Conway, the Hawking Brothers and Johnny ★Chester. She released her debut album *Deniese Morrison* in 1975 and since then has appeared with Conway Twitty, Tom T. Hall, frequently on Nick Erby's *National Country Music Jamboree*, and in NSW clubs. Her crossover country and mainstream repertoire has brought her success with both urban and country audiences, and she has won three ACMA Golden Guitars.

FURTHER REFERENCE

Recordings include her albums *Deniese Morrison* (1975, Fable Records), *Unfinished Business* (1989) and *On The Move* (1991). See also *LattaA*, 130–1; *SmithB*, 310.

Morrison, James   (*b* Boorowa, NSW, 11 Nov. 1962), jazz brass player. He began cornet at the age of seven, formed his first band as a schoolboy and his first big band with brother John (drums) in secondary school. He later added trombone, reeds and bass to his repertoire. Public notice, in the USA and elsewhere, came with his involvement with the Young Northside Big Band in 1979. He graduated from the jazz studies program at the NSW Conservatorium in 1980, joined Don ★Burrows and began teaching in the program in 1983, also becoming musical director for the Pan-Pacific Music Camps.

His celebrity increased rapidly throughout the 1980s as his activities diversified to include overseas tours and concerts, including the Olympic Jazz Festival, Los Angeles, 1984, and Expo 85 in Japan, as well as performances of the classical repertoire with symphony orchestras. At the same time he maintained performance visibility in local venues, including the Regent Hotel and Soup Plus, and through the Morrison Brothers Big Bad Band. More recently, however, he has been less visible outside the concert hall, concentrating instead on his increasing commitments on the international festival circuit. As a composer and guest soloist in touring bands and in his Hot Horn Happening, he has worked in the most eminent company of the internationalist post-bop mainstream, including Jon Faddis, Ray Brown and Lalo Schifrin, with whom he has been particularly associated in jazz/symphonic works. His numerous awards include Germany's prestigious Vierteljahrespreis der Deutschen Schallplattenkritik.

FURTHER REFERENCE

Recordings include *Postcards From Down Under* (1988, WEA Records 255697.1); *Swiss Encounter, James Morrison & Adam Makowicz At The Montreux Jazz Festival* (1989, East West 256731–1); *Snappy Doo* (1990, WEA Records 903171211–1); *This Is Christmas* (1993, East West 4509938632); *James Morrison and the Hot Horn Happening, Live in Paris* (1995, East West

4509992604); *Live at the Sydney Opera House* (1996, East West 0630151462). See also *ClareB*; *OxfordJ*; Eric Myers, 'The Young Lions, James Morrison and Dale Barlow', *JA* (May/June 1981), 5–8; John Shand, 'All Good Fun, The Life and Times of James Morrison', *Australasian Jazz and Blues* 2/4 (1995), 4–6; Eric Myers, 'James Morrison's International Success', *Jazzchord* 29 (Mar./Apr. 1996), 1–2. BRUCE JOHNSON

Morton, Tex [Robert Lane] (*b* Nelson, NZ, 8 Aug. 1916; *d* 23 July 1983), country music singer-songwriter. In his early teens in NZ he busked, worked in a dance band and a sideshow, and cut his first records before he was 16. He came to Australia in 1932, and worked under the name Tex Morton as a tent hand and bit player in Queensland travelling shows, then in a miscellany of other jobs until he won a talent quest as a performer of American country and western music at 2KY Sydney in 1936. He was signed by Regal Zonophone, making nine singles in the next few months, including the classic *Wyoming Willie*; his song *Wrap Me Up In My Stockwhip And Blanket* applied the American idiom to an Australian theme for the first time. He toured Australia with Gladys Moncrieff in the same year. He then assembled the largest and most successful touring rodeo show ever presented in Australia, involving circus, rodeo and singing, which travelled the country 1937–39. He had recorded another 38 singles, increasingly on Australian topics, by 1943; among these *The Black Sheep* (1937), best seller of all his hits, *Mandrake* (1941), *Old Shep* (1941) and *Rover No More* (1941) became enduring country classics.

After the war his travelling show resumed, now including the whole of Ashton's Circus, until he went to NZ in 1949, where he made another 12 singles. He was in the USA and Canada 1949–59, where he performed as a hypnotist, then a character actor on television, as well as recording for the Okeh label, Nashville. In 1959–65 he was again in the Australian outback, in the 1970s appearing on television and occasionally recording albums (including prose recitations) for Festival.

The first national figure in Australian country music, in the late 1930s and early 1940s he was the best-selling recording artist in Australia. At first his songs reflected American themes, but in *Goondiwindi Grey, Sergeant Small* and elsewhere he increasingly sang of Australian bush heroes. Some of the songs he presented as his own (*The Ned Kelly Song, Old Shep*) have since been found in earlier circulation, but his adaptation of American country music to them, and to a host of Australian rural topics, clearly set a pattern for the Australian country style. His touring made the style enormously popular both in cities and remote rural centres, paving the way not just for Buddy ★Williams and Slim ★Dusty but for a generation of younger country artists who first heard the music from him. He was honoured in the ACMA Roll of Renown in 1976 and the Hands of Fame in 1977.

FURTHER REFERENCE
Obit. in *Variety* 311/3 (27 July 1983); *Age* 26 July 1983. Recordings included singles *Wyoming Willie* (Regal Zonophone G22716), *Wrap Me Up In My Stockwhip And Blanket* (Regal Zonophone G22904), *The Black Sheep* (1937, Regal Zonophone G23064), *Mandrake* (1941, Regal Zonophone G24345), *Old Shep* (1941, Regal Zonophone G24376), and *Rover No More* (1941, Regal Zonophone G24394). His albums included *Tex Morton's Australia* (1973, Picture Records), *Regal Zonophone Collection* Nos 1 and 2 (EMI 8142022/2052), *Tex Morton's 50th Anniversary Album* (Festival D193259) and *20 Golden Hits* (Festival D25364). For discography see *WatsonC*, I. *MonashB*; *WatsonC*, I, 9–30.

Mote, Livingstone C. (*b c.*1897), choral conductor. Son of William Mote, for many years choirmaster and leader of the orchestra for the Central Methodist Mission at Centenary Hall, York Street, Sydney, he was conductor of the NSW State Conservatorium choir from 1924, presenting the first Sydney performance of the Vaughan Williams Mass in G Minor, and later conductor of the Royal Philharmonic Society, Sydney.

FURTHER REFERENCE
AMN 18 (Sept. 1928), 25.

Mother Goose [Landing Party]. Pop band (1975–84) formed in NZ. After little success in NZ they moved to Sydney in 1976, and then to Melbourne where their debut single, a comic song, *Baked Beans*, reached No. 23 in the charts in 1977. They released an album, *Stuffed*, and, with a remarkable stage show involving comedy routines, costumed mime and novelty songs, were voted best stage act by *RAM* magazine in 1977. They toured the USA in 1978, then toured Australia and NZ to promote the album *Don't Believe In Fairy Tales* in 1979, settling in Perth in 1982. Despite fine musicianship they were dogged by their novelty image in Australia; learning that their album *This Is The Life* (1982) was popular in Canada, they moved there under the name Landing Party in 1982. Their last single was *Find A Way Out* (1983) and they returned to Melbourne in 1984.

FURTHER REFERENCE
Recordings include *Stuffed* (1977, Mushroom L36312), *Don't Believe In Fairy Tales* (1979, Mushroom L37147), *This Is The Life* (1982, Mushroom L37775), *Find A Way Out* (1983, Parole K9138). For discography, see *SpencerA*. See also *McGrathA*; *SpencerW*; *GuinnessP*, II, 1764.

Motzing, Bill (*b* Pittsburgh, Pennsylvania, USA, 19 Aug. 1937), film composer. He graduated from the Eastman School of Music, University of Rochester, New York, and the Manhattan School of Music in New York, and migrated to Australia in 1972. A musician of great diversity, Motzing was involved extensively in jazz performance in the 1950s, in orchestral and chamber ensemble performance in the 1960s, and more recently as a producer and arranger in the pop and rock recording industries. He is also a conductor and a respected music educator, having taught at the Eastman School of Music, the Cologne Hochschule für Musik, and the Sydney Conservatorium for 12 years, where he held the position of head of the jazz studies program 1976–78. Motzing's interest in a diversity of compositional styles is reflected clearly in his film scores, which include *Newsfront* (1978), *Cathy's Child* (1979), *The Return of Captain Invincible* (1983), *'Undercover'* (1984) and *Young Einstein* (1988). Television mini-series include *Melba*, *The True Believers*, *The Cowra Breakout* and *Vietnam*. He is currently living in the USA.

FURTHER REFERENCE

LimbacherF.   L. THOMPSON

Mount Gambier, pop. (1991) 21 153. Set at the foot of an extinct volcano in the south-eastern corner of SA, it was established as a livestock station in 1841. Settled (as Gambier Town) in 1854, it is a centre for the district's farm produce, timber industry and limestone mining. Adam Lindsay ★Gordon was a horsebreaker in the district and composed his first ballads there in 1867.

A visiting German ensemble gave the first concert in 1857, and beginning with the ★Carandini troupe in 1861, there were sporadic visits by opera companies, bands, and later such singers as Amy ★Castles, Peter ★Dawson and Clara Butt. The residents themselves gave 'Sixpenny Readings' or 'Moonlight Concerts' of vocal and instrumental items interspersed with recitations from 1864, but local ensembles suffered repeatedly from a lack of continuity. The Mount Gambier Choral Society (formed 1863) has had an often interrupted history; there have been short-lived orchestral groups, beginning with the orchestra of the Fortschritts Verein in 1871 and most successfully under Jack Topham (1900–20). The Mount Gambier Philharmonic Society (1870–80) and later groups presented amateur opera, or musical comedy.

Bands have had a more continuous history: a brass band was formed for the Governor's visit in 1867 and its descendants have flourished in the district ever since, the Mount Gambier City Band still meeting today. Local pipers at first provided the only source of dance music in the district and formed the first pipe band in 1899; today the Mount Gambier Blue Lake Highland Pipe Band and at least eight other bands in the district carry on the highland tradition. Competitions began with the Musical Elocutionary and Literary Society from 1905; the present Mount Gambier Eisteddfod has been running continuously each September since 1981, and there is a 'Generations in Jazz' stage band competition each May. The South East Country Music Festival is held at Mount Gambier each February, attracting singers from across the state.

FURTHER REFERENCE

Les R. Hill, *Mount Gambier: the City Around A Cave* (author, 1972).

Moustique. Comic opera in three acts by Henri ★Kowalski, libretto by Marcus Clarke (as *Queen Venus*). First performed at the Allazar Royal, Brussels, in 1883, and in Australia at the Opera House, Sydney, on 2 July 1889.

Moving Pictures. Rock band (1980–87) formed in Sydney comprised originally of Alex Smith (vocals), Andy Thomas (saxophone), Charlie Cole (keyboard, trumpet, vocals), Gary Frost (guitar, vocals), Ian Lees (bass) and Paul Freeland (drums). Building a pub following with their passionate rhythm-and-blues-style rock in Sydney, in 1982 their second single, *What About Me?*, reached No. 1 in the charts in 1982 and the Top 20 in the USA; their next, *Winners*, reached No. 12, and their debut album *Days Of Innocence* reached No. 1 in the album charts and the Top 60 in the USA in the same year. The next year they toured Australia, the USA and Japan and released another album, *Matinee* (1983), which reached No. 16. After this they could not repeat their success, and their last album was *Last Picture Show* (1987).

FURTHER REFERENCE

Recordings include *What About Me?* (Wheatley WBE 648130), *Winners* (Wheatley WBE 846), *Days Of Innocence* (Wheatley WBEX 1005), *Matinee* (1983, Wheatley WBEX 1010), *Last Picture Show* (1987, Wheatley SBLP 1020). For discography, see *SpencerA*. See also *McGrathA*; *SpencerW*; *GuinnessP*, III, 1771.

Moyle, Alice Marshall (*b* Bloemfontein, South Africa, 25 Dec. 1908), Aboriginalist musicologist. She graduated from the University of Melbourne (BMus 1930) and University of Sydney (BA 1954; MA 1957), and was awarded a PhD from Monash University in 1975 for her work on north Australian music. Working as a teaching fellow in the music department at the University of Sydney 1960–63, she was a research officer at the AIAS from 1964 to 1965, a research fellow of the department of music at Monash University 1965–73, and a research fellow and research officer at the AIAS in 1973 and 1974 respectively.

Her work is comprehensive in its scope, including the documentation of Aboriginal sound instruments, and the history of Aboriginal music and dance through film, field recordings, archaeo-musicology, analysis, taxonomy, cataloguing and indexing. Her material is accessible and her publications are used whenever Aboriginal music is studied in schools and tertiary institutions. As an original member and national president (1982–83) of the Musicological Society of Australia, Moyle also contributed to the wider development of musicology in Australia. She collaborated with linguist Judith Stokes to produce a monograph on the clan system of Groote Eylandt. In 1984 her colleagues produced a *Festschrift* to celebrate Moyle's musicological career. She was awarded an honorary DMus from the University of Melbourne in 1995.

FURTHER REFERENCE
Her writings include 'A Handlist of Field Collections of Recorded Music in Australia and Torres Strait', *Occasional Papers in Aboriginal Studies* 6 (1966), 1–227; 'Aboriginal Music on Cape York', *Musicology* 3 (1968–69), 3–20; North Australian Music: A Taxonomic Approach to the Study of Aboriginal Song Performances, PhD, Monash Univ. 1974; *Aboriginal Sound Instruments*, companion book for LP disc (Canberra: AIAS, 1978); 'The Australian "didjeridu": A late musical intrusion', *World Archaeology* 12/3 (1981), 321–31. See also Jill Stubington, 'Alice M. Moyle: An Australian Voice', in *Problems and Solutions: Occasional Essays in Musicology presented to Alice M. Moyle*, ed. J.C. Kassler and J. Stubington (Sydney: Hale & Iremonger, 1984).

MARGARET KARTOMI

Moyle, Richard Michael   (*b* Paeroa, NZ, 23 Aug. 1944), ethnomusicologist, authority on the music of Oceania and Central Australia. He studied at the University of Auckland (MA 1967, PhD 1971), and conducted fieldwork in Samoa, Tonga, Lau, Niue, Northern Cook Islands, Takuu and Central Australia, the latter sponsored by the AIAS. He has lectured at Indiana University, the University of Hawaii and the University of Auckland, where he is also currently director of the Archive of Maori and Pacific Music. Author of eleven books and numerous articles, he is editor and regional co-ordinator for the *Oceania* volume, *The Universe of Music* (UNESCO).

MARGARET KARTOMI

Mucky Duck, The.   Bush band formed in 1977 in WA, comprised of Roy Abbott (acoustic guitar, electric guitar, vocals), Davy Browne (acoustic guitar, mandolin, bodhran drums, vocals), Andy Copeman (bass guitar, synthesiser, cittern, vocals), and Erik Kowarski (fiddle, guitar, vocals).

FURTHER REFERENCE
Their recordings include *From the Bush* (1985, Larrikin LRF 154), and *At Last The Mucky Duck Album* (Grass Roots GR 273804).

Muir, Jim   (*b* Katoomba, NSW, 23 Mar. 1938), country music gospel singer. Learning to play several instruments as a child, he became a Christian evangelist from the age of 17, using music as part of his ministry. Releasing his debut album *Let Me Live* in 1979, he signed with Hadley Records in 1982, then began a weekly program, *Jim Muir's Country*, on 4EB Brisbane and 4YOU Rockhampton. Australia's best-known country gospel singer, he has appeared in Ireland, NZ, the USA (at the Grand Ole Opry) and Canada (at the Calgary Stampede).

FURTHER REFERENCE
Recordings include *Let Me Live* (1979, Unison), *A Thing Called Love* (1986 Hadley GSL/GSC 4) and *Try A Little Kindness* (1990, Hadley GSC 1306). See also *LattaA*, 154–5; *SmithB*, 311.

Mulry, Ted.   See *Ted Mulry Gang*.

Mummery, (Joseph) Browning   (*b* Melbourne, 12 July 1888; *d* Canberra, 16 Mar. 1974), tenor. Originally a mechanic, he took lessons with A.C. Bartleman in Melbourne and sang in church choirs, then appeared with the ★Gonsalez and ★Rigo Opera Co. (1918) and joined the Williamson Opera Co. (1919), touring Australia with Amy ★Castles. Moving to London in 1921, he joined the British National Opera Co. in 1922 and then, after studies in Italy, joined Covent Garden 1926–28, appearing there as Rudolfo with Melba in her farewell of 1926, and recording copiously for HMV. He visited Australia in the Melba-Williamson season of 1928, went to the USA for concerts and work with NBC 1929–32. He was in London with the BBC 1932–33, returned to Australia with the Benjamin Fuller Opera Co. in 1934, made tours of Australia and NZ and then taught in Melbourne. With a lyrical, attractive voice and a studied technique, he was a great favourite with radio audiences in Britain, the USA and Australia. He also made numerous concert and radio appearances, and sang Faust in the first opera broadcast by the BBC.

FURTHER REFERENCE
His HMV recordings and the 19 he made for Zonophone are now rare. See also Roger Covell, *GroveO*; James Griffin, *ADB*, 10; *MackenzieS*, 127–9; *GlennonA*, 58; *AMN* 31 (Oct 1940), 5.

Munro, Charlie (Charles Robert)   (*b* Christchurch, NZ, 22 May 1917; *d* Sydney, 9 Dec. 1985), jazz reeds player, composer. He began piano at the age of seven, later adding reeds, flute and cello to his repertoire. He played in his family's dance band, was conductor of his school orchestra at 13 and began his professional career at 17. He played on ships travelling between NZ, Vancouver and Australia, and with Linn Smith, and settled in Sydney in 1938. He quickly became prominent in dance and pit work, then joined the army and served with the 50–50 (Australian–American) concert party until its disbandment in 1944, when he was posted to other entertainment units. Following his discharge in 1946 he joined Wally ★Norman, through whom he became exposed to bop, a style which he was among the first Australians to assimilate.

In 1950 he joined Bob ★Gibson, with whom he became active in jazz concert performance and recording, and resumed formal study of the cello. In 1954 he began performing, composing and arranging with the ABC dance band, an association that would last until its dissolution in 1976. In the early 1960s he was active with Bryce ★Rohde's groups, as well as groups of his own and Don Andrew's Castilian Players. In 1966 he assembled a large group to perform the Seiber-Dankworth *Improvisation for Jazz Band and Orchestra* with the Sydney Symphony Orchestra under Dean Dixon, and recorded *Eastern Horizons* in 1967, demonstrating an interest in Eastern music well before it became fashionable. His ballet *Count Down*, recorded in 1970, included atonal and freeform exercises. Throughout the 1970s he remained in obscurity, but then emerged in 1979 working with Bruce Cale. He assembled a workshop group in the 1980s which made broadcasts and recorded, led his quintet at Bardwell Park RSL, and was working with the Lucy Brown group at the time of his death.

Munro possessed a comprehensive musical curiosity and command which placed him above pretension. Throughout his career he remained at the forefront of a succession of jazz developments, including bop, modal, freeform, and non-Western music. As a composer and arranger, he showed a broad grasp of the overall context of musical performance and its function. The two recordings nominated by John Clare as the 'most successful' jazz recordings in Australia both display Munro's work; he was invited by leading American bandleader Chico Hamilton to join his group on cello. He was one of the major experimenters in Australian jazz.

FURTHER REFERENCE
Recordings include *Charlie Munro's Music* (1944, Prestophone X-1/X-2); *More Spring,* Bryce Rohde Quartet Featuring Charlie Munro (1990, MBS FM Jazz 6); *Eastern Horizons* (1967, Philips JS-020); *Count Down*, Charlie Munro's Orchestra (1969, Columbia SCXO-7911); *Integrations* (1986, Larrikin LRJ 170). See also *ClareB*; *BissetB*; *OxfordJ*; *GroveJ*; Trevor Graham, 'Charlie Munro's Eastern Horizons', *Music Maker* (Nov. 1967), 4–5, 11, 15; Alan Lee, 'Charlie Munro Talks to Alan Lee', *Music Maker* (May 1972), 4–5; *National Times* 7 Oct. 1978.
BRUCE JOHNSON

Munro, Bill (William Herbert Colyer)   (*b* Adelaide, 1 Oct. 1927), jazz trumpeter. With early training in J.E. Becker's youth bands, he began trumpet in 1940. His first jazz performances were in a school band in 1943, then he joined Malcolm Bills in 1944 and Dave *Dallwitz's Southern Jazz Group, with which he performed at the first Australian Jazz Convention. In the mid-1950s he joined Bruce *Gray, an association which continues to the present. He also formed his own groups and freelanced with Billy Ross, Maurie Le Doeuff, Gordon Coulson and Neville Dunn, demonstrating a broader stylistic command than his commitment to the local traditional jazz movement discloses.

FURTHER REFERENCE
Recordings include *Southern Jazz Group, 1946–1950,* vols 1–4 (Dawn Club DC 12021 to 12024); *Gulgong Shuffle*, Dave Dallwitz Jazz Band, (1978, Swaggie S-1378); *The Bruce Gray and Bill Munro Bands,* the Adelaide Sound (1990, Swaggie Cassette 1). See also *BissetB*; *OxfordJ*.
BRUCE JOHNSON

Murdoch, James Arthur   (*b* 25 Jan. 1930), writer, music consultant. He studied piano at the NSW State Conservatorium and worked for the Sydney *Sun*. In Spain from 1958, he composed the ballet *La Espera* (1959), and worked with the Fires of London from 1962. He returned to Sydney as assistant musical director for the Australian Ballet, became treasurer for the British Society for Electronic Music in London, and worked for the Australian Council for the Arts from 1972. He was founding director of the *Australian Music Centre from 1975, and was later with the Australian Bicentennial Authority. Also involved in film-making, he has produced over 60 documentaries on Australian artists. His book *Australia's Contemporary Composers* (1972) remains a landmark in Australian music studies, and he also wrote *A Handbook of Australian Music* (1983).

FURTHER REFERENCE
His 1972 book is *MurdochA*. See also *CA* (1995–96).

Murdoch, William   (*b* 10 Feb. 1888; *d* Hombury St Mary, Surrey, England, 9 Sept. 1942), pianist, teacher and writer. He studied at the University of Melbourne Conservatorium and went to London in 1906 to study at the Royal College of Music. Making his debut as a solo pianist in London in 1910, he then toured internationally. Especially sought after as a chamber music player, he performed with Lionel Tertis, Albert Sammons, Lauri *Kennedy and W.H. Squire, and took part in the premiere of Elgar's Piano Quintet (1919). He taught at the Royal Academy of Music 1930–36, composed songs, piano pieces and made transcriptions of works by Vivaldi, Handel and J.S. Bach, and was author of books on Brahms (for his 1933 centenary) and Chopin (1934).

FURTHER REFERENCE
Recordings include Elgar, Violin Sonata, A. Sammons, pf (Decca); Ireland, Violin Sonata No. 2, Catterall, pf (Columbia). See also J.A. Provan, *ADB*, 10; *GlennonA*, 84; Ferrucio Bonavia, Frank Dawes, *GroveD*.
CYRUS MEHER-HOMJI

Murphy, Graeme   (*b* Melbourne *c*.1950), dancer, choreographer. He studied at the Australian Ballet School in the 1960s and graduated to join the Australian Ballet, then left the troupe in 1971 to further his career in the USA and Europe. In 1976 he was appointed artistic director of the Dance Co., NSW (later to be renamed the Sydney Dance Co.). With his associate artistic director Janet Vernon he made the troupe one of the foremost dance ensembles in Australia. As a means to that end, the company has commissioned numerous Australian composers to write scores. *Poppy, with music by Carl Vine, and *Nearly Beloved*, scored by Graeme Koehne, have been two of Murphy's most successful collaborations. He was honoured in 1982 with the AM. See *Ballet and Dance Music*.

FURTHER REFERENCE
Michelle Potter, ed., 'Growing in Australian Soil: An Interview with Graeme Murphy, recorded by Hazel de Berg in 1981', *Brolga* 1 (Dec. 1994), 18–29.   JOEL CROTTY

Murphy, Norma (*b* Swan Hill, Vic., 26 June 1944), singer-songwriter. Raised on the Murray River and working as a jillaroo in her youth, she took singing lessons after marriage and a family and sang folk-songs on Swan Hill's Riverboat Restaurant in 1973. Seeking distinctly Australian material, she began writing traditional ballads influenced by those of Banjo Paterson, and released her debut album *Rodeo Queen* in 1981. A successful exponent of both folk and country Australian heritage styles, she has won three ACMA Golden Guitars.

FURTHER REFERENCE
Recordings include her albums *Rodeo Queen* (1981, Country Records), *The Vanishing Horseman* (1986, Selection PRC 042) and *Colours* (1989, Festival D 30043). See also *LattaA*, 132–3; *SmithB*, 311.

Musgrove, George (*b* Surbiton, England, 21 Jan. 1854; *d* Sydney, 21 Jan. 1916), theatrical entrepreneur. Arriving in Australia in childhood, as a young man he worked in accounting for his uncle W.S. *Lyster's opera company. After Lyster's death he produced Offenbach's *La Fille du Tambour Major* at Melbourne in 1880, then joined forces with his rivals J.C. *Williamson and Arthur Garner (from 1882) to present Gilbert and Sullivan operettas, which he had seen at London in 1879. They opened the Princess Theatre, Melbourne, in 1886 and presented musicals, operettas and opera, as well as dramatic works starring Nellie *Stewart, with whom Musgrove was long associated. He imported many front-rank artists and presented such operatic premieres as *Pagliacci* and *Cavalleria Rusticana* in the following years. He leased a theatre at London from 1897 to 1899, and after his partnership with Williamson ended in 1899 he resumed promotion in Australia until two years before his death, including mounting several lavish seasons of Wagner's operas (1900, 1907), and Melba's concert tour of 1902. With a sure eye for the new and significant, he was one of the most important theatrical impresarios in Australia for 30 years.

FURTHER REFERENCE
Obit. in *SMH* 24 Jan. 1916. Nellie Stewart's memoirs are *My Life's Story* (Sydney: John Sands, 1923). See also Alison Gyger, *Opera for the Antipodes* (Sydney: Currency Press,1990); *ParsonsC*; *IrvinD*; Jean Gittins, *ADB*, 5.

Mushroom Records. Independent recording company established 1972 in Melbourne, specialising in rock artists. Founder Michael Gudinski ran dances at the Caulfield Town Hall, Melbourne, from the age of 15 and established Australian Entertainment Exchange, which became one of the leading artist management agencies for rock bands. Concerned that record companies recorded little of the local bands and gave them scant artistic control, he established Mushroom, releasing a triple album of the Sunbury festival. Signing such groups as *Chain, *Skyhooks, *Split Enz, Renee *Geyer, *Ol'55, *Jo Jo Zep, and Billy *Thorpe, he was able to offer an integrated service of management, publishing and recording. He wrote contracts offering much higher royalties to songwriters, invested strongly in building artists' images and, after a long struggle, broke into the US market with Kylie Minogue's *Locomotion*. A key force in transforming the Australian rock industry, Mushroom today represents Kate *Ceberano, *Yothu Yindi, the *Angels, Ross *Wilson and many other major Australian artists, distributes for several smaller independent labels, and is responsible for most of Festival's local catalogue. Through his other ventures Gudinski is involved in the booking of more Australian acts than any other agent.

FURTHER REFERENCE
Rolling Stone (Aust.) 18 Feb. 1982, 58–69; *Australian* 30 Sept. 1989.

Music Education.

1. Specialist Musical Training. 2. Music in General Education. 3. Classroom Music-teaching Methods. 4. Music Education Organisations.

From colonial days Australian music education adhered to British educational practice, first in its adoption of sol-fah and class singing for schools, then in its enduring enthusiasm for a public examinations system offering certificates for the young and the plethora of conservatoriums and music departments offering formal degrees and diplomas for the more advanced. Since the 1970s, however, European, American and Japanese instrumental music approaches and creative classroom methods have gradually taken hold.

1. Specialist Musical Training. (i) Colonial Era and Early Federation. From the earliest colonial times, music was perceived as a desirable artistic pursuit and social accomplishment for the children of the well-to-do settler families. Professional musicians provided tuition in instrumental or vocal music at Sydney from *c*.1810, and private music schools such as the *Adelaide College of Music (founded 1883) catered for this clientele, as well as for young people who showed particular musical talent and wished to undertake vocational training as performers.

These private teaching studios set the scene for the establishment of *conservatoriums: the University of Melbourne Conservatorium under Professor G.W.L. Marshall-Hall in 1895 (the first university conservatorium to be established in the southern hemisphere) and the Elder Conservatorium at the University of Adelaide under the first professor of music, Joshua Ives in 1897. The NSW State Conservatorium of Music was established in 1915 with Henri Verbrugghen as director. In 1900 Marshall-Hall vacated the Ormond chair of music at the University of Melbourne and established the Albert Street Conservatorium as a private institution (now the Melba Memorial Conservatorium of Music, Richmond).

From the early 1880s visiting examiners from British examining bodies such as the Associated Board of the Royal Schools of Music, Trinity College London and London College of Music filled an important legitimating role for private teaching studios and institutions by examining their students for grade certificates and diplomas. The University of Adelaide entered the field in 1887 and University of Melbourne in 1903; they jointly established a Public Music Examinations Board in 1907. By 1914 the Universities of Tasmania, Western Australia and Queensland had become partners, and in 1916 they were joined by the NSW State Conservatorium, allowing the ★AMEB to become a national organisation co-ordinated by a federal council, although still largely operated by state committees.

(ii) The Modern Era.   Departments of music and conservatoriums were progressively established so that by 1994 there were 24 Australian universities offering music courses in some form, and several Technical and Further Education (TAFE) colleges also offering specialist music courses. Special pre-tertiary music training schools were also established to develop the talents of musically gifted students, at the NSW State Conservatorium, the Queensland Conservatorium and the Victorian College of the Arts as well as by state education departments at high schools in Perth and Adelaide. In 1994 the Federal Government announced the establishment of a National Academy of Music, located in Melbourne, as 'a centre of training excellence for musicians of outstanding talent'.

Numerous music teachers in private practice give tuition in instrumental music and singing throughout Australia. In addition, two instrumental teaching methods of Japanese origin were introduced to Australia in 1970: the Yamaha Music Schools offer group tuition to children and beginning adults mainly through 'electone' keyboards, and grade certificate and diploma examinations are offered by the Yamaha Music Foundation of Australia; and the Suzuki Talent Education, introduced to Australia by Harold Brissenden, promotes the teaching of violin, viola, cello, flute, piano and guitar through the 'mother-tongue' approach and group teaching methods.

The Associated Board and London College of Music ceased operations in Australia in the late 1940s and late 1960s respectively, leaving the AMEB and Trinity College London as the two examining bodies until the appearance of the Australian Guild of Music and Speech (AGMS, founded 1970) and Australian and New Zealand Cultural Arts (ANZCA, founded 1983).

The music camp movement in Australia, founded by Professor John ★Bishop and Ruth ★Alexander in 1948,

has provided orchestral and other ensemble performance opportunities for several generations of young instrumental players through the National Music Camp Association (now ★Youth Music Australia). In addition, state and regional music camps are held for young orchestral musicians during school vacations.

Most states have music teacher associations which represent teachers in private practice as well as instrumental and singing teachers in schools. In addition, the Institute of Music Teachers (established 1977) is a national accreditation body for studio teachers and there are also specialist organisations, such as Australian String Teachers' Association, at the national level.

2. Music in General Education. (i) Colonial Era, Early Federation.   School education in NSW and Victoria developed faster than in the less populous colonies. The origin of school music in Australia is essentially that of transplanted British educational practice. Vocal music was introduced to English elementary schools in the early 1840s when the committee of the Council on Education published an English adaptation by John Hullah of the French fixed-doh solmisation method, and was introduced to colonial schools not so much for its intrinsic values as for its capacity to instill moral, patriotic and religious values through the words of school songs. It was also viewed as a healthy recreation for children and a means of making schools attractive to both pupils and parents.

James ★Fisher (1826–91), singing master at Sydney, introduced Curwen's tonic sol-fa (movable-doh) system as the official teaching method to NSW public schools in 1867 and also established singing as part of the ordinary school curriculum. Since then, music teaching in NSW primary schools has generally been the responsibility of generalist classroom teachers. Hugo ★Alpen (1842–1917) was appointed as superintendent of music in 1884 and gradually transferred the teaching of music from tonic sol-fa to a movable-doh staff notation method of his own devising which preceded similar developments in English education by almost a decade. Alpen's successor, Theodore Tearne (1857–1926), was supervisor 1909–22.

The situation in Victoria differed significantly, for singing masters were appointed from the outset as itinerant specialists at the main centres of population. George Leavis ★Allan (1827–97) was appointed as the first singing master in 1853; other appointments followed, and by 1862 an estimated one-third of schoolchildren in Victoria were being taught singing—using Hullah's fixed-doh method—by visiting singing masters. In 1862 the cost of providing specialist music teaching in schools saw the itinerant singing masters initially dismissed and then, after public protest, re-instated under a system of extra fees paid by parents in 1864, effectively making music an extra-curricular subject. By the late 1860s the tonic numeral (staff notation) method—devised by John Waite in England—replaced Hullah's method in Victoria. In 1874 singing was included in the course of free instruction and taught either by itinerant singing masters or by licensed classroom teachers who were paid an additional £10 per annum to give musical instruction. In 1878 Joseph ★Summers (1839–1917) was appointed as inspector of music, a position he held until 1891.

In 1879 Samuel ★McBurney (1847–1909) embarked on a long but ultimately successful campaign for recognition of tonic sol-fa as a school music-teaching method in Victoria. With the onset of the 1890s Depression, the government dismissed all singing masters, abolished the position of inspector of music (to which McBurney was appointed in 1893), and ceased all extra payments to classroom teachers of music. Henceforth singing was to be the responsibility of classroom teachers, although little or no music teaching was evident until John Byatt (1862–1930), an ardent adherent of tonic sol-fa, reorganised school music from 1915.

In South Australia, tonic sol-fa was employed for teaching music in primary schools from the early 1870s, but it was not until 1890, when Alexander ★Clark (1843–1913) was a school inspector, that singing became mandatory in primary schools and a tonic sol-fa syllabus was included in the school curriculum in 1895. This period saw the founding of a choir of children from public schools (later called the Thousand Voice Choir) by the Public Schools Decoration Society in 1891, which presently continues under the SA Public (Primary) Schools Music Society. Frank (Francis Lymer) Gratton (1871–1947), a tonic sol-fa supporter, was appointed the first supervisor of music (1922–36).

In Queensland, music was being taught by itinerant specialists in Brisbane and Toowoomba by the early 1870s, and by 1875 vocal music was a subject in the primary school schedule. In 1908 George ★Sampson was appointed music adviser to the department of public instruction until 1930 when Charles Hall took over this role as lecturer in music at the Teachers College.

The introduction of music to schools in Tasmania was a more gradual process, and it was not until 1905 that singing by the tonic sol-fa method was included in the course of instruction for primary schools. Key figures in the development of school music in Tasmania were Frank ★Gratton, who promoted tonic sol-fa in Launceston and northern Tasmania from 1906 until returning to SA in 1911, and Victor von Bertouch, also a South Australian tonic sol-fa teacher, who was music instructor at the Hobart Teachers College.

(ii) The Modern Era. Secondary education developed in all state education systems from the 1910s, specialist music teachers were appointed to high schools from the 1930s, and directors of music were also appointed at the larger private schools such as Scotch College in Melbourne and St Peter's in Adelaide. Instrumental music in schools during the colonial period had been limited to drum and fife bands, which were viewed as an extension of military

drill; now it became important, with orchestras and concert bands being established in secondary schools from the late 1920s. The Gillies Bequest (1926) was an important factor in promoting instrumental teaching and ensemble performance in Victorian state schools, providing funds for the purchase of instruments.

In NSW, Herbert Fredrind Treharne succeeded Alpen as supervisor of music in 1922. Then in 1948, Terrance Hunt was appointed to supervise music teaching by generalist teachers in primary schools and specialist teachers in secondary schools. Later a School Music Centre was established and from the late 1960s regional music advisers were appointed to promote music in primary schools. By 1970 there were four secondary inspectors in music, but now there are state-wide music co-ordinators in a central performing arts unit as well as regional arts consultants.

In Victoria, Alfred B. Lane became the first supervisor of music in 1923. Under his auspices, itinerant music teachers were appointed to teach in secondary schools and in some primary schools; by 1940 his department was known as the music branch. Doris M. Irwin (1905–94) succeeded Lane in 1943, Helen McMahon followed in 1970, and by 1975 the branch had 107 staff. But in 1978 it was disbanded, and 236 new positions for music specialists and regional music advisers in primary schools were established. With a further shift in official policy in 1982, most of these positions were abolished and the majority of specialist primary music teachers either obtained on-staff 'tagged' music positions or returned as generalist teachers to primary classrooms. In secondary schools, music was part of the ordinary curriculum for Years 7 and 8 by the 1960s as well as being available for elective study through to Year 12. In 1966 the first secondary school inspector of music, Alexandra E. Cameron, was appointed, and in 1972 she was succeeded by Bruce Worland, whose position later became that of senior music development officer until it was phased out with a further devolution of administration to schools. Itinerant instrumental teachers are now appointed at a regional level.

In South Australia, Alva I. Penrose was the supervisor of music 1937–59. John Slee succeeded him (1960–74), during which time the music branch was responsible for supervision of both classroom and instrumental music teaching in schools. Alan Farwell followed as supervisor from 1975 until 1985, after which the branch became the administrative unit for itinerant instrumental teachers until they were re-formed into localised instrumental teaching teams in 1990.

The first supervisor of music appointed in Queensland was Kevin Siddell in 1970. A music section was established to provide itinerant instrumental teachers for the various school regions. Some specialist teachers were appointed to primary schools in addition to those already in secondary schools. The next supervisor, appointed in 1979, was Ann Carroll who is now principal policy officer in a new visual and performing arts unit established in 1991.

In Tasmania, the work of Gratton and Bertouch led to the appointment of specialist singing teachers in primary schools from 1927. Although high schools had been part of the Tasmanian state school system since 1913, it was not until the 1940s that music became part of the secondary school curriculum. The first supervisor, appointed in 1946, was George Limb; Wilfrid King succeeded him in 1950, and John Morriss was supervisor 1972–c.1989, after which a principal curriculum officer in charge of all arts in schools was appointed.

The first superintendent of music in Western Australia was Campbell Egan, who was appointed in 1928 to promote singing and music appreciation in schools. A music branch was established, and during Edgar Nottage's time as superintendent 1955–81 instrumental music—initially recorder playing and then a Suzuki program—developed in secondary schools. Roy Rimmer was appointed as superintendent in 1981, but in 1987 this position was discontinued in favour of music education co-ordinator and instrumental co-ordinator positions. In 1995 a new position of superintendent of the arts was created.

With the devolution of administration of state education from the central departmental authority to regions and then to local schools during the 1980s, most states have now dispensed with music supervisors and centrally administered music-teaching staff. Responsibility for classroom music teaching in state primary schools is either with generalist teachers or on-staff specialists, and in secondary schools, with on-staff specialist teachers. Instrumental teaching at the secondary level is generally provided by visiting teachers assigned to a group of schools. Some states have statewide and/or regional music consultants.

3. Classroom Music-teaching Methods. From c.1920 the music curriculum expanded greatly. The introduction of gramophones to schools ushered in the music appreciation movement, and by the 1930s music appreciation programs were being broadcast by the ABC and its precursors by the Melbourne musician A.E. ★Floyd. Another important impetus to the music appreciation movement was the inauguration of schools' concerts at the Melbourne Town Hall by the conductor Bernard ★Heinze in 1929.

Next followed Music Through Movement, based on Dalcroze eurhythmics. Heather ★Gell (1896–1988) promoted Dalcroze in Adelaide before moving to Sydney to present a series of weekly national broadcasts to schools on ABC radio from 1938. Music Through Movement continues to have an important role in school music and is promoted through Dalcroze Societies in NSW, Victoria and SA.

Percussion bands were introduced to primary music classrooms from the 1920s and later, following the introduction of recorder playing to English schools by Arnold Dolmetsch, recorder groups were established in Australian schools from the 1940s. But it was not until the 1960s that classroom instrumental music and creative music-making

became more firmly established with the Orff-Schulwerk approach. Keith Smith introduced Orff-Schulwerk to Queensland schools, from where it spread to other states. John Morriss also promoted the method, initially in Victoria and later in Tasmania. There are Orff-Schulwerk associations in most states.

Another significant influence on school music was the Kodály method, introduced to Australia in 1971 by Deanna ★Hoermann, who established a highly successful Kodály Pilot Project under the auspices of the NSW department of education in Sydney's western metropolitan region. The Kodály method is now well established throughout Australia as the Developmental Music Program which Hoermann has, with various collaborators, adapted to suit the Australian cultural context. The Kodály Music Education Institute of Australia, established in 1973, has branches in most states and promotes the method through professional development activities for teachers.

As a result of a decision by the Australian Education Council in 1989, a national curriculum for Australian schools was developed and finally published in 1994. Music is included as one of six subject strands within the statement and curriculum profile for the arts in Australian schools, thereby establishing it as an integral component in the general education of young people in Australia. Most state education authorities have developed their own music curriculum frameworks based on the national statement and curriculum profile.

4. Music Education Organisations. The Australian Society for Music Education (ASME) was founded in 1966 and has chapters in all Australian states as well as a national council; it is the representative in Australia of the International Society for Music Education and the publisher of the *Australian Journal of Music Education*. Other national organisations include the Australian Association for Research in Music Education (AARME, formerly the Association of Music Education Lecturers [AMEL]) and more recently the National Affiliation of Arts Educators (NAAE) which promotes music—together with the other arts—in schools. The Callaway International Resource Centre for Music Education (CIRCME) was established at the University of Western Australia in 1989. In addition there are school music and specialist method associations in most states. See also *School and Children's Choirs*.

FURTHER REFERENCE

AJME (1967–82, 1986–); D.M. Bridges, The Role of the Universities in the Development of Music Education in Australia, 1885–1970, PhD, Univ. of Sydney, 1970; L. Lepherd, *Music Education in International Perspective: Australia* (Toowoomba, Qld: Univ. Southern Qld Press, 1994); R.S. Stevens, Music in State-Supported Education in New South Wales and Victoria, 1848–1920, PhD, Univ. Melbourne, 1978.

ROBIN S. STEVENS

Music Hall. A British working-class entertainment, with a chairman who acted as master of ceremonies introducing a sequence of unrelated items, while the customers sat at tables and waiters circulated selling alcohol and food. The entertainment was of frankly vulgar and irreverent mood, with a *mélange* of ribald and sentimental songs, recitations, comedy and animal acts. An early music hall program opened at Tilkes's City Hotel, Sydney in 1857; this was soon imitated elsewhere in the colony. By the late 1860s the Royal Alhambra and the Scandinavian Music Halls opened in Sydney, each with fixed rows of seating, the alcohol now served in an adjacent room. A more sophisticated venue, the Academy of Music, Sydney (later renamed the Alhambra Music Hall), was opened in 1888. Never as popular in Australia as they were in Britain, music halls were being supplanted by the late 1890s by ★vaudeville theatres, which presented a more sophisticated and less narrowly prescribed fare.

FURTHER REFERENCE
Richard Waterhouse, *From Minstrel Show to Vaudeville* (Sydney: UNSWP, 1990), 42; *ParsonsC*; *IrwinD*; *Bulletin* 2 Oct. 1929.

Music-sellers and Retailers

1. Beginnings to 1880. 2. The Boom Years, 1880–1930.
3. Decline, 1930-Present.

Although there are over 50 enterprises printing and selling music in Australia today, most, aside from those that are agents for international publishers, are very small and short-lived, and lack any reliable distribution. The few long-lived, major sellers are both publishers and retailers, and at least until the advent of sound recordings they also played a crucial role in Australian musical life as piano manufacturers, concert promoters, and supporters of Australian composition and many aspects of Australian musical life.

1. Beginnings to 1880. As early as 1811 Sydney possessed a store selling printed music and instruments, and the musicians of Hobart also traded in music and instruments. By 1824 there were at least four stores in Sydney selling instruments, and in April 1828 the most successful, 'professor' John Edwards, claimed to have sold 23 Broadwood pianos to the gentry in the previous three years. Ellard's Music Warehouse in Hunter Street was established in 1832. Francis ★Ellard had learned the music trade in the Dublin firm of Andrew Ellard & Son and imported pianofortes made by the London makers Broadwood and Collard & Collard. In the 1830s William Vincent Wallace (1812–65) sold pianos in his music repository in Hunter Street and a Mr Tyrer imported pianos and harps for his Fancy Repository, also on Hunter Street. Jacob Richard ★Clarke (1822–93) and William Prout Woolcott, 'Music Sellers, Print Sellers, & Publishers', opened a shop at George Street in 1854 selling instruments as well as music by colonial composers.

William Henry ★Paling (1825–95), son of a Dutch piano manufacturer, arrived in Sydney in 1853. He established a music warehouse at Wynyard Square and began teaching and arranging concerts. By 1856 he had obtained an agency for Erard and other European pianos, importing 154 in the following five years. In 1864 he travelled to Europe to obtain instruments and sheet music. On his return he advertised 'large selections of Pianofortes of the best makers … being guided by many years experience respecting the most suitable instruments for this climate'. In 1859 NSW imported musical instruments to the value of £18 984 and only a year later to the value of £26 964. Having become a prominent Sydney businessman and philanthropist, Paling periodically visited European instrument-makers to secure agencies for their products.

In Melbourne by 1850, pianos were sold at Reed's Music Warehouse on Bourke Street. Joseph Wilkie (*d* 1875) had been a piano-tuner with Broadwood, and arrived in Melbourne in 1850. He established himself in Collins Street in that year as 'J. Wilkie, music seller' to tune and repair pianos. Soon afterwards he opened a 'Music and Pianoforte Saloon' in the same street, advertising a stock of sheet music including polkas, quadrilles, negro melodies and musical dictionaries, new pianos by Broadwood and others, violins, flageolets, fifes and flutes. In 1862 another emigrant from Broadwood, J.C. Webster (*d* 1875), joined Wilkie, and in 1863 the music teacher George ★Allan (1826–97) combined with them to form Wilkie, Webster & Allan. In the following years they imported pianos and supplied harmoniums and organs to churches, advertising 'Church Organs of the best English and Foreign Builders imported and erected'. Instruments could be bought on easy terms or hired, and old instruments could be traded in.

Richard Henry Sutton (1830–76) travelled to the Ballarat goldfields in 1854 hoping to find his fortune in gold, but when he discovered the demand for musical instruments he established a music warehouse in Ballarat. After his death in 1876 his wife and sons ran the business, continuing to import French pianos and the first German pianos with iron frames. Alfred Sutton opened a music store in Elizabeth Street, Melbourne, in 1884, at which time the firm became Sutton Bros (then Suttons Pty Ltd, 1894) and opened provincial branches in Bendigo (1892) and Geelong (1903).

The Melbourne partnership of Wilkie, Webster & Allan dissolved in 1875 when Webster died and Allan bought out the remaining business. By 1877 Allan's store had become the largest music warehouse in the southern hemisphere. J.C.W. ★Nicholson (1837–1907) was employed by Allans in Melbourne until 1875 when he opened his own music store on Collins Street in partnership with Elman Ascherberg. By this date Collins Street had become a fashionable boulevard and Melbourne's prosperity was reflected in the abundance of music stores on that street. The *Australasian Sketcher* remarked that because of 'the fine exteriors of some of these places, their spacious and well-arranged inside premises, and the great extent of their stock it would seem that every Victorian must be a born musician, and must devote all his spare money and time to this pursuit'.

Allan decided in 1877 to lease a building at 17–19 Collins Street which had previously housed the small music store of Lee & Kaye. These new premises, costing £8000, were three storeys high; on the ground floor were shelves stacked with cases of music, above was a Grand Salon which could seat 500 and which served as the piano showroom, and above that cabinet organs were displayed. Allan travelled to Europe in 1879 and established trading connections with the major instrument-makers. On his return he advertised his business as the sole agent for many of the leading piano makers with pianos worth £20 000 in stock. In a fire in 1889 Allans and Glens both lost £30 000 worth of sheet music, while Glens also lost 40 pianos worth £14 000.

2. The Boom Years, 1880–1930. William Paling opened an extensive showroom in Sydney at 352 George Street in 1875. In 1876 Nicholson opened a branch in Sydney and when Ascherberg left for London in 1878 the business was renamed Nicholson & Co. The Sydney International Exhibition (1879–80) attested to the demand for instruments in the colony. A local paper reported that 'in Sydney alone the number of pianofortes in use is believed to be larger in proportion to the number of houses than in any European capital, yet the demand rarely slackens'. At the exhibition were displayed concert grand pianos, boudoir grands, semi-grands, patent short-iron grands, upright iron grands and cottage pianos. In 1883 Paling bought large premises costing £45 000 at 356 George Street and formed a limited liability company. He established branches of his business in Toowoomba (1884), Brisbane (1888) and Newcastle (1892). By 1891 he was able to open a new building at 338 George Street with seven storeys of showrooms and teaching rooms.

Overstocking at the time of the exhibition eventually led J.R. Clarke to bankruptcy in 1885, but in the following year Walter Joseph Stent (1863–1930) established a business selling instruments at Elizabeth Street, and later Hunter Street, Sydney. Nicholson & Co. established new branches in Brisbane in 1890 and Perth in 1893 and, recognising more opportunities in Sydney than in Melbourne, moved their head office to 333 George Street in 1894. Nicholsons was by now agent for Steinway, Brinsmead and Mignon pianos as well as Conn saxophones and Crackajack mouth-organs.

A number of other prominent businesses began operation in the 1880s. George Marshall (c.1866–1930) left Palings to open his own piano store. In 1886 Alfred Percy Sykes (d 1936) joined Philip P. Samuel as musical instrument importers in Sydney. By 1887 they opened a branch in Melbourne and when Samuel retired in 1891 Sykes took over the business as A.P. Sykes. Marcus ★Brash & Co.

began trading in Melbourne in 1862 and opened a store at 108 Elizabeth Street in 1880. Paling established a partnership with Richard Jefferies (1841–1920) in Brisbane in 1876 but it dissolved in 1881. William Myers King (1858–1942) left Melbourne in 1886 to move to Brisbane and establish the music business of King & King with his brother. In 1884 Charles Witto-Witto ★Cawthorne (1854–1925) set up a business in Adelaide as 'music-sellers and artists' colormen'. By 1896 he carried sheet music from 60 publishers along with a large stock of instruments. Jacques ★Albert (d 1914) began importing violins in 1890 and when his son joined the business in 1894 they became J. Albert & Son.

By 1900–1 NSW imported more than £350 000 worth of musical instruments. The largest and most influential businesses were Palings in Sydney and Allans in Melbourne. Although troubled by the recession of the 1890s, Allans became a limited liability company. Occupying a Collins Street building four storeys high, it was known that 'budding artists and would-be artists fly to Allan's as naturally as a swallow flies to the south'. On the first floor were up to 100 pianos, including quality pianos by Bechstein, Brinsmead and Erard, as well as less expensive pianos by Lipp, Feurich, Leipsic and Ecke. Advertisements stated that 'No settlement is so remote, no township so lonely as not to contain one of Allan's pianos; and music, the great solace of the bush, is brought within the reach of every householder'. Phonographs became so popular that in 1904 the company rented a building in Little Collins Street as phonograph showrooms. In 1905 Allans bought out the music store of Oscar Flight in Bendigo and in 1910 they purchased the Adelaide firm of Howells, Young & Co. In 1911 they began publishing *Australian Musical News,* a key commentator on musical affairs in Australia for 50 years; by this time they were also publishing music by Australian composers in considerable quantity.

At the onset of war in 1914 NSW imported 40 grand pianos and 3822 uprights, with equal numbers from Germany and Great Britain. The most popular pianos were German because of their better construction and cheaper price. As a result of the war, restrictions were placed on the importation of German goods, prompting businesses to look to Australian manufacturers for supplies. The piano-makers Beale, Carnegie and Wertheim had stores in both Sydney and Melbourne. In 1919 Suttons, Nicholsons, the Australian Implement and House Furnishing Co. of Adelaide, Buhler & Co. of Perth and Findlays of Tasmania became the Concord Company to manufacture pianos and player pianos. Allans, Palings and Suttons joined with the Melbourne piano-makers ★Wertheim to become the Australian Piano Factory, but the venture ended in 1935. With the arrival of the player-piano in the 1920s, sales of pianos declined. In 1922 Allans advertised five brands of player-piano, the Autotone, Playotone, Estey, Faber and Morel, with 'word rolls' for them mostly priced at seven shillings. The popularity of the player can be indicated by the size of imports to Victoria at this time, which increased from £122 871 in 1920 to £293 502 in 1921. In 1928 a Playotone made by Hardman Peck & Co. sold for £255, while others started at £175 and easy terms could be agreed upon with a deposit of £10. At the peak of the boom, Palings had capital of £750 000 and a staff of 450.

3. Decline, 1930 to the Present. Imports quickly fell as a result of the Depression and the new duty and sales tax. NSW in 1930 imported only three pipe organs, seven grand pianos, eight upright pianos and 10 player-pianos. Palings continued to expand, opening branches in Lismore in 1911, Townsville (1923), Cairns (1939), Wollongong (1940), Orange and Bankstown (1941). But businesses were forced to diversify, many turning to sales of whitegoods, and some of the older businesses never recovered. Albert & Son abandoned retailing in 1933, Stent retired in 1925 and George Marshall died in 1930. Nicholsons and Allans merged Sydney operations in 1936 but Allans sold their Nicholsons shares in the mid-1950s. Nicholsons and Palings then merged and a holding company, Music Houses, was formed. By 1956–57 Melbourne possessed 318 establishments selling instruments, records and sheet music, Sydney had 258, Brisbane 69, Adelaide 104, Perth 68 and Hobart 16. Five years later Sydney boasted 100 more while Melbourne had lost 50. The firm of Brashs became a public company in 1958 and in 1960 advertised the largest range of new pianos at its Elizabeth Street store. In 1964 it bought out Suttons and in 1969 acquired Kilners, another firm which had been trading since the 1850s. Recognising the demographical shift it opened branches in the suburbs, a move which Allans was slow to emulate.

By 1970 Allans had a turnover of at least $6 million, a staff of over 300 and branches in Geelong, Bendigo, Adelaide, Hobart and Launceston. A mainstay of the firm's publishing arm was its series for the AMEB, in which it had a monopoly; but increasingly unable to show a profit, it was taken over by Brash Holdings in 1976, which then acquired R.H. Elvy in Sydney (in 1980), B.B. Whitehouse in Brisbane (in 1981) and Edels record stores (in 1984). The publication of *Australian Musical News* had ceased in 1963, and the issue of new works by Australian composers sharply diminished. Palings was taken over by the Billy Guyatt group in 1975. By 1987 Brashs had opened the largest music store in Australia, in Pitt Street, Sydney, and operated 81 stores nationally. In 1991–92 retail sales of recorded music amounted to $850.5 million, while sales of musical instruments and sheet music amounted to $291.7 million, with the majority of sales being made in NSW.

FURTHER REFERENCE
BrisbaneE; Australian Bureau of Statistics, *Retail Industry 1991–92: Commodity Sales Australia*; *Death of an Old Citizen: Mr Jacob Richard Clarke* (Sydney: n.p., 1893); Peter Game, *The Music Sellers* (Melbourne: Hawthorn, 1976); 'Historic Music Firms Join', *AMN* 26 (1 Feb. 1936), 6; *The History, Philosophy and Future of Brash Holdings Limited* (Melbourne: Craftsman Press, 1987); Eve Keane, *Music for a Hundred Years* (Sydney: Ziegler, 1954); Sandra McKay and Bill Birnbauer, 'Playing the Same Tune', *Age*, 9 Dec. 1995, Extra, p. 5; *NSW Year Book* (various); G. Sutton, *Richard Henry Sutton, Esq., 1830–1876* (Melbourne: Suttons, 1954); *Victorian Year Book* (various).

SUZANNE ROBINSON

Music Theatre. Dramatic works were staged in Australia with musical components from the earliest days of European settlement, and many forms of music-theatre thrived in Australia throughout the 19th century. Within a decade of the first settlement, Sideway's Theatre offered music-theatre at Sydney: it will remain uncertain how much music was presented with William Shield's *The Poor Soldier* in 1796, but by 1800 there was clearly music in Henry Fielding's *An Old Man Taught Wisdom,* offered as a support to the main comedy bill. Barnett ★Levey was adding musical interludes to his melodramas at Sydney from 1832, and the Royal Victoria Theatre, Sydney, had a small orchestra for its theatrical programs by 1838.

★Opera was presented regularly from the 1840s, but many other forms of music-theatre also flourished. Dramatic productions in Sydney and Melbourne were often billed with supporting musical burlesques or extravaganzas in the 1850s. English pantomimes were adapted with Australian content from 1850. W.S. ★Lyster's opera company presented the *opéra-bouffes* of Offenbach from 1871, introducing *La Belle Hélène* and Gilbert and Sullivan's *Trial By Jury* in 1876. J.C. ★Williamson presented Gilbert and Sullivan's *HMS Pinafore* in 1879 and George ★Musgrove brought the London company for Offenbach's *La Fille du tambour-major* in 1880; Williamson, Musgrove and Arthur Garner then collaborated and brought the principal Gilbert and Sullivan operettas, to great acclaim, as soon as they were available in the following years. They also had great success with pantomime, musical comedies such as Edwardes' *A Gaiety Girl* in 1893, *The Geisha* in 1898, *The Orchid* in 1904, and operettas of Lehár, Suppé and, from 1903, Victor Herbert.

The advent of the movies, silent from 1914 (but often with elaborate orchestral accompaniment) and 'talkies' from 1929, made live music-theatre after World War I much more fragile. For years promoters would not risk the wartime London hits *Chu Chin Chow* or *The Maid of the Mountains*, and these were not seen in Australia until the 1920s; a few American musicals of greater novelty, such as *No! No! Nanette* (in 1925) or *The Desert Song* (in 1929), came more quickly. The new Broadway hits were surprisingly slow to catch on in Australia, *Show Boat* having only a short run at Melbourne in 1927, and even *West Side Story* doing little better in 1960. The 1930s saw strong success for Australian star Gladys ★Moncrieff, including in Australian works such as Varney Monk's ★*Collits' Inn,* in 1932, but generally the promoters now produced only revivals of Gilbert and Sullivan or old musical standards.

In the years after World War II *Annie Get Your Gun* had an immense success in 1947 and *Oklahoma!* in 1949, but for more than a decade new American or British musicals did not play regularly in Australia. The costs of bringing an imported company were prohibitive, while tax and copyright problems made even the staging of an imported work with a local cast fraught with risk. Australian works such as *The *Sentimental Bloke* in 1961 were very rare. *My Fair Lady* had an unusual success in 1959; *Man of La Mancha* and *A Chorus Line* are two of the few which had successful Australian runs in the 1970s. After the demise of J.C. Williamson's, dedicated music-theatre promoters vanished, and it fell to entrepreneurs like Harry M. *Miller to produce the rock musicals *Hair* or *Jesus Christ Superstar* in the 1970s. Since then the Andrew Lloyd Webber works, the Broadway reworking of *The Pirates* and similar musicals have often been presented in Australia by opera companies or by the venue managements of the capital city concert halls. See *Musical Comedy, Music Hall, Vaudeville.*

FURTHER REFERENCE

John West, 'Musical Theatre', *Parsons C*, which contains a complete index of music-theatre works performed in Australia; idem, *Music Theatre in Australia* (Sydney: Cassell, 1978); Harold Love, ed., *The Australian Stage: A Documentary History* (Sydney: UNSWP, 1984).

Music Theory and Analysis.

1. Theory Pedagogy. 2. Current Developments in Australian Theory and Analysis.

In Australian musical scholarship distinctions such as those between the 'synchronic' and 'diachronic,' or 'internalist' and 'externalist' are not maintained with any rigidity, and this is reflected in the social organisation of musicological disciplines. Whereas separate societies exist in the USA and Britain for the practice of music theory or analysis, these activities are not isolated in Australia from historical scholarship, but remain under the general auspices of the Musicological Society of Australia. This continuing connection between the sub-disciplines of musicology has been seen to facilitate the discovery of interpretive commonality between them (*Kassler 1988–89: 26).

In addition to their interpretive role, music theories codify structural procedures that are applicable to certain styles of contemporary composition. Tonal harmonic relationships, for example, remain current in popular composition, and reappear in 'classical' postmodern works. Serialism also is employed by such Australian composers as Richard Meale and Chris Dench, who have assimilated European modernism. Many of the issues identified in the current discourse of Australian composers have not, however, been addressed in a formal theory.

1. Theory Pedagogy. (i) Orientations. Tonal harmony and counterpoint have formed a prominent part of theory teaching in Australia, which has been strongly influenced by British models. A survey conducted in 1978 on the teaching of traditional harmony by university lecturers (one representing each state), revealed two pedagogic orientations: the first was an emphasis on historically grounded aesthetic appreciation, which finds in harmonic rules a means for imparting understanding of the European repertory of 1650–1925 (*Bartle); harmony is viewed as essential for musical literacy (*Fox), and its study is linked to the imitation of specific styles of the European common-practice period (*Nickson). A textbook by David *Tunley (1978) demonstrates this historical emphasis by presenting harmonic rules through examples from the repertory, without dwelling on details such as 'doubling rules' that are viewed as non-essential to historical understanding; the study of this text is intended for the development of analytic rather than creative skill. The second orientation advocates a more creative approach, motivated by their involvement in the training of teachers for young children (Kay 1978, 1991), or a concern with the practical needs of performers (*Bridges).

(ii) Public Examination Syllabuses. The theory and musicianship examinations administered by the AMEB, Trinity College, and the Associated Board have held an important position in the development of popular conceptions of music theory in Australia because they are prerequisites for the widely used practical examinations, and their graded requirements thus define the minimum knowledge of instrumental and vocal students.

The teaching of theoretical concepts according to the AMEB syllabus has notable idiosyncrasies when it passes beyond the rudiments of notation and scale forms (see Adriaansz, 1972). The recommended harmony textbooks by J.A. *Steele and William *Lovelock present triads and their structural relationships without providing examples from the repertory other than a rare excerpt from a Bach chorale. Until the seventh grade, Bach's vocal four-part harmony is the stylistic model, but instead of using the figured-bass numerals that are grounded in 18th-century practice, the AMEB employs a simplified notation allowing the root position of a triad and its inversions to be labelled with letter names (a,b,c,d), a habit that is also adopted by Tunley.

This practice places emphasis on the vertical transformation of individual chords, rather than on their voice-leading or structural context. As a result the functional discrimination of inversions from one another appears to be dictated by arbitrary rules, and little appreciation is developed for the formation of a tonal context. 'Modulation' appears in this system as a transitory effect of any accidental, other than the leading note of a minor key. Larger-scale tonal connections appear only as an attribute of 'form', which is limited to the progressive identification of binary, ternary, rondo, or sonata designs. Seventh-chords other than applied dominants are not stipulated in the AMEB requirements until the AMusA examination, although they are common in the repertory of less advanced practical students, and aurally familiar to them in popular music. The weak level of reference to musical repertory is not compensated in this program by the practical exercises, which introduce 'creative work' only in the form of writing melodies, whose 'rules' of construction are presented systematically in texts by *Leckie and Lovelock. Many of these shortcomings were recognised by the AMEB in 1986, when it adopted a major report on its theoretical syllabuses by *Bebbington (1986); but although a new syllabus was drafted, it remained unpublished (Bebbington 1988) and none of the 18 recommendations for change have been acted on.

(iii) Music Theory in Schools. The deficiencies of the public examination system have not been unknown in the music programs of schools. Stowasser (1990) comments that the traditional disciplines should not be lost because of past inadequacies in their presentation:

> What is irrelevant is the theoretical and often unaesthetic
> . approaches that are sometimes applied to harmony and
> counterpoint, inherited from nineteenth century England,
> which still prevail in a great many training establishments.
> (1990: 21)

A revision of teaching priorities at school level is evident in the development of programs where harmony and counterpoint do not appear under the distinct rubric of 'music theory' but are integrated with other activities (see, for example, Board of Studies 1994). Teaching material produced by the Australian Music Centre for use in the later school years motivates the consideration of theoretical questions through the study of individual works from the Australian repertory. Smith (1991) gives opportunities for harmonic analysis in a context where tonal harmony is a current compositional practice; *Ford (1991) raises questions about gesture, rhythmic function, mimetic reference, narrative and the role of the performer and in so doing it introduces issues that are currently being explored in music theory; and Fong (1994) introduces questions of cultural representation that are of concern to contemporary composers (Beattie, Carmody 1991). A resource book on Australian Jazz by Roger Frampton (1992) illustrates its theoretical points with taped examples. In all of these resource books theoretical questions are related to cultural concerns, and the development of music theory is stimulated as a response to issues raised in the analysis of individual works.

(iv) Music Theory in Higher Education. Methodologies for teaching tonal theory in tertiary music schools have adapted during the 1980s and 90s to an increasing awareness of the theories of Heinrich Schenker. This change was influenced by Australian scholars who had studied at King's College, London (Malcolm *Gillies) or the City University, New York (Warren Bebbington). Harmony and counterpoint textbooks influenced by Schenkerian concepts (Aldwell and Schachter 1978;

Schachter and Salzer 1969) are the principal means by which students in an undergraduate course gain exposure to concepts of voice-leading as transmitted by the American Schenkerian tradition. Felix Salzer's *Structural Hearing* appeared as an introduction to Schenker's analytical practice in 1962, and the translation of Schenker's *Der Freie Satz* became available (*Free Composition* 1979), but the textbook by Allan Forte and Stephen Gilbert, *Introduction to Schenkerian Theory* (1982), has been the principal text for undergraduate courses in analysis, reinforcing the American Schenkerian emphasis on reductive procedures.

A harmonic practice derived from the teachings of Schoenberg has been influential at the University of Adelaide, where Geoffrey Moon pioneered the first graduate diploma in music theory in 1990, and an approach to structural functions based on the theories of Hugo Riemann has been introduced at the Canberra School of Music by the Swedish theorist Bengt-Olav Palmqvist. Atonal and serial techniques appear in general undergraduate courses as part of the study of 20th century repertory, but do not receive the emphasis given them in the USA. The education of composers is eclectic, and does not give precedence to this or any other technique (Whiffin 1991). A move towards increasing eclecticism in the musical education of all students has been advocated as a response to the cultural diversity of contemporary Australian music (Bebbington 1990). This entails a broadening of theoretical approaches to include a consideration of non-Western cultures and their theories. Rather than a specialised education in individual modal, tonal or atonal theories it demands a flexibility similar to that being developed in materials for secondary schools.

2. Current Developments in Australian Theory and Analysis. Australian scholars have made significant contributions to the history and philosophy of Western music theory (Kassler; Pont) and to the development of new explanatory models (Gillies 1989). Critical response to Australian compositions has not been substantial enough to produce an interpretive theory specific to them, but an incipient theoretical discourse relating to contemporary works has developed through discussions and symposia reported in the journal *Sounds Australian,* and this could lead to further theoretical work. Many issues raised by composers are related to the signification of certain sounds or techniques appropriated from other cultures or schools. Sonic materials taken from Aboriginal or Asian cultures are transformed by their incorporation in a Western composition, and concern has been expressed about the dangers of cultural tokenism (Beattie 1991). Ellis (1991), for example, argues for a greater awareness of the theoretical constructs implied in the structure of Aboriginal song design, rather than an appropriation of the more obvious features of Aboriginal sound (e.g. didjeridu and clapping sticks). This position is countered with support for the composer's freedom in choosing sonic materials (Currie 1991).

The discussion of appropriation suggests the need for analyses that address both signification and structure. For example, a composition by Moya Henderson juxtaposing the sounds of didjeridu, pipe organ and 'car horns' asks for analysis not of its abstract structures alone, but of the role and function of its cultural references (Macarthur, 1991). Signification is an issue even in discussing the reception by Australians of compositional techniques developed in Europe. The 'New Complexity' embraces serial techniques familiar in the Darmstadt school, as well as the complex notations of British composer Brian Ferneyhough. Difficulties in performance are inherent in this style and lead to a redefinition of musical content. Richard *Hames claims that the discomfort experienced by a performer in realising his complex scores is part of the content of the work (1991), an idea that is supported by the semiotic reflections of the composer Liza *Lim (1991).

If performance transforms content so radically, analysts cannot address the score alone in interpreting the work. Neither can they presume the relevance of precompositional procedures to their perceptions, even when the complexity of these procedures yields its own fascination (see Chris *Dench in McCallum 1991b). Instead of seeking the objectivity of score-analysis, or giving an account of compositional procedure, analytic interpreters are compelled to use language in which their own responses are implicated. This may be both personal and metaphorical (Gillies, McCallum, Macarthur, Kassler 1991). Analytical responses to contemporary music necessitate a reassessment of the aesthetic priorities found in structural theories. Inherited oppositions between autonomous structure and cultural reference, abstract organisation and performed embodiment, objective description and personal response, cannot be fully maintained when interpreting this repertory.

The strength of these oppositions in received structural theory may account for the relative paucity of published analyses of contemporary Australian works, but the increasing influence of theoretical approaches developed in other humanistic disciplines has already signalled their demise and provided an impetus for change. Feminism (Macarthur 1991, 1992; Grosz 1989; Kouvaras, 1996), postmodernism (Burt 1992; Kouvaras 1996) and poststructuralism (McCallum 1990rev.) have each suggested a vocabulary for approaching works without making false presumptions of their absolute structural autonomy. Work by ethnomusicologists on the semantic understanding of Aboriginal musicians provides a model from which Western theorists can learn (*Ellis and Barwick, 1987). The development of interpretive music theory may be stimulated by the assimilation of insights from these disciplines. Balancing this broad cultural awareness, a close attention to the analysis of individual works will allow a concern with structural signification to be addressed in concrete compositional circumstances (see Cumming 1996).

FURTHER REFERENCE

(i) Education and Pedagogical Material

Adriaansz, Rebecca, 'The A.M.E.B. System of Theory and Musicianship Examinations: A Critical Appraisal', *AJME* 10 (1972), 31–38.

Bebbington, Warren, Australian Theory and Musicianship Examinations: A Report. Melbourne: AMEB, 1986.

——, Beginning Music. Syllabus; Guide to Teachers. Unpublished ms, AMEB, 1988.

——, 'The Getting of Wisdom? Australian Music in the Music School Curriculum', *SA* 28 (1990), 3–5.

Bartle, Graham, Doreen Bridges, Malcolm Fox, Don Kay, Noël Nickson and Roger Smalley, 'The Teaching of Traditional Harmony', *AJME* 23 (1978), 39–46.

Board of Studies. Verma, Surendra, project editor, *Music: History and Styles, VCE Study Design* (Melbourne: Board of Studies, 1994).

Board of Studies, 'CAT [Common Assessment Task] 1: Analysis of Works', in *Music Performance Study Design* (Melbourne: Board of Studies, 1994).

Board of Studies, 'Music', in *The Arts: Curriculum & Standards Framework* (Melbourne: Board of Studies, 1994), 86–105.

Brumby, Colin, *The Art of Prolonging the Musical Tone* (Brisbane: UQP, [1968]).

Evans, Peter, 'Musical Theory and Practice: The Role of the University', *SMA* 3 (1969), 1–16. (Based on English Experience).

Ford, Andrew, *Australian Classical Music* (Sydney: Sounds Australian, 1991).

Fong, Francis, comp. 'New Australian Music, Foreign Soil', in *World Music in Australia*, rev. and ed. Veronica Crowe (Sydney: Sounds Australian, 1994), 89–106.

Frampton, Roger, *Australian Jazz* (Sydney: Sounds Australian, 1992).

Leckie, A.J., *Melodies and their Treatment* (Melbourne: Allan & Co., 1937).

Moon, Geoffrey, The Tonal System and 19th Century Harmony. Unpublished ms.

Smith, Graeme, *Australian Popular Music* (Sydney: Sounds Australian, 1991).

Steele, J.A. *Handbook of Musical Form* (Melbourne: Allan & Co., n.d.).

——, *Harmony for Students* (Melbourne: Allan & Co., 1958).

——, *Free Counterpoint in Two Parts* (Melbourne: Allan & Co., 1961).

Stowasser, Helen, 'The Music Curriculum in Australian Education', *SA* 28 (1990), 17–21.

Tunley, David, *Harmony in Action: A Practical Course in Tonal Harmony* (London: Faber, 1978).

Whiffin, Lawrence, convenor, 'Australian Tertiary Music Education: Is it Deeply Anachronistic?', in *The Composer Speaks*, ed. Graeme Skinner (Sydney: Sounds Australian, 1991), 57–67.

(ii) Compositional Theory

Beattie, Gordon, convenor, 'Multicultural Influences on Australian Composition', in *The Composer Speaks*, ed. Skinner, 1991, 29–56.

Burt, Warren, 'Postmodernism', *SA* 33 (1992), 17–18.

Carmody, John, convenor, 'Debate: That Australian Composers Should Set out to Develop a Distinctive Australian Music', in *The Composer Speaks*, ed. Skinner (Sounds Australian, 1992), 3–16.

Currie, Neil, 'Issues in the Appropriation of Sources for Musical Composition', *SA* 30 (1991), 15–17.

Ellis, Catherine J., 'Creating with Traditions', *SA* 30 (1991), 13–15.

Ford, Andrew, chair, 'Style Wars: The "New Complexity" and Australian Music', *SA* 28 (1990), 6–14.

——, Transcript of talk with Gerard Brophy, Grahame Dudley and Neil Currie, 'Style Wars II: The Discussion', *SA* 29 (1991), 5–13, 20.

Hames, Richard David, 'Complexity as Process', *SA* 29 (1991), 35–6.

Penberthy, James, 'The Aboriginal influence', *SA* 30 (1991), 23–4.

Schultz, Andrew, 'Other Places, Whose Music?', *SA* 30 (1991), 8–12, 47–8.

Shanahan, Ian, 'The Theory of Bitones', *Ossia* 1 (1989), 17–23.

(iii) Analytical Theory

Cumming, Naomi, 'Encountering Mangrove', *Australasian Music Research* 1 (1996).

Ellis, Catherine J. and Linda M. Barwick, 'Musical syntax and the problem of meaning in a central Australian songline', *MA* 10 (1987), 41–57.

Gillies, Malcolm, *Notation and Tonal Structure in Bartók's Later Works* (New York: Garland, 1989).

——, 'Why Analysis? A Letter from Budapest', *SA* 31 (1991), 10–12, 36.

Hannan, Michael (presenter) with Warren Burt, 'Musicology: Why Don't Australian Musicologists Write about Australian Music, and what can we do about it?', in *The Composer Speaks*, ed. Skinner (Sounds Australian, 1992), 69–91.

Kassler, Jamie, 'Heinrich Schenker's Epistemology and Philosophy of Music: An Essay on the Relations between Evolutionary Theory and Music Theory', in *The Wider Domain of Evolutionary Thought*, ed. D. Oldroyd and I. Langham (New York: Reidel, 1983), 221–60.

——, 'Interpretive strategies in Australian musical scholarship', *MA* 11/12 (1988–89), 24–6.

——, 'I shall remember this', *SA* 31 (1991), 21. [Analysis of Richard Vella's 'You must Remember this']

Lim, Liza, 'The Body transcribes the text, inscribes the sound', *SA* 31 (1991), 21–4

McCallum, Peter, 'Classic preoccupations: Instruments for the obliteration of analysis?', *Music Analysis* 9 (1990), 201–18.

——, 'Why Analysis?', *SA* 31 (1991), 9–10.

——, 'Analysis and Composition: Analysts and Composers' [An interview with Chris Dench], *SA* 31 (1991), 12–14.

McCredie, Andrew. 'Systematic Musicology: Some Twentieth Century Patterns and Perspectives', *SMA* 5 (1971): 1–35.

Platt, Peter, 'A common attitude to the pursuit of music: an Australian opportunity', *MA* 11/12 (1988–89), 2–13.

Whiffin, Lawrence, 'The use of recurring imagery as a structural device and a free approach to serialism in the song cycle *Music in the Mirabell Garden* for soprano and eight instruments by Larry Sitsky', *MA* 10 (1987), 31–40.

(iv) Feminist Theory

Grosz, Elizabeth, 'Feminism and the Critique of Representation', *SA* 21 (1988/89), 29–33.

Kouvaras, Linda, 'Postmodern Temporalities: A Response to Jonathan Kramer', in *Aflame With Music: 100 Years of Music at The University of Melbourne*, ed. Brenton Broadstock et al. (Melbourne: Centre for Studies in Australian Music, Univ. of Melbourne, 1996), 401–11.

Macarthur, Sally, 'Ripping the Beard off Analysis: Writing Moya Henderson and Gillian Whitehead into the Discourse', *SA* 31 (1991), 29–34, 47.   NAOMI CUMMING

Music Therapy. Music therapy is a professional discipline in which the unique potential of music is used by qualified practitioners to meet the needs of clients receiving services in a range of therapeutic contexts. Music therapists use music's expressive, dynamic, evocative, stimulating, relaxing and non-verbal qualities to achieve therapeutic goals. These goals may be in the areas of development of new skills, the promotion of greater understanding of the self, or the enhancement of skills of communication and interaction.

Music therapists must be qualified musicians and therapists. In Australia, graduates of courses accredited with the Australian Music Therapy Association are eligible for registration as music therapists. Accredited courses leading to registration are available at bachelor's level and postgraduate diploma level at the Universities of Melbourne and Queensland. Postgraduate diploma studies are also available at the University of Technology in Sydney and the Nordoff-Robbins Centre, NSW. Accredited courses have satisfied the association's registration board as well as the government education authorities that graduates of the course will have the training, clinical experience and skill development required to enter the music therapy profession.

Australian music therapists work in a diversity of professional settings, including nursing homes, hostels, community programs, prisons, hospitals, rehabilitation services, special schools, hospice care services and private practice. Music therapy is offered to individuals, groups and families depending on which approach is suitable to the identified therapeutic goals. In most settings music therapists work as part of a multi-disciplinary team contributing to the team's understanding of the client's treatment needs and progress.

When people are referred to music therapy, the therapist must identify the client's needs, how best to use music to address them, and the possible outcomes. A series of sessions is planned, usually after an initial assessment. This session plan shows how goals and objectives will be met and the music therapy techniques used are linked to these objectives; the music therapist has the responsibility to evaluate them. During any stage of the treatment, clients, family members and the treatment team may be consulted for feedback and further information, respecting confidentiality at all times. A number of techniques are used: music used in sessions can be chosen or created by the therapist, client or group, and can be listened to, sung, played, composed or improvised. Music, whether improvised or pre-composed, is played live by any combination of the therapist, client or group, and pre-recorded music is also used. No previous musical experience or skills are required for clients to participate in music therapy. Musical experience and preference are identified and respected, as is the client's cultural background.

Prominent Australian music therapists have developed and implemented several unique approaches in music therapy, applying known techniques to new areas and attending to the ongoing challenge of developing and extending the knowledge base of the profession. Ruth ★Bright (1991) has documented her extensive experience in the application of music therapy to address the needs of older adults who have dementia and other neurological or physical disabilities. The benefits of music therapy with people who have some form of mental illness has also been demonstrated by Cullen (1993), Erdonmez and Curtis (1986). O'Callaghan's work (1984) in the development and application of the technique of music profiles with dying patients in hospice care shows a strong commitment to the use of appropriate techniques in music therapy to achieve therapeutic goals. In conjunction with her further work in developing and documenting techniques for use in enhancing communication abilities of people with brain impairment (O'Callaghan 1993), she represents the breadth of specialist music therapy approaches in hospice care in Australia.

Music therapy work with children in hospital has received attention (Dun 1993; Edwards 1994, 1995), while special education contexts, in particular the practice of music therapy to meet needs of children with multiple disabilities, have not been neglected (Shoemark 1993). The use of music therapy with women during childbirth was pioneered by Allison (1993), who continues to research and extend knowledge in this area as well as contributing significantly to the new field of music therapy work with neonates who have special needs.

A small group of Australian music therapy practitioners have completed training and study in the Bonny method of ★Guided Imagery and Music (GIM). Erdonmez describes GIM as 'a method of music therapy in which classical music is used to evoke and stimulate mental imagery and deep emotional states in order to help people in their spiritual and psychological growth' (Erdonmez 1993: 11). The Bonny method of Guided Imagery and Music is open to study and practice by people who have not been registered as music therapists in Australia today. A postgraduate diploma is available at the University of Melbourne.

The discipline of music therapy has developed a significant body of knowledge and practice over the first 20 years of its professional life in Australia. It has embraced the challenge of professional development across a diversity of settings, extending and refining techniques by which to achieve therapeutic goals for clients. It shows strong signs of being able to make further progress towards a healthy, secure, professional status within a wide range of health and education settings in Australia.

FURTHER REFERENCE

Allison, D., The use of programmed music versus non-programmed and no music during childbirth, MMus, Univ. of Melbourne, 1993.

Bright, R., *Music in geriatric care: A second look* (NSW: Music Therapy Enterprises, 1991).

Cullen, I., 'The use of music to enhance group therapy processes with adult acute psychiatric patients', *Australian Journal of Music Therapy* 4 (1993), 36–44.

Dun, B., 'Music therapy at Royal Children's Hospital, Melbourne', in *Music Therapy Collection*, ed. A. Lem (Canberra: Ausdance, 1993), 37–42.

Edwards, J., 'The use of music therapy to assist children who have severe burns', *Australian Journal of Music Therapy* 5 (1994), 3–6.

——, '"You are singing beautifully": Music therapy and the debridement bath', *The Arts in Psychotherapy* 21/1 (1995), 53–5.

Erdonmez, D., 'Guided imagery and music: A case study', in *Music Therapy Collection*, ed. A. Lem (Canberra: Ausdance, 1993), 11–16.

—— and S. Curtis, 'Music therapy: A sound breakthrough', *Mental Health in Australia* 1/16 (1986), 22–5.

O'Callaghan, C., 'Music profiles of dying patients', *Australian Music Therapy Association Bulletin* 7/2 (1984), 5–11.

——, 'Communicating with brain-impaired palliative care patients through music therapy', *Journal of Palliative Care* 9/4 (1993), 53–5.

Shoemark, H., 'The Process of Music Therapy as it Relates to the Development of Children with Multiple Disabilities', in *Music Therapy Collection*, ed. A. Lem, 45–9.

JANE EDWARDS

Musica Viva Australia. Chamber music entrepreneur, founded in Sydney in 1945, which promotes fine ensemble music throughout Australia and beyond. It offers annual subscription concert series and special concerts in seven cities (all state capitals and Newcastle); the concerts are noted for the high quality of their performances, which usually feature touring chamber ensembles of front international rank. In addition, the company manages a touring program in 25 regional centres around Australia, at which the best Australian ensembles are featured, presents an extensive schools visits program featuring more than 25 ensembles annually, and on behalf of the Federal Government and the Australia Council arranges over 25 tours abroad for Australian artists annually. All in all, the company presents more than 2000 concerts annually to a live audience of over 300 000, as well as in broadcasts through the ABC and regional stations, and has the most extensive music touring network established anywhere in the world. The company receives support from the Australia Council and all State Governments, but the greater part of its revenue is from box office and sponsorship.

The origins of Musica Viva are in the Sydney Musica Viva Orchestra, a 17-member string ensemble organised by the Romanian-born violinist Richard *Goldner, which gave a concert in 1945 at the NSW State Conservatorium. Through ample rehearsal and experiments such as the study of string quartets in a string chorus, Goldner hoped to achieve a new standard of interpretation and performance of the masterpieces of the chamber music repertoire. From 1947 a smaller ensemble, comprised of Robert *Pikler and Edward Cockman (violins), Goldner (viola), Theo Salzman (cello) and Maureen Jones (piano), gave 200 concerts a year throughout Australia as the Musica Viva Society. These concerts ceased in 1951, but in 1955 with Regina Ridge as secretary-manager the society began its entrepreneurial activities, importing their first international artists, the Pascal Quartet. In the coming years visits by the Amadeus Quartet and the Smetana Quartet made a deep impression on audiences, and the organisation grew steadily. Today it is an incorporated company, the artistic management in the hands of a board and staff, but it also preserves some of the hallmarks of a musical society, having branches in all its subscription cities and voting members who elect branch committees; these fill important social and fund-raising functions.

The company has focused on the traditional European chamber repertoire, but has also consistently introduced innovative performers such as Philip Glass, Steve Reich or *Southern Crossings to its audiences, and has maintained a strong presence in its tours by early music ensembles and ensembles using period instruments and authentic performance practices. The company also has an exemplary record of commissioning and performing Australian music, having commissioned nearly 60 compositions by Australia's finest composers, including string quartets, piano trios and other chamber works.

Having provided rewarding work to most of the country's outstanding chamber artists and first-rate listening experiences to the national audience for 50 years, it would be difficult to overestimate the importance of the contribution Musica Viva has made to Australian musical life. The current artistic adviser is Stephen *McIntrye and the general manager is Jennifer Bott.

FURTHER REFERENCE
Michael Shmith, ed., *Musica Viva Australia: The First Fifty Years* (Sydney: Playbill, 1996).

Musical Comedy

1. Beginnings to the 1920s. 2. 1930s: The Depression Years. 3. Musicals of the 1950s. 4. Innovations of the 1960s and 70s. 5. The Recent Past. 6. The Future for Musical Comedy.

Dominated by productions imported from London or New York, Australia did not produce its own musical comedies until the 1930s. From the 1960s, however, a considerable body of Australian musicals of increasing originality and independence have appeared.

1. Beginnings to the 1920s. The first productions that approximated the hybrid genre of musical comedy were mounted in Australia in the 1890s. In 1895 a company from the Prince Of Wales Theatre, London, toured Australia with *A Gaiety Girl,* billed as a 'New Musical Comedy'. The following years saw a succession of similar musical comedies imported from London or the USA, including *The Geisha* (1898), *The Girl From Kay's* (1904), *The Girl Behind The Counter* (1909), and *The Sunshine Girl* (1913). There were few productions of such works by Australian authors, but given entrepreneur J.C. *Williamson's penchant for only staging productions already successful in London or New York, the absence of attempts to mount local material is not surprising.

After the war and into the 1920s, lavish musicals continued to be imported, most with American provenance. But American musical comedy was about to undergo a change in form and style. *Showboat* (1927), presented in Australia in 1929, opened not with the routine chorus of pretty, scantily clad women but with black American slaves carrying bales of cotton and singing *Old Man River.* Instead of an inconsequential storyline loosely held together by music, it contained a complicated plot: it was a drama rather than a comedy. In the end, however, the direction of Australian musical comedy was influenced less by *Showboat* and its imitators than by the simultaneous arrival of talkies and the Great Depression, which combined to produce a dramatically reduced demand for live theatre and to force entrepreneurs to cut costs.

2. 1930s: The Depression Years. The Depression brought not just more revivals and less expensive productions but also more opportunities for local works. In these years some amateur musical societies took pride in encouraging local authors, and *Why Not?,* which may lay claim to be Australia's first modern musical comedy, was produced by the Cumberland Musical Society at the Parramatta Town Hall in March 1933. Written by Walter Lynam, its theme was hardly Australian, for it centred on political intrigue in a mythical South American State. Of more significance was the commercial success of *Collits' Inn* in Sydney and Melbourne in 1933–34. Billed as 'Australia's first musical romance', it had lyrics and music by Varney *Monk to a libretto by her Mosman neighbour, T. Stuart Gurr. The work had won second prize in an Australian operetta competition, and had first been staged by a semi-amateur cast at Sydney's Savoy Theatre in 1932; Monk then persuaded film entrepreneur Frank Thring to mount a professional production. More comic business and song-and-dance items were added, a corroboree ballet was incorporated, according to the *Sydney Morning Herald* 'dramatic and breathtaking in its realism' (4 Apr 1934), a revolving stage was used to allow for quick scene changes, and Gladys ★Moncrieff and George Wallace, some of the most famous names of the Australian stage, were recruited for the lead roles.

The plot, with roots in the melodrama and musical comedy genres, was set in convict days at the village of Hartley, at the bottom of a steep descent on the western road from the Blue Mountains. Mixing historical and fictional characters more realistic than the Dad and Dave types that had characterised Australian melodrama, the story involved the love of the innkeeper's daughter Mary for an army captain, John Lake, and the bushranger Robert Keane's love for Mary. Lake departs and Mary loses her memory; Lake inherits a baronetcy and returns; Mary's memory is restored and her love for Lake revived. It was an old-fashioned musical comedy, uninfluenced by the changes to the genre wrought by *Showboat*.

Nevertheless, the success of *Collits' Inn* nurtured Thring's theatrical ambitions. He had intended to make a film from the work; now he announced plans both to purchase a theatre in Sydney to complement his Princess Theatre in Melbourne and to stage a series of locally written musical comedies, beginning with Edmond Samuels' *This is Love*. Although he did not proceed far with the Samuels piece, he presented *The Beloved Vagabond* (libretto and lyrics by British writer Adrian Ross, music by the Australian composer Dudley ★Glass) in 1934–35, based on the romantic novel by W.J. Locke and set in contemporary England and France, and another Australian period musical, *The Cedar Tree* (libretto by Edmund Barclay, music by Monk). Once again with historical characters (including a Flying Pieman) mixed with fictional ones, the music of *The Cedar Tree* included both romantic and patriotic songs, its *March of the Pioneers*, for example, extolling Australia's present beauty and future greatness. It did well at the box office in Melbourne but fared poorly in Sydney.

In a sense Thring was a victim of his own triumph, for the initial successes of his Australian musicals drew imitations, and the failure of *The Cedar Tree* in Sydney was due at least in part to competition from *Blue Mountain Melody* (written by J.C. Bancks, creator of Ginger Meggs, music by Charles Zwar), a rare Williamson offering in Australian musical comedy. Set in the Blue Mountains, Palm Beach and Kings Cross, *Blue Mountain Melody* featured American-style cabaret songs and gangsters with Chicago accents, for, if its locations were Australian, its inspiration came from the American stage and screen. Starring Madge ★Elliott and Cyril ★Ritchard, it enjoyed a six-week Sydney season, a success sufficiently modest to discourage Williamsons from staging another Australian musical work until 1961.

3. Musicals of the 1950s. The production of Australian musical comedies lapsed in the 1940s and enjoyed only a modest revival in the 1950s and early 1960s. The creators of postwar musicals tended either to follow the Broadway formula or self-consciously to reject it in favour of distinctively Australian themes, characters and (sometimes) music. In the former category were *The Highwayman* (1950) and *Lola Montez* (1958); in the latter were ★*Reedy River* (1953), *The Sentimental Bloke* (1961) and *The Ballad of Angel's Alley* (1962). *The Highwayman* (lyrics, music and book by Samuels of *This is Love*) was staged at the King's Theatre, Melbourne, and then at Sydney's Palace in 1951. Set in 19th-century Bendigo, its plot revolves around the attempts by the authorities to trap a bushranger. Described by the *Sydney Morning Herald* as 'imitative and old fashioned in style' (10 March 1951), it seems to have owed something to *Collits' Inn,* not only in its bushrangers and corroborees but also in including vaudevillian Charles Norman in the lead comic role.

Lola Montez had a book by theatre director and television producer Alan Burke, lyrics by businessman Peter Benjamin, who had experience writing for university revues, and music by television producer Peter Stannard. Set in the goldfields, its story focused on a young Irish miner's infatuation with Montez and his love for a young woman who in the Crimea had saved his life. It was first tried out at the University of Melbourne's Union Theatre by the (mostly amateur) Union Repertory Company in February 1958 in co-operation with the ★Elizabethan Theatre Trust. Then with a much larger production of 14 scenes, a chorus line of 40 miners, 'girls of the town', and show folk, it opened at the Trust's Elizabethan Theatre, Newtown, Sydney, in October of the same year. Professionals replaced the amateur performers, and the English musical comedy singer Mary Preston was imported to play the role of Montez. As musicals had proven a financial bonanza for Williamsons, the trust anticipated that success with *Lola Montez* would ease its precarious financial situation. But the work proved ineffectual from every perspective. Billed as 'a gay, virile Australian musical', critics found it essentially derivative of Broadway. It failed to win acclaim and ran at a heavy loss.

Reedy River reflected both the Australian radical nationalist tradition and the new-found public interest in folk music, stimulated by the publication of Vance ★Palmer and Margaret Sutherland's *Old Australian Bush Ballads* in 1950. Claimed as a collective creation by members of Melbourne's New Theatre, the musical celebrated the radicalism of bush workers in the 1890s and featured traditional Australian folk music. The Sydney production also included the first revivalist bush band, the ★Bushwhackers, whose members played such 'authentic' instruments as ★lagerphone and tea-chest ★bush bass. Opening in Melbourne, the musical played in all capitals, and was subsequently performed by many amateur groups, its popularity an indication that the Broadway formula was not the only guarantee of box-office success in Australia.

The Sentimental Bloke had a book by professional diplomat Lloyd Thomson and experienced musical comedy performer Nancy Brown, based on C.J. Dennis's verses about a Melbourne larrikin. The music was by Albert ★Arlen, who had previously composed *Kings Cross Rhapsody* and a musical version of *Clancy of the Overflow*. Williamsons took out an option on the musical in 1957, although it was not staged until it opened in Canberra in 1961. Enjoying profitable runs in Melbourne, Sydney, Adelaide and (particularly) Brisbane, it won critical acclaim for its freshness, innocent charm and authentic colloquialisms. Gloria Dawn was singled out for her performance as Rose of Spadger's Lane. Some of the songs from the musical, including *I Dips Me Lid,* also enjoyed popular success.

In the early 1960s the Melbourne Theatre Co. sought to present more Australian material, including *The Ballad of Angel's Alley* in 1962, a larrikin musical which, if it did not enjoy the success of *Reedy River* or *The Bloke,* nevertheless signalled the determination of sections of the Australian theatre industry to promote local musicals as well as plays.

4. Innovations of the 1960s and 70s. In Australia as elsewhere, the 1960s and 70s were years in which the traditions of the theatre were challenged by new forms. As writers sought to break from the tried-and-true formulas of the past, the distinctions between various types of theatre became blurred, and it became increasingly difficult to differentiate between musical comedy and other genres. *The Legend of King O' Malley* (by Robert Ellis and Michael Boddy) told the story of the Australian-American politician King O'Malley with satire, music and a minimum of scenery, using his debates with Billy Hughes over the proposed introduction of conscription in 1916 to attack Australia's involvement in Vietnam. Directed by John Bell and first performed at Sydney's Jane Street Theatre in 1970, the play's use of songs and instrumental music established a precedent for Bell's subsequent work at the Nimrod Theatre, Sydney, including *Biggles* and *Flash Jim Vaux,* the latter written by Ron Blair in the style of *The Beggar's Opera*.

Apart from *The Legend* perhaps the most successful of the musicals staged by the Nimrod was *The Venetian Twins* (1979, lyrics by Nick Enright, music by Terence ★Clarke). Based on the 18th-century comedy by Carlo Goldoni, it centred on the romantic adventures in Verona of twin brothers, but with many Australian allusions. Its satirical style mocked the traditions of grand opera, musical comedy, Australian popular music and Brechtian theatre.

Ned Kelly Electric Music Show (book by Reg ★Livermore, music by Patrick Flynn) was a highly ambitious attempt to stage a musical that spoke even more directly to Australian themes and traditions. Livermore had enjoyed success with one-man cabaret-style shows like *Betty Block Buster Follies* and *Wonder Woman,* but he had much more difficulty in finding financial support to mount *Ned Kelly*. An album from the piece was released in 1975, but the staging required sets and costumes worth about $500 000, and it was not produced until 1978. Directed by Livermore with Nick Turbin as Ned Kelly, the production was intended as a mixture of rock opera, opera, vaudeville and comedy. It opened in Adelaide to mixed reviews and proved a box-office disaster.

5. The Recent Past. If the 1960s and 70s were marked both by experimentation and the production of a relatively small number of Australian musicals, the 1980s and 90s witnessed both further attempts at new approaches and a return to a more traditional style. The major musicals of these years included *Rasputin* (1987), *History of Australia, The Musical* (1988), *Seven Little Australians* (1988) and *Big Sister* (1990). Whatever form they took, these musicals, with the notable exception of *Rasputin*, were characterised by attempts to present distinctively Australian themes and characters.

Smaller-scale musical comedies in these years were sometimes staged by professional companies. *Dinkum Assorted* (1988), for example, was commissioned and performed by the Sydney Theatre Company. Some were by those who had served apprenticeships in university revues: Dennis Watkins created the highly successful Sydney University revue *Stalin—the Musical* before writing *Beach Blanket Tempest* (1984) and *Burger Brain* (1988) with music by Chris Harriott for the commercial stage. Others included *Last Wake at She-Oak Creek* (1986, The Stables, Sydney), described as a play but including 16 songs; and *Ginger* (1992, The Playbox Theatre, Monash University). Not all of these musicals pursued Australian themes: *Beach Blanket Tempest* provided a retelling of Shakespeare's play of (almost) the same name, only with Prospero as a retired rock and roll singer. It was strongly influenced by the rock musicals and beach and bikini movies of the 1960s and 70s. *Dinkum Assorted* (book and music by Linda Aronson) focused on issues of women's identity; concerned by the unrelieved solemnity of women's theatre and the exclusiveness of its audience, Aronson intended the piece as a celebration of women and of the popular stage. On the other hand *Last Wake at She-Oak Creek* drew on the sentimental Australian tradition of *On Our Selection,* featuring characters like Chookie Greene, while *Ginger* drew on the events at the 19th-century Eureka Stockade and the treatment of convicts (especially women), placing itself within the radical nationalist tradition.

Artists seeking to mount major musical productions often had difficulty finding promoters in these years. Conceived in 1983, *History of Australia* was not staged until 1988, while the production of *Seven Little Australians* was only made possible by a Bicentenary gift from a private sponsor. The $3 million required to perform *Rasputin* was largely underwritten by Harry Vogelsanger, who hoped he was financing the *Crocodile Dundee* of the theatre; as it turned out all three of these productions were financial failures. *Rasputin* had a book by radio journalist David Lucas, and music by a computer business owner, David Tydd, and was directed by a creator of rock video clips,

Steven Hopkins; the theatrical inexperience of the team was reflected in the quality of both the music and the drama. Not even the presence of two well-known rock performers, Angry Anderson and Jon English, was sufficient to make up for these deficiencies.

History of Australia was created by no less than five writers and composers, including the historian-cum-speechwriter Don Watson. The show's central character was the historian Manning Clark, played by Ivar Kants, with cohesion provided by intermittent scenes from his life. The critics found it hard to connect the scenes in any meaningful way; they were also disturbed by the show's left-wing ideological commitment. 'If you are strong on patriotism, jingoism and republicanism', wrote the *Bulletin*, 'this is the *History* for you' (26 January 1988). The opening night, attended by the work's political supporters, drew a standing ovation, but later audiences were both less numerous and enthusiastic. *Seven Little Australians* was a more conventional musical, a family show which, although based on Ethel Turner's novel, fitted comfortably into the conventions of *The Sound of Music*. It played to small houses for three months, surviving mostly through matinees for high schools.

The commercial failure of these three productions made promoters even more cautious, and when Livermore staged *Big Sister—A Larrikin Opera* it was on a smaller scale than he had originally planned, and at an out-of-town venue—Parramatta's Riverside Theatre. Critics were impressed by Livermore's virtuoso female impersonation as Gerri Natwick, a deserted wife who opens a restaurant for truckies, but they found the production fatally flawed by crude humour and poor choreography.

6. The Present. More successful than any of the works of the previous 20 years has been ★*Bran Nue Dae*, billed as the first Aboriginal musical, and written and composed by Jimmy Chi and the Broome band Kuckles. It tells the simple story of an Aboriginal boy's flight back to his home town of Broome in search of love and identity: the theme involves both a celebration of a contemporary Aboriginal culture which is the product of survival and adaptation, and a scepticism towards past, present and future European intentions towards Aborigines. The score reflects the influence of country music, musical comedy, rock opera, the Catholic mass, and traditional Aboriginal music. At the end of the work, even the European characters discover that they are Aborigines. Opening at the Perth Festival in 1990 to considerable critical acclaim, it later toured the hinterland, the other capitals and then went to Europe.

Unlike previous Australian musicals which had located the sources of Australian culture and character in the mythical 19th-century bushman's life, or unintentionally on Broadway or in London's West End, the originality and promise of *Bran Nue Dae* was to place them in an Aboriginal past, with a promise of creative access to all.

See also *Music-theatre; Operetta; Vaudeville*.

FURTHER REFERENCE

(i) Editions

Boddy, Michael, and Robert Ellis, *The Legend of King O'Malley, or, Never say die until a dead horse kicks you* (Sydney: Currency Press, 1987).

Chi, Jimmy, and Kuckles, *Bran Nue Dae: A Musical Journey* (Sydney and Broome: Currency Press/Magabala Books, 1991).

What's the Deal? [Lois Ellis, Tomi Kalinski, Evelyn Krape, Lorraine Milne] *Ginger: A Musical Diversion* (Sydney: Currency Press, 1992).

Herbert, Bob, *The Last Wake at She-Oak Creek* (Sydney: Currency Press, 1988).

Watkins, Dennis, and Chris Harriott, *Burger Brain The First Food Musical*, (Sydney: Currency Press, 1990).

West, John, ed., *Collits' Inn, a Romantic Australian Operetta by T. Stuart Gurr with lyrics and music by Varney Monk* (Sydney: Currency Press, 1990).

(ii) Further Reading

BrisbaneE.

Love, Harold, ed., *The Australian Stage: A Documentary History* (Sydney: UNSWP, 1984).

West, John, *Theatre in Australia* (Sydney: Cassell, 1978).

RICHARD WATERHOUSE

Musicians Union of Australia. Trade union founded in 1927 from several earlier bodies. With about 15 000 members and branches in all states, it aims to protect the interests of professional musicians (mostly orchestral and band instrumentalists), particularly in their pay and working conditions. It provides advice to musicians and government, has a 'Keep Music Live' campaign against the use of backing tapes in the music industry, and administers a policy which protects the work of Australian musicians by controlling the entry of foreign musicians to Australia.

Actors Equity (established 1939) represented singers, and the Australian Theatrical and Amusement Employees Association (founded 1905) represented production crews; these were amalgamated in 1992 as the Media Entertainment and Arts Alliance, with about 35 000 members. Negotiations have recently been under way to merge the Musicians Union with the Alliance.

FURTHER REFERENCE

Lesley Sly, *The Power and The Passion: A Guide to the Australian Music Industry* (Sydney: Warner/Chappell, 1993), 308–11.

Musicological Society of Australia (MSA). Society formed (1963) at the University of Sydney to encourage research and develop public interest in various fields of music. The society now has chapters in all states except Tasmania with about 350 members, and a national executive which moves between the chapters. It organises annual conferences, chapter meetings on various university campuses, and publishes the annual journal *Musicology Australia* and a newsletter.

Musicology

1. Its Development to the Present. 2. Historical Musicology and Editions. 3. Systematic Musicology. 4. Ethnomusicology. 5. Folk and Popular Music Studies. 6. Conclusion.

Scholarly approaches to the discipline of music have been influenced in Australia by the country's geographical position in the Asia–Pacific region, the co-existence within it of tribal Aboriginal music, Western concert hall music, folk music, popular music, and transplanted or multicultural urban music, and its continuing links with the scholarly traditions in Europe and North America.

1. Its Development to the Present. In the early part of the 20th century, a few fieldworkers, music collectors and gentlemen scholars made pioneering studies of Aboriginal and other Australian music, but the first scholarly publications were produced in the 1960s by a small number of specialists in Aboriginal music, especially Alice Moyle, Trevor Jones and Catherine Ellis, whose works were initially built on research into Aboriginal societies and rituals by anthropologists and linguists. In 1964 Roger Covell published a general book on themes in Australian music, but substantial historical research into and teaching of Australian music did not develop until two or three decades later.

Vocational music education at tertiary level, however, began in the 1890s with the creation of the Faculties of Music at the Universities of Adelaide and Melbourne. The courses were based largely on British models and were oriented toward music performance and composition rather than musicology. Unlike in North America, Australia did not experience an influx of émigré musicologists from Europe in the late 1930s and 40s. After the first postwar chair of music had been created in 1947 at the University of Sydney music began to be taught as one of the humanities or liberal arts. Other chairs in music which were subsequently established at the University of Western Australia (1950) and the University of Queensland (1965) remained largely vocational in their educational offerings, though they supported some musicological research.

In the expansionary 1960s and early 1970s, other new chairs were created at Monash (1965), Flinders (1966), NSW (1967), New England (1971) and La Trobe (1974) Universities. They were followed by the University of Tasmania (1984), the University of Wollongong (1985), Macquarie University (1994), James Cook University (1994) and, in the wake of the tertiary amalgamations from the late 1980s, Deakin University (1994) and the Victorian University of Technology (1994). From the late 1970s courses in limited aspects of musicology were also taught in institutions oriented to music practice such as the NSW Conservatorium and the Victorian College of the Arts. The first substantial sequences of courses in musicology proper, however, were taught at the Universities of Adelaide, Sydney, New England and Western Australia and at Flinders and Monash Universities, and the first

courses in ethnomusicology were taught at Monash from the late 1960s. Not until the 1980s were aspects of musicology (normally including ethnomusicology) commonly taught in most Australian universities which offered music.

Musicology was recognised as a nationally significant humanistic discipline from the late 1960s, as evidenced by its acceptance as a member discipline within the Australian Research Council, the Australian Academy of the Humanities (AAH), the Humanities Research Centre (HRC), and the Australian Institute of Aboriginal Studies (recently renamed the Australian Institute of Aboriginal and Torres Strait Islander Studies, AIATSIS). The AAH and HRC offer grants in humanistic disciplines such as musicology and organise annual interdisciplinary seminars in which overseas and Australian musicologists are invited to take part. Musicologists elected to the Australian Academy of the Humanities beginning in the mid-1970s included Andrew *McCredie, David *Tunley, Gordon *Anderson, Margaret *Kartomi, Roger *Covell, Jamie *Kassler, Alice *Moyle, Malcolm *Gillies and Catherine *Ellis. Between them these scholars have published widely on Australian, European and South-East Asian music and theoretical issues in musicology such as historiography, organology, culture contact theory, music as metaphor, aesthetics, the interface with comparative literature, and other interdisciplinary areas.

The breadth of musicological teaching and research in Australia is exemplified by the membership of its professional body, the Musicological Society of Australia (MSA), which from the beginning to the present has included ethnomusicologists as well as historical and systematic musicologists and has encouraged dialogue between them. Due in part to its relatively late start, musicology in Australia has been able to avoid the splits between various branches of the discipline that occurred in Europe and North America. After musicological societies had been formed in the 1960s and 70s in some states of Australia, the MSA acquired its present number of seven chapters and a fully national status from 1978, with a membership varying between 250 and 400. It also became the Australian member body of the International Musicological Society (IMS) and the International Council for Traditional Music (ICTM). National conferences have been held annually on a wide variety of themes and have attracted participants from many countries, especially NZ. The chapters have also held regular state conferences and study weekends and the Victorian chapter has held a postgraduate musicology conference annually since the early 1980s. Besides national and international conferences on Australian music, the MSA has co-hosted international symposia of the International Musicological Society, in Adelaide 1979 and in Melbourne 1988, and the Congress of the International Council for Traditional Music in Canberra (1995). In addition, many other international conferences have been held. Musicological journals that developed since the 1960s included *Studies in Music*

(*SMA*), *Miscellanea Musicologica* (*MMA*), and *Musicology Australia* (formerly *Musicology*, *MA*). In 1992 a new Centre for Studies in Australian Music was established at the University of Melbourne, which began to produce *Australasian Music Research* from 1996. Two monograph series also appeared, the *Music Monograph Series* from the University of Western Australia (UWA Press) and *Australian Studies in the History, Philosophy and Social Studies of Music* from Monash University (Currency Press with Gordon and Breach).

2. Historical Musicology and Editions. Historically oriented Australian musicologists have concentrated on writing on aspects of the history of Australian concert hall music, preparing historical editions of selected music from such countries as England, Italy, France, Germany, Spain and Japan, and more recently writing on aspects of the history of Australian and Asian folk, traditional and popular music. Historical studies of Australian Aboriginal music are still largely in their infancy because of the lack of historical sources gathered to date. However, the number of scholars and students researching Aboriginal music as a whole has burgeoned since 1989, especially at the University of Sydney and Monash University or via AIATSIS, but scholars are still mostly drawn to carry out research into music of Western and Asian countries, where conditions for the collection of library and/or field data are on the whole easier than for material Aboriginal music.

(i) Australian Music History. Following the first conferences devoted to Australian music history and to Percy Grainger (in Melbourne in 1981 and 1982 respectively) and the IMS Symposium in Melbourne during the bicentennial celebrations in 1988, interest in Australian music history began to flourish and substantial courses oriented to Australian history began to be offered at Monash and Melbourne and some other universities. Substantial research on the life and works of Percy *Grainger and a few other Australian composers initially emanated from Melbourne's Grainger Museum, which has become the symbolic centre of Australian music history.

Deconstructionism and gender theory flourished in the 1990s. They first showed fruitful results in the works of such scholars as Sally McArthur, Sarah Weiss, Aline Scott-Maxwell and Kay Dreyfus. Thérèse Radic and others organised national conferences on the topic in Adelaide (1991) and Melbourne (1994). Other themes of Australian historical research include opera, individual women and men in music, 19th-century piano and string ensemble music, historic organs, and new music. Studies of single Australian composers and their works have included those on Peter Sculthorpe, Roy Agnew, Don Banks, Larry Sitsky, Richard Meale and Keith Humble. Only a few rare articles on Australian women in music have appeared from the 1980s, but they began to grow in the 1990s. Regional or statewide histories of Australian

music are also rare; to date only a book on the history of music in SA has appeared (McCredie 1988). Styles of experimental new Australian music have been discussed in various articles and associated disc notes by writers such as Richard Toop, Ros *Bandt and Warren *Burt.

(ii) The Western Tradition. The main fields of interest have been English music from the Renaissance to the present and works (especially opera) of 19th and early 20th-century European composers. Other popular areas are works of 20th-century composers and the German Classical and Romantic periods. Philological research and Medieval and Renaissance research oriented to performance practice has concentrated especially on the music of 13th and 14th-century France and Italy, but pre-13th-century studies are few. Also rare is research in music historiography. Research and editing work has often been associated with performances and radio broadcasts.

Substantial Australian teaching and research into the history of Western music and historiography first began to develop at the University of Adelaide from the late 1960s under Andrew McCredie, whose students and colleagues joined him over the years to produce a substantial body of theses and publications about several historical periods and topics in Australian and European music. Historical research is carried out, however, in many tertiary music institutions. The leading Australian scholar in Medieval music was the late Gordon *Anderson. Other scholars of early music include John *Griffiths, Greta Mary Hair, Jane Hardie, Peter Mackler, Michael Noone, Robyn Smith, John Stinson, Julia Szuster and Carol Williams. Medieval and Renaissance research has recently become increasingly oriented to performance practice with the growing demand for concerts, lecture recitals and festivals in Australian cities.

Largely because of Australia's colonial ties with Britain, historical research into aspects of British music from the Renaissance and the present has absorbed the attention of a number of Australian scholars, the most productive of whom are Richard Charteris, Jamie Kassler, Peter Dennison and Cecil Hall. Research into 17th-century music, notably by David Swale, David Tunley and Margaret Seares, centred on Italy, Spain, and especially France. Music of the High Baroque has been researched by Dene Barnett, Jan Stockigt, Cecil Hill, Graham Pont, John O'Donnell, Ralph Schureck, Robert Huestis, Patrick Brislan and Helen Reeves.

Contributions to pre-Classical and Classical studies include those by McCredie, Warren Bebbington, Michael Burden, Cecil Hill, Graham Strahle, David Galliver and Geoffrey Moon. The demand for operatic performances by national and state opera companies in several Australian cities has instigated the research into and preparation of performing editions of many operas by Richard Divall, Graham Hardie, Andrew McCredie, Warren Bebbington, Sally Kester and Michael Ewans. Broadly historical–analytical or editorial studies of 19th and early 20th-century music include those by Kerry Murphy, Craig De Wilde, Larry ★Sitsky, Richard ★Divall, Roy Howat and Malcolm Gillies. Works on contemporary non-Australian composers include those by Mark ★Pollard and Ros Bandt.

3. Systematic Musicology. (i) Music Theory and Analysis. Until the 1980s the analytical methods taught and practised in Australia were largely empirical and focused on the thematic, motivic and harmonic details of a composer's style in its historical context. A demand for a more rigorous and systematic approach then arose, led by scholars studying either Western music since Debussy or non-Western music, for whom conventional methods of analysis were inadequate. The view has gained acceptance that analytical methods should be allowed to arise freely out of particular pieces, or sometimes a combination of methods chosen for use in full awareness of the theoretical implications. Significant analytical work has been carried out by Malcolm Gillies, Ros Bandt, Alice Scott Maxwell, Larry Sitsky, Lawrence Whiffin, Michael Kassler, Naomi Cumming. (See *Music Theory and Analysis.*)

(ii) Organology, Acoustics, Music Sociology, Aesthetics. Most research into organology and/or acoustics has been carried out at Monash and the University of New England, important contributions having been made by Peter Clinch, Reis Flora, Jamie Kassler, Margaret Kartomi, Neville Fletcher and Dennis Vaughan. Although courses on music sociology, aesthetics and criticism are taught in some universities, research into them has only begun to burgeon in the 1980s and 1990s. A sociologically oriented theme of the 1979 and 1988 IMS symposia in Adelaide and Melbourne was transplanted musical cultures. Papers on aspects of culture contact presented at the Melbourne Symposium were published in Kartomi & Blum 1995. Recently there has been an upsurge of interest in aesthetics, as seen in Kassler 1991.

4. Ethnomusicology. Research has taken a mixture of historical, ethnographic, music-analytical, sociological and aesthetic approaches and has mostly been devoted to the non-Western and folk musics practised in and near the country, including the cultures of the original (Aboriginal) Australians, various migrant groups in the country, and Australia's near neighbours in Papua New Guinea, South-East Asia (especially Indonesia), China, Japan and India. Substantial teaching and research in ethnomusicology began at Monash University in the late 1960s, concentrating on Australian Aboriginal and South-East Asian music. It also developed at Sydney, Adelaide and at the Universities of New England and Queensland. From the early 1990s, most tertiary music institutions have taught some ethnomusicology and included some performance teaching in Indian, Indonesian, African and other traditions.

The task of collecting and researching Aboriginal musics is still vast and urgently in need of concerted effort. Yet mainly because of ethical, budgetary and administrative problems, only a handful of scholars have worked in this field and no native Aboriginal musicologist has yet emerged. Most of the research is sponsored by AIATSIS, the sound archives of which hold the originals of copies of almost all recorded Aboriginal music. To date research has been carried out into the music of (1) northern Australia by Alice M. Moyle, Jill Stubington, Stephen ★Wild, Trevor Jones, Alan Marett, Linda Barwick, Greg Anderson, and others; (2) north-west Australia by Ray Keogh; (3) central Australia by Richard Moyle, Catherine J. Ellis and Stephen Wild; and (4) southern Australia by Catherine Ellis, Helen Payne, Margaret Kartomi, Anthony McCardell, Margaret Gummow and Robin Ryan. Early didgjeridu studies were made by Trevor Jones and more recently by the anthropologist Karl Neuenfeldt, who, like Jill Stubington, Peter Dunber-Hall and Robin Ryan, is publishing on aspects of Aboriginal popular music. Various authors have also published on the musical implications of Aboriginal land rights and interrelationships between Aboriginal dance and music.

Australian studies of the music of Oceania have centred in the University of Queensland, chiefly Gordon Spearritt and Jacqueline Pugh Kitingan, Thomas Aitkin, and Don Niles and Richard Moyle. Australian scholarly interest in South-East Asian music, which has grown since about 1970, has mainly emanated from Monash University, which houses archival recordings of music from all but one of Indonesia's provinces and most other countries of South-East Asia. Research has concentrated on the musics of Indonesia, especially Sumatra, Java, Sunda, Bali, Sulawesi and Maluku Malaysia, the Philippines and an offshore island of southern Taiwan (Lanyu). Organological, historical, anthropological and textual investigations of selected South-East Asian musics have been made by Margaret Kartomi, David Goldsworthy, Catherine Falk, Aline Scott-Maxwell, Lynette Moore, Cheryl Romet, Ashley Turner and Tan Sooi Beng. These scholars are now supervising research by a third generation of graduate students.

Research into North Indian music has been pursued by Reis Flora. Japanese, Korean and Chinese music and/or performing arts have been researched at Sydney, the ANU, Monash, Queensland and Griffith Universities, notably by Allan Marret, Noel ★Nickson, Rosalynd Smith and Colin Mackerras.

5. Folk and Popular Music Studies. The history of Australian folk-songs was neglected until the 1980s and the work of Graeme Smith, Jill Stubington, Peter Dunbar-Hall and Thérèse Radic. But the main collector of Anglo-Australian folk-songs is John Meredith, who published two volumes of folk-songs (see *Folk Music*). Research in musics practised by Australian migrants in Australia began in the 1980s resulting in publications by Peter Parkhill, Alan Marret and Catherine Falk (see *Migrant Music*).

Studies of music in popular culture in Australia began with the founding of a local chapter of the International

Association for the Study of Popular Music (IASPM), beginning at Monash University in the early 1980s. It was not until the 1990s, however, that popular music studies began to flourish. Several national conferences were held and a steady flow of research publications began to appear. Since 1991 most Australian research into music in popular culture has been published in the Australian journal *Perfect Beat* edited by Philip Hayward at Macquarie University. A group research project on Australian, Asian and American popular music was produced by Kartomi and Hayward and a team of researchers at Monash and Macquarie Universities. (See *Popular Music*.)

A small number of Australian jazz studies have appeared. Bruce Clunies Ross's delineation of an Australian style of jazz appeared in 1979, but the main writers have been Jeff Pressing and Bruce ★Johnson. (See *Jazz*.)

6. Conclusion. The growth of national consciousness following Australia's bicentennial year celebrations in 1988 resulted in a greatly increased interest in both Aboriginal/Torres Strait Islander and White Australian music studies and history and fostered the desire to conserve and research the sources and objects of Australia's heritage of multicultural musical expressions. With increased public and private expenditure on the performance of concert hall, community, and multicultural arts has come an increasing demand among musicians for musicological studies of and performing editions of works.

The perceived need for musicological works and critical journalism is also increasing as community listening and performing tastes have broadened to include not only the regular concert hall and popular music repertoires but also a large number of diverse styles of music of South-East Asia, medieval Europe and Japanese music, and the folk and world music of European, Asian and Latin American countries. This broadening of tastes is partially the result of the large intake of postwar migrants and an increasingly diverse multicultural population. The growing interest in Australian music history which has accompanied the growing national consciousness has resulted in the opening up and cataloguing of music holdings in the various depositories around the country. But some other research concentrations are best explained by overseas trends, for example in fields such as the history of 19th and 20th-century Western music and the areas of music analysis, organology and aesthetics and other aspects of systematic musicology.

Musicology in Australia was in a state of rapid growth between 1975 and 1988 and is still growing. Since the late 1980s, many Australian scholars have been avoiding what they see as the 'dry objective' approach of the past. Some have rejected the apparent reliance of the past two generations of scholars on the ethics of objectivity in their choice of topics and methods of research in favour of a more critically humanist approach to the study of music in culture. Sometimes this research approach has been limited to a single issue, such as the relation between gender, the environment, ethnicity, politics or social issues on the one hand and musical creation and reception on the other. Influenced by current literary and cultural studies, they have emphasised social, political and economic issues such as appropriation, the nature of music in popular culture and the encoding of cultural values in musical works. Some ethnomusicologists and historical musicologists had adopted this expanded and tolerant but more subjective and critical approach to the study of music long ago, but it was new to some historical and systematic musicologists. As a result, palaeographic, score-reconstructive and analytical studies have decreased in recent years, while the editing of composers' letters, biography, socially oriented historiography, cultural-organological studies, gender studies, aesthetics, and comparative musicology have provided a new focus in the 1990s.

See also *Libraries and Archives*; *Journals and Magazines*; *Instrument Collections*.

FURTHER REFERENCE
Roger Covell, *Australia's Music: Themes of a New Society* (Melbourne: Sun Books, 1967); Margaret J. Kartomi, 'Musicological Research in Australia 1979–1984', *Acta Musicologica* 56 (1984), 109–145; idem and Stephen Blum, eds, *Music-Cultures in Contact: Convergences and Collisions*. Australian Studies in History, Philosophy and Social Studies of Music (Sydney: Currency Press, 1995); Jamie Kassler, ed., *Metaphor: A Musical Dimension*. Australian Studies in History, Philosophy and Social Studies of Music (Sydney: Currency Press, 1991); Sally Macarthur et al., eds, 'The Woman's Issue', *SA* 40 (1993), 6–46; Andrew McCredie, *Musicological Studies in Australia from the Beginnings to the Present*, 2nd edn (Sydney: Sydney University Press for the Australian Academy of Humanities, 1983).

MARGARET J. KARTOMI

Musicology Australia. Annual journal of the Musicological Society of Australia, first issued irregularly as *Musicology* (from 1964), then from vol. 8 (1985) under its present title. A register of Australian undergraduate theses was included from 1985; the register of Australasian higher degree theses was continued from *Studies in Music* from 1995. A cumulative index appears in vols 11–12 (1988–89). The size and format have changed at least four times.

My Country. Popular song by Arthur S. ★Loam to a text by Dorothea Mackellar, after the poem *My Country*. Introduced in schools in the late 1930s, it is a paean of praise for the Australian native scenery and wildlife, and was still being sung in the 1970s.

My Name is Ben Hall, bushranging ballad. A modern adaptation by John ★Manifold of lines condensed from A.B. Paterson's *Old Bush Songs* (1924), set to the fiddle tune 'The Dear Irish Boy', and first published in *Penguin Australian Song Book* (1964). Here Hall, the Murrurundi farmer driven by harsh police treatment into outlaw life in 1862, has Robin Hood's sense of dash and justice attributed to him.

FURTHER REFERENCE
Edition with commentary in *ManifoldP.*

Myer, Sidney [Baevski, Symcha] (*b* Kritischev, Byelorussia, 8 Feb. 1878, *d* Melbourne, 5 Sept. 1934), retailer, philanthropist. He emigrated to Australia in 1898 and soon afterwards established a retail store which grew into the Myer Emporium. Enormous financial successes enabled him to contribute large sums of money to musical and other cultural activities in Melbourne; his most lasting imprint on musical life was made with the establishment of the Sidney Myer Free Concert Series and the erection of the Sidney Myer Music Bowl, Melbourne.

The idea of a series of free outdoor concerts to be given by the Melbourne Symphony Orchestra was mooted by its conductor Fritz Hart in September 1929. Myer agreed to contribute £1000 annually to support the series, having recently also intervened (together with Bernard Heinze and the University of Melbourne) to save the orchestra from bankruptcy. The first concerts were given at the Royal Botanic Gardens in December 1929, and after two successful seasons when it appeared the concerts had met with an appreciative audience, Myer granted 10 000 £1 shares in the Myer Emporium to the University of Melbourne to fund the concerts in perpetuity. The university continues to administer the fund for these concerts today.

Myer's vision of a Melbourne venue like the Hollywood Bowl was never realised in his lifetime, but was carried to fruition by the Sidney Myer Charitable Trust, which presented the Sidney Myer Music Bowl to the people of Melbourne in 1959. With possibly the largest stage in the world in its time, the Myer Music Bowl was constructed in the Domain, where it continues to host productions of the free Myer orchestral concerts, as well as ballet, opera, and rock music.

FURTHER REFERENCE
Anthea Hyslop, *ADB*, 10; *Herald* 3 Sept. 1929, 4 Dec. 1929, 29 Aug. 1931, 16 Dec. 1932; *Argus* 4 Sept. 1929, 26 Dec. 1930; *Age* 16 Dec. 1932; *Sidney Myer Free Concert Programs* 1935, 1990, 1993; *Myer News* Apr. 1956; Coles Myer Archives, Melbourne; Univ. Melbourne Archives.　　　JOHN WERETKA

Myers, Raymond (*b* Sydney, 1 July 1938), baritone. After winning the ABC Concerto and Vocal Competition in 1962 and the *Sun* Aria in 1963, he appeared with the Elizabethan Theatre Trust Opera Co. and then went to Italy to study with Luigi Ricci at the Rome Opera in 1964. Since then he has appeared with the English National Opera, Glyndebourne, and in Europe, as well as frequently in Australia with the Australian Opera and in concert. An excellent actor as well as a fine vocal talent, his roles have included Rigoletto, Amonasro, Don Fernando, Wozzeck, and Napoleon (*War and Peace).*

FURTHER REFERENCE
Recordings include Wagner in *Faust*, London Symphony Orchestra (1966, Decca 421240–2DM3); and the Doctor in *Macbeth,* London Symphony Orchestra (1970, Decca 440048–2DM02). See also Roger Covell, *GroveO.*

N

Nagel, Charles (*b* 1806; *d* Liverpool, NSW, 1870), playwright. After military service in England, he emigrated to Australia in 1837, bought land and became a magistrate. He wrote plays and music-theatre works, several performed at the Royal Victoria Theatre, Sydney, including the burletta *The Mock Catalani in Little Puddleton* with songs set to his own music and popular songs of the day (1842), the text for Isaac ★Nathan's *Merry Freaks in Troub'lous Times* (1843), and the text and songs for a burlesque *Shaklespericonglommorofunnidogammoniae* (1844). These are the first operatic works composed in Australia.

FURTHER REFERENCE
IrvinD.

Nagorcka, Ron (*b* Hamilton, Vic., 5 Feb. 1948), composer. While at the University of Melbourne he studied organ with Sergio de Pieri and attended classes in contemporary music with Keith ★Humble and Ian ★Bonighton, then went to the University of California, San Diego, in 1974, attending classes with Pauline Oliveros. He returned to Melbourne in 1975 and was associated with the Clifton Hill Community Centre, forming the duo Plastic Platypus with Warren ★Burt and touring Europe in 1979. He presented creative workshops for students in the coming years, and appeared at the Festival d'Automne, Paris (1983), with Roberto Laneri at the Festival of Perth (1986) and in Europe (1987).

Frequently combining electronic improvisation, non-traditional instrumental techniques and the didjeridu to set Australian topics, his works include *Sanctus* for didjeridu, organ voices and electronics (1976), *Atom Bomb* for voices, toy instruments, and tape (1977), *Seven Rare Dreamings* for didjeridu, prepared saxophone, and computer, with slides, masks, and props (1980), and *The Spirit of the Place Part 1—Down the Black Forest* (1983).

FURTHER REFERENCE
Recordings include *Sanctus,* org (1979, Move MS3025); *Theme and Variations*, org (1973, Move MS3008); *Music from a Tasmanian Rainforest* (Aust. Music Centre, CASS 012); *Atom Bomb,* excerpt (1983, NMA Tapes 002); and *Liapatyenna* (1989, NMA Tape 007B). His writings include 'Without the Land There is No Music, Or Why I Live Where I Live', *NMA* 7 (1989), 44–5. See also *Jenkins T*, 132–40; *SA* 34 (Winter 1992), 21–2.

Narelle, Marie [Catherine Mary Ryan] (*b* Temora 1870; *d* London 1941), soprano. A pupil of the Presentation Sisters at Wagga Wagga, her concerts were well known before she studied with Ellen Christian at Potts Point, Sydney, and still later with Snr Steffani and Roberto ★Hazon, also in Sydney. She travelled to Ireland in 1902 where she was immediately successful and where she discovered the then unknown tenor, John McCormack. In 1904 she was principle soprano at the Irish Exhibition at the St Louis World Fair. Invited to make records by the Edison recording company, she made a number of cylinder and disc records which support the epithet applied to her at home and abroad, 'The Australian Queen of Irish Song'. She undertook many concert engagements in the USA and Britain, was noted for a voice not unlike Melba's and for the passion with which she performed songs.

FURTHER REFERENCE
MackenzieS, 74–80   JEFF BROWNRIGG

Nathan, Isaac (*b* Canterbury, England, 1792, *d* Sydney, 15 Jan. 1864), composer, musicologist. Reputedly a grandson of Stanislaus Poniatowski, last king of Poland, whom he resembled, Nathan took rabbinical studies at Cambridge, was articled to Domenico Corri in 1809, and became a singing master and songwriter. His *Hebrew Melodies* (1815–16), with poetry by Byron, brought him fame if no lasting fortune: four years later creditors drove him to Bristol and Wales. He returned to an operatic triumph in 1823 with songs for *Sweethearts and Wives*, which ran for 51 nights at the Haymarket, and the song *Why are you wand'ring here, I pray?* remained in print for almost a century. But apart from *The Illustrious Stranger* (1827), theatrical success thereafter eluded him and he survived on teaching and journalism.

Nathan's four London monographs (1823–36) reveal his erudition, idiosyncrasy and irregular lifestyle, including intimate associations with royalty and the aristocracy, particularly Lady Caroline Lamb whose former husband Lord Melbourne forced him into exile. Arriving at Sydney on 5 April 1841, he became the town's self-appointed musician laureate, composing, performing and mostly publishing almost 50 works, including two operas, *Merry Freaks in Troub'lous Times* (1843/51; never performed publicly) and *Don John of Austria* (1847).

Nathan produced Australia's first glee (1841/45), first musical monographs (1846, 49), first professional arrangements of Aboriginal music and the first song dedicated to an Aborigine. He also became a pioneering music publisher, anthropologist, critic and author of colonial mystery tales as well as the father of Australian opera. Throughout 23 years' residence he wrote voluminously in the Sydney press on music, theatre and the arts in general (including architecture, gastronomy and boxing).

FURTHER REFERENCE

His Overture to *Don John of Austria* has been recorded, Sydney Symphony Orchestra, cond. C. Mackerras (ABC 836 035). His writings include *Essay on the History and Theory of Music* (London, 1823), *Memories of Madame Malibran de Beriot* (London, 1826; reprint AMS Press, 1982), and *The Southern Euphrosyne* (Sydney, n.d.). A list of extant Australian compositions is in G. Pont, *Muse Unruly: The Secret Life of Isaac Nathan* (Sydney: State Library of NSW, 1997). See also *BrewerD*, 57; *IrvinD*; C. Mackerras, *The Hebrew Melodist: A Life of Isaac Nathan* (Sydney: Currawong Press, 1963); idem, *ADB*, 2; Elizabeth Wood, *GroveD*.

GRAHAM PONT

National Anthem. *Advance Australia Fair*, written and first performed in 1878 and attributed to Peter Dodds McCormick, has been the Australian national anthem since 1984, and previously April 1974 to January 1976. Before that the national anthem of Britain, *God Save the Queen* (or King as the gender of the monarch of the time dictated), was in use from the time of British colonisation in the late 18th century to 1974, and 1976–84. However, Australia's national anthem has taken several forms and has been the victim of various political agendas over the past two centuries. Many attempts have been made by writers and composers, as well as through numerous competitions, to find a unique and appropriate anthem to represent Australia.

In the early 19th century many attempts by resident composers to create a definitive national anthem were published. In 1817 words to a national song were written anonymously and published in the *Sydney Gazette and New South Wales Advertiser*, to be sung to the tune of *Rule Britannia*. In the first decades of the 19th century many songs in this genre were written and published: Stephen Hale *Marsh's *Hail to Victoria! Queen of the Southern Seas: National Anthem of Australia* (c.1840s, words by John Rae), Isaac *Nathan's *Long Live Victoria* (c.1850s, words by W.A. Duncan), S. Nelson's *Advance Australia* (c.1850, words by Eliza Postle) and *Commemoration National Anthem* (c. 1851, words by Nathaniel Kentish) to the time of *Rule Britannia* are just a few examples of this genre. In 1859 the Gawler Institute Second Birthday Song Competition, SA, produced the prize-winning *Song of Australia* by Carl *Linger and Caroline Carleton, which was later considered a potential candidate in the 1973 anthem poll. Further competitions were held over the decades producing prize-winning anthems and national songs, but none were considered appropriate or popular enough on a national scale to take the place of *God Save the Queen*.

A period of instability began in the lead-up to the 1972 federal election. Australian Labor Party leader E.G. Whitlam had promised, if elected, to seek an alternative to the then current national anthem. As prime minister in 1973 he instigated a competition for which 3800 entries were received for words and music, but with no positive outcome. Whitlam's quest continued with a public opinion poll later in 1973, run by the Australian Bureau of Census and Statistics. A random sample of 60 000 people were asked to choose between *Advance Australia Fair*, *Waltzing Matilda* and *Song of Australia* as their preference for a national anthem. These three songs were considered to have been sufficiently established and popularised on a national scale to be appropriate to the cause. *Advance Australia Fair* was successful, with 51 per cent of the vote. Whitlam pronounced in 1974 that *Advance Australia Fair* was the national anthem, but both *Advance Australian Fair* and *God Save the Queen* were to be played at state occasions when the Queen was present or to acknowledge the Queen's role as Queen of Australia and head of the Commonwealth at other appropriate occasions.

In 1976, during a period of conservative government, *God Save the Queen* was reinstated by the new prime minister, J.M. Fraser. *Advance Australia Fair* was relegated to non-regal functions in its non-verbal form only. In 1984 the then Labor prime minister, R.J. Hawke, again declared *Advance Australia Fair* as national anthem, to be played at all official and ceremonial functions, while *God Save the Queen* was declared the 'royal anthem,' to be performed at all functions where the Queen or royal family were present.

The anthem question is part of the continuing debate over Australia's future as a republic and the nationalistic fervour mounting towards the centennial celebrations of Australian Federation in 2001. Politicians, community leaders, the media and the general populace regularly debate the issue and this will doubtless continue, as the changing preferences for a national anthem in the past two centuries suggests. See *Patriotic Music*.

FURTHER REFERENCE
Edition of *Advance Australia Fair* with commentary is in *RadicT*. See also Gough Whitlam, *The Whitlam Government 1972–1975* (Ringwood, Vic.: Viking, 1985); Parliament of Australia, Senate and House of Representatives, *Hansard* 1973–74.
                                        GEORGINA BINNS

National Band Council of Australia. Organisation which promotes band performance and composition, and organises the annual Australian National Band Championships. See *Brass Bands*.

National Film and Sound Archive. Established at Canberra in 1984 to collect, preserve and provide access to Australia's screen, radio and recorded sound heritage. The foundations of the archive were the film, radio and sound recording collections formerly housed at the National Library of Australia. The archive is open to the public and maintains libraries of film, video and sound materials, a preservation, repair and copying service, and exhibitions and public programs, notably the SAMI (Sound and Moving Image) interactive exhibition. The development of the archive was invaluable for film and radio, but for music it has placed Australia in a somewhat anomalous position in that its national musical collections are divided between two locations, with scores and printed materials at the National Library and recordings at the archive. The archive's music division has become a strong resource for non-score-based genres, such as popular music and jazz.

National Music Camps Association. See *Youth Music Australia*.

National Opera League. Formed in 1914 by Alfred *Hill and Fritz *Hart to encourage through performance the composition of opera by Australian composers and provide performance opportunities for Australian artists. The league produced Hart's *Pierrette* and Hill's *Giovanni* at both Melbourne and Sydney for short seasons in 1914 to considerable acclaim. The artists and orchestra were paid fully professional rates, and despite the absence of government assistance the season ended with a small surplus, but the league was prevented by the war from going further. A short-lived company, it was nevertheless an auspicious forerunner of the later ventures of Gertrude *Johnson (in Melbourne) and Clarice Lorenz (in Sydney).

FURTHER REFERENCE
John Mansfield Thomson, *A Distant Music: The Life and Times of Alfred Hill 1870–1960* (Melbourne: OUP, 1980), 126–30.

National Opera of Australia. Founded in 1951–55 by Clarice M. Lorenz from the opera school of the NSW State Conservatorium as the National Opera of NSW. With State Government assistance it performed a short season of high quality at the Sydney Tivoli in 1951, conducted by Hans Zander and Joseph *Post. The next year it combined with Gertrude Johnson's *National Theatre Movement, Melbourne, and offered seasons in Sydney, Melbourne and Brisbane. Renamed the National Opera of Australia (a decision which offended Johnson and ended further co-operation), the company presented a third season in Newcastle, Brisbane, Sydney and Melbourne in 1953, now with Sir Eugene *Goossens as conductor, and toured NZ in 1954. The last season was in 1955. Providing the first stage of experience to Ronald *Dowd, Alan *Light, June *Bronhill and other local artists who later had notable careers, the company's artistic success helped lay the basis for the founding of the first full-time national opera company, the *Elizabethan Trust Opera Co. in 1956.

FURTHER REFERENCE
John Cargher, 'The National Operas', *Bravo! 200 Years of Opera in Australia* (Sydney: ABC/Macmillan, 1988), 38–54; *BrisbaneE*, 270–1.

National Theatre Movement (Australian). Founded in Melbourne by soprano Gertrude *Johnson to staunch the haemorrhage of local talent to Europe, it was comprised of opera, drama and ballet schools offering seasons of full-scale productions. Johnson announced her scheme in 1935, attracting prominent financial support, and established her schools with herself as honorary director at St Peter's, Eastern Hill. Her first National Theatre Movement opera season opened with *The Flying Dutchman* at the Princess Theatre in 1938. In the absence of professional competition during the war years the venture flourished, and by 1949 could boast substantial government assistance as well as a large public following.

The largest all-Australian opera producer until that time, the National Theatre provided debuts to a host of Australian singers who later had international careers. The repertoire ranged from standards such as *La traviata, Tannhäuser* and *Madame Butterfly* to new works, such as *Amahl and the Night Visitors* and *Albert Herring*. The musical standards were at first moderate, the conductors including the elderly Gustav *Slapoffski, but later improved under Joseph *Post. As the Australian National Theatre Movement Opera Co., Johnson collaborated with the Sydney-based *National Opera of Australia in 1952, and then mounted a triumphal Royal Command season for the visit of Elizabeth II in 1954, which directly influenced the formation of the *Australian Elizabethan Theatre Trust that year.

In the Trust, Johnson's ambition for a national theatrical company had the potential to be fully achieved; but it was to be nearly a decade before its opera company was secure, and declining its proposals for collaboration, Johnson pressed on with her own venture alone, launching a building appeal for a permanent National Theatre. Inevitably, the best talent was drawn to the more attractive conditions of the Trust (the National

Theatre had never paid singers at professional rates), the National Theatre's productions were increasingly scaled down, and over the next decade gradually receded in the public's mind. After protracted setbacks, including a fire in the uninsured Toorak Village Cinema, which was to be converted into its home, the National Theatre at St Kilda was finally finished and opened in 1974, a few months after Johnson's death. It chiefly presented productions of the fledgling Victorian Opera and Ballet Victoria, for by this time its own schools had lost their position at the centre of the national theatrical life Johnson had done so much to develop.

FURTHER REFERENCE
Thérèse Radic, 'The Australian National Theatre Movement as the Catalyst for The Australian Opera: Tug-Boat to Flagship', in *One Hand On the Manuscript: Music in Australian Cultural History 1930–1960*, ed. Nicholas Brown et al. (Canberra: Humanities Research Centre, ANU, 1995), 201–16; John Cargher, *Opera and Ballet in Australia* (Melbourne: Cassell, 1978), 21–7; *MackenzieS*, 122–6.

Nausicaa. Opera in three acts with prologue by Peggy ★Glanville-Hicks (1960), libretto by Robert Graves and A. Reid after Graves's *Homer's Daughter*. First performed at the Athens Festival on 19 August 1961. Published by Colfrank, New York; ms in *Msl*. Recorded by the Athens Symphony Orchestra (CRI 175).

Neal, Chris (*b* Sydney, 17 Dec. 1946), composer. His studies include an arts degree at the University of Sydney incorporating jazz and orchestration. After a background in jazz piano, rock, music-theatre, record production, and arranging, Neal's career in composition was launched with the production of *Manchild,* a rock musical which toured Australia in the early 1970s with great success. From 1973 to 1979 he was primarily involved in songwriting, record production, and copywriting. His career in film composition began with the score for the 1979 documentary *Mutiny On The Western Front*. He soon established himself as one of Australia's most sought-after film composers, and has worked consistently with directors Carl Schultz, Denny Lawrence and George Ogilvie.

FURTHER REFERENCE
Feature credits include: *Cross Talk* (1982), *Buddies* (1983), *Rebel* and the mini-series *Palace of Dreams* (1985), *Short Changed* (1986), *Around the World in 80 Ways* and *Grievous Bodily Harm* (1988), *Celia, Bullseye,* and *Emerald City* (1989), *Turtle Beach* (1992), and *The Nostradamus Kid (1993)*. Series include: *Palace of Dreams* and *Bodyline* (1984), *The Shiralee* (1987), *G.P.* (1991 to 1994), and *Law of the Land* (1993). Children's programs include: *Johnson and Friends, Liftoff, The Further Adventures of Black Beauty,* and *Butterfly Island*. See also *LimbacherF.*   L. THOMPSON

Neate, Ken(neth) (*b* Cessnock, NSW, 28 July 1914), tenor. After studies at the University of Melbourne Conservatorium, he went to New York in 1940, taking lessons with Emilio de Gorgoza. He was heard at a Metropolitan Opera gala in 1941, but at first chiefly found work in radio. After war service with the Royal Canadian Air Force, he was engaged for principal roles at Covent Garden from 1946, then in Europe from 1951, where he sang mainly for Italian houses, but also in Spain, Egypt, and later France. He appeared in Australia for J.C. Williamsons in 1955 and for the Elizabethan Theatre Trust Opera Co. in 1960, as well as making concert tours. His roles included Don José, the Duke of Mantua, Pinkerton, Otello and Tamino, he sang in the premiere of Henri Tomasi's *Sampiero Corso*. He specialised increasingly in Wagner in later years, singing Loge at the 1963 Bayreuth Festival, and retired in 1975.

FURTHER REFERENCE
David Cummings *GroveO*; *MackenzieS*, 172–3.

Ned Kelly Electric Music Show. Rock musical by Patrick Flynn, book by Reg ★Livermore. A version of the Kelly story told through a lavish mixture of rock opera, vaudeville and comedy. A sound-track album was released in 1975, but the show did not open until a promoter could be found in Adelaide in 1978. See *Musical Comedy*.

Ned Kelly's Farewell to Greta, folk-song. Set at his home near Greta, northern Victoria, as he embarks for the outlaw life in 1878–79, this song is Kelly's farewell to his sister Kate and her reply. Collected by Max Brown and published in *Six Authentic Songs From the Kelly Country* (1955); another version jointly collected by Norm O'Connor, Bob Mitchell and Mary Jean Officer and published in *Gum Sucker's Gazette* (1963).

FURTHER REFERENCE
Edition with commentary in *ManifoldP.*

Neild, James Edward ['Jacques', 'Tahite'] (*b* Doncaster, Yorkshire, England, 6 July 1824; *d* Melbourne, 17 Aug. 1906), music critic. He studied medicine then worked as a surgeon at Rochdale, UK, until coming to the Australian goldfields in 1853. He was soon practising medicine at the Castlemaine diggings, and was a lecturer in forensic medicine at the University of Melbourne from 1865. He became a prolific theatre critic, and was music critic for the *Examiner* (1857–59), *Bell's Life* (1863–66) then the *Australasian* (1865–90) and the *Argus,* under the pen-names 'Jacques' and (from 1870) 'Tahite'. His writing berated performers for any vanity or virtuosity that he judged not strictly in the composer's service. He showed no ear for new developments in composition, but he was the first to recognise Melba's talent and was an important and prodigious witness to music in colonial Melbourne.

FURTHER REFERENCE
Harold Love, *James Edward Neild: Victorian Virtuoso* (Melbourne:
MUP, 1989); Bryan Gandevia, *ADB*, 5; *IrvinD*; Harold Love,
ParsonsC.

Nelson, Sydney   (*b* London, 1800; *d* 1862), popular
music composer, performer. In London he composed the
music for theatre works produced at the English Opera
House, including *The Middle Temple* (1829), *The Grenadier*
(1831), *Cousin Joseph* (1835), *Domestic Arrangements* (1835)
and *The Cadi's Daughter* (1851) before coming to Australia in 1852. In Melbourne he presented musical entertainments with his son and daughters, and collaborated
with William M. ★Akhurst in vaudevilles, including
Ladies' Prerogative, Quite Colonial and *The Rights of Women*.
His songs became popular, especially *The Pilot*, which was
sung in various melodramas based on the Cooper novel
of that name. With his family he also appeared at Sydney
from 1855, where *Cousin Joseph* was given twice (1856,
1860), until 1859 when his daughters Carry and Sara
went to California, making a success at the San Francisco
Opera House.

FURTHER REFERENCE
IrvinD; *Illustrated Sydney News* 21 Apr. 1855.

Nettelbeck, Ted (Theodore John)   (*b* Streaky Bay,
SA, 4 Jan. 1936), jazz pianist. He was pianist with Bruce
Gray (1959–60), then at Melbourne's Embers nightclub
under Frank ★Smith, then the band leader there
(1961–62). In Europe 1962–65, after returning to Adelaide he became central as a performer-composer to the
progressive jazz movement, including work with Schmoe
★Elhay, Billy ★Ross, in solo and duet performances with
Tony ★Gould, Bruce Hancock and Bob ★Sedergreen,
leading groups, and working in more mainstream areas
with Gray and others. He has played frequently at concerts and festivals and worked as support for visitors such
as John Lewis and Phil Woods. He is a lecturer in psychology at the University of Adelaide.

FURTHER REFERENCE
Recordings include *Jazz in South Australia,* Southern Spectrum,
(1987, Larrikin Records LRJ 231); *Jim Mcleod's Jazz Tracks* (1989,
ABC Records 838 832–1); *Reflections in a Bird Bath,* The Ted
Nettelbeck Trio (1995, MBS JAZZ 10). See also *BissetB*; *OxfordJ*.
                                          BRUCE JOHNSON

New Country.   Australian neo-country music style of
the 1990s, developed to appeal to young urban tastes.
Emerging chiefly in the capital cities in the late 1980s, it
mixes traditional country music values with various
retro-American musical trends, such as western swing,
cajun, honky-tonk, tex-mex or polyester country. It
often adds steel or amplified guitar and strong dance
rhythms to the traditional country music resources. The

most notable exponents are the Happening Thang, the
Danglin' Brothers, the Fargone Beauties, Keith ★Glass
and the Tumblers, and Keith Urban; there are also various younger bands developing the style, particularly in
Melbourne and Sydney.

FURTHER REFERENCE
LattaA, 190–8.

New Sydney Woodwind Quintet.   Formed in 1965
from principal players of the Sydney Symphony Orchestra, originally comprised of Neville ★Amadio (flute), Guy
Henderson (oboe), Donald Westlake (clarinet), Clarence
Mellor (french horn) and John ★Cran (bassoon). Several
of the members had played together in the Sydney Sinfonietta, and now they focused on the traditional wind
quintet repertoire but also commissioned new works
from Australian composers. They performed regularly in
Sydney and on tour, appearing at the Manilla Festival of
the Arts in 1969, but by 1979 had largely been superseded
by the Australian Wind Virtuosi, in which two of their
members played.

FURTHER REFERENCE
Recordings include Ivan Smith, *The Death of a Wombat* (1977,
RCA VPK 10159).

Newcastle,   pop. (1991) 262 331. Birthplace of opera
singer John Shaw, popular music pianist Warren ★Carr,
composer David ★Worrall and stringed instrument maker
Ian ★Watchorn, it is the second largest city in NSW, situated at the mouth of the Hunter River north of Sydney.
Founded in 1804 as a penal settlement (Coal River), today
it is a major port and centre for steel and heavy industry.
   Christ Church Cathedral had a small organ from 1872;
the Norman & Beard instrument in the present building
dates from 1906 (rebuilt 1963). A band rotunda was built in
King Edward's Park 1898, the City of Newcastle Band
under William Barkel was a prize-winner at South Street
and elsewhere 1900–30, and the New Steel Works Band
toured Britain in 1924; there remains a strong tradition of
brass bands as well as highland pipe bands in the city. The
Newcastle Eisteddfod was founded in 1875, and continues
to serve the district. The part-time Hunter Symphony
Orchestra, the most successful orchestra outside the Australian capital cities, gave well-patronised concerts under
Ulrich Bernstein from 1985; after his death from illness in
1989 it was placed on a more professional basis and conducted by Roland Peelman at City Hall.
   The Civic Theatre was one of many buildings in the
town to be rebuilt and reopened in 1993 after a major
earthquake shook the city, and it is the venue for visiting
groups such as those of Musica Viva. The University of
Newcastle Conservatorium was founded in 1952, has a
number of distinguished staff and conducts an annual
Keyboard Festival each August with national and interna-

tional guests. The cathedral is the site for many musical performances and an annual church music festival in September. The Newcastle and Hunter Jazz Club conducts an annual festival each August.

Newcastle Conservatorium.

Founded in 1952 as a branch of the NSW State Conservatorium, it has been affiliated with the University of Newcastle since 1988. Since 1981 it has occupied a modified hostel building in the central city with an outstanding concert hall (opened 1988), and focuses on a chiefly practical degree and diploma. An annual keyboard festival, attracting distinguished visiting artists, began in 1989. Directors have been Harold Lobb (1952–68), Keith Field (1970–73), Peter Martin (1975–76), John ★Winther (1977–79) and Michael ★Dudman (1979–94). The present director is Robert Constable.

FURTHER REFERENCE
Kenneth Wiseman, *From Park to Palace: A History of the Newcastle Conservatorium of Music 1952–1986* (Dudley, NSW: K. Wiseman, c.1988).

Newnham, Hartley

(*b* 28 July 1939), countertenor. He has been heard throughout Australia in an unusually wide range of repertoire, from Medieval works with ★La Romanesca to contemporary works with the Seymour Group, including an innovative countertenor *Pierrot Lunaire* in 1982. Various works have been commissioned for him, including Ross Edwards' *Maninyas* and *Il lutto dell'universo*.

FURTHER REFERENCE
As a soloist, his recordings include Ross Edwards, *Maninyas* (1990, MBS MBS 21CD); and *Il lutto dell'universo* (Christophorus SCK 70365).

Newstead, Tony

(*b* Melbourne, 1 Oct. 1923), jazz trumpeter. He began trumpet in 1940, freelancing until joining the RAAF in 1942, and during his war service made contact with a wider jazz community, including playing with the RAAF jazz band. Joining the Varsity Vipers, he recorded with Will McIntyre in 1946, and began leading bands for the Eureka Hot Jazz Society functions; he was president of Melbourne University Rhythm Club in 1947. When the Bell band left for Europe, Newstead assembled groups to take over at the Uptown Club. His Southside (Downtown) Gang played in numerous concerts, clubs and residencies through the early 1950s and in later reunions. He subsequently freelanced, but has been musically inactive since 1985.

FURTHER REFERENCE
Recordings include *Will McIntyre's Jazz Band* (1946, Ampersand 7, 8); *Tony Newstead and His Gang* (1960, Swaggie S-4524); *Take Me To The Circus,* Len Barnard's Famous Jazz Band, (1971, Swag-

gie S-1329); *The Yacht Club Jazz Band* (1977, Swaggie S-1375). See also *BissetB*; *OxfordJ*.   BRUCE JOHNSON

Newton-John, Olivia

(*b* Cambridge, England, 26 Sept. 1948), pop singer, actress. She emigrated to Australia in 1954 and was a member of the schoolgirl quartet the Sol Four. Victory in a solo contest sponsored by Johnny ★O'Keefe saw her return to England, working with Pat ★Carroll in cabaret (1966) and briefly with the pop group Tomorrow. Her first hit was a 1971 country music version of Bob Dylan's *If Not For You*. An American breakthrough followed with *Let Me Be There* (1974), which won a gold record, and in 1973 she won a Grammy as best country vocalist. The categorisation of *Let Me Be There* in both the country and the Hot 100 charts allowed her to win both best female country vocalist and best female pop performance in 1974, and she began a lucrative film career, in 1978 altering her style to accommodate rock and dance audiences. In the film *Grease* her duet with John Travolta *You're The One That I Want* topped the UK singles for nine weeks. Her hit album *Totally Hot* soon followed, and she won the American people's choice award as favourite motion picture actress in 1979. She filmed *Xanadu* (1980), and in 1981 *Physical* was a No. 1 single.

During the late 1980s and early 90s much of her time was spent running her Australian-styled clothing business Blue Koala, and in 1990 she was named goodwill ambassador to the United Nations Environment Program. In 1992 she released her 18th album, *Back to Basics: The Essential Collection 1971–1992*, but the accompanying concert tour was cancelled when she was diagnosed with breast cancer. In 1993 her cancer treatment finished, and she returned to Australia, writing material for a self-produced album, *Gaia: One Woman's Journey,* her songwriting debut. In 1994 she hosted *Wildlife* in Australia, enabling her to travel extensively.

Newton-John's career has spanned country music, disco, easy-listening, and starring roles in musical films and television. She was honoured with the OBE in 1979.

FURTHER REFERENCE
Recordings include *Long Live Love* (1974); *Making A Good Thing Better* (1977); *Gaia: One Woman's Journey* (1993); *Grease* (1978 Sound-track); *Xanadu* (1980, ELO); *Physical* (1981); *Two of a Kind* (1983 Sound-track); *Warm and Tender* (1990); *Olivia Newton-John's Greatest Hists* (1977 US MCA); *Olivia's Greatest Hits* 2 vols (1982 US MCA). See also Fred Dellar, Alan Cackett and Roy Thompson, *The Illustrated Encyclopedia of Country Music,* ed. Ray Bonds (London: Salamander, 1986), 121; *GuinnessP.*

KYLIE MOLONEY

Ngarrindjeri.

People of the Riverine, Coorong and around the Murray River in SA. Modern Ngarrindjeri songs and those in related languages Narrunga and Kaurna were written specifically for children, while also intended for the wider community. They were produced following a songwriting workshop organised by the Ngarrindjeri, Narrunga and Kaurna Languages Project in March 1990. The aim of the workshop was to use the medium of music to keep the languages alive. Some songs are entirely in one language, others in English with key words in the tribal languages. Some seek to imitate or draw upon traditional rhythms and melody shapes, while others use Western-style tunes. See *Aboriginal Music*.

FURTHER REFERENCE
Narrunga, Kaurna and Ngarrindjeri songs (Elizabeth, SA: Ngarrindjeri, Narrunga and Kaurna Languages Project, 1990).

Ngätji. A form of ritual wailing by women in north-eastern and north-central Arnhem Land public ceremonials. See *Clan Songs*.

Nicholls, John Whitburn (*b* Bendigo, Vic., 16 Oct. 1916), organist. Educated at St Paul's Cathedral Choir School and Trinity Grammar School, Melbourne, he was a chorister at St Paul's 1927–31 and subsequently assistant organist. He studied organ with A.E. *Floyd, piano with Roy *Shepherd, and won the Clarke Scholarship in 1936. From 1936 to 1939 he studied with H.G. Ley, Kendal Taylor and R.O. Morris at the Royal College of Music, London. He was then organist and master of the choristers at St David's Cathedral, Hobart, 1940–80, and city organist 1940–81. A choral-orchestral conductor, broadcaster, lecturer and adjudicator, he was also active in the establishment of the Tasmanian Symphony Orchestra under the auspices of the ABC. He was honoured with the MBE in 1980.

FURTHER REFERENCE
GlennonA; *OrchardM*.   IAN BURK

Nicholls, Nev (*b* Tallwood, nr Orange, NSW, 16 Sept. 1930), country music singer-songwriter. Playing guitar and writing traditional country ballads from the age of 12, he was signed by Regal Zonophone, making 15 singles 1952–58, appearing with Tim McNamara and Ted Quigg, and then from 1957 with Kevin King, Chad *Morgan and Reg *Lindsay. His group played in Sydney clubs from 1961, then was resident at the Texas Tavern, Kings Cross, 1968–78. Increasingly attracted to themes of the loneliness of long-distance transport driving, his *Nev Nicholls Roadshow* (1979–) became the largest syndicated truckers' music show on Australian radio. He formed the independent label Nicholls'n'Dimes, which recorded 26 albums of truckers' music (1985–90). Australia's best-known trucking singer, his albums have been enormously successful among truckers. He was honoured in the ACMA Roll of Renown in 1992.

FURTHER REFERENCE
Recordings include his albums *Keep On Truckin'* (1974, RCA), *Just My Trucking Luck* (RCA VCL 10052) and *Blazing Diesels*

(Seven Records). For discography see *WatsonC*, II. See also *LattaA*, 152–53. *SmithB*, 178–9; *WatsonC*, 82–9.

Nicholson, J(ames) C(harles) W(ilson) (*b* 1837; *d* 1907), music publisher, retailer. Nicholson was employed by *Allans in the 1870s and in 1875 established his own business in partnership with Elman Ascherberg, known as Ascherberg & Nicholson. The partnership dissolved in 1878, becoming Nicholson & Co., and branches were founded in Sydney in 1876, Brisbane in 1890 and Perth in 1893. From 1881 the firm published approximately 90 editions of Nicholsons' *Australian Musical Magazine* as well as song, dance and piano albums. From 1894 the head office was located in Sydney. In 1936 Nicholsons and Allans merged, but when Allans sold their interest in the business it was then merged with *Palings and a holding company was formed.   SUZANNE ROBINSON

Nicholson, Ross Edwin (*b* Perth, 8 Feb. 1940), jazz reeds and flute player. After childhood piano lessons he began clarinet at the age of 14, later adding other reeds and flute. He formed a jazz group in 1955, deputised in the Riverside band in 1956, and began attending *Australian Jazz Conventions in 1958. Following a teaching posting in Geraldton 1962–65, he began a decade with JT and the Jazzmen. He played pop music with Abe Walters and Will Upson in the 1970s, then joined the Swan City Jazzmen until the mid-1980s, also freelancing in a range of genres. Ubiquitous in the Perth jazz community since the 1960s, he is currently with the Gumnut Stompers and freelancing.

FURTHER REFERENCE
OxfordJ.   BRUCE JOHNSON

Nickson, A(rthur) E(rnest) H(oward) (*b* Melbourne, 1 Mar. 1876; *d* Melbourne, 16 Feb. 1964), teacher, organist, critic. He studied with Ernest *Wood at St Paul's Cathedral, Melbourne, and was the first organist to win the Clarke Scholarship (1895–99) to the Royal College of Music, where he studied with Walter Parratt, obtaining his FRCO and ARCM. Returning to Melbourne in 1901 he began his life's work, exerting for the next 60 years a profound influence upon Melbourne's musical life. Closely involved in the music of St Peter's Eastern Hill for most of that time, he was also choirmaster at Melbourne Grammar School until 1930, and for some years the school's master-in-charge of music. From 1928 to 1948, as music critic of the *Age,* his thoughtful and scholarly concert reviews were a major feature of Melbourne's musical life. But his main work, spanning the whole of his professional life, was as teacher and lecturer at the University of Melbourne Conservatorium. His lectures in aesthetics were particularly memorable, and his organ lessons of rare inspiration and mastery. Of note was his admiration of the music of Karg-Elert, and his long correspondence with him. Karg-Elert's *Seven*

Pastels from the Lake of Constance were dedicated to him and played by him at St Paul's Cathedral in 1924. As a churchman and idealist he conceived music in terms of ultimate beauty, believing it capable, more than any other art, of reaching the ineffable and sublime. In 'the beautiful, the good, and the true' he found meaning not only for art, but for life itself. This was the essence of his teaching. In 1960 the university conferred on him an honorary DMus, and in 1963 he was made a fellow of the Royal College of Music.

FURTHER REFERENCE
His published essays include *An Ideal in Church Music; The Catholic Spirit in Song; The Mind Beautiful; The Sisters Three; Christ in Art; Tregear.*   HOWARD HOLLIS

Nickson, Noël John Bennie   (*b* Melbourne, 5 Jan. 1919), academic, administrator, composer. He studied at the University of Melbourne and the Royal College of Music, London. He held various music-teaching, lecturing and administrative positions in London and Australia, including at St Paul's School, London, 1949, the NSW State Conservatorium 1951–59, the Royal College of Music 1954, and the University of Melbourne 1959–65, and was appointed foundation professor of music at the University of Queensland, 1965–84. His research interests include the compositions of Dorian Le Gallienne, and as a member of the Cambridge Tang Music project research team from 1980, he has co-authored and co-edited several studies on the music of the Chinese Tang Court and its forms of representation in Japanese courtly music. He has been made a life member of ASME.

FURTHER REFERENCE
ADMR; WWA (1996).   PHILIPPA ROYLANCE

Nilsson, Raymond   (*b* Mosman, Sydney, 26 May 1920), tenor. An arts graduate of the University of Sydney, after war service he taught at Sydney Grammar School and sang as soloist at St Andrew's Cathedral. He studied with Harold ★Williams and Mme Matthay at the NSW State Conservatorium, and after winning the City of Sydney Eisteddfod went to London in 1947. He sang with Sadler's Wells, the Carl Rosa Opera Co. and, from 1952, with Covent Garden, as well as in Europe and the USA and on television. He toured Australia for the Elizabethan Theatre Trust Opera Co. in 1958 and as Camille in *The Merry Widow* with Sadler's Wells in 1960. With a voice of high polish, excellent phrasing and diction and good acting, his roles included Rodolfo, Don José, Alfredo, and Pandarus (*Troilus and Cressida*), as well as the principal role in *The Saint of Bleeker Street;* on the concert platform he featured in many contemporary works, including Schoenberg's *Gurrelieder,* Hindemith's *Mathis der Maler,* and Stravinsky's *Oedipus Rex.* He now lives in retirement in NSW.

FURTHER REFERENCE
Recordings include Bob Bowles in *Peter Grimes,* Covent Garden (Decca 414577–2DH3) and Kodaly, *Psalmus Hungaricus,* London Philharmonic Orchestra (Everest EVC 9008). See also *MackenzieS,* 198–200; *AMN* 46 (May 1956), 10.

Nine Miles from Gundagai (Five Miles from Gundagai; Bill the Bullocky),   folk-song. Sung to 'Camooweal Races' or 'Yellow Rose of Texas', the several versions of this somewhat coarse bullocky song relate a comic incident in which a bullock driver, stranded with a broken axle in pouring rain far from town, cannot eat because his dog has fouled the tucker box. The text was collected by A.V. Vennard and published in *Bush Recitations* in 1937.

FURTHER REFERENCE
Edition and commentary in *EdwardsG.*

Nixon, (Helena) June Rose   (*b* Boort, Vic., 20 May 1942), organist, composer. She was educated at the University of Melbourne, studying organ under Bernard Clarke. In 1967 she was awarded the FRCO and in 1968 was winner of the Australian National Organ Playing Competition. Granted the A.E.H. Nickson and Bentwich scholarships in 1970, she obtained her Choirmaster's Diploma, Royal College of Organists (John Brooke Prize) and ARCM in 1971. Appointed organist and director of the choir at St Paul's Cathedral, Melbourne, in 1973, she received the Percy Jones award for outstanding service to church music in 1995. She is a recitalist and teacher and a widely published composer of organ and choral music.

FURTHER REFERENCE
CohenI; The Organ and Organists of St Paul's Cathedral, Melbourne (Melbourne: St Paul's Cathedral, 1991), 33.   JOHN MAIDMENT

No Fixed Address.   Aboriginal rock group active in the early 1980s, based in Adelaide and led by singer-songwriter Bart Willoughby. With Us Mob they starred in the film *Wrong Side of the Road,* winner of the Australian Film Industry Awards Jury Prize in 1981 Their songs are socially committed and critical of the treatment of Aborigines; their music has a strong reggae influence. Joe Geia was lead singer until 1985.

FURTHER REFERENCE
Recordings include *From My Eyes* (1992, Mushroom Records D19696); and the films *No Fixed Address On Tour* (SBS TV); and *Wrong Side of the Road* (Inma Productions).

P. DUNBAR-HALL

Noble, Patsy Ann [Trisha]   (*b* Sydney, 3 Feb. 1944), pop singer. From the age of 16 she was a regular singer on television's *Bandstand.* Her first two singles did not do well, but she won a TV Logie as best female singer in 1961, and her next single, *Good Looking Boy,* reached No. 6 in the charts in 1962. She went to England the same year, where she recorded seven more singles, including *Don't Ever Change Your Mind* (1963) and *I Did Nothing Wrong* (1964), but did not find enduring chart success. From 1965 she lived in the USA where she sang as Trisha Noble.

FURTHER REFERENCE
Recordings include *Good Looking Boy* (1961, HMV EA 4439), *Don't Ever Change Your Mind* (1963, Columbia DO 4344) and *I Did Nothing Wrong* (1964, Columbia DO 4475). For discography, see *SpencerA*. See also *McGrathA*; *SpencerW.*

Nock, Mike (Michael Anthony) (*b* Christchurch, NZ, 27 Sept. 1940), jazz pianist, composer. He began piano at the age of 10 with lessons from his father, and was subsequently self-taught, also playing saxophone, cornet and drums as a teenager. His first public performance was at the age of 11, then he formed his first band. Moving to Australia at 18, he worked in Melbourne at The Embers with Frank *Smith, who became a significant influence. Based in Sydney, he began playing at *El Rocco in 1960 and formed the influential Three Out Trio with drummer Colin Bailey (subsequently Chris Karan) and bassist Freddie Logan. The group enjoyed great success, with regular work at El Rocco and other engagements including the International Jazz Festival in 1960, a tour of NZ in 1961, and then Europe.

Nock settled in the USA, leading his own groups, notably the seminal fusion group The Fourth Way, and touring and recording prolifically with Coleman Hawkins, Yusef Lateef, Stanley Turrentine, Dionne Warwick, John Handy and others. He returned to Sydney in 1985 and immediately re-established his reputation as a performer-composer and taught at the Sydney Conservatorium. He has won numerous awards including the Australian critics' award three years running (1991–93), hosted his own television series for TVNZ, was the subject of a television documentary, and appeared in *Beyond El Rocco.* He has composed for film, radio and television, for Ten Part Invention, Synergy, and the Australian Chamber Orchestra.

FURTHER REFERENCE
Recordings include *Move*, Three Out Trio (1960, Columbia 330SX-7639); *Almanac*, Mike Nock Quartet (1967, Improvising Artists IA1 37–3851); *The Fourth Way* (1969, reissued 1995, Jazz View Records, COD 022); *In Out and Around*, Mike Nock Quartet (1978, Timeless T1313); *Ondas*, Mike Nock Trio, (1981, ECM 1–1220); *Touch*, Mike Nock Solo (1993, Birdland BL 001). See also *ClareB*; *BissetB*; *OxfordJ*; *GroveJ*; Bruce Johnson, 'Mike Nock, Sinfully Musical', *FM Radio, 2MBS-FM Program Guide* (July 1987), 6–7; Michael Rozek, 'Profile, Mike Nock', *Downbeat* (Apr. 7, 1977), 35; John Shand, 'Mike Nock,' *Australian Jazz and Blues* 1/4 (1994), 11.   BRUCE JOHNSON

Nolan, Col (Colin James) (*b* Sydney, 16 Apr. 1938), jazz pianist. His first jazz work was as pianist with Doc

Willis 1959–60. During the 1960s he led groups at *El Rocco and with Ray Price; he was also with the rock group the *Dee-Jays 1961–62. He led his Soul Syndicate for residencies at the Celebrity Room 1968–69 and at Jason's in the early 1970s. A foundation member of the *Daly-Wilson Big Band, he was later with *Galapagos Duck. He has continued to lead and to freelance, with Errol *Buddle and others, and to do session work with players such as John *Sangster. His venues include Soup Plus and the *Basement. He pioneered the use of the Hammond organ in jazz in Australia.

FURTHER REFERENCE
Recordings include *Ray Price Quartet* (1962, CBS BP-233042); *The Daly Wilson Big Band* (1970, Columbia Co SCXO-7979); *Live at Jason's*, The Col Nolan Soul Syndicate (1973, Avant-Guard SVL-501); *Lord of the Rings Vol 1*, John Sangster (1974, EMI EMC.2525/6), vol. 2 (1976, EMI EMC 2548/9), vol. 3 (1977, EMI EMC 2580/1); *Arrangements*, Col Nolan Quartet (1977, M7 Records MLF-157); *The Galapagos Duck* (1979, Philips 6357 064); *The Main Stream*, Col Nolan (1990, MBS JAZZ 7). See also *ClareB*; *BissetB*; *OxfordJ*.   BRUCE JOHNSON

Norman, Wally (*b* Melbourne, 14 Mar. 1919), jazz trumpeter. He began dance band work in Melbourne in 1939, then moved to Sydney to join Frank *Coughlan, becoming extremely active in dance, nightclub and radio work, with Jim *Davidson and Abe Romain among others. He began at the Roosevelt restaurant in 1944, taking its band leadership from 1945, when Sydney's outstanding progressive musicians worked there. A leader in the exploration of bop, from the mid-1950s he was active as support for visiting performers such as Gene Krupa, Ella Fitzgerald, Louis Armstrong, Mel Tormé and Buddy de Franco. He retired from performance in 1960 to form a theatrical agency.

FURTHER REFERENCE
Recordings include *George Trevare's Jazz Group* (1945, Regal Zonophone RZ G-24954 to 24956); *Les Welch and His Orchestra* (1950, Pacific 10–0017). See also *BissetB*; *OxfordJ*.

BRUCE JOHNSON

Northcote Permanent Orchestra Trust Fund, Lady. Fund established in 1908 at Melbourne. Originally intended to secure the *Marshall-Hall Orchestra on a permanent basis, its founders were Lady Alice Northcote, wife of the Governor-General of Australia, Sir James *Barrett, Baron Carl *Pinschof and others among Marshall-Hall's supporters. They sought to raise money by public subscription, and after the demise of Marshall-Hall's orchestra in 1912, they assisted Alberto *Zelman Jr's Melbourne Symphony Orchestra, tried to establish a Lady Northcote Orchestra, and then assisted Bernard *Heinze's University of Melbourne Conservatorium Orchestra. Melba gave a benefit concert for the fund in 1918, while Percy Grainger, Sir George Tallis and other prominent figures all contributed; the trustees had accumulated £4 000 by 1919. The fund remained the major source of subsidies for orchestral performance in Melbourne until overshadowed by the ABC in 1932, and still survives today, making grants to various musical ventures.

FURTHER REFERENCE
Jim Davidson, *Lyrebird Rising: Louise Hanson Dyer of L'Oiseau-Lyre 1884–1962* (Melbourne: MUP, 1994), 117–31; Chris Cuneen, *ADB*, 2; *AMN* 8 (Nov. 1918), 32.

Noskowski, Ladislas de (*b* Poland, 1892; *d* Sydney, 1969), music critic, diplomat. Noskowski arrived in Australia in 1911. He was an excellent linguist, finding early employment in Australia as a censor and translator for the Australian Army (*c.*1918) and then as a teacher of modern languages in schools. At the same time he was a prolific reviewer of Sydney's musical life, passing informed and balanced judgments on concerts presented in that city. He was especially enthusiastic about opera and was a good judge of singing, like his father from whom he inherited a passion for opera and later an historic record library. His *Sydney Mail* reviews of the 1919–20 Rigo-Williamson opera season are among the best written about that season. In 1925 he co-founded the successful *Australasian Phonograph Monthly*. In the 1930s he became consul-general for Poland, undertaking various diplomatic duties.   JEFF BROWNRIGG

Not Drowning Waving. Experimental popular music band formed in Melbourne in 1984 by David Bridie (piano), John Phillips (guitar) and Tim Cole, who were joined in 1985 by Russell Bradley (drums), Rowan McKinnon (bass) and James Southall (percussion), and in 1989 by Helen Mountford (viola). They composed extended instrumental works which transcended the conventions of mainstream popular music. The group's music borders on popular art, and has often been labelled 'ambient' in an attempt to describe the influence of non-Western cultures on their compositional style. The band gained widespread notoriety with the release of *Tabaran* (1991) and its sound-track for the Australian film *Proof* (1991).

FURTHER REFERENCE
Recordings include *Another Pond* (1984, East West 903173848–2); *The Little Desert* (1984, East West 903173857–2); *Cold and the Crackle* (1987, East West 903173858–2); *Claim* (1989, Reprise 9 26181–2); *Tabaran* (1990, WEA 9031732999–2); *Proof* (1991, Rogue's Gallery RG 001); *Circus* (1993, Reprise 9 45169–2); *Hammers* (1994, Rogue's Gallery RG 002). See also *SpencerW.*   AARON D.S. CORN

Novalis Quartet. String quartet formed (1990) by pianist Jeanell Carrigan and three players of the Sydney Symphony Orchestra: Goetz Richter (violin), Anne-Louise Comerford (viola) and Catherine Hewgill (cello). They have focused on music of the Romantics, reflected in their name—the pseudonym of the early Romantic poet Friedrich von Hardenberg. With a meticulous dedication to ensemble playing, they have appeared regularly in the eastern capital cities and toured for Musica Viva.

Nowra, Louis (*b* Melbourne, 12 Dec. 1950), playwright, librettist. After writing for La Mama Theatre, Melbourne, from 1973, he came to prominence when *Inner Voices* was produced at the Nimrod Theatre, Sydney in 1977. He has written 23 plays, as well as novels, films, and translations, and has been resident playwright at the Sydney Theatre Company (1979–80), and Lighthouse Company, Adelaide (1982–83). Most of his plays contain significant musical content; Sarah *de Jong has composed music for many of his works, and Brian *Howard made an opera of *Inner Voices,* as well as using Nowra as his librettist for his opera *Whitsunday.*

FURTHER REFERENCE
OxfordL; ParsonsC.

NSW Conservatorium Jazz Course. See *Burrows, Don.*

NSW State Conservatorium. See *Sydney Conservatorium.*

Nurlu. Public singing and dancing in the Kimberleys. See *Corroboree.*

O Paddy Dear, and Did You Hear. See *The Ballad of Kelly's Gang.*

Oath of Bad Brown Bill, The. Chamber opera in two acts by Barry ⋆Conyngham, libretto by M. Copland and S. Axelson. First performed at the Victorian Arts Centre Studio on 6 January 1985.

Odamura, Satsuki (*b* Japan, 6 May 1963), koto player. She studied with leading koto exponents Kazue Sawai and Tadao Sawai, completed the Japan National Broadcasting Traditional Music Course (NHK) in 1984, and additional performance courses; she was also a member of the prestigious Sawai Koto Ensemble. Resident in Australia since 1989, Satsuki extensively performs traditional and contemporary Japanese music as well as fusion styles. She teaches in both Sydney and Melbourne and performs widely throughout Australia and internationally. She has inspired Australian composers to write for koto, including Carl Vine (*Gaajin*), Barry Conyngham (*Afterimages*), Liza Lim (*Burning House*), and Peter Sculthorpe (*Little Requiem*). Her solo recording *Like a Bird* was released in 1993, and a further recording of Australian compositions is to be released in 1997. A highly virtuosic musician, Satsuki has been a very influential figure in the propagation of Japanese traditional music in Australia.

FURTHER REFERENCE

Her recording is *Like a Bird* (1993, Tall Poppies TP044).

ADRIAN MCNEIL

O'Donnell, John David (*b* Sydney, 6 Oct. 1948), organist, harpsichordist, choral conductor. After studies in piano (and theory with Alex ⋆Burnard) at the NSW State Conservatorium he went to the UK and studied at Durham University, then took his FRCO, winning the first British national organ competition in 1969. He was organist at St Mary's Cathedral, Sydney, and taught at the NSW State Conservatorium from 1971; he was organist

at St Peter's Eastern Hill, Melbourne, and senior lecturer at the Victorian College of the Arts from 1974, then senior lecturer at the University of Melbourne 1990–95. He has toured the USA 10 times as organist, harpsichordist and lecturer on performance practice, and given recitals on many historic organs in Europe.

As a choral conductor he has specialised in the authentic performance of Baroque and late Renaissance repertoire. He was director of the Tudor Choristers, Melbourne and the Canterbury Fellowship (from 1985), and founded the Ensemble Gombert in 1990, making numerous broadcasts with the ABC. He has published on performance practice in *Musicology, The Diapason, Early Music* and elsewhere, and edited the complete keyboard works of Johann Caspar Kerll (Vienna: Doblinger, 1994).

FURTHER REFERENCE

Recordings include Handel and Telemann trio sonatas, Capella Corelli (1993, Move MD3126); organ works (ABC); and Bach organ works (1993 Milan). His articles include 'Bach's Trills: Some Historical and Contextual Considerations', *MA* 4 (1974), 14–24, and 'The French Style and Overtures of Bach', *Early Music* 7 (1979), 190–6, 336–45. See also *ADMR.*

O'Flaherty, Eliza. See *Winstanley, Eliza.*

O'Hagan, Jack (*b* Melbourne, 29 Nov. 1898; *d* Melbourne, 15 July 1987), popular music songwriter. Without having learned to read music, he published his first song, *Oh, Those Honolulu Girls*, in 1918. He achieved a major success with *On the Road to Gundagai* in 1921, which was recorded by Peter ⋆Dawson in 1922 and used as the theme for the 3DB radio show *Dad and Dave* from 1937; it rapidly entered Australian folklore, recorded by 40 artists in his lifetime. He wrote dance music, stage shows, and over 100 songs, chiefly Australian outback ballads, patriotic fighting songs, or sporting songs. The best known include *Our Don Bradman* (1932) and *Where the Dog Sits on the Tuckerbox*; his *Dreamy Araby* (1922) sold 50 000 copies in sheet music and his *God Bless Australia,* to the tune of

Waltzing Matilda, he hoped would become the national anthem. An immensely successful popular song composer of the interwar years, he was honoured with the MBE.

FURTHER REFERENCE
Obit. in *Age* 16 July 1987. See also *Herald* 28 Oct. 1950.

O'Keefe, Johnny (John Michael) (*b* Sydney, 19 Jan. 1935; *d* Sydney, 6 Oct. 1978), rock and roll singer. Son of a furniture salesman, with only rudimentary musical training he began singing professionally at the age of 17. At first he worked at suburban dances, singing current American covers for promoter Bill McColl, but after seeing Bill Haley in *Blackboard Jungle* in 1955 he soon became interested in the emerging American rock and roll. Alan Dale, leader of the Houserockers, perhaps the earliest of the Haley imitators in Australia, worked for O'Keefe's father, and O'Keefe formed his own rock and roll band, the Dee Jays, along similar lines in 1956. With stage energy akin to Elvis Presley's, he made volatile appearances as a supporting act in Lee ★Gordon's Big Shows at the Sydney Stadium from 1957, first coming to wide attention when he and his band shared the platform with Little Richard's Australian tour. At times his reception by the crowds was bigger than for the visiting American stars. He made his debut single, *You Hit The Wrong Note, Billy Goat,* in the same year.

At this time the Australian Top 40 was in its infancy, and dominated by foreign artists. O'Keefe changed it, and the 22 singles he released in the next six years included several which swept to the top of the charts, beginning with *That'll Be Alright* (1958), *She's My Baby* (1959) and *Shout* (1959). From 1959 he compered ★*Six O'Clock Rock,* and later his own television show *The Johnny O'Keefe Show* (*Sing Sing Sing* from 1963). He tried to break into the US market, appearing as 'The Boomerang Boy' on *The Ed Sullivan Show;* he returned to the USA in 1960 and toured the UK in 1961. Meanwhile, more of his singles sped to the top in Australia: *Ready For You* (1960), *Don't You Know Pretty Baby* (1960), *It's Too Late* (1960), *I'm Counting On You* (1961), *Sing!* (1962), *Move Baby Move* (1963), and *Shake Baby Shake* (1963). In all he was to produce 29 Top 40 hits—more than any other Australian artist has done ever since. These included eight Top 10s and five which reached No. 1.

However, in 1964 with the arrival of Beatlemania, rock and roll was suddenly in rapid decline. Unlike others, O'Keefe would not adapt his style to the changes: he adhered to the music he had developed in the mid-1950s, released *Rock'n'Roll Will Stand* (1964), and banned Beatles haircuts from his TV show. But his show was cancelled before the year was out; for the first few months of 1965 he had no work at all, and for the next two years he often had to play in country rodeos. His singles did not have the same success again until 1969, with *Come On* (1969), *She Wears My Ring* (1969), *Confessions Of A Lonely Man* (1970) and the re-release of *She's My Baby* (1969).

Rock and roll's demise seemed to become for O'Keefe a personal decline. As his music became passé in the late 1960s he was increasingly troubled by depression, with press reports of his being charged for drunken or disorderly conduct, or for various speeding offences. In 1972, on the 20th anniversary of his entry to the profession, he attempted to relaunch his career, but did not recapture his earlier dominating position. His last hit was *Mockingbird* in 1974, and in that year he assembled a touring show, *The Good Old Days of Rock and Roll,* which played the regional club circuit for the next four years. By this time he was regularly using tranquillisers and barbiturates to sleep; ruined by alcohol and drugs, he died aged 43 in 1978, just a few months after his idol, Elvis Presley.

O'Keefe was not a musical innovator or virtuoso; he performed a narrow repertoire of Presley and Haley rock and roll, rhythm and blues, some country and western, and some gospel. It was almost exclusively American material—*Shout!, She's My Baby* and several of his other hits had been recorded before in the USA. His achievement lay more in his stage presence; lacking a natural singing gift he evolved a performance style that was unique, the voice hoarse, harsh, throaty, yet strangely evocative, expressive and compelling, the movements leaping, jumping, exuding a daemonic energy and magnetism. Called 'The Wild One' on stage, in photographs he seems perpetually suspended in the air, two feet above the stage. Promoter Alan Heffernan, who had toured Presley and Frank Sinatra, regarded him as one of the four best live performers in the world. Indisputably, he was one of the greatest live performers Australia has produced.

His magnetism, as well as his downfall, was grounded in his deep identification with the early rock and roll repertoire. 'I'm the sort of guy who is what he sings,' he said. 'My act is not an act. It's me. It's what I am.' He would not vary his previous work: in his last show to be recorded, at Bathurst in 1978, the delivery of his standards was a carbon copy of his recordings of them 20 years before. Nevertheless, he was the most prominent popular music artist in Australia for a decade, and one of the most prolific of recording history: he made 63 singles, 53 EPs, and 113 albums. He changed the face of Australian popular music: when he had finished, Australia was no longer an outpost for Americans but a home in which a local pop musician could become a national figure.

FURTHER REFERENCE
His singles were released on Festival, Lee Gordon, and Leedon. Compilations include *20th Anniversary Album* (1972, Festival L 45137–8); the Bathurst performance of 8 Sept. 1978 is released as *The Last Concert* (Canetoad CTLP 003). For discography, see *Spencer.A.* See also Ted Leane and Henry Plociennik, *Johnny O'Keefe* (Summit Books, 1979); John Bryden-Brown, *JOK: The Official Johnny O'Keefe Story* (Sydney: Doubleday, 1982); Robert Caswell, *Shout: The Story of Johnny O'Keefe* (Sydney: Currency Press, 1986); D. Hudson and B. Ross, *The A to Z of JOK: A Picto-*

rial Discography (Melbourne: Australian Rock and Roll Appreciation Society, 1988); and Michael Sturma, *Australian Rock'n'Roll: the First Wave* (Kenthurst NSW: Kangaroo Press, 1991).

Ol' 55. Rock band (1975–80, 1986–) formed in Sydney. Developed as a nostalgic send-up of early rock and roll bands, it originally combined Frankie J. Holden [Peter Bryan] with Patrick Drummond and Rockpile Jones (guitar, vocals), Jimmy Manzie (bass, vocals) and Geoff Plummer (drums, vocals). At first they released covers of songs from the 1950s and new songs in the 1950s style, such as *Dianna* (1975), *On The Prowl*, which reached No. 16 in the charts in 1976, and their debut album, *Take It Greasy* (1976), which reached No. 2 in the album charts. But after major membership changes in 1977 they featured five-part vocal harmony and a smoother sound, releasing *Stay (While The Night Is Young)* (1977), which reached No. 11 in 1978, and the album *Cruisin' For A Bruisin'* (1978). Several members split to form the Breakers in 1979. The remainder regrouped and released *Two Faces Have I* in 1980, which reached No. 15 in the charts. A group of experienced performers, they presented a show involving comedy, film clips and old-time rock and roll. With substantially new membership the band re-formed in 1986.

FURTHER REFERENCE
Recordings include *Dianna* (1975, Mushroom K6091), *On The Prowl* (Mushroom K6372), *Take It Greasy* (1976, Mushroom L355815), *Stay (While The Night Is Young)* (1977, Mushroom K6936), *Cruisin' For A Bruisin'* (1978, re-released 1983, RCA MLF 234), *Two Faces Have I* (1980 Leo 2079148). For discography, see *SpencerA*. See also *McGrathA*; *SpencerW.*

Old Bark Hut, The, folk-song. Widely known traditional song of a stockman (in some versions a former convict) reduced to the swagman's life and living on rations in a hut of bark. Published by A.B. Paterson in *Old Bush Songs* (1905); republished with music arranged by John Meredith in *Bushwacker Broadsides* (1954); at least four other versions have been collected by Ron Edwards and John Meredith (1966–69).

FURTHER REFERENCE
Edition and commentary in *EdwardsG*; *ManifoldP.*

Olding. Family of performers.
(1) Max(well) Olding (*b* Launceston, Tas., 4 July 1934), pianist, teacher. Max Olding studied piano at the University of Melbourne Conservatorium with Lindsay Biggins and was the 1952 Commonwealth winner of the ABC Concerto Competition. He undertook postgraduate piano studies in Vienna with Viola Thern and in Geneva with Abbey Simon. Appointed senior lecturer in piano at the Queensland Conservatorium in 1961, he became deputy director in 1976 and later acting director, resigning in 1989; he was the founder of the Conservatorium

Symphony Orchestra. He was senior lecturer at the Academy of the Arts, Kelvin Grove Campus, Queensland University of Technology, until his retirement in 1996. He conducted and performed in Australia and South-East Asia, and has long been an AMEB examiner, including federal examiner 1982–83. He is married to fellow pianist Pamela Page (2), and is the father of violinist Dene Olding (3). A pianist of profoundly natural musical gifts and a teacher of many distinguished pupils, in 1970 he was awarded a Churchill Fellowship and in 1991 he was honoured with the AM.

(2) Pamela Page (*b* Petersham, Sydney, 4 Apr. 1934), pianist, teacher. A child prodigy, she featured in a Cinesound documentary and gave her first ABC broadcast at the age of four. She won a scholarship to study with Ronald Kinloch Anderson at Trinity College, London, where she was awarded the Maude Seton Prize for the most outstanding student. Invited by Walter Gieseking to study with him, she joined his master class in Saarbrücken. Returning to Australia in October 1968 she became senior lecturer in piano at the University of Queensland 1979–96. She has performed as soloist with every ABC orchestra and has toured internationally. She is married to Max Olding (1), pianist, and is mother of violinist Dene Olding (3).

(3) Dene Olding (*b* Brisbane 11 Oct 1956), violinist. After studies in Brisbane and at the Julliard School, New York, where he won the Morris Loeb Prize, he became concertmaster of the Florida Orchestra in 1978. He returned to Australia in 1982 as leader of the ★Australia Ensemble and artistic director of the Australian Chamber Orchestra, touring widely in Australia and abroad. In 1985 he won a Churchill Fellowship and studied in Europe with Hermann Knebbers and Gryörgy Pauk, winning a laureate in the Queen Elizabeth of Belgium International Competition. He then became co-concertmaster of the Sydney Symphony Orchestra in 1987. One of the most conspicuously gifted violinists Australia has produced, he has been the soloist in Australian premieres of concertos by Lutoslawski, Elliot Carter, Ross Edwards, Bozidar Kos and others. His recording of Ross Edwards' concerto won an ARIA award.

FURTHER REFERENCE
For Max and Dene Olding, recordings include Violin Sonatas of Beethoven, Brahms, Mozart. For Dene Olding, other recordings include *Dene Olding Violin Concertos* (1993, ABC/Polygram 434900–2). See also *CA* (1995–96); *Australian* 8 July 1994.

RACHEL TEW (§1, §2); Editor (§3)

Olsen, Dennis Hans (*b* Adelaide, 28 Feb. 1938), baritone. He started studying dentistry, then as a pianist was joint winner of the ABC Concerto Competition in 1959, but at first he studied acting at NIDA and pursued an acting career on stage, radio and television. His blend of comic acting and excellent vocal quality came together in Gilbert and Sullivan operas for the Elizabethan Theatre

Trust Opera in 1968–70, where his stunning appearances in the lead comic character parts help to enlarge the company's audiences at that time. He then joined the D'Oyly Carte Co. in London for their tour of 1970–71. He appeared with the Australian Opera in 1977, and since then has been heard widely throughout Australia and beyond, and has also directed opera, operetta and musicals for the Australian Opera and most state companies. The clarity and vigour of his patter-singing combine with excellent comic acting to make his character roles in *HMS Pinafore*, *Pirates of Penzance*, *Iolanthe*, *Mikado*, *The Gondoliers*, and *The Yeoman of the Guard* classics of the Gilbert and Sullivan stage history.

FURTHER REFERENCE
CA (1995–96); John Cargher, *Opera and Ballet in Australia* (Melbourne: Cassell, 1977), 142–7; *Courier-Mail* 21 July 1990; *Age* 22 Aug. 1989.

Olympic Overture. Orchestral work by Clive *Douglas (1956), composed for the Melbourne Olympic Games. It was recorded by the combined Sydney and Victorian Symphony Orchestras under Sir Bernard Heinze (1957, HMV OALP 7526).

On the Road to Gundagai. Popular song (1921), words and music by Jack *O'Hagan. Intended to refer to Bundaberg, O'Hagan changed it to Gundagai at the last minute, although he had never seen the town. Recorded by Peter *Dawson in 1922, it was used as the theme of the 3DB radio show *Dad and Dave* from 1937 and recorded by more than 40 singers. He wrote a sequel, *Where the Dog Sits On the Tucker Box*.

O'Neill, Sharon (*b* NZ, 23 Nov 1952), popular music singer-songwriter. Singing folk-songs in NZ, she was with Chapta (1972–73) and Wellington Shiner (1975–76), then released a soft-rock album, appeared on television and was several times NZ Queen of Pop before she left in 1980. In her first year in Australia, she toured as supporting act to Boz Scaggs, recorded the first of more than 12 Australian singles, *How Do You Talk To Boys* (1980), which reached No. 25 in the charts, and released her album *Words* (1980). She won a *Countdown* award in 1981 and her *Maxine* reached No. 16 in the charts in 1983, while her album *Foreign Affairs* (1983), recorded in the USA, reached No. 17 in the album charts. She was unable to sustain further chart success, but as a songwriter of spare, well-conceived rock and roll ballads, she wrote the sound-track for the movies *Smash Palace* (1983) and *Street Hero* (1984), and the theme for the television series *Sweet and Sour* (1986). She sang with the Wild Colonial Boys (1988) and Jimmy Barnes Band (1991).

FURTHER REFERENCE
Recordings include *How Do You Talk To Boys* (1980, CBS BA 222714), *Words* (1980, CBS SBP 237350), *Maxine* (BCBS BA 223082), *Foreign Affairs* (1983, CBS SBP 237889), and *Edge Of Winter* (1990 Polydor 843883–1). For discography, see *SpencerA*. See also *McGrathA*; *SpencerW*; *GuinnessP*, III, 1865; Ed St John, 'Sharon O'Neill: More Than Just a Pretty Face', *APRAJ* 3/2 (Mar. 1984), 16–17.

Onkel Beckers Geschichte. Operetta in one act, music and libretto by Moritz *Heuzenroeder. First performed at the Albert Hall, Adelaide, on 3 November 1882.

Opera and Opera Companies
*1. Early History to 1860. 2. The Lyster Years, 1861–80.
3. J.C. Williamson and the Imported Companies,
1880–1965. 4. Resident Companies, 1933 to the Present.*

The story of opera in Australia embraces the history of imported touring companies from the 1840s to 1965, ranging from the sadly threadbare to the astonishingly lavish, of resident companies ranging from small amateur ventures to ambitious national institutions, and of a host of hybrids of the two.

1. Early History to 1860. From the early days of European settlement it was common for Australian plays and theatre to be enlivened by musical items; conversely, what may appear from their title to have been operas might have been staged with little or no music. Bishop's *Clari, or The Maid of Milan*, given in Sydney in 1834 and often cited as Australia's first performance of opera, was described as being performed 'without the music', while works such as Shield's *The Poor Soldier* in 1796 comprised a mixture of songs and spoken dialogue in uncertain proportions. Uncertain proportions also dogged Sydney performances in the 1840s of apparently legitimate operas, such as *Il barbiere di Siviglia*, *La Cenerentola*, *La sonnambula*, *Der Freischütz*, and a similar repertoire by Anne *Clarke's dramatic troupe at Hobart. Musical numbers were cut, arranged and interpolated to suit the available forces; it was not uncommon for a woman to substitute for a missing tenor. The absence of scores was a frequent problem, and stories abound of music being reconstructed from someone's memory: reorchestrated from a vocal score, or transcribed in its entirety by dictation. By the mid-1840s, however, at least some of the productions included enough of the original material to qualify as genuine operatic performances.

Most of Australia's early opera was presented by touring companies, although in a country so young the boundaries between 'local' and 'visiting' forces tended to be blurred, especially when (as often happened) members of a visiting company decided to settle in the new land. Familiar faces frequently reappeared in different companies, as their original troupe either disbanded or returned home. In some cases the companies were selected and assembled overseas by an Australian entrepreneur; in others, established troupes merely added Australia to their itinerary. Still others were hybrids: foreign stars would visit and gather a supporting company from local talent, or have it gathered for them by an enterprising local management.

To begin with, operatic performance was sporadic. Sydney, and later Melbourne, heard the ★Gautrot French Operatic company, which specialised in the lighter repertoire, from 1839. In Hobart, Clarke's dramatic company often included performances of opera to give variety to her seasons. It was Hobart's good fortune that so many of the Clarke cast—the young Maria ★Carandini, the two ★Howson brothers, and Theodosia ★Yates-Stirling—were proficient singers, a fact borne out by their subsequent careers. When these four moved to Sydney after a few years, that city gained a core of performers who could be used with visiting artists: Sara ★Flower in 1850, and Catherine ★Hayes and Anna ★Bishop during the mid-1850s. In the guise of various companies, they also gave seasons in Melbourne.

2. The Lyster Years, 1861–80. (i) Lyster and His Contemporaries.

The arrival of William Saurin ★Lyster in 1861 first provided eastern Australia with a steady diet of opera. Settling in Melbourne with a troupe he had assembled in America, he gathered orchestra and chorus together and commenced his first season. By the end of the third, the company had presented 20 different operas, ranging from Balfe and Wallace through the more popular German repertoire and much Italian *bel canto*; the sixth season saw Meyerbeer's *Les Huguenots* added, with more French grand opera in subsequent seasons.

Lyster began touring. Seasons in Sydney provided no problems, with adequate venues available from the outset; Brisbane had to wait until it had built a theatre for its first season in 1865, after an exploratory foray in concert performance the previous year. Adelaide had been civilised for slightly longer, but all these cities shared the problem of transport: the coastal steamers were sufficiently comfortable under ideal circumstances, but bad weather rendered them unreliable and even perilous. Trips to the Victorian goldfields—by a combination of rail and road—were even more uncomfortable.

Lyster's early seasons exhibit a major characteristic of opera performance of the time: the reliability, not to say versatility, of many of its practitioners. His first company was headed by a *prima donna* Lucy ★Escott and *primo uomo* Henry ★Squires, who were to all intents and purposes essential to every performance, in seasons that generally ran six nights a week. The dependence on a single 'star' soprano and, less often, sole tenor was a feature of many other companies, such as those of Annis Montague and Charles Turner, Emelie Melville, Emily Soldene, and Fannie and Martin Simonsen. Italian companies with a double cast, one *drammatico* and one *leggero*, had a much easier time.

Lyster's first company closed in 1868 with the country's premiere of *Un ballo in maschera* at Melbourne, combining forces with a group of visiting Italian singers, the first ripple in a wave of Italians that followed. His next company in 1870 was a composite of Italian stars and many of the *secondo* singers from his first company, bolstered by the expatriate Lucy ★Chambers. With these, and a pile of opera scores acquired in Italy, he was able to present both authentically Italian opera and the ever popular English repertoire. A new trend in the 1870s was the performance by local troupes of French operetta (in English) and English light favourites, while Italian grand opera was left to the visiting companies.

May 1871 brought the first of the latter under the management of Augusto Cagli and Giovanni Pompei, with a large double cast which was both less wearing for the singers and more varied for the audience. This company was the forerunner of a lasting contribution to the country's operatic life by Cagli and Pompei: under the aegis of one or other of the two, companies toured for more than a decade to Melbourne, Sydney, Brisbane, and across the Tasman to NZ.

While Melbourne clearly remained Australia's operatic centre during the 1870s, touring ensured that the other eastern state capitals did not miss out entirely. Sydney, of course, was the second city in operatic terms. Adelaide was well served by Lyster, and also by Simonsen's company; the Italians included it in their itinerary, as did other occasional troupes. Brisbane's operatic fortunes languished for a decade after Lyster's visit in 1865, until the Pompei Co. brought renewed delight with a season of 16 different operas over 26 days. After this Lyster put Brisbane back into his schedule, and the Italians kept it in theirs. Hobart too was part of the usual itinerary: it was no extra trouble to cross the Strait as interstate journeys were also made by steamer.

While most operatic works were available to anyone with the resources to stage them, the newer types, Gilbert and Sullivan and French operetta, raised an issue which had previously never worried the Australian stage—copyright. The rights to stage these profitable new works were in many cases jealously guarded, and many a projected production was taken off at the last minute when litigation threatened. To acquire the Australian rights to one of these works was a coup of the first magnitude. Much of the lighter repertoire, and more recent grand operas such as those of Verdi, were receiving their Australian premieres quite soon after their English ones; even Wagner's *Lohengrin*—in a rather irregular version, to be sure—was given in Melbourne in 1877, only two years after its London premiere. *Carmen* took less than a year for the journey from London to Australia.

(ii) Lyster's Local Successors.

Lyster's death at the end of 1880 removed the single greatest driving force from the Australian operatic scene. There remained some very durable companies, however: the ★Montague-Turner company, arriving shortly after Lyster's demise (its two stars had earlier tested the waters under his management), toured the eastern seaboard for four years, and returned on and off until the mid-1890s. They played not only the capitals but also country centres from Mackay in the north to Launceston in the south. Their repertoire was popular 'English' opera (meaning the favourites of any nationality, sung in English) but as their company was essentially dependent on two principals its scope was relatively limited.

Another family troupe was the *Simonsens. Introduced to Australia by Lyster, Fannie and Martin Simonsen subsequently formed a series of companies, one of which opened in Sydney in 1882 and included three of their daughters, with Martin in overall charge. Their repertoire was rather similar to that of the Montague-Turner company, but with the added attraction of French operetta (Fannie had been Australia's first Grand Duchess of Gerolstein), and the occasional spectacular array of stage effects (*Der Freischütz, La muette de Portici*). For their 1886 season the conductor Roberto *Hazon was engaged and 21 operas were presented, including Australia's first performances of Ponchielli's *La Gioconda* and *I promessi sposi*, Bellini's *I Capuleti e i Montecchi* and two new Donizetti works. The tour lasted well over a year and covered Melbourne, Sydney, Brisbane, Adelaide, and country centres such as Ballarat and Geelong, as well as Tasmania. Despite prodigiously hard work under often appalling conditions, financial pressures finally crushed their efforts in 1892.

3. J.C. Williamson and the Imported Companies, 1880–1965. (i) Until World War II. Lyster's entrepreneurial role was soon taken over by the 'Triumvirate', which originated with his nephew George *Musgrove, whose ideal was to mount lavish imported productions, with long runs transferred from city to city. He was joined in 1882 by Arthur Garner and James Cassius *Williamson.

The Triumvirate was volatile. It lasted for nine years before Musgrove left; a little later Williamson decided to go it alone; eventually Musgrove rejoined him, but the partnership finally disintegrated irrevocably. Specialising in Gilbert and Sullivan, they also managed visiting troupes such as the Cagli (later Cagli and Paoli) Co. which gave seasons in Brisbane, Sydney, Adelaide and Melbourne in 1882–83. One of their biggest triumphs was the 1893 season by an Italian company, hand-chosen by Musgrove, under the direction of Niccolò Guerrera. The Australian premieres of *Cavalleria rusticana* and *I pagliacci* were presented (Pagliaccio sung by the creator of the role, Fiorello Giraud), with Mascagni's cheerful *L'amico Fritz* thrown in for good measure.

The break-up of Musgrove and Williamson proved a bonanza for Australian theatregoers, for it brought a competitive war between them. Musgrove fired the first salvo in 1900–1, with seasons by a company under the dual direction of Gustave *Slapoffski (recruited, along with many of the singers, from the Carl Rosa Co., London) and John Crooks. The 'English' program included the first Australian performances of *Tannhäuser* and *The Flying Dutchman*. Williamson countered spectacularly with an Italian company (which had nearly included Caruso) under Roberto Hazon, playing Sydney, Melbourne and Brisbane, and including the local premieres of *La bohème*, *Otello* and *Fedora*. Musgrove brought out Nellie *Melba for a 1902 concert tour, incorporating scenes from her favourite operas. In 1907 he imported a German cast, which included in its repertoire four operas by Wagner with Australia's first *Die Walküre*, and also *Hänsel und Gretel*. Williamson's 1910 response was unusual—a mainly Italian cast assembled essentially for a single opera, *Madama Butterfly*. It played continuously for four weeks in Sydney, alternating Bel Sorel and Amy *Castles in the title role, before adding other *verismo* works and journeying to other centres. Williamson then followed up in 1911 by bringing back Melba for opera seasons in Sydney and Melbourne, with the young John *McCormack as *primo tenore*. Uncharacteristically Melba agreed to sing three nights a week in six of the season's works; the other six included the novelties *Tosca* and *Samson and Delilah*.

Scarcely had the applause of the Melba season died down when Williamson fired off his next volley: an English company under the management of Thomas *Quinlan, complete with orchestra and chorus, already polished and rehearsed. In quick succession it presented the first Australian performances of *The Tales of Hoffmann*, *The Girl of the Golden West*, *Tristan and Isolde*, and Debussy's *The Prodigal Son*. The rest of its repertoire was a judicious mixture of a little old and much that was fairly new; the staging, costumes and scenery were splendid. The cast included the Australian Lalla *Miranda, on a rare trip home, and much of the original English cast of the Puccini work. Williamson was clearly winning in the operatic wars when his death brought an end to the battle in 1913; Musgrove survived him by less than three years. Williamson's company, 'The Firm', continued, however.

Quinlan was back in 1913 with a feat for the history books: the country's first complete *Der Ring des Nibelungen*, sung in English. Again he brought a complete company, with two conductors, Tullio Voghera and Richard Eckhold. The three complete *Ring* cycles—two in Melbourne, one in Sydney—were part of a repertoire of 28 operas, including premieres not only of three of the *Ring* works (*Die Walküre* had been given in 1907) but also *Manon Lescaut*, *Louise* and *The Mastersingers of Nuremberg*. Quinlan planned to follow this splendid project 18 months later with another season, presenting the Russian repertoire and Richard Strauss, but World War I put an end to his grand scheme.

During the war years, J.C.W.'s fostered local talent in the field of operetta; the most enduring and endearing of its stars was to be 'Our Glad', Gladys *Moncrieff. Fortuitously, Australia became the home of the *Gonsalez company; with a repertoire ranging from *bel canto* to *verismo*, and a few of the traditional French works, this Italian company played from mid-1916 to mid-1917 in an extensive tour. The end of it saw many of the company, such as Count Ercole Filippini, remain in

Australia, as performers, teachers and entrepreneurs. This stockpile of singers proved very useful in 1919 to Frank ★Rigo, formerly stage director of the 1911 Melba-Williamson season, who assembled a company based largely upon the left-behind Italian males, and local female singers, under the musical direction of Slapoffski. The repertoire was mostly conventional, the language however being a democratic mixture of Italian and English (sometimes simultaneously). The significance of the venture lay not only in the season itself but in the local singers whose careers it launched: Browning ★Mummery, Frederick ★Collier, Gertrude ★Johnson and Strella Wilson among others.

After performing in the Rigo season, Count Filippini, late of the Gonsalez company, formed a highly portable troupe which toured outback Queensland and NSW for about 40 weeks. He seems to have been charged with some of Lyster's crusading zeal: in 1923, he founded the South Australian Grand Opera Co. in Adelaide, giving seasons in 1924 and 1925; as the Italo-Australian Co. it toured to Perth in 1926, to Melbourne the following year, and to Tasmania. He eventually established an operatic school in Melbourne, assisted by his Australian-trained wife.

The 1924 Melba-Williamson operatic tour was modelled on the splendid 1911 version. There was no doubt that this was a vehicle for a single star, despite her appearance in only three operas (she was now 63). Certainly, interest was aroused by the inclusion of several *bel canto* works for the company's 'other' *prima donna*, the young Toti Dal Monte, and by the local premiere of *Andrea Chenier*, but the season was essentially Melba's. Her farewell performance on the last night of the season (in *La bohème*), was heard not only by the packed auditorium but by countless radio listeners, for this was also the country's first opera performance to be broadcast live.

It was to be a premature farewell. Another Melba-Williamson company came back in 1928, although by then Melba's contribution was almost entirely entrepreneurial. New works included Puccini's *Il tabarro*, *Gianni Schicchi*, and *Turandot*, Massenet's *Thaïs*, Mascagni's *Lodoletta* and Montemezzi's *L'amore dei tre re*. The company ventured beyond Sydney and Melbourne to Adelaide and Perth, although Brisbane missed a promised season. Dal Monte was back, as was Apollo Granforte, with local lads John Brownlee and Mummery in a solid, carefully assembled, largely Italian cast. The costs for the season were very high, including many expensive productions and £3 000 a week for Melba whether she sang or not. This time she made her real farewell—three times—to the Australian operatic stage.

Running almost at the same time as the Melba tour was another by Gonsalez. It was still a family company and obviously less splendid than the Melba venture; it appeared under the aegis of Sir Benjamin ★Fuller's management, the only real opposition 'The Firm' had after it merged with J. & N. ★Tait. The Gonsalez Co. had a differ-

ent (although less modern) repertoire, substantially cheaper admission prices, and included Brisbane, Toowoomba and provincial NSW centres in its itinerary. Unlike J.C.W.'s, Fuller was able to announce a profit on his venture.

With the Depression gathering, a scaling down of productions became prudent, and J.C.W.'s next company, actually organised and financed by two Sydney men, George Nassoor and S.E. Chatterton, was modest. This 1932 company had a combination of imported Italian principals and Australian singers, with an all-Australian orchestra and chorus (prompting more polyglot performances). The repertoire was standard, and the company was notable for its evenness of talent, although some stars—Lina Pagliughi, the now familiar Granforte, and Brownlee—clearly stood out.

The quality of the 1932 company's local contingent, headed by Brownlee and Molly de Gunst, inspired renewed calls for a resident company. This was not yet feasible, although the number of Australian singers with successful overseas careers enabled Fuller to form a largely Australian cast for his 1934–35 Centenary Royal Grand Opera Co. (the centenary was Melbourne's). The presence of Florence ★Austral and Horace ★Stevens ensured the inclusion of several Wagner works, balanced at the lighter end by *The Pearl Fishers* (an Australian premiere, although in a very odd version) and *Die Fledermaus*. Unfortunately, for social rather than musical reasons the seasons were not as well supported as Fuller had hoped, and the company very nearly foundered; it was said to have made a loss of £30 000.

(ii) After World War II. No further grand schemes were attempted until after World War II, when J.C.W.'s mounted a splendid Grand Opera Season with imported Italian singers in 1948–49; the venture was greatly assisted by the government's remission for the occasion of the infamous entertainment tax (then set at 25 per cent). Franco Ghione was musical director of the troupe, a strong one in which Rina Malatrasi best caught the public's fancy; some local singers also had *comprimario* parts. The repertoire, which was presented to the eastern capitals for nearly a year, had more than a dozen works, from Rossini and Donizetti through Verdi to Puccini. It was ideally chosen to remind a country tired by the war of what opera stood for—melody, spectacle, and grand singing.

Its popularity inspired a repeat performance, and another company of Italians was engaged for a 1955 tour. This included many from the previous group, although with a different conductor, Ermanno Wolf-Ferrari (nephew of the composer) and a young soprano at the threshold of a great career, Gabriella Tucci. But circumstances had changed, and rising costs made it seem unlikely that tours such as these could ever be financially viable again; this one lost more than the Fuller company had in 1934–35. A star of Melba's magnitude was needed to make such a venture possible, if not profitable. One now existed, and although the negotiations took two years, in July 1965 Joan Sutherland opened the Sutherland-Williamson International Grand Opera Co.'s season in Melbourne in *Lucia di Lammermoor*. Although the diva's brilliance tended to cast the rest of the company into the shade in the public mind, it was a very strong troupe. Richard *Bonynge was principal conductor, while many of its Australian singers had, or now have formidable reputations; and no one then could possibly have anticipated the career of one young Italian tenor—Luciano Pavarotti. It was a brilliant swansong for the days of the large touring opera companies.

4. Resident Companies, 1933 to the Present. (i) National Opera Companies.
Conservatoriums and private opera schools had been noteworthy from early days for proffering opera seasons with student singers when no professional troupes were around. The presence of gifted young singers, combined with the Depression's effect on the big managements' nerves, prompted a number of estimable enterprises in the 1930s. In SA Harold Gard and Vera Thrush (both formerly of Filippini's troupe), with Hugh King as musical director, established the Adelaide School of Opera and the State Grand Opera Co. in 1933. This was perhaps the first attempt to establish a national company; the project had an encouraging start, but soon faltered.

Far more durable was that of Gertrude Johnson, who had sung in the Rigo-Williamson season of 1919. In 1935 she founded the *National Theatre Movement in Melbourne, with the idea of providing local training and opportunities for young Australians. It was to be several years before the opera school bore fruit in its first production, but it was the beginning of a potentially genuine national opera company. Similar aspirations were held by Clarice Lorenz, whose *National Opera Co. of NSW gave its first Sydney season in 1951. Although newer than its Melbourne counterpart, it was able to build on firm foundations set by the NSW State Conservatorium. It must have seemed a good idea for the two 'national' bodies to join forces, in a 1952 season to be given in both their home towns and also in Brisbane. With a repertoire ranging from Mozart to Wagner, and Donizetti to Mascagni, they were brilliantly successful, helped by the presence of Brownlee and the newcomer Marie *Collier. Rather than form the basis for a single company, however, the venture merely intensified the rivalry between the two.

The National Theatre's Coronation Festival season of 1953 raised the stakes, performing not only in Melbourne but also touring to other state capitals. The Sydney company, having untactfully modified its name to the National Opera of Australia, responded in kind. This manoeuvring may have gone on indefinitely, had not the *Australian Elizabethan Theatre Trust been established in 1954, with a brief to develop a genuinely national opera company.

With neither the Melbourne nor Sydney company prepared to compromise, in 1956 a new company, the Australian Opera Co., was formed in Sydney. Its first season, of four operas by Mozart, showed that it fully intended to be a national company: it was one of the few to play in Perth, as well as all of the eastern capitals. The following year it was renamed the Elizabethan Trust Opera Co. and in 1970 it became the Australian Opera (now Opera Australia).

The Trust Opera Co. started modestly, with a pattern of seasons in the main capital centres and small troupes touring the provinces. Initially relying on the ABC symphony orchestras in each capital, its viability was improved in 1967 by the formation of the Elizabethan Trust Orchestra to travel with it. A giant step was its move into a world-class venue when the Sydney Opera House was opened in 1973. Since then, although strong ties have been maintained with Melbourne, seasons in the other state capitals have declined or disappeared.

(ii) State and Local Opera Companies.
Local opera in Melbourne at first suffered from the establishment of the Elizabethan Trust Opera Co., with resident singers being attracted by the new Sydney company. As seasons in Melbourne by the latter were reduced, the Victorian Opera Co., formed as a small concern in 1962 by Leonard Spirs, grew in importance, and in 1974 it became the *Victoria State Opera. It, too, acquired a splendid new venue with the opening in 1984 of the Victorian Arts Centre.

After the attempt in 1933 to establish a state-based opera company in Adelaide, opera in SA was chiefly left to the Elder Conservatorium, which presented pro-am performances 1947–58. The mid-1950s saw the South Australian National Grand Opera Co. commence with laudable aims, but like its forebear 20 years earlier, it soon settled for musicals and operetta. Of sterner stuff was the Intimate Opera Group, established about the same time (1957) but with a more practical intent of producing chamber operas. In 1973 the group acquired state backing and changed its name to the New Opera, but retained its emphasis upon flexibility of repertoire and performance style; its triumphs at successive Adelaide Festivals contributed to the decision to declare it, in 1976, the *State Opera of South Australia. Its repertoire then changed towards the more conventional.

George English's Brisbane Opera Society (established 1947) had similar aims to many of its southern counterparts. Its first year, 1948, saw *Maritana* and *The Bohemian Girl* presented (with Donald *Smith in the tenor leads), and the Queensland State Opera scheme instituted, with government-funded scholarships for young singers providing tuition fees and some living allowances. Besides its Brisbane seasons, the company toured northern and outback Queensland, taking *Madame Butterfly* in 1952 and presenting mainstream repertoire in English. Almost contemporaneous with this society was Ruby Dent's Musical and Theatre Guild of Queensland, ostensibly with a lighter repertoire and an amateur charter. In 1950, however, it presented *La bohème*, and at the end of the following year the Queensland National Opera appeared (described later as 'incorporating the Qld Musical Theatre Guild'), presenting *Tosca* in 1953 then *La traviata* before sliding back with *Countess Maritza*.

The next venture was the Opera Group Workshop, established by Colin and Marissa ★Brumby in 1964 and presenting probably the first Haydn opera in Australia, *L'infedeltà delusa*. As the Vocal Arts Ensemble it toured Queensland for the Arts Council, before being renamed the Queensland Opera Co. in 1969. It subsequently underwent a number of changes in management and policy. Meanwhile the Queensland Light Opera Co. had been formed in 1962 by David Macfarlane, presenting the Gilbert and Sullivan repertoire before broadening its aims in the 1970s to include operatic works. When the State Government, which was funding both the Opera Co. and the Light Opera Co., advised amalgamation, the national opera scenario was replayed: no amalgamation occurred and a new company emerged. Without state grants, the original companies disappeared, leaving the field to the new Lyric Opera of Queensland (later ★Opera Queensland) which gave its first season in 1982. Its performance opportunities were greatly enhanced with the opening of the Queensland Performing Arts Complex's Lyric Theatre in 1985.

Perth has been poorly served by most mainstream companies, the distance from the eastern centres being simply too great. It did receive a visit from a company under Henry Bracey (originally one of Lyster's singer-managers, later with the Triumvirate) after its Theatre Royal was erected in 1897, and Williamson and Musgrove sent a Royal Comic Opera Co. Other performances tended to be fortuitous, such as the concert given by J.C.W.'s Italian company on its way home in 1902. Perth shared in the Melba-Williamson tour of 1928, and the inaugural Australian Opera Co. season in 1956; the State Opera of South Australia visited for the 1979 Perth Festival. However, its local company, the ★Western Australian Opera Company, was established as early as most other state companies, presenting from 1967 modest seasons of mostly mainstream repertoire.

Numerous small, semi-professional companies like Canberra Opera or the Metropolitan Opera, Sydney, have appeared and disappeared, some establishing a lasting niche. Their common aim is to provide opportunities for those singers not permanently contracted to the major companies. Conservatoriums and university music schools continue to provide valuable training and experience for younger singers, and generally these smaller performing groups, less governed by shareholders and the box office, present a more adventurous repertoire than the main companies; certainly they have mounted more Australian operas than the commercial companies have.

See also *Musical Theatre*; *Musical Comedy*; *Operetta*; *Entrepreneurs*.

FURTHER REFERENCE

IrvinD; *GroveO*; *ParsonsC*.

Dawson, Jenny, Opera in Colonial Brisbane: The First Twenty-Five Years (1859–1884), MMus, Univ. Qld, 1987.

Dreyfus, Kay, ed., *Report of Symposium: Opera and the Australian Composer* (Melbourne: International Society for Contemporary Music, 1973).

Gyger, Alison, *Opera for the Antipodes: Opera in Australia 1881–1939* (Sydney: Currency Press, 1990).

Hall, James, 'A History of Music in Australia', *Canon* 4 (1951)–7 (1954), 26 parts.

Holmes, Robyn, 'Opera in South Australia', in *From Colonel Light into the Footlights: The Performing Arts in South Australia from 1836 to the Present*, ed. Andrew D. McCredie (Adelaide: Pagel, 1988), 102–32.

Love, Harold, *The Golden Age of Australian Opera: W.S. Lyster and his Companies 1861–1880* (Sydney: Currency Press, 1981).

Opera/Music Theatre in Australia: Report to the Australia Council by the Committee of Inquiry (Sydney: Australia Council, 1980).

Quinn, Michael P., Brisbane Opera Seasons 1901–1928: A Complete Performance Listing with Full Casts, unpub. typescript, Brisbane, 1993.

Simpson, Adrienne, 'The Greatest Ornaments of their Profession'— The New Zealand Tours by the Simonsen Opera Companies, 1876–1889 (Christchurch, NZ: School of Music, Univ. Canterbury, 1993).

Tait, Viola, *A Family of Brothers: The Taits and J.C. Williamson, A Theatre History* (Melbourne: Heinemann, 1971).

Wentzell, Ann K., The First Hundred Years of Music in Australia, 1788–1888, MA, Univ. Sydney, 1963.

West, John, *Theatre in Australia* (Sydney: Cassell Australia, 1978).

Wood, Elizabeth, Australian Opera, 1842–1970: A History of Australian Opera With Descriptive Catalogues, PhD, Univ. Adelaide, 1979.

JENNY DAWSON

Opera Australasia. Monthly magazine of opera and music-theatre in Australia and NZ, with some international coverage.

Opera Australia. Australia's only full-time opera company (founded 1956), based at the Sydney Opera House. It was established by the ★Australian Elizabethan Theatre Trust as the Australian Opera Co., with Joseph ★Post as musical director, and made its debut in *The Marriage of Figaro* on 21 July 1956 at the Theatre Royal, Adelaide. Known as the Elizabethan Trust Opera Co. from 1957, performances were at first accompanied by the ABC orchestras, and given in the Elizabethan Theatre, Newtown, the Tivoli and Her Majesty's, Sydney, or in a variety of interstate and regional venues. The financial basis and artistic standards remained precarious for a decade, especially during the tenure of musical director Karl ★Rankl (1958-60), and the company was periodically close to shutting down.

Operas were first sung in their original language while Dennis ★Vaughan was musical director (1966), and with additional funding from the NSW Government and the first subscription seasons the company began to be more secure from 1967. It was able to form a full-time chorus and orchestra, the Elizabethan Theatre Trust Orchestra, that year, and during the musical directorship of Carlo Felice Cillario (1968–71) began to offer year-round work to its singers. It was freed from the Trust and renamed the Australian Opera in 1970, and with Edward Downes as musical director launched the spectacular new Sydney Opera House with *Boris Godunov* on 28 September 1973.

Bel canto and French repertoire came to the company with the conductorship of Richard *Bonynge (1976–83), whose famous spouse Dame Joan *Sutherland became resident principal artist, bringing great confidence and inspiration to the resident principals. New government funding arrangements averted serious financial crisis in 1987, and today under artistic director Moffatt *Oxenbould (since 1984) the company offers a seven-month season, with a repertoire of over 20 operas a year, as well as outdoor performances and live simulcasts.

Characterised by a strongly talented, chiefly Australian roster of singers, an increasingly original approach to the production of traditional repertoire, and (since 1985) a cautious but steadfast program of development of new Australian works, the company makes annual visits to Melbourne (March–May) and less frequently to other capitals. In 1996 the company combined with the *Victoria State Opera as Opera Australia.

FURTHER REFERENCE
Anthony Clarke, 'Australian Opera'. In *Opera Companies of the World: Selected Profiles*, ed. Robert H. Cowden (Westport Conn.: Greenwood Press, 1992), 7–10; John Cargher, *Bravo! Two Hundred Years of Opera in Australia* (Melbourne: ABC/Macmillan, 1988); Chip Rolley, 'Singing Praises', *Age Magazine* (13 July 1996), 21–44; Ava Hubble, *The Strange Case of Eugene Goosens and Other Tales from the Opera House* (Sydney: Collins, 1988); *ParsonsC*.

Opera Foundation Australia. Philanthropic body founded in 1963 to broaden assistance to young Australian singers and operatic artists of proven potential through scholarships, grants and prizes. Established by Lady Mary Fairfax as a regional branch of the *Metropolitan Opera Auditions program, she added scholarships to La Scala, Milan and Bayreuth in 1965, and incorporated the organisation under its present name in 1974. Other awards followed: the *Bond Family Scholarship (1981–89), *Dame Mabel Brookes Memorial Fellowship and Wagner Scholarship (1982), the *Shell Covent Garden Scholarship and the American Institute of Musical Studies Austrian Scholarship (1987), Lady Galleghan Encouragement Award (1988) and the *Vienna State Opera Award (1994), as well as funds for opera workshops, symposiums and individual awards. With significant private and corporate contributions, the foundation has designed its awards with good sense and considerable vision, distributed more than $1 million to young opera

artists over the years, and played an important role in the launching of many significant Australian singers on the path to notable careers.

Opera Queensland. Founded as the Lyric Opera of Queensland in 1981, its initial aim was to present all forms of opera, and between its inaugural season in 1982 and 1985 the company presented both opera and operetta, mainly in Her Majesty's Theatre. In 1985 the company moved to the newly opened Lyric Theatre and since 1986 has performed grand opera exclusively, in addition to concerts and regional tours of operatic highlights and schools productions. The company presents an annual subscription season of three operas, employing the best international and Australian soloists, conductors and directors in addition to the Queensland Philharmonic Orchestra and a part-time professional chorus of up to 60 members. It gained its present name in 1996.

KERRY VANN

Operetta. The terms opera and operetta appear interchangeably in some discussions of Australian colonial music-theatre. If operetta is defined by a more sentimental, romantic plot and more action taking place through spoken dialogue, then it refers to the works of Offenbach, Gilbert and Sullivan, Lehár, Strauss and others. Offenbach's *The Grand Duchess of Gerolstein* arrived in Australia in 1871, five years after its premiere. It was followed by *La Belle Hélène* in 1876 and others of his works. The Australian demand for Gilbert and Sullivan was immediate: from *Trial By Jury* in 1876 and *HMS Pinafore* in 1879, the Gilbert and Sullivan operettas arrived as soon as they could be obtained. Lehár's works came equally swiftly, *The Merry Widow* arriving in 1908. Victor Herbert's operettas arrived in 1903, before the genre passed into the more transitional American works of Romberg and others. Many of these works remain perennial favourites on the Australian stage.

Some operettas composed in Australia found a local hearing in the same years, including Luscombe *Searelle's *Estrella* (1883), Moritz *Heuzenroeder's *Faust and Gretchen* (1883), Cecil *Sharp's *Dimple's Lovers* (1890), Arundel *Orchard's *The Coquette* (1905), and Fritz *Hart's *The Dead Heat* (1931). More recently, Colin *Brumby has used the term for his *Rita and Dita* series for children. See *Opera*.

Ophelia of the Nine Mile Beach. Comic opera in one act by James *Penberthy (1955). It tells of a woman infatuated with a poet who lives next door and her antics to win his heart. It was first performed at the Tasmanian Festival of Contemporary Music, Theatre Royal, Hobart in July 1965.

Orange, pop. (1991) 29 635. Primary produce centre in central-western NSW, settled 1848. Set on the slopes of Mount Canobolas, it was close to the first Australian find of gold at Ophir in 1851. The Cornish Settlement Sacred Vocal Society was established *c.*1859, beginning a long tradition of strong local choirs and liedertafels, and *Messiah* was given with harmonium accompaniment under Arthur Tipper in 1865. A bell from the post office tower chimed the quarter-hours from 1879. In the early 1900s A.W. Mowle conducted operatic presentations, then R.L. Gregory produced *Messiah* and organist Oliver Frost was prominent in the 1940s. Composer-conductor Robert *Smallwood considerably enhanced community musical life with a number of presentations during his years in residence (1987–90). Roger *Pogson has his organ-building business in the town and composer Edward *Primrose was born there.

Oratorio. Large-scale musical compositions on sacred or semi-sacred subjects for chorus, soloists and orchestra have been a favourite of choirs in Australia since early colonial days. Among the European masterworks of the genre, Handel's *Messiah* has been a staple work since Australian choirs were first formed in the mid-19th century; it is not unusual to find annual performances of this work in even the most remote regional centres. From its premiere in 1900 Elgar's *Dream of Gerontius* also became a mainstay for more than 50 years, at least of capital city choral societies. Works like Haydn's *Creation* or Mendelssohn's *Elijah* have been regularly essayed by the more ambitious choirs, but the challenging Bach *Passions* have appeared less frequently.

A number of colonial composers wrote oratorios or similar compositions for Australian choirs, mostly for large festive occasions. Examples are *Tolhurst's *Ruth*, Charles *Horsley's *Euterpe* (1870), Henri *Kowalski's *Future Life* (1895), and G.W. *Torrance's *The Revelation* (1882). More recently, composers of full-length choral works in Australia have chosen biblical subjects much less frequently, and the works of Malcolm *Williamson, Donald *Hollier, Tristram *Cary or Gordon *Kerry could not so aptly be described as oratorios. See *Choirs and Choral Music*.

Orchard, W(illiam) Arundel (*b* London, 13 Apr. 1867; *d* at sea, 7 Apr. 1961), conductor, administrator. After studies at Durham University he worked as a schoolteacher in England and NZ. He was choirmaster at St George's Cathedral, Perth (1896), then organist and choirmaster at St David's, Hobart, and conductor of the Hobart Philharmonic Society from 1896. After teaching in schools in NZ from 1901, he came to Sydney to conduct the Sydney Liedertafel 1903–16, formed and conducted the Sydney Madrigal and Chamber Society 1908–15, conducted the Great Synagogue choir 1913–23 and the first season of George Plummer's Sydney Symphony Orchestra in 1908. He taught at the NSW State Conservatorium from its founding, becoming director 1923–34 and conducting an annual concert series with the Conservatorium Orchestra; he took the Durham DMus in 1928 and was elected FRCM (1931). He was founding director of music studies at the University of Tasmania 1935–38, then returned to Sydney and was an examiner

for Trinity College, London, for 20 years. He wrote orchestral and choral music, two operettas, *The Coquette* (1905) and *The Emperor* (1906), and an opera, *Dorian Gray* (1919), all performed in Sydney. A sedate, rather punctilious man, his book *Music in Australia: More Than 150 Years of Development* (Melbourne: Georgian House, 1952) is an important early milestone in the serious study of Australian music. He was honoured with the OBE in 1936.

FURTHER REFERENCE
His autobiography is W. Arundel Orchard, *The Distant View* (Sydney: Currawong Publishing, 1943); John Carmody, *ADB*, 11.

Orchestras
1. Theatre Orchestras to the 1850s. 2. The Growth of Symphony Orchestras. 3. Theatre, Semi-Professional and Other Orchestras Today.

Australia has one of the highest ratios of orchestras per capita anywhere in the world. In population the nation is little bigger than the city of New York, yet it has more than double the number of orchestras that renowned capital supports—six full-time symphony orchestras, three full-time theatre orchestras, chamber orchestras, various semi-professional regional orchestras, as well as numerous community and training orchestras.

1. Theatre Orchestras to the 1850s. The earliest evidence of orchestral music being performed in Australia comes from the concerts at Barnett *Levey's Theatre Royal, Sydney, in 1833. These involved *ad hoc* ensembles gathered from among the regimental bandsmen, with the few local teachers and their pupils; the works were often quadrilles, medleys or other trifles in makeshift arrangements for the available instruments, although by 1840 the Caecilian Society was able to present an operatic overture, from Rossini's *Italian Girl in Algiers*. The first professional orchestras were those of the early theatres in Sydney, Hobart and Melbourne, beginning with the Royal Victoria, Sydney, from 1838. These were ensembles often of 20 or more players, whose duties were chiefly to accompany the melodramas, extravaganzas and other entertainments then popular. From the late 1840s they were increasingly called upon to accompany opera; on such occasions the press was often scathing in its assessment of their abilities. By the 1850s there were at least six theatre orchestras of various size in the colony.

2. The Growth of Symphony Orchestras. (i) Melbourne. The Victorian goldrush in the 1850s saw a remarkable growth in the quality of entertainment. Charles Winterbottom established a series of 'Promenade Concerts' in 1853, modelled on Julien's promenade concerts in London. Supported by a regimental band and amateur musicians numbering almost 100, he was able to provide a variety of concert fare, including excerpts from contemporary opera such as Bellini's *Norma*. Tickets were deliberately priced to sell, and not surprisingly the concerts often attracted audiences in excess of 2000. Charles *Horsley, the English composer/conductor, staged a series of orchestral performances in the late 1860s, and by 1888, the year of the Centennial Exhibition, Melbourne was in a position to afford an orchestra of unprecedented quality. Coaxed by an enormous stipend of £5000, the respected British conductor Frederick *Cowen was able to bring to the exhibition 15 key players, including the string and woodwind leaders, a quartet of horns, and a harpist. To these were added 58 local players, assembled by the music-seller George *Allan, who had spent the previous few months in intense rehearsal with them. Although of mixed abilities, the orchestra managed to provide Melbourne with 263 concerts over the year of the exhibition, 211 of them being purely orchestral, introducing to Melbourne most of the standard orchestral repertoire of the day, as well as a number of Cowen's own works.

Cowen's achievement stimulated a petition to the government for the orchestra's continuation, and in 1889 the sum of £3000 was granted to subsidise it for the period of one year. Henceforth known as the Victorian Orchestra, the theatre conductor-composer Hamilton Clarke was appointed its conductor. But Clarke was intractable, lacking the charisma of his predecessor and seemingly incapable of building rapport with his players. The audience appeared to sense this, and already hit by the pains of the economic depression of the 1890s, had neither the time nor the money to patronise an ensemble of low morale. In 1891 the orchestra was forced to disband.

The same year, however, saw the arrival of G.W.L. *Marshall-Hall as the first Ormond professor of music at the University of Melbourne. Although not yet an especially experienced conductor, Marshall-Hall possessed an extraordinarily clear concept of what he wanted from an orchestra, and obtained it through determination and sheer hard work. With the financial backing of Allan, Marshall-Hall gave a concert in 1892 with an orchestra of professionals and local students. The concert was a triumph and led to a subscription series that was to last about 20 years, offering not only the masterwork of the past but also the complex new scores of Richard Strauss, César Franck and Claude Debussy.

Despite its success, the Marshall-Hall Orchestra eventually ran foul of the Musicians' Union for its mixture of paid professional players with unpaid amateurs from Marshall-Hall's Conservatorium. The orchestra collapsed in 1912, and Marshall-Hall left for London, leaving the task of providing Melbourne with orchestral music to the violinist-conductor Alberto *Zelman Jr and his *Melbourne Symphony Orchestra, formed six years earlier. The standard of this ensemble was enough to attract international artists of the calibre of Nellie Melba and Moiseiwitsch to perform as soloists under Zelman's baton. In addition, the orchestra's affiliations with the Orchestral League, the British Music Society and the

Melbourne Philharmonic Society gave it a solid foundation on which to build a subscription base.

By the time of Zelman's death in 1927, Melbourne again had two orchestras: his Melbourne Symphony Orchestra, now under the direction of Fritz *Hart, and the University Symphony Orchestra which, after a decade of neglect, had at last found success with the new Ormond professor, Bernard *Heinze. Innovative and ambitious, Heinze moved quickly to raise the profile of his orchestra, not only by scheduling performances with celebrities like Percy Grainger and Chaliapin, but also by instigating a series of children's concerts modelled on those given by Walter Damrosch and the New York Philharmonic. The success of such ventures proved disastrous for its competitor, and the Melbourne Symphony Orchestra filed for bankruptcy in 1932.

At length a deal was struck with the influential Melbourne retailer Sidney *Myer, who agreed to eliminate all the orchestra's outstanding debts provided it merged with the University Symphony Orchestra, lent its name to the newly amalgamated ensemble, and allowed Hart and Heinze to alternate on the podium as joint conductors. This was agreed, but in the ensuing tussle for leadership of the orchestra Hart was eventually forced out, and he left to accept the post of permanent conductor of the Honolulu Symphony. Nevertheless, ongoing costs still proved a problem for Heinze, who had to wait until 1934 and his group's merger with the *ABC before the orchestra could enjoy a period of financial stability.

(ii) Sydney. An attempt was made to create a permanent professional orchestra in Sydney in 1889, but this and subsequent efforts over the next two years ultimately proved unsuccessful. Late in 1891, however, the Italian composer-conductor Roberto *Hazon founded the Sydney Amateur Orchestral Society. Many new works were introduced during its annual concert series, including some of Hazon's own compositions, and the society became associated with distinguished soloists who visited Sydney at the time, notably virtuoso expatriate violinist Johann Kruse, returning for a visit in 1895, and Paderewski in 1904.

The first professional orchestra in Sydney appeared with George Plummer's *Sydney Symphony Orchestra in 1908. With a personnel consisting largely of professionals and music teachers, this orchestra performed up to six times a year, working in its first year with an array of guest conductors, including Marshall-Hall, Arundel *Orchard, Gustave *Slapoffski and Alfred *Hill, and then with Joseph *Bradley, who arrived from London to become its conductor. Nevertheless, the orchestra suffered from a lack of permanency, and in Bradley the lack of a conductor as spirited as Melbourne had in Marshall-Hall. By 1914 box office receipts were not enough to keep the venture afloat.

The solution to the conducting problem came with Belgian violinist-conductor Henri *Verbrugghen, who arrived to become founding director of the NSW State Conservatorium in 1915. Verbrugghen wanted a permanent orchestra in Sydney, and spent the first few months of his appointment convincing the State Government of the importance of such an ensemble. His lobbying was successful, and the government was persuaded to subsidise a NSW State Orchestra; it had only 36 members for its first concert in April 1916, but by the end of 1917 its number had grown to 70. Achieving excellent quality under Verbrugghen, it gave 25 concerts annually, not only in Sydney, but also in Melbourne, Adelaide and NZ, and with a wide-ranging repertoire. But a change of government in 1922 brought about the withdrawal of the subsidy; the dispersal of the orchestra was inevitable. Dismayed, Verbrugghen resigned from his position at the Conservatorium and left for the United States to take up a conducting post with the Minneapolis Symphony Orchestra.

In the years that followed, the only symphonic music to be heard in Sydney was to come from the student orchestra formed by Orchard, now Verbrugghen's successor at the Conservatorium. To this student body were added the professors, who acted in both a teaching and performing capacity as part of their appointment. Within five years the ensemble was of sufficient standard to impress visiting artists such as Heifetz, who was so happy with this collaboration that he presented the net takings of his concert—about £400—to the Conservatorium to buy music not yet in the orchestra's collection. This was later to become the basis of the Heifetz Library.

The late 1920s were bleak for the Conservatorium orchestra, which by this stage was only giving concerts at the rate of eight per year. This was in part due to the demand for orchestral musicians in the cinemas, which prevented the formation of an established orchestra; later, with the advent of the 'talkies', many saw their livelihood disappear overnight and unemployment became high. The creation of the ABC and its orchestras during the Depression in the 1930s breathed life into a city that had essentially been without a regular symphony orchestra for the better part of 10 years. The ABC developed a plan to build full-time symphony orchestras from its radio ensembles in every capital city, and Sydney was its first success. Amalgamating with the new ABC Sydney Studio Orchestra in 1934, Orchard's orchestra gained in prominence, and within a year the current title Sydney Symphony Orchestra could be bestowed upon it, having been purchased from Plummer, the original owner.

(iii) Other States.   In Brisbane, the English violinist R.T. ★Jefferies arrived in the 1870s with wide experience in solo, chamber and orchestral music, and established a quartet and instrumental ensembles that later provided the foundation for a symphony orchestra. In 1907 the organist George ★Sampson took up the challenge, forming the Sampson Orchestra. Although consisting largely of amateurs, this orchestra managed to provide an annual series of concerts for 30 years, and impressed the State Government and the Brisbane City Council to the extent

that a generous subsidy was provided from 1924. Unlike Verbrugghen's experience in Sydney, the subsidy for Sampson's orchestra began a pattern of financial assistance that had bipartisan support from future Queensland governments; the orchestra became the Queensland State and Municipal Orchestra, and later, under the auspices of the ABC, the ★Queensland Symphony Orchestra.

South Australia was also fortunate in attracting the talents of Carl ★Linger, a composer and conductor perhaps best known today for his anthem *Song of Australia*. Linger arrived in Adelaide in 1849 and conducted the first public concert with the orchestra of the Adelaide Philharmonic. The Adelaide Orchestra Society, a semi-professional ensemble, had a short life under George Oughton from 1879 to 1980 until its finances collapsed. Regular orchestral concerts began in 1891 with Dresden-trained violinist August ★Heinicke's Grand Orchestra from 1891, renamed the Adelaide Grand Orchestra from 1911 until his retirement in 1914. After this it was not until 1920 that regular orchestral concerts were restored, with the birth of the South Australian Orchestra under the baton of Elder professor E. Harold ★Davies, the Conservatorium staff providing the majority of players. The ABC entered the field with its Adelaide Studio Orchestra from 1934 under William ★Cade, later to become the ★Adelaide Symphony Orchestra.

The ★West Australian Symphony Orchestra had its origins in 1928 as a co-operative. The actor Harold Newton, together with his brother Percy, wanted to provide work for the musicians made redundant by the 'talkies' and those unemployed in the Depression, and concerts were given fortnightly until his departure for England in 1934, when George Reed took over the baton. The core players, by this stage in co-operation with the ABC, numbered 35, although the number could be doubled for visiting conductors.

In Hobart William Russell was able to assemble an orchestra for his Choral Society in the 1840s. The Hobart Musical Union gave the first of 30 years of concerts, including orchestral performances, in 1867, and a series of orchestral concerts extending over 12 months was initiated by Otto Linden as part of the Tasmanian Exhibition of 1894. Despite the success of these concerts, the move towards a more permanent orchestra in Hobart did not progress until 1922. Founded by E. Sydney Morris, the Hobart Orchestral Society, as it was then known, had violin teacher J. Glanville Bishop appointed as its first conductor; its inaugural performance was on 19 March 1923. The ABC entered the field with a studio ensemble in 1932, offering orchestral concerts under Clive ★Douglas from 1936 which later led to the establishment of the ★Tasmanian Symphony Orchestra.

3. Theatre, Semi-Professional and Other Orchestras Today.   While it is true to say that orchestral performance in Australia is now dominated by the ABC, there are various other orchestras performing regularly. The

*Australian Opera and Ballet Orchestra, Sydney, and *State Orchestra of Victoria, formerly the Elizabethan Trust Orchestras (founded 1967) are attached to the Opera Australia and the *Queensland Philharmonic Orchestra supports the state companies in Brisbane, carrying on the theatrical music tradition established in the 1830s. The Queensland orchestra has its own subscription series, while its southern counterparts occasionally provide independent programs, largely in the popular vein of the Boston Pops in the United States. The *Australian Chamber Orchestra and the *Australian Brandenburg Orchestra have sought to fill the gaps in the orchestral repertoire, specialising respectively in works for small orchestra and Baroque music in period styles. There are excellent semi-professional orchestras with well-patronised subscription series in smaller cities, notably the Canberra Symphony Orchestra and the *Hunter Orchestra at Newcastle, NSW.

The Australian Youth Orchestra of *Youth Music Australia tours internationally, and there is at least one youth orchestra in every capital city (more than four each in Sydney and Melbourne). The ABC for some years maintained a full-time training orchestra at Sydney, the ABC Sinfonia, and the major music schools each have their own student orchestras. There are many community orchestras in the capital cities, often sponsored by suburban councils, and also many in regional centres. Almost all these make use of their local radio stations to extend their audience; indeed, with the opportunities for broadcast via television, commercial and public radio being more accessible than ever before, there are now few Australians who cannot share in the orchestral experience.

See also *ABC;* entries under individual cities; individual youth orchestras.

FURTHER REFERENCE
Warren Bebbington, 'Australia'. *Symphony Orchestras of the World: Selected Profiles,* ed. Robert R. Craven (Westport, Conn.: Greenwood, 1987), 6–15; Charles Buttrose, *Playing For Australia: A Story About ABC Orchestras and Music in Australia* (Sydney: ABC/Macmillan, 1982); E. Harold Davies, 'The Future of Australian Orchestras', *AMN* 10 (2 May 1921), 413; Eric Irvin, 'Australia's First Public Concerts', *SMA* 5 (1971), 77-86.

ALESSANDRO SERVADEI

Organ-building. The earliest attempts at organ-building in Australia were made at Sydney in 1840 when Johnson & Kinloch built a new two-manual organ for St Matthew's, Windsor, these builders later completing further instruments for other clients in NSW. There were also isolated examples of local organ-building in Adelaide by Samuel Marshall and in Melbourne by Peter Hurlstone; in the latter city James Moyle was engaged in organ-building during the 1850s together with Henry Smith. In the Barossa Valley, SA, several German expatriates built small instruments based on German models. It was not until the 1860s

that the local industry gained momentum at the hands of George *Fincham. Developments mainly took place in Victoria, where a tariff gave protection to the craft; elsewhere in Australia the industry was slow to develop. In Sydney C.J. Jackson and William Davidson were prominent from the end of the 1860s and Charles *Richardson from the 1880s onwards, while in Brisbane Benjamin *Whitehouse completed his first organ in 1888. Fincham & Hobday established themselves at Adelaide in 1881, building 11 organs there; the business was taken over by J.E. *Dodd in 1894. Meanwhile, in Victoria, Fincham faced competition from Alfred Fuller and William Anderson in the 1880s and 1890s. In WA the gifted amateur builder R.C. Clifton built a few organs at the turn of the century. A number of new names entered the organ-building scene in NSW and Victoria early this century, including Griffin, Leggo, Roberts and Taylor. Hill, Norman & Beard opened a factory in Melbourne in 1927, the firm completing more than 800 contracts before its closure in 1974.

The 1930s Depression saw fewer new organs built, but the postwar years saw in an organ-building boom, with many firms working to maximum capacity, building instruments with electric actions. In the 1960s, firms including *Sharp, *Pogson and Fincham began building mechanical action instruments of classical inspiration, later joined by *Smenge in the 1980s. The Melbourne firm of Australian Pipe Organs has specialised in pipemaking for the trade, while other firms have manufactured electrical components, some of which have been exported.

FURTHER REFERENCE
John Maidment, 'Tubular to Tracker', *The Organ Club Golden Jubilee Handbook* (London: The Organ Club, 1976), 83–98; E.N. Matthews, *Colonial Organs and Organbuilders* (Melbourne: MUP, 1969); Graeme Rushworth, *Historic Organs of New South Wales* (Sydney: Hale & Iremonger, 1988).

JOHN MAIDMENT

Organ Historical Trust of Australia. Established (1977) to preserve notable pipe organs in Australia and to promote scholarly research into the history of the organ and its music. The trust holds an annual conference, documents significant organs in Australasia, publishes a quarterly journal, *OHTA News,* and is listing all Australian pipe organs in gazetteer form. To promote high standards of organ conservation it circulates its *Australian Pipe Organ Preservation Standards* (1992). Since 1977 about 100 conservative organ restorations have been completed in NSW, Victoria and Queensland; the nature and extent of this work receives growing international recognition.

FURTHER REFERENCE
Kelvin J. Hastie, 'The Organ in Australia, 1788–1988', *The American Organist* 22/1 (1988) 74–8; John Maidment, 'The Preservation of a National Heritage: Australia's historic organs', *BIOS Journal* 5 (1981) 52–69; idem, 'L'Organ Historical Trust of Australia'

(OHTA): son histoire et son développement', *La Flûte Harmonique* 49/50 (1989), 39–49; Barbara Owen, 'Organ preservation is alive and well "down under"', *The Tracker* 29/3 (1995), 18–23.

KELVIN J. HASTIE

Organs, British.   A few small pipe organs arrived in Australia sporadically from the late 18th century onwards, but it was not until the 1820s that the first commissioned church organs arrived, built by the London firm of John Gray for Sydney and Hobart. In the following two decades, a number of smaller instruments arrived, the largest of which was the 1840 Bevington for St Mary's Cathedral, Sydney. From the 1850s onwards large numbers of British organs were sent out to Australia and by the end of the century all of the illustrious organbuilders of the period were represented, including J. W. Walker & Sons (54 instruments) and Hill & Son (34 instruments), together with many regional builders from Birmingham, Bristol, Huddersfield, Hull and Manchester. In the absence of a strong local organ-building industry, these instruments largely went to NSW, where many survive unscathed and are now of international significance. Principal exports included the town hall organs at Adelaide, Melbourne and Sydney, all built by Hill & Son and the latter the largest in the world at the time of its construction. Major church organs included the T.C. Lewis at St Paul's Cathedral, Melbourne, the Bishop & Son at Sacred Heart Cathedral, Bendigo, and the Forster & Andrews at St Saviour's Cathedral, Goulburn. In the early 20th century, major exports continued (many from the firm of Norman & Beard), culminating in the 1929 organ for Melbourne Town Hall, from Hill, Norman & Beard. More recently, major exports have included the J. W. Walker & Sons organ at Adelaide Town Hall (1990).

FURTHER REFERENCE

John Maidment, 'Australia's Multi-Cultural Organ Heritage', *BIOS Journal* 13 (1989), 79–86; Graeme D. Rushworth, *Historic Organs of New South Wales* (Sydney: Hale & Iremonger, 1988).

JOHN MAIDMENT

Ormond, Francis   (*b* Aberdeen, Scotland, 23 Nov. 1829 *d* Pau, France, 5 May 1889), pastoralist, philanthropist. He financed Ormond College, University of Melbourne, a Presbyterian institution, and founded the Working Men's College (now Royal Melbourne Institute of Technology). His respect for education was fuelled by his religious beliefs; he saw it as the obligation of the wealthy to put their wealth to a proper use through good works which would bring others to God. His first biographer, C. Stuart Ross, wrote in 1913 that Ormond had a good ear and a pleasant singing voice, and that he attended concerts regularly but had no formal knowledge of music. From the few extant letters it seems Ormond saw music as suitable for public celebration: he included a choral and instrumental *conversazione* in plans for the

opening of Ormond College; he also saw it as a worthy domestic occupation, once writing of his household's regime: 'Work and lunch over we have the rest of the day for galleries, driving, walking and music …'. He wanted music included in the curriculum of the Working Men's College and for university students to learn brass instruments, a suggestion that met with derision.

In 1887, after a prolonged public debate over the effects of institutionalising music within academia and after opposing arguments supporting a conservatoire were finally dismissed by him, the University of Melbourne accepted Ormond's gift of £20 000 to endow a chair of music at that institution. The first incumbent, 1891–99, reinstated 1915, was the controversial G.W.L. *Marshall-Hall. His successors were Franklin Sievright *Peterson 1901–1914, William Adolphus *Laver 1915–25, Sir Bernard *Heinze 1926–57, George *Loughlin 1958–79 and Michael *Brimer 1980–89. The present Ormond professor is Warren *Bebbington (1991–).

FURTHER REFERENCE

Don Chambers, *ADB*, 5; Thérèse Radic, Some Historical Aspects of Musical Associations in Melbourne 1888–1915, PhD, Univ. Melbourne, 1978; Peter Tregear, 'The Ormond Chair of Music at the University of Melbourne: An Introduction to its Origins', *Context* 7 (1994), 34–7.

THÉRÈSE RADIC

O'Rourke, Michael   (*b* Queensland, 1944; *d c*.1992), folk-singer, performer, collector. He began writing poetry as a child and won the National Bicentenary Short Story Competition in 1970. From his mother he inherited a strong interest in music and began collecting and performing English, Irish, Scottish and American folk-songs, by the mid-1970s having about 500 songs in his repertoire. After studying philosophy and politics at the University of Sydney, he worked in policy review and co-ordination for the department of Aboriginal Affairs in Sydney. Singing and playing violin, as well as developing his own guitar style from ragtime, bluegrass and Carribean elements, in the 1980s he devoted himself to playing violin and collecting folkmusic, particularly fiddle tunes. He published *O'Rourke's Songbook*, popularised *The Rain in Innisfail* and published *A Poor Immigrant Weariness: 30 Prosems* in 1981. The Fiddler's Convention, in Victoria, which he began, continues to run annually. He was active in Melbourne, appeared in Sydney and Brisbane, and at folk festivals and workshops. He made no recordings.

Osborn, Ethel   (*b* Brisbane, *c*.1900), soprano. After studies with the choral director E.R.B. *Jordan in Brisbane and Roland *Foster at the NSW State Conservatorium, she appeared as a concert soloist in Australia and NZ from 1920. She went to London in 1926, making her debut with the London Symphony Orchestra at the Royal Albert Hall, and then appeared in the British tours of Dame Clara Butt and Kennerley Rumford. With an attractive coloratura voice of unusual ease in the top register, she sang oratorio and cantata, appearing in the Sir Henry Wood Promenade Concerts and for the BBC, but chiefly in provincial centres until 1951, when she returned to teach privately in Brisbane.

FURTHER REFERENCE

MackenzieS,129–31; *AMN* 16 (Sept. 1926), 28.

O'Sullivan, Cathie (*b* Sydney, 1953), folk musician. After studying piano for 13 years, she sang in a choir while studying pharmacy at the University of Sydney and formed a folk-rock band, singing in folk clubs, playing tin whistle and the Celtic harp. She joined the ★Larrikins, touring Australia, NZ, the UK and the South Pacific in the late 1970s, then formed Summerhaze, performing original and traditional folk-songs, reggae and jazz. She toured the USA in 1984 and wrote the music for the musical *Inside Dry Water* (1993). She balances a career as a pharmacist with her musical work.

FURTHER REFERENCE

Recordings include *High Places* (1983 Larrikin LRF 128) with Cleis Pearce, *Artesian Waters* (1980, LRF 047) and *Inside Dry Water* (1994, Larrikin/Jarrah Hill CD JHR 2028). See also *Age* 7 June 1988.

Otterloo, Willem van (*b* Winterswijk, The Netherlands, 27 Dec. 1907; *d* Melbourne, 27 July 1978), Dutch conductor. First studying medicine, he later studied cello and composition at the Amsterdam Conservatoire. He began his conducting career in 1933 as assistant at the Utrecht Symphony Orchestra, becoming associate conductor in 1937. After the war his career progressed and in 1949 he was appointed chief conductor of The Hague Symphony Orchestra, a post he held until 1972. He began his association with Australia in 1962 touring for the ABC and again in 1965. In 1967 he was appointed chief conductor of the Melbourne Symphony Orchestra for two years, during which time he took the orchestra to play at Expo 67 in Montreal. In 1970 he led the orchestra on a highly successful 30-concert tour of the USA and Canada which included a concert at Carnegie Hall. In 1973 he became the chief conductor of the Sydney Symphony Orchestra, taking the orchestra on an eight-week, 33-concert tour of the UK and Europe in 1974. He died tragically in a traffic accident, three days before he was to take up a two-year position with the Melbourne Symphony Orchestra.

As a conductor, both in Europe and Australia, van Otterloo's reputation was for his intense musicality and as a builder of orchestras. His choice of repertoire was wide and varied but centred around the late 19th century, particularly Bruckner. A composer himself, he was encouraging to young Australian composers, including a number of their works in ABC programs. While his

reserved manner on the podium may have lessened his public appeal, his urbane and gentlemanly demeanour endeared him to his players.

FURTHER REFERENCE

His very extensive discography appears in *HolmesC*. In Australia his recordings include works of Debussy and Ravel with the Sydney Symphony Orchestra (RCA); Brahms Symphony No. 4 and Robert Hughes, Sinfonietta with the Melbourne Symphony Orchestra (WRC). See also Herbert Antcliffe and Truus de Leur, *GroveD*.

MICHAEL McNAB

Our Don Bradman. Popular song (1930), words and music by Jack ★O'Hagan. Celebrating batsman Donald Bradman's cricket records that year of 334 runs for Australia in the test match against England at Leeds, and 452 not out for NSW against Queensland. Recorded by Art Leonard (1930, Regal Zonophone G20744). O'Hagan sang the song on radio 3DB the day Bradman scored his triple century at Leeds and 40 000 copies were sold in the coming days.

FURTHER REFERENCE

It was published by Allans Music, Melbourne, 1930; modern edition and commentary in *RadicT*.

Our Man in Havana. Opera in three acts (1963) by Malcolm ★Williamson, libretto by Sidney Gilliat after Graham Greene's novel. First performed at Sadler's Wells, London, on 2 July 1963 and published by Joseph Weinberger. A concert suite (1963) was also made from it for the BBC, published by Joseph Weinberger, 1966.

Outlaw, The. Ballet by Verdon ★Williams, choreography by Edouard Borovansky. Based on the Ned Kelly legend, it was first performed by the Borovansky Ballet at Melbourne in May 1951.

Overlander, The (The Queensland Drover), folk-song. Best known today to a tune similar to the chorus of James Barr's 'Thou Bonnie Wood of Craigie-lea' (published 1818), this traditional drover's song relates the hardships of the nomadic drover's life, plying the stock routes of Queensland. Found in the Hurd Collection (1894–97), it was published by A.B. Paterson in *Old Bush Songs* (1905); a variant was collected by John Manifold and published in *Bandicoot Ballads* (1955). There are at least three other versions, markedly different in their verses but sharing a similar chorus: the earliest, to be sung to 'Dearest Mae', appeared in the *Queenslanders' New Colonial Campfire Songbook* (Sydney, 1865); another, to be sung to the dance tune 'King of the Cannibal Islands', appeared in *Native Companion Songster* (Brisbane, 1889); yet another was collected by A.L. Lloyd (*c*.1930) and recorded in 1957.

FURTHER REFERENCE

Edition and commentary of most of these in *EdwardsG*; *RadicS*, 28.

Overman, Meta   (*b* Rotterdam, Holland, 9 Oct. 1907; *d* Perth, 23 Oct. 1993), composer of Dutch descent. She studied composition in Rotterdam with Edward Flipse and Willem Pijper and had four ballets and an orchestral work commissioned before migrating to Perth in 1951. Her three-act opera *Psyche* (1952) was performed at the 1955 Festival of Perth. Resident in Melbourne for 12 years (1957–69), she was associated with the Grainger Museum, took classes with Keith Humble, and had works performed in concert and on the ABC. Returning to Perth in 1978, she composed mainly for flute. Neo-classic in form, her language displays an early 20th-century European influence. She composed over 60 works.

WORKS (Selective)

(Mss in Wigmore Library, Univ. WA)

Chamber   *Berceuse*, duo-pf (1945), Sonata, va, pf (1956), Sonata for B-flat Clarinet and Piano (1964, Allans n.d), *Seven Miniatures,* fl, ob, cl, bn (1966, Aust Music Fund n.d), *Haiku,* fl, electric pf/pf (1983), *Concertino,* 5 fl (1991).

Vocal and Other   *Psyche,* opera (1952, 3, after Couperin), Perth, 1 March 1955; *Image of the Cross,* cantata, SATB (1953), *Suite of Old Dance Forms,* orch (1959), *Island Songs,* T, pf (1956).

FURTHER REFERENCE

There is a recording of the Piano Sonata, M. Cohen, pf (ABC tape, RRC-70). See also Patricia Thorpe, The Life and Music of Meta Overman, BMus, Univ. WA, 1988; idem, 'Meta Overman—Her Life and Music', *Soundscapes* 1 (1993), 32–3; idem, 'Thoughts on Meta Overman's "Sonata for Viola and Piano"', *SA* 41 (Autumn 1994), 22–3; idem, 'Meta Overman: Her life and Music—A Feminine Response?', in *Repercussions: Australian Composing Women's Festival and Conference, 1994* (Melbourne: National Centre for Australian Studies, Monash University, 1995), 45–8; idem, '"The Image of the Cross" by Meta Overman', *Sing Out* 12/3 (1995), 18–19.

PATRICIA THORPE

Oxenbould, Moffatt Benjamin   (*b* Sydney, 18 Nov. 1943), opera administrator, director. After studying stage production at NIDA he worked as a stage manager in Hobart and Sydney from the age of 19, then for Sadler's Wells Opera, London, 1966–67. In 1967 he joined the Elizabethan Theatre Trust production staff (reorganised as the Australian Opera in 1970), directing *The Rape of Lucretia* (1971) and *Il Trittico* (1973). He became artistic administrator in 1974, succeeding Richard Bonynge as artistic director in 1984, directing productions including *Semiramide* (1983), *La Clemenza di Tito* (1991) and *Idomeneo* (1994). An enormously able and articulate figure, the present style and health of the company owes much to two decades of his influence. His publications include *Joan Sutherland—A Tribute* (1989) and articles in *Opera Australia.*

FURTHER REFERENCE

MonashB; *CA* (1995–96).

P

Packer, Charles (Stuart Shipley) Sandys
(*b* Reading, England, 1810; *d* Sydney, 13 July 1883),
conductor, composer. After studying piano, singing and
composition at the Royal Academy of Music, London,
he embarked on a promising musical career, but was
arrested for forgery in 1839 and transported to Australia
for life. He was imprisoned at Norfolk Island from 1840,
then Tasmania in 1844, where he was allowed to take
pupils and give concerts. After a conditional pardon in
1850, he leased a theatre, then moved to Sydney in 1852
where he became organist of the Vocal Harmonic Society and conducted opera in 1859. His *City of Sydney
Polka* was published in 1854 and his oratorio *Crown of
Thorns, or, Despair, Penitence and Pardon* was performed in
1863. But having secretly married in Hobart, he was
sentenced to five years for bigamy in 1863 (he had been
married prior to his transportation more than 20 years
earlier). At Darlinghurst Gaol he continued to compose
sacred music and organise a church choir. After his
release in 1868 he resumed teaching. One of Sydney's
most talented musicians, he had a number of significant
pupils, but his background made him an outcast from
polite society.

FURTHER REFERENCE
E. Lea-Scarlett, *ADB*, 5.

Packer, Frederick Augustus (*b* Reading, England, 1839; *d* Parramatta, 1 Aug. 1902), organist.
Nephew of Charles *Packer, he learned organ from his
father, the organist at Reading Abbey, and sang in the
choir as a boy. He migrated to Australia in 1852, settling
in Hobart and working as a civil servant 1859–94. He
was organist at St David's Cathedral, a teacher, the principal mover in obtaining the town hall organ, and then
city organist. As a composer he wrote comic operas,
odes and songs.

FURTHER REFERENCE
R.L. Wettenhall, *ADB*, 5.

Paean To The Spirit Of Man. Ballet by John *Antill
(1968).

Page, Pamela. See *Olding (2) Pamela Page.*

Painter, John Galloway (*b* Adelaide, 28 Sept. 1932),
cellist, chamber musician, administrator. He studied piano
with Kathleen Witcombe and George Pearce, and cello
with Harold Parsons and Laurie Kennedy. Joining the
cello section of the Adelaide Symphony Orchestra at the
age of 14, he was principal cellist from 1950 to 1954, and
from 1960 to 1965 was principal cellist and president of
the Sydney Symphony Orchestra and a member of the
ABC String Quartet. His association with the NSW
State Conservatorium began during this period and in
1966 he was appointed lecturer to teach cello and chamber music, play in the Sydney String Quartet, and conduct the chamber orchestra. Following promotion to
senior lecturer in 1972, he was deputy director 1974–81,
in which time he founded and was principal cellist of the
Australian Chamber Orchestra. He was director of the
Conservatorium 1982–85, and director of the Canberra
School of Music 1985–95, from which he retired as
emeritus professor.

Painter's career as performer, teacher, conductor and
adjudicator has taken him to most of the world's music
centres, including in recent years China, Hong Kong and
Japan; he has had an advisory role in federal, state and local
government arts activities, chaired the planning committee for the 1988 ISME Conference, and has long associations with many Australian arts organisations including
the Australia Council, Musica Viva, the Sydney International Piano Competition, the Victorian Institute of Colleges, and NIDA. In 1981 he received an AM for services
to music.

DOREEN BRIDGES

Painters and Dockers. Rock band (1982–)
formed in Melbourne, originally comprised of Paul
Stewart (vocals, trumpet), Chris O'Connor (guitar,

vocals), Dave Pace (trumpet), Mick Morris (saxophone), Phil Nelson (bass) and Colin Buckler (drums). Their debut album was *Love Planet* in 1984, and in 1985 they produced the first of more than seven singles, *Basia*, and a mini-LP, *Kill, Kill, Kill*.

FURTHER REFERENCE
Recordings include *Love Planet* (Big Time BT 7046), *Basia* (Big Time BTS 1448), *Kill, Kill, Kill* (Big Time), *Die, Yuppy, Die* (1987, White K411), *Dirty, Filthy Rock And Roll* (1989, Musicland MUS 72011), *Kiss My Art* (1988, Doc Records L3888), *Nervous Nineties* (1992, MDS DOCKCD 3000) and *Things That Matter* (1994, MDS DOCKCD 6000). For discography, see *SpencerA*. See also *SpencerW*.

Paired sticks. Two sticks, each held in one hand, hit together as an accompaniment to the singing of Aboriginal people. They have been documented throughout all parts of Australia. The sticks produce a resonant, precise beat, which may continue evenly throughout the song or in a carefully repeated pattern of two beats followed by a rest. The person who plays the sticks usually sings. Paired sticks may be painted or carved to resemble animals or plants, whose Dreamtime figures are celebrated in the songs they accompany. Another common decoration is to taper the stick ends. See *Aboriginal Music* §3(i).

GRACE KOCH

Palings. Music publishing and retailing firm, established by William Henry Paling (1825–95). Paling was born in The Netherlands and arrived in Sydney in 1853. He established a music warehouse at 83 Wynyard Square. By 1856 he had become an agent for the French Erard pianos and a recognised composer and concert organiser. He travelled to Europe to obtain instruments and sheet music in 1864, 1870, 1884 and 1893. In 1883 he bought large premises at 356 George Street for £45 000 and registered as a limited liability company. Eight years later he moved to 338 George Street where the new showroom was described as 'the most complete and commodious music establishment to be found in the Southern Hemisphere'. Of the seven floors, one floor each was devoted to pianos and organs, another floor for teaching studios, and on others there were workshops for tuning and repairs and for storage. Palings also established branches in Toowoomba in 1884, Brisbane in 1888, Newcastle in 1892, Lismore in 1911, and Townsville in 1923. By 1926 the firm had capital of £750 000 and a staff of 450.

At the time of the Depression Palings ceased importing instruments and instead became involved in the new medium of radio, acquiring a share in 2UW. Meanwhile structural changes were made to the buildings to accommodate sales of recordings, although the market for these was affected by the onset of war in 1939. At this time the company acquired branches in Cairns, Wollongong, Orange and Bankstown. After the war Palings sold not only instruments, sheet music, records and radios but also refrigerators and washing machines. The company also recognised the potential of the school music market. Palings is now owned by the Billy Guyatt group.

FURTHER REFERENCE
Andrew D. McCredie, *ADB*, 5; Eve Keane, *Music for A Hundred Years: The Story of the House of Paling* (Sydney: Oswald Ziegler, 1954).

SUZANNE ROBINSON

Palmer, (Edward) Vance (*b* Bundaberg, Qld, 28 Aug. 1885; *d* Melbourne, 15 July 1959), author. After making his way as a writer in London from 1904 and touring through Eastern Europe, he worked as a tutor and a bookkeeper in north-west Queensland, then travelled in the USA and served with the AIF in World War I. In short stories, novels, poetry, plays and literary criticism, he explored the Australian way of life, its political issues and national consciousness; his poem *The Forerunners* (1915) and novel *The Passage* (1930) are his best known. His seminal *Old Australian Bush Ballads* (1950), a collection of 13 traditional songs, the music 'edited' (in reality only slightly adjusted) by Margaret *Sutherland, brought wide public attention to Australia's neglected song heritage, and was the earliest and one of the primary sources of the folksong revival in the 1950s. He was crucial in stimulating literary discussion of Australian folk-song, publishing such works as *Legend of the Nineties*, in which he connected the colonial Australian bush balladists with Lawson, Paterson and other later poets who drew on contemporary bush figures and events for their subjects.

FURTHER REFERENCE
ADB, 11; *OxfordF*.

Palmer, Rosina. See *Carandini, Rosina*.

Paolo and Francesca. Opera in five acts, music and text by Claude M. Haydon (*b* South Yarra, Melbourne, 8 Nov. 1884), first performed at Melbourne in 1920.

Parkhill, Peter (*b* Sydney, 26 July 1947), musicologist. After singing traditional English and Scottish ballads and touring Europe 1970–71, he studied musicology at the University of Sydney, and he began collecting the music of various ethnic groups in Sydney, including the Italian, Turkish, Greek, Serb and Croatian communities. Assisted by grants from the Australia Council, he has prepared programs on world music for the ABC and published in *Meanjin*.

FURTHER REFERENCE
His tapes are now at *CAnl*. See also *StubingtonC*, 53–4; *Meanjin* 52/3 (1993), 501–8.

Parkinson, Doug (*b* Newcastle, NSW), rock singer. Parkinson's first band was String'n'Things, then the folk-pop band the A Sound which he formed while still at school. In 1967 he joined Questions, which was placed second in the National Battle of the Sounds. Although considered an exciting rock talent, the band soon dissolved and re-formed as Doug Parkinson In Focus, comprised of Parkinson (vocals), Billy Green (guitar), Rory Thomas (organ), Doug Lavery (drums) and Duncan McGuire (bass). In Focus became renowned for Parkinson's distinctive blues vocals as well as its numerous changes of band members. In 1969 it released a version of the Beatles' *Dear Prudence* which climbed to No. 5 on Australia's Top Five chart, but in 1970 In Focus finally separated after many different configurations. Parkinson travelled to London and formed the Fanny Adams band, without success. He returned to Australia and resurrected In Focus, and in 1973 formed the short-lived rock big band Doug Parkinson's Life Organisation. In that year he also released his first solo album, *No Regrets.* In 1973–75 he worked as NSW promotions manager for WEA Records, though occasionally lending his voice to various performing projects. Later he starred in *Ned Kelly*, *Superstar*, *Big River* and *Buddy*.

FURTHER REFERENCE

For discography, see *SpencerA*. See also *McGrathA*; *GuinnessP*; *SpencerW*; Glenn A. Baker, *Doug Parkinson Notes*, 1966.

ROSE PETERSON

Parsons, Geoffrey Penwill (*b* Sydney, 15 June 1929; *d* London, 26 Jan. 1995), pianist, accompanist. He studied with Winifred Burston at the NSW State Conservatorium from 1941 to 1948, and Friedrich Wührer in Munich in 1956. Intending to study architecture, he won the ABC Concerto Competition in 1947 with the Brahms B-flat Piano Concerto, and in 1950 travelled to Britain to perform with bass baritone Peter ★Dawson. The six-concert tour completed, Parsons remained in London, earning a living initially as a cocktail lounge pianist. A performance of Schubert's *Winterreise* with baritone Gerhard Hüsch in his first London concert since World War II led to his being invited to Munich to be Hüsch's permanent accompanist, where they worked together almost daily. In 1961 he made his first appearance with Elisabeth Schwarzkopf at the Royal Festival Hall at the invitation of Walter Legge, and later became her principal accompanist. The list of singers with whom he worked includes Victoria de los Angeles, Nicolai Gedda, Rita Streich, Birgit Nilsson, Hans Hotter, Janet Baker and Jessye Norman.

Parsons did not confine himself to singers, accompanying some of the greatest instrumentalists, including Nathan Milstein, Paul Tortelier, Wanda Wilkomirska and Ida Haendel. Artists whom he partnered quickly appreciated his exemplary standards of musicianship, and a level of pianistic command that was totally new to the accompanist's role. This led to his increasing recognition as the ideal accompanist in a career that saw him perform in over 40 countries on six continents, including all the major international music festivals. He also recorded widely throughout his career, leaving a vast output. Increasingly Parsons began to partner younger singers such as Thomas Hampson, Olaf Baer and Barbara Bonney. Some of these younger artists were also pupils of his long-time companion, the singer Erich Vietheer: Susan Kessler, Yvonne Kenny, Felicity Lott and Anne Murray among them. The encouragement of younger artists became a feature of the latter part of his career, which saw him accrue honours as the leading exponent of the accompanist's art. He was Prince Consort professor of piano accompaniment at the Royal College of Music. His relationship with Australia was an essential part of his entire career and he became the means for bringing some of the world's most important singers to his native country. He toured Australia 31 times between 1957 and 1993. In 1973 he gave the first recital at the Sydney Opera House with Birgit Nilsson, and his last performance in Australia was with Olaf Baer in *Winterreise* in the University of Melbourne's Melba Hall in 1993.

Musically supportive and pianistically polished, Parsons was the consummate accompanist. He became an honorary member of the Royal Academy of Music in 1975, and of the Guildhall School of Music in 1983. He received the FRCM in 1987, was named the Royal Philharmonic Society's Instrumentalist of the Year in 1992, and was made an OBE in 1977 and an AO in 1990.

FURTHER REFERENCE

Recordings include *Richard Strauss Lieder*, Jessye Norman (1985, Philips 416298–2); *La Chanson d'Eve and Other Songs*, Dame Janet Baker (1989, Hyperion CDA 66320); *Dichterliebe und Liederkreis*, Olaf Baer (1986, EMI CDC 7473972); *Lieder by Brahms, Berg and Le Gallienne*, Lauris Elms (1989, ABC 426191–2); *Liederabend from Ascona, 1967*, Elisabeth Schwarzkopf (1991, Ermitage ERM 109); *Rossini and Meyerbeer*, Thomas Hampson (1992, EMI CDC 54436.2); *Traditional Catalan Songs*, Victoria de los Angeles (1991, Collins 13182); *Schubert Lieder*, Barbara Bonney (1994, Teldec 4509–90873-Z); *Spanisches Liederbuch*, Anne Sophie von Otter and Olaf Baer (1995, EMI 7243.5.55325.2). See also Max Loppert, *GroveD*.

IAN HOLTHAM

Parsons, Gordon (*b* Sydney, 24 Dec. 1926; *d* Sydney, 17 Aug. 1990), country singer-songwriter. Growing up on an isolated farm in northern NSW, Parsons avidly listened to Jimmie Rodgers, Wilf Carter, Tex ★Morton, Buddy ★Williams and Harry Torrani, and when he was 11 his parents bought him a mail-order guitar. At 14 he left home to work as a sleeper-cutter. He made his first public appearances at country dances and his reputation as a singer and yodeller spread. After success on *Australia's Amateur Hour* he gained a recording contract with Regal Zonophone in 1946. Thereafter he toured regularly with all the major travelling shows, including those of Slim

*Dusty, *Rick and Thel, and Tim *McNamara. His strong, pure voice and laconic style won him many fans, and he became a regular on the Sydney country music circuit. In between tours Parsons 'went bush', doing farm and labouring work and writing songs. In 1957 he wrote *A Pub With No Beer*, adapted from a poem by Dan Sheahan. He added additional verses based on characters from his local pub, the Cosmopolitan Hotel at Taylor's Arm (NSW). The song was a massive hit for Slim Dusty. As well as recording for Regal Zonophone in the 1950s and 60s, Parsons also recorded for Hadley and Selection. An early track, *Where the Bellinger River Flows*, remains one of his most popular songs. His talents as a bush balladeer were acknowledged with his induction into the ACMA Hands of Fame in 1979 and the Roll of Renown in 1982.

FURTHER REFERENCE
Recordings include *The Vintage Years, 2 vols* (Hadley 51291, 51292, n.d.); *The Old G.P.* (Selection 021, 1980); *Just Passin' Through* (Selection 706, n.d.). See also *WatsonC*, I; *SmithB*.
            CAROLYN MUNTZ

Pascoe, Clive Brownley (*b* Palmerston North, NZ, 3 June 1941), music educator, administrator. After studies at the NSW State Conservatorium and teacher training, he taught in high schools from 1963, then from 1968 lectured at the Sydney Conservatorium, becoming head of composition in 1974. Meanwhile, he took degrees from Durham University and doctoral studies in music education at the University of Cincinnati. In 1977 he became director of the Australia Council Music Board and since 1982 has been dean of performing arts at the Lismore campus of Southern Cross University, forming the Australian Institute of Contemporary Music, which has published useful guides for the rock music industry and sought to raise the standard of its training. He has published articles in *AJME*, *APRA Journal* and elsewhere.

FURTHER REFERENCE
His writings on the music industry include an article in *APRAJ* 6 (1988), 46–7; his earlier publications include 'Oriental and Occidental Philosophies in Music Education', *AJME* 24 (1979), 7–8. See also *ADMR*.

Paterson, A(ndrew) B(arton) ('Banjo') (*b* Narambla Station, nr Orange, NSW, 17 Feb. 1864; *d* Sydney, 5 Feb. 1941), poet, journalist. Trained as a solicitor, he adopted as a pen-name the name of a racehorse and achieved immediate popular success with *The Man From Snowy River and Other Verses* (1895). A number of his poems passed into folk-song, including 'A Bushman's Song', 'Travelling Down the Castlereagh', 'The Billygoat Overland', as well as, most notably, Australia's national song 'Waltzing Matilda.' He also compiled the seminal anthology of Australian folk-songs, *Old Bush Songs* (first published 1905, with various amended editions to 1931) which, although it is now known to have

relied to a significant extent on texts previously issued in the *Queenslander* in 1894, published numerous traditional bushranger, gold-digger and overlander songs for the first time, and was for a long period the definitive collection of Australian folk-ballads.

FURTHER REFERENCE
His collected songs appear in Douglas Stewart and Nancy Keesing, *Old Bush Songs* (Melbourne: Angus & Robertson, 1957). See also *ADB*, 11; *OxfordL*; *OxfordF*; Philip Butterss, *Songs of the Bush: The First Collection of Australian Folksong* (Kuranda, Qld: Rams Skull Press 1991).

Patriotic Music
1. Pre-Federation. 2. Post-Federation. 3. Wars and Conflict.
4. Competitions

Music used to express national pride is sometimes written specifically for the purpose, and sometimes adopted as patriotic by virtue of its associations or performance environment. In Australia, especially during the 19th century when a significant proportion of the population was of British origin, patriotic devotion was as often felt for 'the mother country', Britain, as for the newly adopted colony. Patriotic music provided a link to the stability and familiarity of Britain, as opposed to the pioneering and often harsh way of life in the new land. As Australia progressed from its colonial phase its participation in foreign wars, Federation, the influx of migrants from non-British backgrounds, and its growing identity as a nation among Pacific and Asian countries, the patriotic music genre shifted to reflect an independent Australia rather than a series of British colonies.

Patriotic music such as the current *national anthem *Advance Australia Fair* (1878) by P.D. McCormick was written for and performed at many celebrations including political, sporting, educational and community occasions to instil a sense of national pride. It has also played the role of propagandist and motivator during both world wars, overseas where Australian troops were fighting and also on the 'home front'. In the commercial sector, patriotic music has been used to advertise and promote products, appealing to a sense of nationalistic pride. The dissemination of patriotic music in Australia has occurred in many forms and media to enable people from all strata of society to perform the music. In the first century of European settlement, newspapers and journals, handwritten manuscripts, and printed music (initially imported from Europe and later printed in Australia) were its main vehicles; in the 20th century the development of electronic media, including radio, sound recordings and television, has contributed to the popularity of this genre of music. The development of the genre can be seen in the many collections of manuscripts, sheet music, sound recordings, and ephemera (concert programs and the like), which have been preserved in Australian libraries.

1. Pre-Federation. The lyrics to what could be considered Australia's first patriotic song were published in 1817 in the *Sydney Gazette and New South Wales Advertiser*. Its title, *Song to the Tune of Rule Britannia*, and the words, by an unknown author, expressed sentiment about the newly settled country and its future, while the musical setting as indicated in the title immediately implied a supporting link to England. As the colonies became established and Australia's population grew, a corresponding demand for published music prompted printing houses to produce suitable music to be learnt and played in the parlours of the colonists. The surviving music sheets reflect the 19th-century British love of ballads and salon music, but there was also a genre of sheet music which was attempting to expound the new country's opportunities and advantages. The songs, *Advance Australia* (*c.*1850s) by S. Nelson with words by Eliza Postle, *Isle of the South* (*c.*1850s) by Sarah Hillam, *Our Australian Sky* (*c.*1850s) by John Bryant with words by John Astbury, *A Garland for Australia* (*c.*1840s) by L.Y. Ball, and *Advance Australia Fair*, are indicative of the type written and performed in the period up to Federation.

2. Post-Federation. Federation of the colonies and the opening of the first Commonwealth Parliament in 1901 saw great celebrations in Melbourne, where the first Parliament was held. Among the music used (which was largely by European composers) was the patriotic hymn *Australia* by Charles Kenningham. The presence of royalty prompted many performances of *Rule Britannia* and *God Save the King*. Despite a lack of appropriate Australian content, it was the ensuing euphoria of the citizens of the newly federated Australia which prompted a plethora of songs. The rise of the Australian Natives Association, with a membership of first-generation, Australian-born settlers promoting and cultivating national feeling, prompted songs such as *The Song of Young Australia* (*c.*1890s) by M. Amati, *Australians True* (*c.*1900) by Henry Walton with words by Hume Cook, and *Australia For Ever* (*c.*1900) by Henry F. Rix.

3. Wars and Conflict. The bulk of Australian patriotic music appears to have been inspired by the actions of Australians on the battlefields, beginning in 1885 when a contingent of soldiers was sent by NSW to the Sudan War. Although arriving too late to see any action, the impetus of the campaign spread into the community. This was the first opportunity for the young colonies to prove themselves as stable, organised and capable of providing assistance in the home country's hour of need. A number of songs and works were written for their departure and return including *The Harp of the Southern Cross* (*c.*1885) by Karl W. Goergs and *Hail Fair Australia* (*c.*1885) by E.M. Boydell. They were sold to raise funds for the contingent and, according to contemporary newspaper reports, sung in the streets and at fund-raising concerts during the campaign. Broadsheets (one survives in the Mitchell Library

entitled *Australian Patriotic Songs*) encapsulated the focus of patriotism, were cheap to print and easily disseminated to those who could not necessarily read music.

In 1899 the Australian colonies committed contingents to the South African War. The songs that were inspired over the four years of the conflict (1899–1902) are of particular interest in their depiction of an evolving Australian identity. The success of the experienced Australian bushmen and their stockhorses on the veldt is reflected in many of the songs: *Australian Kangaroo or The Kangaroo and the British Lion* (*c.*1900) by Alfred Padley, *Tommy Fern the Bushman Bold* (*c.*1900) by W.R. Furlong, *Sons of the Southern Seas* (*c.*1900) by Joseph Gillott with words by Joan Torrance, and *The Bushmen's Corps* (1901) by Joseph Gillott with words by Edward Vidler, and they begin to indicate a breaking away from the imperial mould.

In 1914 the outbreak of World War I once more drew Australian troops into battle, this time a war which affected most Australians. A large body of patriotic songs, both in printed form and through the oral tradition, was produced in response; these reflected many individual incidents in the Australian involvement, emotional and personal sacrifices, recruitment, the anti-conscription campaign and, importantly, the national perception of Australia's particular role in the war during its four-year duration. The music was inevitably bright, with consistent marching beats and catchy melodies composed with amateur musicians in mind. The songs were sung at fund-raising concerts, recruiting drives, around the piano at home and included in pantomimes and vaudeville. Probably the best known was *For Auld Lang Syne! Australia Will be There* (1914) by Skipper Francis. Others include *I'm Glad To Be Back In Australia* (*c.*1917) by H.D. Abbott, *Australia! We Are Proud Of Thee* (1916) by Mme A. Ward, *Though It's Far From Dear Australia* (1915) by A. Grimwood with words by E.T. Luke, *This Little Bit Of The World Belongs To Us* (*c.*1914–18) by 'Dry Blower' and *Defend Australia* (*c.*1914–18) by D.L. Palmer with words by G. Benson.

World War II was fought in an era of change, and action was much closer to home. Radio and the popularity of sound recordings in the interwar years had an impact on the songs that were produced: there were less published, and amateur writers, so prevalent during World War I, were less evident. Popular patriotic music from this period includes *Just A Brown Slouch Hat* (1942) by George Wallace, *Wake Up! Wake Up! Australia* (1942) by Alfred Hill, and *V for Victory* (1941) by Peter Dawson.

Australia's participation in the Vietnam War produced not the same sense of patriotism but protest, which was correspondingly reflected in songs of the period, now influenced by American popular music. It was the response to Australia's participation after the war had ended that produced songs which entered the nation's consciousness such as ★*I Was Only Nineteen* (1983) by J. Schumann and ★*And The Band Played Waltzing Matilda* (1972) by Eric Bogle.

4. Competitions. Many patriotic songs have been produced as a result of competitions, often run in the quest for the definitive national song. The first known of these competitions was held by the Gawler Institute in SA in 1859 to celebrate its second birthday; the winning entry was ★*Song of Australia* by Carl Linger with words by Caroline Carleton. In 1908 the notorious Red Page of the *Bulletin* announced a competition for 'an Australian song'; 74 entries were received and the prize was shared between *The Cross and the Great White Star* by 'Gum Tree' and *An Australian Battle Hymn* by J. Alex Allan. A special award was made to a satirical entry by C.J. Dennis, *A Real Australian Austra-XXXX-laise*, later published in Dennis's *Backblock Ballads and Other Verse* (1913) and adopted by the Australian Expeditionary Forces during World War I. The flexibility of the verse made it susceptible to many changes which kept up with the political and military incidents of the war, and versions of it in soldiers' letters were often severely mutilated by the conservative British censors. It continued to be used in some semblance of its original form in army recruiting advertisements and newspapers up to the Korean War.

In 1907 a competition for an ode was held in conjunction with the Women's Work Exhibition held in Melbourne. The prize was awarded to *God Guide Australia* by Florence Ewart with words by Annie Rentoul. In 1913 the Musical Association of NSW offered prize-money of £200 for a national song. Over 700 sets of verse and 558 musical settings were received. Theodore Torrier was awarded first prize for his *Australian National Song*, later published in the *Commonwealth School Paper* and presumably taught to many a classroom of young Australians. In 1951 the Commonwealth Jubilee National Song Competition was run under the auspices of APRA. Entry numbers were high, with both professional and amateurs contributing. There were state as well as national awards, the first prize being awarded to *Land of Mine* by Henry Krips with words by John Wheeler. In 1973 the Prime Minister, E.G. Whitlam, announced a competition to seek a new national song, but although 2500 verse entries and over 1500 music settings were received, there was no consensus on a winner. Despite the many hundreds of songs inspired by these competitions, few have survived in the current repertoire of patriotic songs.

A sub-genre of patriotic music comprises those not necessarily obvious in their patriotism but which over time have become part of the national ethos. These include folk-songs passed down through oral tradition, often the first that come to mind when Australians are travelling or living overseas or have the desire to sing something redolent of their country. ★*Waltzing Matilda* (1895) is a typical example which is much loved despite its uncertain origins, and since the 1970s has often been put forward as a future national anthem. ★*On the Road to Gundagai* (1921) by Jack O'Hagan, and ★*I Still Call Australia Home* (1980) by Peter Allen are more recent examples.

The past two centuries have produced a melting pot of Australian patriotic music: new songs, 'borrowed' songs, folk-songs, or popular songs transferred from Britain and America with little change. As Australia moves forward into the new millennium through its hosting of the Olympic Games in 2000 and the possibility of a republic, patriotic music will undoubtedly continue to be produced to celebrate these occasions and demonstrate the pride of its people.

FURTHER REFERENCE
Many patriotic songs are edited with commentary in *RadicT*; Georgina Binns, Patriotic and Nationalistic Song in Australia to 1919: A Study of the Popular Sheet Music Genre, MMus, Univ. Melbourne, 1989; Roger Covell, 'Patriotic Songs: An Australian Disease', *Quadrant* 21/5 (May 1977), 16–20.

GEORGINA BINNS

Patrons of Music
1. Vice-regal and Military Patronage to the 1870s. 2. Philanthropists, Businesses, and Public Subscription from the 1880s. 3. The Rise of Government Patronage to the Present.

The principal patrons of music in Australia were first the governors and military commanders in early colonial times, then philanthropists, business families and the public itself from the 1880s, and are largely federal and state governments today. Commercial sponsors have had a much smaller role in Australia than in other free-market countries.

1. Vice-Regal and Military Patronage to the 1870s. The patronage of music in Australia began in a vice-regal and military context. The power of the early governors was such that public entertainment could not proceed without official sanction. Both the theatre and the concert stage were licensed only by gubernatorial consent; neither could exist without the official patronage of the King's representative. Music flourished where particular governors took a personal interest in its private and public performance, as was the case in the 1830s with Sir Richard Bourke, one of whose daughters, Anna Maria Bourke, was a singer appearing on Sydney's public concert platform. Another daughter, Mrs Deas Thomson, acted in his name in the traditional role of the patron, altruistically promoting an art-form through direct monetary support and through the prestige conferred by lending the patron's name to selected activities. In Queensland a similar role was taken by Lady Bowen (neé Roma Diamantina), the pianist wife of the first governor, Sir George Ferguson Bowen. Later in the 19th century the composer Sir William ★Robinson, at various times governor in several states, became the prime mover in establishing a chair of music at the University of Adelaide. In Victoria Lady Alice ★Northcote, wife of the Governor-General, Sir Henry Stafford Northcote, organised the 1907 Australian Women's Work Exhibition with its large musical component and from 1908 lent her name to the trust which ensured the financial basis for the Marshall-Hall Orchestra. Governors were official patrons of the various philharmonic societies and liedertafels in every colony, and lent their names to prestigious concertising wherever it was perceived that the alliance between music and government reflected well on the Crown. The music sanctioned in this way tended to be that of the concert hall and the opera stage.

Until 1870 the bands of the British regiments stationed in Australia—of which there were 22 in addition to that of the First Fleet Marines and the NSW Corps—were put at the disposal of the civilian population through the goodwill of their patrons, the commanding officers of the regiments, who personally paid for their support. These bands, which supplied wind players for the barrack square and the public promenade, also supplied strings and wind for the churches, theatres and concert halls. As performers and teachers they formed a goodwill link between the British military and the Australian civilian population which became a vital element in establishing law and order, as well as the modes by which music was practised in early Australia. In this sense music was used by the ruling elite through its patronage to assist in shaping the culture of the colonies according to the norms of its English masters.

2. Philanthropists, Businesses, and Public Subscription from the 1880s. Early private patronage was largely democratic, the combined effort of large groups of people in country towns and in the cities to raise money, usually by concertising, to further the careers of promising young colonial musicians through further study abroad. Until well into the 20th century, population was not at a level to support careers in music, nor to support the institutions necessary for training. In this way public patronage denuded the country of local talent in a bid for reflected glory when the protégé concerned shone in a European sky, a remarkably frequent occurrence. Musicians as diverse as Melba and Percy Grainger, Ernest Hutcheson and Joan Hammond, Eileen Joyce and Joan Sutherland were the beneficiaries of such patronage. This communal willingness to foster the musically gifted was not confined to propelling the promising into exile for their own good; the mass movements of Australian music, the brass bands and the choirs, owed much to the support groups which clubbed together to raise funds for instruments, music, uniforms and travel costs for the ubiquitous competitions so beloved of Australians.

With the accumulation of wealth peaking in the 1880s, most noticeably in Melbourne, the *de facto* capital of the day, several philanthropists with an interest in music appeared. Sir William *Clarke established the South Province scholarships to the Royal College of Music, London, in 1882. Not to be outdone, Francis *Ormond gave £20 000 in 1887 to establish a chair of music at the University of Melbourne, a gift which may have

prompted the even more generous Sir Thomas *Elder to set up a permanent Royal College of Music scholarship in 1893, to endow a chair of music and conservatorium at the University of Adelaide in 1898, and to provide funds to build Elder Hall there, a concert hall which opened in 1900. Frederick J. Sargood, Carl *Pinschof and his wife Elise *Wiedermann, and Sir James *Barrett belong to the same period in Melbourne.

Before World War II other names appear, again all in Melbourne: Herbert and Ivy *Brookes, George Tallis, and James and Louise Dyer among others. James Dyer set aside funds for orchestral purposes, though part of the Dyer bequest was diverted to the British Music Society in Melbourne. Louise *Hanson-Dyer, his wife, founded the Lyrebird Press in Paris. Melba sponsored a new hall at the University of Melbourne's Conservatorium which bore her name, and gave to orchestral funds in Sydney and Melbourne. Percy Grainger bequeathed his museum to the Australian people in the custodianship of the University of Melbourne. Sidney *Myer left a bequest for free Concerts for the People. The Sydney Moss and Frank Albert bequests made a chair of music at the University of Sydney possible, though it was not established until 1948.

In 1932 Layman Harrison left a bequest for scholarships at the NSW Conservatorium, and in the same vein there were bequests from Sir Samuel and Lady Hordern, Sir Hugh Denison, Miss Nancy Gillespie, Sir William Vicars, Sir Arthur Rickard, Ernest and Alfred Wunderlich, Walter and Eliza Hall, James Chalmers, founder of the Sydney Madrigal Society, and others.

The music warehousing families of *Allans, *Palings and *Alberts also acted as patrons, though their commercial interest in music puts them more into the category of sponsors, for all that they were attempting to act otherwise. The same could be said of the newspaper proprietors, in particular the Murdoch family's establishment of the *Sun* Aria competition. In WA Sir Winthrop Hackett's money helped to bring into being a major concert hall in Perth. Since then private patronage has increased greatly, with the Myer, Pratt and Smorgen families the most recent of the music patrons. Hundreds of small gifts and bequests have funded student scholarships in many institutions over the years, but many have now ceased as inflation and costs have rendered them ineffective.

3. The Rise of Government Patronage to the Present. The Federal and State Governments are now by far the largest patrons of music in Australia. At first grants were made on a merely needs and interest basis. One of the earliest of the needs-based grants was the £3 000 paid by the Victorian Government to maintain the Centennial Exhibition Orchestra of 1888 as the short-lived Victorian Orchestra. In NSW the State Conservatorium was government-funded in 1915 only as a result of the personal interest of Campbell Carmichael, then the minister of education.

Though the Australian Government set up the Commonwealth Literary Fund soon after Federation it was not until the 1960s that the equivalent encouragement for Australian composers appeared as the Australian Music Fund. In 1966 the Australasian Performing Right (*sic*) Association set up the Music Foundation to establish commissions and performance support. For the first time Australian composition received a decisive and highly effective boost. But government support for music had one outstanding channel—the semi-governmental ★ABC which, from its inception in 1932, set out to define public taste not only in what it chose to broadcast but as a national entrepreneur, its policies shaped largely by Sir Bernard Heinze and Sir Charles Moses. Until recent times all the major orchestras in the country were in its employ and in use for the several ABC concert series which dominated the high-art music scene, importing celebrities, performing a largely conservative repertoire, broadcasting nationally, and extending its influence into schools. It had no international equivalent.

State Governments now fund music through programs associated with the state councils for the arts, but it is the ★Australia Council which disburses the largest share of public monies to music. From the private patronage of Gertrude ★Johnson had sprung the Melbourne-based National Theatre Movement, founded in 1935, whose National Theatre Opera Company became the cradle of the Australian Opera. Johnson's success could not be financially sustained without government support and when the 1950s royal visit and the Olympics made it plain that something had to be done about cultural standards, the Australian Elizabethan Theatre Trust came into being in 1954, musically and theatrically taking up where Johnson left off. The trust was supplanted by the Australian Council for the Arts in 1968 and the present Australia Council in 1973, both with music funding as a major part of their brief.

Commercial sponsorship is now being applied across the musical spectrum. Popular music has been governed by commercial interests, with promotion largely in the hands of sponsors primarily with quid pro quo in mind. Concert and operatic music has fared much less well with sponsors in Australia than elsewhere. There were signs of change in the heady economic boom of the 1980s, when Mercedes Benz began to underwrite the Melbourne International Chamber Music Competition, IBM and the national airline Qantas associated with the Australian Youth Orchestra, and the oil companies Shell and Esso identified respectively with the Darwin Symphony Orchestra and various opera ventures. Banks, the media and public utility companies now associate with a number of major ensembles, concerts and competitions. But in the more frugal 1990s both sponsorship and government funding have shrunk to the point where musical activity generally is in jeopardy.

FURTHER REFERENCE
ADB; *OrchardM*.

Blonski, Addette, comp, *Arts for a Multicultural Australia 1973–1991: An account of Australia Council policies* (Sydney: Australia Council,1992).

Covell, Roger, *Australia's Music: Themes of a New Society* (Melbourne: Sun Books 1967).

Davidson, Jim, *Lyrebird Rising* (Melbourne: MUP at the Miegunyah Press, 1994).

McCredie, Andrew D., *From Colonel Light into the Footlights: The Performing Arts in South Australia from 1836 to the Present* (Adelaide: Pagel, 1988).

Niehoff, Pamela, The Pinschofs: Patrons of Arts and Music in Melbourne 1883–1925, MA, Univ. Melbourne, 1991.

Patronage, Power and the Muse: Inquiry into Commonwealth Assistance to the Arts. A Report from the House of Representatives Standing Committee on Expenditure, September 1986 (Canberra: Commonwealth of Australia, 1986).

Radic, Thérèse, Some Historical Aspects of Musical Associations in Melbourne 1888–1915, 3 vols, PhD, Univ. Melbourne, 1979.

——, 'The Australian National Theatre Movement as the Catalyst for The Australian Opera: Tug-Boat to Flagship', in *One Hand on the Manuscript: Music in Australian Cultural History 1930–1960,* ed. Nicholas Brown et al. (Canberra: Humanities Research Centre, ANU, 1995), 201–16.

Rivett, Rohan, *Australian Citizen: Herbert Brookes 1867–1963* (Melbourne: MUP, 1965).

Serle, Geoffrey, *The Creative Spirit in Australia: A Cultural History* (Melbourne: William Heinemann Australia, 1987).

THÉRÈSE RADIC

Paul, Tibor   (*b* Hungary, 1909; *d* 1973), conductor. Paul graduated from the Budapest Academy, studied conducting with Scherchen and Weingartner, and founded and conducted the Budapest Concert Orchestra. Migrating to Australia with his family in 1950, he conducted the ABC's orchestras, leading festivals, youth concerts and tours, was professor of conducting at the NSW State Conservatorium, was resident conductor of the South Australia Symphony Orchestra 1955–58 and of the West Australian Symphony Orchestra 1971–73, and was one of the first conductors of the Sydney Opera Co. and the Australian Opera. He toured overseas, conducted in many European countries and in South Africa. A versatile and accomplished musician, his contribution to musical life in Australia was considerable.

FURTHER REFERENCE

Recordings include dances of Brahms and Dvorak, Vienna Symphony Orchestra (Philips); Liszt works, Vienna Symphony Orchestra (Philips); Alfred Hill Symphony No. 8, West Australian Symphony Orchestra (WRC). See also *HolmesC*; *AMN* 44 (May 1954), 15; *AMN* 46 (Mar. 1956), 6.

J.L. HOLMES

Peake, George   (*b* Exeter, England, July 1853; *d* Melbourne, 13 Apr. 1933), organist, conductor. He arrived in Victoria as a child and studied with G.R.S. Pringle, becoming organist at Holy Trinity Kew. He went to England in 1884, studying piano with E. Silas. Returning in 1886, he was organist under Frederick Cowen at the 1888 International Centennial Exhibition, Melbourne, then conductor of the Royal Melbourne Philharmonic Society 1889–1911, where he was responsible for introducing many new works, such as Elgar's *Apostles* in 1906 and *The Kingdom* in 1908. He was organist at Collins Street Independent Church until 1924. A vigorous figure in Melbourne musical life for a long time, he was was also president of the Musical Society of Victoria and the Victorian Organists Society.

FURTHER REFERENCE
Obit. *Argus* 15 Apr. 1933; *AMN* 21 (May 1933), 13; *AMN* 14 (Feb. 1925), 13.

Pearce, Ian Philp (*b* Hobart, 22 Nov. 1921), jazz trombonist, pianist. He started piano in childhood and became interested in jazz with his elder brother Cedric and neighbour Tom Pickering; with pianist Rex Green they formed the Barrelhouse Four, *c*.1938, with Pearce on trumpet. He also worked in Hobart dance bands and jam sessions at the Stage Door. Mainland postings during World War II gave him a broader exposure to jazz, and he attended the first ★Australian Jazz Convention. Following his discharge in 1947, he studied at the University Conservatorium in Melbourne, where he began working on trombone with Graeme ★Bell and Tony ★Newstead. In 1950 he travelled with Don Banks to England, playing trombone and piano with Mick Mulligan, followed by casual work after the band's demise. Returning to Hobart in 1955, he resumed his association with Pickering, with whom he continued to co-lead a band until the latter's retirement. He also formed his own more mainstream-oriented groups, which broadcast and recorded.

Pearce's stylistic versatility has placed him in high demand as accompanist for visiting musicians, and he has also been significant as composer and arranger. He has played a prominent role as a member and adviser of committees for the promotion of Tasmanian jazz and for locally held Australian Jazz Conventions. In the 1990s he continues to lead his own quartet, producing a vigorous output which belies the fact that, with Pickering, he was the major pioneer of Tasmanian jazz. He was honoured with the AM in 1995.

FURTHER REFERENCE
Recordings include *Jazzmania,* Pearce-Pickering Ragtime Five (1970, Swaggie S 1272); *Tin Lizzie Days,* Pearce Pickering Ragtime Five (1971, Swaggie S 1293); *Tasmanian Jazz Composers* vol. 3 (1994, Little Arthur Productions LACD 03); *Australian Classic Jazz, Duets* (1995, Little Arthur Productions LACD 04). An interview with him is in *WilliamsA*, 29–33. See also *BissetB*; *OxfordJ*; George Melly, *Owning Up* (Harmondsworth: Penguin Books, 1965).

BRUCE JOHNSON

Pearl Tree, The. Opera in two acts by Edgar ★Bainton (1927), libretto by R.C. Trevelyan. First performed at the Sydney Conservatorium on 20 May 1944.

Peart, Donald Richard (*b* Fovant, nr Salisbury, England, 9 Jan. 1909; *d* Sydney, 26 Nov. 1981), musicologist. While studying arts and music at Oxford University he formed a viol consort with Robert Donington and Richard Nicholson, and after studies at the Royal College of Music with Arthur Bent, Ralph Vaughan Williams, R.O. Morris and Constant Lambert, he played viola in the London Philharmonic Orchestra 1937–39. Following war service he resumed work in London and came to Australia as the foundation professor of music at the University of Sydney in 1947. At Sydney he established music primarily as a scholarly discipline, but initiated numerous campus performances of early music, as well as Australian premieres of baroque and contemporary English operas. He also championed contemporary composition, reactivating an Australian branch of ISME (1956) and founding *Musicology* (1963) and *Music Now* (1969).

A charming and humane scholar, the breadth of his enthusiasms had a profound impact on Australian musical scholarship, producing the most prominent of Australia's first generation of musicologists, notably Andrew ★McCredie, Alice ★Moyle, Trevor ★Jones and Catherine ★Ellis, and inspiring the development of a broad range of specialisations in Australia, from ethnomusicology to the avant-garde.

FURTHER REFERENCE
Andrew McCredie, 'Tribute to Emeritus Professor Donald Richard Peart', *MA* 7 (1982), 156–7.

Pekarek, Rudolph (*b* Prague, 1900; *d* Brisbane, 26 Oct. 1974), conductor. After studies at the Prague Conservatory, he founded the Prague Symphony Orchestra, which he conducted 1933–41. Imprisoned during the war, he was first conductor of the Western Australian Symphony Orchestra after its establishment from the ABC Orchestra (1950–54), then the Queensland Symphony Orchestra (1954–68).

FURTHER REFERENCE
His annotated scores are at the Univ. Qld Music library. See also *AMN* 48 (June 1958), 24.

Penberthy, James (*b* Melbourne, 3 May 1917), composer. While studying history and English at the University of Western Australia 1936–37, he worked as a teacher at Wesley College, Perth, then Trinity Grammar, Melbourne, 1938–42. After war service he studied composition at the University of Melbourne under a Commonwealth Reconstruction training scholarship 1947–50; at the same time he served as music director, National Ballet, then went to England, France and Italy on a Victorian State Government Scholarship, 1951–53. He settled in Perth in 1953 and was lecturer in composition for the Adult Education Board, University of Western Australia, founder of the Western Australian Opera Co., musical director of the Western Australian Ballet Co., and president of the Fellowship of Australian Composers. He moved to Sydney as lecturer, NSW State Conservatorium, 1974–75, then was head of music at Northern Rivers College of Advanced Education 1976–80.

Penberthy's compositions include *Dalgerie* (1958) opera, Symphony no. 6 *Earth Mother* (1962) for orchestra, *Colours, Numbers and Objects* (1968) for orchestra, Saxophone Concerto (1970), *Commentaries on Love* (1971) for string orchestra and soprano, *Spheres, Ellipses, Labyrinths* (1971) for orchestra, *Squares, Spirals, Spheres* (1972) for orchestra, Trombone Concerto (1973), *Spectra* (1974) suite for percussion, *Clocks* (1983) for piano, *Three Aboriginal Songs* (1988) for 12 male voices, *Southland* (1991) cantata, Sonatina (1993) for oboe and piano, and Quartet for Piano, Viola, Clarinet and Cello (1993).

Outwardly, Penberthy's prolific output appears to have explored a wide variety of styles and methods of composition, from his earlier music in a traditional European style to works involving chance and computer-assisted composition. In almost every work, however, there is the presence of extra-musical ideas and in particular a concentration on Australian themes and atmosphere.

WORKS (Selective)
Orchestral Violin Concerto (1970), Suite for 21 Strings *Spheres, Ellipses and Labyrinths* (1971), Symphony No. 8 (1972), Symphony No. 9 (1972), Piano Concerto No. 3 (1974), Piano Concerto No. 4 (1982), *Rainbow Music—Symphony on Seven Colours* (1982), Clarinet Concerto (1987), Suite for Orchestra *Pastorale, Waltz, Hymn, Scherzo, Chanson, Canon, Lament, Fanfare* (1987), Horn Concerto (1987), Oboe Concerto (1991).
Chamber Instrumental *Reflections on Bendigo*, vn, pf (1971), *Pastorale*, fl, gui, vc (1975), Saxophone Quartet, 4 sax (1981), String Quartet No. 4, 2 vn, va, vc (1981), Trio, fl, ob, pf (1983), Sonata, vn, pf (1983), Six Easy Pieces, fl, vn, pf (1985), Duo, db, bn (1986), String Quartet No. 5, 2 vn, va, vc (1987) Two Solos, cl, pf (1987), Sonatina, ob, pf (1993), Quartet, pf, va, cl, vc (1993).
Solo Instrumental Three Simple Studies, pf (1971), *Hymn for the Death of Jesus/Devils up There*, org (1972), *Clocks*, pf (1983), Six Preludes, gui (1974), *Reflections*, cl (1983), Three Pieces, ob (1983), Six Pieces, vn (1986), Psalm 130, org (1989).
Brass Band, Wind Ensemble March *Affirmation* (1982), Symphony *The Face of Jesus* (1982).
Theatre *Stations*, opera (1975, 3 acts, Gwen Harwood), *Henry Lawson*, opera (1988/9, 3 acts, Henry Lawson).
Vocal *Femina O-2001*, Mez, tape (1971), *Love Song*, S, 2 hp, tape (1973), *Pastorale*, S, fl, pf (1988), *The Earth Mother*, Bar, pf (1988).

FURTHER REFERENCE
Recordings include *Hymn for the Death of Jesus*, D. Lawrence org (Move MS 3025); *Cantata on Hiroshima Panels*, Adelaide Singers,

SA Symphony Orchestra, soloists, cond. P Thomas (1970, Festival SFC 800–18); *The Beach Inspector and the Mermaid* Suite, WA Symphony Orchestra, cond. T. Mayer (1970, Philips 6508002). A discography to 1972 is in *PlushD*. His writings include: 'The Aboriginal Influence', *SA* 30 (Winter 1991), 23–4. See also David Symons, *GroveD*; Andrew McCredie, *Musical Composition in Australia* (Canberra, Australian Government Advisory Board, 1969), 12–13; *CallawayA*; *MurdochA*.

MICHAEL BARKL

Percussion Instrument Making. Australia has a number of percussion instrument makers. The oldest is Drouyn, at Stones Corner, Brisbane, established by Douglas Drouyn and his sister Dorothy in 1927. They have made drums for military use, kits for bands (for a long period with the trademark 'D-an-D'), Silvertone fifes, and various orchestral drums, which are highly regarded by players and are sold in Australia and abroad. More recently, Chris Brady, of Roleystone, WA, established a business in 1981 making drums from local timbers, which have also become very widely distributed abroad. Marimbas and vibraphones have been made since 1978 by Jim Bailey and John White, Adelaide.

FURTHER REFERENCE
AthertonA.

Pereira, David (*b* Macksville, NSW, 21 Sept. 1953), cellist. After studying with Osric Fyfe and John *Painter at the NSW State Conservatorium, he went to the USA in 1976, studying with Fritz Magg at Indiana University and playing with the Indianapolis Symphony. He returned to Australia as principal cello with the Australian Chamber Orchestra in 1980, and joined the staff of the Canberra School of Music from 1990, conducting the Canberra Youth Orchestra from 1991. A versatile artist, he has been a prominent performer of contemporary music, playing in the Australia Ensemble and Flederman, and having works written for him by Barry Conyngham, Ross Edwards, David Lumsdaine, Richard Meale, Peter Sculthorpe and Carl Vine.

FURTHER REFERENCE
Recordings include Nigel Westlake, *Antarctica* (Tall Poppies TPO 12); *Only Cello* (1992, Tall Poppies TP0 17). See also clippings file, *Msl*.

Perihelion. Contemporary music ensemble formed (1988) as the resident ensemble at the University of Queensland. Members were originally Nigel Sabin (clarinet), Patricia Pollett (viola), Gwyn Roberts (cello) and Colin Spiers (piano). Conceived by Warren *Bebbington as Queensland's first professional contemporary ensemble, the group comprises four contrasting instruments and has commissioned a significant number of Australian works for this unusual combination by Ross *Edwards, Gerard *Brophy, Moya *Henderson, Andrew *Schultz, Sarah

*Hopkins, David *Joseph, Quentin Grant, Nigel Sabin and others. The name is taken from the Greek for the point in a planet's orbit closest to the sun. They have a subscription series in Brisbane, have toured for the ABC, and made four CD recordings.

FURTHER REFERENCE
Recordings include *Tapestry* (1992, Univ. Qld); *Points of Departure* (1995, Tall Poppies, TPO43); and *Andrew Schultz, chamber music* (1994, Tall Poppies TP065).

Perryman, Jill   (*b* Melbourne, 30 May 1933), actress, theatrical singer. Daughter of actors William Perryman and actress Dorothy Duval, she was in the chorus for J.C. Williamsons productions from 1952, and was an understudy or had small roles in *South Pacific, Paint Your Wagon, Can-Can* and *Pyjama Game* (1956). After having a family, she returned to the stage as second lead in *Hello Dolly* in 1965, soon replacing the sick American star Carole Cook in the lead role, to great acclaim; she then triumphed as the star of *Funny Girl* (1966), paving the way for other Australians to be cast in the leading roles of imported musicals. She had more successes in *I Do, I Do* (1969), *No! No! Nanette* (1972), *A Little Night Music* (1973) and *Annie* (1981). She sang in the West Australian Ballet's *The Seven Deadly Sins* (1987) and in the revival of *Hello Dolly* (1995). One of Australia's most notable successes in musicals and variety, she was honoured with the MBE in 1979 and AM in 1992.

FURTHER REFERENCE
ParsonsC; *DPA*; *Herald-Sun* 18 June 1992.

Perth,   pop. (1991) 1 143 378, capital of Western Australia, situated on the Swan River estuary close to Fremantle harbour, which serves as its port. Set near the western seaboard in a vast, largely desert state it is one of the most isolated cities of its size in the world.

Perth was first founded as a British colony in 1829, but scarce resources and extreme isolation retarded its development until the discovery of the Kimberleys pasture land and gold in the 1880s. The harsh conditions had a considerable impact upon social and cultural life, and its music in the 19th century was largely of a domestic or salon nature. Sacred music was heard at St George's church from 1845, but the piano recitals presented from 1846 by Dom Rosendo *Salvado, a Benedictine monk struggling to raise funds for his mission at New Norcia, were the first public musical events of quality. Choral societies, their musical repertoire modelled on that of Victorian Britain, reflected little of either continental European developments or experimentation with a more indigenous musical style. It was not until 1887 that the first orchestra, the Fremantle Orchestral Society, was established. A 'Theatre Royal' was opened at a Perth hotel in 1897, and hosted an opera company managed by one of Lyster's former singers, Henry Bracey.

In the first years of Federation, George Musgrove and J.C. Williamson sent a few theatrical companies to Perth from Melbourne, including their Royal Comic Opera, and the Italian Opera Co. in 1902. After His Majesty's Theatre was opened in 1904, vaudeville and musicals began to be staged. But in general operatic performances were scarce: the Italo-Australian Opera Co. of Frank *Rigo toured from Adelaide in 1928, the Melba-Williamson Opera Co. included Perth in its tour of 1928, and the first Elizabethan Trust Opera season extended to Perth in 1956, one of the rare appearances in the west by the national company.

The earlier tradition of choral music in Perth was kept alive when A.J. *Leckie became organist at St George's Cathedral in 1908; he conducted the Metropolitan Liedertafel and various other choirs until 1948. Today there are several large choirs whose repertoire still depends strongly on British models, and performances of *Messiah* at Christmas and *St Matthew Passion* at Easter are annual events, with major works by Handel, Haydn, Mendelssohn and Britten eclipsing any Australian choral music. The city's principal chamber choir today is based at Collegium Musicum, the University of Western Australia. It has introduced a range of lesser-known repertoire to Perth audiences to balance the work of the larger choral societies.

Various orchestral ventures followed the Fremantle Orchestral Society. In 1928 Harold Newton established a co-operative for players put out of work by the demise of local silent movie orchestras; his orchestra presented numerous concerts in the coming years. He was succeeded by George Reed in 1934, and the ABC established a studio broadcast orchestra in 1936. This became the forerunner of the state's premier orchestra, the *West Australian Symphony Orchestra, for which Henry Krips was appointed conductor from 1947, then Rudolf *Pekarek once it was established in its current form from 1950. This orchestra now has a playing strength of 90 and is jointly funded by the Federal and State Governments. In addition to three major symphonic concert series under the direction of international conductors, it also works with the West Australian Ballet and Opera companies during their annual seasons, and its schedule includes tours to major regional centres, sometimes involving journeys of over 1000 km.

Music education in Perth was long in the hands of private teachers, and Leckie became foundation president of the WA Music Teachers' Association in 1910. The enhancement of the standard of performance was encouraged by the establishment of the WA branch of the AMEB in 1918. Leckie gave lectures at the University of Western Australia from 1931, but a music department and a chair in music were not created until 1959, with Frank *Callaway appointed foundation professor. The University of Western Australia and more recently the *West Australian Conservatorium at Edith Cowan University focus on performance and music education, while the university also offers composition, musicology and training in early music performance practice, and the conservatorium jazz and contemporary popular music. A notable gap in the musical offerings of both institutions is the study of the Aboriginal musical cultures. Both institutions are also heavily involved in the musical training of pre-tertiary students, the former through the West Australian Youth Orchestra, and the latter through the WA Jazz Youth Orchestra.

Australian composition is served by innovative performance ensembles which established a firm reputation in the early 1990s. Three of these, the West Australian Symphony Orchestra Contemporary Ensemble, Nova Ensemble, and Magnetic Pig, play an important role in the commissioning and presentation of new music by West Australian composers, and have been involved in significant music-theatre performances. The state department for the arts (ArtsWA) also plays an important part in supporting professional musicians and in assisting with commissions for new music. A pro-active commissioning policy established in the early 1990s has seen the number and quality of WA compositions increase substantially.

A particular feature of some new works in WA has been the influence of musics from other cultures. Perth has a number of immigrant communities and many of these have worked hard to maintain their musical traditions. In 1983 the Ethnic Music Centre (now Multicultural Arts Centre) was established with funding from both State and Federal Governments to provide support and promotion for immigrant musicians. The centre holds regular musical evenings at which musicians from a variety of ethnic backgrounds present music of their home countries; these range from performances of the classical music of Asia and the Middle East to the traditional music of the Pacific Islands, Africa and of Australia itself. In recognition of the very diverse population mix Perth has had in the last decade, multicultural music is now a growing component of the music taught in WA schools.

Perth has been host to a number of arts festivals. The *Festival of Perth is the longest-running festival of its kind in Australia, bringing to the city each February a number of leading international ensembles and individual artists. Other annual festivals include jazz, multicultural, folk music, Aboriginal arts, and early music, and all make the most of the favourable climate to hold as many activities as possible in the open air. Together with the ABC and Musica Viva, the two universities have sponsored and maintained many of the significant musical activities of Perth, and also run annual concert series for the general public.

FURTHER REFERENCE

J. E. Farrant, Music in Western Australia 1900–1950, PhD, Univ. WA; A. Kornweibel, *Apollo and the Pioneers: The Story of the First 100 Years of Music in WA* (Perth: Music Council of WA, 1973).

MARGARET SEARES

Peters, Jack Vernon   (b Christchurch, NZ, 20 Sept. 1920; d Adelaide, 22 Feb. 1973), organist, teacher. He was educated in NZ and obtained a doctorate of music from the University of New Zealand in 1959. He came to Adelaide in the John *Bishop era as organist and teacher of advanced theory at the Elder Conservatorium, and became a colourful personality in the city's musical scene. Peters was an excellent recitalist, and his playing was at its best inspirational. He was organist and master of the choristers at St Peter's Cathedral 1953–62, city organist from 1967, and then at Pirie Street Methodist Church in its last days. His compositions included two symphonies and a wind quintet as well as choral music.

FURTHER REFERENCE

GlennonA; Andrew McCredie, ed., *From Colonel Light into the Footlights: The Performing Arts in South Australia from 1836 to the Present* (Adelaide: Pagel, 1988).   DAVID SWALE

Peterson, Franklin Sievright   (b Edinburgh, 24 Feb. 1861; d Melbourne, 21 June 1914), music professor. Trained as an organist in Edinburgh and Dresden, Peterson subsequently completed a BMus at Oxford University in 1891. He became well known in the UK as a music journalist and author of music theory textbooks. Appointed to the Ormond professorship at the University of Melbourne in 1901, Peterson had the unenviable task of re-establishing the University Conservatorium after its damaging rift with *Marshall-Hall. He recommended music courses in a new building, introduced a performance major into the bachelor degree, and secured the financial future of the Conservatorium through the creation of an indigenous examination system, later to become the *AMEB. Conservative and reserved by nature, Peterson never earned the respect or recognition accorded to those who preceded or succeeded him, but the erection of the Conservatorium building and Melba Hall remains a lasting monument to his achievements.

FURTHER REFERENCE

Faye Patton, *ADB*, 11.   PETER TREGEAR

Petra String Quartet.   Formed in 1977 from graduates of the Tasmanian Conservatorium as its resident ensemble, originally comprised of Sonia Hyland and Robert Macindoe (violins), Simon Oswell (viola) and Susan Pickering (cello). Conceived by Jan *Sedivka, director of the conservatorium, the quartet focused on Australian compositions, commissioning a number of works and performing a repertoire of Peter *Sculthorpe, Don *Banks, Larry *Sitsky, Ian *Cugley and others. They gave concerts, broadcasts and many school visits and lecture demonstrations of Australian compositions. They toured the eastern states, then Europe in 1980 and appeared at the Adelaide Festival.

FURTHER REFERENCE

Recordings include L. Sitsky, *De Profundis* (1989, Move MD 3084); B. Conyngham and G. Tibbits, quartets (1981, Move MS

3037); and works of M. Sutherland, D. Kay and P. Tahourdin (Canberra School of Music, CSM 7).

Phillips, Linda (*b* Windsor, Vic., 8 June 1899), composer. She studied at the University of Melbourne with Edward ★Goll (piano) and at the Albert Street Conservatorium with Fritz ★Hart (composition), then was music critic on the Melbourne *Sun-News Pictorial* 1950–77 and an adjudicator at the *Sun* Aria competition 1950–78. Confined as a composer to chamber music and songs, many to her own texts, her music falls into two distinct categories: Jewish or Middle Eastern-inspired music, such as *Exaltation (c.*1939), an instrumental piece based on a Chassidic air; and Romantically inclined music, such as *Bush Lyrics (c.*1931). Overall, Phillips has described her music as being 'between the wars lyricism'. She was honoured with the OBE in 1975.

FURTHER REFERENCE
Her memoirs are unpublished. See also Catherine Gerrard, 'A Career in Music', *SA* 41 (Autumn 1994), 19–20; Kerry Murphy, 'Talking with Linda Phillips', *Lip* (1978–79), 129–30.

JOEL CROTTY

Philpott, Ron (Ronald Geoffrey) (*b* Sydney, 21 Nov. 1945), jazz bassist. He began guitar in 1956, later becoming more active on bass. He led a band from 1959 to the mid-1960s, then until the early 1970s played primarily in pop music. Writing for the ★Daly-Wilson Big Band, he joined Judy ★Bailey in 1974 (with whom he appeared in the film *Southern Crossing*), also working with Doug Foskett. In the late 1970s he was active with Bernie ★McGann and John ★Pochée, and with Jack Grimsley's Channel Ten Orchestra. He has prepared curricula and performed for secondary school students, and since 1979 has taught in the Sydney Conservatorium jazz program.

FURTHER REFERENCE
Recordings include *One Moment,* Judy Bailey Quartet (1974, Philips 6357 018); *Colours,* Judy Bailey Quartet (1976, Eureka E-103); *The Julian Lee Orchestra* (1980, Batjazz BAT-2072). See also *ClareB; OxfordJ.* BRUCE JOHNSON

Piano-makers. While a number of craftsmen built or assembled pianos in a small way in the period 1850–90, the golden age of Australian piano manufacture on a large scale was from 1900 until 1930, when the Depression and changing tastes eliminated all but the most hardy manufacturers. ★Beale & Co. was established in Annandale, Sydney, in 1893 and by the 1920s boasted that it was the largest piano factory in the British Empire, with over 60 000 pianos made. Also in Sydney was C.E. ★Davies & Sons who manufactured the Symphony piano from 1946 until 1976. The Melbourne suburb of Richmond had no less than three piano manufacturers. Hugo ★Wertheim built a large factory which opened in 1909 and, like Beale, had an extensive range of models from small uprights to concert grand and player pianos. During 1929 Wertheims reorganised to become the Associated Piano Co., which struggled on until 1935. Francis Howard was established by ★Carnegie & Sons in 1911, making a range of pianos into the 1930s supplemented by radio manufacture from 1927 but still being listed as a piano manufacturer as late as 1959. The international piano manufacturer the Aeolian Co. built a factory in Richmond in 1922 and made pianos and player-pianos until *c.*1929. Also in Melbourne was the Concord Piano and Player Piano Co., 1920–34, backed by a consortium of Australian music warehouses, and in the Melbourne suburb of Camberwell, Zenker & Schultes, established by ★Allan & Co. who operated 1923–29. In Adelaide H.S. Furness & Son began making pianos in a small way from 1905 with their main period of activity and greatest output being 1920–29. Today no pianos are manufactured commercially in Australia.

FURTHER REFERENCE
AthertonA, 38–51. JOHN SEMMENS

Pickering, Tom (Thomas Mansergh) (*b* Burra, SA, 8 Aug. 1921), jazz reeds player. He moved to Hobart in childhood, developing an interest in jazz with Cedric and Ian Pearce, and beginning clarinet in 1936. President of the 7HO Swing Club in 1937, he began tenor saxophone, and co-founded the Barrelhouse Four. He worked in dance bands, building a reputation as a 'hot' soloist. With the Barrelhouse Four he played the revue *Red, Hot and Blue* (1940) and gave ABC broadcasts in 1941. A professional transfer to Westbury in 1941 interrupted his Hobart career, which resumed briefly until his band broke up through wartime postings. A brief period in wartime Melbourne expanded his knowledge of jazz, and in 1945 he reconstituted the Barrelhouse Four, which attended the first ★Australian Jazz Convention. Versions of this band, led by Pickering, remained the mainstay of Tasmanian jazz through the 1950s, playing broadcasts, dances, concerts, and weekly functions at the 7HT Theatrette.

In 1960 Pickering moved to cabaret and also worked in Ian Pearce's Sextet until the early 1970s. Inaugural president of the Hobart Jazz Club in 1961, from 1970 he began co-leading groups with Pearce for ABC recording sessions, producing an extensive documentation of his work as musician, singer, composer. With Ian ★Pearce, Tom Pickering was the pioneer and mainstay of Tasmanian jazz until his retirement from music in the 1990s owing to ill health. He was honoured with the AM in 1982, and has also received literary awards for his creative and critical writing.

FURTHER REFERENCE
Recordings include *Sweet, Soft, Plenty Rhythm,* Pearce-Pickering Barrelhouse Jazz Band (1977, Swaggie S-1404); *Pearce-Pickering Barrelhouse Jazz Band* (1984, Swaggie S-001). An interview with him is in *WilliamsA,* 29–33. See also *BissetB; OxfordJ; WWA.*

BRUCE JOHNSON

Pierrette. Light opera in one act by Fritz ★Hart (1913) on the Pierrot and Pierrette theme, first performed by the National Opera League at Sydney on 3 August 1914, then at Melbourne.

Pikler, Robert (*b* Hungary, 1910; *d* Sydney, 18 Jan. 1984), violinist, violist, conductor. After studying at the Royal Conservatoire, Budapest, he fled the Nazis but was interned in the Far East 1942–45 by the Japanese. He came to Australia as a refugee in 1946, founded and led the Sydney String Quartet, and was one of the initiators of ★Musica Viva, leading its original ensemble. Playing both violin and viola, he was principal viola in the Sydney Symphony Orchestra 1952–66 then joined the staff of the NSW State Conservatorium, forming its chamber orchestra in 1972. Retiring from viola performance in 1969, he focused on conducting, and conducted the Australian Youth Orchestra, Canberra Symphony Orchestra, and other groups. A player deeply imbued with the European tradition, he was a particularly generous teacher and a passionate advocate for Australian talent. He was honoured with the OBE in 1974.

FURTHER REFERENCE
Obit. in *Age* 25 Jan. 1984. Recordings as a conductor with the Sydney Symphony Orchestra (all RCA) included Haydn Symphony No. 55, Mozart *Sinfonia Concertante* K.297b, Mozart Bassoon Concerto, and the Berlioz *Benvenuto Cellini* Overture. See also *HolmesC*; Ann Boyd, *GroveD*; *Age* 17 June 1977.

Pini, Carl (*b* England, 2 Jan. 1934), violinist. Son of the cellist Anthony Pini, he took lessons with his father in London and then in Paris. His first professional engagement was in an orchestra for the Shakespeare Festival at Stratford-upon-Avon; then he played with the English Chamber Orchestra, and, from 1974, the Philharmonia Orchestra, becoming leader of the London String Quartet and the Philomusica of London. Coming to Australia in 1968, he conducted for the ABC from 1970, was leader of the ★Australian Chamber Orchestra and the Carl Pini Quartet, then concertmaster of the Melbourne Symphony Orchestra from 1975 and founder of the ★Melbourne String Quartet. A stylish and profoundly musical player, he has toured widely in Australia, NZ and beyond as a chamber music player and concertmaster.

FURTHER REFERENCE
Recordings include Rubbra, Violin Concerto, Melbourne Symphony Orchestra (1986, Unicorn-Kanchana); I. Farr, *Variations on a Theme of Larry Sitsky* (1972, Festival SFC 80022). See also *CA* (1995–96); *HolmesC*; *Age* 5 Mar. 1990; *Herald-Sun* 18 Mar. 1995

Pinschof, Carl (*b* Vienna, 14 Apr. 1855; *d* Cape Town, South Africa, 19 May 1926), merchant, consul, patron of music. In Melbourne he and his wife Elise ★Wiedermann were founding patrons of the ★Marshall-Hall Orchestra, and he was a founding member of the Lady ★Northcote Permanent Orchestra Trust Fund. The Pinschofs' home in Kew, Studley Hall, was the site for many musical and social gatherings.

FURTHER REFERENCE
Pinschof Papers, Österreichisches Staatsarchiv, Vienna. See also *MackenzieS*; R.F. Middlemann, *ADB*, 2; M.J. Smith, ed., *The Cyclopedia of Victoria,* vol. 1 (Melbourne: Cyclopedia Company, 1903).

KATRINA WATSON

Pintupi. People of the Gibson Desert, west-central Australia. Like the Kukatja, the Pintupi came into continual European contact only two generations ago. By contrast, pre-European contact with neighbouring desert groups was frequent, particularly at shared semi-permanent water sources in time of drought. And like the Kukatja, Pintupi are familiar with the rituals of neighbouring groups and may temporarily add them to their own active repertoire before discarding them or passing them on in turn. Conveyed from the desert after a prolonged drought in the 1960s, many Pintupi have now returned to their homelands, living in family clusters close to readily accessible water, and continuing the small-scale musical activities which characterise the region as a whole.

Conforming broadly to the 'central Australian' style in their manner of performance, accompaniment, use categories (women's *yawulyu* and men's *yilpintji* 'love-magic' rituals, public *turlku* ceremonies, as well as several more restricted types), general structure and associated belief-patterns, Pintupi songs have no unique stylistic identifiers. Rather, they are distinguished by the geographic referents of their poetry, as whole series taking several hours to perform sing the location-specific exploits of Dreamtime ancestors, visually complemented by dramatic representations of individual mythic episodes. To this extent, Pintupi songs project images of self-identity, statements about the Pintupi universe and the human condition within it. Singers frequently report that singing makes them happy, but this state appears not the product of mere singing but of singing together, re-establishing and reaffirming social unity through musical unison. With its attendant need for permissions and co-operation, group singing assumes the nature of a symbol of social cohesion, both reflecting and re-establishing the social order. See also *Aboriginal Music* §2.

FURTHER REFERENCE
Richard M. Moyle, *Songs of the Pintupi: Musical Life in a Central Australian Society* (Canberra: AIAS, 1979); Fred R. Myers, *Pintupi Country, Pintupi Self: Sentiment, Place and Politics among Western Desert Aborigines* (Washington and Canberra: Smithsonian Institution Press and AIAS, 1986).

RICHARD MOYLE

Pipe Bands. Wealthy settlers in Australia had private bagpipers for their entertainment from the 1840s. The first pipe bands were organised with the advent of the Caledonian Societies and Scottish militia units in the 1880s; by 1950 there were 51 pipe bands in Australia, chiefly in Victoria and NSW, based in schools, pipe clubs or the army. Interest has continued to grow: there were 250 bands by 1982. Both country and highland dancing have flourished since the 1950s to the accompaniment of the pipes, and there is a Royal Scottish Country Dance Society. See *Scottish Folk Music*.

FURTHER REFERENCE
Malcolm D. Prentis, *The Scottish in Australia* (Melbourne: AE Press, 1987).

Pipeline. Contemporary music performance group formed (1987) in Melbourne by Simone *de Haan (trombone) and Daryl Pratt (percussion), with Mardi McSullea (flute), Michael Kieran Harvey (piano) and Geoff Dodd (cor anglais). Their concerts focused on live collaborations between performers and composers both from classical and jazz traditions, to create a more fluid relationship between the two via improvisation. They presented concerts, workshops and demonstrations in Melbourne and Sydney of recent Australian, European and American work. They commissioned composers, notably Paul *Grabowsky and Phil Treloar, to write specifically for the individual capabilities of the musicians in the group. With players of virtuosic skill, at their height in the late 1980s they were one of the most innovative and exhilarating contemporary music groups in Australia.

FURTHER REFERENCE
Simone de Haan, 'Pipeline Contemporary Music Project', *Sounds Australian* 18 (Winter 1988), 180–2.

Pitjantjatjara. Desert peoples in far north-west SA, neighbours of *Luritja, *Pintupi and others. After European contact numbers of Pitjantjatjara people moved to missions, including *Yalata, but many returned to the traditional areas in the 1970s and 80s to establish communities, and the Pitjantjatjara Land Rights Act of 1991 granted freehold title to Anangu Pitjantjatjara. Imparja TV, a major outlet for Aboriginal music of all types, is owned and run by Pitjantjatjara and *CAAMA, and the PY Media Association at Ernabella is run by Pitjantjatjara and Yankunytjatjara people. Early research into the music was conducted by T.G.H. *Strehlow (1932–55, 1958–60), with whom Catherine *Ellis worked while completing her PhD research. From the early 1960s Ellis undertook extensive fieldwork in the area, researching both tribal and westernised music-making, especially of the women. She established the *Centre for Aboriginal Studies in Music (CASM) at the University of Adelaide, using Pitjantjatjara elders to teach songs to both Aboriginal and non-Aboriginal students. Other scholars who have worked on Pitjantjatjara song are Guy Tunstil, Margaret Kartomi and Linda Barwick. See *Aboriginal Music*, §2,3.

FURTHER REFERENCE
Catherine Ellis, *Aboriginal Music. Education for Living* (Brisbane: UQP, 1985); idem, 'The Pitjantjatjara Kangaroo song from Karlga.' *MMA* 2(1967), 171–268; idem, 'Time Consciousness of Aboriginal Performers', in *Problems and Solutions*, ed. Jamie C. Kassler and Jill Stubington (Sydney: Hale & Iremonger, 1984), 149–85; idem with Linda Barwick, 'Singers, Songs and Knowledge', *MMA* 15 (1988), 284–301; idem, 'Musical syntax and the problem of meaning in a central Australian songline', *MA 10* (1987), 41–57; idem, 'Classification of Sounds in Pitjantjatjara Speaking Areas', in L. Hiatt, ed., *Australian Aboriginal Concepts* (Canberra: AIAS 1978), Margaret Kartomi, 'Childlikeness in play songs—a case study among the Pitjantjara at Yalata, South Australia', *MMA* 11 (1980), 172–214; idem, 'Delineation of Lullaby Style in Three Areas of Aboriginal Australia', in Kassler and Stubington, 59–93; Guy D. Tunstil, 'An overview of the Centre for Aboriginal Studies in music, 1988', *Australian Aboriginal Studies* 1 (1989), 29–30; idem, 'Melody and rhythmic structure in Pitjantjatjara song', in M. Clunies Ross, T. Donaldson, S. Wild, eds., *Songs of Aboriginal Australia* (Sydney: University of Sydney, 1987), 121–41.

Pirani, Max (*fl.* 1916–50), pianist, composer. An accomplished pianist and chamber music recitalist, Pirani's career was interrupted by two world wars. He gave his first concerts in Melbourne *c.*1913. In 1918 he enlisted in the British Army, returning to Australia after the war to tour with the important Australian violinist Leila *Doubleday, whom he married. His compositions included a *Magnificat*, published in New York in 1917. As the leader of the Pirani Trio he made successful concert tours in Australasia and the UK. Contemporary reviewers speak highly of this group and considered it an important export from Australia.

JEFF BROWNRIGG

Plainsong. See *Anglican Chant, Church Music*.

Play School, It's. Theme-song for the ABC's long-running children's program, which grew from the radio *Kindergarten of the Air* (from 1954) and appeared on television from 1966, offering educational entertainment, usually through song and singing action games. It may be heard on *There's A Bear In There* (ABC Video 8143412/4) and *It's Play School* (ABC Video 813422/4)

Playboys, The. See *Rowe, Normie*.

Plumpton, Alfred (*b* London, ?1841; *d* London, 2 Apr. 1902), music critic, conductor and composer. He arrived in Melbourne in 1878 after touring in Asia as conductor of an opera company. Quickly establishing himself in Melbourne musical circles, in 1882 he became music critic for the Melbourne *Age* and *Leader* newspapers and contributed scholarly articles to the *Victorian*

Review. Highly regarded as a piano teacher, Plumpton was also musical director of Presbyterian Ladies' College and St Francis' Catholic Church, Melbourne. His compositions produced while in Australia include a Mass in G Minor (*c*.1881), a two-act opera, *I Due Studenti* (1887), and the cantatas *Endymion* (1882), *The Apotheosis of Hercules* (1883) and the still extant *Victorian Jubilee Ode* (1885). In 1890 he toured as conductor of Nellie Stewart's Opera Co. and was president of the Society of Musicians of Australasia from 1890 to 1891. In 1892 he left Australia permanently and returned to London with his pianist wife, Madame Tasca.

FURTHER REFERENCE

British Australasian 3 Apr. 1902, 581; James Duff Brown, *British Musical Biography: A Dictionary of Musical Artists, Authors, and Composers Born in Britain and its Colonies* (Birmingham: S.S. Stratton, 1897), 323; H. Morin Humphreys, *Men of the Time in Australia*, Victorian Series, 2nd edn (Melbourne: McCarron, Bird & Co., 1882), clxix; *Table-Talk* 24 Apr. 1902, 3.

JENNIFER ROYLE

Plush, Vincent (*b* Adelaide, 18 Apr. 1950), composer, teacher, writer. He studied at the University of Adelaide 1968–70, then took further study in the USA on a Harkness fellowship, 1981–83. He worked as a radio producer, writer and teacher in Sydney 1971–81, and since mid-1988 he has divided his time between Australia and USA. His compositions reflect his interest in history, literature, theatre and allied arts, often concerning political matters and sometimes Australia's quest for cultural identity. Most frequently performed among his works are the *Australian Folksongs* (1977/8), a music-theatre for baritone and ensemble, *Bakery Hill Rising* (1980) for french horn ensemble, *On Shooting Stars—Homage to Victor Jara* (1981) for six instruments, *Pacifica* (1986/7) for large orchestra, *The Ludlow Lullabies* (1989) for violin and piano, and *Mr Gershwin on Folly Pier* (1995) for saxophone ensemble. In addition to the value of his own compositional work, Plush has made a significant contribution to the promotion of Australian music, both at home and abroad, and to the general knowledge of American music in Australia.

WORKS (Selective)

Orchestral *Pacifica* (1986, rev. 1987), *Pilbara: Homage to Fred Williams,* str orch (1988), *Concord/Eendracht,* large orch (1990–91), *Suite from the ballet 'Louisa',* small orch (1994).
Chamber Instrumental *Aurores,* from *O Paraguay!,* french hn, ens (1979), *Le Piège de Méduse* (arrangement of the instumental dances by Erik Satie), fl, cl, bn, tpt, trbn, perc, vn, db (1979), *Bakery Hill Rising,* solo french hn, 8 hn (live or pre-recorded) (1980, rec. 1989, Canberra School of Music, CSM 9), *On Shooting Stars: Homage to Victor Jara,* fl, cl, pf, perc, vn, vc, with pre-recorded cassettes (1981), *Gallipoli Sunrise,* solo tenor trbn, 7 trbn (live or pre-recorded) (1984), *Fireraisers: A Concertino in the Style of a Vaudeville Entertainment,* fl, cl, bn, pf, perc, accordion, str qrt (1984), *The Wakefield Convocation,* brass quintet (1985), *Helices,* from *The*

Wakefield Chronicles, perc qrt (1985), *The Wakefield Chorales,* brass band (1985–86), *The Wakefield Invocation,* tpt, org (1986), *March of the Dalmatians,* brass band (1987), *The Love Songs of Herbert Hoover,* hn, pf, vn (1987), *Florilegium I,* concertino for va, ens (1988), *Florilegium II,* concertino for marimba, ens (1988), *String Quartet* (1988), *Barcaldine,* 8 vc (1992), *Cristobal Colón— Guamiquiná,* fl, of, cl, bn, hn (1992), *Florilegium II,* solo marimba, fl/pic/alto fl, cl/pic cl/bass cl, pf, vn, vc (1992), *George Gershwin returns to Folly Island,* 8 alto sax (1994).
Solo Instrumental *Chu no mai,* fl (1974–76), *Encompassings,* org, with assistant (1975), *Chrysalis,* org (1977–78), *Stevie's Wonder Music,* fl, tape (1979), *The Wakefield Intrada,* org (1986).
Electronic (all for tape) *Estuary* (1978), *All Ears* (1985), *Metropolis: Sydney* (1987–88).
Vocal/Choral *Three Carols,* S, A, children's choir (1969, 1978, 1982), *Magnificat,* S, fl, 3 SATB vocal quartets (1970), *Australian Folksongs: A Music Theatre Piece in Celebration of Australia's Colonial History and Folk Heritage,* Bar singer/actor, ens (1977–78), *Australian Quadrilles and Dances I,* arr. for nar (optional), ens (1979), *The Maitland and Morpeth String Quartet* (text by Nicholas Enright), narrator/actor, str qrt (1979–85), *Australian Quadrilles and Dances II,* arr. for nar (optional), ens (1981), *The Hymn of the Winstanley Levellers,* SATB (1981), *Letter from the Antipodes: Six Reflections on Colonial Australia* SSAAT-TBarB soli, pf (1984), *The Plaint of Mary Gilmore* (texts from Dame Mary Gilmore) Mez, pf (1984), *Facing the Danger* (based on the poem 'Say No' by Barbara Berman), speaking voice(s) and instrument(s) (1985), *The Wakefield Chronicles: 'An Address to the Citizenry of South Australia'* (based on the writings of Edward Gibbon Wakefield), nar, tpt, trbn, brass quintet, 2 brass bands, org, 4 perc, bell-ringers, hand-bell ringers (1985–86), *The Muse of Fire: A Celebratory Ode* (text by Brian Cartledge, based on the writings of Andrew Torning [1814–1900]), nar, Bar, tpt, fl, pf, large mixed ch (SSAATTBarB), 2 brass bands, children's ch (SA), org (1986–87), *Andrew Torning's March to Victory,* SATB, pf (1987), *The Arraignment of Henry Lawson,* song cycle/dramatic scena, Bar, pf (1988–89), *Funeral rites,* 2 S, A, T, Bar, B, pf (1993), *Cartographies* (text by Rita Dove), ch (1994).

FURTHER REFERENCE

Recordings include *Bakery Hill Rising* Australian Chamber Orchestra (Canberra School of Music, CSM 9); and *Australian Folksongs,* L. Terracini, B (OZM 1003). His writings include: 'Too Close to the Bone?', *SA* 21 (Spring 1990), 19–20; and 'Pacific Overtures', *SA* 31 (Spring 1991), 30–3. See also *BroadstockS*; M. Hannan, 'A Critical Survey of the Music of Vincent Plush', *AMC News* 10 (Summer 1985–86), 22–3; N. Slonimsky, *Baker's Biographical Dictionary of Musicians,* 8th edn (New York: Schirmer, 1992).

MICHAEL BARKL

Pochée, John Kenneth (*b* Sydney, 21 Sept. 1940), jazz drummer. A left-handed drummer on a conventional kit, he began his career with Dave Levy in 1956, becoming active at *El Rocco in 1957. He was in Melbourne 1959–62, with Keith Stirling, Graeme Lyall, Tony Gould, Joe Lane and others. Apart from a season at Melbourne's

Fat Black Pussycat in 1964 and a period in Adelaide, he has since based himself in Sydney, associated with the young progressives at El Rocco, including Bobby ★Gebert, Judy ★Bailey and Bernie ★McGann, with whom he established a significant musical association in the Last Straw. He has also been active in pop music, including as musical director for Shirley Bassey and for the Four Kinsmen during their Australian and overseas tours. With the expansion of opportunities for progressive jazz performance, notably through the Sydney Improvised Music Association and the Jazz Co-ordination programs, Pochée was increasingly able to focus on jazz activity.

Apart from continuing work with the Last Straw and accompanying visitors including Dewey Redman, Richie Cole and Steve Lacey, most significant was the debut of Ten Part Invention in 1986, an uncompromisingly non-commercial big band presenting contemporary Australian compositions, mostly by band members, particularly Roger ★Frampton and Miroslav ★Bukowsky. Through numerous Australasian, US, European and Asian tours and festivals, local performances under the auspices of the Sydney Improvised Music Association, and award winning recordings, Ten Part Invention and its rhythm section the Engine Room were ground-breakers in the current expansion of contemporary jazz performance and Australian composition, generating the public interest and performance support now enjoyed by more recent groups.

FURTHER REFERENCE
Recordings include *One Moment*, Judy Bailey Quartet (1974, Philips 6357 018); *Colours*, Judy Bailey Quartet (1976, Eureka E-103); *At Long Last*, Bernie McGann Trio (recorded 1983, released 1987, Emanem 3601); *Ten Part Invention* (1987, ABC/Phonogram 846 729–2); *At Long Last*, Bernie McGann Quartet (1987, Emanem 3602); *The Last Straw* (1990, Spiral Scratch 0005); *Ugly Beauty*, Bernie McGann (1991, Spiral Scratch 0010); *Tall Stories*, Ten Part Invention (1993, Rufus/Polygram RF006); *McGann x McGann*, Bernie McGann (1995, Rufus/Polygram RF011). See also *ClareB*; *BissetB*; *OxfordJ*; Gail Brennan, 'John Pochée, Not The Bitter End', *JA* (Summer/Autumn 1986), 4–8; *SMH* 20 Mar. 1996.

BRUCE JOHNSON

Poedijono   (*b* Wonogiri, Indonesia, 23 Sept. 1940), Javanese musician, dancer, puppeteer. He studied at the Music Conservatorium in Solo, Central Java and became a dancer and musician at Loro Jonggrang theatre in Prambanan, Central Java, 1960–63. After teaching music and dance at the School of Music and Dance in Denpasar, Bali, 1963–72, he was appointed lecturer in Indonesian music and dance at the music department, Monash University in 1972. He also worked as a part-time lecturer at the Melbourne College of Advanced Education 1978–88, then at the University of Melbourne (since 1989), the Indonesian Consulate and the Victorian College of the Arts. Since 1972 he has directed, performed in and choreographed annual productions of Indonesian dance, drama and music at Monash University, and he regularly performs Javanese shadow puppet plays, leads student cultural tours of Java and Bali, and is a guest teacher of Indonesian music in primary and secondary schools and other tertiary institutions in Australia, New Caledonia, and Hong Kong.

CATHERINE FALK

Pogson, Roger Herbert (Peter)   (*b* Pennant Hills, Sydney, 25 July 1932), organ-builder. Pogson was apprenticed in 1948 to the Sydney builder S.T. Noad, founding his own firm in 1963. At first he built organs with electric action but moved to mechanical action in 1968 for the King's School, Parramatta. At premises in Sydney and Orange from 1982, he has built 20 mechanical action organs for four Australian states and Japan; these are widely known for their excellent craftsmanship, robust sound and imaginative case designs. Pogson is also renowned for his restorations, in particular the Hill organ at Sydney Town Hall, carried out from 1972 to 1982, a project of world significance. He has also built numerous harpsichords and restored stringed instruments.

FURTHER REFERENCE
Kelvin Hastie, 'An Organbuilding Career in Summary: Roger Pogson', *OHTA News* 17/1 (Jan. 1993), 10–12.

JOHN MAIDMENT

Polites, Nick   (*b* Melbourne, 2 July 1927), jazz clarinet, saxophonist. He began performing publicly on clarinet (later adding alto saxophone) in the 1940s, and played at the first ★Australian Jazz Convention with the Jazz Appreciation Society band. He was with Allan Bradley 1947–50, John ★Sangster 1950, and Frank ★Johnson's Fabulous Dixielanders 1951–56, then joined Llew Hird in what became the ★Melbourne New Orleans Jazz Band under Polites' subsequent leadership. Returning to Australia after the band's dissolution abroad, he was freelancing, leading, and with the Yarra Yarra Jazz Band 1964–66 and 1971–73. He continues performing in the Melbourne traditional jazz movement, and has been a trustee of the Australian Jazz Convention.

FURTHER REFERENCE
Recordings include *Frank Johnson's Fabulous Dixielanders, 1951–55* (1982, Swaggie S-1319); *Australian Jazz of the 60's*, The Melbourne New Orleans Jazz Band (1984, EMI YPRX-2166); *The Yarra Yarra New Orleans Jazz Band* (1964, W & G Records, WG-B-1912). See also *OxfordJ*.

BRUCE JOHNSON

Pollard, Mark Clement   (*b* Carlton, Melbourne, 14 Feb. 1957), composer, music educator. He studied composition and music theory at La Trobe University with Jeff Pressing, Theodore Dollarhide and Graham Hair 1975–80, then worked as a tutor at the university

1980–85. He has been lecturer in composition and music craft at the Victorian College of the Arts since 1985. His compositions make strong links with the visual and performing arts and he has received over 30 major commissions from Elision, Pipeline, the Astra Choir, the Australian Chamber Soloists, and the Seymour group among others. His work has been broadcast and performed widely in Australia. Internationally his work has been included at the Warsaw Festival, the Tokyo Nova Festival, the Liverpool Festival, and the Under Capricorn Festival in the USA. His eclectic compositional style embraces such diverse materials as free atonality, improvisation, jazz, pop, the indigenous musics of South-East Asia, and most recently 'the new consonance'.

FURTHER REFERENCE
Recordings include *Krebs*, Larry Sitsky, pf (1988, Move MD 3066); *Carillon for Sacha*, Michael Kieran Harvey, pf (1994, Red House Editions RED9401); *The Quick or the Dead*, Melbourne String Quartet (1994, Move MD 3143); *Under Simple Stars*, Mardi McSullea, alto fl, with electronics (1994, Canberra School of Music, CS1718). His writings include: 'Notturno', *New Music Articles* 2 (1982), 14–22; and 'Accessibility and Innovation: Are They Mutually Exclusive?', *SA* 36 (1992–93), 14–16. See also Pauline Petrus, 'Introducing Mark Pollard', *Soundscapes* Issue 8 (Sept.–Oct. 1994), 44–6.   PAULINE PETRUS

Pommer, Rolph (*b* Ipswich, Qld, 24 Nov. 1914; *d* Ipswich, Qld, 1980), jazz saxophonist. He went to Brisbane in 1932 and became active in dance bands. Leading the Premier Dance Band in 1937, he was with Frank ★Coughlan at Prince's in 1940, moving to Sydney in July that year. He played with Giles O'Sullivan (at the Booker T. Washington Club), Reg Lewis and Wally ★Norman (at the Roosevelt), and following work in Queensland and Wollongong, NSW, he went back to Sydney for work with Ralph Mallen. He was inactive from 1970. He died in obscurity, although idolised by his peers and reportedly described by American alto player Willie Smith as 'the best white alto player in the world'.

FURTHER REFERENCE
Recordings include *George Trevare's Jazz Group* (1945, Regal Zonophone G-24954 to G-24956). See also *OxfordJ*.
                                               BRUCE JOHNSON

Pompili, Claudio (*b* Gorizia, Italy, 12 May 1949), composer. Arriving in Australia in childhood, he worked as a telephone technician and played guitar in a rock band before commencing study in composition with Richard ★Meale and Tristram ★Cary at the Elder Conservatorium in 1979. He went to Italy in 1984, attending classes with Franco Donatoni at Pescara and Salvatore Sciarrino at Perugia, returned to Australia in 1986 as musical director of Doppio Teatro, composing music for its productions, and has been lecturer in composition at the University of New England since 1987. Spanning theatre, electronic and

chamber music, he has had several commissions from Australian contemporary ensembles, and his music includes the sound-track for *Vandalism* (SA Film Commission, 1981), a String Quartet (1982/87), *Fan Tales* for tape collage (1986), *Song for Ophelia* for unaccompanied voice (1989) for a production of *Hamlet*, and *Lo spazio stellato si reflette in suoni* for baroque flute and percussion (1990).

FURTHER REFERENCE
His *Medieval Purity in a Bed of Thorns* has been recorded (1981, Canberra School of Music, CSM 4). See also *SA* 34 (Winter 1994), 26

Poole, Reg   (*b* Tatura, Vic., 24 Sept. 1944), country music singer. Learning the guitar from the age of 10, he appeared on Shepparton television with his band as a teenager, then worked as a dairy farmer. He signed with W&G, releasing a successful first album, *Country Music At Its Best*, in 1974. His Silver Eagle Country Band toured with Jimmy ★Little, Johnny Heap, Chad ★Morgan and others 1970–79. He has recorded for Selection since 1977, and continues touring, as well as running an entertainment agency and broadcasting on 3SR Shepparton. Particularly popular for his ballads of rough-riding, he has won three ACMA Golden Guitars.

FURTHER REFERENCE
Recordings include his albums *The Long Paddock* (1977, Selection PRH 701), *The Cradle To The Saddle* (1980, Selection PRC 708), and *Goin' Rodeoin'* (1978 Selection PRC 001). See also *LattaA*, 142–3; *SmithB*, 36.

Poppy.   Dance work by Carl ★Vine, choreography by Graeme ★ Murphy, first performed at the Theatre Royal, Sydney, by the Sydney Dance Co. on 6 April 1978. Exploring the life and art of Jean Cocteau, it was one of the first full-evening-length dance works to be created in Australia, and helped launch the careers of Vine and Murphy. Vine wrote an instrumental score for the first act, and for the second act an electronic soundscape to underpin Cocteau's drug-induced state of mind. *Poppy* continues periodically to be revived by the Sydney Dance Co., and has been performed by the troupe in Europe, the USA, and South America.   JOEL CROTTY

Popular Music

1. The Colonial Era to 1957. (i) Penal Colony to 1840s. (ii) The Gold Rushes to 1890s. (iii) Sound Recording and Broadcasting to 1950s. 2. Since 1957. Rock and Pop: (i) Early Rock and Roll. (ii) Responses to the Beatles, mid-1960s. (iii) Towards A Local Identity, 1970s–80s. (iv) The Influence of Radio, 1980s–90s. (v) From Local Market to Global Appeal.

The delivery of popular music to Australians has been evident from the first white settlement, with musical tastes tending to reflect Australia's changing social conditions and demography. A commercial imperative is usually evident in popular music: the wide popularity of the piano in Australia from the earliest years of the 19th century brought a need for a suitable repertoire, and musical arrangements for the drawing room or comical songs for the vaudeville stage were thus produced with all the hallmarks of the production line. The phonograph (with cylinder recordings) and gramophone (with disc recordings) appeared in goodly numbers in Australia in the 1890s, and sound recordings became a staple resource of the broadcasting industry, which commenced operation in Australia in the early 1920s. Broadcasting created an appetite for the products it displayed, and the common interests of the record industry and broadcasters brought the two groups together in commercial partnership.

Generally, popular music is linked to singing and to dancing, although music associated with work and ceremonial occasions can also achieve considerable popularity. Sometimes popular songs can take on the mantle of national songs, expressing and endorsing sentiments or beliefs that are widely felt. This is especially apparent during wars or at times when some cohesive force is needed to coalesce national pride. (See *Patriotic Music*)

1. The Colonial Era to 1957. (i) Penal Colony to 1840s.
The popular music of the white invaders of 1788 was British popular song and dance, including 18th-century folk-songs and airs from the pleasure gardens and from the popular theatre. Among the first arrivals, who would have had little to be cheerful about, each group established some sense of their collective identity in songs which expressed the things they shared, usually with new words being added to existing well-known tunes.

The social groupings for which popular music was a commodity included the colonial administration, the army, businessmen and, of course, convicts. The administrators, often with their family in residence, imported the mannerisms of their social class at home. Some degree of gentility was possible even in a penal colony, and pianos and music lessons were a part of the education of youngsters and a diversion for the older folk. The first piano was landed from the ship *Sirius* soon after the establishment of the settlement at Sydney during, in Roger Covell's words, 'Mozart's last years'. Within the army sent to supervise the building of the colony there was a clear hierarchy, based on rank, reflecting a variety of educational and cultural awareness. There was, of course, the need for ceremonial military music, and a band was an essential part of a military resource. It could be adapted to serve ceremonial or recreational ends, the parade ground, formal and religious occasions or Sunday afternoons in the park. Popular arrangements of parlour ballads and tunes from opera were common fare.

The convicts imported traditional tunes orally. Among prisoners the most literate and musically capable seem to have been Irish, many of them political prisoners, who nurtured the unresolved differences of Irish his-

tory in recollected melodies. Some, like Francis MacNamara ('*Frank the Poet*'), composed songs that entered the Australian folk tradition, such as his lament *Morton Bay*, which adapts an Irish tune to new, somewhat high-flown literary words about the convict's lot. There were also work-songs shared spontaneously, although these did not seem to have the wide dissemination and mass appeal necessary to be considered here. Later the convict songs were often filtered through the sensibility of parlour music arrangers. Irish, English and Scottish songs of ambiguous origin, most probably composed or adapted from less musically literate origins, found their way into published collections. Survival of the remnants of genuine folk music and the recollected composed popular music of late 18th-century Britain lingered in pockets where traditions were strong and where the popular music industry of the time found it difficult to reach or was irrelevant. The process of steady change in Australia, the colonisation of a complex collective folk memory made up of genuine folk and composed products, and the growth of its popular music market can all be charted. (See *Folk Music*)

By the 1830s a growing demand for concerts and musical support for a variety of non-military functions like religious and theatrical activities became apparent. Visiting musicians including the Irish composer W. Vincent *Wallace, in Australia to attempt to cure his tuberculosis, gave concerts. Early in 1836 Wallace conducted the band of the 17th Regiment in a concert of popular classics including the *William Tell Overture*. Wallace's most memorable tune, *Scenes That Are Brightest*, which he incorporated in his immensely popular opera *Maritana*, was probably written in Tasmania. The song returned to Australia from the UK after the premiere of his opera, taking a high place among popular songs of the mid- to late 19th century. It was not uncommon for operatic or semi-operatic repertoire by composers like Wallace or Balfe to cross into the parlour repertoire of popular songs and piano arrangements.

(ii) The Goldrushes to 1890s.
From the late 1840s there was a new mix of free travellers and settlers. Cities and inland urban centres developed rapidly, more money began circulating, and with the increased population and a rising level of sophistication in almost everything the service industries, including consumer goods, were in greater demand. The appetite for music, especially the commonplaces of the Anglo-Celtic mainstream, grew like everything else, providing markets that needed to be satisfied.

On the goldfields, music hall entertainers like Charles *Thatcher composed ballads for their own use on the stage. Familiar tunes like the *Lincolnshire Poacher* or *Villikens and his Dinah* were dished up with new, locally relevant words. Thatcher's songs can be heard recreated in the 1980s by Glen *Tomasetti. Thatcher would have had the services of a pianist and perhaps a small orchestra;

Tomasetti, characteristic of her time (1960s–80s), used a guitar. Popular as they may have been in Ballarat at the time of their composition, they quickly fell into obscurity, their revival predicated on historical interest rather than musical worth.

The discovery of gold created conditions conducive to the development of musical commerce. The consolidation of an urban ethos led to the development of a parlour culture: aspidistras, tasselled drapes and parlour pianos. If Oscar ★Comettant, a French music critic who came for the 1888 Centennial Exhibition, was correct, there were over 700 000 pianos in Australia by that year. Popular music in the home was focused around the piano. In the best of Australia's surviving silent films, *The Sentimental Bloke* (1919), Doreen is first noticed by her husband-to-be while singing *The Curse of An Aching Heart* accompanied by a parlour upright. Singing and playing were valued as genteel accomplishments, especially among women. Knowing and understanding the mannerisms which reflected that gentility signalled attainment.

The taste for the piano and its repertoire had several sources. There was the innate musicality of the Irish, anglicised (together with traditional Scottish and Welsh music) as a somewhat exotic specimen to the early Romantic imagination but equally appealing to the genuine Celt. The nationalistic ballads created by Thomas Moore or Robert Burns and the songs drawn from immensely popular ballad operas such as *Maritana* and *The Bohemian Girl* can be found in numerous 19th-century editions designed to be sung at the piano. Songs like *I Dreamt I Dwelt in Marble Hall* and *Scenes That Are Brightest*, which still occupy an ambiguous position somewhere between light opera, folk-song and popular ballad, could be purchased, and the scores of operas reduced to selections for piano. As well as becoming a prestigious symbol for the culturally and socially upwardly mobile, the piano also occupied the increasing hours of leisure, even for the moderately accomplished.

The popular music of marginalised minorities like the large Australian Chinese population had little impact on the cultural mainstream. The music of one goldfields family of Greeks is in many respects a paradigm: Giorgios Morfesis arrived from Ithaca in 1852 in search of gold; later he became the cantor of Australia's first Greek Orthodox church, so it is likely that he recalled and sang songs from his native Ithaca. In 1855 he married an Irishwoman, Bridgit Coal, from the goldfields at Castlemaine, Victoria. Their daughter, Anna Morfesis, married Daniel Dwyer 20 years later and their grandson John Dwyer inherited Irish tunes; in the 1950s his repertoire revealed no traces of his Greek roots.

To these influences must be added, from Dublin after 1846, the extraordinarily pervasive mission of the Sisters of Mercy who taught young women to play. Their missionary work was supported by teaching music to those of their faith and to any others who had the means to pay. The result was a blossoming of musically capable young women, many of whom found support for professional careers among the large Irish Catholic minority. Indeed, by the 1890s the Mercies had initiated the most important flowering of Australian Catholic culture. More than any other single group, they created an Australian musical culture that laid the foundations for some of Australia's first international musical successes. Their teaching generated skills in accompaniment and singing as well as a pervasive patina of Irish sentimentality and sentiment.

The Victorian English spirit and the same style of repertoire is exemplified in the very early sound recordings made in England by Hamilton Hill. Although he is best placed among the recordings artists of the early 20th century, the repertoire he recorded was innately 19th century. Born on the Bendigo goldfields in the 1860s, Hill became an international singing star during the Boer War, recording, among other things, *Good-bye Dolly Grey* and *She Was Only a Bird in a Gilded Cage. Stars of Hope* has all of the hallmarks of Victorian parlour repertoire which was popular in the last 20 years of the 19th century. Its chorus includes the following words:

> Though stars of hope are burning low, Dear
> And all the world is full of woe, Dear
> My heart will still be true
> To the end of the world, with you!

Hill and his wife Beaney Galletly were both vaudeville artists who enjoyed Australian and international careers. Like many other Australian popular singers who left Australia in order to establish careers overseas, he made no sound recordings in Australia.

The piano continued to focus an interest in popular tunes, but as the 19th century drew to a close its ascendancy in the parlour was challenged by the phonograph and its cylinders and later the gramophone and its discs. These machines radically changed the delivery of popular music. In the 20th century popular music was more usually delivered by sound recordings, later the radio, especially the networks sustained by advertising, and later still sound film.

(iii) Sound Recording and Broadcasting to 1950s. Hamilton Hill's recorded repertoire was essentially old-fashioned, but he was no less popular than the large number of Australians who became internationally conspicuous in the new century. Other Australian vaudevillians who became prominent, especially on the vaudeville circuits in the UK and who made large numbers of popular recordings of songs and recitations, were Albert ★Whelan, Florrie ★Forde and Billy ★Williams. Their songs usually derive from the English and American music hall, reflecting current fashions as these appeared. Generally speaking, vaudeville songs tended to be humorous and to have easily remembered choruses; they adapted very well to the two or three minutes of playing time available on a record and were almost always recorded in Europe. Some Australians, like

Leonard Nelson, occupied a significant place at home, recording in Australia for the local recording companies on primitive wax cylinder. Nelson's *Good-bye Melbourne Town* (like his *Good-bye Sydney Town)* was popular on the stage and was recorded at least once in the early 1900s.

Parlour repertoire was more likely to be sentimental. Songs like those by Clifton E. Boanas, which included *Daffodils From My Garden, A Glance* and *Butterflies And Lilac,* are characteristic of the genre. Often Boanas' songs were presented to the audience for whom they were created by singers who were currently popular. Many were published with a prominent acknowledgment that they had been 'Sung by Miss Amy ★Castles'. Castles, who was vigorously promoted by the Catholic Church to displace the 'Protestant tart' Nellie Melba, needed to be successful in opera to achieve the goal set for her, but her opera successes were very few and she was more comfortable with the concert platform and simple, homely, popular ballads.

During her 1909–10 Australian concert tour with the bass baritone Peter ★Dawson, Castles was welcomed in venues where operatic and concert singing was rarely presented by visiting celebrities. The tour commenced in Melbourne and finished in the tiny country town of Nhill. The *Yarrawonga Chronicle* found Amy Castles was 'not superlatively great and she unnecessarily accentuated her weak points': 'It would have been a gracious concession had she sent the audience to their homes with the strains of some popular ballad—such as 'Home, Sweet Home'—thrilling their susceptibilities, but she missed her opportunity'. Earlier the *Chronicle* had noted that Dawson was already well known in Yarrawonga, having been regularly heard there on gramophone records.

★*Home, Sweet Home* is popularly associated with Nellie Melba, who used it in performance and recorded it. Important as the song might have been to Melba, she probably had it in mind when she told Dame Clare Butt that, in Australia, you should 'sing 'em muck. It's all they understand'. Melba was certainly not above presenting popular material in her programs regardless of what she thought of it privately; she included a number of parlour Scottish and Irish songs in her standard concert and encore repertoire and in Europe recorded a number of these.

The earliest evidence of sound recordings being made in Australia is from 1879, when Alexander Sutherland used a tinfoil phonograph based on the published sketches of Thomas Alva Edison's 1877 experiments and patents. Sutherland's experiments were modestly successful. Tinfoil cylinder recordings tended to be destroyed when played back. Replication of an event was possible, but not usefully repeatable beyond one or two playbacks. By the mid-1890s the Edison cylinder record/playback cylinder machines were available in Australia and Australians were making domestic recordings. Some of these were of popular songs, or songs which had been locally composed. Australian companies produced small numbers of cylinders for sale, and for a time in the 1920s there were record-pressing plants such as those of the Vocalion and Brunswick companies making discs from imported masters. By 1926 Australia had factories which were outposts of what would later become multinational sound-recording industries. They were linked to recording studios and had the latest microphone technology; they pressed small numbers of local products as well as substantial quantities of material recorded in America and Great Britain.

Changing musical styles and tastes can be charted among the recordings of Australian performers. Most Australians recording for the mass popular market had to do so in Europe or America, and the earliest recordings of international Australian stars were made in the decade 1900–10. These reflected diverse styles: American 'nigger minstrels', usually white men in black face, were popular on Australian vaudeville circuits in the later part of the 19th century. Some of Whelan's recordings, such as *The Preacher And The Bear,* are a late flowering of this repertoire. Williams recorded parodies of contemporary ragtime songs in 1910, including *Ragtime Wedding.*

In the 1920s American jazz recordings and lengthy visits by American dance bands began to influence local musicians. Jazz was quickly associated with dance, and domestic record-players were advertised (even on film) as being innovative supports for entertaining at home. Guests could be invited to a dance in the home of a record-player's owner. This signalled the gradual decline of the significance of the parlour piano. The lyrics for Williams's 1911 song *Let's Have A Song Upon The Gramophone* describing the beginning of the process of change, becomes an inadvertent valedictory anthem for the piano.

> They were having a merry party in the dear old home
> And everybody shouted with delight
> Songs that were new and some old ones too
> It was a very merry Christmas night
> Dear old Granddad seated in the corner
> Shouted in a manner very strange
> Come on Hannah! Scrap the old 'piana'
> I'll tell you what to do now for a change
>
> Let's have a song upon the Gramophone
> That Billy Williams sings so grand.

Williams re-recorded this song in adaptations for a number of companies; *Let's Have a Song Upon the Gramophone, Lets Have a Song Upon the Pathephone, Lets Have a Song Upon the Homophone* and so on. It is a valuable indicator of the pervasiveness and variety of sound recording players after two decades of its development.

Jazz and jazz recording grew after the 1920s and can be detected in various examples of its manifestations in each decade since that time. It is a multifaceted genre with many different voices: Ray Tellier, for example, began a long run at Melbourne's St Kilda Palais de Danse in mid-1925; his band became more widely influential as a result of the sound recordings it made. These included *Yes Sir! That's My Baby*, a tune redolent of the Charleston era and

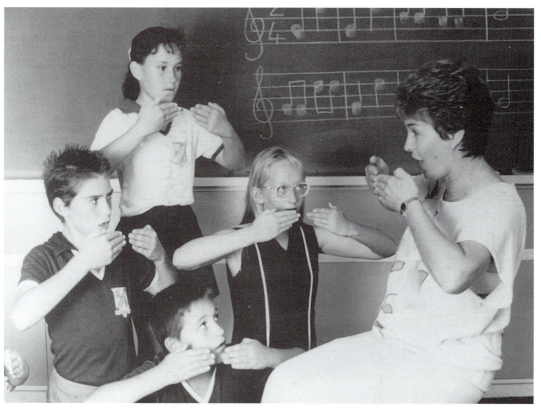

The Kodaly pedagogical approach has strongly influenced music programs in state primary schools, especially in NSW and Queensland. (Courtesy Department of Education Qld)

In tropical far north Australia, the Queensland Education Department's instrumental program and the statewide competition Fanfare has stimulated growth of many school bands and ensembles. Players from Cairns State High School Orchestra, winners of the 1996 Fanfare. (Courtesy Department of Education, Queensland)

Most recently completed of Australia's public music school buildings, the Queensland Conservatorium building, at the Southbank arts complex on the Brisbane River.

(Queensland Conservatorium)

MUSIC SELLERS

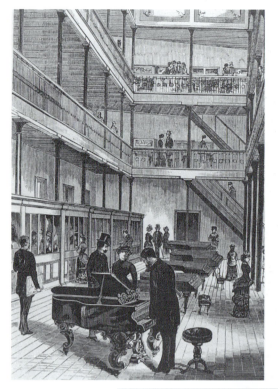

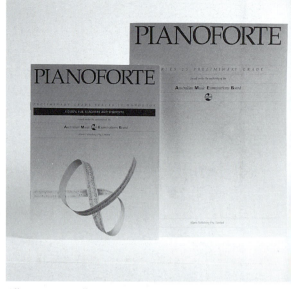

Allans Music, Melbourne, produce the AMEB editions and commentaries universally used by Australian music students. (AMEB)

Left: Palings Music House, Sydney, 1883
(*Illustrated Sydney News*, 7 July 1883)

MUSIC THERAPY

Melbourne music therapist Dianne Allison at work with a visually impaired child.
(Courtesy Dianne Allison)

J.C. Williamson sporadically presented seasons of opera in their early years. *Parsifal* in 1906 was one of their most ambitious ventures. (General Reference Library, State Library of NSW)

The National Theatre Movement Opera Co., Melbourne, was the first company to present regular all-Australian casts. Marjorie Lawrence starred in *Aida* in 1951. (Performing Arts Museum, Melbourne)

The Australian Opera (established 1956, now Opera Australia) is Australia's only year-round professional opera company. Occasionally it has fully staged works by Australians, most notably Richard Meale's *Voss*. Voss (Geoffrey Chard) passes Judd (Robert Eddie) and Mrs Judd (Irene Waugh).
(Opera Australia)

Marie Carandini (*right*), with three of her singing daughters. (Mitchell Library, State Library of NSW)

Nellie Melba, 1892 (State Library of Victoria)

Gladys Moncrieff with Robert Chisholm in Varney Monk's *Collits' Inn*, 1934.

Joan Hammond entertains the British troops in 1941 during World War II. (Courtesy Peter Burch)

Marjorie Lawrence as Brünnhilde in her debut with the Metropolitan Opera New York, 1935.

Joan Sutherland (Opera Australia)

Donald Smith
(John Hearder, courtesy Opera Australia)

Dennis Olsen
(Opera Australia)

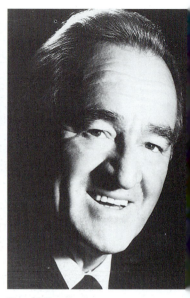

Ronald Dowd
(Opera Australia)

June Bronhill (Opera Australia)

Neil Warren-Smith (Opera Australia)

Marie Collier (Opera Australia)

Marilyn Richardson (Opera Australia)

Yvonne Kenny (Jenifer Eddy)

Bernard Heinze and the first Melbourne Symphony Orchestra at Wilson Hall, University of Melbourne, 1934.
(University of Melbourne)

Sidney Myer, founder of the Myer department stores, whose
patronage helped the Melbourne Symphony Orchestra survive
and develop. (University of Melbourne)

Hobart Symphony Orchestra with conductor J. Glanville Bishop, at the Theatre Royal, Hobart, 1932–33.
(Courtesy J.S. Luckman)

Donald Scotts hangs out his washing on Townsville Railway Station during the Queensland Symphony Orchestra's annual train tour of far north Queensland, c.1960. (ABC Document Archive)

Darwin Symphony Orchestra on a floating stage at Katherine Gorge, NT, conducted by Martin Jarvis, 1990.
(Darwin Symphony Orchestra)

Australian Chamber Orchestra, with leader Richard Tognetti (*front*), 1995. (Greg Barrett, courtesy Australian Chamber Orchestra)

Waltzing Matilda in the Harry Nathan manuscript, one of several sources.
(Mitchell Library; State Library of NSW, courtesy Thérèse Radic)

An early postcard edition of *Advance Australia Fair* with, on the reverse (*below*), the copyright claim of 1915 by Peter Dodds McCormick. (National Library of Australia)

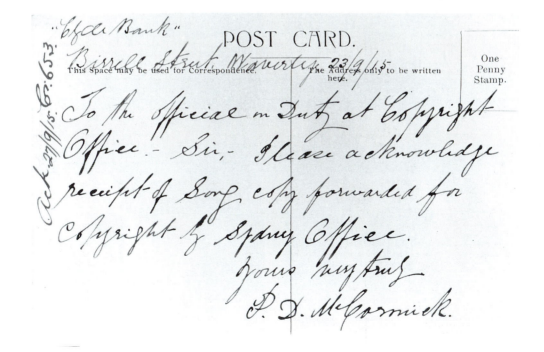

PERFORMERS

Violin: Johann Kruse, *c.*1890 (Latrobe Library Picture Collection)

Violin: Alberto Zelman Jr, *c.*1901 (Don Fairweather)

Violin: Alma Moodie, *c.*1930
(Schloss Wernigerode, Institut für Kunst und Kulturgut, Wernigerode, Germany)

Violin: Ernest Llewellyn
(Antoine Kershaw, courtesy Ruth Llewellyn)

Piano: Nancy Wier, 1970 (ABC Document Archives)

Piano: Isador Goodman, 1962 (ABC Document Archives)

Piano: Eileen Joyce, 1948
(Janet Jevons, courtesy ABC Document Archives)

Piano: Lindley Evans, 1940
(ABC Document Archives)

PERFORMERS

Piano: Stephen McIntyre
(James McFarlane, courtesy ABC Document Archive)

Piano: Roger Woodward
(Courtesy Carmel Gammal)

Piano: Geoffrey Tozer
(Annita Keating, courtesy Edgley Ventures)

French Horn: Barry Tuckwell (Courtesy Michael Shmith)

Trombone: Simone de Haan

Classical guitar: John Williams, 1996. (Julian Nieman, courtesy Harold Holt, London)

Johnny O Keefe and the Dee Jays (Courtesy Glenn A. Baker)

Col Joye, c.1961 (Courtesy Glenn A. Baker)

The Bee Gees (Courtesy Glenn A. Baker)

Billy Thorpe and the Aztecs, 1965 (Courtesy Glenn A. Baker)

Johnny Farnham, 1968 (Courtesy Glenn A. Baker)

Normie Rowe (Courtesy Glenn A. Baker)

John Paul Young (Courtesy Glenn A. Baker)

Skyhooks (Courtesy Glenn A. Baker)

Jimmy Barnes (Courtesy Glenn A. Baker)

Sherbert, 1977 (Courtesy Glenn A. Baker)

Little River Band, 1975 (Courtesy Glenn A. Baker)

Midnight Oil (Courtesy Glenn A. Baker)

Tommy Tycho, pianist, conductor (Tommy Tycho, *Music Maestro Please: The Tommy Tycho Story*, Brolga Publishing)

Simon Gallaher, singer
(David B.Simmonds, courtesy Opera Australia)

RADIO AND MUSIC

Radio stations employed broadcasting orchestras from the outset. Here Bertha Jorgensen (*far left*) leads a broadcast ensemble, *c.*1926. (Courtesy Don Fairweather)

A full-size radio broadcast orchestra for the Australian Broadcasting Company under Percy Code, *c.*1929.

Triple J was founded to promote new Australian rock music: Roy and HG presenting *This Sporting Life*.

RECORDING COMPANIES

Editions L'Oiseau-lyre (Lyre-bird Press) made the first long-playing records in Europe (from 1950). Its Australian founder, Louise Dyer (*rear, left*), listens as her husband Geoff Hanson (*left, front*) supervises a recording session in London. (Courtesy Margarita Hanson)

Michael Gudinski founded Mushroom Records in 1972 to champion Australian rock artists. (Andrzej Liguz, courtesy Mushroom Records)

of a musical style that would become pervasive at first on record. (See *Jazz*)

By the late 1920s infant radio broadcasting stations were established, such as that by an eccentric English inventor and entrepreneur, Noel Pemberton Billing; his station at Brighton in Victoria was 3RPB (Radio Pemberton Billing). Pemberton Billing also made and marketed sound recordings, most of them dance music or jazz, under the World Record (Wocord) label.

The arrival of the 'talkies', the development of the movie musical, together with the gradual decline of the Australian film industry after about 1920 and the growing demand for regular new films, led to the influx of large numbers of American films. From the 1930s onwards Australian audiences relied less on the traditional mixed musical and comedy programs of vaudeville, creating a growing market for films. Vaudeville/variety declined as the movies grew in stature and cinemas proliferated. The first generation who grew up with cinema readily assimilated film culture into their lives, making weekly visits to the movie palaces; their children were more rapacious. Supplying the demand was not difficult. Large numbers of films could be readily imported, and imported culture overtook evolving, more indigenous forms of cultural expression. The local films from this period now appear shallow and parochial, lacking the sophistication evident in most of the expensive products of American and European studios. Recordings lifted from film sound-tracks played on the numerous and constantly improving sound recording machines were supplemented with Australian-made cover versions of popular recordings from overseas. By the time of World War II Australian entertainment had been thoroughly Americanised. Singers like Marjorie Stedeford skilfully copied the prevailing musical fashion without adding much to it. Her version of *Blue Skies* recorded in the 1940s is warmly and competently performed but not distinguishably Australian.

In the later part of 1926 factories at Homebush in Sydney began to record and manufacture substantial quantities of sound recording using the recently developed electrical recording process. After a shaky start in which a very small percentage of Australian performances were considered good enough to publish, Australian Columbia and Regal Zonophone labels soon established a strong representation for Australian artists in record catalogues. Australia demonstrated that it could produce international hit songs in the old mode, and sheet music copies became a stimulus to artists who made recordings. May *Brahe captured the imagination of millions; in 1927 with the publication and first recording of her song *Bless This House*, she had the most recorded Australian song, eloquent testimony to the popularity of the piece.

The music of Jack *O'Hagan, especially such songs as *The Road to Gundagai*, had considerable currency between the wars and continues to be sung and recorded. In O'Hagan's only film appearance (1931) the composer as vocalist delivers several of his most popular songs including *By the Great Big Blue Billabong*. O'Hagan admitted that his musical models tended to be American and that he fashioned lyrics following American precedents. In *The Road to Gundagai*, searching for a word to pick up the sounds of words like 'Mississippi,' he found 'Murrumbidgee,' with the same number of syllables, and composed a ballad where the words have a distinctive Australian ring to them.

Other influences from America in the 1930s generated the roots of an indigenous country music. Tex *Morton was one of the earliest Australians to perform and record US repertoire and Australian modifications of the same themes. The mannerisms of the style, like the Irish folk-songs, the English parlour repertoire, and the nigger minstrel, remain closely attached to their point of origin in the USA. Australians like Smoky *Dawson adopted cowboy hats, Cuban-heeled boots, electric (Hawaiian) guitars and even the vocabulary of American country music. Evolution has caused modest changes in the style, but it is difficult to find peculiar Australianisms beyond place names and other local references. A little later hillbilly music, a popular manifestation of a genre from the south-eastern USA, became popular in Australia. Live acts, broadcasts and recordings like those of Bob Dyer's *The Martins and the Coys* attracted a large following. Dyer's hillbilly, a parodic character in his native America, seemed less of a parody in Australia. Yodeling, another imported American mannerism, was taken up by many performers, probably the most successful being the *McKean Sisters. Joy and Heather McKean married two other highly respected country singers, Reg *Lindsay and Slim *Dusty. Both Lindsay and Dusty were significant adaptors of American cowboy-style country music to an Australian setting, linking it to a powerful yearning for the country among urban audiences and to a equally powerful parochialism in the bush. (See *Country Music*)

During World War II there were more direct American influences on Australian popular music. Dance styles and songs were generally not even derivative. Australians heard original American or English performances or local cover versions that aped the sounds. Big bands provided good copies of what might be heard in London or California. Jim Davidson initially with his New Palais Royal Orchestra and later as Jim Davidson, and His A.B.C. Dance Orchestra, delivered high-quality cover versions of internationally popular tunes, like *Shuffle off To Buffalo*. During the hostilities of World War II he recorded examples of more jingoistic fare, playing, broadcasting and recording songs, including Jack O'Hagan's *Along the Road to Gundagai*.

In the early 1950s the 78 rpm shellac disc record-player had become a standard fixture in Australian homes. But it was radio in the first instance that introduced Australians to rock and roll. The music of Johnny *Devlin and Johnny *O'Keefe has its roots in the first airings of rock music in Australia. Television arrived in 1956 and helped to change the manner in which popular music was presented. Early variety programs like *Sunnyside Up* delivered musical programming which cast a backward glance over many earlier styles. Ron Lees sang standard ballads not unlike those of the late Victorian period. *The Holy City* was characteristic, as were Irish parlour songs like *Macushla*. Syd Halen and 'Honest' John Gilbert had a regular television act reminiscent of vaudeville from the period before World War I, but including a signature tune from the repertoire of Flanagan and Allen, *Underneath The Arches. Sunnyside Up*, although it was in many respects backward-looking, satisfied a market unlikely to find favour with programs targeting young audiences and proselytising the new rock idiom. It was a genre that took to television with a vengeance, and until rock and roll itself became the subject of nostalgic reinvention in American television's *Happy Days* and movies like *Grease*, it never looked back.

2. Since 1957: Rock and Pop.   The arrival of rock and pop music in Australia was a logical extension of the popular music tradition that already flourished in the dance halls and clubs, but its history is distinguished by its convergence with new marketing methods in the mass media—radio, television, recordings—and marked through them by a series of powerful public moments. The Top 40 format for radio stations, the 45 rpm single on the juke-box, and the television dance program transformed the marketing of popular music in the late 1950s and 60s. Later, a more liberal attitude to alcohol accompanied by the liberalisation of social life in general also produced in Australia a rich array of local rock and pop music venues that welcomed a vast number of voices. These included male pub bands as hotels and alcohol mixed with rock in the 1970s, a surge in women's participation in rock bands following mainstream acceptance of feminism in the late 1980s, the remarkable appropriation of regional Aboriginal sounds, images and voices, as well as the techno-beat of the dance club culture reflecting urban experience in the early 1990s.

In general the development of Australian rock and pop has been characterised by a reliance on adapting styles from abroad, notably the USA and the UK. Rock is identified with the immediacy of the live context; its core components rely on the use of strong rhythm patterns, a persistent beat, amplification of pre-existing popular music instruments such as guitar and drum kit, and a strong vocal and visual presence in a public arena. Pop derived its meaning from rock, but its transitory and ephemeral nature often made it the object of derision among advocates of the rock experience, who emphasised an audience and its relationship with the performers and their musical skills. Since the 1980s as the two have merged the distinctions seem less relevant.

(i) Early Rock and Roll.   It was in 1955 that Bill Haley and the Comets first challenged the prevailing class and cultural alliances of global popular music. Haley with the Comets, a white American band from country and west-

ern music, began bringing the black rhythm and blues styles to the mainstream audience, and had a certain success with *Shake, Rattle and Roll* in 1954. In 1955, with the likes of Perry Como, Bing Crosby and Frank Sinatra controlling the airwaves with songs like *White Christmas,* the film *Blackboard Jungle* introduced Haley's *Rock Around the Clock,* the first rock and roll song to reach No. 1 in the US charts. The film cemented the relationship between popular film, music and youth events; in quick succession the films *Rock, Rock, Rock* and *Don't Knock the Rock* appeared, and seemed to confirm the sense of excitement and euphoria that life in the postwar years offered youth, drawing on images which highlighted the bold colours of the American experience.

The dominant feature of Australian rock and roll in the 1950s was its beat, its fashions and its Americanisation of the youth experience. US-born entrepreneur Lee ★Gordon created a sensation in Australia with a tour by Johnnie Ray in 1955; he brought Haley and the Comets to Australia in January 1957. Huge crowds gathered, and the die previously cast for popular musical entertainment was broken: a new American model and style of music gained the upper hand. Gordon identified the similarity in interests between young people in Australia and in America, a task made easier because no Australian recordings in the rock and roll style were receiving radio airplay, while the American ones dominated the airwaves.

But if the nation was mostly peopled by naively insular settlers from Britain, as some accounts of Australia in these years suggest, rock music offered a view of a new world. Black American groups like the Platters toured Australia with Haley, and Little Richard toured in October 1957. Richard was supported by Johnny ★O'Keefe, now the rising star of Australian rock and roll. O'Keefe's had been a frank copy of American rock and roll; at least one account has him being booed as he made his way to the stage to support Little Richard in Sydney in 1957. But his song *The Wild One*, released in March 1958, can be identified as the moment of rock and roll's transition into mainstream Australia as a mass media expression. It was the first Australian recording to reach the Top 40 charts, and appropriated rock and roll as a local Australian youth experience and fashion. It was a moment that still reverberates.

The strength of the mythology surrounding O'Keefe as an icon of the late 1950s and early 1960s cannot be overestimated. Images of him caught in momentary pose as he screamed out *The Wild One* continued to appear every week in the 1980s and 90s in the credits for ABC TV's music television program *Rage*. O'Keefe and his first band the ★Dee Jays, and the slowly expanding live performance circuit in Australia's capital cities, had a special relationship with the unique Australian experience of rock and roll. The first Sydney artists also included the ★Joy Boys—the Jacobsen brothers Colin, Kevin and Keith, with Colin as lead singer taking the stage name of Col Joye. Both O'Keefe and Jacobsen became music entrepreneurs after their first flush of performance achievement, helping others to follow in their wake.

Television's introduction in 1956 produced more new images, with such shows as *TV Disc Jockey*, *The Hit Parade*, *Teenage Mailbag*, *Teen Time*, *Teen Beat*, *Cool Cats*. It was *Bandstand*, introduced on Channel 9 in 1958 and hosted by Brian Henderson, then *Six O'Clock Rock*, which went live to air on ABC TV on 28 February 1959 with O'Keefe and the Dee Jays as resident performers, that took rock and roll into suburban lounge rooms. Radio still had an impact, especially after the advent of the transistor and car radio and with disc jockeys such as Melbourne's Stan ('Stan the Man') Rolfe. Inducted into the Victorian Rock Foundation's Hall of Fame in 1995 for his contribution to Australian music, Rolfe played music being recorded by local and overseas groups before anyone else seemed interested. His impact was considerable.

The television shows served to reveal the large numbers of bands playing in the major cities in the late 1950s and early 1960s, including the *Delltones, the *Allen Brothers, Digby *Richards, Johnny *Devlin and Johnny *Rebb. Elvis Presley had his first No. 1 hit in Australia only in 1959, and from 1960 some artists like Lonnie *Lee borrowed from him the crooning style (if not the suggestive body movements) he had borrowed from black performers. Laurel Lea introduced a ballad style of performance, with Judy Cannon (*Laughing On The Outside*, 1959), Noelene *Batley (*Barefoot Boy*, 1960), Judy *Stone, and *Little Pattie (*He's My Blond Headed Stompie Wompie Real Gone Surfer Boy*, 1964) establishing a female presence that was not prominent in early images of rock and roll mediated by radio and television.

One feature of the new music in the late 1950s and the 1960s was the growth of suburban venues: town halls in the suburbs of all capital cities and regional centres became the locations of Friday and Saturday night youth dances. It was in these venues that some of Australia's longest-serving 'rockers' first performed for their contemporaries: Johnny *Chester, who moved to country music in the 1970s, started out in 1960 with the Chessmen in town halls at Preston and Coburg in suburban Melbourne. In the years 1964–72 Hoadley's *Battle of the Sounds (Battle of the Bands) provided an opportunity for a talent-quest approach to rock. The event signalled the gradual formation of a recording industry and the realisation that a system of artist selection was required to produce the rapid turnaround that made the high volume sales of pop music possible. Melbourne radio station 3UZ incorporated the competition into its Top 40 format.

(ii) Responses to the Beatles, mid-1960s.   Stereo recordings arrived in 1961, and pop instrumentals exploited it, the *Atlantics achieving a No. 1 hit with the single *Bombora* in September 1963. The new-found confidence in the leisure lifestyle was asserted in the Sydney surf music craze of 1962–63. But as the local industry sought to consolidate its position, the arrival of the Beatles (first released in Australia in 1962 but scarcely noticed until 1964) redrew the popular music map. The British popular music invasion of the USA was soon duplicated in Australia, with the proliferation of Merseyside sound appealing especially to Australia, with its close links to Britain. The *Easybeats became brilliant exponents of the Beatles genre, adopting the Beatles' look of suits, longish hair and their more reflective personalities. A massive hit with *Friday On My Mind* (1965) took the Easybeats to the top of the national charts, but a tour to England destroyed the band and their dreams. The Easybeats' songwriting duo Harry *Vanda and George Young then continued their association with Albert's Music and made a significant contribution to Australian popular music, writing songs and producing recordings for new artists into the 1990s.

After the enormous impact of the Australian tour organised by Melbourne entrepreneur Kenn Brodziak in 1964, the Beatles dominated the pop charts in Australia in the mid-1960s, and spelt disaster for O'Keefe, Lee and the early rock artists. Their influence on Australian popular music was twofold: first it established a substantial mainstream pop music market that has endured to the present day; and second it gave birth to numerous Australian bands modelled on them, including the *Groop, the *Twilights (featuring Glenn Shorrock, who later became lead singer of *Little River Band), the Flies, Normie *Rowe and the Playboys (the first Melbourne artists to achieve national chart success), Johnny *Young, and the *Loved Ones. One significant sideline of the Beatles' influence in Australia was a proliferation it caused of English male immigrants in Australian bands in the following years. Many of these went on to become major forces in reworked versions of English rock and pop in the late 1960s and the 1970s.

Another band inspired by the British invasion, Billy *Thorpe and the Aztecs, had a considerable hit with their version of the Rolling Stones' *Poison Ivy* in 1964, over a number of years transforming itself from a rock and roll group into a Merseyside, then a hard-rock band. Meanwhile, from the folk music revival in Melbourne the *Seekers found a more sedate, yet even larger mass audience for a folk-derived genre of acoustic instruments and powerful harmonies, with Judith Durham's congenial vocal style. They had the greatest international chart success of any Australian group for 30 years, their *Hey There Georgie Girl*, *A World Of Our Own* and other hits displacing even the Beatles in the UK charts for a time.

Magazines for the youth market also flourished in the mid-1960s, such as Sydney's *Everybody*, Adelaide's *Young Modern* and Melbourne's *Go-Set*. In these street-level publications newly affluent youth found its own voice, rather than having it represented by older entertainment values, as had taken place on television. They were followed in the 1970s by *RAM*, *Countdown Magazine* and *Rolling Stone* (Aust.).

(iii) Towards a Local Identity, 1970s-80s. The *Sunbury music festivals of 1972–74 mark the moment from which Australian rock began to assert a sense of local identity. At the same time music entrepreneur Michael Gudinski expanded his organisation of local band activities in Melbourne high schools and clubs to establish *Mushroom Records, partly in response to the inequalities imposed on Australian music by multinational record companies. Australian record companies had existed before this, but none with the intense commitment to rock Gudinksi established, built on an identifiable, inner-city rock music scene.

In the early 1970s liberalised liquor licensing laws and the discovery of hotels and universities as venues for rock provided a new vein of activity. A wave of pub-rock bands exploded on the Australian scene, moving from hotel to hotel, living a ritual that had become part of the lifestyle associated with rock music. As popular music it radiated immediacy and disposability; yet it had a harder edge. Pop, on the other hand, began to differentiate itself from rock. *Daddy Cool and *Sherbert began to record and release pop music with a strong sense of playfulness. It was decried as teen music by older and more serious musicians, who sought to establish rock as an art-form. The two blended in the remarkable inner-city scene in virtually every capital city in Australia, and pop and rock collapsed into a single Australian derivative that had its most profound impact in the music of *Skyhooks.

Skyhooks embraced the 1970s post-Vietnam War experience, in which opposition to American views of the world helped redefine an Australian consciousness. Their 1975 album *Living in the 70s* remains a landmark example of the assertive inner-city, pub-rock sound of the 1970s, while their marketing relied on costumes suggestive of androgynous sexual orientation. The genre became known as Oz rock and contributed to an inconclusive debate about 'the Australian sound' in rock music. Changed attitudes to sexual behaviour were part of the shift in values, although Daddy Cool with their song *Baby Let Me Bang Your Box* in 1971 and Skyhooks with *You Just Like Me 'Cause I'm Good in Bed* in 1975 discovered that rock could be the object of significant censorship campaigns. Youth was asserting itself against the tired mores of the mainstream, which in response took umbrage at youth's new-found freedoms. But nothing could stop the emotion-charged atmosphere of rock and pop in the 1970s; an entire generation had been excited by rock and roll and the Beatles, and pop music became the background hum for everyday mainstream life. The *Bee Gees, Helen *Reddy and Olivia *Newton-John all had huge international success.

Nineteen seventy-four brought with it the television program *Countdown, hosted by Ian 'Molly' *Meldrum and broadcast every Sunday evening on the ABC. As a national show it gave a broad overview of the developments in Australian pop music, providing enormous marketing opportunities for bands and ornamented with the visual imagery and associated lifestyle that colour television incorporated as a feature of pop music. Pop bands such as the *Ted Mulry Gang, Sherbert, *Mondo Rock, *Mental As Anything and individual artists like Newton-John, Mark Holden and Sharon *O'Neill appeared alongside star performers from around the world. Dozens of Australian musicians and performers received their early public exposure through the show, and the music video-clip was also tested and used effectively. Some commentators believe the program served as a precursor to later Music Television (MTV) programs. Meldrum provided the local edge for *Countdown*; as a result, the program was a uniquely Australian institution for entertainment and information for and about popular music until its demise in 1987. It consolidated new approaches to the relationship between television and music that were realised in unexpected ways in the 1980s.

Appearing as alternatives to the mainstream, punk rock in the UK and USA, an independent stance representing new voices of nihilism and assertive creativity, produced its local versions in Australia in 1976–77. Australian punk-rock almost matched the force of its English and American versions. Bands like the *Saints, *Birthday Party, *Radio Birdman, and tch,tch,tch ruptured the hold major record company practices had on rock, and broadened the options available to local artists for expression and their careers. The punk explosion assisted the establishment of independent record labels such as Missing Link, Au Go-Go, Mushroom, Waterfront and Regular. Within the pub-rock scene it encouraged innovation, coupled with a keen sense among Australian popular musicians that they wished to claim social space of their own. The music of *AC/DC was similar, using the songwriting talents of Bon Scott and the guitar virtuosity of Angus Young to present a local version of heavy metal; their string of consistently high-selling albums *TNT* (1976), *Dirty Deeds Done Dirt Cheap* (1976), and *Highway to Hell* (1979) convinced Australian supporters of local music that rock and pop could be exported to the rest of the world. Vanda and Young provided songwriting and managerial experience that carried AC/DC into the 1990s in the Australian and international scene. *Rose Tattoo followed a similar trajectory, if without the same longevity.

The most successful Australian artist recently associated with the trend to television-based music marketing is Kylie *Minogue, who appeared as Charlene in the television soap opera *Neighbours*. In 1985 she signed with Mushroom Records and released her first single in Australia, *Locomotion*, in 1987. Known in the UK as the 'Singing Budgie', she and her songs were the incarnation of pop: vacuous, appealing, disposable, simplistic. Nevertheless, sales of her records in Australia, the UK and Japan since her introduction into the pop music scene total nearly 13 million albums and 11 million singles. Her success as a vehicle for selling recordings was almost matched by her male counterpart from the same television series,

Jason ★Donovan, and they were followed by an array of others launched by television soap operas and light entertainment shows, including Toni Peron, Craig McLauchlan and Dannii Minogue.

Largely as a consequence of punk and its immediate offspring new wave, alternative music became popular. In the 1980s this included funk-influenced bands like ★Hunters and Collectors; industrial noise bands like ★Scattered Order; performance art and fringe bands like ★This Is Serious Mum; ambient rock like ★Not Drowning, Waving; and reggae-influenced bands like ★Jo-Jo Zep and the Falcons. The Australian local image and identity meant that some preconceptions about rock and pop as global forms could no longer be applied so simply. John ★Farnham became a substantial star in 1986 with the single *You're the Voice*. His albums *Age of Reason*, *Whispering Jack* and *Chain Reaction* became No. 1 sellers in Australia, while he made little impact on the music scene beyond. Similarly, former ★Cold Chisel lead singer Jimmy ★Barnes had a string of six top-selling albums but little success overseas.

(iv) Influence of Radio, 1980s and 90s. Australian commercial radio has regularly been severely criticised for its inability to play new and locally produced music. Most of the criticism in the 1990s has been directed at the 'classic hits' format, which plays music from the past, decade by decade. The sound is predictably dated, and Australian bands are swamped by 'classics' from overseas. This is not unrelated to the demise of radio's quota for Australian music content which, first introduced in 1942, served to provide a protective apparatus to assist the promotion and development of Australian music and culture. The quota was removed in 1992, when the Broadcasting Services Bill was introduced, to replace the *Broadcasting Act 1942*. A suitable regulatory mechanism for broadcasting to replace it is an ongoing focus for debate.

The failure of commercial radio to play new Australian music was ameliorated but not compensated for by government initiatives to cultivate public and community radio broadcasters. In 1993 HITZ FM began test broadcasting in Melbourne, playing new releases of dance club music; its audience of 15–18-year-olds was so vast that the commercial radio stations successfully appealed to the broadcasting regulator to remove the station from the airwaves. A similar station was licensed in 1994, but by that time it was clear that the established radio hierarchy was fragmenting and finding audiences that would no longer respond to the classic hits formats of commercial concerns.

The move away from mass media radio to niche audience stations had been under way for some time. From 1975 community radio stations played a wide selection of Australian music. Although their impact was not always recognised, there are numerous examples where the alternative sector established and built a fan base for bands, which then moved on to major exposure. In this respect, public radio gives access for Australian music to audiences that could not be reached through major commercial radio broadcasters. Similarly, the ABC's youth radio network, ★Triple-J, provided national access to new Australian music, expanding as the Federal Government released more transmitters for broadcasting in the mid-1990s.

Around CAAMA, in Alice Springs, an Aboriginal and Torres Strait Islander broadcast station was established in 1981 and became a model for other locally based indigenous broadcasters. A variety of indigenous broadcasters now operates. CAAMA was instrumental in recording and promoting the desert music of Aboriginal peoples, on cassette. ★Warumpi Band, ★Yothu Yindi, Sunrise Band, Jimmy ★Chi and Kuckles, and other bands which reached prominence in rock music received early support from CAAMA and equivalent stations. Local music also received a boost with the establishment of ★AusMusic in 1988, and the Victorian Rock Foundation and other state-based promotional organisations developed, sharing a commitment to providing government-subsidised access to popular music experience and related educational opportunities.

(v) From the Local Market to Global Appeal. The opportunities provided by public and government-funded radio for generating musical activity have been significant. Bands like ★Midnight Oil and ★INXS used radio stations like 3RRR in Melbourne and Triple-J in Sydney as stepping stones on their road to global exposure, and the relationship between the growth of the public radio sector and Australian popular music activity became a feature of the 1980s. Consequently major shifts in emphasis began to emerge: popular music became a vehicle for cultural identification along both local and global vectors, a contributor to national identity and development, and an export to global markets which attracted government support and involvement.

Key bands to make the transition from alternative to mainstream and global appeal using the public radio sector aside from Midnight Oil and INXS include ★Icehouse, ★Crowded House, Boom Crash Opera, Cruel Sea, and the ★Divinyls. Others with success abroad were ★Little River Band, ★Air Supply and ★Men At Work. Outside rock and pop other styles were also going global by the 1990s, including locally produced dance music, mixed by local and some British disc jockeys who had made their homes in Melbourne and Sydney. Dance clubs appeared in both cities, and the appropriation into the dance context of old musics from a variety of sources in a timeless musical amalgam set at 160 beats per minute had a huge impact. The ready availability of relatively cheap remixing sequencers encouraged the re-using or remixing of old recordings so that they could be 'sampled' in a single song against a computerised backbeat. Subsequently, rock music and its pub-rock form were challenged by dance and its associated 'rave' events, held to celebrate a rediscovery of the body as an object of pleasure.

The challenge to rock from the dance music scene was dramatic. The fracturing of the Australian rock and popular music world, combined with a proliferation of public radio (there are plans for up to 200 stations by the end of the 1990s) produced new formations. These included such annual events as Big Day Out, which focused on bringing alternative music from overseas and Australia together for a day-long celebration of youth culture. Moreover, overseas stars now make Australia a key destination in their world tours, bringing further pressure on local live music performance.

However, new styles of rock music did emerge, encouraged by the nationalist political orientation of bands like Midnight Oil. Aboriginal music, which had arrived in the mid-1980s, gained power in the mid-1990s. The initial impetus of Aboriginal bands came from ★No Fixed Address, Warumpi Band, ★Scrap Metal and ★Coloured Stone. By 1990 these bands had been joined by Yothu Yindi, Archie ★Roach, Kev ★Carmody, Mills Sisters and ★Tiddas, among others. While their recordings supported the indigenous struggle for Aboriginal recognition, in particular land rights, issues of cultural sovereignty and celebration were also a feature of their music.

Yothu Yindi's 1991 album *Tribal Voice*, which featured the single *Treaty*, stands out as the landmark album. It can also be viewed as the defining moment of the local–global interaction in Australian rock and pop. After nearly 40 years of rock and pop music in Australia, generic definitions became more unstable than ever, as traditional music from Aboriginal Australia was remixed using dance floor rhythms. The international appeal of Yothu Yindi's sound, coupled with the band's numerous tours, suggests that Australian popular music will continue to operate more strongly than ever along its two vectors of apparently contradictory activity—toward the local market and towards export into the global community.

See also *Charts; Country Music; Folk Music; Jazz; Music Hall; New Country; Vaudeville.*

FURTHER REFERENCE
(i) To 1957
BrisbaneE; DPA; MonashB; GuinnessP; IrvinD; MoresbyA.

A bibliography of Australian popular music is in *SnellA*. Many early popular songs are edited with commentary in *RadicT* and *RadicS*. A discography for Australian music is *Australian Record Buyers' Guide*, 4 vols (Sydney: ARIA, 1995). Many references to popular musicians 1911–65 appeared in *AMN,* an index to which is *MarsiI*; since then short articles have appeared in *APRAJ* and since 1991 research articles have appeared in *Perfect Beat.* See also:

Harrison, Tony, comp., *The Australian Film and Television Companion* (Sydney: Simon & Schuster, 1994).

Henderson, Don, *A Quiet Century: 100 Songs and Poems* (Nambour, Qld, Queensland Folk Federation, 1994).

Pinne, Peter, *Australian Performers, Australian Performances: A Discography from Film, TV, Theatre, Radio and Concert 1897–1985* (Melbourne: Performing Arts Museum, 1987).

(ii) Rock and Pop, 1957 to Present
BakerA; CoupeN; GuinnessP; McGrathA; SpencerW. A comprehensive discography for Australian rock music is *SpencerA*; for an index to Australian popular songs see *SnellA*.

Breen, Marcus, ed., *Missing in Action.* Australian popular music in perspective 1 (Melbourne: Verbal Graphics, 1987).

——, *Our Place Our Music: Aboriginal Music.* Australian popular music in perspective 2 (Canberra: Aboriginal Studies Press, 1989).

Coupe, Stuart and Glenn A. Baker, *The Year That Was: '85* (Sydney: Bay Books, 1985).

Coyle, Jackey and Rebecca Coyle, 'Aloha Australia: Hawaiian Music in Australia (1920–55)', *Perfect Beat* 2/2 (1995), 31–63.

Day, David and Tim Parker, *SA Great: It's Our Music. 1956–1986,* (Glandore SA: Day and Parker, 1987).

Hutchinson, Tracee, *Your Names On The Door: Ten Years of Australian Music* (Sydney: ABC, 1992).

Jones, Gavin, *The Australian Rock Information Guide* (Melbourne: RMIT, 1993).

Kent, David, comp., *Australian Chart Book 1970–1992: 23 years of hit singles and albums from the top 100 charts* (Sydney: Australian Chart Book, 1993).

McLean, David, comp., *Collected Stories on Australian Rock'n'Roll* (Sydney: Canetoad Publications, 1991).

Milsom, Wendy and Helen Thomas, *Pay to Play* (Ringwood, Vic: Penguin Books, 1986).

Rogers, Bob and Denis O'Brien, *Rock'n'Roll Australia: The Australian Pop Scene 1964–84* (Sydney: Cassell 1975).

Sturma, Michael. *Australian Rock'n'Roll: The First Wave* (Sydney: Kangaroo Press, 1991).

Walker, Clinton, *Inner City Sound* (Sydney: Wild and Woolley, 1982).

——, *The Next Thing* (Kenthurst, NSW: Kangaroo Press, 1984).

Zion, Lawrence, 'The Impact of the Beatles on Popular Music in Australia 1963–66', *Popular Music* 6/3 1987.

JEFF BROWNRIGG §1;
MARCUS BREEN §2

Port Augusta, pop. (1991) 13 201. City at the head of Spencer Gulf, south-eastern SA. Founded in 1852, it is a rail terminus, a major electricity generator for the state, and service centre for the outback and coastal shipping. The Port Augusta City Band appears to date from the early years of the town; it was re-formed in 1901 and still functions. The Port Augusta Music and Arts Group presented musicals at one time; more recently a Caledonian Band, Gateway Swing Band and Overlanders bush band have flourished. An annual country music weekend began on a small scale in 1993 and is growing, and the annual Beyond Festival began in 1995, presenting an array of cultural events for the three Spencer Gulf cities (Port Augusta, Port Pirie and Whyalla).

Port Fairy, pop. (1991) 2467. Headland town on the mouth of the Moyne River, south-west of Melbourne, Victoria, established 1835 (as Belfast). Originally a whaling station, it now harbours a fishing fleet and is a regional agricultural centre. An organ was installed in St John's Church in 1909. Since 1987 the town has played host to the annual Port Fairy Festival (directed by Michael Easton) each March, which brings artists and an audience from across the state.

Port Jackson Jazz Band grew out of a band founded in Sydney by trombonist Jack Parkes in 1944, though by 1948 all personnel had changed except Ken *Flannery. Significant new members were Ray *Price and Jim *Somerville. The band established a public reputation in March 1948 with concerts at the NSW Conservatorium of Music, which also gave impetus to the jazz concert movement in Sydney. A rural tour ended disastrously, with the band breaking up in Brisbane; Flannery re-formed the band in Sydney, which was rejoined by Somerville in 1949, but the band again became inactive by the end of 1950. After occasional reunions, it was re-formed again in 1955 and remained in more or less continuous existence, albeit with changing personnel, until 1962.

It was Sydney's most celebrated jazz group, with residencies at the Ling Nam restaurant, for sections of the band at the Adams and Macquarie Hotels, for ball seasons at the Empress, and playing support for visiting musicians including Dizzy Gillespie and Coleman Hawkins. The band has subsequently been re-formed for special concerts, as at the Katoomba Festival (1965) and residencies such as at the Stage Door Tavern under the leadership of Dick *Hughes, and as a quartet at the Mosman Rowing Club under Flannery and Somerville. Ray Price also re-formed the band occasionally between 1985 and his death, and it continues to perform for occasional reunion concerts. It has proved the most durable thread in Sydney's postwar traditional jazz tapestry.

FURTHER REFERENCE
Recordings include *Jazzin' At The Con, the Port Jackson Jazz Band* (1957, Jazz Incorporated JL001); *The Famous PIX Sessions, Classic Australian Jazz from the Sixties* (1996, Australian Jazz Reissues AJR–001 A&B). See also *ClareB*; *OxfordJ*; Jack Mitchell, *Back Together Again, The Story of the Port Jackson Jazz Band* (Sydney: Fast Books [1995]).

BRUCE JOHNSON

Portnoj, Henry and Annie, singing teachers. In Vienna Henry had been an accompanist and vocal coach and his wife Annie was a singer; they fled the Nazi entry to Austria in 1938. Teaching in Singapore, with the Japanese invasion of 1942 they settled in Melbourne. After war service Henry established a teaching practice for singers, as well as teaching at the University Conservatorium 1957–59, and trained many young Australian singers to the highest international standards. Teaching as a team, Annie focused on technique while Henry, a soft-spoken man and superb accompanist, focused on musicianship. Moving to Sydney, after Annie's early death from cancer

Henry continued to teach and adjudicate for the ABC. Perceptive operatic teachers of a class uncommon in Australia in the late 1940s and 50s, the Portnojs produced a startling number of singers who went directly from their studio to major careers, including John *Shaw, Clifford *Grant, Neil *Warren-Smith, Jenifer *Eddy, Neil Williams, Robert Simmons, and Gregory *Dempsey.

FURTHER REFERENCE
Neil Warren Smith, *Twenty-Five Years of Australian Opera* with Frank Salter (Melbourne: OUP, 1983), 35–7.

Posselt, Alan (*b* Melbourne, 11 June 1944), sitarist, instrument-maker. His early musical career began as a performer and teacher of the classical guitar; he then studied sitar with Ustad Alauddin Khan (Maihar, India) in the late 1960s and Radhikha Mohan Moitra (Calcutta, India) 1971–82. As a composer, his music includes works for documentary film and dance, most notably works for Australian Dance Theatre, Sydney Dance Co., Ballet Rambert, Nederlands Dans Theatre and Den Norske Opera. From 1978 to 1992 he taught classical guitar and Indian music at the University of New England, Armidale, as well as devising educational programs for schools, universities and radio broadcasts. In addition to regular sitar recitals in India he has performed extensively in Australia and has made two solo sitar recordings. Through his long involvement with performance and teaching, Posselt has played an important role in propagating Indian music in Australia. He is now based in Adelaide.

ADRIAN McNEIL

Post, Joseph Mozart (*b* Sydney, 10 Apr. 1906; *d* Broadbeach, Qld, 27 Dec. 1972), conductor. After studies in piano and oboe at the NSW State Conservatorium he played oboe as a teenager in Sydney orchestras and was chorusmaster for the Williamson Italian Opera tour of 1932, taking the baton for *Aida* at short notice. An unpretentious conductor with a fine technique, extremely capable in opera, he was with the ABC as a conductor from 1933, conducted for the Fuller Grand Opera tour (1935), and the ABC Melbourne Symphony Orchestra and Wireless Chorus (1936). After war service he was assistant conductor of the Sydney Symphony Orchestra and conducted for the National Theatre Movement Opera Co. from 1947, going to Britain for guest appearances with the BBC Symphony, Hallé and other British orchestras in 1950. He was founding musical director with the Elizabethan Trust Opera 1956–57, assistant music director for the ABC, and became director of the Sydney Conservatorium 1966–71.

FURTHER REFERENCE
His recordings include Raymond Hanson and William Lovelock's trumpet concertos, Sydney Symphony Orchestra (RCA); works of Alfred Hill, Robert Hughes and Ian Cugley (EMI), and Richard Meale's *Very High Kings* (World Record Club).

Poulsen, Hans (*b* Denmark, 1945), popular music singer-songwriter. Arriving in Australia in 1966, he briefly played guitar with the 18th Century Quartet, but left to concentrate on songwriting, producing *Rose Coloured Glasses* and *Jamie* for John *Farnham, as well as songs for the *Twilights, Larry's Rebels and Marcia and the Cookies. As a solo performer the first of his 10 singles was *Rocking Chair* (1968), and he had two hits in 1970 with *Boom, Sha La La* (1970), which reached No. 6 in the charts, and *Light Across The Valley* (1970), which reached No. 30. He released the albums *Natural High* (1970) and *Lost And Found* (1973), then he moved to the USA, but contracted cancer, which affected his work for some years. His music was influenced by the San Francisco style of the late 1960s in its setting of texts of peace and love to gentle bluegrass-rock music. In 1981 he returned to Australia and has since recorded several albums of songs for children.

FURTHER REFERENCE
Recordings include *Rocking Chair* (1968, EMI), *Boom, Sha La La* (1970, Fable FB 029), *Light Across The Valley* (1970, Fable FB 029), *Natural High* (1970, Fable FBS A004) and *Lost And Found* (1973, Fable FBS A014). For discography, see *SpencerA*. See also *McGrathA*; *SpencerW*; *GuinnessP* III, 1982; *Age* 11 July 1981.

Power, Lawrence ['Lorenzo Poerio'] (*b* Adelaide, *c.*1900 ; *d* Adelaide, 20 Aug. 1963), tenor. Educated at Adelaide, he won the first Sun *Aria* in 1924, then studied with Peraccini in Milan, and made his debut in *La Favorita* at Lovere in 1926. Under the name Lorenzo Poerio, he appeared in various Italian opera houses 1926–32, such as with La Scala at Malta (1930–31) and with San Carlo, Naples (1931–32). He was at the New York Hippodrome 1933–34, and then on tour in the USA and Canada. A pure, natural lyric tenor of considerable power, he was a memorable Rodolfo and Faust, and his wide repertoire included roles in *Rigoletto*, *Boris Godunov*, *Madame Butterfly*, *Martha*, Rossini's *Moses*, and *Phoebus and Pan*. He returned to Australia in 1939 and appeared in ABC concerts, retiring because of ill health in 1945.

FURTHER REFERENCE
Obit. in *Advertiser*, 21 Aug. 1963. His recordings for HMV are not current. See also K.J. Kutsch and Leo Riemann, *Grosses Sängerlexikon* (Bern: Francke Verlag, 1987); *MackenzieS*, 151–2; *AMN* 30 (Jan. 1940), 11.

Power, Stella (*b* Richmond, Melbourne, 27 June 1896; *d* Melbourne, 16 Jan. 1977), coloratura soprano. While studying with Elise *Wiedermann and Mary Campbell at the Albert Street Conservatorium, she showed considerable promise as a coloratura and was championed by Melba, who arranged a concert debut at the Auditorium, Collins Street, in 1917, and appearances in the USA with the Philadelphia Orchestra and Boston Symphony Orchestra in the same year. She moved to London in 1918, where she made her debut as 'The Little

Melba' with the London Symphony Orchestra under Sir Landon Ronald at the Royal Albert Hall in 1919, then toured English provincial centres 1919–23, appearing in the Chappel Ballad Concerts, Queen's Hall, in 1922 and on tour with Jan Kubelik. She was with the John Murray Anderson operetta tours in the USA from 1924. With a pure tone and unusually wide range, she was unaffected on stage, as comfortable in operetta as in arias from Donizetti or Rossini. She settled in Australia in 1934, appearing in ABC concerts until the war, when she retired to family life.

FURTHER REFERENCE
Obit. in *Age*, 21 Jan. 1977. Her first recording was for Edison, then as 'The Little Melba' for HMV from 1918. See also Frank van Straten, 'Stella Power: The Little Melba', *Victorian Arts Centre Magazine* (June 1987), 21; *MackenzieS*, 132–3; *AMN* 6 (1917), 197; *AMN* 26 (Sept. 1935), 27.

Powning, Graeme (*b* Sydney, 1949), composer, oboist. He studied composition with Raymond Hanson and oboe with Guy Henderson at the Sydney Conservatorium, then studied composition with Nigel Butterley. Appointed lecturer in oboe at the Sydney Conservatorium in 1971, in 1972 he became principal oboe of the Elizabethan Symphony Orchestra, and currently he lectures in oboe at the Newcastle Conservatorium. He has written a considerable number of works, mainly solo and ensemble works for wind instruments, with a large proportion of these being for the complete range of double reeds. Many of these works are written in a light, jovial style with a sense of humour evident in many of their titles, such as *March of the Maudlin Mushrooms* (1993) for solo bassoon and *Flocculent Flummery* (1993) for solo cor anglais.

WORKS (Selective)
(Available through the Australian Music Centre)
Chamber 56 trios, ob, cor anglais (1968–93), 4 trios, fl (1969–89), Sonata, 2 bn (1969), Sonata, ob, cor anglais (1974), 4 trios, bn (1976–94), Quartet, cor anglais, vn, va, vc (1979), Quartet, 3 bn, contra-bn (1979), 5 trios for tpt, hn, trbn (1980–85), Quartet, 4 cors anglais (1980), Sextet, 2 cl, 2 hn, 2 bn (1981), *Octandre*, 8 ob (1981), *Handel on the rocks*, 2 ob, cor anglais, bn (1982), *Divertimento*, ob, ob d'amore, cor anglais, bn (1985), *The pink bassoon*, 4 bn (1985), *Halley's comet*, 2 fl, ob, cl (1986), *Intermezzo*, vn, pf (1986), *Bach goes to town*, 3 cl, b cl (1989), Sonata, cl, bn (1989), Sonata, fl, bn (1990), *A medley*, 8 sax (1992), Quintet, 2 tpt, hn, trbn, tba (1993) Sonata, 2 fl (1993), *Trombone trifles*, 4 trbn (1993), *Lateline lark*, 4 hn (1993), *Z Cars*, pic, side drum (1994).
Solo instrumental *Noah's prayer*, ob, nar (1981), Suite, bass ob (1983), *Improvisation*, alto fl (1985), *Fantasy on Sleeper's Awake*, cor anglais (1986), *Good Friday music*, cor anglais (1987), *Voyage around my cor anglais* (1987), *A Bach burlesque*, ob (1988), *Homage to Rodrigo*, cor anglais (1989), *Four off-stage solos*, tr (1992), *Una furtiva fagotto* (1993), *Pan's peregrinations*, fl (1993).

FURTHER REFERENCE
Recordings include Wind Octet, Melbourne Windpower (Move MD 3082); *Impromptu*, Richard Runnels, hn (Move 3106)
                                                                                        MELINDA J. SAWERS

Predatoras. Opera, words and music by William *Robinson, first performed at Melbourne on 10 January 1894.

Prerauer, Curt (*b* Landeshut, Silesia, Germany, 1901; *d* Sydney, 1967), music critic, pianist, conductor. After studies at Munich University and the Bavarian State Academy of Music under Hugo Leichtentritt, he was chorusmaster at the Oldenburg Opera in 1923 and the Essen Opera in 1924, then assistant to Leo Blech at the Berlin State Opera from 1925. Moving to London in 1933, he worked as a *répétiteur* for the BBC and accompanist on tour for Florence Austral, then came to Australia as conductor for Benjamin Fuller's Royal Grand Opera Co. in 1934 and settled. He conducted the Royal Philharmonic Society, Sydney, taught singing, and was music critic for *Wireless Weekly* and *Tempo.* He was in Europe as accompanist and manager for his wife Maria *Prerauer from 1950, then in Sydney as music critic for *Nation* and the Sydney *Sun,* from 1960. A seasoned operatic coach and a critic with taste born of first-class German training and experience, he also translated a number of Australian literary works into German.

Prerauer, Maria née Wolkowsky ['Marietta'] (*b* Sydney, music critic, columnist, soprano. After studying singing with Curt *Prerauer, she appeared as Giuletta in *The Tales of Hoffmann* for Gertrude Johnson's National Theatre Movement Opera Co. She married her teacher and went to Berlin in 1950, studied with Frida Leider and sang Marie in *Wozzeck* at Covent Garden in 1953. She sang Strauss's *Elektra* and other roles in European houses, but after a perforated eardrum returned to Australia in 1960, making her last appearance replacing the indisposed Joan Hammond at short notice as *Salome* for the Elizabethan Trust Opera Co. that year. She and her husband wrote joint music criticism for *Nation* from 1960, signed 'CM Prerauer'. She was music critic for the *Sunday Australian* in 1971, then music critic and columnist as 'Marietta' for the *Australian* from 1975 (arts editor 1977–91), and contributed to *Opera* (UK). A perceptive but often sharp critic, her gossip column was an unfailing source of reliable inside information in the arts; it was widely and gleefully read. Since 1991 she has written a column for the *Bulletin*.

FURTHER REFERENCE
Who's Who of Australian Writers (Melbourne: D.W. Thorpe, 1995); *Australian* 11 May 1991; *Age* 11 May 1991.

Pretty, Sharman (*b* Launceston, Tas., 12 June 1951), music administrator. After studying oboe at the Elder Conservatorium and at the Freiburg Hochschule für Musik, she played in ACME and as a recitalist and was lecturer in oboe at the Canberra School of Music from 1976. She was a project officer with the Australia Council Music Board from 1985, co-ordinator of studies at the NSW State Conservatorium 1987–88 and general manager of the National Music Camps Association (which she transformed into *Youth Music Australia) 1988–95. A tough, decisive and articulate administrator, her work is informed by high intelligence, considerable vision and a deep musical understanding. She is currently principal of the Sydney Conservatorium and chairman of the AMEB in NSW.

Price, Ray (*b* Sydney, 20 Nov. 1921; *d* Sydney, 5 Aug. 1990), jazz banjo player. He had guitar lessons from Charlie Lees, later concentrating on banjo in a lengthy, intermittent association with the *Port Jackson Jazz Band from 1947. He was a double bass player with the Sydney Symphony Orchestra 1950–56, and the National Ballet. Forming a trio in 1956 (later augmented to quartet), he played a lengthy residency at Adams Hotel until 1966, after which he concentrated on the school concerts he had inaugurated some years earlier. Using a broad cross-section of Sydney's jazz musicians, these provided several generations of schoolchildren with their first exposure to jazz. He retired with ill health in 1982.

FURTHER REFERENCE
Recordings include *Jazzin' At The Con,* the Port Jackson Jazz Band (1957, Jazz Incorporated JL001); *The Ray Price Qintet (sic), Jazz Party No 1* (1975, Dixie Record, RPQ-001); *The Famous PIX Sessions, Classic Australian Jazz from the Sixties* (1996, Australian Jazz Reissues AJR-001 A&B). See also *ClareB; OxfordJ.*
                                                                                        BRUCE JOHNSON

Price, W(illiam) G(eorge) (*b* Newport, Essex, England, *c.*1866; *d* Melbourne, 15 Jan. 1952), organist. Assistant organist at Ely Cathedral, where he trained under E.T. Chipp, Price received his BMus from Oxford University in 1886 and his DMus in 1895. He was later organist at St George's, Belfast, and Belfast city organist. In 1906 he was appointed Melbourne city organist, a post he held until 1930. He served on the staff of the University of Melbourne Conservatorium, teaching counterpoint, canon and fugue, and was well known as a recitalist throughout Australia. His programs included a mix of organ compositions and transcriptions and were much admired.

FURTHER REFERENCE
Table Talk, 13 Sept. 1906, 7; 14 Aug. 1930, 14.
                                                                                        JOHN MAIDMENT

Prima Donna, The. Comic opera in one act by Arthur *Benjamin (1933), libretto by J.C. Cliffe. First performed at the Fortune, London, on 23 February 1949 and in Australia by Intimate Opera Group SA in 1960. A vocal score was published (London, 1935).

Primrose, Edward (*b* Orange, NSW, 24 Oct. 1950), composer. After studying at the NSW State Conservatorium, he studied composition with Don ★Banks, Larry ★Sitsky and Donald ★Hollier at the Canberra School of Music and became lecturer in 20th-century music at Sturt College of Advanced Education, Adelaide. His works include Symphony No. 1, a Chamber Concerto, Trio Sonata, *Divertimento* (1985), *Genus* for vocal ensemble, piano and percussion (1985), and *French Suite*.

Prince Who Couldn't Laugh, The. Children's opera, music and text by Colin ★Brumby (1968), first performed at Brisbane in February 1969. Published by J. Albert & Son, Sydney, 1969.

Pringle, Harry Lempriere (*b* Hobart *c*.1870; *d* 23 Oct. 1914), bass. He studied at the Cathedral School, Hobart, and with Julius Stockhausen in Frankfurt. After six years of training, mainly in Germany, Pringle was engaged by Covent Garden, appearing there 1897–1900 in many Wagnerian roles. He also appeared there in *Fidelio*, *Lucia di Lammermoor* and *The Marriage of Figaro* with singers of the stature of Jean De Reszke, Pol Plançon and Lilian Nordica. During these years he toured the USA with Albani and Patti, also singing at the Met. Returning to Australia for the George ★Musgrove season of 1900–1, he greatly impressed local critics. Pringle was a soloist at the Federation ceremony at the Exhibition Buildings, Melbourne. After 1902 he made a number of sound recordings and appeared in at least one film, *The Lure of London*. In 1910 he created the role of Massakroff in the London production of *The Chocolate Soldier*.

JEFF BROWNRIGG

Pringle, John (*b* Melbourne, 17 Oct. 1938), bass. After work as a pharmacist, he won the *Sun* Aria and studied with Luigi Ricci in Rome, then joined the Australian Opera in 1967, making his debut as Falke in *Die Fledermaus*. He has appeared with the Glyndebourne Touring Company, the Victoria State Opera, various European houses, and in Los Angeles and San Diego, as well as in concert with ABC orchestras and the Orchestra of Paris. His roles include Beckmesser, Golaud, Comte de Nevers, Shadow in *The Rake's Progress*, as well as in operas of Mozart, Verdi and Britten. He was honoured with the AM in 1988.

FURTHER REFERENCE
Recordings include Nevers in Meyerbeer, *Les Huguenots*, Australian Opera (Pioneer PLMCD 00181); Liandro in Prokofiev, *Love for Three Oranges*, Glyndebourne (Castle Vision Video CV 12050); and Robert Storch in Strauss, *Intermezzo*, Glyndebourne (Castle Vision Video CV 12024). See also *CA* (1995–96); Roger Covell, *GroveO*.

Prior, Marina (*b* New Guinea, 1963), theatrical singer. While studying at the Melbourne State College, she was cast in the lead role of the Victoria State Opera's *Pirates of Penzance* (1983), and has since appeared in major musicals, including *Camelot*, *Cats*, *Les Misérables*, *Phantom of the Opera*, and *The Secret Garden*, as well as on television. She has an attractive stage presence with a warm, endearing voice.

FURTHER REFERENCE
Recordings include *Aspects Of Andrew Lloyd Webber* (Sony 472653–2), *Leading Lady* (Sony 469214–2) and *Somewhere: The Songs Of Sondheim And Bernstein* (Sony 478068–2). See also *CA* (1995–96).

Private. Television opera by Felix ★Werder (1969), libretto by Peter Rorke. Commissioned by the ABC, it was first performed at Brussels in 1970 and broadcast by the ABC on 7 November 1971.

Pro Musica Society. Vocal ensemble founded at the University of Sydney. Its origins are in the Coro da Camera, a vocal ensemble created by Donald ★Peart at the university in 1947. From 1953 to 1957 the society presented opera workshops, lunch-hour concerts and productions under Peart's direction, including Australian premieres of little-known Baroque works such as *Acis and Galatea* and *King Arthur* or contemporary works such as *The Rape of Lucretia*. A number of students and young performers who worked with the society went on to significant careers in specialist performance; the society consequently had an impact well beyond its modest setting.

Pryor, Gwenneth Ruth (*b* Sydney, 7 Apr. 1941), pianist. After studying at the NSW State Conservatorium she went to the Royal College of Music, London, winning the Hopkinson Gold Medal and Norris Prize in 1963. She made her Wigmore Hall debut in 1965 and settled in London, giving concerts as a soloist and in chamber music in Europe and the USA, and giving radio broadcasts. She has returned to Australia for ABC concert tours in 1977 and 1981, and now teaches at Morley College and the Royal College of Music.

FURTHER REFERENCE
Recordings include Mussorgsky's *Pictures at an Exhibition*, Schumann's *Carnival* and *Papillons*, Gershwin's Concerto and Malcolm Williamson's concertos, Gervase de Peyer, cl. See also Lyle Wilson, *Dictionary of Pianists* (London: Robert Gale, 1985); *International Who's Who of Music* (Cambridge: Cambridge Biographical Centre, 1995).

Psalmody. See *Anglican Chant*, *Church Music*.

Pseudo Echo. Synthesiser pop band formed in Melbourne (1982) by Brian Canham (vocals), Tony Lugton (vocals) and Pierre Pierre (keyboard, vocals, bass). Drummer Anthony Argiro joined in 1983 but was replaced by Vince Leigh (1985), and keyboard player James Leigh joined in 1984. Pseudo Echo appealed mainly to teen audiences and found Top 10 chart success with *Listening* from *Autumnal Park* (1983), and the singles *Don't Go* and *Love an Adventure* from *Love an Adventure* (1985). But it was their cover of *Funky Town* (1986) that brought their first and only chart-topping success. After recording the album *Race* in 1989 they disbanded.

FURTHER REFERENCE

Recordings include *Autumnal Park* (1984, EMI P 430008); *Love an Adventure* (1985, EMI EMX 430033); *Long Plays 83–87* (1987, EMI EMX 430048); *Race* (1989, EMI EMX 790983). See also *SpencerW.*

AARON D.S. CORN

Pub With No Beer, A.   Country music drinking song (1957) by Gordon ★Parsons after a Dan Sheahan poem. Based on the drinkers of Parsons' hometown pub, Taylor's Arm, near Mount Kalang, NSW, it was recorded by Slim ★Dusty, reaching No. 1 and remaining in the charts for 17 weeks in 1958 and reaching No. 3 in the English Hit Parade in 1959. Dusty quickly followed it with *Sequel to A Pub With No Beer* and *Answer to A Pub With No Beer*. One of the best-selling records in Australia's recording history, it can be heard in numerous Dusty albums.

FURTHER REFERENCE

Recordings include Slim Dusty's *Walk A Country Mile* (EMI CD 7971842) or *Beer Drinking Songs Of Australia* (EMI 7971882). See also *McGrathA*, 105.

Publishers of Music.   All of the largest music retailers in Australia have also acted as publishers. Altogether, Kenneth Snell's index of popular song lists more than 300 Australian publishers of music. Until 1900 most music was published at the composer's expense; in the first two decades of this century the publishing houses of J. ★Albert & Sons, Nicholsons, Palings, Chappell, and D. Davis & Co. were located in Sydney, while Melbourne publishing was dominated by Allans, along with Dinsdale and Lyons Music Store. Popular songs of the 1920s sold up to 100 000 copies. The rise in Australian publishing coincided with the height in popularity of the piano, when one Melbourne dealer reported selling 10 000 copies of a single piano piece. Thereafter sales have declined, but the Australian music publishing industry continues to be dominated by Allans.

Music was circulated among the early settlers of Australia in handwritten manuscript. In 1825 the music master of a Sydney regiment announced that the music for a set of quadrilles 'with proper figures adapted to it, for the Pianoforte, Flute or Violin as also for a full band . . . may be had in manuscript . . . by giving one day's notice. Prices 6s'. The first songs printed in newspapers appeared without musical notation, being set to familiar tunes. By 1826 William Moffitt (1802–74), a bookbinder, stationer and engraver with a business at King Street, Sydney, advertised

that he was able to provide music and account books ruled to any pattern. Francis ★Ellard published a *Minstrel Waltz* in 1836 which was popularly regarded as the equal of imported publications. Yet when the composer Isaac ★Nathan arrived in Sydney he found no printers able to typeset music to his requirements. In the preface to one of his early publications he announced that he had 'worked at my letterpress and music fount, nightly & daily, week after week, for at least twenty hours out of every four & twenty, setting up type of the whole of my musical works, with my own fingers, thus doing the duty of compositor & composer'.

By 1850 several publishers were able to print music. In Hobart, R.V. Hood and J. Walch & Sons printed songs on Australian topics, including *Our Own Tasmanian Home*. In 1854 H. Marsh & Co. announced in the *Illustrated Sydney News* that it had all the equipment from England for carrying on a publishing business, listing polkas, schottisches, waltzes, piano solos and songs in its catalogue. In 1855 the Sydney publishers Woolcott & Clarke published an *Australian Presentation Album* which included *Rain Drops in Australia*, with colour drawings of Willoughby Falls, North Shore on the cover. Their publication of a *City of Sydney Polka* included a list of songs, vocal duets, piano solos, quadrilles, polkas, waltzes and overtures, all published from their premises at George Street. The Australian album was their own idea, believing that 'a book filled with the original productions of our own artistes— is, I think, peculiarly happy, and one which the Australian public will readily appreciate'. The music-seller ★Palings published its first *Christmas Annual* in 1885, priced at one shilling and full of new and popular songs. It gradually became more substantial and more attractive: number 14, for Christmas 1896, included drawings of their premises in George Street and of Linda Falls, Katoomba, songs with words by A.B. Paterson and advertisements for pianos and teachers. In about 1881 the Melbourne firm of Nicholson and Ascherberg began publication of an *Australian Musical Magazine* of songs and piano pieces, priced at one shilling, which continued to 1907. In Sydney the retailers J. Albert & Sons took up publishing, as did the Adelaide retailers Cawthornes.

In Victoria a *School Paper* was regularly published from 1895 by the education department. The first issue included 13 songs and its circulation rate in the first year was over 40 000 a month. By 1905 circulation approached 150 000 and a rival *Commonwealth School Paper* was established in NSW in 1904.

Allans first began publishing music on a large scale in 1891, producing the *Australian Music Year Book* in 1892 which by 1900 was selling 100 000 copies a year at one shilling each. In 1898 Allans began production of the famous Allans Edition which became the Imperial Edition in 1905. From 1906, in collaboration with the AMEB, Allans began publication of large amounts of teaching material. Beginning in 1911, Allans also published the periodical *Australian Musical News*. At the end of World War I Allans was able to acquire its first lino machine from the defence department. Formed in 1920, the Melbourne firm of Kynoch & Wilson imported an engraver from England to manage Allans' requirements. Allans then published vast amounts of music: school music, dance folios, tutors, community songs, hillbilly and western songs. Its nearest rival, Palings, published albums of melody ballads, sonatinas, radio songs, old-time dances, jazz foxtrots and tangos, a Hawaiian song folio and easy waltzes.

By 1905 Alberts was publishing a catalogue of 250 American ballads, coon songs, cakewalks and dance music. Ernest Lashmar (1884–1964) opened a branch of the London publishers Chappell in Melbourne in 1904 before moving to Sydney in 1920. Chappell specialised in scores of successful English and American musicals and by 1963 about 300 items by Australian composers. Boosey & Hawkes also established an Australian office in 1934.

After the slump in the 1930s commissions were rare, with publishers preferring to take over copyright of a work (less 9 per cent), and catering primarily for the educational and pop music market. By 1968 there were only two music engravers in Australia, both employed by Allans. Only about 2 per cent of Allans' publications were engraved, the remainder being photo-reproductions of overseas printings. Palings ceased publishing by 1975, while Alberts specialised in publications by Australian composers. Allans publishes a 500-page catalogue and remains the official publisher of the AMEB.

In the 1980s the *Australian Music Centre became the principal distributor of music for living Australian composers, developing from 1987 an attractive design for its (chiefly facsimile) editions of Australian works. In the same years a few Australian book publishers made small forays into music publishing, Currency Press and Hale & Iremonger of Sydney both producing anthologies of Australian works, and La Trobe University Press, Melbourne, releasing two anthologies of contemporary Australian compositions. With the advent of computerised music typesetting and desktop publishing small independent publishers have proliferated, some little more than backyard operations issuing the music of their proprietor, but others like Red House, Melbourne, producing a small catalogue of new Australian works.

See also *Music-Sellers and Retailers*; *Journals and Music Magazines*.

FURTHER REFERENCE
BrisbaneE; *SnellA*; [Advertisement], *Illustrated Sydney News*, 6 May 1854, 48; Charles H. Bertie, *Isaac Nathan: Australia's First Composer* (Sydney: Angus & Robertson, 1922); Georgina Binns, Patriotic and Nationalistic Song in Australia to 1919: A Study of the Popular Sheet Music Genre, MMus, Univ. Melbourne, 1988; Peter Game, *The Music Sellers* (Melbourne: Hawthorn, 1976); J. Gervase, 'Export Music', *Port of Melbourne Quarterly* 19 (Oct.–Dec. 1968), 44; Louis Lavater, 'Musical Composition in Australia', *Australian National Review*, 1 Aug. 1939, 16; 'Like Printing Notes', *Nation*, 2 Nov. 1963, 13; 'Sydney Half a Century Ago', newspaper cuttings, Mitchell Library, vol. 166, 55–6.

SUZANNE ROBINSON

Puddy, Maude Mary (b Brompton, Adelaide, 27 Mar. 1883; d North Adelaide, 1 Aug. 1974), pianist. After piano lessons with Immanuel *Reimann at the Adelaide College of Music and Bryceson Treharne at the Elder Conservatorium, she went to London in 1905, studying with Busoni and at Vienna with Theodor Leschitizky. She gave concerts in Vienna and Berlin and worked as Leschitizky's assistant, then taught in London from 1913, during the war giving concerts for the troops. She returned to Australia in 1920 and taught at the Elder Conservatorium until 1949, appearing with the Adelaide Symphony Orchestra, in chamber music and on broadcasts. Noted for her beauty of tone and innate musicianship, she was an influential piano teacher in Adelaide for a long time.

FURTHER REFERENCE
Alison Holder, *ADB*, 11.

Purlapa, (Warlpiri) new Aboriginal songs. See *Aboriginal Music*, §2(i).

Purple Hearts, The. Rock band (1963–67) formed in Brisbane when Mick Hadley (vocals), Fred Pickard (guitar) and Bob Dames (bass) arrived together from England and teamed with Lobby *Loyde [Barry Hyde] (guitar) and Adrian 'Red' Redmond (drums, later Tony Cahill). Named for the illicit drug then popular in the UK, they developed a dedicated following in Brisbane and recorded their debut single *Long Legged Baby* in 1965. In 1966 they moved to Melbourne, *Of Hopes And Dreams And Tombstones* reaching No. 24 in the charts and *Early In The Morning* reaching No. 11. They released an EP *Sound of The Purple Hearts* in the same year, but feeling musically stagnant they disbanded in 1967. A group that was the training ground for the *Easybeats and Loyde's later success, their style was loud, insolent hard rock combined with rhythm and blues.

FURTHER REFERENCE
Recordings include *Long Legged Baby* (Sunshine QK 1138), *Of Hopes And Dreams And Tombstones* (Sunshine QK 1213), *Early In The Morning* (Sunshine QK 1448), and *Sound of The Purple Hearts* (Sunshine QX 11175). A compilation is *Let's Meet The Purple Hearts* (1979, Raven RV 02). For discography, see *SpencerA*. See also *McGrathA*; *SpencerW*.

Qasar I. A synthesiser designed in 1972 by Anthony G. Furse and made by his company Creative Strategies. Compactly arranged around a music keyboard, it consisted of an all-digital pitch and waveform generator, an analog filter, and a digital profile generator. A prototype Qasar II was installed at the Canberra School of Music in 1973, but Furse's work was overtaken by the widely marketed Moog synthesisers, and he did not achieve sustained commercial production.

FURTHER REFERENCE
Hugh Davies, *GroveI*.

Qua, Chris (Christopher George) (*b* Orange, NSW, 14 Nov. 1951), jazz bass player, trumpeter. His trumpet teachers included Harry Berry, and he also began bass at school, later studying at the NSW Conservatorium. His first professional engagement was at 15 with Alan Lee. A founding member of *Galapagos Duck, he left in 1980 and toured with the *Daly-Wilson Big Band (1983). In high demand as a freelancer, playing with Bob *Barnard, John *Sangster, Judy *Bailey, Don *Burrows and Tom *Baker among others, he is currently also working with Col *Nolan and drummer Harry Rivers. He has toured with international visitors, including Mose Allison, Ernestine Anderson, Stan Tracey and Scott Hamilton, and he played concert support for Nina Simone, Dizzy Gillespie and Ray Charles.

FURTHER REFERENCE
Recordings include *Ebony Quill*, Galapagos Duck (1973, Philips 6357 015); *The Removalists*, Galapagos Duck (1974, Philips 6357 020); *Tom Baker's San Francisco Jazz Band vol. 1* (1976, Jazz & Jazz J&J 001); vol. 2 (1980, Jazz & Jazz 6357 904); *For Leon Bismark*, John Sangster (1979, Swaggie S-1379); *Music to Midnight*, Bob Barnard with the Kenny Powell Orchestra (1980, ABC L8003); *Stan Tracey and Don Weller Play Duke, Monk, and Bird* (1988, Emanem 3604); *Rhythm of the Heart*, the Bob Bertles Quintet (1995, Rufus Polygram RF 017). An interview with him is in *WilliamsA*, 136–41. See also *OxfordJ*. BRUCE JOHNSON

Quadrille. Fashionable dance in the early 19th century for four couples in a square formation, in which movements follow a prescribed combination of intertwining figures. It was frequently danced to a medley of opera melodies; early colonial bandmasters who composed sets included Joseph *Reichenberg and Kavanagh. A later variation was the lancers, tunes for which were widely dispersed in the folk traditions of bush Australia.

Queensland Ballet. Charles Lisner founded the Lisner Ballet in 1960; two yeas later the troupe was renamed the Queensland Ballet, and became a fully professional company in 1965. Lisner was not only a trained dancer but an accomplished musician, twin skills that were evident in his ballet *The Gift* (1960), in which he provided both the choreography and the music. He retired from the position of artistic director in 1974. Harry Haythorne succeeded him in the following year, and was in turn replaced by Harold Collins in 1978. It has been under Collins's leadership that the company has expanded its creative vision, commissioning scores from a number of Australian composers, including Colin *Brumby, Graeme *Koehne, Wilfred *Lehmann, David Pyle, Antony Slavich and Carl *Vine.

FURTHER REFERENCE
Patricia Laughlin, 'Bold Pioneer of the North', *Dance Australia* 33 (Dec.–Jan. 1987–88), 19–21; idem, 'Harold Collins: A Life of Dance', *Dance Australia* no. 36 (June–July 1988), 16–18; Charles Lisner, *My Journey Through Dance* (Brisbane: UQP, 1982).
JOEL CROTTY

Queensland Conservatorium. Founded by the State Government in 1956, it has been affiliated with Griffith University since 1991, and offers an array of degrees and diplomas chiefly in performance, including a strong vocal school. Originally located at the former South Brisbane Town Hall, it was at Garden Point 1975–95, and now has outstanding modern facilities in the Queensland Performing Arts Complex at South-bank. Directors have been William *Lovelock 1956–59, Basil *Jones 1959–80, Roy *Wales 1981–86 and Anthony Camden 1988–93. The current director is Simone *de Haan.

Queensland Drover, The. See *The Overlander.*

Queensland Light Opera Company. Founded in 1962 as the Brisbane Gilbert and Sullivan Society with *The Mikado*, by 1966 it was staging three productions a year in addition to individual concerts; it closed down in 1981. The company enjoyed enormous public support, playing to several thousand people annually, largely because of its extreme versatility. Its repertoire gradually expanded to include not only musical comedy and light opera but also *opéra bouffe,* grand opera and oratorio. Representative works include *The Merry Widow, Carmen, Brigadoon* and *Cosi Fan Tutte*, staged in leading Brisbane venues such as Her Majesty's Theatre. Since professional principal singers, orchestra and conductor were employed, the company eventually came to rival the *Queensland Opera Company. KERRY VANN

Queensland Opera Company. Formed in 1968 by Colin and Marissa *Brumby to introduce opera to schoolchildren, the company toured Queensland schools for up to 40 weeks a year. Evening performances for adult audiences in both Brisbane and regional Queensland commenced in 1969. At that time the company was not only the first professional opera company in Queensland but also the only full-time opera troupe in Australia apart from the national Elizabethan Trust Opera Co., and by 1976 it had developed into an important venture, rivalling the state companies. During its 13 years it presented 28 operas, including several Australian premieres such as Rossini's *La Cenerentola.* While a policy of singing operas in English contributed to the company's popularity, a policy of including unusual and challenging works contributed to its eventual demise in 1980 as a result of severe financial difficulties.

FURTHER REFERENCE
Kerry Vann, A History of the Queensland Opera Company, BMus, Univ. Queensland, 1984. KERRY VANN

Queensland Philharmonic Orchestra. A 28-piece professional ensemble established in 1978 as the Queensland Theatre Orchestra, the orchestra's primary function was to provide accompaniment for opera, ballet and other music-theatre productions. The conductor until 1987 was Georg *Tintner. Renamed in 1989, the orchestra has grown in stature to give more than 200 performances annually to over 100 000 people and currently numbers 31 full-time musicians. In addition to presenting a Brisbane subscription series, state tours, schools concerts and producing CDs, the orchestra has toured

Japan, Asia and the South Pacific. It maintains a high international standard, engaging the best possible conductors and soloists from within Australia and abroad including James Galway, Claudio Scimone and its president, Sir Neville Marriner. Its artistic director since 1989 has been Anthony Camden. KERRY VANN

Queensland Symphony Orchestra. In 1936 the ABC established a 17-piece studio orchestra in Brisbane to give studio broadcasts and public concerts. After expanding in 1946 to become the 45-piece Brisbane Symphony Orchestra, the QSO was formally inaugurated in 1947, the second full-time professional state orchestra to be formed (after Sydney in 1946). An annual concert season is given in Brisbane at the Performing Arts Centre using the talents of leading international and Australian soloists and conductors. These have included Claudio Arrau, Dame Janet Baker, Sir Yehudi Menuhin, Sir Thomas Beecham and Sir Malcolm Sargent. Other regular activities include schools concerts, concerts of popular classics and the making of recordings. Every year since 1947 the orchestra has undertaken a two-week rail tour of North Queensland, the longest land-based tour undertaken by any orchestra in the world. Currently numbering 71 players, the orchestra's permanent home, since 1977, is the Ferry Road studios.

FURTHER REFERENCE
Charles Buttrose, *Playing for Australia: A Story about ABC Orchestras and Music in Australia* (Sydney: ABC and Macmillan, 1982); Cindy Chen, A History of the Queensland Symphony Orchestra: Its First Thirty Years, BMus(Hons), Univ. Queensland, 1985; Roger Covell, *Australia's Music: Themes of a New Society* (Melbourne: Sun Books, 1967). KERRY VANN

Queensland Youth Orchestra Council. Founded in Brisbane in 1966 by John *Curro, the council provides orchestral and ensemble training to young musicians aged 8–23. Originating in a secondary schools music festival, the organisation was soon the best managed and most active of any youth orchestra in Australia, and now has six ensembles, ranging from the Queensland Youth Symphony to a junior string ensemble, and involving more than 400 players. With core support from the State Government, the council has its administration and excellent rehearsal rooms at the expansive former Queensland Museum, Bowen Hills. From its early days it hosted a national junior concerto competition and has commissioned works from Australian composers. The Youth Symphony has a concert series in Brisbane, makes radio broadcasts, and has toured to the UK, Europe, North America, China and Japan. The Youth Symphony Chamber Players annually tour remote centres in Queensland. John Curro remains its conductor, the longest serving director of any Australian youth orchestra, and has been honoured with the MBE, the AM and an honorary

DMus (University of Queensland) for his extraordinary dedication to the organisation.

Quinlan Opera Company, Thomas. A lavishly equipped touring company organised by the Irish impresario Thomas Quinlan. The company visited Australia twice, staging 15 operas in English, several of which were Australian premieres, including the first *Tristan und Isolde* in 1912, the first *Meistersinger* in 1913, several Mozart works—a rarity at the time—and most remarkably the first (and only) *Ring des Nibelungen* in Australia in 1913. The artists were mostly British, some from Covent Garden, the touring equipment included astonishingly elaborate sets, and unlike previous visiting companies most of the orchestra and chorus were imported as well. Quinlan had planned to return in 1915 with an even more ambitious repertoire, including *Parsifal*, *Salome* and *Elektra*, but the war intervened.

FURTHER REFERENCE
Alison Gyger, *Opera for the Antipodes* (Sydney: Currency Press, 1990), 169–201; *BrisbaneE*, 168,174.

Quinn, Barry (*b* Melbourne, 25 June 1936), percussionist. After studies at the University of Melbourne, he played in jazz bands, radio, television and theatre, then went to London in 1965, playing with the BBC Symphony Orchestra, Peter Maxwell Davies and the Fires of London, as well as doing session work. He returned to Australia in 1972 and became principal percussionist in the Melbourne Symphony Orchestra. He now teaches at the Victorian College of the Arts.

Quiros. Television opera by Peter *Sculthorpe, libretto by Brian Bell. Set in the 17th century, it tells of a Portuguese sea captain's fruitless search for *Terra Australis*. First broadcast on ABC TV on 1 July 1982.

R

Radiators, The. Rock band (1978–) formed in Sydney, originally comprised of former Big Swifty members Brian Nichol (vocals), Stephen 'Fess' Parker (guitar) and Chris Tagg (drums) with Brendon Callinan (keyboards) and Geoff Turner (bass). In 1979 they released the first of more than 15 singles, *Comin' Home*, which reached No. 33 in the charts. In 1980 they were supporting act for the Police tour and released their album *Feel The Heat*. *No Tragedy* reached No. 27 and *Scream Of The Real* reached No. 15 in the album charts and won a gold album in 1983. They are an unusually long-lived pub band with a personal blend of hard-rock sound.

FURTHER REFERENCE

Recordings include *Comin' Home* (WEA 100109), *Feel The Heat* (WEA 600059), *No Tragedy* (EMI EMI968), *Scream Of The Real* (EMI EMX 121), and The *Radiators* (1993, M Records M 003CD). For discography, see *SpencerA*. See also *McGrathA*; *SpencerW*.

Radic, (Maureen) Thérèse (*b* Melbourne, 1935), historian of Australian music, biographer, playwright. She graduated from the University of Melbourne (MusBac 1958; MMus 1969; PhD 1978), and was Australian Research Council research fellow in the department of music, Monash University, 1990–95. She was appointed to the Australia Council in 1984 and chaired the Composing Women's Festival in 1994. She has published three monographs: *G.W.L. Marshall-Hall: Portrait of a Crusader* (1984), *Melba: The Voice of Australia* (1986) and *Bernard Heinze* (1986), two anthologies of Australian folk-song (1983, 1989), and the two-volume *A History of Music in Australia* (in press), as well as contributing entries to *The New Grove Dictionary of Opera* and *The Oxford Companion to Australian Literature*.

MARGARET KARTOMI

Radio and Music

1. The Beginnings to the mid-1930s. 2. The Golden Age, mid-1930s–1950s. 3. The Legacy of Radio.

Most Australians today listen to radio and most listeners, it seems, want to hear music. The musical choice is wide, particularly in the capital cities: classical music and jazz on ABC Classic FM and the Music Broadcasting Society (MBS) stations; music of many cultures from the Special Broadcasting Service (SBS) and some community broadcasters; indigenous Australian music from CAAMA and associated broadcasters; non-mainstream rock from Triple J and some community stations; and from commercial radio there is music usually aimed at specific markets or age-groups: adult contemporary, hits and memories, and easy-listening. It is also fairly easy to find world music, rap, soul, country, heavy metal, blues, folk, gospel and disco.

Surveys have shown that most Australians seem quite content to take what radio programmers give them. But some observers feel that listeners are too complacent and that radio stations, especially the commercial sector, are too conservative (or just occasionally too adventurous) in their programming and often fail to promote local music and musicians or to give airplay to new acts. Nevertheless, since the opening of the airwaves to community broadcasters in the mid-1970s, and in particular since the arrival of regular FM transmission in 1975, Australian music-lovers have had unparalleled variety.

1. The Beginnings to the mid-1930s. Music has always been the basis of radio broadcasting, even being broadcast in Australia before broadcasting officially began. For an experimental transmission in Melbourne on 13 October 1920, the recipient of a Melba scholarship, Miss Laura Walker, gave a recital, and one of her songs was *Advance Australia Fair*. In another radio demonstration on 31 March 1922, the pianist Jascha Spivakovsky, with Madge *Elliott and Cyril *Ritchard from the cast of *A Night Out*, broadcast from Her Majesty's Theatre, Melbourne. In Sydney on 18 March 1923 'Australia's Mary Pickford', Josie Melville, star of *Sally*, broadcast from Charles Maclurcan's private wireless station 2CM at Strathfield.

When wireless regulations were gazetted on 1 August 1923 and broadcasting could officially begin, Australia's first two stations came on air in Sydney: 2SB (later 2BL) on 23 November with an evening concert (and an official opening on 13 December), and 2FC on 5 December. 2FC's official opening on 9 January 1924 was a direct broadcast from the stage of Her Majesty's Theatre of *The Southern Maid*, starring 'Our Glad', Gladys ★Moncrieff, who was to be a regular broadcaster over the next 30 years. 3AR came on air without fanfare in Melbourne on 26 January 1924; and 6WF Perth on 4 June of that year, with a speech by the Premier and 'a long programme of musical items'. Melbourne's second station, 3LO, was fortunate to be able to open with a piece of Australian musical history, a Melba farewell, the charity gala of *La bohème* direct from His Majesty's Theatre, on 13 October 1924. This was heard not only in Melbourne but also in rural Victoria, Sydney, Auckland and even in California.

Much of the music heard in the early broadcasts and the earlier tests and experiments was played either from wind-up gramophones or player-pianos. Sometimes musicians came to the studio to play; at other times outside broadcasts were tried from theatres, dance halls, churches and nightclubs. There were plenty of stunts too, for example, a broadcast of a singer in one town accompanied by a pianist in another. Years were to pass before radio developed from an obsession for 'hams' into a medium of mass entertainment. When broadcasting began, only one Australian home in three had electricity; by 1938 two in every three homes had a radio receiver. At first, good receiving sets were expensive, while crystal sets were cheap but inefficient, and many Australians could not afford to buy radios during the Depression. Reception and transmission in the early days were poor and programs were often interrupted by technical faults, or by programming gaps for, if they ran out of material, stations would simply shut down and reopen later. The idea of a program 'flow' came gradually; in 1935 2UW became the first station to broadcast continuously 24 hours a day. Gradually, as landlines linked stations across the country and a local transcription-disc industry grew, the best city-made programs could be heard nationally, and from the mid-1930s to the late 1950s Australian radio enjoyed its so-called Golden Age.

2. The Golden Age, mid-1930s–1950s. (i) Rise of the ABC.

From 1932 there were commercial stations and the ABC. The ABC was a network of stations publicly owned and (until 1974) funded from licence revenue; by 1938 it had two capital city stations in each state. The commercial stations were privately owned and funded by advertising fees, and often formed loosely organised networks such as the Macquarie or the Major. The music-loving senior management of the ABC, assisted by the indefatigable Bernard ★Heinze, also set about establishing orchestras and organising subscription concerts associated with the network, often coming into conflict with their predecessors in the field, notably the conservatoriums and the entrepreneurs J. & N. ★Tait (allied to J.C. Williamson),

who objected to a publicly funded body competing with free-enterprise private companies. But the ABC hired celebrity conductors, singers and instrumentalists on a scale hitherto unknown.

Much of the ABC's entrepreneurial activity was designed to supply material for its broadcasts, transmissions which were heard in places where no celebrity had ever ventured in person. After a battle with the Taits in 1938, the ABC was obliged by law to broadcast in whole or in part every concert for which it sold tickets, a restriction removed in 1981. Equally important were the ABC's broadcasts from commercial discs, which often introduced Australians to works that had never previously been performed in the country and gave many their first experience of performance standards at the highest level, setting a benchmark for local artists and audiences. Over the years, the ABC's links with such international radio organisations as the BBC and the European Broadcasting Union have helped to keep Australians abreast of musical events overseas.

It soon became fashionable to say that ABC stations were for 'highbrows' and commercial stations were for 'lowbrows'. Certainly, the lengthier classical works were passed over by the commercial broadcasters, it being hard to place advertisements in a Bruckner symphony, but light classics were frequently played on commercial stations, often (but not exclusively) on Sundays. Commercial stations often had long-running 'world-famous tenor' programs. Baritones were also in favour; Peter ★Dawson on his visits home was as likely to appear on a commercial program as an ABC one. On 31 July 1938 for example, Lawrence Tibbett, at the end of his tour for the Taits, gave a half-hour evening recital broadcast on a hook-up of 86 of the 95 Australian commercial stations.

(ii) Radio Music Programs, Performers, Ensembles.

Hector ★Crawford began his summer series of outdoor concerts, *Music for the People*, in 1938. These events in the Botanic Gardens in Melbourne, broadcast for years by commercial station 3DB, attracted huge crowds; admission was free, but a gate collection raised money for charities. Crawford and his sister Dorothy formed their own radio production company in 1945 and made a series of musical serials: *The Melba Story* (first broadcast 1946), *The Blue Danube* (the story of Johann Strauss Jr, featuring the young violinist Desmond Bradley) and *The Amazing Oscar Hammerstein* (the opera entrepreneur, not the lyricist). They also produced *Opera for the People* and *Mobil Quest*. *Mobil Quest* (1949–56) launched the careers of some notable Australian performers, including Joan Sutherland. With the encouragement of Sir Keith Murdoch, managing director of the Herald and Weekly Times which owned the station, 3DB employed its own symphony orchestra 1949–52. Murdoch budgeted £20 000 annually for the orchestra and allowed for an annual loss of £10 000 (one year the orchestra lost only £8000—a 'profit' of £2000). Verdon ★Williams conducted public concerts of symphonic works, William Flynn (known to jazz buffs as Billy O'Flynn) conducted light classics, and Hector Crawford recorded radio shows, including the series *Glenda*. The 3DB orchestra played for Gertrude ★Johnson's National Theatre ballet and opera seasons in Melbourne in mid-1951 (*Swan Lake, Madame Butterfly, The Barber of Seville* and *Rigoletto*) and gave a concert with Yehudi Menuhin.

Throughout its Golden Age radio gave employment to innumerable musical performers, both singers (as soloists, groups and in choirs) and instrumentalists. In the early 1940s Charles ★Mackerras gained valuable experience (and an impressive wage for a teenager) working as an oboist and arranger for the Colgate-Palmolive Radio Unit. Many stations had house ensembles to play dinner music, light classics, even arrangements of symphonic works. A complete list of all the artists who contributed to music-making in these years would require vast space; some of the people who directed instrumental broadcasting ensembles (anything from orchestras and bands to quartets and trios) in these years were: Denis Collinson and Montague Brearley (*Calling the Stars*), Jim Davidson (*Colour Canvas*), Bert Howell (*Shell Show*), Jim Gussey (*Gently Bentley*), Bob Gibson (*Ford Show*), Abe Romain (*Star Parade*), Lou Campara and Gus Merzi (*Bunkhouse Show*), Desmon Tanner (*Music in the Tanner Manner*), Tom King (*Radio Canteen*), Tommy ★Tycho (*Laugh Till You Cry*), Horrie ★Dargie (*Atlantic Show*), Freddy McIntosh (*George Wallace's Barn Dance*), Jay Wilbur, Humphrey Bishop, Bobby ★Limb, Isador ★Goodman, Frank Thorne, Jack Papworth, Clive ★Amadio and Fred Hartley.

The ABC ran dance bands in Sydney and Melbourne, and employed a National Military Band 1933–51. The ABC Melbourne Show Band survived until 1982. The last of the ABC wireless choruses, the Adelaide Singers, disappeared along with the ABC Sydney Show Band in 1976.

(iii) Opera and Radio. Opera has largely been the province of the ABC. In August 1932, its second month of existence, the ABC began a series of broadcasts of the J.C. Williamson Imperial Grand Opera Company; in the New Year it broadcast studio performances by the company, and from October 1933 to May 1934 produced a studio season of abridged operas in Italian. Originally transmitted only in Sydney, these performances were sent on interstate relay in 1934. From October 1934 the ABC covered the season of the Fuller Grand Opera Company, and in November 1935 began a six-month studio season of hour-long versions of grand opera, mostly in English. The conductors were Maurice de ★Abravanel, Percy ★Code and Joseph ★Post. The first Australian performances of Strauss's *Der Rosenkavalier* and Vaughan Williams's *Hugh the Drover* occurred during this radio season. Also in the season were Wagner's *Mastersingers* and *Parsifal*, which the underfunded and short-lived stage company had been unable to perform in the

theatre. Studio opera broadcasts continued throughout the 1930s and 40s.

The mid-1930s were the first high-water mark for opera on radio. The Sutherland-Williamson season of 1965 was not heard on ABC radio, but a collaboration between the ABC and the Australian Opera developed in the late 1970s and peaked in the mid-1980s, and Australian Opera productions in recent times have often been broadcast as simulcasts by ABC radio and television. The Australia-wide coverage of the Australian Opera through radio and simulcasts (and its subsequent marketing on video) has made amends in part for the national opera company's reluctance to travel. In the 1930s the soundtracks of currently showing films were broadcast regularly by both the ABC and the commercial stations, for the Golden Age of radio coincided with the Golden Age of the Hollywood musical.

(iv) Australian Compositions on Radio. In 1926, as radio and the talkies threatened the interests of musical copyright owners, the Australasian Performing Right Association (APRA) was formed. Alberts, Palings, Allans, and several other music merchants and publishers had interests in early radio stations. Because so much music on radio comes from commercial recordings, APRA and the record companies have fought a constant campaign with the commercial broadcasters, today represented by the Federation of Australian Radio Broadcasters (FARB) over royalties, and occasionally quotas and bans have been imposed on FARB members. The record companies feel the radio stations are using recordings as cheap program material, while the stations argue that the record companies are receiving free publicity.

The interests of local composers and performers were advanced from 1942 when all stations were required by legislation to broadcast a minimum of 2.5 per cent Australian compositions. This was raised to 5 per cent in 1956. In 1973 the Australian Broadcasting Control Board required commercial broadcasters to play 10 per cent Australian performances. That quota was raised to 20 per cent in 1976. The ABC, bound by the composition requirement, is not obliged to adhere to the performance quota, but it voluntarily complies.

Australian composers have been wooed by many radio-based competitions over the years. Almost as soon as it began, the ABC held two composers' competitions (1933 and 1935) and gave concert performances of the winning works. In the 1950s the ABC and APRA jointly conducted an annual composers' competition, and in the 1960s they ran a composer-commissioning scheme. At various times, often in conjunction with national anniversaries or state occasions, the ABC and commercial stations have held song competitions, and after the 1951 National Song Competition, the first, second and third prize winners were recorded for EMI by Peter Dawson with an ABC Sydney choir and orchestra conducted by Henry Krips (who composed the winning song). The winner and runner-up in the ABC's Jubilee Song Parade of 1951 were recorded by the English bandleader Geraldo (who had judged the competition) and his orchestra.

The ABC makes in-house disc and tape recordings of Australian musical works for broadcasting purposes, program exchange and distribution to educational institutions. In the days of 78s and LPs ABC recordings were released through such companies as EMI, RCA and Festival. Licensing deals between the ABC and commercial record companies continue in the 1990s, but since 1980 the ABC has had its own internationally distributed commercial record label. The first ABC Shop opened in Sydney in 1981.

The ABC submits Australian works to the annual International Rostrum of Composers in Paris (a UNESCO project inaugurated in 1954) and enters programs for the Italia Prize. Australian musical works that have won the Prix Italia are George English's *Death of a Wombat* (1960) and Nigel Butterley's *In the Head the Fire* (1966). Both were released on LP. In 1989 the prize was awarded to *Collaborations*, a musical program with performances by Jim Denley and five colleagues. The ABC also supports local composers by commissioning new works, holding workshops and schools for composers and conductors, and by organising composer-in-residence programs with ABC orchestras.

(v) Musical Commentary and Quests. Over the years countless on-air 'personalities' have passed their enthusiasm for music on to listeners (some disc jockeys have sought notoriety by smashing recordings they were not enthusiastic about on air). The outspoken *Manchester Guardian* critic, Neville ★Cardus, who came to Australia to cover Beecham's visit in 1940 and stayed until 1947, broadcast and wrote regularly for the ABC; he raised many eyebrows but opened many ears. Of many popular presenters of ABC classical music programs perhaps the most notable was Dr A.E. ★Floyd, who broadcast 1944–72, retiring at the age of 95. Composer-pianist Lindley ★Evans (as 'Mr Melody Man') introduced youngsters to music in the ABC's *Children's Hour*. The ABC has proselytised classical music through articles in its publications, in particular the *ABC Weekly* (1939–59) and *24 Hours* (1976–), and by broadcast talks. Percy ★Grainger and Roy ★Agnew were two prominent radio lecturer-recitalists in the 1930s.

Two forms of musical entertainment that the early radio researcher W.A. McNair identified as having as much human interest as musical appeal were talent quests and community singing programs. The best known of the quests was ★*Australia's Amateur Hour* (1940–58), which toured the country, and was always on the list of the top 10 shows. This and the *Mobil Quest* were but two of innumerable programs of their type, some broadcast locally, some nationally. A talent quest on 3UZ Melbourne, *Radio Auditions*, ran from 1943 to 1983. It has been estimated that during the run of another long-lived Melbourne tal-

ent show, 3KZ's *P and A* (Professional and Amateur) *Parade* (1935–64) about 72 000 hopefuls were auditioned. The ABC hesitated to conduct its own talent quests, but in 1944 established the ★ABC Concerto and Vocal Competition which survives as the Young Performers Awards. For many years the ABC ran a *Young Australia* program as a showcase for budding performers. The concept was revived as a weekly program on ABC Classic FM in 1992.

Community singing, usually in a public hall with a star host and a celebrity vocalist to lead proceedings, gave listeners a chance to attend and partake of the glamour of radio, and afforded stations a chance for promotion and perhaps to raise money for charity. 3LO Melbourne is said to have led the way in 1928. Although interest in radio community singing began to wane in the late 1930s, it endured in *Australia's Hour of Song*, an 'up market' community singalong, broadcast nationally on Sunday nights 1952–55, replacing the *Lux Radio Theatre*. The ABC's *Community Hymn Singing* ran 1948–85. (See *Community Singing*.)

Hit parades became a feature of commercial and ABC radio in the early 1940s. Often the hit tunes were performed by artists in the studio, but from the mid-1950s they were disc-based, and 2UE in Sydney published the first recognised Australian Top 40 chart in March 1958. The end of the Golden Age of radio coincided with the arrival of rock and roll, but television was the reason for the change. Today, commercial stations claim to contribute to Australian musical life by, for example, sponsoring community events (rock concerts, *Carols by Candlelight*, etc.) and by broadcasting promotional interviews with artists. Less frequently, broadcasters organise their own concerts and put them to air.

3. The Legacy of Radio. As in other countries, very little music composed for Australian radio has become 'repertoire'. Few music-lovers could name a radio symphony or radio opera, while musical comedies and revues written for Australian radio seem to have sunk without trace. An Australian folk-rock ballad opera written for radio, *Terry and Frankie* (1972) by Ian McDonald, was released on a Festival LP, guaranteeing that work some permanence, but largely radio has played a reporting rather than an originating role. On the other hand, many radio signature tunes have entered the national consciousness; some of these were composed especially for the programs concerned (e.g. *Mrs 'Obbs*), but most were borrowed from other sources (e.g. the ABC News theme since 1952, *Majestic Fanfare* by Charles Williams).

Most of the music for plays and features has come from mood-music companies. Although the commercial stations have occasionally produced drama with locally composed incidental music, the ABC has led the way; the landmark ABC serial *As Ye Sow* which went to air in 1937 had incidental music by Howard Carr recorded by ABC ensembles at EMI, Homebush. John ★Antill, a pioneer of broadcasting who conducted his Cathedral Quartette at

2SB's opening concert in 1923, composed incidental music for a number of ABC dramatic productions of the 1940s, 50s and 60s. Others who have composed music for ABC productions are Hal Evans, Cecil Fraser, Clive *Douglas, Robert *Hughes, Peter *Sculthorpe and Margaret *Sutherland.

Some of the most enduring Australian radio music has taken the form of advertising jingles: it is strange that while radio's contribution to the musical awareness of Australians has been immeasurably powerful, the most enduring piece of music composed for Australian radio could be the *Aeroplane Jelly Song*, first heard on 2KY in Sydney in 1932—a song probably second only to *Waltzing Matilda* as an unofficial national anthem. See also *ABC*.

FURTHER REFERENCE
Australian Broadcasting Tribunal, *Young Australians and Music* (Melbourne: Australian Government Printer, 1985); idem, *Australian Music on Radio* (Sydney: Australian Government Printer, 1986); Nancye Bridges with Frank Crook, *Wonderful Wireless* (Sydney: Methuen Australia, 1983); Ken Inglis, *This is the ABC* (Melbourne: MUP, 1983); Colin Jones, *Something in the Air* (Sydney: Kangaroo Press, 1995); Jacqueline Kent, *Out of the Bakelite Box* (Sydney: Angus & Robertson, 1983); R.R.Walker, *The Magic Spark* (Melbourne: Hawthorn Press, 1973).   R.J. MAYNARD

Radio Birdman. Punk-rock band (1974–79) formed in Sydney, comprised of former Rats members Rob Younger (vocals), Chris Masuak and Deniz Tek (guitars), Phillip 'Pip' Hoyle (keyboards), Carl Rourke (bass) and Ron Keeley (drums); Johnny Kannis and Mark Sisto (backing vocals) were added later. Tek and Hoyle were two American medical students who introduced the others to the Detroit heavy-rock guitar sound of the late 1960s. At first a part-time student affair, they worked at the few hotels who would tolerate them, playing covers of the Doors, MC5 and similarly loud, obdurate bands. They encouraged a cult following in Sydney, which did not shirk from portraying them as truculent, alienated or even neo-Nazis. After releasing their debut single, *New Race*, in 1977, *Aloha Steve And Danno* in 1978 and their album *Radios Appear* (1977), they went to the UK in 1978, working as supporting act to the Flaming Groovies and releasing an album *Living Eyes* (1981); but they were not successful there, and split amid rancour. The loudest, most pugnacious punk band of their day, their American-derived sound had considerable influence on later Sydney bands.

FURTHER REFERENCE
Recordings include *New Race* (1977, Trafalgar TRS 11), *Aloha Steve And Danno* (1978, Trafalgar TRS 12), *Radios Appear* (1977 Trafalgar TRL 001), *Living Eyes* (1981 WEA 60085). A compilation is *Under The Ashes* (Warner 22559912); there is a bootleg album *Eureka Birdman*. For discography, see *SpencerA*. See also Vivien Johnson, *Radio Birdman* (Sheldon Booth, 1990); *McGrathA*; *SpencerW*; *GuinnessP*, III, 2030; *CoupeN*.

Ragtime. Afro-American music, popularised in the piano works of Scott Joplin in the 1900s. It involves a melody of regular eight-bar phrases and conventional harmony but with persistent off-beat accents set against a heavy 2/4 *oom-pah* (in the left hand). The principal music of American vaudeville until after World War I, American ragtime performers were heard in Australia at the Tivoli variety theatres and in the Brennan-Fuller vaudeville circuit from 1913. American Billy Romaine led ragtime bands in Sydney from 1914; Belle Sylvia and Mabelle Morgan, who succeeded him in 1918, were perhaps the first Australians to include the style in their work; more recently Perth-based pianist John *Gill has been a noted exponent.

Raisbeck, Rosina (*b* Ballarat,Vic.), dramatic soprano. After studies as a mezzo-soprano at the NSW State Conservatorium, she won the ABC Concerto and Vocal Competition and the Sydney *Sun* Aria in 1947, gave concerts in NZ, and moved to London. She made her debut at Covent Garden in the same year as Maddalena in *Rigoletto*, but on Beecham's advice retrained under Dina Borgioli as a dramatic soprano, and sang Ortrud in *Lohengrin*, then Senta in *The Flying Dutchman* at Covent Garden in 1950. She declined engagements to start a family from 1954, then reappeared with Sadler's Wells from 1958, returning to Australia in 1962 and singing in Garnet Carroll musicals, then the Australian Opera from 1966. Aside from Wagnerian roles, her extensive repertoire includes Leonora (*Il trovatore*), Amneris (*Aida*), Kabanicha (*Kát'a Kabanova*), the British premiere of Dallapiccola's *The Prisoner*, Marina (*Boris Godunov*), Maria (*War and Peace*), as well as roles in *Salome*, *The Gondoliers*, *Il Trittico*, and *Mahagonny*.

FURTHER REFERENCE
Recordings include Praskovia in *The Merry Widow*, Australian Opera (1988, Virgin Vision VVD 828). See also *MackenzieS*, 179–81.

Rajah of Shivapore, The. Comic opera in two acts by Alfred *Hill (1914), libretto by D. Souter. Set in India, it tells of the wily characters who deceive a gullible rajah. First performed at the Playhouse, Sydney, 15 December 1917.

RAM. See *Rock Australia Magazine*.

Randall, Bob (*b* *c*.1934, Middleton Pond, Tempe Downs station, NT), Aboriginal singer-songwriter, author, storyteller. He is the composer of *Brown Skin Baby*, a song often covered by Aboriginal performers about the removal of Aboriginal children from their parents. Randall's songs are about issues of Aboriginal life, including the relationship to land and the effects on Aborigines of government policies. A popular performer at numerous festivals of Aboriginal music in the NT, ACT and SA, he was winner of three awards at the Canberra Aboriginal

Country and Western Festival in 1974, for composition, best male vocal, and best group.

FURTHER REFERENCE
Recordings include *Bob Randall* (1984, Imparja Records, unnumbered).

P. DUNBAR-HALL

Randall, Henry. Brand name for a German piano made under Australian licence. See *Carnegie*.

Rankin, Dusty [Roger Hogan] (*b* nr Birchip, Vic., 8 Feb. 1924), country music singer-songwriter. Writing his first song at the age of 16, he learned guitar and polled best on *Australia's Amateur Hour* in 1946. He appeared in Skuthorpe's Rodeo in 1947, his first single, *Where The Murrumbidgee Wends Its Way*, was released in 1948, and he travelled with road shows until 1961, when he settled down as a sheep and wheat farmer. An effortless singer of ballads, many of which are unusually sentimental for country music, he was honoured in the ACMA Roll of Renown in 1996.

FURTHER REFERENCE
Recordings include *Where The Murrumbidgee Wends Its Way* (1948, Regal Zonophone G25261), *The Best Of Dusty Rankin* (Hadley HCSM 3007). See also *WatsonC*, I, 111–17. *SmithB*, 323.

Rankl, Karl (*b* Gaaden, nr Vienna, 1 Oct. 1898; *d* Salzburg, 6 Sept. 1968), Austrian conductor. A pupil of Schoenberg and Webern, he had conducted opera in Berlin and Prague before emigrating to Britain at the outbreak of World War II and becoming conductor at Covent Garden. He came to Australia as music director for the Elizabethan Trust Opera Co. 1958–60, conducting the 1958 season of *Fidelio*, *Carmen*, *The Barber of Seville*, *Lohengrin* and *Peter Grimes* in four states; his own conducting was artistically successful, but a mixed box-office success and his disregard of costs contributed to a large deficit, and after the 1959 season was suspended he resigned.

FURTHER REFERENCE
John Cargher, 'The Rankl Disaster', *Opera and Ballet in Australia* (Melbourne: Cassell, 1977), 62–8; Frank Howes, *GroveD*.

Rantos, Spiros (*b* Corfu, Greece, 7 Nov. 1945), violinist, teacher. After studies at the Athens Conservatorium and the Vienna Hochschule with Edward Melkus, he taught at the Graz Conservatorium and was concertmaster of the Capella Academica, Vienna, from 1968. He was a prize-winner in chamber music competitions at Forte dei Marmi, Italy (1973) and at Colmar, France (1974), then studied with Franca Gulli at Indiana University, USA. He came to Australia in 1976 with the chamber group *Ensemble I for a residency at the Victorian College of the Arts and stayed to teach. He taught at the Darling Downs Institute of Advanced Education,

Queensland, from 1978, where he directed the Toowoomba Youth Orchestra, frequently appearing in recitals with his wife, the pianist Bracchi Tilles. He co-founded the Rantos Collegium in 1984 (later the Melbourne Chamber Orchestra), with which he had a subscription series in Melbourne and toured widely. Moving back to Melbourne in 1985 he taught at the University of Melbourne and conducted the Chamber Strings of Melbourne, taking them on several international tours. He was conductor of the *Melbourne Youth Orchestra 1991–92.

An inspiring teacher and chamber player of style and deep understanding, through his chamber music performances and work with gifted young players he has contributed greatly to Australian string playing. Since 1996 he has taught at the University of Queensland.

FURTHER REFERENCE
Recordings include *Recital* (1983, Grevillea GRV 1050).

Rasp. A large stick or spear-thrower with notches, which is scraped by a smaller stick and is held vertically against the player's chest. It is used by Aboriginal people from the Kimberleys to accompany *dyabi*, songs which offer a commentary on contemporary events. There the rasp is also known as a *dyabi* stick, and is only used to accompany the *dyabi* songs. *Dyabi* songs are sung for entertainment and are individually owned by their composers. See *Aboriginal Music* §3 (i).   GRACE KOCH

Rattle (seed or shell). Segments of the matchbox bean are strung together to form a rattle, which is bunched together in the hand and shaken by Aboriginal dancers in Cape York. These are used especially during Island dance, where the performers wear grass skirts as they dance and sing, sounding the rattles in precision movements. Usually these rattles are used in conjunction with a drum and/or metal tins which are struck rapidly. The same type of rattles are used throughout Torres Strait. Also, in addition to seed rattles, shell rattles have been reported in districts of the Kimberleys. See *Aboriginal Music* §4(i).

GRACE KOCH

Ready, Thelma Constance (*b* Campbelltown, Tas., 23 Sept. 1902), banjo player, bandleader. Encouraged by her father to play the banjo, Ready studied with Albert Durrand and by 1925 was well established as a soloist, broadcasting regularly over 3LO, and teaching and promoting the Ludwig banjo. The Thelma Ready Ladies Orchestra, announced in February 1928, may well have been the first all-girls dance band in Australia. Overturning the 'rule of grace', these five girls played the new instruments of opportunity and, unlike the many preceding all-women's groups, were paid. From a debut at the Mayfair Cafe in St Kilda, the band moved to the Hotel Australia and to No. 9 Darling Street, South Yarra, a smart reception venue.

FURTHER REFERENCE

Australasian Band and Orchestra News; K. Dreyfus, 'Sweethearts of Rhythm', *Stages* (*Magazine of the Victorian Arts Centre Trust*), (Mar. 1995), 34–5.   KAY DREYFUS

Rebb, Johnny [John Dellbridge] (*b* Sydney 1935), rock and roll singer. Singing country and western music from his teens, he formed a rock and roll band and played in local clubs as Johnny Rebb and the Rebels from 1957. In 1958 he was supporting act in the Tommy Sands Show for Lee ★Gordon and released his debut singles, *Johnny B. Goode* and *Hey Sheriff*, which reached No. 28 in the charts. The next year his *Pathway To Paradise* reached No. 10 and *Highway Of Love* reached No. 27, and he began to appear as a regular in *Six O'Clock Rock*. The next few years saw an EP *Hits For Six*, an LP *Some Swing, Some Sweet* and another 14 singles, but he did not match his earlier chart success. Known as 'The Gentleman of Rock' for his conservative appearance and courtesy, he was the first Australian artist to record for Leedon and one of the most memorable of the early Australian rock and roll singers. In the late 1960s he worked in the USA, and he continues to perform.

FURTHER REFERENCE

Recordings include *Johnny B. Goode* (Columbia DO 3967), *Hey Sheriff* (Leedon LS540), *Pathway To Paradise* (Leedon LS558), *Highway Of Love* (Leedon LS584), *Hits For Six* (Leedon LX 10328), *Some Swing, Some Sweet* (Leedon LL 30541). A compilation is *Rock On* (1981, Raven RVLP 04). For discography, see *SpencerA*. See also *McGrathA*; *SpencerW*.

Recorder-making. Australia has produced a number of recorder-makers with international reputations, largely due to the influence of Frederick ★Morgan of Daylesford, Victoria. With the rise in popularity of the transverse flute in the 18th century and the subsequent decline of interest in the recorder, the art of making fine recorders was largely lost until the early music revival this century. Modern makers like Morgan have thus had to research and reconstruct the designs and techniques of the old recorder-makers. The first mass-produced Australian-manufactured recorders were made by the Pan Recorder Co. in Melbourne in the early 1950s. The company made recorders for use in schools, but had ceased production by 1970. Its most famous employee was Morgan, who subsequently worked overseas and returned to Australia to establish a workshop producing instruments modelled on Renaissance and Baroque originals. The second generation of Australian makers is led by Michael Grinter (*b* 1953), who currently makes and sells about 40 recorders a year, mainly into the competitive European market. Grinter also makes Baroque and Classical flutes. Joanne Saunders (*b* 1960) trained with Morgan for three years and has also worked in The Netherlands. Howard Oberg (*b* 1945) of Sydney made some recorders in the 1970s and 80s, but has since concentrated on flutes.

Australian-made recorders are recognised around the world as some of the best available and feature on many recordings. Internationally recognised research into recorder acoustics has also been carried out by Queensland physicist John Martin.

FURTHER REFERENCE

AthertonA, 180–5; Linda Nathan, 'Sounds Australian: Making Musical Instruments in Australia', *Australian Wood Review* 6 (Mar. 1995), 50–3; Joanne Saunders, 'Reflections of a Recorder Maker', *The Recorder: Journal of the Victorian Recorder Guild* 9 (Feb. 1989), pp. 29–30.   PETER NUSSEY

Recording and Recording Companies. The first demonstrations in the Australian colonies of the recording and reproduction of sound were given in mid-1878, less than six months after Thomas Edison unveiled his tinfoil phonograph to the American public on 22 December 1877. Newspaper articles on 'how to make a phonograph' resulted in many tinfoil models being produced in the next two years, including those exhibited at meetings of the Royal Society of Victoria in May and June 1878.

Interest in the invention then waned until the British showman Douglas Archibald arrived in Australia in May 1890 to demonstrate (for a fee) the improved Edison phonograph, which used a wax cylinder record. He played messages from Edison and William Gladstone and proclaimed that 'the voices of the living and the dead will mingle in futurity'. Archibald toured Australasia for two years for entrepreneurs James Macmahon and his brother Charles. The Macmahon brothers also launched Australian motion picture history when they introduced the kinetoscope, a film-viewing machine, in Sydney on 30 November 1894. The following year they converted some kinetoscopes to kinetophones by adding a phonograph. These kinetophones, shown initially at Charters Towers, Queensland, on 16 September 1895, used some locally recorded cylinders.

By the mid-1890s the cylinder phonograph, through technical improvements, was gaining increased public acceptance. At the 1896–97 Warrnambool Exhibition a youthful Thomas Rome displayed a machine on which some of the cylinders were local recordings; the Rome collection was rediscovered after his death in 1974 (aged 101 years) and comprises the earliest known surviving Australian sound recordings. A large number of the early recordings made in Australia were also of Aboriginal speech and song. These include cylinders recorded during the A.C. Haddon Cambridge Anthropological Expedition to Torres Strait in 1898 and recordings made in 1899 of Mrs Fanny Cochrane Smith, who claimed to be the last Tasmanian Aborigine. Other cylinder recordings of Aborigines were made throughout Australia up to 1939, including expeditions to central Australia by (Sir) Walter Baldwin Spencer in 1901–2 and 1912. Beginning in the 1950s, many field recordings of Aboriginal music and language were made, mainly using tape recorders; much of this work has been by AIATSIS, Canberra. The record industry published few recordings of Australia's indigenous people until the 1980s when production increased quite dramatically.

The first marketing of music recorded in Australia took place in 1898 when Melbourne music-sellers ★Allan & Co. offered cylinders of visiting celebrities and performances by staff, made while the customer waited. In Sydney, the Australia Phono Record Company, managed by Edwin Chapman Henderson, issued over 100 titles of local artists from 1903 to 1910, a time when many entertainers were going to London to record. At the end of the 1914–18 war the sale of imported cylinders was in decline and this activity ceased in 1929; in its place in these years a huge variety of acoustic 78 rpm discs were imported from England, Europe (mainly Germany) and America.

The foundations of the modern Australian record industry were laid in the mid-1920s, coinciding with the introduction of electrical recording, where a microphone replaced the acoustic horn. Four disc record manufacturing plants were built 1924–26, three in Sydney and one in Melbourne. First into the field was D. Davis & Co., music publishers, who established a pressing plant at Darlinghurst to make Brunswick records from American masters. The Gramophone Company, of England, built a factory at Erskineville which started operation on 18 January 1926 to issue His Master's Voice (HMV) and Zonophone discs. Later that year, on 14 October, the Columbia Graphophone Company opened their Homebush plant (complete with recording studio) to publish Columbia and Regal recordings. Parlophone set up an Australian branch at the end of 1926 using Columbia facilities to record local performers. In the midst of all this building and investment a young Sydney inventor, Stuart Booty, made the first disc recordings of local musicians in early 1925 at his home studio in Leichhardt for his Vitavox label.

In Melbourne, Noel Pemberton Billing, an English aviation pioneer and eccentric, built a factory for World Records at Brighton, which started pressing overseas masters in early 1925. His company issued many recordings by Australians later in the year before closing down in 1926. Brunswick, HMV, Columbia, and Parlophone had strong competition in the late 1920s, especially from Clifford Industries in Sydney and the Vocalion company in Melbourne. The Depression of 1930–33 forced the closure of Brunswick and all small manufacturers and importers. HMV, Columbia and Parlophone amalgamated in 1933 to form Electrical and Musical Industries (EMI), a group which dominated the Australian market until the arrival of the microgroove long-play disc in 1952. While the 1930s and 40s were not buoyant years, EMI maintained an impressive catalogue, with strong representation from Australian musicians and composers.

After World War II many new record companies were formed, with specialist labels appearing such as Ampersand for jazz, Wattle for folk and Rodeo for hillbilly music.

Diaphon recorded the Civic Symphony Orchestra on 6 July 1951 for the first LP release. The 1950s heralded the arrival and expansion of many publishers, including Capitol, RCA, Festival, Astor, AWA, Philips, ARC and W&G, all in competition with an expanding EMI catalogue. The years 1958–59 saw the advent of stereophonic recording and marked the end of the 78 era. It is estimated that between 1926 and 1959 over 10 000 titles were recorded by Australian recording studios, of which about 6000 were generated at the Sydney studios of EMI. This output has accelerated in subsequent decades.

The LP era fostered an increasing number of independent companies, many specialising in Australian music and composition, such as Swaggie, Mushroom, ★Move, Hadley, Selection, Cherry Pie, ★Tall Poppies and ★Larrikin. The late 1960s saw the emergence of tape recorders as a form of home and mobile entertainment, with cassette sales often rivalling disc sales. Production of LPs virtually ceased in the early 1990s following the introduction of the compact disc to Australia in May 1987. At present there are more than 200 companies publishing and importing sound recordings on more than 1500 labels for the Australian market, which has an annual retail turnover of about $600 million. All the major international companies distribute in Australia, but few take a major interest in Australian works or artists. The ★ABC have developed their ABC Classics label, and Country Music label, specialising in Australian performers and composers.

The record industry is the oldest of the audio-visual media and continues to play an expanding role in both education and entertainment. Its professional bodies in Australia include ARIA, the Oral History Association of Australia, the Australasian Sound Recordings Association, and the Fellowship of Australian Discographers.

See also *Country Music* §4(iv).

FURTHER REFERENCE
The Thomas Rome Collection is in the Performing Arts Museum, Melbourne. For Aboriginal music the largest collection of unpublished recordings is in AIATSIS, Canberra. The major national sound archives are the National Film and Sound Archive, Canberra and the Australian Institute of Recorded Sound, Port Macquarie, NSW. Specialist sound archives include *CAnl* (oral history); Australian War Memorial, Canberra; Australian Archives, Sydney; ABC, Sydney.

PETER BURGIS

Red Onions Jazz Band grew out of a Melbourne group centred on Allen ★Browne, Bill Howard and Brett Iggulden; Howard and Iggulden had been taught trombone and trumpet respectively by Ade Monsbourgh. They performed as the Gin Bottle Jazz Band until, when the name was proscribed for a television appearance, they changed to the Red Onions. Dedication to the classic Dixieland jazz canon and skilful television image projection brought them cult status that centralised them in the traditional jazz boom of the early 1960s. Changes in 1965 produced from their members the successful pop group the *Loved Ones, and stabilised the Red Onions personnel as Browne, Howard, Iggulden, John Scurry (banjo/guitar), Richard Miller, Rowan Smith (piano) and Bill Morris (tuba).

After a residency at the Royal Terminus Hotel they toured Europe and the UK, playing at the Polish Jazz Festival and elsewhere. They returned to Australia in 1968, playing various residencies. Conrad Joyce (bass) replaced Morris for a second trip to Europe in 1970, and Smith remained in the UK when the band returned to Australia. They played further residencies such as that at Prospect Hill Hotel, then in 1972 ceased performing to concentrate on developing material more consistent with the expanding interests of some members. They resumed performing in 1973, but could not break free of the stylistic demands of their established following. They stopped performing, except for occasional reunions, in the mid-1970s. Iggulden later moved to Bellingen, NSW, Scurry and Joyce continue to freelance, and after a period of inactivity Howard resumed work (including with Bob *Barnard) until his death in 1996.

FURTHER REFERENCE
Recordings include *The Red Onion Jazz Band* (1964, W&G Records WG-25/2327); *Big Band Memories*, Red Onion Jazz Band (1967, W&G Records, WG-25–5065); *Crisis*, Red Onion Jazz Band (1993, Newmarket, NEW1015.2). See also *OxfordJ*; Roger Beilby, 'Focus on the Red Onions', *Jazz Down Under* 1/4 (Mar.–Apr. 1975), 22–4   BRUCE JOHNSON

Red Sea, The.   Opera in one act, music and libretto by Malcolm *Williamson (1972). First performed at Dartington College, Devon, on 14 April 1972.

Reddy, Helen   (*b* Melbourne, 25 Oct. 1942), popular music singer. Born into a Melbourne show business family, she made her stage debut at four, and appeared on television in such children's shows as *Swallows Juniors*. She went to New York, her ticket the prize for winning a talent quest in 1966. An appearance on the *Tonight* Show led to her recording her first single, *I Don't Know How To Love Him*, which reached No. 2 in the USA charts in 1971. During the 1970s she had repeated international chart successes, including *I Am Woman* (1973) which reached No. 2, *Delta Dawn* (1973) which was also No. 2, *Leave Me Alone* (1973) which was No. 1, and *Angie Baby* (1975) which was No. 12, as well as various hugely popular albums. She toured Australia in 1973, then in the USA took American citizenship and compèred her own television shows and appeared in films. She was the star of a lavish show at the MGM Grand, Las Vegas, in 1976–77. One of the most successful popular entertainers Australia has produced, by the mid-1970s she had sold 10 million singles and 15 million albums, and won four gold singles and eight gold and three platinum albums. She has won a

Grammy award, as well as awards from *Billboard*, *Cashbox* and *Record World*.

FURTHER REFERENCE
Her early singles were recorded for Capitol. Compilations include *The Best Of Helen Reddy* (EMI 4320602) and *The Most Of Helen Reddy* (EMI 4380142). See also *McGrathA*; *GuinnessP*, III, 2058.

Redgum.   Folk-rock band formed in 1975 at Adelaide by Flinders University politics students Michael Atkinson, Verity Truman, Hugh McDonald, John Schumann and Michael Spicer. The band used acoustic instruments, producing a stridently Australian folk accent in contrast with the bland Los Angeles pop that clogged the airwaves in the 1970s. Their songs expressed left-wing, socialist views. Two early alternative radio hits summed up the importance of the lyrics: *One More Boring Thursday Night in Adelaide* by Schumann and *If You Don't Fight You Lose* by Atkinson had a combination of wit, political fire in the belly and closely observed details of the lives of everyday Australians. *If You Don't Fight You Lose* appeared as graffiti on fences and railway cuttings around Australia, and was adopted as a slogan by several unions in their battles against the Fraser Government.

Diamond Drover by McDonald reflected his rural background and went on to be covered by over 30 other artists here and internationally, including the Irish singer Christy Moore. The band had two varyingly successful tours of Europe. Their biggest hit was *I Was Only 19* in 1984, the No. 1 single in Australia for six weeks, based on the experiences of Schumann's brother-in-law in the Vietnam War; royalties from the work were donated to the Vietnam Veterans Association. They appeared at the Sydney Entertainment Centre, Mit fyn Festival, Denmark, and the Narara Festival in 1983. The band took some pride in steadfastly refusing to appear on television's *Countdown*, and their video-clip for *I Was Only 19* was distinguished by its not showing the band members. Redgum sold over 300 000 records in Australia.

FURTHER REFERENCE
Recordings include *If You Don't Fight You Lose* (1978, Larrikin LP LRF 037); *Virgin Ground* (1980, CBS LP ELPS 4137); *Brown Rice and Kerosine* (1981, CBS LP ELPS 4257); *Caught In The Act* (1983, CBS LP ELPS 4371); *Midnight Sun* (1986, CBS LP ELPS 4570). See also *McGrathA*; *SpencerW*.   THOMAS JUDE SAMMUT

Reed Pipe   (or bone). A whistle made of bamboo, blown during the male initiation ceremony, *Wintjinam*, of the Aboriginal people of Cape York. It was used to signal the approach of unauthorised persons, especially women, to the initiation ground, and heralded the approach of young male initiates. This instrument is no longer in use. A 'rude panpipes made of bone' was also reported by E. Harold Davies in 1927, describing an instrument seen in central Australia among the Aboriginal people; neither were used as accompaniments to singing. Pan-pipes of bamboo are used in the Torres Strait.   GRACE KOCH

Reeder, Haydn   (*b* Melbourne, 27 Feb. 1944), composer. After studying piano at the University of Melbourne Conservatorium and piano and composition (with Schiske, Urbanner, and Cerha) at the Vienna Hochschule für Musik, he worked as an editor and copyist for Universal Edition, London, from 1971. He won the Premio Città di Trieste for his orchestral work *Attract and Repulse* (1976) and his music was soon performed by contemporary groups in Australia and heard on the BBC and European radio. He had two composer fellowships from the Australia Council (1973, 1980), taught at La Trobe University 1983–88 and had a composer fellowship from the Victorian Government in 1989. His works include *Time Limits* for chamber ensemble and tape (1974), *The Three Mirrors* for guitar quartet (1978), an opera, *Siren's Hotel*, after James Joyce *Ulysses* chapter 11 (1986), and *Penumbra* for chamber ensemble (1983).

FURTHER REFERENCE
Masks has been recorded by Larry Sitsky, pf (1988, Move MD3066) and published in *Contemporary Australian Piano* (La Trobe University Press,1985). *The Melbourne Report* 8/2 (Oct. 1992), 32–4.

Reedy River.   Bush ballad with words by Henry Lawson, set to music by Chris Kempster. Theme-song of Dick Diamond's play of that name about the aftermath of the 1891 shearers' strike. Produced by the radical New Theatre, Sydney, in 1953, with its use of folk-songs and dances it became a smash hit around Australia, giving huge impetus to the folk-song revival movement and introducing the *Bushwhackers, the first bush band of the revival movement.

FURTHER REFERENCE
Published in *Reedy River Song Book* (Sydney: New Theatre, 1954).

Reels, The.   Rock band (1976–92) formed at Dubbo, NSW, when songwriters Dave Mason (vocals) and Craig Hooper (guitar, keyboard) joined the Brucelanders. Public recognition followed after radio 2JJ Sydney asked the group to record; they moved to Sydney in 1977 and became the Reels, gaining their first recording contract in 1978. In 1979 the group toured the pub circuit and released their debut single, *Love Will Find A Way*, and first album, *The Reels*. Perhaps the most idiosyncratic band ever to have appeared on the Australian rock scene, in 1980 they began to experiment with the then new synthesiser in the song *After The News*, which was promoted on their Reels by Rail tour, in which the band travelled exclusively by public transport. Similarly idiosyncratic was their Reels Go Primitive tour, which saw the group performing in Fred Flintstone-like costumes. At this stage, the group consisted of David Mason

(vocals), Craig Hooper (guitar), John Bliss (drums), Paul Abrahams (bass) and Colin Newham and Karen Ansell (keyboards).

After the release of *Five Great Gift Ideas From The Reels* at Christmas 1980, they recorded what was to become their most memorable album, *Quasimodo's Dream*. The Kitchen Man tour followed, the audience being invited to dismantle the kitchen set the band used. The release of *Beautiful* came in 1982. After the release of *Pitt Street Farmers* in September 1983, they took a year off, re-forming in 1985 for the first of the Reels by Request tours. The release of *Bad Moon Rising* saw them at No. 11 nationally. Reels by Candlelight tours took place in 1986–87, and their final album, *Neighbours*, was released in February 1988.

FURTHER REFERENCE
Recordings include *The Reels* (1979, Polygram); *Quasimodo's Dream* (1981, Polygram); *Beautiful* (1982, K Tel)*; Unreel* (1983, RCA); *Neighbours* (1988, Regular D19753); *Requiem* (1992, Regular RMD 53370); and mini-albums *5 Great Gift Ideas from The Reels* (1980, Polygram) and *Pitt Street Farmers* (1983, RCA). See also Glenn A. Baker and Stuart Coupe, *The New Music* (Sydney: Bay Books, 1980); *Guinness P*; *McGrathA*; *SpencerW.*
                                                    JOHN WERETKA

Reeves, Adolphus Francis   ('Splinter') (*b* Jarrahdale, WA, 9 Jan. 1924; *d* Tweed Heads, NSW, 23 Jan. 1987), jazz reeds player. He began alto saxophone in 1935, playing professionally in WA before moving to Melbourne in 1941. He was with Frank *Coughlan, and led the Storklub band in 1947. He became a major pioneer of bop, notably through his group the Splintettes, formed in 1948. He left Melbourne in 1954 to work in Surfers Paradise, and won the tenor saxophone *Music Maker* poll in 1955. During the early 1960s he was in Townsville, Queensland, in 1964–70 he was with the Channel Nine Orchestra, Melbourne, then in 1970–81 he was based in Sydney working in clubs and aboard cruise ships. He retired to northern NSW, where he died after a road accident.

FURTHER REFERENCE
Recordings include *Splinter Reeves & His Splintet* (1949, Jazzart JA-16); *Splinter Reeves Splintette* (1950, Jazzart JA-55); *Splinter Reeves And His Splintette* (1953, Jazzart CMS-2). See also *BissetB*; *OxfordJ*.   BRUCE JOHNSON

Reeves, Gabor   (*b* Budapest, Hungary, 8 Feb. 1928), clarinettist. After studying at the Franz Liszt Academy, he emigrated to Australia in 1948, continuing his studies at the NSW State Conservatorium. He was principal clarinet in the Queensland Symphony Orchestra (from 1951), then in the Sydney Symphony Orchestra (from 1954). He worked freelance in London from 1960 and returned to Australia as principal clarinet in the Melbourne Symphony Orchestra in 1963. Teaching clarinet at the Elder Conservatorium from 1964, he was a founding member of the ★University of Adelaide Wind Quintet, then head of woodwind at the NSW State Conservatorium from 1974 (head of performance studies from 1990 and acting principal in 1994). In Sydney he was a foundation member of the Sydney Wind Quintet. He has given solo recitals and played in chamber music throughout Australia and has had several pieces written for him by Australian composers. A dedicated teacher who has given masterclasses in the USA as well as in Australia, his publications include *Playing Scales for Clarinet* (Melbourne: Allans, 1968). He was honoured with the AM in 1995.

Reflections in a Glass-house. Work for speaker, chorus and orchestra (1970) by George ★Dreyfus, libretto by Lynne Strahan. Written for the bicentenary of the voyage to Australia by Captain James Cook, challenging the notions of Australia as a free and lucky country. Published by Allans, Melbourne, *c.*1972.

Reggae. Jamaican popular dance style originating in the 1960s, characterised by a dominant electric bass, against which the other instruments play short ostinato phrases which subdivide the beat in intense patterns. Reggae came to influence some Australian rock bands in the late 1980s, including ★Jo Jo Zep and the Falcons, the ★Tactics, the ★Rockmelons, ★vs Spy vs Spy and others. See also *Aboriginal Music,* §4(iii).

Reichenberg, Joseph (*b* Naples, 1790; *d* Hobart, Jan. 1851), performer, composer. An Italian who joined the British army on campaign in Sicily in 1809, he arrived in Hobart with the 40th Regiment in 1824, and remained to teach at a girls' school at Ross, Tasmania, after his regiment left in 1828. He taught musical instruments, singing and Italian as well as tuning pianos. On an army pension, he returned to Hobart in 1831 where he organised concerts, performed and taught until his death. He was perhaps the first composer to reside in Australia; his *First Set of Quadrilles for Australia* (1826, now lost) for piano, flute, violin, or band, was sold throughout NSW.

Reid, William Duff (*b* Shenley, Hertforshire, England, 13 July 1925), conductor. After studying science, he studied piano, organ, composition and conducting at the Royal College of Music, London, and was organist at St Thomas's Regent Street and the Chapel Royal, Tower of London in 1953. He worked as a *répétiteur* for the Carl Rosa Opera Co. from 1954, then for the Welsh National Opera and the English Opera Group 1957–65. He was conductor of the London Festival Ballet 1965–67, and guest conductor with the Vienna Philharmonic and London Philharmonic Orchestra. He was assistant conductor at Sadler's Wells from 1958 and with them visited Australia with *The Merry Widow* in 1960. He made his debut with the Australian Opera in 1967 and became head of music for the Elizabethan Sydney and Melbourne Orchestras 1967–75, then director of music for the Elizabethan Theatre Trust 1976–87. Over a long period he has proved himself a practical, technically adept conductor and he is esteemed by singers as an excellent and resourceful vocal coach, particularly in modern repertoire.

FURTHER REFERENCE
He has recorded excerpts from *The Merry Widow* with the Sadler's Wells Opera Orchestra (1959, Classics for Pleasure). See also *Holmes C.*

Reimann, Immanuel Gotthold (*b* Hahndorf, SA, 13 Jan. 1859; *d* Norwood, SA, 19 Mar. 1932), piano teacher. He studied with local teachers and at the private Hahndorf Academy, then with Otto Stange. In 1875 he taught at the Hahndorf Academy, later in Adelaide, before leaving for Berlin in 1880. There he enrolled in Kullak's Neue Akademie der Tonkunst, and at the Scharwenka Konservatorium, and after gaining his diplomas returned home and founded the ★Adelaide College of Music in 1883. Following Sir Thomas Elder's bequest to the University of Adelaide in 1897 for a school of music, Joshua ★Ives's 'Report Concerning the Proposed Conservatoire of Music' recommended to the University Council that Reimann and certain of his staff should be engaged, and noted that this 'will turn into an ally one who might be a strong rival'. Reimann was thus the leading piano teacher at the Elder Conservatorium until his death, and eventually became assistant director.

His role in the musical life of Adelaide was wide-ranging. He loved playing chamber music and was director of the ★Adelaide String Quartet Club; from the inception of the AMEB he was an examiner, and edited educational publications for Allans Music; he was president of the Musical Association of South Australia (1930), and from 1891 until shortly before his death was organist and choirmaster at the Flinders St Lutheran Church.

FURTHER REFERENCE
Annagrit Laubenthal, *ADB,* 11.

DOREEN BRIDGES

Renaissance Players, The. Founded in 1966 at the University of Sydney, this group of professional and student musicians has been one of the leading pioneers of early music performance in Australia. The group has a nucleus of nine members and plays music from the ninth century to the present, researched, collected, arranged or composed by founder-director Winsome Evans. More than 40 instruments are used, many by Australian makers. Generally, programs develop themes of satire, comedy, pathos or whimsy and frequently incorporate poetry, mime or dance. The group is famed for its performances at the Sydney University's Great Hall, has also performed throughout Australia and Asia (1974), and has released 16 LP and CD recordings since 1976.

FURTHER REFERENCE

Their recordings include *Adam's Apple* (1977); *The Captive Unicorn* (1978); *The Cat's Fiddlestick* (1981); *The Ring of Creation* (1994); *Songs for a Wise King* (1996).   JOHN GRIFFITHS

Revelation, The. Oratorio (1882) by G.W. *Torrance, set to texts freely chosen from the biblical Revelation. First performed at the Melbourne Town Hall on 27 June 1882. A vocal score was published (Novello & Co., 1899).

Revell, Digger [Gary Hildred] (*b* Dubbo), popular music singer. He started singing rock and roll in 1959, learned guitar and piano, and with the *Denvermen from 1961 appeared regularly on *Six O'Clock Rock* and *Bandstand*, then toured Australia and NZ extensively in 1963. His first solo hit was *I'm Building Castles In the Air,* which reached No. 3 in the charts in 1963, then *My Little Rocker's Turned Surfie* was No. 33 in 1964. After tastes changed with the Beatles he adopted the mod image and *My Prayer* reached No. 12 in 1965. He went to the USA in 1965 but found little success, and returned to Australia to sing country-style songs, touring rural clubs.

FURTHER REFERENCE

Recordings include *I'm Building Castles In The Air* (1963, HMV); *My Little Rocker's Turned Surfie* (1964, RCA); *My Prayer* (1965, RCA); *Reaching For The Stars* (1989, Canetoad). For discography, see *SpencerA*. See also *McGrathA*; *SpencerW.*

Reyne, James. See *Australian Crawl.*

Rhone, Marty [Carl Van Rhoon], pop singer. After singing in local Sydney venues, he worked with the Soul Agents in 1966, making his debut single, *Nature Boy.* Moving to Melbourne in 1967, he appeared on television and in local venues, making five more singles without achieving chart success. During his (conscripted) army service he played flute in the band of the Royal Military College, Duntroon (1970–72), then enrolled in music at the University of Melbourne and appeared in *Godspell* (1972). He made another eight singles, of which *Denim and Lace* reached No. 2 in the charts in 1975. Winning an award at the Tokyo Song Festival in 1976, he released his album *Denim And Lace* in 1976, the single *Mean Pair Of Jeans* and the album *Marty Rhone* in 1977. Going to England, he appeared in *The King And I* in 1978, and he continues to appear as an actor and singer.

FURTHER REFERENCE

Recordings include *Nature Boy* (1966, Spin EK 1221), *Denim and Lace* (M7 MS 115), *Denim And Lace* (M7 MLP 127), *Mean Pair Of Jeans* (M7 MS 209) and *Marty Rhone* (M7 MLF 171). For discography, see *SpencerA*. See also *McGrathA*; *SpencerW.*

Richards, Digby ('Dig') (*b* Dunodoo, NSW, 12 Sept. 1941), popular music singer. He moved to Sydney at the age of 16 as a trainee store manager. Forming the R-Jays, he played at dances and signed with Festival, his debut recording as Dig Richards, *I Wanna Love You*, reaching No. 22 in the charts in 1959 and *My Little Lover* reaching No. 31 in 1960. He appeared regularly on television's *Six O'Clock Rock* and toured with Crash Craddock and Ricky Nelson, having five Top 40 hits in four years. Preparing for a career beyond rock and roll, he took voice lessons at the NSW State Conservatorium and studied guitar; in 1964 he hosted the *Dig Richards Ampol Show* on television. In 1965 he toured South-East Asia and spent the following years in club work, some of it in England (1970). Returning to Australia in 1971 as Digby Richards with a country style, his *People Call Me Country* reached No. 27 in the charts and *Do the Spunky Monkey* (1974) was No. 12. One of the foremost stars of early Australian rock and roll, Richards made 40 singles, seven EPs and eight albums. He survived the changes of taste to make a successful transition into club entertainment.

FURTHER REFERENCE

Recordings include *I Wanna Love You* (1959, Festival FK 3083); *My Little Lover* (1960, Rex RS028); *People Call Me Country* (1972, RCA 102040); *Dig Richards And The R-Jays* (1959, Festival FL 7119); *Harlequin* (1971, RCA SL102035); *Jive After Five* (91988, Festival L19002). For discography, see *SpencerA*. See also *APRAJ* 3/1 (1983), 35; *McGrathA*; *SpencerW.*

Richardson, Charles (*b* Camden Town, London, 25 July 1847; *d* Stanmore, Sydney, 22 May 1926), organ-builder. The son of prominent regional organ-builder W.E. Richardson of Manchester, he trained with Hill & Son and Henry Willis & Sons in London and in Paris with Charles Barker. He was later a partner in his father's business before emigrating to Sydney in 1882, where he began in premises at Darlinghurst, later moving to Paddington, Church Hill and then Stanmore. Richardson built a total of more than 30 instruments for clients throughout NSW and also in Queensland and Victoria. These were mainly of smaller size, but recognised for their solidity of construction and excellent craftsmanship.

FURTHER REFERENCE

Graeme D. Rushworth, *Historic Organs of New South Wales* (Sydney: Hale & Iremonger, 1988), 122–35; idem, *ADB*, 11.
                                                                                 JOHN MAIDMENT

Richardson, Marilyn Ann (*b* Sydney, 10 June 1936), soprano. She studied piano and singing at the NSW Conservatorium. Winning the Adelaide *Advertiser* aria competition in 1969, in 1971 she was awarded a Churchill Fellowship to study in Europe. After tuition with Bernac in Paris, Conchita Badia in Barcelona and theatre classes in Austria, she made her international debut in Basel in the title roles of *Lulu* and *Salome* 1972–75. She returned to Australia to perform the title role in *Aida* in 1975 for the Australian Opera and has been a guest principal artist with that company since then. In addition, she has performed with all of the Australian state companies. While her career has mainly been in Australia, in 1985 she again visited Europe to sing the role of Aida for the English National Opera. Her versatility is reflected in her roles, which include the Marschallin in *Der Rosenkavalier*, the Countess in *Le Nozze di Figaro* and the title roles in *Katya Kabanová*, *Tosca* and *Madama Butterfly*. Since 1990 she has further extended her repertoire to include the Wagnerian roles of Elsa in *Lohengrin*, Isolde in *Tristan und Isolde*, Sieglinde in *Die Walküre* and Eva in *Die Meistersinger von Nürnberg*.

Richardson has given numerous concerts and recitals and has appeared with the ABC orchestras. Specialising in 20th-century music, since 1958 she has given the first Australian performance of over 300 songs and vocal works by composers such as Messiaen, Dallapiccola, Berio and Cage. Additionally she has performed many Australian compositions and has had a number of works composed for her.

FURTHER REFERENCE
Recordings include *Opera arias,* Queensland Symphony Orchestra, cond. V. Kamirski (ABC 434 138); *Italian Opera Arias* (ABC 442 368). See also *CA* (1995–96); *GroveD.*

KERRY VANN

Richardson, Peter   (*b* Sydney, 29 Aug. 1933; *d* Sydney, 11 Mar. 1973), flautist. After studying with Victor McMahon at the NSW State Conservatorium, he was principal flute in the National Opera of Australia tour of 1955, then with the Tasmanian Symphony Orchestra. He returned to Sydney in 1960, teaching privately, working freelance and forming a wind ensemble for ISCM concerts at the University of Sydney in 1965, then teaching at the NSW State Conservatorium and forming the Sydney Baroque Ensemble from 1970 until his untimely death. Skilled in Baroque style and ornamentation, he was also a gifted player of contemporary works; he played in the Australian premiere of Schoenberg's *Pierrot Lunaire* (1959), and at the ISCM presented Boulez's Sonata for Flute and Piano, Richard Meale's *Las Alboradas* (1963) as well as works by Berio, Maderna, Stockhausen and Australian composers.

FURTHER REFERENCE
Obit. by Donald Peart and tribute by Colin Evans in *Music Now* 2/2 (Dec. 1974), 2–6.

Rick and Thel.   Country music duo comprised of Richard Bruce Carey (*b* Sydney, 13 Aug. 1927) and Thelma Carey née Hoctor (*b* Glossodia, NSW, 9 Oct. 1929). They met at a hillbilly club in 1949 and began their duo act as the Sliprail Swingsters, marrying in January 1952. An early triumph came at a Sydney Town Hall Reg Lindsay Show, earning them a standing ovation for *Looking Back to See*. They recorded for EMI from 1954 to

1978, then signed with Hadley Records. National touring began in March 1958 with the All Star Western Show, later with Chad Morgan, and in 1960 with their own Rick and Thel Show. In 1974 they pioneered tours by charter aircraft of the NT and northern Queensland, with mainly Aboriginal audiences from missions and stations. The pair had enormous appeal as fresh-faced sweethearts in the early years, and their show was also popular for Rick Carey's tap-dancing and the slapstick comic character 'Cousin Ratsack'.

FURTHER REFERENCE
Recordings include *She Was Happy Till She Met You* (1953, Regal Zonophone G 25381); *Looking Back to See* (Regal Zonophone G 25440); *Sliprails and Saddles* (OSX 7648); *Mr and Mrs Country Music* (Hadley 1243). For discography see *WatsonC*, 2. See also Monika Allan, *The Tamworth Country Music Festival* (Sydney: Horwitz Grahame, 1988); *SmithB*.

JENNIFER HILL

Rickards, Harry [Benjamin Harry Leete]   (*b* Stratford, London, 4 Dec. 1843; *d* Croydon, London, 13 Oct. 1911), variety actor, theatre owner. At first an engine driver, he worked in English music hall from 1862, having local success with his song *Captain Jinks of the Horse Marines*, but his attempt to run his own music hall ending in bankruptcy. To recover his position he toured Australia (1871–74, 1885–87), then brought his own company to Australia in 1892, leasing the Garrick Theatre, Sydney and renaming it the Tivoli. By 1895 he had Tivoli theatres in most capital cities and was importing major variety artists from London for his circuit, which was to become the major national presenter of pantomime and variety in Australia for more than 50 years. An artist with a fine baritone voice and sure theatrical sense, he was in his last years one of the dominating figures in Australian variety entertainment.

FURTHER REFERENCE
Obit. in *Australasian* 21 Oct. 1911; *Argus* 26 Oct. 1911. See also *ADB*, 11; John West, *Theatre in Australia* (Sydney, 1978).

Riddell, Alistair   (*b* Melbourne, 22 June 1955), composer. After early lessons in classical guitar and lute, he studied music at La Trobe University and from 1981 began experimenting with computer-controlled piano, inspired by the player-piano works of American composer Conlon Nancarrow, producing his first composition *Atlantic Fears* in 1983. After a further course in computer science at La Trobe and a period working as a programmer in 1986, he took doctoral studies in computer music with Paul Lansky at Princeton University. His music is chiefly for computer-processed sounds or computer-driven piano, and he is exploring the application of algorithmic control of signal processing techniques to real-world sound. His works include *Tales from Transitions* (1986) for tape, *Heavy Mouse* (1992) for synthetic sound, the sound installation *Dave Reviews* (1994), and *Legend* (1996) for text and voice sounds. With works heard at computer music venues in New York, London and Europe as well as in Australia, he is currently post-doctoral fellow at La Trobe University

FURTHER REFERENCE

Recordings include *Atlantic Fears* (1983, Canberra School of Music, CSM 4) and *Fantasie,* computer-driven pf (1984, New Albion 028). See also *JenkinsT*, 149–56.

Riedel, Deborah

(b Sydney, 31 July 1958), soprano. After studies at the NSW State Conservatorium and with Audrey Langford and Paul Hamburger in London as a mezzo-soprano, she worked in the Australian Opera chorus from 1983, then won the Sydney Sun *Aria* and made her debut with the Australian Opera in 1986. She soon changed to soprano roles, joining the Australian Opera in 1988. She was with the Frankfurt Opera 1991–93 and has appeared frequently with the Victoria State Opera and in ABC orchestral concerts, as well as abroad with the English National Opera, Covent Garden, Bordeaux, Geneva, Munich, and San Diego Operas. Combining a sparkling voice with excellent acting, she has sung Mimi, Mignon, Zerlina, Susanna, Hansel, Leila in *Pearl Fishers*, Freia in *Das Rheingold*, Nayad in *Ariadne auf Naxos,* as well as Jemmy in *Guillaume Tell,* the Drummer in Ullmann's *Emperor of Atlantis,* and Marianna in *Il Signor Bruschino.*

FURTHER REFERENCE

Recordings include Poulenc, *Dialogue of the Carmelites*, Australian Opera. *CA* (1995–96); Elizabeth Forbes, *GroveO.*

Rigo Opera Company.

Touring company (1919–20) organised by American Frank Rigo (1868–1936). Recruited from the Metropolitan Opera, New York, Rigo came to Australia as stage director for the Melba-Williamson opera season in 1911. He remained after the tour had finished, and in 1919 set up his own opera company from some of the ★Gonzales Co. singers who had remained behind after their tour and a number of principals recruited from local singers, with Gustave ★Slapoffski conducting. The company presented repertory pieces (although Fritz ★Hart conducted his own *Pierrette*), and appeared in Melbourne, then (under J.C. Williamson's management) in Sydney, Adelaide and NZ. Amy ★Castles was featured in her return to the Australian stage, and many fresh local voices were heard in principal parts, but production standards were mixed.

At a time when opera performance in Australia had become less frequent and Australians singing principal parts unknown, Rigo gave a number of important Australian singers their first major roles, including Browning ★Mummery, Frederick ★Collier and Gertrude ★Johnson. He made little money from the venture, and despite

further work as a stage director for Williamson and Fuller, died in straitened circumstances, leaving a 14–year-old daughter.

FURTHER REFERENCE

Obit. in *AMN*, (Sept. 1936), 8. See also Alison Gyger, *Opera for the Antipodes* (Sydney: Currency Press, 1990), 217–30; *BrisbaneE*, 183; Melbourne *Punch* 23 Jan. 1919, 124; Melbourne *Theatre*, (June 1919), 5.

Riptides, The.

Rock band (1979–83) formed in Brisbane, comprised chiefly of Mark Callaghan (vocals), Scott Matheson and Andrew Leitch (guitars), Howard Shawcross (bass) and Dennis Cantwell (drums). The members had mostly studied architecture together at the University of Queensland and worked in other local bands. They recorded a somewhat undeveloped rock debut single, *Sunset Strip*, in 1979 and acquired a dedicated following as a surf band at coast venues. Moving to Sydney in 1980, they became a highly popular pub band, released *Hearts And Flowers* in 1982 and an album, *The Riptides*, and were supporting act to the Simple Minds tour in the same year. There were membership changes, and with a lack of chart success they drifted apart in 1983 after releasing an anthology, *Last Wave*. They re-formed for the album *Resurface* and occasional tours (1988, 1991). With infectious melodies and a relentless dance pulse, often combined with good songwriting from Callaghan, they retained a loyal live following.

FURTHER REFERENCE

Recordings include *Sunset Strip* (Able AB 004), *Hearts And Flowers* (1982, Regular RRSP 716), *The Riptides* (Regular RRLP 1207), *Last Wave* (WEA), *Resurface* (1987, Polygram 832989–1). A compilation is *Wave Rock* (1991, Phonogram 510224). For discography, see *SpencerA*. See also *McGrathA*; *SpencerW*; *GuinnessP*, III, 2094; Donald Robertson, 'Rising Riptides', *Inner City Sound*, ed. Clinton Walker (Sydney: Wild & Woolley, 1982).

Rita and Dita.

Series of children's operettas in one act, music and text by Colin ★Brumby. The first, *Rita and Dita*, after the Grimm Brothers' *Hansel and Gretel*, was first performed at Brisbane on 13 May 1968. A sequel *Rita and Dita and the Pirate* (1968) was published by J. Albert & Son in 1969. *Rita and Dita in Toyland* was first performed at Rockhampton, Queensland, on 23 February 1970, and another, *Rita and Dita and the Jolly Swagman*, after A.B. Paterson's *Waltzing Matilda*, was first performed on 15 February 1971.

Ritchard, Cyril

(b Sydney 1 Dec. 1899; d Chicago, USA, 18 Dec. 1977), dancer, theatrical singer. After studying medicine at the University of Sydney, he worked in the chorus for J.C. Williamsons productions at Sydney from 1917. He had solo roles by 1924 and appeared in the film *The Importance of Being Earnest* in 1929, then worked abroad, becoming renowned in the 1930s for dance routines of the Astaire-Rodgers type with his partner Madge ★Elliot (whom he married in 1935). They toured Australia several times, notably in *Private Lives* (1951) and *The Pleasure of his Company* (1960).

FURTHER REFERENCE
Obit. in *Australian* 19 Dec. 1977. See also *PorterS*, 177–9; John West, *Theatre in Australia* (Sydney, 1978), 172–4.

Ritchie, Stanley (*b* Sydney, *c.*1932), violinist. After studying at the NSW State Conservatorium he won the ABC Instrumental and Vocal Competition in 1952 and studied in Paris, then settled in the USA. He was leader of the Philadelphia Quartet and the Musica Aeterna Orchestra, and a member of the New York Chamber Players, then associate concertmaster of the Metropolitan Opera Orchestra before returning to Australia in 1981 to join the Sydney String Quartet. He moved back to the USA in 1982. A musician of very wide orchestral and chamber experience, he is also an authoritative player of the Baroque violin.

Rites of Passage. Opera (1972–73), music and libretto by Peter ★Sculthorpe, for double chorus, dancers, and two on-stage orchestras (no soloists). Concerned with the progression from birth to death and rebirth, it has no narrative plot; rather six 'chorales' separated by four 'rites' (in an Aboriginal language) and a central interlude. Commissioned by the Australian Elizabethan Theatre Trust for the opening of the Sydney Opera House somewhat prematurely in 1965, it was not performed there until a year after it opened. First performed on 27 September 1974, it was nevertheless the first production of a full-length Australian opera at the Sydney Opera House. Recorded by the Melbourne Chorale with the Victorian College of the Arts Orchestra under John Hopkins (1976, World Record Club R0 3074).

Roach, Archie (*b* 1955, Framlingham Mission, Vic.), Aboriginal singer-songwriter. The removal from his parents as a child by government agencies led to Roach's best-known song, *Took the Children Away*, and other songs are also autobiographical. His festival performances include WOMADelaide, the Corroboree Festival, London (1993), and the Berlin Independence Festival. He has had tours to America, Canada, the UK (1992), America (1993), NZ with Paul Kelly, the UK (1994), and Canada and Europe (1995). He won the ARIA best indigenous album award of 1991 for *Charcoal Lane* and best Australian new talent.

FURTHER REFERENCE
Recordings include *Koorie* (1988, Victorian Aboriginal Cultural Heritage Trust, unnumbered); *Charcoal Lane* (1990, Mushroom Records D30386); *Jamu Dreaming* (1993, Aurora Records D30851). See also A. Roach, *You Have the Power* (Sydney: Angus & Robertson, 1994). P. DUNBAR-HALL

RoadKnight, Margret (*b* Melbourne, 16 July 1943), folk-singer. After singing folk music in her teens, she sang professionally from 1964, appearing in Melbourne clubs, then at national rock, jazz and folk festivals. She sang topical songs for the ABC current affairs program *Open End* (1973) and moved to Sydney in 1974. Her single *Girls In Our Town* reached No. 18 in the charts in 1976. She studied in the USA on an Australia Council grant. She has provided music for five productions with the SA Theatre Co., and was musical director for *Deep Bells Ringing*. In the 1980s she toured Australia for Musica Viva, and appeared in the USA, the UK, Europe, East-Asia and the South Pacific, representing Australia at 10 festivals abroad. One of the most senior Australian folk-singers, often heard at political rallies and marches singing of racism, feminism, the environment or other issues, she has a deep, throaty voice and an eclectic repertoire of folk, blues, gospel and jazz, and has recorded eight albums.

FURTHER REFERENCE
Albums include *Ice* (1978 Infinity/Festival), *Moving Target* (1988, Sandstock SSM 028) and *Fringe Benefit* (1993, Newmarket NEW 10212). See also *CA* (1995–96); *McGrathA*; *SpencerW*; *Age* 26 Apr. 1991.

Rob E.G. [Robert (Robbie) George Porter] (*b* Sydney, 4 June 1942), pop guitarist, entrepreneur. Playing steel guitar from the age of eight, he appeared on television from 1959 playing and singing country music repertoire. He released the steel guitar instrumentals *Your Cheatin' Heart* and *Si Señor*, which reached No. 2 in the charts in 1962, then *55 Days At Peking* which reached No. 1 in 1963, winning him a TV Logie. In all he made 18 singles; by 1964 he was a regular on *Bandstand* and had his own television show, *Surf Sound*, and had released his album *Jezebel* and *Rob E.G. Plays Hawaiian*. With Beatlemania in 1964 tastes for instrumentals evaporated; he moved first to the UK then to the USA in 1965, and went into the business side of popular music. Through his Mega Entertainment he has had a significant role promoting Australian bands there.

FURTHER REFERENCE
Recordings include *Your Cheatin' Heart* (Rex RS 007) and *Si Señor* (Festival FKL 210), *55 Days At Peking* (Festival FK 403, *Jezebel* (Festival) and *Rob E.G. Plays Hawaiian* (Festival FL 31338). A compilation is *5.4.3.2.1* (1988, Festival L19003). For discography, see *SpencerA*. See also *McGrathA*; *SpencerW*; *Australian* 19 Dec. 1992.

Robertson, Harry (*b* Barrhead, Glasgow, Scotland, 16 Sept. 1923; *d* Brisbane, 15 May 1995), ballad singer-songwriter. He served with the British Navy from 1945, learning folk-songs from many parts of the world. He migrated to Australia in 1952, worked as a fitter and turner and became involved with the trade union movement. He was chairman of the first national folk festival (1969), and in a remarkable residency at the Chullora railway workshops, Sydney in 1985–86 taught singing and songwriting to untrained railway labourers. An important figure in the folk-song revival of the 1960s who helped translate the Australian urban and coastal experience into song, he wrote and sang sea shanties, drinking songs, protest songs and love songs, and became the only Australian represented in *The Oxford Book of Sea Songs*.

FURTHER REFERENCE
Recordings include *Whale Chasing Men* (1971, Larrikin LRF 049). See also *Australian* 6 June 1995.

Robinson, Stanford (*b* Leeds, England, 5 July 1904; *d* Brighton, England, 25 Oct. 1984), English conductor. After studies at the Royal College of Music he conducted opera for BBC radio and television broadcast 1936–66, as well as appearing as guest conductor at Covent Garden, Budapest and elsewhere. A capable conductor, especially sympathetic in vocal accompaniment, he came to Australia for the ABC in 1967 and was conductor of the Queensland Symphony Orchestra 1968–69, during this time making early recordings with Kiri Te Kanawa and the New Zealand Little Symphony Orchestra (Decca).

Robinson, Sir William Cleaver Francis (*b* Rosmead, Ireland, 14 Jan. 1834; *d* South Kensington, England, 2 May 1897), British civil administrator, composer. The Governor of WA (1875–77, 1880–83, 1890–95), SA (1883–89) and Victoria (1889 in an acting capacity), Robinson was also a composer, pianist and violinist. He was a keen promoter of the arts and in 1884 raised a substantial sum towards a chair in music at the University of Adelaide. His works include operettas, of which *The Handsome Ransom, or, The Brigand's Bride* (*c*.1893) with libretto by Francis Hart was performed in Perth and Melbourne, and a number of songs, including the patriotic song *Unfurl the Flag* (*c*.1890) to words by Francis Hart, which was performed by schoolchildren on Robinson's return to Perth in 1890. Six of his hymn tunes appear in *78 Australian Hymn Tunes* (1892). Of these, 'Westralia' was especially popular in Perth. See *Australian Hymnody*.

FURTHER REFERENCE
IrvinD; A.H. Kornweibel, *Apollo and the Pioneers: The Story of the First Hundred Years of Music in Western Australia* (Perth: Music Council of WA, 1973); Elizabeth Wood, *GroveD*.

DIANNE GOME

Rock. See *Popular Music* §2.

Rock Australia Magazine (RAM). Fortnightly magazine for rock music fans, published at Darlinghurst, Sydney, 1975–89.

Rockhampton, pop. (1991) 55 768, city situated on the Fitzroy River 40 km from the central Queensland coast. Before European settlement in 1858, the region was home to the peoples of the Darambal language group. Various sites around the district including *ba-dul* (Padygole) functioned as customary locations for corroborees and ceremonial occasions. Decimation of the local Aboriginal population and loss of their culture was recorded as early as 1897, and it was not until the 1980s that the Dreamtime Cultural Centre was established to promote the music and culture of the Aborigines of the central Queensland and coastal regions.

European music-making has had a relatively prominent role in the development of Rockhampton's cultural identity. From the time of the city's first recorded amateur concert at the Rockhampton Court House in 1861, a number of musical societies were established to provide the city's audiences with musical entertainment and local musicians with opportunities for performance (the Rockhampton Choral Society, 1864; the Rockhampton Glee and Madrigal Society, 1865; the Rockhampton Philharmonic Society, 1870; the Rockhampton Instrumental Society, 1875; the Musical Union, 1884; the German Glee Club; the Orpheus Club, 1883; the Liedertafel, 1887; the Royal Flying Squad Orchestra, 1908). Many of these original groups have been disbanded, but several have maintained a profile in community music up to the present (the Musical Union, the Georgian Choir). The establishment of several music halls and theatres in the late 1890s provided venues for local performances, as well as touring soloists and groups including Dame Nellie Melba (1909), Anna Pavlova's ballet company (1927) and Roy Orbison (1974). The first brass band was established in 1862 (the Volunteer Rifle Brigade Band) and in the 1990s brass bands continue to play a prominent role as an informal training ground for young brass players from the local community.

Several prominent musicians have been associated with the musical profile and development of the district, including Viennese violinist Ludwig ★D'Hage (1863–1960), soprano Florence Schmidt, pianist Molly Hourigan (the first Australian to study at the Brussels Conservatoire), and violin prodigy Alma ★Moodie from Mount Morgan, who at 11 was awarded the Brussels Conservatoire prize (1910). In more recent years the increased number and quality of musicians and musical productions have been contingent upon several combined factors: greater provision of studio and school music teachers, the presence of the Rockhampton Performing Arts Centre as a professional concert venue, the prominence of the city's annual Eisteddfod, and most recently the possibility for local musicians to study music to tertiary level at the Central Queensland University.

FURTHER REFERENCE
L. Huf, L. McDonald and D. Myers, eds, *Sin, Sweat and Sorrow: The Making of Capricornia Queensland 1840s-1940s* (Rockhampton:

Univ. Central Queensland Press, 1993); L. McDonald, *Sketches of Old Rockhampton* (Brisbane: QUP, 1981); idem, *Rockhampton: A History of City and District,* 2nd edn (Rockhampton: Rockhampton City Council, 1995); P. Wright, *The Music History of Rockhampton* (Rockhampton: Phil Wright, 1990).

PHILIPPA ROYLANCE

Rockmelons, The. Rock band (1981–) formed in Sydney, originally comprised of Peter Blakeley, Sandy Chick and John Kenny (vocals), Byron and Jonathan Jones and Ray Medhurst (keyboards), Geoffrey Stapleton (keyboards guitar), Stephen Allkins (disc jockey) and Peter Kennard (guitar, percussion). A funk dance band at first playing at local parties, their debut single was *Sweat It Out* (1985). They play reggae, funk, rhythm and blues or soul styles. Their albums include *Form One Planet* (1992).

FURTHER REFERENCE
Recordings include *Sweat It Out* (1985, Truetone 88144), *New Groove* (1987, Truetone TS 2032), *Ain't No Sunshine* (1991, Mushroom D11038), *That Word L.O.V.E.* (1992, Mushroom D11097), *Stronger Together* (1994, Mushroom D11776), *Form One Planet* (1992, Mushroom TVC 93360) and *Choice Rockmelons* (1992, Mushroom Video V81300). For discography, see *SpencerA.* See also *SpencerW.*

Rofe, Esther Freda (*b* Camberwell East, Melbourne, 14 Mar. 1904), composer. She received private composition lessons in Melbourne from Alberto ★Zelman Jr and Fritz ★Hart, and from Gordon Jacob at the Royal College of Music in London. For a brief period in the 1940s, Rofe worked in the commercial music industry with the Colgate-Palmolive radio unit in Sydney. She received commissions from the Borovansky Ballet, the Ballet Guild of Victoria and the ABC. Her choreographic scores, particularly *Sea Legend, Terra Australis* and *Mathinna,* received critical acclaim and undoubtedly helped the ballets become firm favourites with ballet audiences during the 1940s and 50s. In recent years her concert music has gained a growing following among performers.

FURTHER REFERENCE
Pauline Petrus, 'Esther Rofe: Theatre Musician', in *One Hand on the Manuscript,* ed. Nicholas Brown et al. (Canberra: Humanities Research Centre, ANU, 1995), 75–94; Joel Crotty, 'Revisiting Melbourne's Music Heritage', *The View* 4 (1996), 6–12.

JOEL CROTTY

Rohde, Bryce (*b* Hobart, 12 Sept. 1923), jazz pianist, composer. He began piano at the age of 11. After wartime service he was active in Adelaide with Alf ★Holyoak, leading trios and playing solo. He went to Canada in 1953 with Jack ★Brokensha to join the ★Australian Jazz Quartet. Upon its disbandment in Sydney, he led groups at venues such as ★El Rocco, backing Dizzy Gillespie (1960), and travelling to the USA. He was involved in experimentation in Lydian tonal organisation and, returning to Sydney in 1962, he formed an experimental group that included Bruce ★Cale, Charles ★Munro and drummer Mark Bowden, which recorded innovative works. Resettled in California in 1965, he continues to be musically active.

FURTHER REFERENCE
Recordings include *The Australian Jazz Quintet Plus One* (1956, Bethlehem BCP 6012); *The Bryce Rohde Quartet In Concert* (1960, Coronet KLP909); *Straight Ahead*, Bryce Rohde Quartet (1962, Coronet KLL 1742); *More Spring*, Bryce Rohde Quartet Featuring Charlie Munro (recorded 1962, issued 1990, MBS FM Jazz 6); *Corners*, The Bryce Rohde Quartet (1963, CBS BP 233046); *Just Bryce*, The Bryce Rohde Quintet (1965, CBS BP 233196). See also *ClareB*; *BissetB*; *OxfordJ*; *GroveJ*; Jim McLeod, *Jazztrack* (Sydney: ABC Books, 1994), 41–57.

BRUCE JOHNSON

Rolling Stone (Aust.). Magazine with annual Yearbook, published since 1967 in Sydney for rock music fans; bi-weekly until 1979, then monthly. It comprises music news, articles and reviews, as well as features on movies, politics and other matters of youth interest.

Romeo and Juliet. Opera in four acts, music and text by G.W.L. ★Marshall-Hall (1912) after Shakespeare. An excerpt was performed at Her Majesty's Theatre, Melbourne, on 14 December 1912. Published in score (London: Paris & Co., 1914) and duet arrangement (Leipzig: Breitkopf und Härtel, 1914). MS in *PVgm.*

Rosen, Robert (*b* Cernoviti, Romania, 22 Apr. 1921), conductor. After studies with Georges Enesco and at the Royal Conservatorium, Bucharest, he conducted the Bucharest State Opera 1948–64. He came to Australia as musical director of the Australian Ballet in 1964, touring Europe and the USA with the company. He conducted the Sydney Symphony Orchestra in the UK in 1965, and made an expert debut for the Australian Opera in 1966, but oddly was not engaged for its staff, and has appeared with them only sporadically. A gifted teacher, he has conducted the opera studio and taught conducting at the Victorian College of the Arts since 1974, producing a generation of excellent young conductors, and continued to appear as a guest with the Australian Ballet and various ABC orchestras.

Ross, Billy (William John) (*b* Adelaide, 3 Mar. 1934), jazz drummer. He began playing drums in traditional jazz groups in 1950, then moved into more progressive areas with reed player Ian Drinkwater. Spending six months at Melbourne's The Embers under Frank ★Smith, he returned to Adelaide and became associated with progressive activity at The Cellar. From the mid-1960s he spent periods in Sydney with Col ★Nolan, Errol ★Buddle, and recently with Bob ★Gebert and Tom ★Baker. Currently based in Adelaide, he is freelancing mainly in modern groups, with singer Marlene Richards and others, and playing support for visitors such as Red Rodney, Jimmy Witherspoon, Lee Konitz and Johnny Griffin.

FURTHER REFERENCE
Recordings include *Little Jazz Bird* (1991, La Brava 001DDD); *Winter Moon* (1993, La Brava LB 0002); *Doodlin'* (1994, La Brava LB 9504). See also *OxfordJ*.   BRUCE JOHNSON

Roundelay. Ballet by James *Penberthy (1963), choreography by Ray Powell. Commissioned by the Australian Ballet and first performed in 1964.

Routley, Nicholas (*b* Dartford, England, 26 June 1947), conductor, pianist, musicologist. Educated at Cambridge University (BA, MusB, MA and PhD), Routley has taught in the music department of the University of Sydney as a lecturer (now associate professor) since 1975. He is founder-director of the Sydney Chamber Choir and is renowned for his performances of Josquin and contemporary Australian music. He has conducted the Sydney Symphony Orchestra, the Rumanian National Orchestra, the Taiwan Symphony Orchestra, the Hong Kong Sinfonietta and the Hong Kong Chamber Orchestra, and has had similar engagements as a choral conductor in Australia and Asia. He has collaborated with numerous leading Australian singers and instrumentalists as a pianist.

FURTHER REFERENCE
His recordings include *Who Killed Cock Robin?*, Chamber Choir of Sydney University, cond. N. Routley (1982, HMV OASD-7629); *The Hermit of Green Light*, Hartley Newnham, countertenor, N. Routley, pf (1990, MBS Records MBS 21 CD); *Claudio Monteverdi, Vespers of the Blessed Virgin (1610)*, Chamber Choir of Sydney University and Baroque Orchestra, cond. N. Routley (1987, MBS Records MBS 11).   JOHN GRIFFITHS

Rowe, Normie (*b* Melbourne, 1 Feb. 1947), popular music singer. Rowe's professional singing career began in 1964 when radio personality Stan Rofe arranged for him to appear regularly with the *Thunderbirds at dances. By 1965 he was making regular appearances on local television programs and had begun his recording career. Backed by the Playboys (1965–67), his stage repertoire was oriented towards hard rock and his immense teen popularity ensured that his live performances were scenes of hysteria and commotion. But his recording of ballads and pop songs fostered popularity among a more mature and more conservative audience than that of his wilder, more outrageous contemporary Johnny *O'Keefe, and as a result Rowe came to epitomise the clean-cut pop idol of the mid-1960s. Although singles such as *Que Sera Sera* (1965), *It Ain't Necessarily So* (1965), *Tell Him I'm Not Home* (1965) and *Ooh La La* (1967) number among his most popular hits of the 1960s, he also recorded covers of rock classics such as *Shakin' All Over* (1965). His 1966 trip to the UK

did little to further his career, and on his return to Australia in 1967 he was conscripted for army service. After two years in the military, which included active service in Vietnam, he continued his musical career but found it difficult to regain his former popularity. He has, however, maintained celebrity status, with occasional record releases, performances in 1960s nostalgia concerts, television and club appearances, and leading roles in the 1980s and 90s in Australian productions of *Les Misérables* and *Cyrano de Bergerac*.

FURTHER REFERENCE
Recordings include *It Ain't Necessarily So, But It Is* (1965, Sunshine); *Normie Rowe A Go Go* (1965, Sunshine); *A Wonderful Feeling* (1966, Sunshine); *Hit Happenings* (1966, Sunshine); *So Much Love from . . .* (1966, Sunshine); *Normie's Happening Hits* (1967, Sunshine); *Everything's Alright* (1968, Universal); *Normie's Top Tunes* (1969, Universal); *Hello* (1970, Sunshine); *Come Hear My Song* (1974, Summit); *That's the Way I Am* (1975, Summit); *Out of the Norm* (1979, Astor); *Out of the Blue* (1983, Avenue); *Piano Man* (1985, Hammard); *Shakin' All Over* (1986, Raven); *Count Your Blessings* (1992, J&B). See also *CA* (1995–96); *Guinness P*; *SpencerW*.   AARON D.S. CORN

Rowland, Bruce (*b* Melbourne, 9 May 1942), film composer. Self-taught and initially a keyboard player in various rock and roll and jazz bands, Rowland's career was launched in the early 1960s when he toured with the band the Strangers, backing Roy Orbison. Soon afterwards he was offered the position of musical director for the children's show *The Magic Circle Club*, which later became *Adventure Island* and continued until 1969. At this time Rowland was writing as many as 10 songs a week, 50 weeks a year. Between 1969 and 1981 he was mainly involved in writing commercial music for both the Australian and international markets, and has to his credit as many as 3000 jingles. His move into film music in the early 1980s brought him immediate success, and he quickly established himself as one of Australia's foremost film composers. Rowland is the recipient of numerous awards including the Australian Film Institute's Best Film Score Award for *The Man from Snowy River* (1982), *Phar Lap* (1983) and *Rebel* (1985); and APRA's Best Score Award for *The Man from Snowy River*, *Return to Snowy River* and *Phar Lap*. In 1984 his work for the television series *All the Rivers Run* (1983) achieved a Penguin Award. Rowland is currently living and working in both the USA and Melbourne.

FURTHER REFERENCE
His film credits include *The Man from Snowy River* (1982), *Now and Forever* and *Phar Lap* (1983), *Cool Change* (1986), *Bushfire Moon* and *Running from the Guns* (1987), *The Man from Snowy River II* (1988), *Weekend with Kate* (1991), *Gross Misconduct* (1993), and *Lightning Jack* (1994), and more recently, *Andre* — *The Seal* and *North Star*. Mini-series include *Which Way Home* and *All The Rivers Run*. See also *LimbacherF*.

L.THOMPSON

Roy, Ashok Kumar (*b* Dehra Dun, India, 21 June 1936), sarod player. Born into a family of classical musicians, he started musical training at the age of five with his father, Anant Kumar Roy. At 15 he became a disciple of Ustad Ali Akbar Khan and two years later he won the Best Musician's Award at All India Radio (AIR). He went on to join AIR (Delhi) as a staff artist in 1958. Since then he has had a highly distinguished career in India and around the world and has released a number of solo recordings. Resident in Australia since 1987, he is one of the leading exponents of the sarod, and performs and broadcasts extensively, teaching regularly at tertiary institutions. He is artistic director of the Australian Institute of Eastern Music, Sydney. Roy has played an outstanding role in the dissemination of Indian music in Australia.   ADRIAN MCNEIL

Royal South Street Society Eisteddfod. Australia's leading community performing arts competition, founded in 1891 and held annually in mid-August to October at Her Majesty's Theatre, Ballarat. The tradition of such events in Ballarat dates from the Welsh Eisteddfod, organised by Welsh miners at Ballarat from 1855, which from its early days had sections in music, poetry and oratory, judged by visiting experts. In 1879 a group of students at the Dana Street School led by W.D. Hill formed the South Street Debating Society; they began a competition to encourage the performing arts in June 1891 which soon became the principal such event in the town. Today the eisteddfod is held over more than 10 weeks, and nearly 8000 individual or group entrants compete in sections including solo performance (both classical and modern), choir, brass band, school instrumental ensemble, speech and drama, dance, callisthenics, and television auditions. The highlight is the *Herald-Sun* Aria (held since 1924); with prizes currently in excess of $50 000, it attracts national attention and has launched the careers of several of Australia's best-known opera singers. Overall, the competition involves about 68 000 competitors and is a significant source of tourist revenue for Ballarat. Previous section winners in music have included Sir Bernard *Heinze, Peter *Dawson, Amy *Castles, Gladys *Moncrieff, Dame Kiri Te Kanawa, Jonathan *Summers. The society purchased Her Majesty's Theatre in 1964, which they gave to the City of Ballarat in 1987. In a country with a unique passion for eisteddfods, the Royal South Street has been the most important event of its kind; it is quite possibly the largest and most comprehensive community performing arts competition in the world.

Royal Sydney Liedertafel became the Sydney Apollo Club in 1916. See *Liedertafel*.

Rudd, Mike (*b* NZ), rock singer-songwriter. He came to Australia in 1966 with Chants R'n'B, and in 1968 joined Party Machine, which evolved into the alternative band Sons of Vegetal Mother (1969), releasing an EP, *Garden Party* (1970). He formed the heavy-rock band Spectrum with bassist Bill Putt in the same year, writing most of their material, including *I'll Be Gone* (1971), a minor classic of heavy rock. He was in *Ariel 1973–77, Instant Replay 1978–79, the Heaters 1979–82, Living Legend Blues Band 1982 and his experimental band WHY, which toured Germany and released *Woman Of Steel* (1983) and *Mike Rudd's No. 9*. His often experimental songs and 30-year career have made him one of the foremost identities of Australian rock.

FURTHER REFERENCE

Recordings include *Garden Party* (1970, Custom Press MP 465), *I'll Be Gone* (1971, Harvest), *Woman Of Steel* (1983, I.C. KSM 100). For discography, see *SpencerA*. See also *SpencerW*; *GuinnessP*, II, 2160.

Rumsey, David Edward (*b* Sydney, 30 Mar. 1939), organist. Educated at Newington College, Sydney, he began organ studies with Donald *Hollier and continued at the NSW Conservatorium of Music under Norman Johnston. He graduated in 1962 with teaching and performance diplomas and the prize for Student of the Year. Awarded the Vasanta scholarship, he studied in Europe, mainly with Marie-Claire Alain in Paris and Anton Heiller at the Vienna Musik-Akademie, graduating in 1966 with Reifprüfung. In 1966–68 he taught at the Elder Conservatorium, Adelaide, and returned in 1969 to teach at the NSW Conservatorium, in 1975 he was appointed foundation chairman of the department of organ and church music, and in 1993 head of graduate performance studies. Organist to the Sydney Symphony Orchestra from 1969, Rumsey enjoys an international reputation as a recitalist, teacher and organ consultant, and has made a number of recordings.

FURTHER REFERENCE

His recordings include *Olivier Messiaen: Organ Music at Sydney Town Hall* (Tall Poppies); *Camille Saint-Saëns*, Symphony No. 3 'Organ Symphony', Sydney Symphony Orchestra (ABC Classics); *Australian Organ Music* (1997, MBS); *Prevailing Winds*, Daniel Mendelow, tr, and Timothy Dowling, trbn (MBS). See also D. Rumsey, 'Twenty-one Years a Phantom', *Sydney Symphony Orchestra Newsletter* (Nov. 1989).   GRAEME RUSHWORTH

Ruth. Oratorio (*c*.1862) by George *Tolhurst, libretto selected by the composer from the Bible (Ruth Chs 1–2). The first oratorio composed in the colony of Victoria, it was premiered on 21 January 1864 at the Town Hall, Prahran, conducted by the composer's father W.H. Tolhurst. Well received by the audience, it had a mixed review in the *Argus*. The vocal score (London: George Tolhurst, 1867) received a scathing review in the *Musical Times;* nevertheless, after the London premiere on 29 January 1868 the composer was 'overwhelmed with applause' and it went into a second edition (London: Duncan Davison, *c*.1872). It achieved popular notoriety when Percy Scholes (*Mirror of Music*, 1947) hailed it as 'the worst Oratorio ever'. *Ruth* was revived in London in 1973, as part of a 'Grand Musical Entertainment'; the performance, which was broadcast, did not do it justice.

FURTHER REFERENCE
Argus, 13 Jan. 1864, 8; 19 Jan. 1864, 5; 22 Jan. p. 5; *The Monthly Musical Record,* 1 June 1872, 88; *Musical Times,* 1 Feb. 1868, 292–3; 1 Oct. 1868, 552–3; Percy A. Scholes, *The Mirror of Music 1844–1944* (London: Novello, 1947), 95–7.
                                                                ROYSTON GUSTAVSON

Ruth and Naomi.   Opera, in seven scenes, music and libretto by Fritz *Hart (1917) after the biblical story. Excerpt performed by students of the Melbourne Conservatorium at the Melbourne Playhouse on 7 July 1917. Ms in *Msl.*

Rutter, Jane   (*b* Sydney), flautist. She studied at the NSW State Conservatorium and subsequently in Paris with Jean-Pierre Rampal and Alain Marion. After returning to Sydney she became lecturer in flute at the Conservatorium, establishing the jazz chamber ensemble POSH and appearing in concerts for Musica Viva and the Australian Chamber Orchestra. Her first recording, *Nocturnes and Preludes,* was a popular success and in 1989 she was the first Australian classical performer to sign with Warner Records. Her recordings (and their covers) are designed to appeal to a broad audience, and attempt to find a balance between historical authenticity and modern taste.

FURTHER REFERENCE
Her recordings include *Mozart's Flute* (WEA 903172866–2). See also Graham Barry, 'Classical Gasp', *Portfolio* (Feb 1991), 46; *CA* (1995–96).   SUZANNE ROBINSON

Ryan, Ross   (*b* USA, 1951), popular music singer-songwriter. Arriving in Australia in childhood, in his teens he played guitar and sang in bars at Albany, WA, then Perth, appearing as supporting act to Roy Orbison in 1972. Moving to Sydney, he toured with Helen *Reddy and the Hollies in 1973, releasing his debut single *I Don't Want To Know About It,* which reached No. 38 in the charts, and *I Am Pegasus,* which reached No. 9. He toured North America with Reddy in 1974 and released the album *My Name Means Horse.* He formed Ross Ryan Brothers (1979), then Ross Ryan and the Redeemers (1983), and continued to appear in local venues in the 1980s. Mixing folk, country and pop styles, he was one of the most prominent singer-songwriters of the early 1970s.

FURTHER REFERENCE
Recordings include *I Don't Want To Know About It* (EMI EMI 10201), *I Am Pegasus* (EMI EMI 10300), *My Name Means Horse* (EMI EMA 301), *I Thought This Might Happen—Ross Ryan 1973–77* (1977, EMI EMC 2616). A compilation is *The Greats Of Ross Ryan 1973–90* (1990, Axis CDAY 701625). For discography see *SpencerA.* See also *McGrathA; SpencerW; Age* 11 Nov. 1988.

Ryebuck Shearer, The,   folk-song. Field, a shearer from the south, boasts in this traditional song that he can shear more than 100 sheep a day. 'Ryebuck' (or 'rybuck') is slang for 'real' or 'very good'. Collected by John Meredith and published in *Singabout* in 1957.

FURTHER REFERENCE
Edition and commentary *in EdwardsG; ManifoldP.*

Ryrie, Kim.   See *Fairlight CMI.*

S

Saddington, Wendy, rock singer. She sang with Revolution in 1966, ★Chain in 1969 and then Copperwine in 1970–71. She released an album, *Looking Thru A Window*, in 1971, and appeared as support to Jeff ★St John and Doug ★Parkinson. Touring the USA, she returned to Australia in 1978 and formed the Wendy Saddington Band in 1983.

FURTHER REFERENCE
Recordings include *Looking Thru A Window* (1971, Infinity SINL 934255). For discography, see *SpencerA*. See also *SpencerW.*

Saints, The. Rock band (1973–79; 1984–) formed in Brisbane comprised of Chris Bailey (vocals, guitar), Kym Bradshaw (bass until 1977 then Alistair Ward), Ed ★Kuepper (guitar) and Ivor Hay (drums). Although the first Australian punk band to be recognised by the English media, they were firmly rooted in the rhythm and blues tradition, and it was this that eventually saw the group fall from favour, although they have since attained cult status. The release of their debut single *(I'm) Stranded*, under their own recording label, attracted attention immediately; a review in the now defunct British *Sounds* magazine of 1976 catapulted them to public notice in that country. Virtually ignored in their own country, they left for the UK, and remained 18 months (1976–77). In 1977 they were signed to EMI, re-releasing the album *(I'm) Stranded* in May of that year. A further contract with Sire secured an American market for them, and *Eternally Yours* and *Prehistoric Sounds* were released in 1978. Kuepper left the group in 1978 to form his own band, the ★Laughing Clowns. The group continued to perform in various combinations until 1979, when it disbanded after having recorded a further two albums. Bailey kept the group alive in various forms through the 1980s; he also enjoyed a career as solo singer and guitarist. It was in response to this vestige of the original group that Kuepper later formed the Aints (1990). The Saints re-formed in 1984, without Kuepper, and have recorded almost constantly since.

FURTHER REFERENCE
Recordings include *(I'm) Stranded* (1977, EMI 831978–2); *Eternally Yours* (1978, EMI 829555–2); *Prehistoric Sounds* (1978, EMI); *The Monkey Puzzle* (1981, Festival D19353); *Casablanca* (1982, Lost D19354); *A Little Madness to be Free* (1984, RCA D19352); *Live in a Mud Hut* (1985, New Rose); *All Fool's Day* (1986, Mushroom D19355); *Prodigal Son* (1988, Mushroom D38890); *Scarce Saints* (1989, Raven RVCD 04); *Permanent Revolution* (1991, MDS); *Songs of Salvation (1976–1988)* (1991). See also Glenn A. Baker and Stuart Coupe, *The New Music* (Sydney: Bay Books, 1980); *Guinness P*; Colin Larkin, ed., *The Guinness Who's Who of Indie and New Wave Music* (Enfield: Guinness Publishing, 1992); *McGrathA*; *SpencerW.*

JOHN WERETKA

Salamander. See *Thorold Waters.*

Saltbush. Country-rock music group formed in 1975 comprised of Bernie O'Brien (vocals, fiddle, guitar), Ross Nicholson (vocals, guitar), Paul Pyle (vocals, bass), Rod Coe (pedal steel guitar), and Harold Frith (drums); also Ed Bates (1982). Formed in Melbourne, singles such as *Razorback Mountain Blockade* (1979) and the albums *Live At Twin Rivers* (1977) and *Saltbush* (1979) showed the band to be leading innovators of country-rock in the late 1970s. They toured as support act for Slim ★Dusty and Chad ★Morgan in 1978 and represented Australia at the Tulsa Festival, Oklahoma, in 1979. The band won two ACMA Golden Guitars in the same years.

FURTHER REFERENCE
Recordings include *Razorback Mountain Blockade* (1979, Festival K7477) and the albums *Live At Twin Rivers* (1977, reissued EMI EMC 2224) and *Saltbush* (1979, EMI EMC 2538). See also *LattaA*; *SmithB*, 122–3; *SpencerW.*

Salvado. Spanish family of musicians. Pedro Bernard Salvado was cantor and bassoonist at Tui Cathedral, Pontevedra, Spain; his two sons Miguel (1) and Rosendo (2) both became Benedictines and went to Australia.

(1) Frater Frutos San Miguel (de los Santos) Salvado (*b* Tui, 11 July 1811; *d* A Guarda, Pontevedra, 17 Apr. 1894), Benedictine monk, organist. A choirboy at Tui Cathedral, he studied organ from the age of 11, becoming organist at the monastery of San Martin Pinario in 1825. He was ordained a priest in 1835 and became chaplain at San Isidro, Madrid, then (from 1854) chaplain to Queen Isabel II. After the Revolution of 1868 he went with his brother Dom Rosendo (2) to Australia, becoming prior of the monastery at New Norcia in 1870, but after developing an eye condition he returned to Spain in 1879 and retired. He composed the *Invitatorio Santos Salvado,* sung at Monserrat, Madrid, in 1879.

(2) Dom Rosendo Salvado (y Rotea) (*b* Tui, Pontevedra, Spain, 1 Mar. 1814; *d* Rome, 29 Dec. 1900), Benedictine missionary, pianist, composer. He had piano lessons as a child, entered the Benedictine abbey of St Martin, Compostella, as a novice at the age of 15, and after studying the organ at Asturias became organist of the abbey in 1832. After the government seizure of ecclesiastical possessions in 1835, he went to the abbey of La Cava, Naples, where he was ordained a priest in 1839, and attracted wide attention as an organist. Having chosen to become a missionary he was sent to Australia with four monks to create a mission for the education and welfare of Aborigines in 1846. He struggled to establish a settlement which became known as New Norcia on the Victoria Plains north of Perth, but shortages of supplies drove him back to Perth within a few months; there, starving and in rags, he gave a piano recital to raise money for the venture.

The first concert of quality offered in WA, it was highly regarded. He returned to Europe to raise funds in 1849 and wrote his *Memoria storiche dell'Australia* (Rome, 1851), an enthralling account of life in the new colony which appeared in Italian, Spanish and French in the coming years. Returning to Australia in 1853 as bishop of Port Victoria, he brought another 37 monks for his mission. More trips to Europe followed, and by the time he was created Lord Abbot of New Norcia in 1867 the mission's future was secure. In the coming years he formed an orchestra from Aborigines at the mission. He retired to Rome in 1899.

Described as 'the philharmonic monk', he was a unique figure among the pioneers of Australian music, providing the first and for a period the only serious concert music heard in WA. His compositions included a mass, sacred vocal settings, works for the convicts at Fremantle, a 'native corrobory' which was a favourite at his performances, and piano works (a fantasia, march, waltz and variations) of considerable virtuosity.

FURTHER REFERENCE
Rosendo Salvado's memoirs have been translated and edited by E.J. Stormon SJ, as *The Salvado Memoirs* (Perth: Univ. WA Press, 1977), and three piano works have been published as *Obras para piano,* ed. Xoan-Manuel Carreira (A Coruña: Diputación Provincial, 1990). See also Xoan-Manuel Carreira, 'The Piano Music of Rosendo Salvado', *SMA*, 23 (1989), 53–60; Dom William OSB, *ADB*, 2; A.H. Kornweibel, *Apollo and the Pioneers* (Perth: Music Council of WA, 1973), 34–7, 99. For Miguel Salvado, see Baltasar Saldoni, *Diccionario Biográfico-Bibliográfico de efemérides de músicos españoles* (Madrid, 1881; reprint, ed. Jacinto Torres, Madrid: Ministerio de Cultura, 1986); Ernesto Zaragoza-Pascual, 'Músicos benedictinos españoles', *Revista de Musicología* 5 (1982), 25; Joam Trillo and Carlos Villanueva, *La Música en la Catedral de Tui* (A. Coruña, Diputación Provincial, 1987), 463–6.

Salvation Army. Music has been central to this militant evangelical movement since its foundation in the east end of London in 1865. Indoor meetings drew on the atmosphere of the music hall; and outdoor evangelism on the noisy exuberance of the military parade. The first officer appointed to Australia was a cornet player, captain Thomas Sutherland, and on arrival in 1881 he formed the Adelaide I band, establishing the pattern of musical combinations at every local corps (church) centre. The Army's first *Australian Band Journal* began regular publication in 1885; William Gore assumed the editorship in 1905, contributing almost 200 compositions by the time it was superseded by the international *English Band Journal* in 1913. In 1909 Gore's colleague Robert McAnally wrote a complete vocal and instrumental score (now in the National Library, Canberra) for the film feature *Heroes of the Cross* produced by the Salvation Army.

Army vocal compositions were often simply corruptions of secular ballads. As local Songster Brigade choral writing developed through conductor-arrangers such as Arthur Arnott in the 1920s and 30s, it remained firmly attached to its origins in the gospel song, the hymn, and the music hall. Brass composition consists of different types: devotional, martial, and festival. Devotional music developed from hymn tune arrangements into more extended selections linked by thematic motifs. Distinctive marches were the trade mark of Arthur Gullidge, the most prolific and widely published Australian Salvation Army composer of the interwar period. In the 1950s and 60s regular Army music festivals encouraged skilled brass and vocal ensembles. The rhythms of swing, jazz and rock reached salvationists in the 1970s through the vocal music of Howard Davies and the brass arrangements of Barrie Gott.

In the 1980s the Melbourne Staff Band under Colin Woods developed a considerable international reputation. Woods encouraged the talents of composers like Noel Jones and Brian Hogg, and the band also premiered several major works for brass by Brenton ★Broadstock, a composer who received his early training in the Army. In 1990 the Salvation Army in Australia had more than 200 brass bands involving almost 3000 musicians.

FURTHER REFERENCE
John Cleary, *'Salvo': The Salvation Army in the 1990s* (Sydney: Focus Books, in press). JOHN C. CLEARY

Sampson, George (*b* Clifton, England, 24 July 1861; *d* Brisbane, 24 Dec. 1949), organist, conductor. After study with George Risely and Harford Lloyd, he obtained his FRCO and was organist at Bristol and later at St Alban's, Holborn. Arriving in Brisbane in 1898 he was organist of St John's Cathedral until 1946 and city organist until 1949. In 1907 he founded the Sampson Orchestra which, in 1937, became the ABC's *Queensland Symphony Orchestra. He conducted the Brisbane Musical Union (now the Queensland State and Municipal Choir) from 1898 to 1943. A central figure in Brisbane music for over 40 years, he was active as teacher, musical adviser to the University of Queensland and musical adviser and examiner to the department of education. He published textbooks, a little church music and a miniature organ work.

FURTHER REFERENCE
Robert Boughen, *ADB*, 11.   ROBERT BOUGHEN

Sangster, John Grant (*b* Melbourne, 17 Nov. 1928; *d* Brisbane, 26 Oct. 1995), jazz performer, composer. He came to prominence as a trumpeter at the 1948 *Australian Jazz Convention and formed his Jazz Six in 1949. Working with groups associated with the *Bell brothers and Ade *Monsbourgh, he joined the Bell band on drums for its 1950–52 overseas tour. After the band's break-up he remained with Graeme Bell for his tour of Korea and Japan, and then settled in Brisbane in 1955, where he taught himself vibraphone. Returning to Sydney in 1956, he worked with Bell until 1958, when he freelanced until joining the Ray *Price Quartet as trumpeter in the early 1960s.

Although hitherto associated primarily with the traditional movement, he was becoming increasingly interested in progressive styles, apparent in his association with Don *Burrows, in the very open experimental work recorded for the ABC with Bob *Gebert and bassist Ron Carson (1966), and on *Jazz Australia* (1967). He accompanied Burrows at Expo '67 in Montreal (and again at Expo '70 in Japan), and increasingly through the late 1960s worked with electric pop and fusion groups, including Tully and Nutwood Rug. He rented a flat in the same building as the *El Rocco, where he performed with a range of musicians including Dave Macrae (piano), Graeme *Lyall, George Thompson (bass), Alan *Turnbull, Col *Nolan and Judy *Bailey. He played in the pit orchestra for *Hair* for two years, then throughout the 1970s concentrated on composing for film and television, displaying a fascination with musical portrayal of the Australian landscape.

At the same time he was working on his magnum opus, one of the most ambitious original projects to emerge from Australian music, the cycle of songs inspired by Tolkien's *Lord of the Rings*. The first fruit of this was *The Hobbit Suite*, recorded in 1973, and the project continued over several years, producing a further six albums under the title *Lord of the Rings*, as well as other albums recorded as *Landscapes of Middle Earth*. Ranging convincingly from ragtime to freeform and aleatory music, the Tolkien recordings are a magisterial summary of Sangster's assimilation of the jazz-based tradition, and one of the major achievements of Australian music. No other project of such breadth has emerged from Australian jazz, or indeed from jazz internationally. From the 1980s, he continued to compose and record prolifically, and the resumption of his public performances led to an increased appreciation of his work. Suffering from ill health, he moved to Queensland, though he continued to perform until shortly before his death from cancer.

FURTHER REFERENCE
Recordings include *Graeme Bell and His Australian Jazz Band 1949–52* (1982, Swaggie S-1397); *Australia And All That Jazz* (1971, Cherry Pie CPS-1008); *The Hobbit Suite* (1973, Swaggie S-1340); *Lord of the Rings vol. 1* (1974, EMI EMC.2525/6), *vol. 2* (1976, EMI EMC 2548/9), *vol. 3* (1977, EMI EMC 2580/1); *For Leon Bismark* (1977, Swaggie S-1379); *Landscapes of Middle Earth* (1978, EMI EMC2642); *Uttered Nonsense* (1978 Rain Forest Records RFLP 001); *Requiem For A Loved One* (1980, Rain Forest Records RFLP 004 and RFLP 005).

His memoirs are *Seeing the Rafters: The Life and Times of an Australian Jazz Musician* (Ringwood,Vic.: Penguin Books, 1988); an interview with him is in *WilliamsA*, 52–7. See also *ClareB*; *BissetB*; *OxfordJ*; *CA*; *GroveJ*; Norman Linehan, ed., *Bob Barnard, Graeme Bell, Bill Haesler, John Sangster on the Australian Jazz Convention* (Sydney: Australian Jazz Convention Trust Fund, 1981); Eric Myers, 'John Sangster, Music for Fluteman', *JA* (Dec., 1982), 21.   BRUCE JOHNSON

Sargent, Sir (Harold) Malcolm Watts (*b* Ashford, Kent, England, 29 Apr. 1895; *d* London, 3 Oct. 1967), English conductor. He studied at the Royal College of Organists in London, later at Durham University (DMus 1919), and conducted for the D'Oyly Carte Opera Co., the Royal Choral Society; he conducted the Hallé Orchestra and the Liverpool Philharmonic Orchestra and was chief conductor of the Promenade Concerts from 1948 until his death in 1967. Described as Britain's ambassador of music, Sargent made numerous tours overseas to Europe, the USA, South Africa and Australasia. He toured Australia in 1936, 1938, 1939 and in 1945 for the ABC orchestras. He was so popular with Australian audiences that the number of concerts had to be doubled. In Australia he championed the works of English composers such as Elgar, Vaughan Williams, Holst and Walton, giving many premieres of their works, especially their choral works.

FURTHER REFERENCE
For discography see *HolmesC*. See also D Brook, *International Gallery of Conductors* (Bristol: Burleigh Press, 1951); Mária Párkai-Eckhardt, *GroveD*.   NIKOLA SHARP

Saunders, A(lbert) B. (*fl.* 1910–40), songwriter, arranger. Saunders is an obscure composer, who published a substantial body of popular music, mostly with Sydney publishers. Some of his music concerns workingmen's causes including his song *Co-operation,* and he was arranger of *Don't Take The Bread From The Worker* by Herbert William Lennon, the Soviet Union national anthem, the *Internationale,* and other works. Most of Saunders' output as composer is of piano music, usually in dance rhythms from lancers and quadrilles to rags and 'jazz' foxtrots, but there are also some teaching pieces.

FURTHER REFERENCE
A list of some of his works appears in *SnellA.*   JENNIFER HILL

Saunders, Jane   (*b* Bilpin, NSW, *c.*1967), country music singer-songwriter. Listening to American country music and singing in church in childhood, she began performing in her twenties at a Newcastle restaurant, appeared at Tamworth in 1992, then in NSW clubs and as supporting act to Garth Brooks. With a pure voice and hybrid folk-country style, her debut album *Stranger To Your Heart* (1994) produced five Top 10 hits in the country music charts and entered the British country Top 20. She appeared with Lee ★Kernaghan, James ★Blundell and others, and was featured on the ABC *Showcase* tour of Australia and NZ. With Genni Kane and Shanel Del she formed Saunders, Kane and Del and produced *Tea For Three* (1995).

FURTHER REFERENCE
Recordings include *Stranger To Your Heart* (1994, EMI 4795972) and *Tea For Three* (1995, EMI 14798202–4). See also *Australian* 21 Jan. 1995.

Saville, Frances [Fanny Martina]   (*b* San Francisco, California, USA, 6 Jan. 1865; *d* Burlingame, California, 8 Nov. 1935), soprano. Saville came to Australia as a small child. Trained by her mother, Fanny ★Simonsen, she made her professional debut at 15 and was a successful opera and concert singer in Australia until 1891, when she went to study with Marchesi in Paris. Her international opera career began in Brussels in 1892. She sang guest performances with many major European companies, spent two seasons (1895–96 and 1898–99) at the Metropolitan Opera, New York, appeared at Covent Garden in 1897 and 1898 and was a member of the Vienna Opera from 1897 until her retirement in 1903.

FURTHER REFERENCE
Nathan Davis, 'Frances Saville', *The Record Collector* 32/6–7 (1987), 123–38 [includes discography]; Rámon E. Martínez, 'Soprano Parfait', *Encore* 2/1–2 (1985), 24–7; Adrienne Simpson, *Australia's Neglected Prima Donna,* unpub. typescript, Wellington, 1996.   ADRIENNE SIMPSON

SBS Youth Orchestra.   Radio and television broadcast orchestra founded in 1988 in Sydney by Australia's multicultural broadcaster. Formed from teenage players chiefly from Sydney, and conducted since its inception by Matthew Krell, the orchestra makes monthly radio broadcasts and regular television appearances on SBS TV. It has sponsorship from St George Bank and has toured to NZ, the Pacific, and Europe.

Scat.   Jazz singing style made popular by Louis Armstrong in the late 1920s, and developed in the work of Ella Fitzgerald, Sarah Vaughan and others, in which nonsense syllables are used to mimic instrumental improvisation. In Australia a notable exponent from the late 1940s onwards has been Joe ★Lane, but scat has featured in the work of many artists, including vocal ensembles who sing scat arrangements that do not involve improvising.

Scattered Order.   Rock group (1980–) formed at Sydney by Mitch Jones (vocals, bass), Michael Tee (guitar) and Patrick Gibson (guitar, synthesiser), thereafter with a changing collection of others. An alternative studio band with passionless, cynical vocals of black humour, and electronically processed sound set against an unrelenting pulse, their EPs include *Screaming Tree* (1981) and albums *Prat Culture* (1982) and *Professional Deadball* (1991).

FURTHER REFERENCE
Recordings include *Screaming Tree* (1981, M2 M2008), *Prat Culture* (1982, M2 M2020), *Career Of A Silly Thing* (1985, Volition VOLT2), *Comfort* (1988, Volition VOLT14) and *Professional Deadball* (1991, Volition VOLTCD41). For discography, see *SpencerA.* See also *SpencerW.*

Schiemer, Greg   (*b* Dunedoo, NSW, 16 Jan. 1949), composer. After entering a seminary as a novice at the age of 15, he composed hymns and liturgical settings; deciding on a musical career, he studied with Peter ★Sculthorpe at the University of Sydney from 1969, but became increasingly involved in the electronic musical experiments of Phil Connor and Arthur Spring. He taught in high schools 1974–75 while studying a computer technicians' course, then worked as a field technician in computers until he joined the staff of the NSW State Conservatorium in 1984. Generally working with systems and circuits of his own design, he has used computers, synthesisers, tapes, and his own inventions, such as the Tupperware Gamelan (simple electronic circuits in plastic kitchenware), Humming Drums, log dulcimers, and UFO (for Ubiquitous Fontana Oscillators, swung at the end of a rope and undergoing doppler shifts). He provided the music for *Between Silence and Light* for One Extra Company (1980), and his works include *Mandala* for the Tupperware Gamelan (1981), and *Variations* for computer, MIDI, digital sampler and percussion (1986).

FURTHER REFERENCE
Recordings include *Improvisation,* Simone de Haan, trbn (1989, Canberra School of Music, CSM 13) and *Polyphonic Variations* (1989, NMA Tapes 007B). See also *JenkinsT,* 163–70; 'Towards a Living Tradition', *NMA* 7 (1989), 30–8; *Weekend Australian* 26 Mar. 1983.

School and Children's Choirs. Choral singing has a varied history in schools in Australia, ranging from being widely undertaken and well supported by the educational authorities to being virtually neglected. Particularly after World War II, school singing declined, the emphasis resting on radio music programs and instrumental work.

Independent schools were generally supportive, the work of Ruth Flockart at Methodist Ladies' College, Kew, Melbourne, from the 1930s to the 50s being notable. Many denominational boarding schools maintain chapels, some with a choral group. St Peter's Collegiate School, Adelaide (founded 1849), included a choral chapel from its earliest days, and undertook performances of works like Stainer's *The Crucifixion* (1893). Today schools like Pembroke School (Adelaide), St Peter's Lutheran College (Brisbane) and Newington College (Sydney) are well known. The SA Public Schools Decoration Society (now the Public [Primary] Schools Music Society) was formed in 1891 to raise funds for public schools, and held combined schools concerts to this end. These 'Thousand-voice' concerts involved as many as 1600 children performing individual school and combined items, conducted by Alexander ★Clark and later Frances ★Gratton and others. They ran from 1891 to 1939 (except during the 1919 influenza epidemic), were orchestrally accompanied from 1897, and were resumed in 1951. By 1993, 210 schools were involved.

The major city cathedrals either maintain a cathedral school for educating choristers, or offer scholarships to an associated school. St Mary's, Sydney, has an associated Cathedral College to which the choirboys have scholarships. The Choristers of St John's Anglican Cathedral, Brisbane, attend Anglican Grammar School, East Brisbane, where there is also a chapel choir. Founded in 1885 as a choir school, St Andrew's Cathedral School (Sydney) now has a complete syllabus from primary through to matriculation. Composer John ★Antill attended as a chorister (1914–17), when the required uniform for services was the special 'Eton' suit with high starched collar.

Massed children's choirs were often formed to participate in some great occasion, such as a royal visit or a congress like the 1900 Catholic Congress in Sydney, which featured a 1000-voice school choir. The Australian Boys Choral Institute (Melbourne), founded by Vincent J. Kelly in 1939, is one of only a few professional boys' choirs in the world, and the only secular men/boys combination in Australia. A non-profit body, possessing its own premises, it provides (for low tuition fees) a comprehensive training program for auditioned boys. It has made many local and overseas trips. Consisting of 28 voices, it also contains the Vocal Consort, a 16-voice tenor and bass group. In most capital cities there are privately run children's choirs, providing a musical education program to young children through choral music and offering concerts. Gaudeamus and the various choirs of Judith ★Clingan in Canberra and the Sydney Children's Choir are two of many exam-

ples. Youth choirs, for the late teens to mid-twenties age range, also operate in each state. Some, like the Queensland Youth Choir, aim at show-style presentations. The appeal of children as cultural ambassadors is important—the Rosny Children's Choir (1967) took part in the first Australian cultural exchange with the People's Republic of China in 1975. Some choral societies (such as Royal Melbourne Philharmonic, Adelaide Liedertafel, Toowoomba Choral Society) formed youth and children's groups to assist in their concerts and nurture future choristers. See also *Music Education*.

NOEL WILMOTT

Schultz, Andrew (*b* Adelaide, 18 Aug. 1960), composer. After studying at the University of Queensland 1978–82, he went to George Crumb on a Fulbright scholarship at the University of Pennsylvania in Philadelphia 1983, and then David Lumsdaine on a Commonwealth scholarship at Kings College, University of London, 1985–86. Lecturer (later associate professor) at the University of Wollongong from 1986, he has been a fellow at the Institute of Advanced Musical Studies, University of London, 1991–92, and Hazel Hinks fellow at the Villa Montalvo Centre for the Arts, California, 1995.

Schultz's music aims to communicate directly and sensually yet also command an intellectual involvement. His compositions include *L'Oiseau Fantastique* (1983) for clarinet, violin, cello and piano, *L'Oiseau Fantastique II* (1984) for string quartet and piano, *Spherics* (1985) for five players, *Cloud Burning* (1986) for wind, brass and percussion, *Sea-Change* (1987) for piano, *Black River* (1988), a one-act opera for solo, SSTBB and 13 instruments, *Machine* (1989) for four percussion, *Mephisto* (1990) for six instruments, *Dead Songs* (1991) for soprano, clarinet, cello and piano, *The Devil's Music* (1992) for orchestra, *Suspended Preludes* (1993) for double bass and piano, *Silk* (1993) for two sopranos, bass clarinet, double bass and vibraphone, *Willow Bend* (1994) for orchestra, *Chorale, Demon, Beacon* (1995) for koto and four percussion, and *Violin Concerto* (1996) for violin and orchestra. Schultz's opera *Black River* was made into a feature film in 1993. Its social relevance and directness of expression have established its place in Australian music theatre.

WORKS

Orchestral *Garotte* (1981 rev. 1982, rec. 1988, OZM 1002), *Solace,* chamber orch (1981), *Cloud Burning,* wind, brass, perc (1986), *The Devil's Music,* large orch (1992), *Weigenlied,* orch (1994, rec. RS0270), *Willow Bend,* orch (1994, rec. RS0270), Violin Concerto, vn, large orch (1996), *Diver's Lament,* large orch (1996).

Chamber Instrumental *L'Oiseau Fantastique,* cl, vn, vc, pf [synthesiser optional] (1983), *L'Oiseau Fantastique* II, str qrt and pf (1984), *Shadow's Dance,* cl, vn, pf (1985), rev. as *Stick Dance,* cl, marimba, pf (1987), rev. as *Stick Dance 2,* cl, va, pf, arr. N. Saintilan (1989), *Spherics,* fl, trbn (or bass cl), perc, synth/pf, vc (1985), *Barren Grounds,* cl, va, vc, pf (1988), *Sea Call,* 2 tpt, 1 trbn (1988),

Machine, 4 perc (1989), *Collide*, bass cl and marimba, (1990), *Duo Variations*, va, pf (1990), *Mephisto*, fl, cl, vn, va, db, gui (1990), *Silken Weave*, tpt, pf (1993), *Respiro/Simple Ground*, fl, pf (1993), *Suspended Preludes*, db, pf (1993), *Silk Canons*, 2 fl, 2 bass cl, vibr, pf (1994), Septet No.2 *Circle Ground*, fl, cl, 2 vn, va vc, pf (1995), *Chorale, Demon, Beacon*, koto, 4 perc (1995).

Solo Instrumental Piano Sonata (1982), *Sea-Change*, pf (1987), *Attack*, va (1990), *Barcarole*, pf (1992, rec RED9401).

Theatre *Black River*, opera for solo SSTBB, 13-piece ens (1988, 1, Julianne Schultz), Nov 1989, Sydney, *Fast Talking: The Last Words of Dutch Schultz*, solo male v (1988, 1, Dutch Schultz), June 1989, Perth, *A Distant Shore*, Bar, ens (1989, 1, Louis Nowra), May 1991, Newcastle, *Going Into Shadows*, opera (1995, 3, Julianne Schultz).

Vocal/Choral *Reading A View*, 2 S soli, SATB, Orchestra (1985–86), *O Oriensis*, SATB, marimba, pf, org (1986), *Where the Dead Men Lie*, SATB, wind, brass, perc, pf (4 hands) (1987), *Ekstasis*, solo SSATBB (1990), *Dead Songs*, S, cl, vc, pf (1991), *Silk*, 2 S, bass cl, db, vibr (1993), *Sonata sopra Sancta Maria*, S, 2 fl, cl, bass cl, marimba, vc (1994).

FURTHER REFERENCE

His recordings include *Garotte*, Queensland Symphony Orchestra (OZM 1002); *Chamber Music*, Perihelion (Tall Poppies TP 065). His writings include numerous contributions to *SA*. See also *BroadstockS*; C. Dench and I. Shanahan, eds., 'An Emotional Geography of Australian Composition II', *SA* 46 (Winter 1995), 9–31.

MICHAEL BARKL

Scientists. Rock band (1978–87) formed in Perth, originally comprised of Kim Salmon (vocals, guitar), Roddy Radalj (guitar), Boris Sudjovic (bass) and James Baker (drums). Evolving from three of Perth's earliest punk bands, by 1979 they toured capital city venues and released the first of their seven singles, *Frantic Romantic*. Their success not building, they reduced to a trio in 1980, and re-formed with a largely different membership at Sydney in 1981. Developing a neo-1960s acid-rock sound, they were resident at Vaucluse Hotel in 1982 and made *We Had Love* (1983) and a mini-LP, *Blood Red River* (1983), which was released successfully in Europe. They went to London in 1984, supporting Nick ★Cave and the Bad Seeds and other expatriate bands, and appearing at the Pandora's Box Festival, Holland.

Back in Australia, *Heading For A Trauma* (1985) and the mini-LP *Atom Bomb Baby* (1985) confirmed them as leaders of grunge, but after a national tour in 1987, membership departures led to their disbanding. A band which matured considerably during its course, it was a significant exponent of savage neo-acid rock in the mid-1980s and a training ground for the ★Hoodoo Gurus and Beast of Bourbon.

FURTHER REFERENCE

Recordings include *Frantic Romantic* (White Rider SMX 46959), *We Had Love* (1983, Au Go Go ANDA 29), *Blood Red River* (1983, Au Go Go ANDA 27), *Heading For A Trauma* (1985, Au Go Go ANDA 39), and *Atom Bomb Baby* (1985, Au Go Go ANDA 37). A compilation is *Absolute* (1991, Polydor 849882). For discography, see *SpencerA*. See also *McGrathA*; *SpencerW.*

Score. Independent recording company, see *Mann, Peter.*

Scotney, Evelyn Mary (*b* Ballarat, Vic., 1887; *d* London, 5 Aug. 1967), lyric soprano. She studied under Elise ★Wiedermann at the Albert Street Conservatorium in Melbourne, in Paris with Mathilde Marchesi and in Rome with Tosti. Her career was made in America: she joined the Boston Opera Co. in 1911 and the Metropolitan Opera Co. in 1920, where she sang with Caruso. She was acclaimed especially in *Lucia di Lammermoor*. Returning to England in the 1920s, she sang with Beecham's British National Opera Co. and at fashionable At Homes in partnership with Welsford Smithers, who wrote many songs for her. She continued singing until *c.*1939, touring the USA, Australia and Britain.

FURTHER REFERENCE

Her recordings for HMV are not current. For an index to references in *AMN*, see *MarsiI*. See also *BiographicalR*; *GlennonA*, 29; *MackenzieS*, 133–4.

KAY DREYFUS

Scott, Alan (*b* Caboolture, Qld, 30 Jan. 1930; *d* Southern Highlands, NSW, 11 Dec. 1995), folk-singer, collector. Younger brother of folklorist Bill Scott, he played in the ★Bushwhackers at Sydney from 1954, was founding secretary of the Bush Music Club, and a contributor to and publisher of its magazine *Singabout*. First with John ★Meredith then from 1955 on his own, he made field recordings in NSW, including of Duke ★Tritton singing *Shearing in the Bar*, publishing *Authentic Australian Bush Ballads* (1960) with Meredith, and *A Collector's Songbook* (1970). He performed regularly at folk clubs, concerts and festivals, contributed to *Australian Tradition*, *Stringybark and Greenhide*, and *Cornstalk Gazette*. An important early performer-collector in the 1950s folk-song revival, he represented NSW in the Australian Folk Trust 1987–91.

FURTHER REFERENCE

His collection is now at *CAnl*. Recordings include the singles *Drover's Dream* (1955, Wattle), *Bush Music Club* (1958), *Dinky Di* (1964), *Native Mate* (1988), *Battler's Ballade* (1991, Fanged Wombat) and *Travelling Through The Storm* (Sandstock FWD 002). See also *OxfordF*; *Australian* 19 Jan. 1996.

Scott, Bill (*b* Bundaberg, Qld, 4 Oct. 1923), folklorist. After leaving school at the age of 14, he joined the navy in the war years, then worked in various jobs until becoming a bookseller and publisher in 1956. He was field editor for Rigby Publishing 1959–74, then trade manager with Jacaranda Press. Collecting folk-songs, he published *Folksongs from Queensland* with John Manifold (1959), *Bushranger Ballads* (1976) and *The Second Penguin Australian Songbook* (1980). From 1974 he wrote books on Australian folklore, novels, history, magazine articles and radio programs. His articles have appeared in *Australian Tradition, Stringybark and Greenhide, Overland, Quadrant* and elsewhere. A key member of the Queensland folk movement, he was honoured with the OAM in 1992.

FURTHER REFERENCE
Recordings include *The Billygoat Overland* (1958, Wattle), *Folksongs From Queensland* (1959, Wattle) and *Hey Rain!* (Sandstock RRP 026C). See also *OxfordF*; Walter McVitty, *Authors and Illustrators of Australian Children's Books* (Rydalmere, NSW: Hodder & Stoughton, 1989), 200–1.

Scott, Craig Blakefield (*b* Sydney, 20 Oct. 1956), jazz bass player. He began bass as a teenager, studying at the NSW Conservatorium jazz program in the late 1970s, then worked with Dave *Levy and Keith *Stirling. He joined Don *Burrows in 1981, through the 1980s working with James *Morrison and Julian *Lee, and playing in schools concerts with the Sydney Jazz Quintet, apart from a period of further study in the USA with Todd Coolman and Rufus Reid. Touring with Mike *Nock (1980) and Joe Henderson, he played support for numerous visiting musicians, including Red Rodney and Urbie Green. Currently he is on the full-time staff of the Sydney Conservatorium, where he has taught since 1984. He took an MMus in 1996.

FURTHER REFERENCE
Recordings include *David Baker String Ensemble* (1980, Larrikin LRJ-066); *You Must Believe in Spring*, Bob Bertles (1985, Larrikin LRJ 147); *Lorraine Silk Trio* (1983, EMI Custom Records YPRX 2135); *Babinda Trilogy*, Don Burrows (1990, WEA Records 903172626, 1/2/3); *Stories*, Bill Risby (1994, Risby Music, War 001); *The Singer*, Kerrie Biddell (1995, Origin/Polygram OR 015); *Soundpoint*, Ian Cooper (Larrikin CDLRJ 310). See also *OxfordJ*. BRUCE JOHNSON

Scott, Norm (*b* 1 Jan. 1907; *d* 2 July 1989), country music performer, teacher. Playing a home-made ukulele from the age of 12, then banjo and guitar, he sang country and Hawaiian music professionally from 1924. His Norm Scott Hawaiian Studios at Sydney sold hillbilly guitars, ukuleles, and other country instruments, and offered tuition from a phalanx of teachers by correspondence. Renamed the Hawaiian Club from 1928, the *McKean Sisters and a vast number of other young country artists passed through his hands before he sold the business in the 1950s. His radio show on 2GB featured the young Tex *Morton, Buddy *Williams and many others. In the late 1930s he formed the Singing Stockmen with his brother Arthur; they recorded eight singles for Regal Zonophone, which were among the earliest country recordings in Australia.

One of the seminal figures in early country music, he then formed the Country Band with Dick Carr (steel guitar), George Raymond (fiddle) and Hal Carter (accordion).

FURTHER REFERENCE
Recordings included Night *Time In Nevada* (1937, Regal Zonophone G23534), *There's A Home In Wyoming* (1939, Regal Zonophone G23775) and *Colorado Sunset* (Regal Zonophone G23777). See also *WatsonC*, I, 31–4.

Scottish Folk Music. The mid-19th century saw a great migration of Scots from their native home to Australia and other parts of the New World, due to the Highland clearances in Scotland, mass evictions, whereby with successive famines the Highland economy had collapsed and the lairds and chieftains were forced to sell huge portions of their lands to their creditors. All the tenants on these lands had to leave; and when they set off for the New World they took with them their culture, the mainstay of which was music. The new settlers arrived with fiddles, whistles, flutes, concertinas and, of course, the bagpipes. And as was done in the old country, many, in fact any, social occasion was accompanied by music. This type of gathering is still evident in some of the inner suburban pubs and bars of major cities, and is currently enjoying a renaissance. Although the music is no longer identifiable as pure Scottish, having been interwoven with Welsh and Irish as a matter of survival, this blend of Celtic melodies, with ballads, airs and *presto* jigs and reels, is now gaining audiences and recognition from people seeking their Celtic roots.

Pipers, on the other hand, have been able to maintain their technique and melody lines without the same type of cross-pollination, at least until recent years, when pipers in Australia started following the world trend towards incorporating Irish styles and tunes. The pipe band movement in Australia has been the dominating and motivating force behind the survival of the piping culture. A Highland pipe band of the 21st Regiment was stationed at Hobart in 1834, and dancing to the bagpipes was popular at social functions in the 1840s. Caledonian societies formed in settlements with Scottish families in the 1880s and were active in capital cities in World War I. From as early as the 1860s, Highland Gatherings (festivals of sports, music and dance) have been the focus of pipers and pipe bands alike. Many of these take the form of competitions, and are spread throughout the year, the dates varying from state to state. At Easter in even-numbered years the Australian Pipe Band Championship is held in each capital city in rotation. While the overall numbers of pipers and pipe bands are diminishing, concerted efforts are being made to ensure that this trend does not continue. Like many other groups in Australia's multicultural society, the Scots have a survival tradition, and a musical inheritance for the next generations.

CHRISTOPHER SINCLAIR

Scrap Metal. Rock group founded in 1976 in Broome, WA, comprised of the three Pilgrim brothers Allan (guitar), Stephen (vocals, guitar), and Phillip (drums), their cousin Michael Teh (bass), and one white member Duncan Cambell (keyboard). Formed in Sunburn, they played at Broome's garrulous Roebuck Bay Hotel, mixing Irish folk-song, country and tribal Aboriginal elements, and later rock. In 1986 they travelled to Darwin to promote their self-produced cassette *Just Looking*, and after finding national interest in their album *Broken Down Man* in 1988 they toured with ★Midnight Oil. In 1990 they appeared on an ABC special, *From Broome To The Big Smoke*, and toured the eastern states. Blending rock, country, reggae and pop, their blithe music reflects the tolerant, easy mood of Broome, with its heterogeneous social mix.

FURTHER REFERENCE
Recordings include *Broken Down Man* (1988, Larrikin ASJ001); *Scrap Metal* (1990, ABC 846519–1/2). For discography, see *SpencerA*. See also Glenn A. Baker, 'Scrap Metal: Living the Aboriginal Side', *Faces, Places and Barely Human Races* (Sydney: Random House, 1995); *SpencerW*.

Screaming Tribesmen, The. Rock band (1981–) formed in Brisbane originally comprised of Ron Peno (vocals), Mick Medew (guitar, vocals), John Hartley (bass), and Murray Shepherd (drums). They released their debut single, *Igloo*, in 1983, then moved to Sydney in 1984 with a significantly different membership drawn from former members of the New Christs and Hitmen, and made the mini-LP *Date With A Vamppyre* (1985). More recent work includes the single *I've Got A Feeling* (1987), and the albums *Bones And Flowers* (1987), *High Time* (1990) and *Formaldehyde* (1993). At first a loud, pugnacious hard-rock band, their work has recently become more mainstream.

FURTHER REFERENCE
Recordings include *Igloo* (1983, Citadel CITE 004), *Date With A Vamppyre* (1985, Citadel CITE P902), *I've Got A Feeling* (1987, Survival 6510217), *Bones And Flowers* (1987, Survival 4601201), *High Time* (1990, Survival 4671012) and *Formaldehyde* (1993, Survival SUR 527CD). For discography, see *SpencerA*. See also *SpencerW*; *Rolling Stone* (USA) 9 Feb. 1989, 125.

Sculthorpe, Peter Joshua (*b* Launceston, Tas., 29 Apr. 1929), composer. Arguably the most significant composer in Australia today, he has been prolific and influential since the late 1950s. His originality and 'Australian' aesthetic gained support from local critics especially in the 1960s and 70s; he now enjoys a substantial international reputation, and his influence continues through his many students.

1. His Life. Peter Sculthorpe was raised in rural northern Tasmania and, encouraged by his mother, took a youthful interest in music and literature. He studied piano at the University of Melbourne Conservatorium (BMus, 1950), where he was involved in contemporary music activities along with fellow students Keith ★Humble, Don ★Banks, George ★Dreyfus, James ★Penberthy and others. Several early compositions won him prizes, performances and the support of Bernard ★Heinze, then Ormond professor at the university. After his graduation he returned to Tasmania and wrote many short works, including incidental music for plays, while running a sporting goods shop with his brother Roger and teaching music at the Council for Adult Education.

The watershed in his career was the composition in 1954 of the Sonatina for solo piano, which marked for him a new direction technically and aesthetically and formed the basis of his mature style. It was also the first work sent to represent Australia at an ISCM Festival (Baden-Baden, 1955) and led eventually to his enrolling for doctoral studies under Edmund Rubbra and Egon Wellesz at Wadham College, Oxford (1958–60). In England he consolidated his new direction, and was befriended by English composers such as Wilfrid Mellers and Peter Maxwell Davies. He returned to Tasmania when his father fell ill, after his death writing *Irkanda IV* (1961) in his memory.

Sculthorpe first came to critical notice through the first Australian Composers' Seminar (Hobart, 1963), at which several of his works were heard. In 1963 he was appointed to the University of Sydney as lecturer (since 1991 professor, personal chair). He attracted wide public attention with his *Sun Music* series (composed and premiered 1965–69), especially when several were choreographed by Robert Helpmann for the Australian Ballet and broke all box-office records in 1968. The expressionist vision of the Australian environment in the ballet was acclaimed as a musical parallel to the landscapes of painter Russell Drysdale and the novels of writer Patrick White; both artists were friends of Sculthorpe.

In the late 1960s Sculthorpe became interested in the music and philosophy of Japan and Bali, and spent a short but significant period in a Zen Buddhist monastery in 1970. Public recognition increased with his involvement in the Sydney ABC youth concerts—for which he composed the quasi-theatre piece *Love 200*, which combines popular idioms with his own style—his first full-length dramatic work *Rites of Passage,* several scores for Australian historical feature films and his extensive use of Australian imagery in instrumental works. Growing international recognition, particularly in the USA, accompanied evocative orchestral works such as *Mangrove* (1979), *Earth Cry* (1986) and *Kakadu* (1988).

Today Sculthorpe receives a steady stream of commissions and requests for new arrangements of existing works. His many successful students include Anne ★Boyd, Brenton ★Broadstock, Barry ★Conyngham, and Ross ★Edwards. His work has been the subject of one of the few substantial monographs on an Australian composer (Hannan, 1982); he lectures widely about his music and aesthetics, publishes occasional articles, and since 1985 has been at work on an autobiography. He has been composer-in-residence at Yale University 1966 and visiting professor at Sussex University, UK 1972–73. He has won the first Alfred Hill Memorial Award (1963), the first John Bishop Memorial Award (1967), a Radcliffe Music Award (1968), an AFI Award (1980), an APRA Award (1985), a Sounds Australian Award (1990), and an ARIA Award (1991). He has been honoured with the MBE (1970), OBE (1977), AO (1990), and four honorary doctorates from universities.

2. His Music. In the mid-1950s Sculthorpe came to consider his student experiments with European styles and techniques, especially serialism, irrelevant to Australia and its culture. Thus he turned to local sources of inspiration: Aboriginal music, mythology, words and place-names; the events and musical history of European settlement in Australia; and the music and philosophy of Australia's geographical neighbour, Asia. His new direction was first articulated clearly in an article in *Music Now* in 1969, where he wrote that Australia's immigrant culture, being relatively immature, is primarily visual and concrete rather than aural and abstract; hence he considered there to be a preponderance of extra-musical reference in typically Australian music.

Important imagery includes flatness, vastness, stasis, heat and haze. These are evoked by the main features of Sculthorpe's language: falling phrases and intervals, especially minor seconds and thirds and their compounds; a predominantly linear conception; extended, evolving, but usually non-developmental melodic phrases; the technique of *fuori di passo*, in which a melodic line is played slightly out of phase by two or more instruments; strong tone centres, often established through pedal-points; formal structures comprised of blocks of contrasting material; clear but not necessarily regular rhythmic articulation; and textural and timbral exploration through extended playing techniques and sound masses reminiscent of Penderecki and Ligeti. Aural imagery includes the imitation of tropical birdsong, primarily by stringed instruments. 'Australian-ness' is also seen in his choice of texts for vocal setting, which range from traditional Aboriginal texts to contemporary non-indigenous poets.

The concreteness of Sculthorpe's musical conception lies in the dramatic nature of even his instrumental works, and in his pragmatism: works are usually written for specific performers, taking into account their idiosyncrasies, and sometimes with their collaboration or input. He often revises works after their official or unofficial premieres, treating first performances as a stage in the compositional process. He has also evolved a theory of dualism in culture and music, important to his consistent attempts to explore the conflicts inherent in being of European descent in Australia. In particular, he has pitted colonial music against his own 'Australian' style in works like *Port Essington*. The dualities of the private versus the public, the personal versus the cultural, are also explored, for example, in *Requiem* for solo cello, where ideas derived from Gregorian chant are juxtaposed with more fluid, passionate and rhapsodic writing.

Sculthorpe's path has essentially been highly consistent, and experiments with other styles and techniques have generally been tangential. Electronic media, used only sporadically, remain subservient to acoustic instruments; Asian music, although an abiding interest, primarily influenced his works of the late 1960s and 70s. In the last decade, Sculthorpe has further pursued his interest in Australian colonial musical history through transcriptions.

WORKS

(Mss with composer)

Confusion can arise regarding the titles of Sculthorpe's works because of his practice of renaming and withdrawing works, and transcribing and re-using material. Many works effectively exist in several versions; Hayes (1993) provided accurate details of works completed to that time.

Principal publisher: Faber

Orchestral *The Fifth Continent* speaker, orch (ms, 1963, D.H. Lawrence), *Sun Music I–IV* (1966, 1973, 1973, 1973), *From Tabuh Tabuhan* str, perc (1968), *Lament for Strings* (1978) [arr. vc, str (c.1991)], *Music for Japan* (1979), *Port Essington* 2 vn, vc, str (1980), *Mangrove* (1982), *Sun Song* (ms, 1984), *Autumn Song* (1986), *Earth Cry* (1991), *Nangaloar* (1991), *Kakadu* (1992), *Memento Mori* (1993), *Third Sonata for String Orchestra* (1994). Many other works arr. from own chamber works. Arrangements for symphonic band (two) and big band (two).

Concertos *Irkanda IV* vn, str, perc (1968) [arr. str, perc (1964), fl, str trio (c.1990), str qrt (1991), fl, str qrt (ms, 1992)], Piano Concerto (ms, 1983), *Nourlangie* gui, perc, str (ms, 1989), *Little Nourlangie* org, orch (1990).

Chamber Str Quartets: Nos 1–4 (1947–50) lost, No. 5 (*Irkanda II*) withdrawn, No. 6 (1966), [No. 7] *Red Landscape* (1966), [No. 8] *String Quartet Music* (1974, rev. 1979), No. 9 (1978) [arr. Second Sonata for Strings (1988/90)], No. 10 (1993) [arr. Sonata for Strings (1983)], [No. 11] *Jabiru Dreaming* (c.1990), *Little Serenade* (ms, 1977, [arr. pf duet (ms, 1979)], *Hill Song No. 1* (ms, 1992). *The Loneliness of Bunjil* str trio (1964), *Tabuh Tabuhan* wind quintet, 2 perc (1968), *Dream* any insts (ms, 1970), *How the Stars Were Made* 6 perc (ms, 1971), *Crimson Flower* gamelan (ms, 1973), *Dua Chant* SAT recs (1978), *Landscape II* pf qrt (1979), Sonata for va & perc (1979), *Cantares* 10 gui, str qrt (c.1980), *Tailitnama Song* arr. fl, vn, vc, 2 perc (1981) [arr. vc, pf (1989), vn, pf (1991)], *Djilile* vc, pf (1986) [arr. pf (1986/89), 4 perc (1990)], *Songs of Sea and Sky* cl, pf (1987) [arr. fl, pf (1987)], *Sun Song* 4 perc (1989), *Dream Tracks* pf trio (1992), *Tropic* cl, vn, perc, 2 gui, db (1992), *Chorale* 8 vc (1994), *From Ubirr* str qrt, didjeridu (1994), *Parting* vc, pf (1995).

Solo Instrumental Pf: *Left Bank Waltz* (c.1962) [arr. pf duet (ms, 1979)], Sonatina (1964), *Haiku* (1968), *Landscape* (ms,

1971; rev. 1981), *Koto Music* [*I*] (ms, 1973; rev. 1981), *Koto Music II* (ms, 1976; rev. 1981) [both arr. hp (ms, 1979)], [*Five*] *Night Pieces* (1973) [arr. hp (ms, 1979)], *Mountains* (1982), Three Pieces for Prepared Piano (ms, 1982), *Callabonna* (1989), *Nocturnal* (1989).Vn: *Irkanda I* (1977), Sonata (ms, 1954–55), *Alone* (ms, 1976). Vc: *Requiem* (1982), *Threnody* (1992), *Simori* (ms, 1992), *Cello Dreaming* (1993). Gui: *From Kakadu* (1994), *Into the Dreaming* (1994).

Dramatic Incidental music to 10 plays (1951–56). Operas: *Rites of Passage* 2xSATB, 2 orchs (ms, 1972–73, 11 sections, Sculthorpe after Boethius, traditional Aranda), *Quiros* (ms, 1982, 3, Brian Bell) [several numbers also arr. separately]. Ballet: *Sun Music* SATB, orch (ms, 1968). Films: *They Found a Cave* (ms, 1962), *The Age of Consent* (ms, 1968), *Essington* (ms, 1974), *Manganinnie* (ms, 1980), *Burke and Wills* (ms, 1985), four documentaries. Several short radio and television pieces.

Choral *Night Piece* SATB, pf (1966, Chris Wallace-Crabbe), *Autumn Song* SATBarB (1968, Roger Covell), *Sea Chant* vv, pf (1968, Roger Covell) [arr. vv, orch (ms, 1975), pf duet (ms, 1979)], *Music for Mittagong/Fun Music I* vv, wind, str, perc (ms, 1968), *Sun Music for Voices and Percussion* SATB, pf, 3 perc (c.1969), *Ketjak* 6 vv, tape (ms, 1972), *Child of Australia* speaker, sop, SATB, orch (ms, 1987, Thomas Keneally) [several numbers arr. separately], *Saibai* vv, org (1987), *Morning Song for the Christ Child* SATB, opt. gong (ms, 1988) [arr. str qrt (ms, 1970), pf duet (ms, 1979)], *The Birthday of Thy King/Awake Glad Heart* SATB (1988, after Henry Vaughan) [arr. 2 tpt, str (1992)], *Haughty Sortie* vv, pf (ms, 1990, Edna Sculthorpe).

Vocal Three songs v, pf (ms, 1962, Edna & Peter Sculthorpe), Two Shakespeare Songs v, pf (ms, 1962), *Love 200* 2 singers, rock band, orch (ms, 1970, Tony Morphett) [several numbers arr. separately], *Eliza Fraser Sings* S, fl/a.fl/pic, pf (ms, 1978, Barbara Blackman), *The Song of Tailitnama* S, 6 vc, 2 perc (1974, traditional Aranda) [arr. med vc, pf (1984), S, pf (1994), Ct, pf (1994); see also *Tailitnama Song* under Chamber], *From Nourlangie* S, va, vc, pf (1994) [arr. str qrt (1994)].

Transcriptions *Colonial Dances* 2 pf (Essie Thomas & Ernesto Spagnoletti; ms, 1977), *The Dream* str (Michael Balfe, *The Bohemian Girl*, 1843; 1985), *Ballad* S, orch (W.V.Wallace, *Maritana*, 1845; ms, 1987), *It's You* SATB (two Gershwin songs; ms, 1989), *Two Grainger Arrangements* str, perc (Chinese arr. Grainger, 1935 & Faeroe Island arr. Grainger; 1989), *Rose Bay Quadrilles* pf (William Stanley, 1856; 1989), *Koo-ee* str qrt (Isaac Nathan, 1849; 1991), *National Country Dances* pf (F. Ellard, 1854; 1991), Second Impromptu pf (M. Hauser, 1857; 1991).

WRITINGS

'Sculthorpe on Sculthorpe', *Music Now* 1.1 (1969), 7–13; 'The Constant Presence of Duality', *24 Hours*, May 1993, 62–6; comprehensive list to end of 1992 in Hayes.

FURTHER REFERENCE

Michael Hannan, *Peter Sculthorpe: His Music and Ideas, 1929–1979* (Brisbane: UQP, 1982); Deborah Hayes, *Peter Sculthorpe: A Bio-Bibliography*. (Westport, Conn.: Greenwood Press, 1993).

PATRICIA SHAW

Seal, Andrew (*b* Wiesbaden, Germany, 1834; *d* Brisbane, 1904), band leader, cornettist. He studied music with his father, played cornet in a theatre orchestra from the age of 14 and migrated to Australia with his brother Auguste (*b* 1821) who played trombone and double bass. He played cornet in W.H. Paling's concerts at Sydney and took a wind quartet to Brisbane in 1857, giving concerts at the Botanic Gardens, as well as playing at balls and hotels, then toured the region from Ipswich to Warwick. He opened a music shop in Brisbane in 1858, but this failed and he went back to Sydney, soon returning with a new wind quintet. In 1861 he formed the Queensland Volunteer Band, which he conducted with notable success until he was replaced in 1869, after which he formed another quartet. One of the first professional musicians of substance to reside in Queensland, as a composer he wrote more than 20 works, including the cantata *Life and Death of a Soldier*, works for solo wind, two patriotic choruses, *Federation* and *Australia's Golden Shore,* songs, marches, and an overture for band.

FURTHER REFERENCE

Warren Bebbington, 'Music in 19th-Century Brisbane: The German Impact', in *The German Presence in Queensland*, ed. Manfred Jurgensen and Alan Corkhill (Brisbane: QUP, 1988), 267–75; C.G. Austin, 'Early History of Music in Queensland', *Journal of the Royal Historical Society of Queensland* 6/4 (1962–63), 1052–68.

Searelle, (William) Luscombe (*b* Devon, England, 1853; *d* 18 Dec. 1907), impresario, conductor, composer. Raised in NZ from the age of nine, he worked as a pianist, then conductor and composer at Christchurch, but after conducting a pirated *HMS Pinafore* with his own sequel, *The Wreck of the Pinafore* (1880), he had to flee legal action. He came to Australia, bringing his *The Fakir of Travancore* (1881) without great success. He staged his *Estrella* (1883) in the UK and briefly in the USA, but once he returned to Australia it became a smash hit with the Montague-Turner Opera Co. in 1884. His *Bodabil* (1884) and *Isadore* (1885) were less successful. Bankrupt in 1886, he left for the USA. He took an opera troupe complete with prefabricated iron theatre to Johannesburg and the Rand goldfields, South Africa, in 1889, but had little further success. Producing rather clichéd, mundane scores, his other works include a cantata, *Australia*.

FURTHER REFERENCE

The Encyclopaedia of the Musical Theatre, comp. Kurt Gänzl (Oxford: Blackwell Reference, 1994); *MackenzieS*, 278; *IrvinD*; *BrewerD*, 84.

Sedergreen, Bob (Robert Alexander) (*b* Acre, Haifa, British Palestine, 24 Aug. 1943), jazz pianist. He moved to the UK then Australia in childhood and took formal lessons in piano (later adding trumpet). Becoming active in the jazz movement, he embraced a wide range of styles from blues to experimental, with Ted *Vining, Brian *Brown, Onaje, and Peter Gaudion's Blues Express among others. He formed Blues on the Boil in 1985 and Art Attack in 1988. A founding jazz improvisation teacher at the Victorian College of the Arts, he has been musical director for numerous visitors including Dizzy Gillespie, Lee Konitz and Phil Woods.

FURTHER REFERENCE

Recordings include *Jimmy Witherspoon Sings The Blues* (1980, Aim Records, AIM 1005); *The Ted Vining Trio Live at PBS-FM* (1981, Jazznote JNLP 029); *The Planets*, Brian Brown (1985, Larrikin LRJ 151); *Waltz for Stella*, Onaje (1985, Larrikin LRJ 174); *Blues on the Boil* (1986, Larrikin LRS 187). See also *ClareB*; *BissetB*; *OxfordJ*; Adrian Jackson, 'Interview, Bob Sedergreen', *JA* (Dec. 1981), 22–4.   BRUCE JOHNSON

Sedivka, Beryl   (*b* Aylesbury, England, 27 Nov. 1928), pianist. She studied with Marcel Ciampi, Solomon and Franz Reizenstein and graduated from the Paris Conservatoire with a diploma of music. In 1954 she won the Harriet Cohen International Medal, under the name of Diana Merrien. Since arriving in Australia in 1961 she has participated in several Meet-the-Composer chamber music concerts at the Odeon in Hobart and has performed as a soloist and in many concerto performances with the Tasmania Symphony Orchestra. She has worked at the Tasmanian Conservatorium of Music since 1966 as lecturer in advanced piano studies.

FURTHER REFERENCE

Corliss Gustavson, Pianists of Australia, MMus., Univ. Queensland, 1977.   KERRI-ANN SHEPPARD

Sedivka, Jan   (*b* Slany, Czechoslovakia, 8 Sept. 1917), violinist, teacher. After studying with O. Ševčik and J. Kocian at the Prague Conservatoire, he studied with Jacques Thibaud at the École Normale, Paris, from 1938, then with Max Rostal in London. He was a member of the London Czech Trio and London International Trio, and taught at Trinity College, London, the Surrey College of Music, and Goldsmith's College. Bringing eight of his pupils, he came to Australia in 1961 and taught at the Queensland Conservatorium until 1965, then at the Tasmanian Conservatorium from 1968 (as its director from 1972). He has given masterclasses at most of Australia's music schools, as well as in China and elsewhere. He appeared widely as a recitalist, often with his wife, pianist Beryl Sedivka; as a concerto soloist a number of works were written for him, notably by Larry Sitsky. He was a member of the Australia Council Music Board 1975–80 and federal chairman of the AMEB.

A charismatic personality and remarkably successful pedagogue, he built a string school at Tasmania which for nearly 30 years has been the most important in Australia, producing a startling number of successful professional players. He has been honoured with the AM (1987), the

FTCL, a DLitt (Univ. Tasmania), the Gold Medal of the Prague Academy of Musical Arts, and the Sir Bernard Heinze Award (1996).

FURTHER REFERENCE

Recordings include Larry Sitsky, Violin Concerto No. 2, Tasmanian Symphony Orchestra (1989, Move). See also *WWA* (1996); *Bulletin* 18 June 1993.

Seekers, The.   Folk-pop group formed (1964) in Melbourne, comprised of Judith Durham (lead vocals; *b* Melbourne 1943), Keith Potger (vocals, guitar; *b* Colombo, Sri Lanka, 1941), Bruce Woodley (vocals, guitar; *b* Melbourne, 1942), and Athol Guy (vocals, double bass; *b* Melbourne, 1940). After settling their membership during 1962–63, they worked their way to London on board a cruise ship, arriving in mid-1964. At once the pace quickened considerably: they signed with the Grade Agency, performed live and made television appearances. Soon afterwards the group were introduced to songwriter and performer Tom Springfield, who wrote and produced many of their best-known songs. These included *I'll Never Find Another You*, *A World Of Our Own* and *The Carnival Is Over*, each of which reached the Top 10 during 1965 in England, Australia and the USA. Other hits from this high point in the group's career include *Someday Oneday* (1966), *Morningtown Ride* (1967) and *Georgie Girl* (1967), the group's most successful single in the USA, which peaked at No. 2 on the charts.

Their appearance at Melbourne's Myer Music Bowl in March 1967 drew an estimated crowd of 200 000, but the group separated the following year when Durham indicated she wanted to pursue more eclectic singing interests. The name of the Seekers was kept alive over the following years by Keith Potger, who formed the New Seekers, active in the 1970s. Additionally, the male members of the quartet have appeared and recorded with singers Louisa Wisseling during the 1970s and Julie Anthony in the late 1980s. In 1993 the original membership re-formed for an extensive Silver Jubilee tour in Australia, NZ and the UK.

Performing a range of folk, traditional and popular material, the Seekers were the first Australian group to achieve international success, and paved the way for other Australian acts to follow. They were inducted into the Australian Rock'n'Roll Hall of Fame.

FURTHER REFERENCE

Recordings include *The Silver Jubilee Album* (EMI 781408–2); *The Seekers Complete* (EMI 814639–2); *This Is The Seekers* (EMI 814440–2); *A World Of Our Own* (Pol ID00482). See also *GuinnessP*; *McGrathA*.   WILLIAM VAN PINXTEREN

Selby, Kathryn   (*b* Sydney, 20 Sept. 1962), pianist. She studied at the NSW State Conservatorium with Nancy Salas. Churchill and Australia Council fellowships enabled her to continue her studies in the USA, and she studied at the Curtis Institute and graduated from Bryn Mawr College and the Julliard School. She won awards at the Van Cliburn International competition and the William Kappell competition and has performed widely with orchestras in the USA and Europe, and at several American and Australian festivals. Chamber music coach at the Sydney Conservatorium 1989–95, she was co-founder of Trio Oz and the Academy Chamber Players (Philadelphia), and co-founder and manager of the Macquarie Trio.

FURTHER REFERENCE
Recordings include Gershwin works (Naxos).
                                                    CYRUS MEHER-HOMJI

Sentimental Bloke, The (1). Ballet (1952) by John Tallis (*b* 1911), choreography by Laurel Martyn based on the C.J. Dennis story. First Performed by the Victorian Ballet Guild in 1952.

Sentimental Bloke, The (2). Ballet (1955) by John ★Antill based on the C.J. Dennis story. Antill also arranged *A Sentimental Suite* (1955) for orchestra.

Sentimental Bloke, The (3). Musical comedy (1961) by Albert ★Arlen, book by Lloyd Thomson after the C.J. Dennis story. The song ★*I Dips Me Lid* from the show became widely popular. First performed in Canberra in 1961, then nationally by J.C. Williamsons.

Sentimental Bloke, The (4). Opera (1965) in two acts by George ★Dreyfus, libretto by Graham Blundell after the C.J. Dennis story. First performed at the Victorian Arts Centre Playhouse on 12 December 1985. Vocal score published (Melbourne, 1985).

Serena, Clara [Clara Serena Hulda Kleinschmidt] (*b* Lobethal, SA, 9 June 1890; *d* Adelaide, 11 Aug. 1972), contralto. She studied with Guli Hack at the Elder Conservatorium, Adelaide, and subsequently with Blower and Visetti at the Royal College of Music, London, as the recipient of the 1908 Elder Overseas Scholarship. When war broke out in 1914 she abandoned a proposed operatic debut in Cologne and returned temporarily to Adelaide. Her career reached its peak in the 1920s when she emerged as one of the leading contraltos in Britain. She appeared with considerable success at Covent Garden in such roles as Alkestis and Amneris, but was equally accomplished as a concert, oratorio and recording artist.

FURTHER REFERENCE
GlennonA, 30; *MackenzieS*, 134–6.
                              WAYNE HANCOCK (with M. Elphinstone)

Seven Deadly Sins, The. Opera in two acts by Colin Brumby (1970), libretto by Thomas Shapcott. First performed at the SGIO Theatre, Brisbane, on 12 September 1970 by the Queensland Opera Co.

Severed Heads. Rock band (1980–) formed in Sydney, originally comprised of Paul Derring, Tom Ellard, Richard Fielding and Steven Jones. Beginning with the album *No Vowels, No Bowels* (1980), they gained a wide following as an atmospheric dance act, and have toured Europe, the USA and Japan. They have made at least 16 albums, including *Since The Accident* (1983), *Big Bigot* (1986), *Cuisine* (1991) and *Gigupus* (1994). The first Australian band to enter the *Billboard* (USA) dance charts, they combine electronically processed sound with a relentless dance pulse and multimedia presentation.

FURTHER REFERENCE
Recordings include *No Vowels, No Bowels* (1980, Terse YPRX 1706), *Since The Accident* (1983, EMI INK 2), *Big Bigot* (1986, Volition VOLT 7), *Cuisine* (1991, Volition VOLTCD 40) and *Gigupus* (1994, Volition). For discography, see *SpencerA*. See also *SpencerW*; *Melody Maker* 17 Nov. 1989, 29.

Seymour Group, The. Contemporary music performance ensemble, founded in 1976 in Sydney, at present comprised of Christine Draeger (flute) Margery Smith (clarinet), Anthony ★Fogg (piano until 1994), Ian Cleworth (percussion) and Peter Morrison (cello); various guest artists have included Joan ★Carden, John ★Pringle, and Merlyn Quaife, and their conductors have included Stuart ★Challender, Myer ★Fredman and David Stanhope. Their diverse offerings have embraced chamber music, electronic music, contemporary jazz, chamber opera and music-theatre, always emphasising Australian works. Commissioning more than 50 works from Australian composers of all styles, they have given many young composers their first experience of professional performance. Their activities have focused on a subscription series at the Seymour Centre, Sydney, but they presented *Le Chat Noir* at the Brisbane Biennial and in Canberra in 1991 and the premiere of Graeme Koehne's opera *Love Burns* at the Adelaide Festival in 1992.

FURTHER REFERENCE
Recordings include *The Owl: Aria for Edward John Eyre* (1993, Vox Australis VAST 011–2); and A. Schultz, *Black River* (1993, video Film Australia).

Seymour, Peter (*b* Melbourne, 1932; *d* Sydney, 20 Mar. 1987), choral conductor. After studying singing, piano and percussion at the University of Melbourne, he went to London in 1960, studying singing with Max Worthley, singing in oratorio and teaching. He returned to Australia as director of music at Sydney Grammar School (1966–77). In 1968 he became music director for the Sydney Philharmonia Society, building it into the leading choral organisation in Australia, conducting many new Australian and European works as well as an intensive schedule of standard repertoire, and making numerous radio broadcasts. He founded and conducted the Sydney Youth Orchestra in 1972, was chairman of the National

Music Camps Association from 1977, and was chorusmaster and conductor for the Australian Opera from 1978, then its musical co-ordinator from 1981. His sudden illness and death from cancer at the height of his powers deprived Australia of an articulate conductor of boundless energy and enthusiasm. He had been honoured with the OBE in 1977.

Shake-A-Leg Songs.   Secular dance-songs of western Cape York peoples, north Queensland. See *Aboriginal Music* §3(iv).

Shanahan, Ian   (*b* Sydney, 13 June 1962), composer, recorder player. He studied at the University of Sydney, 1980–85 and 1989 to the present. President of the Fellowship of Australian Composers 1989–92, he has been associate lecturer in performance, University of Western Sydney (Nepean), since 1996. Shanahan's works, stimulated by an interest in mathematics, proportion and cosmology, include *Echoes/Fantasies* (1984) for bass clarinet and percussion, *Cycles of Vega* (1990) for E-flat clarinet and percussion, *Lingua Silens Florum* (1991) for prepared alto recorder, and *Lines of Light* (1993) for recorder player, percussion and synthesisers.

FURTHER REFERENCE
Recordings include *Legends*, fl (AMC 002); *Solar Dust, Echoes/Fantasies* (JADE 1013). His writings include (with C. Dench), 'An Emotional Geography of Australian Composition II', *SA* 46 (Winter 1995), 9–31. See also *BroadstockS*; C. Beaumont, Ian Shanahan: A glimpse into his world-view of music through an analysis of *Cycles of Vega*, BMus(Hons), Univ. Sydney, 1993.   MICHAEL BARKL

Shanks, Donald Robert   (*b* Brisbane, 5 July 1940), bass. After singing in Gilbert and Sullivan operettas he appeared with the Elizabethan Theatre Trust Opera Co. (later the Australian Opera) from 1964, toured with the Sutherland-Williamson Co. 1965 and appeared at Covent Garden 1974, the Paris Opera 1976 and the Canadian Opera 1983–86. He has sung with the Queensland Lyric Opera and Victoria State Opera, and made numerous concert appearances in Australia in oratorio. His repertoire of more than 70 roles ranges from the comic Osmin, Baron Ochs and Don Pasquale to Nabucco, Zaccaria, Raimondo (*Lucia di Lammermoor*), Phillip (*Don Carlos*), Sarastro, Boris Godunov, Bluebeard, and the Wagnerian roles Daland, Gurnemanz and Hunding. He was honoured with the OBE in 1976 and the AO in 1987.

FURTHER REFERENCE
CA (1995–96); Ann Carr-Boyd/Elizabeth Forbes, *GroveO*.

Shapcott, Thomas W.   (*b* 21 Mar. 1935), poet, novelist. After working as an accountant 1961–78 and studying arts at the University of Queensland, he went freelance as a critic, editor, and anthologist and was director of the Australia Council Literature Board 1983–90. His poems and novels include *Time On Fire* (1961), *Inwards To The Sun* (1969), *Shabbytown Calendar* (1975), and *Mona's Gift* (1993). He has always been interested in musical composition, and has written texts for over 20 musical works, notably by Colin ★Brumby, from choral works such as *We Reach Among Bells* (1968), *Bring Out Your Christmas Masks* (1969), *A Ballade for Saint Cecilia* (1971), *Celebrations and Lamentations* (1971) and *This is the Vine* (1972) to the operas *Ishtar's Mirror* (1972) and *The Seven Deadly Sins* (1970).

FURTHER REFERENCE
WWA (1996); *OxfordL*; W. Wilde, *Australian Poets and their Work* (Melbourne: OUP, 1996).

Sharp, Cecil   (*b* London 22 Nov. 1859; *d* London, 28 June 1924), folk-song collector. After studying at Cambridge University, he came to Australia in 1883 and worked as an associate to the chief justice of SA. He taught at the Adelaide College of Music 1889–92 and was deputy cathedral organist. With Guy Boothby as librettist he wrote the operetta *Dimple's Lovers* (1890) and the comic opera *Sylvia, or The Marquis and the Maid* (1890), both performed at Adelaide. Returning to the UK in 1892, he embarked on the career that made him famous as a folk-song collector.

FURTHER REFERENCE
Maud Karpeles, *Cecil Sharp: His Life and Work* (London, 1967); *ADB*, 11; *IrvinD*; Elizabeth Wood, *Quadrant* (May–June 1973).

Sharp, Ronald William   (*b* Sydney, 8 Aug. 1929), organ-builder. Without any formal training in organbuilding, Sharp built his first organ in 1959 for the chancel of St Mary's Cathedral, Sydney, using electric action. Shortly afterwards he adopted mechanical actions, culminating in his first major work in this style for Knox Grammar School, Sydney (1965). He later built organs for Wollongong Town Hall, NSW, the Perth Concert Hall, Ormond College at the University of Melbourne, and St John's, Canberra. He is best known for the monumental instrument in the Sydney Opera House which was opened in 1979, the largest mechanical action organ in the world and the focus of international attention. Sharp's approach to organ-building has been based upon an entirely fresh and intuitive approach, an original synthesis of style and sound. His instruments are characterised by a vibrant and warm sound unique in the history of organ-building. They have been widely acclaimed and frequently recorded.

FURTHER REFERENCE
Cecil Clutton, 'Ronald Sharp: Australian Organbuilder', *The Organ* 50/198 (Oct. 1970), 64–8; Ronald Nagorcka, From Schnitger to Sharp, BA(Hons), Univ. Melbourne, 1971.
                                            JOHN MAIDMENT

Shaw, John (*b* Newcastle, NSW, 12 Oct. 1921), baritone. While working as an accountant in Newcastle, Hector ★Crawford suggested he move to Melbourne for lessons with Henri and Annie ★Portnoj, and he sang there with the National Theatre Movement Opera Co. 1945–55. After a prodigious feat in singing 15 baritone roles with the Italian Grand Opera Co. touring Australia in 1955, he was appointed principal baritone in the newly founded Elizabethan Theatre Trust Opera 1956–57. He appeared there with Joan ★Hammond, on whose recommendation he was engaged without audition by Covent Garden, where he sang high baritone roles 1958–74, making guest appearances throughout Europe and North America. He was with the Australian Opera 1974–89. A commanding stage presence with a voice of great power and vivacity, his roles ranged from Rigoletto and Scarpia to Telramund and Amfortas; he sang in the premiere of Walton's *The Bear* at Aldeburgh, Ruprecht in the London premiere of Prokofiev's *The Fiery Angel*, and at the opening of the Sydney Opera House in Prokofiev's *War and Peace* (1973). He was honoured with the OBE in 1977 and the AO in 1986.

FURTHER REFERENCE
Recordings include Colonel Calverley in *Patience*, Glyndebourne (EMI CMS7 64406–2); *Lucia di Lammermoor* (GDS, not current); *Aida* (Italiana Opera, not current). See also Roger Covell, *GroveO*; *MackenzieS*, 216–19; *AMN* (Feb 1969), 9.

Shearer's Dream, The, shearer's ballad. With words by Henry Lawson, it is the comical fantasy of a sheep shearer, set to a tune resembling 'Covent Gardens'. Collected by John Meredith and published in *Singabout* (1958); also well known as recorded by A.L. Lloyd in 1958 to the tune 'The Girl I Left Behind'.

FURTHER REFERENCE
Edition and commentary in *EdwardsG*.

Shearston, Gary (*b* Tenterfield, NSW, 1939), folk singer-songwriter. While working as a journalist he took occasional singing engagements, appearing on children's television programs, becoming a full-time folk-singer in 1963 and working in Sydney's folk clubs and coffee lounges, at trade union meetings, and for the Aboriginal Advancement League. He released the first of 12 albums, *Folk Songs And Ballads Of Australia* (1964), and his single *Sydney Town* reached No. 30 in the charts in 1965. *Sometime Lovin'* was also a chart success; he released *Garry Shearston Sings His Songs* (1966) and he hosted the television program *Just Folk* in 1966. From 1967 he worked in Italy and the UK, his single *I Get A Kick Out Of You* reaching No. 12 in Australia in 1974, and he released the album *The Springtime It Brings On The Shearing* (1977). He was in the USA for four years, and when he returned to Australia in 1989 he released *Aussie Blue* and won a Tamworth Songwriters' Association award in 1990. One of

the best known figures in the popularisation of Australian folk-song in the mid-1960s, he was one of very few folk-singers to achieve Top 40 chart success. He has entered the Anglican priesthood and is currently at a parish at Hay, NSW.

FURTHER REFERENCE
The early singles were recorded for CBS and *I Get A Kick Out Of You* for Pickwick. Currently available is *The Springtime It Brings On The Shearing* (1977, Larrikin LRF 022TC) and *Aussie Blue* (1989, Larrikin). See also *McGrathA*; *Age* 4 Sept., 25 Oct. 1989; *Australian Tradition* 3/1 (Mar. 1966), 3–4.

Shegog, Kevin (*b* Launceston, Tas., 20 Aug. 1933), country singer-songwriter. He grew up on a farm at Lower Turners Marsh, 40 km from Launceston, Tas. His father played fiddle and button accordion at bush dances. At the age of eight he began playing guitar and singing, influenced by Buddy ★Williams, Hank Snow and Tex ★Morton. When he was 10 he sang at his first dance, and by the age of 14 he was performing throughout the district and at charity shows in Launceston. In 1955 he moved to Victoria, singing with the country and western group the Gold Toppers. He signed with W&G records in 1960 and first made the Top 40 in January 1961 with his own composition *Little Kangaroo*. Because of strong sales in country areas, Shegog was one of the most popular recording artists of the early 1960s. At the height of his popularity he appeared on the big touring shows of ★Rick and Thel, but has not undertaken large-scale touring since. He worked regularly in Melbourne, country Victoria and Tasmania until 1980 when he retired from full-time performing. He is noted for his deep and powerful voice and his fine songwriting. *One Small Photograph*, which he wrote and recorded early in his career, has become a country standard.

FURTHER REFERENCE
Recordings include *Wolverton Mountain* (W&G 1455, 1962); *Cowboy Boots* (W&G 1756, Nov. 1963); debut album *Kevin Shegog* (W&G 1387, n.d.); *Kevin Shegog's Greatest Hits* (W&G 1991, 1978). *WatsonC*, II 175–7.

CAROLYN MUNTZ

Sheik of Scrubby Creek, The. See *Chad Morgan*.

Shell Aria. Vocal competition founded in 1955 as part of the Australian National Eisteddfod at Canberra. Winners have included Jenifer ★Eddy, Yvonne ★Minton and Raymond ★Myers.

Shell Covent Garden Scholarship. Awarded annually (since 1984) after national competition for a singer under 32 who is an Australian citizen and has been resident in Australia for the preceding 12 months. The winner is provided with fares, accommodation and tuition fees for a year's study at the National Opera Studio, London. Previous winners have included Lisa Gasteen and Miriam Gormley. Sponsored by Shell (Aust.) and administered by Opera Foundation Australia, the prize is currently valued at $35 000.

Shephard, David (*b* London 1935), clarinettist. After studies with John Davies at the Royal Academy of Music he worked freelance in London from 1955. He toured Australia as soloist with the band of the Irish Guards in 1957 and returned to settle in 1958 as clarinettist in the Queensland Symphony Orchestra. He was principal clarinet in the orchestra from 1961, teaching at the Queensland Conservatorium and the University of Queensland. He taught at the Canberra School of Music from 1970, then the Elder Conservatorium from 1974. As a member of the *University of Adelaide Wind Quintet, he toured Australia for Musica Viva and the ABC as well as in South-East Asia. A seasoned player and dedicated teacher, he has given clarinet masterclasses widely and is director of the SA State Music Camp. Since 1994 he has been director of the Elder Conservatorium and chairman of the AMEB.

Shepherd, Roy (*b* Melbourne, 1908; *d* 20 June 1987), pianist. After taking lessons from Jessie F. Valentine from the age of seven, he studied at the University of Melbourne Conservatorium with F.W. Homewood, won the South Street Eisteddfod, Ballarat, and for three years running the ANA Competitions, Melbourne, and gained his LTCL. He won an Albert Street Conservatorium Scholarship (1924) and the Clarke Scholarship (1925) and went to London, studying at the Royal College of Music with Herbert Fryer and Harold Samuel. He then studied with Alfred Cortot at the École Normale, Paris, in 1929 and returned to Australia in 1931. He gave recitals of modern French repertoire, began taking pupils at the University of Melbourne Conservatorium, and toured as accompanist to John Brownlee in 1932. He was music director of Geelong College 1936–38 and director of music at Lord Somers Camp for 20 years. He gave recitals with violinist Harry Hutchins 1945–46, but by this time had largely ceased performing to concentrate on teaching, becoming the first full-time senior lecturer (later reader) in music at the University of Melbourne in 1959.

One of the most productive piano teachers Australia has produced, his pupils over 40 years included Keith *Humble, Bruce *Hungerford, Dennis *Hennig, Max *Cooke, and a remarkably large number of others who found significant careers as pianists. He published editions with his own fingering and pedalling of the Debussy *Preludes* (Melbourne, Allans Music, 1969) and other works, and was in Europe 1962–63, but otherwise was at the University of Melbourne teaching and examining for the AMEB well beyond his official retirement in 1974.

FURTHER REFERENCE
Melbourne University Gazette (Mar. 1959), 9; *AMN* 15 (Dec. 1925), 31, 47; *AMN* 27 (Apr. 1937), 32.

Shepparton, pop. (1991) 30 511, city at the confluence of the Goulburn and Broken Rivers, north-east of Melbourne. The central city of the Goulburn Valley, it was established in 1853 as McGuires Punt. Early musical activity in the district involved local church groups, and several choirs emerged in the 1880s, such as the Wesleyan Church Choir and the Methodist Church Choir. Concerts and competitions organised by local music teachers appear in the 1890s and local dances were held in the Public Hall (later Parish Hall), High Street. By 1900 the Star Theatre was the largest musical venue in the town and amateur groups such as the Shepparton Musical Society (1908) and the Orrvale Choral Society (1913) used it for music-theatre productions, particularly Gilbert and Sullivan. Brass bands developed early and include the Shepparton Union Brass Band (1890), the Shepparton Town Band (*c*.1920) and the Shepparton Model Band (*c*.1920). Today band music is provided by the City of Shepparton Pipe Band and the Shepparton Brass Band.

In 1933 violinist Arthur Lilley formed and conducted the Shepparton Symphony Orchestra, which continued until the early 1980s under his direction, finally disbanding in the mid-1980s. A valued asset, the orchestra accompanied visiting artists and also took part in local theatrical productions. Concerts by professional touring groups such as the Melbourne Symphony Orchestra were organised by the Shepparton Musical Advancement Society (now the Shepparton Performing Arts Association) and held at the Shepparton Civic Centre (established in the 1960s). Host of the annual Shepparton Piano Awards, the region has benefited from groups like the Goulburn Valley Youth Orchestra and Choir, which contributed to the implementation of strong music programs in both primary and secondary schools.

FURTHER REFERENCE
AMN 21 (June 1932), 15; *Shepparton News* 12 Feb. 1996; W.S. James, *History of Shepparton* (Shepparton: Borough of Shepparton, 1934), 84–90; Raymond West, 'Those were the days', *A Story of Shepparton, Victoria, and (To Some Extent) its District* (Melbourne: Waterwheel Press, 1962), 60. The Shepparton Symphony Orchestra papers are in the possession of Mavis Lilley; concert programs are held by the Shepparton Historical Society.

JENNIFER ROYLE

Sherbet [The Sherbs]. Rock band formed in Sydney (1969) by vocalist Daryl *Braithwaite (*b* Melbourne, 11 Jan. 1949), the songwriting team of Garth Porter (keyboards, vocals) and Clive Shakespeare (*b* 3 June 1957, guitar, vocals), Alan Sandow (*b* 28 Feb. 1958, drums) and Bruce Worrall (bass). Worrall left the band in 1972 and was replaced by Tony Mitchell (*b* 21 Oct. 1951). British bands Slade and Sweet were among Sherbet's primary influences during their early recording career, and evidence of this can be found in their fourth single release, *You've Got the Gun* (1972). Their management worked hard during this early period to build a media profile by booking tours to population centres all over Australia, some of which had never before hosted a rock concert. By the time they had released their third album, *Slipstream*, in 1974, they had attracted a massive teen and pre-teen audience. *Slipstream* hit No. 3 in the national charts and the singles *Slipstream* and *Silvery Moon* both hit No. 5. The following year saw Sherbet continue to dominate the charts with albums *Sherbet's Greatest Hits* and *Life is for Living* peaking at No. 1 and No. 3 respectively in 1975, and four hit singles *Summer Love* (No. 1), *Life* (No. 4), *Only One You/Matter of Time* (No. 5) and *Child's Play* (No. 4). Their most popular album, *Howzat*, (1976) topped the national charts, as did the single *Howzat*, which also hit No. 4 in the UK.

Later in 1976, Shakespeare left Sherbet and was briefly replaced by ex-*Daddy Cool member Gunther Gorman before Harvey James joined the band permanently. After recording *Photoplay* in 1977, Sherbet attempted to break into the US market. The vehicle for this was their 1978 self-titled album, which was renamed *Highway* for US audiences. Having made little impact in the USA, the band returned to Australia and renamed themselves the Sherbs with the intent of attracting a more mature audience. Unfortunately, this change of direction not only alienated the band from its teen audience, but also failed to impress older audiences. Although the Sherbs released three critically acclaimed albums, *The Skill* (1980), *Defying Gravity* (1981) and *Shaping Up* (1982), their former popularity had dwindled drastically, and in 1984 they disbanded.

As Sherbet in the 1970s, they had enjoyed 11 national Top 10 hit singles, with another eight in lower positions on the Top 40 chart. Porter joined his former colleague Shakespeare in production work, and in 1988 Braithwaite launched a successful solo singing career.

FURTHER REFERENCE
Recordings include *Time Change a Natural Progression* (1972, Infinity INL 34725); *On with the Show* (1973, Infinity L 35007); *Slipstream* (1974, Infinity L 35275); *Sherbet in Concert* (1975, Infinity L 35443); *Sherbet's Greatest Hits* (1975, Infinity L 35525); *Life is for Living* (1975, Infinity L 35652); *Howzat* (1976, Sherbet L 35905); *Photoplay* (1977, Razzle L 36268); *Caught in the Act . . . Live* (1977, Razzle L 36417); *Sherbet* (1978, Sherbet L 36617). As The Sherbs: *The Skill* (1980, Razzle L 37394); *Defying Gravity* (1981, Razzle); *Shaping Up* (1982, Razzle). See also *GuinnessP*; *SpencerW*.   AARON D.S. CORN

Sherwin, Amy   (*b* Huon Valley nr Judbury, Tas., 1855; *d* London, 20 Sept. 1935), soprano. She learned piano and singing from her mother, and later studied with F.A. *Packer in Hobart. She first appeared in *Puss In Boots* at Del Sarte's Rooms, Hobart and made her opera debut as Norina in *Don Pasquale* with the visiting Pompei and Carlo Opera Co. in Hobart in 1878. Later that year she went to NZ, then San Francisco where she sang Violetta and *La Favorita,* then sang elsewhere in the USA, including New York (1880). She settled in London, sang Lucia

at Covent Garden, and as the 'Tasmanian Nightingale' became a favourite concert artist, especially in Patti's concerts and at the Proms. She visited Australia in 1887 and engaged John *Lemmone for her tours, sang at the 1888 International Centennial Exhibition, Melbourne, then toured Hong Kong, China and Japan. In the 1890s she chiefly gave concerts in Europe and toured, revisiting Australia in 1897–98, with Jan Kubelik in 1902, and on her final tour in 1906. After this she retired from the concert platform, struggling to support a completely dependent invalid daughter, and died in ill health and straitened circumstances. With a clear, bell-like tone, which had great beauty in the top register, she was the most widely travelled singer of her day, and set a standard to which the young *Melba aspired.

FURTHER REFERENCE
Obit. in *AMN* 1 Oct. 1935. See also Judith A. Bowler, *Amy Sherwin: The Tasmanian Nightingale* (Hobart: the author, 1982); A Fysh, *Amy Sherwin* (Hobart, 1965); Deirdre Morris, *ADB*, 6; *MackenzieS*, 69–83.

Ship of Heaven, The.   Musical fantasy in two acts by Alfred *Hill (1923), the text by Hugh McCrae. With no narrative, the work stages verse by McCrae on a variety of fanciful themes. First performed by Doris Fitton's Independent Theatre Co. at the Savoy Theatre, Sydney on 7 October 1933.

Shorrock, Glen   (*b* Kent, England, 30 June 1944), popular music singer. After singing in the vocal trio the Checkmates at Adelaide from 1962, he sang with the *Twilights 1965–69, then *Axiom 1969–71. Going to England in 1971, as a soloist he released *Let's Get the Band Together* (1971), and with Esperanto was supporting act to Cliff Richard in 1974. He joined the *Little River Band 1975–82 and from 1988, released a solo album, *Villain Of The Peace* (1982), and his *We're Coming To Get You* reached No. 6 in the charts in 1983. After appearing in *The Rocky Horror Show* and *Evita,* and producing cabaret shows, he formed Blazing Saddles with Brian *Cadd in 1993. For 20 years the lead vocalist in three of Australia's most successful bands, he has had a long career of prominence in popular music. He was honoured in the ARIA Hall of Fame in 1991.

FURTHER REFERENCE
Recordings include *Let's Get the Band Together* (1971, Mam MAM 9673), *Villain Of The Peace* (1982, EMI ST I2222), and We're *Coming To Get You* (EMI EMI 1059). A compilation is *Glen Shorrock The First 20 Years* (1985, EMI EME 261014/5). For discography, see *SpencerA*. See also *CA* (1995–96); *McGrathA*; *SpencerW*; *Australian* 18 Mar. 1996.

Siede, Auguste   (*b* Melbourne?; *d* London, 6 Sept. 1925), music critic. Son of Julius *Siede, he was pianist for the Melbourne Liedertafel from 1889, then deputy conductor from 1897, resigning in favour of the English organist Ernest ★Wood in 1905. He was organist at various Melbourne churches, musical adviser to the state education department and music critic for the *Age*.

FURTHER READING
Obit. in *Australasian* 31 Oct. 1925. See also *OrchardA*, 56, 117, 185.

Siede, Julius (*b* Dresden, Saxony, 1825; *d* Melbourne, 23 Apr. 1903), flautist, conductor, composer. He studied flute with A.B. Fursteneau and composition with Karl Reissiger, making his debut at the age of 12. As a flautist he toured Europe from 1846, and the USA with sopranos Jenny Lind in 1850 and Anna Bishop in 1851–52. He arrived in Australia with Bishop in 1856, then gave concerts in Melbourne from 1857 and played for the ★Lyster Opera Co. from 1861. He conducted the Headquarters Band from 1863, for Lyster 1865–71, and the Melbourne Liedertafel 1879–90, appearing with them at the 37th Commemoration festival of Sydney University in 1888.

A gifted and able conductor, he handled the very wide range of opera Lyster introduced to Australia very capably. His compositions are well crafted but quite pedestrian; they include three overtures, two cantatas and part songs for the Liedertafel, band music and chamber works, some first heard in Lyster's performances. He also orchestrated *Les Huguenots* for the Lyster forces in 1862.

FURTHER REFERENCE
Thérèse Radic, *ADB*, 6. His *Chinese Street Serenade* has been recorded in an orchestral arrangement (Pearl).

silverchair. Rock group founded (1992) at Newcastle High School, comprised of Daniel Johns (vocals, guitar), Chris Joannon (bass) and Ben Gillies (drums). Formed as Innocent Criminals, they won the Youth Rock Encouragment Award in 1993, and in 1994 won a contest which provided the means for a video-clip and recording at Sydney 2JJJ. They signed with Murmur Records, and a No. 1 single and double platinum EP followed while they were still aged 16 and attempting to finish their school studies. The youngest band ever to achieve national chart success in Australia, their stage performances are potent and their music, influenced by Pearl Jam and Led Zeppelin, is infectious grunge with a keen melodic sense.

FURTHER REFERENCE
Recordings include *Frogstomp* (1995, EPIC 67247). See *Rolling Stone* (Aust.) 508 (Apr. 1995), 72–3.

Simmonds, Mark Bentley (*b* Christchurch, NZ, 21 July 1959), jazz saxophonist. He emerged in the late 1970s underground contemporary movement, with an eclectic background that covered rock-based music from

work in the groups ★Ol' 55 and the ★Dynamic Hepnotics. A founding member of Keys Music Association, he worked with most of Sydney's major contemporary jazz musicians emerging during the 1980s, and his Free-boppers bands have presented some of the most authoritative and uncompromising work in contemporary styles over the last decade. The expansion of performance opportunities, especially through the Sydney Improvised Music Association, has brought him increasing visibility and recognition, including an ARIA award for his recording *Fire*.

FURTHER REFERENCE
Recordings include *Dedication to Horst Liepolt*, Serge Ermoll Concert Ensemble (1980, Janda Jazz JJ 1002); *The March of the Five Limbs*, Keys Music Association (*c.*1980, KMA LP 8301–2); *Age of Elegance,* the Umbrellas (1990, The Sound of Music SOM 1002); *Fire*, Mark Simmonds Freeboppers (1994, Birdland BL 002). See also *ClareB*; John Shand, 'No Slaves, Mark Simmonds', *Australian Jazz and Blues*, 1/5 (1994), 7–10.

BRUCE JOHNSON

Simonsen. Family of three generations of operatic artists. Martin (1) and his wife Fanny Simonsen (2) arrived in 1865 (for their daughter see *Frances Saville*, and their granddaughter see *Frances Alda*).

(1) Martin Simonsen (*b* Hamburg, 30 Jan. 1830; *d* Melbourne, 28 Nov. 1899), violinist, conductor and impresario and **(2) Françoise ('Fanny') Simonsen** (*b* Paris, 10 Feb. 1835; *d* Melbourne, 18 Sept. 1896), soprano, singing teacher, impresario, arrived in Australia with a touring concert party in 1865 and joined W.S. ★Lyster's opera company the following year. Fanny's versatility and acting skill quickly made her popular with audiences; Martin's volatile temperament restricted his conducting opportunities, but he was considered one of the best violinists in the colonies.

After alternating between Europe and Australia for some time, the couple settled in Melbourne in 1876 and immediately formed their own travelling opera troupe. For the next 15 years they were major figures on the Australasian touring circuit, not only as performers but as entrepreneurs (see *Simonsen Opera Companies*). They recruited several touring companies from the talent available in Melbourne as well as importing two high-quality Italian opera troupes (1886–88 and 1891–92) and a short-lived and inept Spanish dance ensemble (1888). Since the couple's financial acumen did not match their musical skills these enterprises were seldom profitable, but they were important in maintaining the tradition of grand and Italian opera that Lyster had established.

From *c.*1878 Fanny was also one of Melbourne's leading singing teachers. Her pupils included Ada ★Crossley and her own daughter, Frances ★Saville, and granddaughter, Frances ★Alda, both of whom had international careers. After his wife's sudden death Martin gave way to depression, exacerbated by ill health and increasing blindness, and eventually took his own life.

FURTHER REFERENCE

Harold Love, *The Golden Age of Australian Opera* (Sydney: Currency Press, 1981); Adrienne Simpson, *The Greatest Ornaments of their Profession: The New Zealand Tours by the Simonsen Opera Companies 1876–1889* (Christchurch: Canterbury University Music Department, 1993); idem, 'Footlights and Fenians', *Australasian Drama Studies* 24 (1994), 182–96; idem, *Opera's Farthest Frontier* (Auckland: Reed, 1996).

ADRIENNE SIMPSON

Simonsen Opera Companies. Fanny and Martin *Simonsen formed their first touring company in 1876, disbanding it in 1877. In the decade following the death of W.S. *Lyster in 1880 they travelled throughout Australasia with a succession of ensembles ranging from small-scale troupes playing a mixed English and *opéra bouffe* repertoire (1880–81, 1882–83, 1888 and 1889) to large companies of imported Italian singers (1886–88 and 1891–92). The couple kept grand opera alive at a time when lighter genres dominated the musical theatre; they were responsible for the Australian premieres of *Die Fledermaus* (1877), *La gioconda* (1887), *I due studenti* by Alfred *Plumpton (1887), and several lesser-known Donizetti operas.

FURTHER REFERENCE

Alison Gyger, *Opera for the Antipodes* (Sydney: Currency Press, 1990); Adrienne Simpson, 'On Tour with the Simonsens', in *Opera in New Zealand—Aspects of History and Performance,* ed. A. Simpson (Wellington: Witham Press, 1990), 19–32; idem, 'The Simonsen Opera Company's 1876 Tour of New Zealand', *Turnbull Library Record* 23 (1990), 99–121; idem, *The Greatest Ornaments of their Profession: The New Zealand Tours by the Simonsen Opera Companies 1876–1889* (Christchurch: Canterbury University Music Department, 1993); idem, *Opera's Farthest Frontier* (Auckland: Reed, 1996).

ADRIENNE SIMPSON

Sinclair, John Stewart (*b* Melbourne 1915; *d* Williamstown, Melbourne 8 Jan. 1991), music critic. He studied painting at the National Gallery School, Melbourne, and became a member of the group of painters associated with John and Sunday Reed of 'Heide'. Working as a journalist on the *Herald,* he became music critic in 1947 and continued in this position until 1985, when he was dismissed after making an error of fact in one of his reviews; he spent the rest of his life in straitened conditions. Over nearly 40 years, Sinclair developed a concise journalistic style which matched the popular image of the *Herald* very well and became one of its ornaments. The general accuracy of his comments and his outstanding concern for the good of music in Melbourne and for the welfare of performing musicians were recognised throughout the musical community and made a strong contribution to the well-being of musical life in Melbourne.

FURTHER REFERENCE

Obit. in *Age* 11 Jan. 1991. KENNETH HINCE

Sing Out. Quarterly journal, founded in 1984, of the Australian National Choral Association, incorporating the Australian Choral Conductors Association *Newsletter* from 1988. It contains reviews, choral news and articles. A cumulative index was included with issue 13/2 (July 1996).

Singing Kettles, The. Country music vocal group. Formed as a trio by Bill, Ross and Max Kettle at Lilydale, Tasmania, in 1963, they came to radio attention with *White Silver Sands* in 1963, and moved to Tamworth in 1969. After Max's death (22 Jan. 1971) they moved to Sydney and continued as a duo until 1988, touring widely in country venues. Featuring close, high harmonies, they made over 15 albums; *Kettle Country* (EMI) was their most successful.

FURTHER REFERENCE

The original trio may be heard on *18 Of Our Best* (Hadley HCDM 1311) and *The Best Of The Singing Kettles* (Hadley HCSM 304). See also *SmithB*, 335.

Single-Headed Skin Drum. Cylindrical drum made from a hollow tree trunk and traditionally covered with a drum head of wallaby skin, goanna, or other natural hide. It is played as an accompaniment to traditional Aboriginal songs or hymns in the Cape York area of Queensland. In Torres Strait the body of the drum is in an hourglass shape, as in drums from Papua New Guinea. The tension on the head of the drum, which regulates the pitch, is modified by small pellets of wax, which may be moulded or flattened on the head to change the sound quality, or by warming the drum head by the fire. See *Aboriginal Music* §3(i). GRACE KOCH

Sippe, George (*b* Norwich, *c*.1790; *d* Sydney, 10 Apr. 1842), conductor. He arrived in Australia in 1826 in the 57th West Middlesex Regimental band, and after his discharge in 1831 worked freelance. He played flute, piano, cello, and occasionally sang. He appeared as a singer at the first public concert in Sydney at Freemason's Tavern, George Street, on 9 June 1826, for Barnett *Levey at the Royal Assembly Rooms, Sydney, conducting the Overture to Cherubini's *Lodoïsk* in 1829, and as a cellist he appeared in Levey's 1833 concerts. He was under contract to Mrs Levey at the Theatre Royal in 1838, successfully suing her for unpaid wages when the theatre closed.

FURTHER REFERENCE

Eric Irvin, 'Australia's First Public Concerts', *SMA* 5 (1971), 77–86; John T. Spurway, *Australian Biographical and Genealogical Record vol. 1, 1788–1841* (Sydney: Society of Australian Genealogists, 1992).

Sirocco. Cross-cultural style ensemble consisting of six players who play tupan, darabuka, timbales, diary, congas, gongs, cymbals, bells, woodblocks, seed-pods, Aboriginal clapsticks, flute, cabreet, bagpipes, didjeridu, kaval, tin whistle, bombarder, targotino, hammer, dulcimer, electric guitar, violin, viola, Uigher revop, Irish harp and synthesiser. Blending rock and roll and music of the folk traditions of various countries, it has toured widely in Australia and beyond.

FURTHER REFERENCE
Recordings include *The Breath of Time* (ABC 842738); *Earth Dance* (1983, Arika AR 006TC); and *Voyage* (1986, Larrikin TC LRF 184).

Sister Janet [Mead] (*b* Adelaide, 1937), church musician. A member of the Sisters of Mercy, she studied piano at the University of Adelaide and while teaching at St Aloysius College, Adelaide, presented popular rock masses at the Catholic cathedral. She released a single, *The Lord's Prayer*, in 1974, written by a member of her congregation, Arnold Strauls. It reached No. 3 in the charts and became an international best-seller, winning an American gold record and becoming the first Australian record to sell over a million copies in the USA. She then released an album, *With You I Am* (1974), which reached No. 19 in the album charts and remains available, and her *Rock Mass* (1975). She declined all offers to tour, including one to replace Judith Durham in the *Seekers, and gave her royalties to charity. She continues to work as a religious sister with homeless men in Adelaide.

FURTHER REFERENCE
Recordings were released with Festival, including *With You I Am* (1974, Festival C35148). See *SpencerA*. See also *McGrathA*; *Sunday Age* 7 Nov. 1993.

Sisters Of Mercy. The religious of this Catholic order arrived in Australia in small groups, first in WA (1846), later in Sydney (1857), Brisbane (1861) and Adelaide (1880), spreading their mission to many Australian towns. Capable music teachers were numerous in their ranks, and by the 1890s they had established many convent schools where musical training was offered. They taught the piano, violin and singing, and their pupils frequently won prizes in music examinations. Students of the Sisters of Mercy who became professional musicians have included Ella *Caspers and Amy *Castles, but many Australians owe them their basic musical training.

JEFF BROWNRIGG

Sitsky, Larry [Lazarus, Lazar] (*b* Tianjin, China, 10 Sept. 1934), composer, pianist, musicologist, of Russian Jewish parentage. Sitsky grew up in European concessions of Tianjin, showing precocious pianistic talent. In 1951 his family fled China, settling in Sydney. He studied piano with Winifred Burston at the NSW Conservatorium

1952–58, then with Egon Petri at San Francisco Conservatorium 1959–61, when he began composing seriously. A chief study piano teacher at the Queensland Conservatorium and visiting lecturer in contemporary music at the University of Queensland 1961–65, since 1966 Sitsky has taught keyboard, music history and composition at the Canberra School of Music, heading each department in turn; he was appointed professor at the Australian National University in 1994. He has held visiting composer fellowships (USSR, 1977 and 1988; China, 1983; University of Cincinnati, 1989–90).

Sitsky's eclectic background is reflected in his diverse interests and influences: the folk music, spiritualism and philosophies of Judaism, eastern Europe and Asia; Romanticism; 19th-century composer-pianists (Chopin, Liszt and others); his own pianistic heritage (Anton Rubinstein via Busoni to Petri and Burston); Bach, Beethoven and Bartók; and the Second Viennese School. These diverse influences result in great variety of compositional styles, ranging from aggressively avant-garde (String Quartet No. 1, 1969) to neo-Romantic (Trio No. 4, 1986). Sitsky's characteristic technique is a quasi-serial manipulation of note- and chord-rows and/or pre-existing melodies. Textures are typically dense, contrapuntal, rhythmically complex, and often rhapsodic. The composer generally retains a sense of tone-centredness, especially in recent works, where folk influences are strong (Violin Concerto No. 2, 1983 [Armenian]; Trio No. 5, 1986 [Chinese]).

Sitsky's most significant and characteristic output is dramatic music (with poet Gwen Harwood), piano and chamber music, and concertos. He often writes for unusual instruments or combinations, such as for theremins (*Legions of Asmodeus*, 1975), Baroque trio (*Agharti*, 1986), double-keyboard piano (Fantasia No. 10, 1992). Prolific in all genres and one of Australia's most commissioned composers, he maintains active parallel careers as concert pianist, teacher and writer on music. As a pianist, he favours unusual 19th- and 20th-century chamber repertoire and large-scale Romantic concertos, including the Busoni. As a teacher and writer, Sitsky is idiosyncratically serious yet irreverent and generally polemical, often criticising the musical establishment.

Sitsky earned a reputation as an *enfant terrible* with the deliberately provocative Wind Quartet (1963) at the inaugural Australian Composers' Seminar, Hobart; he remained an important figure in the 1960s and 1970s avant-garde. He is also known for meticulous professionalism, but he is now a somewhat marginalised composer, perhaps because of his eclecticism and his relative isolation in Canberra. As a scholar he has written three books on piano music, and a large number of magazine, journal and newspaper articles for such publications as *PNM*, *Quadrant* and *24 Hours*. His numerous awards include the Alfred Hill Prize (1969), the A.H. Maggs Award (1971), fellowships from the Music Board, Australia Council (1974, 1984), the Spivakovsky Prize (1981), the Advance Australia Award (1989) and a Fulbright (1988–89).

WORKS (Selective)

(All mss in *CAnl*)

Principal publishers: Ricordi, Allans, Seesaw, Australian Music Centre.

Orchestral *Apparitions* (1975), *Prelude* (1967), *Symphonic Elegy* (1973), *A Song of Love* (1974), *Concerto for Orchestra* (1987).

Concertos Three for vn (1972, 1983, 1987), one each for 2 solo pfs (1971), wind quintet (1973), cl (1981), trbn, perc & kbd (1982), gui (1984), pf (1991), vc (1994).

Chamber Vast output for 1–10 instruments, especially pf, including 10 fantasias (most for pf), six 6 trios, three string quartets, three solo flute sonatas.

Electronic *Dimensions*, pf, 2 tape recorders (1964); *Concert Aria*, low v, ens, tapes, synth (1972).

Dramatic *Fall of the House of Usher*, opera (1965, 1, Harwood after Poe), 19 Aug. 1965, Hobart, *Lenz*, opera (1970–74, 1, Harwood), 14 Mar. 1974, Sydney, *Fiery Tales*, opera (1974, 1, Harwood after Boccaccio and Chaucer), 23 Mar. 1976, Adelaide, *The Golem*, opera (1976–80, 3, Harwood), 14 Oct. 1993, Sydney, *Voices in Limbo*, radio drama (1977, 1, Harwood), 12 Aug. 1981, ABC FM broadcast; six short films; one each ballet, monodrama, dramatic scena.

Choral *Five Improvisations*, SATB, pf (1977); *The Ten Sephiroth of the Kabbalah*, SATB, 3 perc (1977).

Vocal Five sets/cyles for voice and piano including *A Whitman Cycle* (1972); seven sets/cycles for voice and chamber ensembles, including *Eight settings after Li-Po* (1974), *Music in the Mirabell Garden* (1982, Georg Trakl, trans. James McAuley), *In Pace Requiescat* (1989, after Poe).

Transcriptions of works by Bach, Busoni, Bartók, Gershwin, Liszt, A. Rubinstein and traditional tunes.

FURTHER REFERENCE

Recordings include Concerto *Mysterium Cosmographicum* for vn, orc, SSA, Sonata, Jan Sedivka vn (YPRX 2041); Violin Concerto No. 2 *Gurdjieff*, Tasmanian Symphony Orchestra, Jan Sedivka, vn (Move MD 3091); *Fall of the House of Usher*, excerpt, B. Hansford, West Australian Symphony Orchestra, cond. H.-H. Schonzeler (1971, Festival SFC 800–24); and various works in the *Anthology of Australian Music on Disc* (Canberra School of Music, CSM 8, 11, 12, 13, 14). As a pianist he can be heard in *Contemporary Australian Piano Music*, incl. his own *Arch* and *Fantasia No. 1 (In Memory of Egon Petri)* (Move MD 3066). A discography of recordings to 1972 is in *PlushD*.

His views on composition are in *Music Now* 1/4 (Apr. 1971) and *SA* 13 (Nov.–Dec. 1986). As a scholar his writings include *Busoni and the Piano* (Westport, Conn.: Greenwood Press, 1986); *The Classic Reproducing Piano Roll*, 2 vols (Westport, Conn.: Greenwood Press, 1989); and *Music of the Repressed Russian Avant-Garde, 1900–1929* (Westport, Conn.: Greenwood Press, 1994); there is an annotated thematic catalogue of piano music of Anton Rubinstein (Westport, Conn.: Greenwood Press) forthcoming. See also *ADMR*; Robyn Holmes, Patricia Shaw and Peter Campbell, *Larry Sitsky: A Bio-Bibliography* (Westport, Conn.: Greenwood Press, 1997); Elizabeth Wood, *GroveD*.

PATRICIA SHAW

Six O'Clock Rock. National popular music show (1959–62) broadcast by ABC TV. Based on the BBC *6.05 Special*, there were both jazz and rock and roll segments, the bands of each style placed on opposite sides of the set, with teenage couples dancing in between. After a few weeks the show came to be hosted by Johnny ★O'Keefe, whose band the ★Dee Jays was the resident rock and roll act. The show canvassed the whole range of popular music, from jazz and country music to rock and roll, with local artists being required to perform live (and often with only a few hours' notice) whatever current hits O'Keefe decreed. American stars touring with Lee ★Gordon's Big Shows appeared without fee to promote their acts. Although O'Keefe enforced a smart dress code, the show's image was lusty and untamed relative to *Bandstand*, its glossy competitor on commercial television. It launched the careers of Lonnie ★Lee, Johnny ★Rebb, Digby ★Richards, Judy ★Cannon, Lucky Starr, Johnny ★Devlin, Noeleen ★Bailey and many other Australian pop stars of the period.

FURTHER REFERENCE

A compilation from the show is *The Living Legends Of Six O'Clock Rock* (1989, Starlite, ST 804). See also Lonnie Lee, *Six O'Clock Rock: The Facts* with Suzanne Aufder-Heide (Liverpool, NSW: Starlite International, 1989).

Skyhooks. Rock group (1973–80; 1990) founded in Melbourne, originally comprised of Steve Hills (vocals to 1974, then Graeme 'Shirley' Strachan), Bob 'Bongo' Starkie (guitar), Peter Starkie (guitar), Red Symons (guitar), Greg Macainsh (bass), and Freddie Strauks (drums). With satirical songs on Australian topics by Macainsh, the band began playing in Melbourne pubs with immediate success. Adding Strachan in 1974, they presented a glam-rock image of outrageous costumes and make-up. Their debut album *Living In The 70s* reached No. 7 and stayed in the charts for 40 weeks, despite six of its 10 tracks having been banned from radio airplay for obscenity. Twelve Top 40 hits followed, including *Horror Movie*, which reached No. 1, *Million Dollar Riff* No. 2, and *Women In Uniform* (1978) No. 8. Skyhooks toured Australia in 1975, then the USA in 1976, their album *Ego Is Not A Dirty Word* achieving critical acclaim. They returned to the pub circuit in the same year to recapture their connection with local audiences, but with the departure of Symons in 1977 and Strachan in 1979, both tired of constant touring, the band's essence slowly dissipated, and they played for the last time at Kalgoorlie, WA, in June 1980. A reunion tour in 1983 to launch a nine-disc compilation of their recordings was a huge success; they gave a tenth anniversary concert in October 1984, and re-formed for a time from 1990.

With their combination of topical, truly Australian lyrics, a quirky sense for off-beat comedy, and carefully developed stage presence, their music had great influence in the development of Australian rock music with specifically local themes. The pre-eminent Australian band of the late 1970s, they made 17 singles and 11 albums.

FURTHER REFERENCE
Recordings include *Living In The 70s* (1974, Mushroom K5628); *Horror Movie* (1974, Mushroom K5753); *Ego Is Not A Dirt Word* (1975, Mushroom L35575); a compilation *Skyhooks Boxed Set*, 9 discs (1983, Mushroom L8085–9). For discography, see *SpencerA*. See also Maree Barkla, *Skyhooks: The Other Side* (Newstead, Vic: Maree Publications, 1990); Jenny Brown, *Skyhooks: Million Dollar Riff* (Melbourne: Dingo, 1975); *GuinnessP*, III, 2289; *McGrathA*; *SpencerW*.

Slapoffski, Gustave ('Slap') (*b* London, 20 Aug. 1862; *d* Windsor, Melbourne, 3 Aug. 1951), conductor. He was a choirboy at Christ Church Cathedral, Oxford, and a child prodigy on the violin. He studied composition at the Royal Academy of Music with Prosper Sainton and Arthur Sullivan, then was musical director of the Princess Theatre, Manchester, from 1879. After playing violin then conducting for the Carl Rosa Co., he came to Australia in 1900 for Musgrove's company, conducting *Lohengrin*, *Tannhäuser*, *The Flying Dutchman*, *La bohème* and *Fedora* that year and numerous Gilbert and Sullivan works thereafter. He conducted for the Melba tour of 1902, the operetta *The Fortune Teller* in 1903, the Australian premieres of *Die Walküre*, *Die Meistersinger* and *Hansel and Gretel* in 1907 and of *The Merry Widow* for J.C. Williamson in 1908. He appeared in the first season of the Sydney Symphony Orchestra and with John Wren's National Opera Co., Sydney, in the same year, with the ★Rigo Grand Opera Co. in 1919, and in his old age for Sir Benjamin ★Fuller's opera tour in 1935 and the ★National Theatre Movement Opera Co. from 1939.

A forthright, at times unpolished character, he was a resourceful and dynamic conductor, working with his left hand, having injured his right in earlier years. His wife was Lillie Williams, who had sung with the Carl Rosa Co. and appeared with him in many Musgrove engagements.

FURTHER REFERENCE
Diane Langmore, *ADB*, 11. His memoirs appeared in the Sydney *Mail* in 1934.

Slater, Joe (John Joseph) ['Felix Le Roy', etc.] (*b* 1872; *d* Manly, Sydney, 16 May 1926), Sydney composer, lyricist, publisher of popular music. Slater was associated with Sydney theatre from boyhood, and had a close association with vaudeville entrepreneur and performer Harry ★Rickards and his Tivoli circuit. He established his own Joe Slater Publishing Co. in Leichhardt around 1915. Slater was enormously prolific, and published many sentimental ballads and patriotic songs under his own name; he also wrote under pseudonyms. His songs appeared with many publishers from the late 1890s on; successes include *Only a Leaf* and *Like a Bird With a Broken Wing* (both recorded by Regal). Slater was also composer of the music

for one of prominent local vaudeville comedian Fred Bluett's best-loved sketches, *The Hobble Skirt*, performed in drag.

FURTHER REFERENCE
Obit. in *SMH* 17 May 1926. A list of some of his works appears in *SnellA*. See also *Theatre*, 1 Feb. 1911, 36.

JENNIFER HILL

Sloane, Sally [Sarah Frost] (*b* Parkes, NSW, 1894; *d* Wodonga, Vic., 20 Sept. 1982), traditional song and bush-dance performer. Her grandmother came from Ireland in 1838, and her mother played concertina, button accordion, jaws harp, and piano. She learned her mother's instruments, as well as fiddle, tin whistle and mouth organ. Through her stepfather William Clegg, a railway construction worker, she learned Australian bush songs, adding to them a large repertoire of her mother's Irish songs, music hall and popular songs, as well as jigs, hornpipes, reels, waltzes, polkas, mazurkas, varsoviennas, set tunes for the lancers, and quadrilles. John ★Meredith recorded her work 1954–61, gathering from her more than 150 works. One of the most prolific performers of traditional Australian music, she was a major source of Australian traditional songs and bush dances.

FURTHER REFERENCE
She may be heard on *Australian Traditional Singers and Musicians* (1957, Wattle) and *A Garland For Sally* (1983, Larrikin LRF 136). Meredith's transcriptions are in *MeredithF*, I, 161–98. See also *OxfordF*.

Small, Joe (*b* England, 1831; *d* at sea, 1875), music hall entertainer. Arriving in Australia as a child in 1836, he appeared as a singer on the Victorian goldfields at the Beechworth diggings in 1852, and then worked with Charles ★Thatcher, in the coming years singing in all the major goldfields, as well as very widely in town venues throughout Australia and NZ. Appearing as an Irish comedian, he sang his own topical songs, comic songs and sentimental ballads, such as *The Unfortunate Man* and *Paddy's Trip To Australia*. He published his songs in *Colonial Songster* (*c*.1857) and *The New Zealand and Australian Songster and Goldfield Diary* (1866). One of the most successful of the goldfields entertainers, he retired from the stage to pursue business interests in the 1870s, dying at sea *en route* to Hong Kong.

FURTHER REFERENCE
Colonial Songster (Castlemaine, Vic.: Hodgson, *c*.1857). *The New Zealand and Australian Songster and Goldfield Diary* has been reprinted (Christchurch, NZ: Nag's Head Press, 1970).

Small, Judy (*b* Coffs Harbour, NSW, 1953), folk-singer, songwriter. While working as a community relations officer, she started writing folk-songs in Celtic and modern styles. She went abroad in 1982, singing at the

Vancouver folk festival with Eric ★Bogle, and since then has appeared at folk festivals in Europe and the UK and regularly toured in the USA and NZ, appearing with Odetta, Billy Bragg, Arlo Guthrie, Pete Seeger and many others. Her songs have been recorded by Bogle, Ronnie Gilbert and others. Grounded in the folk ballad style but absorbing blues, country, jazz and rock influences, her songs often deal with women's experiences, peace and justice, or are wryly humorous. She was honoured with a Mo award in 1990.

FURTHER REFERENCE
She has published the *Judy Small Songbook* (Sydney: Orlando, 1986). Albums include *Judy Small The Best Of The 80s* (1993 Crafty Maid CMM 007CD), *Second Wind* (1993, Crafty Maid CMM 008 CD) and *Global Village* (1995, 009 CD). See also *Age* 15 July 1987; *Age* 24 Feb. 1983

Smalley, Roger (*b* Swinton, nr Manchester, England, 26 July 1943), composer. Entering the Royal College of Music in 1961, he studied composition with Peter Racine Fricker and John White. He also studied with Alexander Goehr (London, 1962), Stockhausen (Cologne, 1965–66) and Boulez (Darmstadt, summer 1965). His earliest works, up to 1967, follow Peter Maxwell Davies' lead in their combination of serial, *cantus firmus*, and Medieval parody techniques. The works of the late 1960s and early 1970s are more influenced by Stockhausen. *The Song of the Highest Tower* is the first of several works to investigate 'moment form', while the live use of electronics in *Transformation* and *Pulses for 5 x 4 Players* heralded Smalley's formation of the electronic instrument ensemble Intermodulation with Tim Souster, Peter Britton and Robin Thompson.

In the 1960s and early 1970s he was composer-in-residence and then research fellow at King's College, Cambridge, and active as a critic of contemporary music, writing mostly for periodicals such as the *Musical Times* and *Music and Musicians*. He emigrated to Australia in 1976 to take up a position in the department of music at the University of Western Australia, and Intermodulation was disbanded. He is now an associate professor at the university, and during 1995 he was composer-in-residence with the West Australian Symphony Orchestra. He is also a pianist, and artistic director of the West Australian Symphony Orchestra 20th-Century Ensemble.

He had previously spent one term at Perth as artist-in-residence in 1974, during which time *Accord* was conceived. This pivotal work, regarded by Smalley as his 'real' opus 1, consolidates the move since the early 1970s to a vertically oriented approach to composition, in which lines are generated from related chords (the opposite occurs in the Davies-influenced works). Many of the works written since, including the Symphony and the Concerto for Piano and Orchestra, employ material and techniques derived from it. The harnessing of the expressive and structural potentialities of intervallic differentiation has proved especially fruitful, prompting a further broadening of his harmonic palette in a number of works based on music by Chopin (Variations on a Theme of Chopin, the Piano Trio, and *Poles Apart*). Another recent feature has been the stimulus of visual images: *Diptych (Homage to Brian Blanchflower)* is based on some of the eponymous Perth artist's work, while *Close to the Edge* was inspired by the miniatures of another WA artist, Lesley Duxbury. Both works are powerful evocations of Australian landscapes and seascapes, continuing a rich interaction with Australian themes begun in one of the first pieces Smalley completed on Australian soil, *Didgeridoo*.

WORKS (Selective)
Principal publishers: Faber Music and the Australian Music Centre (AMC).
Orchestral *Gloria tibi Trinitas I* (1965; rev. 1969, Faber), *Pulses for 5 x 4 Players*, brass, perc, ring modulator (1969; rev. 1985–86, Faber), *Beat Music*, soprano sax, electric va, perc, electric org, orch (1970–71), *Konzertstück* solo vn, orch (1979–80, AMC), Symphony (1979–81, Faber), Concerto for Piano and Orchestra (1984–85, AMC), *Diptych (Homage to Brian Blanchflower)* (1990–91, AMC), *Chimera* (1994, AMC), *Close to the Edge* (1995, AMC), Oboe Concerto (1996, AMC).
Chamber *Piano Pieces I–V* (1962–65, Faber), *Transformation*, pf, electronics (1968–69; rev. 1971, Faber), *Zeitebenen*, live electronic ens, 4-channel tape (1973, Faber), *Accord*, 2 pf (1974–75, Faber), *Echo II*, vc, tape-delay (1978, Faber), *Strung Out*, 13 solo str (1987–88, AMC), Variations on a theme of Chopin, pf (1988–89, AMC), *Ceremony II*, fl/picc, E-flat cl/bass cl, perc, pf, vn, vc (1989; rev. 1990, AMC), *Poles Apart*, fl, bass cl, vn, va, vc (1990–92, AMC), Piano Trio (1990–91, AMC).
Tape *Didgeridoo*, 4-channel tape (1974)
Choral *Missa Brevis*, 16 solo vv (1966; rev. 1967, Faber), *The Song of the Highest Tower*, solo vv, ch, orch (1967–68, Faber).

FURTHER REFERENCE
Recordings include *Ceremony II*, Seymour Group (ABC 434 901); Piano Concerto, Symphony (OZM 1001); *Impulses*, Flederman (Canberra School of Music, CSM 1). See also Judy Thönell, ed., *Poles Apart: The Music of Roger Smalley* (Perth: CIRCME and EVOS, 1994); Stephen Walsh, *GroveD*.

CHRISTOPHER MARK

Smallman, Greg, guitar-maker. Based at Glen Innes, NSW, he sees himself more as a developer than a producer, and makes only three guitars a year. He has focused on research into increasing guitar resonance, and several of his experiments have influenced other makers. His innovations include a unique system of lattice bracing, where the fan struts are varied in height, strength and direction, allowing greater control of the sound. He has also experimented with carbon fibre attached to each side of the balsa ribs. John ★Williams has purchased three of his guitars.

FURTHER REFERENCE
AthertonA, 86–9.

Smallwood, Robert (*b* Melbourne, 22 July 1958), composer, conductor. He studied composition with Barry ★Conyngham and Peter ★Tahourdin at the University of Melbourne, where he founded and directed the New Audience Ensemble 1979–84; then he became music director of the Astra Chamber Music Society 1983–84. He attended classes in Sienna with Franco Ferrara and Peter Maxwell-Davies and was conductor-in-residence at Royal Northern College of Music, Manchester, in 1985. He was musician-in-residence at Orange, NSW, 1987–90; there he considerably enhanced the local musical life, directing an array of community ensembles. Since then he has freelanced in Melbourne. A number of his works are straightforward scores for the large community groups he has worked with, such as *Wake Up My Soul* for adult and children choirs, soloists, orchestra, and organ (1987, rev. 1990), or *Living Land* for handbells, choruses, wind band, brass band, and strings (1988); more recently he has written a musical, *Red Dirt* (1991).

FURTHER REFERENCE
His *Solo*, cl, has been recorded (cassette, Australian Music Centre). See also *BroadstockS*, 213–15.

Smeaton, Bruce (*b* Brighton, Melbourne, 1938), film composer. Self-taught, Smeaton launched his career by writing music for commercials. He completed more than 2500 jingles before moving exclusively into screen composition and establishing himself as one of Australia's foremost composers for film and television. He has won numerous prizes for his work in commercial and screen composition, and contributed significantly to the development and recognition of Australian film music through his role as president of the Australian Guild of Screen Composers, and 12 years board membership of APRA. Since 1989 Smeaton has developed his interest in computer music. The film score for *Wendy Cracked a Walnut* (1989) was composed using a sophisticated daisy-chain of 17 computers designed to produce digital music to image, marking an important technical development in Australian film composition.

FURTHER REFERENCE
His other film credits include: *The Cars that Ate Paris* (1974), *Picnic at Hanging Rock* (1975), *The Devil's Playground*, *Eliza Fraser*, and *The Trespassers* (1976), *The Chant of Jimmie Blacksmith* (1978), *… Maybe This Time* (1980), *Monkey Grip* and *Squizzy Taylor* (1982), *'Undercover'* (1984), *Evil Angels*, *Roxanne*, and the television mini-series *The Alien Years* (1988), *Naked Under Capricorn* (1989) and *The Private War of Lucinda Smith* (1990). See also *LimbacherF*.   L.THOMPSON

Smenge, Knud (*b* Herning, Denmark, 12 Dec. 1937), organ-builder. Apprenticed to the prominent Danish firm of Marcussen & Son and later head voicer with Bruno Christensen & Son, Smenge arrived in Australia in 1979 as head voicer for George ★Fincham &

Sons, where he was responsible for initiating changes in the firm's organ-building style. He began his own firm in 1981 at premises at West Melbourne, later moving to North Melbourne and in 1991 to his present factory at Healesville, Victoria, which is the best equipped of its type in the country. He has completed contracts for 34 new organs in a period of 15 years for buildings in all Australian states and Hong Kong. Major instruments may be found at St George's Cathedral, Perth; the Newcastle Conservatorium, the University of Tasmania, St John's Southgate, South Melbourne; and Newington College, Sydney. These are notable for the exclusive use of mechanical key action, solid timber cases, mahogany windchests and high percentage tin pipework, employing craftsmanship of an exemplary order. Smenge's instruments have a forthright, articulate sound and use the principle of open toe voicing; they have been widely used for recordings and recitals.

FURTHER REFERENCE
David Kinsela, 'The Organ at Newington College, Sydney', *Victorian Organ Journal* (Oct. 1985), 3–12; (Dec. 1985), 13; unpub. list of Smenge organs compiled by John Maidment (1995).
                                 JOHN MAIDMENT

Smetanin, Michael (*b* Sydney, 1 Oct. 1958), composer. After studying at the NSW State Conservatorium 1979–81, he went to Louis Andriessen at the Royal Conservatorium in The Hague, 1982–84. He has lived and worked in Sydney since 1985 and was composer-in-residence for Musica Viva in 1988. Smetanin's compositions, which display modernist elements combined with Andriessen-inspired European minimalism, include *Ladder of Escape* (1984) for seven bass clarinets and two contrabass clarinets, *Black Snow* (1987) for large orchestra, *Red Lightning* (1988) for string quartet, *Minimalism isn't dead, it just smells funny* (1990) for four percussion, *The Burrow* (1993) opera, and *Women and Birds in Front of the Moon* (1994) for orchestra.

WORKS (Selective)
Orchestral *Zyerkala* (1981), *After the first circle* (1982), *Black Snow* (1987), *Blitz* (1989), *Shakhmat/supremat*, solo fl, str orch (1995), *Strip*, str orch (1991), *Women and birds in front of the moon*, orc, pf (1994).

Chamber Instrumental *Undertones*, bass cl, perc, pf (1981), *Per Canonem*, 2 fl, 2 alto sax, 2 trbn, 2 perc, 4 pf (1982–84), *Lichtpunkt*, fl/alto fl/pic, bass cl, perc, pf, 2 vn, vc (1983), *The Speed of Sound*, 4 perc (1983), *Aufstand*, 2 pf (1983), *Ladder of Escape*, 7 bass cl, 2 contra-bass cl (solo performance version exists for solo bass cl and 8 parts on pre-recorded tape) (1984, rec. 1986, Attacca Records CD Babel 8635–4), *Track*, 2 fl/pic, 2 alto sax, tpt, 2 perc, 2 pf, 2 electric pf, 2 bass gui (1984–85), *Vault*, fl/alto fl/pic, cl/bass cl, gui, perc, vn, db (1986), *Bellevue II* (To the memory of Andy Warhol), tenor sax, trbn, perc (1987), *Red Lightning*, str qrt (1988), *Music for Children and Dancers*, fl, ob, cl, bn, hn (1988), *Fylgjir*, chamber ens (1989), *Minimalism isn't dead, it just smells funny*, 4 perc, tape (1990), *Spray*, amplified alto fl, bass cl, pf (1990, rec. 1991, Attacca Records), *Strange Attractions*, fl, bcl, pf, vn, va, vc (1990), *Sharp*, bass cl, pf, va, vc (1991, rec CSM30), *Hot Block*, elec gui, perc, elec (1991), *Obsession: and the three minute single*, tenor sax, elec gui, drum set, pf, vc, db (1995).

Solo Instrumental *Something's missing here (ik mis heir iets) — a postcard from Holland… No.4*, pf (1988), *Sting*, mandolin (1987, rec. 1990, Jade 1013), *Stroke*, pf (1987), *Nontiscordardime I*, bass fl (1991, rec. ABC4467382), *Nontiscordardime II*, pic (1991, rec ABC4467382), *Nontiscordardime III*, fl (1992, rec. ABC4467382).

Theatre *The Burrow*, opera (1993, 5 scenes, Alison Croggon) 21 Feb. 1994, Melbourne.

Vocal/Choral *3 Songs*, 3 female voices, pf (1981), *Adjacent rooms*, S, Mez, A, T, 2 Bar, pf, marimba, vibr (1992), *Cossack Song*, SATB (1992), *Poem*, 2 S, A, T, Bar, B (1992), *The skinless kiss of angels*, Mez, Bar, fl/pic, ob/english hn, cl/pic cl, bass cl, tpt, trbn, hp, pf, perc, mandolin, gui, vn, va, vc, 2 db (1992, rec ABC4466252), *If you're not afraid…* , S, Bar, fl, ob, cl, bass cl, elec gui, elec mandolin, pf, perc, va, vc (1993).

FURTHER REFERENCE

Recordings include *Minimalism isn't dead, it just smells funny*, Synergy (1990, ABC 442 350); *Ladder of Escape, Harry Sparnaay* (Babel 8945); and *Sting* (JADE 1013). See also BroadstockS; M. Hindson, An investigation into correlations between the poster design Red Lightning by Ignaty Nivinsky and the eponymous String Quartet by Michael Smetanin, MMus, Univ. Melbourne, 1994; I. Shanahan and C. Dench, eds, 'An Emotional Geography of Australian Composition', *SA* 34 (Winter 1992), 8–32; S. Smith, New dimensions in percussion: *Black Snow* by Michael Smetanin, MMus, Univ. NSW, 1994.   MICHAEL BARKL

Smith, Arthur Edward   (*b* Islington, London, 1880; *d* Canberra, 16 May 1978), violin-maker. Apprenticed to an engineering design firm at Maldon, Essex, he designed and built his first violin to improve on the instrument he had for his own playing in a local amateur group. From 1905 he worked for the Maldon instrument-dealer C.W. Jeffreys, repairing and making violins. He first came to Australia in 1909, but soon left for San Francisco where he worked with the Belgian violin-maker Carl Rothammer 1910–12. Back in Australia, he opened a shop in George Street, Sydney, in 1912 (then in Hunter Street from 1915), importing professional quality stringed instruments and repairing them. He continued to make violins, developing machinery to produce local parts that could match those imported from Europe.

By the 1930s his fame as a maker had grown significantly, and visiting virtuosos Yehudi Menuhin, Ruggerio Ricci, Isaac Stern and Zlatko Balokovic all bought his instruments. He retired in 1970 at the age of 90, after making his 200th instrument, and his daughter Kitty Smith and grandson Daffyd Llewellyn continued as makers of his prototypes. The most outstanding violin-maker Australia has produced, he trained Guy ★Griffin, Harry ★Vatiliotis and other significant makers, and has had considerable influence on instrument-making in Australia.

FURTHER REFERENCE
AthertonA.

Smith, Broderick   (*b* England, 17 Feb. 1948), singer, harmonica player. Smith emigrated to Australia with his parents in 1959. His early musical career was spent playing blues and rhythm and blues in several Sydney bands including the Adderly Smith Blues Band 1966–67, Sundown 1970, and Carson 1971. In 1973 he co-starred as Tommy's father in the Melbourne stage production of the Who's rock opera *Tommy*; he formed the Dingoes with Kerryn Tolhurst (guitar), Chris Stockley (guitar), John Stongie (bass) and John Lee (drums), and successfully rose to national acclaim with Top 40 albums *The Dingoes* (1974), *Five Times the Sun* (1977) and *Orphans of the Storm* (1979). The Dingoes recorded and toured in Canada and the USA with some success, but ultimately failed to break into the American market, returned to Australia and disbanded in 1979.

Smith has since led various blues-influenced bands including Hired Hands (1979), the Doors of Perception (1987), the Noveltones (1988–) and the Blues Power Band (1991), and has become a mainstay of Melbourne's pub-rock scene. In 1981 his Big Combo released a self-titled album that reached No. 23 in the national charts. Despite his excellent blues and soul voice, Smith's solo albums *Broderick Smith* (1983), *Suitcase* (1992), *Songster* (1995) and *Crayon Angels* (1996) have failed to attract mass market recognition.

FURTHER REFERENCE

Recordings with the Dingoes include *The Dingoes* (1974, Mushroom L 35110); *Five Times the Sun* (1977, A&M L 36237); *Orphans of the Storm* (1979, A&M L 36721); with Broderick Smith's Big Combo *Smith's Big Combo* (1981, Wheatley WBEX 1006); solo albums *Broderick Smith* (1983, Wheatley); *Suitcase* (1992, Mushroom D 30825); *Songster* (1995, EMI 4798332); *Crayon Angels* (1996, EMI 4835692). See also *GuinnessP*; *McGrathA*; *SpencerW.*

AARON D.S. CORN

Smith, Donald   (*b* Bundaberg, Qld, 27 July 1922), tenor. His career began with light opera in Brisbane, and after the war he sang on radio in Bundaberg then Brisbane. In 1947 he won a State Government scholarship and toured Queensland with the State Government Opera Scheme. In 1948 he made his debut with the Brisbane Opera Co. and in 1951 the visiting Italian Grand Opera Co. invited him to participate on its Australian tour. After winning the Mobil Quest (1952) and the Joan Hammond Scholarship (1953) he studied for two years at the London Opera School and in Italy. On returning to Australia in 1955 he toured with the Italian Opera Co. and joined the Elizabethan Theatre Trust Opera Co. in 1958. In 1963 he was engaged by Sadler's Wells and subsequently by the Royal Opera, Covent Garden (1965). Until 1968 he performed leading roles with both companies as well as appearing for Scottish Opera and through-out the USA. He returned to Australia in 1969 to become a principal artist with the Australian Opera, and on retiring from the Australian Opera in 1980 he taught at the Queensland Conservatorium until *c*.1990.

With an extraordinarily robust Italianate voice, Smith is generally regarded as the greatest tenor Australia has produced and one of the finest in all opera of recent times. His impressive list of roles includes Radamès in *Aida*, Cavaradossi in *Tosca* and Don José in *Carmen*. He was the first resident artist of the Australian Opera to receive the OBE (1973) and in the same year was the first singer to perform in the Concert Hall and Opera Theatre of the newly constructed Sydney Opera House.

FURTHER REFERENCE
Recordings include *Donald Smith Sings Opera, Operetta and Oratorio*, Tasmanian Symphony Orchestra, Queensland Symphony Orchestra, cond. V. Cavdarski (EMI 166283–2); Saint-Saëns *Samson et Dalila*, Bavarian Radio Chorus, Berlin Radio Symphony Orchestra, cond. C. Davis (Polygram 4262432). See also *MackenzieS*, 200–1. KERRY VANN

Smith, Frank (Francis Percival) (*b* Sydney, 30 July 1927; *d* Melbourne, 18 Feb. 1974), jazz reeds player, bandleader. He became prominent mainly on alto saxophone in nightclub, dance and concert work in the 1940s, with Reg Pedersen, Doug Cross, Marsh Goodwin and others. With Col Anderson at Bondi Esplanade in 1948, until 1950 he worked at Christy's, Romano's and the Trocadero under Frank *Coughlan. He was at the Roosevelt 1951, with Warren Gibson on the Metronome dance circuit 1952, then returned to Romano's under Bela Kanitz 1953–54. Throughout this period he was also active in specifically jazz settings, notably in concerts with Ralph Mallen, Enso Toppano, Joe Singer and Jack Allan, with whom he recorded with visiting American cornettist Rex Stewart (1949); he was also active at *El Rocco during its early years. Playing at the opening of the Embers in Melbourne in 1959, he returned as leader of his quintet after its closure owing to fire damage and remained until 1961 during which time his group played support for numerous visiting American musicians. In the 1960s he concentrated on studio work such as television and jingle production, forming his own music production company in 1971. He played at Wrest Point Casino, Hobart, in 1973, but had returned to Melbourne at the time of his death.

One of the outstanding progressive jazz musicians of his time, in informal workshops he was a source of great musical insight, and imparted a sense of commitment which many of his colleagues recall as the most significant influence on their own careers. Although sparsely recorded, Smith is revered for his inspirational influence.

FURTHER REFERENCE
Recordings include *Rex Stewart & His Sydney Six* (1949, Wilco 0–106); *The Troc, 1936–1956* (1991, MBS JAZZ 8, Linehan Series); *Music Maker 1957 All Stars* (Parlophone PMDO-7511);

The Embers Quintet (1959, Columbia Co. 330SX-7625); *Don Burrows, The First 50 Years, vol. 1 1944–1965* (1993, ABC/Polygram 514 296–2); *Bruce Clarke* (*c*.1968, Cumquat CQR 12–02). See also *ClareB*; *BissetB*; *OxfordJ*; *GroveJ*. BRUCE JOHNSON

Smith, Ian Leslie (*b* Bletchley, England, 23 Apr. 1948), jazz trumpeter and drummer. He settled in Melbourne as a child and began drums at school (later adding trumpet, tuba, bass, and singing). Beginning by sitting in with the Melbourne Dixieland Band in 1963, he was also in a rock group in 1967, then formed the New Harlem Jazz Band in 1968. Leaving the band in 1979, he worked with numerous other groups, and toured internationally with Tom Baker, the New Melbourne Jazz Band, the Cathay Pacific Jazz Australia Band, and Hotter Than Six, of which he has been a member since 1993. He has played support for Turk Murphy, Ralph Sutton and Kenny Davern, and directed workshops for the Victorian Jazz Club.

FURTHER REFERENCE
Recordings include *The New Harlem Jazz Band, With Guest Alex Frame* (1976, Jazznote JNLP 019/S); *Never Swat a Fly*, The New Harlem Jazz Band (1977, Jazz & Jazz 6357 902); *Cooking Up A Storm*, The Hotter Than Six Jazz Band (1995, Newmarket NEW 1074.2). See also *OxfordJ*. BRUCE JOHNSON

Snow Queen, The. Opera by Grahame *Dudley (1985), libretto by Nick Enright, orchestrated by David Morgan.

Snowy. Ballet by John *Antill (1961).

Snugglepot and Cuddlepie. Ballet by Richard *Mills, choreography by Petal Miller Ashmole with designs by Hugh Coleman, first performed at the Sydney Opera House by the Australian Ballet on 29 April 1988. The ballet was an adaptation of May Gibbs's *The Complete Adventures of Snugglepot and Cuddlepie* (1940). The story revolves around the kidnapping of Ragged Blossom by the evil Banksia Men and her rescue by Snugglepot and Cuddlepie in association with various bush creatures. Mills wrote an atmospheric orchestral score which he considered to be 'unequivocally theatrical', and Ashmole aimed to create a ballet for 'the child in every one of us'. The work was to find its home in the Australian Ballet's education programs rather than in the troupe's general repertoire. Published by Boosey & Hawkes (Aust.) and recorded by the Queensland Symphony Orchestra, cond. R. Mills (ABC 422 933–2). JOEL CROTTY

Somerville, Jim (James Anquetil) (*b* Sydney, 14 Nov. 1922), jazz pianist. He began his professional career in 1941, working as a pianist in a wide range of settings: composing and performing for theatrical productions, playing at the Booker T. Washington Club 1942–44, and as bandleader of the 2KY Swing Club in 1944. In 1947 he began a long but intermittent association with Ray *Price and the *Port Jackson Jazz Band, sometimes as leader. Later he worked in nightclubs, such as the Roosevelt and André's. Since the 1960s, in addition to jazz performance he has freelanced in concert, session and club work, including with John McCarthy at the Paddington-Woollahra RSL among others. He has been periodically active as a jazz journalist.

FURTHER REFERENCE
Recordings include *The Ellerston Jones Septet* (1947, Kinelab, unnumbered); *Ray Price and his Dixielanders* (1954, Diaphon DPS-20). See also *OxfordJ*.   BRUCE JOHNSON

Song Company, The.   Full-time small vocal ensemble founded in 1984 in Sydney by Charles *Colman. Singing repertoire from the 16th century to modern popular arrangements and commissioned works by Australian composers, the group's extensive rehearsal practices ensured from the outset an admirable blend and brilliance. From the ensemble's inception it toured Australia and South-East Asia extensively for Musica Viva, appeared at two Adelaide Festivals and the New Zealand International Festival (1988). It has commissioned works from Barry *Conyngham, Gillian *Whitehead, Nigel *Butterley and others. Now reduced to a sextet, it has a subscription concert series in Sydney. The only fully professional vocal ensemble in Australia, its musical director since 1990 has been Roland Peelman.

FURTHER REFERENCE
Recordings include *The Green CD*, works of R. Edwards, M. Whitacker, M. Wesley-Smith, et al. (Tall Poppies TP 064); *The Laughter of Mermaids*, works of A. Schultz, M. Whitacker, et al. (1994, Vox Australis VASTO 16–2); Rossini, *Petite Messe Solennelle* (2MBS MBS 20CA).

Song of Australia.   Patriotic song (1858) by Carl *Linger, words by Carol Carleton. Winning a song competition in Adelaide, it was first performed on 12 December 1859 and achieved enduring popularity in SA, sung in government schools from 1880. It was revived in wartime, and in the 1970s was regarded as a possible national anthem, before the official sanction of *Advance Australia Fair*.

FURTHER REFERENCE
First published Penman & Galbraith, Sydney, 1859; numerous reprints and arrangements; modern edition and commentary in *RadicT*.

Song of the Maypole.   Children's opera by George *Dreyfus, libretto by Frank Kellaway, first performed at Canberra in 1967.

Sorlie, George Brown   (*b* Liverpool, England, 7 Feb. 1885; *d* Sydney 19 June 1948), vaudeville entertainer, entrepreneur of West Indian ancestry. Arriving in Australia as a small child, he sang as a boy in Melbourne vaudeville, by the age of 11 earning enough to support his mother.

He had a song and dance act at Harry Clay's Newtown Theatre, Sydney, from 1903, and was corner man in Harry *Rickard's vaudeville circuit from 1905. Real success came in 1914 when he developed a song and dance duo with Billy Brown in the Fuller circuit, and from 1917 he had his own travelling melodrama show (a variety show from 1931), presented in a tent theatre, which continued successfully in NSW and Queensland for nearly 30 years. A favourite purveyor of musical entertainment in rural areas in the interwar years, he was affectionately known as the 'King of the Road'.

FURTHER REFERENCE
Obit. in *Argus* 21 June 1948. See also *ADB*, 12; Harold Love, *The Australian Stage* (Sydney: UNSWP, 1984), 126, 182, 303.

Sounds Australian.   Quarterly journal of the Australian Music Centre, originally *AMC News*, appearing under its present title from No. 15 (October 1987) to discuss issues pertaining to the practice of musical composition in Australia.

Soundscapes.   Magazine for fine music published from 1994 six times a year by Gore & Osment Publications, Rushcutters Bay, Sydney, containing music news, reviews, and articles on classical music in Australia and abroad. Incorporates AMEB *Intrada*.

Souter, David H.   (*b* Aberdeen, Scotland, 30 Mar. 1862; *d* Sydney, 22 Sept. 1935), cartoonist, writer. Apprenticed in the UK as a housepainter and signwriter, he was briefly with the magazine *Bon Accord* in 1880; later he went to South Africa, and in 1887 settled in Melbourne. He drew cartoons for *Tribune* and *News of the Week*, then for the *Bulletin* 1895–1935, as well as writing children's verses, publishing books, and editing a literary journal. He wrote the libretto for the operas *The Grey Kimona* (1902) and Alfred *Hill's *Rajah of Shivapone*.

FURTHER REFERENCE
Obit. in *SMH* 24 Sept 1935. See also *ADB*, 12.

South Australia.   See *Bound for South Australia*.

South Sea's Sisters, The.   Festival masque by Richard Henry Horne (1866) with incidental music for soloists (S,T,B), chorus and orchestra, by Charles *Horsley, performed at the opening of the Melbourne Intercolonial Exhibition on 29 October 1866. Unpublished.

South Street Eisteddfod.   See *Royal South Street Society Eisteddfod*.

Southern Crossings.   World music ensemble formed (1986) in Sydney, comprised of Michael *Atherton, Michael Askill, and John Napier, who play a wide variety of folk and traditional instruments. Their repertoire embraces music from Turkey, China, India, Korea,

Mexico, Africa, and Australian traditional music. They have appeared widely in Australia and South-East Asia. Their recordings include *Southern Crossings* (SSMo 26).

Spearritt, Gordon Donald (*b* Bundaberg, Qld, 30 Jan. 1925), musicologist. He graduated from the University of Melbourne Conservatorium (BMus 1950); the University of Queensland (BA 1953), Harvard University (MA 1966 on Renaissance English vocal composer Richard Nicholson), and was awarded the first PhD in Music from the University of Queensland (1980) for his work on the music of the Iatmul people of the Middle Sepik River, Papua New Guinea. An AMEB examiner and experienced choral conductor, he also wrote music theory books to furnish the needs of private teachers in remote areas. He worked at the University of Queensland from 1957 to 1987 (reader 1972, dean of the faculty of music 1974–75, and head of the department of music 1980–85), where he was instrumental in designing undergraduate and postgraduate courses, and vastly extended the music library. His students have carried out fieldwork in Papua New Guinea and Bougainville, and helped to establish a computerised sound-cataloguing and duplicating project at the Institute of Papua New Guinea Studies, Port Moresby.

An authority on the music of Papua New Guinea, Spearritt was elected president of the Musicological Society of Australia 1978–79. He has published many articles on the past and future of Papua New Guinea music research, logical musical systems in Papua New Guinea, music of Petspets villages in north-west Bougainville, the pairing of musicians and instruments in Iatmul society, and problems in transcribing drum and flute music in Papua New Guinea. He issued two discs of and companion essays about music from the Middle Sepik. In 1994 he was honoured with the AM.

FURTHER REFERENCE

His writings include 'Logical Musical Systems in Papua New Guinea', in *International Musicological Society: Report of the Twelfth Congress*, ed. Daniel Heartz and Bonnie Wade (Kassel: Bärenreiter, 1981), 123–7; 'Problems in Transcription: Drum Rhythms and Flute Music of Papua New Guinea', in *Problems and Solutions: Occasional Essays in Musicology Presented to Alice M. Moyle*, ed. Jamie C. Kassler and Jill Stubington (Sydney: Hale & Iremonger, 1984), 33–50. His recordings include *Music of Oceania: Papua Niugini—The Middle Sepik* and *The Iatmul of Papua Niugini* (Musicaphon BM30 SL2700, BM30 SL2701, Kassel: Bärenreiter, 1981). See also Warren Bebbington and Royston Gustavson, eds, *Sound and Reason: Music and Essays in Honour of Gordon Spearritt* (Brisbane: UQP, 1992).   MARGARET KARTOMI

Spectrum [Murtcepts; Indelible Murtcepts]. Rock band (1969–73) formed in Melbourne, originally comprised Mike Rudd (vocals, guitar), Lee Neale (organ), Bill Putt (bass) and Mark Kennedy (drums, Ray Arnott from 1970). With Rudd and Putt writing the material, they focused on experimental work and concert events such as the Sunbury rock festival (1969). To improve their appeal at dance venues, from 1971 they also worked in a more accessible guise as the Indelible Murtcepts, releasing *I'll Be Gone*, which reached No. 1 in the charts, *But That's All Right* (1971), and the album *Spectrum Part I* which reached No. 10 in 1971. Their album *Milesago* reached No. 16 in 1972, then in 1973 they released the single *Indelible Shuffle* (1973) and the album *Warts Up Your Nose* (1973). Pitched at an alternative, drug-tripping audience, their obscure lyrics and lengthy, at times turgid improvisations gained them critical acclaim, while in their more commercial Murtcepts guise they were greatly popular. Their farewell concert in 1973 was released as *Terminal Buzz* (1973).

FURTHER REFERENCE

Recordings include *I'll Be Gone* (Harvest HAR 9329), *But That's All Right* (1971 Harvest HAR 9667), *Milesago* (Harvest SHDW 5051), *Indelible Shuffle* (1973, EMI EMI 10218), *Warts Up Your Nose* (1973 EMI OCSD 7597), *Terminal Buzz* (1973 EMI SDELP 10081/2). For discography, see *SpencerA*. See also *SpencerW*; *GuinnessP*, III, 2341.

Speer, Stewart ('Stewie') (*b* Melbourne, 26 June 1928; *d* Sydney, 16 Sept. 1986), jazz and rock drummer. He began drums at the age of 13, playing in brass bands, then with Doc Willis. He joined Max Collie 1955–58 and was a founding member of Brian ★Brown's quartet 1956–60. Moving to Sydney in 1961 he played in nightclubs, ★El Rocco, and was with Col Nolan in 1965. Returning to Melbourne in 1957 to join Max ★Merritt, he was incapacitated by a road accident which permanently limited his mobility. He was with Merritt 1970–80 in England, then settled in Sydney, gradually resuming freelance work, with Bernie ★McGann and others. Speer was one of Australia's most respected drummers.

FURTHER REFERENCE

Recordings include *The Brian Brown Quintet* (1956, Score Records POL-006); *Tony Newstead And His Gang* (1960, Swaggie S-4524); *Col Nolan And The Soul Syndicate* (1966, CBS BP-233319); *Tribute to Stewart*, Barry Duggan/Stewart Speer Quartet (Recorded 1981, issued 1989, BDLP 001); *Jazz Live at Soup Plus* (1987, 2MBS-FM Jazz-4). See also *ClareB*; *BissetB*; *OxfordJ*.   BRUCE JOHNSON

Spencer, Don. Children's entertainer. Featured on ABC *Playschool* since the 1970s, he is a singer-composer of numerous songs in country and bluegrass styles which seek to inculcate pride in Australia by introducing Australian topics and themes to small children in an amusing way. With country music songwriter Allan ★Caswell he has produced four albums for children, including *Feathers, Fur or Fins*. His songs may be heard on *Don Spencer's Australian Animal Songs* (ABC Video 8143912/4) or *Don Spencer's Songs About Australia For Kids* (1995, ABC 8145664).

Spivakovsky, Jascha (*b* Smiela, Russia, 18 Aug. 1896; *d* Melbourne, 23 Mar. 1970), pianist. He studied with M. Mayer-Mahr in Berlin and his concert career began after he won the coveted Bluethner prize in 1910. After World War I, a series of concerts with the Berlin Philharmonic Orchestra that traced the history of the concerto from Bach to Brahms did much to advance his career. He toured Australia and NZ in 1921 and 1929 with phenomenal success. Further tours of Europe, the UK and Scandinavia were undertaken during the 1920s. In 1930 Spivakovsky formed the Spivakovsky-Kurtz trio with his younger brother Tossy and cellist Edmund Kurtz, and when the trio toured Australia in 1933 Spivakovsky settled in Melbourne with his Adelaide-born wife Leonore. He was engaged to teach piano at the University of Melbourne Conservatorium, and a highly successful Australian tour in 1947 preceded his return to the international concert circuit. Illness cut short his international career in 1960, but he continued to perform in Australia until his death in 1970.

Spivakovsky's playing was noted for its superb tonal quality and extraordinary legato technique. His substantial repertoire ranged from music of the Baroque era to that by the foremost composers of his time. Critics regarded him as a musician of the highest order who used his substantial imaginative, intellectual and physical powers in interpretations that were remarkable for the clarity and maturity of their conception.

FURTHER REFERENCE

AMN 51 (1967), 7; George Kehler, *The Piano In Concert*, 2 vols (Metuchen: Scarecrow Press, 1982); Michael Spivakovsky, 'Jascha Spivakovsky: The Early Years', *Music and the Teacher* 2 (1985), 3–12; idem, 'Jascha Spivakovsky: Continuing The Biographical Outline', *Music and the Teacher* 4 (1985), 3–9; idem, 'Jascha Spivakovsky: A Musical Life', *Journal of the Australian Jewish Historical Society* 11 (1990), 128–41.

CATHERINE STEVENS

SPK. Rock band (1978–) formed in Sydney around Sinan Leong (vocals) and Graeme Revell (synthesiser, vocals). They have released numerous singles, including their debut *No More* (1978) and *See Saw* (1981), and the albums *Kollective* (1983) and *Machine Age Voodoo* (1984). They moved to London where they were well received, then released the single *Breathless* (1988) and the album *Oceania* (1987). One of Australia's first electronically processed industrial noise bands, their later work is more rhythmic and accessible, if still metallic and often athematic.

FURTHER REFERENCE

Recordings include *No More* (1978, Side Effects SER 1), *See Saw* (1981, M2 M2009), *Kollective* (1983, Side Effects SER 02), *Machine Age Voodoo* (1984, WEA 240515–1), *Breathless* (1988, Regular K524), *Oceania* (1987, SPK SLR 11). A compilation is the triple CD *SPK* (1992, MDS SPKBOX 1). For discography,

see *SpencerA*. See also *SpencerW*; *Melody Maker* 17 Nov. 1984, 12–13, 20.

Split Enz. Rock band formed (1972) in Auckland, NZ, as Split Ends by (Brian) Tim ★Finn (vocals, piano), Mike 'Jonathan' Chunn (bass), Phil Judd (voice, guitar, mandolin) and Paul 'Wally' Wilkinson (guitar). Miles Golding (violin) and Michael Howard (flute) were also early members. Geoff Chunn was the band's original drummer but he was shortly replaced by Paul 'Emlyn' Crowther. The band also sported long-standing 1974 recruit Geoffrey 'Noel' Crombie, a spoons player-cum-percussionist who was largely responsible for the group's theatricality and eclectic costume, set and make-up designs. Refusing to play the pub circuit in their early career, by touring university campuses they pioneered park concerts. They reached the finals of NZBC TV's *New Faces* contest (1973). Rob Gillies (saxophone, trumpet) and Tony 'Eddie' Rayner (keyboards) joined the band in early 1974.

Moving to Australia in 1975, they changed their name to Split Enz, and signed with Mushroom to record their first album, *Mental Notes*. They moved to the UK in 1976 for guitarist Phil Manzanera to produce *Second Thoughts* and signed with Chrysalis. During a 1977 US tour, Judd left the group and was replaced by Finn's brother Neil (*b* Te Awamutu, NZ 27 May 1958). Shortly before *Dizrythmia* was released (1977), Wilkinson, Chunn and Crowther also left and were replaced by Nigel Griggs (*b* 18 Aug. 1949, bass) and Malcolm Green (*b* 25 Jan. 1953; drums). In 1978 Judd rejoined the group but soon left, as did Gillies. Later that year Chrysalis dropped the group, and after recording *Frenzy* they returned to Australia and re-signed with Mushroom. In 1979, Split Enz released their best-selling album *True Colours* which topped the Australian charts, as did the single *I Got You*. Despite the loss of Green in early 1981, this success was followed by two more Australian chart-toppers, *Corroboree* (1981), which was released outside Australia as *Waiata*, and *Time and Tide* (1982).

Six Months in a Leaky Boat from *Time and Tide* reached No. 2, but was banned in the UK by the BBC, who feared that the song may have referred to the British fleet preparing to engage Argentina in the Falklands War. After celebrating their tenth anniversary with a concert at Te Awamutu NZ in 1983, Paul Hester became the group's new drummer. The band then recorded *Conflicting Emotions* (1983) and, after the departure of Finn for a solo career, their final album was *See Ya Round* (1984). They disbanded and Neil Finn, Hester and Nick Seymour formed ★Crowded House (1985). Split Enz re-formed briefly in 1989 to tour Australia with Crowded House, and in 1993 celebrated their 20th anniversary with a short reunion tour of NZ and the release of a commemorative album. In 1996 *EnzSO* was released, featuring the vocal talents of the Finn brothers and orchestral arrangements of Split Enz's most popular songs.

FURTHER REFERENCE

Recordings include *Mental Notes* (1975, Mushroom L 35588); *Second Thoughts* (1976, Mushroom L 35981); *Dizrythmia* (1977, Mushroom L 36347); *Frenzy* (1979, Mushroom L 36921); *True Colours* (1980, Mushroom L 37167); *Corroboree* (1982, Mushroom RML 53001); *Time and Tide* (1982, Mushroom RML 53012); *Conflicting Emotions* (1983, Mushroom RML 53107); *See Ya Round* (1984, Mushroom RML 53146); *Anniversary* (1994, Mushroom D 98010); *EnzSO* (1996, Epic 483870–9). See also M. Chunn, *Stranger than Fiction: The Life and Times of Split Enz* (Wellington: GP Publications, 1992); *GuinnessP*; D. Rees and L. Crampton, eds, *Rock Movers and Shakers* (Santa Barbara, CA: ABC-CLIO, 1991); *SpencerW*.

AARON D.S. CORN

Spooner, Danny (*b* London, 16 Dec. 1936), folksinger. A barge deckhand from the age of 13, he worked aboard boats on the River Thames until 1962, when he emigrated to Australia. After working as a labourer in Sydney, he sang at Frank Traynor's folk club, Melbourne, 1963–67, releasing *A Wench And A Whale And A Pint Of Good Ale* (1965), then sang at La Mama and the Pram Factory, as well as presenting educational programs using folk-song for ABC radio. He was in residence at the University of Melbourne 1968–78, lecturing and singing on campuses in Australian and NZ, and releasing *Danny Spooner And Friends* (1978), then toured English campuses and folk venues from 1978. Back in Melbourne in 1982, he trained as a teacher and taught in schools from 1987; he is currently at Mowbray College, Melton. Singing and accompanying himself on guitar, concertina or spoons, he continues to appear at folk festivals and to give workshops and lectures on Australian topics illustrated with folk-songs.

FURTHER REFERENCE

A Wench And A Whale And A Pint Of Good Ale (1965, POL 038), *Danny Spooner And Friends* (1978, Anthology AR 002), *I Got This One From* (1986, Sandstock SSM 017) and *All Around Down Under* (Sandstock 036). See also Ian Hawthorne, *One Man's Eye* (Bacchus Marsh Vic.: Joval Publications, 1990), 57.

Sports, The. Rock band formed in Melbourne (1976) by Steve Cummings (vocals), Ed Bates (guitar), Andrew Pendlebury (guitar), Jim Niven (keyboards, vocals), Robert Glover (bass) and Paul Hutchins (drums). Their early work was influenced by rockabilly and rhythm and soul, but their debut album *Reckless* (1978), produced by *Black Sorrows' founder Joe *Camilleri, embraced a more conventional rock idiom. Later, in 1978, Bates left the band and was replaced by guitarist Martin Armiger. *Who Listens to the Radio* (1978) reached No. 35 in the national charts and skirted the US Top 40, providing the Sports with their first taste of chart success. Their second album, *The Sports Don't Throw Stones* (1979), reached No. 8 and went double gold, selling over 40 000 copies, and yielded the No. 26 hit *Don't Throw Stones*. In

1980 their third album *Suddenly* hit No. 13, despite changes in band personnel that saw Hutchins replaced in turn by Ian McLennan and ex-*Skyhooks drummer Freddie Strauks. Niven also quit and was not replaced, although ex-Skyhooks guitarist Red Symons did play keyboards on the Sports' tour of east-coast Australia in March 1980.

In early 1981 the band simplified their name to Sports for the release of their final studio album *Sondra*. Although this album reached No. 20, and the singles *Strangers On A Train* (1980) and *How Come* (1981) had hit No. 22 and No. 21 respectively, by December 1981 they had disbanded. Cummings embarked on a fruitful solo career, collaborating occasionally with Pendlebury who has also recorded three solo albums, and the Church's Steve Kilbey. Armiger moved into television, stage and music production.

FURTHER REFERENCE

Recordings include *Reckless* (1978, Mushroom L 36571); *The Sports Don't Throw Stones* (1979, Mushroom L 36844); *Suddenly* (1980, Mushroom L 37131); *Sondra* (1981, Mushroom L 37552); *The Sports Play Dylan (and Donovan)* (1981, Mushroom L 20007); *All Sports* (1982, Mushroom RML 53027); *Missin' Your Kissin'* (1988, Raven). See also *GuinnessP*; *McGrathA*; *SpencerW*.

AARON D.S. CORN

Springfield, Rick (*b* Guildford, NSW, 23 Aug. 1949), pop singer-songwriter. Playing guitar from the age of 14, he worked in a Melbourne club band in his teens, played with Jordy Boys, Rock House, MPD, and then joined *Zoot in 1969. He wrote several of Zoot's hits, and went solo in 1971, his debut *Speak To The Sky* reaching No. 5 in the Australian charts and No. 14 in the USA, and his debut album *Beginnings* reaching No. 20. Moving to the USA in 1972, he was groomed for the teenage scene, but a contractual dispute kept him inactive for two years. There he developed a new career as a television actor, appearing with a lead role in the soap *General Hospital*, then re-launching his recording career with a series of hits (1981–82), *Jessie's Girl* reaching No. 1 in Australia. He played a rock singer in the film *Hard to Hold* (1984) and had successful albums throughout the 1980s. He has made more than 25 singles.

FURTHER REFERENCE

Recordings include *Speak To The Sky* (1971, Sparmac SPRO 11); *Jessie's Girl* (1981, Wizard 2544473); *Beginnings* (1972, Sparmac SPL003); *Working Class Dog* (1976 Wizard ZL218); *Living In The Land Of Oz* (1983, RCA VPL1 0441); a compilation is *Greatest Hits* (1990, BMG PD90394). For discography, see *SpencerA*. See also *GuinnessP*, III, 2350–1; *McGrathA*; *SpencerW*.

Squires, Henry (*b* Bennington, Vermont, USA, 7 May 1825; *d* Paris?), American tenor. After lessons with G.W. Warren and James Maeder and concert appearances at New York in 1851–52, he made his debut in the Teatro Nuovo, Naples, as Manrico in the still new *Il trovatore* in

1853. He then sang principal roles in Sicily and other Italian houses, and with the Tully National English Opera Co. on its tour of Britain in 1857. He returned to the USA in 1858 for a season at the Metropolitan Opera under management that soon failed, and then sang at theatres in various American cities until, in the New Orleans Co., he came under W.S. *Lyster's management. With Lyster he appeared at Maguire's Opera House, San Francisco, and on tour 1859–60; then, with the Civil War impending, he accompanied Lyster to Australia in 1861. As principal tenor of Lyster's first Australian company, he sang more than 40 roles in Australia in the following years.

With a refined, sweet tone, secure intonation, and an elegant if at times reserved stage presence, his repertoire embraced major works of Donizetti, Verdi, Auber, Rossini and Meyerbeer, for most of which he gave the Australian premieres. He returned to California with Lyster for a season at the Metropolitan Theatre, San Francisco, in 1869, then joined the tour of Carlotta Patti and Sarasate, making with them his last concert appearance at Steinway Hall, New York, in the same year. Financially comfortable from his years in Australia, he then married Lucy Escott, with whom he had been associated throughout his career (she had been principal soprano in the Lyster company), and at the age of 44 retired to Paris.

FURTHER REFERENCE
Harold Love, *The Golden Age of Australian Opera: W.S. Lyster and His Companies* (Sydney: Currency Press, 1981), 14ff.

St George and the Dragon.
Opera in one act, music and libretto by Fritz *Hart (1930) after a Cornish mummers' play. First performed at St Kevin's Hall, Melbourne, on 10 July 1931.

St John, Jeff
[Jeff Newton] (*b* Sydney, 22 Apr. 1946), rock singer. In 1965 he joined the jazz–rock band Syndicate, which became known as Jeff St John and the Id, *Big Time Operator* (1966) reaching No. 12 in the charts. They toured as support for the Yardbirds, Roy Orbison and the Walker Brothers, but he left in 1967 over musical differences, forming Yama. In 1969 he formed Jeff St John and Copperwine, adding Wendy *Saddington in 1970, and *Teach Me How To Fly* reached No. 16 and the album *Joint Effort* No. 17. From 1972 he launched a solo career, working in the UK and the USA with mixed success. In 1977 he released *A Fool in Love*, which reached No. 9 in the charts and in 1978 he toured Australia. He formed Jeff St John's Asylum in 1982. Confined to a wheelchair, he had an individual, forceful voice, mixing Chicago blues, jazz and rock. He was one of the first to introduce American soul influences into Australia. His bands had good live followings, but sustained chart success eluded him.

FURTHER REFERENCE
Recordings include *Big Time Operator* (1966, Spoin EK1606); *Teach Me How To Fly* (1970, Chart CH214); *A Fool In Love* (1977,

Asylum 100060); *Joint Effort* (1970, Spin SEL 933742); compilations are *Best Of Jeff St John* (1972, Spin SEL 934500) and *Survivor 1965–1975* (1977, Infinity L36478). For discography, see *SpencerA*. See also *GuinnessP*, III, 2356; *McGrathA*; *SpencerW*.

Stafford, Jean
(*b* Latrobe, Tas., 1 Jan. 1950), country music singer. After recording an EP with Dusty Rankin at the age of 15, she won a Tasmanian talent quest in 1970, making her debut album, *Flowers For Mama*, in 1974. She won three ACMA Golden Guitars in the coming years, producing albums such as *Born Again* (1980), and was crowned Queen of Country Music at the 2NBC-FM *Spectrum* show in 1989. The same year she sang at the International Fan Fair, Nashville, and was engaged by United Music Group (USA); living in the USA since then she has produced five albums, hosted her own television show, and toured with the Grand Ole Opry star Jim Ed Brown. A talented singer of American and Australian repertoire, her *Classic Jean Stafford* (1990) won a gold record within six months of its release.

FURTHER REFERENCE
Recordings include *Flowers For Mama* (1974, Hadley HCS 51216). *Born Again* (1980, Hadley HCS 51246), *Classic Jean Stafford* (1990 RRR JSR 1990/CD). See also *LattaA*, 160–1; *SmithB*, 41–2.

Stanton, Barry
(*b* England, 23 Jan. 1941), rock and roll singer. Arriving in Australia as a child, after singing in a local band and winning a talent quest he formed Barry Stanton and the Boppers (1957) when he was 16, then the Bel Aires (1958). From 1959 he appeared on *Six O'Clock Rock* and toured interstate with Johnny *O'Keefe and Lonnie *Lee. In 1960 he released his debut single *Don't Let Go*, then *Don't You Worry About That* which reached No. 32 in the charts, and *Beggin' On My Knees* which reached No. 16 in 1961. He was a popular figure on television and in concert, releasing the EPs *Barry Stanton Sings*, *Teenage Idol* and *Little Miss Heartbreaker*, and retiring after Beatlemania changed tastes in 1964. He resurfaced for O'Keefe's rock and roll revival tour of 1974–75. At his height he was one of the best of the early Elvis Presley-style rock and roll artists in Australia. In the 1980s he began singing Presley nostalgia on the cabaret circuit, and released *Tribute To The King: Rare Songs 1957–1965*.

FURTHER REFERENCE
Recordings include *Don't Let Go* (Leedon LS593), *Don't You Worry About That* (Leedon LS603), *Beggin' On My Knees* (Leedon LK128), *Barry Stanton Sings* (Leedon LEP 6302), *Teenage Idol* (Leedon LX 10363), *Little Miss Heartbreaker* (Leedon LX 10706), and *Tribute To The King: Rare Songs 1957–1965* (1988, Canetoad CTLP 001). For discography, see *SpencerA*. See also *McGrathA*; *SpencerW*; Paul Hughes in *Collected Stories on Australian Rock and Roll*, ed. David McLean (Sydney: Canetoad Publications, 1991), 137–41.

Stars. Rock band (1975–79) formed in Adelaide, originally comprised of already seasoned players Mick Pealing (vocals), Mal Eastick (guitar, then Andy Durant [*d* 6 May 1980]), Graeme Thomson (bass) and Glyn Dowding (drums). They built a large following as a rock band with a Wild West image at Adelaide and toured as supporting act for *Little River Band. They moved to Melbourne in 1976, and with Durant providing their songs they released *Quick On The Draw*, which reached No. 25 in the charts. They toured as supporting act for Joe Cocker (1977), the Beach Boys (1978), and Linda Ronstadt (1979), releasing *West Is The Way* (1978), *Last Of The River Boats* (1979) and their live album *Paradise* (1978). Tired of touring, with Durant ill from cancer and the audience's taste for rock with a Western flavour ebbing, their *Land Of Fortune* album did not do well. In spite of their crisp rock sound with a country ambience, they could not sustain their brief chart success and disbanded in 1979.

FURTHER REFERENCE
Recordings include *Quick On The Draw* (Mushroom), *West Is The Way* (1978, Mushroom), *Last Of The River Boats* (1979, Mushroom) and *Paradise* (1978, released 1980 Mushroom 1157). For discography, see *SpencerA*. See also *McGrathA*; *SpencerW*; David Day and Tim Parker, *SA Great: It's Our Music 1956–1986* (Glandore, SA: Day and Parker, 1987), 166–71.

State Opera of South Australia. Professional opera company founded in 1976 in Adelaide. The company had its genesis in the local singers collective, the Intimate Opera Group (1957–72), followed by a professional ensemble known as New Opera, South Australia (1973–76). These two companies performed chamber-sized opera classics as well as new works, but with the establishment of the State Opera of South Australia in 1976 came a change in focus to grand opera. The company mainly performs standard 19th-century repertoire, but there have been significant productions of more innovative operas at some Adelaide Festivals: most notably Britten's *Death in Venice* (1980), Janáček's *The Makropoulos Affair* (1982) and John Adams's *Nixon in China* (1994). Its best-known general director has been an American, Bill Gillespie (1988–95).

JULJA SZUSTER

State Orchestra of Victoria. Theatre orchestra founded in 1987 in Melbourne, comprised of 69 full-time players. The orchestra's origins are in the Australian Elizabethan Theatre Trust (Melbourne) Orchestra, formed in 1969 to accompany the Trust Opera Co. and Australian Ballet performances. With significant funding from the Australia Council and the State Government, the orchestra's management was passed to the Victorian Arts Centre Trust in 1987 and the present name adopted. The orchestra accompanies the seasons of the Australian Ballet, and the Melbourne seasons of Opera Australia, but

also offers about six concert performances annually, notably a free outdoor series at the Myer Music Bowl. A problem for the orchestra has been the shifting demands of conductors of the various companies it serves, and the orchestra at first had little success in finding an artistic director to give it continuity. Nevertheless, it has achieved admirable standards. The current artistic adviser is Anthony Conolan.

FURTHER REFERENCE
Recordings include Ballet music *Madame Butterfly*, cond. J. Lanchbery (ABC); *Popular Classics* (1995, Morning Melodies).

Steel, Anthony Gerald (*b* Sheffield, England, 28 Oct. 1932), festival director, administrator. Educated at Oriel College, Oxford, he worked for the London Mozart Players, for the London Symphony Orchestra as assistant to general manager Ernest Fleischmann, and as planning manager for South Bank Concert Halls before settling in Australia as general manager (later director) of the Adelaide Festival Centre Trust in 1972. Appointed to direct the 1978 Adelaide Festival, his brilliantly imaginative programming was an immediate success. He became general manager of the Los Angeles Philharmonic Orchestra, where Fleischmann was now executive director, 1978–79, but he returned to direct four more Adelaide Festivals, the 1988 Brisbane World Expo on Stage, two Brisbane Biennial Festivals, and the 1990–91 Australian Theatre Festival, Canberra. His events have been characterised by striking and highly appealing juxtapositions of European and Asian performing arts presentations. He was honoured with the AM in 1978, and a long involvement with the Australia Council culminated in a term as chairman of the Performing Arts Board 1987–90. Since 1994 he has been artistic director of the Festival of Sydney and Carnivale.

FURTHER REFERENCE
ParsonsC; *WWA* (1996); *Age* 4 Aug 1993.

Steele, J(ames) A(rthur) (*b* Kyneton, Vic., 1894; *d* Melbourne, 21 June 1970), music educator. Trained at the University of Melbourne Conservatorium under Franklin *Peterson, Steele taught harmony, counterpoint and piano at the Conservatorium for nearly 50 years, 1916–65. A quiet man, highly regarded by staff and students alike, he was awarded an honorary DMus in 1959. He published *Harmony for Students,* (1952), *Free Counterpoint in Two Parts* (1955) and *Advanced Harmony for Students* (1956), and composed several didactic pieces for the piano.

PETER TREGEAR

Steele, Suzanne (*b* England, 1937; *d* 13 Dec. 1986), soprano. After appearing in the Old Vic Company's *A Midsummer Night's Dream* tour of the USA with Robert Helpmann at the age of 16, she joined

Drury Lane as an extra with a visiting Italian opera company and then the chorus of Sadler's Wells, making her debut in a major role in *Hansel and Gretel*. She toured Australia with Sadler's Wells in 1962, appearing as Euridice in *Orpheus in the Underworld* and *The Merry Widow*, and remaining as regular singer on the ABC TV *World of Song*. She returned to London in 1964, appearing on the BBC, at Covent Garden and in East Germany in the coming years. She settled in Australia in 1967, singing for J.C. Williamsons as star of *Man of La Mancha* (1967–68, 1971–72), for the Australian Opera from 1972, in *La belle Hélène* for the Victoria State Opera (1977), and regularly in *Music for the People* and *Carols By Candelight* at the Myer Music Bowl. A vivacious stage actress with a sweet tone, her roles included Musetta, Esmeralda, Santuzza, Cherubino, Papagena, Diana (*Orpheus in the Underworld*), and Metella (*La vie parisienne*).

FURTHER REFERENCE
Obit. *Victorian Arts Centre Magazine* (Oct. 1987), 25.

Stella. Opera in one act, music and text by G.W.L. ★Marshall-Hall (1910). Set in a Melbourne seaside town, it tells of the destruction of a young woman's happiness by the Victorian moral prejudice of the community. First performed at Her Majesty's Theatre, Melbourne on 4 May 1912, then (abridged) at the London Palladium in 1914. A modern edition has been published, edited by Suzanne Robinson (Melbourne: Centre for Studies in Australian Music, University of Melbourne, 1992), and revived at the University of Melbourne in 1996. MS in *PVgm*.

Stevens, Horace Ernest   (*b* Prahran, Melbourne, 26 Oct. 1876; *d* South Yarra, Melbourne, 18 Nov. 1950), bass-baritone. A choir soloist at the age of eight, he became a chorister at St Paul's Cathedral, Melbourne, in 1891. Following his father's profession, he practised dentistry for 20 years before choosing to make singing his career. After serving in World War I he was invalided to London in 1918 and, encouraged by Sir Henry Wood, made his debut in Mendelssohn's *Elijah* in the following year. With his severe looks and massive voice his success was immediate. Becoming widely known at oratorio festivals in England and the USA, he began his operatic career in the 1924 London premiere of Samuel Coleridge Taylor's *Hiawatha*. Assisted by a powerful dramatic sense, he was particularly successful in Wagnerian roles and in 1934 returned to Australia as part of Benjamin Fuller's Grand Opera Co. He settled in Melbourne, and sang in the first Melbourne performance of Alfred Hill's *Auster* in 1936. From 1938 until his death he gave lessons at the University of Melbourne Conservatorium.

FURTHER REFERENCE
Obit in *Age* 20 Nov. 1950. See also *Moresby A*, 64–6; James Griffin, *ADB*, 12; Desmond Shawe-Taylor, *GroveD*; Ron White,

'Three Melbourne Singers and the European Tradition', *Australasian Sound Archive* 1 (Aug. 1986), 14–16; for a list of references in *AMN* see *Marsi I*.

JENNIFER ROYLE

Stewart, D. Henry   (*b* NZ, 1885–92; *fl.* Sydney, 1905–30), composer. His family settled in Sydney when he was five, and he studied piano with Charles Heunerbein. Stewart became a piano teacher and composer, and later publishing editor for W.H. ★Paling, composing and arranging for them under various pseudonyms. Under his own name he wrote mostly piano pieces, his greatest successes being *Valse brillante* (written at the age of 17), *Silvery Shadows (Barcarolle)*, *Silver Stream* and *Repentance* (all published by Palings). Stewart's piano works were popular teaching and eisteddfod pieces, but he also wrote an unpublished concerto for two pianos and two comic operas.

FURTHER REFERENCE
A list of some of his works appears in *SnellA*. See also *AMN*, 1 May 1923, following p. 464.   JENNIFER HILL

Stewart, Nellie (Eleanor Towzey)   (*b* Sydney, 20 Nov. 1858; *d* Sydney, 21 June 1931), actress, singer. Daughter of the comedian Richard Stewart [Towzey] and the singer Theodosia ★Yates, she made her debut as an actress at the age of five. After touring abroad with her family, she was lead in Coppin's *Sinbad the Sailor* in 1880 at Melbourne. She then took the lead in Offenbach's *La fille du Tambour Major* for producer George Musgrove, with whom she became closely associated for the rest of her career. She sang Marguerite in *Faust* in 1888 and pantomime and numerous comic opera roles in Australia and England. At Melbourne in 1902 she first played Nel Gwynne in *Sweet Nell of Old Drury,* which was to become her most famous role. One of the major figures of her era in Australian drama, pantomime and operetta, she continued to play youthful roles until she was 70.

FURTHER REFERENCE
Her autobiography is *My Life's Story* (1923). See also M. Skill, *Sweet Nell of Old Sydney* (1973); *ADB*, 12.

Stirling, Keith Alexander   (*b* Melbourne, 5 Jan. 1938), jazz trumpeter. He began trumpet at the age of eight, later taking lessons from Freddie Thomas. Joining Brian ★Brown's quintet at Jazz Centre 44 in Melbourne in 1960, he began commuting to Sydney to play at ★El Rocco, where he led a band with Bob ★Bertles. He was based temporarily in Adelaide, playing at the Cellar with Billy ★Ross and Bob ★Gebert, then in Perth from 1965, playing with Jim Cook and others. Returning to Sydney, he worked in pit orchestras including that of the Moscow Circus, and nightclubs where he backed Carmen McRae, Stevie Wonder and Tony Bennett. In Melbourne during the early 1970s he worked mainly in studios with

Bruce Clarke, then went back to Sydney to teach in the Conservatorium jazz program. In 1978–79 with an Australia Council grant he studied in the USA, notably under Lee Konitz.

Back in Sydney he formed a succession of groups with performances at local venues such as the Basement, at festivals and concerts, and as support for American visitor Johnny Griffin. He also worked in other groups which included the *Daly-Wilson Big Band, Don *Burrows, and tours with Georgie Fame. In the late 1980s he was resident in Newcastle playing mainly in clubs, then returned to Sydney, working on the Hilton Hotel circuit, with touring shows such as Billy Fields, visitors such as Lester Bowie, and extensive studio work with pop groups, film and television, including the mini-series *Come In Spinner*.

Stirling's career has coincided with major phases in Australian jazz's progressive movement. He continues to perform with jazz groups and to present guest lectures and workshops.

FURTHER REFERENCE
Recordings include *Bruce Clarke Big Band* (1973 Cumquat CQR 12–01); *Stratusphunk*, the Bruce Clarke Quintet (1974, Cumquat CQR 12–04); *The Daly Wilson Big Band* (1976, Hammard HAM-014); *The Tony Ansell Orchestra* (1979, Batjazz BAT-2069); *The Jazz Action Sessions vol. 1* (1983, 2MBS-FM JAZZ-2/3). See also *ClareB*; *BissetB*; *OxfordJ*; Eric Myers, 'Keith Stirling, An Enigma,' *JA* (July/Aug. 1983), 4–7.   BRUCE JOHNSON

Stirling String Quartet. Founded in Perth in 1990 as the resident quartet of the WA Academy of Performing Arts, comprised of Pál Eder and Erika Tóth (violins), Alan Bonds (viola) and Suzanne Wijsman (cello), all teaching staff at the academy. They have toured regularly for Musica Viva and appeared on ABC radio and television. They are the only full-time string quartet resident in WA.

Stoltz Music Scholarship, Robert. One of the most valuable music scholarships in Australia. Awarded annually after a national competition, the scholarship provides one year's fully funded study at the Vienna Conservatorium, including travel, fees, accommodation and all expenses—benefits worth in excess of $40 000. Named for the Viennese song composer Robert Stoltz, it is funded by Apex Clubs and the finals are held each year in Melbourne.

Stone, Judy (*b* Sydney), popular music singer. She taught herself to play guitar in country and western style in her teens, then met Col *Joye in 1960 and concentrated on pop singing, her duets with him becoming popular. She toured with Joye and the *Joy Boys, was a regular on the television show *Bandstand*, and signed with Festival Records. Her debut single *I'll Step Down* reached No. 5 in the charts in 1962. She toured Japan (1965) with Joye and *Born A Woman* reached No. 3 in 1966. After marrying Leo *de Kroo in 1966 she was in club work in Australia and

abroad, then her *Would You Lay With Me In A Field Of Stone* reached No. 2 in 1974. In 1981 she won female country performer of the year at the Queensland Country Music Awards. She worked in China from 1986, being the first foreign artist to record in the Beijing Opera House. With a sweet, endearing voice, she combines popular, country and soul elements in a urbane cabaret style that has found continuing popularity. She has made more than 25 singles, 13 EPs and 14 albums.

FURTHER REFERENCE
Recordings include *I'll Step Down* (1962, Festival FK191); *Born A Woman* (1966, ATA ATAK1458); *Would You Lay With Me In A Field Of Stone* (1974, M7 MS046); *Col and Judy,* with Col Joye (1963, Festival FL 31026); a compilation is *Greatest Hits* (1994, AVM AVM003). For discography, see *SpencerA*. See also *McGrathA*; *SpencerW*; *SmithA*.

Stoneham, Reg(inald) A. A. (*fl*. 1910–40), songwriter. Little is known of his life except that he lived in St Kilda, Melbourne, from 1918 to 1928. Stoneham was prolific, publishing widely, usually with local publishers and sometimes by himself. He wrote most of his own lyrics and his output includes location and patriotic songs, songs on the new technologies—for example the gramophone and motor bike—and the exotic. He also undertook commercial commissions promoting, for example, Tintex hair dyes and dried fruit. Some of his songs were recorded, including *The Drover* and *Sleepy Seas* (both Regal Zonophone). Stoneham also wrote dance and salon pieces for the piano.

FURTHER REFERENCE
A list of some of his works appears in *SnellA*.
                                        JENNIFER HILL

Strachan, 'Shirley'. See *Skyhooks*.

Strahan, Lynne (*b* Dunedin, NZ, 2 Oct. 1938), poet, critic. After studies at the University of Melbourne, she wrote under the pseudonyms Lynne Duncan and Marion Watt, producing poetry and criticism, including *Half Open Doors* with Pat Grimshaw (1982), *Last Voyage of the Araminta* (1985), *Out of the Silence* (1988), and *At the Edge of the Centre* (1994). She has written librettos for several works of George *Dreyfus, including *Reflections in a Glass House* (1969), *Grand Aurora Australis Now Showing* (1972), *Silver Sticks and Salt Petre* (1974) and *Gilt-Edged Kid* (1970).

Stralia, Elsa [Elsie Mary Fischer] (*b* Adelaide, 1 Mar. 1881; *d* Melbourne, 31 Aug. 1945), soprano. A pupil of Elise *Wiedermann in Melbourne and *Slapoffski in Sydney, she left Australia in 1910 to study in Milan and London. She created a favourable impression in opera at Covent Garden (making her debut in 1913), at the Carlo Felice, Genoa, and at Drury Lane with the Beecham Opera Co. Stralia was a regular concert soloist with major

British orchestras, and also made successful appearances with the Lamoureux Orchestra, Paris, and the New York Symphony Orchestra under Walter Damrosch. Her extensive concert tours included visits to Australia in 1925 and 1934. Her recordings for Columbia reveal a vibrant, technically superb dramatic soprano voice.

FURTHER REFERENCE
ADB, 12; *GlennonA*, 37; *MackenzieS*, 109–11.
WAYNE HANCOCK (with M. Elphinstone)

Streets of Forbes, The, bushranging ballad. Attributed to its subject's brother-in-law, John McGuire, this bushranging song tells the story of Ben Hall, the Murrurundi farmer who was purportedly driven by harsh government treatment into outlaw life in 1862, and killed in 1865 by police who then paraded his body through the town of Forbes, NSW. The tune was collected by John Manifold.

FURTHER REFERENCE
Edition with commentary in *ManifoldP.*

Strehlow, T(heodor) G(eorge) H(enry) (b Hermannsburg, NT, 6 June 1908; *d* 3 Oct. 1978), linguist and collector of Aboriginal artefacts. Lecturer, research fellow, reader and professor in Australian linguistics, Adelaide University, 1934–73. His seminal work on the ethnomusicology of central Australian song verse, *Songs of Central Australia*, was published in 1971. It details the rhythmic and metrical forms of over 4000 Aboriginal song verses from central Australia, as well as their language and verbal structure and the occasions on which they were sung. Other major works are: *Aranda Phonetics and Grammar* (1944), *Aranda Traditions* (1947) and *Journey to Horseshoe Bend* (1969).   DAVID F. HUGO

Studies in Music. Annual journal (1967–92) published by the University of Western Australia to report the results of musicological studies in Australasia. Founded by Frank *Callaway, it maintained a high standard of presentation and content, included a register of graduate theses in Australasian universities, and for some years also contained musical supplements presenting editions of rare repertoire.

Sturt 1829 [Kaela]. Symphonic poem by Clive *Douglas (1954) on the theme of Charles Sturt's explorations of the Murrumbidgee and Murray rivers. Recorded by the Victorian Symphony Orchestra, conducted by the composer (HMV OALP 7511).

Stylus. Rock band (1974–79) formed in Sydney, drawing on former Mason's Cure members, originally comprised of Peter Cupples (vocals, guitar), Sam McNally (keyboards), Ron Peers (guitar), Ashley Henderson (bass) and Peter Lee (drums). In 1975 they released their debut

single *Summer Breeze*, which reached No. 31 in the charts and the album *Where In The World*, which reached No. 19. They toured extensively, appearing as supporting act to George Benson (1978), and releasing their single *So Much Love* (1977) and the album *Part Of It All* (1979). The most impressive of the Australian soul-funk bands of the 1970s, their work was of a consistently high quality, but despite critical acclaim they could not break into radio or the international market and disbanded in 1979.

FURTHER REFERENCE
Recordings include *Summer Breeze* (Atlantic 100029), *Where In The World* (WEA 600024), *So Much Love* (1977, Crystal Clear CC 278) and *Part Of It All* (1979, Oz OZS 1012). For discography, see *SpencerA.* See also *McGrathA*; *SpencerW.*

Sullivan, Chris, folklorist. Looking for material to perform, he began collecting folk-song and oral history in 1981, working with John *Meredith, Dave *de Hugard and others. With an interest in bush-dance tunes and non-tribal Aboriginal music as well as folk-song, he has been assisted by fellowships from AIATSIC, the Australia Council, the National Library of Australia and other bodies. He presented *Old Times Come Back Again* for ABC-FM in 1992. He has gathered 700 tapes, the single largest body of field recordings collected in Australia.

FURTHER REFERENCE
His tapes are now in *CAnl.* See also *StubingtonC*, 56; *24 Hours* (Jan. 1992), 54–5.

Summer Carol. Opera in one act by Colin *Brumby, libretto by Thomas Shapcott. First performed by the Canberra School of Music at Llewellyn Hall, Canberra, on 10 August 1991.

Summer of the Seventeenth Doll. Opera in two acts by Richard *Mills (1996), libretto by Peter Goldsworthy after the play by Ray Lawler. First performed in 1996 by the Victoria State Opera.

Summers, Jonathan (*b* Melbourne, 2 Oct. 1946), baritone. After studies with Bettine McCaughan in Melbourne and Otakar Kraus in London, he made his debut with Kent Opera in 1975 and sang with Covent Garden from 1977, as well as English National Opera, Scottish Opera and Glyndebourne. He first sang with the Australian Opera in 1981, and his guest appearances have since embraced almost all most major houses in Europe and the USA. With excellent acting and a clarion sound, his roles include Rigoletto, Balstrode, Mozart's Figaro, Don Carlos, Falstaff, Michele, Sharpless, Marcello, and Enrico.

FURTHER REFERENCE
Recordings include 12 complete operas, notably Balstrode in *Peter Grimes*, Covent Garden (Philips 432578–2PM2); Yamadori

in *Madame Butterfly*, Philharmonia (Sony MZK 35181); the Priest in *Samson et Dalila*, Covent Garden (Castle Vision); the Baron in *La traviata* (Decca 430491–2DH2); videos of *Il trovatore*, Australian Opera, and Faninal in the Covent Garden *Rosenkavalier* (Castle Vision Video CV 12017); concert works *Carmina Burana* (Angel); and Vaughan Williams *Sea* Symphony (EMI CDC7 49911–2). See also *CA* (1995–96); Elizabeth Forbes, *GroveO*.

Summers, Joseph (*b* Charlton, Somerset, England, 1839; *d* Perth, 10 Oct. 1917), composer, church musician, school music inspector. He studied with Goss, Gauntlett and Sterndale Bennett (taking the Oxford BMus and Canterbury DMus) and emigrated to Melbourne in 1865. Organist at St Peter's, Eastern Hill, 1868–79, then at All Saints, St Kilda, 1879–96, he was conductor of the Melbourne Philharmonic Society 1872–74. As school inspector of music for the Victorian department of education 1878–91, he opposed the tonic sol-fa method, supporting instead the teaching of staff notation in schools. He moved to Perth in 1897. He composed chiefly choral music, including hymns, anthems, patriotic songs and an oratorio, *The Two Worlds* (*c*.1899).

FURTHER REFERENCE

His memoirs are *Music and Musicians: Personal Reminiscences, 1865–1910* (Perth: Galway Printing Company, 1910). See also R.S. Stevens, *ADB*, 6.

R.S. STEVENS

Sun Aria. The popular name of two unrelated vocal competitions, both of which have been the starting points for the careers of many distinguished Australian singers.
(1) Herald-Sun Aria, Ballarat. Established as the *Sun Aria* in 1924. The reception given to the 1924 Melba-Williamson Grand Opera Co. inspired Thorold *Waters, music critic of the *Sun* newspaper and editor of *Australian Musical News*, to persuade the management of his newspaper to establish a substantial national vocal prize to assist young Australian singers. There were at first three competitions, held at Ballarat, Bendigo and Geelong, but from 1934 it was administered solely by the Royal South Street Eisteddfod Society, Ballarat, with a final in the Melbourne Town Hall. At a time when local operatic opportunities were scarce, a steady succession of winners went on to sing as soloists in the leading opera houses of the world, including Laurence *Power (1924), Marjorie *Lawrence (Geelong, 1928) and Kiri Te Kanawa (1965). The value of the prize has steadily increased from £23 in 1924 to $50 000 in prize-money in 1995.
(2) Sun Aria, Sydney. Founded (1933) largely at the instigation of Roland *Foster, singing teacher at the NSW State Conservatorium, as part of his City of Sydney Eisteddfod. From the outset it was sponsored by the Sydney *Sun* newspaper. Winners have included Raymond *Nilsson, Rosina *Raisbeck, Joan *Sutherland, June *Bronhill and Heather *Begg.

FURTHER REFERENCE

For the *Herald-Sun* Aria, an index to references in *AMN* is in *MarsiI*. An interview with Linda Phillips, longtime adjudicator of the award, is by Lloyd Jenkins in Oral History Tape No. 110 (1983), Ballarat Municipal Library; Archival Records, Royal South Street Society, Her Majesty's Theatre, Ballarat, Vic.

KAY DREYFUS §1; editor §2

Sun Music. Six related works by Peter *Sculthorpe, considered typical of his style and aesthetic in the late 1960s. Significant stylistic differences exist between the Penderecki-influenced *Sun Musics I & II* (1965, 1969), the Balinese-influenced *Sun Music III* (1967), the more diverse *Sun Music IV* (1967) and the almost purely percussive *Sun Music for Voices and Percussion* (1966). Their approachable style, brevity (9–13 minutes), generally favourable reception, publication and recording have ensured frequent performances, especially of the orchestral works *Sun Musics I–IV*. The 44-minute ballet *Sun Music* (1968) incorporates material from all but *Sun Music II*. See Hayes for clarification of the several title changes.

FURTHER REFERENCE

Michael Hannan, *Peter Sculthorpe: His Music and Ideas, 1929–1979* (Brisbane: QUP, 1982); Deborah Hayes, *Peter Sculthorpe: A Bio-Bibliography* (Westport, Conn.: Greenwood Press, 1993).

PATRICIA SHAW

Sunbury. Rock music festival (1972–74), held each Australia Day weekend outside the picturesque town of Sunbury on Jackson's Creek, north-west of Melbourne. Planned in imitation of the American Woodstock festival, 40 000 people attended the first festival, mainly teenagers who camped in tents or slept in the open for the three nights of the event. Officially alcohol-free (until being licensed in 1974), the site was nevertheless always littered with the debris of obvious drinking and drug-taking. Popular bands of the time were featured, including in 1972 Max Merritt and the Meteors, Daddy Cool, Spectrum, La De Das, Billy Thorpe, Wild Cherries, and Chain.

The styles broadened in 1973 to include jazz and folk; there was a 36-piece orchestra and new artists included Margret RoadKnight, Coloured Balls, Kush and (the audience favourite) Johnny O'Keefe. At the 1974 festival, a second stage was added for theatre (from the Pram Factory and Monash University) and dance (from the Victorian Ballet), and artists included Linda George, Ayers Rock, Ariel, Matt Taylor, Sherbert, Lobby Loyde, Captain Matchbox, Richard Clapton and Skyhooks.

Overall, the festivals received mixed reviews: the site was acoustically poor, the stage was built in a natural trough with sound bouncing between the surrounding slopes, the toilets and facilities were primitive, and the catering was limited to crude junk food. The musical performances were often excellent, but few felt the transforming experience of Woodstock.

FURTHER REFERENCE

Adrian Rawlins, *Festivals in Australia. An Intimate History* (Spring Hill, Qld.: DTE, 1982); *Go-Set* (Jan.–Feb. 1972, 1974).

Sunnyboys. Rock band (1980–84; 1987–) formed in Sydney, originally comprised of Jeremy Oxley (vocals, guitar), Richard Burgman (guitar), Peter Oxley (bass) and Bill Bilson (drums). They formed Wooden Horse while at school together in Kingscliff, northern NSW, then moved to Sydney, establishing Sunnyboys in 1980. Their debut single *Happy Man* and *Alone With You* both reached No. 26 in the charts in 1981 (the Top 10 in Sydney), and their album *The Sunnyboys* (1981) was well received. They produced another eight singles and five albums, including *Days Gone By* (1985), and went to the UK in 1984, but failed to make an impact and disbanded. They re-formed in 1987 with a largely new membership. In spite of their distinctive, light rock sound, reminiscent of the 1960s but with the energy of new-wave, they could not sustain their early success.

FURTHER REFERENCE

Recordings include *Happy Man* (Mushroom K8335), *Alone With You* (Mushroom K8476), *The Sunnyboys* (1981, Mushroom L37696), *Days Gone By* (1985, Mushroom), *Play The Best* (1991, Mushroom D24501). For discography, see *SpencerA*. See also *McGrathA*; *SpencerW*; *GuinnessP*, III, 2417; *CoupeN*.

Sutherland, Dame Joan (*b* Sydney, 7 Nov. 1926), soprano. She won the Sydney *Sun* Aria competition in 1949 and the Mobil Quest in 1950. Her stage debut was in 1951 in the title role of Eugene ★Goossens' *Judith* at the NSW State Conservatorium, and she travelled to the UK and studied at the Royal College of Music Opera School. Joining the Company of the Royal Opera House Covent Garden in 1952, she made her debut as the First Lady in *Die Zauberflöte*. At Covent Garden she created the role of Jenifer in Tippett's *The Midsummer Marriage* and among other roles sang Amelia in *Un ballo in maschera*, Aida, Agathe in *Der Freischütz*, the Countess in *Le nozze di Figaro*, Gilda in *Rigoletto*, Eva in *Die Meistersinger von Nürnberg*, the heroines in *Les contes d'Hoffmann*, Madame Lidoine in *Dialogues of the Carmelites* and Penelope Rich in *Gloriana*. Her husband, Richard ★Bonynge, recognised the potential in her voice to sing the great *bel canto* roles and he coached and encouraged her in this repertoire. In 1959 she sang Donizetti's *Lucia di Lammermoor* for the first time and was hailed as one of the greatest singers since Melba and Tetrazzini. A major international career followed in the leading opera houses of the world and in the recording studio. In 1959, after performances of Handel's *Alcina* in Venice, she was given the sobriquet *La Stupenda,* which remained with her throughout her subsequent career.

She returned to Australia in 1965 to head the Sutherland-Williamson International Grand Opera Co. and again in 1974 to sing *Les contes d'Hoffmann* with the Australian Opera. From 1976 until her retirement from the stage in 1990 she returned regularly to the Australian Opera in many of her greatest roles. Her vast repertoire included Handel's *Alcina*, *Rodelinda* and Cleopatra; Mozart's Countess Almaviva, Donna Anna, Pamina, Queen of the Night and Elettra; Bellini's *Norma*, Elvira in *I puritani*, *La sonnambula* and *Beatrice di Tenda*; Donizetti's Lucia, *Lucrezia Borgia*, *Maria Stuarda*, *Anna Bolena* and *La fille du régiment*; Rossini's *Semiramide*; Verdi's Amalia in *I Masnadieri*, Leonora in *Il trovatore*, *La traviata;* Meyerbeer's Marguerite de Valois, Gounod's Marguerite, Thomas's Ophélie, Delibes' *Lakmé*, Massenet's *Esclarmonde* and Sita in *Le roi de Lahore*, Puccini's *Suor Angelica*, Johann Strauss's Rosalinde and Lehár's *The Merry Widow.*

Sutherland's unique vocal quality, seamless legato, secure coloratura, great dynamic range and a career which lasted for more than 40 years have ensured that she is regarded as one of the greatest singers of all time. Since her retirement she has appeared in the Australian film *On Our Selection* and has worked with young singers as a master teacher in Australia's National Vocal Symposium. She was awarded the CBE in 1961, the AC in 1975, created DBE in 1979 and awarded the OM in 1991. She has three honorary doctorates.

FURTHER REFERENCE

Sutherland's recorded output is vast; a discography to 1987 is in Norma Major, *Joan Sutherland*, pp. 242–51. Her studio recordings were made almost exclusively by Decca; there are also numerous live recordings, including those released on ABC video. Recital discs include *The Art of the Prima Donna* (1960, Decca 425 493–2) and *The Age of Bel Canto* (1963, Decca 421 881–2). There are more than 40 complete studio opera recordings, including all of the Bellini and Donizetti operas mentioned above.

Her memoirs are *Joan with Richard Bonynge: The Joan Sutherland Album* (Sydney: Craftsman House, 1986). A chronological list of all opera performances and major concerts and recitals to 1989 is in Moffatt Oxenbould, *Joan Sutherland: A Tribute*, pp. 102–27.

See also Brian Adams, *La Stupenda* (Melbourne: Hutchinson, 1980); Richard Bonynge, *Joan Sutherland and Richard Bonynge with The Australian Opera* (Sydney: Craftsman House, 1990); Russell Braddon, *Joan Sutherland* (Sydney: Collins, 1962); *CA* (1995–96); Rupert Christiansen, *Prima Donna: A History* (London: Bodley Head, 1984); Quaintance Eaton, *Sutherland and Bonynge: An Intimate Biography* (New York: Dodd Mead, 1987); Edward Greenfield, *Joan Sutherland* (Sheperton, Surrey: Ian Allen, 1972); Jerome Hines, *Great Singers on Great Singing* (New York: Doubleday, 1982); *MackenzieS*; Norma Major, *Joan Sutherland* (London: Queen Anne Press, 1987); *MonashB*; Moffatt Oxenbould, *Joan Sutherland: A Tribute* (Westgate, NSW: Honeysett Publications, 1989); Harold Rosenthal, *Opera at Covent Garden* (London: Gollancz, 1967); *WWA* (1996).

MOFFATT OXENBOULD

Sutherland, Margaret Ada (*b* Adelaide, 20 Nov. 1897; *d* Melbourne, 12 Aug. 1984), composer. Her father was a writer and amateur pianist, while other relatives included musicians, artists and academics. Resident in Melbourne from 1902, Sutherland studied at the Marshall-Hall (now Melba) and University of Melbourne conservatoriums where her chief teachers were Edward Goll (piano) and Fritz Hart (composition). From 1923 she spent two years in England and Europe, during which time (perhaps influenced by Goll's enthusiastic championing of his music) she sought out and studied composition informally with Arnold Bax. Returning to Melbourne in 1925, she launched herself as a composer when friends arranged concerts (in Melbourne and Adelaide) of her own works written before and during her period of overseas study, the most notable of these being her Sonata for violin and piano which had won praise from Bax.

She was married at this time to Melbourne psychiatrist Norman Albiston and had two children (b 1929 and 1931) but the marriage was unsuccessful and ended in 1948. In the years 1926–35 she wrote little, concentrating (in her professional career) upon performance and piano teaching. After 1935, when her children had reached school age, her creative output increased markedly, also encouraged perhaps by the publication in 1934–36 of a number of works including the Violin Sonata by her friend Louise ★Hanson-Dyer's Éditions de L'Oiseau-lyre in Paris. After her divorce her rate of compositional output increased further, and during the next 20 years (1948–68) she produced her best-known works. Her creative career ended prematurely, in 1968, when a stroke, together with failing eyesight, made further composition impossible.

Sutherland's musical style was, in earlier years, influenced by post-impressionist and English 'pastoral' composers. Later the predominant stylistic character became more neo-classical, although earlier affinities never entirely disappeared. Her work is now generally recognised as among the most progressive as well as significant of all composers working in Australia before 1960.

In addition to her composition, performing and teaching, Margaret Sutherland was also a notable champion of other Australian composers and of Australia's artistic development generally. During the 1940s, 50s and 60s she was associated with numerous organisations including the Council for the Encouragement of Music and the Arts (CEMA), the advisory board of the Australian Music Fund and the Australian Music Advisory Committee for UNESCO. She was also one of the chief instigators of a movement from the early 1940s to ensure that the site of the present Victorian Arts Centre would be preserved for this purpose.

For many years Sutherland's work received only limited recognition. Since the 1960s, however, the number of performances and recordings of her music has increased considerably. She was also honoured with an honorary DMus from the University of Melbourne in 1969 as well as the OBE in 1970 and the AO in 1981.

WORKS (Selective)
Principal publishers: L'Oiseau-lyre, Kurrajong, Albert.
Mss in Australian Music Centre.

Orchestra   *Suite on a Theme of Purcell* (1938), *The Passing,* Mezz, ch (SSAA), orch (1938), Prelude and Jig, str (1939), Concertino, pf, orch (1940), *Pavan* (1945), Concerto for Strings (1948), Concerto, fl, hp, orch (1948), *Haunted Hills* (1950), *Four Symphonic Concepts* [*Triptych* 1–3; *Vistas* 4] (1951), *Open Air Piece* (1953), *Threesome (Homage to John Sebastiano)* (1953), *Pastoral* (1954), *Walking Tune* (1955), *Bush Ballad* (1954), *Adagio and Allegro Giocoso*, 2vn, orch (1955), *Ballad Overture* (1956), *Rondel* (1956), Concerto Grosso (1958), *Outdoor Overture* (1958), Violin Concerto (1960, Sydney: Albert, 1978), *Concertante*, ob, str (1961), *Fantasy*, vn, orch (1962), *Three Temperaments* (1964).

Instrumental   Sonata, vn, pf (1925; Paris: L'Oiseau-lyre, 1935), Trio, cl, va, pf (1934), *Burlesque*, 2pf (1934), *The Argument*, cl, 2vn, va, vc (1935), String Quartet No. 1 (1937), Sonata, vc/sax, pf (1938/1942), Two Pieces, 'Cavatina' and 'Rhapsody', vn, pf (1938), Sonatina, pf/hpd (1939), Three Pieces, hpd (1939), *House Quartet* (Quartet in G minor), vn/cl, va, vc/hn, pf (1942), *Nocturne*, vn, pf (1944), *Six Profiles*, pf (1947; London: Augener, 1953), Sonata, cl/va, pf (1947; Sydney: Currency, 1993), *Serenade*, ob, 2vn, va, vc (1950), *Contrasts*, 2vn (1953), *Discussion* (String Quartet No. 2) (1954), *Divertimento*, vn, va, vc (1958), Sonatina, vn/ob, pf (1955; Melbourne: Kurrajong, 1958), Trio, ob, 2vn (1954; Melbourne: Kurrajong, 1958), Quartet, cor anglais, vn, va, vc (1956; Sydney: Albert, 1974), Sonatina, pf (1956), Six Bagatelles, vn, va (1956), *Pavan and Canonical Piece*, 2pf (1957; Melbourne: Kurrajong, 1958), Movement, 2pf (1958), *Little Suite*, fl, cl, bs (1960), Quartet, cl, vn, va, vc (1967), String Quartet No. 3 (1967), *Extension*, pf (1967), *Chiaroscuro I&II*, pf (1968), *Voices I&II*, pf (1968).

Stage   *Dithyramb*, ballet (1937, 1, Verchina), Melbourne, May 1940; *The Selfish Giant*, ballet (1947, 1, Martyn), Melbourne, 1947; *The Young Kabbarli*, chamber opera (1964, 1, Casey), Hobart, 19 Aug. 1965.

Songs   Over 30, including *Five Songs* (1936; London: OUP, 1948), *The Orange Tree*, v, cl, pf (1938; Melbourne: Lady Northcote Permanent Orchestra Trust Fund, 1954), *Four Blake Songs* (1957), *Six Songs: Settings of Poems by Judith Wright* (1951–62; Melbourne: Allans, 1967).

Other Works   Miscellaneous short (including educational) choral, instrumental, and piano works.

FURTHER REFERENCE
Obit. in *APRAJ* 3/3 (Dec 1984). Recordings include *Haunted Hills*, Melbourne Symphony Orchestra, cond. P. Thomas, Violin Concerto, Melbourne Symphony Orchestra, L. Dommett, vn, Concerto Grosso, S. Copland, vn, J. Gilmore, va, Max Cooke, hpd, Melborne Symphony Orchestra, cond. J. Hopkins, Concerto for Strings, Queensland Symphony Orc, cond. P. Thomas (1995, ABC 446 2852); Quartet No. 1, Petra Str Quartet (Canberra School of Music, CSM 7); and *Little Suite*, wind trio (Move MD 3071). A discography of recordings to 1972 is in *PlushD*. See also *CohenI*; J.D. Garretty, Three Australian Composers: The Place of Contemporary Australian Music in World Trends, with Particular Reference to the Work of Margaret Sutherland, Robert

Hughes and Dorian Le Gallienne, MA, Univ. Melbourne, 1963; Christina Green, 'Margaret Sutherland—Australian Composer', *SA* 21 (Autumn 1989), 13–15; *LePageW*; *MurdochA*; David Symons, *GroveD*.   DAVID SYMONS

Sverjensky, Alexander (*b* Russia, 1900), pianist. After studies at the St Petersburg Conservatoire with Alexander Glazunov, he escaped the Bolshevik revolution in 1919 and went to Harbin, China. In 1922 he became accompanist to another émigré, former star of the Imperial Opera Lydia Lipkovskaya, and they toured China and the Philippines, coming to Australia in 1924. In Sydney he made a deep impression with his perceptive playing of the works of Balakirev, Rachmaninov and Scriabin, and he settled there, giving solo and chamber music recitals presenting unusual juxtapositions of Baroque, Classical and contemporary repertoire. At a concert in 1926 he introduced Prokofiev's music to Australia, and gave many Russian works their Australian premieres. He appeared with the ABC Sydney Orchestra from 1933, founded a piano trio in 1936, and became president of the Musical Association of NSW. He taught at the NSW State Conservatorium 1938–65.

An imaginative artist of wonderful subtlety and tone-colours, he promoted standards of virtuosity and precision still far from characteristic in Australia. His students included Roger *Woodward, Malcolm *Williamson, Richard Farrell, Romola *Costantino, and others who went on to notable careers.

FURTHER REFERENCE
The Theatre (Sydney), Apr. 1924, 17 and Apr. 1926, 30; *AMN*, 39 (Nov. 1948), 29; *AMN*, 40 (May 1950), 17.

Swanee. Rock band (1978–) formed in Sydney by John 'Swanee' Swan. Brother of Jimmy *Barnes, Swan first performed with a backing band in 1978 and recorded the singles debut *Crazy Dreams* in 1979. With a frequently changing membership, numerous musicians have appeared in the band. Swan's *If I Were A Carpenter* reached No. 5 in the charts in 1981 and *Lady What's Your Name* reached No. 13 in 1981. His albums include *Into The Night* (1980), *Days Gone By* (1984) and *This Time Is Different* (1982) which won a gold album. Featuring Swan's harsh, muscular vocal lead, the band plays rock music with an alignment to soul and rhythm and blues.

FURTHER REFERENCE
Recordings include *Crazy Dreams* (WEA 10098), *If I Were A Carpenter* (WEA 100176), *Lady What's Your Name* (WEA 100214), *Into The Night* (1980, WEA 600076), *Days Gone By* (1984, WEA 251771) and *This Time Is Different* (1982, WEA 600121). For discography, see *SpencerA*. See also *McGrathA*; *SpencerW*.

Swanton, Lloyd (*b* Sydney, 14 Aug. 1960), jazz bass player. He graduated from the NSW Conservatorium jazz

program and joined the Benders in 1980, then studied bass in London with Thomas Martin and in Los Angeles with Buell Neidlinger. He has been a major and prolific figure in the new wave of jazz musicians since the early 1980s, playing with the Necks, Clarion Fracture Zone, Bernie *McGann and his own group The catholics, formed in 1991. He has toured nationally and internationally, worked with numerous visiting musicians including Dewey Redman, Sting, Nat Adderley and George Coleman Jr, performs as a solo improviser and teaches. He has won multiple awards, for performance, record production, composition and film music.

FURTHER REFERENCE
Recordings include *The March of the Five Limbs*, Keys Music Association (*c.*1980, KMA LP 8301–2); *Distance*, the Benders (1985, Hot Records HTLP 1015); *Wizards of Oz* (1988, Polygram 834531–2); *The Last Straw* (1990, Spiral Scratch 0005); *Ugly Beauty*, Bernie McGann, (1991, Spiral Scratch 0010); *Sex*, the Necks (1989, Spiral Scratch 0002); *Next*, the Necks (1990, Spiral Scratch 0004); *Aquatic*, the Necks (1994, Fish of Milk 0002); *The catholics* (1993, Spiral Scratch 0011); *Simple*, The catholics (1994, Rufus Polygram RF009). See also John Shand, 'Fun Music Rules—No 'K', Lloyd Swanton', *Australian Jazz and Blues* 1/6 (1994), 6–10.   BRUCE JOHNSON

Swing. A jazz style pioneered in the USA by Fletcher Henderson and flourishing from the early 1930s until the end of World War II. Usually an ensemble of 12–16 players, divided into four sections (trumpets, trombones, saxophones/clarinets, and rhythm), played written arrangements involving repeated riffs or dialogues between the sections; opportunities for solo improvisation were therefore more confined than in earlier jazz. Through American band recordings released in the early 1930s, swing rapidly became popular in Australia, led by such bands as Frank *Coughlan and the Trocadero Orchestra from 1936, and Jim *Davidson's ABC Dance Band from 1937. See *Jazz*.

Swy. Street opera in one act by James *Penberthy, libretto by D. Kevans. First performed on the Parliament House lawns, Canberra, in March 1975.

Sydney, pop. (1991) 3 538 448. Capital of NSW and largest metropolitan area in Australia, situated in picturesque Sydney Harbour, one of the major ports of the South Pacific, on Australia's south-eastern coast.

1. Musical Life to 1850. 2. After 1850. 3. The 20th Century.

1. Musical Life to 1850. (i) Aboriginal Music. The history of Sydney's music begins with the music of the Aborigines of the area, but written observations are scarce. One account relates to the year 1791, when Captain John Hunter attended a corroboree at Port Jackson:

Their music consisted of two sticks of very hard wood, one of which the musician held upon his breast, in the manner of a violin, and struck it with the other, in good and regular time; the performer, who was a stout strong voiced man, sung the whole time, and frequently applied those graces in music, the piano and forte; . . . [children] beat time with the flat of their hand [and] also sung with the chief musical performer. (Hunter 1968:144–45)

Further interest was shown by the colonists throughout the 1800s, including transcriptions by John Lhotsky and Isaac *Nathan, but more sophisticated understanding by the European community had to await the work of the anthropologists and ethnomusicologists in the 20th century.

(ii) Concert Life.   In the early days of Sydney's European settlement, music had to struggle against a prevalent apathy towards the arts in general, which saw music merely as entertainment, along with horse-racing and the theatre. But there were also those who saw the cultivation of music, as well as of literature and the fine arts, as basic to the development of a truly civilised society, and as an antidote to the view of Botany Bay as merely a rowdy convict prison. Given music's precarious position in this community, it comes as no surprise that early musicians and entrepreneurs such as John Philip *Deane (1796–1849) and Barnett *Levey (1798–1837) had to spread their efforts across a wide range of activities.

A violinist in the concerts of London's Philharmonic Society, Deane settled first in Hobart in 1822, establishing himself as an importer of musical instruments, auctioneer and hotel proprietor, and later as a teacher of piano and violin and as organist of St David's Church of England. He also organised concerts and opened a small theatre, but ran into financial difficulties and in 1836 moved to Sydney. Here the Deane family remained a hub of musical activity for many years.

Levey's activities were even more eclectic. General merchant, publican, estate agent, jeweller, watchmaker, flour miller, property developer, theatre manager, actor, comic singer and bookseller, he also opened one of the first lending libraries in Australia. But Levey's main ambition was to build a theatre and concert hall, and the progress of Sydney's early music making owes much to the success of this venture. In 1829 Levey opened an Assembly Room in his Royal Hotel, with boxes and seats sold by subscription for a series of concerts; he promoted more musical entertainments in 1832, combining theatrical farce, melodrama and musical items. Although opposed by the governor of NSW, Sir Ralph Darling, Barnett Levey's Theatre Royal was finally opened in 1833, under the more enlightened administration of Sir Richard Bourke.

Given the problems of a musical career within the civilian population, those best suited to this *métier* were the trained instrumentalists of the regimental bands, who were paid by the British Government to provide music for military functions and for public entertainment. Since the foundation of the colony, the bands played for both private and public functions, including balls, race meetings, ceremonial occasions and open-air concerts: this music helped engender goodwill between the colonial administration and the public, and also catered to their nostalgia. It was these musicians who formed the nucleus of music-making in the early years, with a secure living and the authority of their professional training. The experience was so valuable for some bandsmen that they chose to remain in Sydney after their period of duty to teach and to play in community orchestras. It is of interest also that the later development of civilian bands, early in the 20th century (e.g. Tooth's Brewery Band), was to follow the trends of the British countryside rather than those of London, since it was in the provinces that the band movement in Britain had its roots (Bythell 1991: 161).

Even outside the milieu of the regimental bands, Sydney's music in the earliest days was mostly a male preserve. 'Decisions in British courts and parliaments meant that the early Australian population was predominantly male. In 1825 the aggregate female population was less than a quarter of the male equivalent' (Vamplew 1987:25). The earliest teachers, as shown by advertisements in the *Sydney Gazette*, were the barrack master Robert McIntosh (1814), offering lessons 'on the Piano Forte . . . Violin, Clarionet, Houlboy, and other wind instruments'; John Scarr (1823), who offered 'instruction in music and singing'; and John Edwards (1825). Music shops were opened by Robert Campbell (1824) and John Wood (1826); part of their stock-in-trade would have been the *Australian Quadrilles*, composed probably by Joseph *Reichenberg, bandmaster of the 40th Regiment, and the collection of marches and waltzes by Mr Kavanagh, bandmaster of the 3rd Regiment, titled *Original Australian Music* (1826). While women began to appear in Sydney's musical life as teachers, amateur pianists, and even as patrons (for example: Miss Bourke, daughter of Sir Richard, later Lady Deas-Thomson), it was only gradually that they were to join the ranks of Sydney's performers. A Miss Cooney and a Mrs Edmonds had been noted by the *Monitor* in 1829 as providing vocal solos in Levey's concerts, and the singers Mrs Taylor, Mrs Jones and Mrs Meredith are named among those who left him in 1834 in a dispute over payment. In that same year Mrs *Clarke, Mrs Ellard and Mrs Boatwright sang in the Philharmonic Society's first concert. It was not until the arrival of Mrs Chester in 1835 'from the Theatres Royal, Drury Lane and Covent Garden' and her appearance in Sir Henry Bishop's *Clari, Maid of Milan* (libretto by John Howard Payne) that the popular Mrs Maria Taylor had any rival. Whatever excellence she might achieve in teaching or in domestic music-making, the dual role of actress and singer remained the one role in which a female musician might aspire to the highest regard.

(iii) Instrument-makers. The colonists' need for musical instruments is typified by the arrival of a piano with the First Fleet in January 1788, belonging to the surgeon George Worgan (see *Worgan's Piano*). Musical instruments had been imported as early as 1815, including pianos, violins, flutes, flageolets, clarinets, french horns, barrel organs, cymbals and tambourines. Seeking to satisfy this demand, John Benham, an English carpenter who had migrated to Australia in 1831, began to manufacture pianos. The oldest of these instruments to survive (presently in the collection of the Powerhouse Museum) is an English-style 'cottage piano' with a compass of six octaves, built in 1834 from local timbers. Much later, Octavius *Beale built up a successful piano-manufacturing business (1893–1960) which produced over 95 000 instruments and employed, in its heyday, over 300 workers.

The demand for church organs, likewise, provided a stimulus for local industry. William Johnson (from London) and John Kinloch (from Perthshire, Scotland) entered into partnership and produced Australia's first locally built pipe organ in 1840 for the Francis Greenway church in Windsor, outside Sydney. Today, following the endeavours of the Organ Historical Trust of Australia, Sydney boasts the greatest number in the world of unaltered 19th-century organs. The Sydney Town Hall instrument, which in 1890 was the largest in the world, remains the biggest surviving 19th-century organ. The largest organ with a mechanical action is the Sydney Opera House instrument, built locally by Ronald *Sharp and opened in 1979.

Violin-making achieved prominence in Sydney only in 1912, with the formation of A.E. *Smith and Co., producing instruments for famous performers including Yehudi Menuhin, David Oistrakh and Isaac Stern, until its closure in 1965. Smith also became internationally famous as an instrument repairer, built up a dynasty of luthiers (his daughter Kitty and grandsons Roderick Smith and Daffyd Llewellyn), and trained many others. (Atherton 31–33, 42–46, 55–58).

(iv) Opera. The beginnings of opera reflected the popularity of ballad opera in London, with its spoken dialogue and tuneful songs, but suffered from weak accompaniment, in some cases consisting simply of fiddle, fife, tambourine and bass drum. The earliest recorded music-theatre work to be produced in Sydney was William Shield's comedy *The Poor Soldier* (libretto: John O'Keefe), presented at Sidaway's Theatre in 1796 (13 years after its first London production under the title *The Shamrock: or, The Anniversary of St. Patrick*). In 1800 there followed Henry Fielding's ballad opera *An Old Man Taught Wisdom; or, The Virgin Unmasked.* Built by convict labour for Robert Sidaway, a prosperous emancipist ex-burglar, the theatre cost £100; admission was one shilling, and could be paid in money, flour or meat. Even more enterprising was a theatre constructed at Emu Plains prison

farm, about 56 km from Sydney, through the perseverance of a Cockney convict, Jemmy King. Here, between 1825 and 1830, were produced the ballad operas *The Mock Doctor; or, The Dumb Lady Cured* (Henry Fielding), and *The Devil to Pay; or, The Wives Metamorphosed* (Charles Coffey and John Mottley).

It was not until the opening of Levey's Theatre Royal in 1833 that the performance of full-length musical works with singers and something resembling an orchestra became feasible. Its first year included productions of *The Devil to Pay*, William Jackson's comic opera *The Lord of the Manor* (General John Burgoyne), Samuel Arnold's comic dialogue opera *Inkle and Yarico* (George Colman the younger), his dialogue opera *The Mountaineers* (Colman the younger) and the afterpiece *The Children in the Wood* (Thomas Morton), Henry Bishop's melodrama *The Miller and His Men* (I. Pocock) and his adaptation of Mozart's *Le nozze di Figaro*. Press reviews were mostly negative, given that Mrs Taylor and Mrs Jones were the only really accomplished singers and that the orchestra failed to reach the standard of the regimental bands. In 1835 two operettas of Nathan were produced: *The Illustrious Stranger; or, Married and Buried* and *Sweethearts and Wives* (both by James Kenney).

Along with the music of the bands, the theatre was to have a strong influence on Sydney's musical life, helping to form cultural taste and, incidentally, to promote the phenomenon of the actress/singer, and later the prima donna, as cultural hero in the new country. As already noted, music in the theatre, at least until mid-century, consisted frequently of tuneful ballads in a spoken play and incidental music for farces, melodramas and burlesques: preference in stage music was for the melodious ballad rather than for characterisation, scene development and originality. Catering to this trend in Britain was the work of Michael William Balfe (1808–70), whose grand operas *The Bohemian Girl* (Alfred Bunn), *The Siege of Rochelle* (Edward Fitzball), *The Enchantress* and *The Daughter of St Mark* (both by Bunn), were successfully presented between 1846 and 1852 at the Royal Victoria Theatre— the first permanent theatre in Australia.

Another English composer, Isaac Nathan (1790–1864), had arrived in Sydney in 1841. Having built a reputation in London as a singing teacher and composer, he lost no time in establishing himself in the colony, where, in addition to his operettas of 1835, he composed two operas: a comedy, *Merry Freaks in Troublous Times* (1843; libretto by Charles Nagel) and a three-act opera *Don John of Austria* (1847; Jacob L. Montefiore). This latter work, performed under Nathan's direction at the Royal Victoria Theatre on 7 May 1847, is believed to be the first Australian opera to receive a full performance in this country.

A further stimulus to operatic standards had been the arrival in 1836 of the soprano Eliza Wallace (later Mrs Bushelle), who appeared in 1843 in Dibdin's ballad opera *The Waterman* and Bellini's *La Sonnambula;* the following January she sang in Henry Bishop's *Guy Mannering* (Sir

Walter Scott) and took the title role in an English version of Rossini's *La Cenerentola*. In 1845 the Royal Victoria company was augmented by the arrival from Hobart of the soprano Madame Maria ★Carandini (née Marie Burgess) and the brothers ★Howson: Frank (baritone) and John (tenor). With the recent addition of up-to-date stage machinery, under the supervision of the mechanist James Belmore, the theatre was now considered equal to at least the minor houses of London.

(v) Music in the Church.

In 1820 a choir trained by Mrs Catherine Fitzpatrick became the first St Mary's Cathedral choir, at the celebration of Father J.J. Therry's first mass in Sydney. About 15 years later, at the Pulteney Hotel in Bent Street, this choir was to participate in Sydney's first public concert to include choral music; it was organised by Joseph Cavendish, musical director of the Theatre Royal and, later, St Mary's Cathedral organist. The program comprised vocal solos, trios, glees and choruses, with a few instrumental and orchestral items.

In 1836 a musical festival was held at St Mary's Cathedral, conducted by William Vincent ★Wallace, with excerpts from Handel's *Messiah* and Haydn's *Creation*; this was one of three concerts promoted in order to raise £1000 for an organ. Built by Bevington & Son in London, this instrument arrived in 1841, noted by the *Australasian Chronicle* as 'one of the most powerful in the British Empire, its compass being equal to that in Westminster Abbey' (Lea-Scarlett 1970:39). The newly appointed organist and choirmaster was Nathan, who over the next 23 years was to exert such a pervasive influence on Sydney's musical life as composer, conductor, impresario and even music publisher.

2. After 1850 (i) Concert and Operatic Life.

By 1856 the population of Sydney had risen to over 69 000, and visiting artists had become more numerous. Consequently, concert and operatic life grew more varied and musical organisations began to proliferate. While still following English models, the blueprint for Australia's theatre builders was the popular Drury Lane theatre, rather than the more exclusive Her Majesty's or Covent Garden (Love 1981:125–6).

Resting on strong foundations laid in the previous decades, the new musical organisations included the St Mary's Choral Society (1853); the Sydney Philharmonic Society (1854); the Sydney Choral Society (1857); the Sydney Vocal Harmonic Society (1858); the People's Vocal Music Association (1860); the Orpheonist Society (1862); the Sydney Liedertafel (1881); the Orpheus Club; the Metropolitan Liedertafel (1888); and the Summer Hill Choral Society (1889). In the teaching of sight-singing, John Churchill Fisher had introduced Curwen's tonic sol-fa system at Fort Street Public School in 1855, but by 1864 Mr Chizlett, a follower of John Hullah, was teaching the continental fixed sol-fa in Sydney schools (Brewer 58–9).

(ii) Visitors.

Among the arrivals during this first half century, those who made a strong impression include the soprano Mrs Chester (1835); Wallace and his sister Eliza (1836); and a small French operatic troupe headed by Monsieur ★Gautrot, opera singer and violinist (1839). Once the colony began to establish a firm foundation of performance venues, appreciative audiences and expectation of financial gain, however, touring musicians were to visit Sydney in increasing numbers, and the most successful had a strong influence on Sydney's musical awareness. The 1850s, for example, saw the appearance of the contralto Sara ★Flower, 'from the Nobility Concerts in London', who remained to make her mark in opera; the bassoonist Mr Winterbottom, from Jullien's orchestra, who organised a series of promenade concerts; and the soprano Anna Bishop, who after a successful career in Italy and the United States remained in Sydney for two years, introducing Donizetti's *Lucrezia Borgia* and *Linda di Chamounix*, and Flotow's *Martha*, to the repertoire.

The 1860s saw the arrival of the ★Lyster Opera Company (1861–63). In 1885 the French pianist Henri ★Kowalski settled in Sydney, conducting the Sydney Philharmonic Society (1886–89) and co-founding the Orpheus Club with Leon ★Caron (1887–91), as well as teaching and making concert appearances. A most auspicious concert took place in 1885, followed by a benefit concert in the next year: this was the up-and-coming Melbourne soprano Nellie Armstrong, before her study in Paris with Mathilde Marchesi and her debut in Brussels as Nellie Melba.

3. The 20th century.

The progress of the new century saw the initial cautiousness towards the arts gradually replaced by a strong appetite for the visual arts, ballet and music. In 1936 the impresarios J. and N. Tait toured Colonel de Basil's Ballet Russe de Monte Carlo. In 1938 George Bell ('arguably the most influential single teacher who ever worked in Australia') was elected president of the newly formed Contemporary Art Society in Melbourne, and his influence spread to Sydney through his students Russell Drysdale, Sali Herman and David Strachan (Hughes 132). In the following year a comprehensive exhibition of modern French and British painting toured the country.

In 1915 the NSW State Conservatorium of Music had been founded, and in 1916 the Belgian violinist and conductor Henri ★Verbrugghen (1873–1934) was appointed director, and conductor of the NSW State Orchestra. It was not until 1947 (the same year in which Eugene Goossens took up a dual appointment as director of the Conservatorium and permanent conductor of the Sydney Symphony Orchestra) that a department of music was established at the University of Sydney. In 1948 Donald ★Peart (1909–81) was appointed to the chair, which he held until 1974. Peart was to reinvigorate the Sydney chapter of ISCM (1956), became the first president of the Musicological Society of Australia (1964) and of the

NSW chapter of the Australian Society for Music Education (1968). Integral to the curriculum of the new department was the study of ethnomusicology, at first emphasising Australian Aboriginal music, and later including Indonesian and Japanese musics. Today, the University of NSW and the University of Western Sydney also boast thriving music departments.

On the orchestral front, recommendations made by visiting conductors Sir Hamilton Harty (1934) and Eugene Ormandy (1944), brought out by the ABC, were able to bring about improvements in the standard of the *Sydney Symphony Orchestra and to help build a larger audience for orchestral music. But it was the prolonged residence of Eugene *Goossens (1947–56) which was crucial in leading the orchestra towards its present standard, and in expanding its repertoire by eclectic and sophisticated programming. Outstanding Australian conductors of the Sydney Symphony Orchestra have included Joseph *Post and Stuart *Challender; local conductors who have achieved an international reputation include Sir Charles *Mackerras and, more recently, Simone *Young. Other outstanding performing groups include the Brandenburg Orchestra (dir. Paul Dyer), the Australian Chamber Orchestra (dir. Richard Tognetti), the Renaissance Players (dir. Winsome Evans), the Seymour Group (cond. Mark Summerbell), Synergy, the Philharmonia Choir (cond. Anthony Walker), the Contemporary Singers (cond. Elliott Gyger), the Sydney Chamber Choir (cond. Nicholas Routley) and the Song Company (cond. Roland Peelman).

Following the death of Lyster in 1880, Sydney's operatic fare consisted of touring companies, some of which were imported by the impresarios J.C. Williamson and Sir Benjamin Fuller. The culmination of Sydney's fascination with opera came with the establishment in 1954 of the *Australian Elizabethan Theatre Trust and the first performance, in 1956, of the Australian Opera Co. (becoming the Elizabethan Trust Opera Co. in 1957 and the Australian Opera in 1970). Since 1956 Sydney has been assured of virtually continuous performances of opera. Since 1973 the Australian Opera has had a permanent performing base in the opera theatre of the Sydney Opera House. A national company based in Sydney, the Australian Opera (now Opera Australia) gives over 200 performances a year, spending seven months of the year in Sydney (Gyger 1990).

The cultural ambience of the 20th century has also become increasingly favourable to Australia's composers; symptomatic of the growing interest in national identity has been the establishment by James Murdoch (1976) of the *Australia (later Australian) Music Centre, for the dissemination of Australian music. Composers born or currently active in Sydney include, among those born 1880–95, Edgar *Bainton, Frank *Hutchens, Roy *Agnew, Lindley *Evans; those born 1904–15, John *Antill, Raymond *Hanson, Miriam *Hyde, Dulcie *Holland; those born 1926–35, Eric

*Gross, Peter *Sculthorpe, David *Lumsdaine, Malcolm *Williamson, Richard *Meale, Bozidar *Kos, Nigel *Butterley; those born 1938–50, Ann *Carr-Boyd, Michael *Atherton, Ian Fredericks, Ross *Edwards, Alison *Bauld, Moya *Henderson, Barry *Conyngham, Martin *Wesley-Smith, Anne *Boyd, Greg *Schiemer; and those born after 1950, Carl *Vine, Colin Offord, Michael *Whiticker, Jim Franklin, Caroline Szeto, Elena Kats-Chernin, Ian *Shanahan, Elliott *Gyger, Kirsty Beilharz.

FURTHER REFERENCE

AthertonA; *BrewerD*; *GroveO*

Bertie, Charles, *Isaac Nathan: Australia's First Composer* (Sydney: Angus & Robertson, 1922).

Bythell, Duncan, 'The brass band in Australia: The transplantation of British popular culture, 1850–1950', in *Bands: The Brass Band Movement in the 19th and 20th Centuries*, ed. Trevor Herbert (Milton Keynes: Open University Press, 1991, 145–164).

Carr-Boyd, Ann, 'Peart, Donald', *GroveD*.

Duffy, C.J., *Catholic Religious and Social Life in the Macquarie Era* (Sydney: Catholic Press Newspaper Co., 1966).

Gyger, Alison, *Opera for the Antipodes* (Sydney: Currency Press, 1990).

Hall, James, 'A history of music in Australia', *The Canon* 4 (1951), 6–12; 5 (1952), 1–11; 6 (1953), 1–7; 7 (1954), 3–6.

Hughes, Robert, *The Art of Australia* (Ringwood, Vic.: Penguin, 1970).

Hunter, Captain John, *An Historical Journal of Events at Sydney and at Sea 1787–1792*, ed. John Bach (Sydney: Angus & Robertson, 1968).

Irvin, Eric, 'Sydney's early opera performances', *Opera* (Sept. 1969): 764–72.

——, *Theatre comes to Australia* (Brisbane: UQP, 1971).

Lea-Scarlett, E.J., 'Music-making in early Sydney', *MMA* 5 (1970), 26–57.

Love, Harold, *The Golden Age of Australian Opera* (Sydney: Currency Press, 1981).

Osric [Hall, Humphrey; Cripps, Alfred J.], *The Romance of the Sydney Stage* (Ms *c*.1912, publ. Sydney: Currency Press, 1996).

Sametz, Phillip, *Play On!* (Sydney: ABC, 1992).

Skill, Marjorie, *Sweet Nell of Old Sydney* (Sydney: Urania, 1973).

Vamplew, Wray, ed., *Australians. Historical Statistics* (Sydney: Fairfax, Syme, Weldon & Associates, 1987).

Wentzel, Ann K., The first hundred years of music in Australia: 1788–1888, MA, Univ. Sydney, 1963.

White, Eric Walter, *A History of English Opera* (London: Faber and Faber, 1983).

Wood, Elizabeth, 'Kowalski, Henri', *GroveD*.

GRAHAM HARDIE

Sydney Conservatorium. Founded in 1915, it is Australia's largest music school. Originally established by the State Government as the NSW State Conservatorium, it was merged with the University of Sydney in 1990. Offering diplomas and a degree chiefly in performance (including large opera and jazz programs), but also in composition or music education, and a Conservatorium High School (opened 1918), it is housed at the modified Greenway Building, Macquarie Street, originally the Government House stables, built in 1821. The directors have been Henri *Verbrugghen (1915–21), W. Arundel *Orchard (1923–33), Edgar *Bainton (1933–46), Sir Eugene *Goossens (1947–56), Sir Bernard *Heinze (1957–65), Joseph *Post (1966–70), Rex *Hobcroft (1971–82), John *Hopkins (1986–91) and Ronald Smart (1992–94). The current principal is Sharman *Pretty.

Sydney Dance Company. Founded as Ballet In A Nutshell in 1966 by Suzanne Musitz, in 1967 the name of the troupe was changed to Athletes and Dancers and then again in 1970 to the Dance Company, NSW. By 1972 a number of government grants enabled it to develop into a full-time performing troupe. In 1976 Graeme *Murphy became artistic director, and three years later the troupe was renamed the Sydney Dance Co. Under Murphy's tutelage the company has become one of the most prominent troupes in Australia, and has successfully toured overseas on a number of occasions. An impressive list of Australian composers have been commissioned by it, including Roy Ritchie, Carl *Vine and Graeme *Koehne. (See *Ballet and Dance Music*).

FURTHER REFERENCE
Edward H. Pask, *Ballet in Australia* (Melbourne: OUP, 1982).
JOEL CROTTY

Sydney Festival. Founded in 1976, it evolved from the Waratah street festival, and is held annually in January over three weeks, at venues ranging from the Opera House and the Entertainment Centre to the outdoor Domain. Subsidised by the state and municipal governments, the event offers an array of international as well as Australian artists, and has a strong musical component.

Sydney Improvised Music Association (SIMA). Established in 1984 to promote contemporary jazz performance, which had been moribund, and free improvised music through performances. At first SIMA presented occasional concert series subsidised by the Australia Council and the State Government, then in 1989 achieved its goal of weekly concerts from its base at the Strawberry Hills Hotel, Surry Hills. It now presents over 130 performances annually, promotes national tours for local and visiting performers, and runs the non-profit Farside Music Projects agency. SIMA is a decisive force in the current resurgence of Australian contemporary jazz.
BRUCE JOHNSON

Sydney International Piano Competition. Held every four years, it has become one of the major international piano competitions, attracting applicants between the ages of 18 and 32 from most countries. Administered

by the Sydney Conservatorium, the prize is currently $15 000; many smaller awards are made during the competition and engagements follow for the finalists.

Sydney Jazz Club. Founded by Harry *Harman in 1953 as a vehicle for his Paramount Jazz Band. Enjoying great success, the club moved into the Ironworkers Building, George Street, in 1955 and establishing a journal, *Quarterly Rag* (1955–67, revived 1976). Black Opals was added as the second house band in 1958. Problems of overcrowding led to its brief dormancy in 1967, followed by its move to a succession of venues, including Abraham Mott Hall in the Rocks through the 1970s, then Vanity Fair Hotel as its unofficial venue until the hotel's closure in 1985. Australia's most durable and oldest surviving jazz club, the major focus of Sydney's traditional movement since its foundation, the Sydney Jazz Club continues to present performances and related events.

FURTHER REFERENCE
Recordings include *The Paramount Jazz Band and The Black Opal Jazz Band* (1959, Sonic SLA-115); *The Sydney Jazz Club, 1953–1993* (1993, MBS JAZZ 9, Linehan Series). See also *OxfordJ*; Bruce Johnson, 'The Sydney Jazz Club, 30 Years On', *JA* Part 1 (July/Aug. 1983), 8–9, Part 2 (Spring 1983), 24–5.
BRUCE JOHNSON

Sydney, Lorna (*b* Perth, *c*.1910), mezzo-soprano. Appearing first as a pianist in Perth at the age of 16, she studied at the University of Western Australia and sang Nedda and Santuzza on the same evening with a visiting Italian opera company in Perth. Lotte Lehmann heard her and invited her to Vienna to study in 1937; internment by the Nazis deferred her career until after the war, when she joined the Vienna State Opera and had her debut as Carmen in 1946. Over the next 20 years she sang nearly 50 roles at Vienna, as well as in the USA and on television, in operas by Gluck, Verdi, Wagner and R. Strauss among others; she became a favourite Carmen and Clytemnestra. An authoritative presence on stage, she combined a voice of unusual beauty and range with excellent musicianship. She was also a prominent lieder recitalist in Europe, the USA, and Africa, made regular tours of Australia for the ABC from 1947, and frequently taught in American colleges from 1965.

FURTHER REFERENCE
Her recordings included Handel, Bach, Brahms, Schumann and Mahler. *MackenzieS*, 170–1; *GlennonA* 42; *AMN* 37 (May 1947), 16.

Sydney Metropolitan Opera. Part-time company founded in 1989 to produce and commission chamber opera and music-theatre by Australian composers. Each year the company has workshops of two or three works and productions of at least one. Its most significant success has been Andrew *Schultz's *Black River*, which was made into a film and received various awards. The artistic director is John Wregg and musical director Mark Summerbell.

Sydney String Quartet. Formed (1966) as the resident quartet of the NSW State Conservatorium of Music, its members were Harry *Curby and Robert *Pikler (violins), Robert Ingram (viola) and John *Painter (cello). Carl *Pini was leader 1969–71; the group was re-formed in 1974 with Curby and Dorel Tincu (violins), Alexander Todicescu (viola) and Nathan *Waks (cello). They toured widely for Musica Viva, as well as abroad, making their Carnegie Hall debut in 1980. Curby resigned and was replaced by John Harding in 1980, Tincu died in 1981 and was replaced by Stanley *Ritchie, then (from 1983) Laszlo Kiss. By 1993 the membership had largely changed—Ronald Thomas and Tony Galt (violins), Todicescu (viola) and Georg Pederson (cello), and its activities have now reduced.

FURTHER REFERENCE

Recordings include *Australian String Quartets: by W. Lehmann, A. Ford, D. Banks, A. Hill* (1990, ABC/Polygram 426992–2); Janáček, String Quartets (1978, Cherry Pie LA 07724); and *Serenades* (1978, VP CD 6776).

Sydney Symphony Orchestra (1). Semi-professional orchestra formed (1908) by George Plummer. Consisting of 65 players, it gave a season of five or six concerts each year, conducted in the first year by W. Arundel *Orchard, shared by Orchard, G.W.L. *Marshall-Hall, Gustave *Slapoffski and Joseph *Bradley in the next, then in the following years solely by Bradley. It provided the only regular symphonic concerts in Sydney before the formation of the NSW State Orchestra in 1919. In 1946 the title was sold to the ABC for their Sydney Symphony Orchestra (2).

Sydney Symphony Orchestra (2). Established as a full-size symphony orchestra in 1946, the orchestra is the largest and busiest in Australia. Funded through the ABC as a subsidiary company, it has 104 full-time players and presents 150 concerts annually, mostly at its home in the Concert Hall of the Sydney Opera House. It offers 17 subscription series, as well as children's, schools, family, and outdoor concerts, and regularly makes visits to outer metropolitan and regional centres.

The orchestra's origins are in the 15-piece full-time broadcast ensemble the ABC inherited when it purchased its Sydney radio station in 1932; under the title National Broadcast Symphony Orchestra this group played at the opening broadcast of the ABC, conducted by W. Arundel *Orchard. Expanded to a core of 25 full-time players, with additional forces from the NSW State Conservatorium, and now with the title ABC Symphony Orchestra,

it gave impressive concerts under the visiting Irish conductor Sir Hamilton Harty in 1934. With Bernard *Heinze as adviser (later chief conductor), the core ensemble was increased to 45 players and a subscription season was inaugurated in 1936. Plans for a full-size symphony orchestra had to be shelved during the war, but in 1946 with assistance from the State Government and the city council the core was expanded to 72, the title Sydney Symphony Orchestra was purchased from George Plummer (who had founded the 1908 group of that name), and a permanent symphony orchestra was at last a reality. The British conductor Sir Eugene *Goossens made a dazzling debut as a guest, and was engaged as chief conductor (and jointly as director of the Conservatorium) in 1947. Magnetic and exceptionally gifted, Goossens startled the public with performances of great excitement; the number of subscriptions series grew to five, outdoor concerts were introduced, premieres of new works were given, and the first series of recordings was made (1952, EMI). But after giving the orchestra a dazzling decade, Goossens departed abruptly in 1956 amidst an absurd scandal involving charges that he had imported pornographic literature.

Conductors of less flamboyance followed—Nicolai Malko 1957–61, Dean Dixon 1964–67, and Moshe Atzmon 1969–71—and it was not until Willem van *Otterloo (1973–78) that the orchestra regained some of the lustre it had enjoyed under Goossens. After Otterloo's death in a car accident, he was succeeded by Louis Frémaux 1979–81, Sir Charles *Mackerras 1982–85, Zdenek Macal 1986, and Stuart *Challender 1987–91. The present chief conductor is Edo de Waart. The orchestra has had five international tours to Asia, the UK, NZ and Europe, and it is extensively recorded on the ABC Classics label.

FURTHER REFERENCE

Recordings include Mahler, Symphony No. 2, cond. S. Challender (1990, ABC 434778–2); works of Tchaikovsky, Brahms, Chabrier, cond. S. Challender (ABC 426289); R. Smalley, Piano Concerto, cond. P. Thomas, R. Smalley, pf, (1987, Oz Music OZM 1001); C. Vine, Symphonies, cond. S. Challender (1990, ABC 426995–2); works of A. Hill, N. Butterley, D. Banks and R. Hughes, cond. W. van Otterloo (1978, RCA VRL 10191). See also Phillip Sametz, *Play On!: 60 Years of Music-Making with the Sydney Symphony Orchestra* (Sydney: ABC, 1992); Charles Buttrose, *Playing for Australia: A Story about ABC Orchestras and Music in Australia* (Sydney: ABC/Macmillan, 1982); Warren Bebbington, 'Sydney Symphony Orchestra', in *Symphony Orchestras of the World: Selected Profiles*, ed. Robert R. Craven (Westport, Conn.: Greenwood Press, 1987), 10–15; Ava Hubble, *The Strange Case of Eugene Goosens and Other Tales from the Opera House* (Sydney: Collins, 1988), 46–72.

Sydney Wind Quintet. Ensemble formed (1980) from staff at the NSW State Conservatorium, comprised of Michael Scott (flute), Gabor *Reeves (clarinet), Josef Hanic (oboe), Anthony Buddle (french horn) and Gordon Skinner (bassoon). They have toured widely in Australia with Musica Viva and in 1983 through South-East Asia. They have focused on the wind quintet repertoire but have also commissioned a number of Australian works.

Sylvia. Comic opera in two acts by Cecil *Sharp (1890), libretto by Guy Boothby. Subtitled *The Marquis and the Maid,* it was first performed at the Theatre Royal, Adelaide on 4 January 1890.

Symphony Pianos. See *Davies, Charles Edwin.*

Synergy. Percussion ensemble formed (1974) from members of the Sydney Symphony Orchestra, at present comprised of Michael Askill (director), Ian Cleworth, Rebecca Lagos and Colin Piper, and from 1996 associated with the Sydney University of Technology. They focus on works by major contemporary composers such as John Cage, Iannis Xenakis, Pierre Boulez and Karlheinz Stockhausen, as well as commissioned Australian works. They have presented their own subscription seasons, toured Australia for Musica Viva and appeared in the UK, Paris, NZ, Hong Kong and Japan. With the Sydney Dance Company they presented *Synergy With Synergy,* and with the Sydney Symphony Orchestra the premiere of Toru Takemitsu's *From Me Flows What You Call Time.* The longest running of Australia's contemporary performance groups, they have commissioned over 30 new percussion works from Australian composers and played nearly 50 premieres.

FURTHER REFERENCE
Recordings include *Taiko,* music of Ian Cleworth and Sen Amano (1996, Black Sun 15021–2); *Synergy Percussion* (1991, Vox Australis VAST 001–2); *Matsuri* (1994, Celestial Harmonies 13081); and *Synergy with Samuels* (Tall Poppies TP O30).

T

Tactics, The. Rock band (1978–82; 1984–) formed in Canberra, originally comprised of David Studdert (vocals, guitar), Ingrid Speilman (keyboards), Angus Douglas (guitar), Geoff Marsh (bass) and Robert Whittle (drums). After moving to Sydney in 1977, they attracted a regular following in suburban venues, and released their EP *Long Weekend* (1979), then their debut album *My Houdini* (1981). Their singles included *Gold Watch* and *Fatman* (1985), and their albums *Glebe* (1981) and *The Bones Of Barry Harrison* (1982). After membership upheavals they disbanded in 1982, but re-formed with a largely new group in 1984. With all their material written by Studdert, they focused on political and social issues, set to a singular blend of reggae and indulgent neo-1960s rock.

FURTHER REFERENCE

Recordings include *Long Weekend* (1979 Folding Chair PRS 2653), *My Houdini* (1981, Green Records LRF 064), *Gold Watch* (Green), *Fatman* (1985, Waterfront DAMP 19), *Glebe* (1981, Green LRGH 094), *The Bones Of Barry Harrison* (1982, Green LRF 113), and *The Great Gusto* (1990, Regular L30161). For discography, see *SpencerA*. See also *McGrathA*; *SpencerW*; *CoupeN*; Clinton Walker, ed., *The Next Thing* (Kenthurst, NSW: Kangaroo Press, 1984), 142; idem, 'Tactical Triumphs', *Inner City Sound*, 110–13.

Tahite. See *Neild, James Edward*.

Tahourdin, Peter Richard (*b* Bramdenn, Hampshire, England, 27 Aug. 1928), composer. After studies with Richard Arnell (composition) and Rowland Dyson (trumpet) at Trinity College London, he worked freelance as a composer, teacher and broadcaster; his two *Sinfoniettas* (1952–1959) were broadcast by the BBC, his ballet *Pierrot the Wanderer* was televised by CBC Toronto in 1955, and his one-act opera *Inside Information* (Charmian Landon, 1955) was staged by Trinity College in 1959. He came to Australia in 1964 and was visiting composer at the University of Adelaide in 1965, writing a ballet, *Illyria*, on commission for the Australian Ballet. After a year in Canada studying electronic music and composition at Toronto University, he returned to the Elder Conservatorium in 1967; a number of electronic works, such as *Three Mobiles* (1973) followed. He was lecturer, then senior lecturer, at the University of Melbourne 1973–88. His music is polished and articulate in traditional idioms, including five symphonies, two choral works, a quartet (1982) and numerous small ensemble works, such as the four *Dialogues* for two instruments (1971–84).

FURTHER REFERENCE

Recordings include Symphony No. 2, SA Symphony Orchestra, cond. H. Krips (1970, Festival SFC 800–23); *Three Mobiles*, 4-channel tape (1973, LPMUMS S001); Quartet for Strings (1982, Canberra School of Music, CSM 7); and *San Diego Canons*, elec (Canberra School of Music, CSM 5). *PlushD* lists other works on ABC tapes. See also Elizabeth Wood, *GroveD*; *GlennonA*, 177–8.

Tait Ltd, J. & N. Firm of concert and theatrical entrepreneurs (1908–76) founded in Melbourne by John and Nevin Tait. After working as casual concert assistants for their older brother Charles at *Allans Music, they began importing concert artists from Europe to tour Australia from 1903, at first presenting concerts in the Athenaeum Hall then, from 1913, in their Auditorium in Collins Street. Forming a company in 1908 with their brother Frank, they staged musicals, produced their own films (from 1906) and established radio station 3AW (from 1928). In 1916 they were joined by their brother E.J. (Edward), who had been working for J.C. *Williamson; they merged their theatrical productions with Williamsons in 1920, but continued to promote concerts.

Prior to the ABC's dominance of concert presentation after 1936, the Taits were the primary importers to Australia of leading concert celebrities, presenting Clara Butt, Amelita Galli-Curci, Chaliapin, Toti Dal Monte, Paderewski, Menuhin, Grainger and many more; merged with Williamsons, they became the leading promoters of musicals in Australia until they closed in 1976. E.J. Tait was managing director of Williamsons 1939–47, then his brother (Sir) Frank held the position until his death in 1965.

FURTHER REFERENCE
An excellent family memoir is by Viola Tait, *A Family of Brothers* (Melbourne: Heinemann, 1971). See also *ParsonsC*; *BrisbaneE*, 143.

Takeover, The. Opera (1969) for schools in one act by George ★Dreyfus, libretto by Frank Kellaway, on the theme of Aboriginal land rights. Commissioned by Musica Viva and first performed on 6 October 1969 in Canberra; vocal score published (Melbourne 1969).

Tale of Two Cities, The. Opera in prologue and three acts by Arthur ★Benjamin (1949–50), libretto by J.C. Cliffe after the Dickens novel. First heard on the BBC on 17 April 1953, and first staged at Sadler's Wells, London, on 23 June 1957. A vocal score was published (London, 1954).

Taman Shud. Rock band (1967–72) formed in Sydney, originally comprised of Lindsay Bjerre (guitar, vocals), Alex 'Zac' Zytnik (guitar to 1970, then Tim Gaze), Kevin Stevenson (reeds), Richard Lockwood (winds), Peter Baron (bass), Dannie Davidson (drums) and Larry Duryrea (congas). Drawing members from local bands along the NSW coast, they first appeared at Intermedia Circus, Sydney, and gained a following among the surfing and emerging hippie groups. Their album *Evolution* (1969) was the sound-track to a surfing film. They released the EP *Bali Waters* (1970) and the album *Goolutionists And The Real People* (1970). One of the first Australian bands to merge the surfing craze with hippy themes of political and environmental issues, they were notable for their long instrumental solos and gentle, blues-based rock sound.

FURTHER REFERENCE
Recordings include *Evolution* (1969, CBS SBP 233761), *Bali Waters* (1970 Warner EPW 207) and *Goolutionists And The Real People* (1970, WEA WS 200001). A compilation is *Permanent Culture* (1994, Polydor 523442). For discography, see *SpencerA*. See also *McGrathA*; *SpencerW*; *GuinnessP*, III, 340.

Tamworth, pop. (1991) 31 716. Birthplace of country music singer Deniese ★Morrison and national centre of country music, it is on the Peel River, central-eastern NSW. Established in 1848 and at first chiefly a coach station, it is now a service centre for the surrounding farming district. The Tamworth Musical Society was founded in 1888, and continues to present musical productions each year.

Local country singers became an important attraction at the Tattersalls Hotel in 1964, and Radio 2TM commenced its *Hoedown* broadcasts in 1965. This led to the first Tamworth Country Music Jamboree (later Festival) in 1966, which rapidly expanded the following year. Opal Records was established to market country music in 1971, and the annual Australasian Country Music Awards (ACMA) began as part of the festival in 1973. Held each

Australia Day, the festival is now the largest music festival of any kind in Australia and has had a major effect on the shape and life of the town itself. Attracting over 10 000 people, it offers an elaborate program ranging from bush ballads to rockabilly. The Country Music Association of Australia, founded in 1992, is based at Tamworth.

The Tamworth Regional Conservatorium was founded in 1984 and occupies the restored Dominican Convent; the most securely established of Australia's regional music centres, it has a branch at Gunnedah, offers part-time tuition in an array of instruments, maintains the Tamworth Youth Orchestra, and presents regular concerts and operetta.

Tapu. Comic opera in two acts by Alfred ★Hill (1902–3), libretto by Arthur H. Adams. It deals with the adventures of an Australian politician in NZ who tangles with a Maori tohunga (priest). First performed by Pollard's Opera Co. at the Opera House, Wellington, NZ on 16 February 1903, it had 19 performances at Sydney in a much altered version for J.C. Williamsons in 1904.

Tarczynski, Stanislaw Victor (*b* Warsaw, Poland, 7 Apr. 1882; *d* Melbourne, 18 June 1952), violinist. After studying violin at the Warsaw Conservatorium, he was leader of the Moscow Grand Opera in 1902, worked for the Polish periodical *Mloda Muzyka* in 1903, then studied at Berlin. He gave concerts at Dresden and Prague, and became leader of the Ysaÿe Symphony Orchestra, Brussels. After one of his left-hand fingers became paralysed he went to Egypt to recover, then arrived in Australia on a recital tour in 1912. Prevented from returning to Europe by the war, he played in Melbourne theatres, taught at the University of Melbourne Conservatorium 1922–36 and the Albert Street Conservatorium. He was leader of the Melbourne Symphony Orchestra and for J.C. Williamsons in most visiting opera companies in Australia and NZ between the wars, and leader of the Adelaide String Quartet 1936–41. A greatly gifted violinist, he also published *Mazourka mélancolique* (1915) and an edition of the Kayser *Studies for Violin* Op. 20.

FURTHER REFERENCE
L.K. Paszkowski, *ADB*, 12.

Tartuffe. Opera in two acts with epilogue (1959–60) by Arthur ★Benjamin, libretto by J.C. Cliffe after Molière. The orchestration was completed posthumously by A. Boustead and first performed at Sadler's Wells, London, on 30 November 1964.

Tasmanian Conservatorium. Founded with state education department funds in 1964, it has been located since 1965 on the campus of the University of Tasmania, with which it became affiliated, and now offers degrees and diplomas, chiefly in practical music (including a strong string school) and music education. Directors have been Rex ★Hobcroft 1964–71, Jan ★Sedivka 1972–82, David ★Cubbin 1983–90 and Simone ★de Haan 1991–96.

Tasmanian Symphony Chamber Players.

String ensemble which appears unconducted, founded (1981) by William Hennessy with a core of players from the Tasmanian Symphony Orchestra. It presents work for string orchestra, soloist and orchestra, or chamber ensemble, ranging from traditional repertoire to new works by Australian composers; since 1987 it has also focused on stylish readings of Baroque repertoire with harpsichordist Geoffrey ★Lancaster directing from the keyboard. Immediately acclaimed for its first-class ensemble playing and polished, energetic interpretations, it has toured widely for Musica Viva. The current leader is Barbara Jane Gilby.

FURTHER REFERENCE

Recordings include *18th-Century Virtuoso String Music* (1991, ABC 432530); A. Ford, *Whispers*, 1994, Tall Poppies TO 053); Vivaldi, *Four Seasons* (ABC 838 904B).

Tasmanian Symphony Orchestra.

Founded in Hobart in 1948, the orchestra has 46 full-time players, gives over 60 concerts annually, principally of the smaller symphonic repertoire, and supports Tasmanian performances of opera and ballet. Funded by the ABC, it offers a statewide subscription series, with concerts in Launceston, Burnie and Devonport as well as at its rather cramped home in the Odeon Theatre, Hobart. It also supports the ★Tasmanian Symphony Chamber Players, who have toured nationally.

The origins of the orchestra are in the broadcast ensemble of 11 full-time players attached to the ABC's Hobart radio station in 1932. With very generous subsidies from the State Government as well as from the Launceston and Hobart city councils, the core was expanded to 31 in 1948 and the orchestra was securely established. To offset the limitations of its size, it has sought to establish a reputation for versatility, and has been more involved than its mainland counterparts in Baroque and contemporary repertoire (through New Music Tasmania), or in special projects such as composers' schools, conductors' workshops, or session recording (for video-clips, television theme-music). It won the Sidney Myer Performing Arts Award in 1995. The current principal conductor is David Porcelijn.

FURTHER REFERENCE

Recordings include *Rita Hunter* (1991, ABC 432250); Mozart, *Bass arias*, cond. D. Franks, C. Coad, B (ABC 432 697B) L. Sitsky, Violin Concerto, cond. V. Cavdarski, J. Sedivka, vn (c.1978, Caxton YPRX 2041); Paganini, Violin Concerto No. 1, cond. Shalom Ronly-Riklis, Adele Anthony, vn (1989, ABC 8388903–2); and M. Williamson, Two Piano Concerto, cond. B. Tuckwell,

M. Williamson and S. Campion, pfs (1982, ABC 426483–2). See also Charles Buttrose, *Playing for Australia: A Story about ABC Orchestras and Music in Australia* (Sydney: ABC/Macmillan, 1982).

Taste. Rock band (1975–77), formed in Melbourne, comprised of Ken Murdoch (vocals, guitar, keyboards), Joey Amenta (guitar), Michael Gemini (bass), and Virgil Donati (drums). Growing from Cloud Nine, a high school band which went professional in 1972, they released their debut single *Say When* (1973), then *Tickle Your Fancy* reached No. 22 in the charts in 1976 and *A Little Romance* reached No. 28 in 1977. Two of their albums became minor classics of rock: *Tickle Your Fancy* (1976) and *Knights Of Love* (1977). With Murdoch's songs, they made a heavy rock sound, stressing their two guitars.

FURTHER REFERENCE

Recordings include *Say When* (1973, Warner), *Tickle Your Fancy* (Bootleg BL 264), *A Little Romance* (Bootleg BL 302), *Tickle Your Fancy* (1976, Bootleg 2475709) and *Knights Of Love* (1977, Philips 6357/050). For discography, see *SpencerA*. See also *SpencerW.*

Tate, Henry (*b* Prahran, Melbourne, 27 Oct. 1873; *d* Melbourne, 6 June 1926), composer, critic. Tate's musical childhood followed the usual path of choral singing and piano lessons. On leaving school in the 1890s he pursued part-time studies at the University of Melbourne Conservatorium, with G.W.L. Marshall-Hall for piano and composition and later Franklin Peterson for analysis and counterpoint. For most of his life Tate made his living in the business world, including real estate and insurance; in his last three years, 1924–26, he was music critic for the Melbourne *Age*, to which he also contributed articles on chess.

Belonging to a group of nationalistic writers and artists calling themselves the Australian Institute of Arts and Literature, Tate shared the ideals of the landscape painter David Davies (1862–1939), 'the landscape turned into a metaphor of the psyche', a 'sense of identity between man's moods and Nature's' (Hughes 1970:75–6), and the poet Bernard O'Dowd (1866–1953). In his *Australian Musical Possibilities* Tate quotes from O'Dowd's developing mythology of Australia's destiny, *The Bush:*

All that we love in olden lands and lore
Was signal of her coming long ago!
. . . She is the Eldorado of old dreamers,
The sleeping Beauty of the world's desire.

His passionate belief in this mythology is manifest in many of his compositions, including *Dawn* (for orchestra), which 'seeks to embody both the material sounds of a dawn in the bush, and the mytho-historical stimulus of the 'dawn' of Australia in the minds of the men of the olden times' (Tate 1924:55), and the operetta *The Dreams of Diaz*. Piano pieces and songs, some of which are set to the composer's own poems, evoke the spirit of the bush, and often incorporate Australian birdcalls.

Tate strongly supported research into Aboriginal music, but apparently made no attempt to incorporate this music into his own compositions. His suggestions for developing a distinctively Australian music are set out in two booklets: *Australian Musical Resources: Some Suggestions* (1917), and *Australian Musical Possibilities* (1924). In the latter he focuses on the sounds and rhythms of the bush:

> The wind in the trees calls for strings. Its undertones lie in the region of the double basses and cellos, and the violins and violas will readily match the long tremolo of the leaves. The superb contrapuntal figures of the birds indicate wood-wind effects. (Tate 1924:30)

Since the enthusiastically received performance of the symphonic poem *Dawn* under Bernard Heinze in March 1926, little has been heard of Tate's music. One reason may be that his impact took effect in the context of a largely amateur musical society, and this challenging and evocative spirit, as Elizabeth Wood has pointed out, has since become the victim of a restrictive professionalism.

FURTHER REFERENCE
His writings are *Australian Musical Resources* (Melbourne: Sydney J. Endacott, 1917) and *Australian Musical Possibilities* (Melbourne: Edward A. Vidler, 1924). See also John Carmody, *ADB*, 12; Roger Covell, *Australia's Music: Themes of a New Society* (Melbourne: Sun Books, 1967); Graham Hardie, 'Henry Tate (1873–1926): Towards an Australian music', *MMA* 12 (1987), 201–6; Robert Hughes, *The Art of Australia,* rev. edn. (Harmondsworth: Penguin Books, 1970); Elizabeth Wood, *GroveD*.

GRAHAM HARDIE

Taylor, Matt (*b* Brisbane, 12 July 1948), blues guitarist. Playing guitar and harmonica while he was still at school, he appeared in Melbourne with Bay City Union from 1966, then from 1968 with various groups including ★Wild Cherries and ★Chain (1970–71). He made his solo single *I Remember When I Was Young* which reached No. 26 on the charts in 1973 and the album *Straight As A Die* which reached No. 13 in 1973. He appeared at the Sunbury pop festival in 1974 and released *Old, New, Intuitive* (1975), then toured with Ralph McTell in 1977, joined Western Flyer 1977–79, and formed the Matt Taylor Band in 1979, releasing *Always Land On Your Feet* (1984). One of Australia's best blues guitarists and a characteristic vocal tone, he has had a career spanning more than 20 years. Based in Perth, he has now performed with Bourbon Blues Band (1990), the Blues Power Band (1991), his own band Phil Manning, and Matt Taylor's Chair (1993), releasing with them the album *Trouble In The Wind* (1992).

FURTHER REFERENCE
Recordings include *I Remember When I Was Young* (Mushroom K5251), *Straight As A Die* (Mushroom L34955), *Old, New, Intuitive* (1975 Mushroom L35609), *Always Land On Your Feet* (1984 Forever MTB 001) and *Trouble In The Wind* (1992, Aim AIM 1036). For discography, see *SpencerA*. See also *McGrathA*; *SpencerW*.

Ted Mulry Gang (TMG). Rock band (1972–86) formed in Sydney, comprised of Ted Mulry (vocals, guitar, piano, bass), Les Hall and Gary Dixon (guitars), and Herm Kovak (drums). At first a trio backing Mulry, they built a young teenage following and in 1973 toured North America. In 1975 their album *Here We Are* won a gold album and the single *Jump In My Car* reached No. 1 in the charts. They toured nationally in 1976, releasing the album *Struttin'* which reached No. 9, *Steppin' Out* (under their newly abbreviated name TMG) which won a double gold album, and *Dark Town Strutter's Ball* (1976). They toured as supporting act to Sherbert in the same year. Their single *My Little Girl* reached No. 10 in the charts. Directing their light-hearted rock to young teenagers, they have been one of the longest-running popular bands in Australia.

FURTHER REFERENCE
Recordings include *Here We Are* (Albert APLP 007), *Jump In My Car* (Albert AP 10830), *Struttin'* (Albert APLP 018), *Steppin' Out* (Albert APLP 0211), *Dark Town Strutter's Ball* (1976, Albert AOP 11004), *My Little Girl* (Mushroom K6811) and *TMG Live* (1979, Mushroom L37078). For discography, see *SpencerA*. See also *SpencerW*.

Terra Australis. One-act ballet by Esther ★Rofe (1946), choreography by Edouard Borovansky, dealing with the relationship between Blacks, Whites and the Australian land. First performed by the Borovansky Ballet at Melbourne in May 1946.

Thalben-Ball, Sir George Thomas (*b* Sydney, 18 June 1896; *d* London, England, 18 Jan. 1987), organist. He spent his first three years in Sydney, then his parents returned with him to England. Educated privately and at the Royal College of Music, he was organist at the Temple Church, London, for 58 years until retirement in 1981. He was familiar to BBC Promenade audiences, and is remembered for presenting Handel organ concertos on a grand scale with extravagant cadenzas. Organ professor and examiner at the Royal College of Music, he was Birmingham city and university organist 1949–82. He made a recital tour of Australia in June–September 1951 as guest of the Commonwealth Jubilee celebrations; he visited Australia again in April–May 1971. He was regarded as the finest English organist of his time; his death severed the last living link with the great English Romantic school of organ and church music.

FURTHER REFERENCE
Peter Jewkes, 'Dr Sir George Thalben-Ball 1896–1987: An Appreciation', *Sydney Organ Journal* 18/2 (1987), 4–6; J. Rennert, *George Thalben-Ball* (London: David & Charles, 1979).

GRAEME RUSHWORTH

Thatcher, Charles Robert (*b* Bristol, England, 1831; *d* Shanghai, China, 1878), popular music singer-songwriter, actor, satirist. He was taught to play the flute as a boy, and from 1857 was employed in London in theatre orchestras. In 1852 he sailed for Australia, eager to try his luck in the Victorian goldfields. Finding the hard manual work of gold-digging physically difficult and unrewarding, he gained employment as a flautist at the Royal Victoria Theatre, Sandhurst. Here his talent for inventing topical lyrics, which he sang to popular melodies, was discovered. His fame soon spread, and the *Argus* (23 January 1854) wrote of his songs, 'they are really good, full of point and local allusions, humorous and well written, and elicit tremendous applause'. The local allusions in his songs were frequently of a personal, libellous nature, and often caused scandals. Many were published, usually in collections. He married the singer Annie Vitelli in 1861, and they travelled to New Zealand's gold-mining towns, again performing for the diggers. They returned to Victoria in 1867, where he went on a solo tour of the goldfields, performing his 'lecture', *Life on the Goldfields*, which detailed in song and prose the early days of the goldrush. After several more peripatetic years in Victoria and NZ, he returned to England, where he set up a curio shop (which had been his father's occupation), travelling widely to collect items for sale, and dying of cholera on such an expedition at Shanghai in 1878.

FURTHER REFERENCE
His published lyrics include *Victorian Songster* (1855); *Thatcher's Colonial Songster* (1857); *Thatcher's Colonial Minstrel* (1859); *Adelaide Songster* (1866); *Thatcher's Colonial Songs: Forming a Complete Comic History of the Diggings* (1864, facsimile edn. Adelaide, Libraries Board of South Australia, 1964). See also Hugh Anderson, *Goldrush Songster* (Ferntree Gully, Vic.: Rams Skull Press, 1958); idem, *The Colonial Minstrel* (Melbourne: Cheshire, 1960); idem, *Charles Thatcher's Gold-Diggers' Songbook* (Rams Skull Press, 1980); idem., *ADB*, 6.   ISOBEL McLENNAN

Theatre Organists. In the 1920s and 30s, 32 theatre pipe organs were installed in Australian theatres (American Wurlitzer or English Christie), and over the years 90 resident organists were appointed, including 10 Americans and 16 women. Early-model Wurlitzer theatre organs began arriving in Australia to accompany silent films from *c*.1918. One was installed in the Grand Theatre, Adelaide, and local organist Horace Weber (1887–1968) was engaged to play it. With no overseas recordings yet available to influence him, Weber adopted an orchestral approach, which he later developed on larger organs at Melbourne's Hoyts de Luxe (1922) and Capitol (1924), then at Sydney's State and Perth's Ambassadors in the 1930s. His last appointment was at the Melbourne Regent 1948–49. Notable among many Weber pupils were Charles Tuckwell, Geoff Robertson, Les Waldron, Lionel Corrick and Barry Brettoner (who opened several organs in England and Denmark in the 1930s).

The coming of sound films in 1928 changed the organist's role to soloist, accompanist to stage acts and as part of orchestras in major theatres. The best organists became nationally known through interchange between capital cities and radio broadcasts, including, aside from those already mentioned, Knight Barnett, Arnold Colman, Stanley Cummins, Reubert Hayes, Owen Holland, Stanfield Holliday and Les Richmond. The longest residencies at the one theatre were held by Noreen Hennessy (Prince Edward, Sydney, 1944–63), Knight Barnett (Regent, Adelaide, 1949–67), Aubrey Whelan (State, Melbourne, 1940–55), and Horace Weber (Capitol, Melbourne, 14 non-consecutive years, 1924–44). The closing of large cinemas by the 1960s created a hiatus, relieved by the formation of the Theatre Organ Society, which resulted in theatre organs being installed in public venues in all States and heard in public concerts. They totalled 17 in 1996. Organists on the concert circuit include Tony Fenelon, David Johnston, John Atwell, Gordon Hamilton, Ray Thornley, Neil Jensen, Margaret Hall and Gordon McKenzie, with John Giacchi and Chris McPhee heading the new generation. The influence of American visiting artists and recordings is often discernible in loudness and thick registration.   ERIC WICKS

(Theme from) Rush. Orchestral work by George *Dreyfus, 1974. This orchestral theme music for the 1974 ABC TV series about life on the Australian goldfields instantly caught the public imagination, and the first recorded version, by the Melbourne Showband, quickly climbed the popular music charts — the only Australian instrumental number ever to do so. It won a gold record, awards and prizes, and is now an evergreen. The piece has retained popularity through air-play from 17 recordings and other commercial exploitations. Strictly European and classical in style, its upward sweeping motive is reminiscent of Siegfried's sword motive. The scoring is Brahmsian and the music unfolds through the use of a developing variation technique.

FURTHER REFERENCE
G. Dreyfus, *The Last Frivolous Book* (Sydney: Hale & Iremonger, 1984).   KAY DREYFUS

Thin Men, The. Popular vocal group (1961–68) formed in Melbourne, originally comprised of former Moontones and Planetones members Johnny Edwards (tenor), Johnny Florence, Ron Patrick and Adrian Usher (baritones), and Tony Lee (bass). They released their debut single *I Can't Get You Out Of My Mind* in 1961, then *A Little Bit Now* reached No. 32 in the charts in 1962. They sang vocal arrangements of rock and roll and pop at dances and on the television shows *Sunnyside Up* and *Teen Scene*, then released *Till The Cheque Comes In* in 1966. They worked in the Sydney club circuit with guitar backing in the 1970s, releasing *Leah* in 1974 and backing such artists as Shirley Bassey, Neil Sedaka and Jerry Lewis. Perhaps the longest-lived vocal group in Australia, they made a polished, homogenous sound but never repeated their one chart success.

FURTHER REFERENCE

Recordings include *I Can't Get You Out Of My Mind* (W&G SI419), *A Little Bit Now* (W&G SI544), *Till The Cheque Comes In* (HMV EA 4809) and *Leah* (Earth ESP 001). For discography, see *SpencerA*. See also *McGrathA*; *SpencerW.*

This Is Serious Mum.   See *TISM.*

Thomas, Patrick   (*b* Brisbane, 1 June 1932), conductor. Thomas studied flute, piano, organ and voice, making his debut at the age of 13 as a flautist in the ABC Instrumental and Vocal Competition finals. Early work included posts as organist and choirmaster for Methodist and Presbyterian churches in Brisbane, and playing flute in the Queensland Symphony Orchestra 1951–55; he resigned from the orchestra in 1955 to work as an accountant. In 1963 he passed a conducting test set by the ABC, and was appointed coach and conductor of the Australian Elizabethan Theatre Trust Opera Co. He came to wider attention in 1964 by conducting 150 performances of opera and ballet for the Elizabethan Theatre Trust and the Australian Ballet, with ABC and freelance orchestras, and in 1965 the ABC appointed him assistant conductor of the South Australian Symphony Orchestra. He was also appointed musical director of the Adelaide Singers and the Adelaide Philharmonic Choir. He conducted the Tasmanian Symphony Orchestra for their 1968 season, and was appointed chief conductor of the Queensland Symphony Orchestra in 1973. He became the ABC's conductor-in-residence, a position created for him in 1978, which involved conducting all six orchestras, workshopping new Australian compositions, and having responsibility for the schools concerts program. He has undertaken many overseas engagements, more recently as a freelance conductor, including work in Europe, NZ, North America, Russia and South Africa. Thomas has been a strong supporter of Australian music and young performers, and conducts new Australian compositions for recordings and live performances. He was awarded the Sir Bernard Heinze prize in 1990 and was honoured with the MBE in 1978.

FURTHER REFERENCE

For discography see *HolmesC*. See also Charles Buttrose, *Playing for Australia: A Story about ABC Orchestras and Music in Australia* (Sydney: ABC and Macmillan, 1982); *GlennonA.*

NATASHA LANGFORD

Thomas, Wilfrid   (*b* London, 2 May 1904; *d* London, 16 Aug. 1991), radio broadcaster, baritone. His family settled in Australia when he was a boy. He worked in a shipping firm from the age of 14, took singing lessons, then sang solo in *Messiah* at the Melbourne Town Hall in 1925. He moved to Sydney, working as a singer, announcer and actor on radio 2FC while studying singing with Roland ★Foster at the NSW State Conservatorium, then joined the Westminster Glee Singers and toured Asia, Africa and

the UK. He settled in London, working with the BBC, and returned to Australia as director of light entertainment for ABC radio in 1943, but soon reverted to broadcasting. His *Wilfrid Thomas Show* (from 1942) featured a broad array of music and continued for 40 years, broadcast in many countries. One of the best-known and longest-serving music broadcasters Australia has produced, he was honoured with the AO in 1976. As a singer his *Rose, Rose I Love You* won a gold record in 1951.

FURTHER REFERENCE

Obit. in London *Times* 23 Aug. 1991, *Independent* 20 Aug. 1991. His autobiography is *Living on Air: Some Memories of Wilfrid Thomas* (London: Frederick Muller, 1958).

Thompson, Lawrie (Lawrence Edward)   (*b* Melbourne, 3 Apr. 1941), jazz drummer. He began drums at the age of 17, freelancing with Frank ★Johnson, Bob ★Barnard and others, and also leading the Southern City Jazz Band. Moving to Sydney to join Graeme ★Bell in 1964, he spent a period in London from 1968. Returning to Australia, he became involved in club and session work, and from the early 1970s increased his jazz freelancing, taking regular work with Col ★Nolan, Don ★Burrows, and Bob Barnard. His work with Bell included *Salute to Satchmo* (1977) and tours of China (1990); he was with ★Galapagos Duck 1980–*c*.1982, and played support for visitors such as Billy Eckstine and Ernestine Anderson.

FURTHER REFERENCE

Recordings include *Graeme Bell and his All Stars* (1964, Festival FL-31395); *Don Burrows Quartet* (1974, Cherry Pie CPS-1017–2); *Bud Freeman with Bob Barnard's Jazz Band* (1976, Swaggie S-1367). See also *OxfordJ.*

BRUCE JOHNSON

Thoms, Shirley   (*b* Toowoomba, Qld, 12 Jan. 1925), country singer-songwriter. Thoms grew up on a cane farm, listening to Buddy ★Williams, Tex ★Morton and Harry Torrani. In 1940 she began her career on Bundaberg radio 4BU, singing *The Mocking Bird Yodel*. After winning a talent quest in Brisbane, she signed with the Regal Zonophone label. From 1941 to 1946 she recorded 32 original tracks, including her most popular song, *Where the Golden Wattle Blooms*. She was the first Australian female to make solo country records and the first Queenslander to appear on disc. During the 1940s Thoms toured with George Sorlie's road show, Vernon's Varieties, Sole Brothers Circus and an army entertainment unit. Her fresh voice and youthful charm earned her the title 'Australia's Yodelling Sweetheart'. Thoms married in 1950 and shortly afterwards gave up her career. In 1970 she was brought to Tamworth by John ★Minson to appear at a 200th anniversary concert. Thoms subsequently recorded two albums for Hadley Records in 1970 and 1972. She then retired completely from the entertainment business, working as a veterinary surgeon. Thoms' early work remains very popular and Hadley have reissued all her 78 rpm singles on a set of three LPs. While her earlier compositions owe a heavy debt to the popular hillbilly singers of the time, Thoms gradually developed her own style. Melodies became more complex, lyrics more personal. Honours from Tamworth include induction into the ACMA Hands of Fame and a place on the Roll of Renown.

FURTHER REFERENCE

Recordings are *Australia's Yodelling Sweetheart* (Hadley 1204, 1970); *Shirley Thoms* (Hadley 1214, 1972); *The Complete Shirley Thoms Collection—Vols 1–3* (Hadley 1251, 1252, 1253). See also *WatsonC*, I 48–53, which includes discography.

CAROLYN MUNTZ

Thomson, Warren (*b* Melbourne 1932), music administrator, examiner. After studies in piano at the University of Melbourne Conservatorium, he taught at Trinity Grammar School, Melbourne, was president of the Victorian Music Teachers' Association and became an active AMEB examiner. He was head (later associate professor) of extension studies at the NSW State Conservatorium 1976–95, serving through most of that period as chairman of the NSW Music Examinations Board and adjudicator for an array of competitions and scholarships, including the Sydney International Piano Competition and the International Tchaikovsky Competition, Moscow. He was at various times chairman of the AMEB and its federal examiner.

Deeply committed to the value of a national public examinations system in music, he was a dominant presence in the AMEB for a long period. He recorded AMEB piano works (Cherry Pie), edited AMEB piano examination albums, keyboard works of Bach and others, and with May *Clifford published *Backgrounds, Styles and Composers* (all Allans Music, Melbourne). He was honoured with the OAM.

Thornton, Barry (*b* Junee, NSW, 14 June 1934), country music guitarist. Playing guitar from the age of 15, he entered local talent quests and joined Slim *Dusty's show from 1953. Associated with Dusty for 20 years, his guitar playing helped define the Australian traditional country sound; his comic character Mulga Dan also became well known. He recorded his first EP, *Talking Guitar*, in 1970 and he has produced albums almost annually since his first solo album, *The Country Way*, in 1981. He now tours with his own band, which includes his son Brian, also a guitarist. He was honoured in the ACMA Roll of Renown in 1991.

FURTHER REFERENCE

Recordings include *The Country Way* (1981, Selection PRC 029); those currently available include *The Big Heart Of The North* (Selection PRC 051), *Bazza's Best* (Selection PRC 058) and *Barry Thornton's Country Dance* (Selection CPCD 075). See also

Monika Allan, *The Tamworth Country Music Festival* (Sydney: Horwitz, Grahame, 1988), 77.

Thorpe, Billy   (*b* Manchester, England, 29 Mar. 1946), rock singer-songwriter. He began singing while at high school in Brisbane, and worked in vaudeville with George Wallace and Reg *Lindsay from 1958, then as support to Johnny *O'Keefe and Col *Joye. In 1964 he moved to Sydney and joined the Aztecs, an instrumental band looking for a vocalist. Despite the arrival of the Beatles in Australia that year, Thorpe's third single with the Aztecs, *Poison Ivy*, reached No. 1, and they achieved nine gold records over the next 18 months, *Twilight Time* reaching No. 3. There were numerous membership changes in the band, and by 1966 all original members had left, but Thorpe remained. He presented *It's All Happening* on Channel 7 in 1966 and *The Sunday Club* on ABC radio in 1967, and his regular performances in 1968 of rhythm and blues covers at the Whisky a Go Go nightclub, frequented by US servicemen on leave from Vietnam, further cemented his reputation.

He moved to Melbourne and built a new following with hard-driving blues, loud boogie and his own explicit lyrics, appearing at Sunbury and other festivals and on the pub circuit. *Most People I Know* reached No. 3 in 1972, but a trip to the UK that year was not a success. The Aztecs finally disbanded in 1975, after which Thorpe turned to a quieter, more melodic style. He settled in the USA in 1976, achieving gold albums (1978–82), several hits in Canada, and returning on various Australian tours. In the 1980s he ran a toy business, wrote music for Brian *Cadd and Barry *Gibb, for films and television, and words for children's books. In 1991 he formed Zoo and toured the USA and Australia.

Surviving more than 30 years in popular music, Thorpe was one of the few artists to shine brightly against the Beatlemania of the mid-1960s in Australia. His distinctive, throaty voice of potency and range, and his full-blooded, raucous songs, became a significant influence on such later Australian groups as *AC/DC, *Rose Tattoo and *Cold Chisel. He won the TV Logie for best male voice in 1964, *TV Week* best songwriter, most popular group and band of the year in 1972, and has been honoured in the ARIA Hall of Fame.

FURTHER REFERENCE

Recordings include *Poison Ivy* (1964, Linda Lee LL007); *Twilight Time* (1965, Parlophone A8164); *Most People I Know* (1972, Havoc); *Live At Sunbury* (1972 Havoc); *Rock Classics,* 7 discs (1974 MLX064); *Children Of The Sun* (1979, Capricorn L36890); a compilation is *20 Greatest Hits* (1994, Sony 4654002); a remastered compilation is *Lock Up Your Mothers*, 3 discs (1994, Mushroom D80968). For discography, see *SpencerA*. See also Paul McHenry *Thorpie!* (Golden Square, Vic.: Moonlight, 1994); Billy Thorpe, *Sex and Thugs and Rock'n'Roll: A Year in Kings Cross, 1963–64* (Sydney: Pan Macmillan, 1997); *GuinnessP*, III, 2488–9; *Age* 3 July 1994; *McGrathA*; *SpencerW*.

Thousand Miles Away, A, pastoral ballad. Attributed to Queensland station owner Charles Augustus ★Flower, *c.*1879, and sung to the air 'Ten Thousand Miles Away' (now familiar from George Dreyfus's adaptation in the Theme from *Rush*), it tells of sending beef to Brisbane from the rugged far west of Queensland. Found in the Hurd Collection (1894–97), and published by A.B. Paterson in *Old Bush Songs* (1905), another version was collected by A.L. Lloyd (1957).

FURTHER REFERENCE
Edition and commentary in *EdwardsG.*

3DB Orchestra. See *Radio and Music.*

Three Scenes from Aboriginal Life. Children's opera by Larry ★Sitsky, libretto by Gwen Harwood. First performed at the Canberra School of Music in October 1991.

Thunderbirds, The. Rock and roll band (1957–65) formed in Melbourne originally comprised of Billy Owens, Billy O'Rourke and Judy Cannon (vocals), Colin Cook (guitar), Laurie Bell (guitar, vocals), Graeme Lyall (saxophone), Murray Robertson (piano), Peter Robinson (bass), and Harold Frith (drums). Formed by Frith, at first they played at Earl's Court, St Kilda, and at dances. Their early sound with a vocal trio can be heard on the EP *The Thunderbirds* (1959). They soon appeared on television, becoming an instrumental group in 1960, and their single *Wild Weekend* (1961) reached No. 8 in the USA *Cashbox* Top 100 in 1963, the first Australian recording to succeed in the American charts. They recorded *New Orleans Beat* (1961), the EP *The Thunderbirds Play Their Big 6* and the live album *Quite A Party*, and appeared as backing group to Johnny ★O'Keefe, Johnny ★Chester and Normie ★Rowe, as well as to visiting stars Cliff Richards, Roy Orbison and many others. The most professional and versatile band of their era, they appeared with all the major soloists of the first decade of rock and roll.

FURTHER REFERENCE
Recordings include *The Thunderbirds* (1959, Rex RE 1007), *Wild Weekend* (1961 W&G S1103), *New Orleans Beat* (1961, W&G S1170), *The Thunderbirds Play Their Big 6* (W&G E1191) and *Quite A Party* (Gem 38). A compilation is *The Thunderbirds: The W&G Instrumental Story vol. 2* (Canetoad CTLP 011). For discography, see *SpencerA.* See also *McGrathA*; *SpencerW*; Geoff Jeremy and Ian B. Allen in *Collected Stories on Australia Rock'n'Roll,* ed. David McLean (Sydney: Canetoad Publications, 1991), 48–51.

Tibbits, George Richard (*b* Boulder, WA, 7 Nov. 1933), composer, architectural historian. Formerly senior lecturer in architectural history, University of Melbourne, he works in deliberate isolation from the country's intense musical politics. His early influences include Indonesian

and Indian music; in the 1950s he produced brutalist work based on urban life, which he rejected in the 1960s for lyricism. In 1965 he visited England and subsequently became interested in European rock and pop groups. Later works turned to parody and collage of antique models. He won the Albert H. Maggs award for composition in 1976. His music in general is notable for intellectual irony and an avoidance of pretension.

WORKS
Orchestral *Pili,* wind quintet, 2 str qrt (1966), *Fanfare for the Great Hall,* orch in groups (1968), *Neuronis Nephronicus and his Lowly Queen,* small orch (1968), *I Thought you were all Glittering with the Noblest of Carriage* (1969), *Serenade,* small orch (1969), *Beside the Rivering Waters of ...* (1970), *Antediluvia,* str (1971), *The Rose Garden of the Queen of Navarre,* mandolins (1975), *Violin Concerto* (1975), *Symphony: The Castle in the Air* (1979/84).
Vocal *Five Songs,* A, pf (1969), *Golden Builders,* S, small chorus, ens (1972), *Five Bells,* 5 str qrt (1972), *Shadows,* hpd, str orch (1974), *The Ice Fishermen–Lake Erie,* T, orch (1969/1973; reworked in 1981 for T, str qrt, brass qrt, db), *Battue; near Alberton, on a massacre of Aborigines,* dramatic work, Bar, cor anglais, 2 hn, tpt, trbn, str (1976).
Chamber and Instrumental *Silip,* fl, celeste, (1963), Quintet, fl, cl, va, vc, pf (1964), Trio, fl, va, hpd (1964), *Qashq,* fl, cl, hn, pf (1966), *Homage to Stravinsky,* fl, va, pf (1968), String Quartet No. 1 (1968); *Variation,* pf 4 hands (1969), *Stasis,* pf (1970), *Fantasy on the ABC,* org (1975), *Gateau,* wind quintet (1975), String Quartet No. 2 (1978; lost), String Quartet No. 3 (1983); String Quartet No. 4 (1989).

FURTHER REFERENCE
Recordings include *Five Songs,* v, pf, *Five Bells,* and other works, E. Campbell, S, A. Fogg, pf (Canberra School of Music, CSM 15); Second String Quartet, Petra String Quartet (Move MS 3037). Other recordings to 1972 are listed in *PlushD.* See also T. Radic, *GroveD*; *MurdochA.*

THÉRÈSE RADIC

Tiddas. Melbourne-based female vocal trio consisting of Lou Bennett, Sally Dastey, and Amy Saunders, active since 1990. The name of the group is from the Melbourne Aboriginal (Koori) word *tidda,* sister. Songs are socially committed, most often on Aboriginal and gender themes. The members of Tiddas worked at first with the Aboriginal rock band Djambi. Regular appearances and recordings with Kev Carmody, Ruby Hunter and Archie Roach followed, and they toured to Canada and Europe with these three in 1995.

FURTHER REFERENCE
Recordings include *Sing About Life* (1993, Phonogram/Mercury 518 3482); *Inside My Kitchen* (1996, ID Records 5327992).

P. DUNBAR-HALL

Tie Me Kangaroo Down, Sport. Comic song (1960), words and music by Rolf ★Harris. A parody of the

'Dying Stockman' ballads, it was recorded by Rolf Harris (Columbia) and reached No. 7 in the Australian charts in 1960, No. 9 in the UK and No. 3 in the USA. It was published by Castle Music, Sydney, 1960. A cover version 'Tie My Hunting Dog Down, Jed', was recorded by Arthur 'Guitar' Boogie in the USA.

Tintner, Georg (*b* Vienna, 24 May 1917), conductor. He began studying piano at the age of six and later composition. From the age of nine he spent five years as a member of the Vienna Boys' Choir, and entered the Vienna State Academy where he studied conducting with Felix Weingartner. He became assistant conductor at the Vienna Volksoper at 19. Tintner left Austria in 1938, and in NZ he was appointed conductor of Auckland Choral Society and Auckland String Players. He moved to Australia as conductor of the National Opera of NSW in 1954. In 1964 he became musical director of the NZ Opera and Ballet Co., and in 1966–67 was musical director of the Municipal Orchestra, Cape Town. In London he conducted at Sadler's Wells and leading British orchestras for the BBC. In 1970 he was appointed musical director of the WA Opera Co., in 1971 became senior resident conductor of the Australian Opera, and was music director of the Queensland Theatre Orchestra between 1976 and 1987.

Conducting without a baton and invariably from memory, Tintner has appeared many times with all major Australian and NZ orchestras and opera companies. In late 1987 he moved to Canada where he is musical director of Symphony Nova Scotia. He has prestigious awards from Canada and Vienna and two honorary doctorates.

FURTHER REFERENCE
He is currently recording the complete orchestral and choral works of Bruckner for Naxos. For discography see *HolmesC*. See also John Cargher, *Bravo! Two Hundred Years of Opera in Australia* (Melbourne: Macmillan, 1988); idem, *The Australian Opera: The First Twenty Years* (Sydney: Friends of the Australian Opera, 1971); A. Carr-Boyd, *GroveD*; Neil Warren-Smith, *25 Years of Australian Opera* (Melbourne: OUP, 1983).   HELEN GAGLIANO

Tintookies, The. Marionette musical by Kurt Herweg (1956), the story and puppetry by Peter Scriven. Set in the Australian bush, it was a full-scale theatrical work of a kind rare in modern puppetry. First performed by Peter Scriven's puppet company at the Elizabethan Theatre, Sydney in June 1956.

TISM (This Is Serious Mum). Rock band (1984–) formed in Melbourne. The release of their single *Defecate On My Face* (1986) caused not unexpected controversy, foreshadowing them as exponents of black humour and absurdist rock. They appear in masks, keeping their identities a secret. Their debut album was *Great Trucking Songs Of The Renaissance* (1988) and they followed this with the singles *Martin Scorsese Is Really Quite A Joyful Fellow* (1989) and *Let's Form A Company* (1991).

FURTHER REFERENCE
Recordings include *Defecate On My Face* (1986, Elvis), *Great Trucking Songs Of The Renaissance* (1988, Elvis LP 2001), *Martin Scorsese Is Really Quite A Joyful Fellow* (1989, Elvis), *Let's Form A Company* (1991, Phonogram). There is a video, *Incontinent In Ten Continents* (Shock EO1) and a compilation, *Gentlemen Start Your Egos* (1991, Shock SHOCKCD 0017). For discography, see *SpencerA*. See also *SpencerW*; *Melody Maker* 28 Mar. 1992, 38.

Tiwi Music. Music of the indigenous people who inhabit Bathurst and Melville Islands, off the coast of the NT. There is no Tiwi word or concept which can be directly translated using the European word or concept 'music.' *Kuruwala* is commonly translated as 'to sing' and *yoi* as 'to dance'. These terms however, need further clarification as Tiwi and European classification systems and conceptual orders differ. The terms *kuruwala* and *yoi* embrace multidimensional performance events: both may be used to refer to the whole event or to any particular element of the event (for example, the song, singing, the dance, dancing, the rhythmic pattern and the song text). Thus the Tiwi *yoi* incorporates many separate European categories. At the same time *yoi* and *kuruwala* divide several discrete European categories; European and Tiwi classifications thus intersect in an interesting way.

Although all Tiwi music is primarily vocal music with percussion accompaniment, the music which is performed during *yoi* is stylistically different from the music which is performed during *kuruwala*. *Yoi* songs are performed during various ceremonies and informally for relaxation and enjoyment. There is a large repertoire of *yoi* songs which individuals inherit the right to perform from their patrilineal relatives; alternatively individuals may compose their own songs about any subject they choose. Although both men and women are able to compose and/or perform *yoi* songs, men are the more prolific. The songs are always sung as an accompaniment to dance and never for their own sake. A typical *yoi* song begins with a soloist who introduces a short text and rhythm (the melodic line is the same for all *yoi* songs) to a chorus who gradually join in the singing. The chorus also provides the percussion accompaniment, which may consist of handclapping, buttock-slapping and clapsticks. Once the chorus has learned the song the soloist often stops singing and concentrates on dancing. Each song lasts only for around one minute, but usually many songs are performed in succession.

Kuruwala songs are musically more elaborate than *yoi* songs, and there are several different types. One type, *Kulama,* are performed exclusively during the annual Kulama Yam Ceremony, and are only composed by men, but are performed by both men and women. The subject a composer may choose to sing about is not restricted, although there are specific stages during the ceremony where it is appropriate to sing songs which express specific emotions (for example, grief, anger or respect for one's mother-in-law). The *kulama* men compose the songs well in advance, as great emphasis is placed on originality and creative ability. *Kulama* songs are in verse form, and consist of between three and 10 verses, and may take between two and 10 minutes to perform. The composer sings the vocal solo and accompanies himself with *murukungwa* (fighting clubs). Ideally his female relatives will join in the singing after the first couple of verses, combining the textual material the composer has already introduced with their own melodies.

FURTHER REFERENCE
A. Grau, Dreaming, Dancing, Kinship: The Study of *Yoi*, the Dance of the Tiwi of Melville and Bathurst Islands, North Australia, PhD, Queen's University, Belfast, 1983; idem, 'Sing a Dance: Dance a Song: The Relationship between the Two Types of Formalised Movements and Music among the Tiwi of Melville and Bathurst Islands, North Australia', *Dance Research* 1/2 (1983), 32–44; A.J. Reynolds, Tiwi music: an examination of *yoi* and *kunuwala*, BMus(Hons), ANU, 1994.

AMANDA JANE REYNOLDS

Tjijiku Inma.   (Pitjantjatjara) play ceremonies. See *Aboriginal Music* §2(iv).

TMusA.   Teacher of Music, Australia. A diploma awarded by the *AMEB based on written and practical examinations in studio music teaching methods, taken after the completion of prerequisites in the AMEB's advanced practical and theoretical examinations. Unlike classroom teacher training qualifications, the award does not certify completion of a course and has no formal status with Australian education authorities, but it nevertheless tests knowledge very relevant to studio music teaching, takes more than a year to complete, and has served as the primary qualification of many private music teachers in Australia.

Tognetti, Richard   (*b* Canberra, 4 Aug. 1965), violinist. He studied with Alice Waten at the NSW State Conservatorium 1976–84, with Igor Ozim at Berne Conservatory 1987–89, winning the Tschumi Prize in 1989. He has been director and leader of the Australian Chamber Orchestra since 1989, and co-director of the Huntington Festival. With the Australian Chamber Orchestra he has appeared on 12 international tours, including the Musikverein's international chamber orchestra series (1990), the BBC Proms (1992), the Concertgebouw Summer Festival (1992), at Carnegie Hall (1993, 1995), and at the Teatro Colón (1993). He has been soloist with the Sydney and Melbourne Symphony Orchestras. Works commissioned for the orchestra and given under his direction include *Lament* (Sculthorpe), *Strung Out* (Smalley), *Figures in a Landscape* (Smalley), *Sono Petal* (Dean), *Shakhmat/Supremat* (Smetanin), and works arranged for them include *Kaddisch* (Ravel), *String Quartet No. 1* (Janáček), *String Quartet No. 2* (Szymanowski), and *Black Angels* (Crumb).

FURTHER REFERENCE
For recordings, see *Australian Chamber Orchestra*. See also *CA* (1995–96).

CLIVE O'CONNELL

Tolhurst, George   (*b* Maidstone, England, 1827; *d* Barnstaple, England, 18 Jan. 1877), composer. Arriving in Melbourne in December 1852 with his father William Henry Tolhurst, he became a teacher of vocal music at the Denominational School Board July–August 1854, professor of vocal music at St Patrick's College 1859, singing master for the National Board February 1862 to October 1863, and organist at St James' Cathedral from 1864. His anthem *God Preserve our Sovereign's Viceroy* was premiered at Geelong in the presence of the Governor in March 1858. He maintained a piano studio at St Kilda until March 1866, when he left for London with his wife and children. A strong personality and prolific composer, his compositions, which display a lack of both skill and originality, were well received by the public. He is remembered solely for his oratorio, *Ruth*.

WORKS (Selective)
A Christmas Song (Southwark: Blackman, [1846]); *England, the Land of the Free* (Southwark: Blackman, [1846]); *Where There's a Will, There's a Way* (London: Jefferys, [1849]); 'O, Call It By Some Better Name', *Illustrated Journal of Australasia* 3 (1857), 176–8; 'God Preserve Our Sovereign's Viceroy', *Illustrated Journal of Australasia* 3 (1857), 276–8; 'The 'Post' Galop', *Illustrated Melbourne Post* 25 June 1864, 16; 'Christmas in Australia', *Illustrated Melbourne Post* 24 Dec. 1864; *Ruth* (London: George Tolhurst, [1867]); *There's Sunshine in the Sky* (London: Duncan Davison, [1872]); *The Little Brown Jug* (London: George Tolhurst, [1875]); *Pray Without Ceasing* (London: Broome, [1876]).

FURTHER REFERENCE
His writings include 'The Wagner Controversy—Poetic Basis', *Musical Times* 1 Apr. 1874, 459. See also *Age* 5 Nov. 1859, 5; *Argus* 10 Dec. 1860, 6; *Melbourne Directory*, annual, 1858–66; *Musical Times* 1 July 1858, 275; 1 Sept. 1864, 355; 1 Mar. 1868, 316.

ROYSTON GUSTAVSON

Tomasetti, Glen(ys) Ann   (*b* Melbourne, 21 May 1929), folk singer-songwriter. After studying literature and history at the University of Melbourne, she began performing traditional songs during the folk-song revival in the 1950s, then wrote songs commenting on current issues, releasing *Glen Tomasetti Sings* (1961). She co-founded *Traynor's, a folk music coffee lounge at Frank Traynor's Jazz Agency in 1964, then broadcast *World of Folkmusic* for radio (1965) and *Folk Music and Legends* (1967), and released her *Ballad of Bill White* (1966). From 1969 to 1970 she was resident songwriter for the current affairs program *This Week,* and wrote anti-Vietnam War and anti-conscription songs sung at political rallies in the coming years. After completing an MA on Australian folklore she wrote a first novel and has been increasingly known as a writer.

FURTHER REFERENCE
Recordings include *Gold Rush Songs* (1975, Museum of Victoria SMV 001) and *Songs From A Seat In The Carriage*. See also *OxfordF; OxfordL; Who's Who of Australian Writers.*

Toop, Richard (*b* Chichester, England, 1 Aug. 1945), musicologist. He studied at Hull University and worked as a pianist, conductor and freelance translator. From 1973 he was Stockhausen's teaching assistant at the Cologne Hochschule für Musik, and came to Australia in 1975 as lecturer (later head of musicology) at the NSW State Conservatorium. He has written brilliantly thought-provoking and clever music criticism and commentary for a number of Australian publications and has published his research on Stockhausen and postwar European compositional techniques in *Perspectives of New Music, Studies in Music* and elsewhere. His influence on young composers in Sydney has been considerable, and he has played an important part in introducing recent European ideas such as the new complexity to Australia.

FURTHER REFERENCE
ADMR.

Toowoomba, pop. (1991) 75 991. City on the edge of the Darling Downs and the Great Dividing Range, inland from Brisbane, founded in 1853. In 1866 'grand lyrical entertainments' were given in Mrs Gentle's Horse and Jockey Inn, while a School of Arts attracting, for example, the Melbourne Opera Co. catered for more serious music-lovers. A music shop from the Palings chain, Paling, Kay & Jeffries, was set up in 1878; Kay and Jefferies were prominent in the 1880s as concert organisers in Toowoomba. A significant German population produced by 1858 the first of several German bands, from which developed the current Municipal Band. The Germans also formed a Glee Club which developed by 1878 into the Verein Teutonia, and a highly successful 40-voice Liedertafel established in 1902.

Toowoomba has a long vocal and choral tradition. A Toowoomba Operatic Co. operated early in the century. The Toowoomba Musical Union, formed in 1879, became in 1933 the Choral Society, now featuring senior and junior departments. The Toowoomba Philharmonic Society was established in 1903 under foundation conductor Stanley Hobson, developing from the earlier Austral Choir. Toowoomba has produced several nationally recognised musicians including Leonard *Dommett, Elsie *Hall, Geoffrey Saba and Richard *Mills. Current groups include the amateur Toowoomba Concert Orchestra and the Sinfonia, a semi-professional training orchestra attached to the University of Southern Queensland, which boasts a small but active music department. The Toowoomba Chamber Music Society hosts concerts by local and visiting artists. There are also the Darling Downs Youth Orchestra and the Toowoomba Jazz Society. The Toowoomba Eisteddfod (commenced 1942) has grown to become one of the largest in Australia.

FURTHER REFERENCE
Robert Dansie, *History of Toowoomba . . . A Series of Articles: Ceremonies and Celebrations* (Toowoomba: Toowoomba Education Centre, 1978–82); idem, *1880: Events and News Reports in Toowoomba A Century Ago* (Toowoomba: Toowoomba Education Centre, 1980); idem, *A Deserving Class of People: Toowoomba's German Heritage 1855 to 1885* (Toowoomba: Toowoomba Education Centre, 1980); idem, *To Foster the Arts and Science: Austral—the Beginning 1903–4* (Toowoomba: Toowoomba Education Centre, 1991).   PHILLIP GEARING

Torrance, Revd George William (*b* Rathmines, Dublin, 1835; *d* Kilkenny, Ireland, 20 Aug. 1907), composer, organist. He studied music in Dublin and Leipzig and was ordained a Church of England priest in 1866. After his arrival at Williamstown in 1869 he was at Christ Church, South Yarra, 1870–71, St John's, Latrobe Street, 1871–77, 1895–97, All Saints, Geelong, 1877–78 and Holy Trinity, Balaclava, 1878–95. From 1872 to 1876 he was acting principal of Trinity College, later affiliated with the University of Melbourne. He returned to Ireland in 1897, where he held further clerical positions in and around Ossory.

In Melbourne Torrance was highly regarded as an organist, conductor, examiner, scholar and as a fine composer. He was honorary organist at his own parish, Holy Trinity, Balaclava, 1880–82, an adviser on church organs, examiner for the Royal College of Music and convenor of the inaugural choir at St Paul's Cathedral. He presented a lecture on music (outlining something of his vision for colonial music) at the opening of the Melbourne Social Science Congress in November 1880. Composition was a lifelong interest for Torrance and took the form of oratorios, anthems, service settings, hymns, an opera, songs and madrigals, many of which were published in Australia, Ireland and England. His third oratorio, *The Revelation*, was premiered in the Melbourne Town Hall on 27 June 1882, and a concert of his music was given at the same venue on 28 February 1881 to raise funds for the St Paul's Cathedral School of Music. Torrance was awarded the DMus in 1879 by the University of Dublin and the University of Melbourne. (See *Church Music* §1, *Hymnody.*)

WORKS (Selective)
Oratorio: *The Revelation* (Novello, 1899). Service Music: *Magnificat & Nunc Dimittis* (MS Trinity College, University of Melbourne, n.d.), *Of the Father's Love* (London: Novello, 1898), *Lord, I have loved the habitation of thy house*, anthem (London: Novello, 1901). Hymns include *Adoration, Advent, Euroclydon, Gladness, Melbourne, Nativity* and *Trust* in *The Church Hymnal* (Dublin: APCK, 1883); Heber and Trust in *78 Australian Hymn Tunes* (London: Novello, [1892]).

FURTHER REFERENCE

R. Stevens, *ADB*, 6; R.P. Stewart, *GroveD*; J.D. Brown and S. Stratton, *British Musical Biography* (Birmingham: Stratton, 1897); J.D. Champlin and W.F. Apthorp, *Cyclopedia of Music and Musicians* (New York: Scribner, 1890); E.A.C. Farran, 'Dr George William Torrance', *Victorian Historical Magazine* 39 (1968), 113–26; J.A. Grant, ed., *Perspective of a Century . . . Trinity College* (Melbourne: Council of Trinity College, 1972); E.N. Matthews, *Colonial Organs and Organ-Builders* (Melbourne: MUP, 1969); A. Sutherland, et al., *Victoria and its Metropolis*, vol. 2 (Melbourne: McCarron, 1888).   DIANNE GOME

Torres Strait Islands. Islands off north-eastern Australia, in the waters between Papua New Guinea and Cape York Peninsula, populated by Australia's only indigenous Melanesian minority group. Many Islanders also live in Australian mainland cities and towns, and wherever they live, they express their culture and identity through music and dance performances. Their cultural and geographical groupings fall into four broad categories: western, 'top' western (northern), central and eastern. People of the first three groupings speak the Western language, Kala Lagaw Ya, or its dialects; people of the eastern islands speak Meriam Mir, an indigenous Papuan language. The lingua franca of Torres Strait is a creole language, referred to by Islanders as Broken, Kriol or occasionally as Pizin. Most Torres Strait Islanders also have English as a second language; teaching in the schools is given in English.

The music of Torres Strait Islanders is primarily vocal and accompanied by instruments. Because the people are generally bilingual or even multilingual, song texts can be in a variety of languages. The introduction of Christianity has had a profound influence; before the arrival of the first representatives of the London Missionary Society (LMS) in 1871, Islander music culture reflected the diversity of the cultural and geographical groupings across the Strait.

1. Pre-Christian Music and Dance. Members of the 1898 Cambridge Anthropological Expedition, led by Alfred Cort Haddon, made the earliest moving film and phonograph recordings of dance and music performances in eastern Torres Strait, but in the 1960s, when the Australian anthropologist Jeremy Beckett recorded music performances in Torres Strait, he reported: 'There have been no new compositions in traditional style for at least thirty years' (Beckett 1972:1). Nevertheless, Beckett was able to record sacred songs dating from the pre-Christian period, many of which used archaic language texts. Formerly, ritual dance and chant were performed for cult ceremonies, and men wore elaborate ceremonial masks for dances performed in religious rituals. Haddon (1893: 134) believed that dance masks were not worn for secular dances.

In addition to the single-headed skin drum (usually obtained from Papua), Islanders played flutes, pan-pipes and jaws harps (Myers in Haddon 1912:238). Other musical instruments included whistles, shell trumpets, bamboo clappers, bamboo rattles, and a variety of rattles made of the dried fruits of trees and climbing plants. Haddon (1912: 284) observed that songs 'may be accompanied by drum-beating on ceremonial or festive occasions, and may be sung, spoken in recitative in a humming tone, or even muttered'. Both Haddon (1912: 289) and, later, the missionary W.H. Macfarlane (1922), emphasised the importance of dances and laments performed at death ceremonies in pre-Christian times. Written accounts dealing with early music and dance refer mainly to men's performances; almost nothing is known of women's or children's music. In some Islander communities, men's dance from this period is still remembered and performed; it is referred to as 'Old Fashioned Dance' *(lagae kab,* Kala Lagaw Ya; *kab kar,* Meriam Mir, meaning 'the dance of the island'), and is accompanied only by drums and the dancers' rattles (Beckett and Mabo [*c*.1987]: 7, 10).

2. Since Christianity. (i) Sacred Music. The Christian missionaries not only altered the music cultures through the introduction of Protestant hymnody, thereby producing a degree of uniformity in the performance of sacred music, but also through the influence of individual Pacific Islander pastors prohibited performances of some dance-forms while condoning others. Nowadays, dance and music are arguably the most significant visual and aural expressions of Islander beliefs, knowledge and behaviour, for they have come to symbolise Islander life itself. Churches, particularly the Anglican Church of Australia (which accepted responsibility from the LMS in 1915) and the Roman Catholic Church, support and encourage performances of both sacred and secular music; the Pentecostalist sects have also recently had influence, especially through the prohibition of the performance of secular dances and the encouragement of the singing of evangelical songs with English texts.

(ii) Secular Music and Dance. The early missionaries were LMS representatives from islands in both Polynesia and Melanesia. Pacific Islanders who visited or settled in Torres Strait brought with them their own musical traditions, influences of which can be seen today in the contemporary secular music and dance of the Torres Strait Islanders. Dance genres based on Pacific Islander dance either retain song texts in Pacific Islander languages or are locally composed using vernacular texts. Such dances include the *taibobo,* an adaptation of chants and dances from Rotuma, and 'sit-down' dances based on Samoan dance (Beckett and Mabo *c.* 1987:6). In the early 20th century, Islanders developed a song and dance form termed in Kala Lagaw Ya *kasa girer* (gammon dance) or in Meriam Mir *segur kab wed* (play dance and song) (Mabo 1984:34; Beckett 1981:3); this Island Dance is now the most popular form of contemporary dance performed by Islanders throughout Torres Strait (Beckett 1987:56). Island Dance spread north to Papua, and south to Cape York Peninsula.

Some Torres Strait Islander festivals and ceremonies are also the result of Pacific Islander influence, but such events have been transformed or adapted by the local people to meet their own cultural needs and values. Likewise, the instrumental accompaniment for some dances, provided by a length of bamboo, rolled mat or kerosene tin (each of which is beaten with two sticks), and later by the guitar and ukulele, are based upon Pacific Islander usage (Beckett and Mabo *c.* 1987:10). Dancers are usually accompanied by a separate group of singers and instrumentalists, although occasionally dances may be performed with drum accompaniment only. Musical instruments for dance consist of a tubular, hand-held, single-headed skin drum (beaten with the bare hand) and a small length of bamboo, or a small bamboo slit-drum, beaten with two sticks.

Texts for Island Dance songs cover a wide range of topics; many dances are performed solely for entertainment and, depending on the occasion, can be competitive. Generally speaking, the melody of a song and its accompanying dance movements have more importance than the meaning of the song text. New dance songs continue to be composed, and songs that have been retained in the repertoire are sometimes updated with new choreography. Both men and women perform dances in which they shake or strike hand-held rattles; clapping is also a feature of some dances, although it is usually only male dancers who incorporate body-slapping in their dance movements. For some Island dances, the dancers substitute bamboo clappers for the hand-held rattles; in others, elaborate dance gear forms part of the dancers' accoutrements.

The most important festival for Islanders is the Coming of the Light, an annual celebration commemorating the arrival of the first missionaries in Erub (Darnley Island) on 1 July 1871; other festivals include the biennial Torres Strait Cultural Festival in May, and the Torres Strait Music Fest in June. Within individual island communities, occasions for feasting, singing and dancing include Christmas, New Year, NAIDOC week (a national celebration of Australia's indigenous peoples), and tombstone unveiling ceremonies. Islander musicians and dancers also perform at multicultural festivals held in mainland locations, and young Islanders on the mainland have the opportunity to engage in other kinds of music and dance. Reggae has recently been especially popular, and the career of Christine ★Anu, a pop singer of Islander descent, is followed with interest. In the Torres Strait itself, the Torres Strait Islander Media Association (TSIMA) plays an increasingly important role in recording and broadcasting performances of Islander music. Several audio recordings have been commercially released by TSIMA; these include contemporary songs, both secular and sacred.

(iii) Contemporary Sacred Songs. New religious songs first introduced by the Pacific Islander missionaries had parts for female as well as male voices; these hymns, composed in the vernacular in two-part harmony, with the two parts moving independently and usually accompanied by a single-skin drum, are structurally comparable to the *himene* of the Society Islands and Cook Islands though simpler and less exuberant (Beckett 1981:2). The contemporary Anglican hymnody of the Torres Strait Islanders, although usually sung in Torres Strait languages, continues to exhibit musical characteristics of the early hymns first taught by the Polynesian pastors. The lead singers are women, whose combined musical knowledge forms a valuable repository of language texts and sacred music repertoire. As well as these Polynesian-style hymns, members of the Anglican Church sing Sankey-type hymns, with alternating stanza and refrain.

Other kinds of sacred songs are sung in English and are primarily of two types: hymns from the Australian Anglican hymnal, and *koras* (Kriol, chorus, indicating evangelical songs). *Koras* became popular from the 1960s onwards, largely as a result of the influence of the Pentecostal churches; in the Anglican Church they are accompanied by drums and acoustic guitars, but in the Pentecostal churches by electric guitars and modern drum kits. Islanders continue to create their own sacred songs in various styles, using both English and vernacular language texts. The Anglo-Catholic affiliation of the Anglican Church in Torres Strait means that, like the Roman Catholic Church, services often include a sung mass, and this too may be locally composed. In addition, hymns with vernacular texts provide an important resource of language knowledge and cultural heritage. As a result of the influences of the different Christian churches, the variety of sacred song types in Torres Strait is extensive and the repertoire continues to grow. See also *Aboriginal Music*, §4(i).

FURTHER REFERENCE

Anglican Church of Australia, *Island Language Hymns* (The Diocese of Carpentaria, Torres Strait Region, [Thursday Island], 1995).

——, *Hymns and Songs of Torres Strait* [Audiocassette, n.d., Impact MCI 104]

Beckett, Jeremy, *Torres Strait Islanders: Custom and Colonialism* (Cambridge: CUP, 1987).

——, comp. *Traditional Music of Torres Strait*. With musical analysis and transcriptions by Trevor A. Jones. [Audiodisc and booklet.] (Canberra: AIAS, 1972).

——, and Bryan Butler, eds, *Modern Music of Torres Strait*. [Audiocassette and booklet.] (Canberra: AIAS, 1981).

——, and Koiki Mabo, Dancing in Torres Strait. Unpub. paper (18pp), James Cook University, *c.*1987.

Choksy, Lois, and Frank York, 'Music in the Islands of the Torres Strait', *Bulletin of the International Kodály Society* 18/2 (1993), 27–33.

Egan, Ted, coll. *Traditional Music of the Torres Strait* [Audiocassette]. (Aboriginal Arts Board, Sydney, 1976).

Townsville

Haddon, Alfred Cort, 'The secular and ceremonial dances of Torres Straits', *Internationales Archiv für Ethnographie* 6 (1893), 131–62.

——, ed. *Reports of the Cambridge Anthropological Expedition to Torres Straits*, vol. 4. (Cambridge: CUP, 1912).

Laade, Wolfgang, *Traditional Songs of the Western Torres Strait, South Pacific* (New York: Ethnic Folkways Library, 1977).

Lawrie, Margaret, *Myths and Legends of Torres Strait*. With accompanying audiodisc 'Songs from Torres Strait'. (Brisbane: UQP, 1970).

Mabo, Koiki, 'Music of the Torres Strait', *Black Voices* 1/1 (1984), 33–6.

Macfarlane, W. H., 'The death dance of the Murray Islanders', *Australian Board of Missions Review* 13/3 (1922), 42–4.

Mairu-Kaczmarek, Annie, 'Music on Badu Island—Torres Strait', *Black Voices* 4/1 (1988), 36–8.

Pilot, Boggo, comp., *The Diocese of North Queensland, Eastern and Western Hymn Book and Liturgy, Torres Strait Island Ministry* (Arr. by Rev. Boggo Pilot. Townsville, [*c.*1973]).

Savage, Stephanie, ed., *Torres Strait Music Resource Kit* (Cairns: Queensland Education Department Regional Equity and Development Centre, in press).

York, Frank, *Children's Songs of the Torres Strait Islands*. With accompanying audiocassette (Bateman's Bay, NSW: Owen Martin, 1990).

——, and Lois Choksy, 'Developing a culturally appropriate music curriculum for Torres Strait Island [*sic*] schools', in Heath Lees, ed., *Musical Connections: Tradition and Change* ([Auckland]: International Society for Music Education, 1994), 111–19. HELEN REEVES LAWRENCE

Townsville, pop. (1991) 82 809, city and port, with its sister city Thuringowa situated at the mouth of the Ross Creek on Cleveland Bay, eastern Queensland. Before European settlement in 1864, the Townsville region was home to the peoples of the Wulgurukabba language group; records by anthropologists Houzé and Jacques (1884) include rudimentary descriptions of the indigenous music.

Early audiences were drawn to Townsville in its initial role as a conduit for the Charters Towers goldfields. John Melton Black figured in early theatrical ventures. In 1866–68 the first (unnamed) visiting artists appeared at the Criterion Hotel; in 1869 the Exchange Hotel hosted Marie Carandini; in 1869 the Theatre Royal opened with a vaudeville entitled *Le Chalet*, accompanied by Signor Panizza, a local music teacher, but it closed in 1870. The Olympic Theatre, Townsville's first purpose-built theatre, operated between 1874 and 1877, hosting three concerts by Anna Bishop in 1875. The Musical Union's first concert was in 1876 and the Townsville Liedertafel was established by 1885. In 1877 the School of Arts Theatre opened with a variety show by the Townsville Orpheus Glee Club (formerly the Amateur Dramatic Club). It hosted performances by violinist Remenyi (1886), Hart and Searelle's Opera Co., the Lynch Family Bellringers, and the Carandinis once again.

In 1891 Her Majesty's opened; it hosted the Geisha and Lilliputian Opera companies, Henry Cowan's Minstrel Co., Melba (1909), and a Chinese Opera. The Orchestral Society gave monthly orchestral concerts in Queen's Gardens. In 1900 the Theatre Royal opened, venue for many local productions such as the Townsville Popular Variety Minstrels, the Townsville Review Co., the Dampiers, Amelita Galli-Curci, and Anna Pavlova (1929). There were also live musical items during reel changes of silent films (Quintrell's Pictures, 1909). Soprano Gladys *Moncrieff made her debut there in *The Pirates of Penzance* in 1905. The first Eisteddfod was held in the Theatre Royal in 1906, after the Musical Union (previously the West End Musical Union and the City Choir) formed the Townsville Competitive Choir with choristers from the churches. From this grew the Townsville Choral and Orchestral Society in which the Foley, Nott and Pease families have been prominent. Ernest Toy and pianist Aggie Rawes (Gladys Raines) made their debuts at the Eisteddfod. In 1930 the Wintergarden Theatre opened, and a concert version of *Carmen* with Adeline Bertheau and Jim Gilchrist was staged by the Choral and Orchestral Society in 1933.

By the 1960s the Choral and Orchestral Society was staging operettas such as *The Desert Song*. Numerous amateur groups such as the Townsville Brass and the Townsville Youth Orchestra have been supplemented by annual visits of the Queensland Symphony Orchestra and the Elizabethan Theatre Trust. Musica Viva toured from the early 1960s until 1987. In 1973 the Theatre Royal closed, and the Wintergarden and the newly revived His Majesty's became the main venues. More recent developments which have accelerated audience exposure to quality music and created performance opportunities for local musicians include the opening of the Civic Theatre (1978), the North Queensland Concerto Competition (1980), the Community Music Centre (1983), the community radio station 4TTT-FM (1982), the department of music at James Cook University and the annual Australian Festival of Chamber Music (established 1991).

FURTHER REFERENCE

Lynne Clancy, *History of the Townsville Choral and Orchestral Society* (Townsville: Townsville Choral and Orchestral Society, 1992); Harold Love, 'Stock Companies, Travelling Stars and the Birth of "The Firm" (1854–1900)', in *The Australian Stage: A Documented History*, ed. Harold Love (Sydney: UNSWP, 1984); Dorothy M. Gibson-Wilde, 'Entertainment in Townsville', in *Peripheral Visions: Essays on Australian Regional and Local History*, ed. Brian J. Dalton (Townsville: James Cook University, 1991), 197–222; idem, with John Matthew, *The Show Must Go On!*, Program notes to 10th Anniversary Concert, Townsville Civic Theatre, 1988; Emile Houzé and Victor Jacques, 'Les Australiens du Musée du Nord', *Bulletin de la Société Royale Belge d'Anthropologie et de Préhistoire de Bruxelles* 3 (1884), 53–154 [see 141–2]; Gladys Moncrieff, *My Life of Song* (Brisbane: Rigby, 1971); *A Historical Listing of Concerts and Theatrical Performances in Townsville*, pamphlet, Townsville Library Service Local History Collection, n.d.

PETER GORE-SYMES

Tozer, Geoffrey (*b* northern India, 5 Nov. 1954), pianist. He began performing at the age of seven and appeared with the Melbourne Symphony Orchestra at the age of eight. The youngest person to be awarded a Churchill fellowship (aged 14), he went to London where he first performed with the BBC Symphony under Sir Colin Davis, and was the youngest participant in the Leeds International Piano Competition in 1969. Joint winner of Alex de Vries Belgian Prize and first prize in the Royal Overseas League Music Festival, London (both 1970), he won the bronze medal in the Rubinstein International Piano Competition (1977) and studied piano in London with Eileen Ralf.

A tireless exponent of the works of Nikolai Medtner, his recordings of this composer's three concertos received the *Diapason d'Or* award (France) in 1992 and a Grammy Award (USA) nomination in 1993; he has also recorded piano concertos of Alan Rawsthorne, Liszt, Rimsky-Korsakov, Tchaikovsky (No 3), the complete works for piano and orchestra by Respighi and Stravinsky's *Capriccio*, as well as solo works by Liszt, complete sonatas of Korngold and solo piano works by Busoni. He is also renowned as a skilled concert improviser. He has toured China, Japan, South-East Asia, India, the UK and Europe. An inaugural recipient of the Australia Council creative fellowship in 1989, he now lives in London.

FURTHER REFERENCE

Recordings include *For Children* (Tall Poppies TP001); Medtner works (Chandos); Tchaikovsky Concerto No. 3 (Chandos); Respighi complete works for piano and orchestra (Chandos); Stravinsky's *Capriccio* (Chandos); Korngold complete sonatas (Chandos); Busoni works (Chandos).

CYRUS MEHER-HOMJI

Trad. Australian jazz revival style of the post-World War II years, at first chiefly derived from the Dixieland style of the early 1920s, but diversifying after 1950. Its chief early exponent was Graeme ★Bell and his bands from 1946; he was associated with the founding of the annual Australian Jazz Convention (1946–), held each December, where the style may still heard. See also *Dixieland*.

Trailblazers, The. Country music performance organisation. Formed in Melbourne in the late 1940s as a non-commercial collective, it was conceived and managed by Bill Earl. Its members comprised more than a dozen part-time artists, including the young Les Partell and the Hawking Brothers. They performed in various combinations on radio 3XY, at charity concerts, in professional development sessions and similar ventures. In 1956 they mounted a continuous two-day concert outdoors at the Moomba Festival in 1956, its members working in shifts, and from 1958 their radio program was syndicated to 50 stations. At their height they were the major influence in country music throughout the southern states.

FURTHER REFERENCE

Recordings include the EP *Country Hall of Fame* (Planet PZ 102) and the album *The Trailblazers' Stage Show* (Planet PP 015). For discography, see *WatsonC*, II. See also *WatsonC*, II, 109–17.

Transposed Heads, The. Opera in one act, music and libretto by Peggy ★Glanville-Hicks (1954) after the Thomas Mann story. First performed by the Louisville Opera Co., Kentucky, USA, on 3 Apr. 1954 and in Australia at the Adelaide Festival in 1976. A vocal score was published (New York, 1953). It was recorded by the Louisville Co. (LOU 545–6) and the ABC (1992, ABC 434 139–2).

Travelling Man, The. Opera in one act, music and text by Fritz ★Hart after Gregory. First performed by the Melbourne Conservatorium in 1920.

Travelling Showman, The. Country music ballad (1970) by Tex ★Morton. Perhaps an autobiographical narrative, Morton recorded the song in NZ; it has been reissued on *The Travelling Showman* (EMI CD 8142092).

Traynor, Frank (*b* Melbourne, 8 Aug. 1927; *d* Melbourne, 22 Feb. 1985), jazz trombonist, bandleader. He learned piano, switching to trombone by the time he formed his first band in 1947. Playing with the bands of Len ★Barnard, Neville Sherburn and Frank ★Johnson, he formed his Jazz Preachers in 1958 as the house band for the Melbourne Jazz Club. By 1960 the Preachers had achieved great celebrity, with numerous residencies including at Traynor's folk and jazz club (1961–76). They also played at balls, school concerts, festivals, on television, and recorded prolifically. Traynor was also an energetic jazz proselytiser through his writing, teaching, and his production of lecture-recitals.

FURTHER REFERENCE

Recordings include *Jazz From The Pulpit,* Frank Traynor's Jazz Preachers (1963, W&G Records WG-B-1722); *Favourites,* Frank Traynor's Jazz Preachers (1979, Roseleaf Records/EMI YPRX-1632-B). See also *OxfordJ*; Marcus Breen, 'Jazz in Discussion, Interviews with Frank Traynor and Bruce Clarke', in *Missing in Action: Australian Popular Music in Perspective*, ed. M. Breen (Verbal Graphics, Vic., 1987), 98–106.

BRUCE JOHNSON

Trent, Jackie (*b* Newcastle-Under-Lyme, Staffordshire, England, 6 Sept. 1940), popular music singer-songwriter. Singing from the age of nine, she began a professional career on leaving school and became one of the UK's top recording artists, appearing on the television shows *Morecombe and Wise* and *Des O'Connor*. She hosted her own television show, and recorded *Where Are You Now,* which reached No. 1 in the UK charts in 1965. She married songwriter Tony Hatch in 1967; their single *The Two Of Us* (1967) became an international chart success, then *Bye Bye, My Love* and *That's You* also entered the charts in 1968. They came to Australia in 1982, establishing the songwriting partnership Mr and Mrs Music at Sydney, and writing for film and television. They have produced *My Country* (1982) and the theme for the television show *Neighbours* (1985).

FURTHER REFERENCE
Melbourne *Herald* 12 Feb. 1986.

Tribe, Kenneth Wilberforce   (*b* 6 Feb. 1914), solicitor. He joined the fledgling board of *Musica Viva in 1950, and during a term of 36 years (chairman 1974–86) profoundly influenced its remarkable growth into a vast network for the promotion of fine chamber music concerts around Australia. His combination of passionate commitment to music and admirable clarity of thought made him sought after for board roles, and he served as a member of the Australia Council Music Board 1974–77, ABC Commissioner 1978–83, management co-ordinator for the Australian Opera 1979–81, chairman of Nimrod Theatre 1983–87, and chairman of the Australian Chamber Orchestra Foundation 1986–89, as well as being on the boards of competitions, benevolent trusts, and several leading music schools. His report as chairman of the National Committee of Inquiry into Orchestras, *Study into the Future Development of Orchestras in Australia* (the 'Tribe Report' 1985), while never fully implemented, remains a significant commentary on Australia's musical outlook. He was honoured with the AM in 1975, the AO in 1982 and the AC in 1989.

Triffids, The.   Country-rock band (1978–) formed in Perth, originally comprised of Dave McComb (vocals, bass), Rob McComb (violin, guitar), Phil Kakulas (guitar, vocals), Margaret Gillard (keyboards), Andrew McGowan (guitar), Byron Sinclair (bass), and Alan McDonald (drums, vocals). McComb and McDonald had played together from 1976, and with their new band they played at Perth venues from 1978, in 1983 making their debut album *Treeless Plain* and touring the eastern states. They released *Born Sandy Devotional* which reached No. 27 in the UK album charts in 1986, and *In The Pines* (1987) featured folk and country material. They gradually acquired a wide following in Europe, appearing at the Glastonbury Festival in England and making a live recording at the Stockholm Festival, *Stockholm Live* (1990). With fine songwriting suggesting the Australian countryside and evocative vocals from McComb, they combine folk and country influences with rock.

FURTHER REFERENCE
Recordings include *Treeless Plain* (Hot HOT 1003), *Born Sandy Devotional* (White Records L38521), *In The Pines* (1987, White L38718), *Stockholm Live* (1990 Mushroom L30231). A recent

album is *Australian Melodrama* (1994, White D31182). For discography, see *SpencerA*. See also *SpencerW*; *BakerA*, 28–32; *GuinnessP*, IV, 2532.

Triple J.   Non-commercial youth radio station, founded (1975) by the ABC at Sydney to play new Australian rock music. At first broadcasting as 2JJ on the AM band, from 1980 it moved to FM as 2JJJ. Concentrating on unsigned Australian bands, the station was the first to air Nirvana, Pearl Jam, and Right Said Fred!, as well as many Australian bands. With a formula of 35 per cent Australian content, their programs include live field recordings, and 'the Hottest 100', an independent charting of Australian and new foreign artists. Starting its expansion to other centres in 1989, by 1996 it was a national network, heard in all capital cities and 44 regional centres.

Tristan and Iseult.   Opera in 13 scenes by Gillian *Whitehead, libretto by Malcolm Crowthers and Michael Hill. First performed at Maidment Theatre, Auckland, NZ, in May 1978.

Tritton, Harold Percival Croydon ('Duke')   (*b* Fivedock, Sydney, 1886; *d* Concord, Sydney, 1965), traditional singer, songwriter. He grew up in Sydney but spent most of his life working in the outback, travelling and learning songs on the way. In 1952 he responded to a request for material from the *Bulletin* for Nancy Keesing and Douglas Stewart, then became a key figure in the folk music revival, performing and giving workshops for the Sydney Bush Music Club and assisting John *Meredith with his folk-song collecting. He also wrote songs in the traditional bush ballad style, including *Shearing In The Bar* and *The Rouseabout's Prayer*. With a strong, clear voice and prodigious memory, he was a highly significant source of songs, verse and yarns, recalling children's songs, dances and whipping-tunes from as early as the 1890s.

FURTHER REFERENCE
His autobiography was published in the *Bulletin* and then as *Time Means Tucker* (1964, reprint Sydney: Akron Press, 1984). See also John Meredith, *Duke of the Outback* (Ascot Vale, Vic.: Red Rooster Press, 1983).

Trocadero Ballroom.   Opened on 3 Apr. 1936 at George Street, Sydney, the Trocadero was financed by Ezra Norton, with support from entrepreneur James C. Bendrodt. With space for 2000 dancers, it became Australia's primary dance venue, its link with American-influenced pop music strengthened by the patronage of US servicemen during World War II. In the postwar years it retained its pre-eminence, for example an official reception venue for Elizabeth II in 1954. Following Norton's death in 1967 the public dances were discontinued, and the final private function, on New Year's Eve 1969, used bandleader Frank *Coughlan, who had also opened the ballroom more than 32 years before. Demolished in 1971, it was replaced by a cinema complex.

FURTHER REFERENCE

Recordings include *The Troc* (1991, MBS Jazz 8, Linehan Series). See also Joan Ford, *Meet Me At The Trocadero* (Cowra, NSW: Joan Ford, 1995).

BRUCE JOHNSON

Truman, Ernest Edwin Philip (*b* Weston-Super-Mare, Somerset, England, 29 Dec. 1869; *d* Sydney, 6 Oct. 1948), organist. He began formal music studies at the age of 13 with A.J. Bath at Dunedin, NZ, and in 1885 moved to Sydney and studied piano with Julius Buddee. Truman enrolled at the Royal Conservatorium of Music, Leipzig, Germany, in 1888 and graduated in 1893 with a diploma. During this time he also qualified as ARCO and LRCM. He returned to Sydney in 1893 and served as occasional organist at several city churches. In 1909 he was appointed Sydney city organist, a post he held for 26 years, giving over 3000 concerts. His programs comprised organ music as well as transcriptions; his own transcriptions of complete operas and operettas were greatly enjoyed. He also wrote an operetta, *Club Life*, to a text by A.B. Paterson. A gifted musician, he was also a respected teacher of piano and organ, and accompanied many distinguished singers.

FURTHER REFERENCE

Graeme D. Rushworth, *ADB*, 12; idem, *Historic Organs of New South Wales* (Sydney: Hale & Iremonger, 1988), 397–8; *McCredieM*; Elizabeth Wood, *GroveD*.

GRAEME RUSHWORTH

Trumby. Country music ballad by Joe Daly, a stockman in north-west NSW. The story of an Aborigine who, unable to read a warning sign, drinks from a waterhole that has been poisoned to kill dingoes, and dies. It was recorded by Slim *Dusty, Barry *Thornton, Lindsay *Butler and Reg *Poole; Dusty found it was a great favourite with Aboriginal audiences in the Kimberleys, where its performance increased enrolments in government literacy classes.

FURTHER REFERENCE

It has been reissued in The *Best of Slim Dusty* (EMI TCOSX 7807) and is published in *Slim Dusty Songbook* (Melbourne: Anne O'Donovan, 1984), 42–45.

Tuckwell, Barry Emmanuel (*b* Melbourne, 5 Mar. 1931), french horn player, conductor. He had perfect pitch and studied at the NSW State Conservatorium. He played french horn with the Sydney Symphony Orchestra 1947–50, before going to Britain and playing with the Hallé Orchestra, among others. In 1955 he became the principal horn with the London Symphony Orchestra, a position he held for 13 years; as solo horn he featured on most of the orchestra's recordings during this period. Since then he has appeared as a horn soloist and with his own wind quintet. As a conductor Tuckwell has worked with many international orchestras, and was conductor of the Tasmanian Symphony Orchestra 1980–83 and conductor of the Maryland Orchestra

from 1982. He was professor of horn at the Royal Academy of Music, London, 1963–74, and has written several books on horn playing. Tuckwell has been called 'the leading horn player of his generation' and in Italy *Il Corno d'Oro* (the Golden Horn). He lives in Maryland, USA, with his American wife, Sue, having now retired from regular musical appointments. He was honoured with the OBE (1965), AC (1992) and an honorary DMus from the University of Sydney.

FURTHER REFERENCE

Recordings include Telemann, *Horn Concerto in D*, Cherubini, *Sonata No. 2 in F for Horn and Strings*, Forster, *Horn Concerto in E-flat*, Weber, *Horn Concertino in E minor*, L. Mozart, *Horn Concerto in D*, M. Haydn, *Horn Concerto in D*, Punto, *Horn Concertos*, and F. Haydn, *Horn Concerto in D*, Barry Tuckwell, hn, English Chamber Orchestra and the Academy of St Martin-in-the-Fields, cond. Neville Marriner (1996, EMI). His writings include *The Horn* (New York: G. Schirmer, 1983) and *Playing the Horn* (London: OUP, 1978). See also *CA* (1995–96); Magnus Magnusson, *Chambers Biographical Dictionary* (Edinburgh: Chambers, 1990); Niall O'Loughlin, *GroveD*; *WWA* (1996).

ROBERT PETERSON

Tully. Rock band (1969–72) formed in Sydney, originally comprised of Terry Wilson (vocals, flute), Colin Campbell (guitar), Michael Carlos (keyboards), Graham Colon (guitar, bass, vocals), Ken Firth (bass), Bobby Gebert (piano), Richard Lockwood (flute, saxophone, clarinet), and Robert Taylor (drums). Gaining a following in Sydney surfing venues, their debut album *Tully* (1970) revealed them as a thoughtful, creatively important band. They released only two more albums, *Love Is Hard* (1972), and the sound-track for the film *Sea Of Joy* (1972), each exploring its own sound world. The first Australian band to use the Moog synthesiser, they also employed sitar, violin and various woodwind instruments, producing gentle, entrancing music with long, well-played instrumental passages.

FURTHER REFERENCE

Recordings include *Tully* (1970, Columbia SCX O7926), *Love Is Hard* (1972, Harvest SHVL 607) and *Sea Of Joy* (1972, Harvest SHVL 605). For discography, see *SpencerA*. See also *McGrathA*; *SpencerW*.

Tunley, David Evatt (*b* Sydney, 3 May 1930), musicologist. Educated at the NSW State Conservatorium and the Universities of Durham (BMus 1958, MMus 1963) and Western Australia (DLitt by examination, 1970), from 1958 to 1994 he held positions in the department of music at the University of Western Australia as lecturer (later personal chair) in music. He won first prize in a competition for Australian composers at the Wangaratta Arts Festival, Victoria (1962) and studied composition with Nadia Boulanger 1964–65. As president of the Musicological Society of Australia 1980–81, he hosted their Seminar on Music and Dance in 1980. Tunley was chair of the Music Board of the Australia Council; he worked as a visiting scholar at Wolfson College, Oxford (1966), the Rockerfeller Study Centre in Bellagio, Italy (1987), and Christ Church, Oxford (1993).

Tunley's writings and performing editions reflect his interest in French Baroque music, especially the 18th-century French cantata and the music of Couperin. He contributed to *The New Grove Dictionary of Music and Musicians* (30 entries), as well as to *Die Musik in Geschichte und Gegenwart*, *The New Oxford History of Music* and *The New Oxford History of Opera*; published on music education; edited the journal *Studies in Music* 1967–92; and is preparing a book on Campoli. A *Festschrift* was published in 1995 to mark the occasion of his 65th birthday, and he was elected a fellow of the Australian Academy of the Humanities (1980), was made a *Chevalier dans l'Ordre des Palmes Académiques* (1983) and received the AM (1987).

FURTHER REFERENCE
His writings include, with Frank Callaway, eds, *Australian Composition in the Twentieth Century: A Symposium* (Melbourne: OUP, 1980); *Harmony in Action* (London: Faber Music, 1984); *Alfredo Campoli: A Biography* (OUP, forthcoming). His editions include *The 18th Century French Cantata*, 17 vols. of facsimile editions with scholarly commentaries (New York: Garland, 1990–91); *Romantic French Song 1830–1870*, 6 vols of facsimile editions with scholarly commentaries, translations, etc. (New York: Garland, 1994–95). His compositions include *Two Preludes for Piano* (1962); *Concerto for Clarinet and Strings* (1966); *A Wedding Masque* (rev. 1970). See also Frank Callaway, ed., *Essays in Honour of David Evatt Tunley* (Perth: Callaway International Resource Centre for Music Education, 1995).   MARGARET KARTOMI

Turklu (Pintupi), public singing and dancing in the Gibson desert. See *Corroboree*.

Turnbull, Alan Lawrence (b Melbourne, 23 Nov. 1943), jazz drummer. He had drum lessons from Graham Morgan, and began playing at ★Jazz Centre 44 in Melbourne at the age of 14. After working with Frank ★Smith at the Embers in 1961, he settled in Sydney, and apart from a visit to Europe worked at ★El Rocco from the late 1960s, particularly with Don ★Burrows, with whom he toured extensively, to the Montreux and Newport festivals and elsewhere. He toured Australia and the USA with the Australian Jazz Orchestra in 1988. An influential teacher and ubiquitous freelancer with broad experience of film, television and club work, he has also played support for numerous visitors, including Phil Woods, Cleo Laine, Johnny Griffin, George Cables and Sonny Stitt.

FURTHER REFERENCE
Recordings include *Don Burrows Quartet* (1971, Cherry Pie CPS 1009); *Australian Pops Orchestra* (1975, Cherry Pie CPS-1020); *Don Burrows Quintet* (1976, Cherry Pie CPF-1023); *Jazz Co-op* (1976, 44 Records 44 6357 706); *Buddles Doubles*, Errol Buddle (1977, M7 Records MLF 216); *Moontrane*, Bob Bertles (1979,

Batjazz BAT 2070); *Don Andrews And Friends* (1979, 44 Records, 44 6357 722); *Horn*, Dale Barlow (1990, Spiral Scratch 0003). See also *OxfordJ*; *ClareB*; *BissetB*; John Shand, 'Alan Turnbull talks to John Shand', *JA* (May/June 1982), 22–3.
BRUCE JOHNSON

Turner, Charles. See *Montague-Turner Opera Company.*

Turner, Geraldine (b Brisbane, 23 June 1950), theatrical singer, dancer. She made her stage debut as a dancer in pantomime at the age of nine. After studying singing at the Queensland Conservatorium, she appeared in musicals with the Queensland Theatre Co. and from 1971 for J.C. Williamsons in *No! No! Nanette*, *Kismet* and *A Little Night Music*. She has sung for the Victoria State Opera in *La Belle Hélène* and *HMS Pinafore*, won a Green Room Award for her appearance as Nancy in *Oliver* (1984), and played the lead in *Anything Goes* (1988). With an adaptable voice and durable talent, she has been one of Australia's most successful performers in musicals and operetta. Her albums include *Torch Songs And Some Not So Tortuous*, *Anything Goes* and *Old Friends*. She was awarded the AM in 1988 and a Mo Award in 1990.

Turner, Walter James Redfern (b South Melbourne, 13 Oct. 1884; d Hammersmith, London, 18 Nov. 1946), writer, music critic. Son of W.J. Turner, organist at St James Cathedral, Melbourne, he worked as a clerk, then went to England in 1907 to seek his fortune as a writer. He wrote satirical pieces for *New Age* and music criticism for the *Musical Standard,* then during his war service published the first of his 16 volumes of poetry. As well as becoming one of the leading writers in London, he was music critic for the *New Statesman* 1915–40, *Truth* 1920–37 and *Modern Mystic* 1937. He published short stories, drama, and other writings; his books on music included *Facing the Music: Reflections of a Music Critic* (London: G. Bell, 1933), *Music and Life* (London: Methuen Press, 1921), and studies of individual composers. Outspoken and independent in his music notices, he was the first Australian to succeed as a music critic abroad, and one of the first English-speaking critics to appreciate Stravinsky, Hindemith and the composers of the Second Viennese School.

FURTHER READING
Obit. in London *Times* 23 Nov. 1946. C.W.F. McKenna, *W.J. Turner, Poet and Music Critic* (London: Gerrards Cross, 1989).

24 Hours. Monthly magazine of fine music reviews and articles published by the ABC, together with the ABC-FM radio programs and ABC concert details.

Twilights. Rock group (1963–69) founded in Adelaide, comprised of Glen ★Shorrock (vocals), Clem McCartney (vocals), Terry Britten (guitar), Peter Brideoake (guitar, harmonica), John Bywaters (bass), and

Frank Barnard (drums to 1965, then Laurie Pryor). They began as a vocal trio, the Checkmates, and then merged with the Hurricanes in 1964. Building a large following with their performance of British covers by the Beatles, the Yardbirds, the Animals and the Who, some of them Britten originals, they moved to Melbourne in 1965. In 1966 they won the national Battle of the Sounds, while *Bad Boy* reached No. 4 in the charts and *Needle In A Haystack* No. 1. They went to the UK, returning in 1967 with a new image and sound influenced by Traffic and the Beatles' *Sergeant Pepper's* album, their *Cathy Come Home* reaching No. 4. They regained their local following by mixing their original numbers with new, more sophisticated material, but a television series in 1968 failed, a second album was not a success, and with the departure of Pryor and management strife the band disbanded in 1969. Shorrock went on to success with *Axiom and *Little River Band, while Britten's songs have been recorded by Cliff Richard, Tina Turner, Christie Allen and others. Incorporating droll skits with increasingly multifarious musical material, the close vocal harmony of Shorrock and McCartney and the fine Britten songs gave them enormous popularity in Australia in the mid-1960s.

FURTHER REFERENCE
Recordings include *Bad Boy* (1966, Columbia D04698); *Needle In A Haystack* (1966, Columbia D04717); *Cathy Come Home* (1967, Columbia D05030); *The Twilights* (1966, Columbia 330SX 7779); a compilation is *The Way They Played* (1978, EMI EMA 327). For discography, see *SpencerA*. See also *GuinnessP* IV, 2549; *McGrathA*; *SpencerW*.

Two Suitors, The.   Chamber operetta for children in one act, music and libretto by Colin *Brumby (1969). First performed at Rockhampton, Queensland, on 23 February 1970.

Tycho, Tommy   (*b* Budapest, Hungary, 11 Apr. 1928), popular music pianist, conductor. Son of opera singer Helen Tehel, he was a child prodigy, making his debut playing Gershwin with the Hungarian Philharmonic at the age of 10 and writing a concerto when he was 14. He studied at the Budapest Conservatorium and Franz Liszt Academy, but in the turbulence of Hungary in 1951 he migrated to Australia. Working as a storeman in Sydney, he was soon arranging and playing for radio, and made a deep impression substituting for a sick pianist in Lee Gordon's Johnny Ray tour in 1956; after that he was increasingly in demand as a show pianist. He was musical director for the ATN7 Orchestra (1958–73) and toured as accompanist in the Australian tours of Jack Benny, Jerry Lewis, Frank Sinatra, Roy Orbison and many others.

From 1973 he increasingly appeared as a light music conductor with ABC orchestras and major variety shows, conducting three Royal Command Variety Performances before Elizabeth II. He wrote television and film scores, including *Young Einstein* and *Reckless Kelly*. An ebullient entertainer of great musical gifts whose influence in Australian popular music has been felt over a long period, he was honoured with a Mo award, the MBE in 1977 and the AM in 1987.

FURTHER REFERENCE
His autobiography is *Music Maestro Please: The Tommy Tycho Story* (Melbourne: Brolga, 1995). See also *Australian* 4 Nov. 1995.

Tyrrell, Edward H.   (*fl.* 1900–37), songwriter, composer. Little is known of Tyrrell's life, though he seems to have been teaching piano in Newcastle in 1925, publishing almost exclusively with the Sydney firm W.H. Palings. Many of his compositions are patriotic: he wrote many songs and marches during World War I, including the very successful *Somewhere In France* and *Coo-ee, Coo-ee, You're Wanted At The Dardanelles*. He also wrote salon and teaching pieces for solo piano.

FURTHER REFERENCE
A list of some of his works appears in *SnellA*.

JENNIFER HILL

Tzipine, Georges   (*b* Paris, 22 June 1907), French conductor. After studying at the Paris Conservatoire, he appeared with the major French orchestras from 1948. He was conductor of the Victorian Symphony Orchestra 1961–65, providing an eclectic repertoire which proved popular with the audiences. Since then he has been professor of conducting at the Paris Conservatoire, appearing as a guest with Paris orchestras and making numerous recordings, chiefly of French composers.

FURTHER REFERENCE
Recordings principally with EMI. *HolmesC*; Christiane Spieth-Weissenbacher, *GroveD*.

U

Ubar. Aboriginal hollow log ceremony, northern Arnhem Land. See *Hollow Log*.

Uncanny X-Men. Rock band (1982–87) formed in Melbourne, originally comprised of Brian Mannix (vocals), Ron Thiessen, Chuck Hargreaves and Brett Kingman (guitars), Steve Harrison (bass), and Nick Manthandos (drums). Releasing a mini-LP, *Salive One* (1982), they toured as supporting act to Joan Jett in 1982, then released their debut single, *How Do You Get Your Kicks*, in 1983. Developing a clever live show sending up well-known bands in the brazen punk vein, they produced *50 Years* and the album *Cos Life Hurts* in 1985 and *What You Get Is What You Give* in 1986.

FURTHER REFERENCE
Recordings include *Salive One* (1982 Mushroom L20022), *How Do You Get Your Kicks* (Mushroom K9034), *50 Years* (1985, Mushroom K9671), *Cos Life Hurts* (Mushroom RML 53165) and *What You Get Is What You Give* (CBS SBP 8204). For discography, see *SpencerA*. See also *McGrathA*; *SpencerW.*

University Choirs and Choral Societies. Most major Australian universities have student-based choral or musical societies, while the music schools in universities and other tertiary institutions have also promoted choral activity.

1. Student Choral Societies. Sydney University Musical Society (SUMS) was established in 1878, Queensland (QUMS, 1912), Melbourne (MUCS, 1939) and others followed suit, through to 1991 (MUSCUTS, University of Technology, Sydney). Unauditioned, these highly social groups are comprised of people of all skill levels. Standards vary considerably according to the quality of the personnel, the conductor, and the support the society receives. Semesterisation and continual assessment have also affected the societies. Nevertheless, despite a sometimes precarious existence, they have presented many important musical events. For example, QUMS undertook the first

Bach Festival held in the southern hemisphere (1930), at which performances of the B Minor Mass, the *Christmas Oratorio* and several cantatas were combined with organ and chamber music recitals, church sermons on Bach, and public lectures delivered by Robert *Dalley-Scarlett. The societies have also commissioned works, been associated with many major musical identities, and participated in major events.

Many of these societies are members of the Australian Intervarsity Choral Societies' Association (AICSA), which was originally formed to facilitate contact with federal funding bodies and provide support to members. AICSA has produced a combined societies' library catalogue, and issues a regular newsletter, *Erato*. Meetings of member societies are conducted during the annual Intervarsity Choral Festival (IVCF). The two-week IVCF originated in 1949, and is held in each capital city (except Darwin) on a roster. Some festivals in the 1950s numbered up to 350 participants, but more recently numbers ranged from 120 to 240. Within a non-competitive social environment, good musical standards are sought, and an increasingly challenging mix of modern and classical repertoire is selected. Concerts have included Venetian poly-choral music, stage works, commissions, 'classics' like Verdi's *Requiem*, and less familiar pieces like Howells' *Hymnus Paradisi* and Walton's *Belshazzar's Feast*. Works have been commissioned from Colin *Brumby, Theodore Dollarhide, Martin *Wesley-Smith, and others. Festival conductors have included Gordon *Spearritt, Hugh *Brandon, Percy *Jones, David Carolane, Georg *Tintner, Peter *Seymour, Warren *Bebbington and Rodney Eichenberger. There have also been a number of collaborations with the ABC.

2. University College and Music School Choirs. Significant choral work takes place in many university colleges and music schools. The University of Melbourne, for example, has a number of denominational residential colleges with choral chapels. Trinity (1872, Anglican) was a male-only residence until 1974, and the opening of the

Horsfall Chapel (1917), and the installation of an organ (1923), prompted the appointment of college organists. The revival of its glee club eventually led to a sung Compline service each weeknight. For a time the choir of the Canterbury Fellowship was the major college group (having moved from St John's Church, Latrobe Street, in 1956) but the chapel choir has developed further, and is an important part of university musical life. Ormond College (Presbyterian, 1881) only established its chapel in 1967, and obtained an organ in 1973. A chapel choir was founded in 1982. It sings in the chapel each Sunday, has given many recitals and broadcasts, issued recordings, and toured overseas.

The university and conservatorium choral groups—large choirs, small chamber choirs and early music ensembles—are essentially teaching ensembles. They tend to be somewhat more wide-reaching in repertoire than local choral societies—at the University of Melbourne Percy Jones, for example, conducted the first Australian performance of Monteverdi's *Vespers* (1610) in 1966. They are generally open to non-music students after audition, and in some cases participation can gain a student academic credit. Lack of men's voices (especially tenors) can lead to problems in balance and repertoire selection, a problem often met by allowing outside participants. The Brisbane Chorale (1983) and the Canberra School of Music Choir are two such groups.

The Adelaide University Bach Choir (1900, as the University Choral Class) is the oldest surviving institutional choir. The NSW Conservatorium Select Choir (1916) was formed by Henri *Verbrugghen to study composers like Purcell and Palestrina, who were considered beyond the powers of existing choral groups. Enthusiasm for 'high class choral music' was required, as were a good voice, true intonation and good sight-reading. The first concerts (1916) featured J.S. Bach's *Jesus, Priceless Treasure* sung from memory. In 1920 it performed the Beethoven 9th Symphony and *Missa Solemnis* in Melbourne as part of a highly acclaimed Beethoven festival, and later toured NZ. In 1923 Arundel *Orchard took over the Select Choir, which had been languishing since Verbrugghen left. 'Like all such bodies', he wrote, 'it was largely held together by the personal contact of the Conductor who had formed it'. Rehearsals were undertaken for a year to prepare the Bach B Minor Mass for performance in April 1925, and in 1929 he performed *The Dream of Gerontius*, with soloists who had sung the work in England under Elgar's direction.

The establishment of the music department at the University of Western Australia in the 1950s led to a collaboration with the ABC that made the university a centre for much of Perth's choral activity. The University Choral Society (1930) performed a number of large works from 1962, including the Perth premiere of Verdi's *Requiem* (1962). This group is distinguishable from the student choral club, PUCS (1960). Performances by the UWA Collegium Musicum (1976) included Machaut's *Messe de Nostre Dame* (1977). At the University of Queensland QUMS and the small music department were closely linked throughout the 1950s and 60s, QUMS being the only choral group on campus; since then the gradual establishment of a Department Choir has seen the two bodies pursue their own goals. Currently there are four choral groups on campus.

Postwar music summer schools conducted by various universities (Queensland, New England, Sydney) usually included choral classes. Teacher-training colleges also formed choirs as part of the teaching program and these often combined with other choral groups. New music departments and conservatoriums in Darwin, Townsville, Mackay and elsewhere are gradually making an impact on local choral music. See also *Choirs and Choral Music*.

FURTHER REFERENCE
Jenny Dawson, A History of the Queensland University Musical Society 1912–1980, BMus(Hons), Univ. Qld, 1980.

NOEL WILMOTT

University Conservatorium, Melbourne. See *University of Melbourne Music Faculty*.

University of Adelaide Wind Quintet. One of the most successful chamber ensembles to exist in Adelaide (1964–80). The original members were David *Cubbin (flute), Jiri Tancibudek (oboe), Gabor *Reeves (clarinet), Tom Wightman (bassoon) and Stan Frey (horn). All had been principals in either the South Australian or the Melbourne Symphony Orchestras, and were appointed to full-time lectureship positions at the Elder Conservatorium, University of Adelaide. The ensemble gave regular concerts in Adelaide and toured interstate, with two successful international tours in 1969 and 1973. The group commissioned a number of works from Australian composers including Sculthorpe, Werder, Meale and J.V. Peters.

FURTHER REFERENCE
Recordings include music of Mozart, Danzi, Hindemith and Mozart (W&G BS 5008). JULJA SZUSTER

University of Melbourne Music Faculty. Founded in 1895, it is the oldest music school in Australia. Originally named the University Conservatorium, it was created following a bequest from pastoralist and parliamentarian Francis *Ormond which established a chair of music (from 1891). At first housed in rented premises in Carlton, since 1909 it has been in Royal Parade on the edge of the campus at the Conservatorium building, with its fine recital venue, Melba Hall. In the 1950s the focus shifted away from a performance diploma, and now over half the students are in academic BMus specialisations, combine music with other disciplines, or are in graduate programs. Directors (usually occupants of the Ormond chair of music) were G.W.L. *Marshall-Hall (1895–1900, 1915), Franklin *Petersen (1901–14), William *Laver (1915–25), and Bernard *Heinze (1926–57); deans have been George *Loughlin (1958–74), Max *Cooke (1975–80), Michael *Brimer (1981–85) and Ronald *Farren-Price (1986–90). The present dean is Warren *Bebbington.

FURTHER REFERENCE
Peter Tregear, *The Conservatorium of Music: An Historical Essay* (Melbourne: Univ. Melbourne Faculty of Music, 1997).

University of NSW Opera Company.   Part-time company founded (1968) at Kensington, Sydney, and directed by Roger *Covell. It gives short annual seasons of unusual and new works by professional singers, such as the revival of Glanville-Hicks's *Transposed Heads* in 1971.

Up There, Cazaly.   Football song (1979), words and music by Mike Brady and Noel Delbridge. Commissioned by the Seven TV network to promote its coverage of Australian Rules football in 1980, the song refers to early football hero Roy Cazaly (1921–63), player for St Kilda and (from 1921) South Melbourne, whose supporters would chant 'Up there, Cazaly!' Recorded by Brady and Peter Sullivan as Two Man Band (1979, Fable FB 1052), it sold 200 000 copies in 11 weeks, becoming one of the biggest-selling singles in Australian recording history. The duo released various sequels, *One Day in September* (1980), *There's A Bit Of Cazaly In Us All* (1981) and *We're Gonna Grab That Cup* (1983).

FURTHER REFERENCE
Published by Remix Music, 1979. Edition and commentary in *RadicS*, 93.

V

v Spy v Spy. Rock band (1980–) formed in Sydney, originally comprised of Mike Weiley (guitar, vocals), Cliff Crigg (drums, vocals) and Marcus Phelan (drums). With clever lyrics and a surprisingly full sound for a trio, their musical debt to reggae, their debut single was *Do What You Say* in 1982. They have since been prodigious, their releases including the album *Meet Us Inside* in 1984, 12 singles including *Harry's Reasons* (1986), and other albums including *Trash This Planet* (1989) and *Spy File* (1992).

FURTHER REFERENCE
Recordings include *Do What You Say* (Green LRS 703), *Meet Us Inside* (Powderworks SML 10501), *Harry's Reasons* (1986, Powderworks POW 0336), *Trash This Planet* (1989, WEA) and *Spy File* (1992, East West 403176549–2; also video). For discography, see *SpencerA*. See also *SpencerW*; *Melody Maker* 26 Mar 1983, 18.

Valentines. Pop band (1966–70) formed in Perth, comprised chiefly of Bon Scott (vocals, *d* 1980), Vince Lovegrove (vocals), Wyn Milson (guitar), John Cooksey (bass), and Russ Kennedy (drums). Winning the Perth Battle of the Bands in 1967, they moved to Melbourne and developed a strong following, releasing the first of their seven singles, *Each Day I Have To Cry* (1967). In 1969 they choreographed their stage presentation, adding matching outfits and theatrical effects, and their *My Old Man's A Groovy Old Man* reached No. 23 in the charts. After legal problems over marijuana possession, they modified their show again towards a more leathery image, releasing *Juliette* in 1970, but they disbanded later that year. They combined a bubblegum pop sound with a surprisingly untamed stage act, incidentally providing a training ground for Scott's later work with ★AC/DC.

FURTHER REFERENCE
Recordings include *Each Day I Have To Cry* (1967, Clarion MCK 1773), *My Old Man's A Groovy Old Man* (Philips BF 427), and *Juliette* (Philips BF 469). A compilation is *The Valentines* (1987, Clarion CLR 501). For discography, see *SpencerA*. See also *McGrathA*; *SpencerW.*

Van Diemen's Land, folk-song. Presenting a gallery of convicts transported to 'the fatal shore' of Tasmania and their various subsequent misfortunes, this is one of Australia's oldest traditional convict songs. It became known throughout the colonies and spread back to Britain. Various versions were published in broadsides *c.*1830, then in the English Folk Dance and Song Society *Journal* (1902); more recent publication began with John Manifold's arrangement in *Bandicoot Ballads* (1951).

FURTHER REFERENCE
Edition and commentary in *EdwardsG*; *ManifoldP.*

Vanda and Young. Popular music production and songwriting duo, of Harry Vanda [Johannes Vandenberg] (*b* 22 Mar. 1947) and George Young (*b* 6 Nov. 1947). They worked together from 1964, forming the enormously successful ★Easybeats, for which Young co-wrote the songs. After the group disbanded in 1970, they released recordings as a duo under various names, notably ★Flash and the Pan. Their songs were recorded by Rod Stewart, David Bowie, Suzie Quatro, Bay City Rollers, John ★Farnham and Johnny ★O'Keefe, and they won *TV Week* awards five times (1974–78) for their songs and producing. Since then they have produced and written songs for ★AC/DC, John Paul ★Young, Stevie Wright and others.

FURTHER REFERENCE
Recent work includes the album *Their Music Goes Round* (1992, Albert). See also *SpencerW*; *McGrathA.*

Vast. Ballet by Barry ★Conyngham (1988), choreography by Graeme ★Murphy. Commissioned for a national tour to celebrate the Australian Bicentennial, its four acts represent features of the vast Australian continent. It was first performed by the combined forces of the WA and Queensland Ballets, the Australian Dance Theatre and the Sydney Dance Co. in 1988. Recorded by the Australian Youth Orchestra, cond. J. Hopkins (1990, ABC 432 528–2), and published (Universal Edition, 1987).

Vatiliotis, Harry [Charalambos Andrea] violin-maker. After attempting to make violins from textbooks, he was apprenticed to A.E. *Smith at Hunter Street, Sydney (1953–55, 1958–65). After Smith's shop closed, he established his own business at Concord, Sydney. Using imported timbers, he has made over 300 violins and 40 cellos. He also teaches instrument-making at the University of Sydney. Australia's most prolific maker of violins, his instruments are today in high demand among professionals.

FURTHER REFERENCE
AthertonA.

Vaudeville. The earliest use of the term 'vaudeville' in Australia occurs from 1852 in playbills for the light musical plays of Sydney Nelson; it was not until the popularity of British *music hall began to wane in the late 1890s that musical and variety entertainments without a book on the American vaudeville model came to be popular in Australia. Typically, these amusements consisted of a black-face minstrel first half and a variety second half presenting singers, dancers, comics, acrobats, ventriloquists, animal acts, and male or female impersonators. Often most of the featured artists were imported star performers, such as Marie Lloyd, and later W.C. Fields or Harry Houdini, but local artists also became vaudeville stars, including George Wallace, Florrie *Forde, Jim Gerald and 'Mo' (Roy Rene).

Harry *Rickards established the first vaudeville circuit in Australia from 1892, when his Tivoli Minstrels and Specialty Co. opened in Sydney; in 1893 he bought the Garrick Theatre (built on the site of the older Scandinavian Music Hall) and renamed it the Tivoli, and by 1900 he had Tivoli theatres in most capital cities. Known as the 'King of Vaudeville', on his death in 1911 Hugh McIntosh took control of his circuit. Another entrepreneur, James Brennan, built the vast National Amphitheatre, Sydney, in 1906; in 1912, when he had theatres in most capital cities, he was taken over by Sir Benjamin *Fuller. By 1915 the Fuller circuit controlled 36 theatres in Australia and NZ. Whereas the Tivoli circuit featured more imported acts, the Fuller circuit emphasised comedy, their second halves typically being a loosely strung narrative of comic episodes. Harry Clay and the former comedian J.C. Bain also had small suburban networks in Sydney for a time, but Fuller's and the Tivoli were the chief presenters of vaudeville in Australia.

The advent of the movies, silent from 1914 and 'talkies' from 1929, brought a lower-priced entertainment which eventually supplanted vaudeville. George *Musgrove led a dazzling vaudeville revival at the Tivoli circuit in the 1920s, but most vaudeville theatres had been converted into cinemas by the early 1930s. During World War II Will Mahony presented vaudeville at the Cremorne Theatre, Brisbane, largely aimed at American troops stationed there; the Sydney and Melbourne Tivolis, the last variety houses in Australia, finally shut in 1966.

FURTHER REFERENCE
Richard Waterhouse, *From Minstrel Show to Vaudeville* (Sydney: UNSWP, 1990), 116–35; Celestine McDermott, 'National Vaudeville', in *The Australian Stage: A Documentary History*, ed. Harold Love (Sydney: UNSWP, 1984), 135–43; Charles Norman, *When Vaudeville Was King: A Soft Shoe Stroll Down Forget-Me-Not Lane* (Melbourne: Spectrum, 1984); F.H. Parsons, *A Man Called Mo* (Melbourne: Heinemann, 1973); *The Tivoli Story: 55 Years of Variety* (Melbourne: Tivoli Co., 1956).

Vaughan, Denis Edward (*b* Melbourne, 6 June 1926), conductor, musicologist. After organ and double bass study at the University of Melbourne Conservatorium, with G. Thalben Ball at the Royal College of Music, London (Tagore Gold Medal, 1949) and André Marchal in France, he played in the Royal Philharmonic Orchestra 1950–53, gave annual harpsichord concerts at the Royal Festival Hall 1948–58, and gave organ recitals in Europe. He made his conducting debut as Beecham's assistant at the Royal Festival Hall in 1953, then formed the Orchestra of Naples, with which he toured Europe and made 23 recordings, including the complete Schubert, 12 Haydn and 11 Mozart symphonies. He was music director for the Australian Elizabethan Theatre Trust in 1966, conducted at the Munich State Opera 1972–80, directed the South Australian Opera 1981, and has appeared in opera and concert in Europe and North America. A conductor who obtains clean, animated playing informed by a knowledge of period performance practice, as a scholar he has published on Verdi, Puccini, and musical copyright in *Proceedings RMA*, *Musical Times*, *Opera News*, *Gramophone* and elsewhere.

FURTHER REFERENCE
His recordings as a conductor with the Orchestra of Naples include Mozart *Il re pastore*, Symphonies K.128–196, Haydn Symphonies Nos. 82–92, and the complete Schubert symphonies (RCA). He appears as harpsichordist in Alfred Deller's Monteverdi *Ballo delle ingrate* (Vanguard) and as organist in the *Elizabeth Schwarzkopf Christmas Album* (EMI). See also *HolmesC*; Stanley Sadie, *GroveD*; *ADMR*.

Veitch, Patrick Lee (*b* Beaumont, Texas, USA, 26 Mar. 1944), music administrator. He studied English literature at North Texas State University and attended the Graduate School of Business, Columbia University. After working in advertising at New York from 1965, then in public relations for Manhattan College, he was marketing director for the Metropolitan Opera from 1973. He came to Australia to advise the Australian Opera on fund-raising and was appointed general manager in 1981.

During his term with the opera free outdoor performances and educational programs were expanded, radio-television simulcasts and surtitles were introduced, the first recordings and videos were made, and better business methods were adopted, but there were also acrimonious and often widely publicised exchanges with the Australia

Council over funding. He encountered internal problems, and resigned to become managing director for J.C. Williamsons 1986–87; since then he has worked as a producer of musicals and arts festivals.

FURTHER REFERENCE
Age, 12 Feb. 1981, 28 Oct 1986; John Cargher, *Bravo! 200 Years of Opera in Australia* (Sydney: ABC/Macmillan, 1988), 160–1.

Vella, Richard (*b* Melbourne 1954), composer. He began writing pop songs at the age of 16 and studied music at Monash University, then La Trobe University (from 1976) with Keith *Humble, Graham *Hair and Warren *Burt. Collaboration with the Modern Dance Ensemble was an important formative influence, and he moved to Sydney to work with One Extra Dance Co., throughout the 1980s composing for various theatrical productions. He was in the USA in 1983 on an Australia Council grant, working with Kenneth Gaburo and others, and composer-in-residence at the Playbox Theatre, Melbourne, in 1986; he also co-founded New Music Articles Publications and taught at the NSW State Conservatorium 1983–91, then at Macquarie University. In 1988 he joined Currency Press as music editor, and in 1990 founded Calculated Risk Opera Productions. Since 1993 he has worked on multimedia productions with the Australian Film, Television and Radio School. Lyrical and accessible, with a strong rhythmic focus, his music consciously explores a variety of styles and genres, often within a single work, by using multiple time structures and textures.

FURTHER REFERENCE
Recordings include *A Piano Reminisces* (1994, Red House RED 9401); *Mercury Pieces*, D. Heskovitch, pf (1992, Tall Poppies TP020). See also *BroadstockS.*

Venetian Twins, The. Musical by Terence Clarke, book by Nick Enright. Set in 18th-century Verona but with various references to modern Australia, it recounts the romantic escapades of twin brothers. First performed at the Nimrod Theatre, Sydney in 1979. See *Musical Comedy.*

Venetians, The. Rock band (1983–89) formed in Sydney, originally comprised of Rick Swinn (vocals), Peter Watson (guitar, vocals, synthesiser), Matthew Hughes (keyboards), Dare Skeet (guitar, vocals, bass, synthesiser) and Tim Powles (drums). Their 10 singles included *Sound On Sound* (1983), their albums *Step Off The Ledge* (1985) and *Calling In The Lions* (1986), then in their last three years the singles *Inspiration* (1986), *Must Believe* (1988) and the album *Amazing World* (1988).

FURTHER REFERENCE
Recordings include *Sound On Sound* (1983, Parole K9071), *Step Off The Ledge* (1985, Parole L38226), *Calling In The Lions* (1986,
Parole RML 53204) *Inspiration* (1986, Parole K9944), *Must Believe* (1988, Parole K0573) and *Amazing World* (1988, Parole L38911). For discography, see *SpencerA.* See also *SpencerW.*

Vennard, A(lexander) V(index) ('Bill Bowyang') [Frank Reid] (*b* 1884; *d* 1947), journalist, publisher. Under his pen-name Bill Bowyang he edited 'On the Track', a popular column in the *North Queensland Register*, 1922–47. Songs appearing in the column were republished in his *Old Bush Recitations* (1933) and various other volumes, making him a significant collector of Australian folk-song.

FURTHER REFERENCE
OxfordF.

Verbrugghen, Henri Adrien Marie (*b* Brussels, 1 Aug. 1873; *d* Northfield, Minn., USA. 12 Nov. 1934), conductor. Verbrugghen studied at the Brussels Conservatoire and subsequently worked as an orchestral violinist in Belgium and Britain. He was appointed professor of violin, chamber music, orchestra and opera in Glasgow in 1904 and made a solo appearance with the Berlin Philharmonic. In 1915 he was chosen as the foundation director of the NSW State Conservatorium, arriving in Sydney later that year. Verbrugghen oversaw the first staff appointments, which included the three other members of the Verbrugghen String Quartet. Among Australians, he appointed Alfred *Hill to teach harmony and counterpoint and Arundel *Orchard to teach history. A conservatorium orchestra (later the NSW State Orchestra), consisting of staff, professionals and students, was formed in 1916 and Verbrugghen issued a prospectus proposing 12 concerts and 24 chamber music concerts; in that year eight lecture-concerts were given. He also selected a choir of 50.

The orchestra increased the number of concerts each year, by 1919 offering a prodigious total of 132 performances in Sydney, and in the following year touring country towns and other states. In 1919 the NSW Government guaranteed £11 500 to establish a permanent orchestra of 70 and hailed it as the first state-supported orchestra in the Empire. Verbrugghen programmed works by Australians Fritz *Hart, Mirrie Solomon (*Hill) and Alfred Hill, among others, and reports of performances particularly praised the orchestra's unanimity of tone. In Melbourne in that year the orchestra performed six concerts on consecutive nights, a record for that city. When it toured NZ in 1919 the concerts were described as a revelation, leading Verbrugghen to consider the possibility of conducting a world tour.

In 1920 Verbrugghen's contract expired and there was a change of government in NSW, the new government being less interested in subvention of the cost of an orchestra. A concert was given in Sydney on 24 December 1921, before a further tour of NZ, but Verbrugghen was not to return. Although subscribers raised £2000 towards a permanent orchestra, Verbrugghen was offered a position with the Minneapolis orchestra for £200 a week. He remained in Minnesota until his death. As a conductor he was praised for 'finesse, imagination and a genial manner', and should be credited with popularising orchestral music in Sydney.

FURTHER REFERENCE
John Carmody, *ADB*, 12; D.C. Parker, *GroveD*.

SUZANNE ROBINSON

Verbrugghen Quartet. String quartet formed in Glasgow, Scotland, in 1903, which came to Australia as resident ensemble of the NSW State Conservatorium following Henri Verbrugghen's appointment as its founding director in 1916. Comprised of Verbrugghen and Jenny Cullen (violins), David E. Nichols (viola) and James Messens (cello), it played first-rate period instruments, gave regular recitals in Sydney and toured interstate, setting a new high standard for chamber music playing in Australia. The group moved to the USA with Verbrugghen in 1923, after which the NSW State Conservatorium Quartet was established with local players (Gerald Walenn, Lionel Lawson, Alfred Hill and Gladstone Bell) to carry on the tradition.

Vercingétorix. Lyric opera in three acts by Henri *Kowalski, libretto (in French) by M. Mainiel. Subtitled *Love and Patriotism*, it was first performed at the Garden Palace, Sydney, on 1 April 1881, then with an English text by J. Lake at the Melbourne Town Hall on 24 September 1881. Libretto published by W.H. Williams, Melbourne, 1881.

Victoria State Opera. Formed (1962) by Leonard Spira from the amateur Victorian Light Opera Co., which had given seasons of Gilbert and Sullivan operettas. As the Victorian Opera Company it presented short seasons which attracted increasing critical notice, but it remained a tiny, perilous venture, and languished after Spira's departure in 1968. With the appointment of Richard *Divall as its conductor in 1972, and with Dame Joan *Hammond as artistic director, it was soon transformed: fare including Baroque, modern and neglected 19th-century works established a strong contrast to the repertoire of the Australian Opera. Renamed the Victoria State Opera in 1976, its home from 1984 was the State Theatre at the Victorian Arts Centre, where, despite periodic financial crises, it presented at least four operas a year of a quality which at times rivalled those of the Australian Opera, as well as large-budget musicals and concert spectaculars. Divall remained as principal guest conductor. In 1996 the company merged with the Australian Opera as Opera Australia.

FURTHER REFERENCE
Robert H. Cowden, ed., *Opera Companies of the World: Selected Profiles* (Westport, Conn.: Greenwood Press, 1992), 5–7; John Cargher, *Bravo! 200 Years of Opera in Australia* (Sydney: ABC/Macmillan, 1988), 190–207.

Victorian College of the Arts. Founded by the State Government in 1973, it has been affiliated with the University of Melbourne since 1990. Its School of Music is located in a modern building close to the Victorian Arts Centre and focuses on a degree and diplomas in performance, including strong opera and jazz programs. The college also maintains a specialist secondary school in music and the arts. Deans have been John *Hopkins (1973–85), John *O'Donnell (1986–87), and Nicholas *Braithwaite (1988–90). The present dean is Gillian Wills.

Victorian Folk Music Club. Launched (1959) as the Victorian Bush Music Club. After the huge popularity of the musical *Reedy River*, which incorporated performances by the Melbourne Bushwackers (later renamed the Billabong Band), and the example of the Sydney Bush Music Club (founded 1954), a greatly successful woolshed dance featuring the Billabong Band during the 1956 Melbourne Olympics produced a following for regular singabouts, and these led eventually to the club's formation. Monthly sessions of singing, dancing and yarning took place at the Toorak scout hall (later the Armadale scout hall), folk tuition groups and concerts were organised, and a newsletter and the *Gumsuckers Gazette* (*Australian Tradition* from 1964) were published. At its height the club (renamed the Victorian Folk Music Club in 1963) presented mass folk concerts at the annual Moomba festival, published books and recordings, and managed its own concert party. *Australian Tradition* ceased publication in 1975, but the club continues to offer dances, workshops, weekly folk nights and a biannual woolshed ball, and to publish songbooks and recordings.

FURTHER REFERENCE
Australian Tradition (June 1969) 10th anniversary issue.

Victorian Jazz Club (VJC). The most durable of a succession of traditional jazz clubs in Melbourne, beginning with the Southern Jazz Society, which was established in 1949 by Shirley Wood, under the presidency of Will McIntyre, a house band led by Len *Barnard, and a newsletter, *Southern Rag*. The society was succeeded by the Melbourne Jazz Club, which emerged in 1958 from record sessions at the home of Jess and Bill *Haesler, with Pat and Frank *Traynor. This club was dormant by 1967, and the VJC was established 1968, its functions held in a succession of hotels including Prospect Hill, Manor House, Museum, and Whitehorse Inn. Presenting a radio program, publishing a newsletter and a journal, *Jazzline*, it organises performances and related jazz events.

FURTHER REFERENCE
OxfordJ, 207–10.

BRUCE JOHNSON

Victorian Rock Foundation. Government-funded agency established (1987) to develop and promote the local rock music industry. It conducts workshops on skills necessary to success in the music industry, provides a liaison between bands and funding sources, and since 1988 has organised an annual 10-day Melbourne Music Festival.

Vienna State Opera Award. Awarded annually since 1994 for a singer by nomination from the Australian opera companies. The award provides travel, accommodation and tuition for a year at the Vienna State Opera. Administered by Opera Foundation Australia, the prize is currently valued at $35 000.

Vietnamese Music. There are over 122 300 Vietnamese in Australia, most arriving since 1975 as refugees or migrants; the largest communities are in Sydney and Melbourne. In Australia they have preserved and developed three main categories of Vietnamese music: traditional, contemporary and popular.

1. Traditional music. Various genres of Vietnamese traditional music have been transplanted into Australia. Folk-songs exist in both authentic and westernised forms. Authentic folk-songs such as lullabies, village songs and sung poetry are performed by elderly people and traditional musicians; westernised folk-songs are performed mostly by pop singers and younger members of the community, and are characterised by the lack of traditional tonal and microtonal ornaments, the temperisation of pitches, and the use of Western instruments and harmony in the accompaniment. Two genres of classical music, the *nhac Hue* and *nhac Tai Tu,* have been preserved by a small number of traditional musicians, prominent among them Dang Kim Hien, Le Tuan Hung, Le Thi Kim, Nguyen Anh Dung and Nguyen Anh Tuan, based in Melbourne.

The South Vietnamese music-drama *cai luong* has been maintained by a number of amateur troupes in Melbourne, such as the Hoa Tinh Thuong and the Lac Hong. This theatrical form combines spoken dialogues, sung poetry, South Vietnamese classical songs, new songs in traditional styles, folk-songs and westernised popular songs.

The main characteristics of Vietnamese traditional music are melodies based on modes (each defined by tonal material, specific ornaments for each pitch level, and melodic motives and contours), heterophonic texture in multi-part music, and performance by a process of elaborating a skeletal melody. Musical instruments used in both folk and classical music are: dan tranh (zither), dan nguyet (moon lute), dan bau (monochord), dan nhi (two-string fiddle), dan ty ba (four-string pear-shaped lute), sao (flute), sinh tien (coin clapper), phach (wooden sticks), song lang (wooden foot clapper), wood blocks and drums. In the music drama, the modified Western electronic guitar (with curved finger board), the moon lute and the foot clapper are used in all troupes in Australia.

2. Contemporary art music. Works by composers of Vietnamese descent in the 1980s and 90s exhibit two main compositional trends, Romantic-nationalistic and experimental. The Romantic-nationalistic compositions, such as

Memories of the Highlands (1984), *Full Moon Festival* (1984) for classical guitar and *Vietnamese Dance Suite* (1991) for wind, brass and percussion by Hoang Ngoc Tuan, or *String Waves* (1990) for violin and string orchestra and *Melorhythm* (1993) for 13 violins and 2 cellos by Le Tuan Hung, were written for Western instruments and based on Vietnamese folk melodies, rhythmic structures and modes. Experimental compositions, such as *Reflection* (1991), *Spring* (1991), *Prayer for Land* (1991), *Homeland Now and Then* (1994), *Calm Water* (1995), *Longing for Wind* (1995) by Le Tuan Hung, *Silent Tears* (1995) by Dang Kim Hien and *Paper and Strings* (1991) by Le Thi Kim, are characterised by the exploration of old and new possibilities of sound-making on voice or instruments, the experimental combination of Vietnamese, non-Vietnamese instruments, and/or non-conventional sound-generating devices, and the high level of flexibility in performance. Many of these compositions are written in graphic or skeletal notations.

3. Popular music. Vietnamese popular music in Australia is dominated by songs written in Western style and American or French pop songs sung with original and Vietnamese lyrics. Original popular songs are characterised by the use of Western harmony, the tempered scale, ABA song form and dance rhythms such as Cuban bolero, tango, cha cha, rumba, or waltz. The rock group with electronic guitars, keyboard and a drum kit is the standard accompanying ensemble.

FURTHER REFERENCE
Recordings include *Quivering String*, Back to Back Zithers (1992, Move 3141); *Musical Transfiguration: A Journey across Vietnamese Soundscapes*, Le Tuan Hung, Le Thi Kim (1993, Move 3128); *Landscapes of Time: Contemporary Sound Art of Vietnam*, Le Tuan Hung, Dang Kim Hien (1996, Move 3197). See also Le Tuan Hung, 'Dan Tranh Music outside Vietnam: The Case of a Transplanted Tradition', in Music and Socio-Political Change: A Study of Dan Tranh Music in Central and South Vietnam between 1890 and 1990, PhD, Monash Univ., 1990, 206–36.

LE TUAN HUNG

Vine, Carl Edward (*b* Perth, 8 Oct. 1954), composer. Playing piano and trumpet as a child, after studying science at the University of Western Australia, as well as with Stephen ★Dornan (piano) and John ★Exton (composition) and a brief period at the BBC Tape Transcription Unit, London, he won the Perth Music Festival instrumental prize (1972) and the ABC Instrumental and Vocal Competition (1974), then worked as a pianist in Sydney with AZ Music, the Seymour Group and other contemporary ensembles. He was co-founder of ★Flederman (1979–88), which commissioned a large body of new Australian work and performed it widely in Australia and abroad. During the same years he was pianist and composer-in-residence with the Sydney Dance Co. (1978), the London Contemporary Dance Theatre (1979), the NSW State Conservatorium (1985), the Australian Chamber Orchestra (1987) and the WA Conservatorium

(1989). He taught at the Queensland Conservatorium 1980–82, but mainly works freelance.

His earliest works were mainly electronic, but he came to prominence as a composer of vibrant, imaginative music for dance, incidental music for plays, and films. His work with the Sydney Dance Co. led to *Poppy* (1978), the first full-length Australian dance work, and he has since composed 13 commissions for dance companies. These are works of great vitality and wit, written with deep understanding of the dancers' needs. His years with Flederman produced a number of chamber works, including *Café Concertino* (1984), increasingly an Australian classic; these are virtuosic works, with complex manipulations of the rhythmic pulse, yet their texture is never opaque and is always superbly crafted with a player's understanding of technique. More recently he has produced orchestral works for the ABC, including a concerto and four symphonies, works which suggest he is becoming increasingly tonal, without losing the individual eloquence of his earlier voice. One of the most widely performed and commissioned composers in Australia, he is both a first-rate performer and one of the most articulate and gifted composers Australia has produced.

WORKS (Selective)

Orchestral *Curios* (1980), *Micro Symphony* (1986, rec. 1991, ABC Classics 426955–2), Percussion Concerto, perc, orch (1987), Symphony No. 2 (1988, rec. 1991, ABC Classics 426955–2), Symphony No. 3 (1990, rec. 1991, ABC Classics 426955–2), *Celebrare Celeberrime* (1993), Symphony No. 4 (1993), *Esperance*, chamber orch (1994), Symphony No. 5 *Percussion Symphony*, 4 percussionists, orch (1995).

Chamber Instrumental *Miniature II*, 2 va (1974), *Tempi*, str qrt (1976), *Everyman's Troth*, va, vc, clavichord (1979), *Occasional Poetry*, trbn, pf (1979), *Scene Shift*, pf (4 hands, or pf duet), trbn, db (1979), *Images*, fl, vc, trbn, perc, pf, hpd (1981), *Miniature III*, fl, trbn, pf, perc (1982, rec. LRF 156; Tall Poppies TP013), *Sinfonia*, fl, cl, vn, vc, pf, perc (1982), *Café Concertino*, fl, cl, vn, va, vc, pf (1984, rec. Tall Poppies TP013), String Quartet No. 2 (1984), *Elegy*, fl, vc, trbn, pf (4 hands), perc (1985, rec. Tall Poppies TP013; Anthology of Australian Music on Disc CSM 1), *Suite from Hate*, trbn, hn, 2 pf, perc (1985), *Defying Gravity*, perc qrt (1987, rec. Anthology of Australian Music on Disc CSM 2), *Miniature IV*, fl, cl, vn, va, vc, pf (1988), *Concerto Grosso*, vn, fl, ob, hn, str (1989), Sonata, fl, pf (1992), *The Battlers Suite*, ob, hn, hp, str (c.1993), *GAIJIN*, koto, str, tape (1994), String Quartet No. 3 (1994).

Solo Instrumental *Miniature I*, va (1973), Trio, org (1975), *Tergiversative Blues*, lute (1977), *Free Game*, tba, electronics (1979), *Love Song*, trbn, tape (1986), *Percussion Concerto*, perc, tape (1987, rec. Tall Poppies TP013), *Piano Sonata*, pf (1987, rec. Tall Poppies TP013), *5 Bagatelles*, pf (1994), *Inner World*, vc, tape (1994).

Incidental Music for Theatre *New Sky*, mime by Judith Anderson (1981), *Signal Driver*, play by Patrick White (1982), *Shepherd On The Rocks*, play by Patrick White (1987), *Ham Funeral*, play by Patrick White (1989).

Dance *Poppy*, S, fl, cl, 2 hn, bn, trbn, perc, pf, tape (1978), *Everyman's Troth*, va, vc, clavichord (1978), *Knips Suite*, 2 vn, va, vc (1979), *Scene Shift*, trbn, db, 2 pf (1979), *Donna Maria Blues*, tape (1980), *Daisy Bates*, chamber ens (1982), *Hate*, trbn, hn, 2 pf, perc (1982), *A Christmas Carol*, orch (1983), *Prologue+Canzona*, str orch (1986, rec. Anthology of Australian Music on Disc CSM 9), *Legend*, orch (1988), *On The Edge*, tape (1989), *The Tempest*, orch, tape (1991), *Beauty and the Beast*, electronic montage (1993).

Vocal/Choral *Aria*, S, fl, vc, pf, celeste, perc (1984), *After Campion*, SSAATTBB, 2 pf (1989).

FURTHER REFERENCE

Recordings of his works include *Micro Symphony* and Symphony Nos 2 and 3, Sydney Symphony Orchestra (1990, ABC 426995–2); *Café Concertino*, Australia Ensemble (Tall Poppies TP 002); *The Battlers* (Tall Poppies TP024); *Elegy*, Flederman (Canberra School of Music, CSM 1); Defying Gravity (Canberra School of Music, CSM 2), Prologue and Canzona (Canberra School of Music, CSM 9), l; Piano Sonata *Miniature III*, *Love Song*, Percussion Concerto *Carl Vine* in Chamber *Music vol. 1* (Tall Poppies TP 013). The text of his 1993 Goossens Lectures, 'Art For Whose Sake', is in *24 Hours* (Aug. 1993), 44–50. See also *CA* (1995–96); *BroadstockS*, 239–42; Rosemary Johnson, *ContemporaryC*; *SMH* 24 Jan. 1986.; *APRAJ* 7/1 (Oct. 1989), 12–4.

Vining, Ted (Edward Norman) (b Melbourne, 22 Aug. 1937), jazz drummer. He began drums as a teenager playing at the Lido, and led a trio for television. In 1959 he began a lengthy association with Alan Lee. He was in Sydney in 1965, then returned to Melbourne and became active with Brian ★Brown. Forming a trio with Bob ★Sedergreen and bassist Barry ★Buckley, he was active in Sydney 1979–81, then Brisbane, where he was Queensland jazz co-ordinator. He returned to Melbourne in 1986, reuniting the Trio and his group Musiiki Oy, then worked in Adelaide 1992–94, after which he returned to Melbourne. He teaches in the Victorian College of the Arts jazz program.

FURTHER REFERENCE

Recordings include *The Ted Vining Trio Live at PBS-FM* (1981, Jazznote JNLP 029); *Yours Is My Heart Alone*, Ted Vining Trio (1995, Newmarket NEW 1076.2); *Spoon Relief*, *The Big One* (1995, Newmarket NEW 1083.2). See also *OxfordJ*; *BissetB*; Neville Meyers, 'Ted Vining, In The Jazz Wilderness', *JA* (Spring 1983), 12.   BRUCE JOHNSON

Violin-making. Scotsman William Henry ★Dow (1835–1927) and Englishman John ★Devereux (b 1810) were the earliest violin-makers of note to work in Australia. Dow arrived from Tayport, Scotland, in 1854, Devereux from London in 1864. Both worked in Melbourne producing instruments of excellent quality, Dow being very prolific, making about 250 violins, violas and cellos. Arthur Edward ★Smith (1880–1978) was, in the opinion of most violin experts, the finest Australian maker. Born in London, Smith migrated to Melbourne in 1909, later settling in Sydney where he set up the A.E. Smith Co. His violin shop became a veritable Mecca for violin enthusiasts, and his best instruments are wonderful examples of the violin-maker's art and are, in the opinion of many, as fine as any made in Europe in the first half of the 20th century. Many famous violinists bought Smith violins, among them Yehudi Menuhin, Isaac Stern and David Oistrakh. In 1949 Smith received diplomas of honour for both the violin and viola which he exhibited at The Hague, the only 'British' maker to obtain this double distinction. His influence was enormous and today there are excellent violin-makers in every major city.

The traditions of Smith are faithfully observed by many, particularly with regard to the choice of European woods, spruce and maple. But there are an increasing number of makers who use Australian timbers and passionately believe that instruments made from native trees are tonally equal, if not superior, to their European counterparts. As many as 20 species of Australian trees have been used in violin-making, and instruments made from some of these woods are extremely beautiful in appearance, especially when enhanced by a fine translucent varnish and mulga wood fittings. Violin-making in Australia is attracting many young artisans who serve apprenticeships with established makers before furthering their knowledge of the craft in Europe or America. Meanwhile the violins of Dow, Devereux and especially Smith are highly prized and sought after by discerning players throughout the world.

FURTHER REFERENCE
AthertonA.   CHRISTOPHER MARTIN

Violins of Saint-Jacques, The.   Opera with prologue and three acts by Malcolm ★Williamson (1966), libretto by William Chappell after the story by P. Leigh Fermor, commissioned by Sadler's Wells Opera, London. First performed at Sadler's Wells on 29 November 1966 and published by Joseph Weinberger in 1972.

Vivian, Alan   (*b* USA, 18 Sept. 1952), clarinettist. He settled in Australia in childhood, and after playing as a freelance jazz player and in the ABC Training Orchestra became bass clarinettist in the Melbourne Symphony Orchestra in 1974, clarinet in the Vienna Staatsoper in 1976, the Sydney Symphony Orchestra in 1978, and principal clarinet with the Australian Chamber Orchestra from 1982. He has been senior lecturer at the Canberra School of Music since 1983, playing with the Canberra Wind Soloists.

Vogel, Peter.   See *Fairlight CMI.*

Vogt, Dieter   (*b* Basel, Switzerland, 23 Mar. 1945), jazz trumpeter, bass player. He began trumpet at the age of 12, later adding bass to join Oscar Klein. Migrating to Sydney in 1966, he became active in a broad range of jazz, rock and pop groups, including playing trumpet with Jeff ★St John. He played bass in the USA in 1973, then returned to Sydney, playing in sessions, touring, concert and festival work, with Billy Burton, the ★Daly-Wilson Big Band, Judy Bailey, the Nolan/Buddle quartet and Winifred Atwell among others. Also playing support for visiting

musicians such as Mark Murphy, he is currently bassist with Bob ★Henderson, Keith ★Hounslow, George ★Brodbeck and Graeme ★Bell, whom he joined in 1982.

FURTHER REFERENCE
Recordings include *The Daly Wilson Big Band* (1971, Festival SFL-934453); *No Worries*, Len Barnard's Famous Jazz Band (1971, Swaggie S-2192); *For The Record*, Peter Boothman (1975, 44 Records 44 6357 705); *The Nolan-Buddle Quartet* (1975, M7 Records MLF-100); *Riverboat Days*, Bob Barnard and Friends (1975, Swaggie S-1366); *The Julian Lee Orchestra* (1980, Batjazz BAT-2072); *At Last*, Keith Hounslow's Jazzmakers (1988, Emanem Records 3605). See also *OxfordJ.*   BRUCE JOHNSON

Vogt-Evans, Linda Caprice   (*b* Northcote, Melbourne, 28 Sept. 1922) flautist, teacher. After studying flute with Leslie ★Barklamb in Melbourne, she played with the Sydney Symphony Orchestra 1942–52. While raising a family, she did jazz session work and occasionally appeared with the ABC; she studied with James Pellerite at the NSW State Conservatorium then toured Australia and South-East Asia for Musica Viva in 1973, and was associate principal flute with the Elizabethan Trust Sydney Orchestra 1973–74. She was founder and president of the Sydney Flute Society (now Flute Society of NSW) from 1973, director of the first and fifth national flute conventions (1973, 1983), and a foundation member of the Australian Flute Association from 1981. She established Zephyr Music in 1976, a publisher of educational music. A dedicated flute teacher who has contributed to music camps and masterclasses over a long period, she was honoured with the AM in 1987.

Voices in Limbo.   Radio opera by Larry ★Sitsky, libretto by Gwen Harwood. First heard on the ABC in 1977.

Voss.   Opera (1986) in two acts by Richard ★Meale, libretto by David Malouf, after the Patrick White novel. Set in colonial NSW in the mid-19th century, it tells of a disastrous attempt to cross the Australian continent from east to west by a German explorer, Voss, loosely based on the last expedition of F.W.L. Leichhardt, who disappeared in 1848. It was the first full-length work commissioned from an Australian composer by the Australian Opera. First performed on 1 March 1986 by the Australian Opera, Adelaide. Recorded by the Australian Opera, with the Sydney Symphony Orchestra, cond. S. Challender (1987, Philips 420928–1).

FURTHER REFERENCE
Michael Ewans, 'Voss: White, Malouf, Meale', *Meanjin* 48/3 (Spring 1989), 513–25.

Voyageur.   Ballet by Dorian ★Le Gallienne (1954), choreography by Laurel Martyn. First performed by the Victorian Ballet Guild in 1954 and recorded by the Ballet Guild Orchestra under Harold Badger (W&G AL 660).

Wa Wa Nee.   Rock band (1986–) formed in Sydney, originally comprised of Paul Gray (vocals, keyboard), Steve Williams (guitar, vocals), Paul Greenwood (bass, trumpet), Elizabeth Lord (backing vocals), Mark Gray (bass) and Phil Whitacker (drums, *d* Jan. 1989). Their debut singles *Stimulation* (1986) and *Sugar Free* and their album *Wa Wa Nee* were released in 1986 to quick success, introducing them as a heavy metal band of the glossy funk genre. They followed these with the album *Ultra Mixes* in 1987, the single *I Can't Control Myself* in 1988, and the album *Blush* in 1989, sustaining an enthusiastic following.

FURTHER REFERENCE
Recordings include *Stimulation* (1986, BCBS BA 3373), *Sugar Free* (CBS BA 3516), *Wa Wa Nee* (CS SBP 8206), *Ultra Mixes* (CSB 4605771, *I Can't Control Myself* (CBS 653162), and *Blush* (CBS 463345–1) . For discography, see *SpencerA*. See also *SpencerW*; *Musician* 112 (Feb. 1988), 122.

Wagga Wagga,   pop. (1991) 40 875. Birthplace of violinist Carmel *Kaine, it is set on the Murrumbidgee River, south-eastern NSW, settled in the 1830s. It is a service centre for the Riverina wheat and sheep district and site of a major RAAF base. The Wagga Wagga Eisteddfod commenced in 1920, by 1928 attracting entrants from all over NSW and Victoria, and today the tradition continues with the City of Wagga Eisteddfod each September and other events. A Wagga Wagga Philharmonic Society was formed in 1915. The Wagga Wagga Male Choir could afford a grand piano in 1950, and the Wagga Wagga Music Club was a centre for visiting artists from Sydney in the 1950s. An excellent Civic Theatre was opened in 1963, used for musicals by the School of Arts. The Riverina Music Centre offers tuition in an array of instruments, and there is an annual Riverina Summer School for Strings in January. Jazz Plus, the Wagga Wagga Country Music Association and the Riverina Country Music Club all offer monthly events.

Wagner Societies of Australia.   Four independent Wagner Societies exist in Australia, in Sydney, Melbourne, Adelaide and Perth. Formed from 1980, the primary aim of each is to promote the music of Richard Wagner and encourage its wider understanding. Funds are raised to donate sponsorships to Wagnerian performances, while the Sydney society additionally provides sponsorship for the Bayreuth Scholarship. Some societies meet monthly, others four to five times a year. Activities are open to both members and non-members and include lectures and seminars on subjects related to Wagner's music, concerts and video presentations. An annual dinner is held, generally near Wagner's birthday in May.   KERRY VANN

Wakooka.   Ballet by John *Antill (1957), choreography by Valrene Tweedy. Set on an outback sheep station, it was first performed by the Elizabethan Trust Ballet Co. in 1957.

Waks, Nathan   (*b* Sydney, 23 Jan. 1951), cellist, administrator. After studies at the Sydney Conservatorium and the Paris Conservatoire, he won the ABC Instrumental and Vocal Competition in 1968. He played with the BBC Symphony Orchestra 1969, was principal cello with the Sydney Symphony Orchestra 1970, then the Elizabethan Theatre Trust (Sydney) Orchestra 1971–75. A particularly gifted chamber music player, he was in the Fidelio String Quartet in these years, then the *Sydney String Quartet 1975–85, and with the *Mittagong Trio became artist-in-residence at the Hong Kong Academy of the Performing Arts 1985–87. Moving towards music management on his return to Australia, he was artistic adviser to the Australian Chamber Orchestra in 1989, a record producer for Sony Classic International from 1991, producing records for John Williams and others, and, after conducting an inquiry into the ABC concert music department, was appointed its director in 1993.

FURTHER REFERENCE
CA (1995–96); *WWA* (1996).

Wales, Roy Frederick   (*b* England), English choral conductor, administrator. After studies at the University of

London, Trinity College and the Guildhall School of Music, he took a doctorate in choral conducting from the University of Washington. He came to Australia as director of the Queensland Conservatorium in 1981, formed and directed the Brisbane Chorale, making it the leading choir in Queensland, and conducted numerous choral workshops around the state. A choral conductor of boundless energy, vision and wry humour, his single-minded approach to managing the Conservatorium eventually polarised the staff, and he returned to England in 1987.

Wallace, W(illiam) Vincent (*b* Waterford, Ireland, 11 Mar. 1812; *d* Vieuzos, Hautes-Pyrénées 12 Oct. 1865), Irish composer. A violinist at the Theatre Royal, Dublin, from his early teens and organist at Thurles Cathedral from 1830, he arrived in Australia in November 1835, first giving a concert in Hobart, then settling at Sydney in 1836, where he gave concerts, taught and opened a music shop. The first musician of exceptional talent to take up residence in Australia, he was described by the press as 'the Australian Paganini'. With lively competition from J.P. ★Deane and the patronage of the governor, Sir Richard Burke, he helped transform the quality of concert music heard in Sydney. His business was not a success, however, and in the face of mounting debts he fled the country in 1838, abandoning his wife and son. In the following years he toured the Americas and Europe as a violinist until 1845, when his opera *Maritana* opened at Drury Lane, London, bringing him immense fame.

FURTHER REFERENCE
Osric [Humphrey Hall and Alfred John Cripps], *The Romance of the Sydney Stage* (ms, 1911; pub. Sydney: Currency Press, 1996), 38; Nigel Burton *GroveD*; Catherine Mackerras, *ADB*, 2; *GlennonA*, 180; *BrewerD*; Kathleen Hellyer, William Vincent Wallace: Life and Works, PhD, Bryn Mawr College, 1980.

Walters, Oscar W., popular music songwriter. He published at least 15 songs 1948–60 with Allans, Davis & Co., Chappell & Co. and others, including *My Love Song To A Tree* (1945), *Before We Say Goodbye, I Fell In Love With An Angel, Glowing Embers* (1953), and *Dreams Are Such Wonderful Things* (1960).

FURTHER REFERENCE
A list of his songs is in *SnellA*.

Waltzing Matilda. Best known of all Australian songs, there have been several unsuccessful attempts to have it declared the ★national anthem. The words are by A.B. 'Banjo' ★Paterson (*c*.1895), the music of the most widely known version was arranged by Marie Cowan (1900), but the authorship has long been disputed.

On 24 April 1894 Christina Macpherson, a member of a Victorian grazier family, attended the Warrnambool races where she heard Godfrey Parker's (alias bandmaster Thomas Bulch's) arrangement of *Craigielea,* composed *c*.1805 by James Barr, words by Robert Tannahill, published in 1818. It is thought that it was a version of this tune that Miss Macpherson put to words by poet-lawyer Paterson when they met at Dagworth station in mid-western Queensland in 1895. An attempt was made to cut the tune into paper rolls for an instrument resembling a barrel-organ as Dagworth had no piano. The song was further developed at Oondoroo station with baritone Herbert Ramsay's assistance, and during the Winton race meeting in May at 'Aloha', the home of Mrs Fred Riley, and at the North Gregory Hotel. Copies of the song circulated, entering the bushman's repertoire as well as that of the squattocracy, forking into two versions, one known as the Queensland or Buderim version which was used locally.

Folklorist Richard Magoffin has recently unearthed two early manuscripts of the song both said to be in Christina's hand. What is thought to be the earlier of the manuscripts was located in 1986 by Diana Baillieu, a grand-niece of Christina Macpherson. The second manuscript comes from the Bartlam-Roulston family of Hobart. The Bartlam-Roulston copy is said to date from 1895, a copy made by Christina for Mr and Mrs J.R.Y.B. Bartlam during the Winton races held on 28 and 29 May. Her song was never published. The Mitchell Library houses a rival claimant—a manuscript by Harry Nathan, organist and choirmaster, a descendant of composer Isaac ★Nathan, himself said to have been the bookkeeper at Dagworth who taught Christina Macpherson to cut music rolls and helped in her attempts to reproduce *Waltzing Matilda* in 1895. There are other claimants to being the original version, notably a song from the Marlborough Wars, called variously *The Bold Fusilier* or *The Brave Fusilier*. Words for this have appeared, but none known to be from the period. The tune is today's *Waltzing Matilda,* which is improbable, given that no known song of the day resembles its pared down, unornamented melodic usage, which is more typically late Victorian.

In 1900 Paterson sold *Waltzing Matilda* to his publisher, Angus & Robertson. The poem was bought by the tea merchant James Inglis, always on the look-out for suitable advertising verses. For most of the 1890s his firm's name had been appearing at the end of bush verses in the *Bulletin*. His *Billy Tea*, with its swaggie and kangaroo on the packet, had become a household name. Inglis had a Scottish-born manager, William Cowan, a performer with the Sydney Liedertafel and the Philharmonic Society, and he asked him to look at the verses with an eye to setting them to music. Inglis may have obtained a copy of the Macpherson tune from Paterson and passed it to Cowan. Cowan took words and music, if this was the case, to his Australian wife Marie, neé Barr, who played the piano and who was said to be very fond of Scottish songs. It was she who gave us the version of *Waltzing Matilda* now in general use, to words altered from the Paterson original to emphasise the Billy tea connection. When it was proposed to sell the tea with a free copy of the music thrown in,

Marie is said to have been horrified; but with her school-girlish music privately printed and her name on the cover as the arranger, the die was cast. Though it has frequently been claimed she died young, in fact she died in 1919, aged 64. No other music by her is known. Given her family ancestry, interests and connections it is more than likely that she knew of *Craigielea* independent of Macpherson's manuscript, and came to her own conclusions. She could also have known Nathan's version, or he hers.

In 1911 *Waltzing Matilda* was published and further disseminated through the *Australasian Students' Song Book*. During World War I it was used for recruitment drives, entering the repertoire of military brass bands both at home and abroad: the words appear in a 1918 soldier's songbook distributed by the army. It was taken up by early film, its patriotic associations established, and first recorded in 1927 by the Queensland tenor John Collinson, but it was not until the English examiner for the Royal Schools of Music, Thomas Wood, published it in his travel book *Cobbers* in 1934 as (quite mistakenly) the only example of Australian folk-song that it achieved real international status. In 1938 Peter ★Dawson's recording of it soared into 20 reprints to become one of the world's 10 most recorded songs. Over 500 artists here and overseas have recorded it.

FURTHER REFERENCE
Richard Magoffin, *Fair Dinkum Matilda* (1973), rev. as *Waltzing Matilda: Song of Australia* (1983), and as *Waltzing Matilda: the Story Behind the Legend* (Sydney: ABC, 1987); John S. Manifold, *Who Wrote the Ballads?* (Sydney: Australasian Book Society, 1964); Sydney May, *The Story of 'Waltzing Matilda'* (Brisbane: Smith & Paterson, 1955); Oscar Mendelssohn, *A Waltz With Matilda* (Melbourne: Lansdowne Press, 1966); Harry Hastings Pearce, *On the Origins of Waltzing Matilda* (Melbourne: Hawthorn Press, 1971); idem, *The Waltzing Matilda Debate* (Charters Towers, Qld: Rams Skull Press, 1974); Thérèse Radic, 'And his Ghost may be Heard: The Songlines of "Waltzing Matilda"', *Journal of Australian Studies: Australian Frontiers* 49 (Sept. 1996), 39–47; idem, 'The Matilda Knot', *Victorian Journal of Music Education* 2 (1995), 3–11; idem, 'National Icon', *The Centre for Studies in Australian Music Newsletter* 3 (June 1996), 1–4; Thomas Wood, *Cobbers* (London: OUP, 1934).

THÉRÈSE RADIC

Wanam. Cape York clan songs. See *Aboriginal Music* §3(iv).

Wangga. Public singing and dancing in north-western NT. See *Corroboree*; *Aboriginal Music* §3(iii).

Warburton. Town in the Great Victoria Desert, 250 km west of the WA–SA–NT border, which grew from the United Aboriginal Mission for the Ngaanyatjarra and other peoples of the region, established in 1934. In 1970 the mission handed the administration to the government, and in 1972 the Warburton Community Council

was formed to self-manage the community. From 1975 many people moved back to the desert camps. The town holds an annual Desert Dust-Up, a three-day sporting and cultural festival for Ngaanyatjarra children from remote schools. In 1992 it was one of the largest Western Desert communities with *c.*1100 Aboriginal residents. See *Aboriginal Music*.

Ward, Russel Braddock (*b* Adelaide, 9 Nov. 1914; *d* Texas, Qld, 13 Aug. 1995), folklorist. Collecting folksongs, ballads and yarns, he completed a doctorate at the Australian National University in 1953, from which he published *The Australian Legend* (1958), an influential work which sought the national archetype through Australian folk-song in the character of the convict and colonial bushman. He taught at the University of New England from 1956, was a founder of the Australian Folklore Society and was a popular lecturer on ballads and folk-song at folk festivals. His 17 books include *The Penguin Book of Australian Ballads* (1964) as well as historical works. One of the first scholars to make serious use of Australia's folk music sources, he was honoured with the AM in 1987.

FURTHER REFERENCE
Obit. in *Australian* 6 Sept. 1995. His memoirs are *A Radical Life: Autobiography of Russel Ward* (Melbourne: Macmillan, 1988). See also *OxfordF*, 34–41, 363; *WWA* (1996).

Ward 13. Rock band (1978–82) formed in Sydney, comprised of John Arthurs (vocals), Leigh Hamilton Johnston and Ron Roberts (guitars), Steve Lunn (guitar, saxophone), Andrew Ross (keyboards), Peter Mullens (bass) and Tim Powles (drums). A hard-rock band, piercing and truculent, once they began to record in 1980 they did so at white heat, in less than two years releasing an EP, *Robot Wizards* (1980), six singles including *See Venice And Die* (1981) and *Slow Dancer* (1981), and the album *Flash As A Rat* (1981). In 1982 they made the mini-LP, *Too Much Talk*, before dissolving.

FURTHER REFERENCE
Recordings include *Robot Wizards* (1980, Survival ES 013), *See Venice And Die* (1981, EMI EMI 446), *Slow Dancer* (1981, EMI EMI 605), *Flash As A Rat* (1981, Survival EMX 106), and *Too Much Talk* (Polygram 6437160). For discography, see *SpencerA*. See also *McGrathA*; *SpencerW*.

Warlow, Anthony (*b* 11 Nov. 1961), stage musicals singer, actor. After studying singing at the Sydney Conservatorium he appeared as Puck in *A Midsummer Night's Dream* for the Australian Opera in 1980. He studied in NZ in 1981 and took minor operatic roles, until appearing in the musical *Guys and Dolls* at Adelaide in 1985. Since then he has had a solo show, *A Song to Sing-O*, appeared in *Countess Maritza* for the Australian Opera (1987), and had the leads in the Melbourne production of

Phantom of the Opera, My Fair Lady (1993) and *Secret Garden* (1996). He has a rich tone and striking stage presence.

FURTHER REFERENCE

Recordings include *Back In The Swing* (Polygram 5195632), *Centre Stage* (Polygram 8474342), *Midnight Dreaming* (Polygram 5236122) and *On The Boards* (Polygram 5134022). See also *CA* (1995–96).

Warlpiri. People traditionally living in and around the Tanami Desert, NT, in north-western central Australia. Warlpiri language and culture, including music, predominantly belongs to the central Australian–Western Desert region, although it is influenced more than most of such cultures by northern Aboriginal traditions, particularly religious ceremonies. An example of northern influence is the important Warlpiri *kajirri* religious cult which is closely related to the Arnhem Land *kunapipi* cult. Other elements of the religious tradition, for example male initiation, women's religious ceremonies *(yawulyu)*, love-magic rites *(yilpinji)*, and so-called fire ceremonies *(jarriwanpa, ngajakula)* are closely related to central Australian and Western Desert traditions.

The Warlpiri believe that songs, along with dances and sacred visual designs, originate either in the Dreaming *(Jukurrpa)* or with spirit-agents, either spirits of deceased kin or other spirits. Songs are usually received from spirit-agents while the recipient is cut off socially from the community, for example when he or she is sick or camping alone. The spirit-agent appears to the person and teaches them the songs. The recipient is then obliged to teach others, usually people of their own clan because songs are owned by clans. Songs originating in the Dreaming are believed to have always been in the Warlpiri song repertoire.

Songs are organised into named series according to the particular ancestral Dreamings to which they belong and are about. Song texts concern the activities of spiritual ancestors in the creative epoch of the Dreaming, when the physical features and social organisation of the world were established. For example, there are song series about the Rain Ancestor, the Kangaroo Ancestor and the Fire Ancestor, each ancestor believed to be responsible for the phenomenon after which it is named. A song series can be identified by the general melodic shape or contour, which every song in the series follows. The text of each song, consisting of three to six words, is also fixed and set to a particular rhythm and repeated several times in the course of a single performance of a song.

Songs are usually performed by groups of people singing in rhythmic unison but not always in melodic unison. Mostly men and women sing separately, although there is one category of songs, *purlapa,* which may be sung by women and men together. Men accompany themselves usually by striking together the tips of two boomerangs or two sticks, while women strike with cupped hands the hollow between the thighs

when kneeling, which produces a loud thud. Occasionally, both women and men use handclapping as accompaniment. The rhythms produced by these means are very regular and provide a steady rhythmic background to the singing.

Singing is an essential component of all religious ceremonies, and most singing is done in these contexts. Children's songs, often performed in make-believe ceremonies, are not considered by adults to be the same phenomenon as adult songs because they are merely made up by children. Only when children reach puberty are they introduced to adult songs in the context of adult religious ceremonies, and for several years they can only listen to and absorb the songs. Gradually they are permitted to sing first the least sacred songs and then more sacred ones, especially those owned by their own clan which they have special responsibility to perform and pass on to the next generation.

The only songs which are regularly sung solo or in groups of two or three singers are love-magic songs *(yilpinji)*. A person will sing *yilpinji* to a personal item belonging to a desired member of the opposite sex. This imbues the item with the power of the Dreaming associated with the particular *yilpinji*, and when it is returned to its owner he or she is believed to become overwhelmed with desire for the perpetrator of the love-magic. This is an example of the spiritual power which is believed to be activated by the singing of all Warlpiri songs, which is why singing is central to Warlpiri religious life. See also *Aboriginal Music* §2.

STEPHEN WILD

Warma. Public singing and dancing in parts of Cape York, Queensland. See *Corroboree*.

Warner, Dave (*b* Perth), singer-songwriter. He formed the rock band From the Suburbs with other Perth musicians in 1978. Dubbed 'Suburban Rock' or 'Ocker Rock', their early albums gained Warner notoriety for his articulate singing style and satirising of Australian suburban life. Although his debut releases, *Mug's Game* and the single *Suburban Boy*, reached No. 23 and No. 31 respectively (1978), by the time *This is My Planet* (1981) was released he had faded into obscurity. His later work included *The Dark Side of the Scrum* with the Happy Hookers band, and the re-formation of From the Suburbs to record *Meanwhile Out in the Suburbs* (1989) and *Suburban Sprawl* (1990).

FURTHER REFERENCE

Recordings with From the Suburbs include *Mug's Game* (1978, Mushroom L 36759); *Correct Weight* (1979, Mushroom); *Free Kicks* (1979, Mushroom L 36910); *This is My Planet* (1981, Mercury 6437 146); *Dave Warner and the Happy Hookers* (J&B); *Meanwhile Out in the Suburbs* (1989, Musicland); *Suburban Sprawl* (1990, Mushroom); and with the Happy Hookers *The Dark Side of the Scrum* (J&B). See also *GuinnessP*; *McGrathA*; *SpencerW.*

AARON D.S. CORN

Warren-Smith, Neil [Neil Smith]   (*b* St Kilda 1930; *d* 28 July 1981), bass baritone. While working as a butcher Smith had lessons with Ethel Manders and Henry Thomas and won the Melbourne Eisteddfod in 1947. He sang in St Paul's Cathedral choir and at the first *Music for the People* concert in 1948, was a finalist in the Mobil Quest and as Neil Warren-Smith toured Australia in concert. He studied with Henry and Annie ★Portnoj, then made his operatic debut as Leporello in *Don Giovanni* with the National Theatre Movement Opera Co., Melbourne, in 1955, joined the Elizabethan Theatre Trust Opera Co. (later the Australian Opera) from its inception in 1956. He appeared at Sadler's Wells, the English National Opera and in NZ (1974–75), but turned down further offers from London, making his career exclusively in Australia with the national and state companies. Combining an imposing, centred voice with mature acting skills, he sang the roles of Bartolo, Don Giovanni, Don Pasquale, Sparafucile (*Rigoletto*), Rocco (*Fidelio*), Sarastro, Gianni Schicchi, Baron Ochs, and Kutuzov (*War and Peace*). He was honoured with the OBE.

FURTHER REFERENCE
His memoirs are *Twenty-Five Years of Australian Opera* with Frank Salter (Melbourne: OUP, 1983). See also Roger Covell, *GroveO.*

Warriors, The.   Work for orchestra, three pianos and 'tuneful percussion' by Percy ★Grainger, completed in 1916. Subsequently arranged by the composer for two pianos, six hands (1922), it was first performed in Norfolk, Connecticut, with the composer conducting the Norfolk Festival Orchestra on 7 June 1917. Commissioned by Beecham for the Ballets Russes and subtitled 'Music to an Imaginary Ballet', *The Warriors* is Grainger's largest and most ambitious composition, requiring up to three conductors for any given performance. Although never choreographed during his lifetime, Grainger invented a colourful program to complement the work, involving 'shining black Zulus', 'flaxenhaired Vikings' and 'cannibal Polynesians', among many others.   ALESSANDRO SERVADEI

Warrumbungle Mare, The.   Country music ballad by Coral Dasey after a poem by Charles Shaw ('Old Timer') originally published in the *Bulletin*. It tells of an untameable red mare who ran wild in the Warrumbungle foothills, and a rider who set out to catch her and was never seen again. In the traditional bush ballad style, it was recorded by Reg Poole in *From The Cradle To The Grave* and earned him an ACMA Golden Guitar in 1981; there is also a recording by Stan Coster on *My Country*.

FURTHER REFERENCE
Published in Charles Shaw, *The Warrumbungle Mare and Other Poems* (Sydney: Dymocks, 1943), 3–5. Recordings include Reg Poole, *From The Cradle To The Grave* (Selection CDPRC 708); Stan Coster, *My Country* (Hadley CASOLLP 535).

Warumpi Band.   Aboriginal rock group from Papunya (Warumpi), NT, active in the 1980s, re-formed in the mid-1990s. Members include Sammy Butcher, E. Ellis, Alan Murphy, George Rurrambu, Kenny Smith, and non-Aboriginal Neil Murray. One of the first Aboriginal groups to gain widespread recognition throughout Australia, it was the first rock group to release a recording commercially in an Aboriginal language, the single *Jailanguru Pakarnu/Kintorelakatu* (1984), also on their second album, *Warumpi Band Go Bush!* (1987). Their songs are influenced by country styles and reggae, and include instruments of traditional Aboriginal music, the didjeridu and boomerangs. Their song topics cover local Aboriginal identity, problems of Aboriginal life (alcohol in *Nyuntu Nyaaltjirriku* or looking after children in *Wima Tjuta*), dispossession of indigenous people (*Secret War*), and the importance of land and specific places (*Warumpinya, Fitzroy Crossing* and *Kintorelakutu*). Their lyrics are in both English and Aboriginal languages, including Luritja and Gumatj. In 1986 they toured parts of northern Australia with ★Midnight Oil, and in 1995 they toured to Germany and France.

FURTHER REFERENCE
Recordings include *Warumpi Band* (1983, CAAMA unnumbered); *Big Name—No Blankets* (1988, Festival Records 38935); *Too Much Humbug* (1996, CAAMA 260); *Warumpi Band Go Bush!* (1987, Festival Records 38707); and the film *Midnight Oil: Black Fella-White Fella* (1987, Sony Music Video 200440 2).

P. DUNBAR-HALL

Watchorn, Ian Donald   (*b* Newcastle, NSW, 13 Apr. 1955), period stringed instrument maker. He established a workshop in Sydney from 1976 to make historic copies of period lutes using plans from the English Lute Society, as well as violins, viola da gambas, and bows. He worked in Canberra from 1979, then with an Australia Council grant went to Germany in 1982 to study musical instrument conservation at the Germanisches Nationalmuseum, Nuremberg, with Friedemann Hellwig and John Henry van der Meer. From 1984 he was employed as a conservator at the museum, returning to Australia as conservator and (acting) curator of musical instruments at the Powerhouse Museum, Sydney, in 1987. He moved to Melbourne in 1989 and re-established his private studio.

His instruments have been purchased by such early music performers as Wieland Kuijken, Hajo Bäss of the Musica Antiqua Cologne, and Peter Lissauer of the London Baroque Soloists, as well as by universities and museums in Australia and Europe. William Bower has six of his lutes. He has published articles in *The Strad, Holz Aktuell*, and *Studien zur Aufführungspraxis, Kultur- und Forschungsstätte*. He is one of the most learned and experienced makers of early instruments Australia has produced.

Waters, Edgar   (*b* Sydney 1925), folklorist, historian. From the mid-1950s he edited and extensively annotated many of the pioneering folk-song recordings for Wattle

Records, and wrote for *Australian Tradition*. He completed a doctorate in 1962 at the Australian National University on Australian folk-song and popular verse and then lectured at the University of Papua New Guinea. He is now consultant to the National Library of Australia and working on folk-song recordings for *Australia's Heritage in Sound*.

FURTHER REFERENCE
OxfordF; *StubingtonC*, 56.

Waters, Thorold ['Salamander'] (*b* London, 1876; *d* Melbourne, 29 Jan. 1956), music critic, tenor. He came to Australia at the age of 12 and worked as a journalist in his teens in Sydney and Dunedin, NZ, publishing occasional verse and short stories in the *Bulletin* as Thorold Dalrymple. He was briefly editor of the Bathurst *National Advocate* in 1898, then a correspondent for the *Age* at Melbourne from 1900. In Melbourne he studied singing with William Parkinson and appeared in local oratorio performances. He went to the UK in 1904, studied at the London Opera School, and appeared in concerts at the Royal Albert Hall, on provincial tours and with the Denhof-Beecham Opera Co. (1913). After war service in Egypt he worked for the *Pall Mall Gazette*, returned to Australia to work for the new Melbourne *Sun News-Pictorial* from 1923, and was managing editor of the *Australian Musical News* 1923–48. A knowledgeable but outspoken music critic, he was also a popular vocal adjudicator and radio broadcaster, and largely responsible for establishing the *Sun* (now *Herald-Sun*) Aria in 1924. His memoirs are *Much Besides Music* (Melbourne: Georgian House, 1951).

FURTHER REFERENCE
Obit. in *AMN* 46 (Feb. 1956), 6. An index to his numerous contributions to *AMN* is in *MarsiI*.

Watson, Eric (*b* Casino, NSW, 1926), country music record producer, scholar, advocate. Writing traditional country ballads from the age of 12, his songs were recorded from the 1950s by Jimmy *Little, Slim *Dusty, Buddy *Williams and others. In 1975 he developed the country music division of Larrikin Records, Sydney, then in 1978 used its catalogue as the foundation of his Selection label. He moved his company to Tamworth (1981) and then to his cattle property at nearby Theresa Creek (1986). His label has recorded established country figures such as Reg *Poole, Gordon *Parsons and Dusty Rankin, and has been critical in developing the careers of numerous younger bush ballad and heritage style artists, including Norma Murphy, Barry Thornton and Terry Gordon. He discovered Owen *Blundell, Glen Jones and Evelyn *Bury. A passionate advocate of traditional Australian country style, his two-volume *Country Music in Australia* (1976, 1983) is a standard work in the field. He was honoured with a special ACMA Wrangler award for services to country music in 1977.

FURTHER REFERENCE
Country Music in Australia, vol. 1, 2nd edn (NSW: Rodeo Publications, 1976), vol. 2 (NSW: Cornstalk Publishing, 1983).

Watson, Gordon (*b* Sydney), pianist, teacher. He lived in London most of his professional life. He graduated from the NSW Conservatorium in 1946, where he would later become head of piano. From 1946 to 1948 he studied with Egon Petri at Mills College in San Francisco, where he was awarded a scholarship for composition by Darius Milhaud. He also studied with Laurence Godfrey Smith. He gave his debut recital in January 1949 at Wigmore Hall and his first BBC broadcast later that year, which was to inspire many more radio broadcasts, with the ABC and elsewhere. With an interest in the works of modern composers and a love for 12-tone music, he developed a reputation in London and Europe for his many first performances, which included the Strauss *Passacaglia* for left hand, Milhaud's Piano Concertos Nos. 1 and 3, and Valen's Piano Sonata No. 2. Humphrey Searle dedicated his new piano concerto to Watson, and he also worked with Clifford Curzon in London and Richard Farrell in San Francisco and New York.

Watson's style is strong and incisive, with great attention to detail. His recordings include works by Bartók, Searle, Vaughan Williams, Britten, Warlock, and Constant Lambert's piano concerto, and he is a specialist in Liszt.

FURTHER REFERENCE
For an index to references in *AMN*, see *MarsiI*.   TOM LIOLIOS

Watson, Joe (*b* Boorowa, NSW, 15 Aug. 1881; *d* Boorowa, 1977?), traditional singer, entertainer. He worked as a bullock boy and rouseabout from 1895, then joined Paddy Doolan's travelling magic lantern show from 1897. He learned about 400 songs from Doolan, which they sang as the slides were shown. On the road for 22 years, from bushmen he learned political and sporting songs such as *The Ballad of the Kelly Gang* and *A Bushman's Song*, and rare versions of English songs, and compiled and sold illustrated song-books. In later years he settled as a publican in Boorowa, playing in the local brass band. An important source of traditional songs, recitations and verse, Warren Fahey collected material from him in 1973–74.

FURTHER REFERENCE
Fahey's recordings of Watson are now in *CAnl*. Watson may be heard on *Bush Traditions* (1976 Larrikin LRF 007). See also Warren Fahey, *Joe Watson: Australian Traditional Singer* (Sydney: Australian Folklore Unit, 1975).

Watson, Richard Charles (*b* Adelaide, 1902), bass. After studies with Clive *Carey at the Elder Conservatorium, in 1926 he won a scholarship to the Royal College of Music, London, where he studied with W. Johnstone-Douglas. He made his debut as soloist in Delius's *Appalachia* at Queen's Hall in 1929, and became principal bass at Covent Garden that year, but went over to the D'Oyly Carte Opera Co. from 1933 to specialise in Gilbert and Sullivan. He visited Australia for operetta roles (1935–37) and again for J.C. Williamsons during the war, 1940–44; he taught at the University of Adelaide 1944–46 but returned to D'Oyly Carte 1946–51 and continued to tour Europe and the USA in opera, operetta and recital. From 1951 he was director of the Regina Conservatory, University of Saskatchewan, Canada, but in 1955 Williamsons attracted him back to the stage in Australia, and he resumed his teaching at Elder Conservatorium until 1966. With a rich, powerful tone and an excellent comic sense, he was outstanding in all the major Gilbert and Sullivan bass roles, but he also sang many repertory opera parts, including Don Basilio, Don Alhambra, Kruschina in the *Bartered Bride*, Kothner in *Meistersinger*, and Mephistopheles in *Faust*.

FURTHER REFERENCE
His recordings for Decca and HMV are now rare. See also *MackenzieS*, 154; *GlennonA*, 61–3; *AMN* 27 (Dec. 1946), 11–12.

WATT. Electronic music performance group formed in 1975 by Martin *Wesley-Smith at the NSW State Conservatorium. Using live electronics, tape, film, and video they presented new electronic music by Australian composers. They appeared in Tokyo in 1978.

Webb Brothers, The. Country music group (founded 1953), comprised of brothers Fabian (guitar, harmonica, vocals), Marius (rhythm guitar, vocals) and Berard (guitar, mandolin, harmonica, vocals), graziers from the Gympie district in Queensland. Fabian took guitar lessons at school and taught Marius, while Berard studied piano and violin. Success in talent quests led to a recording contract in 1954, and their debut single, *Call of the Bellbird*, written by chief songwriter Berard, became their signature tune. The Webb Brothers concentrated on farming in the 1960s, but returned to country music with renewed enthusiasm after being featured on ABC TV's *Big Country* in 1972. They toured NZ in 1974 and 1976. Successes at the Australasian Country Music Awards in Tamworth included a Golden Guitar for best country music group in 1976, and induction into the ACMA Hands of Fame in 1978. In September 1981 a meat substitution scandal prompted Marius to write *The Colonel Put the Lickin' in the Chicken But Who Put the Roo in the Stew?* The song reached No. 29 in the charts and earned the group an ACMA Golden Guitar for top selling record in 1982. The Webb Brothers continue to perform occasionally. Their enduring popularity can be attributed to their down-to-earth bush style and evident love of performing.

FURTHER REFERENCE
Recordings include *Call of the Bellbird* (Rodeo 105, 1954); *The Old Palmer River Song* (Festival 5544, 1975); *Clancy of the Overflow* (W&G 2632, 1978); *Silver Jubilee Album* (1982). See also *WatsonC*, II, 64–67.   CAROLYN MUNTZ

Weber, Horace George Martin (*b* Parkside, SA, 9 May 1887?; *d* Fitzroy, Vic., 4 Oct. 1968), church and cinema organist. Weber was born into a musical family and was a chorister and assistant organist at St Peter's Cathedral, Adelaide. After piano studies he was organist at Napier Cathedral, NZ, and North Adelaide Baptist Church before beginning his career as cinema organist in Adelaide in 1919. He later held positions in several leading Melbourne cinemas at various periods up to the mid-1940s and was regarded as the doyen of his profession. From 1949 he was organist at Armadale Baptist Church, Victoria, performing many recitals which included both serious and popular repertoire.

FURTHER REFERENCE
Age, 5 Oct. 1968; Joyce Gibberd, *ADB*, 12.   JOHN MAIDMENT

Wedderburn Old Timers, The. Old-time dance band founded (*c.*1974) in Bendigo, in 1992 comprised of Lionel Collison (violin), Jack Condon (stroh-viol), 'Grummy' Ross (drums), Elma Ross (piano), Lindsay Holt (*d* 1995, button accordion), Trevor Holt (banjo), Calvert Hargreaves (double bass), Peter Ellis (concertina, tin whistle, spoons, mouth-organ) and Ian Johnston (button accordion, squeeze box). Formed for a tourist promotion, they soon appeared on radio, toured Australia and released three albums. Playing traditional instruments and pre–World War I dance tunes such as the schottische, valetta waltz, gay lords, lancers and polka mazurka, they appear at barn dances with their own caller.

FURTHER REFERENCE
Albums include *Live At Fenton's Creek* (Newmarket Music CD OTOCD 001). Clippings file in *Msl*.

Weddings, Parties, Anything. Folk-rock band (1985–) formed in Melbourne, comprised chiefly of Michael Thomas (guitars, bass, vocals), Paul Thomas (guitar), Mark Wallace (piano accordion, vocals), David Steel (guitars, vocals, harmonica), and David Adams (drums) but changing frequently. While resident at a suburban hotel in Melbourne, they released an EP, *Summons In The Morning*, then toured interstate with Stevie Ray Vaughan. Their single *Away Away* reached No. 41 in the charts in 1987 and they made their debut album *Scorn Of The Women*, then began several tours of North America and the UK.

With Thomas's narrative ballads of football, domestic violence, or local issues, they combine traditional folk music styles with pub-rock. Among later work, they recorded the singles *Streets Of Forbes* (1989) and *Step Out* (1989) and the albums *Difficult Loves* (1992) and *King Tide* (1993).

FURTHER REFERENCE
Recordings include *Summons In The Morning* (Suffering Tram Records), *Away Away* (WEA 7–258395), *Scorn Of The Women* (WEA 254705–1), *Streets Of Forbes* (1989, WEA 7–257447), *Step*

Out (1989, Warner), *Difficult Loves* (1992, Warner 4509900922) and *King Tide* (19093, rooART 4509937732). There is also *Through the Hungry Years: A Weddings, Parties, Anything Songbook* (Hobart: Production House, 1992). For discography, see *SpencerA*. See also *SpencerW*.

Weir, Nancy Mary (*b* Melbourne, 13 July 1915), pianist, teacher. She studied with Ada ★Corder in Melbourne 1926–30, Artur Schnabel in Berlin 1930–32, and Harold Craxton at the Royal Academy of Music 1933–36. Achieving fame as a child prodigy, she was featured in Australia's first indoor 'talkie'. Following her orchestral debut at 13 with the Melbourne Symphony Orchestra under Fritz ★Hart, the Lord Mayor of Melbourne instituted a public fund to send her to Europe. She established a career as a soloist and chamber musician in the UK from 1936 to 1954 with Proms appearances under Sir Henry Wood, membership of the Bangor Trio, and performances and broadcasts with BBC orchestras. She served with RAF Intelligence in North Africa and Italy, 1942–46, reaching the rank of flight officer.

She toured Australia in 1951, and in 1952 helped found the Australian Musical Association in London. Returning to Melbourne in 1954, she performed and broadcast extensively for the ABC as soloist and chamber musician, and was the only Australian soloist in the Arts Festival of the 1956 Melbourne Olympic Games. In 1958 she gave concerts and classes in China for the Chinese Association for Cultural Relations. She joined John Glickman and John Kennedy in the Ormond Trio in the early 1960s, in 1963–64 toured Europe, the Middle East and Asia with John Kennedy and Joan Dargarvel, and made four solo recordings for Spotlight Records. She tutored at the National Music Camps and taught at the University of Melbourne Conservatorium 1956–66. Appointed lecturer (later senior lecturer) at the Queensland Conservatorium 1966–80, she founded and led the Student Symphonic Safari Orchestra, which toured Queensland and the NT 1969–73, and the Kindy Konzerts for young children, and organised concerts in Queensland hospitals. Founder and president of the Bach Society of Queensland, after her retirement from the Conservatorium in 1980 she restored Brisbane's Rialto Theatre and other historic buildings as concert venues.

Weir brought to Australian music an intimate knowledge of European musical traditions and international performing standards. Her broadcasts and performances throughout rural and metropolitan Australia made her one of the country's best-known pianists in the 1950s and 60s. She also contributed to raising the standards of Australian tertiary music training. Her students include Rodney Sigston, who won the 1961 ABC Competition; and Piers ★Lane. Her awards include the AO, an honorary DMus. from Griffith University, the FRAM, and the University of Melbourne Conservatorium Centennial Award.

FURTHER REFERENCE
MoresbyA, 118–19.   BELINDA McKAY

Werder, Felix (*b* Berlin, 24 Feb. 1922), composer, music critic. He initially studied with Boas Bischofswerder and Nado Nadel and then, after leaving Germany in 1934 to escape Nazi persecution, attended Shoreditch Polytechnic in London. Other teachers were Sundberg and ★Goossens. Arriving in Australia in 1941 as a refugee, he served time in the army from 1944 to 1946, then worked as a musician, arranger, schoolteacher, conductor, and lecturer in music. Since 1952 he has lectured on contemporary music, including electronic music, for Council of Adult Education classes. From the 1950s to the early 1960s he became a leading figure of the Australian avant-garde, contributing towards the formation of a characteristic Australian voice along with composers such as ★Meale, ★Sculthorpe, ★Butterley, ★Dreyfus, ★Sitsky and ★Brumby. In 1963 he was appointed music critic for the *Age*, and continued in this position until 1975, proving to be an idiosyncratic, amusing writer, and an outspoken if at times eccentric champion of certain causes, particularly new music and early music performance practice. In 1976 he was honoured with the AM.

Werder is an exceptionally prolific composer, with a substantial list of chamber music, orchestral works and operas. His music is both intriguing and challenging in its emotional intensity, and it has been performed in Australia, Europe, England and America. He draws predominantly from European musical currents since the 1920s, with his main influences being the atonal school of Schoenberg, the German expressionist school, and the modality and cantillation of Hebrew chants. Werder has always held a reputation for being radical and non-conformist, and holds strong personal ideas and philosophies about his musical intentions. His predominantly European reference is obvious, but he has successfully assimilated his Jewish, Germanic, and Australian identities into his music.

WORKS (Selective)
Orchestral Symphonies No. 1, op. 6 (1948–51), No. 2, op. 33 (1959), No. 3, *Laocoon*, op. 67 (1965, rec. ABC), No. 4, op. 107 (1970), No. 5, op. 118 (1971), No. 6 (n.d.), No.7, *Pique Dame* (1994); Concertos for fl, op. 15 (1954), pf, op. 18 (1955), vn, op. 19 (1956), cl, op. 47 (1962), va, op. 53 (1963), vn, op. 72 (1966, rec. 1966, Festival LP SFC 80020), *Tower Concerto*, op. 91 (1968, rec. ABC), *Prom Gothic*, op. 123, org, orch (1971), *Sans souci*, op. 143, fl, orch (1974); *Actomos*, op. 5, chorale prelude, str (1948, rev. 1952), *Abstract '67*, 3 groups (1967, rec. ABC), *Concert Music*, fl, perc, str (1971, LP Mopoke GYS004).
Chamber 12 string quartets, including no. 4 (1955, rec. HMV OASD 7553), no. 6 (1962, rec. World Record Club LP S/2474), no. 9 (1968, rec. HMV OASD 7563); Piano Quartet, op. 12 (1954, rec. W&G AL660), *Fantasia in Three Parts*, op. 17 (1955, rec. Festival SFC 80020), *Music for Clarinet, Horn and String Trio*, op. 31 (1959, rec. W&G A/1635), *Concert Music for Five*, wind quintet (1964, rev. 1970, rec. HMV OASD 7558), *Music for Clarinet and String Quartet*, op. 63 (1965, rec. HMV OASD 7553), *Three Night Pieces*, op. 121 (1972, rec. Thorofon, Germany, CD CTH 2086), *Sonata No. 3 for Violin and Piano* (1986, rec. Canberra School of

Music CSM 17), *The Peter Clinch Saxophone Quartet* (1992, rec. Quadrella CD PCSQ001).

Keyboard *Reverberations* (Toccata), org (1972, rec. Move MS 3008), *Reverberations II*, org (Move MS 3025), *A Little Piano Music* (1987, Tall Poppies TP020), *The Hands—The Dream*, pf (1990, rec. Tall Poppies TP 020).

Opera *Kisses for a Quid*, op. 39 (1960, A. Marshall), 1961, Melbourne, *The General*, op. 69 (1966, 1, L. Radic), unperformed, *Agamemnon* (1967, Werder after Aeschylus, rec. Enzo Marciano Studios, LP SSM007), 1977, Melbourne, *The Affair*, op. 99 (1969, L. Radic), 1974, Sydney, *Private*, op. 103 (1969, P. Rorke), 1970, Melbourne, *The Vicious Square*, op. 120 (1971, 3, P. Rorke), unperformed, *The Conversion*, op. 138 (1973, after Wedekind), Melbourne, *The Director* (1980, Werder), 1980, Melbourne.

Music-Theatre *Banker*, 2 synth, perc, gui, pf (1971, rec. Discovery Stereo, CD GYS.001), 1973, Melbourne, *Medea* (1985, after Euripides), 1985, Melbourne, *Business Day: Concerto for Cash Register*, chamber orch, cash register, vv (1989, Werder after Marlowe), 1989, Perth.

Vocal *Four Songs after Poems of Walter von der Vogelweide* (1989, rec. Scalaton 6058), *Requiem*, S, fl, ob, cl, vn, pf, perc, brass (rec. LP QW075), Cantata *Peace*, Mez, Bar, small orch (1967, L. Radic).

Electronic *Machine Messages* (1992, rec. Australian Computer Music Association, ACMA vol. 1).

FURTHER REFERENCE
A discography of recordings to 1972 is in *PlushD*. His writings include '20th-century Rococo', *Opera Australia* 1/1 (Jan. 1974), 20–1. See also *CallawayA*; Andrew McCredie, *GroveD*; *McCredieM*; *MurdochA*.   PAULINE PETRUS

We're Happy Little Vegemites. Advertising jingle for Vegemite, a yeast extract spread with distinctive dark colour and piquant taste, developed (as Parwill) in 1923 by Fred Walker & Co. and now a universal favourite in Australia. First heard on radio, the tune remains a perennial in television commercials.

Wertheim. Firm of piano manufacturers founded in Melbourne by Hugo Wertheim (1854–1919). Arriving in Australia, Wertheim established himself as a merchant, selling sewing machines, washers, mangles, bicycles, gramophones, records, music and Hapsburg pianos. He established his store at William Street, Melbourne, from 1900, and began making Australian pianos using staff trained by Steinway and Bechstein, then opened a factory at Richmond, Melbourne, in 1908. His instruments had durable iron frames, used local timbers and featured native floral motifs.

At its height, his business employed 300 people and covered all aspects of piano manufacture, offered a range of models, and supplied pianos to town halls and conservatoriums throughout the country. After his death his son Herbert continued the business, combining with ★Allans, W.H. ★Palings, and Suttons to form the Australian Piano Company in 1929, but with the 1930s Depression and the radio increasingly supplying music

in the home, the company had ceased to manufacture instruments by 1935.

One of the most successful of Australia's piano manufacturers, Wertheim made instruments that were durable and resonant. Lyric House, the showroom opened by Herbert Wertheim in Collins Street, still stands. Many of his instruments are still in circulation; a fine example is in the Powerhouse Museum, Sydney.

FURTHER REFERENCE
AthertonA.

Wesley-Smith, Martin (b Adelaide, 10 June 1945), composer. After singing with his twin brother Peter in the folk group the Wesley Three, he studied composition with Peter ★Tahourdin, Peter Maxwell-Davies, Richard ★Meale and Jindrich Feld at the University of Adelaide, wrote music for ABC radio's *Let's Have Music* and taught at Bedford Park Teacher's College in 1971, then took doctoral study at York University (DPhil, 1974). He joined the NSW State Conservatorium staff in 1974, developing its electronic studios, becoming an expert in the possibilities of the Fairlight CMI, and directing ★WATT contemporary ensemble. He has since taught at the University of Hong Kong and in China. His choral cantata *Boojum!* was commissioned for the Adelaide Festival in 1986, and he was Australia Council Don Banks fellow in 1987. An eclectic composer and a leading exponent of electronic and computer music, he writes effectively and often humorously for music-theatre and for choir. His music includes successful works for children, such as *Boojum!* (1986, after Lewis Carroll), or on political or environmental topics, such as *Kdadalak (For the Children of Timor)* (1977).

WORKS (Selective)
Orchestral *Sunday Arvo*, closing theme (1989), *Beta-Globin DNA 3* (1990).

Chamber *Tiger, Tiger*, 2 vn (1970, Sydney: J. Albert & Son, 1974), *Doublets*, str qrt (1974), *Doublets 2 (a)*, alto/soprano/tenor sax, live electronics, tape (1974), *Snark-Hunting*, fl, melodion/pf/celeste, perc, vc, tape (1984), *White Knight and Beaver*, trbn, vn/va, tape (1984), *Doublets 2 (f)*, va, live electronics, tape (1987), *Beta-Globin DNA*, performer(s), tape (1987).

Solo Instrumental *Small Bitonal Study*, pf (1968, Sydney: J. Albert & Son, 1974), *Guitar Music I* (1973), *Pat-a-Cake*, trbn, tape (1980, Sydney: Purple Ink, 1980), *For Marimba and Tape* (1982), *For Clarinet and Tape* (1983), *Oom Pah Pah Oom Pah*, pf (1989), *Three Little Piano Pieces* (1991), *Balibo*, fl, tape (1992).

Theatre *Machine: A Music Mime*, children's ch, 3 perc, tape (1972, [London]: Universal Edition, 1978), *Media Music Two*, 4 tape recorder players, mixer operator, lighting technician (1973), *Sh…*, orch, audience participation (1973), *Boojum! In Concert: Nonsense, Truth and Lewis Carroll* (1986, Peter Wesley-Smith), *Quito*, 2 S, A, T, Bar, B, computer music, audio visuals, puppets (1994, Peter Wesley-Smith).

Choral *Three Shakespearean Songs*, SATB (1965), *I'm a Caterpillar of Society (Not a Social Butterfly)*, SATB (1977); v, pf, or v, fl, bass cl, pf (1985), *Who Killed Cock Robin?*, SATB (1979), *Lost in Space*, primary school ch, pf (1982), *Songs for Snark-Hunters*, SATB, pf (1985), *The Lilyfield Post Office Song*, arr. barbershop qrt, TTBarB (1988), *Lines by a Cowhand In Love*, barbershop qrt, TTBarB (1988), *Songlines*, 2 S, T soli, SATB, org (optional) (1988), *Songs for Kids*, high v, fl/pic/alto fl, cl/bass cl, pf, vc (1990), *Songs of Australia,* SATB, pf, perc (1988), *These are the Songs of Australia*, S, A soli, TTBB (1988), *When we are Old and Gay*, T solo, SATB, pf (1988), *Tiananmen Square*, S, T soli, SATB (1989), *Several Australian Conservation Songs*, SSATBarB (Sydney: Sounds Australian, 1991), *Songs for Kids*, female (or unbroken male) vv, pf (1991), *The Hunting of the Snark*, SSAA, pf (n.d.), *Let's Have Music,* children's vv (n.d.), *M. C. Pig*, SATB, pf (n.d.), *Old Coat: A Love Song*, S solo, TBarBarB; or S solo, SATB; or SSATBarB; or SATB (n.d.), *Recruiting Song (The Crooked Back Whackers' League)*, SATB (n.d.), *Several Australian Barbershop Quartets*, TTBarB (n.d.), *Songs for Kids*, SATB; or SSATBarB (n.d.), *Together*, SATB (n.d.), *Trust*, SATB soli (n.d.).

Solo Voice (with pf)   *The Wild West Show* (Universal Edition, 1971), *Climb the Rainbow* (1976), *Jubjubby* (from *Boojum! In Concert*) (1985), *Ten Songs* (c.1992).

FURTHER REFERENCE
Recordings include *Boojum!* (1992, Vox Australis VAST010–2); *Wattamolla Red Electronic Music* (1995, Tall Poppies TP072); *The Green CD*, Song Company (1995, Tall Poppies TP064); *Songs for Snark-Hunters* (Oz Music, OZM 2006). See also *MonashB*; Andrew Ford, *Composer to Composer* (Sydney: Allen & Unwin, 1993); *MurdochA*; *Sing Out* 8/2 (1991), 10–11.

Wesley-Smith, Peter   (*b* 10 June 1945), law professor, writer. After being tutor in history at the University of Adelaide, he taught law, becoming professor and dean of law at the University of Hong Kong. His books including *Constitutional and Administrative Law in Hong Kong*, 2 vols (1987–94) and *Sources of Hong Kong Law* (1994), and works of fiction *Ombly-Gombly* (1969), and *Hocus Pocus* (1973). Involved in the folk music revival of the 1960s playing in the Wesley Three with his twin brother, the composer Martin ★Wesley-Smith, he has written texts for a number of his brother's works, including the children's opera *Pie in the Sky* (1971), the music-theatre work *Boojum!* (1986), the musical *Noonday Gun* (1986), the choral cantata *Songs of Australia* (1988) and *Quito* (1994).

FURTHER REFERENCE
Who's Who of Australian Writers.

West Australian Ballet.   Founded in 1952 by Kira Bousloff and the composer James ★Penberthy. Being the company's music director, Penberthy was in a position to have a number of his original choreographic compositions realised. In 1969 the troupe turned professional and Bousloff retired from the directorship, having developed a strong foundation for the future artistic directors, namely Rex Reid (1969–73), Luis Moreno (1973–77), Robyn Haig (1977–79), Garth Welch (1979–83) and Barry

Moreland (since 1983). Other composers who have been commissioned by the troupe include Brian ★Howard, Graeme ★Koehne, Roger ★Smalley, Peter Sluik, Carl ★Vine and Verdon ★Williams. (See *Ballet and Dance Music*).

FURTHER REFERENCE
Edward H. Pask, *Ballet in Australia* (Melbourne: OUP, 1982).
JOEL CROTTY

West Australian Conservatorium.   Founded in 1985 and forming part of Edith Cowan University since 1991, it offers degrees focusing on performance (including music-theatre and jazz programs) and music education. Its origins are in the music department of the Mt Lawley Teachers College, later the WA Academy of the Performing Arts (from 1980), where it developed with classical and jazz divisions. Set in an extensive modern performing arts building at Mt Lawley, its deans have been Richard ★Gill (1986–91), Ed Applebaum (1991–92), and Brian ★Howard (1992–95). Its current dean is Graeme Ashton.

West Australian Opera Company.   Founded in its present form in Perth in 1967 by James ★Penberthy and Giuseppe Bertinazzo, in the first 18 months it presented *Carmen, La Bohème, Faust,* and *Amahl and the Night Visitors.* The Opera (WA Arts) Orchestra was formed in 1970 and in 1980 His Majesty's Theatre became the company's permanent home. Financial support comes from public and private sources. Lindy Hume was appointed first artistic director in 1992 with productions since of *Carmen, Heloise and Abelard, Orpheus in the Underworld, The Burrow, The Magic Flute, The Elixir of Love, Alcina* and *Die Fledermaus.* The company combines with touring principals of the Australian Opera.

FURTHER REFERENCE
John Cargher, *Bravo! 200 Years of Opera in Australia* (Sydney: ABC/Macmillan, 1988).   PATRICIA THORPE

West Australian String Quartet.   Formed in 1978 as the Arensky String Quartet with George Ermolenko, Ashley Arbuckle (Alan Bonds), Berian Evans, and Gregory Baron. Renamed the West Australian String Quartet in 1982, it resided at the University of Western Australia (with leader Graham Wood) and from 1984 at the WA Academy of Performing Arts (with leader Paul Wright). It disbanded in 1989, re-forming in 1990 as the ★Stirling String Quartet, with Alan Bonds the only remaining long-standing member. The quartet has performed regularly at Festivals of Perth, throughout Western Australia (supported by the WA Arts Council), and interstate and overseas for Musica Viva. Commissions include Smalley's String Quartet (1979).   PATRICIA THORPE

West Australian Symphony Orchestra.   Founded in Perth in 1949, the orchestra has 90 full-time players, and gives over 130 performances annually. It is funded by the ABC and offers a subscription series, with concerts at the Perth Concert Hall and tours regularly to regional cities, including centres in the remote north-west of WA such as Broome and Port Hedland. It also supports performances of ballet and the WA Opera and maintains an Educational Chamber Orchestra (ECHO), which also tours regional centres.

The origins of the orchestra are in a co-operative of 35 players begun by actor-conductor John Hayward [Harold Newton] in 1928 to provide concert work for silent movie musicians put out of work by the advent of 'talkies'. Hayward was succeeded by George Reed in 1934, and from his musicians the ABC created the ABC (Perth) Orchestra in 1936 with a full-time core of 17. The war prevented further progress, but in 1947 Henry ★Krips was appointed resident conductor, and with subsidies from the State Government as well as from the Perth and Fremantle city councils, the core was expanded to 40 in 1949, augmented with casuals to 55 in concerts, and the orchestra was securely established. Rudolf ★Pekarek was appointed conductor, and several long-running appointments followed with John Farnsworth ★Hall (1954–65), Thomas Mayer (1966–71) and David ★Measham (1972–81). The current conductor is Vernon Handley.

FURTHER REFERENCE
Recordings include *West Australian Symphony Orchestra*, cond. D. Measham, D. Franks (1986, ABC C-38547); V. Williams, *On Wenlock Edge*, cond. D. Measham (1980, Unicorn-Kanchana KP 8001); and W. Lovelock, Saxophone Concerto, cond. V. Williams, P. Clinch, sax (1975, ABC AC1009). See also Charles Buttrose, *Playing for Australia: A Story about ABC Orchestras and Music in Australia* (Sydney: ABC/Macmillan, 1982).

West Australian Youth Orchestra Association.

Founded at the University of Western Australia in 1975, the association seeks to assist young musicians in the pursuit of excellence through ensemble playing. Originally a youth orchestra of 50 or so players, the association now operates seven ensembles ranging from the Western Australian Youth Orchestra to the Amati Ensemble, a primary school string orchestra, and involves about 220 players aged 8–23. With core support from the State Government, as well as assistance from sponsorship and the Australia Council, the ensembles rehearse each Saturday at the WA Conservatorium. The Youth Orchestra performs regularly at the Perth Concert Hall and has appeared at the Festival of Perth and the Leeuwin Estate and has toured to Singapore (1989). The Babies Proms, interactive concerts for small children inaugurated by then musical director Richard ★Gill in 1986, have been an enduring success, and several groups tour each year to regional centres in WA. The current musical director is Peter Moore.

West, Haydn Scarr   (*b* Wellington, NZ; *d* Ballarat, Vic., 20 Oct. 1942), choral conductor and teacher. West settled in Ballarat at the age of eight. He trained under

G.W.L. Marshall-Hall with Franz Dierich (violin) and David Coutts (piano), Nellie Billings and August Siede. He returned to Ballarat at the age of 18 to assist his father, Hautrie, himself a distinguished musician, as organist of St Patrick's Cathedral. For 30 years from 1906, when he founded the Ballarat Choral Union, to 1936, when he won his 41st First Prize, he dominated competitive choral singing as conductor, adjudicator and teacher, mainly through Ballarat's South Street Eisteddfod. Out of 75 entries, his various choirs were only twice unplaced.

FURTHER REFERENCE
K. Dreyfus, 'The South Street Eisteddfod and Local Music-Making in Ballarat in the 1920s and 1930s', *Victorian Historical Journal* 66/2 (Nov. 1995), 99–121.   KAY DREYFUS

West, John   (*b* Concord, Sydney, *c*.1923), radio broadcaster. He joined the ABC at 17 and remained there for his whole career, apart from his period of war service with the RAAF. He wrote and hosted *The Showman* for ABC radio from 1964; covering show business and especially the latest Broadway musicals, the program ran for 26 years. He produced another long-running program, *Sentimental Journey*, from 1978, playing nostalgic popular music and taking listeners' requests. A cultured presence on radio with a vast knowledge of musicals and the history of theatre, he wrote *Theatre in Australia* (Sydney: Cassell, 1978).

FURTHER REFERENCE
Jeremy Eccles, 'John West's Sentimental Journey', *24 Hours* (Aug. 1991), 50–1; *Age* 18 Oct. 1984.

Westlake, Nigel   (*b* Perth, 6 Sept. 1958), composer, clarinettist. After studying clarinet with his father, Donald Westlake, 1972–78, and bass clarinet with Harry Sparnaay in Amsterdam in 1983, he worked as clarinettist with the Magic Puddin' Band 1980–83, the Australia Ensemble 1987–92, Attacca 1992, and as composer-in-residence with ABC Radio (1987). His compositions include *Onomatopoeia* (1984) for bass clarinet and digital delay, *The Flying Fruit Fly Circus* (1986) theatre music, *Malachite Glass* (1990) for four percussion and bass clarinet, *Antarctica* (1992) for guitar and orchestra, *Music for High Tension Wires* (1994) for string quartet, *Invocations* (1995) for bass clarinet and chamber orchestra, the feature film *Babe* (1995), and extensive work in radio and television. Westlake's attractive blend of minimalism, improvisation and elements from popular music has firmly established his presence in both concert music and music for radio and screen.

WORKS (Selective)
Orchestral *Cudmirrah Fanfare* (1988), *Vortex*, orch (1991), *Threnody*, solo vc, str (1991), *Antarctica*, solo gui, orch (1992), *Out of the blue...*, str orch (1994), *Celluloid Heroes—Suite for Orchestra* (1994/5), Concerto for bass clarinet and chamber orchestra (1995).

Chamber Instrumental *Hinchinbrook Riffs*, jazz rock ens (1978), *Trellis Music*, jazz rock ens (1979), *Nursery Crimes*, v, cl, bn, ob (1980), *Excuse me, sir, look at the balloon*, jazz rock ens (1980), *Minus the dingus*, jazz rock ens (1980), *Sir Globular Thread*, jazz rock ens (1981), *Le Cirque de Domain*, perc qrt, tape (1985), *Omphalo Centric Lecture*, perc qrt (1985), *Lapsang Souchong*, soprano sax, perc, electronics (1987), *Our Mum was a Waterfall*, soprano sax, perc, electronics (1987), *Angola*, bass cl/soprano sax, perc, electronics (1987), *Omphalo*, bass cl/soprano sax, perc, electronics (1987), *Parliamentary Fanfare*, brass ens (1988), *Refractions at Summercloud Bay*, fl, cl, vn, va, vc (1988), *Moving Air*, perc qrt (1989), *Winter in the Forgotten Valley*, gui qrt (1989), *Blue on Gold*, gui, vn, fl (1990), *Entomology*, fl, cl, vn, vc, pf, perc, tape (1990), *Touching Wood*, 2 gui, bass cl, perc (1990), *Malachite Glass*, 4 perc, bass cl (1990), *Call of the Wild*, bass cl, perc, tape (1992), *High tension wires*, 2 vn, va, vc (1994), *Songs from the forest*, 2 gui (1994).

Solo Instrumental *Onomatopoeia*, bass cl, digital delay (1984), *Fabian Theory*, perc, digital delay (1987), *The Devil's Marbles*, giu, elec (1993).

Vocal/Choral *Stone the Crows*, v, jazz rock ens (1981)

Theatre *The Flying Fruit Fly Circus*, incidental circus music (1986), *Richard III* (1992, Bell Shakespeare Co.), *Romeo and Juliet* (1993, Bell Shakespeare Co.), *Macbeth* (1994, Bell Shakespeare Co.).

Music for Television, Radio, Film and Video 'Pepperminati', documentary (1982), *Stone the Crows*, short radiophonic work (1983), *Time and tide*, short radiophonic work (1983), *Our Mum was a Waterfall*, short radiophonic work (1983), 'Marathon', documentary (1983), 'The Health Report' theme, ABC Radio (1984), 'Real Life', documentary (1984), 'Making it in Japan', documentary (1984), 'Music Line' theme, ABC Radio (1985), 'That's Democracy', documentary (1985), 'The Greatest Little Show on Earth', documentary (1986), 'The Food Programme' theme, ABC Radio (1987), 'Newsvoice' theme, ABC Radio (1987), Parliamentary Fanfare, ABC Radio (1987), 'News in brief' theme, ABC Radio (1987), Radio National station theme, ABC Radio (1987), 'Late Night Live' theme, ABC Radio (1987), *24 Hours* magazine promotion theme, ABC Radio (1987), 'Listener Feedback' theme, ABC Radio (1987), 'Andi Ross' theme, ABC Radio (1987), 'Books & Writing' theme, ABC Radio (1987), 'Radio National Morning' theme, ABC Radio (1987), 'Fictions' theme, ABC Radio (1987), 'Sunday Night' theme, ABC Radio (1987), 'Candy Regentag', feature film (1987), 'Backchat' theme, ABC TV (1987), ABC Radio National promotion, ABC TV (1987), 'Roads to Xanadu', ABC TV (1987–88), Logo theme, Film Australia (1988), 3 Station Identification themes, SBS TV (1989), 'AIDS Means Business Too', Corporate video (1989), 'Arts Review' theme, ABC TV (1989), MLC Corporate video (1990), 'Newsbreak' theme, SBS TV (1990), 7 'Tonight's Lineup' themes, SBS TV, (1990), 'Midwives' (1990), 'Toxic' (1990), 'Backsliding' (1991), 'Antarctica', Imax film (1991), 'Dateline', SBS TV (1992), 'News Theme' SBS TV (1992), 'Five Station Identification Themes', SBS TV (1993–4), 'Breaking Through', 3D Imax film (1993), 'Celluloid Heroes', 4-part TV series, 'Babe', feature film (1995).

FURTHER REFERENCE
Recordings include *Omphalo Centric Lecture*, Michael Askill, perc (SCCD 1021); *Grand China* and other works, N. Westlake, cl (ABC 846 219; *Synergy Impact*, Synergy (ABC 442 350). See also *BroadstockS*; J. Cashman, Aspects of Nigel Westlake's *Onomatopoeia*: The Performed and the Processed, BMus, Univ. Sydney, 1992; B. Mackay, 'Nigel Westlake, Composer/Performer', *SA* 23 (Spring 1989), 20–2; B. Webster, 'Nigel Westlake', *APRAJ* (Aug. 1990), 14–16.   MICHAEL BARKL

Wheatley, Glen Dawson (b 23 Jan. 1948), manager. After a career performing in several rock bands, notably the ★Masters Apprentices 1968–71, he became a manager, representing ★Little River Band, ★Australian Crawl and John ★Farnham, and managing director of the Hoyts Media group.

Wheeler, John (*fl.* 1940–70), songwriter. Based in Sydney, he wrote carols, children's songs and art song texts, set to music by Alfred ★Hill, William ★James, Dulcie ★Holland, Werner ★Baer, Oscar W. Walters, Claude McGlyn and others. His works include the texts for Hill's symphonic sketch *Green Water* (1969) and *A Little Town I Love* (1948), James's popular *Australian Christmas Carols*, *Eastern Stranger* for SA choir (reissued 1973), and Baer's *Under the Coolabah Tree: Songs for Young Australians* (1955).

Whelan, Albert [Albert Waxman] (b Melbourne, 4 May 1875; d London, 1962), popular music singer, entertainer. The tenth child of a successful Polish-born banker in Melbourne, Whelan was first an accountant and a mechanic before he became a goldminer at Coolgardie, WA. He was unsuccessful on the goldfields as a miner but developed an act as a singing clown. Returning to Melbourne, he successfully auditioned for the first Australian production of *Belle of New York*, playing Ichabod Bronson. Moving to the UK in 1900, his first appearances were in vaudeville as a dancer. In 1901 he was selected to play Bronson in a revival of *Belle* at the Adelphi Theatre. His career flourished and his acts included singing, dancing, whistling and playing the piano. He developed an elegant style which included a white tie, cape, top hat and gloves. He is credited with being the first vaudeville artist to use a signature tune, *Der Lustige Bruder*. Songs like *The Preacher and the Bear* and *The Three Trees*, like the many other things he recorded, were widely popular from 1910 to the 1950s. His last appearances were on British television.
                                                          JEFF BROWNRIGG

Where The White Faced Cattle Roam. Country music bush ballad (1942) by Buddy ★Williams. Recorded by Williams on 18 May 1942 as the B-side of the single *What A Pal My Mother Might Have Been To Me* (Regal Zonophone G24596), it became very popular, and was also recorded by Barry Thornton, Eddie Tapp, and Lindsay Butler. Reissued on *Buddy Williams Remembers* vol. 1 (1965, RCA L101594).

Whistle, Folded Leaf. See *Gumleaf.*

Whitehead, Gillian (*b* Hamilton, NZ, 23 Apr. 1941), composer. After studies at the Universities of Auckland, Wellington and Sydney, she met Peter Maxwell-Davies at his classes in Adelaide in 1966, and went to the UK to study with him in 1967; his ensemble Pierrot Players played several of her works. In the following years she had several commissions from the Arts Council of Great Britain, and was composer-in-residence at the University of Newcastle-Upon-Tyne, UK, 1978–80, while continuing to write works for NZ performance, often on Maori subjects. She returned to Australia in 1981, and since then has been lecturer at the NSW State Conservatorium. Her music is complex, frequently employing Maxwell-Davies' technique of generating materials from a number grid, yet the spare instrumentation and evocative colours make for an articulate language. She often features the voice, and there are choral works, vocal settings, a chamber opera, *Tristan and Iseult* (M. Crowthers and M. Hill, 1978), a children's opera, *The Tinker's Curse* (J. Aiken, 1979), a dance work, *Requiem* (1981), and a full-length opera, *Bride of Fortune* (dell'Oso, 1988), for the WA Opera.

WORKS (Selective)
Orchestral   *Te tangi a Apakura*, str (1975), *Tirea*, ob, vn, vc, hpd, str (1978), *Hoata*, chamber orch (1979), *Resurgences* (1989).
Chamber   *Okuru*, vn, pf (1979), *Antiphons*, 3 tpt, 2 hn, 3 trbn, tuba (1980), *Ahotu (o matenga)*, ens (1984), *Windstreams*, perc (1985), *Napier's Bones*, 24 perc, improvised jazz pf (1989), *Angels Born at the Speed of Light*, str qrt (1990), *Moon, Tides and Shoreline*, str qrt (1990).
Piano   *Fantasia on 3 Notes* (1966), *La cadenza sia corta* (1974), *Voices of Tane* (1976), *Tamatea Tutahi* (1980), *5 Bagatelles* (1986).
Stage   *Tristan and Iseult*, chamber opera (1975, M. Crowthers, M. Hill), *The Tinker's Curse*, children's opera (1979, J. Aiken), *Requiem*, Mez, org, dancers (1981), *The King of the Other Country*, chamber opera (1984, F.Adcock), *The Pirate Moon*, chamber opera (1986, A.M. dell'Oso), *Bride of Fortune*, chamber opera (1988, A.M. dell'Oso), *Angels Born at the Speed of Light* (1992, C. McQueen, choreography B. Judge).
Choral   *Missa brevis*, SATB (1963), *The Inner Harbour*, chamber orch, perc (1979), *Low Tide: Aramoana*, Mez, SATB, 3 tpt, 2 trbn, timpani (1982), *The Virgin and the Nightingale*, 5 songs, S, Mez, C, T, Bar or B, ch or sextet (1986), *Moments*, SATB (1993).
Solo Voice   *Pakuru*, S, fl, cl, va, vc, hpd, perc (1967), *Whakatauki* (Maori proverbs), male v, chamber ens (1970), *Bright Forms Return*, Mez, str qrt (1980), *Hotspur*, S, ens (1980), *Pao*, S, cl, pf (1981), *Eleanor of Aquitaine*, Mez, ens (1982), *Out of this Nettle: Danger*, Mez, ens (1983), *These Isles your Dream*, Mez, va, pf (1983), *Awa Herea*, S, pf (1993).

FURTHER REFERENCE
Recordings include *Manutaki*, ens (1986, Tall Poppies). See also J.M. Thomson *GroveW*; Sally Mays, *ContemporaryC*; *CohenI*; *LePage.*

Whitehead, James (*b* Newchurch, Lancashire, England, 1912; *d* Adelaide, Jan. 1979), cellist. His mother was an opera singer, and he studied cello from the age of 10 with Walter Haffon in Manchester. He won a scholarship to the Royal College of Music, then played principal cello in the Boyd Neel String Orchestra 1933–53. He also played at the Glyndebourne Opera and conducted Bach cantatas with his own orchestra and choir. He served with the RAF during the war, then was principal cellist with the Zurich Tonhalle Orchestra 1945–49. He arrived in Australia in 1959 and taught at the Elder Conservatorium, becoming a member of the Elder Quartet and ★Elder Trio. He conducted the Adelaide Choral Society and retired in 1977.

FURTHER REFERENCE
Recordings include Elgar, Cello Concerto and Rachmaninov, Cello Sonata (1980 Sarec SAC 2002).

Whitehouse Bros.   A firm of Brisbane organ-builders tracing its origins to the 1880s when Benjamin B. Whitehouse, who had emigrated from Britain in 1883, was responsible for installing imported organs and constructing the first Queensland-built organ. In 1897 he was joined by his English-trained brother Joseph Howell Whitehouse, trading as B.B. Whitehouse & Co. from 1903, and then Whitehouse Bros from 1921 when the firm established its factory in Red Hill. Using imported metal pipework, the firm had the unique distinction until the 1990s of building organs for all states in Australia. Many had a reliable tubular-pneumatic action, sliderless windchests, and colourful symphonic voicing. The firm was later managed by Joseph's son Joseph and grandson Kevin before its dissolution in 1982.

FURTHER REFERENCE
Robert K. Boughen, *ADB*, 12; Geoffrey Cox, *Gazetteer of Queensland Pipe Organs* (Melbourne: Society of Organists, 1976).
JOHN MAIDMENT

Whiticker, Michael (*b* Gundagai, NSW, 26 Apr. 1954), composer. He studied at the NSW State Conservatorium of Music 1979–82, with Isang Yun and Witold Szalonek at the Höchschule der Künste in West Berlin, 1983–84, the University of NSW 1986, and at the University of Wollongong 1988, 1991–93, and 1996. Working in Sydney 1985–89, then West Berlin 1989–91, and Batlow, NSW, 1991, he was composer-in-residence with the Melbourne Symphony Orchestra, 1992–93, and has been lecturer in composition at the University of Western Sydney (Nepean) since 1994. His works include *Plangge* (1987) for percussion quartet, the chamber opera *Gesualdo* (1987), *In Prison Air* (1988) for guitar and tape, *After the Fire* (1991) for harp, *Purgatorio-Paradisio* (1992) for six voices and tape, and *Wild is the Wind* (1993) for bass clarinet, winds, brass and percussion. Whiticker's work displays both the composer's concern for technique and rigour, and a desire to establish a wide community base for composers through education, participation and improvisation.

FURTHER REFERENCE
Recordings include *Kiah*, fl (AMC 002); *As Water Bears Salt* (1981, VAST 016–2); *The Hands, The Dream*, pf (1989, Tall Poppies TP020). See also *BroadstockS*; D. Menzies, 'Michael Whiticker, Composer-in-Residence', *Encore: Newsletter of the Melbourne Symphony* (Aug. 1992); I. Shanahan and C. Dench, eds, 'An Emotional Geography of Australian Composition', *SA* 34 (Winter 1992), 8–32.   MICHAEL BARKL

Whitsunday. Opera in three acts by Brian *Howard, libretto by L. Nowra. First performed at the Sydney Opera House Drama Theatre on 2 September 1988.

Whittaker, Douglas Robert (*b* Melbourne, 1925; *d* Canberra, 10 Jan. 1974), flautist. After studies with Leslie *Barklamb at the University of Melbourne, he became principal flute in the WA Symphony Orchestra in 1949. He went to London in 1950, playing in the Sadler's Wells Orchestra, then as co-principal flute in the BBC Symphony Orchestra from 1952. He also played with the London Bach Orchestra and the Leonardo Ensemble, and gave premieres of concertos by Goffredo Petrassi, André Jolivet and Gunther Schuller; a sonatina was written for him by Alan Richardson. With the Soho Concertante from 1964 he focused on the music of J.C. Bach, Handel and Mozart. He toured Australia for the ABC in 1969 and in 1973 was appointed to the staff of the Canberra School of Music but died of a heart attack shortly after his arrival. His gold flute, made by Albert Cooper, was sold to the Australia Council, who then loaned it to several fine Australian players; there were recurring mechanical problems with it, however, and in 1996 it was sold in London to an English collector for £32 000.

Whyalla, pop. (1991) 25 863. Second largest city in SA, situated on the arid west coast of the Spencer Gulf, Eyre Peninsula, southern SA. Founded (1901) as Hummock Hill, it has a busy steelworks and chemical industry, and is a major port for iron ore and steel brought from the Middleback Ranges. The Whyalla Citizens Band was formed in 1912, a bandstand being built in front of the Whyalla Institute in 1925, and the Band Hall opened in 1939, by which time the band was a regular competition winner in band championships. The City of Whyalla Pipe Band (formerly Mount Laura Pipe Band) also continues to thrive. The Whyalla Choral Group presents 'Classics in the Foyer' at the Middleback Theatre, and the Whyalla Players Theatrical Group (founded 1956) presents an annual musical and pantomime. Many local musical activities have been supported by the steel industry, principally BHP.

FURTHER REFERENCE
Colin Stanton, *Hummock Hill to Whyalla* (Whyalla, n.d.); Sue Scheiffers, *A Ribbon of Steel* (Whyalla: Whyalla Jubilee 150 Committee, 1985).

Wickety Wak. Comedy rock band (1969–) formed in Brisbane, from 1985 comprised of Tony Jeffrey (vocals), Greg Doolan (guitar, vocals), Rob Rosenlund (keyboards, vocals), Pani Gilbert [Pahnie Jantzep] (bass) and Peter Mackay (drums). In the earlier years 'Molly' *Meldrum, Beeb Birtles, Rick Springfield and others took part, but the membership has completely changed. Appearing in cabarets and clubs, they do nostalgic send-ups of well-known pop stars, made effective by their mellifluous vocal harmonies and able rock playing.

FURTHER REFERENCE
Recordings include *Moonlight Marvel* (1982, Hot Wax VDH 001) and *Bend Me Shape Me* (1985, Hot Wax WAX 1626); their albums include *New Horizons* (1983, Hot Wax WAX 200), *Second Helpings* (1985, Hot Wax WAX 201) and *Wacked About Australia* (1987, Hot Wax, WAX 202). For discography, see *SpencerA*. See also *McGrathA*; *SpencerW.*

Wiedermann, Elise (*b* Vienna, 31 Aug. 1851; *d* Melbourne, 24 July 1922), soprano. A pupil of Mme Marchesi, Mme Wiedermann established a career as an opera singer in Europe, notably at the Vienna State Opera, which was curtailed by her marriage in Melbourne in 1883 to Carl *Pinschof, the honorary consul for Austria-Hungary. In 1895 she became the principal teacher of singing at the new University of Melbourne Conservatorium and subsequently at the Albert Street Conservatorium from 1900. Her students included Florence *Austral and Elsa *Stralia. As teacher and friend of both artists and musicians, including Arthur Streeton, Tom Roberts and Marshall-Hall, Wiedermann was an invaluable patron of music in Melbourne.

FURTHER REFERENCE
MackenzieS; Raoul F. Middlemann, *ADB*, 2; Thérèse Radic, *Melba: The Voice of Australia* (Melbourne: Macmillan, 1986), 159–60.   SUZANNE ROBINSON

Wiegand, Chevalier August (*b* Liège, Belgium, 16 Oct. 1849; *d* Oswego, USA, 27 May 1904), Belgian organist. Wiegand was appointed organist of St Giles', Liège, when only six. Admitted to the Conservatorium of Liège in 1859, he studied organ with Jules Duguet, receiving numerous prizes and medals. He taught there for six years from 1870 then started a career as concert organist. His organ studies continued with Jacques Lemmens in 1879–81 and Alphonse Mailly. Wiegand presented 517 organ recitals between 1878 and 1890 in the principal cities of Europe. He arrived in Sydney in June 1891 to take up an appointment as city organist, and was also appointed organist to St Patrick's, Sydney.

He returned to Europe in 1900. His vast repertoire included all standard works for organ as well as an endless array of orchestral and instrumental transcriptions and compositions of his own.

FURTHER REFERENCE
His writings include A. Wiegand, *The Largest Organ in the World and the Musical Artists of Sydney* (Sydney: Maddock, 1892); idem, *Biography, List of Organ Recitals and Press Extracts* (Oswego, New York: Times Book and Job Print, 1903). See also A. Armstrong, 'Guilmant, Wiegand, Courboin, and Father Barry', *The American Organist* 28/6 (1994), 54–9.   GRAEME RUSHWORTH

Wiggles, The. Children's entertainment band formed in Sydney (1991), comprised of Greg Page (vocals), Murray Cook (guitar), Jeff Fatt (keyboards) and Anthony Field (drums). Page, Cook and Field had studied pre-school teaching at Macquarie University, while Field and Fatt had played with the rock band *Cockroaches. They set out to apply child development theory to pop music and offer educational entertainment to small children. Writing child action songs with pre-school level language, set to catchy tunes often grounded in early paraphrases of rock and roll, they developed a stage show combining music with slapstick sketches, creating the characters Dorothy the Dinosaur, Henry the Octopus, and Captain Feathersword. They released their first album in 1991, winning a gold record for *Here Comes A Song* and in the next four years platinum albums for *The Wiggles*, *Yummy Yummy* and *Big Red Car*. Through appearances on ABC TV and extensive touring, they have become Australia's most popular pre-school entertainers. Combining entertainment of endearing simplicity and magnetic enthusiasm, they may be heard on *Here Comes A Song* (ABC 8143442/4) and *Wake Up Jeff* (ABC 8146722/4) or in their various ABC videos. They won two APRA children's songwriting awards (1994–95) and an ARIA children's award in 1995.

Wilcannia. Town on the Darling River in Paakantji country, north-east of Broken Hill, NSW. It has become home to people of other descents, particularly after the closure of the government mission downstream at Menindee where Paakantji and Ngiyampaa (Wangaaypuwan) were institutionalised, with others, 1933–49. Recordings 'in language', held by AIATSIS, range from occasional songs with known, often local composers, such as Granny Moysey, to ceremonial songs from distant traditions, such as those sung by George Dutton. Wilcannia also became home to Dougie *Young, self-styled 'wine-loving mug', maker of witty hillbilly-inspired songs in English about the quirks of Wilcannia identities and their ways of life.   TAMSIN DONALDSON

Wild Cherries. Rock band (1964–68) formed in Melbourne, originally comprised of John Bastow (vocals, harmonica), Rob Lovett (guitar, vocals), Malcolm McGee (guitar, vocals), Les Gilbert (bass, organ) and Kevin Murphy (drums). At first a rock band influenced by rhythm and blues, they became more experimental from 1967 with the addition of Lobby *Loyde, releasing *Krome Plated Yabby* and *That's Life*, which reached No. 37 in the charts. Their EP *Krome Plated Yabby* followed in 1967, and the single *I Don't Care* in 1968, but when Gilbert left they soon disbanded. Loyde's trio version of the band, which he revived in 1971, was short-lived. One of the most influential heavy rock bands of the mid-1960s, their adventurousness within the rock idiom and their feral antics on stage are fondly remembered.

FURTHER REFERENCE
Recordings include *Krome Plated Yabby* (Festival FK 1879), *That's Life* (Festival FK 2052), *Krome Plated Yabby* (Festival FK 11422), *I Don't Care* (1968, Festival FK 2535). A compilation is *That's Life* (1979, Raven). For discography, see *SpencerA*. See also *McGrathA*; *SpencerW*.

Wild Colonial Boy, The, folk-song. Often sung to 'The Wearing of the Green', this is the most widely disseminated of all Australian folk-songs; in one waltz-time version it is well known in Britain and other English-speaking countries. Set in central Victoria in the early 1860s, it recounts the exploits of the mythical Jack Doolan, a dashing bushranger who fights troopers to the death. Perhaps inspired by the real-life exploits of the escaped convict Jack Donahoe (killed by NSW troopers in 1830), it was published in *The Colonial Songster* (1881), and variants of this version were later collected by Percy *Jones and John *Manifold. Another version was published by A.B. *Paterson in *Old Bush Songs* in 1905, of which five variants have since been collected; a version set to 'Friar and the Nun' was collected and published by Manifold in 1951, for which four variants have since been collected; 15 other versions have been collected, mainly by John *Meredith and Ron *Edwards, including two under the titles 'Jack Dowling' or 'John Doolan'.

FURTHER REFERENCE
For a commentary, see Ron Edwards, *The Overlander Songbook* (Ferntree Gully, Vic.: Rams Skull Press, 1956); an edition of the most important versions is in *EdwardsG*; see also *ManifoldP*; *RadicS*, 6.

Wild Colonial Boys. Folk band (1968–70) formed in Melbourne, originally comprised of Declan *Affley (guitar, banjo, vocals), Tony Lavin (vocals, bush bass, bones), Jacko Kevans (accordion), Jim Fingleton (spoons, concertina) and Bob McGuiness (mandolin, fiddle). Founded by Affley and Lavin on the model of the Dubliners (Ireland) but playing Australian music, they appeared in the movie *Ned Kelly* (with Mick Jagger) and moved to Sydney in 1969, playing at folk clubs and on television and touring NSW.

FURTHER REFERENCE
Their recordings include *Glenrowan to the Gulf* (1970, EMI SOEX 9631).

Wild Rover No More, street ballad about the repentant resolution of a young man to forsake carousing and return to his parents. A popular ballad, perhaps of British origin, it was first published in Ashton's *Modern Street Ballads* (1888). Another version was published by A.B. Paterson in *Old Bush Songs* (1905); further versions were collected by Percy Jones (1953), A.L. Lloyd (1958), John Meredith (1958), and others.

FURTHER REFERENCE
Edition and commentary in *Edwards G*.

Wild, Stephen Aubrey (*b* Perth, WA, 17 Jan. 1941), ethnomusicologist. He graduated from the University of Western Australia (BA 1963, MA 1967), Indiana University (PhD 1967), and was lecturer in the department of music, Monash University, 1969–73. An authority on the music of the Warlpiri, central Australia, the Anbarra, Arnhem Land, and WA Aboriginal music, since his appointment to AIATSIS he has been a visiting music professor at the University of Illinois, the University of Washington, Seattle, lecturer at the Canberra School of Music and a visiting fellow at the Australian National University. He co-ordinated the International Council of Traditional Music World Conference in Canberra, January 1995.

MARGARET KARTOMI

Willcock, Fr Christopher John (*b* Sydney, 8 Feb. 1947), composer. He studied composition at the University of Sydney 1964–74 and entered the Society of Jesus in 1969, was ordained a priest in 1977, earning doctorates in theology and liturgy in France. His published works include *Psalms for Feasts and Seasons* (1977, rev. 1990), *Psalms for the Journey* (1991), *God Here Among Us* (1995) and *In Remembrance of You* (1996). Intended for liturgical use, his work has been influential in changing liturgical perceptions and practice in Australia. His unpublished concert works include *Friday 3.30* for choir and string orchestra (1986), the song cycle *New Song in an Ancient Land* (1993), and the a cappella *John Shaw Neilson Triptych* (1995).

FURTHER REFERENCE
Noel Ancell, Christopher Willcock, Australian Liturgical Composer, MA, Monash Univ., 1992. NOEL ANCELL

Williams, Billy [Richard Isaac Banks, sometimes Curly Banks] (*b* Melbourne, 1878; *d* Shoreham, England, 1915), vaudeville chorus singer. Having become too portly to continue a career as a jockey, Williams began singing in the working men's clubs of Melbourne and Collingwood. His singing act was seen by visiting English vaudevillian Tom Wootwell, who gave Williams some copyright songs for the young Australian to perform. Williams made his professional debut with the touring American Cogill Brothers and later worked for J.C. Williamsons, travelling to the UK late in 1899. On the English vaudeville circuit he started as a clown but quickly found that audiences were attracted to

his voice and that he could lead them in songs with easily remembered, attractive choruses. He composed the words for many of his songs. A partnership with Welsh composer Fred Godfrey saw the creation of many successful songs with words by Williams. In 1906 expatriate Australian vaudeville and pantomime artist Florrie Forde introduced him to the London Edison Bell recording studios. His first recording, *John Go and Put Your Trousers On*, was an instant success and he went on to record almost 150 songs, many of them smash hits. Williams adopted a distinctive personal costume consisting of a velvet suit and spats. With his hair curled into the 'bubble cut' he was considered eccentric, but songs like *The Hobnailed Boots That Father Wore* (1907), *I Must Go Home Tonight* (1909), *When Father Painted the Parlour* (1911) and *The Kangaroo Hop* (1912) remained popular after his early death. A major figure on the English vaudeville stage and an even more significant sound-recording artist, Williams has been an enduring star of Australian popular music and one of its most important figures. Some of his records having been almost continually available commercially since he made them in the first two decades of the 20th century. JEFF BROWNRIGG

Williams, Gerald (*b* Sydney, 1930), conductor. After studies in piano with Alexander *Sverjensky and in conducting with Eugene *Goossens at the Sydney Conservatorium, he conducted the Ballet Rambert in London 1954–56, in Basel, Vienna and Hilversene from 1962, and became conductor at the Stadt-Theater, Hildesheim, in 1975.

Williams, Harold ('Buddy') (*b* Newtown, Sydney, 5 Sept. 1918; *d* 12 Dec. 1986), country music singer-songwriter. Placed in an orphanage at Glebe and then raised from the age of seven by foster parents on a Dorrigo dairy farm, he ran away at the age of 15 and busked along the NSW north coast until he was signed by EMI in 1939; his first single, *That Dappled Grey Bronco Of Mine*, achieved huge success. He toured in a rodeo show in 1940, then during his war service and long convalescence (he was severely wounded in Borneo) he continued to write and record, producing some of his most enduring classics, including *Where The White Faced Cattle Roam* (1942) and *The Overlander Trail* (1946). On his recovery he formed a travelling tent rodeo show (1946–54), then his Country and Western Variety Show (1955–75), for more than 30 years touring the whole of Australia, from capital cities to the most remote centres.

With an unusually clear, natural voice and a guitar style that was widely emulated, he continued to appear as a solo vocalist with guitar until his album *Aussie On My Mind* (1973); he was unsurpassable in traditional ballads dealing with the Australian bush, to which he responded with straightforward lyrical warmth and endearing ardour. He was the first Australian-born country music artist to achieve national prominence; in his hands the music emerged from dependence on American themes. Despite indifferent health in later years, he kept touring and working until his death. He was honoured in the ACMA Roll of Renown in 1977 and won an ACMA Golden Guitar in 1980.

FURTHER REFERENCE
Recordings include singles *That Dappled Grey Bronco Of Mine* (Regal Zonophone GT 23854), *Where The White Faced Cattle Roam* (1942, Regal Zonophone G24596), *The Overlander Trail* (1946, Regal Zonophone G25052) and *Aussie On My Mind* (1973, RCA MSL 102227); re-releases of his music include *Under Western Skies* (EMI 701692–2), *Buddy Williams 1939–1940* (1992, Kingfisher KF AUS-22) and *Buddy Williams 1941–1942* (1992, Kingfisher KF AUS-23). For discography see *WatsonC*, I. See also *WatsonC*, I, 37–48.

Williams, Harold John ['Geoffrey Spencer', etc] (*b* Woollahra, Sydney, 3 Sept. 1893; *d* Gordon, Sydney, 5 June 1976), baritone. During his war service he sought a transfer to London in 1918 to study with Charles Phillips of the Royal Academy of Music, funded his own debut at Wigmore Hall in 1919, then sang in the Tillet ballad concerts 1920–21. He was soon appearing with the British National Opera Co., then Covent Garden and the English National Opera Co., giving noble, stirring accounts of Wolfram, Iago, Boris Godunov or Mephistopheles. In concert and oratorio he was increasingly in demand for *Messiah*, *The Kingdom*, or the annual *Song of Hiawatha* at the Royal Albert Hall; his Prophet in *Elijah* and Angel of Agony in *The Dream of Gerontius* were classics of oratorio performance. He was heard at every Proms season between 1921 and 1951, many Edinburgh Festivals and the Three Choirs Festival, and he sang solo at the coronations of George VI (1938) and Elizabeth II (1952). He visited Australia for the Taits in 1929 and for ABC concerts and oratorios in 1940–44. Renowned for his clear diction in English repertoire, rich, dark colours and superb breathing, he returned to teach at the NSW State Conservatorium from 1952, and sang concerts and opera until his voice gave out during *Elijah* at Melbourne in 1953.

FURTHER REFERENCE
Recordings included *Elijah*, cond. M. Sargent (not current); Valentin in *Faust*, cond. T. Beecham (Dutton Laboratories 2CD AX2001); and *Messiah*, cond. T. Beecham (1927, Pearl GEMMCD 59456). See also *MackenzieS*, 142–4; John Carmody, *ADB*, 12; *GlennonA*, 64.

Williams, Harry and Wilga. Leaders of the group Country Outcasts, one of the best-known Aboriginal country music groups of the 1970s and 80s. Wilga (née Munro) was originally from Tamworth and played bass guitar in the group. Harry was from Cowra, NSW, and also at times a rugby league player and actor, appearing in popular television series such as *Matlock* and the film *Blackfire* (produced by Bruce McGuinness, 1972), the first known film made by an indigenous Australian. He is the composer of many songs, among them *My Homemade*

Didjeridu and *Streets of Old Tamworth*. The Country Outcasts were formed in 1972, won a number of country music contests and toured throughout Australia and to New Guinea. In 1982 Harry and Wilga set up their own recording company in Canberra to support Aboriginal performers. The Outcasts also included Ian Mackay and Bert Williams, and during the 1980s the singer Laurie Ingram (*b* Tumut, NSW, 1935), later to form his own group, the Bidgee Wanderers.

FURTHER REFERENCE
Recordings include *Harry Williams and the Country Outcasts* (RCA, 1979); *Harry and Wilga Williams and the Country Outcasts*; and the film *Country Outcasts* (Film Australia, 1991).

P. DUNBAR-HALL

Williams, John Christopher (*b* Melbourne, 24 Apr. 1941), classical guitarist. Taught to play the guitar from the age of seven by his English father Len Williams during his residence in Melbourne (1939–52), Williams subsequently studied at the Royal Academy in London and the Accademia Chigiana in Siena with Andrés Segovia. He made his London debut at Wigmore Hall in 1958, and his first LP recording was released shortly thereafter. Since then he has toured the world continuously as recitalist and as soloist with the world's major orchestras. He has toured Australia almost every year since the early 1970s and has increasingly strengthened his ties with this country, having been artist-in-residence at various Australian institutions and encouraged performers, composers and luthiers.

Williams is noted for his superb technical mastery and his controlled musical expression. His unpretentious attitude to the guitar has produced some collaborations not customary within the concert tradition: during the 1970s and 80s his group Sky achieved great popularity with a repertoire that fused classical, jazz and pop idioms. Subsequently he has undertaken successful joint ventures with flamenco guitarist Paco Peña and the Chilean ensemble Inti Illimani. He has recorded the standard guitar repertoire and commissioned new works, and has also stimulated numerous compositions by Australian composers, recently culminating in an internationally released CD of solo works and concertos by Peter Sculthorpe and Nigel Westlake. Since the 1980s he has played guitars built by Australian luthier Greg ★Smallman in his concerts and recordings.

FURTHER REFERENCE
His many recordings include *From Australia*, John Williams, gui, London Symphony Orchestra, cond. Paul Daniel, Australian Chamber Orchestra, cond. Richard Hickox (1994, Sony Classical SK 53361).

JOHN GRIFFITHS

Williams, Kim(berley) Lynton (*b* 26 May 1952), administrator. A composition graduate of the University of Sydney, where he first showed administrative flair organising ISCM concerts 1971–74, on graduation he taught briefly at the NSW State Conservatorium, but was soon appointed administrator for Rostrum Australia (1974–75). He was manager of programming/planning for Musica Viva from 1978 and its general manager from 1980. A highly talented arts administrator, he became chief executive of the Australian Film Commission from 1984, of Southern Star Entertainment from 1988, and general manager of ABC Pay TV from 1992. Since 1995 he has been chief executive of Fox Studios Australia.

FURTHER REFERENCE
CA (1995–96); *WWA* (1996).

Williams, (George Edward) Verdon Garrett (*b* Brunswick, Melbourne, 17 Mar. 1916; *d* Unley Park, Adelaide, 19 Feb. 1997), conductor, composer, arranger. He studied piano with Waldemar Seidal and Percy Grainger and cello with Henri Touzeau at the University of Melbourne Conservatorium. He worked for the ABC intermittently between 1937 and 1975 in various administrative and music positions including conductor residencies with the WA Symphony Orchestra 1960–75 and the Tasmanian Symphony Orchestra 1969–71; he was conductor of the 3DB Orchestra 1949–52; conductor, pianist, *répétiteur* and touring music director for the National Theatre Opera and Ballet Companies 1951–55; and music development officer with the SA department of further education 1975–81. He composed a number of scores for ballet, and his skills as an arranger are widely acknowledged within the music fraternity. He was honoured with the AM in 1992.

FURTHER REFERENCE
For discography, see *HolmesC*.   JOEL CROTTY

Williams, Warren (*b* Maroubra, Sydney, *c*.1940), rock and roll singer-songwriter. The son of a music teacher, he formed the Squares in 1958, playing at local dances, but after meeting Johnny ★O'Keefe appeared solo on *Six O'Clock Rock*, *Bandstand* and *Teen Time*. The first of his 15 singles, *Where My Baby Goes*, was released in 1959, and *A Star Fell From Heaven* reached No. 24 in the charts in the same year. He appeared as supporting act for Fabian and toured interstate with O'Keefe, Col ★Joye and others, releasing *It's Party Time* in 1964. With Beatlemania and the change of taste in 1964, he sang in the club circuit, released an EP, *Warren Williams Sings Famous Tenor Solos*, and began writing ballads, which were recorded by Petula Clark, Digger ★Revell, Noelene ★Batley and others. He still performs in the Williams Family Show with his four children. A cultivated musician with a fine tenor voice, he successfully made the change from early rock and roll stardom to adult, middle-of-the-road ballads.

FURTHER REFERENCE
Recordings include *Where My Baby Goes* (Festival FK 3118), *A Star Fell From Heaven* (Leedon LK 120), *It's Party Time* (Leedon

LK 551), and *Warren Williams Sings Famous Tenor Solos* (Festival). A compilation is *Teenage Love: The Festival File vol. 4* (1988, Festival L19004). For discography, see *SpencerA*. See also *McGrathA*; Damian Johnstone and Warren Williams in *Collected Stories on Australian Rock and Roll,* ed. David McLean (Sydney: Canetoad Publications, 1991), 367–8.

Williamson, J(ames) C(assius) (*b* Mercer, Pennsylvania, USA, 26 July 1844; *d* Paris, 8 July 1913), theatrical entrepreneur. After working as a comic actor in New York from 1863, with his wife the actress Maggie ★Moore he successfully toured Australia, the UK and the USA with his own show, *Struck Oil*, 1874–79. He then purchased the Australian rights to Gilbert and Sullivan's *HMS Pinafore*, and brought it to Melbourne (first under George ★Coppin's management) in 1879. In the following years he won the rights to produce all the Gilbert and Sullivan works in Australia, and became the country's principal presenter of operetta, then opera, pantomime and musicals. He arranged Melba's dazzling opera tour of 1911. He was at various times in partnership with Arthur Garner (1882–91), George ★Musgrove (1882–90, 1892–99), George Tallis and Gustavo Ramaciotti (1904–7), then he formed J.C. Williamson Ltd with Sir Rupert Clarke in 1907.

Always noted for first-rate talent and high-quality productions, he was the dominating entrepreneur in Australian music-theatre for more than 30 years. After his death 'The Firm', as it was known, continued to import opera and musicals. Merged with J. & N. ★Tait from 1916, it arranged Melba's opera tours of 1924 and 1928 and the memorable Sutherland-Williamson season of 1965. Abandoning opera after the emergence of the Elizabethan Trust in the 1950s, it survived to present American musicals until 1976.

FURTHER REFERENCE
John G. Dicker, *JCW: a Short Biography of James Cassius Williamson* (Sydney 1974); *ParsonsC*; *IrvinD*; Helen M. Van der Poorten, *ADB*, 6; H.G. Stephens, *The JC Williamson Memorial* (Sydney: The Bookfellow, 1913).

Williamson, John Robert (*b* Quambatook, Vic., 1 Nov. 1945), popular singer-songwriter. Raised on a wheat farm at Croppa Creek, NSW, he began playing folk music in a Moree restaurant in 1969, then won the *New Faces* TV talent quest in Melbourne and was signed to Fable Records, his country-style *Old Man Emu* becoming No. 1 in the national charts in 1970. In the 1970s he worked in Sydney venues, in a duo with rock guitarist Tommy ★Emmanuel, in country-rock, and in rock bands; for a time he hosted a regional variety show, *Travelin' Out West*, for Newcastle television. He became increasingly interested in the environment and conservation issues, and in 1986 he released his album *Mallee Boy*, which became the biggest-selling country music album in Australian recording history. The 15 albums that followed, including

Boomerang Cafe (1988), *Warragul* (1989) and *True Blue* (1992), also achieved very wide popularity. He also started writing for children, his song *Goodbye Blinkey Bill* dealing with the threat to the koala and his *JW's Family Album* (1990) having great success.

An unassuming presence on stage, playing folk guitar and amplified foot-box, backed only by fiddle and acoustic bass, his themes of rural lifestyle (*Cootamundra Wattle)*, of the commercial abuse of Australia's environment *(Rip, Rip Woodchip* 1989), or of its endangered species seem an inspired match for his personal blend of folk, country and other idioms. He wrote *Australia Calling* (1992), a jingle used by the national telephone company to stave off foreign competition. He has achieved a unique position by sustaining Australian country and marginal styles before a mainstream audience. He published *True Blue: Stories and Songs of Australia* (1995), and his 21 albums include *Mulga To Mangoes* (1994) and *Australia Calling—All The Best vol. 2* (1992). He has won 13 ACMA Golden Guitars, two ARIA awards and eight Mo awards and was honoured with the AM in 1992.

FURTHER REFERENCE
Recordings include *Mallee Boy* (1986, Festival), *Boomerang Cafe* (1988, Emusic), *Warragul* (1989, Emusic EMI 7801422), *True Blue* (1992), *JW's Family Album* (1990), *Mulga To Mangoes* (1994, EMI 8301732) and *Australia Calling—All The Best vol. 2* (1992, EMI 7806442). He has published *True Blue : Stories and Songs of Australia* (1995). See also *MonashB*; *LattaA*; *CA* (1995–96); *Age* 4 Feb. 1990.

Williamson, Malcolm Benjamin Graham Christopher (*b* Sydney, 21 Nov. 1931), composer, pianist, organist, conductor. He entered the NSW State Conservatorium at the age of 11 to study piano, french horn and, later, composition with Sir Eugene Goossens. In 1953 at the age of 22 he left Australia to live in London in order to study with Elizabeth Lutyens and Erwin Stein, a pupil of Schönberg, supporting himself by working as a church organist and nightclub pianist. In Paris he first heard the work of Messiaen and Boulez, two subsequently major influences. He was a lecturer in music at the Central School of Speech and Drama, London, 1961–62. His early *Symphony for Organ* was commissioned for the opening of Coventry Cathedral in 1961, and in 1963 he was awarded the Bax Memorial Prize. He performs in his own works and is a notable soloist, appearing with all the major English orchestras. He has a special interest in writing works for the young and is particularly interested in music therapy for handicapped children. In 1970–71 he was composer-in-residence at Westminster Choir College, Princeton, and was a visiting professor at Strathclyde University 1983–86.

His style, frequently described as eclectic, has been influenced by Messiaen, Boulez, Stravinsky, Bartók, Hindemith, Sibelius, Honegger, Britten, and more pertinently, jazz and popular music from Gershwin on. In spite of this,

he has long seen himself as part of the Australian tradition represented by Alfred Hill, Roy Agnew and Margaret Sutherland, seeing his prolific output as characteristically Australian. Much of his oeuvre consists of music for voices or voices and organ in quasi-sacred contexts, but he has achieved recognition also for his operas and other theatre works and for a small number of orchestral pieces. Critical response to his work has been polarised and unbalanced, but the effect has been to confirm the composer in his continuing commitment to a double stream of work, the larger derived from popular styles, the other coming from an austere personal creativity. This defiance of his critics has been deliberate and sustained. He has held office in a number of key organisations in Britain, notably as a member of the executive committee of the Composers' Guild of Great Britain, the Society for the Promotion of New Music, and the London branch of the ISCM. He has been a lecturer at the Royal Academy of Music, the Guildhall School of Music, Morley College and a series of English universities. In 1975 he succeeded Sir Arthur Bliss as Master of the Queen's Music.

In 1975 and again in 1981 he returned to Australia, on the first occasion to take up a Creative Arts Fellowship at the ANU, and on the second to lecture there. At this time he became a fierce advocate of government support for the arts here. In Australia he is probably best known for the music to the ballet *The Display*, a work commissioned by the Australian Ballet and premiered in 1964 with choreography by Sir Robert Helpmann and designs by Sir Sidney Nolan. He was appointed CBE in 1976.

WORKS (Selective)

Orchestral   Symphony No. 1, *Elevamini* (1956–57), *Santiago de Espada*, overture (1957), *Sinfonia Concertante*, 3 tpt, pf, str (1958–62), *Our Man in Havana*, suite (1963), *The Display*, suite (1964), *Concerto Grosso* (1965), *Symphonic Variations* (1965), *Epitaphs for Edith Sitwell*, str (1966), *Sinfonietta* (1967), Symphony No. 2, *Pilgrim på havet* (1968), *A Word from Our Founder* (1969), Symphony No. 3, *The Icy Mirror*, S, Mez, 2 Bar, ch, orch (1972), *2 Pieces* from *The Bridge That Van Gogh Painted*, str (1975), Symphony No. 4 (1977), *The House of Windsor*, suite (1977), *Fiesta* (1978), *Ochre* (1978), *Fanfarade* (1979), Symphony No. 5, *Aquerò* (1980), *Ode for Queen Elizabeth*, str (1980), Symphony No. 6 (1982), *In Thanksgiving—Sir Bernard Heinze* (1982), Symphony No. 7, str (1984), *Cortège for a Warrior* (1984), *Lento for Strings* (1985), *Bicentennial Anthem* (1988).

Concertos   Pf No. 1 (1958), Pf No. 2 (1960), Org (1961), Pf No. 3 (1962), Vn (1965), 2 pf, str (1972), *Au Tombeau du Martyr Juif Inconnu*, hp, str (1976), *Lament* in memory of Lord Mountbatten (1980), Pf No. 4 (1994).

Chamber Music   String Quartet No. 1, *Winterset* (1948), String Quartet No. 2 (1954), *The Merry Wives of Windsor*, chamber ens (1964), *Variations*, vc, pf (1964), Concertino, wind quintet, 2 pf (8 hands) (1965), *Serenade*, fl, pf, vn, vc (1967), *Pas de Quatre*, fl, ob, cl, bn, pf (1967), Pf Quintet (1968), *Partita on themes of Walton*, va (1972), pf trio (1976), String Quartet No. 3 (1993), *Day that I have loved*, hp (1994).

Brass *Canberra Fanfare*, brass, perc (1973), *Adelaide Fanfare*, brass, org (1973), *Konstanz Fanfare*, brass, perc, org (1980), *Richmond Fanfare*, brass, perc, org (1980), *Fontainebleau Fanfare*, brass, perc, org (1981), *Concertino for Charles*, sax, band (1987), *Fanfare of Homage*, military band (1988), *Ceremony for Oodgeroo*, brass quintet (1988), *Fanfares and Chorales*, brass quintet (1991).

Piano Sonata No. 1 (1956), Sonata No. 2 (1957, rev. 1971), Sonata No. 3, fortepiano (1958), *Travel Diaries* (1960–61), Sonata No. 4 (1963), *5 Preludes* (1966), Sonata for 2 pf (1967), *Haifa Watercolours* (1974), *The Bridge That Van Gogh Painted and the French Camargue* (1975), *Ritual of Admiration* (1976), *Himna Titu* (1984), *Springtime on the River Moskeva* (1987).

Organ *Fons Amoris* (1956), *Résurgence du Feu (Pâques 1959)* (1959), Symphony (1960), *Vision of Christ Phoenix* (1961, rev. 1978), *Elegy—J.F.K.* (1964), *Epitaphs for Edith Sitwell* (1966), *Peace Pieces* (1971), *Little Carols of the Saints* (1972), *Mass of a Medieval Saint* (1973), *Fantasy on 'This is My Father's World'* (1975), *Fantasy on 'O Paradise!'* (1976), *The Lion of Suffolk* (1977), *Offertoire* from *Mass of the People of God* (1981).

Operas *Our Man in Havana* (1963, 3, S. Gillatt after G. Greene), London, 2 July 1963, *The English Eccentrics* (1964, 2, G. Dunn after E. Sitwell), Aldeburgh, 11 June 1964, *The Happy Prince* (1965, 1, Williamson after O. Wilde), Farnham, 22 May 1965, *Julius Caesar Jones* (1965, 2, Dunn), London, 4 Jan. 1966, *The Violins of Saint-Jacques* (1966, 3, W. Chappell after P. Leigh Fermor), 29 Nov. 1966, *Dunstan and the Devil* (1967, 1, Dunn), Cookham, 19 May 1967, *The Growing Castle* (1968, 2, Williamson after A. Strindberg), Dynevor Castle, 13 Aug. 1968, *Lucky-Peter's Journey* (1969, 3, E. Tracey after Strindberg), London, 18 Dec. 1969, *Genesis* (1971), *The Red Sea* (1972, 1, Williamson), Dartington College, Devon, 14 Apr. 1972.

Cassations (Audience and Orchestra or Pf) *The Moonrakers* (1967), *Knights in Shining Armour* (1968), *The Snow Wolf* (1968), *Genesis* (1971), *The Stone Wall* (1971), *The Winter Star* (1973), *The Glitter Gang* (1974), *La Terre des Rois* (1974), *The Valley and The Hill* (1977), *The Devil's Bridge* (1982).

Ballets *The Display* (1964), *Sun into Darkness* (1966), *Bigfella Toots Squoodge and Nora* (1967), *Perisynthyon* (1974), *Heritage* (1985), *Have Steps Will Travel* (1988).

Chorus and Orchestra *Our Man in Havana*, suite (1963), *The Brilliant and the Dark* (1966), *Ode to Music* (1973), *Jubilee Hymn* (1977), *Mass of Christ the King* (1978), *Songs for a Royal Baby* (1979), *A Pilgrim Liturgy* (1984), *The True Endeavour* (1988), *The Dawn is at Hand* (1989).

Solo Voice and Orchestra *Hasselbacher's Scena (Our Man in Havana)*, B (1963), *6 English Lyrics*, low v (1966), *Hammarskjöld Portrait*, S, str (1974), *Les Olympiques*, Mez, str (1976), *Tribute to a Hero*, Bar (1981), *Next Year in Jerusalem*, S (1985).

Accompanied Choral (additional soloists are indicated; accompanied by organ unless stated otherwise) *Adoremus*, Christmas cantata, A, T (1959), *Dawn Carol* (1960), *Ascendit Deus* (1961), *Tu es Petrus*, speaker (1961), *Agnus Dei*, S (1961), *Dignus est Agnus*, S (1961), *Procession of Psalms* (1961), *Easter Carol* (1962), *Jesu, Lover of My Soul*, solo qrt, double ch (1962), *12 New Hymn Tunes* (1962), *Harvest Thanksgiving* (1962), *Wrestling Jacob*, S (1962), *The Morning of the Day of Days*, S, T (1962), *Te Deum* (1963), *An Australian Carol* (1963), *Epiphany Carol* (1963), *6*

Christmas Songs for the Young, pf with optional perc (1963), *Mass of St Andrew* (1964), *6 Evening Hymns* (1964), *A Psalm of Praise (Psalm 148)* (1965), *I will lift up mine eyes (Psalm 121)*, echo ch (1970), *Cantate Domino (Psalm 98)* (1970), *In Place of Belief*, pf duet (1970), *Te Deum*, optional brass (1971), *6 Wesley Songs for the Young*, pf (1971), *O Jerusalem, The King of Love, Who is the King of Glory*, and *Together in Unity*, congregation (1972), *Canticle of Fire* (1973), *The World at the Manger*, S, Bar (1973), *Communion Hallelujahs* (1975), *16 Hymns and Processionals* (1975), *This is My Father's World* (1975), *Love Chorales*, pf or org or gui (1975), *Dove Chorales* (1975), *Above Chorales* (1975), *Mass of St James* (1975), *20 Psalms of the Elements*, congregation (1975), *This Christmas Night* pf (1977), *Kerygma* (1979), *Little Mass of St Bernadette*, boys vv (1980), *Mass of St Margaret of Scotland*, congregation (1980), *Mass of the People of Go* (1981), *Now is the Singing Day*, Bar, Mez, str, pf (4 hands), perc (1981), *Our Church Lives* (1980), *Mass of St Etheldreda* (1990).

Unaccompanied Choral *2 Motets* (1954), *Dawn Carol* (1960), *Symphony for Voices*, A, ch (1962), *Planctus*, male vv (1962), *A Young Girl* (1964), *A Canon for Stravinsky* (1967), *Sonnet* (1969), *Love, the Sentinel* (1972), *The Musicians of Bremen*, 2 Ct, T, 2 Bar, B (1971–72), *3 Choric Hymns* (No. 2, 1980, Nos 1 and 3, 1947), *Galilee* (1987), *Easter in St Mary's Church* (1987), *Requiem for a Tribe Brother* (1992).

Voice and Piano (unless stated otherwise) *A Vision of Beasts and Gods*, high v (1958), *Celebration of Divine Love*, high v (1963), *3 Shakespeare Songs*, high v (1964), *A Christmas Carol*, low v (1964), *North Country Songs*, low v, orch or pf, optional ch (1965), *6 English Lyrics*, low v (1966), *From a Child's Garden*, song-cycle, high v (1967–68), *The Death of Cuchulain*, 5 male vv, perc (1971), *Vocalise in G minor*, Mez (1973), *Pietà*, S, ob, bn, pf (1973), *White Dawns*, low v (1985), *Vocalise in G*, Mez (1985), *The Mower to the Glowworms*, low v (1986), *The White Island*, low v (1986), *Day that I have Loved*, low v (1986), *The Feast of Eurydice*, song-cycle, female v, fl, perc, pf (1986).

Film and Television *The Timber Getters* (1948), *Arid Lands* (1960), *The Brides of Dracula* (1960), *North Sea Strike* (1964), *September Spring* (1964), *Rio Tinto Zinc (1965), Crescando* (1969), *The Horror of Frankenstein* (1969), *Churchill's People*, television (1975), *The House of Windsor*, television (1977), *Watership Down* (1978), *The Masks of Death* (1984).

FURTHER REFERENCE

Recordings include Concerto for Two Pf, Tasmanian Symphony Orchestra, M. Williamson, S. Campion, pfs (ABC 426 483); *Peace in Solitude, Peace in Childhood*, D. Kinsela, org (SCCD 1022); *Richmond Fanfare*, Elizabethan Philharmonic Orchestra (MBS 18CD); and *The Happy Prince*, Guildhall Chamber Choir, soloists, cond. M. Dods (1966, Argo ZRG 2800). A discography of various recordings to 1972 is in *PlushD*. For his views on composition see 'How Australian Can Australian Music Become', *Music Now* 1/4 (Apr. 1972). See also *CallawayA*; Phillip Gearing, Malcolm Williamson's Organ Symphony: An Analysis of Serial Technique, MMus, Univ. Qld, 1989; Belinda Kendall-Smith, Pitch Processes in the Major Symphonies of Malcolm Williamson, PhD, Univ. Qld, 1995; *MurdochA*; Steven Walsh, *GroveD*.

THÉRÈSE RADIC

Willmore, Henrietta née Percival [Mrs Mallalieu] (*b* London, 27 Mar. 1842; *d* Wynnum, Brisbane, 22 Aug. 1938), pianist, organist. She arrived in Australia in 1864 and appeared as an accompanist, soloist, and in collaboration with R.T. *Jefferies in concerts at Brisbane. She taught music at Brisbane schools and privately from 1867. After studying organ with Walter Willmore (her second husband), she became organist at St John's Cathedral 1882–85, at Wickham Terrace Presbyterian Chruch, and elsewhere. She gave recitals in Sydney in 1890 and South Africa in 1896, and appeared in chamber music at Brisbane from 1911.

FURTHER REFERENCE
Betty Crouchley, *ADB*, 12.

Willoughby, Bart (*b* 1961, Ceduna, SA), singer-songwriter, didjeridu player. Lead singer of *No Fixed Address and *Mixed Relations, he was musical director of the film *Jindalee Lady*. He began studies at CASM in 1978, and wrote songs influenced by reggae, committed to calls for Aboriginal rights. He performed with Yothu Yindi early in their career and on tour in America and Canada.

FURTHER REFERENCE
He may be seen in the films *No Fixed Address on Tour* (SBS TV) and *Wrong Side of the Road* (Inma Productions).
P. DUNBAR-HALL

Wills, Ron (*b* Sydney, 1918), record producer, collector, broadcaster. He worked in a record store from the age of 11, began collecting jazz records from Australia and abroad, and reviewed records for the *Australian Music Maker* 1934–37, then for *Tempo* 1937–52. From 1936 he broadcast jazz recordings from radio 2UW Sydney and founded their first Swing Club. He served in the navy during the war, then managed a Sydney record store. Joining EMI in 1950, then RCA (1964–78), he became artist and repertoire manager and produced records for Smoky *Dawson, Buddy *Williams, Slim *Dusty, Gordon *Parsons, Dusty *Rankin and others. He launched the record careers of many younger figures, including Johnny *Ashcroft, *Rick and Thel, Rolf *Harris, Frank *Ifield and Chad *Morgan. He was honoured with an ACMA Golden Guitar for services to the recorded music industry in 1985. His record collection is now in the National Library of Australia.

FURTHER REFERENCE
His memoir, 'Reminiscing in Tempo: A Personal Recollection of Jazz, Music and the Record Business in Australia 1923–1933', remains unpublished.

Wilson, Ross (*b* Melbourne, 18 Nov. 1947), rock singer-songwriter. In his teens he sang in Pink Finks 1964–66, then the rhythm and blues-influenced Party Machine until 1969 and Progression. In 1969 he formed the experimental Sons of the Vegetal Mother, which evolved into *Daddy Cool in 1970, for whom he was both vocalist and songwriter. He was with Daddy Cool until 1976 (save for a period in Mighty Kong, 1974), his *Eagle Rock* staying at No. 1 for eight weeks and winning *Go-Set* single of the year. Then he formed *Mondo Rock, finding more success, his *Living In The Land Of Oz* reaching No. 30 in the charts. With Glen *Wheatley he formed Oz Records and produced the *Skyhooks recordings. He formed Ross Wilson's Rockhouse (1985–86) and the hard-funk band Raw (1992–93), and made a solo recording *Bed Of Nails* in 1989, which reached No. 20 in the charts, and *Dark Side Of The Man*, which reached No. 26. A gifted singer-songwriter, he was the driving force in two of Australia's leading bands in the 1970s. Now an influential figure in Australian rock music, he has produced recordings for *Jo Jo Zep, the Johnnys, and the *Dynamic Heptonics.

FURTHER REFERENCE
Recordings include *Living In The Land Of Oz* (1976, Oz Oz002); *Bed Of Nails* (1989, WEA 257714); *Dark Side Of The Man* (1989, WEA 256405–1); and *Retrospective* (1988, EMI EMX 748315). For discography, see *SpencerA*. See also *GuinnessP*, IV, 2711; *Age* 22 Aug. 1992; *McGrathA*; *SpencerW.*

Wilson, William Horatio ['Euterpe'] (*b* Wales, 1839; *d* Brisbane, 1902), music critic. An amateur violinist and organist at Toowong church, he wrote for the Brisbane *Courier* as 'Euterpe' from 1879. The first regular music critic in Queensland, he was president of the Brisbane Musical Union, the Brisbane Liedertafel and the Brisbane Orchestral Society and hence hardly in a position to write independent criticism of their activities. An advocate of the oratorios of Handel, Haydn, and Mendelssohn and an opponent of lighter works, he welcomed songs of euphoric enthusiasm for colonial life, but had little ear for other innovations. He composed the anthem *O How Amiable Are Thy Dwellings* (Melbourne: Allans).

FURTHER REFERENCE
Warren Bebbington, 'Music in 19th-Century Brisbane: The German Impact', *The German Presence in Queensland*, ed. Manfred Jurgensen and Alan Corkhill (Brisbane: Univ. Queensland, 1988), 273.

Windmill, The. Operetta in two acts by Moritz *Heuzenroeder, libretto by C.H. Smith after Melville. First performed at the Albert Hall, Adelaide, on 18 June 1891.

Winstanley, Eliza [Mrs O'Flaherty] (*b* England, 1818; *d* Sydney, 2 Dec. 1882), actress, theatrical singer. Appearing in the lead role in *Clari, or the Maid of Milan* at Sydney in 1834 at the age of 16, she was soon acclaimed as an acting talent, especially in Shakespeare. She married the theatre violinist H.C. O'Flaherty in 1841 and appeared with him at Hobart and Launceston, then managed a theatre with him at Sydney in 1842. She went to England in 1846, appearing at the Princess Theatre and on provincial tours, then to the USA. She was with Charles Kean's troupe in London, and after her husband's death in 1854 became a successful editor and writer of fiction, drawing on her theatrical experiences. A notable actress in melodramatic and tragic roles, she also appeared in many musicals. She returned to Australia in 1880, two years before her death.

FURTHER REFERENCE
ADB, 2; *IrvinD*; *ParsonsC*.

Winther, John   (*b* Copenhagen, 1933), pianist, administrator. Trained as a pianist and conductor, he worked for the Royal Danish Opera, becoming its general manager from 1963, and came to Australia as general manager of the Australian Opera in 1973. At the Opera he assumed more complete control than his predecessors had achieved, and he resigned in 1977 once the board began to assert itself in matters he regarded as his own province. Thereafter he became director of the Newcastle Conservatorium, then of the Canberra School of Music (from 1980), dramatically improving the performance profile of both institutions. He gave numerous recitals as a solo pianist and concerto artist for the ABC in these years, appeared at the Adelaide Festival, and established the ★Mittagong Trio, with which he toured Australia. In 1985 he became head of piano (later dean) at the Hong Kong Academy of Performing Arts; he has lived at Magnetic Island since 1992.

As an administrator, he was a visionary if rather authoritarian leader. His years at the Australian Opera achieved some of the best artistic standards the company has seen and swiftly brought order to its troubled financial affairs. As a pianist, particularly in Chopin or Schubert, he is both a soloist of very high calibre and a chamber musician and lieder accompanist of first-rate artistry.

FURTHER REFERENCE
Recordings include Schubert, *Winterreise*, Ronald Dowd, Bar (1990, ABC 426 991–2) and *Lauris Elms* (1995, ABC 442 371–2). See also John Cargher, 'The Managerial Glass Slippers', *Bravo! 200 Years of Opera in Australia* (South Melbourne: Macmillan, 1988), 157–60; *Age* 31 Aug. 1977; *Australian* 26 Mar. 1977.

Wion, John   (*b* Rio de Janeiro, Brazil, 22 Jan. 1937), flautist. After studying with Leslie ★Barklamb at the University of Melbourne Conservatorium, he went abroad in 1958, taking lessons from Julius Baker, William Kincaid, Claude Monteux and Marcel Moyse. He played with the American Symphony 1963–65 and became principal flute in the New York City Opera from 1965, and a member of the Bronx Arts Ensemble from 1977. Elected President of the National Flute Association (USA) 1984–85, he has taught at Mannes College, New York, and was professor of flute at Harrt School of Music 1992–93. The most internationally successful flautist Australia has produced, he regularly returned to Australia on tour. He has

published *Opera Excerpts for Flute*, 4 vols (1990–93) and contributes to the *Instrumentalist* and *Flute Talk*.

FURTHER REFERENCE
Recordings include *John Wion Plays French Flute Solos* (HMP 2W91514) and *John Wion Plays Solo Flute* (Musical Heritage Society MHS 513074). See also *International Who's Who of Music* (1995); *Australian* 10 Mar. 1983.

Wirth Brothers.   Musicians and circus proprietors. Their father John Wirth (1834–80) arrived in Victoria in 1855 and travelled the eastern states as an itinerant performer. Philip Peter Jacob Wirth (*b* Sydney, 29 June 1864; *d* Coogee, NSW, 29 Aug. 1937) played trombone and was a horse trainer, while his brother George Wirth (*b* Sydney, 30 July 1867; *d* Sydney, 16 Oct. 1941) played tenor horn and was a clown; they were both acrobats as well. From 1858 they toured as Werth's Band with the Jones National Circus. They joined Ashton's Circus *c.*1870 and played at bush dances and city balls, from 1881 as Wirth's Touring Band. They set up their own circus troupe in 1882, which by 1887 was the leading circus in Australia. After an accident, George Wirth retired from performing to manage the business, and they toured the world during the 1890s, returning to Perth in 1900. They leased the Olympia building, Melbourne (site of the present Arts Centre), in 1907, presenting elaborate circus entertainment for many years; by this time they were both wealthy men. The circus outlived them and continued until 1963.

FURTHER REFERENCE
Their autobiographies are George Wirth, *Round the World With a Circus* (1925) and Philip Wirth, *The Life of Philip Wirth* (1934). See also Mark Valentine St Leon, *ADB*, 12.

Wise Shoemaker, The.   Children's operetta in one act, music and text by Colin ★Brumby (1967), first performed at Brisbane in May 1968.

With My Swag on My Shoulder,   folk-song. Set to 'Dennis O'Reilly', this traditional gold-digger's song recounts the changing fortunes of an immigrant who comes to Victoria in the goldrush of the 1850s and slowly descends into the life of a swagman. Published by A.B. Paterson in *Old Bush Songs* (1905), and with its music by John Meredith 1956; another version was collected by John Manifold and published 1964.

FURTHER REFERENCE
Edition and commentary in *EdwardsG*.

Woden Valley Youth Choir.   Founded in Canberra (1969) by public servant Don Whitbread, who has been its conductor since its inception. The choir caters for children and youngsters 9–19, divided into a performing choir (of about 70 voices) and training choir (of 30), singing a repertoire ranging from classical to jazz and popular music. They perform regularly in Canberra and have toured abroad five times, to the USA, Japan, NZ, the UK and Europe. With a policy of free membership, staff are entirely unpaid; for his service with the group, Whitbread was honoured with the OAM in 1980.

Wojtowitz, Christian (*b* 9 Apr. 1948), cellist. After studying with Sela Trau and Jan ★Sedivka at the Tasmanian Conservatorium, he was awarded a Churchill fellowship in 1969 and studied at the Paris Conservatoire with Pierre Fournier and André Navarra. He was principal cellist in the Elizabethan Theatre Trust (Melbourne) Orchestra, taught at the Canberra School of Music, then at the Tasmanian Conservatorium, founding the ★Tasmanian Symphony Chamber Players. As well as his stylish and sensitive playing of traditional repertoire, he has made a significant contribution to contemporary music, having been cellist in the Australian Contemporary Music Ensemble, ★Flederman and ★Pipeline, and premiered numerous works written for him.

FURTHER REFERENCE
Recordings include *The Legend of Moinee*, Tasmanian Symphony Orchestra, cond. R. Mills (1993, Vox Australis VASTO 13–2).

Wollongong, pop. (1991) 211 417, city in the Illawara district of coastal NSW. As it is confined between a rugged escarpment and a coast without natural harbours, Wollongong's initial musical development was restricted to individual settlements. Improving roads and the building of the Temperance Hall in 1871 made Wollongong the Illawarra's musical centre, but most of the town's concerts, minstrel shows and band recitals remained amateur, mainly held in local halls. Visits by professional companies, such as Carandini's in 1878, were rare. Brass bands and choirs were important in the mining areas and an eisteddfod, which still continues, was established in 1894.

The rail-link to Sydney in 1888 started to reverse the city's isolation. Although public music-making diminished during the 1930s Depression, after World War II there was considerable growth and an influx of European migrants, but their music tended to remain outside the mainstream and to be centred on churches and clubs. Jazz and folk music also developed, with major local festivals. By the 1980s, with a freeway connection to Sydney and the availability of electronic ticket-sales, popular music entrepreneurs and even the ABC and Musica Viva had withdrawn from Wollongong: most people now travel to Sydney concerts. Nonetheless, a new performing arts centre was opened in 1988.

Wollongong's early composers were choir or bandmasters whose work was for their own immediate use; some were private teachers who initially provided the only music education in the district. A branch of the NSW State Conservatorium was established in the city in the 1970s, widening horizons and raising standards; in 1984 its control was transferred to Wollongong Univer-

sity, which established a School of Creative Arts with a strong musical component.

FURTHER REFERENCE
P.G. Roberts, Wollongong's Music, 1817–1989, MMus, Univ. NSW, 1994.   P.G. ROBERTS

Wollongong Conservatorium. Founded in 1972 as a branch of the NSW State Conservatorium, it has been affiliated with the University of Wollongong since 1984, and offers tuition on an array of instruments as well as contributing to the university's BCA (Bachelor of Creative Arts) in composition and performance.

Woman Who Laughed At Faery, The. Comic opera in one act, music and libretto by Fritz ★Hart. First performed by students of the Melbourne Conservatorium at the Melbourne Playhouse on 25 September 1929.

Women in Australian Music. European settlement in 1788 brought with it the social customs which generally restrained women from full participation in musical life. To some extent these still cast their shadow over women today; but the course of Australia's development has provided at least some opportunities for women in music which were achieved only with difficulty elsewhere.

For 30 years before public musical life began in Australia, the early settlers heard music chiefly in their homes. There it was largely the province of the women, who fostered it with a distinctive tenacity. From little more than a decade after the First Fleet arrived, music features in the correspondence of the colony's women, and by the 1820s their letters are effusive about progress at the piano, music written or shared, or their singing, dancing, and soirées for family and friends. 'I have sent for a piano from the Cape', wrote Georgina Molloy characteristically in 1832, 'and hope to send you some most beautiful Spanish airs from a Mrs Smith, a Spanish lady who plays divinely on the guitar'. Music was for these women both a memento of the European society from which they had been torn and a medium for civilising their rude surroundings. They populated the early church choirs and choral societies in abundance.

With the advent of professional musical life in the 1830s, women grasped an important share of the entrepreneurial possibilities. One of the earliest entrepreneurs of consequence was Anne ★Clarke, who presented opera and music-theatre at Hobart from 1834, and the most intrepid of all the operatic pioneers was Maria ★Carandini, who after singing in many operatic premieres at Sydney and Melbourne, toured with her company from the 1850s, and over 25 years introduced opera to almost every settlement in Australia. In the 1890s Fanny ★Simonsen's Opera Co. was overshadowed by more successful organisations, but the main opera presenters of the 1950s (and the two principal forerunners of the Australian Opera) were again women, Gertrude ★Johnson at Melbourne and Clarice Lorenz at Sydney.

To be sure, the theatre has always provided an escape from the social constraints which kept women out of other spheres of public performance. But it remains surprising that female opera singers in Australia achieved far more international success than their male counterparts. Most of the Australian opera singers prominent abroad have been women, from Lucy *Chambers, Amy *Castles, Amy *Sherwin and Nellie *Melba in the 19th century, through Marjorie *Lawrence, Florence *Austral and Joan *Hammond in the war years, to Marie *Collier, Joan *Sutherland and Yvonne *Kenny in recent times, and including over 20 women who have sung principal roles at Covent Garden, Sadler's Wells and the European opera houses. The position is similar with popular music singers, Australia's most internationally successful solo artists being almost entirely women, from Eliza *Winstanley, Nellie *Stewart and Florrie *Forde in the 19th century through Gladys *Moncrieff, Madge *Elliot and Jenny *Howard in the war years to Lana *Cantrell, June *Bronhill, Helen *Reddy, Olivia *Newton-John and Kylie *Minogue in recent times.

The conflicts of career and family were resolved by these artists in a variety of ways. Some like Melba put career first at the expense of husbands or lovers; others like Elsie *Morison virtually abandoned their careers after marriage (Morison married conductor Rafael Kubelik). Still others briefly interrupted their activities to start a family, then courageously pressed on: Carandini seems scarcely to have paused as she produced eight children, five of whom joined her company as singers.

Beyond the theatre, the traditional rules of decorum which kept women from the professional concert platform seem to have acted in Australia as strongly as elsewhere. Save for pianists Elsie *Hall, Nancy *Weir, Ada *Corder, Una *Bourne and Eileen *Joyce and more recently violinist Alma *Moodie and flautist Jane *Rutter, there have been few international successes among female Australian instrumentalists. Few women played in Australia's 19th-century theatre orchestras and bands.

Yet almost by misadventure, the gender make-up of the symphony orchestras has always differed dramatically from those in Europe or the USA (which were, at least until very recently, all male). When resident symphony orchestras were founded in Australia in the early 1900s, they were at first chiefly semi-professional, allowing the involvement of a sizeable number of music school students, who were overwhelmingly female. Later, when the fully professional ABC orchestras were in the process of formation, World War II drew many able male musicians into military service, providing many opportunities for female players and in the Melbourne Symphony Orchestra for a female concertmaster (Bertha *Jorgensen). To be sure, no Australian orchestra acquired a female conductor: few women have made headway in conducting until Simone *Young and Nicolette Fraillon in the 1990s.

The private music teaching profession in Australia was at first largely male, the early 'professors' who advertised in the press only occasionally offering the services of a wife or daughter as associate in their practices. This changed with World War I, and today males are vastly outnumbered in private practice. Nevertheless, music schools have been much slower to change, and rarely made female appointments (other than in singing) until the 1980s. A woman was not appointed to a university chair in music until 1985 (Catherine *Ellis, University of New England), and the first women to direct music schools were Gillian Wills (Victorian College of the Arts, from 1989) and Sharman *Pretty (Sydney Conservatorium, from 1995). Yet there had long been women among the most prominent scholars: Doreen Bridges (music education), Margaret *Kartomi (ethnomusicology), Alice *Moyle (Aboriginal music), Kay *Dreyfus and Thérèse *Radic (Australian music), and Elizabeth Wood has become a noted exponent of feminist musicology in the USA.

A significant number of the Australian composers with international success have been women, from Margaret *Sutherland through Peggy *Glanville-Hicks to Anne *Boyd and Alison *Bauld. Interestingly, these have had scant recognition within Australia, where the situation for women composers has recently been discouraging. The proportion of women successful in the first ABC composition competitions in the 1930s was significant, but ever since seems to have declined. Whereas Mona *McBurney, Florence *Ewart and Esther *Rofe all had productions of major theatrical works in Australia, since the end of World War II obvious theatrical talents such as Moya *Henderson or Gillian *Whitehead have seldom been presented by the major companies, and most who have written for orchestra have gone unperformed (at least within Australia). Some, like Ros *Bandt and Sarah *Hopkins, have created new idioms of their own; but many others of excellent talent have had to find careers writing for chamber ensembles or solo performers, or producing educational miniatures for children and the AMEB.

In other genres, the situation has been even less impressive. Although the earliest Australian ragtime players were female (Belle Sylvia and Mabelle Morgan from 1918), as was Shirley *Thoms, one of the major pioneers of country music, and Thelma *Ready led an all-female dance band, jazz and country music have had a much smaller proportion of major female artists than in the USA. Aside from Jeannie *Lewis and Margret *Road-Knight, the major artists of the folk music revival were largely male. Rock music has been perhaps the least conducive of the pop genres to female talent; despite the early success of Debbie *Byrne, Patsy-Anne *Noble and Judy *Stone, there were few sustained chart successes by women in Australia, until the late 1980s brought forward Sharon *O'Neill, Deborah *Conway, Jenny Morris, Christina Amphette, Linda Morris and Kate *Ceberano.

Advocacy for women in music increases. Australia has had an executive member of the International League of Women Composers since 1984 (Betty *Beath). The growth of interest in gender studies in the 1990s brought forth symposia and conferences on women in music, notably the Composing Women's Conferences in 1991 (Adelaide) and 1994 (Melbourne), and courses on women in music in several Australian universities. (See also entries under individual names.)

FURTHER REFERENCE

Jamie Kassler, 'The "Woman Question" in Music', in *The Woman Composer*, ed. Sally Macarthur, No. 21 of *SA* (Autumn 1989), 22–5; Thérèse Radic, 'Composing Women: Setting the Record Straight', in *Repercussions: Australian Composing Women's Festival and Conference, 1994*, ed. Thérèse Radic (Melbourne: National Centre for Australian Studies, Monash Univ., 1995), 151–5; *LePageW*; *GroveW*; J.W.C. Cumes, *Their Chastity Was Not Too Rigid: Leisure Times in Early Australia* (Melbourne: Longman Cheshire, 1979).

Wood, Ernest   (*b* Sheffield, England, *c.*1861; *d* Melbourne, 9 May 1914), conductor, church musician, organist. Wood held positions as assistant organist at Lincoln Cathedral and organist at St Peter's, Eaton Square, London, before his appointment in 1888 as organist of St Paul's Cathedral, Melbourne. He trained the new cathedral choir and established a tradition of excellence in English church music. He was also an adjudicator, prominent recitalist, teacher and conductor of the Royal Melbourne Liedertafel, conducting the first performances of Bach's *St Matthew Passion* and Brahms's *German Requiem* in Melbourne.

FURTHER REFERENCE

Obit. in *Australasian* 16 May 1914; *Argus* 11 May 1914; and *Church of England Messenger* 22 May 1914. See also *The Organs and Organists of St Paul's Cathedral, Melbourne* (Melbourne: St Paul's Cathedral, 1991), 29.   JOHN MAIDMENT

Woodward, Roger   (*b* Sydney, 20 Dec. 1942), pianist. He attended the NSW State Conservatorium High School, studying organ and harpsichord, and subsequently studied piano with Alexander ★Sverjensky, conducting with Eugene ★Goossens and composition with Raymond ★Hanson. He was expelled from the Conservatorium twice but regarded his piano studies as 'great training for life'. In 1964 he won the ABC Concerto Competition, controversially electing to play Prokofiev's Piano Concerto No. 3. A recital he gave in Sydney in that year was described in the press as a display of 'intoxicated brute strength'. He furthered his studies at the Warsaw State Academy of Music on a Polish Government scholarship, studying with Zbigniew Drzewiecki and later Witold Rowicki. In 1968 he won the International Chopin Festival competition in Warsaw and the International Gaudeamus Competition in The Netherlands in 1970, the year of his London debut.

He began to perform premieres of contemporary works, including those by Xenakis and Stockhausen. At the opening of the Sydney Opera House in 1973 he performed works by the Australian composers ★Ahern, ★Sitsky, ★Boyd, ★Meale, ★Sculthorpe, ★Fowler and ★Werder.

After a recital of Beethoven the press reported his 'clangorous power, enormous stamina, physical excitement, conspicuous and dramatic contrasts of dynamics'. In 1985 he first performed the complete works of Chopin, and has since frequently performed all 32 of Beethoven's piano sonatas. Several leading Australian and European composers have dedicated works to Woodward, and he considers the premiere of Xenakis's *Keqrops* with Zubin Mehta and the New York Philharmonic in 1986 as his greatest concert. In 1989 he was commissioned by the French Government to compose and perform his own work, *Sound by Sound*, for the bicentenary of the French Revolution, and in 1990 he instituted the first Sydney Spring International Festival of New Music and Visual Arts. Woodward continues as the festival's artistic director, with the intention of highlighting Australian composers and performers. He has recorded 35 albums and videos of new works and popular classics and has collaborated with the American jazz pianist Cecil Taylor, and Graeme Murphy and the Sydney Dance Company. In 1994 he gave his first recital of the works of Debussy and since then has been contracted to perform the complete Debussy piano works for ABC Classics.

Described as the 'sacred monster of the avant-garde', Woodward has a reputation as a peerless interpreter of new music, with a virtuosic and controversial technique. In 1976 he became a fellow of the International Frederic Chopin Society in Warsaw and was awarded an OBE in 1980.

FURTHER REFERENCE

Recordings include Prokofiev works (ABC 426 806); *Contemporary Australian Piano Music* (RCA VRLI-0083); *Rustle of Spring* (Warner 903177472–2); *Keyboard Music*, by Takemitsu (Etcetera KTC 1103). See also *CA* (1995–96); Miriam Cosic, 'Woodward Takes Stock', *SMH* 18 Aug. 1995, 15; Megan Cronly, 'Sounding Out', *Follow Me Gentlemen* (June/Aug. 1987), 40–3; Ross Edwards, 'Roger Woodward and Music Rostrum', *Music Now* 2/2 (Dec. 1974); Dominic Gill, *GroveD*.

SUZANNE ROBINSON

Wookey, Paul   (*b* 21 May 1950), folk-singer, guitarist. He first played in rock bands, then bluegrass and country music. His first professional performance was at Frank ★Traynor's, Melbourne, and he was a regular at the Troubadour, faithfully recreating folk-songs. From 1977 he was with the Hawking Brothers, and toured extensively in Australia as a supporting artist to John Hammond, Vince Gill and others. In the 1980s he toured with Chris Duffy (banjo) and is currently based at Tamworth. Combining blues, bluegrass and folk styles he also plays jazz and country, he has won an ACMA Golden Guitar.

FURTHER REFERENCE

Recordings include *Mountain Breakfast* (1988, Troubadour YPRX 1855) and side work on such albums as the Hawking Brothers *Country Travellin'* (1978).

Woolley, Emmeline Mary Dogherty (*b* Hereford, England, 16 June 1843; *d* Darlinghurst, Sydney, 18 Mar. 1908), pianist, teacher. Arriving in Australia in childhood, she studied piano in Italy in 1858, theory and composition with Alessandro Kraus, singing with Pietro Romani, then piano with Julius von Kolb at Munich. She returned to Sydney in 1863, teaching and becoming organist at St John's, Darlinghurst. She formed and conducted the female St Cecilia Choir from 1884, and gave concerts with her pupils. Her cantata *The Captive Soul* was performed on 11 June 1895. With a bright and enlightened style, she was one of the best-trained piano teachers active in Sydney in the later colonial days.

FURTHER REFERENCE
Martha Rutledge, *ADB*, 12.

Worgan's Piano. The first piano to be landed in Australia was brought by George Bouchier Worgan, doctor of music, who came to Australia on the First Fleet in 1788 as surgeon on Captain Phillip's ship *HMS Sirius*. When he returned to England in 1791 his house and piano were occupied by the prominent John and Elizabeth Macarthur; Elizabeth learned to play on the instrument. The instrument still survives in private hands in Sydney.

World Music in Australia. Aside from the classical and folk music traditions of the majority Anglo-Celtic community, Australia has had significant flowerings of the music of other cultures whose members have settled.

The oldest and most entrenched are the musical customs and ceremonies of the Chinese, who arrived in Victoria and Queensland as indentured labourers from 1848, then in large numbers with the goldrush of the 1850s, reaching a peak in 1888 when restrictive legislation was enacted against them. The White Australia policy was enacted in 1901 which, together with various assistance schemes for British immigrants, constricted the diversity for a long period. From 1938 European refugees from the Nazis began arriving, and from 1946 intensive European immigration made Melbourne the largest Greek city outside Greece; similarly large communities arrived from other parts of Europe, particularly Italy and Yugoslavia. Italian and Greek popular musical traditions flourished widely, while in smaller communities the music of Latvia, the Ukraine and elsewhere was cultivated. There has always been a musical interchange with NZ, although this has chiefly affected composers and performers of mainstream repertoire.

With the relaxation of the White Australia policy in 1966, communities from East-Asia began to form, and Perth became the largest Burmese city outside Burma. Asian immigration intensified with the end of the Vietnam War in 1975, and today both the classic and folkloric musical traditions of Vietnam may be found in enclaves in Australian cities. Much smaller but very musically active communities are from India, Turkey, Latin America, Lebanon and Japan.

A number of organisations cultivate world music, including the Brisbane Ethnic Music and Arts Centre (BEMAC); the Australian Institute of Eastern Music and La Peña, Sydney; La Boite, Melbourne; the Multicultural Arts Council of WA and the Ethnic Music Centre, Perth; and the multicultural arts networks in SA. See also entries under *Migrant Music, African, Eastern European, Gamelan, Greek, Hmong, Indian, Irish, Italian, Jewish, Scottish Folk Music* and *Vietnamese*.

FURTHER REFERENCE
Francis Fong, comp., *World Music in Australia* (Sydney: Australian Music Centre, 1994); *Ethnic Arts Directory*, 3rd edn (Sydney: Australia Council, 1984).

World Of Our Own, A. Song (1965) by Tom Springfield. Recorded by the *Seekers (1965, W&G), it was No. 1 in the Australian charts for 27 weeks, No. 1 and then No. 2 for six months in the UK, and No. 4 in the USA. It was one of three songs Springfield wrote for the Seekers (the others were *I'll Never Find Another You* and *The Carnival Is Over*) which challenged the Beatles and the Rolling Stones for dominance of the international charts in 1965.

Worrall, David (*b* Newcastle, NSW, 25 Oct. 1954), composer. After studying composition with Ross *Edwards and Peter *Sculthorpe at the University of Sydney and Richard *Meale and Tristram *Cary at the University of Adelaide, he won the Albert Maggs Award (1980), and taught at the University of Melbourne Conservatorium (from 1980) and at the Canberra School of Music from 1986, establishing the Australian Centre for the Arts and Technology. He founded Floating Exceptions (now Polymedia Inc.) to create sound and light works in a portable geodesic dome.

Focusing on algorhythmic composition, stochastic modelling, spatial manipulation of sound and polymedia, his works are chiefly for tape or live electronics. They include the dance work *Windows* for lighting designer and electronics (1988), *Chromachron* for electronics and computer (1993), ... *with fish scales scattered* ... for tape (1982), and *Butterflies Flutter By* for tape (1987). *Air* uses a flute with electronics (1993) and *Cords 26* is for live electronics in the geodesic dome (1990). He won the 2MBS-FM award for radiophonic composition in 1985.

FURTHER REFERENCE
There are recordings of ... *with fish scales scattered* ... (1989, Canberra School of Music, CSM 5); *Butterflies Flutter By* (1989, Canberra School of Music, CSM 4); *Air* (1994, Canberra School of Music, CSM18); and *Cords 26* (1994, Canberra School of Music, CSM 20). His writings include 'Credo: Unreliable Processes', *SA* 24 (Summer 1989–90), 4–5. See also *BroadstockS*, 56–7; *SA* 34 (Winter 1992), 10–11.

Worsley, Tony (*b* Hastings, England, 25 Dec. 1944), rock singer. Worsley and his family migrated to Australia in 1958, settling in Brisbane. After finishing his schooling, he worked as a sailmaker; he became a rock singer when the band which regularly performed in the café in which he was working as a dishwasher found itself without a vocalist. In 1964 he joined the Blue Jays for what was to become a two-year partnership, with Bobby Johnson (drums, bass), Paul Shannon (saxophone, organ), Mel Clarke (rhythm, banjo), Ray Eames (lead guitar, piano) and Ray Nicholls (bass, harmonica). The addition of Worsley, the 'first Australian beat star to sport outrageously long hair' (Glenn A. Baker), gave the group's performances a sexual euphoria which did its part to alter the early Australian rock scene. In 1965 the group acted as support group to the tour of the Kinks, Manfred Mann and the Honeycombs. They also signed with Sunshine Records, releasing two national hits, *Just A Little Bit*, which reached No. 31 nationally, and *Velvet Waters* which reached No. 14. After the March 1966 release of *Something's Got A Hold On Me*, Worsley left the Blue Jays and disappeared from the scene.

FURTHER REFERENCE
Recordings include *Tony Worsley and the Fabulous Blue Jays; My Time of Day; Just a Little Bit/If I* (1965, Sunshine); *Velvet Waters* (1965, Sunshine); *Missing You* (1965, Sunshine); *Something's Got A Hold On Me* (1966, Sunshine). For discography, see *SpencerA*. See also David Day and Tim Parker, SA Great: Its Our Music 1956–1986 (Glandore, SA: Day and Parker, 1987); *McGrathA*.

JOHN WERETKA

Worthley, Max (*b* Adelaide *c*.1909), tenor. He studied with Mrs H. Kugelberg and at the Elder Conservatorium, then worked as a bank clerk while appearing in ABC concerts and radio until 1939. After war service, he studied in London from 1947, appearing with the English Opera Group, Covent Garden, and in numerous BBC broadcasts. He returned to Australia because of family illness in 1953, teaching at the Elder Conservatorium, touring for ABC concerts and in South-East Asia, and joining the Elizabethan Theatre Trust Opera Co. in 1956. He was in Germany studying from 1958 and working with the BBC again in 1960. His pure tone and impeccable taste shone in such roles as Basilio, Tamino, Rodolfo, Ottavio (*Don Giovanni*), and *The Bartered Bride*. He sang many contemporary works, including the Captain in *Wozzeck* under Kleiber at Covent Garden, Phyllis Tate's *Phoenix and the Turtle*, Anthony Hopkins' *Prayers from the Ark*, Britten's *Seven Michelangelo Sonnets*, and the premieres of his *Prima Donna* and *Let's Make An Opera*. He became a member of the Deller Consort in 1961 and toured Australia with them in 1964; he taught at the University of Arkansas from 1967.

FURTHER REFERENCE
Recordings include Monteverdi, *Lament d'Arianna* (Vanguard VANG 08.5063.71). See also *MackenzieS*, 187–90; *AMN* 49 (Feb. 1959) 20.

Wreckery, The. Rock band (1984–89) formed in Melbourne, originally comprised of Hugo Race (guitar, vocals), Edward Clayton-Jones (keyboard, guitar, vocals), Charles Todd (saxophone), Ted O'Biegly (bass) and Ross Casinader (keyboard, guitar, violin, percussion). They quickly acquired a partisan following, their album *I Think This Town Is Nervous* (1985) revealing them as an obdurate, opaque combination of jazz, blues, and elementally heavy rock. They followed this with a few more recordings, including the singles *No Shoes For This Road* (1987) and *Everlasting Sleep* (1987), before disbanding in 1989.

FURTHER REFERENCE
Recordings include *I Think This Town Is Nervous* (1985, Hot HOTM 4), *No Shoes For This Road* (1987, Rampart RR 023), *Everlasting Sleep* (1987, Rampart RR 041), *Collection* (1988, Rampart RR 067) and *Laying Down The Law* (1988, Citadel CITLP 516). For discography, see *SpencerA*. See also *SpencerW*.

Wright, Frank Joseph Henry (*b* Smeaton, Vic., 2 Aug. 1901; *d* London, 16 Nov. 1970), bandsman. Born into a musical family, Wright studied cornet with Percy *Code, whom he later succeeded as bandmaster of the City of Ballarat Band. A South Street cornet champion (1919), he left Ballarat in 1933 as local employment opportunities diminished. In England he was appointed director of music for the London County Council (1935–70), being responsible for the summer season's musical entertainments in London's 106 parks. He composed a number of original works for band, but his reputation was principally based on his many arrangements of classical works, a number of which have been recorded. He was known internationally as an adjudicator.

FURTHER REFERENCE
Obit. in *British Bandsman* 3585 (28 Nov. 1970); *Brass Band News* 12 (Dec. 1970). See also biographical file, Ballarat Municipal Library; *Conductor* Jan. 1971 (memorial edition); *Australian Band Leader* Oct. 1974; Ballarat *Courier* 16 Jan. 1982.

KAY DREYFUS

Wyndham-Read, Martyn, folk-singer. He came to Australia in 1960 and worked as a jackeroo at Emu Springs station, where he heard Australian folk-songs. He moved to Sydney and performed with Gary *Shearston, Brian *Mooney and Don Aynton, and appeared at the major Melbourne folk venues 1962–63. An important populariser of Australian songs in the early years of the folk revival, he returned to England to live in 1967, but makes regular visits to Australia.

FURTHER REFERENCE
Recordings include *A Wench And A Whale And A Pint Of Good Ale* (1970, Leader LER 2009), *Mussels On A Tree* (Larrikin FECD 84CD) and *Australian Songs* (W&G B2957). See also *Stringybark and Greenhide* 2/1 (Feb. 1980), 3; 6/1 (1985), 12.

Y

Yalata. Small town on the south-east edge of the Nullarbor Plain, SA, supporting a population of Pitjantjatjara Aborigines who live either in the town or in *wiltja* camps in the surrounding spinifex country. It was a Lutheran Mission until 1976; since then it has been run by a local self-governing council when the self-determination policy was implemented (its Lutheran church now has a Pitjantjatjara minister). The people moved out of the spinifex into Ooldea between 1920 and 1952, after which they migrated south to the Yalata area as a result of the British atomic tests at Maralinga.

Studies of aspects of the people's music culture carried out at Ooldea in the early 1940s by the Berndts, at Yalata in the late 1960s by Kartomi, and at Yalata in the 1980s by Brady indicate that their musical lives have been in a state of continual flux. In the late 1960s they practised a rich musical life, performing frequent sacred ceremonies (secret male, secret female and mixed ceremonies), children's play ceremonies, children's play-songs, lullabies, and musical story-telling sessions for children, with church hymns and hit parade pop songs being kept quite separate in their minds. The adults' singing styles ranged from the very calmly sung lullabies to vigorously sung sacred ceremonial songs featuring intricately ornamented melodic descents. The children's play ceremonial songs served as part of the pre-initiation enculturation process. Most of the singing by the children was in an energetic, non-ornamented melodic style, often accompanied by rhythmic thigh-slapping or stick-beating, as in the adult music. From 1982 most of the people at Yalata moved to Oak Valley, which became the symbolic centre of their ceremonial business, though sometimes the religious ceremonies are also still performed in the Yalata area.

In the 1980s the Yalata-born women at Oak Valley revived their detailed knowledge of their main ceremonial song cycle—the Seven Sisters, which their mothers still knew well in the 1960s—by inviting Pitjantjatjara women from the north (from Ernabella, for example) to visit and teach it to them in detail. In the 1990s the men,

women and children still perform their songs and ceremonies including initiation ceremonies.

FURTHER REFERENCE
R.M. Berndt and C.H. Berndt, 'Children's Songs from Ooldea, Western South Australia', *Mankind* 4/9–10 (1952–54), 12; M. Brady, 'Leaving the Spinifex; The Impact of Rations, Missions and the Atomic Tests on the Southern Pitjantjara', *Records of the South Australian Museum* 20 (1987), 35–45; idem, *Diet and Dust in the Desert* (Canberra: AIATSIS, 1991), 90; M.J. Kartomi, 'Tjitji Inma at Yalata', *Hemisphere* 14/6 (1973), 33–7, reprinted as 'A Children's Ceremony at Yalata', in *The Australian Aboriginal Heritage*, ed. R.M. Berndt and E.S. Phillips (Sydney: Australian Society for Education through the Arts/Ure Smith, 1973), 54–8, and in *From Earlier Fleets. Hemisphere: An Aboriginal Anthology* (Canberra: Department of Foreign Affairs, 1978); idem, 'Childlikeness in Play Songs—A Case Study Among the Pitjantjara at Yalata, South Australia', *MMA* 11 (1980), 172–214; idem, 'Songs of Some Aboriginal Australian Children's Play Ceremonies', *SMA* 15 (1981), 1–35; idem, 'Delineation of Lullaby Style in Three Areas of Aboriginal Australia', *Problems and Solutions: Occasional Essays in Musicology Presented to Alice M. Moyle,* ed. J. Kassler and J. Stubington (Sydney: Hale & Iremonger, 1984), 59–83.

MARGARET J. KARTOMI

Yarrabah. Former Anglican mission established in 1892, located on a peninsula just south of Cairns, north Queensland. It is the home of the Yidiny people, although Aboriginal people from other parts of Queensland were relocated there. In 1966 Yarrabah people performed songs in two general styles for Alice Moyle: 'traditional' and Torres Strait. Traditional songs, sung by only one man, were accompanied by sticks; dancers with body painting and headdresses of cane and feathers performed with the singer. These songs are similar to the Gama songs of the Dyirbal people to the south. The Yarrabah singers tried to ensure that the words of the traditional songs would be passed on to the young people, and set texts to Torres Strait tunes, which were very popular with the youth.

FURTHER REFERENCE
A. Moyle, *Songs from Yarrabah* (1970, AIAS).

GRACE KOCH

Yates, Theodosia [Mrs Stirling, Mrs Guerin]   (*b* England, 1815; *d* July 1904), singer, actor. After working as an actress in Drury Lane, she came to Tasmania with Anne ★Clarke's troupe as Mrs Stirling in 1842. There she appeared in plays, burlesque and opera, and married the violinist James Guerin. After Clarke's company disbanded in 1845, she went to Sydney and appeared in many theatrical productions, including the operas *Fra Diavolo*, *Maritana* and *Jean de Paris*. Her husband died, and in 1857 she married Richard Towzey who became an actor as Richard Stewart; for the next 20 years they appeared throughout Australia, then on tour in India, the USA and the UK. Their daughter was the actor Nellie ★Stewart.

FURTHER REFERENCE
IrvinD; *PorterS*, 70–71; P. McGuire, *The Australian Theatre* (London: OUP, 1948).

Yirrkala.   Settlement on Gove Peninsula, north-east edge of Arnhem Land, NT. It began as a Methodist mission in 1935, with many different Aboriginal groups forced together. Richard A. Waterman made recordings at Yirrkala in 1952, and Trevor Jones also conducted fieldwork there. These groups were the earliest agitators for land rights, but in the mid-1970s control of the mission was handed to a town council of representatives from the principal clans. Several outstation communities were established in the following years, with about 10 by 1980. Yirrkala is the home community for Mandawuy Yunupingu, lead singer of ★Yothu Yindi and principal of Yirrkala school (1990–91), as well as other members of Yothu Yindi. Their CD *Tribal Voice* records songs from the Rirratjingu and Gumatji clans of north-east Arnhem Land; they also incorporate Yolngu language in pop songs, and *Homeland Movement* records traditional songs of the Rirratjingu and Gumatj clans of Yirrkala. See *Aboriginal Music*.

FURTHER REFERENCE
Yothu Yindi recordings include *Homeland Movement* (1989, Mushroom Records D38959); *Tribal Voice* (1991, Mushroom Records D30602). A video *Djungguwan at Gurka'wuy* (Film Australia, 1980–89) shows Aboriginal ceremonies in Yirrkala region. See also Richard A. Waterman, 'Music in Australian Aboriginal Culture—Some Sociological and Psychological Implications', *Journal of Music Therapy* (1955), 40–9.

Yodelling.   Singing in which zigzag patterns of wide intervals, rapidly alternating high falsetto and lower chest voice notes, are set to nonsense syllables. Of ancient origin, it can project the voice over long distances and has traditionally been used as a signalling device in the Swiss and Austrian Alps, the mountains of China and the Americas.

In Australia a similar technique is found in some Aboriginal music, but it was first heard frequently in vaudeville, with appearances by Swiss yodellers in the early 1900s. It became ubiquitous among country music singers from the 1930s, where it spread in imitation of the American hillbilly tradition of the 1920s, which came to Australia through the recordings of Jimmy Rodgers, Goebel Reeves and others. Harry Cash's *The Black Yodel* (1927) was probably the first recording of yodelling in Australia, and 'The Whispering Yodeller', Gill Harris, recorded cowboy yodels in the same years. But Tex ★Morton's *Happy Yodeller* and Buddy ★Williams's first recording, *Rambling Yodeller* (1939), were more influential for developments in country music. At the height of its popularity in the 1940s, Shirley ★Thoms was billed as 'Australia's Yodelling Sweetheart', but as country music became more sophisticated only the more traditional country balladists continued to feature it in their work.

There was a resurgence of yodelling in the 1980s. Swiss yodelling, using a stronger delivery than the American hillbilly style, was revived in country music by Mary Schneider, whose albums of yodels by Minna Reverelli, Harry Torrani and George Van Dusen include *The Magic of Yodelling* and *Can't Stop Yodelling*. Rex ★Dallas also studied the Swiss techniques, producing *Yodelling Mad* (1979) and *Duelling Yodellers* (1988). Specialists appeared among younger traditional country artists, including Wayne Horsburgh, with his *Yodelling For You* (1985), Kathryn Pitt, who released *Where Did The Yodellers Go?* (1988) and especially 'The Snowy Mountain Yodeller', Owen ★Blundell. The one aspect of country music which allows for technical display, these singers have preserved the technique into the 1990s, at a time when in the USA it has faded into insignificance.

Yoi   (Tiwi), public singing and dancing on Bathurst and Melville Islands. See *Corroboree*.

Yolngu.   People of north-east Arnhem Land, active in the performance of a number of traditional ceremonial and modern secular song forms. ★Clan songs (*manikay*) are the most prevalent Yolngu song genre, performed widely at public ceremonial and secular events. Yolngu also perform sacred songs (*dhuyu manikay*) during closed men's ceremonies and at certain points during public ceremonies. Both clan songs and sacred songs are integral to Yolngu ancestral liturgy. There are also a number of overlapping thematic elements in the two genres; however, knowledge concerning the meaning of sacred songs is more esoteric, ostensibly restricted to mature men.

As with clan song repertoires, the sacred songs of each clan pertain to events of the ancestral past that occurred on their own land. Sacred song cycles are also conceived in terms of long ancestral journeys which link together all of the co-owning clans and their respective lands. But the subject matter of clan songs pertains to more localised events and shorter journeys, focused more on the respective lands of individual clans. A correlate musical distinction may be seen in the melodic features of the two genres: when performing clan songs, each clan uses its own set of idiomatic melodic characteristics, whereas when performing their portion of a sacred song cycle all the co-owning clans use a single set of melodic elements. Instrumentation provides another musical distinction between clan songs and sacred songs: songs of both genres are sung by men accompanying themselves on clapsticks, but only clan songs make use of didjeridu accompaniments. In public performances, both genres may involve dancing by men and women.

One of the distinctive features of Yolngu clan song performance is that each clan maintains a distinct, emblematic set of melodic characteristics (*dhambu*); another is the intricate rhythms created by didjeriduists in their combined use of blown fundamental, blown overtone, vocal resonance and guttural shrieks. These are not entirely new, but involve combinations of old and new thematic, textual and/or musical elements. All new-song verses are acknowledged as the creations of contemporary (or late) Yolngu singers; their creation is inspired by some event in everyday life and, through a metaphoric or physical affinity, some aspect of the inspiring contemporary event is linked to an ancestral song subject, resulting in a juxtaposed or fused thematic content. For example, on one occasion a young child's incessant crying inspired his father to create a new-song verse that combined a brief reference to this event with text concerning Tawny Frogmouth, an ancestral bird who always cries for the dead. New-song verses usually involve some new musical element, such as contemporary vocal or didjeridu rhythms or a new clapstick pattern. Often, but not always, sparing additions of new words also comprise part of new-song verse creation. Despite their contemporary component, new-song verses are still regarded as part of ceremonial clan song repertoire and in certain contexts are performed together with purely ancestral verses.

Since the coming of Methodist missionaries in the 1930s, Yolngu have also engaged in the performance of a number of types of Christian song. Today these include Christian texts in both Yolngu and English, with musical styles ranging from hymn settings to gospel and rock-influenced song (with electric keyboards and guitars) to songs performed with vocal harmonies and simple guitar-strummed accompaniments influenced by Pacific island song styles. Christian youth groups in the Yirrkala area often create 'action dances' to be performed with their songs. These are stationary dances in which choreographed arm movements are used to physically portray key words of the songs.

A popular, non-ceremonial song and dance form that developed at Yirrkala during the mission era (late 1930s to early 1970s) is *djatpangarri*. Its songs are purely recreational in nature and were first created and performed by young men at impromptu concerts at Yirrkala's beach camp. The subject matter of *djatpangarri* variously pertains to every-

day or contemporary phenomena (birds, the sea tide, cricket players, stage comics), some of which are also the subject of clan songs. At another level, *djatpangarri* may allude to personal relations between individuals through reference to the names of particular secondary kinship groups that the individuals belong to. The basic components of *djatpangarri* (male voice, clapsticks, didjeridu, dance) are the same as for clan songs. There are a number of musical differences, however, the most notable being that most *djatpangarri* employ a five-note descending scale roughly analogous to the first five notes of the Western minor scale, a musical construct not associated with clan song melodies. See also *Aboriginal Music* §3(iii).

STEVEN KNOPOFF

Yorta Yorta Man. Country music ballad (1988) by Jimmy *Little. The song reflects Little's early life at Cummeragunja, NSW, the Aboriginal reserve on the Murray River opposite Barmah, Victoria. Little's recording has been re-released on *Kings Of Country* (1993, Birubi Records) and is also recorded on his *Yorta Yorta Man* (Monitor 1995).

Yothu Yindi. Aboriginal (Yolngu) rock group based in Yirrkala and Galiwinku, north-east Arnhem Land, NT, full-time as a band since 1986. The lead singer, Mandawuy Yunupingu, was named Australian of the Year in 1993. Their recordings include traditional Yolngu songs of the Gumatj and Rirratjingu clans alongside rock songs which themselves combine elements of Yolngu traditional music and rock music. The songs are critical of the treatment of Aborigines, appealing for changes to political systems (*Treaty*), or they present Yolngu culture. They have made extensive national and international tours. Membership varies and at times includes non-Aboriginal Australians, or musicians from Papua New Guinea. In 1991 they won the MTV Award for the best Australian rock video (*Treaty*); in 1992 they won ARIA awards for best single, song of the year, and cover artwork (all for *Treaty*); then best indigenous record for the album *Tribal Voice* in 1993, and best indigenous record and best video (for *Djapana*).

FURTHER REFERENCE

Recordings include *Homeland Movement* (1989, Mushroom Records D38959); *Tribal Voice* (1991, Mushroom Records D30602); *Freedom* (1993, Mushroom Records D93380), *Birrkuta—Wild Honey* (1996, Mushroom Records TVD 93461). See also J. Stubington and P. Dunbar-Hall, 'Yothu Yindi's "Treaty": *Ganma* in music', *Popular Music* 13/3 (1993), 243–59; L. Thompson, *Aboriginal Voices: Contemporary Aboriginal Artists, Writers and Performers* (Sydney: Simon & Schuster, 1992); M. Yunupingu, 'Black and White', *Rolling Stone* 471 (June 1992), 33–4.

P. DUNBAR-HALL

Young, Brian (*b* Ayr, Qld, 2 Sept. 1935), country music singer. After working as a rodeo rider, he toured with *Rick and Thel from 1959 and released an EP in

1961. In 1968 he went farming and lived in the bush in Queensland and Tasmania; he rejoined Rick and Thel in 1975, releasing the first of his eight albums, *Young Country*, in 1976. Since 1977 he has had his own touring show, which tours seven months of the year, reaching very remote areas, particularly Aboriginal communities. Playing rock music as well as country numbers and often giving younger artists touring experience, his is the last surviving full-time travelling country music show in Australia. He was honoured in the ACMA Hands of Fame in 1978 and with an ACMA Heritage Award in 1991.

FURTHER REFERENCE
Recordings include *Young Country* (1976, Hadley OLLP 502TC), *Gotta Wander, Gotta Travel* (1978, Hadley CASOLLP 507), *Pull Up A Stump* (1983, Hadley CASOLLP 521) and *Thistles On The Hillside* (1991, LBS). See also *LattaA*, 174–5; *Smith*, 358.

Young, Charles (Frederick) Horace Frisby (*b* Yorkshire, England, 5 Apr. 1819; *d* Sydney, 29 Jan. 1874), burlesque performer, dancer, actor. The son of an actor, he appeared with his family's troupe from an early age, coming to notice in *Oliver Twist* in Surrey in 1838. He served in the navy, arrived at Hobart in 1843, stayed to work in theatre and married the dancer Eliza Thomson in 1845. They worked in George *Coppin's productions. He managed the Queen's Theatre, Melbourne, from 1849, gaining a wide following as a burlesque performer. He went to England in 1857, appearing in major burlesque venues, and returned to Australia in 1861, becoming the leading actor in Sydney for comic roles, but descending into alcoholism and mental disturbance in his last years. An adaptable talent, at his height he was matchless in burlesque, combining singing, dancing and comedy.

FURTHER REFERENCE
Obit. in *Illustrated Sydney News* 28 Feb. 1874. See also *ADB*, 6; P. McGuire, *The Australian Theatre* (London: OUP, 1948).

Young, Douglas ('Dougie'; 'Young Dougie') Garry (*b* Mitchell, Qld, *c*.1935; *d* Newcastle, NSW, 1991), Aboriginal singer-songwriter. Active in Wilcannia, NSW, from the 1950s, he was recorded by Jeremy Beckett in 1962 and 1964 (originally released on a Wattle disc in 1966), by Glen Vallance in Walgett in 1969, and Anthony Wallis in 1979. Of his songs 14 survive on these recordings, 13 of them in his own performances; they are reflections of the country town lives of Aborigines, with particular reference to alcohol, bouts in jail, and Aboriginal identity. One later song, *Treaty* (1979), deals with Aboriginal politics. Much of the detail of the songs is autobiographical.

FURTHER REFERENCE
Recordings include *The Songs of Dougie Young* ([1993], AIATSIS/National Library of Australia 19CD). See also J. Beckett, ' "I

Don't Care Who Knows": The songs of Dougie Young', *Australian Aboriginal Studies* 2 (1993), 34–8. P. DUNBAR-HALL

Young, Florence Maude (*b* Melbourne, 2 Oct. 1870; *d* Melbourne, 11 Nov. 1920), theatrical singer. She made her stage debut with Nellie *Stewart's Opera Co. in 1890 and then began a series of appearances in operetta, including *The Gondoliers*, *La Mascotte* and *Dorothy*. She was principal boy in pantomime for J.C. Williamson from 1895, and went to the UK with George Musgrove's company in 1897, then to South Africa. She studied for operatic roles with Mme Marchesi in Paris in 1899, but returned to Australia and musical comedy in 1901, appearing in many productions, including *San Toy*, *The Country Girl*, and *The Geisha* in later years. An excellent principal boy with a voice of considerable quality, she was one of Australia's most popular performers in pantomime and operetta until the years of World War I.

FURTHER REFERENCE
Obit. in *Age* 12 Nov. 1920; *Argus* 12 Nov. 1920. See also *ADB*, 12.

Young, Gary (*b* New York, 1947), rock drummer. He grew up in Melbourne and played with the Silhouettes from the age of 15, then the Rondells in 1966, Laurie Allen Revue 1967–68 and Ram Jam Big Band 1968–69 before joining *Daddy Cool in 1970. A founding member of *Jo Jo Zep and the Falcons 1976–81, he has worked with more than 20 bands since, including Phil *Manning 1983, *Black Sorrows 1984–85, the funk-blues band Relax With Max 1986, Keith *Glass and Mick Hamilton. A drummer with a career of more than 30 years in rock music, he has played styles from early rock and roll to progressive rock, rockabilly and western swing.

FURTHER REFERENCE
SpencerW; *McGrathA*.

Young, John Paul (*b* Glasgow, Scotland, 21 June 1950), pop singer. Arriving in Australia in 1966 and apprenticed as a sheetmetal worker, he sang in Elm Tree, then joined the cast of *Jesus Christ Superstar* in 1972. He had his first hit (as John Young) the same year with *Vanda and Young's *Pasadena*. In 1975, after two unsuccessful releases, his *Yesterday's Hero* reached No. 1 in the charts, and a series of eight Top 20 singles and two Top 20 albums followed, mostly songs by Vanda and Young. He formed the All Stars in 1975 as a touring band, with Kevin *Borich, Vince Maloney (of the *Bee Gees and the *Aztecs), Phil *Manning and other first-rate musicians. Using his full name (John Paul Young) to avoid confusion with another rising singer Johnny Young, his *I Hate The Music,* reached No. 3 in 1976 and the album *JPY* reached No 10.

He toured South Africa in 1977 to a tumultuous reception; *Standing In The Rain* was No. 1 there in 1978, reaching the Top 5 in Holland and Germany, the Top 40 in France and the Top 100 in the USA. *Love Is In the Air* was No. 3 in Australia in 1978 and in the US Top 40, as well as charting in Europe. He toured Europe, the UK and the USA that year, appearing on the British *Top Of The Pops.* Returning to Australia for a national tour, he had three singles in the Australian Top 20 in six months. In 1983 he retired from the scene; *Soldiers of Fortune*, which reached No. 17, was his final single.

One of Australia's most successful pop artists of the late 1970s, his cheerful, carefree manner brought him a vast following, especially among teenage girls. Combining a dependable backing band with excellent Vanda and Young material, he produced consistently impressive results. His *Love Is In the Air* has enjoyed a revival after its use in the film *Strictly Ballroom*.

FURTHER REFERENCE
Recordings include *Yesterday's Hero* (1975, Albert AP 10688), *I Hate The Music* (1976, Albert AP11037), *Love Is In The Air* (1978, Albert AP11710), *Soldiers Of Fortune* (1983, IC KSS1039), *Hero* (1975, Albert ABLP 013) and *JPY* (1976, Albert APLP019); a compilation is *Classic Hits* (1989, CBS 465240). For discography, see *Spencer.A.* See also *GuinnessP*, IV, 2756; *McGrathA*; *SpencerW.*

Young Kabbarli, The.　Chamber opera in one act by Margaret *Sutherland (1965), libretto by Maie Casey. It is based on the life of Daisy Bates (1863–1951), the social worker who spent her life as a protector of the outback Aborigines. First performed at the Hobart Festival of Contemporary Opera and Music on 19 August 1965. Recorded by HMV and published in Sydney, 1972.

Young Performers Award, ABC.　Largest and most prestigious national performance competition in Australia. Its origins are in the *ABC Instrumental and Vocal Competition (founded 1944), renamed in 1989. Open to singers and instrumentalists under 30 years resident in Australia for one year, it is awarded annually after heats, state finals, and a national final with an ABC orchestra. The competition also assesses performers for a number of Australia Council International Study Grants. The current value is $19 500, with ABC concert engagements usually following for the winners.

Young, Simone　(*b* Sydney, 2 Mar. 1961), conductor. After studying piano at the NSW State Conservatorium she worked as a *répétiteur* with the Australian Opera from 1982 and the Cologne Opera from 1987, becoming assistant conductor at Cologne from 1989. She was assistant to Daniel Barenboim at Bayreuth and elsewhere from 1991 and made her British debut at Covent Garden conducting *Rigoletto* in 1994. Appearing at the Berlin Staatsoper and the Bavarian State Opera, she was the first woman to conduct the Vienna Volksoper, the Vienna Staatsoper and the Paris Opera. She has conducted at the Metropolitan Opera, New York, at other major houses in the USA and Europe, and returned to Australia as guest conductor with ABC orchestras from 1995, appearing at the Melbourne

International Festival. With a repertoire which includes, aside from the standard operatic works, a specialisation in the works of Wagner, she has had a meteoric rise to international prominence. She won a Mo award in 1995.

FURTHER REFERENCE
Recordings include an operetta (WDR/EMI). See also *CA* (1995–96).

Younger, Montague Thomas Robson　(*b* Sydney, 25 June 1836; *d* North Sydney, 26 Dec. 1899), organist, conductor. He took lessons from Stephen Hale *Marsh and Charles *Packer and was organist at St Thomas's, North Sydney, from the age of 12. Working in his father's ironmongery until 1865, he was organist at St Peter's, Cooks River, then went to Ipswich in Queensland, becoming organist at St Paul's church and conductor of the Ipswich Philharmonic Society. He returned to Sydney in 1869 as the first organist at St Andrew's Cathedral, and taught at the Sydney College of Music. He was Sydney city organist 1901–7. An accomplished, natural performer, he also published a number of rather commonplace compositions.

FURTHER REFERENCE
E.J. Lea-Scarlett, *ADB*, 6.

Youth Music Australia.　Ensemble training organisation (founded 1948) based in Sydney, which administers the Australian Youth Orchestra, Camerata Australia, annual national music camps and other activities. Ruth *Alexander (of Melbourne Girls' Grammar School) had admired the orchestral music camps organised by Joseph E. Maddy in Michigan, USA, and joining with John *Bishop (then at Scotch College) and Percy *Jones (University of Melbourne Conservatorium) a Victorian School Music Association music camp was held in conjunction with the National Fitness Council at Point Lonsdale, Victoria, in January 1948. Teenage players came from far afield to play in the camp orchestra, and orchestral musicians donated their services as tutors.

From 1952 regular summer camps were held at Geelong Grammar School, in 1955 organised independently as the National Music Camp Association, and in 1957 the Australian Youth Orchestra was formed. The enterprise attracted wide attention. Sir Eugene *Goossens, Georges *Tzipine and other conductors resident with the ABC came to conduct, and many players from ABC orchestras come to tutor. The camps engendered great loyalty. The staff returned year after year, and Bishop, Bernard *Heinze, and later John *Hopkins became long-standing conductors. The Australian Youth Orchestra began touring and issuing recordings.

The association was renamed Youth Music Australia in 1992 and today, with very substantial assistance from the Federal Government and private sponsors, the annual camp offers an array of orchestras, as well as embracing training in orchestral management, new music, and chamber repertoire; the Australian Youth Orchestra regularly tours to Asia, Europe and the Americas, and conductors of international standing are engaged; a chamber orchestra, Camerata Australia, also tours nationally and internationally; a Summer Academy presents advanced training in the chamber orchestra repertoire; and other ventures have included contemporary music workshops and regional community music festivals. Enjoying great affection from former campers now in all walks of life across Australia, the organisation remains an important training ground for Australian orchestras.

FURTHER REFERENCE

Recordings of the Australian Youth Orchestra include *Music for Australia Day* (ABC 834740–2), *Christmas Under Capricorn* (Tall Poppies TP 016) and works of Tchaikovsky and Glinka (ABC 426210–2); and Camerata Australia in *Camerata Australia* (Youth Music Australia). See Christopher Symons, *John Bishop: A Life for Music* (Melbourne: Hyland House, 1989), 135–78; June Epstein, *Concert Pitch: The Story of the National Music Camp Association and the National Youth Orchestra* (Melbourne: Hyland House, 1984).

Yu, Julian   (*b* Beijing, China, 1957), composer. He studied composition at the Central Conservatory of Music, Beijing, later joining the staff there. In 1980–82 he studied with Joji Yuasa at the Tokyo College of Music, then in 1985 migrated to Australia. Awarded a Composition Fellowship to study with Hans Werner Henze and Oliver Knussen at Tanglewood in 1988, he won the Koussevitzky Tanglewood Composition Prize and received a commission from Henze. Since 1987 Yu has won various major composition prizes, including the inaugural and second Paul Lowin Orchestral Prizes, the Vienna Modern Masters Recording Award, the International New Music Composers' Competition for three consecutive years, the Tenth Irino Prize, second prize in the 56th Japan Music Concours, the 35th Premio Musicale Città di Trieste, the Albert H. Maggs Composition award, and the Adolf Spivakovsky Composition Prize.

His works have been included in ISCM World Music Days in Zurich and Mexico, in the Asian Composers' League festivals in NZ, Seoul and Taiwan, and in the Huddersfield Festival and the 2nd Munich Biennale. His orchestral works have been performed by the Tanglewood, BBC, Hiroshima, Sydney and Melbourne Symphony Orchestras. His music is founded in the traditional Chinese practice of embellishing earlier work until it takes new shape and individuality, but he also uses advanced Western techniques, with unswerving logic expressing in vivid orchestration what he sees as an outward reflection of order of the inner life.

WORKS (Selective)

Publisher: Universal Edition.

Stage   *The White Snake*, puppet opera, chamber ens (1989, 3 and epilogue, composer), 27 Apr. 1990, Munich.

Orchestral   *Wu-Yu* (1987, Vienna Modern Masters VMM 3022), *Great Ornamented Fuga Canonica* (1988), *First Australian Suite*, chamber orch (1990), *Hsiang-Wen* (1991), *Three Symphonic Poems* (1994).

Other   *Scintillation II*, pf, 2 vibraphone, glockenspiel (1987; rec. ABC Classics 442350–2), *Reclaimed Prefu*, 2 pf (1989), *Passacaglissimi*, fl, cl, str qrt (1994).

FURTHER REFERENCE

Recordings include *Scintillation II*, Synergy (ABC 442 350); *Wu-Yu*, Orchestra (1987, Vienna Modern Masters VMM 3022). See also *BroadstockS*.

THÉRÈSE RADIC

Yunupingu, Mandawuy Bakamana   (*b* Yirrkala, NT, 17 Sept. 1956), bandleader. After training as a teacher he taught at Yirrkala mission, becoming lead singer of the Aboriginal rock band ★Yothu Yindi in 1991, recording *Tribal Voice* and *Freedom*, and appearing extensively in Australia and abroad. A vibrant stage presence, his distinctive vocal tone is closely identified with the Yothu Yindi sound.

Yurisich, Gregory   (*b* Mount Lawley, WA, 13 Oct. 1951), baritone. After a few months' study with Molly McGurck in Perth, he won the state finals of the ABC Instrumental and Vocal Competition. He made his debut as Paolo (*Simon Boccanegra*) with the Australian Opera in 1974, and sang for them until 1987, then with the Frankfurt Opera 1988–90, as well as in guest appearances at English National Opera, Covent Garden, Glyndebourne, Brussels and New York. With a warm, liquid tone and effective acting, his repertoire includes Figaro, Simon Boccanegra, Marcello, Don Alfonso, Don Profundo, Pizarro, Scarpia and Escamillo, and he has been particularly notable in comic parts, such as Pooh-Bah, Dr Bartolo, Masetto, Bottom, and the four villains in *Tales of Hoffmann*. He sang at the premieres of Stephen Oliver's *Timon of Athens* and John Buller's *Bakaxi*.

FURTHER REFERENCE

Recordings include Leporello in *Don Giovanni*, cond. R. Norrington (EMI CDS7 54859–2); Sulpice in *Fille du régiment*, Australian Opera (MCEG Video VVD 829); Frank in *Die Fledermaus*, Australian Opera (MCEG Video VVD 781); and Stanker in *Stiffelio*, Covent Garden (Covent Garden Pioneer Video CGP 03). See also *CA* (1995-96); Elizabeth Forbes, *GroveO*.

Z

Zavod, Allan (*b* Melbourne, 20 Sept. 1947), composer, jazz pianist. A graduate of the University of Melbourne Conservatorium, Zavod was heard playing jazz piano by Duke Ellington in the late 1960s. Ellington helped to arrange a scholarship for him to study at the Berklee School of Music in Boston. There Zavod completed his doctorate and later held a post as professor of music. Through the 1970s he played, recorded and toured the world with the Glenn Miller Orchestra, the Woody Herman Orchestra, the Maynard Ferguson Big Band, Billy Cobham, Don Ellis, George Benson and others, and in 1984 he recorded and toured with Frank Zappa. Returning to Australia in the late 1980s, Zavod has since won the Asian Broadcast Union's popular song contest in Kuala Lumpur with his composition *Time Can't Keep Us Apart*, performed by Kate ★Ceberano, and established an impressive career in film composition.

FURTHER REFERENCE

His film credits include *Death of a Soldier* (1985), *The Big Hurt* and *The Right Hand Man* (1986), *The Time Guardian* and *The Howling III* (1987), *Sebastian and the Sparrow* (1988), *Garbo* and *Fatal Sky* (1990), *Shotgun Wedding* (1992), *Art Deco Detective* and the television series *A Country Practice* (1994), and *Back in Business* and the television series *Bush Patrol* and *State Coroner* (1996). See also *LimbacherF.*
L.THOMPSON

Zelman, Alberto (*b* 1832 Trieste, Austrià; *d* Melbourne, 28 Dec. 1907), conductor. Educated in Trieste, Zelman worked in Italy as an opera conductor before being engaged by the Cagli-Pompei opera company to tour Australia, where he also appeared as pianist playing his own works. He settled in Melbourne, marrying one of his piano students, teaching, conducting for ★Lyster's operas, directing choirs and bands, and composing. For Lyster's production of *Lohengrin* in 1877 Zelman reconstituted the orchestral score from memory. At the 1888 Centennial Exhibition he deputised as conductor for Cowen. In 1889 he became conductor of the Melbourne Liedertafel but resigned in the following year because of ill health.

SUZANNE ROBINSON

Zelman, (Samuel Victor) Albert ('Alberto') Jr (*b* North Melbourne, 15 Nov. 1874; *d* Melbourne, 3 Mar. 1927), violinist, conductor, teacher. Eldest son of Alberto ★Zelman Sr, Melbourne's 'brainiest musician', Zelman was a prodigy who gave his first performance at the age of six. As a teenager he formed his own orchestra and learned to play each instrument, but never undertook formal theory and harmony instruction. At the age of 17 he accompanied Amy ★Sherwin on her tour of Australia and NZ; he then joined the ★Marshall-Hall Orchestra and began conducting light opera. He gained an increasing reputation as a soloist, presenting Australian premieres of works by Delius and Elgar. He was a member of the Melbourne String Quartet and the British Music Society Quartet and a member of staff at both the Albert Street (1901–10) and University of Melbourne (1910–15) Conservatoriums. His students included several of those employed in the radio broadcasting orchestras in the 1920s. In 1906 Zelman founded the amateur ★Melbourne Symphony Orchestra, rivalling the Marshall-Hall Orchestra, and became conductor of the Melbourne Philharmonic from 1911. His orchestra accompanied Melba in her concerts in 1921 and gave the first children's concerts in Melbourne. In 1922 Alberto and his wife, soprano Maude Harrington, travelled to Europe, where Zelman made recordings and conducted the London Symphony and Berlin Philharmonic Orchestras, although to mixed acclaim.

A talented conductor, musician and teacher, Zelman was a modest and unassuming man whose talents many believe were not recognised. A light burns continually in Zelman's memory at the Savage Club in Melbourne.

FURTHER REFERENCE

The Zelman papers are at *Msl*. For Alberto Zelman Sr, see Thérèse Radic, *ADB*, 6; *MackenzieS*, 269–70. For Alberto Zelman Jr, see Don Fairweather, *Your Friend Alberto Zelman* (Melbourne: Zelman Memorial Symphony Orchestra, 1984); Thérèse Radic, *ADB*, 12. For an index to references in *AMN* see *MarsiI*.

SUZANNE ROBINSON

Zoot. Rock band (1965–71) formed in Adelaide, originally comprising Daryl Cotton (vocals), John D'Arcy and Beeb Birtles [Gerard Birtlekamp] (guitar, vocals), and Teddy Higgins (drums). At first a high school band, they went professional, backing John *Farnham, Bev *Harrell and others, and moved to Melbourne in 1967, adopting pink costumes and instruments, which led to a teenage craze for 'zoot suits'. Their *One Times Two Times Three Times Four* reached No. 32 in the charts in 1969. In 1970 they disposed of their pink trademark and explored gentler material, releasing their version of *Eleanor Rigby*, which reached No. 4 in the charts. Although their playing matured from basic rock to more sophisticated repertoire, they were unable to shake off their lurid teeny-bopper image and disbanded in 1971; but they proved a training ground for the notable later success of Rick *Springfield (a member from 1969), Birtles and Cotton (in *Little River Band).

FURTHER REFERENCE

Recordings include *One Times Two Times Three Times Four* (Columbia DO 8605), *Just Zoot* (1969 Columbia SCX O7916), *Four Shades Of Pink* (Columbia SEG O70191) and *Eleanor Rigby* (Columbia DO9317). A compilation is *Zoot Locker* (1980, EMI EMY 502). For discography, see *SpencerA*. See also *SpencerW*; *McGrathA*; David Day and Tim Parker, *SA Great: It's Our Music 1956–1986* (Glandore, SA: Day and Parker, 1987), 68–87.